Managing Human Resources

Sixth Canadian Edition

Monica Belcourt, PhD, CHRP
Director, School of Human Resource Management
York University

George Bohlander
Professor Emeritus of Management
Arizona State University

Scott Snell
Professor of Business Administration
University of Virginia

NELSON

EDUCATION

NELSON

EDUCATION

Managing Human Resources, Sixth Canadian Edition
by Monica Belcourt, George Bohlander, and Scott Snell

Vice President, Editorial Director:
Evelyn Veitch

Editor-in-Chief, Higher Education:
Anne Williams

Acquisitions Editor:
Amie Plourde

Marketing Manager:
Kathaleen McCormick

Developmental Editor:
Karina Hope

Photo Researcher/Permissions Coordinator:
Kristiina Bowering

Senior Content Production Manager:
Imoinda Romain

Production Service:
Elm Street Publishing Services

Copy Editor:
Karen Rolfe

Manufacturing Manager:
Joanne McNeil

Design Director:
Ken Phipps

Managing Designer:
Franca Amore

Interior Design:
Greg Devitt

Cover Design:
Carianne Sherriff

Compositor:
Integra Software Services Pvt. Ltd.

Printer:
R.R. Donnelley

Library and Archives Canada Cataloguing in Publication

Belcourt, Monica

Managing Human Resources Monica Belcourt, George Bohlander, Scott Snell—6th Canadian ed.

Includes bibliographical references and index.
ISBN: 978-0-17-650178-5

1. Personnel management—Textbooks. 2. Personnel management—Canada—Textbooks. I. Bohlander, George W. II. Snell, Scott, 1958– III. Title.

HF5549.B333 2010
658.3   C2009-905439-6

ISBN-13: 978-0-17-650178-5
ISBN-10: 0-17-650178-9

Cover photos, back row: Andresr/iStockphoto. **Front and middle rows, from left to right:** © Justin Horrocks/iStockphoto; © Steve Cukrov/iStockphoto; © Justin Horrocks/iStockphoto; © Adam James/iStockphoto; © Justin Horrocks/iStockphoto; © Lise Gagne/iStockphoto; Andresr/iStockphoto; © Jaroslaw Wojcik/iStockphoto; Neustockimages/iStockphoto; © Francisco Romero/iStockphoto; © Justin Horrocks/iStockphoto.

To my son, Brooker Belcourt, for his intelligent and insightful observations on the complexities of human behaviour

To my wife, Ronnie Bohlander, and to our children, Ryan and Kathryn

To my wife, Marybeth Snell, and to our children, Sara, Jack, and Emily

FEATURES

THE INTEGRATED LEARNING SYSTEM

The Integrated Learning System (ILS) anchors chapter concepts, provides a framework for study, and links all of the instructor resources.

Icons that identify the learning outcomes appear throughout the text and end-of-chapter materials.

The ILS provides structure for instructors preparing lectures and exams and helps students learn quickly and study efficiently.

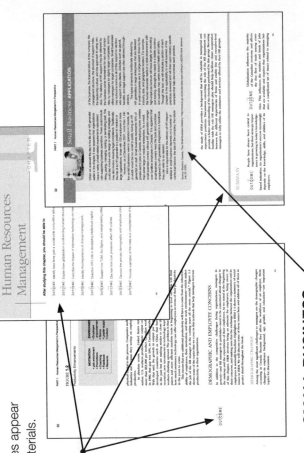

HIGHLIGHTS IN HRM

This popular boxed feature provides real-world examples of how organizations perform HR functions. The Highlights are introduced in the text discussion and include topics such as small business and international issues.

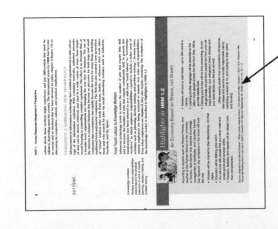

SMALL BUSINESS APPLICATION

Small Business Application takes the principles and prescriptions of a functional area, such as recruitment, and demonstrates how these can be applied in a small business setting.

REALITY CHECK

Reality Check presents an interview with a Canadian expert in the field, illustrating how the material in the chapter is used in the real world.

THE BUSINESS CASE

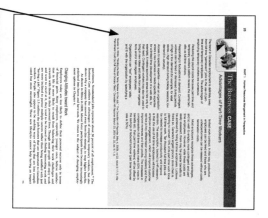

The Business Case features the business or financial implications of the adoption of HR practices. It also helps students build the skills necessary to recommend practices and projects, based on the projected costs and benefits, to senior management.

ETHICS IN HRM

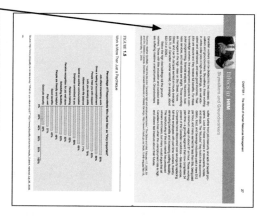

Ethics in HRM provokes debate and discussion among students around the often grey areas of human resources management, including drug testing of employees and electronic surveillance of employees at work.

USING THE INTERNET

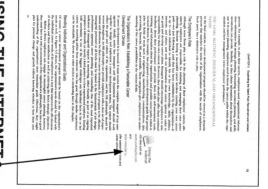

The Internet is referenced in all chapters, with new government, research, and business Internet links and addresses.

KEY TERMS IN MARGIN

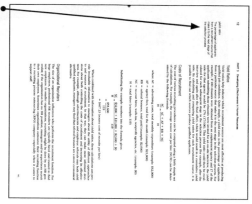

Key terms appear in boldface and are defined in margin notes next to the text discussion. The key terms are also listed at the end of each chapter and in the glossary.

CAREER COUNSEL

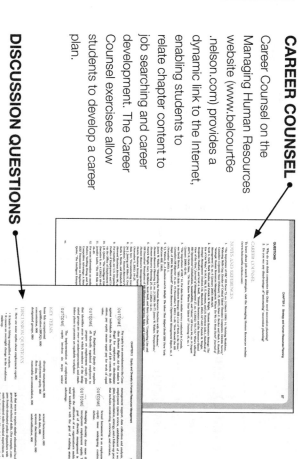

Career Counsel on the Managing Human Resources website (www.belcourt6e .nelson.com) provides a dynamic link to the Internet, enabling students to relate chapter content to job searching and career development. The Career Counsel exercises allow students to develop a career plan.

DISCUSSION QUESTIONS

Discussion questions following the chapter summary offer an opportunity to focus on each of the learning outcomes in the chapter and to stimulate critical thinking. Many of these questions allow for group analysis and class discussion.

INTERNET EXERCISE

Internet Exercise requires the use of the content available on the Internet in order to develop a solution.

BIZFLIX EXERCISES

Short film clips taken from popular movies provide real-world examples of HR in action. BizFlix Exercises encourage students to see and consider the HR issues and content in the world around them.

HRM EXPERIENCE EXERCISES

These skill-building exercises help students gain practical experience when dealing with employee/management concerns. Students can work through the exercises on either an individual or team basis.

CASES

Two or more case studies per chapter present current HRM issues in real-life settings that encourage consideration and critical analysis. The end of the text features five real cases used in Excalibur, the Canadian University Tournament in Human Resources.

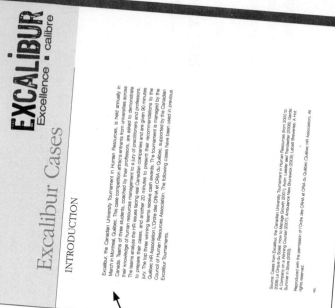

BRIEF CONTENTS

PART 1 HUMAN RESOURCES MANAGEMENT IN PERSPECTIVE

1 THE WORLD OF HUMAN RESOURCES MANAGEMENT   3

2 STRATEGY AND HUMAN RESOURCES PLANNING   43

PART 2 MEETING HUMAN RESOURCES REQUIREMENTS

3 EQUITY AND DIVERSITY IN HUMAN RESOURCES MANAGEMENT   95

4 JOB ANALYSIS, EMPLOYEE INVOLVEMENT, AND FLEXIBLE WORK SCHEDULES   137

PART 3 DEVELOPING EFFECTIVENESS IN HUMAN RESOURCES

5 EXPANDING THE TALENT POOL: RECRUITMENT AND CAREERS   173

6 EMPLOYEE SELECTION   225

7 TRAINING AND DEVELOPMENT   271

8 APPRAISING AND IMPROVING PERFORMANCE   321

PART 4 IMPLEMENTING COMPENSATION AND SECURITY

9 MANAGING COMPENSATION   369

10 PAY-FOR-PERFORMANCE: INCENTIVE REWARDS   405

11 EMPLOYEE BENEFITS   439

12 SAFETY AND HEALTH   473

PART 5 ENHANCING EMPLOYEE–MANAGEMENT RELATIONS

13 EMPLOYEE RIGHTS AND DISCIPLINE 511

14 THE DYNAMICS OF LABOUR RELATIONS 547

PART 6 EXPANDING HUMAN RESOURCES MANAGEMENT HORIZONS

15 INTERNATIONAL HUMAN RESOURCES MANAGEMENT 583

16 CREATING HIGH-PERFORMANCE WORK SYSTEMS

(SEE THE *MANAGING HUMAN RESOURCES* WEBSITE: HTTP://WWW.BELCOURT6E.NELSON.COM)

Excalibur Cases 629

Glossary 642

Name Index 651

Organization Index 653

Subject Index 657

CONTENTS

PREFACE   xxxiii

ABOUT THE AUTHORS   xii

PART 1
HUMAN RESOURCES MANAGEMENT IN PERSPECTIVE

CHAPTER 1   THE WORLD OF HUMAN RESOURCES
             MANAGEMENT

WHY STUDY HUMAN RESOURCES MANAGEMENT?   4

Highlights in HRM 1.1: A Day in the Life of an HR Generalist   5

COMPETITIVE CHALLENGES AND HUMAN
RESOURCES MANAGEMENT   5

*Challenge 1: Competing, Recruiting,
and Staffing Globally*   6

Challenge 2: Embracing New Technology   8

Highlights in HRM 1.2: An Economy Based on
Brains, not Brawn   8

Highlights in HRM 1.3: Automation of Talent
Management Functions   10

Challenge 3: Managing Change   11

Challenge 4: Managing Talent, or Human Capital   12

Challenge 5: Responding to the Market   14

Reality Check: Six Sigma   16

Challenge 6: Containing Costs   17

DEMOGRAPHIC AND EMPLOYEE CONCERNS   20

Demographic Changes   20

Highlights in HRM 1.4: Social Issues in HRM   21

The Business Case: Advantages of Part-Time Workers   26

Ethics in HRM: Skywalkers and Groundworkers   27

Highlights in HRM 1.5: Work–Life Harmony   28

THE PARTNERSHIP OF LINE MANAGERS AND HR DEPARTMENTS 29

Responsibilities of the Human Resources Manager 29

Competencies of the Human Resources Manager 30

Role of the Line Manager 31

Small Business Application 32

SUMMARY 32

KEY TERMS 33

DISCUSSION QUESTIONS 34

INTERNET EXERCISE 34

HRM EXPERIENCE: BALANCING COMPETITIVE CHALLENGES AND EMPLOYEE CONCERNS 34

BIZFLIX EXERCISES: *BABE:* HERDING SHEEP, BABE'S WAY 35

CASE STUDY 1: THE GLOBAL MANAGEMENT CONSULTING FIRM ACCENTURE BRINGS EMPLOYEES FACE TO FACE 35

CASE STUDY 2: INTERGENERATIONAL ISSUES 36

CAREER COUNSEL 37

NOTES AND REFERENCES 37

CHAPTER 2   STRATEGY AND HUMAN RESOURCES PLANNING 43

STRATEGIC PLANNING AND HUMAN RESOURCES 44

Strategic Planning and HR Planning: Linking the Processes 45

STEP ONE: MISSION, VISION, AND VALUES 45

STEP TWO: ENVIRONMENTAL ANALYSIS 46

Highlights in HRM 2.1: WestJet: Mission, Vision, and Values 47

Competitive Environment 47

External Supply of Labour 49

STEP THREE: INTERNAL ANALYSIS 50

The Three Cs: Culture, Capabilities, and Composition 50

Highlights in HRM 2.2: Spotting Trends in the Global Economy 51

Highlights in HRM 2.3: The Measurement of Human Capital 54

Ethics in HRM: The Employment Contract 56

The Business Case: Hiring Contract Workers Pays 56

Forecasting: A Critical Element of Planning — 57

Reality Check: HR Planning for Registered Nurses — 58

Highlights in HRM 2.4: HR Planning and Strategy Questions to Ask — 60

Assessing a Firm's Human Capital Readiness: Gap Analysis — 62

Highlights in HRM 2.5: Succession-Planning Checklist — 64

STEP FOUR: FORMULATING STRATEGY — 64

Corporate Strategy — 66

Highlights in HRM 2.6: Key HR Activities Associated with Merger or Acquisition Phases — 67

Business Strategy — 68

Functional Strategy: Ensuring Alignment — 70

STEP FIVE: STRATEGY IMPLEMENTATION — 70

Taking Action: Reconciling Supply and Demand — 72

Highlights in HRM 2.7: Managing Labour Shortages — 72

STEP SIX: EVALUATION AND ASSESSMENT — 75

Evaluation and Assessment Issues — 75

Highlights in HRM 2.8: Ten Measures of Human Capital — 76

Measuring a Firm's Strategic Alignment — 77

Ensuring Strategic Flexibility for the Future — 79

Small Business Application — 80

SUMMARY — 81

KEY TERMS — 81

DISCUSSION QUESTIONS — 82

INTERNET EXERCISE — 82

HRM EXPERIENCE: CUSTOMIZING HR FOR DIFFERENT TYPES OF HUMAN CAPITAL — 82

BIZFLIX EXERCISES: *U-571*: SETTING STRATEGY — 83

CASE STUDY 1: STAFFING, DOWN TO A SCIENCE AT CAPITAL ONE — 83

CASE STUDY 2: MATCHING TALENT WITH TASKS: DOLE IMPLEMENTS SUCCESSION — 85

CAREER COUNSEL — 87

NOTES AND REFERENCES — 87

CONTENTS

APPENDIX: CALCULATING TURNOVER AND ABSENTEEISM   90

EMPLOYEE TURNOVER RATES   90

Computing the Turnover Rate   90

Determining the Costs of Turnover   91

EMPLOYEE ABSENTEEISM RATES   91

Computing Absenteeism Rates   91

Highlights in HRM 2.A1: Costs Associated with the
Turnover of One Computer Programmer   92

Costs of Absenteeism   93

Absenteeism and HR Planning   93

PART 2
MEETING HUMAN RESOURCES REQUIREMENTS

CHAPTER 3   EQUITY AND DIVERSITY IN HUMAN
RESOURCES MANAGEMENT   95

EMPLOYMENT EQUITY   96

Status of Designated Groups   97

Highlights in HRM 3.1: Barriers to the Advancement
of Women   97

Highlights in HRM 3.2: Outreach Efforts   98

Highlights in HRM 3.3: What's in a Name?   99

Ethics in HRM: Ethics: Equality or Equity   100

Benefits of Employment Equity   101

THE LEGAL FRAMEWORK   101

The Charter of Rights and Freedoms   101

The Canadian Human Rights Act (CHRA)   101

The Enforcement of Provincial Human Rights Laws   106

PAY EQUITY   106

THE *EMPLOYMENT EQUITY ACT* (1995)   107

*Administration and Enforcement of the
Employment Equity Act*   108

THE IMPLEMENTATION OF EMPLOYMENT
EQUITY IN ORGANIZATIONS   108

Highlights in HRM 3.4: Implementation Criteria
for Federal Contractors Program   109

Step 1: Senior Management Commitment   109

Step 2: Data Collection and Analysis	111
Highlights in HRM 3.5: Suggestions for Inclusion	112
Step 3: Employment Systems Review	113
Highlights in HRM 3.6: Participation in the Federal Public Service	115
Highlights in HRM 3.7: The Duty to Accommodate	116
Step 4: Establishment of a Workplan	117
Step 5: Implementation	117
Step 6: Evaluation, Monitoring, and Revision	117
SEXUAL HARASSMENT	118
Highlights in HRM 3.8: The Cost of Sexual Harassment	118
Highlights in HRM 3.9: Questions Asked in Auditing Sexual Harassment	120
Highlights in HRM 3.10: The Aftermath of Sexual Harassment	121
Highlights in HRM 3.11: Basic Components of an Effective Sexual Harassment Policy	122
MANAGING DIVERSITY	122
CREATING AN ENVIRONMENT FOR SUCCESS	123
The Business Case: The Economic Values of Diversity	124
Reality Check: Diversity Achievements at Air Canada	125
Small Business Application	127
SUMMARY	128
KEY TERMS	129
DISCUSSION QUESTIONS	129
INTERNET EXERCISE	130
HRM EXPERIENCE: PREVENTING SEXUAL HARASSMENT	130
BIZFLIX EXERCISES: *LEGALLY BLONDE:* SEXUAL HARASSMENT	130
CASE STUDY 1: FIGHTING FIRES	131
CASE STUDY 2: WHAT WENT WRONG?	132
CAREER COUNSEL	132
NOTES AND REFERENCES	132
CHAPTER 4 JOB ANALYSIS, EMPLOYEE INVOLVEMENT, AND FLEXIBLE WORK SCHEDULES	137
RELATIONSHIP OF JOB REQUIREMENTS AND HRM FUNCTIONS	138

Recruitment 138

Selection 139

Training and Development 139

Performance Appraisal 139

Compensation Management 139

The Business Case: Flying for Love or Money 140

JOB ANALYSIS 140

Gathering Job Information 140

Reality Check: Job Analysis at EDS Canada Inc. 142

Controlling the Accuracy of Job Information 142

Ethics in HRM: Inflation 143

Approaches to Job Analysis 143

Job Descriptions 147

Highlights in HRM 4.1: Job Description for an HR
Employment Assistant 148

Problems with Job Descriptions 149

JOB DESIGN 149

Behavioural Concerns 150

Highlights in HRM 4.2: Empowered Employees
Achieve Results 152

Industrial Engineering Considerations 153

Ergonomic Considerations 154

Designing Work for Group/Team Contributions 154

Flexible Work Schedules 159

Highlights in HRM 4.3: Why Students Value Flexible
Scheduling 160

Highlights in HRM 4.4: Flextime and Work–Life Balance 163

Small Business Application 164

SUMMARY 164

KEY TERMS 165

DISCUSSION QUESTIONS 165

INTERNET EXERCISE 166

HRM EXPERIENCE: ESTABLISHING GROUND
RULES FOR TEAM SUCCESS 166

BIZFLIX EXERCISES: *INTOLERABLE CRUELTY:*
JUST DOING MY JOB 167

CASE STUDY 1: DUCKS UNLIMITED CANADA | 167

CASE STUDY 2: BUT MY JOB HAS CHANGED | 168

CAREER COUNSEL | 169

NOTES AND REFERENCES | 169

PART 3
DEVELOPING EFFECTIVENESS IN HUMAN RESOURCES

CHAPTER 5   EXPANDING THE TALENT POOL: RECRUITMENT AND CAREERS | 173

RECRUITING TALENT EXTERNALLY | 174

Outside Sources for Recruitment | 175

Highlights in HRM 5.1: Guidelines for Setting Up an Online Job Posting System | 177

The Global Labour Market | 181

Improving the Effectiveness of External Recruitment | 181

RECRUITING TALENT INTERNALLY | 183

Advantages and Limitations of Recruiting from Within | 183

Methods for Identifying Qualified Candidates | 185

Highlights in HRM 5.2: The Assessment Centre Program of the Public Service Commission | 187

CAREER MANAGEMENT: DEVELOPING TALENT OVER TIME | 188

The Goal: Matching Individual and Organizational Needs | 189

Identifying Career Opportunities and Requirements | 190

Reality Check: Career Edge Making a Difference | 196

Career Development Initiatives | 197

The Business Case: The Value of Career Development Programs | 197

Ethics in HRM: Individual Investment or Organizational Investment? | 199

Highlights in HRM 5.3: E-Mentoring | 202

DEVELOPING A DIVERSE TALENT POOL | 203

Recruitment and Development of Women | 203

Eliminating Women's Barriers to Advancement | 204

Glass Ceiling Audits | 204

Preparing Women for Management 205

Accommodating Families 205

Advancement of Minorities to Management 205

OTHER IMPORTANT TALENT CONCERNS 206

Managing a Multigenerational Workforce 206

Highlights in HRM 5.4: The Four Generations 206

Employing Dual-Career Couples 207

Small Business Application 207

SUMMARY 208

KEY TERMS 209

DISCUSSION QUESTIONS 209

INTERNET EXERCISE 210

HRM EXPERIENCE: CAREER MANAGEMENT 210

BIZFLIX EXERCISES: *IN GOOD COMPANY:* CARTER MANAGES HIS CAREER 210

CASE STUDY 1: HUMAN RESOURCES CAREER PROGRESSION 211

CASE STUDY 2: RECRUITMENT CHANNELS 212

CASE STUDY 3: PREPARING A CAREER DEVELOPMENT PLAN 213

CAREER COUNSEL 214

NOTES AND REFERENCES 214

APPENDIX: PERSONAL CAREER DEVELOPMENT 217

DEVELOPING PERSONAL SKILLS AND COMPETENCIES 217

CHOOSING A CAREER 217

Highlights in HRM 5.A1: Career Competencies at Caterpillar 218

Use of Available Resources 218

Accuracy of Self-Evaluation 218

The Significance of Interest Inventories 218

CHOOSING AN EMPLOYER 219

Questions to Ask Yourself Before You Accept a Job Offer 220

BECOMING AN ENTREPRENEUR 220

KEEPING A CAREER IN PERSPECTIVE 221

Developing Off-the-Job Interests 221

Balancing Marital and/or Family Life 221

Planning for Retirement 222

KEY TERM 222

NOTES AND REFERENCES 222

CHAPTER 6 EMPLOYEE SELECTION 225

MATCHING PEOPLE AND JOBS 226

Person–Job Fit: Beginning with Job Analysis 227

Person–Organization Fit 227

The Selection Process 227

Obtaining Reliable and Valid Information 228

SOURCES OF INFORMATION ABOUT
JOB CANDIDATES 231

Application Forms 231

Ethics in HRM: Writing It Wrong 232

Online Applications 233

Biographical Information Blanks 233

Background Checks 233

Polygraph Tests 234

Highlights in HRM 6.1: Sample Reference-
Checking Questions 235

Honesty and Integrity Tests 235

Graphology 237

EMPLOYMENT TESTS 237

Nature of Employment Tests 238

Classification of Employment Tests 238

Highlights in HRM 6.2: Testing at Steelcase 241

THE EMPLOYMENT INTERVIEW 242

Interviewing Methods 242

Highlights in HRM 6.3: Sample Situational Interview
Question 244

Highlights in HRM 6.4: Too Funny for Interviews 244

Highlights in HRM 6.5: Behavioural Interviews at BMO 245

The Business Case: Behavioural Interviews Bring
Big Returns 246

Guidelines for Employment Interviewers 248

Employment Equity: Are Your Questions Legal? 250

Highlights in HRM 6.6: Appropriate and Inappropriate
Interview Questions 251

Medical Examination 252

Drug Testing 253

REACHING A SELECTION DECISION 253

Reality Check: Selection at The Bay 254

Summarizing Information about Applicants 255

Decision-Making Strategy 255

Final Decision 257

Small Business Application 258

SUMMARY 258

KEY TERMS 259

DISCUSSION QUESTIONS 259

INTERNET EXERCISE 260

HRM EXPERIENCE: DESIGNING SELECTION
CRITERIA AND METHODS 260

BIZFLIX EXERCISES: *BOWFINGER:* THE
LOOKALIKE 260

CASE STUDY 1: JOB CANDIDATE ASSESSMENT
TESTS GO VIRTUAL 261

CASE STUDY 2: APTITUDE TESTS AT AN
ELECTRONICS CORPORATION 263

CASE STUDY 3: SEARCHING FOR SPIES 264

CAREER COUNSEL 265

NOTES AND REFERENCES 265

CHAPTER 7   TRAINING AND DEVELOPMENT 271

THE SCOPE OF TRAINING 272

Investments in Training 272

Ethics in HRM: Mandatory or Voluntary? 273

A Systems Approach to Training 274

PHASE 1: CONDUCTING THE NEEDS ASSESSMENT 274

Highlights in HRM 7.1: Notes on Rapid Needs Assessment 276

Organization Analysis 276

Task Analysis	277
Highlights in HRM 7.2: A Competency Assessment for a Managerial Position	278
Person Analysis	279
PHASE 2: DESIGNING THE TRAINING PROGRAM	280
Instructional Objectives	280
Trainee Readiness and Motivation	280
Principles of Learning	281
Characteristics of Instructors	284
PHASE 3: IMPLEMENTING THE TRAINING PROGRAM	285
Training Methods for Nonmanagerial Employees	285
Highlights in HRM 7.3: Internship Program at Durham College	287
Highlights in HRM 7.4: Making the Most of Internships	288
Methods for Management Development	293
PHASE 4: EVALUATING THE TRAINING PROGRAM	296
Criterion 1: Reactions	297
Reality Check: A Classic Four-Level Evaluation	297
Criterion 2: Learning	298
Criterion 3: Behaviour	298
Criterion 4: Results, or Return on Investment (ROI)	299
Highlights in HRM 7.5: Calculating Training ROI: Examples	300
The Business Case: Return on Training Investment	300
Highlights in HRM 7.6: Benchmarking HR Training	301
SPECIAL TOPICS IN TRAINING AND DEVELOPMENT	302
Orientation Training	302
Highlights in HRM 7.7: Wowing the Candidate	303
Highlights in HRM 7.8: Checklist for Orienting New Employees	304
Basic Skills Training	304
Team Training and Cross-Training	305
Ethics Training	306
Diversity Training	307
Small Business Application	308
SUMMARY	308
KEY TERMS	309
DISCUSSION QUESTIONS	309

INTERNET EXERCISE   310

HRM EXPERIENCE: TRAINING AND LEARNING
PRINCIPLES   310

BIZFLIX EXERCISES: *BACKDRAFT*: PROBIE'S
TRAINING EXPERIENCES   311

CASE STUDY 1: SERVICE AT THE CHATEAU
WHISTLER   311

CASE STUDY 2: PEOPLE DEVELOPMENT
STRATEGIES AT CREDIT UNION CENTRAL
OF SASKATCHEWAN   313

CASE STUDY 3: ORIENTATION AT BELL CANADA   314

CAREER COUNSEL   315

NOTES AND REFERENCES   315

CHAPTER 8   APPRAISING AND IMPROVING PERFORMANCE   321

PERFORMANCE APPRAISAL PROGRAMS   322

The Purposes of Performance Appraisal   323

Why Appraisal Programs Sometimes Fail   324

DEVELOPING AN EFFECTIVE APPRAISAL PROGRAM   326

What Are the Performance Standards?   326

Legal Issues   328

Who Should Appraise Performance?   329

Putting It All Together: 360-Degree Appraisal   332

Reality Check: Canadian Tire 360-Degree Matrix   334

Training Appraisers   336

The Business Case: Rank and Yank   338

PERFORMANCE APPRAISAL METHODS   339

Highlights in HRM 8.1: Supervisor's Checklist for the
Performance Appraisal   340

Trait Methods   340

Highlights in HRM 8.2: Graphic Rating Scale with Provision
for Comments   341

Highlights in HRM 8.3: Example of a Mixed-Standard Scale 342

Behavioural Methods   343

Highlights in HRM 8.4: BARS and BOS Examples   344

Results Methods   345

Highlights in HRM 8.5: Sample Items from Behaviour
Observation Scales   345

Highlights in HRM 8.6: Personal Scorecard 348

Which Performance Appraisal Method to Use? 349

APPRAISAL INTERVIEWS 350

Three Types of Appraisal Interviews 350

Conducting the Appraisal Interview 351

Ethics in HRM: Stretch Goals 354

Improving Performance 355

Small Business Application 357

SUMMARY 358

KEY TERMS 359

DISCUSSION QUESTIONS 359

INTERNET EXERCISE 359

HRM EXPERIENCE: PERFORMANCE DIAGNOSIS 360

BIZFLIX EXERCISES: *SEABISCUIT: GEORGE RIDES SEABISCUIT* 360

CASE STUDY 1: JUST-IN-TIME FEEDBACK 361

CASE STUDY 2: BANK OF MONTREAL'S BALANCED SCORECARD 362

CAREER COUNSEL 362

NOTES AND REFERENCES 363

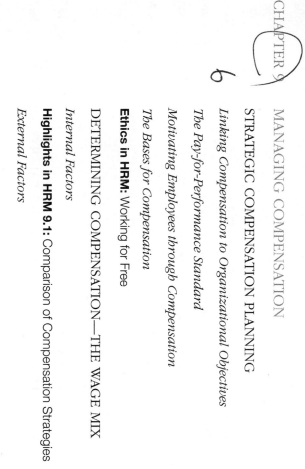

PART 4
IMPLEMENTING COMPENSATION AND SECURITY

CHAPTER 9

6

MANAGING COMPENSATION 369

STRATEGIC COMPENSATION PLANNING 370

Linking Compensation to Organizational Objectives 371

The Pay-for-Performance Standard 372

Motivating Employees through Compensation 372

The Bases for Compensation 375

Ethics in HRM: Working for Free 375

DETERMINING COMPENSATION—THE WAGE MIX 376

Internal Factors 376

Highlights in HRM 9.1: Comparison of Compensation Strategies 377

External Factors 379

The Business Case: Labour Market Rates — 379

JOB EVALUATION SYSTEMS — 381

Job Ranking System — 381

Job Classification System — 381

Point System — 382

Highlights in HRM 9.2: Point Values for Job Factors of the American Association of Industrial Management — 383

Highlights in HRM 9.3: Description of Education Factor and Degrees of the American Association of Industrial Management — 383

Work Valuation — 384

Job Evaluation for Management Positions — 384

THE COMPENSATION STRUCTURE — 385

Wage and Salary Surveys — 385

Highlights in HRM 9.4: Compensation Surveys for HR Professionals — 386

The Wage Curve — 387

Pay Grades — 388

Rate Ranges — 389

Competence-Based Pay — 390

GOVERNMENT REGULATION OF COMPENSATION — 391

The Canada Labour Code — 391

Employment Standards Acts — 392

Other Legislation — 392

SIGNIFICANT COMPENSATION ISSUES — 392

Equal Pay for Work of Equal Value — 392

Measuring Comparability — 392

Reality Check: Pay Equity — 393

The Business Case: Cashing Out — 394

The Issue of Wage-Rate Compression — 395

Small Business Application — 395

SUMMARY — 396

KEY TERMS — 397

DISCUSSION QUESTIONS — 397

INTERNET EXERCISE — 397

HRM EXPERIENCE: WHY THIS SALARY? — 397

BIZFLIX EXERCISES: *THE WEDDING DATE:*
HOW MUCH IS NICK MERCER'S JOB WORTH?   398

CASE STUDY 1: PAY DECISIONS AT
PERFORMANCE SPORTS   399

CASE STUDY 2: CANADA POST   400

CAREER COUNSEL   401

NOTES AND REFERENCES   402

CHAPTER 10 3

PAY-FOR-PERFORMANCE: INCENTIVE REWARDS   405

STRATEGIC REASONS FOR INCENTIVE PLANS   406

Incentive Plans as Links to Organizational Objectives   407

REQUIREMENTS FOR A SUCCESSFUL
INCENTIVE PLAN   408

Setting Performance Measures   409

Highlights in HRM 10.1: Setting Performance
Measures—The Keys   409

Administering Incentive Plans   410

INDIVIDUAL INCENTIVE PLANS   410

Piecework   410

Standard Hour Plan   412

Bonuses   412

Merit Pay   412

Lump-Sum Merit Pay   413

Incentive Awards and Recognition   414

Highlights in HRM 10.2: Customize Your Noncash
Incentive Awards   414

Sales Incentives   415

Ethics in HRM: Counter-Productive Compensation   415

INCENTIVES FOR PROFESSIONAL EMPLOYEES   417

The Executive Pay Package   417

Executive Compensation: Ethics and Accountability   420

Highlights in HRM 10.3: The "Sweetness" of Executive Perks   421

GROUP INCENTIVE PLANS   421

Team Compensation   421

Highlights in HRM 10.4: Lessons Learned: Designing
Effective Team Incentives   423

Gainsharing Incentive Plans   423

ENTERPRISE INCENTIVE PLANS   425

Profit-Sharing Plans   426

Employee Stock Option Plans   426

Highlights in HRM 10.5: Employee Stock Option Plans   427

Reality Check: Pay-for-Performance at Lombard Canada   428

Employee Stock Ownership Plans (ESOPs)   429

The Business Case: Organizational Benefits of Incentive Plans   430

Small Business Application   430

SUMMARY   431

KEY TERMS   432

DISCUSSION QUESTIONS   432

INTERNET EXERCISE   432

HRM EXPERIENCE: AWARDING SALARY INCREASES   433

BIZFLIX EXERCISES: *SCENT OF A WOMAN*: FREDDIE
BISCO'S INCENTIVES   433

CASE STUDY 1: OUT BUT RICH AT HOME DEPOT   434

CASE STUDY 2: TEAM-BASED INCENTIVE REWARDS:
IT'S NOT ALL ROSES   434

CAREER COUNSEL   435

NOTES AND REFERENCES   435

CHAPTER 11   EMPLOYEE BENEFITS   439

EMPLOYEE BENEFITS PROGRAMS   440

HRIS and Employee Benefits   440

Requirements for a Sound Benefits Program   441

Communicating Employee Benefits Information   443

Highlights in HRM 11.1: Crafting an Effective Benefits
Communication Program   444

CONCERNS OF MANAGEMENT   446

The Business Case: Managing the Costs of Benefits   446

Reality Check: Benefits Planning: From Entitlement
to Self-Responsibility   447

EMPLOYEE BENEFITS REQUIRED BY LAW   448

Canada and Quebec Pension Plans (CPP/QPP)   448

Ethics in HRM: Benefits Fraud   449

Employment Insurance (EI)   449

Workers' Compensation Insurance 450

Provincial Hospital and Medical Services 451

DISCRETIONARY MAJOR EMPLOYEE BENEFITS 452

Health Care Benefits 452

Highlights in HRM 11.2: A Team Approach to Cost Containment 453

Payment for Time Not Worked 454

Life Insurance 455

Retirement Programs 455

Pension Plans 456

Highlights in HRM 11.3: Whose Money Is It? 458

EMPLOYEE SERVICES: CREATING A WORK–LIFE SETTING 459

Creating a Family-Friendly Setting 459

Employee Assistance Programs 459

Highlights in HRM 11.4: Yukon Government's Public Service Commission 460

Counselling Services 460

Child and Elder Care 460

Highlights in HRM 11.5: CIBC Cares 461

Other Services 462

Highlights in HRM 11.6: Perks at Intuit 462

Small Business Application 464

SUMMARY 464

KEY TERMS 465

DISCUSSION QUESTIONS 465

INTERNET EXERCISE 466

HRM EXPERIENCE: UNDERSTANDING EMPLOYER BENEFIT PROGRAMS 466

BIZFLIX EXERCISES: ERIN BROCKOVICH: ERIN GETS BENEFITS, WITH DENTAL 466

CASE STUDY 1: EVALUATE THE WORK–LIFE CLIMATE IN YOUR COMPANY 467

CASE STUDY 2: TRUE NORTH'S FAMILY-FRIENDLY BENEFITS: AN UNEXPECTED BACKLASH 468

CAREER COUNSEL 469

NOTES AND REFERENCES 469

CHAPTER 12

SAFETY AND HEALTH

SAFETY AND HEALTH: IT'S THE LAW 473

Acts and Regulations 474

Duties and Responsibilities 475

Highlights in HRM 12.1: Health and Safety Checklist for New Employees 475

Highlights in HRM 12.2: A World Leader in H&S 477

Penalties for Employer Noncompliance 478

WORKERS' COMPENSATION 479

CREATING A SAFE WORK ENVIRONMENT 480

Promoting Safety Awareness 480

Enforcing Safety Rules 481

Investigating and Recording Accidents 482

Ethics in HRM: Bury the Record 483

Reality Check: CN Centre for Occupational Health and Safety 483

CONTROLLING AND ELIMINATING HEALTH HAZARDS 484

Health Hazards and Issues 485

Highlights in HRM 12.3: Are You Ready? 485

Workplace Violence 489

Terrorism 490

BUILDING BETTER HEALTH 492

Ensuring Healthful Employees 493

Promoting Workplace Fitness and Health 493

The Business Case: Investing in Employee Health 494

Employee Assistance Programs 494

Highlights in HRM 12.4: Depression in the Workplace 495

MANAGEMENT OF STRESS 496

What Is Stress? 497

Job-Related Stress 497

Coping with Stress 498

Small Business Application 498

SUMMARY 500

KEY TERMS 500

DISCUSSION QUESTIONS 501

INTERNET EXERCISE 502

HRM EXPERIENCE: REDUCING EMPLOYEE STRESS 502

BIZFLIX EXERCISES: *8 MILE*: WORKING AT NORTH DETROIT STAMPING 502

CASE STUDY 1: WORKPLACE SAFETY AND YOUNG WORKERS 503

CASE STUDY 2: RETURN TO WORK: WHAT WORKS? 504

CASE STUDY 3: THE SILENT SAFETY ISSUE 505

CAREER COUNSEL 507

NOTES AND REFERENCES 507

PART 5
ENHANCING EMPLOYEE–MANAGEMENT RELATIONS

CHAPTER 13

4

EMPLOYEE RIGHTS AND DISCIPLINE 511

THE THREE REGIMES OF EMPLOYMENT LAW 512

The Common Law of Employment 512

Statutory Employment Regulation 513

Highlights in HRM 13.1: Take Notice! 514

Collective Bargaining Legislation and Labour Arbitration 514

UNDERSTANDING THE INDIVIDUAL EMPLOYMENT CONTRACT 515

The Business Case: The Danger of Changing a Contract Term Without the Employee's Agreement 516

THE RULES GOVERNING DISMISSAL 516

Dismissal of a Nonunion Employee: Wrongful Dismissal 516

Dismissal of Unionized Employee: Just Cause 518

EMPLOYEE PRIVACY RIGHTS 519

Privacy Issues at the Workplace 519

Highlight in HRM 13.2: Overview of Regimes Governing Dismissals 520

Employee Conduct Outside the Workplace 523

Reality Check: Privacy Issues with New Technologies 524

Ethics in HRM: Supervising or Super-Spying? 525

Highlights in HRM 13.3: The Long Arm of the Employer 526

DISCIPLINARY POLICIES AND PROCEDURES 527

The Results of Inaction   527

Setting Organizational Rules   528

The Hot-Stove Approach to Rule Enforcement   529

Defining Discipline   529

Investigating the Disciplinary Problem   530

Approaches to Disciplinary Action   531

Informing the Employee   533

Highlights in HRM 13.4: Volkswagen Canada's Positive
Discipline Program   534

Alternative Dispute Resolution Procedures   535

MANAGERIAL ETHICS IN EMPLOYEE RELATIONS   538

Small Business Application   539

SUMMARY   539

KEY TERMS   540

DISCUSSION QUESTIONS   540

INTERNET EXERCISE   541

HRM EXPERIENCE: LEARNING ABOUT
EMPLOYEE RIGHTS   541

BIZFLIX EXERCISES: IN GOOD COMPANY: FIRING
AN EMPLOYEE   542

CASE STUDY 1: DISMISSING AN EMPLOYEE FOR
ABSENTEEISM   542

CASE STUDY 2: IMPROVING PERFORMANCE
THROUGH A PROGRESSIVE DISCIPLINE POLICY   543

CAREER COUNSEL   544

NOTES AND REFERENCES   544

CHAPTER 14   THE DYNAMICS OF LABOUR RELATIONS   547

GOVERNMENT REGULATION OF LABOUR RELATIONS   548

The Industrial Relations Disputes and Investigation Act   548

Highlights in HRM 14.1: Test Your Labour Relations Know-How   549

THE LABOUR RELATIONS PROCESS   549

Why Employees Unionize   549

Highlights in HRM 14.2: Homeworkers: Canada's Invisible
Labour Force   551

Organizing Campaigns   552

CONTENTS

Highlights in HRM 14.3: Is a Union Being Organized?   552

Reality Check: Magna's Unique HR Culture   555

How Employees Become Unionized   555

Highlights in HRM 14.4: Unfair Labour Practices   556

Highlights in HRM 14.5: Strategies to Remain Union-Free   556

Contract Negotiation   556

Decertification   556

Impact of Unionization on Managers   557

STRUCTURES, FUNCTIONS, AND LEADERSHIP OF LABOUR UNIONS   558

The Canadian Labour Congress   558

International and National Unions   558

Local Unions   559

Ethics in HRM: Inflation   559

LABOUR RELATIONS IN THE PUBLIC SECTOR   560

Political Nature of the Labour–Management Relationship   561

Strikes in the Public Sector   561

THE BARGAINING PROCESS   562

Preparing for Negotiations   562

Developing Bargaining Strategies and Tactics   563

Interest-Based Bargaining   565

Management and Union Power in Collective Bargaining   565

Highlights in HRM 14.6: Building Trust Through IBB   566

The Business Case: The Benefits of IBB   567

Resolving Bargaining Deadlocks   569

THE COLLECTIVE AGREEMENT   569

The Issue of Management Rights   569

Highlights in HRM 14.7: Items in a Collective Agreement   570

Union Security Agreements   570

ADMINISTRATION OF THE COLLECTIVE AGREEMENT   570

Negotiated Grievance Procedures   571

The Grievance Procedure in Action   571

Rights Arbitration   573

Small Business Application   573

SUMMARY   574

KEY TERMS 575

DISCUSSION QUESTIONS 575

INTERNET EXERCISE 576

HRM EXPERIENCE: LEARN ABOUT UNIONS 576

BIZFLIX EXERCISES: *BREAD & ROSES*: JOIN THE UNION; GET BREAD AND ROSES 576

CASE STUDY 1: UNIONIZATION IN THE SERVICE SECTOR 577

CASE STUDY 2: WALMART STORES IN CANADA 578

CASE STUDY 3: THE NEGOTIATING CLIMATE 579

CAREER COUNSEL 580

NOTES AND REFERENCES 580

Answers to Highlights in HRM 14.1 581

PART 6

EXPANDING HUMAN RESOURCES MANAGEMENT HORIZONS

CHAPTER 15 INTERNATIONAL HUMAN RESOURCES MANAGEMENT 583

MANAGING ACROSS BORDERS 584

How Does the Global Environment Influence Management? 586

Highlights in HRM 15.1: Understanding the Importance of Cultural Differences 588

Ethics in HRM: Bribery Abroad 588

DOMESTIC VS. INTERNATIONAL HRM 589

INTERNATIONAL STAFFING 589

Reality Check: Selecting for Service 590

Recruiting Internationally 592

Highlights in HRM 15.2: Reference Checking 593

Highlights in HRM 15.3: Importing Culture 594

Selecting Employees Internationally 595

Highlights in HRM 15.4: Skills of Expatriate Managers 598

TRAINING AND DEVELOPMENT 599

Content of Training Programs 600

Highlights in HRM 15.5: Stressors and Coping Responses in the Developmental Stages of Expatriate Executives   604

Highlights in HRM 15.6: Repatriation Checklist   606

COMPENSATION   607

Compensation of Host-Country Employees   607

Compensation of Host-Country Managers   609

Compensation of Expatriate Managers   609

PERFORMANCE APPRAISAL   611

Who Should Appraise Performance?   611

Home- vs. Host-Country Evaluations   611

Performance Criteria   612

Providing Feedback   612

The Business Case: The Costs of Employing Expatriates   613

THE LABOUR ENVIRONMENT WORLDWIDE   614

Collective Bargaining in Other Countries   614

International Labour Organizations   615

Labour Participation in Management   615

Small Business Application   616

SUMMARY   617

KEY TERMS   618

DISCUSSION QUESTIONS   618

INTERNET EXERCISE   618

HRM EXPERIENCE: A CANADIAN (EXPATRIATE) IN PARIS   619

BIZFLIX EXERCISES: *MR. BASEBALL:* TOLERANCE OF CULTURAL DIFFERENCES   619

CASE STUDY 1: CULTURAL CONUNDRUM   620

CASE STUDY 2: RECRUITING AND RETAINING INTERNATIONAL EMPLOYEES   621

CAREER COUNSEL   622

NOTES AND REFERENCES   622

CHAPTER 16

CREATING HIGH-PERFORMANCE WORK SYSTEMS

(SEE THE *MANAGING HUMAN RESOURCES* WEBSITE:
HTTP://WWW.BELCOURT6E.NELSON.COM)

EXCALIBUR CASES

629

CASE 1: LE CIRQUE DU SOLEIL: HOW TO MANAGE GROWTH 630

CASE 2: AVON: LEADER AND TRENDSETTER 632

CASE 3: GARDA: A COMPANY ON A WINNING COURSE! 633

CASE 4: AMBULANCE NEW BRUNSWICK 635

CASE 5: LABATT BREWERIES: A HOT SUMMER IN STORE 639

GLOSSARY 642

NAME INDEX 651

ORGANIZATION INDEX 653

SUBJECT INDEX 657

PREFACE

The sixth Canadian edition of *Managing Human Resources* will place your students at the forefront in understanding how organizations can gain sustainable competitive advantage through people. The role of HR managers is no longer limited to service functions such as recruiting and selecting employees. Today, HR managers assume an active role in the strategic planning and decision making at their organizations. Using human resources effectively is critical to the success of any work organization. In this edition of the book, we've made improvements that make these points more strongly.

In the first chapter, we begin by explaining the key challenges to HRM in developing the flexible and skilled workforce needed to compete effectively. Side by side with the competitive challenges, HRM must also address important employee concerns by managing a diverse workforce, recognizing employee rights, and adjusting to new work attitudes. This chapter also discusses the important partnership with line managers and the competencies required of HR management. Then the textbook continues with the introduction, explanation, and discussion of the individual practices and policies that make up HRM. We recognize the manager's changing role and emphasize current issues and real-world problems and the policies and practices of HRM used to meet them.

Although we focus on the HR role of managers, we do not exclude the impact and importance of the HR department's strategic role in developing, coordinating, and enforcing policies and procedures relating to HR functions. Whether the reader becomes a manager, a supervisor, or an HR specialist, or is employed in other areas of the organization, *Managing Human Resources* provides a functional and practical understanding of HR programs to enable readers to see how HR affects all employees, the organization, the community, and the larger society.

Issues of strategy and talent have become such central concerns of HR today that we have reinforced these concepts throughout this edition. The second chapter of the book specifically addresses the issues of HR strategy and planning. Chapter 5 focuses on expanding and managing the talent pool in organizations. The detailed coverage of these topics solidifies *Managing Human Resources* as perhaps the premier text for thought leadership, especially the global talent pool.

Organizations in today's competitive world are discovering that it is *how* the individual HR functions are combined that makes all the difference. Managers typically don't focus on HR issues such as staffing, training, and compensation in isolation from one another. Each of these HR practices is combined into an overall system to enhance employee involvement and productivity. *Managing Human Resources* ends with a final online chapter that focuses on development of high-performance work systems. We outline the various components of the system, including work-flow design, HR practices, management processes, and supporting technologies. We also discuss the strategic processes used to implement high-performance work systems and the outcomes that benefit both the employee and the organization as a whole.

WHAT'S DYNAMIC IN THE SIXTH CANADIAN EDITION

Many new features and much new information are provided in this revision. We introduce overall text improvements that more accurately reflect HRM in today's business world and help the reader understand HRM issues more effectively.

- The sixth Canadian edition reflects the body of knowledge required by students to pass the national knowledge exam, given by the Canadian Council of Human Resource Associations, as one of the steps toward the granting of the HR designation, the CHRP (Certified Human Resources Professional). The lead author, Dr. Monica Belcourt, participated in the development of the standards for the national certification process. This text covers more than 90 percent of the material being tested on the national knowledge exam. As a CHRP herself, Dr. Belcourt is very familiar with the competencies required for the profession and has written the text with these required professional competencies (RPCs) as the foundation for learning about HR.

- **Small Business Application.** New to this edition is the inclusion of a section in each chapter that takes the principles and prescriptions of a functional area, such as recruitment, and demonstrates how these can be applied in a small business, of which there are about 1 million in Canada. This feature was written by Angus Duff, a PhD candidate in Human Resources Management at York University, and a former manager of HR, with extensive experience in small and large businesses.

- **HRM Experience.** We build upon a popular feature in previous editions of *Managing Human Resources* by including many new experiential exercises to explore significant issues in HR. These skill-building exercises will help students gain practical experience when dealing with employee/management concerns such as pay for performance, effective team building, employee benefits, reducing employee stress, employee rights, balancing competitive challenges and employee concerns, customizing HR for different types of human capital, designing selection criteria and methods, and assessing the strategic fit of high-performance work systems (HPWS). Students can work through the new exercises on either an individual or a team basis.

- **Human Resources Information Systems (HRIS).** Throughout the text, we have specifically highlighted the use of HRIS to facilitate the managing of employees and the efficient performance of HR functions. For example, the impact of information technology on HR and the role of HRIS in such areas as compensation, recruitment and selection, training, job analysis, and safety are discussed.

- **Diversity.** Because we believe that diversity issues are an integral part of every HRM activity, updated and expanded coverage is included throughout the text.

- **HRM Strategy.** The increasingly important role HRM plays in strategic planning is covered in Chapter 2. However, elsewhere we also discuss the role of human capital and Six Sigma, HR benchmarking, balanced scorecard and performance diagnosis, global HR strategy, as well as strategic alignment and implementing high-performance work systems.

- **Contemporary employment issues** such as global sourcing, offshoring, alternative work arrangements, temporary workers, and the like are covered throughout the book.

- **Global and international concerns** are covered in great detail. This includes issues such as the World Trade Organization, China, and the impact of globalization of HR; multinationals, joint ventures and the like; and global rights issues such as data protection, rights, and intellectual property. Although these issues have perhaps been peripheral to HRM in the past, they are increasingly seen as front and centre to many organizations.

- A complete and thorough review and update of legislation and court cases governing HRM has been completed by Dr. David Doorey, a professor of employment and labour law at the School of Human Resources Management at York University. Dr. Doorey has a BA and Masters in Industrial Relations from the University of Toronto; a LLM from the London School of Economics and a LLB and PhD from the Osgoode Law School. He practised labour and employment law in British Columbia and Ontario. Check out his blog http://www.yorku.ca/ddoorey/lawblog for current insights into these issues.

- **Comprehensive cases.** Five comprehensive cases are found at the end of the book. This exciting feature includes real cases used in Excalibur, the Canadian University Tournament in Human Resources, whereby university students from across Canada are asked to demonstrate their knowledge of HR to a jury. After students have developed solutions to the problems faced by dynamic companies such as Cirque du Soleil and Avon, the instructor can compare their responses to the one generated by the winning university team, and the answer prepared by an HR professor.

- We have readdressed the important role of compensation in HRM by heightening our discussion of pay for performance, extended health care cost savings, strategic pension planning, and effective employee awards.

- We have expanded discussions of major issues, including

balanced scorecard	performance diagnosis
child and elder care	person–organization fit
competency assessment for training	privacy legislation
conflict resolution techniques	role of human capital
cumulative trauma disorders	safety issues for youth
interest-based bargaining	strategic compensation planning
offshoring and outsourcing	violence and terrorism in the workplace

- Many new Highlights in HRM boxes, Reality Checks, Ethics in HRM, and the Business Case boxes have been added. As a former president of the Human Resources Professionals Association of Ontario, Dr. Monica Belcourt, is very involved in the HR profession, with access to some of the thought leaders in HR in Canada.

- **Internet.** The ever-growing role of the Internet in HR activities is evident throughout the text. A few examples include online recruiting and online recruitment in Chapter 5; web-based training and e-learning in Chapter 7; and online 360-degree performance appraisal in Chapter 8.

- Most chapters have at least one new end-of-chapter case study highlighting chapter content. These cases have been selected to provide students with both current and practical HR problems and issues.

- **Ancillaries.** A new NETA Guide to Classroom Engagement and a NETA test bank play a strategic role in the Integrated Learning System. A new set of PowerPoint presentation slides makes teaching and preparation easier and more convenient. For more on the ancillaries, see page xxxvii.

FEATURES OF THE BOOK

Use of the Integrated Learning System continues for the sixth edition and ancillaries. This integrated structure creates a comprehensive teaching and testing system. Designed to facilitate understanding and retention of the material presented, each chapter contains the following pedagogical features:

- **Learning outcomes** listed at the beginning of each chapter provide the basis for the Integrated Learning System. Icons that identify the learning outcomes appear throughout the text and all ancillaries.

- **Highlights in HRM** is a popular boxed feature that provides real-world examples of how organizations perform HR functions. These popular boxed features are introduced in the text discussion and illustrate how a concept is actually used in the workplace.

- **Reality Check** presents an interview with a Canadian expert in the field, illustrating how the material in the chapter is used in the real world.

- **Ethics in HRM** provokes debate and discussion among students, as they struggle with the often grey areas of human resources management, such as drug testing of employees and electronic surveillance of employees at work. Following the Enron scandal and scandals closer to home, Canadians are preoccupied with the ethics of those working in organizations.

- **The Business Case** features the business or financial implications of the adoption of HR practices. The Business Case will help students build the skills necessary to recommend HR practices and projects, based on the projected costs and benefits, to senior management.

- **Small Business Application** provides information about how the concepts in the chapter can be applied to a small business.

- **Career Counsel** on the *Managing Human Resources* website (http://www.belcourt6e.nelson.com) provides a dynamic link to the Internet, enabling students to relate chapter content to job searching and career development. The Career Counsel exercises allow students to develop a career plan.

- **The Internet** is referenced in all chapters, with new government, research, and business Internet links and addresses.

- **Key terms** appear in boldface and are defined in margin notes next to the text discussion. The key terms are also listed at the end of the chapter and appear in the glossary at the end of the text.

- **Figures**, with an abundance of graphic materials and flowcharts, provide a visual, dynamic presentation of concepts and HR activities. All figures are systematically referenced in the text discussion.

- **Summary** includes a paragraph or two for each learning outcome, providing a brief and focused review of the chapter.

- **Discussion questions** following the chapter summary offer an opportunity to focus on each of the learning objectives in the chapter and to stimulate critical thinking. Many of these questions allow for group analysis and class discussion.

- **Internet exercise** requires the use of the content available on the Internet in order to develop a solution.

- **HRM Experience**, an experiential activity (described earlier), is included in each chapter.

- **BizFlix** is a feature that encourages students to see the HR issues and content in the world around them. BizFlix are short film clips taken from popular movies that provide real-world examples of HR in action.

- **Two or more case studies** per chapter present current HRM issues in real-life settings that allow for student consideration and critical analysis.

- **Chapter 16, Creating High-Performance Work Systems**, and all Career Counsels, appear on the Internet at the *Managing Human Resources* website (http://www.belcourt6e.nelson.com). The Career Counsel sections help students with job search strategies and value assessment and salary negotiation tactics.

- **Excalibur case.** Five longer cases are provided at the end of the main text. These cases use material covered in more than one chapter and an opportunity to integrate principles to solve real organizational problems.

ANCILLARY TEACHING AND LEARNING MATERIALS

For Students

- **Online Study Guide to Accompany *Managing Human Resources*.** In partnership with Captus Press, Nelson is pleased to offer an online study guide prepared by Dr. Monica Belcourt (to access, visit http://www.belcourt6e.nelson.com). Complete with chapter summaries, multiple-choice questions, short-answer questions, and progress checks, this supplement will enhance your learning experience. Equally important, the study guide provides the opportunity to practise taking multiple-choice tests in preparation for the National Knowledge Examination, given by the Canadian Council of Human Resource Associations (CCHRA), a first step in becoming a CHRP (Certified Human Resource Professional).

- **Internet course.** For students seeking extra help, a full online HRM course is available from Captus Press. Supplement classroom teaching by accessing the Internet server and listening to lectures given by Dr. Monica Belcourt. You can then scroll to areas of interest and access necessary information. Please contact Captus Press directly for information on the cost of these options (http://www.captus.com).

- **InfoTrac® College Edition.** With InfoTrac, students can receive anytime, anywhere online access to a database of full-text articles from hundreds of popular and scholarly periodicals, such as *Canadian Business*, *Canadian Business Review*, *BusinessWeek*, *Canadian Labour*, *HR Magazine*, and *HR Professional*, among others. Students can use its fast and easy search tools to find relevant news and analytical information among the tens of thousands of articles in the database—updated daily and going back as far as four years—all at a single website. InfoTrac is a great way to expose students to online research techniques, with the security that the content is academically based and reliable. An InfoTrac College Edition subscription card is packaged free with all new copies of *Managing Human Resources*.

- **Website.** A comprehensive website includes practice quizzes, chapter web links, study tips, and information on degrees and careers in human resource management (http://www.belcourt6e.nelson.com).

- **Online exam prep for National Knowledge Exam.** The Canadian Council of Human Resources Associations (CCHRA) offers an online preparation course for the National Knowledge Exam, the first exam leading to the designation of CHRP (Certified Human Resource Professional). The course includes a diagnostic test that assesses knowledge of the Required Professional Capabilities (RPCs) and links to appropriate content in this text and others. There are also three practice exams, online multimedia lectures, and quizzes. For more information, contact, the CCHRA website (http://www.cchra-ccarh.ca), or Captus Press (http://webclients.captus.com/cchra/).

FOR INSTRUCTORS

NETA Products

Nelson Education
Testing Advantage

The **Nelson Education Teaching Advantage (NETA)** program is designed to ensure that instructors and students have access to research-based resources that enable the success of Canadian students and educators.

Engagement: NETA Guide to Classroom Engagement

The *NETA Guide to Classroom Engagement to accompany Managing Human Resources*, Sixth Canadian Edition, includes a range of activities that give instructors a practical, user-friendly way to incorporate interactive learning activities in both large and small classrooms. The *Guide* is focused on four core principles: student-centred learning, deep learning, active learning, and creating positive classroom environments. All of these principles are based on decades of research into what helps students learn best and are designed to foster classroom engagement. Each *NETA Guide* includes a section outlining the research underlying these principles, which will help you create engaging classrooms. The *Guide* was written by Dr. Roger Fisher and created in partnership with an interdisciplinary board of scholars of teaching and learning. All *NETA Guide* authors have been trained in the principles underlying the program. The *NETA Guide to Classroom Engagement to accompany Managing Human Resources*, Sixth Canadian Edition, was authored by Natasha Koziol, University of Western Ontario and contains the rich learning activities, as well as updates to the instructor's manual, including learning outcomes that anchor the integrated learning system, detailed lecture outlines, and answers to the end-of-chapter material.

Editorial advisory board:

Norman Althouse, Haskayne School of Business, University of Calgary

Scott Follows, Manning School of Business Administration, Acadia University

Glen Loppnow, Department of Chemistry, University of Alberta

Tanya Noel, Department of Biology, York University

Gary Poole, Director, Centre for Teaching and Academic Growth and School of Population and Public Health, University of British Columbia

Dan Pratt, Department of Educational Studies, University of British Columbia

Brenda Chant-Smith, Department of Psychology, Trent University

Assessment: NETA Test Bank

In most post-secondary courses, a large percentage of student assessment is based on multiple-choice testing. Many instructors use multiple-choice reluctantly, believing that it is a methodology best used for testing what a student *remembers* rather than what she or he has *learned.* Nelson Education Ltd. understands that a good quality multiple-choice test bank can provide the means to measure *higher-level thinking* skills as well as recall. Recognizing the importance of multiple-choice testing in today's classroom, we have created the Nelson Education Teaching Advantage program to ensure the value of our high quality test banks. The testing component of our NETA program was created in partnership with David DiBattista, a 3M National Teaching Fellow, professor of psychology at Brock University, and researcher in the area of multiple-choice testing. NETA for test banks ensures that subject-matter experts who author test banks have had training in two areas: avoiding common errors in test construction, and developing multiple-choice test questions that "get beyond remembering" to assess higher-level thinking. All NETA test banks include David DiBattista's guide for instructors, "Multiple Choice Tests: Getting Beyond Remembering." This guide has been designed to assist you in using Nelson test banks to achieve your desired outcomes in your course. See the Instructor's Resource CD button "NETA Guidelines" for this valuable resource. The *NETA Test Bank to accompany Managing Human Resources*, Sixth Canadian Edition, was authored by Professors Parbudyal Singh and Mary Jo Ducharme, Professors of HRM at the School of HRM at York University.

- **Computerized NETA Test Bank in ExamView®.** The computerized testing software contains all the questions from the test bank and allows the instructor to edit, add, delete, or randomly mix questions for customized tests.
- **PowerPoint® Presentation Slides.** Created by Dr. Monica Belcourt and Amina Malik, a doctoral candidate in HRM at York University, specifically for the new edition, these presentation slides will add colour and interest to lectures.

- **Instructor's Resource CD (ISBN 0-17-647868-X).** The Instructor's Manual, Test Bank, Computerized Test Bank, and PowerPoint slides are provided on a single CD-ROM.

- **Real to Reel DVD Package (ISBN 0-324-59264-7).** The video package consists of two separate sets of DVDs:

  – **BizFlix DVD.** BizFlix are short film clips taken from popular Hollywood movies that provide real-world examples of the human resource management concepts students are learning. End-of-chapter BizFlix exercises in the text stimulate students to see how the filmed scenarios apply to chapter topics.

  – **Workplace DVD.** This collection features both small and large companies with innovative HR practices, many of which have been recognized for their excellence in HR practices.

- *JoinIn*™ **on TurningPoint®.** Transform any lecture into a truly interactive student experience with *JoinIn*. Combined with your choice of several leading keypad systems, *JoinIn* turns your ordinary PowerPoint® application into powerful audience response software. With just a click on a handheld device, your students can respond to multiple-choice questions, short polls, interactive exercises, and peer review questions. You can take attendance, check student comprehension of difficult concepts, collect student demographics to better assess student needs, and even administer quizzes without collecting papers or grading. In addition, we provide interactive text-specific slide sets that you can modify and merge with any existing PowerPoint lecture slides for a seamless classroom presentation. This interactive tool is available to qualified college and university adopters.

- **Website.** A comprehensive website includes practice quizzes, chapter web links, study tips, and information on degrees and careers in human resource management. We have also included a link for instructors that contains downloadable ancillaries and supplementary cases and solutions. The website can be found at http://www.belcourt6e.nelson.com.

- **Nelson ePacks.** Nelson provides cartridge content for this title that's compatible for all versions of BlackBoard (and the former WebCt). Visit the Instructor's Resource area at http://www.belcourt6e.nelson.com for details.

ACKNOWLEDGMENTS FOR THE SIXTH CANADIAN EDITION

In preparing the manuscript for this edition, we have drawn on not only the current literature but also the current practices of organizations that furnished information relating to their HR programs. We are indebted to the leaders in the field who have influenced us through their writings and personal associations. We have also been aided by our present and former students, by our colleagues at the Human Resources Professionals Association of Ontario with whom we have been associated, by HR managers, and by our academic colleagues. I am particularly appreciative of the review of legislation and court cases by Dr. David Doorey. Dr. Doorey also revised Chapter 13, Employee Rights and Discipline. Because of his feedback and contribution, the reader is assured that the "legal content" is accurate and current.

As we will see, while the human resources management principles outlined in each chapter apply to both large and small organizations, the delivery of human resources practices in small organizations are largely by managers and business owners rather than HR practitioners. The Small Business Application feature was written by Angus Duff, a PhD candidate in Human Resources Management at York University, and a former human resources manager. As an HR practitioner, Mr. Duff has provided HR support to organizations as small as 25 employees, and as large as 20,000. Using the material discussed in each chapter, Angus outlined how it could be used in a small business, of which there are over 1 million in Canada. Small business represents nearly 50 percent of all private-sector jobs and we estimate that managers in small businesses are managing over 5 million employees, without the assistance of a HR generalist. Thus, this feature is extremely useful for this segment.

We would like to express our appreciation to the following reviewers who have helped shape the text:

Julie Aitken Schermer, University of Western Ontario
Gordon Barnard, Durham College
Kathleen Boies, Concordia University
George Broderick, Kwantlen Polytechnic University
Stéphane Brutus, Concordia University
Julie Bulmash, George Brown College
Joan Condie, Sheridan College
Tim DeGroot, McMaster University
Cathy Fitzgerald, Okanagan College
Gary Gannon, Durham College
Lisa Guglielmi, Seneca College
Robert Isaac, University of Calgary
Don MacCormac, University of PEI
Colleen Marshall, Confederation College
Teal McAteer, McMaster University
Ty Menna, University of Lethbridge
Marc Mentzer, University of Saskatchewan
Ed Ng, Trent University
Jessica Nicholson, McMaster University
Robert Oppenheimer, Concordia University
Carolin Rekar-Munro, Durham College
Maria Rotundo, University of Toronto
Sudhir Saha, Memorial University
Aaron Schat, McMaster University
Basu Sharma, University of New Brunswick
Pat Sniderman, Ryerson Polytechnic University
Indira Somwaru, Seneca College
Trudy Temple, University College of the Fraser Valley
Krista Uggerslev, University of Manitoba
Chantal Westgate, McGill University
Diane White, Seneca College
Deborah Zinni, Brock University

We appreciate the efforts of the team at Nelson who helped to develop and produce this text. They include Jackie Wood, Executive Editor; Imoinda Romain, Senior Content Production Manager; and Karen Rolfe, copy editor; as well as the wonderful sales representatives who have enthusiastically supported the book. The most important person in the production of a text would have to be Developmental Editor Karina Hope, who managed the entire process professionally and facilitated the production of an excellent text. Thank you, Karina.

Our greatest indebtedness is to our spouses—Michael Belcourt, D. Comm, Ronnie Bohlander, and Marybeth Snell—who have contributed in so many ways to this book. They are always sources of invaluable guidance and assistance. Furthermore, by their continued enthusiasm and support, they have made the process a more pleasant and rewarding experience. We are most grateful to them for their many contributions to this publication, to our lives, and to our families.

ABOUT THE AUTHORS

MONICA BELCOURT

Monica Belcourt is the founding Director of the School of Human Resources Management at York University. Additionally, she is a full Professor, Human Resources Management, and founding Director of the Graduate Program in HRM at the Atkinson Faculty of Liberal and Professional Studies, York University. She has an extensive and varied background in human resources management. After receiving a B.A. in psychology from the University of Manitoba, she joined the Public Service Commission as a recruitment and selection specialist. During her tenure with the federal government, she worked in training, HRM research, job analysis, and HR planning.

Dr. Belcourt alternated working in HRM with graduate school, obtaining an M.A. in psychology from York University, an M.Ed. in adult education from the University of Ottawa, and a Ph.D. in management from York University. She also holds the designation of Certified Human Resource Professional (CHRP). Her research is grounded in the experience she gained as Director of Personnel for the 63,000 employees at CP Rail; as Director of Employee Development, National Film Board; and as a functional HR specialist for the federal government. She has taught HRM at Concordia University, Université du Québec à Montréal, McGill University, and York University, where she founded and managed the largest undergraduate program in HRM in Canada. She created Canada's first degrees in human resources management: B.HRM, B.HRM (honours), and a Master's in HRM. A full description of these degrees can be found at http://www.yorku.ca/laps/shrm.

Dr. Belcourt is Director of the International Alliance for Human Resources Research (IAHRR), which is a catalyst for the discovery, dissemination, and application of new knowledge about HRM. The IAHRR programs are described at http://www.yorku.ca/hrresall. Her research interests focus on strategic HRM, and she has published more than 100 articles, several of which received best paper awards. A practitioner publication is *Making Government the Best Place to Work: Building Commitment*, published by the Institute of Public Administration of Canada. Dr. Belcourt is Series Editor for the Nelson Series in Human Resources Management: *Performance Management through Training and Development; Occupational Health and Safety; Human Resources Management Systems; Recruitment and Selection in Canada; Compensation in Canada; Strategic Human Resources Planning; Research, Measurement and Evaluation in HRM; The Canadian Labour Market; International Human Resources Management: A Canadian Perspective and Industrial Relations in Canada.*

Active in many professional associations and not-for-profit organizations, Dr. Belcourt was the President of the Human Resources Professionals Association of Ontario, served on the national committee for HR certification, and was a board member of CIBC Insurance and the Toronto French School. She is a frequent commentator on HRM issues for Workopolis, CTV, *Canada AM*, CBC, *The Globe and Mail*, *Canadian HR Reporter*, and other media. She has been recognized as a champion of HR by *Canadian HR Reporter*. In 2009, the Human Resources Professional Association honoured Dr. Belcourt with the award of Right Management HR Academic of the Year—an award given for outstanding contributions to the HR profession and for thoughtful leadership.

GEORGE BOHLANDER

George Bohlander is Professor Emeritus of Management at Arizona State University (ASU). He received his MBA from the University of Southern California and his PhD from the University of California at Los Angeles. His areas of expertise include employment law, compensation work teams, public policy, and labour relations. He has received the Outstanding Undergraduate Teaching Excellence Award presented by the College of Business at ASU and also received the prestigious ASU Parents Association Professorship for his contributions to students and teaching.

Dr. Bohlander is an active researcher and author. He has published over 50 articles and monographs in professional and practitioner journals such as *National Productivity Review*, *HR Magazine*, *Labor Law Journal*, *The Journal of Collective Bargaining in the Public Sector*, and others. Dr. Bohlander continues to be a consultant to public and private organizations including the U.S. Postal Service, BFGoodrich, McDonnell Douglas, Banner Health Services, and Del Webb. He is also an active labour arbitrator.

SCOTT SNELL

Scott Snell is Professor of Business Administration at the University of Virginia's Darden Graduate School of Business. He teaches in the Leadership and Organization area and specializes in strategic human resource management. In recent years he has worked with companies such as American Express, AstraZeneca, CIGNA, Deutsche Telekom, Heineken, Shell, and the World Bank to address the alignment of human resource issues and strategic management. Professor Snell is the author of over 50 publications in professional journals and edited texts and has co-authored four books: *Managing Human Resources*; *Management: Leading and Collaborating in a Competitive World*; *M: Management*; and *Managing People and Knowledge in Professional Service Firms*. He has served on the boards of the Society for Human Resource Management Foundation, the Academy of Management's Human Resource Division, the *Human Resource Management Journal*, the *Academy of Management Journal*, and the *Academy of Management Review*.

Prior to joining the Darden faculty in 2007, Dr. Snell was Professor and Director of Executive Education at Cornell University's Center for Advanced Human Resource Studies and Professor of Management in the Smeal College of Business at Pennsylvania State University. He received a BA in Psychology from Miami University, as well as MBA and PhD degrees in Business Administration from Michigan State University. Originally from Lodi, Ohio, he now lives in Charlottesville, Virginia, with his wife and three children.

CHAPTER 1

The World of Human Resources Management

After studying this chapter, you should be able to

[OUTCOME] 1 Identify how firms gain a sustainable competitive advantage through people.

[OUTCOME] 2 Explain how globalization is influencing human resources management.

[OUTCOME] 3 Describe the impact of information technology on managing people.

[OUTCOME] 4 Identify the importance of change management.

[OUTCOME] 5 Describe HR's role in developing intellectual capital.

[OUTCOME] 6 Explain how TQM, Six Sigma, and reengineering affect HR systems.

[OUTCOME] 7 Discuss how cost pressures affect HR policies.

[OUTCOME] 8 Discuss the primary demographic and employee concerns pertaining to HRM.

[OUTCOME] 9 Provide examples of the roles and competencies of today's HR managers.

There's an old joke that goes . . .

The organization of the future will be so technologically advanced that it will be run by just one person and a dog. The person will be there to feed the dog, and the dog will be there to make sure that the person doesn't touch anything.

In the past, observers feared that machines might one day eliminate the need for people at work. In reality, just the opposite has occurred; people are more important in today's organizations than ever before. As Ed Gubman, author of *The Talent Solution*, points out, "In many fast-growing economies, it may be easier to access money and technology than good people." Competitive advantage belongs to companies that know how to attract, select, deploy, and develop talent.[1]

We use a lot of words to describe how important people are to organizations. The terms *human resources, human capital, intellectual assets,* and *talent management* imply that it is people who drive the performance of their organizations (along with other resources such as money, materials, and information). Successful organizations are particularly adept at bringing together different kinds of people to achieve a common purpose. This is the essence of **human resources management (HRM)**.

human resources management (HRM)

The process of managing human talent to achieve an organization's objectives

WHY STUDY HUMAN RESOURCES MANAGEMENT?

OUTCOME 1

As you embark on this course, you may be wondering how the topic of human resources management relates to your interests and career aspirations. The answer to the question "Why study HRM?" is pretty much the same regardless of whether you plan on working in a HR department or not. Staffing the organization, designing jobs and teams, developing skillful employees, identifying approaches for improving their performance, and rewarding employee successes—all typically labelled HRM issues—are as relevant to line managers as they are to managers in the HR department. See Highlights in HRM 1.1 for a day in the life of an HR professional.

To work with people effectively, we have to understand human behaviour, and we have to be knowledgeable about the various systems and practices available to help us build a skilled and motivated workforce. At the same time, we have to be aware of economic, technological, social, legal, and global issues that either facilitate or constrain our efforts to achieve organizational goals.[2] Because employee skills, knowledge, and abilities are among the most distinctive and renewable resources on which a company can draw, their strategic management is more important than ever. As Thomas J. Watson, the founder of IBM, said, "You can get capital and erect buildings, but it takes people to build a business."[3]

While "competing through people" may be a theme for human resources management, the idea remains only a framework for action. On a day-to-day basis, managers focus on specific challenges and issues that pertain to human resources. Figure 1.1 provides an overall framework for human resources management. From this figure, we can see that HR managers have to help blend many aspects of management; at this point, we will simply classify them as either "competitive challenges" or "employee concerns." By balancing sometimes competing demands, HR personnel help firms get the most from their employees by providing a work environment that meets employees' short-term and long-term needs. We will use this framework as a basis for our discussion throughout the rest of this chapter.

Highlights in **HRM** 1.1

A Day in the Life of an HR Generalist

Deena Durack is an HR generalist. Responsible for 15 manager groups and 1,200 employees at a local hospital, Deena's days are filled with recruitment; new hire documentation; benefits administration; collective agreement interpretation; payroll changes; educational loans; redeployment; management, employee, and retirement counselling; job fairs; and special projects. Beginning with recruitment, Deena develops job postings for available positions that are based on the job descriptions and are posted internally or externally on the hospital's website, sent to professional associations, and sometimes, but not often, sent to various newspapers. Around 25 résumés arrive every day that must be screened for qualifications; knowledge, skills and abilities (KSAs); and work history. The résumés that pass are sent to the hiring manager and she arranges interviews. Half of Deena's day is then spent on developing interview questions about the job and creating a scoring guide on which to evaluate the candidates. A salary range will be given beforehand to the hiring manager that is based on either market data from a salary survey or on the recommendation of the compensation analyst. If the candidate is successful, references will be checked and Deena will write a letter of offer that includes benefits information.

Deena also advises employees about their benefits. As part of her labour relations duties, Deena will give advice on the interpretation of the collective agreement with respect to the rights and duties of employees and managers. Here, she will handle general questions on scheduling hours of work and attendance issues. Scheduling issues can be anything from whether an employee should be paid premiums for working shifts or whether the manager has to pay premiums

on certain weekends. Attendance support questions are varied. For example, Deena may run a report for a manager on number of absences. Patterns of absences are analyzed to determine if the absenteeism is to be considered punitive or if there are valid reasons for absenteeism. If an employee is missing many hours, the manager will speak with that individual to determine if there is a way she or he can help through scheduling changes or, if necessary, arranging for the individual to contact the Employee Assistance Program (EAP) if there are problems outside work. This is all done with the coordination of the HR manager and the departmental manager.

As another part of her job as a generalist, Deena goes to job fairs to promote the organization and market positions that are currently available. She sits on the Corporate Events Committee where she organizes and chairs the staff and children's holiday parties as well as the company picnic. She is also a member of the Staff Recognition Committee where discussions and decisions are made on yearly service awards and on the types of gifts to be purchased for employees who are retiring.

Special projects can also come up for a generalist. Deena developed a new manager's manual to orient managers to HR processes and sat on the bargaining committee for a new collective agreement. Her busy day may also include creating voluntary exit packages when the hospital is in a redeployment process and meeting with employees to advise them on their rights concerning their severance packages. And then there is the human side of being a generalist. Daily, a manager or an employee will come to her office just to talk. As a generalist she will sit and listen and may offer advice.

COMPETITIVE CHALLENGES AND HUMAN RESOURCES MANAGEMENT

Professional organizations such as the Human Resources Professionals Association (HRPA) and the Human Resource Planning Society (HRPS) conduct ongoing studies of the most pressing competitive issues facing firms. By seeking the input of chief executives and HR managers, these organizations keep a finger on the pulse of

FIGURE **1.1**

Overall Framework for Human Resources Management

COMPETITIVE CHALLENGES	HUMAN RESOURCES	EMPLOYEE CONCERNS
• Globalization	• Planning	• Background diversity
• Technology	• Recruitment	• Age distribution
• Managing change	• Staffing	• Gender issues
• Human capital	• Job design	• Job security
• Responsiveness	• Training/development	• Educational levels
• Cost containment	• Appraisal	• Employee rights
	• Communications	• Privacy issues
	• Compensation	• Work attitudes
	• Benefits	• Family concerns
	• Labour relations	

major trends. For the past decade or so, there has been a constant theme around the following issues:

- Competing, recruiting, and staffing globally
- Embracing new technology
- Managing change
- Managing talent, or human capital
- Responding to the market
- Containing costs

These trends extend beyond "people issues" per se, but they all focus on the need to develop a skilled and flexible workforce in order to compete in the 21st century.

CHALLENGE 1: COMPETING, RECRUITING, AND STAFFING GLOBALLY

To grow and prosper today, companies are aware that they will likely to have to seek business opportunities in global markets. Competition—and cooperation—with foreign companies has become an important focal point for business. China could surpass the United States to become the largest economy in the world by 2041, and India could be the third largest. These countries can produce goods and provide services at a fraction of the cost of Canadian workers. As the vice-president and chief economist of the Conference Board of Canada stated, "There are billions of people in Asia who want to get to where we are, and they're prepared to work longer and harder. So we have to work smarter."[4]

The Impact of Globalization

[OUTCOME 2]

By partnering with firms in other regions of the world and using information technologies to coordinate distant parts of their businesses, companies have shown that they can offer customers "anything, anytime, anywhere" around the world. Even well-known products are losing or have lost their national identities. BMW has traditionally been a German brand, but now the automaker builds cars in South Carolina.[5] Two of Canada's mining giants were bought by a Swiss firm and a Brazilian firm. Canadian companies such as Thomson, which bought Reuters, and TD Bank, which bought Bank of America, illustrate the extent of global ownership.[6]

The manufacturing of cars in Canada provides a good example of the impact of globalization. There is no such thing as a Canadian car. Most parts—up to 85 percent—of cars manufactured in Canada come from other countries. On the other hand, Canadian content represents about 10 percent for cars assembled outside Canada.[7] A recent study suggests that about 37 percent of Canada's workforce will be affected by globalization, with knowledge workers and manufacturing jobs taking the brunt of the impact of the competition by lower-wage countries.[8]

Numerous free-trade agreements forged between nations in the last half century have helped quicken the pace of globalization. The first major trade agreement of the 20th century was made in 1948, following World War II. Called the General Agreement on Tariffs and Trade (GATT), it established rules and guidelines for global commerce between nations and groups of nations. Since GATT began, world trade has increased more than twenty-sevenfold in terms of volume. This is three times faster than the world's overall output has grown during the same period. GATT paved the way for the formation of the European Union in 1986; the North American Free Trade Agreement (NAFTA) in 1994, encompassing the United States, Canada, and Mexico; and the Asia-Pacific Economic Cooperation (APEC) in 1989, which loosened trade restrictions among Pacific Rim countries. The World Trade Organization (WTO), headquartered in Lausanne, Switzerland, now has more than 150 member countries, and new free-trade agreements seem to be forged annually.[9]

Globalization and Corporate Social Responsibility

Even though globalization has led to a great improvement in people's living standards in the last half century, free-trade agreements still stir fierce debate—especially when it comes to jobs. Manufacturing jobs have been lost to low-wage nations such as China and India. Other people worry that free trade is creating a "have/have not" world economy, in which the people in developing economies and the world's environment are being exploited by companies in richer, more developed countries.

This has sparked anti-free-trade protests in many nations. Concerns such as these, coupled with numerous scandals plaguing corporations in recent years, have led to a new focus on corporate social responsibility, or good citizenship. Companies are discovering that being socially responsible both domestically and abroad helps the bottom line. Moreover, prospective workers are saying corporate responsibility is now more important to their job selection. One of HR's leadership roles is to spearhead the development and implementation of corporate citizenship throughout the organization.[10]

How Globalization Affects HRM

For all of the opportunities afforded by international business, when managers talk about "going global," they have to balance a complicated set of issues related to different geographies, including different cultures, employment laws, and business practices. Human resources issues underlie each of these concerns. They include such things as dealing with employees today who, via the Internet, are better informed about global job opportunities and are willing to pursue them, even if it means working for competing companies. Gauging the knowledge and skill base of international workers and figuring out how best to hire and train them, sometimes with materials that must be translated into a number of different languages, is also an issue for firms. Relocating managers and other workers to direct the efforts of an international workforce is a challenge as well. HR personnel are frequently responsible for implementing training programs and enhancing their firms' managers' understanding of other cultures and practices as well as dealing with the

---

globalization
The trend toward opening up foreign markets to international trade and investment

Using the Internet
To learn more about the effects NAFTA has had, go to
http://www.nafta-sec-alena
.org

corporate social responsibility
The responsibility of the firm to act in the best interests of the people and communities affected by its activities

Using the Internet
Sources of information about companies and their programs to promote corporate social responsibility can be found on this news service at
http://www.csrwire.com

culture shock these workers might experience and pay differentials that must be adjusted, depending upon the country. The international arena for HRM has become so crucial and so involved that we have devoted an entire chapter (Chapter 15) to discussing its competitive, cultural, and practical implications.

CHALLENGE 2: EMBRACING NEW TECHNOLOGY

Advancements in information technology have enabled organizations to take advantage of the information explosion. With computer networks, unlimited amounts of data can be stored, retrieved, and used in a wide variety of ways, from simple record keeping to controlling complex equipment. The effect is so dramatic that, at a broader level, organizations are changing the way they do business. The use of the Internet to transact business has become so pervasive for both large and small companies that e-commerce has rapidly become the norm for many firms, including traditional brick-and-mortar companies. The Web has also created a new generation of "virtual" workers who work from home, hotels, or wherever their work takes them and who search for jobs via social networking websites such as Linked-In, Facebook, and My Space.

From Touch Labour to Knowledge Workers

Advanced technology tends to reduce the number of jobs that require little skill and to increase the number of jobs that require considerable skill. In general, this transformation has been referred to as a shift from "touch labour" to "**knowledge workers**," in which employee responsibilities expand to include a richer array of activities such as planning, decision making, and problem solving.[11] In many cases, current employees are being retrained to assume new roles and responsibilities. Even when employees are displaced, they also require retraining. The workplace of the knowledge worker is described in Highlights in HRM 1.2.

[OUT**3**OME]

knowledge workers
Workers whose responsibilities extend beyond the physical execution of work to include planning, decision making, and problem solving

---

Highlights in **HRM 1.2**

An Economy Based on Brains, not Brawn

According to experts such as Richard Florida, who teaches at the Rotman School at the University of Toronto, Nick Bontis who teaches knowledge management at McMaster, and Canadian futurist Dan Tapscott, the workplace of the future will look like this:

- Workers will be chained to their BlackBerrys, not their desks.
- Education will be lifelong, jobs won't.
- You will work with people that you never meet and create goods and services online.
- Freedom, flexibility, and respect will be valued more than compensation.

- Workers will have to read faster—up to 300 words a minute.
- Learning another language will be essential as five billion more people access the Net from Asia, Africa, and the Middle East.
- Clearing your in-box will be time consuming, as you will get e-mails not just from people but from your car (need electricity), your refrigerator (need cheese) and your store (shoes you like just arrived).

Other experts predict that corporations will become mini-states and assume a socially responsible role by identifying workers at 16, and paying for their tuition and housing.

Source: Adapted from Dianne Rinehart, "When Brains Replaces Brawn," *The Globe and Mail*, October 1, 2007, B12; Shannon Klie, "What Will Working World Look Like in 2020? *Canadian HR Reporter* (September 22, 2008), vol. 21, iss. 16; 1, 2.

Technology, transportation, communications, and utilities industries tend to spend the most on training. Knowledge-based training has become so important that Manpower Inc., one of the largest employment agencies in the world, offers free information technology training through its Manpower Training and Development Center (www.manpowergic.com), an online university for its 2.5 million employees worldwide. The Manpower site features more than 6,000 hours of online instruction in technology applications, along with professional development and business skills and telecommunications courses. In fact, Manpower is so focused on developing technical skills in potential employees that it has set up the system so that some training and career planning information is available to those who simply send the company a résumé. "Just-in-time" learning delivered via the Internet to employees' desktops when and where they need training has become commonplace. "Virtual" learning has emerged as well. IBM and Manpower are among the companies that have built training facilities, offices, and meeting rooms inside the online reality game Second Life. The spaces these companies build online enable them to do some things more easily and cheaply than they can in the real world—for example, bringing people from several continents into one room for training.[12]

Influence of Technology in HRM

Information technology has, of course, changed the face of HRM in North America. Perhaps the most central use of technology in HRM is an organization's **human resources information system (HRIS)**. Organizations determined to improve productivity and lower costs are finding HR a good place to start. Because HR affects the entire workforce—everyone who works for the company must be hired, trained, and paid, usually through HR—the impact of HRIS has been dramatic. It has become a potent weapon for lowering administrative costs, increasing productivity, speeding up response times, and improving decision making and service to managers and employees.

The most obvious impact has been operational—that is, automating routine activities, alleviating administrative burdens, reducing costs, and improving productivity internal to the HR function itself. The most frequent uses include automating payroll processing, maintaining employee records, and administering benefits programs. One of the big trends in recent years has been toward HRIS "self-service"—setting up systems, usually on an Intranet, to allow managers to access employee records themselves for administrative purposes and to allow employees to access and change their own benefits and other personal information. Merck's HR system was redesigned to enable line managers and employees to enter, retrieve, and edit data in order to make better decisions faster. This has helped alleviate many of the paper burdens Merck's HR group previously faced and offered greater convenience to both managers and their employees.

Today, however, software applications are available to automate far more HR activities than just payroll, records, and benefits information. All sorts of routine HR activities have seen some sort of automation. Companies are now using software to recruit, screen, and pretest applicants online before hiring them as well as to train, track, and promote employees once they have been hired. For example, Merck's staffing management system supports the hiring process by tracking applicants' information, scanning résumés, and making the information immediately accessible to line managers so they can search systematically for the people whose skills they want. Managers can search online for internal and external talent by running searches of candidates who have been categorized by skill set.[13]

Corning, Inc. uses HR software, among other things, to set the developmental goals of its employees once they have been hired and to gauge how well they are meeting them. Employees can look online to see their own goals and mark their progress as well as see everyone else's goals in the command chain, from the CEO down to their immediate supervisors. This "cascading" of goals has helped Corning's

---

human resources information system (HRIS)

A computerized system that provides current and accurate data for purposes of control and decision making

Highlights in HRM 1.3

Automation of Talent Management Functions

Source: *IDC/CLO Magazine Talent Management Survey, 2007.* Reprinted by permission of MediaTec Publishing.

employees align their personal goals with the organization's overall objectives in order to reach higher levels. "Like any large company, we tended to get 'silo-ed' and fragmented the more we grew," said one vice-president at a company using a system similar to Corning's. "We needed a better way to pull our global team together and get people focused on what the priorities are for our business." Similarly, Merck worked with a software vendor to develop a system that provides coaching tips and learning tools and resources for employees and managers based on their goals.[14]

Highlights in HRM 1.3 shows the extent to which various functions are being automated. According to a survey by Cedar Group, a technology consulting firm, prepackaged, or "canned," HR Web-based solutions are as commonly used as custom-designed systems. Generally, companies also have the choice of hosting the applications on their own servers or having "Software as a Service" vendors (or *SaaS* vendors) such as IBM or PeopleSoft do it for them.

So what sort of system should HR professionals choose from among the many options available? Experts say the first step in choosing a HRIS is for HR personnel to evaluate the biggest "headaches" they experience, or the most time-consuming tasks, and then choose the applications that can have the strongest impact on the firm's financial measures—that is, the ones that get the "biggest bang for the buck." These applications are more likely to get "buy-in" from the firm's top managers. HR managers should then calculate the costs based on average salaries, or HR hours, that could be saved by using an HRIS, along with the hours of increased productivity that would occur as a result.

Other factors that need to be evaluated include the following:

- *Fit of the application to the firm's employee base.* If many of the firm's employees work on a factory floor, is the system appropriate, or does HR need to install kiosks in employee areas? How will the information be secured? Will employees need to be assigned passwords? Can they access the information from off-site (for example, from their homes)?

- *Ability to upgrade or customize the software.* What sorts of costs will be involved to upgrade the software in the coming years?
- *Compatibility with current systems.* Does the HRIS link into existing, or planned, information systems easily and inexpensively?
- *User friendliness.* Does the software provide additional features such as links to learning resources or help for managers who might need it?
- *Availability of technical support.* Should the HRIS system be supported internally, or should the vendor host it? What are the vendor's technical support capabilities?
- *Time required to implement and train staff members to use the HRIS, including HR and payroll personnel, managers, and employees.* Who is responsible for training employees, and how will it be done?
- *Initial costs and annual maintenance costs.* Is a "suite" of applications needed or just a few key applications? Experts advise HR managers to price each application separately and then ask vendors for a "bundled" price. [15]

When an effective HRIS is implemented, perhaps the biggest advantage gained is that HR personnel can concentrate more effectively on the firm's strategic direction instead of on routine tasks. This can include forecasting personnel needs (especially for firms planning to expand, contract, or merge), planning for career and employee promotions, and evaluating the impact of the firm's policies—both those related to HR functions and other functions—to help improve the firm's earnings and strategic direction. "We wanted our HR teams to focus on people issues instead of data problems," explains Sandra Hoffman, CIO of MAPICS, an HR applications provider.

The initial drive to adopt HRIS was related to cutting HR costs. But HR managers have since discovered that the systems allow them to share information with line managers, who, by having access to it, have been able to come up with better production practices and cost control solutions. As a result, HR managers are now requiring their application providers to provide them with software to meet certain goals, including lowering a company's total spending on employee health care and improving its customer service. [16] Home Depot Canada, Inc. uses HR software to train its 28,000 sales associates and to schedule their hours at their 2,000 stores. [17]

CHALLENGE 3: MANAGING CHANGE

Technology and globalization are only two of the forces driving change in organizations and HRM. Today, being able to manage change has become paramount to a firm's success. As one pundit put it, "No change means chance." Successful companies, says Harvard Business School professor Rosabeth Moss Kanter, develop a culture that just keeps moving all the time. [18] Given the pace of today's commerce, organizations can rarely stand still for long. In highly competitive environments, where competition is global and innovation is continuous, being able to manage change has become a core competency sought by organizations.

Types of Changes

Programs focused on total quality, continuous improvement, downsizing, reengineering, outsourcing, and the like are all examples of the means organizations are using to modify the way they operate in order to be more successful. Some of these changes are reactive change, resulting when external forces have already affected an organization's performance. Other changes are proactive change, initiated by managers to take advantage of targeted opportunities, particularly in fast-changing industries in which followers are not successful. In 2000, Alan Lafley, the CEO of

OUTCOME 4

reactive change
Change that occurs after external forces have already affected performance

proactive change
Change initiated to take advantage of targeted opportunities

Procter & Gamble, was looking to change the company by transforming P&G's culture into one that was "curious, collaborative, and courageous, while still retaining its core values." "You need both an external mirror and a rear view of the direction in which you're headed," Lafley wrote in his book *The Game Changer*.[19]

Managing Change through HR

Two-thirds of firms believe that managing change is their biggest challenge, according to a recent survey by the research institute Roffey Park. Moreover, more than 80 percent of organizations reported some form of change initiative currently going on in their companies. Yet many companies lack formal change management programs.[20] This is unfortunate because successful change rarely occurs naturally or easily. Most of the major reasons change efforts fail come down to HR issues. Some of the top reasons are as follows:[21]

1. Not establishing a sense of urgency
2. Not creating a powerful coalition to guide the effort
3. Lacking leaders who have a vision
4. Lacking leaders who communicate the vision
5. Not removing obstacles to the new vision or motivating employees
6. Not systematically planning for and creating short-term "wins"
7. Declaring victory too soon
8. Not anchoring changes in the corporate culture, or failing to maintain the momentum of the change

Formal change management programs help to keep employees focused on the success of the business.

Most employees—regardless of occupation—understand that the way things were done five or ten years ago is very different from how they are done today (or will be done five or ten years from now). Responsibilities change, job assignments change, and work processes change. This change is continuous—a part of the job—rather than temporary. Nevertheless, people often resist change because it requires them to modify or abandon ways of working that have been successful or at least familiar to them. As Dr. Marilyn Buckner, the immediate past president of the Human Resource Planning Society, put it: "Nontechnical, unattended human factors are, in fact, most often the problem in failed change projects." To manage change, executives and managers, including those in HR, have to envision the future, communicate this vision to employees, set clear expectations for performance, and develop the capability to execute by reorganizing people and reallocating assets. Organizations that have been successful in engineering change typically build into their change management planning these key elements:

• They link the change to the business strategy.
• They create quantifiable benefits.
• They engage key employees, customers, and their suppliers early.
• They integrate required behaviour changes.
• They lead clearly, unequivocally, and consistently.
• They invest to implement and sustain change.
• They communicate continuously and personally.
• They sell commitment to the change, not communication about the change.[22]

CHALLENGE 4: MANAGING TALENT, OR HUMAN CAPITAL

The idea that organizations "compete through people" highlights the fact that success increasingly depends on an organization's ability to manage talent, or **human capital**. The term *human capital* describes the economic value of employees' knowledge, skills, and capabilities. Although the value of these assets may not show

- "If you look at our semiconductors and melt them down for silicon, that's a tiny fraction of the costs. The rest is intellect and mistakes." (Gordon Moore, Intel)
- "An organization's ability to learn, and translate that learning into action rapidly, is the ultimate competitive business advantage." (Jack Welch, General Electric)
- "Successful companies of the 21st century will be those who do the best jobs of capturing, storing and leveraging what their employees know." (Lew Platt, Hewlett-Packard)

Staffing programs focus on identifying, recruiting, and hiring the best and the brightest talent available. A jobs fair is one resource, and often brings in many applicants for few positions.

Human Capital and HRM

Human capital is intangible and cannot be managed the way organizations manage jobs, products, and technologies. One of the reasons for this is that the employees, *not* the organization, own their own human capital. If valued employees leave a company, they take their human capital with them, and any investment the company has made in training and developing those people is lost.

To build human capital in organizations, managers must continue to develop superior knowledge, skills, and experience within their workforce. Staffing programs focus on identifying, recruiting, and hiring the best and the brightest talent available. Training programs complement these staffing practices to provide skill enhancement, particularly in areas that cannot be transferred to another company if an employee leaves.[24] In addition, employees need opportunities for development on the job. The most highly valued intelligence on the part of employees tends to be associated with competencies and capabilities they learn from experience and are not easily taught.[25] Consequently, managers have to do a good job of providing employees with developmental assignments and ensuring their job duties and requirements are flexible enough to allow them to grow and learn. Beyond the need to invest in employee development, organizations have to find ways of using the knowledge that currently exists within their firms. Too often, employees have skills that go unused. As Robert Buckman, who served as CEO of Buckman Laboratories for 22 years, a period of unprecedented growth for the company, noted, "If the greatest database in the company is housed in the individual minds of the associates of the organization, then that is where the power of the organization resides. These individual knowledge bases are continually changing and adapting to the real world in front of them. We have to connect these individual knowledge bases together so that they do whatever they do best in the shortest possible time."[26]

In companies such as Texas Instruments, Procter & Gamble, and HSBC, managers are evaluated on their progress toward meeting developmental goals. These goals focus on skill development and gaining new competencies and capabilities. In a growing number of instances, pay is attached to this knowledge and skill acquisition. Skill-based pay, for example, rewards employees for each new class of jobs they are capable of performing. We will discuss skill-based pay (or pay-for-knowledge) more in Chapter 9. Developmental assignments, particularly those involving teamwork, can also be a valuable way of facilitating knowledge exchange and mutual learning. Effective communication (whether face to face or through information technology) is instrumental in sharing knowledge and making it widely available throughout the organization. As Dave Ulrich, professor

human capital
The knowledge, skills, and capabilities of individuals that have economic value to an organization

up directly on a company's balance sheet, it nevertheless has tremendous impact on an organization's performance. The following quotations from notable CEOs illustrate this point:[23]

of business at the University of Michigan, noted: "Learning capability is g times g—a business's ability to *generate* new ideas multiplied by its adeptness at *generalizing* them throughout the company."[27]

HR programs and assignments are often the conduit through which knowledge is transferred among employees. A survey by the Human Resource Planning Society revealed that 65 percent of responding companies believed that their HR groups play a key role in developing human capital. Arvinder Dhesi, the new head of talent for the insurance company Aviva, explains that his firm's goal is to treat *everyone* as talent and not just focus on a few. "We talk about the sum of people's experiences as well as their skills," says Dhesi, who notes that Aviva is rolling out new software that will create a "talent profile" of each of the firm's 39,000 employees worldwide. Similarly, Boeing Satellite Systems has created a "lessons learned" site on its Intranet where all areas of the company can store the knowledge they have learned. As information and intellectual capital are posted to the company's electronic newsgroups, they can be analyzed and consolidated by editorial teams. Executives at Boeing estimate that this form of intellectual capital has reduced the cost of developing a satellite by as much as $25 million.[28]

HR managers and line managers each play an important role in creating an organization that understands the value of knowledge, documents the skills and capabilities available to the organization, and identifies ways of utilizing that knowledge to benefit the firm. We will address these issues throughout the text, but particularly in Chapters 5 and 7 on career development and training.

CHALLENGE 5: RESPONDING TO THE MARKET

Meeting customer expectations is essential for any organization. In addition to focusing on internal management issues, managers must also meet customer requirements of quality, innovation, variety, and responsiveness. These standards often separate the winners from the losers in today's competitive world. How well does a company understand its customers' needs? How quickly can it develop and get a new product to market? How effectively has it responded to special concerns? "Faster, Leaner, Better"—the vision at pharmaceutical company AstraZeneca—requires the organization to constantly align its management processes with customer needs. Management innovations such as total quality management (TQM) and process reengineering are but two of the comprehensive approaches to responding to customers. Each has direct implications for HR.

Total Quality Management, Six Sigma, and HRM

Total quality management (TQM) is a set of principles and practices whose core ideas include understanding customer needs, doing things right the first time, and striving for continuous improvement. TQM techniques were developed in the mid-1940s by Dr. W. Edwards Deming after studying Japanese companies rebuilding following World War II. The TQM revolution in North America began in the mid-1980s, led by companies such as Motorola, Xerox, and Ford. But since that time, criteria spelled out in the Malcolm Baldrige National Quality Award have provided the impetus for both large and small companies to rethink their approach to HRM. Currently, the Baldrige Award is given annually in each of six categories: manufacturing, service, small business, education, health care, and nonprofit.[29]

When TQM initiatives work, it is usually because managers have made major changes in their philosophies and HR programs. More recently, companies such as Motorola, GE, Dow Chemical, and Honeywell have adopted a more systematic approach to quality, called Six Sigma, which includes major changes in management philosophy and HR programs. Six Sigma is a statistical method of translating a customer's needs into separate tasks and defining the best way to perform each

[OUTCOME]

total quality management (TQM)
A set of principles and practices whose core ideas include understanding customer needs, doing things right the first time, and striving for continuous improvement

Six Sigma
A process used to translate customer needs into a set of optimal tasks that are performed in concert with one another

task in concert with the others. By examining the optimal process, Six Sigma can have a powerful effect on the quality of products, the performance of customer service, and the professional development of employees. What makes Six Sigma different from other quality efforts is that it catches mistakes before they happen. In a true Six Sigma environment, variation from standard is reduced to only 3.4 defects per million.[30]

The importance of HR to Six Sigma begins with the formation of teams and extends to training, performance management, communication, culture, and even rewards. As individuals progress through Six Sigma training, they can move up from "Green Belt" to eventually achieve "Black Belt" status. Many of Dow's key HR slots require black belt certification, for example. If this all sounds a bit hokey, take note of the successful companies that have made cultural—and performance—transformation as a result: Motorola credits Six Sigma with $16 billion in savings over the course of 12 years; Ford reports that it saved more than $4 billion in one year alone; and Motorola is so committed to Six Sigma that it now conducts Six Sigma training for employees of other firms who attend its Motorola University.[31] The most important quality improvement techniques stress employee motivation, change in corporate culture, and employee education. Organizations known for product and service quality strongly believe that employees are the key to that quality. Read Reality Check about the Six Sigma effect at Goodyear Canada.

One of the reasons that HR programs are so essential to programs such as Six Sigma is that they help balance two opposing forces. According to Laurie Broedling, an organizational psychologist and human resources expert, "One set of forces (the need for order and control) pulls every business toward stagnation, while another set of forces (the need for growth and creativity) drives it toward disintegration." Six Sigma's focus on continuous improvement drives the system toward disequilibrium, while Six Sigma's focus on customers, management systems, and the like provide the restraining forces that keep the system together. HR practices help managers balance these two forces. Like human resources information systems, TQM has helped HR departments progress from a focus on functional activities to strategic planning. Better business thinking builds more strategic HR thinking.[32]

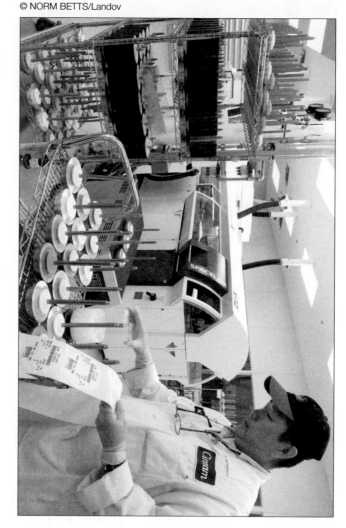

© NORM BETTS/Landov

Many Canadian companies use business process reengineering to improve productivity at their plants.

Reality CHECK

Six Sigma

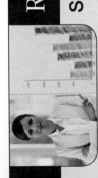

Goodyear Canada is in the midst of a major business transformation. Already there are 19 Black Belts (full-time project leaders) and seven Green Belts (part-time project leaders) working in offices, warehouses, and the eight Canadian tire and rubber products manufacturing plants. Projects currently under way are projected to yield $10 million in waste reduction, capital equipment purchase avoidance, and increased sales through elimination of production bottlenecks.

Goodyear's tire manufacturing facility in Medicine Hat, Alberta, needed to produce more rubber from its Banbury rubber mixer in order to meet its daily quota and lessen its dependence on rubber produced by outside sources. In buying material, the factory was paying freight charges to get the rubber to the factory. By optimizing the Banbury uptime and increasing the Banbury output, the factory could reduce the amount of rubber it needed to purchase. Using the tools of Six Sigma, the factory determined that it could stagger shift rotations so that an operator was always available to keep the Banbury mixer running. The company was also able to increase the batch weight sizes of some of the compounds by 4 percent to 11 percent. In addition, staging batches and reducing the gate delay realized gains of two to three seconds per batch. Although three seconds does not sound like a great amount, over the course of a week, it adds about 150 minutes of productivity. After six months, the factory increased its Banbury mixer output

by more than 5 percent, generating savings of over $110,000. The Medicine Hat plant estimates that it can save $250,000 to $400,000 annually by implementing the new procedures.

Gary Blake, Goodyear Canada Six Sigma champion, and a Black Belt, says that it is a problem-solving model that applies rigorous statistical thinking to reduce defects, improve cycle time, and increase customer satisfaction. The methodology is being applied not only to traditional manufacturing processes, but also to transactional processes—supply chain, purchasing, invoicing, sales, and marketing. A Six Sigma team follows five major steps known as DMAIC to clearly Define the scope of the project, Measure customer requirements and process outputs, Analyze the current situation and set clear goals, Improve the process through planned experimentation, and finally Control to validate and lock in the improvement—then sustaining it so that there is no backslide. The model moves the organization to whatever goals are required by the customer. Six Sigma derives its name from the Greek letter *sigma*, which is sometimes used to denote variation from a standard, and the statistical concept that if you measure the defects in a process, you can figure out how to get rid of them and get ever closer to perfection. A Six Sigma company cannot produce more than 3.4 defects per million opportunities. For a process with only one specification limit, this results in six process standard deviations between the mean of the process and the customer's specification limit.

Reengineering and HRM

In addition to TQM and Six Sigma programs, some companies take a more radical approach to process redesign called reengineering. Reengineering has been described as "the fundamental rethinking and radical redesign of business processes to achieve dramatic improvements in cost, quality, service and speed."[33] Reengineering often requires that managers start over from scratch in rethinking how work should be done, how technology and people should interact, and how entire organizations should be structured. HR issues are central to these decisions. First, reengineering requires that managers create an environment for change, and as we mentioned previously, HR issues drive change. Second, reengineering efforts depend on effective leadership and communication processes, two other areas related to HRM. Third, reengineering requires that administrative systems

reengineering
Fundamental rethinking and radical redesign of business processes to achieve dramatic improvements in cost, quality, service, and speed

be reviewed and modified. Selection, job descriptions, training, career planning, performance appraisal, compensation, and labour relations are all candidates for change to complement and support reengineering efforts. We will return to these issues and speak more directly to the organizational development tools necessary for reengineering in later chapters.

CHALLENGE 6: CONTAINING COSTS

Companies today are facing sharply rising costs, including higher product transportation costs and skyrocketing employee extended health care costs. As a result, many firms are under extreme pressure to improve their productivity in order to maximize their efficiency and keep their prices competitive. Like other functional department managers, HR managers are under pressure to show top managers the "bottom line" financial results their departments are achieving. Labour costs are one of the largest expenditures of any organization, particularly in service- and knowledge-intensive companies. Organizations are taking many approaches to lowering labour-related costs. In addition to shifting some of the rising costs of health care back onto employees, firms are also downsizing, outsourcing, offshoring, and engaging in employee leasing in an attempt to enhance productivity. Each of these efforts has a big impact on HR policies and practices.

Downsizing

Downsizing is the planned elimination of jobs. For example, when L.L. Bean saw that sales had fallen, the company undertook a number of efforts to identify what it called "smart cost reductions." Bean's TQM activities helped the company target quality problems and saved an estimated $30 million. But the cuts were not enough, and ultimately Leon Gorman, president of the firm, and Bob Peixotto, vice-president of HR and quality, realized the company needed to eliminate some jobs. Instead of simply laying off people, however, the company started early retirement and "sweetened" voluntary separation programs. Then the company offered employee sabbaticals for continuing education.[34]

These efforts, combined with better employee communication, helped soften the blow of layoffs at L.L. Bean. But the pain of downsizing has been widespread throughout North America. Virtually every major corporation has undergone some cycle of downsizing. Historically, layoffs tended to affect manufacturing firms and line workers in particular, but beginning in the 1990s, the layoffs began to encompass white-collar workers in greater numbers in knowledge-intensive industries. Engineering, accounting, information technology, and architecture have been among the hardest hit professions.[35]

But downsizing is no longer being regarded as a short-term fix when times are tough. It has now become a tool continually used by companies to adjust to changes in technology, globalization, and the firm's business direction. For example, in a study that surveyed 450 senior HR executives at companies that had downsized, only 21 percent said that financial difficulties had spurred the cutbacks. In fact, 34 percent of the executives said that the downsizing was done to strengthen their companies' future positions; 21 percent said it was done to achieve fundamental staff realignment; and 17 percent said it was due to a merger or acquisition.

Whatever the reason, while some firms improve efficiency (and lower costs) with layoffs, many others do not obtain such benefits. A study by Watson Wyatt of 750 companies showed that companies with excellent recruiting and retention policies provide a nearly 8 percent higher return to shareholders compared to those that do not. Those with a strong commitment to job security earned an additional 1.4 percent for shareholders.

OUTCOME 7

downsizing
Planned elimination of jobs

Advocates of a no-layoff policy often note that layoffs may backfire after taking into account such hidden costs as the following:

- Severance and rehiring costs
- Accrued vacation and sick day payouts
- Pension and benefit payoffs
- Potential lawsuits from aggrieved workers
- Loss of institutional memory and trust in management
- Lack of staffers when the economy rebounds
- Survivors who are risk averse, paranoid, and political

In contrast, companies that avoid downsizing say they get some important benefits from such policies:

- A fiercely loyal, more productive workforce
- Higher customer satisfaction
- Readiness to snap back with the economy
- A recruiting edge
- Workers who are not afraid to innovate, knowing their jobs are safe[36]

More than one executive has concluded that you do not get dedicated and productive employees if at the first sign of trouble you show them that you think they are expendable.

To approach downsizing more intelligently, some companies have made special efforts to reassign and retrain employees for new positions when their jobs are eliminated. Others, such as Rogers Communications, Inc., offered their employees a four-day work week for reduced pay on a voluntary basis.[37] This is consistent with a philosophy of employees as assets, as intellectual capital.

Outsourcing, Offshoring, and Employee Leasing

Over the past 25 years, the employment relationship between companies and employees has shifted from relationship-based to transaction-based. Fewer people are working for one employer over the course of their lifetimes and, as we have explained, the Internet has created a workforce that is constantly scanning for new opportunities. In addition, more people are choosing to work on a freelance, or contract, basis or to work part-time, especially women and senior citizens. Outsourcing is evidence of this trend.[38] Outsourcing simply means hiring someone outside the company to perform business processes that could be done within a firm. Companies hire accounting firms to take care of their financial services. They hire advertising firms to handle promotions, software firms to develop data-processing systems, and law firms to handle their legal issues. Maintenance, security, catering, and payroll are often outsourced in order to increase the organization's flexibility and lower its overhead costs.

The interest in outsourcing has been spurred on by executives who want to focus their organization's activities on what they do best. In fact, some management experts predict that companies will one day strip away every function not regarded as crucial. Even now, many firms are outsourcing what would seem to be their core functions. Drug companies such as GlaxoSmithKline are outsourcing their research and development functions to smaller firms that can more cheaply and nimbly create new products for them. Procter & Gamble hopes to outsource half of its product development by the year 2010. The Portables, makers of tradeshow displays and based in Richmond, BC, has outsourced its manufacturing to China.[39] Outsourcing is changing the way HR departments operate as well. The practice has been one of the most prominent HR trends of the last ten years and will continue to be until the last dollar of excess costs has been wrung out.[40]

Offshoring, also referred to as "global sourcing," involves shifting work to overseas locations. Almost half of 500 senior finance and HR leaders surveyed said their firms are either offshoring or are considering offshoring in the next three years,

outsourcing

Contracting outside the organization to have work done that formerly was done by internal employees

offshoring

The business practice of sending jobs to other countries

according to a study by Hewitt Associates. Spending on offshore services has been rising worldwide.[41] Cost reduction is among the key motivators for these decisions—companies estimate that they can save 40 to 60 percent on labour costs by reallocating work to countries such as India, where highly educated workers can perform the same jobs as Canadian workers at half the price. Other labour markets include the Philippines, Russia, China, Mexico, Brazil, Hungary, and Bosnia. However, a new attitude is emerging. According to Atul Vashistha, the coauthor of the book *Offshore Nation*, CEOs these days are not asking how much offshoring can save them so much as they are asking by how much it can grow their businesses. In some cases, the decisions reflect the allocation of work across the multiple countries in which the company does business. In other cases, managers are finding that if they save money by offshoring, they can rescue failing businesses, make better use of their skilled labour, and deliver products more cheaply and quickly because they have people across the globe working 24-7 on them.[42]

But hidden costs can sometimes chew up much of the financial gains from offshoring, including those associated with finding foreign vendors, productivity lost during the transition, domestic layoff costs, language difficulties, international regulatory challenges, and political and economic instability that can threaten operations. In Chapter 2, you will learn about the other ways firms can gain a competitive edge besides just cutting labour costs. Nonetheless, offshoring will continue to be a key employment strategy as global economies continue to shift. The key is for top managers, finance departments, and the offshoring consulting firms they hire to begin working in conjunction with their companies' HR departments early in the game. "Companies can minimize hidden costs and maximize their returns by enabling HR [to] have a seat at the table early so they can carefully address issues such as skill and language requirements, labour costs by market, alternative talent pools, workforce training, retraining and change management," says Mark Arian, a corporate restructuring and change practice leader for Hewitt. To minimize problems, line and HR managers have to work together with the firm's other functional groups to define and communicate transition plans, minimize the number of unknowns, and help employees identify their employment options.[43]

As an alternative to downsizing, outsourcing, and offshoring, many companies, especially small ones, have decided to sign employee leasing agreements with professional employer organizations (PEOs). A PEO—typically a larger company—takes over the management of a smaller company's HR tasks and becomes a co-employer to its employees. The PEO performs all the HR duties of an employer—hiring, payroll, and performance appraisal. Because PEOs can co-employ a large number of people working at many different companies, they can provide employees with benefits that small companies cannot afford, such as adoption assistance. In addition, many PEOs offer their employees flextime, job sharing, part-time employment, consulting arrangements, seasonal work, and on-call work. The value of employee leasing lies in the fact that an organization can essentially maintain its working relationships with its employees but shift some employment costs to the PEO, in return for a fee.[44]

Productivity Enhancements

The results of pure cost-cutting efforts such as downsizing, outsourcing, and employee leasing can be disappointing, however, if managers use them as simple solutions to complex performance problems. Overemphasizing labour costs misses the broader issue of improving a firm's productivity. Employee productivity is the result of a combination of employees' abilities, motivation, and work environment, and the technology with which they have to work. Since productivity can be defined as "the output gained from a fixed amount of inputs," organizations can increase their productivity either by reducing their inputs (the cost approach) or by increasing the amount that employees produce, by adding more human and/or physical capital to the process. Companies such as Toyota achieve low

employee leasing
The process of dismissing employees who are then hired by a leasing company (which handles all HR-related activities) and contracting with that company to lease back the employees

FIGURE **1.2**

Productivity Enhancements

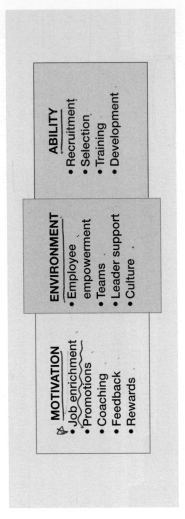

MOTIVATION
• Job enrichment
• Promotions
• Coaching
• Feedback
• Rewards

ENVIRONMENT
• Employee empowerment
• Teams
• Leader support
• Culture

ABILITY
• Recruitment
• Selection
• Training
• Development

costs in their industries not because they scrimp on employees, but because they are the most productive.

In absolute terms, the United States remains the world's most productive nation. U.S. workers produce more output collectively than any other country—more than $63,000 per worker. Canadian workers average $48,000, a gap of 25 percent. In 1980, that gap was 10 percent, so Canadian workers are becoming less competitive.[45] With that said, the growth in output per worker is now climbing faster in less-developed countries such as China that have lacked expertise and technology in the past but are making strides to close the gap. Even during the 2001–2002 recession, new investments in technology kept the productivity of North American workers climbing upward. The problem is that this rapid investment in faster computers and more efficient machine tools is beginning to level off. This will limit how much assistance technology can offer employees in terms of their productivity in the years to come.

This means that any additional productivity will have to come from the enhanced ability of employees, their motivation, and their work environment—which makes the job of the HR manager in the coming years all the more crucial.[46] Figure 1.2 shows some of the topics that we cover in this textbook that help managers increase productivity in their organizations.

DEMOGRAPHIC AND EMPLOYEE CONCERNS

In addition to the competitive challenges facing organizations, managers in general—and HR managers in particular—need to be concerned about changes in the makeup and the expectations of their employees. As we noted at the beginning of this chapter, HRM involves being an advocate for employees, being aware of their concerns, and making sure that the exchange between the organization and its employees is *mutually* beneficial. Highlights in HRM 1.4 shows a summary of social issues in HRM. We will discuss some of these issues here and address all of them in greater detail throughout the book.

DEMOGRAPHIC CHANGES

Among the most significant challenges to managers are the demographic changes occurring in Canada. Because they affect the workforce of an employer, these changes—in employee background, age, gender, and education—are important topics for discussion.

[OUTCOME]

Highlights in **HRM 1.4**

Social Issues in HRM

Changing Demographics: The coming decades will bring a more diverse and aging workforce to developed countries such as Canada. This has major implications for all aspects of HRM because it alters traditional experience and expectations regarding the labour pool. Among the issues in this area are

- Globalization
- Shrinking pool of skilled entry-level workers
- Rising health care costs for employees
- Outsourcing, offshoring, and the use of temporary and part-time employees
- Diversity strategies
- Retirement issues
- Continual skills development and retraining

Employer/Employee Rights: This area reflects the shift toward organizations and individuals attempting to define rights, obligations, and responsibilities. Among the issues here are

- Relationship employment versus transactional-based employment
- Concern for the privacy of employees

- Employer-employee ethics
- Equal pay for work of equal value
- Whistle-blowing
- Legal compliance
- Mandated benefits

Attitudes toward Work and Family: Because of the increase of working women as well as employee mobility and a growing concern about family issues, there is demand for recognizing and supporting family-related concerns. Among the issues are:

- Day care and elder care
- Job sharing
- Job rotation
- Parental leave
- Flextime
- Alternative work schedules
- Telecommuting

The Diversity/Immigration Challenge

Figure 1.3 shows the current composition of the population of Canada. Minorities in Canada are increasing relative to the population. Between 2001 and 2006, minorities increased by 27.2 percent, compared to a 5.4 percent increase in the population of Canada for the same period. British Columbia and Ontario lead the country in the percentage of their visible minorities populations at 24.8 percent and 22.8 percent of their respective populations.

How a shortage of immigrant labour could undercut competitiveness is not lost on Canadian businesses that need talent on both ends of the spectrum (low-level jobs as well as those requiring high levels of education). To accommodate the shift in demographics, demand, and labour trends, these businesses know it's absolutely vital to increase their efforts to recruit and train a more diverse workforce. They realize that immigrants are not only critical to their very survival but also add to their strength and allow them to better attract and serve a larger customer base. Hotel chain Marriott and Big Four accounting firm Deloitte & Touche are examples. Chapter 15 in more detail what companies are doing to cope with this difficult situation.[47]

Age Distribution of Employees

Canada's population was 33,505,000 in 2009. About 14 percent are 65 or over, and this number is expected to increase significantly over the next ten years as an additional 3.7 million Canadians will turn 65 in this period.[48]

FIGURE **1.3**

Composition of the Population of Canada (millions)

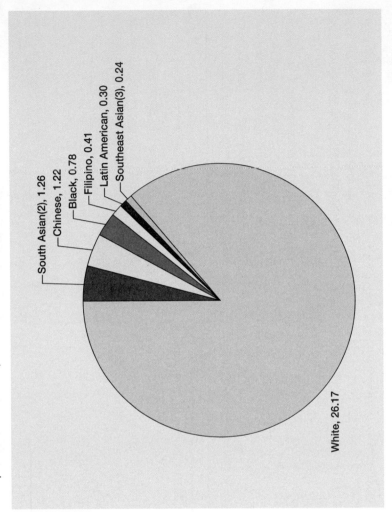

- South Asian(2), 1.26
- Chinese, 1.22
- Black, 0.78
- Filipino, 0.41
- Latin American, 0.30
- Southeast Asian(3), 0.24
- White, 26.17

Source: Statistics Canada, Ethnic Origin and Visible Minorities, 2006 Census, 97-562-XWE2006002, Released April 2, 2008 http://www.statcan.gc.ca/bsolc/olc-cel/olc-cel?catno=97-562-X2006002&lang=eng.

The echo boom generation in Canada, comprising people born roughly between 1977 and 1997, represents 20 percent of the population of Canada. These workers will be needed to fill the workforce demands created by the retirement of 8.6 million baby boomers.[49]

The imbalance in the age distribution of the labour force is having a significant effect on employers. Companies are finding that large portions of their workforces are nearing retirement. Beyond the sheer number of employees they will have to replace, managers are concerned that the expertise of these employees is likely to be drained too rapidly from the company. As a stopgap measure, employers are making positive efforts to attract older workers, especially those who have taken early retirement. Workers are taking them up on the offer. Many baby boomers say they expect to work past traditional retirement age. Good health and longer life expectancies play the biggest role in extended work lives. But some retirees have returned to the workforce because of economic needs.

Home Depot and McDonald's Canada are among the companies making efforts to attract older workers. Recruiting older workers may sound counterintuitive because they incur higher health care costs. But older workers also have fewer dependants and offer other cost savings. "Our over-50 employee turnover is ten times less than those under 30," says Smith. "So when you think about the savings you have in training costs, transitions costs, and recruitment costs, you save a lot more on that for the over-50 workers than you do for others."[50]

Like the baby boom, the "echo boom" is also having an effect in Canada. "Echo boomers," or "millennials," are people born roughly between 1977 and 1997. This wave of workers is generally regarded as having a good work ethic and technological know-how. Similar to the trends with baby boomers, those who constitute this new population bulge are experiencing greater competition for advancement from others of approximately the same age. This situation challenges the ingenuity of managers to develop career patterns for employees to smooth out gaps in the numbers and kinds of workers.[51]

Gender Distribution of the Workforce

Women make up 43 percent of the workforce in Canada, and the educational attainment of women is also increasing relative to men. Today, 54 percent of university graduates are women. Employers wanting to attract the talent that women have to offer are taking measures to ensure they are treated equally in the workplace in terms of their advancement opportunities and compensation. In addition, more companies are accommodating working parents by offering them parental leave, part-time employment, flexible work schedules, job sharing, telecommuting, and child and elder care assistance.

Education of the Workforce

The 2006 Census confirmed that higher education is a gateway to higher earnings, as did all previous censuses. For men and women of all ages, full-time full-year earners with a university degree earned substantially more than their counterparts who did not have a high school diploma. Figure 1.4 shows the extent to which more years of education result in increased earnings.

Experts estimate that the value of a college or university degree is $1 million over the course of a career, according to the Association of Universities and Colleges of Canada. The unemployment rates of those with only high school education average 12–20 percent higher than degree holders of the same age.[52] It is important to note, however, that while the complexity of jobs is increasing significantly, the skills gap is huge and widening. More than 3 million Canadians (aged 16–65) have problems reading printed material. The BHP Ekati Diamond Mine in the Northwest Territories realized that a large number of candidates had not completed high school, and so the company hired educators to deliver training in basic math and literacy, using actual workplace documents and manuals as teaching tools. Many employers are using

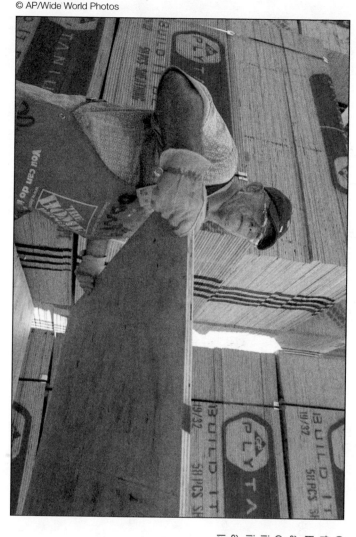

Changing demographics throughout the world will bring a more diverse and aging workforce to developed countries. This has major implications for HRM because it alters traditional experience and expectations regarding the labour pool.

FIGURE **1.4**

Education of the Workforce

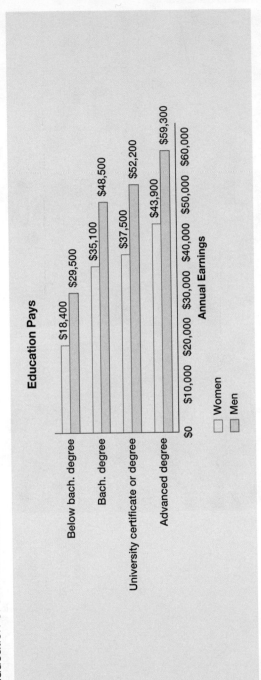

Education Pays

	Annual Earnings
Below bach. degree	Women $18,400 / Men $29,500
Bach. degree	Women $35,100 / Men $48,500
University certificate or degree	Women $37,500 / Men $52,200
Advanced degree	Women $43,900 / Men $59,300

$0 $10,000 $20,000 $30,000 $40,000 $50,000 $60,000

☐ Women ☐ Men

Source: Data from Statistics Canada, 2006 Census; http://www40.statcan.gc.ca/l01/cst01/labor50a-eng.htm, retrieved July 30, 2009.

Using the Internet

The Conference Board of Canada and the National Literacy Council provide tools and advice for Canadian companies facing literary issues at **http://www.conferenceboard .ca/workplaceliteracy**

managing diversity
Being aware of characteristics common to employees, while also managing employees as individuals

a tool, the Test of Workplace Essential Skills (TOWES), developed at the Bow Valley College in Calgary, Alberta, to assess employee competence in three essential skills: reading text, document use, and numeracy. The test results provide managers with information about the gaps in existing skills sets in employees; managers can then turn to educators or institutions for remedial training. As a result of skills gaps, businesses now spend millions of dollars on basic skills training for their employees.[53]

It is not only workers with four-year degrees that employers want to hire. Companies are having trouble finding trained and certified workers such as pipe fitters, motorcycle mechanics, and air traffic controllers. As the baby boomers retire, the problem will likely worsen. HR departments will have to offer higher compensation packages to attract qualified candidates, and recruiting and selection systems will have to function much more competitively in order to identify talent. Given the economic downturn and rise in unemployment Canada has experienced recently, this might sound strange. But demographic shifts can, and will, have a huge impact on HR and society. HR managers are interested in these trends because the economy and job market are critical to HR's operations. For example, given that visible minorities and women have increased their share of the labour force, HR managers frequently analyze how each group is represented in both fast-growing and slow-growing occupations—a topic to which we will return in Chapter 3.

But these are only the initial efforts to provide an overall environment that values and utilizes a diverse workforce. Managing diversity means being acutely aware of characteristics *common* to employees, while also managing these employees as *individuals*. It means not just tolerating or accommodating all sorts of differences but supporting, nurturing, and utilizing these differences to the organization's advantage.[54] While there are important social reasons for including a broader spectrum of workers, there are some essential business reasons as well.

Cultural Changes

The attitudes, beliefs, values, and customs of people in a society are an integral part of their culture. Naturally, their culture affects their behaviour on the job and the environment within the organization, influencing their reactions to work assignments, leadership styles, and reward systems. Like the external and internal environments of which it is a part, culture is undergoing continual change. HR policies and procedures therefore must be adjusted to cope with this change.

Employee Rights

Over the past few decades, federal legislation has radically changed the rules for management of employees by granting them many specific rights. Among these are laws granting employees the right to equal employment opportunity (Chapter 3), union representation if they desire it (Chapter 14), a safe and healthful work environment (Chapter 12), pension plans regulated by the government (Chapter 11), equal pay for men and women performing essentially the same job (Chapter 9), and privacy in the workplace. An expanded discussion of the specific areas in which rights and responsibilities are of concern to employers and employees will be presented in Chapter 13.

Concern for Privacy

HR managers and their staffs, as well as line managers in positions of responsibility, generally recognize the importance of discretion in handling all types of information about employees. The *Personal Information Protection and Electronic Documents Act* (PIPEDA) is a federal law that deals with the collection, use, and disclosure of personal information (note that Quebec is the only province with similar laws, although Ontario, British Columbia, and others have draft legislation in place). This law requires federally regulated organizations holding personal information on customers or employees to obtain their consent before it uses, collects, or discloses this information. Employer responses to the issue of information privacy vary widely. IBM was one of the first companies to show concern for how personal information about employees was handled. It began restricting the release of information as early as 1965 and in 1971 developed a comprehensive privacy policy. The Royal Bank, the Hudson's Bay Company, and Zero Knowledge Systems in Montreal are among other employers that have developed privacy programs.

Globalization has added another twist to privacy compliance. For example, EU countries prohibit the transfer of personal data to countries with inadequate data protection laws, such as China. In addition to implementing privacy policies, most companies now try to limit the use of SIN numbers on time sheets, log-in sheets, and other employment forms. Some companies lock up employee files, conduct background checks on employees who have access to others' files, educate employees in fraud prevention, and contract with outside firms specializing in identity theft.[55]

Although PIPEDA protects people's electronic communications such as their e-mail, the rules are different when it comes to the privacy that employees can expect with regard to their electronic communications at work. Workers are learning the hard way that their employers have a right to monitor their e-mail and Internet use, for example. The information employees post on the Web—either on social networking sites or on job-hunting sites such as Monster.com—have also become subject to scrutiny by employers. Electronic surveillance in the workplace is also becoming an issue. In Chapter 13, we will discuss the content of privacy programs, along with the privacy employees can expect while on the job, and recommend some privacy guidelines.

The Changing Nature of the Job

The era of the full-time permanent job seems to have disappeared. The number of self-employed is also increasing, accounting for 18 percent of employment and 75 percent of new job growth. Nearly half of all the jobs created in the last two decades have been nonstandard—that is, part-time, temporary, or contract work. As job security erodes, so do pension plans and health care benefits, especially for

The Business CASE

Advantages of Part-Time Workers

The trend in Canadian employment is definitely away from full-time "permanent" jobs to the use of part-time and temporary employees. The advantages of employing temporary workers are numerous:

Reducing the payroll costs because part-time and temporary workers seldom receive the same benefits as full-time workers.

Responding to fluctuations in demand. Contingent workers can be hired or dismissed during periods of high or low demand (for example, for retail stores—high demand during holiday seasons; low demand in January).

Access to specific expertise—when an organization enters a new business or needs specific expertise for a limited time (development of a website, for example), it makes economic sense to hire only for that need. Contingent workers may also be used to bring in new ideas and skills from other organizations and/or train regular employees.

Organizations can "test" employees' skills and fit with the organization by specifying a

limited work contract. In this way, productive employees can be hired and those who are underperformers can be released without costly termination costs.

Most employers recognize these advantages, and so wish to employ more contingent and part-time employees. However, while these costs are easily assessed, there may be greater benefits to be achieved by hiring full-time employees. Loblaws thinks so. Canada's largest grocery store chain is planning to convert 10 percent of its part-time work force to full-time work. Ten thousand full-time jobs will be created to increase productivity and improve retention. The assumption, backed by HR research, is that the use of full-time employees will increase employee engagement, which will improve customer service (a key differentiator among retailers) and thus, improve revenues and then profits. The increases in compensation (full-time workers make 50 percent more in benefits etc. than part-time workers) will be offset by the savings of reduced turnover (part-timer turnover rate is 50 percent).

Source: G. White, "Finding the Best Temp Worker for the Job," *The Canadian HR Reporter*, (May 4, 2009), Vol. 22, Iss. 9: 17; S. Klie "Part-timers Could Go Full Time at Grocery Giant," *Canadian HR Reporter* (March 23, 2009) Vol. 22, Iss. 6: 1, 8.

part-timers. Nonstandard jobs represent about 30 percent of all employment.[56] The Business Case outlines the advantages of employing temporary workers, but also shows why a company has moved away from this strategy, to reap higher benefits.

As shown in Ethics in HRM, labour force participants have become increasingly polarized into haves and have-nots. We return to the subject of changing employment options in Chapter 4.

Changing Attitudes toward Work

Employees today are less likely to define their personal success only in terms of financial gains. Many employees, especially younger ones, believe satisfaction in life is more likely to result from balancing their work challenges and rewards with those in their personal lives. Though most people still enjoy work and want to excel at it, they tend to be focused on finding interesting work and are more inclined to pursue multiple careers rather than being satisfied with just "having a job." Figure 1.5 outlines the job features that are important to Canadian workers. People also appear to be seeking ways of living that are less complicated but more meaningful. These new lifestyles cannot help having an impact

Ethics in **HRM**

Skywalkers and Groundworkers

Canadian workers can be divided into two classes: skywalkers and groundworkers. Skywalkers, those working in white-collar jobs in high-rise buildings, are well educated and well trained, and earn good incomes. Their jobs are secure and they receive full benefits. For these knowledge workers, the employment prospects in computer programming, financial analysis, insurance, business services, and real estate are bright. Those working as managers in the high-rises on Bay Street, Howe Street, and rue St-Jacques earned an hourly average of $30.70. (A Canadian worker earned, on average, about $22.04 in 2009.)

Below the high-rise buildings toil the groundworkers. Those with little education and outdated skills are suffering massive unemployment. Groundworkers

suffer further from job insecurity and lack of benefit programs. Look for these workers in restaurants, hotels, and shops. The "McJobs" they hold in the accommodation, food, and beverage industries paid a mere $12 per hour, and many earned far less than this, being paid the minimum wage of about $7 an hour. Those working part-time—a growing segment that now comprises 34 percent of the Canadian workforce—fare even worse. Companies have discovered cost savings by replacing full-time employees with part-time workers, thereby eliminating benefits and increasing staffing flexibility. This restructuring of the job market has produced winners and losers, but many would argue that all Canadians lose when the unemployment rate is high and citizens feel insecure about their futures.

Sources: Heather Scoffield, "Hold the McJobs: Canada's High End Employment Boom," *The Globe and Mail*, February 17, 2006, B1 and B4; Statistics Canada, *Statistics Canada Measures of Weekly Earnings*, http://www4.hrsdc.gc.ca/.3ndic.1t.4r@-eng.jsp?iid=18, retrieved May 11, 2009.

FIGURE **1.5**

Work Is More Than Just a Paycheque

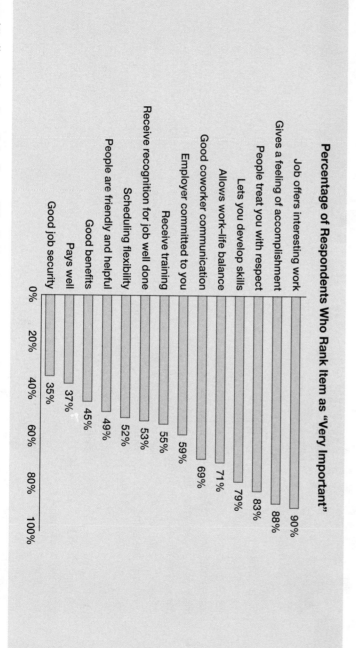

Percentage of Respondents Who Rank Item as "Very Important"

Item	Percentage
Job offers interesting work	90%
Gives a feeling of accomplishment	88%
People treat you with respect	83%
Lets you develop skills	79%
Allows work-life balance	71%
Good coworker communication	69%
Employer committed to you	59%
Receive training	55%
Receive recognition for job well done	53%
Scheduling flexibility	52%
People are friendly and helpful	49%
Good benefits	45%
Pays well	37%
Good job security	35%

0%   20%   40%   60%   80%   100%

Source: http://www.jobquality.ca Online Survey: "What Do You Value in a Job?" *Canadian Policy Research Networks* (2004). http://www.jobquality.ca/surveys/results_8.shtml, retrieved July 26, 2009.

on the way employees must be motivated and managed. Consequently, HRM has become more complex than it was when employees were concerned primarily with economic survival.

Balancing Work and Family

Work and the family are connected in many subtle and not-so-subtle social, economic, and psychological ways. Because of the forms that the family now takes—such as the two-wage-earner and the single-parent family—work organizations are finding it advantageous to provide employees with more family-friendly options. "Family friendly" is a broad term that can include flexible work hours, day care, elder care, part-time work, job sharing, pregnancy leave, parental leave, executive transfers, spousal involvement in career planning, assistance with family problems, and telecommuting. A survey by HR consulting firm Hewitt Associates found that 64 percent of employers now offer flexible work hours, 46 percent permit job sharing, and 39 percent allow telecommuting.[57] Other companies are exploring the use of four-day workweeks to lessen their employees' commuting costs (particularly with rising gasoline prices).

Companies with programs such as these calculate that accommodating their employees' individual needs and circumstances is a powerful way to attract and retain top-calibre people. Aetna Life and Casualty, for example, cut its turnover by 50 percent after it began offering six-month parental leaves, coupled with an option for part-time work when employees return to the job.[58] With that said, family-friendly companies have to balance the benefits they provide to families versus their single employees. The majority of employees have no children under 18. A Conference Board survey of companies with family-friendly programs found that companies acknowledge that childless employees harbour resentment against employees with children who are able to take advantage of these programs.[59]

See Highlights in HRM 1.5 for a discussion with Nora Spinks, an expert in work–life harmony.

Highlights in HRM 1.5

Work–Life Harmony

Nora Spinks, president and CEO of Work–Life Harmony, a consulting company specializing in work–life balance issues, comments on the demographic issues affecting employee behaviour: "Women are in the workplace to stay; they have fewer and shorter career breaks and have more opportunities to make or influence organizational decisions. There is a high proportion of the aging 'boomer' workforce that are asking, 'What is my legacy?' They are rethinking priorities and lifestyles and reducing the number of hours they are working. At the same time, the nexus generation [i.e., the generation born in the 1980s] is entering the workforce and managerial positions with a fresh perspective and different outlook on the work experience. They see work as a means to having a life, not as life in and of itself. The boomers tend to live to work, the nexus

generation work to live. Growing up, they witnessed people give up a life for the sake of a job, only to see them ultimately lose employment in periods of downsizing and restructuring. They don't want the same experience.

"A recent international study of students found that young people about to enter the workforce wanted to have a challenging career with plenty of opportunity to grow personally and professionally, and they wanted to be able to take advantage of those opportunities while achieving work–life balance. It is up to organizations, executives, and managers to create the kinds of environments to make that possible. It is the only way for them to meet increasing customer/client demands, meet the challenges of global competition, and reach their organizational objectives."

THE PARTNERSHIP OF LINE MANAGERS AND HR DEPARTMENTS

We have taken a good deal of time upfront in this book to outline today's competitive and social challenges to reinforce the idea that managing people is not something that occurs in a back room called the HR department. Managing people is every manager's business, and successful organizations combine the experience of line managers with the expertise of HR specialists to develop and utilize the talents of employees to their greatest potential. Addressing HR issues is rarely the exclusive responsibility of HR departments acting alone. Instead, HR managers work side by side with line managers to address people-related issues of the organization. While this relationship has not always achieved its ideal, the situation is rapidly improving. HR managers are assuming a greater role in top management planning and decision making, a trend that reflects the growing awareness among executives that HRM can make important contributions to the success of an organization.

RESPONSIBILITIES OF THE HUMAN RESOURCES MANAGER

Although line managers and HR managers need to work together, their responsibilities are different, as are their competencies and expertise. The major activities for which a HR manager is typically responsible are as follows:

1. *Advice and counsel.* The HR manager often serves as an in-house consultant to supervisors, managers, and executives. Given their knowledge of internal employment issues (policies, labour agreements, past practices, ethics and corporate governance, and the needs of employees) as well as their awareness of external trends (economic and employment data, new legal and regulatory issues, and the like), HR managers can be an invaluable resource for making decisions. For example, larger companies have begun appointing "chief ethics officers" to help their employees wade through grey areas when it comes to right and wrong. The firm's top HR manager is in a good position for this job. In smaller companies, however, this task frequently falls on the shoulders of individual HR managers. HR managers are also being relied on more heavily to advise compensation committees, which are more closely scrutinizing executives' pay than they have in years past.

2. *Service.* HR managers also perform a host of service activities such as recruiting, selecting, testing, planning and conducting training programs, and hearing employee concerns and complaints. Technical expertise in these areas is essential for HR managers and forms the basis of HR program design and implementation. Moreover, managers must be convinced that the HR staff is there to help them increase their productivity rather than to impose obstacles to their goals. This requires not only the ability on the part of the HR executive to consider problems from the viewpoint of line managers and supervisors, but also skill in communicating with the managers and supervisors.

3. *Policy formulation and implementation.* HR managers generally propose and draft new policies or policy revisions to address recurring problems or to prevent anticipated problems. Ordinarily, these are proposed to the senior executives of the organization, who actually issue the policies. HR managers may monitor performance of line departments and other staff departments to ensure conformity with established HR policies, procedures, and practices. Perhaps more important, they are a resource to whom managers can turn for policy interpretation.

[OUTCOME]

4. *Employee advocacy.* One of the enduring roles of HR managers is to serve as an employee advocate—listening to employees' concerns and representing their needs to managers—to make certain that the interests of employees and the interests of the organization are aligned with one another. Effective employee relations provide a support structure when disruptive changes interfere with workers' normal daily activities.

In the process of managing human resources, increasing attention is being given to the personal needs of the participants. Thus, throughout this book, we will not only emphasize the importance of the contributions that HRM makes to the organization, but also give serious consideration to its effects on the individual and on society. This is important because employees and the public at large are demanding that employers demonstrate greater social responsibility in terms of managing their human resources. Complaints that job stress is devitalizing the lives and injuring the health of employees are not uncommon. Charges of discrimination against women, visible minorities, physically and mentally disabled people, and the elderly with respect to hiring, training, advancement, and compensation are being levelled against some employers. Issues such as equal pay for work of equal value, living wages, the high cost of extended health care and dental benefits, day care for the children of employees, elder care for their parents, and alternative work schedules are concerns that many employers must address as their workforces grow more diverse. All employers are finding that privacy and confidentiality of information about employees are serious matters and deserve the greatest protection that can be provided.

Where employees are organized into unions (covered in Chapter 14), employers can encounter costly collective bargaining proposals, threats of strike, and charges of unfair labour practices. Court litigation, demands for corrective action by governmental agencies, and sizable damage awards in response to employee lawsuits are still other hazards that contemporary employers must try to avoid. (We will discuss these issues in detail in Chapter 13.) Good managers recognize the contributions that their HR departments make to their organizations. These managers expect HR personnel to assume a broader role in the overall strategy of their organizations.

COMPETENCIES OF THE HUMAN RESOURCES MANAGER

As top executives expect HR managers to assume a broader role in overall organizational strategy, many of these managers will need to acquire a complementary set of competencies. These competencies are summarized here and shown in Figure 1.6.

1. *Business mastery.* HR professionals need to know the business of their organization thoroughly. This requires an understanding of its economic and financial capabilities so that they can become a key member of the team of business managers in order to develop the firm's strategic direction. It also requires that HR professionals develop skills at external relations focused on their customers.

2. *HR mastery.* HR professionals are the organization's behavioural science experts. HR professionals should develop expert knowledge in the areas of staffing, development, appraisal, rewards, team building, and communication.

3. *Change mastery.* HR professionals have to be able to manage change processes so that their firms' HR activities are effectively merged with the business needs of their organizations. This involves interpersonal and problem-solving skills, as well as innovativeness and creativity.

4. *Personal credibility.* Like other management professionals, HR professionals must establish personal credibility in the eyes of their internal and external customers. Credibility and trust are earned by developing personal relationships with one's customers, demonstrating the values of the firm, standing up for one's own beliefs, and being fair-minded when dealing with others.

Using the Internet

Canadian HR professionals abide by a code of ethics which can be found on

http://www.cchra.ca

The HR required professional competencies can also be found on this site.

FIGURE **1.6**

Human Resource Competency Model

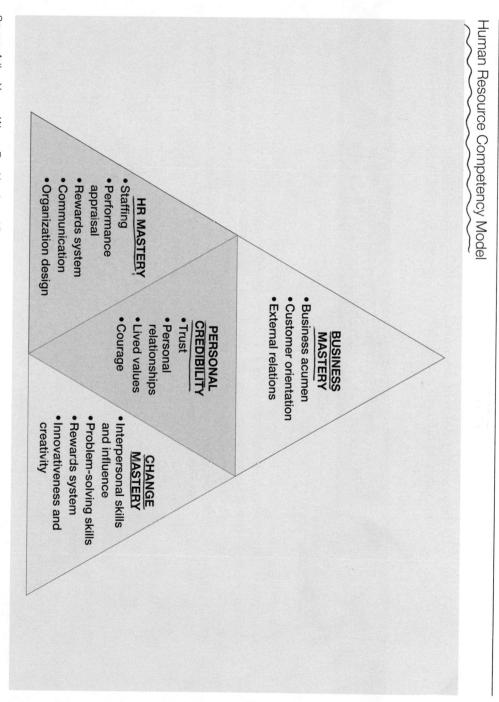

Source: Arthur Yeung, Wayne Brockbank, and Dave Ulrich, "Lower Cost, Higher Value: Human Resource Function in Transformation." Reprinted with permission from *Human Resource Planning*, Vol. 17, No. 3 (1994), Copyright 1994 by The Human Resource Planning Society, 317 Madison Avenue, Suite 1509, New York, NY 10017, Phone: (212) 490-6387, Fax: (212) 682-6851.

Good HR managers help their organizations build a <u>sustained competitive advantage</u>. At lower levels in the organization, a rapidly growing number of companies, including Ford Canada and UPS Canada are assigning HR representatives to their core business teams to make certain that HR issues are addressed on the job and that their HR representatives, in turn, are knowledgeable about core business issues rather than simply focusing on employee-related administrative functions.

ROLE OF THE LINE MANAGER

As much as we might say about the role of the HR department, in the final analysis managing people depends on effective supervisors and line managers. As one executive at Merck put it, "Human resources are far too important to be left to the personnel department." Although HR managers have the responsibility for coordinating programs and policies pertaining to people-related issues, managers and employees themselves are ultimately responsible for performing these functions.

We understand that most readers of this book will be line managers and supervisors, rather than HR specialists. This text is, therefore, oriented to *helping people manage people more effectively*, whether they become first-line supervisors or chief executive officers. Students now preparing for careers in organizations will find that the study of HRM provides a background that will be valuable in managerial and supervisory positions. Discussions concerning the role of the HR department can provide a better understanding of the functions performed by this group. Becoming familiar with the role HR managers play should help facilitate closer cooperation between the different departments of firms and enable line and executive-level managers to fully utilize the assistance and services offered by their HR groups.

Small Business APPLICATION

When we reviewed the day in the life of an HR generalist earlier in the chapter, it was apparent that organizations have a variety of staff-related requirements associated with supporting business operations. These could include hiring, paying, managing, training, or terminating staff. This could also involve work design or staffing strategies, and may also involve ensuring legal compliance. Traditionally, the role of an HR generalist is a position in medium or large organizations, those with 100 employees or more.

However, as of December 2007, more than 1 million small businesses were in operation in Canada, all of which would be too small to justify having an HR generalist on staff. Small business represents 48 percent of private-sector jobs in Canada, employing more workers than either large or medium enterprises. As a result, small business owners without HR generalists manage over 5 million employees in Canada. It is apparent that small business owners need the tools and practices employed by HR generalists integrated in a handbook they can refer to as needed.

Who is responsible for the delivery of HR responsibilities in small business depends on a number of contextual factors: the size of the company, the nature of the business, the financial status of the company, the management structure, the structure of support roles, the leadership culture, and the approach to using vendors. The delivery of HR support may be delivered by the business owner themselves for very small companies, by managers for slightly larger companies, and by office managers for larger companies. Small businesses may outsource some or all of this support to vendors who support many clients. Activities such as payroll, benefits, and legal support are often delivered through vendors.

The types of services traditionally delivered by HR generalists in large enterprises that are delivered in small companies are to a large extent driven by the industry, size, and geographic location. For example, the human resources needs in a retail environment with high employee turnover will focus largely on recruiting and training, although the needs in a stable construction business may centre around health and safety. Through this text, we will dedicate a section of each chapter to the applicability to small business of the practices reviewed and will draw upon industry-specific examples that help demonstrate each practice.

Source: Statistics Canada, "Key Small Business Statistics," http://www.ic.gc.ca/eic/site/sbrp-rppe.nsf/eng/h_rd02395.html, retrieved July 26, 2009.

SUMMARY

[OUTCOME 1] People have always been central to organizations, but their strategic importance is growing in today's knowledge-based industries. An organization's success increasingly depends on the knowledge, skills, and abilities of its employees.

[OUTCOME 2] Globalization influences the majority of the Canadian economy and affects the free flow of trade among countries. This influences the number and kinds of jobs that are available and requires that organizations balance a complicated set of issues related to managing people in different geographies, cultures, legal environments, and business conditions. HR functions such as staffing, training, compensation, and the like have to be adjusted to take into account the differences in global management.

OUTCOME 3

Advanced technology has tended to reduce the number of jobs that require little skill and to increase the number of jobs that require considerable skill, a shift we refer to as moving from touch labour to knowledge work. This displaces some employees and requires that others be retrained. In addition, information technology has influenced HRM through human resources information systems (HRIS) that streamline HR processes, make information more readily available to managers and employees, and enable HR departments to focus on the firm's strategies.

OUTCOME 4

Both proactive and reactive change initiatives require HR managers to work with line managers and executives to create a vision for the future, establish an architecture that enables change, and communicate with employees about the processes of change.

OUTCOME 5

In order to "compete through people," organizations have to do a good job of managing human capital: the knowledge, skills, and capabilities that have value to organizations. Managers must develop strategies for identifying, recruiting, and hiring the best talent available; for developing these employees in ways that are firm-specific; for helping them to generate new ideas and generalize them through the company; for encouraging information sharing; and for rewarding collaboration and teamwork.

OUTCOME 6

In order to respond to customer needs better, faster, and more cheaply, organizations have instituted total quality

management (TQM) and reengineering programs. Each of these programs requires that HR be involved in changing work processes, training, job design, compensation, and the like. HR issues also arise when communicating with employees about the new work systems, just as with any change initiative. Better business thinking builds more strategic HR thinking.

OUTCOME 7

In order to contain costs, organizations have been downsizing, outsourcing, offshoring, leasing employees, and enhancing productivity. HR's role is to maintain the relationship between a company and its employees while implementing the changes.

OUTCOME 8

The workforce is becoming increasingly diverse, and organizations are doing more to address employee concerns and to maximize the benefit of different kinds of employees. Demographic changes, social and cultural differences, and changing attitudes toward work can provide a rich source of variety for organizations. But to benefit from diversity, managers need to recognize the potential concerns of employees and make certain that the exchange between the organization and employees is mutually beneficial.

OUTCOME 9

In working with line managers to address the organization's challenges, HR managers play a number of important roles; they are called on for advice and ethics counsel, for various service activities, for policy formulation and implementation, and for employee advocacy. To perform these roles effectively, HR managers must contribute business competencies, state-of-the-art HR competencies, and change-management competencies. Ultimately, managing people is rarely the exclusive responsibility of the HR function. Every manager's job is managing people, and successful companies combine the expertise of HR specialists with the experience of line managers to develop and utilize the talents of employees to their greatest potential.

KEY TERMS

corporate social responsibility, 7
downsizing, 17
employee leasing, 19
globalization, 7
human capital, 12
human resources information system (HRIS), 9

human resources management (HRM), 4
knowledge workers, 8
managing diversity, 24
offshoring, 18
outsourcing, 18
proactive change, 11

reactive change, 11
reengineering, 16
Six Sigma, 14
total quality management (TQM), 14

DISCUSSION QUESTIONS

1. Are people always an organization's most valuable asset? Why or why not? Name other strategic or valuable assets of organizations.

2. Suppose your boss asked you to summarize the major people-related concerns in opening an office in Tokyo. What issues would be on your list?

3. In groups, create a list of the ways in which you have encountered technology in your job search, hiring, training etc. Assess your experiences; were they primarily positive or negative? Why?

4. The auto sector is undergoing rapid changes. Describe these changes, and then prepare a list of how auto manufacturers are responding to the impact that these are having on employees.

5. Can you think of a situation in which, if a particular person left an organization, the organization's expertise would drop rapidly?

6. In groups, debate the proposition: *Employees are an expense and their numbers should be reduced.*

7. If you were managing a small business, and had to cut costs, which would be your preferred option and why: downsizing or outsourcing?

8. What are the pros and cons of having a more diverse workforce? Is Canada in a better position to compete globally because of its diverse population? Find examples from a school or work project where having a diverse team made a difference, and explain that difference.

9. In your opinion, what is the most important role of HR managers? Should HR professionals be the "voice" for employees or the "spokesperson" for managers? Explain your view. Should HR professionals be licensed, like accountants and lawyers?

INTERNET EXERCISE

Go to a job board such as careerbuilder.ca or monster.ca, and find three HR generalist jobs. Make a list of the tasks that the successful candidates would be expected to do. Go to Highlights in HRM 1.1, and compare these tasks to the description of "A Day in the Life of an HR Generalist." What are the similarities and differences? Also make a list of the education, experience, and skill requirements for these jobs. Are they identical across all jobs? What might account for any differences?

HRM EXPERIENCE

Balancing Competitive Challenges and Employee Concerns

Human resources management is not just the responsibility of the personnel department. If people are a competitive resource, then line managers play an increasingly important role in managing the workforce. But this is not an either/or situation. Rather than seeing line managers assume the responsibilities of HR managers, we see both groups working together to handle workforce issues. But how exactly do these two groups work together?

Assignment

1. Working in teams of four to six individuals, identify what role the HR department would play in terms of the following activities and what role line managers would play. Where would overlaps occur, and would there be any likely problems?

    a. Recruiting and selection
    b. Training and development
    c. Compensation
    d. Performance evaluation
    e. Labour relations

2. How would potential problems be resolved?

3. Write the groups' findings on flip charts and post for all to see. One member from each team should explain his or her findings to all class members.

4. Point out the similarities and differences across the teams. Save these points and revisit them—possibly revising them—as you study subsequent chapters in this text.

BIZFLIX EXERCISES

BABE: HERDING SHEEP, BABE'S WAY

This chapter's introduction to human resources management emphasized its role in helping managers bring together different types of people to reach a common purpose. An earlier chapter section, "Demographic and Employee Concerns," highlighted those differences. Watch this scene from *Babe* while recalling those discussions.

Babe is a charming Australian film featuring eccentric, quiet Farmer Hoggett (James Cromwell), who trains a pig he won at the fair to herd his sheep. His eccentricity turns to determination when he enters the pig in the Australian National Sheepdog Championships. The Academy Award-winning visual effects include a seamless mixture of animatronic doubles, computer images, and live animals.

This scene comes from the "A Pig That Thinks It's a Dog" segment that appears about 40 minutes into the film. Farmer Hoggett's sheepdogs, Rex (voiced by Hugo Weaving) and Fly (voiced by Miriam Margolyes), along with Babe (voiced by Christine Cavanaugh) the pig, accompany him to his sheep herd. Hoggett needs to gather the sheep into a pen so he can shear their wool. Before leaving for the pasture, Farmer Hoggett saw Babe carefully divide some chickens into two groups based on their color. Hoggett suspects that perhaps Babe has some herding skills.

What to Watch for and Ask Yourself

- Are Babe's methods of herding sheep different from those used by the sheep-dogs? If yes, what are the differences?
- Does Babe discover that he cannot successfully herd sheep as a sheepdog herds them? What does he do?
- Does Farmer Hoggett accept Babe for what he is—a pig, not a sheepdog?

CASE STUDY 1

THE GLOBAL MANAGEMENT CONSULTING FIRM ACCENTURE BRINGS EMPLOYEES FACE TO FACE

A team of Filipino IT professionals is responsible for creating Accenture's own social networking tool that allows collaboration among the company's workers worldwide. Aptly called Accenture People, it resembles popular social networking sites, much like Facebook, and allows employees to create their own profiles. But more than a listing of hobbies and other personal interests, these profiles provide a glimpse of each employee's role in Accenture, including technical expertise and the projects in which he or she was involved.

For a global company with numerous business units like Accenture, the idea is to simply make everyone more familiar with each other's background and then encourage knowledge sharing. In the Philippines alone, Accenture has around 15,000 workers doing management consulting, system integration, and BPO (business process outsourcing). In terms of size, the Philippines is behind only the United States and India in Accenture's global network. "One of the challenges for us is collaboration," said Michael Duff, project manager for Accenture Philippines, who leads a six-person team that developed Accenture People. "Different teams within Accenture have been using tools before that allow people to share knowledge on projects. This time, we put everything into a single system," added Duff, who has been with Accenture for more than eight years.

The idea for a Web-based tool like Accenture People resulted from a leadership development program held in the United States. Since a local team was responsible for some of Accenture's presence on the Internet—including the main Accenture Web page and Accenture Careers—the task of building a social networking tool fell to Duff's team. Accenture People was launched only last December, but Duff estimates about one-third of Accenture's entire global workforce of about 175,000 people have already created profiles. That includes Accenture's chairman and CEO Bill Green.

Duff recalls an instance when someone working for Accenture in London got in touch with him and asked for his help on a particular technology both were using. Like Friendster or MySpace, employees can create blogs and participate in discussion forums—usually best practices and "tips and tricks" on tasks such as programming code, according to Duff—to ask for help on certain projects. For less technical matters, the search button alone makes for a very useful tool for Annbel Tierro, who heads Accenture's system integration unit in the Philippines.

"I get to do a lot of conference calls in a day. It helps to at least have an idea what the person I am talking to looks like or what his or her interests are," said Tierro. "We have speakers who regularly come here, so even before they arrive, at least I am already familiar with their roles and achievements in the company."

Source: Reprinted from Lawrence Casiraya, "Filipino Team Builds Accenture's Internal 'Facebook,'" Inquirer.net (February 14, 2008).

QUESTIONS

1. How does the Accenture People site help Accenture better serve its customers?

2. How successful do you think Accenture will be at getting its employees to create their profiles?

3. Can you see any drawbacks related to employees creating their own profiles?

CASE STUDY 2

INTERGENERATIONAL ISSUES

When Jason Traynor was a junior human resources administrator at Peregrine Incorporated, he faced serious challenges with a workforce of different ages. The reason for many of the issues was that General Motors had recently sold off the fabrication plant as part of its new business strategy to get out of auto parts manufacturing and focus solely on assembling vehicles. With the sale of the plant came the condition that any GM employee would be allowed to return to the main GM autoplex as positions came open through employee attrition. Once a GM employee left, he had to be replaced. More times than not, GM would "call out" (recruit) 30 to 40 employees with only two or three days' notice to Peregrine. With no pool of candidates available, Peregrine had to react quickly as not to disrupt production at General Motors.

Due to time constraints, prescreening was minimal. There were often no interviews, reference checks, or selection instruments. On several occasions, people would be selected on Friday night for a Monday morning start. The majority of the new hires were young and right out of high school. These new employees, with limited postsecondary education and little, if any, factory experience were earning $28 an hour, plus benefits, which equalled approximately $85,000 per year. The job was so lucrative that many opted out of pursuing further education. The biggest challenge came when the 18- to 19-year-olds were thrown into a working environment of preretirement 60-year-old factory workers. There was conflict and complaints about everything from the type of music choice on the shop floor to clothing tastes and inappropriate sexual comments.

One of the greatest challenges began when the senior employees began interacting with the junior employees and the new employees would attempt to "use" the system in the same way that a 25-year employee did. The junior employees learned very quickly how to manipulate the collective agreement to their advantage. Activities such as punch card fraud, not badging in or out, and leaving the facility unauthorized while still on the clock were quickly becoming the norm. According to Jason Traynor, "This is not the kind of behaviour you want in your new hires." Having new employees acting as though they had put in 20 years of service often created conflict between the two generations as many of the senior employees felt that these "kids" had not paid their dues and were simply riding the coattails of the senior membership. Addiction problems were rampant among the new employees—many having never been exposed to the readily available supply of drugs and alcohol. Linked to this were the increasing levels of casual absenteeism. Many new hires were terminated and a great deal of time and energy was spent with the union, which fought to reinstate these employees.

An independent third-party consulting company was asked to help manage these issues. Self-directed workshops were initiated to teach the workers about teamwork and quality. Employee assistance programs were created to help struggling employees. A labour council was started to deal with conflict on the factory floor. The company adopted aptitude testing and joint interviewing with the union in an attempt to select employees that were more qualified.

In the end, Peregrine eventually failed and went out of business.

QUESTIONS

1. Based on your experiences working with students/colleagues of different ages, do you believe that there are generational differences in attitudes toward work? Do a search to see if there is any evidence for these beliefs.

2. As the demand for autos declined, and GM and Chrysler faced bankruptcy, the benefits given to auto workers were reduced. Check out the compensation packages for new auto workers, and decide if the package is attractive enough for young workers to leave school, as these young workers did.

CAREER COUNSEL

Most students are legitimately worried about jobs and career prospects. Career Counsel is a feature at the end of each chapter designed to help students manage their working lives and prepare for a career. The assessment exercises are designed to encourage introspection and self-discovery. We encourage you to complete these exercises on the *Managing Human Resources* website and compile them into a separate career planning workbook. Start by accessing http://www.belcourt6e.nelson.com.

NOTES AND REFERENCES

1. Edward L. Gubman, *The Talent Solution: Aligning Strategy and People to Achieve Extraordinary Results* (New York: McGraw-Hill Professional Publishing, 1998).

2. "Retiring Workforce, Widening Skills Gap, Exodus of 'Critical Talent' Threaten Companies: Deloitte Survey," *Canadian Corporate News* (February 15, 2005); "The Importance of HR," *HRfocus* 73, no. 3 (March 1996): 14.

3. T.J. Watson, Jr., *A Business and Its Beliefs: The Ideas That Helped Build IBM* (New York: McGraw-Hill, 1963).

4. Jennifer Rivkin, "The New Rules of Growth" *Profit*, vol. 24, Issue 5, 2005: 58.

5. "U.S. Firms Extend Global Reach," *Workforce Management* 83, no. 13 (December 1, 2004): 138; Susan Meisinger, "Going Global: A Smart Move for HR Professionals," *HR Magazine* 49, no. 3 (March 2004): 6; "In Bev Flattens SAB Miller," *The New York Times* (June 13, 2003).

6. Anonymous "Lie Back and Forget the Maple Leaf," *The Economist*, April 5, 2008.

7. Helmar Drost and Richard Hird, *An Introduction to the Canadian Labour Market*, 2nd edition, Thomson Nelson, 2006.

8. HRPAO, "Globalization of Knowledge Work Threatens 2.4 Million Canadian Jobs," http://www.hrpao.org/hrpao/knowledgecentre, retrieved December 19, 2005.

9. World Trade Organization, *World Trade Report, 2007* (Geneva: WTO Publications): 34; "One Ninth of All U.S. Production Is for Export," *PPI Trade Fact of the Week* (March 19, 2008).

10. Nancy R. Lockwood, "Corporate Social Responsibility: HR's Leadership Role," *HR Magazine* 49, no. 2 (December 2004): S1–11.

11. "China Engineers Next Great Leap with Wave of 'Knowledge Workers,' *Milwaukee Journal Sentinel* (Knight-Ridder/Tribune News Service), December 31, 2003; "Edward Yourdon's New Book Helps 'Knowledge Workers' Put Emotion Aside to Look at the Facts of the New Economic Reality," *PR Newswire* (October 4, 2004); Marshall Goldsmith, "Supervisors of the Smart," *BRW* 30, no. 20 (May 22, 2008): 57.

12. Ben Worthen, "Measuring the ROI of Training," *CIO* 14, no. 9 (February 15, 2001): 128–36; Hashi Syedain, "Out of this World," *People Management* 14, no. 8 (April 17, 2008): 20–24.

13. Scott A. Snell, Donna Stueber, and David P. Lepak, "Virtual HR Departments: Getting Out of the Middle," in R. L. Heneman and D. B. Greenberger (eds.), *Human Resource Management in Virtual Organizations* (Columbus, OH: Information Age Publishing, 2002); Samuel Greengard, "How to Fulfill Technology's Promise," *Workforce* (February 1999): *HR Software Insights* supplement, 10–18.

14. Drew Robb, "Building a Better Workforce: Performance Management Software Can Help You Identify and Develop High-Performing Workers," *HR Magazine* 49, no. 10 (October 2004): 86–92.

15. Robb, "Building a Better Workforce," 86–92; "How to Implement an Effective Process for a New HR Management System," *HRfocus* (January 2005): 3–4; "New Study Finds HRIS Key to Reducing Costs," *Payroll Managers Report* 7, no. 5 (May 2007): 13.

16. Bruce Shutan, "HRMS Flexibility Unlocks Secret to Success," *Employee Benefits* (August 1, 2004); "New Study Finds HRIS Key to Reducing Costs," *Payroll Managers Report* 7, no. 5 (May 2007): 13.

17. Dan McLean "Home Depot wins with IT. Others, not so much," *The Globe and Mail*, June 21, 2007, B9

18. John P. Kotter, "Ten Observations," *Executive Excellence* 16, no. 8 (1999): 15–16.

19. "Lessons from Industry about Managing Change," *Seybold Report: Analyzing Publishing Technologies* 8, no. 10 (May 10, 2008): 10.

20. Jennifer J. Laabs, "Change," *Personnel Journal* (July 1996): 54–63; Louisa Peacock, "Change Management Is Biggest Challenge," *Personnel Today* (February 12, 2008): 47.

21. Edward E. Lawler III, Alec Levenson, and John W. Boudreau, "HR Metrics and Analytics: Use and Impact," *Human Resource Planning* 27, no. 4 (December 2004): 27–36; Louisa Peacock, "Change Management Is Biggest Challenge," *Personnel Today* (February 12, 2008): 47; J.P. Kotter, "Leading Change: Why Transformation Efforts Fail," *Harvard Business Review* (March/April 1995): 59–67.

22. Lee G. Bolman and Terry E. Deal, "Four Steps to Keeping Change Efforts Heading in the Right Direction," *Journal of Quality and Participation* 22, no. 3 (May/June 1999): 6–11; "Coaching Employees through the Six Stages of Change," *HRfocus* 79, no. 5 (May 2002): 9; Stefan Stern, "Forever Changing," *Management Today* (February 7, 2005): 40; Dennis Smillie, "Managing Change, Maximizing Technology," *Multi-Housing News* 40, no. 1 (January 2005): 4.

23. Donald C. Busi, "Assignment Reviews (ARs): Moving toward Measuring Your Most Valuable Asset," *Supervision* 66, no. 1 (January 2005): 3–7.

24. David Lepak and Scott Snell. 2003. "Managing the Human Resource Architecture for Knowledge-Based Competition." In S. Jackson, M. Hitt, and A. DeNisi (eds.), *Managing Knowledge for Sustained Competitive Advantage: Designing Strategies for Effective Human Resource Management.* (SIOP Scientific Frontiers Series, 127–154); David Lepak and Scott Snell, "Examining the Human Resource Architecture: The Relationship among Human Capital, Employment, and Human Resource Configurations," *Journal of Management* 28, no. 4 (2002): 517–543; Steve Bates, "Study Links HR Practices with the Bottom Line," *HR Magazine* 46, no. 12 (December 2001): 14; Ann Pomeroy, "Cooking Up Innovation: When It Comes to Helping Employees Create New Products and Services, HR's Efforts Are a Key Ingredient," *HR Magazine* 49, no. 11 (November 2004): 46–54.

25. Gary S. Becker, *Human Capital* (New York: Columbia University Press, 1964); Charles A. O'Reilly III and Jeffrey Pfeffer, "Cisco Systems: Acquiring and Retaining Talent in Hypercompetitive Markets," *Human Resource Planning* 23, no. 3 (2000): 38–52.

26. For more on Buckman Labs and its approach to managing human capital, visit the organization's website at http://www.buckman.com. The company is also well known for its knowledge management initiatives, called Knowledge Nurture, as well as its knowledge management system, called K'Netix; see http://www.knowledge-nurture.com.

27. Dave Ulrich, Steve Kerr, and Ron Ashkenas, *The GE Work-Out: How to Implement GE's Revolutionary Method for Busting Bureaucracy & Attacking Organizational Problems* (New York: McGraw-Hill Professional Publishing, 2002).

28. Benoit Guay, "Knowledge Management Is a Team Sport," *Computing Canada* 27, no. 3 (July 13, 2001): 23; Pimm Fox, "Making Support Pay," *Computerworld* 36, no. 11 (March 11, 2002): 28; "Visions of the Future," *Human Resources* (January 2008): 22.

29. C.W. Russ Russo, "Ten Steps to a Baldrige Award Application," *Quality Progress* 34, no. 8 (August 2001): 49–56; "Nonprofits Aim to Apply for Baldrige Award," *Quality* 43, no. 11 (November 2004): 11–13.

30. The term *Six Sigma* is a registered trademark of Motorola. It is based on the Greek letter sigma, used as a symbol of variation in a process (the standard deviation). For more information, see Peter S. Pande, Robert P. Neuman, and Roland R. Cavanagh, *The Six Sigma Way: How GE, Motorola, and Other Top Companies Are Honing Their Performance* (New York: McGraw-Hill, 2000).

31. Joseph A. Defeo, "Six Sigma: Road Map for Survival," *HRfocus* 76, no. 7 (July 1999): 11–12; Michele V. Gee and Paul C. Nystrom, "Strategic Fit between Skills Training and Levels of Quality Management: An Empirical Study of American Manufacturing Plants," *Human Resource Planning* 22, no. 2 (1999): 12–23; Linda Heuring, "Six Sigma in Sight," *HR Magazine* 49, no. 3 (March 2004): 76–81; Paul Teague, "A Take-Charge Approach Worth Imitating," *Purchasing* 136, no. 11 (August, 16 2007): 14.

32. Ed Gubman, "HR Strategy and Planning: From Birth to Business Results," *Human Resource Planning* 27, no. 1 (March 2004): 13–21.

33. M. Hammer and J. Champy, *Reengineering the Corporation* (New York: HarperCollins, 1994). See also Michael Hammer, *Beyond Reengineering: How the Process-Centered Organization Is Changing Our Work and Our Lives* (New York: HarperBusiness, 1996); William M. James, "Best HR Practices for Today's Innovation Management," *Research-Technology Management* 45, no. 1 (January–February 2002): 57–61.

34. Up to Speed: L.L. Bean Moves Employees as Workloads Shift," *Chief Executive* (July–August 1996): 15; Darrell Rigby, "Look Before You Lay Off," *Harvard Business Review* 80, no. 4 (April 2002): 20–21.

35. "WorldatWork Finds One-Third of Companies Downsized after 9/11," *Report on Salary Surveys* (December 2002): 2; Jeanne Whalen, "Glaxo Is Eliminating R&D Jobs as Part of Cost-Cutting Plan," *The Wall Street Journal* 251, no. 137 (June 12, 2008).

36. Stephanie Armour, "Some Companies Choose No-Layoff Policy," *USA Today*, December 17, 2001, B-1; Gene Koretz, "Hire Math: Fire 3, Add 5," *BusinessWeek Online* (March 13, 2000); Michelle Conlin, "Where Layoffs Are a Last Resort," *BusinessWeek Online* (October 8, 2001); Lynn Miller, "Downsizing Trend Brings New Change to HR Directors," *HR Magazine* 45, no. 1 (January 2001); Norman E. Amundson, William A. Borgen, Sharalyn Jordan, and Anne C. Erlebach, "Survivors of Downsizing: Helpful and Hindering Experiences," *Career Development Quarterly* 52, no. 3 (March 2004): 256–272.

37. Tavia Grant "Not a cure-all, but creativity is saving some jobs," *The Globe and Mail,* January 24, 2009, B15.

38. Gubman, "HR Strategy and Planning," 13–21.

39. Jeff Hale "Ask what another country can do for you," *The Globe and Mail,* February 22, 2007, B11.

40. Gubman, "HR Strategy and Planning," 13–21; Thomas W. Gainey, Brian S. Klaas, and Darla Moore, "Outsourcing the Training Function: Results from the Field," *Human Resource Planning* 25, no. 1 (2002): 16–23, 873, 881; Denise Pelham, "Is It Time to Outsource HR?" *Training* 39, no. 4 (April 2002): 50–52; Tom Anderson, "HR Outsourcing Expected to Surge this Year," *Employee Benefit News* (February 1, 2005); Jessica Marquez, "More Piecemeal Approach to HRO Emerging," *Workforce Management,* 87, no. 8 (May 5, 2008): 10.

41. Karyn Siobhan Robinson, "HR Needs Large Role in Offshoring," *HR Magazine* 590, no. 45 (May 2004): 30–32; Nick Heath, "Global Outsourcing to Grow in 2008," *BusinessWeek* (January 10, 2008).

42. Pete Engardio, Michael Arndt, and Dean Foust, "The Future of Outsourcing," *BusinessWeek* (January 30, 2006): 50.

43. Pam Babcock, "America's Newest Export: White-Collar Jobs," *HR Magazine* 49, no. 4 (April 2004): 50–54.

44. Elliot Spagat, "Procter & Gamble to Outsource about 80% of Back-Office Work," *The Wall Street Journal Online* (June 14, 2002); "Outsourcing HR," *IndustryWeek* 249, no. 10 (May 15, 2000): 71; Carolyn Hirschman, "For PEOs, Business Is Booming," *HR Magazine* 45, no. 2 (February 2000): 42–47; Brian Klaas, "Trust and the Role of Professional Employer Organizations: Managing HR in Small and Medium Enterprises," *Journal of Managerial Issues* 14, no. 1 (Spring 2002): 31–49; Chris Pentilla, "Got It Covered: If You Can't Afford to Offer Employee Benefits on Your Own, Why Not Join Forces with a PEO?" *Entrepreneur* 32, no. 2 (February 2004): 66–68; Milan Yager, "Outsource to Gain Human Resources Expertise," *Hotel & Motel Management* 223, no. 7 (April 21, 2008): 14.

45. Neil Reynolds "US workers leave competition in the dust," *The Globe and Mail* September 24, 2007, B2.

46. Patrick Barta and Andrew Caffrey, "Productivity Leap Shows Potential of U.S. Economy—Rise at 8.6 Percent Pace, Positive For Profits, Doesn't Bode Very Well for Employment," *The Wall Street Journal,* May 8, 2002: A1; Jon E. Hilsenrath, "The Economy: Big U.S. Service Sectors Boosted Late 1990s Surge in Productivity," *The Wall Street Journal,* April 22, 2002: A2; Karen Lowry Miller, "Economy: Out of Steam—A Dip in U.S. Productivity Provokes Anxious Questions," *Newsweek International* (February 21, 2005): 34; Milan Yager, "Outsource to Gain Human Resources Expertise," *Hotel & Motel Management* 223, no. 7 (April 21, 2008): 14.

47. Irwin Speizer, "Diversity on the Menu: Rachelle Hood, Denny's Chief Diversity Officer, Has Boosted the Company's Image. But That Hasn't Sold More Breakfasts," *Workforce Management* 83, no. 12 (November 1, 2004): 41; Patrick Purcell, "Older Workers: Employment and Retirement Trends," *Journal of Pension Planning & Compliance* 34, no. 1 (Spring 2008): 32–48.

48. Statistics Canada, "Canada's Changing Labour Force, 2006 Census: Overview of Canada's Changing Labour Force," June 29, 2009, http://www12.statcan.ca/census-recensement/2006/as-sa/97-559/p2-eng.cfm, retrieved August 5, 2009.

49. Ibid.

50. "Work force reflects how much gray matters," *The Kansas City Star* (via Knight- Ridder/Tribune Business News), March 6, 2005; Kevin G. Hall, "Age-old dilemma," *Fort Worth Star-Telegram* (via Knight- Ridder/Tribune News Service), March 7, 2005, C3–C4; Milan Yager, "A Workforce That Doesn't Retire," *Accounting Today* 22, no. 6 (March 31, 2008): 26–27; Mark L. Alch, "Get Ready for a New Type of Worker in the Workplace: The Net Generation," *Supervision* 69, no. 6 (June 2008): 18–21.

51. Bureau of Labor Statistics, *Women in the Labor Force: A Databook* (2007 Edition)

52. Wallace Imen, "The value of a degree: A million bucks," *The Globe and Mail,* May 24, 2005, C1.

53. Uyen Yu, "Northern Mine Develops Essential Skills in its Workforce," *Canadian HR Reporter,* July 18, 2005: 8; David Hayes, "Canadian Organizations Move to Develop Workplace Literacy and Numerical Skills," *Canadian HR Reporter,* July 18, 2005: 7;

Conrad Murphy, "Assessing Essential Skills to Recruit and Train," *Canadian HR Reporter*, July 18, 2005: 11.

54. Kathleen Iverson, "Managing for Effective Workforce Diversity," *Cornell Hotel and Restaurant Administration Quarterly* 41, no. 2 (April 2000): 31–38; Gail Johnson, "Time to Broaden Diversity Training," *Training* 41, no. 9 (September 2004): 16.

55. "Avoiding Identity Theft," *Aftermarket Business* 114, no. 12 (December 2004): 10.

56. Personal correspondence with Leah F. Vosko, Canada Research Chair in Feminist Political Economy York University, who studies precarious (i.e., nonstandard) employment.

57. Hewitt Canada, "Employers Missing Opportunity to Boost Employee Attraction and Retention," (August 14, 2008), http://www.hewittassociates.com/Intl/NA/en-CA/AboutHewitt/Newsroom/PressReleaseDetail.aspx?cid=5486, retrieved July 26, 2009.

58. Todd Raphael, "The Drive to Downshifting," *Workforce* 80, no. 10 (October 2001): 23; Jim Olsztynski, "Flexible Work Schedules May Make More Sense: One in Six Americans Qualifies as a Caregiver Who May Benefit from Flextime," *National Driller* 26, no. 2 (February 2005): 16–19; Karen Springen, "Cutting Back Your Hours," *Newsweek*, 151, no. 19 (May 12, 2008): 60

59. Leah Carlson, "Flextime Elevated to National Issue," *Employee Benefit News* (September 15, 2004).

CHAPTER 2

Strategy and Human Resources Planning

After studying this chapter, you should be able to

[OUTCOME] 1 Identify the advantages of integrating human resources planning and strategic planning.

[OUTCOME] 2 Understand how an organization's competitive environment influences its strategic planning.

[OUTCOME] 3 Understand why it is important for an organization to do an internal resource analysis.

[OUTCOME] 4 Describe the basic tools used for human resources forecasting.

[OUTCOME] 5 Explain the linkages between competitive strategies and HR.

[OUTCOME] 6 Understand what is required for a firm to successfully implement a strategy.

[OUTCOME] 7 Recognize the methods for assessing and measuring the effectiveness of a firm's strategy.

One of the clichés about the annual reports of companies is that they often claim that "people are our most important asset." Although we might believe this to be true, the fact is that historically managers often have not acted as though they themselves really believed it. In the past, executives often tried to remove human capital from the strategy equation by substituting capital for labour where possible or by creating hierarchical structures that separated those who think from those who actually do the work. But much is changing today.

In a survey, nearly 80 percent of corporate executives said the importance of HRM in their firms has grown substantially over the years, and two-thirds said that HR expenditures are now viewed as a strategic investment rather than simply a cost to be minimized. Indeed, research shows that strategically designed and implemented HR systems increase the value of firms, something executives are keenly interested in accomplishing. They are also demanding their human resources groups push past short-term projections and provide detailed forecasts for needs and the associated costs over a two- to three-year horizon.[1]

[OUTCOME] 1

strategic planning
Procedures for making decisions about the organization's long-term goals and strategies

human resources planning (HRP)
The process of anticipating and providing for the movement of people into, within, and out of an organization

strategic human resources management (SHRM)
The pattern of human resources deployments and activities that enable an organization to achieve its strategic goals

STRATEGIC PLANNING AND HUMAN RESOURCES

As we explained in Chapter 1, "competing through people" is the theme for this book. But the idea remains only a premise for action until we put it into practice. To deliver on this promise, we need to understand some of the systems and processes in organizations that link human resources management and strategic management. A few definitions may be helpful upfront.

Strategic planning involves a set of procedures for making decisions about the organization's long-term goals and strategies. In this chapter, we discuss strategic plans as having a strong external orientation that covers major portions of the organization. The plans especially focus on how the organization will position itself relative to its competitors in order to ensure its long-term survival, create value, and grow. **Human resources planning (HRP)**, by comparison, is the process of anticipating and providing for the movement of people into, within, and out of an organization. Overall, its purpose is to help managers deploy their human resources as effectively as possible, where and when they are needed, in order to accomplish the organization's goals. **Strategic human resources management (SHRM)** combines strategic planning and HR planning. It can be thought of as the pattern of human resources deployments and activities that enable an organization to achieve its strategic goals.

HR planning is an essential activity of organizations. Consider CNA Financial Corp. an insurance company, for example. CNA Financial discovered via HR planning that it would run short of underwriters—a key skill pool in the company—in just two years time if its turnover rate continued at the current pace. The global strategies firms are increasingly pursuing, such as mergers, joint ventures, offshoring, the relocation of plants, product innovation plans, and downsizing, are also making HR planning more critical and more complex for managers. The good news, according to the president and CEO of the Human Resource Planning Society, is that the increased global competitiveness, which in many industries has led to the commoditization of products based on price, is making talent the "great differentiator" among firms. After all, it is relatively easy for a competitor to copy your product and make it more cheaply. But duplicating the talents of your employees will prove much more difficult.[2] The dramatic shifts in the composition of the labour force that are occurring also require that HR managers become more involved in planning because these changes affect the full range of a company's HR practices (such as employee recruitment, selection, training, compensation, and motivation).

STRATEGIC PLANNING AND HR PLANNING: LINKING THE PROCESSES

As organizations plan for their future, HR managers must be concerned with meshing HRP and strategic planning for the organization as a whole. Via strategic planning, organizations set major objectives for themselves and develop comprehensive plans to achieve those objectives. HRP relates to strategic planning in several ways, but at a fundamental level, we can focus on two issues: strategy formulation and strategy implementation. HRP provides a set of inputs into the strategic formulation process in terms of what is possible, that is, whether a firm has the types and numbers of people available to pursue a given strategy. For example, when Indigo executives contemplated the move into Web-based commerce to compete with Amazon.com, one of the issues they had to address was whether they had the talent needed to succeed in that arena.

In addition to strategy formulation, HRP is important in terms of strategy *implementation*. In other words, once the firm has devised its strategy, the company's executives must make resource allocation decisions to implement that strategy, including decisions related to the firm's structure, processes, and human capital.[3] Companies such as GE and IBM have taken strides to combine these two aspects of strategic management.[4] All the available evidence suggests that the integration of HRP and strategic planning tends to be most effective when there is a reciprocal relationship between the two processes. When this occurs, a firm's top management team recognizes that strategic planning decisions affect—and are affected by—HR concerns. Figure 2.1 shows how companies align their HRP and strategic planning in this way. As we look at trends in the best of companies, there is surprisingly little distinction between strategic planning and HRP. The planning cycles are the same, and HR issues are viewed as being integral to the management of the business. As James Walker, a noted HRP expert, puts it, "Today, virtually *all* business issues have people implications; *all* human resource issues have business implications."[5] HR managers, along with the other top executives of their firms, are therefore important facilitators and strategic partners of the planning process.[6] This is an important point we will return to in the rest of this chapter. Traditionally, authors—and too many HR managers—have treated HRP and strategic planning as separate activities. That is why in this chapter, we lay out a step-by-step process to show how a firm's HRP and strategy efforts can be integrated.

STEP ONE: MISSION, VISION, AND VALUES

The first step in strategic planning is establishing a mission, vision, and values for the organization. The **mission** is the basic purpose of the organization, as well as its scope of operations. It is a statement of the organization's reason for existing. The mission often is written in terms of general clients it services. Depending on the scope of the organization, the mission may be broad or narrow. For example, the mission of Google is "to organize the world's information and make it universally accessible and useful."[7] The **strategic vision** of the organization moves beyond the mission statement to provide a perspective on where the company is headed and what the organization can become in the future. The mission and vision of Tim Hortons is as follows:

> Our guiding mission is to deliver superior quality products and services for our customers and communities through leadership, innovation and partnerships. Our vision is to be the quality leader in everything we do.

Although the terms *mission* and *vision* often are used interchangeably, the vision statement ideally clarifies the long-term direction of the company and its strategic intent.

mission
The basic purpose of the organization as well as its scope of operations

strategic vision
A statement about where the company is going and what it can become in the future; clarifies the long-term direction of the company and its strategic intent

FIGURE 2.1

Linking Strategic Planning and Human Resources

BUSINESS/CORPORATE

- Identify purpose and scope
- Clarify long-term direction
- Establish enduring beliefs and principles

- Opportunities and threats (OT)
- Environmental scanning (legal, etc.)
- Industry/competitor analysis

- Strengths and weaknesses (SW)
- Core competencies
- Resources: People, process, systems

- Corporate strategy
- Business strategy
- Functional strategy: Alignment

- Design structure, systems, etc.
- Allocate resources
- Leadership, communication, and change

- Assessment and benchmarking
- Ensuring alignment
- Agility and flexibility

HUMAN RESOURCES

- Capture underlying philosophy
- Establish foundation of culture
- Guide ethical codes of conduct

- Demographic trends
- External supply of labour
- Competitor benchmarking

- Culture, competencies, composition
- Forecast demand for employees
- Forecast supply of employees

- Productivity and efficiency
- Quality, service, speed, innovation
- External fit/alignment and internal fit

- Reconcile supply and demand
- Downsizing, layoffs, etc.
- HR practice: Staffing, training, rewards, etc.

- Human capital metrics
- Balanced scorecard

Mission, Vision, and Values → External Analysis → Internal Analysis → Strategy Formulation → Strategy Implementation → Evaluation

SWOT Analysis

core values
The strong and enduring beliefs and principles that the company uses as a foundation for its decisions

OUTCOME 2

environmental scanning
Systematic monitoring of the major external forces influencing the organization

Organizational core values are the strong enduring beliefs and principles that the company uses as a foundation for its decisions. These are the underlying parameters for how the company will act toward customers, employees, and the public in general. In many cases, the values capture the underlying philosophy of the company culture and give direction to its employees. The values also place limits on what behavior is seen as ethical and acceptable. Highlights in HRM 2.1 shows the mission, vision and values of WestJet.

STEP TWO: ENVIRONMENTAL ANALYSIS

The mission, vision, and values drive the second component of the strategic management process: analysis of external opportunities and threats. Changes in the external environment have a direct impact on the way organizations are run and people are managed. Some of these changes represent opportunities, and some of them represent real threats to the organization. Because of this, successful strategic management depends on an accurate and thorough evaluation of the environment. Environmental scanning is the systematic monitoring of the major external forces influencing the organization.[8] Managers attend to a variety of external issues; however, the following six are monitored most frequently:

1. Economic factors and development information, including general, regional, and global conditions
2. Industry and competitive trends including new processes, services, and innovations

Highlights in **HRM 2.1**

WestJet: Mission, Vision, and Values

Our mission:

To enrich the lives of everyone in WestJet's world by providing safe, friendly, affordable air travel.

Our vision:

WestJet will be the leading low-fare airline that:

People want to work with...

Customers want to fly with...

and Shareholders want to invest with.

At WestJet we have legendary values:

* We are positive and passionate about everything we do.
* We take our jobs seriously, but not ourselves.
* We embrace change and innovation.

* We are friendly and caring toward our People and our Customers, and we treat everyone with respect.
* We provide our People with the training and tools they need to do their jobs.
* We celebrate our successes.
* We personify the hard-working "can-do" attitude.
* We are honest, open, and keep our commitments.
* We are team WestJet!

At WestJet we keep the spirit alive by:

* Being successful in the air.
* Being successful on the ground.
* Celebrating new markets.
* Providing legendary service.
* Experiencing legendary growth.
* Creating internal "magic" and external "wow."

Source: http://www.westjet.com/guest/en/aboutUs/corporateProfile/westJetCulture.shtml

3. Technological changes, including information technology, innovations, and automation.

4. Government and legislative issues, including laws and administrative rulings.

5. Social concerns, including child care, elder care, the environment, and educational priorities.

6. Demographic and labour market trends, including the age, composition, and literacy of the labour market, and immigration.

By scanning the environment for changes that will likely affect an organization, managers can anticipate their impact and make adjustments early.

COMPETITIVE ENVIRONMENT

Many factors in the general environment—factors a firm cannot directly control—can affect its strategic decisions. This is why analyzing the firm's competitive environment is central to strategic planning. The competitive environment includes the specific organizations with which the firm interacts. As Figure 2.2 shows, the competitive environment includes the firm's customers, rival firms, new entrants, substitutes, and suppliers. In strategic planning, firms analyze the competitive environment in order to adapt to or influence the nature of competition. A general rule of thumb about this analysis is: The more power each of these forces has, the less profitable (and therefore attractive) the industry will be. Let us look at each of the five forces.

FIGURE **2.2**

Five Forces Framework

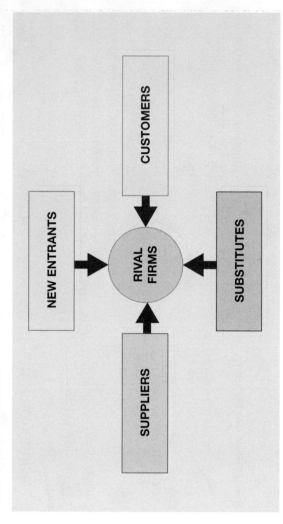

Customers

One of the most important assessments a firm can make is identifying the needs of its customers. At a fundamental level, a firm's strategy should focus on creating customer value—and different customers often want different things. For example, in the hotel industry, business travellers may want convenient locations with meeting facilities. Vacationers may want resort locations with swimming pools, golf courses, and luxury spas. Other travellers may just want an inexpensive room next to the highway. The point is that increasingly, "one size does not fit all," and organizations need to know how they are will provide value to customers. That is the foundation for strategy, and it influences the kind of skills and behaviour that will be needed from employees. For example, actions and attitudes that lead to excellent customer service can include the following:

- Speed of delivering normal orders
- Willingness to meet extraordinary needs
- Merchandise delivered in good condition
- Readiness to take back defective goods and resupply new goods quickly
- Availability of installation and repair services and parts

Rival Firms

In addition to customer analysis, perhaps the most obvious element of industry analysis is examining the nature of competition. The first question to consider is: Who is the competition? Often the answer is clear to everyone, but sometimes it is not. For example, for many years, Toys "R" Us viewed its main competitors to be other toy stores such as FAO Schwarz or KB Toys. However, other retailers such as Zellers and Walmart soon moved into this space very successfully. This had a direct effect on HRP for Toys "R" Us. While in the past, Toys "R" Us had been successful with a volume-based approach (that is, "stack it high, and let it fly"), bigger retailers soon gained an advantage—who can beat Walmart's volume and cost advantage? As a consequence, Toys "R" Us had to modify its strategy to compete more on customer service and the expertise of its employees. But did Toys "R" Us have the number and kind of employees required to compete in this way? Were its staffing, training, performance management, and compensation practices aligned with this strategy?

New Entrants

As we suggested previously, new companies can sometimes enter an industry and compete well against established firms, and sometimes they cannot. To protect their position, companies often try to establish entry barriers to keep new firms out of the industry. However, when new firms do enter an industry, it is often because they have a different—and perhaps better—way to provide value to customers. For example, when WestJet entered the airline business, it distinguished itself by providing excellent service and low prices in regions where customers did not have many options. The HR implications of this are clear. When we look at the challenges faced by traditional airlines because of the threat of carriers such as WestJet, we can clearly see that new entrants can change the "rules of the game" in an industry. The impact on labour costs, productivity, skills required, and work design are important considerations in both strategic planning and HRP.

Substitutes

At times, the biggest opportunity or threat in an industry is not with direct competition, but from substitution. In the telephone industry, for example, cellular technology and VOIP (Voice-Over-the-Internet Protocol) are rapidly substituting for landline phone systems. These substitutes offer the same service or function as traditional firms, but through a different method. That implies that firms may need to adjust their employee skill bases in order to support different technologies, or they may need to think about how they will compete in different ways. As an example, think about how the travel business has changed over the years. Travel agents used to be the key resource for flights, hotels, rental cars, and the like. The focus was almost exclusively on transactions. However, with the advent of online reservation systems, travel agents have had to adapt their approach. Today, they are as likely to compete based on the service they provide and the expertise they have about particular locations.

Suppliers

Organizations rarely create everything on their own, but instead have suppliers that provide them with key inputs. These inputs can include raw materials for production, money (from banks and stockholders), information, and people. This last factor—people, or labour as it is historically called—has direct implications for strategic planning and HRP. Because of its central role in both strategic planning and HRP, we explore it next in much more detail.

EXTERNAL SUPPLY OF LABOUR

Many factors influence the labour supply, including demographic changes in the population, national and regional economics, education level of the workforce, demand for specific employee skills, population mobility, and governmental policies. Consider these labour force statistics:

- About 18 million people are in the workforce; a participation rate of 67 percent. This rate will decline in the coming decades because of the aging baby boomers and declining fertility rates.
- The largest gains in employment are in the service sector. The beneficiaries of this gain are women, who tend to be overrepresented in this sector, and as a result, their participation rate in the labour force is increasing more rapidly than that of men.
- In 2007, about one in five workers was employed part-time, a rate that has doubled over the last three decades. A quarter of these part-time workers would prefer full-time work.

- The hours that Canadians work per week has been trending downward and now hover around 33 hours a week.
- The vast majority (81 percent) of Canadians held permanent jobs (i.e., jobs that did not have a specified end date). The holders of these jobs were paid on average $21 an hour, compared to $16 an hour for those in temporary jobs. The number of Canadians holding two or more jobs has tripled over the last three decades, and accounts for 5 percent of all workers.
- One in three Canadians will be 55 or older by 2027. The median age of retirement is 61.
- The number of immigrants to Canada averages 225,000 annually, and about 70 percent of these locate in Toronto, Vancouver, and Montreal (cities that are home to only 34 percent of Canada's population).[9]

These labour force trends illustrate the importance of monitoring demographic changes as a part of environmental scanning. Fortunately, labour market analysis is aided by various published documents. Statistics Canada and Human Resources and Skills Development Canada (HRSDC) publish many studies on the labour force, as do various provincial governments. In addition, local chambers of commerce and city planning departments can assist both large organizations and new business ventures by providing them with a labour market analysis of their areas. Offshore consulting firms such as IBM and Accenture can be a good source for information about labour trends in other countries.

These sources of information are invaluable; in a rapidly changing environment, it is extremely risky to be caught off-guard. Such changes are important for many reasons, some related to operational issues and some to strategic issues. HRP has to focus on both. At an operational level, the change in labour supply directly influences hiring plans that must take into account the demographic composition of the population in the area in which the organization is located or plans to locate. Similarly, with a "maturing" workforce, HRP must consider the implications for recruitment and replacement policies.

From a strategic standpoint, changes in the labour supply can limit the strategies available to firms. High-growth companies in particular may find it difficult to find the talent they need to expand their businesses. While unemployment rates vary by sector, the shortage of talent in high-skill jobs continues to create real challenges for firms.

In Highlights in HRM 2.2, David Foot, a demographer at the University of Toronto, explains why HR professionals must become aware of the need to scan.

STEP THREE: INTERNAL ANALYSIS

As organizations conduct external analyses of environmental opportunities and threats, they also analyze their internal strengths and weaknesses. Internal analysis provides strategic decision makers with an inventory of organizational skills and resources as well as performance levels.

To be sure, many resources combine to give organizations a competitive advantage. But in contrast to the past, the advantages due to physical assets are being supplanted by intangible assets, including people. As James Brian Quinn noted, "With rare exceptions, the economic and producing power of firms lies more in its intellectual and service capabilities than in its hard assets—land, plant, and equipment."[10]

THE THREE Cs: CULTURE, CAPABILITIES, AND COMPOSITION

In the context of human resource planning, internal analysis focuses especially on "the three Cs": culture, capabilities, and composition.

[OUTCOME 3]

Highlights in **HRM 2.2**

Spotting Trends in the Global Economy

Every human resource professional recognizes that anticipating trends is an important part of the job. Furthermore, senior HR professionals want to influence strategy, not just respond to strategies determined by the "real players" at the boardroom table.

David Foot, a famous Canadian economist and demographer at the University of Toronto, says that HR professionals are often ill equipped to contribute to their organization's strategy. He contends that HR people are experienced in dealing with micro issues, but often lack the big-picture or macro perspective that is necessary to deal with corporate or strategic issues.

Having worked with executives and boards of directors, he is very familiar with the issues facing them and with the inability of HR managers to advance the HR view of the implications of strategic decisions. He offers this example: A company is thinking about going global—say, by expanding into Mexico. The HR person has very little knowledge about the labour market of that country (where there are many young people but relatively few seniors). Furthermore, he or she is likely to be preoccupied with important micro issues, such as how to hire employees and what the local health and safety rules are, when he or she ought to be considering, for example, Mexico's regional unemployment and education rates by region to determine plant location.

Other executives can think strategically when faced with changes in the environment. Foot asks: "How many HR professionals could answer the question, 'How does the exchange rate impact HRP?' Those with a macro perspective would immediately determine: (1) How much business is internal/external? (2) Have the financial people bought insurance against exchange rate fluctuations? (3) If the Canadian dollar depreciates, and there will be more demand for our products, what are the opportunities to access labour in external markets such as Poland or Mexico? How can we recruit these people faster than other companies? This mindset is crucial to being at the boardroom table.

"Let me give you another example of reactionary micro thinking. Low unemployment rates traditionally result in demands from business for higher immigration levels to ease labour shortages. But this traditional HR response will become increasingly inappropriate in the new millennium because more immigrants will only compete with the children of boomers who will be entering the labour force. A proactionary macro-thinking HR person will, therefore, be able to advise the CEO that this is likely to be a short-term, not a long-term, labour shortage and to think internally rather than externally for new workers. This information could be crucial in influencing the company's strategic planning for the next five years."

Culture: Auditing Values, Beliefs, and Attitudes

Think about our initial discussion (in Step One) of mission, vision, and values. Because managers increasingly understand that their employees are critical to their success, they often conduct **cultural audits** to examine the attitudes and beliefs of their workforces as well as the activities they engage in. At one level, this analysis focuses on whether a firm's critical values are embraced and demonstrated by employees throughout the organization. Employee surveys, for example, can measure how employees feel on a number of critical issues and can be very useful for upward assessment and feedback of (and for) management. However, these audits can go much deeper. Sears, for example, found that positive employee attitudes on ten essential factors—including workload and treatment by bosses—are directly linked to customer satisfaction and revenue increases.[11]

Cultural audits essentially involve discussions among top-level managers of how the organization's culture reveals itself to employees and how it can be influenced or improved. The cultural audit may include questions such as the following:

- How do employees spend their time?
- How do they interact with each other?

cultural audits
Audits of the culture and quality of work life in an organization

- What is their morale level?
- Are employees empowered?
- What is the predominant leadership style of the firm's managers?
- How do employees advance within the organization?

By conducting in-depth interviews and making observations over a period of time, managers are able to learn about the culture of their organization and the attitudes of their employees. With the increased diversity of the Canadian workplace, cultural audits can be used to determine whether there are different groups, or subcultures, within the organization that have distinctly different views about the nature of the work and how it should be done, the quality of the company's managers, and so on. Before any HRP can take place, managers have to gain a clear idea of how employees view their organization.

Capabilities: People as a Strategic Resource

A growing number of experts now argue that the key to a firm's success is based on establishing a set of core capabilities—bundles of people, processes, and systems that distinguish an organization from its competitors and deliver value to customers. McDonald's, for example, has developed core capabilities in management efficiency and training. FedEx has core capabilities in package routing, delivery, and employee relations. Royal Dutch Shell has core capabilities in oil exploration and production.[12] Core capabilities tend to be limited in number, but they provide a long-term basis for technology innovation, product development, and service delivery.

In many cases, people are a key resource that underlies a firm's core capabilities. Particularly in knowledge-based industries such as the software and information services industries, success depends on "people-embodied know-how." This includes the knowledge, skills, and abilities of employees. As a result, a number of companies that previously relied on standard plans for recruiting and managing their employees are designing more tailored plans for them. These personalized plans are designed to address the individual needs of employees so they will be in a better position to help implement their firms' strategies. Microsoft goes so far as to ask certain types of employees to design their own career paths. For example, the company offers software engineers both a management-focused and technical specialist career track and allows them to move back and forth between the two.

Organizations can achieve a sustained competitive advantage through people if they are able to meet the following criteria:[13]

1. *The resources must be valuable.* People are a source of competitive advantage when they improve the efficiency or effectiveness of the company. Value is increased when employees find ways to decrease costs, provide something unique to customers, or some combination of the two. To improve the bottom line, RBC and Enbridge are among the companies that utilize employee empowerment programs, total quality and continuous improvement efforts, and flexible work arrangements to motivate and spark the creativity of their workers.

2. *The resources must be rare.* People are a source of competitive advantage when their knowledge, skills, and abilities are not equally available to competitors. Companies such as Microsoft and Four Seasons Hotels therefore invest a great deal to hire and train the best and the brightest employees in order to gain an advantage over their competitors.

3. *The resources must be difficult to imitate.* People are a source of competitive advantage when the capabilities and contributions of a firm's employees cannot be copied by others. Disney, Southwest Airlines, and Starbucks are each known for creating unique cultures that get the most from employees (through teamwork) and are difficult to imitate.

core capabilities

Integrated knowledge sets within an organization that distinguish it from its competitors and deliver value to customers

These four criteria highlight the importance of people and show the closeness of HRM to strategic management.

Composition: The Human Capital Architecture

A related element of internal analysis for organizations that compete on capabilities is determining the composition of the workforce. That is, managers need to determine whether people are available, internally or externally, to execute an organization's strategy. Managers have to make tough decisions about whom to employ internally, whom to contract externally, and how to manage different types of employees with different skills who contribute in different ways to the organization. The Province of British Columbia recognizes the value of human capital as described in Highlights in HRM 2.3.

Figure 2.3 shows that different skill groups in any given organization can be classified according to the degree to which they create strategic value and are unique to the organization. As a general rule, managers often consider contracting externally (or outsourcing) skill areas that are not central to the firm's core competence. HRP plays an important role in helping managers weigh the costs and benefits of using one approach to employment versus another.

Evidence from research suggests that employment relationships and HR practices for different employees vary according to which segment they occupy in this matrix. Here are some general trends:

Strategic knowledge workers. This group of employees tends to have unique skills that are directly linked to the company's strategy and are difficult to replace (such as R&D scientists in pharmaceuticals company or computer scientists in

4. *The resources must be organized.* People are a source of competitive advantage when their talents can be combined and deployed to work on new assignments at a moment's notice. Companies such as IBM and GE have invested in information technology to help allocate and track employee assignments to temporary projects. Teamwork and cooperation are two other pervasive methods for ensuring an organized workforce.

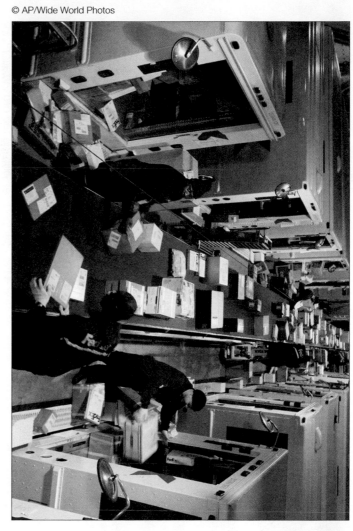

Couriers and package handlers, core employees of the human capital architecture at FedEx, are only a part of the FedEx network.

Highlights in HRM 2.3

The Measurement of Human Capital

The Office of the Auditor General of British Columbia recognized that human capital is critically important to the delivery of high-quality service to the province's citizens. So it set out to measure whether training and development (T&D) were being used to increase human capital in the B.C. public service. As a first step, it defined human capital as the collective brainpower in an organization. This brainpower consists of

- *facts* acquired through informal and formal education
- *skills* gained through training and practice
- *experience* gained through reflection on past successes and mistakes
- *value judgments* based on individual perceptions
- *social networks* developed through relationships with coworkers, colleagues, and customers

The audit took several measures, including a large-scale survey of a random sample of full-time employees and an in-depth audit of three ministries. Some of the data generated by this audit are the following:

- Thirty-six percent of government employees had received no formal training.
- The average B.C. government employee received 17 hours of training (compared to a Canadian benchmark of 29 hours).

- Less than 1 percent of payroll was spent on training (compared to the 4 percent that the best employers spend).
- Forty percent of employees had had their jobs redefined.
- Forty-three percent of senior managers would reach age 55 in the next five years and be eligible to retire.
- Thirty-three percent of employees with less than one year of employment did not feel they had been trained properly to carry out their duties.

The audit revealed that most T&D decisions were based on requests made from individual employees, and that most programs they attended consisted of one- and two-day courses outside the organization. It had never been ascertained whether these courses increased employees' skills or helped the organization achieve its goals. There was no way of knowing how effective this training was; nor was there any accounting for T&D expenditures.

Government employees generally believed that training was of great value to them and their organizations. Paradoxically, they also believed that they weren't being supported in their work; and only half thought they had the tools and resources they needed to do their jobs.

Sources: Adapted from J. McCannel and L. McAdams, "The Learning Culture in Public Service," *Public Sector Management* 11, no. 1 (2000); http://www.ipac.ca/Public_SectorMagazine. Used by permission.

a software development company). These employees typically are engaged in knowledge work that involves considerable autonomy and discretion. Companies tend to make long-term commitments to these employees, investing in their continuous training and development and perhaps giving them an equity stake in the organization.

Core employees. This group of employees has skills that are quite valuable to a company, but are not particularly unique or difficult to replace (such as salespeople in a department store or truck drivers for a courier service). These employees tend to be employed in traditional types of jobs. Because their skills are transferable, it is quite possible that they could leave to go to another firm. As a consequence, managers frequently make less investment in training and development and tend to focus more on paying for short-term performance achievements.

Supporting labour. This group of employees typically has skills that are of less strategic value to the firm and are generally available in the labour market (such as clerical workers, maintenance workers, and staff workers in accounting and human

FIGURE 2.3

Mapping Human Capital

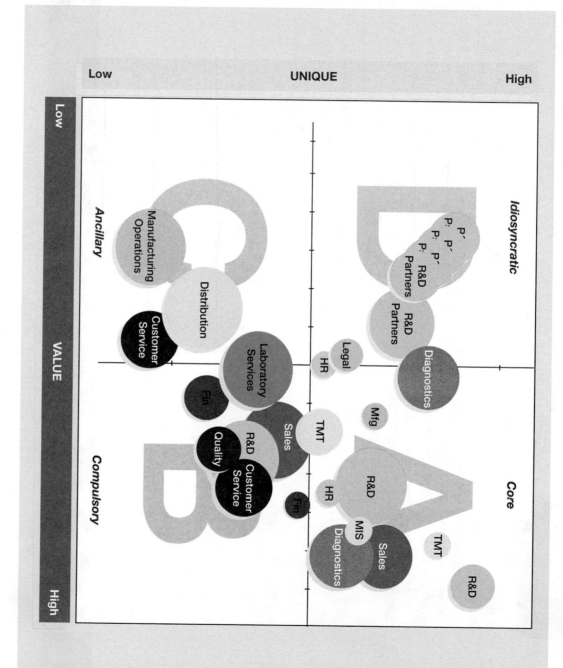

resources). Individuals in these jobs are increasingly hired from external agencies on a contract basis to support the strategic knowledge workers and core employees. The scope of their duties tends to be limited, and their employment relationships tend to be transaction-based, focused on rules and procedures, with less investment in development. Ethics in HRM describes some issues associated with contract employees. The Business Case outlines the advantages to the employer of hiring contract labour.

Alliance partners. This group of individuals has skills that are unique but frequently are not directly related to a company's core strategy (such as lawyers, consultants, and research lab scientists). Although companies perhaps cannot justify their internal employment, given their indirect link to strategy, these individuals have skills that are specialized and not readily available to all firms. As a consequence, companies tend to establish longer-term alliances and partnerships with them and nurture an ongoing relationship focused on mutual learning. Considerable investment is made in the exchange of information and knowledge.[14]

Ethics in HRM

The Employment Contract

The number of organizations substituting part-time workers for full-time employees is growing. Employees—even those with excellent track records and many years of service—are considered expendable as organizations revise their strategies to become more competitive and more profitable. When yet another reorganization occurs, management reveals the new plan with excitement. However, while management thinks it is telling employees, "We will provide you with meaningful, challenging, and skill-building work that will be good for your résumé—you are responsible for your own employment," employees are hearing, "We will work you to the bone, pay you enough to prevent you from quitting, and fire you when we no longer need you. Oh, and by the way, you are our most valuable resource."

Some employment contracts are extremely one-sided, with employers determining when to hire and when to fire, without obligation or guilt. This kind of contract works when people need jobs more than organizations need employees. However, as some sectors continue to experience rapid growth, and as the labour market for certain skills becomes tighter, employees are making contractual demands that place them in the driver's seat. They are demanding signing bonuses, stock equity, retention bonuses, and sufficient notification with predetermined buyouts for termination. Furthermore, the courts are ruling that if an employee is retained for a series of uninterrupted contracts, then that contract worker is de facto an employee.

The Business CASE

Hiring Contract Workers Pays

As you can see, the employer can save a lot of money by hiring only contract employees. The use of contract workers has the additional benefits of functional flexibility (employers can hire the workers with the exact skills needed) and numerical flexibility (workers can be added or discharged as work demand fluctuates). Contract workers (also called temporary workers or "temps") are defined as paid workers with a specified end date for their job or completion of a task or project. In 2006, 22 percent of all Canadian workers were temporary or permanent part-time workers.

Employers want to hire people on contract for several reasons, including

- The ability to terminate their contracts easily
- No obligation to pay benefits

- Reduced need for training and development investments
- Less pay is required because contract workers rarely benefit from seniority provisions
- Typically, contract workers are not entitled to paid sick leave or vacation pay
- No obligation on the part of the employer to pay into a pension plan
- Typically contract employees do not participate in company incentive compensation programs that award merit pay or bonuses.

A growing organization must decide whether to hire full-time or part-time employees, and the chart below will assist in this decision.

continued

The Advantages and Limitations of Part-Time Employment

Advantages for the Employer	Advantages for the Employee
Work scheduling flexibility	Control over personal time
Reduced compensation costs	More variety in jobs
Increased ability to add/reduce programs	Home office tax advantages

Limitations for the Employer

Limitations for the Employer	Limitations for the Employee
No organizational loyalty	No job security
Costs of continuous replacement	Limited benefits
Costs of continual training	Stresses of continuous learning
Strategic competencies can quit	Lack of training and career progression

Sources: Adapted from Helmar Drost and H. Richard Hird, *An Introduction to the Canadian Labour Market,* 2nd edition, Thomson Nelson, 2006; Barbara Moses, "Loss of Loyalty Cuts Both Ways," *The Globe and Mail,* November 6, 1997, B17; R. S. Echlin, "Courts Apply Smell Test in Judging Contract Workers as Long Term Employees," *The Globe and Mail,* November 22, 1999, B1.

FORECASTING: A CRITICAL ELEMENT OF PLANNING

While internal analysis of the three Cs (culture, capabilities, and composition) may reveal a great deal about where the organization is today, things change. In an important sense, strategic planning is about managing that change. Managers must continually forecast both the needs and the capabilities of the firm for the future in order to do an effective job at strategic planning. As shown in Figure 2.4, managers

FIGURE **2.4**

Model of HR Forecasting

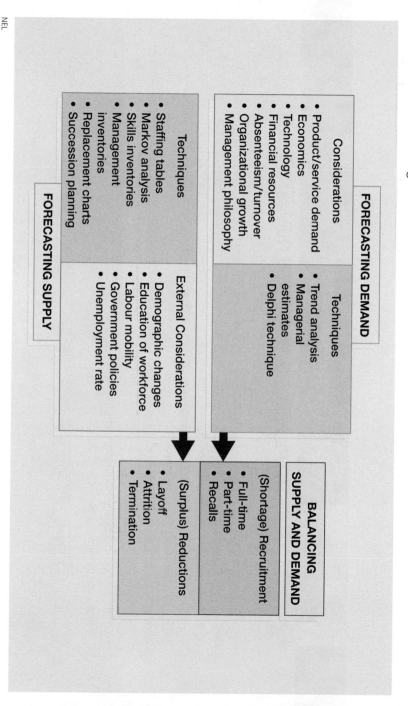

focus on (at least) three key elements: (1) forecasting the demand for labour, (2) forecasting the supply of labour, and (3) balancing supply and demand considerations. Careful attention to each factor helps top managers meet their human resources requirements.

Consider for a moment the high costs of not forecasting—or forecasting poorly. If job vacancies are left unfilled, the resulting loss in efficiency can be very costly, particularly when you consider the amount of time it takes to hire and train replacement employees. As pointless as it may sound, we have seen situations in which employees are laid off in one department while applicants are hired for similar jobs in another department. Poor forecasting that leads to unnecessary layoffs also makes it difficult for employees to accurately assess their own career prospects and development. When this happens, some of a firm's more competent and ambitious workers will be inclined to seek other employment where they feel they will have better career opportunities.[15]

On the plus side, accurate forecasting provides the kind of information managers need to make sound decisions. It can help them ensure that they have the right number and right kinds of people in the right places at the right times, doing things that provide value to both the organization and the employees.

Reality Check describes the labour market forecasts for nurses and provides some solutions for the anticipated shortages.

Forecasting a Firm's Demand for Employees

If a key component of forecasting is predicting the number and types of people an organization needs to meet its objectives, the question remains: "How can this be done?" A variety of factors, including a firm's competitive strategy, technology, structure, and productivity, can affect the demand for labour. For example, as we noted in Chapter 1, the use of advanced technology is generally accompanied by less demand for low-skilled workers and more demand for knowledge workers. External factors such as business cycles—economic and seasonal trends—can also play a role. For example, retailers such as The Bay and Canadian Tire rely heavily on temporary employees between November and January, during the holiday season. There are two approaches to HR forecasting: quantitative and qualitative, which we

OUTCOME

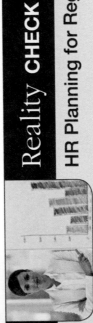

Reality CHECK

HR Planning for Registered Nurses

The Canadian Nurses Association released a study that showed that Canada could have a shortfall of 60,000 registered nurses by 2022. There are currently 217,000 registered nurses (RNs) in Canada, the single largest group of health care workers. The majority of these work in acute care hospitals.

Proposed solutions:

- Faster processing by the Federal government to allow temporary foreign workers into Canada.

- Reduce absenteeism (which currently is 14 days a year, almost double the average Canadian worker) would result in the equivalent of an additional 7,000 RNs.

- Increase enrollment in nursing schools by adding about 1,000 new spaces a year. Couple this with reducing the attrition rate in the nursing school. About one in four nurses do not complete their studies or do not practice after graduating.

Source: A. Picard, "Six Steps Urged to Reverse RN Shortfall" *The Globe and Mail*, May 12, 2009, L1; D. Harder, "Rules Eased in B.C., Alberta for Temp Foreign Workers," *Canadian HR Reporter* (November 5, 2007): 1.

discuss next. An organization's demands will ultimately determine which technique is used. Regardless of the method, however, forecasting should not be neglected, even in relatively small organizations.

Quantitative approaches Quantitative approaches to forecasting involve the use of statistical or mathematical techniques. One example is trend analysis, whereby a firm's employment requirements are forecasted on the basis of some organizational index. Trend analysis is one of the most commonly used approaches for projecting HR demand and is typically done in several stages.

First, select an appropriate business factor. This should be the best available predictor of human resources needs. Frequently, sales or value added (the selling price of the firm's products minus the costs of the materials and supplies used to make them) is used as a predictor in trend analysis. Second, plot a historical trend of the business factor in relation to the number of employees. The ratio of employees to the business factor will provide a labour productivity ratio (for example, sales per employee). Third, compute the productivity ratio for at least the past five years. Fourth, calculate human resources demand by multiplying the business factor by the productivity ratio. Finally, project the firm's human resources demand out to the target year. This procedure is illustrated in Figure 2.5 for a hypothetical building contractor.

Other, more sophisticated statistical planning methods include modelling or multiple predictive techniques. Whereas trend analysis relies on a single factor (such as sales) to predict employment needs, the more advanced methods combine several factors, such as interest rates, gross national product, disposable income, and sales, to predict employment levels. Forecasting methods such as these are usually used by larger companies with the help of analysts and statisticians. However, advances in data collection technology and computer software are making it easier and more affordable for smaller businesses to use more sophisticated forecasting techniques.

Qualitative approaches Admittedly, forecasting is frequently more an art than a science, providing inexact approximations rather than absolute results. The ever-changing environment in which an organization operates contributes to this

trend analysis

A quantitative approach to forecasting labour demand based on an organizational index such as sales

Using the Internet

See if there are labour shortages or surpluses for the job that you want at:

**http://www.labourmarket
information.ca/standard.
asp?ppid=578&lcode=E**

FIGURE **2.5**

Example of Trend Analysis of HR Demand

Year	Business Factor (Sales in Thousands)	Labour Productivity (Sales/Employee)	Human Resources Demand (Number of Employees)
2002	$2,351	14.33	164
2003	$2,613	11.12	235
2004	$2,935	8.34	352
2005	$3,306	10.02	330
2006	$3,613	11.12	325
2007	$3,748	11.12	337
2008	$3,880	12.52	310
2009*	$4,095	12.52	327
2010*	$4,283	12.52	342
2011*	$4,446	12.52	355

*Projected figures

situation. For example, estimating changes in the demand for a firm's products or services is a basic forecasting concern, as is anticipating changes in national or regional economics. A firm's internal changes are critical, too. For example, a community hospital anticipating internal changes in its technology or how the facility is organized or managed must consider these factors when it forecasts its staffing needs. Also, the forecasted staffing needs must be in line with the organization's financial resources.

In contrast to quantitative approaches, qualitative approaches to forecasting are less statistical. Management forecasts are the opinions (judgments) of supervisors, department managers, experts, or others knowledgeable about the organization's future employment needs. Another qualitative forecasting method, the Delphi technique, attempts to decrease the subjectivity of forecasts by soliciting and summarizing the judgments of a preselected group of individuals. HR personnel can do this by developing a list of questions to ask the managers in their companies. Highlights in HRM 2.4 contains a list of good questions to ask. The final forecast thus becomes a collective, or group, judgment. Ideally, forecasting should include the use of both quantitative and qualitative approaches. Numbers without context—including the context supplied by skilled HR professionals who understand the business and can analyze and interpret the data—are less useful. "The most important software is the one running between your ears," explains Matthew C. Brush, the director of human capital planning at Corning, Inc. Indeed, in small organizations, forecasting may be as informal as having one person who knows the organization and anticipates its future HR requirements.[16]

Forecasting the Supply of Employees

Just as an organization must forecast its future requirements for employees, it must also determine whether sufficient numbers and types of employees are available to staff the openings it anticipates having. As with demand forecasts, the process involves both tracking current employee levels and making future projections about those levels.

management forecasts

The opinions (judgments) of supervisors, department managers, experts, or others knowledgeable about the organization's future employment needs

Highlights in HRM 2.4

HR Planning and Strategy Questions to Ask

Business Managers

Workforce planning requires that HR leaders periodically interview their managers to gauge future workforce needs. Here are some sample questions to ask:

- What are your mission, vision, and values?
- What are your current pressing business issues?
- What are our organizational strengths?
- What are our competitors' organizational strengths? How do we compare?
- What core capabilities do we need to win in our markets?
- What are the required knowledge, skills, and abilities we need to execute the winning strategy?

- What are the barriers to optimally achieving the strategy?
- What types of skills and positions will be required or no longer required?
- Which skills should we have internally versus contract with outside providers?
- What actions need to be taken to align our resources with strategy priorities?
- What recognition and rewards are needed to attract, motivate, and retain the employees we need?
- How will we know if we are effectively executing our workforce plan and staying on track?

Sources: Adapted from Agilent Technologies for The Conference Board and the Society for Human Resource Management.

Staffing tables and Markov analysis. An internal supply analysis can begin with the preparation of staffing tables. **Staffing tables** are graphic representations of all organizational jobs, along with the numbers of employees currently occupying those jobs (and perhaps also future employment requirements derived from demand forecasts). Another technique, called a **Markov analysis**, shows the percentage (and actual number) of employees who remain in each of a firm's jobs from one year to the next, as well as the proportions of those who are promoted, demoted, or transferred or exit the organization. As Figure 2.6 shows, a Markov analysis can be used to track the pattern of employee movements through various jobs and to develop a transition matrix for forecasting labour supply.

Forecasting the supply of human resources available to a firm requires that its managers have a good understanding of employee turnover and absenteeism. We have included formulas for computing turnover and absenteeism rates in an Appendix to this chapter. The calculations are easily made and used by managers of both large and small organizations.

Skill inventories and management inventories. Staffing tables, a Markov analysis, turnover rates, and the like tend to focus on the *number* of employees in particular jobs. Other techniques are more oriented toward the *types* of employees and their skills, knowledge, and experiences. **Skill inventories** can also be prepared that list each employee's education, past work experience, vocational interests, specific abilities and skills, compensation history, and job tenure. Of course, confidentiality is a vital concern in setting up any such inventory. Nevertheless, well-prepared and up-to-date skill inventories allow an organization to quickly match forthcoming job openings with employee backgrounds. When data are gathered on managers, these inventories are called *management inventories.* All of this analysis is made simpler these days through the use of HR information systems and enterprise systems provided by companies such as Oracle-PeopleSoft and SAP.

Replacement charts and succession planning. Both skill and management inventories—broadly referred to as talent inventories—can be used to develop

staffing tables
Graphic representations of all organizational jobs, along with the numbers of employees currently occupying those jobs and future (monthly or yearly) employment requirements

Markov analysis
A method for tracking the pattern of employee movements through various jobs

skill inventories
Files of personnel education, experience, interests, skills, and so on that allow managers to quickly match job openings with employee backgrounds

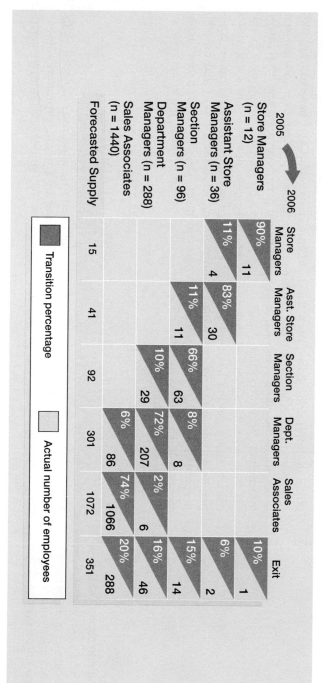

FIGURE **2.6**

Hypothetical Markov Analysis for a Retail Company

2005	2006	Store Managers	Asst. Store Managers	Section Managers	Dept. Managers	Sales Associates	Exit
Store Managers (n = 12)		90% / 11					10% / 1
Assistant Store Managers (n = 36)		11% / 4	83% / 30				6% / 2
Section Managers (n = 96)			11% / 11	66% / 63	8% / 8		15% / 14
Department Managers (n = 288)				10% / 29	72% / 207	2% / 6	16% / 46
Sales Associates (n = 1440)					6% / 86	74% / 1066	20% / 288
Forecasted Supply		15	41	92	301	1072	351

Transition percentage   Actual number of employees

External factors such as business cycles—economic and seasonal trends—can play a role in forecasting the demand for and supply of employees.

replacement charts
Listings of current jobholders and people who are potential replacements if an opening occurs

succession planning
The process of identifying, developing, and tracking key individuals for executive positions

human capital readiness
The process of evaluating the availability of critical talent in a company and comparing it to the firm's supply

employee **replacement charts**, which list current jobholders and identify possible replacements should openings occur. Figure 2.7 shows an example of how an organization might develop a replacement chart for the managers in one of its divisions. Note that this chart provides information on the current job performance and promotability of possible replacements. As such, it can be used side by side with other pieces of information for **succession planning**—the process of identifying, developing, and tracking talented individuals so that they can eventually assume top-level positions.

In a recent study conducted by the Society for Human Resources, three out of four chief executives said succession planning was their most significant challenge for the future. Software developers are responding to this need with new succession planning and talent management software. Software developer Taleo, for example, offers an application based on a firm's organizational chart and baseball-card-like representations of its employees. Clicking on the cards flips them over to show statistics about the employees such as their individual performance review data, career information, and succession data.

This type of automated system is a relatively new development with which managers are getting acquainted. With or without software, however, more companies will need to engage in succession planning. One study found that only 50 percent of companies have succession plans in place, despite the apparent acute need for it. Highlights in HRM 2.5 shows a checklist for evaluating the "success" of succession planning.[17]

ASSESSING A FIRM'S HUMAN CAPITAL READINESS: GAP ANALYSIS

Once a company has assessed both the supply and demand for employee skills, talent, and know-how, it can begin to understand its **human capital readiness**. Any difference between the quantity and quality of employees required versus the quantity and quality of employees <u>available</u> represents a gap that needs to be closed. Figure 2.8 shows how Chemico, a specialty chemical manufacturing company, approaches its assessment of human capital readiness. Similar to our discussion in the preceding sections, managers begin by identifying a company's core capabilities and the key people and processes that are critical to those capabilities. Chemico's executive team identified eight key job "families" that comprise about 100 employees of the firm's 1,500-member staff (in other words, less than 10 percent of its workforce). For each of these critical job families, managers identified the critical knowledge, skills, and behaviours necessary to build the core capabilities. They then determined the number of people required for these positions, as well as the number who are currently qualified.

As the lower portion of the figure shows, the company's human readiness ranged between 0 percent for supply chain management design specialists and 75 percent for call centre representatives.

Once the assessment of the firm's human capital readiness is complete, managers have a much better foundation for establishing their strategy going forward and the specific requirements for developing the talent needed to implement the strategy.[18]

FIGURE **2.7**

An Executive Replacement Chart

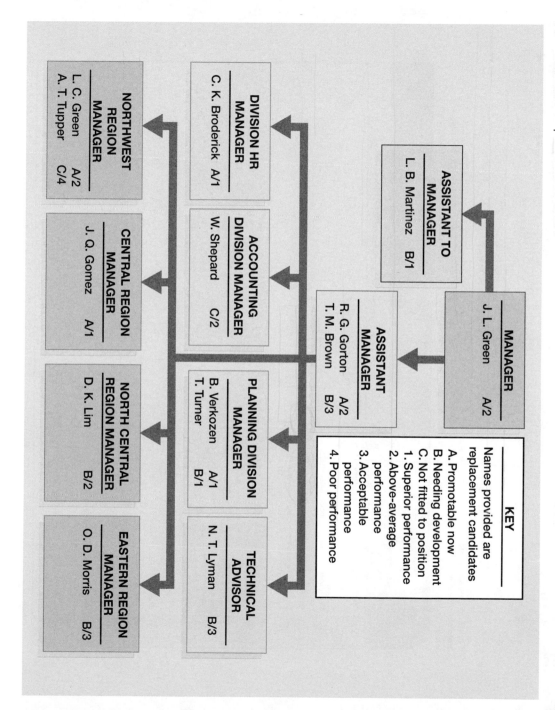

KEY

Names provided are replacement candidates

A. Promotable now
B. Needing development
C. Not fitted to position
1. Superior performance
2. Above-average performance
3. Acceptable performance
4. Poor performance

MANAGER
J. L. Green   A/2

ASSISTANT TO MANAGER
L. B. Martinez   B/1

ASSISTANT MANAGER
R. G. Gorton   A/2
T. M. Brown   B/3

DIVISION HR MANAGER
C. K. Broderick   A/1

ACCOUNTING DIVISION MANAGER
W. Shepard   C/2

PLANNING DIVISION MANAGER
B. Verkozen   A/1
T. Turner   B/1

TECHNICAL ADVISOR
N. T. Lyman   B/3

NORTHWEST REGION MANAGER
L. C. Green   A/2
A. T. Tupper   C/4

CENTRAL REGION MANAGER
J. Q. Gomez   A/1

NORTH CENTRAL REGION MANAGER
D. K. Lim   B/2

EASTERN REGION MANAGER
O. D. Morris   B/3

Highlights in HRM 2.5

Succession-Planning Checklist

RATE THE SUCCESS OF YOUR SUCCESSION PLANNING

For each characteristic of a best-practice succession-planning and management program appearing in the left column below, enter a number to the right to indicate how well you believe your organization manages that characteristic. Ask other decision makers in your organization to complete this form individually. Then compile the scores and compare notes.

Characteristics of a Best-Practice Succession-Planning and Management Program	How Would You Rate Your Organization's Succession Planning and Management Program on the Characteristic?				
Your organization has successfully...	Very Poor (1)	Poor (2)	Neither Poor Nor Good (3)	Good (4)	Very Good (5)
1 Clarified the purpose and desired results of the succession-planning and management program.					
2 Determined what performance is required now for all job categories in the organization by establishing competency models.					
3 Established a means to measure individual performance that is aligned with the competencies currently demonstrated by successful performers.					
4 Determined what performance is needed in the future by establishing future competency models for all job categories.					
5 Created an ongoing means by which to assess individual potential against future competency models.					
6 Established a means by which to narrow gaps through the use of individual development plans (IDPs).					
7 Created a means to follow up and hold people accountable.					
8 Created a means by which to document competence and find organizational talent quickly when needed.					
9 Created and sustained rewards for developing people.					
10 Established a means by which to evaluate the results of the succession planning and management program.					

Total (add up the scores for items 1–10 and place in the box on the right)

SCORES

50–40 Congratulations. The succession-planning and management program in your organization conforms with best practices.

39–30 Pretty good. Your organization is on the way toward establishing a first-rate succession-planning and management program.

29–20 Okay. While your organization could make improvements, you appear to have some of the major pieces in place for a succession-planning and management program.

19–10 Not good at all. Your organization is probably filling positions on an as-needed basis.

9–0 Give yourself a failing grade. You need to take steps immediately to improve the succession-planning and management practices of your organization.

Source: From William J. Rothwell, "Putting Success into Your Succession Planning," *The Journal of Business Strategy* 23, no. 3 (May/June 2002): 32–37. Republished with permission—Thomson Media, One State Street, 26th Floor, New York, NY 10004.

STEP FOUR: FORMULATING STRATEGY

The forecasting techniques discussed previously provide critical information for strategic planning. Recall that we noted at the beginning of the chapter that HR analysis is an input to strategy formulation. However, a word of caution is needed

OUTCOME

FIGURE 2.8

Assessing a Firm's Human Capital

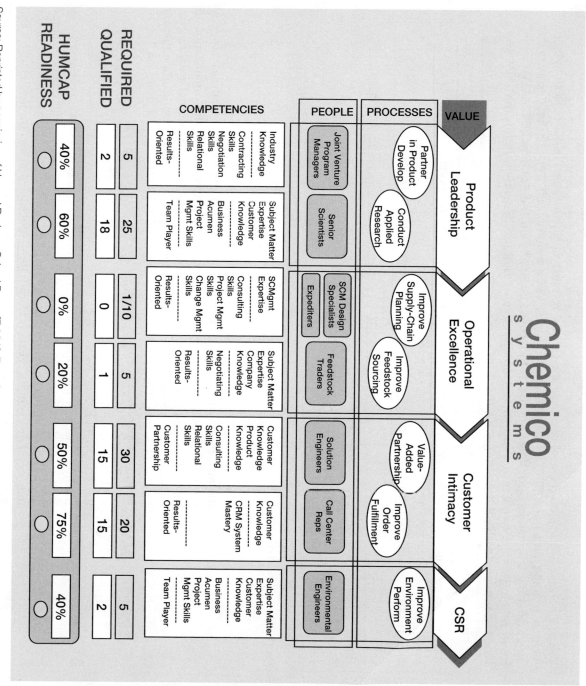

Source: Reprinted by permission of Harvard Business School Press. [Exhibit]. From *Strategy Maps: Converting Intangible Assets into Tangible Outcomes* by Robert Kaplan and David Norton, 2006. Copyright © 2006 by the Harvard Business School Publishing Corporation; all rights reserved.

here. Because HR forecasting techniques take us deep into the specifics of labour supply and demand, we need to be careful not to lose sight of the larger strategic picture. One of the biggest concerns among executives is that (at times) HR managers cannot "see the forest for the trees" because they become mired in the administrative details of their planning models. SWOT analysis, discussed shortly, helps managers combine various sources of information into a broader framework for analysis.

After managers have analyzed the internal strengths and weaknesses of the firm, as well as external opportunities and threats, they have the information they need to formulate corporate, business, and HR strategies for the organization. A comparison of *strengths, weaknesses, opportunities,* and *threats* normally is referred to as a **SWOT analysis.** SWOT analysis helps executives summarize

SWOT analysis

A comparison of strengths, weaknesses, opportunities, and threats for strategy formulation purposes

FIGURE **2.9**

An Example of a SWOT Analysis

Valero Energy Corporation (Valero) is one of the largest refiners in North America. Its core activities include refining and marketing of petroleum products. With a combined throughput capacity of approximately 3.3 million bpd, Valero is the 15th largest company on the Fortune 500 list. Valero's large refining capacity gives it a significant competitive advantage. However, rising material and labour costs could affect the company's margins.

STRENGTHS	WEAKNESSES
Large refining system	Weak performance in Canada
Leader in conversion capacity and feedstock flexibility	Litigations
Strong revenue growth and capital expenditure	High dependence on the United States
OPPORTUNITIES	THREATS
Growing diesel demand	Material and labor cost
Strategic refocus	Stringent regulations
Rising petrochemical capacity in the Middle East	

Source: DataMonitor.com, June 2007.

the major facts and forecasts derived from external and internal analyses. Strategy formulation builds on SWOT analysis to use the strengths of the organization to capitalize on opportunities, counteract threats, and alleviate internal weaknesses. In short, strategy formulation moves from simple analysis to devising a coherent course of action. Figure 2.9 is an example of a SWOT analysis done on Valero Energy Corporation.

CORPORATE STRATEGY

In any industry, firms decide where and how they will compete. Corporate strategy focuses on domain selection, that is, the markets in which they will compete. Some firms choose a concentration strategy that focuses on only a limited portion of the industry. For example, Visteon Corporation specializes in electronics, climate, and power train technologies for the automotive industry. In contrast, Henry Ford at one time had fully integrated his company from the ore mines needed to make steel all the way to the showrooms where his cars were sold.

Growth and Diversification

Emerging and growing companies execute their strategies differently than mature companies or those in decline. As companies grow, their strategic choices tend to focus on geographic, volume, and product expansion. HRP is a vital input to these decisions. Growth hinges on three related elements: (1) increased employee productivity, (2) a greater number of employees, and (3) employees developing or acquiring new skills. Thus, a firm's staffing, training, employee motivation efforts, and the like can either enable the company to grow or limit its potential.

As companies diversify into new businesses, managers inevitably are faced with a "make or buy" decision. That is, should they develop the capabilities in-house or contract externally? For example, when IBM entered the personal computer market in the early 1980s, it contracted with (start-up companies) Intel and Microsoft to make the hardware and operating systems for its PC. The decision did not rest solely on human resources issues; but they were an important part of the equation. Interestingly, IBM got out of the PC business altogether in 2005, by selling its PCs product lineup to Chinese computer manufacturer Lenovo. Instead, IBM is focusing on developing custom technology services for businesses, which it believes will be more profitable in the long run and a harder product for competitors to imitate. To help accomplish this new strategy, the company spent the first part of the decade buying up dozens of business service–related companies and their talent. Some companies diversify far beyond their core businesses. GE, for example, has diversified from its original base in electrical and home appliance products to such wide-ranging industries as health, finance, insurance, truck and air transportation, and even media, with its ownership of NBC. In order to manage such a diverse portfolio, GE has invested heavily in the development of general management skills and leadership ability. CEO Jeffrey Immelt has stated that GE's future depends on pursuing businesses that leverage human capital (in contrast to its traditional focus on manufacturing). This new strategy is strongly linked to human resources. In fact, the strategy is viable only because the company has done such an enviable job developing talent over the years.

Mergers and Acquisitions

In addition to strategies of growth and diversification, corporate Canada has seen a host of mergers and acquisitions in recent years.

While there are some important competitive reasons for mergers such as these, it is unfortunate to note that many of them have not gone well. Not surprisingly, perhaps, the failure rate among firms is very high. Some estimates suggest that only about 15 percent of all mergers achieve their objectives (measured by return on investment, shareholder value, and the like). Often the failure is due to cultural inconsistencies, as well as conflicts among the managers of each firm. Clearly, these concerns point directly to the importance of effective HRP prior to—and during—the merger process. Highlights in HRM 2.6 shows key HR activities associated with different phases of a merger or acquisition.

Highlights in **HRM 2.6**

Key HR Activities Associated with Merger or Acquisition Phases

HR Issues   Key HR Activities

Stage 1—Precombination

- Identifying reasons for the M&A
- Forming M&A team/leader
- Searching for potential partners
- Selecting a partner
- Planning for managing the process
- Planning to learn from the process
- Participate in preselection assessment of target firm

- Assist in conducting thorough due diligence assessment
- Participate in planning for combination
- Assist in developing HR practices that support rapid learning and knowledge transfer

Stage 2—Combination

- Selecting the integration manager(s)
- Designing/implementing transition teams
- Creating the new structure/strategies/leadership

continued

Stage 3—Solidification and Assessment

- Retaining key employees
- Managing the change process
- Communicating to and involving stakeholders
- Developing new policies and practices
- Assist in recruiting and selecting integration manager(s)
- Assist with transition team design and staffing
- Develop retention strategies and communicate to top talent
- Assist in deciding who goes
- Facilitate establishment of a new culture
- Provide assistance to ensure implementation of HR policies and practices

- Solidifying leadership and staffing
- Assessing the new strategies and structures
- Assessing the new culture
- Assessing the concerns of stakeholders
- Revising as needed
- Learning from the process
- Participate in establishing criteria and procedures for assessing staff effectiveness
- Monitor the new culture and recommend approaches to strengthen it
- Participate in stakeholder satisfaction
- Assist in developing and implementing plans for continuous adjustment and learning

Source: From Susan E. Jackson and Randall S. Schuler, *Managing Human Resources Through Strategic Partnerships*, 9th ed. (Mason, OH: Thomson/South-Western, 2006), 50. © 2006 South-Western, a part of Cengage Learning, Inc. Reproduced by permission. http://www.cengage.com/permissions.

value creation
What the firm adds to a product or service by virtue of making it; the amount of benefits provided by the product or service once the costs of making it are subtracted

Strategic Alliances and Joint Ventures

Sometimes firms do not acquire or merge with another firm, but instead pursue cooperative strategies such as a strategic alliance or joint venture. Especially when firms enter into international joint ventures, the issues of culture (both company culture and national culture) become paramount. On the front end, HR plays a vital role in assessing the compatibility of cultures and potential problems. As the alliance is formed, HR helps select key executives and develops teamwork across the respective workforces. In addition, HR is typically involved in the design of performance assessment and mutual incentives for the alliance. Of course, one of the controversial issues related to such alliances is the inevitable issue of outsourcing or offshoring work to other locations.

BUSINESS STRATEGY

While we think about corporate strategy as domain selection, business strategy is viewed in terms of domain navigation. It is more focused on how the company will compete against rival firms in order to create value for customers. We can think of **value creation** in a cost/benefit scenario (that is, value = benefits − costs). Companies can increase the value they offer customers by decreasing the costs of their goods and services or by increasing the benefits their products provide (or some combination of the two). Their business strategies reflect these choices.

Low-Cost Strategy: Compete on Productivity and Efficiency

A low-cost strategy means keeping your costs low enough so that you can offer an attractive price to customers (relative to competitors). Organizations such as McDonalds have been very successful at using a low-cost strategy. Critical success factors for this strategy focus on efficiency, productivity, and minimizing waste. These types of companies often are large and try to exploit of economies of scale in production and distribution. In many cases, their large size allows them to sell their products and services at a lower price, which leads to higher market share, volume, and (it is hoped) profits.

However, even a low-cost leader must offer a product or service that customers find valuable. As Gordon Bethune, the former CEO of Continental Airlines, put it, "You can make a pizza so cheap that no one will buy it."[19] Ultimately, organizations need to use a cost strategy to increase value to customers, rather than take it away.

A low-cost strategy has several links to HRP. The first has to do with productivity. A common misconception about low-cost strategies is that they inevitably require cutting labour costs. On the contrary, there are several good examples of companies that pay their employees "top dollar," but gain back cost advantages because of excellent productivity. That is, they get a terrific "bang for the buck." Either they produce more from the workforce they have, or they can produce the same amount with a smaller workforce.

The second way that low-cost strategies are linked to HRP pertains to outsourcing. In some cases, companies seeking low cost may consider contracting with an external partner that can perform particular activities or services as well (or better) at a lower cost. This decision directly links strategic planning to HRP. Decisions such as these often result in layoffs, transfers, and the like. As noted previously, organizations need to have a clear understanding of their core processes and skills in order to make these decisions. Too often, firms approach outsourcing decisions based on costs alone, but this can lead to detrimental effects in the long run if the skills base of their employees suffer and their core capabilities are subsequently eroded.

Differentiation Strategy: Compete on Value Added

While decreasing costs is one important way to enhance customer value, another involves providing something unique and distinctive to customers. A differentiation strategy is often based on high product quality, innovative features, speed to market, or superior service. Four Seasons Hotels' commitment to quality and luxury, FedEx's focus on speed and flexible delivery, Holt Renfrew's commitment to fashion and customer service, and Apple's emphasis on innovation and product development are all easily identifiable examples of differentiation strategies.

© Tony Freeman/PhotoEdit

The use of part-time employees helps to contain labour costs at fast food restaurants.

Each of these strategies is rooted in the management of human resources. Companies that focus on service, for example, need to identify and support ways to empower employees to serve customers better. In contrast to the company that emphasizes low cost and efficiencies, you may find that differentiating companies will bend the rules a bit more, allow more flexibility to let you "have it your way," and customize products and services around the customer's particular needs. In place of rigid rules, service-oriented companies often try to embed their values in the cultural values of the company. For example, one quality Starbucks looks for in prospective employees is the ability to make good decisions on their own.

FUNCTIONAL STRATEGY: ENSURING ALIGNMENT

In addition to formulating corporate and business-level strategies, managers also need to "translate" strategic priorities into functional areas of the organization (such as marketing, manufacturing, human resources, and the like). This involves all aspects of the business, but in particular there needs to be a clear alignment between HR and the requirements of an organization's strategy. In this regard, HR policies and practices need to achieve two types of fit: external and internal.[20]

External Fit/Alignment

External fit (or *external alignment*) focuses on the connection between the business objectives and the major initiatives in HR. For example, as we noted earlier, if a company's strategy focuses on achieving low cost, its HR policies and practices need to reinforce this idea by reinforcing efficient and reliable behaviour on the part of employees, enhanced productivity, and the like. On the other hand, if the organization competes through innovation and new product development, then its HR policies and practices would be more aligned with the notion of fostering creativity and flexibility.

Internal Fit/Alignment

In addition to external alignment, or fit, managers need to ensure that their HR practices are all aligned with one another internally to establish a configuration that is mutually reinforcing. The entire range of the firm's HR practices—from its job design, staffing, training, performance appraisal, and compensation—needs to focus on the same workforce objectives. Unfortunately, often one HR practice, such as training, might be focused on teamwork and sharing, while another HR practice, such as the firm's appraisal and compensation programs, reinforces the ideas of individual achievement. Charles Schwab and Company faced this very situation. The company has a reputation in the financial services industry for developing a culture of teamwork that has been important to its strategy. However, when it changed its compensation strategy to provide more rewards to its high-performing brokers, the firm sent mixed signals to its employees. Which is more important: teamwork or individual high flyers?[21]

STEP FIVE: STRATEGY IMPLEMENTATION

As the old saying goes, "well begun is half done"—but only half. Like any plan, formulating the appropriate strategy is not enough. Managers must also ensure that the new plans are implemented effectively. This is easier said than done. One recent survey revealed that about half of managers say there is a gap between their organization's ability to develop a vision and strategy and actually execute

FIGURE **2.10**

The 7-S Model

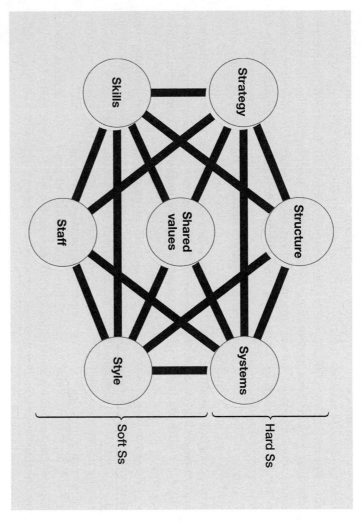

Source: McKinsey & Company

it. Recently organizations have been paying more attention to implementation and execution. [22]

Figure 2.10 shows the now classic 7-S framework and reveals that human resources management is instrumental to almost every aspect of strategy implementation, whether it pertains to structure, systems, style, skills, staff, or shared values. While *strategy* lays out the route that the organization will take in the future, organizational *structure* is the framework in which activities of the organization's members are coordinated. If the strategy requires employees to be reorganized or redeployed, HR will be intimately involved. Closely related to structure are *systems* and processes. These include formal and informal procedures that govern the everyday activities of a firm. As organizations consider reengineering and redesign their processes to implement their strategies, HR helps ensure that the best workflow models are in place and—importantly—that employees are involved in sharing their advice, too.

Shared values were discussed earlier in the chapter as a guiding parameter for strategic planning. They arise again as an important issue in implementation as well.

Strategic change often requires employees and managers to modify, or abandon, their old ways of doing things. HR managers play a central role as guardians of the corporate culture—the principles on which the company is founded and the fundamental ideas around which the business is built. This is tightly connected to the issue of *style*, which refers not only to the leadership approach of top managers, but also the way in which employees present themselves to the outside world (to suppliers, customers, and so on).

Skills and *staff* relate directly to the concerns of human resources management and point to the critical role that HR plays in strategy implementation. At a fundamental level, HR's role in strategy implementation focuses on reconciling (1) human resources demanded and (2) human resources available.

TAKING ACTION: RECONCILING SUPPLY AND DEMAND

Through HRP, organizations strive for a proper balance between demand considerations and supply considerations. Demand considerations are based on forecasted trends in business activity. Supply considerations involve determining where and how candidates with the required qualifications can be found to fill a firm's vacancies. Because of the difficulty in locating applicants for the increasing number of jobs that require advanced training, this aspect of planning has been receiving much more attention. Greater planning effort is also needed to recruit members of designated groups for managerial jobs and technical jobs that require advanced levels of education.

In an effort to meet their human resources demands, organizations have many staffing options, including hiring full-time employees, having current employees work overtime, recalling laid-off workers, using temporary or contract employees, and outsourcing or offshoring some of their business processes. Highlights in HRM 2.7 outlines how one Nova Scotia company deals with a projected labour shortage.

However, when forecasts show a surplus of employees, organizations often restrict their hiring, reduce their employees' work hours, and consider layoffs, demotions, and/or terminations. Some organizations try to reduce their workforces by relying on attrition, which is a gradual reduction of employees through resignations, retirements, and deaths. Over the past few decades, early retirements have become a more and more common means for organizations to reduce their excess labour supply. Organizations sometimes encourage employees to accept early retirement by offering "sweetened" retirement benefits. The various types of benefits are discussed in Chapter 11.

Organizational Downsizing, Outsourcing, and Offshoring

As we have discussed, organizations have to be constantly prepared to exit and enter new lines of business, restructure, outsource, offshore, and sometimes downsize. Because of either economic or competitive pressures, General Motors,

Highlights in **HRM 2.7**

Managing Labour Shortages

Dexter, a construction company based in Bedford, Nova Scotia, was facing a skills gap in its labour market. The demands in this sector have changed and there is less need for manual labourers and a greater demand for technicians with computer literacy skills. For example, a heavy equipment operator or surveyor used to operate by observing and using pen and paper; now much of this work is dictated by GPS (Global Positioning Systems) and integrated software. Ron Hyson, director of HR for Dexter, decided to partner with the Nova Scotia Community College to recruit, select, and train employees in the required skills. About 350 candidates applied for the two-year

training program, were tested, and then interviewed. A final group of 30 was selected to receive training in all fields of construction. They were cross-trained in surveying and heavy equipment operations and were given courses in management development, job costing, and safety. The training methods were varied. About 40 percent of the time, trainees were in the classroom. The remaining time was spent in the field in six to eight functional areas, such as surveying. Work terms of six months, consisting of rotations in each area for four weeks, were used to help the students determine their interests and abilities. At the end of the program, the trainees are guaranteed employment.

Air Canada, and Nortel are among the many firms that have eliminated thousands of jobs—either because they had too many employees or employees with the wrong skill sets.[23] In many cases, downsizing is part of a longer-term process of restructuring to take advantage of new technology, corporate partnerships, and cost minimization.

Making Layoff Decisions

Decisions about employee layoffs are usually based on seniority and/or performance. In some organizations, especially those with collective agreements, seniority may be the primary consideration. In other organizations, such factors as ability and fitness may take precedence over seniority in determining layoffs. There are several options available to employers when it comes to dealing with surplus employees: layoffs, attrition, and termination.

Layoff Strategies

Employee layoff decisions are usually based on seniority and/or ability. With unionized organizations, the criteria for determining an employee's eligibility for layoff are typically set forth in the collective agreement. As a rule, job seniority receives significant weight in determining which employees are laid off first. Similar provisions in the collective agreement provide for the right of employees to be recalled for jobs they are still qualified to perform. Organizational policy as well as provisions in the collective agreement should therefore establish and define clearly the employment rights of each individual and the basis on which layoff selections will be made and re-employment effected. The rights of employees during layoffs, the conditions concerning their eligibility for recall, and their obligations in accepting recall should also be clarified. It is common for collective agreements to preserve the re-employment rights of employees laid off for periods of up to two years, provided that they do not refuse to return to work if recalled sooner.

While it has become customary for employers to recognize seniority in unionized employees, nonunion employees are not always given the same consideration. Due to the demand for a technically skilled workforce, the ability of employees to change jobs and learn new skills, as well as their performance and competencies, is given a great deal of weight in layoff decisions. The most important reason for using seniority as a basis for layoffs is the objective nature of the decision: number of years of work, not perception of ability, is the basis for the decision. The system is fair, and employees themselves can calculate their own probability of being employed.

One of the major disadvantages of overemphasizing seniority is that less competent employees receive the same rewards and security as more competent ones; the seniority system ignores talent and effort. The payroll is also higher than under other systems, because more experienced workers tend to earn more money. Also, the practice of using seniority as the basis for deciding which workers to lay off may well have a disproportionate impact on women and visible-minority workers, who often have less seniority than other groups.

Under the umbrella of layoff strategies are several work reduction options: reduced workweek, reduced shifts, transfers to related companies, and so on. Under the reduced workweek, employees work about 20 to 30 hours per week. This option allows the organization to retain a skilled workforce and lessens the financial and emotional impact of a full layoff, and at the same time reduces the costs of production. Some organizations have worked out arrangements so that employment insurance benefits make up most of the difference of the lost wages. However, it is sometimes difficult to predict how much work is available each week; also, overhead fixed costs such as rent and administration continue, independent of the number of hours worked.

Reduced shift work is based on a similar concept of reducing costs by reducing the number of hours worked. Some plants operate three shifts a day and may shut down the midnight to 8:00 a.m. shift to save money. In some rare cases, organizations can transfer laid-off employees to a sister company. Layoffs are the fastest way to achieve workforce reduction; attrition is the slowest.

Attrition Strategies

Some organizations have adopted a no-layoff policy. These firms view people as their most important asset and recognize that their competencies and attitudes are valuable and cannot be easily replaced. They prefer to reduce the workforce through attrition. Attrition refers to the "natural" departure of employees through quits, retirements, and deaths. The turnover rates of an organization vary greatly by industry and by occupation. For example, university professors rarely quit, while turnover among fast-food workers can reach 300 percent a year. Most organizations can easily estimate how many people will leave the organization and so can slowly reduce the workforce through natural means.

Attrition must be supplemented by other practices. Hiring freezes are usually implemented at the same time as the organization adopts a strategy of workforce reduction through attrition. A hiring freeze means that organizations will not hire new workers as planned, or will hire only in areas critical to the success of the organization. Sometimes the practice is to not replace the worker who has left or been fired.

These practices have several advantages. Organizations can control and predict compensation expenses. But the savings go beyond the salaries and benefits redeemed from departing employees. Take, for example, the costs of employing a manager earning $60,000 a year. Her benefits probably cost another $20,000. However, the costs of replacing her would include recruitment costs ($5,000), paperwork and time in hiring costs ($1,000), and orientation and training expenses ($7,000). Thus, the organization can save significantly by not replacing workers.

However, the disadvantages are significant. Current employees may be overburdened with the work of those who left; their skills may not match the skill sets of the departed workers; and, of course, no new skills or ideas are infiltrating the organization. The major disadvantage of reduction through attrition is that the organization cannot control who leaves and who stays. Valuable employees may be retiring, while less-needed ones are still on the job. And the process takes a very long time compared to layoffs, which can be accomplished in days.

Some organizations attempt to accelerate attrition by offering incentives to employees to leave. These incentives include cash bonuses for people to leave during a specified time, accelerated or early retirement benefits, and free outplacement services. However, the buyout process must be carefully managed. Employees with valuable skills who can easily find another job may be the first to cash in. People in key positions should not be targeted for this program. Another disadvantage is that buyouts require a great deal of money upfront, which may work against the goal of cost reduction. For example, Ontario Hydro paid out millions in buyouts for a few thousand employees. To sustain a no-layoffs policy, some organizations ask for volunteers to transfer into divisions where employee shortages are developing. This causes other problems. For example, highly competent employees who have years of experience, expertise, and contacts in one position may not be as productive in another division. Skill match is a recurrent problem. Mandatory transfers allow the employer to match employee skills with vacant positions more accurately. However, there may be associated morale problems as individuals move into jobs or divisions they do not like or leave their team and its working style. In addition, union contracts may forbid or inhibit these types of transfers.

If the surplus of employees is deemed to be permanent, terminations may be the only option.

attrition

A natural departure of employees from organizations through quits, retirements, and deaths

hiring freeze

A practice whereby new workers are not hired as planned, or workers who have left the organization are not replaced

Termination Strategies

Termination is a practice initiated by an employer to separate an employee from the organization permanently. Termination is different from firing, in which an employee is released for such causes as poor performance, high absenteeism, or unethical behaviour. The purpose of termination is to reduce the size of the workforce and thereby save money.

A termination strategy begins with the identification of employees who are in positions that are no longer considered useful or critical to the company's effectiveness. The managers of these employees are contacted about redeployment or termination options. Next the employee is told the news, with varying degrees of advance notice. CIBC gives three months' notice, allows the employee and the manager to prepare a redeployment plan, and allows up to six months for retraining and repositioning. At CIBC, the emphasis is on retaining competent employees whose jobs have been eliminated; the title of the program, Employment Continuity, reflects this strategy.

Employers cannot terminate without some form of compensation to the employee. **Severance pay**, a lump-sum payment given to terminated employees, is calculated on the basis of years of service and salary. Every province has legislation such as the *Employment Standards Act*, which establishes minimum standards for termination and severance pay. The legal minimum varies by province; for example, a clerk making $500 a week with eight years' service would receive about $4,000 in severance pay. A typical severance package would include

- A lump-sum severance payment
- An extension of group benefits such as medical and dental plans for a pre-determined period
- An option for the employee to convert group life insurance to a private policy
- Some pension plan options

These payments, if accepted by the employee, immediately discharge the employer from further obligations. Most employers now refer to "ballpark," "reasonable range," or "reasonable offer" court decisions. The ballpark approach offers some degree of certainty to both employers and employees, and thus helps minimize costly court battles.

Some organizations adopt "golden parachutes," a form of severance pay, to protect their employees (especially their executives) from the downsizing effects of mergers, acquisitions, and leveraged buyouts. Golden parachutes are guarantees by the employer that detail the compensation and benefits that employees will receive in termination situations. Golden parachutes encourage managers to work actively with the company during a restructuring, and reduce the possibility of legal challenges on termination. But they are costly.

STEP SIX: EVALUATION AND ASSESSMENT

At one level, it might seem that assessing a firm's effectiveness is the final step in the planning process. That is true. But it is also the first step. Planning is cyclical, of course, and while we have somewhat conveniently placed evaluation at the end of this chapter, it actually provides the inputs to the next cycle in the planning process. Measurement, benchmarking, alignment, fit, and flexibility issues are central to the evaluation process.

EVALUATION AND ASSESSMENT ISSUES

In order to evaluate their performance, firms need to establish a set of parameters that focus on the "desired outcomes" of their strategic planning, as well as the metrics they will use to monitor how well the organization delivers against those outcomes. Because strategic management is ultimately aimed at creating a

termination
Practice initiated by an employer to separate an employee from the organization permanently

severance pay
A lump-sum payment given to terminated employees

[OUTCOME 7]

benchmarking

The process of comparing the organization's processes and practices with those of other companies

competitive advantage, many firms evaluate their performance against other firms. Benchmarking is the process of identifying "best practices" in a given area—for example, productivity, logistics, brand management, training, and so on—and then comparing your practices and performance to those of other companies. To accomplish this, a benchmarking team would collect information on its own company's operations and those of other firms in order to uncover any gaps. The gaps help determine the causes of performance differences, and ultimately the team would map out a set of best practices that lead to world-class performance. Interestingly, the target company for benchmarking does not need to be a competitor. For example, when Xerox wanted to learn about excellent customer service, it benchmarked L.L. Bean. By working with a noncompeting company, Xerox was able to get access to information a competitor would not divulge.

In the context of HR strategy, the metrics fall into two basic categories: human capital metrics and HR metrics. Human capital metrics assess aspects of the workforce, whereas HR metrics assess the performance of the HR function itself. The Saratoga Institute (now an arm of PriceWaterhouseCoopers) publishes the annual *Human Capital Benchmarking Report*, which includes benchmarking information from almost 900 companies (see Highlights in HRM 2.8). The Institute's clients can use the information from studies of such areas as

Highlights in **HRM 2.8**

Ten Measures of Human Capital

The ten areas to measure, as recommended by Jac Fitzenz, chair of the Saratoga Institute (now part of PriceWaterhouseCoopers) will not all apply to your company, but some will:

1. **Your most important issues.** These are the targets of all lower-level measures. Focus on them and ensure that your metrics lead in a direct line to them.

2. **Human capital value added.** How do your workers optimize themselves for the good of the company and for themselves? This is the primary measure of an individual's contribution to profitability.

3. **Human capital ROI.** This is the ratio of dollars spent on pay and benefits to an adjusted profit figure.

4. **Separation cost.** How many people are leaving? From which departments? What does it cost the company? The average cost of separation for an employee is at least six months' equivalent of revenue per employee.

5. **Voluntary separation rate.** Lost personnel equal potential lost opportunity, lost revenue, and the cost of workers having to fill the gaps under greater stress. Cutting the separation rate saves

the cost of hiring and keeps customer service quality high.

6. **Total labor-cost/revenue percentage.** This is total benefits and compensation cost as a percentage of organizational revenue and shows how much of what you are taking in through revenue goes to support the company's total labor cost, including temporary, seasonal, and contract or contingent workers. This metric can help you track changes in your workforce. Best approach: Compare it to your revenue factor and compensation, benefits, and contingent off-payroll costs. If the metric is rising, determine whether compensation or benefits costs are up or revenue is down. This will help you decide what actions to take.

7. **Total compensation/revenue percentage.** This is the percentage of the company's revenues allocated to the direct costs of employees. It excludes costs for off-payroll employees. Before creating strategies to address concerns, compare this metric to your revenue factor, compensation costs, and benefits costs to analyze what is happening with workers.

continued

8. **Training investment factor.** Basic skills are crucial: Workers who cannot read, write, do simple calculations, or talk intelligently with customers need to have these skill deficiencies addressed.

9. **Time to start.** Recruitment will continue to be a challenge. The amount of time it takes from approval of a job requisition until the person is on the job is a challenge. The amount of time it takes from approval

10. **Revenue factor.** This is the basic measure understood by managers.

Source: "The Top 10 Measures of Human Capital Management," *HRfocus* 78, no. 5 (May 2001): 8. Copyright © 2001. Reprinted by permission of IOMA.

Using the Internet

Look at the studies being conducted by the HR Benchmarking Association at:

http://www.hrba.org

---

pay structure, return on investment per employee, turnover rates, and cost-per-hire and time-to-fill for key employees. This kind of detailed information clarifies potential bases of competitive advantage and reveals a path for developing future HR strategies.[24]

With that said, benchmarking alone will not give a firm a competitive advantage. According to author and HRM consultant Mark Huselid, a competitive advantage is based on the unique combination of a company's human capital, strategy, and core capabilities—which differ from firm to firm. This means that HR managers cannot simply rely on the benchmarks and strategies of other firms. Instead, they must develop their own. If they can successfully do so and implement them, they can achieve a sustained competitive advantage.[25]

MEASURING A FIRM'S STRATEGIC ALIGNMENT

Earlier in the chapter, we discussed the importance of strategic alignment and fit as an element of strategy formulation and implementation. As an element of evaluation, some very useful techniques help managers assess the extent to which they have achieved these objectives.

Strategy Mapping and the Balanced Scorecard

One of the tools for mapping a firm's strategy in order to ensure strategic alignment is the **balanced scorecard (BSC)**. Developed by Harvard professors Robert Kaplan and David Norton, the BSC is a framework that helps managers translate their firms' strategic goals into operational objectives. The model has four related cells: (1) financial, (2) customer, (3) processes, and (4) learning. The logic of the BSC is firmly rooted in human resources management. People management and learning help organizations improve their internal processes and provide excellent customer service. Internal processes—product development, service, and the like—are critical for creating customer satisfaction and loyalty, and they are also important for ensuring productivity to contain costs for better financial performance. Customer value creation, in turn, drives up revenues, which enhances profitability.

Figure 2.11 shows how this might work at Starbucks. In each cell, Starbucks would identify the key metrics that help translate strategic goals to operational imperatives. For example, under customer metrics, Starbucks might look at percentage of repeat customers, number of new customers, growth rate, and the like. Under people metrics, managers might measure the numbers of suggestions provided by employees, participation in Starbucks' stock-sharing program, employee turnover, training hours spent, and the like. Each of these cells links vertically;

balanced scorecard (BSC)
A measurement framework that helps managers translate strategic goals into operational objectives

FIGURE **2.11**

Building the Metrics Model

Strategic Theme: "The Third Place"		Objectives	Measures	Targets	Initiatives
Financial	Long-Term Shareholder Value / Asset Utilization / Grow Revenues	• Profitability • Grow revenues • Improve cost structure	• Market value • Revenue • G&A as % of sales	• 20% CAGR • 30% CAGR • 5% CAGR	• Intl. growth • Cdn. growth • Corp. layoffs
Customer	Attract & Retain Customers / The "Third" Place / Premium Coffee	• New customers • More value to current (now) customers	• # Customers • New stores • Repeat customers • Same store sales	• 20 mill/week • 1,500/yr • 15% 2/wk • 13% growth	• Store Develop • New Products • Customer loyalty program • New partners
Internal	Fill Orders / Engage Cust	• Friendly service • Accurate orders • Fast fulfillment	• Customer FB • First time right • Order fulfillment	• 90+ satisf. • 99+% acc. • <3 minutes	• Customer engagement • Automation • Cycle time opt.
People	Store Manager / Baristas	• Store manager stability • Barista engagement	• Average tenure • Voluntary turnover • Engagement survey	• Mgr >3 yrs • Barista 80% • 85% rating	• 40 hrs. training • MUG Awards • Beanstock

People management issues such as rewards, training, and suggestions can be linked to efficient processes (brewing the perfect cup, delivering top-notch customer service, and so forth). These processes then lead to better customer loyalty and growth. Growth and customer loyalty in turn lead to higher profitability and market value.

Measuring Internal Fit

Recall that internal fit means that HR practices are all aligned with one another to establish a configuration that is mutually reinforcing. Figure 2.12 shows an example of how organizations can assess the internal fit of their HR practices. There are essentially three steps. First, managers need to identify the key workforce objectives they hope to achieve. Often this information can come from the people/learning cell of the BSC and might include loyalty, customer service, productivity, and creativity. Second, managers would identify each of the HR practices used to elicit or reinforce those workforce objectives (job design, staffing, training, appraisal, compensation, and so on). Third, managers would evaluate each HR practice on a scale of –5 (not supportive) to 5 (supportive). By tallying up the ratings across managers, organizations can get a very clear idea of which HR practices are working together to achieve the workforce objectives and which are not.

An important caveat to this analysis is that internal fit is a necessary, but insufficient, cause of strategic alignment. A company could have nearly perfect alignment among its HR practices, and they still might not be aligned with the competitive strategy. For that reason, it is important for managers to assess both internal fit and external alignment.

ENSURING STRATEGIC FLEXIBILITY FOR THE FUTURE

Apart from the need to establish and measure fit between HR and strategy, HR is also focused on ensuring flexibility and agility when the environment changes.

FIGURE 2.12

Assessing Internal Fit

ORGANIZATION	WORKFORCE OBJECTIVES				
	SALES PRODUCTIVITY	CUSTOMER SERVICE	MERCHANDISE INFORMATION	STOCK MAINTENANCE	TOTAL
Structure/Workflow					
• Cross-functional teams	3	2	0	−1	4
• Rotation (Depts.)	3	3	−1	−1	4
Staffing					
• Test battery	2	2	1	1	6
• Select for experience	5	3	2	2	12
Training					
• Retail selling skills	4	5	1	1	11
Rewards					
• Results appraisal	5	−4	−2	−5	−6
• Individual incentives	5	−5	−3	−5	−8
Leadership					
• Corporate	3	3	1	0	7
• Store manager	4	2	2	2	10
Technologies					
• Merchandise IS	5	2	5	1	13
• Daily postings	4	−3	4	−1	4
SYSTEM COHERENCE	43/55	10/55	10/55	26/55	57/220

FUNCTIONAL COHESION

+5 Strongly supports the priority
0 Neutral
−5 Strongly counterproductive

organizational capability
The capacity of the organization to act and change in pursuit of sustainable competitive advantage

Ultimately, successful HRP helps increase **organizational capability**—the capacity of the organization to continuously act and change in pursuit of sustainable competitive advantage.[26]

Flexibility can be achieved in two primary ways: coordination flexibility and resource flexibility. *Coordination flexibility* occurs through rapid reallocation of resources to new or changing needs. Through HRP, managers can anticipate upcoming events, keep abreast of changes in legal regulations, forecast economic trends, recognize competitor moves, and the like. With advance notice, managers can move people into and out of jobs, retrain them for new skill requirements, and modify the kinds of incentives they use. Use of a contingency workforce composed of part-timers, temporary employees, and external partners also helps achieve coordination flexibility.[27] *Resource flexibility*, on the other hand, results from having people who can do many different things in different ways. Cross-training, job rotations, team-based work modes, and the like are all focused on establishing a flexible workforce.

We will draw on these ideas throughout this text. But at this point we want to close the chapter by emphasizing that strategic planning is a process designed to ensure superior performance today, as well as establishing the capability and agility to respond tomorrow. As the great hockey player Wayne Gretzky used to say, "I don't skate to where the puck is. I skate to where the puck is going to be."

Small Business **APPLICATION**

Small businesses, by their size, provide for a much closer alignment between organizational and people strategies. What is different for small business is threefold: (1) access to resources to analyze the competitive landscape and market opportunities, (2) access to internal and available talent to pursue markets or opportunities, and (3) being less constrained by existing internal processes or structures in the pursuit of new strategies.

As we have seen, the development and integration of HR in the strategic planning process requires a scan of market opportunities and the competitive landscape. This research requires time, money, and expertise that may not be readily available in small companies. So how do small companies develop and pursue strategy? Typically, small companies grow around a core competency, a single business activity that has been established to address a specific market need or specific large client requirement. From that centre, all research regarding market opportunities and threats are focused on identifying opportunities that are aligned with this core competency, and guarding potential threats to the core business.

Let's use a small printing company with 50 employees as an example. This company has been created out of a need to provide printing services to a packaged-goods company. From this, the company has grown to take on additional clients. However, the packaged-goods company still accounts for 40 percent of the revenue and profitability for the company. With this in mind, the strategic planning exercise focuses on (1) What does the company need to do to grow the business with the existing clients and identify new clients? (2) What risks are there of client or profitability erosion from the existing client base? (3) What changes, if any, are required in the talent the company has in place to sell and deliver printing services to meet these needs?

The challenge for small business is that by the very nature of size, the range of talent available within the existing organization will be constrained. As a result, any change in strategic direction may require retraining or recruitment of talent, both of which will take time and money and will depend on the availability of training services or talent available to hire. These factors will need to be considered in the development of strategy.

SUMMARY

OUTCOME 1 Strategic human resources management (SHRM) integrates strategic planning and human resources planning (HRP).

It can be thought of as the pattern of human resources deployments and activities that enable an organization to achieve its strategic goals. HRP and strategies becomes especially critical when organizations consider global strategies, including mergers, joint ventures, offshoring, the relocation of plants, product innovations, and downsizing, or when dramatic shifts occur in the composition of the labour and type of people needed to meet organizational objectives. Supply analysis involves determining whether sufficient employees are available within the organization to meet demand and also whether potential employees are available on the job market.

OUTCOME 2 Analyzing the firm's competitive environment is central to strategic planning. The competitive environment includes the specific organizations with which the firm interacts. Firms analyze the competitive environment in order to adapt to or influence the nature of competition.

OUTCOME 3 Conducting an internal analysis to gauge the firm's strengths and weaknesses involves looking at a firm's "three Cs"—its culture, capabilities, and composition. An internal analysis enables strategic decision makers to inventory the organization's skills and resources as well as their performance levels. An organization's success increasingly depends on the knowledge, skills, and abilities of employees, particularly as they help establish a set of core capabilities that distinguish an organization from its competitors. When employees' talents are valuable, rare, difficult to imitate, and organized, a firm can achieve a sustained competitive advantage through its people.

OUTCOME 4 HRP is a systematic process that involves forecasting demand for labour, performing supply analysis,

and balancing supply and demand considerations. Forecasting demand requires using either quantitative or qualitative methods to identify the number by HR functions. (Supply analysis involves determining whether sufficient employees are available within the organization to meet demand and also whether potential employees are available on the job market.)

OUTCOME 5 As organizations plan for their future, top management and strategic planners must recognize that strategic planning decisions affect—and are affected by—HR functions. On one hand, HRP plays a reactive role in ensuring that the right number and type of employees are available to implement a chosen business plan. On the other hand, HRP can proactively identify and initiate programs needed to develop organizational capabilities on which future strategies can be built. HRP and strategic planning tend to be most effective when there is a reciprocal relationship between the two processes.

OUTCOME 6 Formulating a HR strategy is only half of the HR battle; the strategy must also be implemented. Employment forecasts must be reconciled against the internal and the external supplies of labour the firm faces. This can include having current employees work overtime, hiring full-time, part-time, or contract employees; downsizing; outsourcing; and offshoring. If there is a labour shortage, the firm might have to reformulate its long-term and short-term strategic plans.

OUTCOME 7 Firms need to establish a set of parameters that focus on the "desired outcomes" of strategic planning, as well as the metrics they will use to monitor how well the firm delivers against those outcomes. Issues of measurement, benchmarking, alignment, fit, and flexibility are central to the evaluation process. Firms use benchmarking, strategy mapping, and the balanced scorecard (BSC) as tools to gauge their outcomes.

KEY TERMS

attrition, 74
balanced scorecard (BSC), 77
benchmarking, 76
core capabilities, 52
core values, 46
cultural audits, 51
environmental scanning, 46
hiring freeze, 74
human capital readiness, 62
human resources planning (HRP), 44
management forecasts, 60
Markov analysis, 61
mission, 45
organizational capability, 80
replacement charts, 62
severance pay, 75

skill inventories, 61
staffing tables, 61
strategic human resources
management (SHRM), 44

strategic planning, 44
strategic vision, 45
succession planning, 62
SWOT analysis, 65

termination, 74
trend analysis, 59
value creation, 68

DISCUSSION QUESTIONS

1. Identify the three key elements of the HRP model and discuss the relationships among them.

2. What environmental forces influence the future of community colleges and universities? List these and discuss the implications for the demand for faculty.

3. What criteria must be met if firms are to achieve a competitive advantage through their employees?

4. Which approach do you think should be relied on more heavily for strategy formulation—the quantitative or qualitative approach?

5. Explain the difference between a firm's corporate strategy and business strategy. Why do firms need to look at both aspects?

6. Choose a Canadian organization such as Nortel or Air Canada. What downsizing options were used and why?

7. Why is organizational capability important to a firm, and how can HR managers enhance it?

INTERNET EXERCISE

The number-one issue for some employers is finding and keeping good employees. Replacing employees costs money, but exactly how much? Go to http://www.uwex.edu/ces/cced/economies/turn.cfm and use this online employee turnover calculator to determine the cost to your employer if you (or a member of your student group who has a job) quit your job.

HRM EXPERIENCE

Customizing HR for Different Types of Human Capital

Part of strategic planning in HR is mapping an organization's human capital. When we look at the strategic value of a person's skills as well as their uniqueness, we soon discover that organizations comprise different kinds of workers who have very different kinds of skills. Some are core knowledge workers; some are more traditional job-based employees; some are contract workers; and some are external partners. In this context, it is unlikely that we would manage all of these employees the same way (as much as we might want to for fairness). There are differences in HR practices for different groups. That is not bad, but it makes the job of HR managers more difficult.

Assignment

The following are descriptions of three different employees. How would you characterize each worker? What role does each play when it comes to the organization's strategy?

Andrea Bascomb is a highly talented computer programmer for MiniFluff, Inc. She is among the elite set of engineers in the computer industry that is doing leading-edge work on advanced computer modelling.

In truth, CEO Bill Ding believes that the future of the company rests on the innovative work that Andrea and her team are doing. He worries that someone might lure Andrea away to work for them. So he wants to give her all the room she needs to grow and stay committed to MiniFluff.

Calvin Duff is a salesperson on the retail side of MiniFluff. He has daily contact with customers and is responsible for making sales and communicating with service personnel. Make no mistake: To many customers, Calvin and his coworkers are the "face" of MiniFluff. Always on the lookout for a better situation, Calvin has thought about working for PeachTree Computing, MiniFluff's main competitor. In truth, other

continued

salespeople have found that they can leave MiniFluff and get "up to speed" easily at other firms. Their skills are very transferable, and the transition is not difficult. Bill Ding and other managers at MiniFluff recognize this fact, so they try to keep salespeople loyal and productive, recognizing that many of them do eventually leave.

Evelyn Frank is a part-time secretary for MiniFluff. She handles routine typing and filing work for the company, particularly in peak periods in the summer and around the holidays. She usually works for a few weeks at a time and then takes time off. The executives at MiniFluff have considered either outsourcing the job to an agency or automating it through a new computer system. But for now things are steady.

BIZFLIX EXERCISES

U-571: SETTING STRATEGY

Watch the scene from *U-571*. It shows several aspects of strategic planning described earlier in this chapter.

This action-packed World War II thriller shows a U.S. submarine crew's efforts to retrieve an Enigma encryption device from a disabled German submarine. After the crew gets the device, a German vessel torpedoes and sinks the U.S. submarine. The survivors must now use the disabled German submarine to escape from the enemy with their prize. The film's almost nonstop action and extraordinary special effects look and sound best with a home theatre system.

The scene comes from the "160 Meters" segment toward the film's end. Lt. Andrew Tyler (Matthew McConaughey) is now the submarine's commander following the drowning death of Lt. Commander Mike Dahlgren (Bill Paxton), the original commander. Lt. Tyler says, "Chief," Chief Petty Officer Henry Klough (Harvey Keitel) approaches the map table. The film continues to its dramatic end with the execution of the strategy Tyler describes.

What to Watch for and Ask Yourself

• Does Lt. Tyler analyze the submarine's external environment? Does he engage in environmental scanning as described earlier in this chapter?
• What is Lt. Tyler's assessment of the submarine's strengths and weaknesses?
• Does Lt. Tyler consider threats and opportunities in forming his strategic plan? Has he done a SWOT analysis as described earlier in this chapter?

CASE STUDY 1

STAFFING, DOWN TO A SCIENCE AT CAPITAL ONE

When the financial services industry tumbled into crisis in June 2007, Capital One chairman and CEO Richard Fairbank issued a mandate to strip $700 million out of the company's operating costs by 2009. The cost reduction plan includes consolidating and streamlining functions, reducing layers of management, and eliminating approximately 2,000 jobs. The mandate did not set off a mad scramble in workforce planning, however. Instead, the planning staff simply added new defined variables to their simulations and modified their projections for the company's talent needs.

"The key to workforce planning is to start with the long-term vision of the organization and its future business goals and work back from there," says Matthew Schuyler, chief human resources officer for Capital One and its 27,000 employees. "We anticipate the strategic needs of the business and make sure that we have the workforce required to meet those needs. The $700 million mandate gives us goals and boundaries that we didn't have before. We made the adjustments."

Capital One and other leading companies are now developing a set of best practices for workforce planning that reach into the future for each business unit and evolve with corporate strategic planning. In an increasingly unstable global business environment, the value of a long-term vision is clear, but effective workforce planning requires dedicated resources, heavy analytics, and, perhaps most important, the full engagement of business unit leaders and line managers.

WORKING BACKWARD

The workforce planning at Capital One stems from a process executed by a metrics and analytics group of 20 people, plus hundreds of executives, managers, and analysts pulled from all the business lines and corporate functions. Leaders and analysts from the business lines work in blended teams with human resources generalists and members of the metrics group to build models for each line and the entire world force. The models flow to Schuyler, who reports directly to the CEO. "You have to garner your long-term vision of the organization from your seat at the table and from the time you spend with business leaders, immersed in places where you can get data," Schuyler says. "You have to probe the business leaders and know the business leaders and know what their endgame looks like." Planning varies by business line. Some lines are stable, while others are restructuring or moving through rapid growth.

Part of Schuyler's job is to ensure that senior business line leaders are engaged in the process. "Their door is open," he notes. "Your ticket through the door is to show business leaders the bundles of money they can save if their workforce is the right size with the right mix and the right skills. Once you're inside, you have to act on the promise." The potential cost savings come from minimizing the inherent costs associated with the size of the workforce, plus savings from lower recruiting and severance costs and avoiding the costs of a disengaged workforce. "The cost of disengagement is difficult to quantify, but business leaders intuitively understand the cost," Schuyler says. "There is a toll paid when a workforce is disempowered, disengaged, and not sufficiently busy."

Workforce planning at Capital One forecasts not only the head count required to meet future business needs, but also the staffing mix—the ratio of internal to external resources—and the skills mix, including any changes in that mix that are required as the business moves forward. Schuyler also looks at any changes in "spans of control," which determine the number of organizational layers, optimal methods for staffing managerial positions, and the related costs. The planners also document both rational and emotional employee engagement, which affect current and future productivity and recruiting, training, and turnover costs.

The responsibility for workforce planning at Capital One resides in human resources, but the hard work takes place inside the business units, where the blended teams operate. This grounding in the business units keeps workforce planning focused on corporate goals. Workforce planning really gets traction when it is linked to the line managers who understand business needs and can project their business growth and productivity changes. The time frames for workforce planning at Capital One vary by unit and function. The legal function, for example, is very stable and can easily plan out two to four years. The credit card division, however, is rapidly evolving, so its forecasts stretch out two to four years but are reviewed every quarter. Likewise, the demand for some jobs follows the business cycle. Collections and recoveries work at Capital One was stable and predictable several years ago, for example. "But because of the current economic conditions, this work is now more important, and we had to ramp up very quickly," Schuyler explains.

MANAGING DEMAND AND SUPPLY

Schuyler refuses to choose between overshooting and undershooting staffing. "The beauty of workforce planning is that it allows the flexibility to be right on target," he says. "We don't have to wait for the next budget cycle to get it right."

That flexibility derives from a more sophisticated approach to planning that looks at a range of possible scenarios about business conditions and then calculates the labor needed to match them. Capital One's workforce planning models allow business leaders to anticipate the talent requirements for each business option and the human resources and labour cost consequences of the choices they make. Especially for companies that are just beginning to implement a workforce planning process, the best approach is to focus first on the critical roles in the organization and then expand out to cover more positions in greater detail. Avoid the tendency to drown managers in data, by breaking the data down on a critical-jobs basis. At Capital One, the workforce planning process reaches down through the entire executive structure for each business unit—five or six levels of leadership plus groups of managers. Business leaders see the talent management costs and consequences of the business options at hand. Each option carries its own implications for internal and external staffing levels, recruiting, training, promotions, engagement, attrition, and total compensation costs over time. More important, workforce planning allows business leaders and line managers to see how different approaches to talent management can actually expand their business options and boost performance. "If workforce planning is done right, human resources can help business leaders think about what their endgame can be," Schuyler says.

Source: Excerpted from Fay Hansen, "The Long View," *Workforce Management* 87, no. 7 (April 21, 2008): 1, 19. Used by permission.

QUESTIONS

1. Why do you think it is important for Capital One to calculate the "disengagement" factor of its employees when it comes to workforce planning?

2. What merits do you see to breaking down the planning process by business units through multiple layers of leaders? Do you see any drawbacks of doing so?

CASE STUDY 2

MATCHING TALENT WITH TASKS: DOLE IMPLEMENTS SUCCESSION

With 61,000 workers in more than 90 countries, Dole Food Company has talent all over the world. Only a few hundred of those employees are in top management at the 151-year-old company. The trouble is, Dole doesn't have comprehensive knowledge of who these managers are or what they can do. If a key job opens up in North America, the business unit leader wouldn't know if the perfect candidate worked in another Dole unit in Canada. Dole has no way to match its top managerial talent with its executive needs.

But that is changing. The highly decentralized company is launching a succession planning process, supported by Web-based software, through which Dole executives hope to rectify their inability to promote the best and the brightest across the corporation. The process itself requires a change of culture and could become an agent for further culture change. "The idea of succession planning is contrary to being highly decentralized," says Sue Hagen, vice president of HR for North American operations, who led the effort.

Hagen talked informally to all corporate executives and the leaders and staffs of each business unit to generate consensus for succession planning for corporate positions—corporate officers, business unit presidents, and their direct reports. "The initial group would be about 100," she says. Next year, another few hundred will be included.

"The reaction was mostly positive," Hagen says. Hagen's next step was to hold a series of in-depth interviews with the executives to determine which succession planning processes were needed and how often they should be conducted. The goal was to reflect as much of their thinking as possible. "One division wanted to review succession plans on their people six times a year. Another didn't want to do it at all," she says. Hagen compromised. Succession planning will be conducted twice a year. She also identified four competencies on which everyone would be evaluated: accountability, business acumen, multifunctionality (cross-training), and vision/originality.

Many human resource management system (HRMS) software suites have an optional succession planning module, but neither Dole nor its business units have a HRMS. "Since most employees are farm or factory workers, there is not much need for the detailed information a HRMS provides," says Hagen. "It would be overkill. In a way, the succession planning software Dole adopted will become a mini HRMS for top personnel," she adds.

Hagen also wanted an application service provider (ASP) model. Outsourcing, including payroll, is common at Dole. Hagen didn't want to own and support technology, and she didn't want the small corporate information technology staff to have to work on it.

The users of the system—top managers—access the program from the Web with a password. They fill out a resume, including career interests, and note any mobility restrictions. They assess themselves on the four competencies. When they are done, the system automatically notifies their manager, who does an assessment and indicates whether he or she thinks the individual could be promoted. The manager also assesses overall potential and the risk of losing the user. This assessment then goes automatically to the division head, then to the divisional HR director, and then to Hagen. Hagen will use the information to create a career development plan for each individual, including seminars she'll organize. She'll also direct business unit leaders to potential candidates in other units when they have appropriate openings. "The beauty is, for the first time we'll have a database that ties together these talent metrics and can serve as a clearinghouse for people available for opportunities," Hagen says. "Dole's corporate management hopes all business units will eventually adopt similar succession planning processes and software," Hagen says. "I view this as a pilot, a very visible pilot," she says. "To get the buy-in of individual business units, we'll show them that this was adopted by their senior management and that it works."

Source: Excerpted from Bill Roberts, "Matching Talent with Tasks: Dole Implements Succession Planning to Get Ready for Changes at the Top," *HR Magazine* 47, no. 11 (November 2002): 91–95. Reprinted with permission of *HR Magazine*. Published by the Society for Human Resource Management, Alexandria, VA.

QUESTIONS

1. Why do you think companies like Dole need succession planning?

2. Do you see any disadvantage of "automating" succession planning?

CAREER COUNSEL

To learn about job search strategies, visit the *Managing Human Resources* website (http://www.belcourt6e.nelson.com).

NOTES AND REFERENCES

1. "The Importance of HR," *HRfocus* 73, no. 3 (March 1996): 14; "Retiring Workforce, Widening Skills Gap, Exodus of 'Critical Talent' Threaten Companies: Deloitte Survey," *Canadian Corporate News* (February 15, 2005); Brian E. Becker and Mark A. Huselid, "Strategic Human Resources Management: Where Do We Go From Here?" *Journal of Management* 32, no. 6 (January 2006): 898–925.

2. Scott A. Snell, Mark Shadur, and Patrick M. Wright, "Human Resources Strategy: The Era of Our Ways," in M. A. Hitt, R. E. Freeman, and J. S. Harrison (eds.), *Handbook of Strategic Management* (Oxford, UK: Blackwell, 2002), 627–649; Patrick M. Wright, Benjamin Dunford, and Scott A. Snell, "Human Resources and the Resource-Based View of the Firm," *Journal of Management* 27, no. 6 (2002): 701–721," What's Affecting HR Operations? Globalization, Sustainability, and Talent," *HRfocus* 84, no. 8 (August 2007): 8; Doris Sims, "Do You Know Where Your Talent Is?" *Training* 45, no. 1 (January 2008): 42–46.

3. "The Importance of HR," 14. For data from a similar survey conducted in Canada, see David Brown, "HR's Role in Business Strategy: Still a Lot of Work to Be Done," *Canadian HR Reporter* 14, no. 19 (November 5, 2001): 1–20; "How Should the HR Dept. of 2004 Be Structured?" *Human Resource Department Management Report*, no. 3 (November 2003): 1.

4. T. J. Watson, Jr., *A Business and Its Beliefs: The Ideas That Helped Build IBM* (New York: McGraw-Hill, 1963).

5. James W. Walker, "Integrating the Human Resource Function with the Business," *Human Resource Planning* 14, no. 2 (1996): 59–77; James W. Walker, "Perspectives," *Human Resource Planning* 25, no. 1 (2002): 12–14.

6. Patrick Wright, Gary McMahan, Scott Snell, and Barry Gerhart, "Comparing Line and HR Executives' Perceptions of HR Effectiveness: Services, Roles, and Contributions," *Human Resource Management* 40, no. 2 (2001): 111–23; Ryan Langlois, "Fairmont Hotels: Business Strategy Starts with People," *Canadian HR Reporter* 14, no. 19 (November 5, 2001): 19–25.

7. Bala Iyer, "Deconstructing Google," *Computerworld* 42, no. 15 (April 7, 2008): 32–33.

8. Jay J. Jamrog and Miles H. Overholt, "Building a Strategic HR Function: Continuing the Evolution," *Human Resource Planning* 27, no. 1 (March 2004): 51; Gary L. Nielson, Karla L. Martin, and Elizabeth Powers, "The Secrets to Successful Strategy Execution," *Harvard Business Review* 86, no. 6 (June 2008): 60–70.

9. For example, see U.S. Department of Labor, Bureau of Labor Statistics, Geographic Profiles of Employment and Unemployment. The data and information are accessible via the Office of Employment Projections home page at http://www.bls.gov/emp.

10. J. B. Quinn, "The Intelligent Enterprise: A New Paradigm," *Academy of Management Executive* 6, no. 4 (2002): 48–63.

11. Jennifer Laabs, "The HR Side of Sears' Comeback," *Workforce* 78, no. 3 (March 1999): 24–29.

12. For more information on methods to identify a firm's core capabilities, see Khalid Hafeez, YanBing Zhang, and Naila Malak, "Core Competence for Sustainable Competitive Advantage: A Structured Methodology for Identifying Core Competence," *IEEE Transactions on Engineering Management* 49, no. 1 (February 2002): 28–35; Jane Wollman Rusoff, "Outsourced Solutions: Quinn, "The Intelligent Enterprise," 48–63;

Brokerage Firms Looking to Focus on Their Core Competencies Find the Most Value in a Resource-Rich Clearing Partner," *Research* 27, no. 11 (November 2004): 37–40.

13. Snell, Shadur, and Wright," Human Resources Strategy," 627–649; Wright, Dunford, and Snell, "Human Resources and the Resource-Based View of the Firm," 701–721; David Collis and Cynthia Montgomery, "Competing on Resources," *Harvard Business Review* 86, no. 7/8 (July–August 2008): 140–150; Susan Cantrell, "The Work Force of One," *The Wall Street Journal* 249, no. 140 (June 16, 2007): R10.

14. D. P. Lepak and S. A. Snell, "The Human Resource Architecture: Toward a Theory of Human Capital Development and Allocation," *Academy of Management Review* 24, no. 1 (1999): 31–48; David Lepak and Scott Snell, "Examining the Human Resource Architecture: The Relationship among Human Capital, Employment, and Human Resource Configurations," *Journal of Management* 24, no. 1 (January 1999): 31; Mike Berry, "HR Must Push for Change to Drive Human Capital Strategy," *Personnel Today* (April 6, 2004): 4; Brian E. Becker and Mark A. Huselid, "A Players or A Positions? The Strategic Logic of Workforce Management," *Harvard Business Review* 83, no. 12 (December, 2005): 110–117.

15. Stephenie Overman, "Gearing Up for Tomorrow's Workforce," *HRfocus* 76, no. 2 (February 1999): 1, 15; Kathryn Tyler, "Evaluate Your Next Move," *HR Magazine* 46, no. 11 (November 2001): 66–71; Bill Leonard, "Turnover at the Top," *HR Magazine* 46, no. 5 (May 2001): 46–52.

16. Carolyn Hirschman, "Putting Forecasting in Focus," *HR Magazine* 52, no. 3 (March 2007): 44–49.

17. "Talent Management: Now It's the Top Priority for CEOs & Their Organizations," *HRfocus* 85, no. 2 (February 2008): 8–9; "Finding Top Talent," *Community Banker* 17, no. 4 (April 2008): 15; Paul Bernthal and Richard Wellins, "Trends in Leader Development and Succession," *Human Resource Planning* 29, no. 2 (2006): 31–40; Sarah Needleman, "Demand Rises for Talent-Management Software," *The Wall Street Journal* 251, no. 12 (January 15, 2008): B8.

18. Robert Kaplan and David Norton, *Strategy Maps: Converting Intangible Assets into Tangible Outcomes* (Boston: Harvard Business School Press, 2006), Chapter 8.

19. John Huey, "Outlaw Flyboy CEOs," *Fortune* 142, no. 11 (November 13, 2000): 237–50; "Visions of the Future," Human Resources (January 2008): special section, 22.

20. Brian Becker, Mark Huselid, and Dave Ulrich, *The HR Scorecard: Linking People, Strategy And Performance* (Cambridge, MA: Harvard Business School Press, 2001). See also Shari Caudron "How HR Drives Profits" *Workforce*, 90, no. 12 (December 2001): 26–31.

21. "A Singular Sensation for Schwab Brokers," *BusinessWeek Online* (January 24, 2002).

22. Larry Bossidy, Ram Charan, and Charles Burck, *Execution: The Art of Getting Things Done* (New York: Crown Business, 2002); Stacey L. Kaplan, "Business Strategy, People Strategy and Total Rewards—Connecting the Dots," *Benefits & Compensation Digest* 44, no. 9 (September 2007): 1–19; Gary L. Neilson, Karla L. Martin, and Elizabeth Power, "The Secrets to Successful Strategy," *Harvard Business Review* 86, no. 6 (June 2008): 60–70; Mark Vickers, "HR Growing Pains: Getting from Awkward to Accomplished," *Human Resource Planning* 30, no. 4 (2007): 20–24.

23. Jesse Drucker, "Motorola to Cut 7,000 More Jobs and Take $3.5 Billion in Charges," *The Wall Street Journal* (June 28, 2002): B6; Dennis K. Berman, "Planning to Outsource," *HRfocus* 81, no. 5 (May 2004): 1; David Koenig, "American Airlines Workers Brace for Job Cuts," Associated Press (July 3, 2008).

24. Ray Brillinger, "Best Practices: Human Resources Benchmarking," *Canadian HR Reporter* 14, no. 12 (June 18, 2001): 12; Chris Mahoney, "Benchmarking Your Way to Smarter Decisions," *Workforce* 79, no. 10 (October 2000): 100–103; Brian E. Becker and Mark A. Huselid, "Strategic Human Resources Management: Where Do We Go From Here?" *Journal of Management* 32 no. 6 (January 2006): 898–925. Lisa Bransten, "U.S. Examining Sun Microsystems over Complaint," *The Wall Street Journal* (June 25, 2002): B6; Matthew Miklave and A. Jonathan Trafimow, "Expecting Problems from This Dismissal," *Workforce* 80, no. 12 (December 2001): 81–83;

25. Brian E. Becker and Mark A. Huselid, "Strategic Human Resources Management: Where Do We Go From Here?" *Journal of Management* 32 no. 6 (January 2006): 898–925.

26. P. M. Wright and S. A. Snell, "Toward a Unifying Framework for Exploring Fit and Flexibility in Strategic Human Resource Management," *Academy of Management Review* 22, no. 4 (1998): 756–772; Snell, Shadur, and Wright, "Human Resources Strategy," 627–649; Wright, Dunford, and Snell, "Human Resources and the Resource-Based View of the Firm," 701–721.

27. R. Sanchez, "Strategic Flexibility in Product Competition," *Strategic Management Journal* 16 (1995): 135–159; Wright and Snell, "Toward a Unifying Framework," 756–772.

Appendix

CALCULATING TURNOVER AND ABSENTEEISM

Throughout this chapter we have emphasized that HRP depends on having an accurate picture of both the supply of and the demand for employees. Two factors, employee turnover and absenteeism, have a direct impact on HRP strategy and recruitment processes. In this Appendix, we provide a detailed discussion of turnover and absenteeism, methods for measuring them, and suggestions for managing their impact.

EMPLOYEE TURNOVER RATES

Employee turnover refers simply to the movement of employees out of an organization. It is often cited as one of the factors behind the failure of Canadian employee productivity rates to keep pace with those of foreign competitors. It is also one of the chief determinants of labour supply. Even if everything else about an organization stays the same, as employees turn over, its supply of labour goes down. This involves both direct and indirect costs to the organization.

COMPUTING THE TURNOVER RATE

The following formula for computing turnover rates is often used:

$$\frac{\text{Number of separations during the month}}{\text{Total number of employees at mid-month}} \times 100$$

Thus, if there were 25 separations during a month and the total number of employees at mid-month was 500, the turnover rate would be:

$$\frac{25}{500} \times 100 = 5 \text{ percent}$$

Turnover rates are computed on a regular basis to compare specific units such as departments, divisions, and work groups. Another method of computing the turnover rate is one that reflects only the avoidable separations (S). This rate is computed by subtracting unavoidable separations (US)—for example, due to child-birth, return to school, death, or marriage—from all separations. The formula for this method is as follows:

$$\frac{S - US}{M} \times 100 = T \text{ (turnover rate)}$$

where M represents the total number of employees at mid-month. For example, if there were 25 separations during a month, 5 of which were US, and the total number of employees at mid-month (M) was 500, the turnover rate would be

$$\frac{25 - 5}{500} \times 100 = 4 \text{ percent}$$

In looking at the impact of turnover on HRP and recruitment, it is vitally important to recognize that quantitative rates of turnover are not the only factor to be considered. The *quality* of employees who leave an organization is equally important. If poor employees leave, what experts refer to as "functional turnover," this can prove to be beneficial to the organization. The costs of keeping unproductive workers may be far more than the costs to recruit and train a new, more effective performer.

DETERMINING THE COSTS OF TURNOVER

Replacing an employee is time consuming and expensive. Costs can generally be broken down into three categories: separation costs for the departing employee, replacement costs, and training costs for the new employee. These costs are conservatively estimated at two to three times the monthly salary of the departing employee, and they do not include indirect costs such as low productivity prior to quitting and lower morale and overtime for other employees because of the vacated job. Consequently, reducing turnover could result in significant savings to an organization. Highlights in HRM 2.A1 details one organization's costs associated with the turnover of a single computer programmer. Note that the major expense is the cost involved in training a replacement.

EMPLOYEE ABSENTEEISM RATES

How frequently employees are absent from their work—the absenteeism rate—is also directly related to HRP and recruitment. When employees miss work, the organization incurs direct costs of lost wages and decreased productivity. It is not uncommon for organizations to hire extra workers just to make up for the number of absences totalled across all employees. In addition to these direct costs, indirect costs may underlie excessive absenteeism. A certain amount of absenteeism is, of course, unavoidable. There will always be some who must be absent from work because of sickness, accidents, serious family problems, or other legitimate reasons. However, chronic absenteeism may signal deeper problems in the work environment.

COMPUTING ABSENTEEISM RATES

Managers should determine the extent of the absenteeism problem, if any, by maintaining individual and departmental attendance records and by computing absenteeism rates. Although there is no universally accepted definition of "absence" or a standard formula for computing absenteeism rates, one frequently used method is

$$\frac{\text{Number of worker-days lost through job absence during period}}{\text{Average number of employees} \times \text{number of workdays}} \times 100$$

Highlights in HRM 2.A1

Costs Associated with the Turnover of One Computer Programmer

Turnover costs = Separation costs + Replacement costs + Training costs

Separation costs

1. Exit interview = cost for salary and benefits of both interviewer and departing employee during the exit interview = $30 + $30 = $60

2. Administrative and record-keeping action = $30 Separation costs = $60 + $30 = $90

Replacement costs

1. Advertising for job opening = $2,500
2. Pre-employment administrative functions and record-keeping action = $100
3. Selection interview = $250
4. Employment tests = $40
5. Meetings to discuss candidates (salary and benefits of managers while participating in meetings) = $250

Replacement costs = $2,500 + $100 + $250 + $40 + $250 = $3,140

Training costs

1. Booklets, manuals, and reports = $50
2. Education = $240/day for new employee's salary and benefits × 10 days of workshops, seminars, or courses = $2,400
3. One-to-one coaching = ($240/day per new employee + $240/day per staff coach or job expert) × 20 days of one-to-one coaching = $9,600
4. Salary and benefits of new employee until he or she gets "up to par" = $240/day for salary and benefits × 20 days = $4,800

Training costs = $50 + $2,400 + $9,600 + $4,800 = $16,850
Total turnover costs = $90 + $3,140 + $16,850 = $20,080

Source: Adapted from the book *Turning Your Human Resources Department into a Profit Center™* by Michael Mercer, PhD (Barrington, IL: Castlegate Publishers, Inc.). Copyright 2002 Michael Mercer. Reproduced with permission from Michael Mercer, PhD, http://www. DrMercer.com.

If 300 worker-days are lost through job absence during a month having 25 scheduled working days at an organization that employs 500 workers, the absenteeism rate for that month is

$$\frac{300}{500 \times 25} \times 100 = 2.4 \text{ percent}$$

Job absence can be defined as the failure of employees to report to work when their schedules require it, whether or not such failure to report is excused. Scheduled vacations, holidays, and prearranged leaves of absence are not counted as job absence.

COSTS OF ABSENTEEISM

Traditional accounting and information systems often do not generate data that reflect the costs of absenteeism. Consequently, their usefulness in HRP is often limited. To accentuate the impact of absenteeism on organizational performance, managers should translate the data into dollar costs. A system for computing absenteeism costs for an individual organization is available. Organizations with computerized absence reporting systems should find this additional information easy and inexpensive to generate. The cost of each person hour lost to absenteeism is based on the hourly weighted average salary, costs of employee benefits, supervisory costs, and incidental costs.

For example, XYZ Company, with 1,200 employees, has 78,000 person hours lost to absenteeism; the total absence cost is $560,886. When this figure is divided by 1,200 employees, the cost per employee is $467.41. (In this example, we are assuming the absent workers are paid. If absent workers are not paid, their salary figures are omitted from the computation.)

ABSENTEEISM AND HR PLANNING

While an employer may find that the overall absenteeism rate and costs are within an acceptable range, it is still advisable to study the statistics to determine whether there are patterns in the data. Rarely does absenteeism spread itself evenly across an organization. It is very likely that employees in one area (or occupational group) may have nearly perfect attendance records, while others in a different area may be absent frequently. By monitoring these differential attendance records, managers can assess where problems might exist and, more importantly, begin planning ways to resolve or improve the underlying causes. For example, incentives could be provided for perfect attendance. Alternatively, progressive discipline procedures might be used with employees having a record of recurring absenteeism.

NEL

CHAPTER 3

Equity and Diversity in Human Resources Management

After studying this chapter, you should be able to

[OUTCOME] 1 Explain the reasons for equity-seeking legislation.

[OUTCOME] 2 Identify the legal framework including the *Charter* and human rights legislation.

[OUTCOME] 3 Describe pay equity and strategies for implementing it.

[OUTCOME] 4 Discuss the *Employment Equity Act* with respect to its origins, its purpose, and its continued enforcement.

[OUTCOME] 5 Describe how employment equity is implemented in organizations.

[OUTCOME] 6 Discuss sexual harassment as an employment equity issue.

[OUTCOME] 7 Explain and give examples of diversity management.

Managers and human resource professionals are expected to manage employees in ways that comply with and respect the laws and regulations of Canada. These rules have been written to protect employees and employers. In some cases, the laws have been created because of previous situations where employees were not treated fairly. In other cases, the laws simply reflect the values of society. Human rights legislation and employment equity legislation, introduced in this chapter, arose because of both of these cases. But they are not the only laws that govern the employment relationship. In other chapters you will become familiar with other legislation, always introduced in the context of the functions, such as the regulations governing the handling of hazardous material in Chapter 12, which addresses occupational health and safety. It is important to know that managers (and employees) cannot do whatever they want at work, without suffering consequences. The consequences range from criminal charges, costly and time-consuming litigation, negative publicity for the organization, and a decrease in organizational morale and commitment. Therefore, following the laws and regulations is just good business, as you will see in the discussion of equity and diversity.

Canada is one of the most diverse countries in the world—a kaleidoscope of cultures, languages, and nationalities consisting of more than 200 different ethnic groups. Nearly 20 percent of our citizens were born outside Canada, with more than nine out of ten of these immigrants making their homes in urban centres. By 2016, about one in every five citizens will be a visible minority.[1] The workplace must not only reflect this reality but also accommodate this diversity. Discrimination based on race, age, or sex is illegal in every jurisdiction. In the field of HRM, perhaps no topic has received more attention in recent decades than employment equity. **Employment equity,** or the treatment of employed individuals in a fair and nonbiased manner, has attracted the attention of the media, the courts, practitioners, and legislators. Employment equity is not just the absence of discrimination but the proactive programs to ensure that the organization's workforce is representative of the population. Employment equity legislation affects all aspects of the employment relationship. When managers ignore the legal aspects of HRM, they risk incurring costly and time-consuming litigation, negative public attitudes, and damage to organization morale.

Employment equity is not only a legal topic; it is also an emotional issue. It concerns all individuals regardless of their sex, religion, age, national origin, race, or position in an organization. Supervisors should be aware of their personal biases and how these attitudes can influence their dealings with subordinates. It should be emphasized that covert as well as blatantly intentional discrimination in employment is illegal.

In this chapter we emphasize the legislation governing employment equity, and describe the organizational response to this legislation. Today, compliance with employment equity involves managing diversity with the goal of utilizing fully the organization's human capital.

employment equity

The employment of individuals in a fair and nonbiased manner

EMPLOYMENT EQUITY

Central to Canada's economic growth and prosperity in a highly competitive global marketplace will be a barrier-free environment in which all Canadians can fully explore and develop their career potential. Labour force statistics (see Chapter 1) indicate changing patterns of immigration, rising labour force participation rates for women, and an aging population with a proportionally higher incidence of disabilities. Women, visible minorities, and people with disabilities make up over 60 percent of Canada's labour force, and their numbers continue to rise.[2] Members of designated groups (as defined by federal legislation) entering Canada's labour pool constitute a vital resource, and their full participation in the workplace will be fundamental to an organization's ability to understand and respond to the needs of a rapidly changing marketplace. As a society, we have moved beyond principle to imperative in ensuring equal access to employment opportunities.

By definition, *equity* means fairness and impartiality. In a legal sense, it means justice based on the concepts of ethics and fairness, and a system of jurisprudence administered by administrative tribunals. The implementation of employment

OUTCOME 1

equity has involved establishing policies and practices designed to ensure equitable representation in the workforce and to redress past discriminations. (Note that in the United States, the term *affirmative action* is used, and includes quotas, which are not typically part of employment equity here in Canada). There are four **designated groups** in Canada (as recognized in the federal *Employment Equity Act*) that have not received equitable treatment in employment.

STATUS OF DESIGNATED GROUPS

Women, Aboriginal people, visible minorities, and people with disabilities face significant (albeit different) disadvantages in employment, even though they make up about 60 percent of Canada's workforce. Some of these disadvantages include high unemployment, occupational segregation, pay inequities, and limited opportunities for career progress.

Women tend to be concentrated in occupations that are accorded lower status and pay. In 2006, women constituted 43 percent of the total workforce but were not equally represented in all occupations. Women are underrepresented as semi-professionals and technicians; as supervisors in trades; and in natural and applied sciences. Women are also underrepresented in management positions and as members of boards. As well, it is still the case that female earnings lag those of men. The census found that women working full-time earned 85 cents for every dollar earned by men in 2005. (StatsCan did find that in cases of identical education, experience, and occupation, men and women earn the same.[3]

Women cite the top barriers to women's advancement in Highlights in HRM 3.1.

According to the 2006 Census, over 1 million people self-identify as Aboriginal in Canada, approximately 3.8 percent of the total Canadian population. Among people who identify themselves as Aboriginal, 60 percent are First Nations, 33 percent Métis, and 4 percent Inuit. Their unemployment rate is more than twice the national average at around 13 percent. In 2006, 45 percent of Aboriginal people

designated groups

Women, visible minorities, Aboriginal people, and persons with disabilities who have been disadvantaged in employment.

Highlights in **HRM 3.1**

Barriers to the Advancement of Women

1. Commitment to personal and family responsibilities
2. Lack of mentoring opportunities
3. Lack of female role models
4. Stereotyping and preconceptions of women's roles and abilities
5. Exclusion from informal networks of communication
6. Failure of senior leaders to assume accountability for women's advancement

What can companies do to retain women? Here are seven strategies:

1. Equal pay—people talk about pay and it is important that women know that they are receiving equal pay for work of equal value.

2. Flex schedules—accommodate women with child and elder care responsibilities by offering them four 10-hour days, half days, or a flexible arrival times.
3. Forty-hour workweeks—Many professionals are willing to work and accomplish but unwilling to put in 80-hour weeks.
4. Part-time and job sharing—an ideal solution for new mothers.
5. Mentoring—pair a promising woman professional with a senior manager to help her develop a career strategy.
6. Focus on the family—allow women to get the work done but on a schedule that accommodates their family responsibilities.
7. Offer opportunities—all employees will stay in jobs if they are learning.

Source: D. De Marco "Retaining Gen X Women Becoming Crucial," *Canadian HR Reporter* (December 3, 2007), vol. 20, iss. 31: 31; A. Tomlinson, "Wall Street Rougher than Bay Street," *Canadian HR Reporter* 15, no. 5 (March 11, 2002): 1, 14.

aged 25 to 54 were postsecondary graduates; 14 percent had a trade credential, 19 percent had a college diploma, and 8 percent had a university degree. Employment rates tend to rise with higher educational attainment.[4] The median income for the Canadian population is $29,000 while the median for Aboriginal people is $18,000. In western Canada they will account for a substantial portion of labour market growth. However, many Aboriginal people face major barriers to employment, which are often compounded by low educational achievement and lack of job experience, as well as by language and cultural barriers. In urban centres, many Aboriginal workers are concentrated in low-paying, unstable employment. Economic self-sufficiency and participation in the economy are seen as essential to Aboriginal development. Interestingly, Aboriginal values such as cooperation and consensus decision making have become more closely aligned with management approaches.[5] A study in one Canadian company showed that the creation of an Aboriginal networking group, based on cultural concepts such as talking circles and collective decision making, resulted in Aboriginal people with strong feelings of belonging and a sense of professional purpose, and this in turn made them willing to help recruit other Aboriginal people.[6] Highlights in HRM 3.2 describes how Manitoba Hydro and SaskTel reach out to the Aboriginal population.

Highlights in HRM 3.2

Outreach Efforts

Human Resources Development Canada awarded Manitoba Hydro its Vision award for creativity and innovation in its employment equity programs. Currently, Aboriginal people make up 8.3 percent of Manitoba Hydro's workforce. In northern Manitoba, where there is a greater concentration of Aboriginal people, 27.4 percent of the corporation's workforce is Aboriginal. The goal is to get the overall corporate representation of Aboriginal people up to 10 percent, and up to 33 percent in the north. The creative ways in which these goals are being reached include the following:

- A zero-tolerance policy of workplace harassment and discrimination
- An outreach and partnership program with Aboriginal organizations to provide information about employment and training opportunities
- Partnerships with postsecondary institutions to provide educational programs and career information and to brand Manitoba Hydro as an employer of choice
- A review of training programs to ensure that there are no systemic barriers
- Systematic recruitment efforts to introduce Aboriginals by means of internships, co-op placements, summer employment, and part-time work

The most successful program is the pre-employment training designed to facilitate the entry of Aboriginal people into Manitoba Hydro's training programs, which are more like apprenticeship programs. The pre-employment training provides academic upgrading, a rotation through three trades to familiarize candidates with these jobs, and workshops to deal with the concerns and issues about being away from home. A recent addition to the program is the utility's "Building the Circle Camp" which introduces girls in Northern Manitoba to opportunities in engineering, technology, and trades.

SaskTel is a Crown corporation providing cellular, phone, Internet, and multimedia services to 13 cities and more than 500 remote communities in Saskatchewan, many of them inhabited by First Nations and Métis people. SaskTel cares about the Aboriginal population both as customers and employees (8 percent of SaskTel's workforce is Aboriginal and the company has a target of 13.5 percent, the provincial labour force rate). The company's call centre can offer service in three different First Nations languages.

Sources: Shannon Klie, "Short Circuiting the Labour Supply," *Canadian HR Reporter*, vol. 21, iss. 22 (December 15, 2008): 6; Laura Bogomolny, Peter Evans, Andy Holloway, Zena Olijnyk, Erin Pooley, and Andrew Wahl, "The Best Workplaces in Canada," *Canadian Business* (April 10–23, 2006): 74; Cheryl Petten, "Manitoba Hydro Recognized for Employment Equity Efforts," *Windspeaker 20*, no. 4 (August 2002): 31.

It is estimated that one in seven Canadians has a disability. This rate increases with (age,) with about 5 percent of those between 15 and 24 having a disability, and 18 percent of those aged 45 to 64 having one. People with disabilities represent 14 percent of Canada's population, but again, their workforce representation is low at 1.6 percent.[7] About one-third of those with disabilities became disabled as adults, resulting in 70 percent of them forced to make career changes. People with disabilities face attitudinal barriers, physical demands that are unrelated to actual job requirements, and inadequate access to the technical and human support systems that would make productive employment possible. Seventy percent of those with disabilities need some kind of workplace accommodation, and in 80 percent of the cases the cost is less than $500.[8] Employers can seek to redress attitudinal barriers by focusing on (abilities) not disabilities.

The (visible minority) population in Canada experienced a growth rate of 27.2 percent since the 2001 Census, compared to an overall population growth of 5.4 percent. Visible minorities represent about 16.2 percent of Canadians, and 15.4 percent of the labour force. Visible minority groups vary in their labour force profiles and in their regional distributions. Studies have shown that Latin Americans and Southeast Asians experience lower-than-average incomes, higher rates of unemployment, and reduced access to job interviews, even when they have the same qualifications as other candidates. See Highlights in HRM 3.3 for a study documenting this. Systemic barriers that negatively affect employment for visible minorities include culturally biased aptitude tests, lack of recognition of foreign credentials, and excessively high language

Highlights in **HRM 3.3**

What's in a Name?

Metropolis, an immigration and diversity research network, sent out 6,000 résumés tailored to the job requirements of 2,000 online postings from employers across 20 occupational categories. These included administrative, financial, marketing, programming and retail. All résumés included a university degree and two- to four-years' experience. The only difference on these résumés was the name of the applicant. Some had names like Tara Singh, and others had names like Emily Brown. The results were a wake-up call for Canadians who pride themselves on being less biased than other nationalities. Those with English names received callbacks 16 percent of the time, compared to 11 percent for applicants with Pakistani, Indian, and Chinese names who had the same level of education and experience. According to the study's author, UBC Economics Professor Oreopoulos, "The findings suggest that a distinct foreign-sounding name may be a significant disadvantage on the job market—even if you are a second- or third-generation citizen," He adds "'In cases

where the employer requires the hire to be very good at English, then consciously or unconsciously, they may have a concern when looking at their résumé. The other possibility is preference-based discrimination: the employer, consciously or unconsciously, prefers to have applicants of the same ethnicity working for them."

Those who had been educated outside Canada received callbacks 8 percent of the time, and those who had no Canadian work experience only 5 percent, confirming that Canadian work experience is very important to employers. While immigrants had unemployment rates of 11.5 percent in 2006 (compared with 4.9 percent for the Canadian-born population), second-generation immigrants of Chinese and Indian origin have statistically above-average incomes and educations. A new online tool, Roadmap, from the Toronto Region Immigrant Employment Council, will help employers hire, integrate, and retain skilled immigrants. For more information, visit http://www.hireimmigrants. ca/roadmap.

Source: M. Jimenez "Right Resume, Wrong Name," *The Globe and Mail,* (May 21, 2009), 1; Anonymous, University of British Columbia, "Employers Discriminate Against Applicants with Non-English Names, UBC Study Suggests" *NewsRx Health & Science* (June 21, 2009), 198; D. Karp, "Job Seekers with Asian Names Face Discrimination; Canadians with English Names Are Called Back More Often for Job Interviews, UBC study finds," *The Vancouver Sun,* (May 21, 2009), A1.

FIGURE **3.1**

Representation of Designated Groups in the Labour Force

	Representation in the Canadian Population (%)	Representation in the Workforce (%)
Women	50.9	43.0
Aboriginal people	3.8	2.6
People with disabilities	14.3	1.6
Members of visible minorities	16.2	15.4

Source: Adapted from 97-562-XCB2006017, referring to "Labour Force Activity (8), Visible Minority Groups (15), Immigrant Status and Period of Immigration (9), Highest Certificate, Diploma or Degree (7), Age Groups (9) and Sex (3) for the Population 15 Years and Over of Canada, Provinces, Territories, Census Metropolitan Areas and Census Agglomerations, 2006 Census—20% Sample Data (table). Topic-based tabulation. 2006 Census of Population." 89-628-XIE, referring to "Participation and Activity Limitation Survey 2006: Tables. Ottawa: Statistics Canada, 2007." 97-558-XIE2006001, referring to "Aboriginal Peoples in Canada in 2006: Inuit, Métis and First Nations, 2006 Census: Findings."

Using the Internet

WorkAble Solutions provides job seekers and employers with information on the benefits of hiring persons with disabilities

http://www.workable solutionsbc.ca

requirements. Recent statistics indicate that although visible minorities—73 percent of recent immigrants are visible minorities—tend to be better educated, they also have the highest unemployment rates.[9] The unemployment rate of recent immigrants (12.1 percent) was still nearly twice that of the Canadian-born population (6.4 percent).[10] As such, there are targeted efforts to recruit them to ensure representation.

Figure 3.1 shows the workforce representation of the designated groups in the Canadian population. Ethics in HRM describes some of the issues in employment equity.

Ethics in **HRM**

Ethics: Equality or Equity

The Public Works department of the federal government sent its managers an e-mail telling them persons recruited externally must be from designated groups. The federal Department of Fisheries ran an ad on the government's website that stated explicitly that those who can apply are "persons working or residing in Canada and Canadian citizens living abroad, who are members of the visible minority groups." The *Employment Equity Act* defines visible minorities as being persons, other than Aboriginal people, who are non-Caucasian in race or non-white in colour. The decision to restrict applicants to visible minorities is part of the government's efforts to have its employees look more like the Canadian population. About 16.2 percent of Canadians identify themselves as visible minorities, and they represent about 15.4 percent of the labour

market. However, in 2006, only 7.3 percent work in the public service. Therefore, the government decreed that about 3 percent of job postings would be restricted to visible minorities. Unlike the United States, quotas are not in place. But words such as *benchmarks*, *targets*, and *goals* have the same impact. Critics argue that candidates should be judged on merit, not colour, and that other programs to increase minority candidates would be better: provide more education and training for minorities or create an office culture that values diversity. The public service has a good track record in increasing the number of francophones and women, and restricted competitions may not be the best route. But the commissioner of the public service counters that treating all people the same way does not always lead to equitable results, and special measures are necessary.

Sources: T. Blackwell, "White Males Need Not Apply," *The National Post*, November 19, 2005, A1; E. Greenspon, "Don't Apply," *The Globe and Mail*, May 29, 2003, A21.; M. Wente, "Whites Need Not Apply," *The Globe and Mail*, May 30, 2003, A16;

BENEFITS OF EMPLOYMENT EQUITY

Employment equity makes good business sense. It contributes to the bottom line by broadening the base of qualified individuals for employment, training, and promotions, and by helping employers avoid costly human rights complaints. Employment equity enhances an organization's ability to attract and keep the best-qualified employees, which results in greater access to a broader base of skills. It also enhances employee morale by offering special measures such as flexible work schedules and work sharing. Finally, it improves the organization's image in the community.[11]

The Charter of Rights and Freedoms, the federal Canadian Human Rights Act, and pay equity and employment equity acts are the governing pieces of legislation dealing with employment equity.

THE LEGAL FRAMEWORK

THE CHARTER OF RIGHTS AND FREEDOMS

The Constitution Act of 1982, which contains the Canadian Charter of Rights and Freedoms, is the cornerstone of equity legislation. The Charter guarantees some fundamental rights to every Canadian, including

- Fundamental freedoms (s. 2) that comprise the standard rights of freedom of speech, press, assembly, association, and religion
- Democratic rights (ss. 3 to 5), covering franchise rights
- Mobility rights (s. 6), concerning the right to move freely from province to province for the purposes of residence and/or employment
- Legal rights (ss. 7 to 14), conferring standard procedural rights in criminal proceedings
- Equality rights (s. 15), guaranteeing no discrimination by law on grounds of race, ethnic origin, colour, religion, sex, age, sexual orientation, marital status, citizenship, Aboriginal residence, or mental and physical ability
- Language rights (ss. 16 to 23)[12]

Although the Charter has offered many Canadians opportunities with regard to their own individual rights and responsibilities, it has also been a source of disappointment. The enactment of the Charter created high expectations on the part of various groups, especially unions, which believed that under Section 2 all employees would have a fundamental right to associate, to bargain collectively, and to strike. However, in 1987 the Supreme Court of Canada, in ruling on a challenge to federal public-sector laws relating to compulsory arbitration, back-to-work legislation, and wage restraint legislation, declared that Section 2 of the Charter does not include the right to bargain collectively and to strike. In the Court's view, these were not fundamental freedoms, but rather statutory rights created and regulated by legislation. As a result of this ruling, governments can weaken the collective bargaining process by limiting salary increases, legislating strikers back to work, and imposing compulsory arbitration. However, a 2007 case in B.C. ruled that indeed, the Charter does in fact protect the right to bargain collectively. It is important to note that the Charter protects only the right of government and public-sector employees, not private-sector employees.

THE CANADIAN HUMAN RIGHTS ACT (CHRA)

The Canadian Human Rights Act (CHRA) was passed by Parliament on July 14, 1977, and became effective in March 1978. This act proclaims that every individual should have an equal opportunity with other individuals to

© B. Busco/The Image Bank

OUTCOME 2

Workplace accommodation for persons with disabilities is usually inexpensive.

make for himself or herself the life that he or she is able and wishes to have, consistent with his or her duties and obligations as a member of society, without being hindered in or prevented from doing so by discriminatory practices based on race, national or ethnic origin, colour, religion, age, sex or marital status, or convictions for an offence for which a pardon has been granted or by discriminatory employment practices based on physical handicap.[13]

The act applies to all federal government departments and agencies, to Crown corporations, and to other businesses and industries under federal jurisdiction, such as banks, airlines, railway companies, and insurance and communications companies.

For those areas not under federal jurisdiction, (which is the vast majority of workplaces) protection may be available under provincial human rights laws. Provincial laws, although very similar to federal ones, do differ from province to province. Every province and territory has a human rights act (or code), and each has jurisdiction prohibiting discrimination in the workplace.

The prohibited grounds of discrimination in employment include race, religion, sex, age, national or ethnic origin, physical handicap, and marital status (see Figure 3.2 for a complete listing). Employers are permitted to discriminate if employment preferences are based on a **bona fide occupational qualification (BFOQ)** or BFOR (bona fide occupational requirement) and it is not possible to accommodate the employee without causing undue hardship. A BFOQ is justified if the employer can establish necessity for business operations. In other words, differential treatment is not discrimination if there is a justifiable reason. For example, according to the Ontario provincial legislation, adherence to the tenets of the Roman Catholic Church was deemed a BFOQ for employment as a teacher in a Roman Catholic school.[14] Business necessity also relates to the safe and efficient operation of an organization. There is an ongoing debate as to whether male guards should be allowed to work in women's prisons and whether members of the Sikh religion, whose religion mandates the wearing of turbans, must wear hard hats at construction sites, etc. The duty to accommodate is an important part of human rights legislation and is discussed more thoroughly later in the chapter, under special measures and reasonable accommodation.

© Jese Luis Pelaez, Inc./CORBIS

When looking for employees, employers need to assess abilities.

bona fide occupational qualification (BFOQ)
A justifiable reason for discrimination based on business reasons of safety or effectiveness

FIGURE **3.2**

Prohibited Grounds of Discrimination in Canada

This document provides comparative information on the grounds of discrimination covered by federal, provincial, and territorial human rights legislation in Canada. In some instances, prohibited grounds for employment differ from those for the provision of services.

Prohibited Ground	Jurisdiction	Comments
Race or colour		
Employment	all jurisdictions	
Provision of Service	all jurisdictions	
Religion		
Employment	all jurisdictions	Yukon's Act reads "religion or creed, or religious belief, religious association or religious activity"
Provision of Service	all jurisdictions	Yukon's Act reads "religion or creed, or religious belief, religious association or religious activity"

continued

103

Prohibited Ground	Jurisdiction	Comments
Physical or mental disability		
Employment	all jurisdictions	Quebec uses the phrase "handicap or use of any means to palliate a handicap"
Provision of Service	all jurisdictions	Quebec uses the phrase "handicap or use of any means to palliate a handicap"
Dependence on alcohol or drugs		
Employment	all except Yukon and Northwest Territories	Policy to accept complaints in British Columbia, Alberta, Saskatchewan, Manitoba, Ontario, New Brunswick, and Prince Edward Island Included in "handicap" ground in Quebec Previous dependence only in New Brunswick and Nova Scotia
Provision of Service	all except Yukon, Northwest Territories, and Quebec	Previous dependence only in New Brunswick and Nova Scotia Included in "handicap" ground in Quebec
Age		
Employment	all jurisdictions	British Columbia: 19–65 Alberta: 18+ Saskatchewan: 18–64 Ontario: 18–65 Newfoundland: 19–65 Quebec: except as provided for by law For tenancy only in British Columbia Saskatchewan does not include accommodation In Ontario, applies to those 18 years and older, although 16- and 17-year-olds who have left the care of parents or guardians are protected regarding accommodation In Quebec, except as provided for by law
Provision of Service	all except British Columbia, Alberta, and Newfoundland	
Sex (includes pregnancy and childbirth)		
Employment	all jurisdictions	British Columbia includes breast feeding Alberta uses the term "gender" Manitoba includes gender-determined characteristics Ontario recognizes the protection of transgendered persons and accepts complaints related to "gender identity"; Ontario accepts complaints related to female genital mutilation In Quebec, pregnancy as such is considered a ground of discrimination
Provision of Service	all jurisdictions	Alberta uses the term "gender" Manitoba includes gender-determined characteristics Ontario recognizes the protection of transgendered persons and accepts complaints related to "gender identity"; Ontario accepts complaints related to female genital mutilation In Quebec, pregnancy as such is considered a ground of discrimination

continued

Prohibited Ground	Jurisdiction	Comments
Marital status		
Employment	all jurisdictions	Quebec uses the term "civil status"
Provision of Service	all jurisdictions	Quebec uses the term "civil status"
Family status		
Employment	all except New Brunswick and Newfoundland	Saskatchewan defines being in a parent-child relationship Quebec uses the term "civil status"
Provision of Service	all except New Brunswick and Newfoundland	Saskatchewan defines as being in a parent-child relationship Quebec uses the term "civil status"
Sexual orientation		
Employment	all jurisdictions	The Supreme Court of Canada read sexual orientation into the *Alberta Human Rights, Citizenship, and Multiculturalism Act* in 1998
Provision of Service	all jurisdictions	The Supreme Court of Canada read sexual orientation into the *Alberta Human Rights, Citizenship, and Multiculturalism Act* in 1998
National or ethnic origin (including linguistic background)		
Employment	all except British Columbia and Alberta	Saskatchewan and Northwest Territories use the term "nationality" Ontario's Code includes both "ethnic origin" and "citizenship"
Provision of Service	all except British Columbia and Alberta	Saskatchewan and Northwest Territories use the term "nationality" Ontario's Code includes both "ethnic origin" and "citizenship"
Ancestry or place of origin		
Employment	Yukon, British Columbia, Alberta, Saskatchewan, Manitoba, Northwest Territories, Ontario, and New Brunswick	
Provision of Service	Yukon, British Columbia, Alberta, Saskatchewan, Manitoba, Northwest Territories, Ontario, and New Brunswick	
Language		
Employment	Yukon, Ontario, and Quebec	Ontario accepts complaints on the grounds of ancestry, ethnic origin, place of origin, and race New Brunswick will accept language-related complaints filed on the basis of ancestry, although not an enumerated ground
Provision of Service	Yukon, Ontario, and Quebec	Ontario accepts complaints on the grounds of ancestry, ethnic origin, place of origin, and race New Brunswick will accept language-related complaints filed on the basis of ancestry, although not an enumerated ground
Social condition or origin		
Employment	Quebec, Northwest Territories	New Brunswick and Newfoundland

continued

Prohibited Ground	Jurisdiction	Comments
Provision of Service	Quebec, Northwest Territories, New Brunswick and Newfoundland	
Source of income		
Employment	Alberta, Saskatchewan, Manitoba, Quebec, Prince Edward Island, and Nova Scotia	Defined as "receipt of public assistance" in Saskatchewan Included under social condition in Quebec
Provision of Service	British Columbia, Alberta, Saskatchewan, Manitoba, Ontario, Prince Edward Island, and Nova Scotia	Applies to tenancy only (not public services or facilities) in British Columbia Defined as "receipt of social assistance" in Saskatchewan Ontario bans discrimination in accommodation on the grounds of receipt of public assistance Included under social condition in Quebec Applies to occupancy or accommodation only in Nova Scotia
Assignment, attachment, or seizure of pay		
Employment	Newfoundland	Included under social condition in Quebec
Provision of Service	Newfoundland	Included under social condition in Quebec
Based on association		
Employment	Yukon, Manitoba, Ontario, New Brunswick, Nova Scotia, Northwest Territories, and Prince Edward Island	Northwest Territories has prohibition on basis of "political association"
Provision of Service	Yukon, Manitoba, Ontario, New Brunswick, Nova Scotia, Northwest Territories, and Prince Edward Island	Northwest Territories has prohibition on basis of "political association"
Political belief		
Employment	Yukon, British Columbia, Manitoba, Quebec, Nova Scotia, Prince Edward Island, New Brunswick, and Newfoundland	Newfoundland has prohibition on basis of "political opinion"
Provision of Service	Yukon, Manitoba, Quebec, Nova Scotia, Prince Edward Island, New Brunswick, and Newfoundland	Yukon includes political activity and political association Newfoundland has prohibition on basis of "political opinion"
Record of criminal conviction		
Employment	Yukon and Quebec	Yukon's Act reads "criminal charges or criminal record"
Provision of Service	Yukon, British Columbia, Quebec, and Prince Edward Island	Yukon's Act reads "criminal charges or criminal record"
Pardoned conviction		
Employment	Federal, Yukon, and Northwest Territories	
Provision of Service	Federal, Yukon, and Northwest Territories	

Source: Canadian Human Rights Commission "Prohibited Ground of Employment Discrimination by Jurisdiction." http://www.chrc-ccdp.ca/publications/pgd_mdi-en.asp. Reproduced with the permission of the Minister of Public Works and Government Services, 2009.

Enforcement of the *Canadian Human Rights Act*

The Canadian Human Rights Commission (CHRC) deals with complaints concerning discriminatory practices covered by the Canadian *Human Rights Act*. The CHRC may choose to act on its own if it believes that sufficient grounds exist for a finding of discrimination. It also has the power to issue guidelines interpreting the act.

Individuals have a right to file a complaint if they feel they have been discriminated against. (The CHRC may refuse to accept a complaint if it has not been filed within a prescribed period of time, if it is deemed trivial, or if it was filed in bad faith.) The complainant must first complete a written report describing the discriminatory action. A CHRC representative reviews the facts and determines whether the claim is legitimate. Once a complaint has been accepted by the CHRC, an investigator is assigned the task of gathering more facts from both the complainant and the accused. The investigator then submits a report to the CHRC recommending a finding of either substantiation or nonsubstantiation of the allegation. If the allegation is substantiated, a settlement may be arranged in the course of the investigation. If the parties are unable to reach agreement, a human rights tribunal consisting of up to three members may be appointed to further investigate the complaint. If the tribunal finds that a discriminatory practice did take place, or that the victim's feelings or self-respect have suffered as a result of the practice, it may order the person or organization responsible to compensate the victim. Former employees of Majestic Electronics received $300,000 in compensation because they were harassed after they refused to obey the racist and sexist orders of the company president.[15]

Any person who obstructs an investigation or a tribunal, or who fails to comply with the terms of a settlement, can be found guilty of an offence, which may be punishable by a fine and/or jail sentence. If the guilty party is an employer or an employee organization, the fine can be as high as $50,000.[16]

THE ENFORCEMENT OF PROVINCIAL HUMAN RIGHTS LAWS

Provincial human rights laws are enforced in a manner very similar to that of the federal system. At the provincial level, employers tend to be small and medium-sized businesses, many of which lack an HR professional who is knowledgeable about human rights legislation. Employers and employees alike may have little experience in matters of discrimination. The Ontario legislation now permits employees to file complaints directly to the Human Rights Tribunal.

The majority of cases are resolved at the investigation stage. If no agreement can be reached, the case is presented to the province's human rights commission. The members of the commission study the evidence and then submit a report to the minister in charge of administering human rights legislation. The minister may appoint an independent board of inquiry, which has powers similar to those of a tribunal at the federal level. Failure to comply with the remedies prescribed by the board of inquiry may result in prosecution in provincial court. Individuals may be fined between $500 and $1,000 and organizations or groups between $1,000 and $10,000. These levies vary from province to province.

PAY EQUITY

As a result of a 1978 amendment to the Canadian *Human Rights Act*, pay equity became enacted as law in the federal jurisdiction. Pay equity law makes it illegal for employers to discriminate against individuals on the basis of job content. The goal of pay equity is to eliminate the historical wage gap between men and women and to ensure that salary ranges reflect the value of the work performed. In 2002, women aged 15 and over who had employment income made 79.3 cents for every $1 earned by their male counterparts (the gap was smaller for younger women).[17]

Using the Internet

The Canadian Human Rights Commission deals with complaints concerning discriminatory practices covered by legislation. This site includes a summary of the duty to accommodate

http://www.chrc-ccdp.ca/preventing_discrimination/toc_tdm-en.asp

CHRC

[OUTCOME]

By definition, pay equity means equal pay for work of equal value. It is based on two principles. The *first* is equal pay for equal work—pay equality.[18] Male and female workers must be paid the same wage rate for doing identical work. The *second* is equal pay for similar or substantially similar work (equal pay for work of comparable worth). This means that male and female workers must be paid the same wage rate for jobs of a similar nature that may have different titles (e.g., "nurse's aide" and "orderly"). Professor Marc Mentzer at the Edwards School of Business at the University of Saskatchewan suggests that these key points help in understanding the differences between pay equality and pay equity:

- Pay equality (in which employers are required to pay women the same as men doing the same job) is required by law in every jurisdiction in Canada. Pay equality is about fair pay for individual women employees. For example, a female electrician must be paid the same as a male electrician.

- Pay equity is about fair pay for entire occupations, which are dissimilar, within an organization, such as comparing nurses (as a group) to electricians. Pay equity is required of all federally regulated employers, both private and public sectors. Provincially, it varies from Ontario and Quebec adopting pay equity legislation that applies to both private-sector and public-sector employees, to other provinces such as Saskatchewan, that have no pay equity legislation at all.

Implementation of pay equity is based on comparing the work of female-dominated job classes to the value of work performed in male-dominated jobs by males. Comparisons require the use of a gender-neutral, unbiased comparison system to evaluate the jobs in an establishment.[19] Comparisons must be based on the amount and type of skill, effort, and responsibility needed to perform the job and on the working conditions where it is performed. The comparison must be done in such a way that the characteristics of "male" jobs, such as heavy lifting and "dirty" working conditions, are valued fairly in comparison to the characteristics of "female" jobs, such as manual dexterity and caring for others.[20]

The federal pay equity legislation applies to that section of the workforce under its jurisdiction and covers all organizations regardless of number of employees. The federal pay equity system is complaint-based, meaning that complaints can be raised by an employee, a group of employees, or a bargaining agent.[21] Some recent decisions included compensating high school secretaries at rates similar to the male job class of audio-visual technicians and comparing a female job class of law clerk with that of the male job class of investigator.[22] However, at the time of publication, there are plans to replace this system with a proactive model, such as the one used in Ontario, where employers take the initiative to ensure jobs of equal value receive equal pay. A more comprehensive review of pay equity is provided in Chapter 9.

THE *EMPLOYMENT EQUITY ACT* (1995)

Employers and Crown corporations that have 100 employees or more and that are regulated under the *Canada Labour Code* must implement employment equity and report on their results. Under the act, the employer is required to

- Provide its employees with a questionnaire that allows them to indicate whether they belong to one of the four designated groups
- Identify jobs in which the percentage of members of designated groups falls below their availability in the labour market
- Communicate information on employment equity to its employees, and consult and collaborate with employee representatives
- Identify possible barriers in existing employment systems that may be limiting the employment opportunities of members of designated groups

[OUTCOME]

- Develop an employment equity plan aimed at promoting an equitable workplace
- Make all reasonable efforts to implement its plan
- Monitor, review, and revise its plan from time to time
- Prepare an annual report on its employment equity data and activities.[23]

The concept of employment equity is rooted in the wording of federal and provincial employment standards legislation, human rights codes, and the *Charter*. Employment equity involves identifying and removing systemic barriers to employment opportunities that adversely affect women, visible minorities, Aboriginal people, and people with disabilities. Employment equity also involves implementing special measures and making reasonable accommodation.[24]

Under the Federal Contractors Program (FCP) contractors who bid for goods and services contracts with the federal government valued at $200,000 or more, and that employ 100 people or more, are required to implement an employment equity program. This is not a law, but contractors that do not cooperate may not be allowed to bid. (For a list of this program's implementation criteria, see Highlights in HRM 3.4.) To assist in the process, the federal government provides professional consulting services to employers throughout Canada regarding how to implement employment equity. Federally regulated employers must conduct a workforce analysis to identify underrepresentation of members of designated groups; review their employment systems, policies, and practices to identify employment barriers; and prepare a plan outlining the steps they will take to remove any identified barriers. Most provinces have similar legislation governing employment equity.

Winners of merit awards for initiatives in employment equity include Scotiabank, for increasing the number of visible minorities in its workforce to 19 percent, and the Saskatchewan Wheat Pool, for its partnerships with the Aboriginal community—particularly its investment in an MBA program in Aboriginal Business. In the face of threats to employment equity legislation, employers are showing willingness to keep the practice alive. As Robert Rochon, director of employment equity for National Grocer Co., puts it: "Regardless of any legislative requirement, [employment equity] is a good business decision for us. When you consider the changing face of Canada, it just makes good business sense to reflect the customers that you serve."[25]

ADMINISTRATION AND ENFORCEMENT OF THE *EMPLOYMENT EQUITY ACT*

Human Resources Development Canada is responsible for administering the FCP. The CHRC is mandated under the *Canadian Human Rights Act*[26] to prohibit discrimination in the establishments of federally regulated businesses.[27]

The CHRC is authorized to conduct on-site compliance reviews. Failure to comply may result in fines ranging from $10,000 for first offenders to $50,000 for repeat offenders.

THE IMPLEMENTATION OF EMPLOYMENT EQUITY IN ORGANIZATIONS

The implementation of employment equity in an organization follows the precepts of any change management program. Thus, successful implementation must employ strategic planning, which must be incorporated into an overall business strategy. The FCP outlined in Highlights in HRM 3.4 provides a good overview of what a plan should incorporate. The process involves six main steps: senior management commitment; data collection and analysis; employment systems review; establishment of a workplan; implementation; and a follow-up process that includes evaluation, monitoring, and revision.

[OUTCOME] 5

Highlights in **HRM 3.4**

Implementation Criteria for Federal Contractors Program

1. Communication by the organization's CEO to employees, unions, and/or employee associations of the commitment to achieve equality in employment through the design and implementation of an employment equity plan.

2. Assignment of senior personnel with responsibility for employment equity.

3. Collection and maintenance of information on the employment status of designated-group employees by occupation and salary levels and with regard to hiring, promotion, and termination in relation to all other employees.

4. Analysis of designated-group representation within the organization in relation to their representation in the supply of qualified workers from which the contractor may reasonably be expected to recruit employees.

5. Elimination or modification of those human resource policies, practices, and systems, whether formal or informal, shown to have or likely to have an unfavourable effect on the employment status of designated-group employees.

6. Establishment of goals for the hiring, training, and promotion of designated-group employees. Such goals will consider projections for hiring, promotions, terminations, layoffs, recalls, retirements, and, where possible, the projected availability of qualified designated-group members.

7. Establishment of a work plan for reaching each of the goals in 6.

8. Adoption of special measures where necessary to ensure that goals are achieved, including the provision of reasonable accommodation as required.

9. Establishment of a climate favourable to the successful integration of designated-group members within the organization.

10. Adoption of procedures to monitor the progress and results achieved in implementing employment equity.

11. Authorization to allow representatives of the CHRC access to the business premises and to the records noted in 3 in order to conduct on-site compliance reviews for the purpose of measuring the progress achieved in implementing employment equity.

Source: Federal Contractors Program (FCP) – Criteria for Implementation, Human Resources and Skills Development Canada, 2006. Reproduced with the permission of the Minister of Public Works and Government Services Canada, 2008.

STEP 1: SENIOR MANAGEMENT COMMITMENT

Commitment to an employment equity plan necessitates a top-down strategy. A more supportive culture is created when the CEO or owner-operator publicly introduces written policy describing the organization's commitment to employment equity. This policy must be strategically posted throughout the organization and sent to each employee. For example, the CEO, all members of the board of directors, as well as the staff at the Law Society of Upper Canada are fully committed and all have received equity and human rights training. The world's largest food service company, Compass Group, has employment equity as a top priority, by making it a topic at every board meeting, where workforce data are reviewed and built into the performance scorecard of all managers.[28]

An employment equity policy statement may raise many questions, so it is important to be thorough in this process in order to keep concerns to a minimum. The policy statement should be supplemented with a communiqué explaining what employment equity is, the rationale for the program, and its implications for current and future employees. Assurances must be given at this time that all information provided will be treated confidentially and will not be used to identify individuals other than for the purpose of employment equity program activities. The communiqué should also list the names of individuals responsible for administering the

109

110

program and outline any planned activities the employer may deem necessary to establish the program (e.g., analysis of the workforce or of policies and procedures).

This commitment to employees and candidates for employment applies to all aspects of the employment relationship, including recruitment, work assignment, training opportunities, compensation, promotions, transfers, and terminations.

Communication tools may include periodic information sessions, workplace posters, departmental or small group meetings conducted by line management, orientation and training programs, newsletters, and vehicles such as videos, brochures, employee handbooks, and memos from the union. An innovative approach to communications was taken at the Centre de recherche industrielle du Québec (CRIQ) where employees decided to create a video to demonstrate that seemingly harmless comments and attitudes can have devastating consequences for members of designated groups. Their goal was to sensitize people without lecturing or pointing fingers. The employees acted in the video, selected its music, and directed and produced it. Its title was *Moi... des préjugés? (Me... prejudiced?)*. The video depicts the experiences of a black man, a person who is deaf, and a woman, all of whom are seeking employment with a company, and who are confronted with opinions and attitudes that have everything to do with prejudice and nothing to do with the requirements of the job.[29]

Assignment of Accountable Senior Staff

Senior management must place the responsibility for employment equity in the hands of a senior manager, a joint labour–management committee, and an employment equity advisory committee with mechanisms for union consultation (or, in nonunionized settings, for consultation with designated employee representatives). Senior management must designate line management responsibility and accountability. Anyone given responsibility for employment equity must be knowledgeable about the problems and concerns of designated groups; have the status and ability needed to gain the cooperation of employees at all levels in the organization; have access to financial and human resources required to conduct planning and implementation functions; have sufficient time to devote to employment equity issues; monitor and be in a position to report to the CEO on the results of employment equity measures; and be prepared to serve as the employment equity contact person with federal and provincial government agencies.

Among the employment areas committee members may be required to review are employment practices, advertising and recruitment policies, company-sponsored training, the organization of work schedules and facilities, and systems for promotion to management positions. While committees are usually given responsibility for making recommendations and reporting on issues, ultimate authority generally rests with senior management.

Employers covered by the *Employment Equity Act* are legally obligated to consult with designated employee representatives or, in unionized settings, with bargaining agents. Consultation means that the employer must supply sufficient information and opportunity to employee representatives or bargaining agents to enable them to ask questions and submit advice on the implementation of employment equity.

The labour movement in Canada generally supports the concept of employment equity, so long as unions are fully informed and involved from the beginning with respect to an employer's planning process. This makes sense considering that unions are the legitimate representatives of employee interests in unionized settings. Supportive mechanisms for achieving employment equity

First Nations University is a unique university in Canada that caters to the advanced education needs of Aboriginal people.

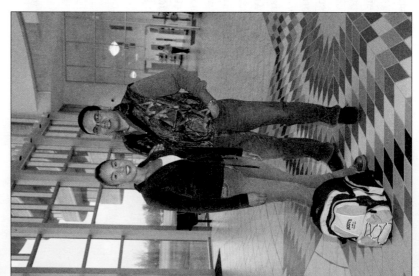

have been reported by Human Resources Development Canada.[30] Many employers and unions have successfully negotiated family-friendly policies such as parental leave, child care provisions, and flexible hours.

STEP 2: DATA COLLECTION AND ANALYSIS

The development of an internal workforce profile is an important tool in employment equity planning. Without this information, an organization would not be able to determine where it stands relative to the internal and external workforce. Profiles must be based on both stock data and flow data. Profiles provide a snapshot of the organization. They show where members of designated groups are employed in the organization, at what salaries and status, and in what occupations on a particular date. Flow data refer to the distribution of designated groups in applications, interviews, hiring decisions, training and promotion opportunities, and terminations. They provide information on the movement of employees into and through the organization. Computerized reporting systems and tracking software are available from Human Resources Development Canada to assist employers in gathering, reporting, and analyzing their internal workforce data.

Most of the information necessary for equity planning (e.g., salary, sex, access to benefits, seniority status, and occupational and career history within the organization) is contained in existing personnel files. Information pertaining to the distribution of members of designated groups in the employer's organization must be accumulated by the employer through a self-identification process. Under the *Employment Equity Act*, employers may gather data on members of designated groups as long as employees voluntarily agree to be identified or identify themselves as members of designated groups, and as long as the data are used only for employment equity planning or reporting purposes.

Creating a climate of trust in the management of the program is a major challenge. Employers can encourage participation and confidence in the program by providing focused employment equity training to managers and by providing opportunities for managers to be recognized for their contributions to the development and administration of effective employment equity strategies. Companies such as Pratt & Whitney have introduced equity and diversity training for their supervisors. Cameco Corporation in northern Saskatchewan has committed to improving the job prospects of Aboriginal people as part of its long-term employment strategy, based on economics, not just a keen sense of social responsibility. Mentoring, basic training, educational support, and family assistance programs mean a lot to those employees who may be the first in their families to have full-time paid employment.[31]

If an employer administers a self-identification questionnaire, confidentiality and a clear commitment at senior levels to the concept of employment equity should be communicated. Having employees self-identify is crucial to the success of the program, but problems may arise with self-identification. Under some provincial employment equity acts, terms such as *Aboriginal* and *racial minority* are not defined. Some employees, who have "hidden" disabilities such as epilepsy or partial deafness, may not wish to label themselves for fear of future discriminatory treatment. Some minorities, such as Aboriginals people, have never disclosed their ethnic origins for similar reasons.

If too many employees with nonvisible disabilities do not identify themselves as disabled, the program could end up being designed to recruit more employees with disabilities, leaving another segment of the employee population underrepresented. Thus, because inaccurate data were accumulated on one group, the other group will not benefit from the employment equity efforts. An additional concern is that individuals with disabilities may need some form of accommodation to help them perform their jobs better. If they do not self-identify, they have denied themselves certain basic rights. Highlights in HRM 3.5 outlines words and actions that

stock data
Data showing the status of designated groups in occupational categories and compensation levels

flow data
Data that provide a profile of the employment decisions affecting designated groups

are appropriate in dealing with persons with disabilities. A self-identification form should contain the following:

- An explanation of the employer's employment equity policy, the purpose of the employment equity program, and the need for the information requested
- An indication that the information supplied will be confidential and will be used only for employment equity purposes by those individuals identified as responsible for the program
- The categories for self-identification, with brief explanations and examples
- An indication that the form has been reviewed by the relevant human rights agency
- Space for comments and suggestions
- The name of the contact person for information and suggestions[32]

Once the personal information forms have been completed, all occupations within the organization must be cross-referenced to the National Occupational Classification (NOC). This manual was created by Statistics Canada for use in statistical surveys and for other purposes. Personal data are organized under the four-digit NOC classifications. When building a workforce profile, employers should first refer to the four-digit unit groups and then determine which one each job belongs in. For example, secretaries and stenographers are classified in unit group 4111, which in turn can be assigned to the "clerical workers" group.

A full workforce analysis can be generated once all the information has been loaded and the reports are complete. This utilization analysis will include

Highlights in HRM 3.5

Suggestions for Inclusion

Person who is blind, or person with a visual impairment

Identify yourself and anyone with you; if you have met before, explain the context of the meeting; speak in a normal tone of voice and indicate to whom you are speaking if in a group; remove obstacles; describe the surroundings ("There is a door on your right"); if offering to guide, ask the person to take your arm above the elbow and walk about a half-step ahead; plan ahead to obtain material in audio cassettes or Braille.

Person with a physical disability or person with a mobility impairment

Rearrange furniture or objects to accommodate a wheelchair or other mobility aids; avoid leaning on a mobility aid; push someone in a wheelchair only when asked; give directions that include distance and physical objects such as curbs.

Person who is deaf, deafened, or person with a hearing impairment

Speak clearly and at a pace that allows the sign language interpreter to interpret and to allow for questions; write notes or use gestures for one-on-one discussions; face the person to facilitate lip-reading; speak clearly, slowly, and directly to the person, not the interpreter; reduce or eliminate background noise.

Person who is unable to speak, or person with a speech impairment; person with a learning, developmental, or psychiatric disability

When needed, offer assistance and provide guidance, repeat information when necessary, speak directly to the person and listen actively.

Sources: Treasury Board of Canada Secretariat, *Creating a Welcoming Workplace for Employees with Disabilities*; David Brown, "Focus on Ability not Disability," *Canadian HR Reporter* 13, no. 22 (December 18, 2000): 12.

a distribution of members of designated groups according to occupations and salary levels throughout the organization. Comparisons will show which designated groups exhibit underutilization and which groups exhibit concentration in specific occupations or levels, in proportion to their numbers in the labour market.[33]

STEP 3: EMPLOYMENT SYSTEMS REVIEW

"Employment systems" or "employment practices" are the means by which employers carry out personnel activities such as recruitment, hiring, training and development, promotion, job classification, discipline, and termination. Some of these practices are found in personnel manuals and collective agreements, while others remain more informal and based on traditional practices.

An important legal principle is that employers are accountable even when discrimination is the unintended result of employment systems that block the progress of particular groups of employees or potential employees for reasons unrelated to qualifications, merit, or business requirements. This unintentional discrimination is referred to as systemic discrimination.

Systemic Barriers in Employment Practices

Systemic discrimination refers to the exclusion of members of certain groups through the application of employment policies or practices based on criteria that are neither job related nor required for the safe and efficient operation of the business. Systemic discrimination can create legal concerns for an organization. Many employment barriers are hidden, unintentionally, in the rules, procedures and even facilities that employers provide to manage their human resources. (See Figure 3.3 for examples of systemic barriers, along with possible solutions.) Inequity can result if these barriers encourage or discourage individuals based on their membership in certain groups rather than on their ability to do a job that the employer needs done. In one case, the Supreme Court of Canada ruled that a physical fitness test discriminated against women and required the employer to reinstate the woman as a firefighter.[34]

underutilization
Term applied to designated groups that are not utilized or represented in the employer's workforce proportional to their numbers in the labour market

concentration
Term applied to designated groups whose numbers in a particular occupation or level are high relative to their numbers in the labour market

systemic discrimination
The exclusion of members of certain groups through the application of employment policies or practices based on criteria that are not job related

FIGURE 3.3

Employment Practices

Examples of Systemic Barriers

1. Recruitment practices that limit applications from designated groups, e.g., word of mouth, internal hiring policies.
2. Physical access that restricts those who are mobility impaired, e.g., no ramps, heavy doors, narrow passageways.
3. Job descriptions and job evaluation systems that undervalue the work of positions traditionally held by women.
4. A workplace environment that does not expressly discourage sexual or racial harassment.

Examples of Possible Solutions

1. Word of mouth could be supplemented by calls to community organizations representing designated groups or to the local Canada Employment Centre.
2. Facility upgrading.
3. Rewrite job descriptions, rationalize evaluation systems, provide special training for supervisors.
4. Issue a company policy against these practices, with guidelines and follow-up through appraisal and discipline procedures, and develop complaint and problem-solving mechanisms for an employee to use.

Source: *Employment Equity: A Guide for Employers*, Employment and Immigration Canada, Human Resources and Skills Development Canada, 1991. Cat. No. 143-5-91, May 1991, p. 19. Reproduced with permission of the Public Works and Government Services Canada, 2009.

Another example of systemic discrimination occurs when an employer's workforce represents one group in our society and the company recruits new employees by posting job vacancies within the company or by word of mouth among the employees. This recruitment strategy is likely to generate candidates similar to those in the current workforce, thereby unintentionally discriminating against other groups of workers in the labour market. A better approach might be to vary recruitment methods by contacting outside agencies and organizations. The Toronto Police Force has established an eight-member recruitment task force to boost its community representation, in part by educating visible minority groups about career opportunities in the force.[35]

The following employment practices and issues may need to be reviewed: job classifications and descriptions, recruitment processes, training and development, performance evaluation systems, promotions and upward mobility, levels of compensation, access to benefits, termination processes, discipline procedures, facilities (e.g., building design, barrier-free access), and access to assistance.

The usual test for identifying systemic barriers involves using the following criteria to assess the policy:

- Is it job related?
- Is it valid? (i.e., does it, or the required qualification, have a direct relationship to job performance?)
- Is it consistently applied?
- Does it have an adverse impact? (i.e., does it affect members of designated groups more than those of dominant groups?)
- Is it a business necessity?
- Does it conform to human rights and employment standards legislation?[36]

If the employee profiles indicate that certain types of people are underrepresented, then special measures may be undertaken to correct this imbalance.

Special Measures and Reasonable Accommodation

Special measures are initiatives designed to accelerate the entry, development, and promotion of members of designated groups from among the interested and qualified workforce. For example, some special measures may include targeted recruitment or special training initiatives aimed mainly at correcting, over a specified period of time, employment inequities stemming from past discrimination. These measures are intended to hasten the achievement of fair representation of the four designated groups in an employer's workforce. Highlights in HRM 3.6 describes the special measures used by the federal government.

Reasonable accommodation involves adjusting employment policies and practices so that no individual is denied benefits, disadvantaged with respect to employment opportunities, or blocked from carrying out the essential components of a job because of race, colour, sex, or disability. Human rights tribunals across Canada have placed employers under a duty to demonstrate a degree of flexibility in meeting the reasonable needs of employees. It is no longer acceptable for employers to simply assume that all employees will "fit in" no matter what their special needs. Employers must find the means to alter systems to meet the needs of their employees as long as this does not cause "undue hardship to the employer." Reasonable accommodation may include redesigning job duties, adjusting work schedules, providing technical, financial, and human support services, and upgrading facilities. The City of Toronto developed award-winning facilities in its Barrier Free Access program, which was designed to allow people with disabilities accessible passage throughout city facilities. The Canadian military has adopted a policy that allows Aboriginal service men to wear their hair in traditional braids.

Reasonable accommodation benefits all employees. When a company provides compensation for child care expenses for employees taking company-sponsored

reasonable accommodation

Attempt by employers to adjust the working conditions or schedules of employees with disabilities or religious preferences

114

Highlights in **HRM 3.6**

Participation in the Federal Public Service

The goals of the Employment Equity (EE) program in the federal government are to

- Establish a workforce of qualified employees that reflects the diversity of the Canadian population which they serve
- Ensure equal access to job opportunities
- Correct conditions that have historically impeded the full participation of designated groups

Discussions with Alonia Lawrence, Chief Employment Equity Advisor of the Public Service Commission, indicated that although visible minorities represented 8.7 percent of the labour force, they represented only 6.8 percent of the federal employee population in 2002. To accomplish the EE goals, the Public Service Commission (PSC) has established a number of special measures, which include the following:

- *Outreach.* The recruiting teams of the federal government have established a visible presence within the visible minority communities. Through contacts with visible minority associations, such as the Association of Black Law Enforcers, recruiters make presentations and hold information sessions about the recruitment processes used by the federal government to fill jobs. Recruiters talk about the structured interviews and tests, procedures that may be unfamiliar to visible minority candidates.

- *Creation of specific tool.* The brochure "So You're Thinking of Working for the Federal Government" was developed specifically for the visible minority communities. Workshops that explain the types of tests used, such as the managerial in-basket or the written communications test, are held within these communities. The PSC has also introduced tools for

use by managers and human resources professionals in developing and implementing employment equity strategies and approaches. New tools include "Improving Employment Equity Representation: Tips and Tools," "Guidelines for Assessing Persons with Disabilities," and "Guidelines for Fair Assessment in a Diverse Workplace."

- *Composition of recruitment teams.* An effort was made to place visible minorities on the recruitment teams, particularly because selection decisions could be made on perceptions of "fit," and culture plays a large role in this. In 2002, the PSC established an inventory of 100 visible minorities, trained in interviewing processes, who were invited by managers to sit on selection boards. The federal government, like other public-sector employers, has been finding it difficult to recruit visible minorities in areas of law enforcement, such as correctional officers. However, building relationships with visible minority communities is beginning to result in greater interest in federal government jobs.

Is the process working? Yes; the number of visible minorities working in the federal public service has increased from 5.9 percent in 2001 to 7.3 percent in 2006. Career development is vital to the retention of good employees, and in 2001 the PSC launched a career assignment program for visible minorities. Because visible minorities represent only 4.1 percent of the executive group, for example, the Career Assignment Program develops participants for executive-level positions. The ultimate goal is to match participation rates in the labour market. However, with the special measures adopted by the PSC, progress is slow but certain.[37]

courses, it does more than remove a barrier to women; it also assists any employee with sole-parenting responsibilities. The flexible work schedules adopted by some companies in northern Canada benefit Aboriginal employees, who are prepared to work atypical hours in exchange for significant breaks away from the work site to take part in traditional hunting and fishing activities. Many other employees also benefit from these flexible work schedules. Highlights in HRM 3.7 recounts two court cases on accommodation.

Special arrangements should be made to accommodate people who are visually impaired, illiterate, or unfamiliar with the English language by using tools such as

Highlights in HRM 3.7

The Duty to Accommodate

- Two employees of the Ford Motor Company of Oakville, Ontario, became members of a religious group that observed its Sabbath from Friday sunset to Saturday sunset. Both employees were required to work two Friday nights out of four, which they refused to do. They tried, but failed, to make alternative arrangements with other workers. They were disciplined and ultimately terminated for unauthorized absenteeism. After a 71-day hearing, the Human Rights Commission decided it would constitute undue hardship on Ford to accommodate the religious absences of these employees.

- The Ontario Human Rights Commission found that the City of Ancaster, Ontario, had discriminated against a part-time firefighter when they turned him down for a full-time job because he had partial vision in one eye. As such he was unable to obtain a class F driver's licence, a job requirement for driving ambulances that are driven by firefighters. The tribunal felt that the city should have accommodated him by assigning him to firefighter duties exclusively.

Source: Laura Cassiani, "Law Takes Tough Stand on Accommodation," *Canadian HR Reporter* (February 26, 2001): 1, 5.

Braille forms, confidential interviews, or translation. Leah Levy, the founder of the Gulf Islands Dog Biscuit Company, found it easy to accommodate deaf employees by installing a white board for messages and a light indicating when the doorbell rang.[38] Suggestions for an accessible workplace are found in Figure 3.4.

FIGURE 3.4

Suggestions for an Accessible Workplace

- Install easy-to-reach switches.
- Provide sloping sidewalks and entrances.
- Install wheelchair ramps.
- Reposition shelves so materials are easy to reach.
- Rearrange tables, chairs, vending machines, dispensers, and other furniture and fixtures.
- Widen doors and hallways.
- Add raised markings on control buttons.
- Provide designated accessible parking spaces.
- Install hand controls or manipulation devices.
- Provide flashing alarm lights.
- Remove turnstiles and revolving doors or provide alternative accessible paths.
- Install holding bars in toilet areas.
- Redesign toilet partitions to increase access space.
- Add paper cup dispensers at water fountains.
- Replace high-pile, low-density carpeting.
- Reposition telephones, water fountains, and other needed equipment.
- Add raised toilet seats.
- Provide a full-length bathroom mirror.

Source: Statistics Canada website: http://www.statcan.ca/english/Pgdb/labor20a.htm, table 282–0002.

STEP 4: ESTABLISHMENT OF A WORKPLAN

The workforce analysis and the review of employment systems will provide the employer with a useful base from which to develop a workplan with realistic goals and timetables. A narrative statement or summary of the conclusions drawn from the examination of the workforce analysis forms part of the employment equity workplan. The summary should include any restrictions faced in hiring due to collective agreements, staff movements, or the need for specialized skills in a particular profession. The identification of restrictions helps form an overall employment equity strategy.

The plan should be considered a working tool designed to achieve results. It is a document that describes how proposed actions are to be achieved. The plan should be an integral part of the organization's overall operational plans and must include

- Numerical goals with time frames (numerical goals can be expressed in numbers—for example, *42 percent of our personnel should be women*)
- Explanations about the proposed improvement in the hiring, training, and promotion of the four designated groups to increase their representation and improve their distribution throughout the organization;
- Descriptions of specific activities to achieve the numerical goals
- An outline of monitoring and evaluation procedures to follow program implementation.

Numerical goals must be realistic numbers related to the workforce analysis. The goals must catalogue opportunities for hiring, training, and promotion and must demonstrate a valid effort to correct underrepresentation or concentration of all designated groups in specific occupations or occupational categories. Non-numerical goals include activities such as implementation of barrier-free design, targeted recruitment and advertising, modification of employment policies or practices, and provision of developmental training.

The overall goal for an organization is to achieve a representative workforce. An organization's workforce is representative when it reflects the demographic composition of the external workforce. A nonrepresentative workforce is an indicator of the need for evaluation and action to remove the barriers that block or discourage certain groups from employment and advancement. Workplan initiatives in conjunction with special measures and reasonable accommodation should contribute to the overall success of this goal.

STEP 5: IMPLEMENTATION

The implementation of employment equity is idiosyncratic in that no two plans will be the same. Each strategy should be designed to meet the needs of the particular organization. The success of plan implementation depends on senior management's commitment to the process, how the roles and responsibilities are defined, the resources available, the effectiveness of the communications strategy, the acceptance of plan initiatives and objectives, and the availability of training. The plan, in essence a living document, will be affected by the changes in the internal and external environment throughout the implementation period. Therefore, its strategies may be modified or eliminated when results are not achieved or if resource restraints or economic conditions necessitate a different strategy. The implementation is guided and monitored by those responsible and accountable for its outcome.

STEP 6: EVALUATION, MONITORING, AND REVISION

By monitoring progress, the employer will be able to evaluate the overall success of the equity initiatives used to achieve a representative workforce, as well as respond to organizational and environmental changes. Annual progress reports provided to all employees communicate initiatives and achievements. Interim reports on special projects heighten program visibility and acceptance; they also promote management commitment and accountability. Research suggests that the wage gaps between white men and the designated groups are closing more rapidly in organizations with formal employment equity programs than in organizations without such programs.[39]

The monitoring activity is an essential component in the planning cycle. Only through monitoring can an employer determine whether goals are being attained and problems resolved, whether new programs are succeeding, and whether strategies have been effective. If the employer finds, upon review of the program, that there are negative results, alterations to the existing plan will have to be made with new goals. In this regard, the planning process is evolutionary, in that the achievement of employment equity involves organizational changes and builds on experience.

SEXUAL HARASSMENT

[OUTCOME]

Please note that although this section deals only with sexual harassment, many of the prescriptions apply equally to other forms of harassment based on, for example, race or religion. The two main sources of the employer's duty to prevent harassment in the workplace are

Highlights in HRM 3.8

The Cost of Sexual Harassment

In 2002, sexual harassment complaints topped the list of complaints heard by provincial human rights commissions; 64 percent of working women say they have experienced some form of sexual harassment throughout their careers (up from 48 percent in the previous year). Harassment affects productivity, retention, morale, turnover, and absenteeism rates. It also affects an employee's self-esteem, home life, and stress levels. Some 48 percent of women executives say they left a job because of inhospitable organizational culture and harassment.

An employee at the Victoria Tea Company in Ontario was found guilty of sexual harassment and ordered to pay the victim $50,600. A supervisor at SkyCable in Brandon, Manitoba, was ordered to pay $100,000 in damages for creating a poisoned work atmosphere. The four women employees testified that the supervisor had made inappropriate remarks, sexual advances, and derogatory comments on an ongoing basis. The poisoned work environment generated by his conduct took a toll on their psychological

and physical health and caused them significant pain and suffering. The supervisor's remarks were clearly persistent, repetitious, and serious enough to create a hostile work environment for all the complainants. The Canadian Human Rights Tribunal ruled that the supervisor must compensate the four women for lost wages, hurt feelings, and legal costs. But what exactly is sexual harassment? According to Canadian legal cases, the following behaviours define sexual harassment:

- Sexually degrading words or remarks used to describe an individual or group
- Inquiries or comments about an individual's sex life
- Sexual flirtations, advances, and propositions
- Demands for sexual favours
- Verbal threats or abuse
- Leering
- Unwanted gestures
- Display of sexually offensive material
- Sexual assault

Sources: "Sexual Harassment Endangered Health," *Tribunal OH & S Canada* 18, no. 6 (September 2002): 10; Laura Cassiani, "Sexual Harassment Persists Despite Workplace Fallout," *Canadian HR Reporter* 14, no. 7 (April 9, 2001): 1.

1. Human rights legislation, which prevents harassment *only* on the basis of the designated grounds in the legislation (sex, race, religion, etc.).

2. Common law obligation to treat workers with decency and respect. This is a fairly new development in the common law. However, it applies to all forms of harassment that make the workplace intolerable to the worker. If the employer fails to stop the harassment, it is in breach of the employment contract. The employee could quit and sue for constructive dismissal ("reasonable notice").[40]

Sexual situations in the work environment are not new to organizational life. Sexual feelings are a part of group dynamics, and people who work together may come to develop these kinds of feelings for one another. Unfortunately, however, often these encounters are unpleasant and unwelcome, as witnessed by the many reported instances of sexual harassment.[41]

According to one study, only four of every ten Canadian women who suffer sexual harassment at work take any formal action, and only one out of every two women believes that a complaint would be taken seriously in her workplace.[42] This belief is reinforced by cases such as the one involving a female Sears employee who was shot to death by her manager. Fifteen months earlier, she had complained to her employer that she was being sexually harassed by her manager. The company maintained that his behaviour did not constitute sexual harassment and that he was merely a "persistent pursuer." In keeping with this position, Sears made no effort to stop the manager's behaviour.[43] The City of Richmond has only four women among the more than 200 firefighters and none of them are on active duty. At least one has complained of harassment, saying that she found obscenities on her locker, and feces in her boots, and that her water pressure was not turned on during a fire inside a building.[44] Sexual harassment costs, as Highlights in HRM 3.8 shows.

Many organizations are developing policies to deal with sexual harassment in the workplace. Such policies are intended as preventive measures against not only damage to reputation and employee morale, but also the kind of litigation that Magna International faced when it was sued on the grounds that Magna employees had attempted to win contracts from purchasing officers for the Big Three automakers by wooing them with gifts and entertainment, including trips to topless bars.[45] Some organizations have put policies in place to attempt to deal with the issue. For example, the sexual harassment policy at B.C. Hydro focuses on avoidance and resolution rather than punishment after the fact. In another organization, the Canadian Armed Forces, 90,000 members have been trained to recognize and avoid harassment of all kinds.

Highlights in HRM 3.9 provides a sample of questions that can be used during a sexual harassment audit. An instrument like this one, which is essentially a test, is a valuable tool for determining what employees know and do not know about sexual harassment.

The Ontario *Human Rights Code* identifies three kinds of sexual harassment:

1. When someone says or does things to you of a sexual nature and you do not want or welcome it. This includes behaviour that a person should know you do not want or welcome (for example, your supervisor makes you feel uncomfortable by talking about sex all the time). The *Human Rights Code* says that when you show that you do not welcome or want the remarks or actions, the person must stop doing those things right away.

sexual harassment
Unwelcome advances, requests for sexual favours, and other verbal or physical conduct of a sexual nature in the working environment

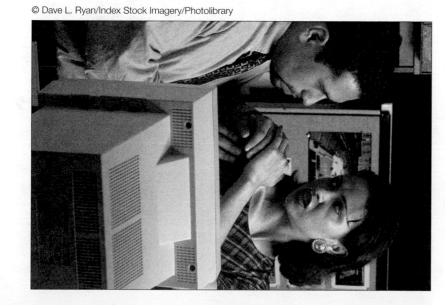

Sexual harassment encounters are unpleasant, causing personal and organizational hardships.

© Dave L. Ryan/Index Stock Imagery/Photolibrary

Highlights in HRM 3.9

Questions Asked in Auditing Sexual Harassment

Activity	Is This Sexual Harassment?			Are You Aware of This Behaviour in the Organization?		
Employees post cartoons on bulletin boards containing sexually related material.	Yes	No		Uncertain	Yes	No
A male employee says to a female employee that she has beautiful eyes and hair.	Yes	No		Uncertain	Yes	No
A male manager habitually calls all female employees "sweetie" or "darling."	Yes	No		Uncertain	Yes	No
A male manager fails to promote a female employee when she will not grant sexual favours.	Yes	No		Uncertain	Yes	No
Male employees use vulgar language and tell sexual jokes that are overheard by, but not directed at, female employees.	Yes	No		Uncertain	Yes	No
A male employee leans and peers over the back of a female employee when she wears a low-cut dress.	Yes	No		Uncertain	Yes	No
A supervisor gives a female (male) subordinate a nice gift on her (his) birthday.	Yes	No		Uncertain	Yes	No
Two male employees share a sexually explicit magazine while observed by a female employee	Yes	No		Uncertain	Yes	No

2. A person who has authority or power to deny you something such as a promotion or a raise makes sexual suggestions or requests that you do not want or welcome (for example, your teacher says you must have sex with him or her or you will not pass the course). Even if you do not complain about a sexual suggestion or request, it can still be sexual harassment unless it is clear that you welcome or want it.

3. A person with authority or the power to deny you something important punishes you or threatens to do something to you for refusing a sexual request (for example, your employer fires you, or threatens to fire you, because you refuse to go on a date).

For sexual harassment policies to succeed, confidentiality is necessary, and so is a method for filing complaints. Highlights in HRM 3.10 describes a company whose method for filing complaints became a problem. Without organizational commitment to zero tolerance with respect to harassment, any such policy will be meaningless. Highlights in HRM 3.11 presents some suggestions for an effective sexual harassment policy.[46]

The concepts of harassment in the workplace are being broadened to include psychological harassment, such as bullying. Laws in Quebec and Saskatchewan ban psychological harassment, which is defined as any repeated, hostile, or unwanted

Using the Internet

For more information on the law requiring Ontario employers to have a harassment policy, go to http://www.yorku.ca/ddoorey/lawblog/?p=1042

Highlights in **HRM** 3.10

The Aftermath of Sexual Harassment

Sexual harassment has been making headlines for decades, and companies have invested vigorously in programs for its prevention in the workplace. Due to its continued sensitivity and the need to protect individuals and companies, "ABC Manufacturing" (a real organization that preferred not to be identified) will be profiled in order to depict how sexual harassment is still a prevalent and problematic issue in today's workplace.

ABC Manufacturing is a reputable company with a business history built around strong business ethics and core values. As part of its corporate mandate on how ABC Manufacturing does business, it invested in diversity training for all employees. The program goes beyond training on the human rights codes; it stressed mutual respect in the workplace and the business case for diversity. In fact, ABC had previously won awards for its progressive diversity programs. The key to the success of the company's program is the open-door policy. Employees were comfortable going to the human resources department with their concerns, including reporting allegations of sexual harassment. In 99 percent of cases, the complainants were satisfied with the resolutions of their cases. Resolutions included punishments ranging from agreed misunderstandings to terminations.

ABC Manufacturing first devised its policy on sexual harassment from the understanding of "here's the law." The policy then developed into a comprehensive diversity plan to respect all individuals regardless of race, gender, religion, age, sexual orientation, culture, or nationality. It also included the linkage to the business strategy. This integrated approach and training seemed effective. All complaints were resolved within the organization, avoiding potential outside legal cost and time. Then, two years ago, ABC Manufacturing got a call from the Human Rights Commission with a complaint of sexual harassment. Management was confused. Apparently, a temporary student worker had filed a report about a permanent employee who had called her frequently at home. Checking their records, there had been no report made at ABC or at the temp agency that had placed her. The accused employee was called in and questioned about the incident in which he denied having done anything wrong. To get him to his story, the permanent employee was asked to provide records of phone calls from his home. He promptly

went on stress-mitigated sick leave and retained legal counsel that prevented ABC from investigating the matter further. The complainant also refused to discuss the matter directly with ABC Manufacturing.

With no other alternatives to investigate the alleged harassment, ABC was forced to speak through the lawyer of the accused employee and the Human Rights Commission. The alleged victim asked for an extraordinary amount of money that ABC would not pay without any facts. The permanent employee now on sick leave refused to speak of the matter for it was not in his best interests. As ABC learned more of the facts of her complaint, corporate lawyers recommended to pay off the temporary worker but asserted that the company was to accept no responsibility since it could not validate the story. Further complicating matters, without the facts the permanent employee could not be disciplined while on sick leave or terminated. After one and a half years of legal quagmire, the Human Rights Commission proposed that ABC pay a nominal sum with an apology to the victim. Although the Commission did not find fault with ABC's handling of the situation, it believed that the incident took place. The Commission also believed that there was potential for future incidents due to the imbalance of power between the permanent and temporary employees. ABC paid the sum of money requested but, instead of an apology, put out an assurance that it would rectify the situation in the company policy. The worker is still on sick leave collecting benefits and will not return without a full restitution of his reputation. Given the circumstances, this cannot happen since the facts were never divulged and the matter with the temporary worker has been settled. Resolving this situation with the permanent worker will require more legal manoeuvring.

ABC thought that it had a world-class diversity program firmly embedded within the corporation. As pointed out by the Human Rights Commission, ABC management found that there was a flaw in the execution of its policy. The company had made sure that every permanent employee underwent its best-in-class diversity training program. Due to co-employment liabilities, ABC did not give the temporary worker the diversity training. Legally, temporary employees work for the agency that assigned them to the company. The agency did not provide the worker with diversity training

continued

either. As such, the temporary workers did not know their rights, procedures, or ABC's open-door policy in human resources. Without knowledge of an effective course of action, the temporary worker went to the Human Rights Commission for resolution of her complaint. Upon further investigation, however, ABC learned that this was not an isolated incident. There were other incidents, involving temporary student workers,

which were not reported. ABC reacted quickly to this finding and while it does not take on the responsibility of training temporary workers in diversity, the company ensures that all employees, permanent or temporary, are fully aware of their rights and ability to contact human resources. This mandatory training became part of the new employee orientation program for both permanent and temporary employees.

Highlights in HRM 3.11

Basic Components of an Effective Sexual Harassment Policy

1. Develop a comprehensive organization-wide policy on sexual harassment and present it to all current and new employees. Stress that sexual harassment will not be tolerated under any circumstances. Emphasis is best achieved when the policy is publicized and supported by top management.

2. Hold training sessions with supervisors to explain their role in providing an environment free of sexual harassment, and institute proper investigative procedures when charges occur.

3. Establish a formal complaint procedure whereby employees can discuss problems without fear of retaliation. The complaint procedure should spell out how charges will be investigated and resolved.

4. Act immediately when employees complain of sexual harassment. Communicate widely that investigations will be conducted objectively and with appreciation for the sensitivity of the issue.

5. When an investigation supports employee charges, discipline the offender at once. For extremely serious offences, discipline should include penalties up to and including discharge. Discipline should be applied consistently across similar cases and among managers and hourly employees alike.

6. Follow up on all cases to ensure a satisfactory resolution of the problem.

conduct; verbal comments; actions; or gestures that affect an employee's dignity or psychological or physical integrity. This protection requires employers to create policies to prevent this type of harassment.[47] Ontario recently introduced a law requiring employers to develop and post a harassment policy in the workplace and to develop a system through which employees can report incidents of harassment.

MANAGING DIVERSITY

Managing diversity goes beyond Canadian employment equity legislation's four designated groups in addressing the need to create a fair work environment. The terms *diversity management* and *employment equity* are often used interchangeably, but there are differences. Diversity management is voluntary; employment equity is not. Managing diversity is a broader, more inclusive concept encompassing factors such as religion, personality, lifestyle, and education. By managing diversity, organizations hope to gain a strategic and competitive advantage by helping all employees perform to their full potential.[48]

[OUTCOME 7]

diversity management
The optimization of an organization's multicultural workforce in order to reach business objectives

The City of Toronto led by example when it recognized "non-Christian City of Toronto staff" by giving them two days of paid time off for religious holidays if they agreed to work Christmas Day and Good Friday (Christian holidays) at straight time.[49] Also, McDonald's Restaurants of Canada used multi-age teams and found the diversity of ages led to a remarkable synergy.[50]

Organizations such as CN, the Bank of Montreal, and Warner-Lambert are pioneers in the diversity movement. According to Marie Tellier, CN's assistant vice-president of employment equity, the hiring, development, and good management of a diverse workforce whose values and expectations are different from their managers is no longer an option—it is an economic necessity. In the context of an increasingly diverse labour force, diversity management is not only a legal obligation, but also a necessity imposed by market laws, competition, and the need to be the best to survive.[51]

Statistics show that the ethnocultural profile of Canada has been changing since the 1960s and will continue to change dramatically over the next 20 years. European immigrants who led the first wave of immigrants in the early years of the 20th century have been surpassed by immigrants from Asia, including the Middle East.[52] A new study by Statistics Canada has found an immigrant's country of origin and arrival date in Canada are strongly correlated with his or her chances of finding a job. Immigrants born in Southeast Asia and aged 25 to 54 had employment levels close to or better than those of their Canadian-born counterparts, regardless of when they arrived in Canada.[53] The goal of diversity management is to have the workforce at all levels resemble the population.

CEOs in Canada recognize that ethnic groups possess expertise such as language skills, knowledge of foreign cultures and business practices, and natural trade links with overseas markets that can be used to capture market share in emerging economies and new Canadian markets. Ebco, a manufacturing company in Richmond, British Columbia, which has won awards for excellence in race relations, is doing business in Germany and Taiwan because it was able to tap the networks and skills of its employees, who trace their origins to 48 different countries. The spending power of these groups is another motivating factor to incorporate them into all levels of the workforce.[54] According to Edgar Ware, ethnocultural business manager at Digital Equipment of Canada, "We have an obligation to the cultural fabric. We want to look like the people we sell to."[55] Digital's goal is to balance a diversity strategy with the organization's business plan.

Besides the moral issues surrounding diversity, there is a critical economic need for Canada to increase its share of world trade and expand its trade portfolio (see the Business Case). Our export market is dominated by the United States, Japan, and the United Kingdom. If Canadian business continues to rely heavily on these markets, our export growth and standard of living may not keep pace with other international markets.[56] Developing countries in emerging markets will require new investments in infrastructure, public systems, and productive capital. Given the multicultural background of many of its workers, Canada is in an excellent position to provide these services.[57] Canadian companies such as Nortel and SNC-Lavalin have already begun to tap the potential of these emerging markets.

CREATING AN ENVIRONMENT FOR SUCCESS

Transforming an organizational culture into a culture that embraces diversity can be a complex and lengthy process. Diversity initiatives should be taken slowly so that everyone can understand that this change is an evolutionary process and that expectations should be realistic. Individuals must fully understand the time, effort, commitment, and risk involved, and the need for a systematic approach.[58]

The Business CASE

The Economic Values of Diversity

Although employment equity and its partner, employment diversity, were launched on moral grounds, increasingly, these initiatives are sustained on business grounds. The first principle to understand is that members of the designated groups are consumers, not just potential employees. For example, the purchasing power of people with disabilities is estimated to be $120 billion. Racial minorities control more than $76 billion of combined purchasing power. Women control 80 percent of the consumer dollars spent in North America. People with disabilities account for about $50 billion annually in spending power.

The second business fundamental is that employees who are members of the designated groups represent an organizational resource that facilitates the understanding and linkages to these markets by helping various departments to understand the lifestyles, consumption needs and wants, purchasing preferences, media usage habits,

and brand loyalty of these groups. Business is increasingly international and employees who speak other languages and understand other cultures are a valuable resource.

A study of nearly 1,000 companies operating in the European Union reported that a diverse workforce brings these benefits to business: (in rank order)

- Access to new labour pool
- Benefits related to a company's reputation
- Commitment to equality and diversity as company values
- Innovation and creativity
- Compliance with laws
- Competitive advantage
- Economic effectiveness
- Marketing opportunities
- Enhanced customer satisfaction

Sources: Terrence Belford "Hire Local, Think Global," *The Globe and Mail*, January 26, 2009, E1; European Commission, "Business Case for Diversity," Directorate-General for Employment, Social Affairs, and Equal Opportunity, Luxembourg, 2005; Aparita Bhandari, "Ethnic Marketing—It's More Than Skin Deep," *The Globe and Mail*, September 7, 2005, B3; B. Siu, "Beyond Quotas: The Business Case for Employment Equity," *Canadian HR Reporter* (June 4, 2001): 20.

Leadership is one of the most important variables in an organization's ability to successfully incorporate diversity into its business strategy. In a Conference Board of Canada survey, 86 percent of respondents indicated that responsibility rested with human resources.[59] The initiative should not be perceived as a human resources program or policy, but rather as a business imperative. In the words of Prem Benimadhu, vice-president of human resources research for the Conference Board, "Building a facially and culturally diverse workforce has been perceived as a human resources issue. But as long as it is, it's not going to be in the mission statement of organizations."[60] Only 6 percent of firms surveyed by the Conference Board study mentioned ethnic and cultural diversity in their mission statements.

Diversity initiatives should be linked directly to the business objectives and goals of the most senior levels of management. Reality Check demonstrates how the BMO Financial Group has woven its program into its organizational fabric.

Organizations seeking to incorporate the value of diversity into their corporate philosophy must make use of appropriate internally and externally focused communications. For example, the National Bank of Canada participates annually in Montreal's La semaine des communautés culturelles, a week dedicated to the celebration of Montreal's multiculturalism. The bank believes that its visible demonstrations of commitment to ethnocultural diversity in the community it serves help raise the bank's profile.[61]

Reality CHECK

Diversity Achievements at Air Canada

In 2008, Air Canada was at the top of Mediacorp's list for Canada's Best Diversity Employers. Over 30 percent of its 27,000 full-time employees are visible minorities. The main driver of this commitment to diversity was not because, as a Crown corporation, it was subject to the federal legislation. For Air Canada, it simply made good business sense to be able to access the expertise and languages of a diverse workforce, because it has operations in countries around the world. According to Jo Steiner, director of employee and labour strategy, the organization proactively recruits from the four designated groups. For example, if the airline is recruiting new flight attendants, it contacts Aboriginal employment centres. When visiting schools, the recruiter is often accompanied by an Aboriginal pilot or a female mechanic. In preparation for the 2008 Olympic Games in Beijing, Air Canada prepared to accommodate the transportation of Canada's Paralympics team. In this way, the airline learned much about how to accommodate the needs of employees and passengers with

disabilities. Employees have now become comfortable with dealing with a diverse workforce. When a deaf mechanic joined one team, his coworkers learned sign language.

Air Canada's commitment speaks to the advantages of becoming adept at diversity. According to the associate Dean, Beatrix Dart, at the Rotman School of Management, University of Toronto, there are sound business reasons to pursue diversity:

- The shrinking pool of labour, and the forthcoming retirement of boomers, makes accessing diverse pools an imperative.
- Business is increasingly international, and having employees fluent in other languages and with cultural savvy is a tremendous asset.
- The organization must reflect the communities it serves, and all these communities are potential customers.

Source: D. Harder "Diversity Takes Flight at Air Canada," *Canadian HR Reporter,* vol. 21, iss. 9: 17; T. Belford, "Hire Local, Think Global," *The Globe and Mail,* January 26, 2009, E1.

Cross-functional teams established to promote the diversity initiative are used successfully as communication vehicles by many leading-edge organizations. Toronto's Sunnybrook Health Sciences Centre has implemented the Patient Diversity Task Force to examine and report on the barriers faced by its patients, residents, and families.[62] Other organizations seek to raise the awareness of ethnocultural diversity.

Training is essential to the success of diversity implementation. A number of companies, including Imperial Oil and Connaught Laboratories, have incorporated diversity training. Cultural etiquette is an important aspect of diversity training that aims to explain the differences, or diversity, in people.

The Department of National Defence includes diversity training in its basic officer training course.[63] A consortium of European and North American businesses is attempting to develop a global diversity standard, by which companies will be able to use software to rate the success of their diversity programs.[64]

Figure 3.5 outlines some of the key factors in a diversity management strategy.

Of even greater importance than training is the need to incorporate elements of diversity into all core training programs and to tailor those elements to meet the needs of specific business units or groups of employees.[65]

An added advantage of implementing a diversity initiative relates to its impact on employee retention. Retention of well-qualified and skilled employees is an important goal, considering the amount of resources—in both time and money—spent on recruiting and hiring new employees. Canadian organizations spend an average of 28 hours recruiting a new management or professional employee, 42 hours recruiting a new executive, and 20 hours recruiting a new technical/supervisory employee.[66] Maintaining

FIGURE **3.5**

Model of Diversity Management Strategy

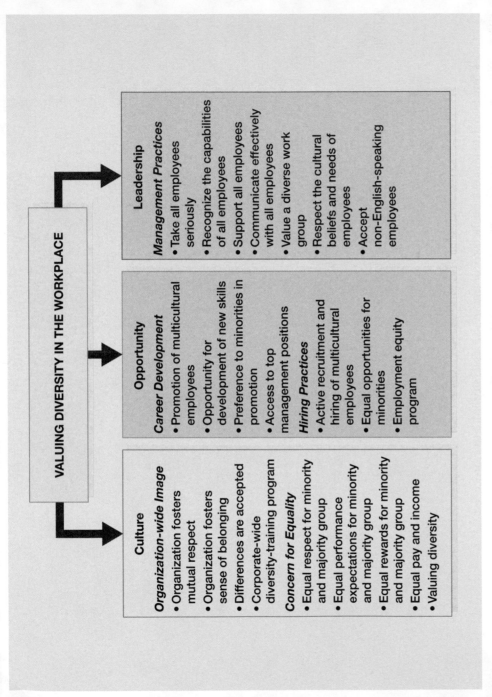

Source: From "Managing for Effective Workforce Diversity" by Kathleen Iverson from *The Cornell Hotel and Restaurant Administration Quarterly* 41, no. 2 (April 2000): 31–38. Reproduced by permission of the Cornell Hotel and Restaurant Administration Quarterly.

a balanced and diversified workforce during periods of downsizing continues to be a major challenge. See Figure 3.6 for a summary of the benefits of diversity management.

Much the same as is required under employment equity, an overall review of policies and employment practices must be considered. In this regard, the use of an employee attitude survey may prove beneficial in finding areas of systemic or perceived discrimination. The evaluation criteria used most often by Canadian organizations are staff attitudes, increases in promotions for minority employees, reduction in turnover of minority employees, reduction in number of harassment suits, recruitment statistics for minorities, and improvements in productivity.[67]

A final element in achieving success is monitoring progress and providing qualitative and quantitative evidence of change. For example, during their performance appraisals, all salaried employees at Levi Strauss & Co. (Canada) are evaluated on their ability to meet both business and aspirational goals. Aspirational goals are based on the company's core values, which include valuing diversity, following ethical management practices, and encouraging new behaviours, recognition, communications, and empowerment. These aspirations are the shared values and behaviours that will drive the company toward its mission of "sustained responsible

FIGURE **3.6**

Why Diversity?

The primary business reasons for diversity management include . . .

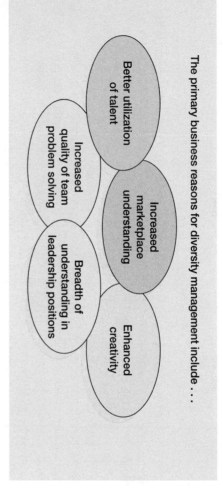

- Better utilization of talent
- Increased marketplace understanding
- Increased quality of team problem solving
- Breadth of understanding in leadership positions
- Enhanced creativity

Source: Survey data from Gail Robinson and Kathleen Dechant, "Building a Business Case for Diversity," *Academy of Management Executive* 11, no. 3 (August 1997): 21–31.

commercial success."[68] When management measures performance as a function of diversity initiatives, values are instilled in the minds of all employees, and it is demonstrated that change and diversity are part of day-to-day business. To achieve success in diversity, it is vital to set an example and to create an atmosphere that respects and values differences. Canadian organizations have recognized the competitive advantage of embracing diversity in their business strategies.

Small Business **APPLICATION**

As we have already said, small businesses are bound to the same legislation regarding workplace standards as are large companies. While there are some exclusions, such as for employers of less than 100 employees being excluded from the *Employment Equity Act*, small business needs to ensure that practices applying to recruitment, pay, and workplace standards treat all Canadians fairly and equitably and in accordance with the *Charter*. In addition to legal compliance, equitable treatment of staff is good business.

But how does small business achieve this? Through the operation of three principles: (1) diverse and inclusive recruitment, (2) equal pay for work of equal value, and (3) maintaining an harassment-free workplace.

To illustrate how this plays out small companies, let's use an example of a retail store in Surrey, British Columbia. Retail business relies on the local community as the primary source of customers, as well as employees. Part of successfully being able to serve clients comes as a result of understanding the needs of customers and providing an environment sensitive to their specific needs. As such, in order to serve the diverse population of Surrey, this store is well served by hiring staff that reflects this diverse population. The

continued

same is true for gender and people with disabilities. Given equivalent qualifications, many organizations will hire candidates from the designated groups to ensure that their organizations' employees are representative of the Canadian population.

So what strategies can this small business employ to maintain a diverse workforce? Firstly, management can ensure that all people involved in the selection and support of employees recognize the value of maintaining a diverse representative workforce. Secondly, they can employ simple attraction strategies such as placing an "Employee Wanted" sign in the window of the store to draw from the diverse local community. Lastly, they can take measures to ensure the management of an inclusive workplace. This can include ensuring equitable wage treatment of staff based on position and performance, as well as providing workplaces that are supportive to all employees.

While equal pay for equal work is quite complex in large organizations, in small companies often the exercise is quite easy. In our retail store in Surrey, we could set salary ranges for retail staff based on the regional norms for this work and then set guidelines within that range based on work experience and performance history.

Finally, harassment in the workplace, whether sexual or bullying in nature, is both illegal and destructive.

Employers have the obligation to provide a safe work environment, free from such activity. Small employers are bound to the same legal requirements as large companies in this regard. In addition to legal compliance, protecting workplaces from such behaviour guards employers from productivity decreases in the form of absenteeism, turnover, and decreased work performance.

Ensuring a harassment-free workplace requires a leadership commitment to this priority, a monitoring of the environment to ensure that harassment is not taking place, and immediate and effective actions to address harassment in the workplace if it is discovered. In the case of our retail store in Surrey, BC, it is the store manager who is responsible for both hiring and ensuring that the workplace is harassment-free. Recognizing that they would not have an HR generalist to support them, this store could employ a three-prong approach to ensuring an inclusive workplace. Firstly, the store manager could participate in diversity and harassment training offered by many third-party training providers. Secondly, the store can seek to eliminate bias in hiring selection by involving someone other than the store manager in the selection process. Lastly, the store can measure turnover and conduct exit interviews to assist in the identification of problems needing resolution.

SUMMARY

[OUTCOME 1]   Employment equity refers to the employment of individuals in a fair and nonbiased manner. Four groups in Canada—women, visible minorities, Aboriginal people, and persons with disabilities—tend to be concentrated in a few occupations that are accorded lower status and pay.

[OUTCOME 2]   The Canadian *Human Rights Act* applies to all federally governed departments and agencies, and all organizations incorporated under federal jurisdiction. The act prohibits discrimination on the basis of grounds such as race, religion, sex, age, national or ethnic origin, physical handicap, and marital status. The *Charter of Rights and Freedoms* guarantees some fundamental rights to every Canadian, including freedom from discrimination. The Canadian Human Rights Commission (CHRC) enforces the act through a formal complaint procedure.

[OUTCOME 3]   Pay equity is an amendment to the Canadian *Human Rights Act* that makes it illegal for employers to discriminate against individuals on the basis of job content. By definition, pay equity means equal pay for work of equal value.

[OUTCOME 4]   The *Employment Equity Act* requires all federally regulated employers to prepare an employment equity plan that identifies areas in which members of the designated groups are over- or underrepresented, and establishes plans to promote an equitable workplace.

[OUTCOME 5]   The implementation of employment equity involves six steps: senior management support, data collection and analysis, an employment system review, establishment of a workplan, implementation, strategy, and a

Managing diversity does more than incorporate employment equity. The goal of diversity management is to optimize the utilization of an organization's multicultural workforce with the goal of realizing strategic advantage.

[OUTCOME] **7**

Sexual harassment is an employment equity issue undergoing continued debate.

follow-up process that includes monitoring, reviewing, and revision.

KEY TERMS

bona fide occupational qualification (BFOQ), 102
concentration, 112
designated groups, 97

diversity management, 122
employment equity, 96
flow data, 111
reasonable accommodation, 115

sexual harassment, 119
stock data, 111
systemic discrimination, 113
underutilization, 112

DISCUSSION QUESTIONS

1. Here are some myths about employment equity:

   - It leads to hiring unqualified workers.
   - It causes an overnight change in the workforce makeup.
   - It is a plan that would make Calgary's workforce look like Toronto's.
   - This program lays off white males to make room for designated group members.
   - It's a program mainly for racial minorities.
   - Employers who implement the plan can destroy hard-won seniority provisions that protect all workers.
   - It's the end of hiring for white males.

   In groups, determine if group members share these beliefs. As human resource professionals, how would you work with employees who held these beliefs?

2. While the process for filing a complaint of discrimination appears clear, many would choose not to do so. List the reasons alleged "victims" of discrimination in employment might not file a complaint.

3. Find a male class job (i.e., a job in which the majority of workers are male) and a female class job that seem to require similar educational background and technical skills. (For example, compare female-dominated police dispatchers with male-dominated radio technical supervisors, or female-dominated health technicians to male-dominated transportation workers.) Then,

   using an Internet salary compensation index, calculate the pay rates. Are there differences? How would you account for these differences?

4. List as many jobs as you can in which you could hire only male applicants, based on a BFOQ.

5. Have you ever encountered questions, such as . . .

   "Do you really think you could handle this job? You know it takes a lot of energy and enthusiasm. Besides, we are looking for someone with career potential."

   "You don't need this training program. At your age, what would be the benefit be?"

   "Well, you are getting on. What do you expect at your age?"

   Such comments reflect ageism—an attitude that makes assumptions about older persons and their abilities and puts labels on them. About 15 percent of Canada's workforce is 55 and over. They are often stereotyped and not hired or promoted. Using what you have learned in this chapter about hiring and accommodating the four designated groups, design a recruitment and retention program for older workers.

6. After receiving several complaints of sexual harassment, the HR department of a city library decides to establish a sexual harassment policy. What should be included in the policy? How should it be implemented?

7. Describe how an organization can make best use of a multicultural workforce.

INTERNET EXERCISE

Read the interview with Zabeen Hirji, senior vice-president, Human Resources, RBC Financial Group on http://www.jobquality.ca/interviews/interview_rbc.shtml. Make a list of all RBC's diversity management initiatives. Based on your readings, make suggestions to improve the bank's program. Now go to the RBC website, and assess the success of RBC's programs by the numbers of women, etc. in management groups.

HRM EXPERIENCE

Preventing Sexual Harassment

Over the past decade, the problem of sexual harassment has captured the attention of managers and employees. While it is widely known that sexual harassment is both unethical and illegal, incidents of sexual harassment continue to plague business. Unfortunately, when these cases arise, they cause morale problems among employees, embarrassment to the organization, and costly legal damages. Consequently, all managers and supervisors play a central role in preventing sexual harassment complaints. It is important that managers understand the definition of sexual harassment, who is covered by sexual harassment guidelines, and how to prevent its occurrence. This skill-building exercise will provide you with knowledge in each of these areas.

Assignment

1. Working in teams of female and male members, develop a list of behaviours that could be classified as quid pro quo harassment or hostile environment. Explore the possibility that some sexual

harassing behaviours might be viewed differently by female and male employees. Give examples.

2. Many sexual harassment incidents go unreported. Fully discuss why this can occur and what might be done to reduce this problem.

3. The cornerstone to addressing sexual harassment is achieving organizational awareness through training. Develop a sexual harassment training program for a company of 250 employees that covers, at a minimum, the following: (1) who should attend the training sessions, (2) the content outline for the training program (the list of materials your team wants to teach), (3) specific examples to illustrate the training materials, and (4) how to investigate sexual harassment complaints.

4. This chapter will assist you with this assignment. You can obtain additional materials from employment equity publications and websites of the federal government and from various HR magazines.

5. Be prepared to present your training outline to other class members.

BIZFLIX EXERCISES

LEGALLY BLONDE: SEXUAL HARASSMENT

Review the earlier section "Sexual Harassment" before watching this scene from *Legally Blonde*. Several aspects of that discussion appear in the scene.

Elle Woods's (Reese Witherspoon) boyfriend, Warner Huntington III (Matthew Davis), wants to go to Harvard Law School instead of keeping their relationship alive. Elle pursues him vigorously by applying to and getting accepted to Harvard Law School. This is a charming comedy, dedicated to blonde women everywhere in the world. It is filled with stereotyping, giving many delightful twists to its surprise conclusion.

This scene comes from the "Poor Judgment" segment near the end of the film. It follows the successful use of Elle's hunch about key witness Enrique Salvatore (Greg Serano) in Brooke Windam's (Ali Larter) trial. The film continues after she leaves Professor Callahan's (Victor Garber) office. Elle sees Emmett (Luke Wilson) in the building lobby and tells him she is quitting the internship.

What to Watch for and Ask Yourself

- Does Professor Callahan sexually harass Elle? If yes, what is the evidence in these scenes?
- Did Elle behave appropriately or inappropriately in Professor Callahan's office?

CASE STUDY 1

FIGHTING FIRES

In British Columbia, the competition for firefighting jobs is fierce, with more than 1,600 people applying for about 60 jobs. At one time, the provincial Ministry of Forests required all job applicants to pass this physical fitness test:

- Lift a 23-kilogram bar in an upright rowing motion 18 times.
- Carry pumps and hoses, weighing as much as 50 kilograms, over a timed distance.
- Perform a shuttle run, which involves darting back and forth at an increasingly faster pace between cones situated 20 metres apart.

The B.C. Government and Service Employees Union argued that the average man, with training, could easily pass the test, whereas the average woman, even with training, could not. Only 35 percent of women who applied for the firefighter's job passed the test; about 70 percent of the men did.

The University of Victoria scientists who designed the tests argued that most women could reach the standard, although they would have to work harder than most men to do so. Female firefighters said they had to train year-round to pass the test, but they took this as a personal responsibility and as the cost of qualifying for the job. Their safety, as well as that of their colleagues and the public, depends on their strength and endurance. The B.C. Ministry of Forests spokeswoman suggested that lowering the standards would be a mistake: "Already male firefighters are asking if blazes will be designated as 'guy' fires and 'girl' fires. We want the fittest people."

QUESTIONS

1. Did the standards result in safer and more effective firefighting crews or were they inadvertently keeping women out of a traditionally male job?
2. Was this a BFOQ? The ministry was challenged on the basis of sex discrimination. What did the Supreme Court rule, and what was its reasoning?
3. Female applicants had the chance to train and try the test at B.C. university campuses. Was this special preparation discriminatory?
4. Did the changes made fix the underlying problems? Explain.

CASE STUDY 2

WHAT WENT WRONG?

Early in her appointment as a member of the executive team in a large institution, Debra became aware of hostility between several subordinates and herself. Those who had been unsuccessful applicants for her job said publicly that her experience was inappropriate for the position. Shortly after that, she heard rumours suggesting that her appointment was predicated on a sexual relationship with her boss.

Rumours proliferated through e-mail chat and comments were made at national meetings. When Debra confronted her superior about the situation, he suggested that the rumours reflected professional jealousy and were not worthy of a response. While she made numerous attempts to squelch the insinuations, at no time did her boss address the rumours or condemn those who made remarks. Over the course of several months, Debra sensed that he enjoyed hearing the insinuations. As time passed, she began to feel that her authority was being undermined.

Six months into the appointment, her boss's marriage ended. The event refuelled the rumour mill. Shortly afterward, Debra's superior was replaced. Upon his arrival, her new boss requested Debra's resignation. While performance was not an issue, he stated that she did not fit in well with the new executive team. When Debra brought in her lawyer to discuss concerns about sexual harassment, the organization settled quickly to avoid public trial or publicity. Now on leave, Debra is reluctant to return to the organization, and she is aware that prospective employers know of her experience and that rumours will make it difficult to secure a similar position.

Source: *Sexual Harassment Is Still A Management Issue*, The Conference Board of Canada, Ottawa 2001. Used by permission.

QUESTIONS

1. What went wrong?
2. What should have been done?

CAREER COUNSEL

Find out how to handle prohibited questions during a job interview by visiting the *Managing Human Resources* website (http://www.belcourt6e.nelson.com).

NOTES AND REFERENCES

1. http://www12.statcan.ca/census-recensement/2006/as-sa/97-557/index-eng.cfm, retrieved July 29, 2009.
2. Human Resources Development Canada, "Annual Report, Analysis of Employers' Reports," http://www.hrdc-drhc.gc.ca/LEEP/Annual_Reports/03. http://www.hrsdc.gc.ca/eng/lp/lo/lswe/we/ee_tools/reports/annual/index-we.shtml, retrieved July 30, 2009.
3. Statistics Canada, Labour Force Survey 2006; Human Resources Development Canada, *Annual Report, Employment Equity Act, 2003*, Labour Standards and Workplace Equity, Cat. No. MP31-5/2002; http://www.12.statcan.ca/english/census06/reference/consultation/92-135/labourforce.cfm
4. Human Resources Development Canada, "Workplace Equity," http://info.load-otea.hrdc-drhc.gc.ca/workplace_equity/leep/annual/2002/, retrieved August 4, 2009. http://www.hrsdc.gc.ca/eng/lp/lo/lswe/we/information/overview.shtml, retrieved July 30,

2009; Shannon Kie, "Feds Pledge Big Money but No Plan to Tackle Aboriginal Unemployment" *Canadian HR Reporter*, (January 30, 2006): 3.

5. L. Redpath and M. O. Nielsen, "A Comparison of Native Culture, Non-Native Culture and New Management Ideology," *Canadian Journal of Administrative Studies* 14, no. 3 (1996): 327–339.

6. Deborah Zinni, Barry Wright, and Mark Julien, "Want to Retain Aboriginal Employees?" *HR Professional* (August/September 2005).

7. Alar Prost and David Redmond, "Employers Need Help with Integration," *Canadian HR Reporter* (December 19, 2005): 7.

8. Ibid.

9. Statistics Canada, 2006 Census Ethnic and Visible Minorities, http://www.statcan.gc.ca/daily-quotidien/080402/dq080402a-eng.htm, retrieved July 30, 2009

10. Ibid.

11. *Employment Equity: A Guide for Employers*, Employment and Immigration Canada, Cat. No. LM-143-5-91, May 1991, 9.

12. Victor S. Mackinnon, "The Canadian Charter of Rights and Freedoms," *Public Administration: Canadian Materials* (North York: Captus Press, 1993): 179–180.

13. *Canadian Human Rights Act*, Canadian Human Rights Commission, 1978, Paragraph 2, Subsection (a).

14. A.P. Aggarwal, *Sex Discrimination: Employment Law and Practices* (Toronto: Butterworths Canada, 1994).

15. "Firm Pays $300,000 in Racial Harassment Settlements," *Human Resources Management in Canada*, Report Bulletin No. 72 (February 1989) (Scarborough, ON: Prentice-Hall Canada): 1–2.

16. *Canadian Human Rights Act*, Paragraph 60, Section 2(a), (b).

17. Human Resources Development Canada, *Annual Report, Employment Equity Act, 2001*, Labour Standards and Workplace Equity, Cat. No. LT-020-12-01.

18. Russel J. G. Juriansz, *Equal Pay Legislation and Ontario's New Pay Equity Act* (Toronto: Blake, Cassels & Graydon, 1995), 3–5.

19. Susan Riggs, "Comparing Apples and Oranges: Job Evaluations," *Worklife* 8, no. 1 (1991): 7–10

20. "Achieving Pay Equity First Goal, But through Co-operation: Commissioner," *Pay Equity Commission Report* 1, no. 1 (March 1988): 6.

21. Morley Gunderson and Roberta Edgecombe Robb, "Equal Pay for Work of Equal Value: Canada's Experience," *Advances in Industrial and Labour Relations* 5 (1991): 151–168. See also John G. Kelly, *Pay Equity Management* (Toronto: CCH Canadian, 1988): 45–54.

22. David Brown New Rules Proposed for Pay Equity" *Canadian HR Reporter*, May 31, 2004: 1, 2.

23. *Introduction to Employment Equity* (Ottawa: Human Resources Development Canada, 1996).

24. *Employment Equity Act*, http://laws.justice.gc.ca/en/E-5.401/48928.html, retrieved July 30, 2009.

25. Kelly Toughill, "Firms back equity: To some it's 'good business' despite Harris's vow to scrap it," *Toronto Star*, June 21, 1995, A2.

26. *Canadian Human Rights Act*, S.C. 1976–77, c. as amended.

27. R. G. L. Fairweather, Canadian Human Rights Commission, *The Standing Committee on Legal and Constitutional Affairs*, May 29, 1986, 10.

28. Shenaz Mode "Employment Equity: An Important Piece in the Human Rights Puzzle," *HR Professional* (April/May 2005): 26.

29. *Towards Equity: 1993 Merit Awards*, Employment Equity Branch, Human Resources Development Canada (June 1994): 17–18.

30. *Workplace Innovations Overview—1996*, Bureau of Labour Information, Human Resources Development Canada: 1–84.

31. *Towards Equity: 1993 Merit Awards*: 11–12; Laura Cassiani, "Canada's Quiet Labour Crisis," *Canadian HR Reporter* 14, no. 3 (February 12, 2001): 1, 8.

32. L. Young, "Employers Need to Scrutinize All Job Testing for Human Rights Violations, Supreme Court Rules," *Canadian HR Reporter* (October 4, 1999): 3.

33. Ibid, 18.

34. Aggarwal, *Sex Discrimination*.

35. Nicholas Keung, "Police recruit ethnic officers to boost force," *Toronto Star*, July 25, 1997, A7.

36. *Employment Equity: A Guide for Employers*: 1995, c4.

37. Interview with Aloma Lawrence, 2006.

38. Wendy Stueck, "Business taps talents of disabled workers," *The Globe and Mail*, May 18, 2004, B4.

39. Joanne Leck, Sylvie St. Onge, and Isabelle La Lancettee, "Wage Gap Changes among Organizations Subject to the Employment Equity Act," *Canadian Public Policy* 21, no. 44 (December 1995): 387–400.

40. David Doorey, "Employer Bullying: Implied Duties of Fair Dealing in Canadian Employment Contracts" (2005), *Queen's Law Journal*, Vol. 30 (2005): 500.

41. Seymour Moskowitz, "Adolescent Workers and Sexual Harassment," *Labor Law Journal* 51, no. 3 (Fall 2000): 78–84. For an excellent reference guide on sexual harassment, see William Petrocelli and Barbara Kate Repa, *Sexual Harassment on the Job: What It Is and How to Stop It* (Berkeley, CA: Nolo Press, 1998).

42. "Sexual Harassment," *CACSW Fact Sheet*, Canadian Advisory Council on the Status of Women, March 1993.

43. "Inquest Probes Murder-Suicide Involving Harassment Victim," *Sexual Harassment, Workplace Diversity Update* 5, no. 3 (March 1997): 4.

44. Shannon Kari "B.C. Fire chief vows policy to combat sexual harassment," *The Globe and Mail*, May 31, 2005, A1.

45. Malcolm McKillop, "A manager's guide to sexual impropriety," *The Globe and Mail*, October 7, 1997, B23.

46. For a good review of sexual harassment policy, see Dana S. Connell, "Effective Sexual Harassment Policies: Unexpected Lessons from Jacksonville Shipyards," *Employee Relations Law Journal* 17, no. 2 (Autumn 1991): 191–205.

47. Katherine Harding, "Taking aim at bullies," *The Globe and Mail*, March 19, 2003, C1.

48. Christine L. Taylor, "Dimensions of Diversity in Canadian Business: Building a Business Case for Valuing Ethnocultural Diversity," *Conference Board of Canada Report* (April 1995): 143–195.

49. Paul Moloney, "Toronto okays non-Christian holidays for staffers," *Toronto Star*, May 17, 1995, A6.

50. S. Hood, "Generational Diversity," *HR Professional*, June–July 2000: 19.

51. Jennie Constantinides, "Diversity Management: At CN, the 'Token' Will Be Broken," *Human Resources Professional* 7, no. 4 (April 1991): 29–30.

52. Statistics Canada, *Canada's Ethnocultural Portrait*; Anderson, "Immigration Shifts Population Kaleidoscope."

53. Statistics Canada, *Canada's Ethnocultural Portrait*.

54. Jana Schilder, "The Rainbow Connection: Employers Who Promote Diversity May Discover a Pot of Gold," *Human Resources Professional* 11, no. 3 (April 1994): 13–15.

55. Ibid.

56. Doug Nevison, "Profiting in the Pacific Rim: Can Canada Capture Its Share?" *Conference Board of Canada Report*, 1994: 117–194.

57. World Bank, 1993.

58. R. Roosevelt Thomas, Jr., "Beyond Race and Gender," *AMACOM*, 1991: 34.

59. Taylor, "Dimensions of Diversity in Canadian Business": 13;

60. John Spears, "The many colours of money: Diversity boosts profit, firms told," *Toronto Star*, May 9, 1995.

61. Taylor, "Dimensions of Diversity in Canadian Business," 15.

62. *Continuing in-patient focused care excellence*, Sunnybrook Community and Public Affairs, Sunnybrook Health Science Centre, Toronto, April 1995.

63. P. Lungen "Military addresses racism issue," *Canadian Jewish News* 30, No. 7, (February 17, 2000), 6.

64. Leslie Young, "Global Diversity Standard in Works," *Canadian HR Reporter*, April 5, 1999: 1.

65. Claudine Kapel, "Variation Is the Theme: Organizations That Value Diversity Glimpse Profits in Improved Productivity," *Human Resources Professional* 1, no. 3 (April 1994): 9–12.

66. Taylor, "Dimensions of Diversity in Canadian Business."

67. Ibid, 18.

68. Young, "Global Diversity Standard in Works," *Canadian HR Reporter,* April 5, 1999: 1.

CHAPTER 4

Job Analysis, Employee Involvement, and Flexible Work Schedules

After studying this chapter, you should be able to

[OUTCOME 1] Discuss the relationship between job requirements and the performance of HRM functions.

[OUTCOME 2] Indicate the methods by which job analysis typically is completed.

[OUTCOME 3] Identify and explain the various sections of job descriptions.

[OUTCOME 4] Provide examples illustrating the various factors that must be taken into account in designing a job.

[OUTCOME 5] Discuss the various job characteristics that motivate employees.

[OUTCOME 6] Describe the different group techniques used to maximize employee contributions.

[OUTCOME 7] Differentiate and explain the different adjustments in work schedules.

A global business environment forces organizations to "reengineer" themselves to gain competitive advantage and profitability.[1] The goal is to become more efficient and effective. To achieve success, companies such as Canadian Pacific and Ducks Unlimited are breaking into smaller units and getting leaner and flatter. There is emphasis on smaller scale, less hierarchy, fewer layers, and more decentralized work units.[2] As organizational reshaping takes place, managers want employees to operate more independently and flexibly to meet customer demands. To do this, they require that decisions be made by the people who are closest to the information and who are directly involved in the product or service delivered.[3] The objective is to develop jobs and basic work units that are adaptable enough to thrive in a world of high-velocity change.

In this chapter, we will discuss how jobs can be designed so as to best contribute to the objectives of the organization and at the same time satisfy the needs of the employees who are to perform them. Clearly, the duties and responsibilities present in jobs greatly influence employee productivity, job satisfaction, and employment retention.[4] Therefore, the value of job analysis, which defines clearly and precisely the requirements of each job, will be stressed. Importantly, we will emphasize that these job requirements provide the foundation for making objective and legally defensible decisions in managing human resources. The chapter concludes by reviewing several innovative job design and employee contribution techniques that increase job satisfaction while improving organizational performance. Teamwork and the characteristics of successful teams are highlighted. Stacy Sullivan, director of HR at Google, notes that "the work environment and the sense of team spirit have become a critical job element."

RELATIONSHIP OF JOB REQUIREMENTS AND HRM FUNCTIONS

A **job** consists of a group of related activities and duties. Ideally, the duties of a job should consist of natural units of work that are similar and related. They should be clear and distinct from those of other jobs to minimize misunderstanding and conflict among employees and to enable employees to recognize what is expected of them. For some jobs, several employees may be required, each of whom will occupy a separate position. A **position** consists of different duties and responsibilities performed by only one employee. In a city library, for example, four employees (four positions) may be involved in reference work, but all of them have only one job (reference librarian). Where different jobs have similar duties and responsibilities, they may be grouped into a **job family** for purposes of recruitment, training, compensation, or advancement opportunities.

RECRUITMENT

Before they can find capable employees for an organization, recruiters need to know the job specifications for the positions they are to fill.[5] A **job specification** is a statement of the knowledge, skills, and abilities required of the person performing the job. In the HR department for the City of Calgary Alberta, the job specification for senior personnel analyst includes the following:

1. Appropriate university degree, preferably at the master's level
2. Four to five years of corporate management experience
3. Working knowledge of employment equity, human rights legislation, statistical analysis, investigative procedures, and organizational development

---

OUTCOME 1

job
A group of related activities and duties

position
The different duties and responsibilities performed by only one employee

job family
A group of individual jobs with similar characteristics

job specification
A statement of the needed knowledge, skills, and abilities of the person who is to perform the job

Because job specifications establish the qualifications required of applicants for a job opening, they serve an essential role in the recruiting function. These qualifications typically are contained in the notices of job openings. Whether posted on organizational bulletin boards or HRIS Internet sites or included in help-wanted advertisements or employment agency listings, job specifications provide a basis for attracting qualified applicants and discouraging unqualified ones.

SELECTION

In addition to job specifications, managers and supervisors use **job descriptions** to select employees and orient them to jobs. A job description is a statement of the tasks, duties, and responsibilities of a job. (See "Job Descriptions" later in this chapter.)

In the past, job specifications used as a basis for selection sometimes bore little relation to the duties to be performed under the job description. Examples of such non-job-related specifications abounded. Applicants for the job of labourer were required to have a high school diploma. Firefighters were required to be at least six feet tall, and applicants for skilled craft positions—plumbers, electricians, machinists—were required to be male. These kinds of job specifications discriminated against members of designated groups, many of whom were excluded from these jobs.

job description
A statement of the tasks, duties, and responsibilities of a job to be performed

TRAINING AND DEVELOPMENT

Any discrepancies between the knowledge, skill, and abilities (often referred to as KSAs) demonstrated by a jobholder and the requirements contained in the description and specification for that job provide clues to training needs. Also, career development as a part of the training function is concerned with preparing employees for advancement to jobs where their capacities can be utilized to the fullest extent possible. The formal qualification requirements set forth in high-level jobs indicate how much more training and development are needed for employees to advance to those jobs.

PERFORMANCE APPRAISAL

The requirements contained in the description of a job provide the criteria for evaluating the performance of the holder of that job. The results of performance appraisal may reveal, however, that certain requirements established for a job are not completely valid. As we have already stressed, these criteria must be specific and job related. If the criteria used to evaluate employee performance are vague and not job related, employers may find themselves being charged with unfair discrimination.

COMPENSATION MANAGEMENT

In determining the rate to be paid for performing a job, the relative worth of the job is one of the most important factors. This worth is based on what the job demands of an employee in terms of skill, effort, and responsibility, as well as the conditions and hazards under which the work is performed. The systems of job evaluation by which this worth may be measured are discussed in Chapter 9. As the Business Case outlines, job analysis has financial implications and could cause workplace problems if handled poorly.

The Business CASE

Flying for Love or Money

The two unions representing pilots who fly for Air Canada and its regional airline, Air Canada Jazz, fought over pay scale. Pilots for both carriers must meet the same job requirements. However, those who fly for the mainline service earn about $140,000 to $200,000 annually while those who fly for the regional airline earn on average $75,000 to $100,000. The 3,100 Air Canada pilots feel that the pay differential is justified because they fly bigger planes (carrying 150 to 250 passengers) at longer distances (flight times of up to 14 hours) with the latest technology. The 1,400 Air Canada Jazz pilots carry smaller passenger loads

over shorter distances (flight times of 60 to 90 minutes). However, this entails many more takeoffs and landings, which are considered the most difficult and stressful part of the flight. Air Canada pilots dispute this, saying compensation is not determined by the number of takeoffs and landings; if it were, then bush pilots would be making the most money. Accurate job descriptions would normally help to resolve this contentious and costly debate, but it was collective bargaining that resolved the issue. The association representing the pilots at Jazz won a concession that allowed Jazz pilots to operate Air Canada jets.

Source: John Partridge, "Air Canada, the Pilots and All That Jazz," *The Globe and Mail*, June 14, 2003: B1, B4. Paul Vieira and Nicolas Van Praet "Air Canada Will Keep Flying: Tentative Deals Will Save Airline $1.1 Billion," *Edmonton Journal* (June 2, 2003), A1.

[OUTCOME 2]

job analysis

The process of obtaining information about jobs by determining the duties, tasks, or activities of jobs

JOB ANALYSIS

Job analysis is sometimes called the cornerstone of HRM because the information it collects serves so many HRM functions. **Job analysis** is the process of obtaining information about jobs by determining the duties, tasks, or activities of those jobs.[6] The procedure involves systematically investigating jobs by following a number of predetermined steps specified in advance of the study.[7] When completed, job analysis results in a written report summarizing the information obtained from the analysis of 20 or 30 individual job tasks or activities. HR managers use these data to develop job descriptions and job specifications. These documents, in turn, are used to perform and enhance the different HR functions such as the development of performance appraisal criteria or the content of training classes. The ultimate purpose of job analysis is to improve organizational performance and productivity. Figure 4.1 illustrates how job analysis is performed, including the functions for which it is used. As contrasted with job design, which reflects subjective opinions about the ideal requirements of a job, job analysis is concerned with objective and verifiable information about the actual requirements of a job. The job descriptions and job specifications developed through job analysis should be as accurate as possible if they are to be of value to those who make HRM decisions. These decisions may involve any of the HR functions—from recruitment to termination of employees.

GATHERING JOB INFORMATION

Job data may be obtained in several ways. The more common methods of analyzing jobs are through interviews, questionnaires, observation, and diaries.

- *Interviews*. The job analyst may question individual employees and managers about the job under review.

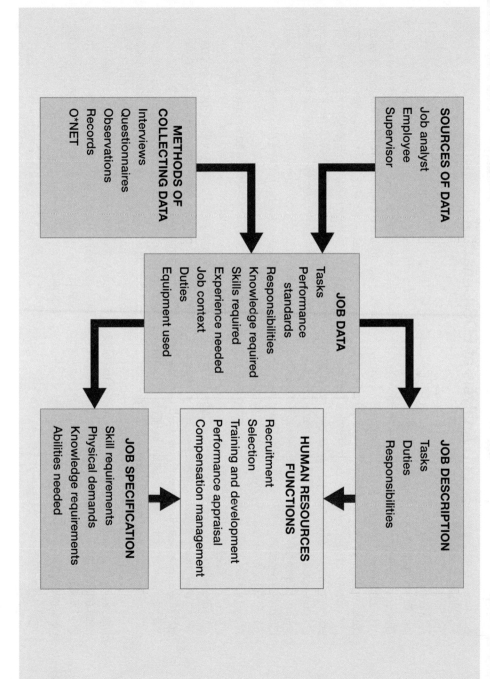

FIGURE **4.1**

The Process of Job Analysis

- *Questionnaires.* The job analyst may circulate carefully prepared question-naires to be filled out individually by jobholders and managers. These forms will be used to obtain data in the areas of job duties and tasks performed, purpose of the job, physical setting, requirements for performing the job (skill, education, experience, physical and mental demands), equipment and materials used, and special health and safety concerns.

- *Observation.* The job analyst may learn about the jobs by observing and recording on a standardized form the activities of jobholders. Videotaping jobs for later study is an approach used by some organizations.

- *Diaries.* Jobholders themselves may be asked to keep a diary of their work activities during an entire work cycle. Diaries are normally filled out at specific times of the work shift (such as every half hour or hour) and main-tained for a two- to four-week period.

Although HR specialists, called job analysts, are the personnel primarily responsible for the job analysis program, they usually enlist the cooperation of the employees and managers in the departments where jobs are being analyzed (see the Reality Check). These managers and employees are the sources of much of the information about the jobs, and they may be asked to prepare rough drafts of the job descriptions and specifications the job analysts need.

Reality CHECK

Job Analysis at EDS Canada Inc.

As the senior human resources specialist at EDS Canada Inc., Don Weatherbee is responsible for conducting job analyses. While new job codes and classifications are normally developed by head office in Texas, there are three cases that warrant job analysis in Canada. The first is to comply with pay equity legislation that states that men and women should be paid equally for performing work of equal value. In order to comply with pay equity, jobs are analyzed and weighted for Specialized Knowledge, Effort, Responsibility, and the Working Environment. Salary survey companies are often retained to do this type of analysis since they are the experts in ensuring that the pay grades are in compliance with the act.

The second occasion is when new jobs are created, which need to be classified and their compensation rates assessed. In one example, EDS Canada Inc. did not have an entry-level position in HR and so the task force developed an HR administrator position. On another occasion, a business services consultant position needed to be developed at the top end of the business analyst family. Because these positions were new to EDS Canada Inc., the full range of duties needed to be assessed and coded.

The third occasion occurs when, through acquisitions and transitioning people to EDS Canada Inc., job analysis is needed to verify what the employees do since job titles are frequently poor indicators of what a person actually does. For example, when EDS Canada Inc. won a contract bid to do IT outsourcing for a land registry company, a job analysis was needed in order to create new job codes for the employees who were transitioning to the company.

Information for both the employees and their supervisors is gathered on a job summary questionnaire (JSQ). This is done to ensure that there is no artificial inflation of job duties. There is one form for management and another form for professional, technical, clerical, trades, and services. The management questionnaire is more detailed as it includes areas of responsibilities, supervision given to direct reports, and previous work history that explains how it relates to the present job. Each questionnaire is designed to determine the percentage of time spent on each task, what that task is, for whom the task is done, how it is accomplished, and why it is done.

Using the Internet

For a general information site on job analysis, consult HR-Guide at

http://www.hr-guide.com/jobanalysis.htm

CONTROLLING THE ACCURACY OF JOB INFORMATION

If job analysis is to accomplish its intended purpose, the job data collected must be accurate. Care must be taken to ensure that all important facts are included. A job analyst should be alert for employees who tend to exaggerate the difficulty of their jobs in order to inflate their egos and their paycheques (see Ethics in HRM).[8] When interviewing employees or reviewing their questionnaires, the job analyst must look for any responses that do not agree with other facts or impressions the analyst has received. One job analyst noted, "When in doubt about the accuracy of employee responses, always double-check the data with others."[9] Furthermore, when job information is collected from employees, a representative group of individuals should be surveyed. For example, the results of one study indicated that the information obtained from job analysis was related to race. In another study, the experience level of job incumbents influenced job analysis outcomes.

A job analyst who doubts the accuracy of information provided by employees should obtain additional information from them, their managers, or other individuals who are familiar with or perform the same job. It is common practice to have the descriptions for each job reviewed by the jobholders and their managers.

Ethics in **HRM**

Inflation

At some point in your working life, you will be asked to describe your job, perhaps when being interviewed by a job analyst or by answering questions on a form. Most employees have a reasonable expectation that their answers will affect their lives in significant ways. The information obtained may be used to reclassify the job to either a higher or lower pay level. Most employees believe that standards of performance may change—and the employer will expect them to work faster or to do more—although that is not the goal of job analysis.

As a result of these beliefs and expectations, employees have a vested interest in "inflating" their job descriptions, by making the job sound very important and very difficult. Thus night clerks in hotels become auditors and receptionists become administrators. Making a job sound more important than it is may reflect an employee's sincere belief in the significance of his or her contribution or an attempt to lobby for higher pay.

The NOC and Job Analysis

Commonly referred to as the NOC, the National Occupational Classification is compiled by the federal government. The purpose of the NOC is to compile, analyze, and communicate information about occupations. This information can be used for employment equity, human resource planning, and occupational supply and demand forecasts and analyses.

The NOC is a composite of the Canadian labour market and has helped bring about a greater degree of uniformity in the job titles and descriptions used by employers in different parts of the country. This uniformity has facilitated the movement of workers from regions that may be experiencing widespread unemployment to areas where employment opportunities are greater. Also, the NOC code numbers facilitate the exchange of statistical information about jobs and are useful in reporting research in the HR area, in vocational counselling, and in charting career paths through job transfers and/or advancements. Some professional associations provide a job classification system that is intended to be more current than the NOC.[10]

APPROACHES TO JOB ANALYSIS

The systematic and quantitative definition of job content that job analysis provides is the foundation of many HRM practices. Specifically, the job analysis serves to justify job descriptions and other HRM selection procedures. Several different job analysis approaches are used to gather data, each with specific advantages and disadvantages.[11] Four of the more popular methods are the position analysis questionnaire, critical incident method, task inventory analysis, and competency-based analysis.

The Position Analysis Questionnaire System

The **position analysis questionnaire (PAQ)** is a quantifiable data collection method covering 194 different worker-oriented tasks. Using a five-point scale, the PAQ seeks to determine the degree, if any, to which the different tasks, or job elements, are involved in performing a particular job.

A sample page from the PAQ covering 11 elements of the Information Input Division is shown in Figure 4.2. The person conducting an analysis with this questionnaire would rate each of the elements using the five-point scale shown in the

Using the Internet

The NOC contains standardized and comprehensive descriptions of about 25,000 occupations at **http://www5.hrsdc.gc.ca/NOC/English/NOC/2006/Welcome.aspx**

position analysis questionnaire (PAQ)

A questionnaire covering 194 different tasks that, by means of a five-point scale, seeks to determine the degree to which different tasks are involved in performing a particular job

FIGURE **4.2**

A Sample Page from the PAQ

INFORMATION INPUT

1 INFORMATION INPUT

1.1 Sources of Job Information

Rate each of the following items in terms of the extent to which it is used by the worker as a source of information in performing his job.

	Extent of Use (U)
NA	Does not apply
1	Nominal/very infrequent
2	Occasional
3	Moderate
4	Considerable
5	Very substantial

1.1.1   Visual Sources of Job Information

01 U   Written materials (books, reports, office notes, articles, job instructions, signs, etc.)

02 U   Quantitative materials (materials which deal with quantities or amounts, such as graphs, accounts, specifications, tables of numbers, etc.)

03 U   Pictorial materials (pictures or picturelike materials used as sources of information, for example, drawings, blueprints, diagrams, maps, tracings, photographic films, x-ray films, TV pictures, etc.)

04 U   Patterns/related devices (templates, stencils, patterns, etc., used as sources of information when observed during use; do not include here materials described in item 3 above)

05 U   Visual displays (dials, gauges, signal lights, radarscopes, speedometers, clocks, etc.)

06 U   Measuring devices (rulers, calipers, tire pressure gauges, scales, thickness gauges, pipettes, thermometers, protractors, etc., used to obtain visual information about physical measurements; do not include here devices described in item 5 above)

07 U   Mechanical devices (tools, equipment, machinery, and other mechanical devices which are sources of information when observed during use or operation)

08 U   Materials in process (parts, materials, objects, etc., which are sources of information when being modified, worked on, or otherwise processed, such as bread dough being mixed, workpiece being turned in a lathe, fabric being cut, shoe being resoled, etc.)

09 U   Materials not in process (parts, materials, objects, etc., not in the process of being changed or modified, which are sources of information when being inspected, handled, packaged, distributed, or selected, etc., such as items or materials in inventory, storage, or distribution channels, items being inspected, etc.)

10 U   Features of nature (landscapes, fields, geological samples, vegetation, cloud formations, and other features of nature which are observed or inspected to provide information)

11 U   Man-made features of environment (structures, buildings, dams, highways, bridges, docks, railroads, and other "man-made" or altered aspects of the indoor or outdoor environment which are observed or inspected to provide job information; do not consider equipment, machines, etc., that an individual uses in his work, as covered by item 7)

Source: *Position Analysis Questionnaire*, copyright 1969, 1989 by Purdue Research Foundation, West Lafayette, IN 47907. Reprinted with permission.

upper right-hand corner of the sample page. The results obtained with the PAQ are quantitative and can be subjected to statistical analysis. The PAQ also permits dimensions of behaviour to be compared across a number of jobs and permits jobs to be grouped on the basis of common characteristics.

The Critical Incident Method

The objective of the **critical incident method** is to identify critical job tasks. Critical job tasks are those important duties and job responsibilities performed by the job-holder that lead to job success. Information about critical job tasks can be collected through interviews with employees or managers or through self-report statements written by employees.

Suppose, for example, that the job analyst is studying the job of reference librarian. The interviewer will ask the employee to describe the job on the basis of what is done, how the job is performed, and what tools and equipment are used. The reference librarian may describe the job as follows:

I assist clients by answering their questions related to finding books, periodicals, or other library materials. I also give them directions to help them find materials within the building. To perform my job, I may have to look up materials myself or refer patrons to someone who can directly assist them. Some individuals may need training in how to use reference materials or special library facilities. I also give library tours to new patrons. I use computers and a variety of reference books to carry out my job.

After the job data are collected, the analyst then writes separate task statements that represent important job activities. For the reference librarian, one task statement might be, "Listens to clients and answers their questions related to locating library materials." Typically, the job analyst writes five to ten important task statements for each job under study. The final product comprises written task statements that are clear, complete, and easily understood by those unfamiliar with the job. The critical incident method is an important job analysis method because it teaches the analyst to focus on employee behaviours critical to job success.

Task Inventory Analysis

The **task inventory analysis** method can be considered a job-oriented type of job analysis. The technique was pioneered by the U.S. Air Force to analyze jobs held by Air Force specialists. Unlike the PAQ, which uses a standardized form to analyze jobs in different organizations, a task inventory questionnaire can be tailor-made to a specific organization.

The technique is developed by identifying—with the help of employees and managers—a list of tasks and their descriptions that are components of different jobs. The goal is to produce a comprehensive list of task statements that are applicable to all jobs. Task statements then are listed on a task inventory survey form to be completed by the person analyzing the job under review. A task statement might be, "Inventories current supplies to maintain stock levels." The job analysis would also note the importance and frequency of use of the task to the successful completion of the job.

Competency-Based Analysis

The traditional approach to job analysis assumes a static job environment in which jobs remain relatively stable apart from incumbents who might hold these jobs. Here, jobs can be meaningfully defined in terms of tasks, duties, processes, and skills necessary for job success. This assumption, unfortunately, discounts technological advances that are often so accelerated that jobs, as they are defined today,

critical incident method
A job analysis method by which important job tasks are identified for job success

task inventory analysis
An organization-specific list of tasks and their descriptions used as a basis to identify components of jobs

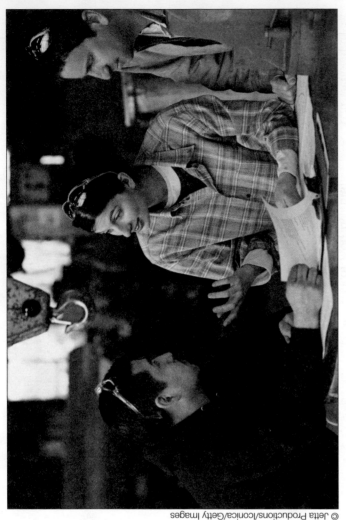

© Jetta Productions/Iconica/Getty Images

Task inventory analysis uses employees to develop lists of job tasks and descriptions common to all jobs.

may be obsolete tomorrow. The following statement by two HR professionals highlights this concern: "Typically, job analysis looks at how a job is currently done. But the ever-changing business market makes it difficult to keep a job analysis up to date. Also, companies are asking employees to do more, so there is a question of whether 'jobs' as we know them are obsolete." Furthermore, the need to respond to global change can alter the nature of jobs and the requirement of individuals needed to successfully perform them. Therefore, in a dynamic environment where job demands rapidly change, obsolete job analysis information simply hinders an organization's ability to adapt to change.

When organizations operate in a fast-moving environment, managers may adopt a competency-based approach to job analysis.[12] This job analysis method relies on building job profiles that look at the responsibilities and activities of jobs, and the worker competencies necessary to accomplish them. The objective is to identify "key" competencies for organizational success. Competencies can be identified through focus groups, surveys, or interviews and might include such things as interpersonal communication skills, decision-making ability, conflict resolution skills, adaptability, or self-motivation. An organization's job descriptions, recruitment requirements, and performance evaluation system will reflect the competencies needed by employees.

HRIS and Job Analysis

Human resource information systems have greatly facilitated the job analysis process. Available today are various software programs designed specifically to analyze jobs and to write job descriptions and job specifications based on those analyses. These programs normally contain generalized task statements that can apply to many different jobs. Managers and employees select those statements that best describe the job under review, indicating the importance of the task to the total job where appropriate. Advanced computer applications of job analysis combine job analysis with job evaluation (see Chapter 9) and the pricing of organizational jobs. Computerized job analysis systems can be expensive to initiate, but where the organization has many jobs to analyze, the cost per job may be low. HR publications such as *Canadian HR Reporter* contain advertisements from numerous software companies offering HRIS job analysis packages.

JOB DESCRIPTIONS

As previously noted, a job description is a written description of a job and the types of duties it includes. Since there is no standard format for job descriptions, they tend to vary in appearance and content from one organization to another. However, most job descriptions will contain at least three parts: job title, job identification section, and job duties section. If the job specifications are not prepared as a separate document, they are usually stated in the concluding section of the job description. Highlights in HRM 4.1 shows a job description for a HR employment assistant. This sample job description includes both job duties and job specifications and should satisfy most of the job information needs of managers who must recruit, interview, and orient a new employee.

Job descriptions are of value to both the (employees) and the (employer). From the employees' standpoint, job descriptions can be used to help them learn their job duties and to remind them of the results they are expected to achieve. From the employer's standpoint, written job descriptions can serve as a basis for minimizing the misunderstandings that occur between managers and their subordinates concerning job requirements. They also establish management's right to take corrective action when the duties covered by the job description are not performed as required.

Job Title

Selection of a job title is important for several reasons. First, the job title is of psychological importance, providing status to the employee. For instance, "sanitation engineer" is a more appealing title than "garbage collector." Second, if possible, the title should provide some indication of what the duties of the job entail. Titles such as *meat inspector, electronics assembler, salesperson,* and *engineer* obviously hint at the nature of the duties of these jobs. The job title also should indicate the relative level occupied by its holder in the organizational hierarchy. For example, the title *junior engineer* implies that this job occupies a lower level than that of *senior engineer.*

Job Identification Section

The job identification section of a job description usually follows the job title. It includes items such as the departmental location of the job, the person to whom the jobholder reports, and the date the job description was last revised. Sometimes it also contains a payroll or code number, the number of employees performing the job, the number of employees in the department in which the job is located, and the NOC code number. "Job Statement" usually appears at the bottom of this section and distinguishes the job from other jobs—something the job title may fail to do.

Job Duties, or Essential Functions, Section

Statements covering job duties are typically arranged in order of importance. These statements should indicate the weight, or value, of each duty. Usually, but not always, the weight of a duty can be gauged by the percentage of time devoted to it. The statements should stress the responsibilities all the duties entail and the results they are to accomplish. It is also general practice to indicate the tools and equipment used by the employee in performing the job. Remember, the job duties section must list only the essential functions of the job to be performed.

Job Specifications Section

As stated earlier, the personal qualifications an individual must possess in order to perform the duties and responsibilities contained in a job description are compiled in the job specification. Typically, the job specification covers two areas: (1) the skill required to perform the job and (2) the physical demands the job places on the employee performing it.

[OUTCOME 3]

148

Highlights in HRM 4.1

Job Description for an HR Employment Assistant

Job Identification

JOB TITLE: Employment Assistant

Division: Western Region

Department: Human Resources Management

Job Analyst: Virginia Sasaki

Date Analyzed: 12/3/09

Report to: HR Manager Job Code: 11–17

Date Verified: 12/17/09

Job Statement

Brief Listing of Major Duties

Performs professional human resources work in the areas of employee recruitment and selection, testing, orientation, transfers, and maintenance of employee human resources files. May handle special assignments and projects in Employment Equity, employee grievances, training, or classification and compensation. Works under general supervision. Incumbent exercises initiative and independent judgment in the performance of assigned tasks.

Essential Functions

Essential Functions and Responsibilities

1. Prepares recruitment literature and job advertisements for applicant placement.
2. Schedules and conducts personal interviews to determine applicant suitability for employment. Includes reviewing mailed applications and résumés for qualified personnel.
3. Supervises administration of testing program. Responsible for developing or improving testing instruments and procedures.
4. Presents orientation program to all new employees. Reviews and develops all materials and procedures for orientation program.
5. Coordinates division job posting and transfer program. Establishes job posting procedures. Responsible for reviewing transfer applications, arranging transfer interviews, and determining effective transfer dates.
6. Maintains a daily working relationship with division managers on human resources matters, including recruitment concerns, retention or release of probationary employees, and discipline or discharge of permanent employees.
7. Distributes new or revised human resources policies and procedures to all employees and managers through bulletins, meetings, memorandums, and/or personal contact.
8. Performs related duties as assigned by the human resources manager.

Job Specifications

Job Specifications and Requirements

1. Four-year college or university degree with major course work in human resources management, business administration, or industrial psychology OR a combination of experience, education, and training equivalent to a four-year degree in human resources management.
2. Considerable knowledge of principles of employee selection and assignment of personnel.
3. Ability to express ideas clearly in both written and oral communications.
4. Ability to independently plan and organize one's own activities.
5. Knowledge of human resources computer applications desirable.

Skills relevant to a job include education or experience, specialized training, personal traits or abilities, and manual dexterities. The physical demands of a job refer to how much walking, standing, reaching, lifting, or talking must be done on the job. The condition of the physical work environment and the hazards employees may encounter are also among the physical demands of a job.

Job specifications should also include interpersonal skills or key competencies necessary for job success. For example, behavioural competencies might include the ability to make decisions on imperfect information, decisiveness, the ability to handle multiple tasks, and conflict resolution skills. Behavioural competencies can be assessed by asking applicants situational interview questions (see Chapter 6). For example, a manager could ask an applicant about a time when he or she had to make a critical decision quickly.

PROBLEMS WITH JOB DESCRIPTIONS

Managers consider job descriptions a valuable tool for performing HRM functions. Nevertheless, several problems are frequently associated with these documents, including the following:

1. If they are poorly written, using vague rather than specific terms, they provide little guidance to the jobholder.
2. They are sometimes not updated as job duties or specifications change.
3. They may violate the law by containing specifications not related to job success.
4. They can limit the scope of activities of the jobholder, reducing organizational flexibility.

Writing Clear and Specific Job Descriptions

When writing a job description, it is essential to use statements that are terse, direct, and simply worded. Unnecessary words or phrases should be eliminated. Typically, the sentences that describe job duties begin with a present-tense verb, with the implied subject of the sentence being the employee performing the job. The term *occasionally* is used to describe duties that are performed once in awhile. The term *may* is used in connection with duties performed only by some workers on the job.

Managers may find that writing job descriptions is a tedious process that distracts from other supervisory responsibilities. Fortunately, software packages are available to simplify this time-consuming yet necessary task. One program provides an initial library of more than 2,500 prewritten job descriptions. Since the program works much like a word processor, text can be easily deleted, inserted, or modified to user demands.

JOB DESIGN

It is not uncommon for managers and supervisors to confuse the processes of job analysis and job design. Job analysis is the study of jobs as currently performed by employees. It identifies job duties and the requirements needed to perform the work successfully. Job design, which is an outgrowth of job analysis, is concerned with structuring jobs in order to improve organization efficiency and employee job satisfaction. Job design is concerned with changing, modifying, and enriching jobs in order to capture the talents of employees while improving organization performance.[14] For example, companies such as Harley-Davidson and PageNet, which are engaged in continuous improvement, or process reengineering, may revamp their

OUTCOME 4

job design

An outgrowth of job analysis that improves jobs through technological and human considerations in order to enhance organization efficiency and employee job satisfaction

FIGURE **4.3**

Basis for Job Design

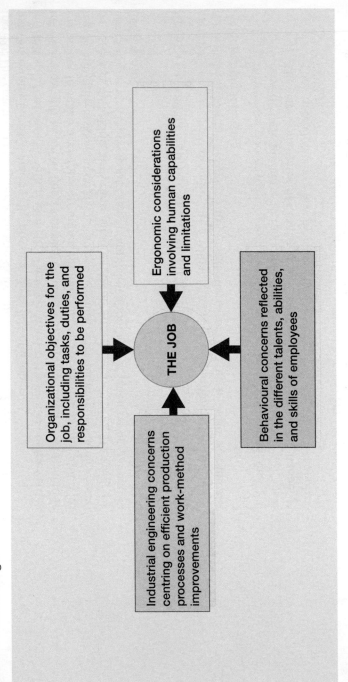

jobs in order to eliminate unnecessary job tasks or find better ways of performing work. Job design should facilitate the achievement of organizational objectives. At the same time, the design should recognize the capabilities and needs of those who are to perform the job.

As Figure 4.3 illustrates, job design is a combination of four basic considerations: (1) the organizational objectives the job was created to fulfill; (2) industrial engineering considerations, including ways to make the job technologically efficient; (3) ergonomic concerns, including workers' physical and mental capabilities; and (4) behavioural concerns that influence an employee's job satisfaction.[15]

BEHAVIOURAL CONCERNS

Two job design methods seek to incorporate the behavioural needs of employees as they perform their individual jobs. Both methods strive to satisfy the intrinsic needs of employees. The job enrichment model and the job characteristics model have long been popular with researchers and practitioners as ways to increase the job satisfaction of employees.

Job Enrichment

Any effort that makes work more rewarding or satisfying by adding more meaningful tasks to an employee's job is called **job enrichment**. Originally popularized by Frederick Herzberg, job enrichment is touted as fulfilling the high motivational needs of employees, such as self-fulfillment and self-esteem, while achieving long-term job satisfaction and performance goals.[16] Job enrichment, or the vertical expansion of jobs, may be accomplished by increasing the autonomy and responsibility of employees. Herzberg discusses five factors for enriching jobs and thereby motivating employees: achievement, recognition, growth, responsibility, and performance of the whole job versus only parts of the job. For example, managers can use these five factors to enrich the jobs of employees by

job enrichment
Enhancing a job by adding more meaningful tasks and duties to make the work more rewarding or satisfying

- Increasing the level of difficulty and responsibility of the job
- Allowing employees to retain more authority and control over work outcomes
- Providing unit or individual job performance reports directly to employees
- Adding new tasks to the job that require training and growth
- Assigning individuals specific tasks, enabling them to use their particular competencies or skills

These factors allow employees to assume a greater role in the decision-making process and become more involved in planning, organizing, directing, and controlling their own work. Vertical job enrichment can also be accomplished by organizing workers into teams and giving these teams greater authority for self-management.

In spite of the benefits to be achieved through job enrichment, it must not be considered a panacea for overcoming production problems and employee discontent. Job enrichment programs are more likely to succeed in some jobs and work situations than in others. They are not the solution to problems such as dissatisfaction with pay, employee benefits, or employment security. Moreover, not all employees object to the mechanical pacing of an assembly line, nor do all employees seek additional responsibility or challenge. Some prefer routine jobs because these jobs are predictable and concise.

Job Characteristics

Job design studies explored a new field when behavioural scientists focused on identifying various job dimensions that would improve simultaneously the efficiency of organizations and the job satisfaction of employees. Perhaps the theory that best exemplifies this research is the one advanced by Richard Hackman and Greg Oldham.[17] Their job characteristics model proposes that three psychological states of a jobholder result in improved work performance, internal motivation, and lower absenteeism and turnover.[18] A motivated, satisfied, and productive employee (1) experiences *meaningfulness* of the work performed, (2) experiences *responsibility* for work outcomes, and (3) has *knowledge of the results* of the work performed. Hackman and Oldham believe that five core job dimensions produce the three psychological states. The five job characteristics are as follows:

1. *Skill variety:* The degree to which a job entails a variety of different activities, which demand the use of a number of different skills and talents by the jobholder
2. *Task identity:* The degree to which the job requires completion of a whole and identifiable piece of work, that is, doing a job from beginning to end with a visible outcome
3. *Task significance:* The degree to which the job has a substantial impact on the lives or work of other people, whether in the immediate organization or in the external environment
4. *Autonomy:* The degree to which the job provides substantial freedom, independence, and discretion to the individual in scheduling the work and in determining the procedures to be used in carrying it out
5. *Feedback:* The degree to which carrying out the work activities required by the job results in the individual being given direct and clear information about the effectiveness of his or her performance

The job characteristics model appears to work best when certain conditions are met. One of these conditions is that employees must have the psychological desire for the autonomy, variety, responsibility, and challenge of enriched jobs. When this personal characteristic is absent, employees may resist the job redesign effort. In

OUTCOME 5

job characteristics model
A job design theory that purports that three psychological states (experiencing meaningfulness of the work performed, responsibility for work outcomes, and knowledge of the results of the work performed) of a jobholder result in improved work performance, internal motivation, and lower absenteeism and turnover

addition, job redesign efforts almost always fail when employees lack the physical or mental skills, abilities, or education needed to perform the job. Forcing enriched jobs on individuals lacking these traits can result in frustrated employees.

Employee Empowerment

Job enrichment and job characteristics are specific programs by which managers or supervisors can formally change the jobs of employees. A less structured method is to allow employees to initiate their own job changes through the concept of empowerment. **Employee empowerment** is a technique of involving employees in their work through the process of inclusion. Empowerment encourages employees to become innovators and managers of their own work, and it involves them in their jobs in ways that give them more control and autonomous decision-making capabilities (see Highlights in HRM 4.2). As described by one manager, employee empowerment involves "pushing down decision-making responsibility to those close to internal and external customers."

employee empowerment
Granting employees power to initiate change, thereby encouraging them to take charge of what they do

Highlights in HRM 4.2

Empowered Employees Achieve Results

In today's highly competitive and dynamic business environment, employers as diverse as Home Depot and RBC have turned to their employees to improve organizational performance. Empowered employees have made improvements in product or service quality; reduced costs; and modified or, in some cases, designed products.

- At Kraft Foods, employees participated in work redesign changes and team building that increased productivity, reduced overhead, and cut assembly time.
- Avon Products empowered its minority managers to improve sales and service in inner-city markets. Grounded in the belief that minority managers better understand the culture of inner-city residents, Avon turned an unprofitable market into a highly productive sales area.
- At a Ford factory one group of employees made a suggestion that resulted in savings of $115,000 annually on the purchase of gloves used to protect workers who handle sheet metal and glass. The group figured out how to have the gloves washed so they could be used more than once.
- Home Depot's Special Project Support Teams (SPST) work to improve the organization's business and information services. Employees with a wide range of backgrounds and skills collaborate to address a wide range of strategic and tactical business needs.

- American Airlines' "Rainbow Team" of gay employees brought in $192 million in annual revenue by targeting the gay community.

While defining empowerment can become the first step to achieving it, in order for empowerment to grow and thrive, organizations must encourage these conditions:

- *Participation.* Employees must be encouraged to take control of their work tasks. Employees, in turn, must care about improving their work process and interpersonal work relationships.
- *Innovation.* The environment must be receptive to people with innovative ideas and encourage people to explore new paths and to take reasonable risks at reasonable costs. An empowered environment is created when curiosity is as highly regarded as is technical expertise.
- *Access to information.* Employees must have access to a wide range of information. Involved individuals decide what kind of information they need for performing their jobs.
- *Accountability.* Empowerment does not involve being able to do whatever you want. Empowered employees should be held accountable for their behaviour toward others, producing agreed-on results, achieving credibility, and operating with a positive approach.

Employee empowerment grows in an organizational culture that promotes satisfaction, support, and recognition.

industrial engineering
A field of study concerned with analyzing work methods and establishing time standards

Additionally, employee empowerment succeeds when the culture of the organization is open and receptive to change.[19] An organization's culture is largely created through the philosophies of senior managers and their leadership traits and behaviours. Effective leadership in an empowered organization is highlighted by managers who are honest, confident, trusting, and receptive to new ideas and who exhibit dignity and respect for employees as partners in organizational success. Conversely, organizations or managers who are autocratic and control-oriented seldom empower their employees or welcome organizational change. Chris Argyris, noted Harvard professor, critically states, "Managers love empowerment in theory, but the command and control model is what they trust and know best."

INDUSTRIAL ENGINEERING CONSIDERATIONS

The study of work is an important contribution of the scientific management movement. **Industrial engineering**, which evolved with this movement, is concerned with analyzing work methods and establishing time standards.[20] Specifically, it involves the study of work cycles to determine which, if any, elements can be modified, combined, rearranged, or eliminated to reduce the time needed to complete the cycle. Next, time standards are established by recording the time required to complete each element in the work cycle, using a stopwatch or work-sampling technique. By combining the times for each element, observers can determine the total time required. This time is subsequently adjusted to allow for the skill and effort demonstrated by the observed worker and for interruptions that may occur in performing the work. The adjusted time becomes the time standard for that particular work cycle.

Industrial engineering constitutes a disciplined and objective approach to job design. Unfortunately, the concern of industrial engineering for improving efficiency and simplifying work methods may cause the behavioral considerations in job design to be neglected. What may be improvements in job design and efficiency from an engineering standpoint can sometimes prove psychologically unsound. For example, the assembly line with its simplified and repetitive tasks embodies sound principles of industrial engineering, but these tasks are often not psychologically rewarding for those who must perform them. Thus, to be effective, job design must also provide for the satisfaction of behavioural needs.

ergonomics

An interdisciplinary approach to designing equipment and systems that can be easily and efficiently used by human beings

ERGONOMIC CONSIDERATIONS

Consider this statistic. In North America, millions of workplace injuries occur yearly from motions such as lifting, bending, and typing. These injuries cost employers through lost productivity, medical benefits, and lost time payments. Therefore, ergonomics is an important element of job design.

Ergonomics is the study of people at work and the practice of matching the features of products and jobs to human capabilities, preference, and the limitations of those who are to perform a job. Ergonomics focuses on ensuring that jobs are designed for safe and efficient work while improving the safety, comfort, and performance of users. In short, it seeks to fit the job to the person rather than the person to the job. Additionally, ergonomics attempts to minimize the harmful effects of carelessness, negligence, and other human fallibilities that otherwise may cause product defects, damage to equipment, or even the injury or death of employees.[21] Alan Hedge, professor of ergonomics at Cornell University, notes, "The goal of sound ergonomics is to boost employee performance while reducing injuries and errors."[22]

Equipment design must consider the physical abilities of operators to use the equipment and to react through vision, hearing, and touch to the way the equipment operates. For example, there is substantial variation in the way individuals move depending on their physical size, gender, age, and other factors. Designing equipment controls to be compatible with both the physical characteristics and the reaction capabilities of the people who must operate them and the environment in which they work is critically important. Ergonomics also considers the requirements of a diverse workforce, accommodating, for example, women who may lack the strength to operate equipment requiring intense physical force or Asian Americans who may lack the stature to reach equipment controls. Managers must adapt the workplace to the labour force or risk sacrificing quality and productivity.

Ergonomics improves productivity and morale and yields positive return on investment (ROI). Peter Budnick, president of ErgoWeb, Inc, notes, "At our company we look at ergonomics as much more than a musculoskeletal issue. Injuries are one of the natural outcomes of poor workplace design. But so is lost productivity, loss of efficiency, errors and increased waste. We really look at ergonomics as a broad approach to improving human performance."[23] Ergonomics has proven cost-effective at organizations such as Compaq Computer and Pratt and Whitney. Ergonomics has recently focused on elimination, or at least reduction, of many repetitive-motion injuries, particularly those related to the back and wrist. For example, with the increased use of computers, ergonomics has particular application at employee workstations. Figure 4.4 provides a checklist of potential repetitive-motion problem areas for employees using computers.

DESIGNING WORK FOR GROUP/TEAM CONTRIBUTIONS

Although a variety of group techniques have been developed to involve employees more fully in their organizations, all of these techniques have two characteristics in common—enhancing collaboration and increasing synergy. In increasing the degree of collaboration in the work environment, these techniques can improve work processes and organizational decision making. In increasing group synergy, the techniques underline the adage that the contributions of two or more employees are greater than the sum of their individual efforts. Furthermore, research has shown that working in a group setting strengthens employee commitment to the organization's goals, increases employee acceptance of decisions, and encourages a cooperative approach to workplace tasks.[24] Two collaborative techniques are discussed here: employee involvement groups and employee teams.

FIGURE 4.4

Computer Workstation Ergonomics Checklist

Use the following list to identify potential problem areas that should receive further investigation. Any "no" response may point to a problem.

1. Does the workstation ensure proper worker posture, such as
   - Thighs in the horizontal position?
   - Lower legs in the vertical position?
   - Feet flat on the floor or on a footrest?
   - Wrists straight and relaxed?

2. Does the chair
   - Adjust easily?
   - Have a padded seat with a rounded front?
   - Have an adjustable backrest?
   - Provide lumbar support?
   - Have casters?

3. Are the height and tilt of the work surface on which the keyboard is located adjustable?

4. Is the keyboard detachable?

5. Do keying actions require minimal force?

6. Is there an adjustable document holder?

7. Are armrests provided where needed?

8. Are glare and reflections minimized?

9. Does the monitor have brightness and contrast controls?

10. Is there sufficient space for knees and feet?

11. Can the workstation be used for either right- or left-handed activity?

Source: The National Institute for Occupational Safety and Health (NIOSH), *Elements of Ergonomics Programs: A Primer Based on Workplace Evaluations of Musculoskeletal Disorders* (Washington, DC: U.S. Government Printing Office, March 1997).

Employee Involvement Groups

Groups of five to ten employees doing similar or related work who meet regularly to identify, analyze, and suggest solutions to shared problems are often referred to as **employee involvement groups (EIs)**. Also widely known as *quality circles (QCs)*, EIs are used principally as a means of involving employees in the larger goals of the organization through their suggestions for improving product or service quality and cutting costs.[25] Generally, EIs recommend their solutions to management, which decides whether to implement them.

The employee involvement group process, illustrated in Figure 4.5, begins with EI members brainstorming job-related problems or concerns and gathering data about these issues. The process continues through the generation of solutions and recommendations that are then communicated to management. If the solutions are implemented, results are measured, and the EI and its members are usually recognized for the contributions they have made. EIs typically meet four or more hours per month, and the meetings are chaired by a group leader chosen from the group. The leader does not hold an authority position but instead serves as a discussion facilitator.

Although EIs have become an important employee contribution system, they are not without their critics. First, in order to achieve the results

employee involvement groups (EIs)

Groups of employees who meet to resolve problems or offer suggestions for organizational improvement

FIGURE **4.5**

The Dynamics of Employee Involvement Groups

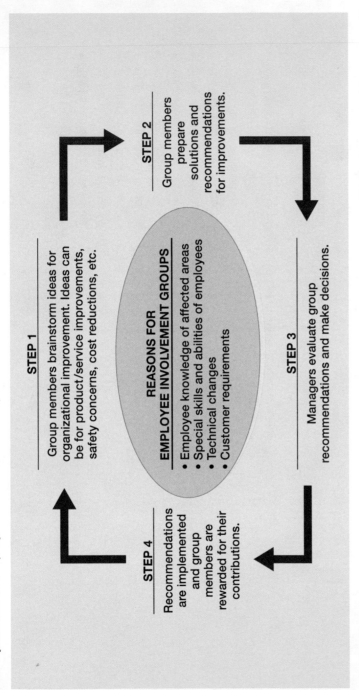

STEP 1

Group members brainstorm ideas for organizational improvement. Ideas can be for product/service improvements, safety concerns, cost reductions, etc.

STEP 2

Group members prepare solutions and recommendations for improvements.

REASONS FOR EMPLOYEE INVOLVEMENT GROUPS

- Employee knowledge of affected areas
- Special skills and abilities of employees
- Technical changes
- Customer requirements

STEP 3

Managers evaluate group recommendations and make decisions.

STEP 4

Recommendations are implemented and group members are rewarded for their contributions.

Source: Adapted from materials prepared by The Family and Relationship Center, 7946 Ivahoe Avenue, La Jolla, CA 92037.

desired, those participating in EIs must receive comprehensive training in problem identification, problem analysis, and various decision-making tools such as statistical analysis and cause-and-effect diagrams. Comprehensive training for EIs is often cited as the most important factor leading to their success. Second, managers should recognize the group when a recommendation is made, regardless of whether the recommendation is adopted. This approach encourages the group to continue coming up with ideas even when they are not all implemented by management. Third, some organizations have found that EIs run out of ideas, and management must feed them ideas to keep the process going. Finally, and most important, managers and supervisors must exhibit a participative/democratic leadership style in which employees are encouraged to work collaboratively with management to improve organizational performance.

Employee Teams

During the past decade, perhaps one of the more radical changes to how work is done is the introduction of organizational teams. Jim Barksdale, president and CEO of Netscape Communications, states, "These days it seems as if every time a task needs to be accomplished within an organization, a team is formed to do it." This statement simply emphasizes the increasing importance of teams to organizational success in an ever-dynamic business climate. At such diverse organizations as FedEx, Hewlett-Packard, and LucasFilm, producer of the *Star Wars* and *Indiana Jones* films, the benefits of employee teams have included more integration of individual skills, better performance in terms of quality and quantity, solutions to unique and complex problems, reduced delivery time, reduced turnover and absenteeism, and accomplishments among team members.[26]

Using the Internet

The Employee Involvement Association has interesting content on this issue at http://www.eianet.org

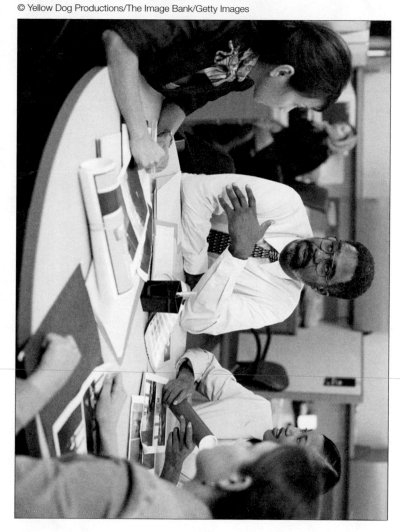

Teams create synergy through the integration of their members' knowledge, skills, and abilities and the acceptance of individual diversities.

employee teams
An employee contributions technique whereby work functions are structured for groups rather than for individuals and team members are given discretion in matters traditionally considered management prerogatives, such as process improvements, product or service development, and individual work assignments

Employee teams are a logical outgrowth of employee involvement and the philosophy of empowerment. Although many definitions of teams exist, we define a work team as a group of individuals working together toward a common purpose, in which members have complementary skills, members' work is mutually dependent, and the group has discretion over tasks performed. Furthermore, teams seek to make members of the work group share responsibility and accountability for their group's performance. Inherent in the concept of employee teams is that employees, not managers, are in the best position to contribute to workplace performance. With work teams, managers accept the notion that the group is the logical work unit for applying resources to resolve organizational problems and concerns.[27]

Teamwork also embraces the concept of *synergy*. Synergy occurs when the interaction and outcome of team members is greater than the sum of their individual efforts.[28] Unfortunately, synergy may not automatically happen, but rather, it must be nurtured within the team environment.[29] Figure 4.6 lists the factors contributing to a synergistic team setting.

Teams can operate in a variety of structures, each with different strategic purposes or functional activities. Figure 4.7 describes common team forms. One form, self-directed teams, is often championed as being the highest form of team structure. Self-directed teams, also called *autonomous work groups, self-managed teams,* or *high-performance teams,* are groups of employees who are accountable for a "whole" work process or segment that delivers a product or service to an internal or external customer. For example, in a manufacturing environment, a team might be responsible for a whole product (e.g., a computer screen) or a clearly defined segment of the production process, such as the building of an engine for a passenger car. Similarly, in a service environment, a team is usually responsible for entire groupings of products and services, often serving clients in a designated geographical area. Typical team functions include setting work schedules, dealing directly with external customers, training team members, setting performance targets, budgeting, inventory management, and purchasing equipment or services. To operate efficiently, team members acquire multiple skills enabling them to perform a variety of job tasks.

FIGURE **4.6**

Synergistic Team Characteristics

Team synergy is heightened when team members engage in these positive behaviours.

- *Support.* The team exhibits an atmosphere of inclusion. All team members speak up and feel free to offer constructive comments.

- *Listening and clarification.* Active listening is practised. Members honestly listen to others and seek clarification on discussion points. Team members summarize discussions held.

- *Disagreement.* Disagreement is seen as natural and is expected. Member comments are nonjudgmental and focus on factual issues rather than personality conflicts.

- *Consensus.* Team members reach agreements through consensus decision making. Consensus decisions require finding a proposal that is acceptable to all team members, even if not the first choice of individual members. Common ground among ideas is sought.

- *Acceptance.* Team members are valued as individuals, recognizing that each person brings a valuable mix of skills and abilities to team operations.

- *Quality.* Each team member is committed to excellent performance. There is emphasis on continuous improvement and attention to detail.

To compete in today's national and international markets, managers increasingly form virtual teams. **Virtual teams** use advanced computer and telecommunications technology to link team members who are geographically dispersed—often world-wide. Management may form a project team (see Figure 4.7) to develop a new pharmaceutical drug and have the team operate in a virtual environment to achieve its goal. For a major telecommunication client, IBM used a global team to develop a Web-based tool for launching new services. The team included members from Japan, Brazil, and Britain and delivered a finished product in two months, a considerable reduction in product delivery time.[30] Although virtual teams have many benefits, they are

virtual team
A team with widely dispersed members linked together through computer and telecommunications technology

FIGURE **4.7**

Forms of Employee Teams

Cross-functional teams: A group staffed with a mix of specialists (e.g., marketing, production, engineering) and formed to accomplish a specific objective. Cross-functional teams are based on assigned rather than voluntary membership.

Project teams: A group formed specifically to design a new product or service. Members are assigned by management on the basis of their ability to contribute to success. The group normally disbands after task completion.

Self-directed teams: Groups of highly trained individuals performing a set of interdependent job tasks within a natural work unit. Team members use consensus decision making to perform work duties, solve problems, or deal with internal or external customers.

Task force teams: A task force is formed by management to immediately resolve a major problem. The group is responsible for developing a long-term plan for problem resolution that may include a charge for implementing the solution proposed.

Process-improvement teams: A group made up of experienced people from different departments or functions and charged with improving quality, decreasing waste, or enhancing productivity in processes that affect all departments or functions involved. Team members are normally appointed by management.

not without problems.[31] Paulette Tichenor, president of Organizational Renaissance, a team-training organization, notes these concerns with virtual teams: language and cultural barriers, unclear objectives, time conflicts due to diverse geographical locations, and selecting people who can work in a collaborative setting.[32]

Navi Radjou, an expert in network innovations, notes, "One problem with distributing work is that you lose the intimacy of talking things through at the local café." To reduce this problem, companies such as Nokia are careful to select people who have a collaborative mindset. At Nokia, team members are encouraged to network online and to share their pictures and personal biographies. In another example, Accenture, a worldwide consulting organization, yearly involves 400 managers in virtual team leadership training. The goal is to create team effectiveness and to promote understanding of cross-cultural differences.

Regardless of the structure or purpose of the team, the following characteristics have been identified with successful teams:

- Commitment to shared goals and objectives
- Motivated and energetic team members
- Open and honest communication
- Shared leadership
- Clear role assignments
- Climate of cooperation, collaboration, trust, and accountability
- Recognition of conflict and its positive resolution

Unfortunately, not all teams succeed or operate to their full potential. Therefore, in adopting the work team concept, organizations must address several issues that could present obstacles to effective team function, including overly high expectations, group compensation, specialized team training, career movement, and conflict resolution. For example, new team members must be retrained to work outside their primary functional areas, and compensation systems must be constructed to reward individuals for team accomplishments. Importantly, research shows that teams achieve greater effectiveness when team members initially establish team ground rules, or team norms, for operational and behavioural success. HRM Experience, at the end of the chapter, presents an exercise to set team ground rules.

Another difficulty with work teams is that they alter the traditional manager–employee relationship. Managers often find it hard to adapt to the role of leader rather than supervisor and sometimes feel threatened by the growing power of the team and the reduced power of management. Furthermore, some employees may also have difficulty adapting to a role that includes traditional supervisory responsibilities. Therefore, from our experience in working with teams, extensive attention must be given to training team members as they move through the four stages of team development—forming, storming, norming, and performing.[33] Complete training would cover the importance of skills in (1) team leadership, (2) mission/goal setting, (3) conduct of meetings, (4) team decision making, (5) conflict resolution, (6) effective communication, and (7) diversity awareness.[34]

FLEXIBLE WORK SCHEDULES

Flexible work schedules are not a true part of job design because job tasks and responsibilities are not changed. Nevertheless, we discuss adjustments in work schedules here because they alter the normal workweek of five 8-hour days in which all employees begin and end their workday at the same time. Employers may depart from the traditional workday or workweek in their attempt to improve organizational productivity and morale by giving employees increased control over the hours they work.[35]

Speaking on the importance of flexible work schedules, Lois Brakon, codirector of the Families and Work Institute, notes, "Flexible schedules are going to be the way good, competitive businesses work." Flexible work schedules may be assigned by the organization or requested by individual employees—and are

OUTCOME 7

Highlights in HRM 4.3

Why Students Value Flexible Scheduling

When students choose an employer, they consider work–life balance to be the fourth most important factor in their selection decision. The first three considerations are opportunities for advancement, good people to work with, and good people to report to. Students do want to be challenged, but many are not interested in committing to an 80-hour workweek. Flexible work arrangements, such as flextime, job sharing, a compressed workweek, and telecommuting, offer the following advantages:

- Reduces the time and cost of travelling to work. Students with high debt loads would be attracted to these cost savings.
- Enables the student to complete his or her degree part-time. Through job sharing or the compressed

workweek, students can attend classes and earn money to help pay for their education, while at the same time acquiring work experience and contacts that may prove helpful in obtaining that first job after graduation.

- Provides the option for work–life balance. Students have a broad range of interests, from volunteering with disadvantaged youth to extreme skiing, and flexible work arrangements allow them the time to enjoy these activities.

One size fits all does not apply to a diverse workforce. To attract employees of various ages and lifestyles, the key is flexibility. By 2009, 90 percent of employers will offer flex hours and 71 percent will offer employees the option to work from home on a part-time basis.

Source: Adapted from Graham Donald, "What Students Want," *Canadian HR Reporter* (December 9, 2006): 15, 21; Manny Campione and Laura Williams, "Diverse Labour Force Demands Diverse Options," *Canadian HR Reporter* (October 23, 2006): 14.

---

particularly valuable to students (see Highlights in HRM 4.3). The more common flexible work schedules are the compressed workweek, flextime, job sharing, and telecommuting.

Compressed Workweek

Under the compressed workweek, the number of days in the workweek is shortened by lengthening the number of hours worked per day. This schedule is best illustrated by the four-day, 40-hour week, generally referred to as 4/10 or 4/40. Employees working a four-day workweek might work 10 hours a day, Monday through Thursday. Although the 4/10 schedule is probably the best known, other compressed arrangements include reducing weekly hours to 38 or 36 hours or scheduling 80 hours over nine days (9/80), taking one day off every other week. Managers cite the following reasons for implementing compressed workweek schedules:

- Recruitment and retention of employees[36]
- Coordinating employee work schedules with production schedules
- Accommodating the leisure time activities of employees while facilitating employee personal appointments (medical, dental, financial)
- Improvements in employee job satisfaction and morale[37]

Flextime

Flextime, or flexible working hours, permits employees the option of choosing daily starting and quitting times, provided that they work a certain number of hours per day or week. With flextime, employees are given considerable latitude in scheduling their work. However, there is a "core period" during the morning and

flextime

Flexible working hours that permit employees the option of choosing daily starting and quitting times, provided that they work a set number of hours per day or week afternoon when all employees are required to be on the job. Flexible working hours are most common in service-type organizations—financial institutions, government agencies, and other organizations with large clerical operations.

Flextime provides both employees and employers with several advantages. By allowing employees greater flexibility in work scheduling, employers can reduce some of the traditional causes of tardiness and absenteeism.[38] Employees can adjust their work to accommodate their particular lifestyles and, in doing so, gain greater job satisfaction. Employees can also schedule their working hours for the time of day when they are most productive. In addition, variations in arrival and departure times can help reduce traffic congestion at the peak commuting hours. In some cases, employees require less time to commute, and the pressures of meeting a rigid schedule are reduced.

From the employer's standpoint, flextime can be most helpful in recruiting and meeting the challenges of age diversity in the workforce.[39] It has proved invaluable to organizations wishing to improve service to customers or clients by extending operating hours. Qwest, a telecommunications company, uses flextime to keep its business offices open for customers who cannot get there during the day. Research demonstrates that flextime can have a positive impact on the performance measures of reliability, quality, and quantity of employee work.

There are, of course, several disadvantages to flextime. First, it is not suited to some jobs. It is not feasible, for example, where specific workstations must be staffed at all times. Second, it can create problems for managers in communicating with and instructing employees. Flextime schedules may also force these managers to extend their workweek if they are to exercise control over their subordinates.

Job Sharing

The arrangement whereby two part-time employees perform a job that otherwise would be held by one full-time employee is called **job sharing**. Job sharers usually work three days a week, "creating an overlap day for extended face-to-face conferencing." Their pay is three-fifths of a regular salary. Employers note that without job sharing two good employees might otherwise be lost.

Job sharing is suited to the needs of families in which one or both spouses desire to work only part-time.[40] It is suited also to the needs of older workers who want to phase into retirement by shortening their workweek. For the employer, the work of part-time employees can be scheduled to conform to peaks in the daily workload. Job sharing can also limit layoffs in hard economic times. A final benefit is that employees engaged in job sharing have time off during the week to accommodate personal needs, so they are less likely to be absent.

Job sharing does have several problems, however. Employers may not want to employ two people to do the work of one because the time required to orient and train a second employee constitutes an added burden. Additionally, managers may find it more difficult to supervise two employees particularly when one job sharer is not dependable, job sharers cannot effectively work together, or they simply distrust one another.[41] The key to making job sharing work is good communications between partners, who can use a number of ways to stay in contact—phone calls, written updates, e-mail, and voice mail.

Telecommuting

Telecommuting is the use of personal computers, networks, and other communications technology to do work in the home that is traditionally done in the workplace. A variant of telecommuting is the *virtual office*, where employees are in the field helping customers or are stationed at other remote locations working as if they were in the home office.[42] Both managers and HR professionals note the following advantages of telecommuting.[43]

---

job sharing

The arrangement whereby two part-time employees perform a job that otherwise would be held by one full-time employee

telecommuting

Use of personal computers, networks, and other communications technology to do work in the home that is traditionally done in the workplace

- Increased flexibility for employees—better work–life balance
- Reduced absenteeism
- Retention of valued employees who might otherwise quit
- Reduced "carbon footprints" through minimizing daily commuting
- Increased productivity (e.g., reduced wasted office time)
- Lower overhead costs and reduced office space

While telecommuting offers significant benefits to employers, it also presents potential drawbacks. These include the loss of creativity as employees are not interacting with one another on a regular basis, the difficulty of developing appropriate performance standards and evaluation systems for telecommuters, and the need to formulate an appropriate technology strategy for allocating the necessary equipment.[44] Traditional line managers accustomed to managing by observation may find supervising distributed employees stressful. Additionally, managers may believe that telecommuting negatively affects employee–supervisor relationships through loss of knowledge or information, training or development, and a sense of connectedness.[45]

Employers wishing to have their employees telecommute must comply with wage and hour laws, liability and workers' compensation regulations, equipment purchase or rental agreements with employees, and all employment equity regulations (see Chapter 3). Employees who are denied the opportunity to work from home may feel discriminated against and resent home telecommuters. Figure 4.8 presents suggestions for establishing a successful telecommuting program. Highlights in HRM 4.4 features work–life balance expert, Nora Spinks.

FIGURE **4.8**

Keys for Successful Telecommuting

- *Identify jobs best suited to distance work.* Those involving sales, customer service, and auditing are logical choices.
- *Select responsible employees.* Employees who are self-starters, motivated, and trustworthy and who can work independently are ideal candidates. Establish employee feedback procedures and performance review methods for employee evaluation.
- *Establish formalized telecommuting procedures.* Telecommuting guidelines could cover hours of availability, office reporting periods, performance expectations, and weekly progress reports or e-mail updates.
- *Begin a formal training program.* Training for both telecommuters and managers should include the technical aspects of equipment usage and relationship factors such as how and when to contact the office or availability and location of support facilities.
- *Keep telecommuters informed.* Physical separation can make telecommuters feel isolated and invisible. Department and staff updates, inclusion of telecommuters on project teams, required attendance at meetings, and "chat room" discussions all keep telecommuters "in the loop."
- *Recognize when telecommuting isn't working.* State in telecommunicating policies that the arrangement may be terminated when it no longer serves company needs or if the employee's performance declines.

Source: Adapted from Barbara Hemphill, "Telecommuting Productivity," *Occupational Health and Safety* 73, no. 3 (March 2004): 16.

Highlights in HRM 4.4

Flextime and Work–Life Balance

Nora Spinks, president and CEO of Work–Life Harmony Enterprises, works with employers to create organizational cultures that enable employees to achieve work–life balance. The firm's goal is to develop successful work environments where individuals and organizations have the ability to reach their full potential and where employees have full and satisfying lives outside their work.

Spinks asserts that employers benefit from these family-friendly policies: "The most effective and productive employees are those who do work they enjoy; are challenged; have access to the necessary resources to meet that challenge; have control over how they work; receive recognition, rewards, and compensation based on the effort they put forth; and feel their life outside work is respected and valued. These employees are highly resilient. In today's world of work, individual and organizational resiliency is critical for success. People in resilient, adaptable, responsive environments have the ability to change, the capacity to adapt to change, the energy to drive change and the flexibility to react positively to change, regardless of the intensity or the factors outside of their immediate control such as market forces, economic pressures, and social or political circumstances."

Today's most popular employee-support initiative is workplace flexibility: flextime with core hours and flexible start and end times, compressed workweeks (full workload completed in less than five days per week), and/or permanent part-time hours with equal status, pro-rated benefits, and the same development opportunities as full-time employees. Gaining in popularity are creative alternatives such as extended workweeks (full workload completed in six days) and self-funded or radical sabbaticals (setting aside a portion of pay for a period of time and taking an extended leave while collecting the banked salary—e.g., 2.5 years working at 85 percent pay and six months away from the workplace on a self-funded sabbatical).

Employees are using the time gained from workplace flexibility to fulfill family responsibilities, create a

balanced lifestyle, continue their education, make a contribution to their community, or volunteer in developing countries.

Spinks argues strongly for these policies: "Establishing control over hours of work has very specific, well-documented results: reduction in illness, injury, absenteeism, presenteeism (physically present, but mentally and emotionally absent), turnover, conflict, and unhealthy lifestyles and behaviours such as smoking, drinking, and drugs.

"When you work too hard or too long, you tend to rely on substances such as nicotine, caffeine, or sugar boosters to get you through the day. When you are tired all the time, your ability to solve problems and resolve conflicts is decreased significantly. When you are rundown, you become uninterested and disengaged. Employees who have control over their working hours have more energy, more time, and are more engaged at home, at work, and in the community. Employers, customers, and coworkers benefit during the day, and employees, their family, friends, and community benefit at the end of the day.

"When I started in this field many years ago, employers had no understanding of the issues. I received several letters from companies saying, 'Thank you for your interest, but all our charitable dollars have been allocated for this year.' So we began to build the business case for supportive work environments. In the '80s and '90s, progressive HR departments began to implement programs and policies to address the issues. Now, employers across all sectors, from all industries, are beginning to see the strategic advantages of a family-friendly, employee-supportive work environment. I now work with CEOs in boardrooms, integrating these concepts into corporate strategy.

"I think there are many reasons why employers are embracing these policies now: labour force demographics, tight labour markets, and an increasing body of evidence documenting the costs and benefits of supportive work environments and the high costs of work–life imbalance and stress in the workplace."

Small Business APPLICATION

As we have seen, to effectively provide performance feedback, train, or recruit new employees, developing and optimizing job requirements acts as the cornerstone. While this is not different in small companies, what is different is that in small enterprises (1) these job requirements may be less structured than in large companies, (2) requirements may be more individualized to factor the individual talents of team members, (3) these requirements are less likely to be written down.

For example, let's say that we have a small Internet development company with 25 employees. These 25 employees are involved either in selling, website development, or website maintenance, for a variety of clients. While there may be general classifications of roles in that some people will be involved in sales, some in development, and some in maintenance, it will likely be the case that every employee in the company, rather than having specific duties, will be drawn upon based on his or her skills and how busy that person is. For example, a client may have identified it they would like to have a new feature added to its website. The employee responsible for the support of this site may not be the best person on the team to develop this new feature. The entire team will be consulted to determine not just who has or could

develop the skill to do this. The end result is that the determination of what is to be done and who is to do it is based on situational requirements and the allocation of talent at that point in time.

This highlights a primary challenge in all organizations: that organizations hire individuals, but then manage teams to deliver on changing requirements. In small enterprises, especially, while the core job requirements will consist of a collection of tasks generally associated with the performance of the role, employees will be required to support requirements outside a prescribed job requirement. Small enterprises often neglect actions such as written job requirements or written performance reviews. These acts may be deemed to be unnecessary formalities that are counter to the informal culture in small companies. The advantages to both the company and employees are two-fold. Firstly, documenting job requirements increases operational efficiency in recruiting and training future employees. Secondly, performance evaluations result in improving the effectiveness and morale of existing staff. What is different in small enterprises is that each of these will be carried out by a manager without the support of a human resources professional.

SUMMARY

OUTCOME 1   Job requirements reflect the different duties, tasks, and responsibilities contained in jobs. Job requirements, in turn, influence HR functions performed by managers, including recruitment, selection, training and development, performance appraisal, compensation, and various labour relations activities.

OUTCOME 2   Job analysis data may be gathered using several collection methods—interviews, questionnaires, observations, and diaries. Other more quantitative approaches include the position analysis questionnaire system, critical incident method, task inventory analysis, and

competency-based analysis. It is the prevailing opinion of the courts that HRM decisions on employment, performance appraisal, and promotions must be based on specific criteria that are job related. These criteria can be determined objectively only by analyzing the requirements of each job.

OUTCOME 3   The format of job descriptions varies widely, often reflecting the needs of the organization and the expertise of the writer. As a minimum, job descriptions should contain a job title, a job identification section, and a job duties, or essential functions, section. A job specification section also may be included. Job descriptions should be written in clear and specific terms with consideration given to their legal implications.

OUTCOME 4

Job design is a combination of four basic considerations: organizational objectives; industrial engineering concerns of analyzing work methods and establishing time standards; ergonomic considerations, which accommodate human capabilities and limitations to job tasks; and employee contributions.

OUTCOME 5

In the job characteristics model, five job factors contribute to increased job performance and satisfaction—skill variety, task identity, task significance, autonomy, and feedback. All factors should be built into jobs, since each factor influences different employee psychological states. When jobs are enriched through the job characteristics model, employees experience more meaningfulness in their jobs, acquire more job responsibility, and receive direct feedback from the tasks they perform.

OUTCOME 6

To improve the internal process of organizations and increase productivity, greater efforts are being made by organizations to involve groups of employees in work operations. Employee involvement groups are composed of employees in work units charged with offering suggestions for improving product or service quality or fostering workplace effectiveness. Employee teams stress employee collaboration over individual accomplishment. Teams rely on the expertise and different abilities of members to achieve a specific goal or objective. Self-directed teams are characterized by their willingness to perform traditional managerial tasks.

OUTCOME 7

Changes in work schedules—which include the compressed workweek, flextime, job sharing, and telecommuting—permit employees to adjust their work periods to accommodate their particular lifestyles. Employees can select from among these HR techniques to accommodate diverse employee needs while fostering organizational effectiveness.

KEY TERMS

critical incident method, 145
employee empowerment, 152
employee involvement groups (EIs), 155
employee teams 157
ergonomics 154
flextime, 160
industrial engineering, 153

job analysis, 140
job characteristics model 151
job description, 139
job design, 149
job enrichment 150
job family, 138
job sharing, 161
job specification, 138

job, 138
position analysis questionnaire (PAQ), 143
position, 138
task inventory analysis 145
telecommuting, 161
virtual team, 158

DISCUSSION QUESTIONS

1. Place yourself in the position of general manager of a service department. How might formally written job requirements help you manage your work unit?

2. Discuss the various methods by which job analysis can be completed. Compare and contrast these methods, noting the pros or cons of each.

3. Working with a group of three or four students, develop different job descriptions based on your personal knowledge of a job. Compare the descriptions, highlighting similarities and differences.

4. Explain how industrial engineering and ergonomics can both clash with and complement each other in the design of jobs.

5. The job characteristics model has five components that enhance employee jobs—skill variety, task identity, task significance, autonomy, and feedback. Give an example illustrating how each component can be used to improve the organization and the job of the employee. (Suggestion: Consider your present or a recent job to answer this question.)

6. Figure 4.7 shows the different forms of employee teams. Provide an example of where each type of team can be used. How do teams create synergy?

7. Does a four-day (10 hours a day) workweek result in higher productivity? Help the environment? Debate these issues.

INTERNET EXERCISE

The Canadian Centre for Occupational Health and Safety http://www.ccohs.ca/oshanswers/hsprograms/telework.html is an excellent source for information on telecommuting. Using this information, develop a case that you could present to your employer to allow you to telecommute.

HRM EXPERIENCE

Establishing Ground Rules for Team Success

Professional trainers understand that setting ground rules for teams is a cornerstone for continued team success. Ground rules—or team norms—are agreed-on formal rules that guide group member behaviour. Norms established prior to the team's task regulate the behaviour of group members. Ground rules simply state how members want to be treated and how members agree to treat others. When team members follow the established norms, the norms help maintain order and promote positive behaviour, and can be used to correct undesirable actions. Remember, because teams operate in different settings, different norms may be appropriate in different arrangements.

Assignment

1. Working within your team, select what you believe are the ten most important norms for team behaviour.

2. From the following Behaviour List, have each team member *silently* select two lists of ten items each of the behaviours they believe most critical for team success. The first list of ten items (your A list) is considered the most important for group conduct. The second list (the B list) is desired items but those not of major importance.

3. In a group discussion, have all team members select a final list of ten items from both lists. These become your team's final norms. Select no more than ten items. During your discussion, items can be modified or combined to meet your team's specific needs.

4. Prepare a written document of chosen behaviours and have all team members sign the form. You have now established a written contract for positive team conduct.

Behaviour List

While working in our team, individuals should…

1. Do their fair share of the work.
2. Check to ensure that everyone clearly understands what is to be done.
3. Encourage planning, including short-range agendas as well as long-range goals.
4. Encourage open and candid opinions about issues.
5. Listen willingly and carefully to other people's ideas, even if those people have a different viewpoint.
6. Prepare thoroughly before meetings.
7. Make team members feel at ease in discussion.
8. Ask questions when they do not clearly understand tasks or procedures.
9. Propose specific analyses of the pros and cons of decisions faced by the team.
10. Follow through on task assignments.
11. Help other members when assistance is requested.
12. Treat all team members as equals.
13. Paraphrase or restate what someone else says in order to check meaning.
14. Openly voice opinions and share ideas.
15. Be flexible in arranging meeting schedules.
16. Compliment others for things they have said or done.
17. Be willing to meet whenever it is necessary to discuss a problem.

continued

18. Deal with conflict directly, bringing it to the attention of the team.
19. Express enthusiasm about what the team is doing.
20. Encourage budgeting of the team's time.
21. At the end of a meeting, restate their own responsibilities to check for agreement.
22. Be serious about the team's work.
23. Arrive on time for regularly scheduled meetings.
24. Be willing to listen to other team members' ideas.
25. Get the team's approval on important matters before proceeding.

BIZFLIX EXERCISES

INTOLERABLE CRUELTY: JUST DOING MY JOB

This chapter discussed several aspects of job analysis and job design. Try to apply much of that discussion to this scene from the film *Intolerable Cruelty*. Use the following questions below as guides to your viewing.

Ruthless, beautiful Marilyn Rexroth (Catherine Zeta-Jones) matches the brilliance of divorce attorney Miles Massey (George Clooney). Conflict rises and falls as the two try to outwit each other in this charming romantic comedy. The film twists and turns in typical Coen brothers (coscreenwriters; Joel Cohen, director) fashion as it reaches its predictable end.

This scene comes from "The War Room" segment that occurs about 20 minutes into the film. It follows Rex Rexroth's (George Herrmann) escapade with a young woman (Kristen Dattilo). His wife, Marilyn Rexroth, hired private detective Gus Petch (Cedric the Entertainer) to videotape the event. He now needs some legal help. Miles Massey meets his new client and discusses the case. The film continues with a group of women sitting by The Waters swimming pool talking about their ex- and present husbands.

What to Watch for and Ask Yourself

• What knowledge, skills, and abilities (KSAs) are required for the successful performance of Miles Massey's job?
• Recall the earlier chapter section "Job Analysis." Apply some observations from that section to this scene. What duties, tasks, and activities do you infer from the scene for Massey's job?
• Job design views certain job characteristics as important for a person's motivation and satisfaction (see the earlier section "Job Design"). Which of the five core job dimensions appear(s) in Miles Massey's job?

CASE STUDY 1

DUCKS UNLIMITED CANADA

Ducks Unlimited Canada, a not-for-profit environmental agency, has as its goal the protection of wetland habitats in Canada. Relying on its 100,000 members, 7,000 volunteers, and 330 employees, this charitable organization has saved more than 7.29 million hectares (18 million acres) in Canada. Ducks Unlimited has no problem attracting biologists, scientists, and accountants, because its recruits are committed to a conservation ethic and are dedicated to protecting the environment. It has also helped recruitment that Ducks Unlimited has reorganized itself to flatten its management structure. Its goal was to empower the employees and facilitate decision making. People working in the field no longer have to go up and down the power ladder to obtain approvals at every step. Field employees feel more in control of what they are doing.

The human resources administrator cites many advantages to an empowered workforce: increased retention, increased motivation, and decreased absenteeism and sick days.

Source: Adapted from "Taking Care of the People," *Canadian Health Care Manager* 6, no. 3 (April–May 1999): 5–9.

QUESTIONS

1. What arguments could be advanced both for and against the use of employee empowerment?

2. Empowerment is mainly a motivational tool, but at Ducks Unlimited the employees arrive dedicated and committed to the environmental cause. Does Ducks Unlimited need to implement empowerment?

3. How might a manager at a traditional organization react to the implementation of empowerment?

CASE STUDY 2

BUT MY JOB HAS CHANGED

Job descriptions are a critical tool used for job orientation and training and, importantly, in annual employee performance evaluations. When the duties and responsibilities listed in the job description do not reflect current job content, employee/management disagreements can arise, as this case illustrates.

Both employees and managers agree that Brenda Batten has been an exceptional employee. As a senior technical representative (STR) for Blackhawk Aironics, she is valued for her knowledge in airplane instrumentation. One manager described her as "simply an expert in the complex technology of satellite weather systems."

In May 2007, Blackhawk Aironics implemented a new work reorganization plan. STRs such as Brenda now work largely by telecommuting with managers and engineers at company headquarters and with customers scattered throughout North America. Additionally, under the new work plan, STRs were given more freedom to deal directly with customers and engineers without supervisory intervention. This freedom greatly facilitated customer service needs and demands in an aviation market everyone considers highly dynamic.

Brenda's current job description reflects the technical dimensions of her position but not the telecommuting requirements now performed. Personal competencies such as decision making, self-motivation, problem solving, and communication skills are not covered.

In May 2008, Brenda met with her manager, Martin Eaton, for her annual performance review. Unfortunately, unlike past meetings, which were highly satisfactory, this meeting quickly developed into a disagreement. At the centre of the controversy were the factors to be used to measure Brenda's new job demands. Martin wanted to place major emphasis on the tasks and duties listed in her current job description. As he explained to Brenda, "I hardly see you anymore, and I have no objective criteria or performance data by which to measure those behaviours you now use." Brenda, in response, acknowledged that some things in the current job description were still important aspects of her job, but overall the current job description did not capture the full scope of her new duties and responsibilities. Brenda concluded that she was satisfied with Martin's evaluation of the technical aspects of her job, but she was clearly not pleased with the overall evaluation of her performance. As she told Martin, "It's simply not fair; you just don't know what I do now."

QUESTIONS

1. Given the facts of this case, is it possible for Brenda and Martin to reach a satisfactory result? Explain.

2. How could an organization go about identifying and measuring the personal competencies of employees?

3. How could the company prevent this problem from occurring in the future? Explain.

Source: Based on an actual case known to the authors. All names and locations are fictitious.

CAREER COUNSEL

Complete the exercise on the *Managing Human Resources* website to find your dream job (http://www.belcourt6e.nelson.com).

NOTES AND REFERENCES

1. Narasimhaiah Gorla, Ravi Chinta, and Tam Wai Chu, "An Enhanced Business Process Re-engineering Model for Supply Chain Management and a Case Study," *Journal of Information Technology Case and Application Research* 9, no. 2 (2007): 5.

2. Michael Hammer, "The Process Audit," *Harvard Business Review* 85, no. 4 (April 2007): 111.

3. Peter Coy, "COG or Co-worker?; The Organization Man Isn't Extinct or Even Endangered—But the Role Has Been Refined Over the Past 100 Years," *Business Week*, Issue 4047 (August 2007): 58.

4. Arnold B. Bakker, Evangelia Demeroob, and Willem Verbeke, "Using the Job Demands Resources Model to Predict Burnout and Performance," *Human Resources Management* 43, no. 1 (Spring 2004): 83.

5. Valerie L. Myers and Janice L. Dreachslin, "Recruitment and Retention of a Diverse Workforce: Challenges and Opportunities," *Journal of Healthcare Management* 52, no. 5 (September/October 2007): 290.

6. Paul Lyons, "Charting Skills for Quality Improvement," *The Journal of Quality and Participation* 30, no. 1 (Spring 2007): 30.

7. George T. Milkovich and Jerry M. Newman, *Compensation*, 9th ed. (Boston: McGraw-Hill Companies, 2007).

8. Frederick P. Morgeson, Kelly Delaney-Klinger, Melinda S. Mayfield, Philip Ferrara, and Michael A. Campion, "Self-Presentation Processes in Job Analysis: A Field Experiment Investigating Inflation in Abilities, Tasks, and Competencies," *Journal of Applied Psychology* 89, no. 4 (August 2004): 674.

9. Interview with job analyst Carol Tucker, Mesa, Arizona, May 10, 2006.

10. http://www5.hrsdc.gc.ca/NOC/English/NOC/2006/Welcome.aspx.

11. A detailed description of different job analysis techniques is beyond the scope of this text. For those interested in more comprehensive information or job analysis tools, see Michael T. Bannick, Edward L. Levine, and Frederick P. Morgeson, *Job and Work Analysis: Methods, Research, and Applications for Human Resource Management*, 2nd ed. (Thousand Oaks, CA: Sage, 2007).

12. Jessica Marquez, "A Talent Strategy Overhaul at Pfizer," *Workforce Management* 86, no. 3 (February 12, 2007): 1.

13. Marqie Mader-Clark, *Job Description Handbook* (Berkeley, CA: Nolo Press, 2006).

14. Gensheng Liu, Rachna Shah, and Roger G. Schroeder, "Linking Work Design to Mass Customization: A Socio-technical Systems Perspective," *Decision Sciences* 37, no. 4 (November 2006): 519.

15. Pooja Garg and Renu Rastogi, "New Models of Job Design: Motivating Employees' Performance," *The Journal of Management Development* 25, no. 6 (2006): 572.

16. For Herzberg's important article on job enrichment, see Frederick Herzberg, "One More Time: How Do You Motivate Employees?" *Harvard Business Review* 46, no. 2 (January–February 1968): 53–62.

17. For the original article on the job characteristics model, see J. Richard Hackman and Greg R. Oldham, "Motivation through the Design of Work: Test of a Theory," *Organizational Behavior and Human Performance* 16, no. 2 (August 1976): 250–279.

18. Jed DeVaro, Robert Li, and Dana Brookshire, "Analyzing the Job Characteristics Model: New Support from a Cross-Section of Establishments," *The International Journal of Human Resource Management* 18, no. 6 (June 2007): 986.

19. Richard E. Wilmot and Robert Galford, "A Commitment to Trust," *Communication World* 24, no. 2 (March/April 2007): 34.

20. Denise Robitaille, "Invaluable Contributions," *Industrial Engineering* 39, no. 1 (January 2007): 32.

21. Laura Baron, James Vander Spek, and Wendy Young, "The Economics of Ergonomics," *Journal of Accountancy* 222, no. 6 (December 2006): 34.

22. Julian Faraway and Matthew P. Reed, "Statistics for Digital Human Motion Modeling in Ergonomics," *Technometrics* 49, no. 3 (August 2007): 277.

23. Bernie Knill, "Practical Ergonomics for Plant People," *Material Handling Management* 57, no. 2 (September 2002): 53.

24. Andrew J. DuBrin, *Fundamentals of Organizational Behavior*, 4th ed. (Cincinnati, OH: South-Western, 2007), Chapter 10.

25. Keith Ayers, "Get Employees to Help you Increase Productivity and Profitability," *Rural Telecommunications* 26, no. 5 (September/October 2007): 26.

26. Brian Hindo, "The Empire Strikes at Silos," *BusinessWeek*, August 20, 2007, 63.

27. Roy C. Herrenkohl, *Becoming a Team: Achieving a Goal* (South-Western, 2004).

28. Vojko Potocan and Bostjan Kuralt, "Synergy in Business: Some New Suggestions," *Journal of American Academy of Business* 12, no. 1 (September 2007): 199.

29. Leigh Thompson, "Improving the Creativity of Organizational Work Groups," *The Academy of Management Executive* 17, no. 1 (February 2003): 96.

30. Michael Mandel, "Which Way to the Future," *BusinessWeek*, August 20, 2007, 45.

31. Laura A. Hambley, Thomas A. O'Neil, and Theresa J. B. Klien, "Virtual Team Leadership: The Effects of Leadership Style and Communication Medium on Team Interaction Styles and Outcomes," *Organizational Behavior and Human Decision Processes* 103, no. 1 (May 2007): 1.

32. Interview with Paulette Tichenor, Arizona State University, Tempe, Arizona, January 18, 2007.

33. For a discussion of the stages of team development, see Don Hellriegel and John W. Slocum, Jr., *Organizational Behavior*, 11th ed. (Cincinnati, OH: South-Western, 2007).

34. Stephen B. Knouse, "Building Task Cohesion to Bring Teams Together," *Quality Progress* 40, no. 3 (March 2007): 49.

35. Michelle Conlin, "Smashing the Clock," *BusinessWeek*, December 11, 2006, 60. See also Susan Meisinger, "Flexible Schedules Make Powerful Perks," *HR Magazine* 52, no. 4 (April 2007): 12.

36. Kathy Gurchiek, "Good News for Moms Reconsidering Work," *HR Magazine* 51, no. 7 (August 2006): 39.

37. James A. Breaugh and N. Kathleen Frye, "An Examination of the Antecedents and Consequences of the Use of Family-friendly Benefits," *Journal of Management Issues* 19, no. 1 (Spring 2007): 35.

38. Rita Zeidner, "Bending with the Times," *HR Magazine* 53, no. 7 (July 2008): 10.

39. Nancy Sutton Bell and Marvin Narz, "Meeting the Challenges of Age Diversity in the Workplace," *The CPA Journal* 77, no. 2 (February 2007): 56.

40. "Have You Considered Job Sharing as a Retention Tool?," *HRfocus* 83, no. 9 (September 2006): 10.

41. Susan Berfield, "Two for the Cubicle," *BusinessWeek*, July 24, 2006, 88.

42. Tammy Dewar, "Virtual Teams—Virtually Impossible," *Performance Improvement* 45, no. 5 (May/June 2006): 22.

43. www.wikipedia.org/wiki/telecommuting, retrieved July 30, 2009.

44. Wendell Joice, "Implementing Telework: The Technology Issue," *Public Manager* 36, no. 2 (Summer 2007): 64.

45. Marjorie Deruen, "The Remote Connection," *HR Magazine* 52, no. 3 (March 2007): 111.

CHAPTER 5

Expanding the Talent Pool: Recruitment and Careers

After studying this chapter, you should be able to

[OUTCOME] **1** Explain the advantages and disadvantages of external recruitment.

[OUTCOME] **2** Explain the advantages and disadvantages of recruiting from within the organization.

[OUTCOME] **3** Discuss how job opportunities can be inventoried and employee potential assessed.

[OUTCOME] **4** Explain how career management programs integrate the needs of individual employees and their organizations.

[OUTCOME] **5** Describe the conditions that help make a career management program successful.

[OUTCOME] **6** Explain why diverse recruitment and career development activities are important to organizations.

In earlier chapters, we stressed that many HR challenges centre on the idea that organizations increasingly compete on the basis of their employees' talents and capabilities. Even though the unemployment rate ticked upward in 2009, employers still face a labour shortage in the coming years. As you have learned, as the baby boomers begin retiring, the demand for labour is expected to far outstrip supply.

The greater competition for talent means that recruiting has become more important for managers. Today, many jobs require higher skill levels. No longer can managers rely on unsolicited applications to fill these positions. To stay apace of their competitors and expand their operations around the world, companies are also looking globally for workers. It is therefore essential that organizations do a good job of broadening their pools of talent—the number and kinds of people able to contribute to the success of the organization and the variety of ways in which they recruit and retain them.

Of course, unlike physical assets, human assets (employees) can decide to leave the firm of their own accord as well as join it. The Internet has helped make workers better informed about opportunities and allowed them to telecommute or work off-site. As a result, rival firms are in a better position to lure good employees away. Flatter organizational structures within firms mean that there are fewer positions for promotion. Consequently, individuals often must look for advancement opportunities outside their companies. At the same time, as economic cycles lead organizations first to hire—and then to lay off—and then to hire again, employment security can be assured only when individuals take control of their own careers. The upshot is that individuals are less likely to work in the same job for extended periods, and in fact, most are unlikely to spend their entire careers with only one firm. In other words, today's labour market—for both employees and employers—has become more "free agent" oriented.[1]

In this chapter, we will discuss various sources and approaches to expanding the talent pool in organizations. Specifically, we will discuss both external sources of recruitment and internal sources (such as promotion, transfers, and the like). But beyond recruiting itself, we will also discuss the approaches that organizations take toward career management over time. As organizations consider the long-term implications for managing their talent, career development is taking on new importance. Finally, at the end of the chapter, we devote special attention to the recruitment and career development of those in designated groups.

RECRUITING TALENT EXTERNALLY

Recruitment is the process of locating potential individuals who might join an organization and encouraging them to apply for existing or anticipated job openings. During this process, firms make an effort to inform the applicants fully about the qualifications they need for particular jobs and the career opportunities the organizations offer employees. Whether a particular job vacancy will be filled by someone from within the organization or from outside will depend on the availability of personnel, the organization's HR policies, and the requirements of the job to be staffed.

Unless managers intend to reduce the size of the workforce, any job vacancy is a cue that a replacement from outside must be found to replace a departing employee. An old adage goes something like this: "When the president or CEO of the organization retires, a chain reaction of promotions occurs. Everyone moves up a slot, and someone new is hired into a starting position in the mailroom." Of course, this almost never occurs, but the story illustrates a philosophy for how some companies approach recruiting. More realistically, when there is an opening, managers must make careful decisions about whether to fill the position, and if so, who to bring into the position, and how best to approach the decision. The question therefore is not whether to bring people into the organization, but rather at which level they are to be brought in. In the past few years, some of Canada's largest companies, including CN, have brought in outsiders to be their new chief executive officers (CEOs). Stock prices rose and fell based on a CEO's appointment, and hiring someone from the outside was seen as essential for revitalizing the organization. The problem is that although outside CEOs might be charismatic, they sometimes lack the knowledge and skills they need to be successful in a new industry or are a bad fit with their new companies' culture. Perhaps this why two out of five CEOs fail in their first 19 months on the job.[2]

OUTSIDE SOURCES FOR RECRUITMENT

The outside sources from which employers recruit will vary with the type of position to be filled. A computer programmer, for example, is not likely to be recruited from the same source as a machine operator. Trade schools can provide applicants for entry-level positions, though these recruitment sources are not as useful when highly skilled employees are needed. Some firms keep detailed statistics by job type on the sources from which their employees are hired. This helps human resources managers make better decisions about the places to begin recruiting when different job openings arise.

The condition of the labour market may also help determine which recruiting sources an organization will use. During periods of high unemployment, organizations might be able to maintain an adequate supply of qualified applicants from unsolicited résumés alone. A tight labour market, one with low unemployment, might force the employer to advertise heavily and/or seek assistance from local employment agencies. How successful an organization has been in reaching its employee diversity goals can be still another factor in determining the sources from which to recruit. Typically, an employer at any given time will find it necessary to use several recruitment sources.

Several studies have suggested that an employee's recruitment source can affect that employee's subsequent tenure and job performance in both large and small organizations.[3] In general, applicants who are referred by a current employee, if hired, tend to remain with the organization longer and perform better. Employers are cautioned, however, that relying on only one or two recruitment sources to secure job applicants could have an adverse effect on designated groups.

Advertisements

One of the most common methods of attracting applicants is through advertisements. Although websites, newspapers, and trade journals are the media used most often, radio, television, billboards, posters, and e-mail are also used. Advertising has the advantage of reaching a large audience of possible applicants. Some degree of selectivity can be achieved by using newspapers and journals directed toward a particular group of readers. Professional journals, trade journals, and the publications of unions and various fraternal or nonprofit organizations fall into this category. Preparing recruiting advertisements is not only time consuming, but also requires creativity in terms of developing their design and message content. Well-written advertisements highlight the major assets of the position while showing the responsiveness of the organization to the job, career, and lifestyle needs of applicants. Also, there appears to be a correlation between the accuracy and completeness of information provided in job advertisements and an organization's recruitment success. The more information disclosed, the better. Among the information typically included in advertisements is that the recruiting organization is an equal opportunity employer.

However, even when a job opening is described thoroughly in an advertisement, many unqualified applicants will still apply. This can create a burden for HR personnel who have to sift through stacks of inquiries and résumés in an effort to locate qualified candidates. In fact, for each vacant position, HR staff and managers typically review 20 to 100 résumés. Fortunately, software developers are designing new tools companies can use to prescreen applicants online, digitize their résumés, distribute the data into company databases, and automate the process of candidate referrals from in-house personnel. Other software developers have created talent search software, which can be customized to search the Web for valuable but "passive" job candidates, based on information they post on industry blogs, mailing lists, association sites, and so forth.[4]

Unsolicited Applications and Résumés

Many employers receive unsolicited applications and résumés from individuals who may or may not be good prospects for employment. Even though the percentage of acceptable applicants from this source generally is not high, it is a source that cannot be ignored. In fact, it is often believed that individuals who contact employers on their own initiative will be better employees than those recruited through college or university placement services or newspaper advertisements.

Good public relations dictate that any person contacting an organization for a job be treated with courtesy and respect. If there is no present or future possibility of employment in the organization, the applicant should be tactfully and frankly informed as much. Telling an applicant to "fill out an application, and we will keep it on file" when there is no hope for his or her employment is not fair to the applicant. Research has shown that a candidate who has been treated well by a potential employer will, on average, tell one other person. On the other hand, a candidate who has been treated poorly—perhaps receiving a tardy rejection letter or no letter at all—will, on average, tell 11 other people.[5]

Internet Recruiting

Looking on the Internet is the most commonly used search tactic by job seekers and recruiters to get the word out about new positions. Both companies and applicants find the approach cheaper, faster, and potentially more effective. The top one—Workopolis—makes up about half of the people recruited from this source. Staffing experts say it is also a good idea to post your firm's jobs at free association and trade group sites, where your specific talent pool is most likely to congregate.[6] Of course, most large companies post job openings on their own corporate websites, usually under a link titled "Careers." Some companies are now posting podcasts that profile the working lives of their different employees, Highlights in HRM 5.1 provides guidelines for setting up an online posting system.

Employee Referrals

The recruitment efforts of an organization can be greatly aided by employee referrals, or recommendations from the firm's current employees about potential candidates. In fact, word-of-mouth recommendations are the way most job positions are filled. (Apparently there is truth to the phrase, "It's not what you know, but who you know.") Managers have found that the quality of employee-referred applicants is normally quite high, since employees are generally hesitant to recommend individuals who might not perform well. Companies can also create referral portals on their own website with products such as Referred Hire. The software creates a secure domain where employees can log in to recommend friends and professional acquaintances.[7]

There are several suggested ways to increase the effectiveness of employee referral programs, whether conveyed online or via word-of-mouth.

Highlights in **HRM 5.1**

Guidelines for Setting Up an Online Job Posting System

Below is a list of best practices for online recruitment:

- Links to careers from the home page résumé
- About the company: benefits
- Attachment of formatted résumé
- A university recruiting section
- Job search by job category
- Job search by key word
- Complete job description
- One click to apply
- Preassessment tool customized for each position
- Choice of cut-and-paste form or résumé builder
- Attachment of formatted résumé
- Application automatically connected to a job
- Anonymous application
- E-mail to a friend
- Profiling

- Reuse of candidate information for multiple applications
- Online user feedback

To begin building an electronic job posting system, organizations need an e-mail software program with the capability to display job postings and accept recruiting requests for available openings.

Designing and Administering the System

To design and administer the system, organizations need

- An automated process to enter job postings into the system and to delete listings once they are filled
- The capability to automatically calculate each listing's expiration date

Sources: "Canadian Employers Lagging behind in Use of Corporate Websites for Recruitment," *Canadian HR Reporter*, November 19, 2001; Condensed from Sharon M. Tarrant, "Setting Up an Electronic Job-Posting System," *Training and Development*, January 1994, 39–42.

- *Up the ante.* Companies pay high commissions to employment agencies and search firms. So why not do the same thing with employees when they provide a good referral? Other recruitment incentives used by organizations include complimentary dinners, discounts on merchandise, all-expenses-paid trips, and free insurance. When employers pay higher bonuses for "hot" skills, employees are more likely to focus on people they know in that area.

- *Pay for performance.* Some firms save part of the referral bonus until the new hire has stayed for six months. This encourages referring employees to help the new hires succeed.

- *Tailor the program.* Companies typically need more of certain types of skills than others, but the referral programs do not always reflect this. Part of a good referral program is educating employees about the kinds of people the organization wants to hire. This includes some communication of the skills required and also a reaffirmation of the values and ethics sought in applicants.

- *Increase visibility.* One of the best ways to publicize a referral program is to celebrate successes. Some companies use novel approaches such as "job of the month" or "celebrity endorsements" from managers. The idea is to keep everyone thinking about bringing in good people.

- *Keep the data.* Even if a referral does not get the job, it might be a good idea to keep the résumé on file just in case another vacancy arises.

- *Rethink your taboos.* Some companies are reluctant to take on certain potential hires, such as former employees, relatives, and the like. In a tight labour market, it is a good idea to broaden the search.

- *Widen the program.* Just as it may make sense to consider hiring former employees, it may make sense to ask them for referrals even if they are not candidates for the jobs themselves. A number of companies have mailing lists of "corporate friends" that can be used to seek potential candidates.
- *Measure results.* No surprise here. After the program is implemented, managers need to take a hard look at the volume of referrals, qualifications of candidates, and success of new hires on the job. These results are then fed back to fine-tune the program.[8]

Some potential negative factors are associated with employee referrals. They include the possibility of corporate "inbreeding" and systemic discrimination. Since employees and their referrals tend to have similar backgrounds, employers who rely heavily on employee referrals to fill job openings may intentionally or unintentionally screen out, and thereby discriminate against, members of designated groups. Furthermore, organizations may choose not to employ relatives of current employees. The practice of hiring relatives, referred to as **nepotism**, can invite charges of favoritism, especially in appointments to desirable positions. HR personnel hiring globally, however, need to realize that in other cultures, including Asia and the Middle East, nepotism is the norm. Even in North America, nepotism gets mixed reviews, in part, because family members are in an ideal position to pass job knowledge and skills on to one another. Many corporate dynasties (Ford Motor Company and the Bata Shoe Company) have been built on nepotism, and labour unions would not have flourished without it. In recent years, a number of law firms and universities have dropped restrictions against hiring spouses on the basis that they are prejudicial.[9]

nepotism

A preference for hiring relatives of current employees

Executive Search Firms

In contrast to public and private employment agencies, which help job seekers find the right job, executive search firms (often called "headhunters") help employers find the right person for a job. Firms such as Korn/Ferry and Ray Bernstein seek out candidates with qualifications that match the requirements of the positions their client firm is seeking to fill. Executive search firms do not advertise in the media for job candidates, nor do they accept a fee from the individual being placed.

The fees charged by search firms can range from anywhere from 25 to 40 percent of the annual salary for the position to be filled. For the recruitment of senior executives, this fee is paid by the client firm, whether or not the recruiting effort results in a hire. It is for this practice that search firms receive the greatest criticism. Nevertheless, as we noted earlier, hiring new CEOs from outside the organization has become commonplace. A large number of these new CEOs are placed in those positions through the services of an executive search firm. However, newer data suggest that CEOs who are promoted from within their organizations actually outperform those hired from the outside. In light of the numerous CEO-related scandals and bankruptcies that have occurred in recent times, human resources personnel are increasingly being called on to demand more from executive search firms and to assist boards of directors in the careful selection of top executives. In some instances, executive search firms have been criticized for selling the "Superman" qualities of outside CEOs—for which firms pay a premium.

After studying thousands of organizations, Harvard Business School professor Joseph Bower found that CEOs recruited internally know the company and its people but are often blind to the need for radical change. By contrast, CEOs recruited outside the company see the need for change but cannot make it happen because they are unfamiliar with the organization or industry. Bower believes companies need to develop what he calls "inside-outsiders," or internal candidates who have an outside perspective. These employees might have spent much of their time away from the company's headquarters or main operations and therefore experienced different opportunities and threats.

Educational Institutions

Educational institutions typically are a source of young applicants with formal training but relatively little full-time work experience. High schools are usually a source of employees for clerical and blue-collar jobs. Community colleges, with their various types of specialized training, can provide candidates for technical jobs. These institutions can also be a source of applicants for a variety of white-collar jobs, including those in the sales and retail fields. Some management trainee jobs are also staffed from this source.

For technical and managerial positions, colleges and universities are generally the primary source. Some employers fail to take full advantage of college and university resources because of a poor recruitment program.[10] Consequently, their recruitment efforts fail to attract many potentially good applicants. Another common weakness is the failure to maintain a planned and continuing effort on a long-term basis. Furthermore, some recruiters sent to college campuses are not sufficiently trained or prepared to talk to interested candidates about career opportunities or the requirements of specific openings. This is a grave mistake because research shows that students' perceptions of recruiters have a big impact on the companies for which they choose to work.

Attempting to visit too many campuses instead of concentrating on selected institutions and the inability to use the campus placement office effectively are other recruiting weaknesses. Mismanaging applicant visits to an organization's headquarters and the failure to follow up with individual candidates or obtain hiring commitments from upper-level managers are among other mistakes that have caused employers to lose well-qualified prospects. To attract high-demand graduates, in addition to offering higher pay, firms sometimes employ innovative recruitment techniques such as work-study programs, internships, low-interest loans, and scholarships. Figure 5.1 lists the factors that students from Canadian colleges and universities consider when choosing employers.

FIGURE **5.1**

Taking the Student Pulse

Opportunities for advancement	86.7%
Good people to work with	82.2%
Good training opportunities/developing new skills	82.1%
Good people to report to	79.6%
Challenging work	71.8%
Work–life balance	70.2%
Good initial salary level	70.1%
Job security	69.1%
Opportunities to have a personal impact	68.8%
Good health and benefits plan	63.2%
Strong commitment to employee diversity	49.5%
Commitment to social responsibility	48.6%
Organization is a leader in its field	47.1%
Opportunity to travel	36.1%

Source: Graham Donald. "People and Opportunities the Biggest Draw for Students," *Canadian HR Reporter* (April 25, 2005): 9.

Professional Associations

Many professional associations and societies offer a placement service to members as one of their benefits. Listings of members seeking employment may be advertised in their journals or publicized at their national meetings. A placement centre is usually established at national meetings for the mutual benefit of employers and job seekers. The Human Resource Professional Association (HRPA), for example, helps employers and prospective HR employees come together.

Labour Unions

Labour unions have been a principal source of applicants for blue-collar and some professional jobs. Some unions, such as those in the maritime, printing, and construction industries, maintain hiring halls that can provide a supply of applicants, particularly for short-term needs. Employers wishing to use this recruitment source should contact the local union under consideration for employer eligibility requirements and applicant availability.

Public Employment Agencies

Each province maintains an employment agency that is responsible for administering its employment insurance program. The agency is called the Department of Human Resources Development, or something similar, and maintains local public employment offices in most communities of any size. Individuals who become unemployed must register at one of these offices and be available for "suitable employment" before they can receive their weekly employment insurance cheques. This requirement means that public employment agencies are able to refer those applicants with the required skills who are available for employment to employers with job openings.

Human Resources and Skills Development Canada (HRSDC) has developed a nationwide computerized job bank that lists job openings, and provincial employment offices are connected to this job bank. The computerized job bank helps facilitate the movement of job applicants to different geographic areas. Most of these offices now have a local job bank book that is published as a daily computer printout. Job openings are listed along with other pertinent information, such as number of openings, pay rates, and job specifications. The local job bank makes it possible for the agency's employment interviewers to keep a list of all the job openings in the geographic area for which the applicants assigned to them might qualify. Also, applicants looking for a specific job can review the computer printout and apply directly to the organization that has the opening. HRSDC provides all kinds of labour market information including occupational profiles, industry profiles, and job outlooks.

In addition to matching unemployed applicants with job openings, public employment agencies may assist employers with employment testing, job analysis, evaluation programs, and community wage surveys.

Private Employment and Temporary Agencies

Charging a fee enables private employment agencies to tailor their services to the specific needs of their clients. However, it is common for agencies to specialize in serving a specific occupational area or professional field. Depending on who is receiving the most service, the fee may be paid by the employer, the job seeker, or both. It is not uncommon for private employment agencies to charge an employer a 25- to 30-percent fee, based on the position's annual salary, if the employer hires an applicant found by the agency.

Private employment agencies differ in the services they offer, their professionalism, and the calibre of their counsellors. If counsellors are paid on a commission

Using the Internet

Go to HRSDC at

http://www.hrsdc.gc.ca/ eng/home.shtml

for extensive information about jobs and careers

basis, their desire to do a professional job may be offset by their desire to earn a commission. Thus, they may encourage job seekers to accept jobs for which they are not suited. Because of this, job seekers would be wise to take the time to find a recruiter who is knowledgeable, experienced, and professional. When talking with potential recruiters, individuals should discuss openly their philosophies and practices with regard to recruiting strategies, including advertising, in-house recruiting, screening procedures, and costs for these efforts. They should try to find a recruiter who is flexible and who will consider their needs and wants.

In addition to placing permanent workers, many private agencies hire and place workers in temporary positions. "Temps" are typically used for short-term assignments or to help when managers cannot justify hiring a full-time employee, such as for vacation fill-ins, for peak work periods, or during an employee's maternity leave or sick leave. Increasingly, temps are being employed to fill positions once staffed by permanent employees. This practice adds flexibility because temporaries can be laid off quickly, and with less cost, when work lessens. Some companies use a just-in-time staffing approach in which a core staff of employees is augmented by a trained and highly skilled supplementary workforce. The use of temporaries thus becomes a viable way to maintain proper staffing levels.

THE GLOBAL LABOUR MARKET

As we explained in Chapter 2, companies are no longer simply offshoring work to save labour costs. They are also looking abroad to develop better products around the clock via a global workforce and attract the best talent wherever it may be. Emerging countries such as China and India are also heating up the competition for talent as firms there attempt to staff the burgeoning high-tech industries in these nations. The staffing firm Manpower recently surveyed 36,000 employers in 27 countries around the world and found that 41 percent are having difficulty filling positions due to a lack of suitable talent. It is not only technical positions firms are trying to fill but also lower-skilled positions, too. Resorts and vacation areas are among the businesses having trouble finding employees to staff their operations.

Recruiting abroad can be very complicated, however. In addition to having to deal with myriad local, national, and international laws, employers also have to take into account the different labour costs, pre-employment and compensation practices, and cultural differences associated with the countries in which they are recruiting. In volatile areas of the world, security is a concern. Because locals are often unfamiliar with foreign firms and their brands, companies often find the need to develop an employment brand and advertise it to potential recruits. For example, Genpact, a company that helps firms globalize, has set up "storefronts" in eight Indian cities in which it recruits employees. Candidates can walk in and chat with company representatives about what Genpact does and the kinds of opportunities it offers; they can leave their résumés and come back later for voice and accent testing, when necessary.

IMPROVING THE EFFECTIVENESS OF EXTERNAL RECRUITMENT

With all of the uncertainties inherent in external recruiting, it is sometimes difficult to determine whether an organization's efforts to locate promising talent are effective and/or efficient. However, managers can do several things to maximize the probability of success. These include calculating yield ratios on recruiting sources, calculating costs of recruitment, training organizational recruiters, and conducting realistic job previews.

Yield Ratios

yield ratio
The percentage of applicants from a recruitment source that make it to the next stage of the selection process

Yield ratios help indicate which recruitment sources are most effective at producing qualified job candidates. Quite simply, a **yield ratio** is the percentage of applicants from a particular source that make it to the next stage in the selection process. For example, if 100 résumés were obtained from an employment agency and 17 of the applicants submitting those résumés were invited for an on-site interview, the yield ratio for that agency would be 17 percent (17/100). This yield ratio could then be recalculated for each subsequent stage in the selection process (for example, after the interview and again after the final offer), which would result in a cumulative yield ratio. By calculating and comparing yield ratios for each recruitment source, it is possible to find out which sources produce qualified applicants.

Costs of Recruitment

The cost of various recruiting procedures can be computed using a fairly simple set of calculations. For example, the average source cost per hire (SC/H) can be determined by the following formula:

$$\frac{SC}{H} = \frac{AC + AF + RB + NC}{H}$$

where   AC = advertising costs, total monthly expenditure (example: \$32,000)

AF = agency fees, total for the month (example: \$21,000)

RB = referral bonuses, total paid (example: \$2,600)

NC = no-cost hires, walk-ins, nonprofit agencies, etc. (example: \$0)

H = total hires (example: 119)

Substituting the example numbers into the formula gives

$$\frac{SC}{H} = \frac{\$32,000 + \$21,000 + \$2,600 + \$0}{119}$$

$$= \frac{\$55,600}{119}$$

$$= \$467.23 \text{ (source cost of recruits per hire)}$$

When combined with information about yield ratios, these calculations can provide invaluable information to managers about the utility of different approaches to and sources of recruitment. In that way, they can make more informed decisions about both controlling the costs of recruitment and increasing its effectiveness. For example, although advertisements and employee referrals may both yield qualified applicants, managers may find that referral bonuses are a more economical alternative.

Organizational Recruiters

The size of an organization influences who performs the recruitment function. For large employers, professional HR recruiters are typically hired and trained to find new employees. In smaller organizations, recruiting might be done by an HR generalist; if the organization has no HR position, managers and/or supervisors recruit their own employees. Sometimes organizations outsource their recruiting function to a recruiting process outsourcing (RPO) company—especially when it comes to support staff.

Regardless of who does the recruiting, it is imperative that these individuals have a good understanding of the knowledge, skills, abilities, experiences, and other characteristics required for the job. All too often, a new person in the HR department or a line manager is given a recruiting assignment, even before that person has undergone interview training, before he or she fully understands the job being recruiting for, or comprehends the values and goals of the organization. It is important to remember that recruiters significantly influence an applicant's job decision. Because recruiters can often enhance the perceived attractiveness of a job and an organization, they are often a main reason that applicants select one organization over another. On this basis, we can conclude that personable, enthusiastic, and competent recruiters have an impact on the success of an organization's recruitment program.

Realistic Job Previews

Another way organizations may be able to increase the effectiveness of their recruitment efforts is to provide job applicants with a **realistic job preview (RJP)**. A RJP informs applicants about all aspects of the job, including both its desirable and undesirable facets. In contrast, a typical job preview presents the job in only positive terms. The RJP might also include a tour of the working area, combined with a discussion of any negative health or safety considerations. Proponents of RJPs believe that applicants who are given realistic information regarding a position are more likely to remain on the job and be successful because there will be fewer unpleasant surprises.

In fact, a number of research studies on RJPs report these positive results:

- Improved employee job satisfaction
- Reduced voluntary turnover
- Enhanced communication through honesty and openness
- Realistic job expectations

Some companies are taking their RJPs online. For example, the North Shore Health Region, in British Columbia, realized that it had unique attributes that could give a competitive advantage in recruiting nurses. Recruitment materials were prepared that captured the main appeal of this employer: a small, friendly full-service hospital. This message was reinforced in all recruitment efforts and was based on research with existing employees.[11]

RECRUITING TALENT INTERNALLY

While we typically think about recruiting being focused on attracting potential employees from outside the organization, most managers try to follow a policy of filling job vacancies above the entry-level position through promotions and transfers. By filling vacancies in this way, an organization can capitalize on the investment it has made in recruiting, selecting, training, and developing its current employees, who might look for jobs elsewhere if they lack promotion opportunities. Indeed, experienced employees take with them years of corporate know-how that is hard to replace. Some signs that the firm needs to work harder at grooming internal talent are shown in Figure 5.2. To lessen the chances of losing top performers, some managers actively identify high-potential "at risk" employees and take steps to retain these people.[12]

ADVANTAGES AND LIMITATIONS OF RECRUITING FROM WITHIN

Promotion-from-within policies at Loblaws and RBC have contributed to the companies' overall growth and success.[13] Promoting employees rewards them for past performance and is intended to encourage them to continue their efforts. It also gives other employees a reason to believe that if they perform similarly, they will

realistic job preview (RJP)
Informing applicants about all aspects of the job, including both its desirable and undesirable facets

2 OUTCOME

FIGURE **5.2**

Warning Signs of a Weak Talent "Bench"

1. It takes a long time to fill key positions.
2. Key positions can be filled only by hiring from the outside.
3. Vacancies in key positions cannot be filled with confidence in the abilities of those chosen for them.
4. Replacements for positions often are unsuccessful in performing their new duties.
5. Promotions are made on the basis of whim, favouritism, or nepotism.

Source: Adapted from William Rothwell, *Effective Succession Planning* (New York: AMACOM, 2000).

be promoted, too. This can improve morale within the organization and support a culture of employee engagement. This may be particularly true for members of designated groups who have encountered difficulties in finding employment and have often faced even greater difficulty in advancing within an organization. The connection is so important that most organizations have integrated promotion policies as an essential part of their employment equity programs.

If an organization's promotion policy is to have maximum motivational value, employees must be made aware of that policy. The following is an example of a policy statement that an organization might prepare.

"Promotion from within" is generally recognized as a foundation of good employment practice, and it is the policy of our organization to promote from within whenever possible when filling a vacancy. The job vacancy will be posted for five calendar days to give all qualified full- and part-time personnel an equal opportunity to apply.

While a transfer lacks the motivational value of a promotion, it sometimes can serve to protect employees from layoffs or broaden their job experiences. Furthermore, the transferred employee's familiarity with the organization and its operations can eliminate the orientation and training costs that recruitment from the outside would entail. Most important, the transferee's performance record is likely to be a more accurate predictor of the candidate's success than the data gained about outside applicants.

Side by side with the potential advantages of internal recruitment, managers need to be aware of potential limitations as well. For example, jobs that require specialized training and experience cannot be easily filled from within the organization and may need to be filled from the outside. This is especially common in small organizations where the existing talent pool is limited. Also, for certain openings it may be necessary or advantageous to hire individuals from the outside who have gained from another employer the knowledge and expertise required for these jobs.

Even though a company's HR policy might encourage job openings to be filled from within the organization, potential candidates from the outside should be considered in order to prevent the "inbreeding" of ideas and attitudes. Indeed, excessive reliance on internal sources can create the risk of "employee cloning." Applicants hired from the outside, particularly for certain technical and managerial positions, can be a source of creativity and innovation, and may bring with them the latest knowledge acquired from their previous employers.

From a different perspective, it is not uncommon for firms to attempt to gain secrets from their competitors by hiring away their employees. Procter & Gamble sued a rival papermaker when it hired former employees who had a great deal of knowledge about the making of Charmin toilet paper and Bounty paper towels—both P&G products. Amazon.com was sued by Walmart, which accused it of hiring away employees who had in-depth knowledge about Walmart's sophisticated inventory systems.[14]

METHODS FOR IDENTIFYING QUALIFIED CANDIDATES

The effective use of internal sources requires a system for locating qualified job candidates and for enabling those who consider themselves qualified to apply for the opening. Qualified job candidates within the organization can be located in a number of ways, which we discuss next.

Inventorying Management Talent

As we discussed in Chapter 2, more firms are electronically capturing the qualifications of each of their employees and using this information to identify potential candidates for available jobs. Companies such as PeopleSoft and SAP are leaders in developing automated staffing and skills management software. Similar to the skills inventories mentioned earlier, these information systems allow an organization to rapidly screen its entire workforce to locate suitable candidates to fill an internal opening. These data can also be used to predict the career paths of employees and to anticipate when and where promotion opportunities might arise.[15]

Skill inventories are an important tool for succession planning. They provide an indication of the skills employees have as well as their interests and experiences. In this way, they help managers pay better attention to the developmental needs of employees, both in their present jobs and in managerial jobs to which they may be promoted. An equally important part of this process is identifying high-potential employees who may be groomed as replacements for managers who are reassigned, retire, or otherwise vacate a position. At GE, for every position at or above a director level, two or three people are usually identified who can easily step in when the current jobholder moves on.[16]

Job Posting and Bidding

Organizations communicate information about job openings through a process referred to as **job posting and bidding**. The jobs are frequently posted on a firm's Intranet or on regular bulletin boards where employees congregate. Job openings can also be announced in employee publications, special handouts, direct mail, and public address messages. Many companies have developed online job posting systems whereby employees looking for upgraded positions can post their names, résumés, and the positions in which they are interested. As a position becomes available, the list of employees seeking that position is retrieved, and the records of these employees are reviewed to select possible candidates for interviews. The employees can be electronically notified about interview schedules and track their progress electronically through the various hiring stages.[17] Job bidding is more effective when it is part of a career development program in which employees are made aware of the opportunities available to them within the organization. For example, HR departments can provide new employees with information on the progression of employees doing their particular jobs, training requirements for each job, and skills and abilities they need to advance within their organizations.

Identifying Talent through Performance Appraisals

Performance appraisals are discussed more fully in Chapter 8. For our purposes here, we want to note that managers measure and evaluate employee performance for several reasons, none of which is more important than making promotion and career decisions. Successful performers are often good candidates for a promotion.

$\begin{bmatrix} 3 \\ \text{OUTCOME} \end{bmatrix}$

job posting and bidding
Posting vacancy notices and maintaining lists of employees looking for upgraded positions

In contrast, poorly performing employees may need—and benefit from—a transfer to another area or even a demotion or, in a worst-case scenario, termination.

But performance appraisals are not just used for "racking and stacking" the best talent. Identifying and developing all employees is a role that all managers should take seriously. As they conduct formal appraisals, they should be concerned with their subordinates' potential for managerial or advanced technical jobs and encourage their growth in that direction. In addition to immediate managers, others in the organization should have the power to evaluate, nominate, and sponsor employees with promise. A tool called a **9-box grid** is helping firms such as General Mills and others do this by allowing appraisal and assessment data to be compiled into a single visual reference. The grid is a comparative diagram that allows managers to readily see both an employee's actual performance as well as potential performance. This can then help managers determine the developmental needs of the employee and what the person's next steps within the organization might be. Figure 5.3 is an example of a 9-box grid.

Using Assessment Centres

There are other very effective ways to assess a person's career potential. Pioneered in the mid-1950s by Douglas Bray and his associates at AT&T, assessment centres are considered one of the most valuable and time-honoured methods for evaluating personnel. An **assessment centre** is a process (not a place) by which individuals are evaluated as they participate in a series of situations that resemble what they might be called on to handle on the job. The popularity of the assessment centre can be attributed to its capacity for increasing an organization's ability to select employees who will perform successfully in management positions or to assist and promote the development of skills for their current position. The centres use a variety of methods, including in-basket exercises, leaderless group discussions, and other approaches.

- *In-basket exercises.* This method is used to simulate a problem situation. The participants are given several documents, each describing some problem or situation requiring an immediate response. They are thus forced to make

9-box grid

A comparative diagram that includes appraisal and assessment data to allow managers to easily see an employee's actual and potential performance.

assessment centre

A process by which individuals are evaluated as they participate in a series of situations that resemble what they might be called on to handle on the job

FIGURE **5.3**

An Example of a 9-Box Grid

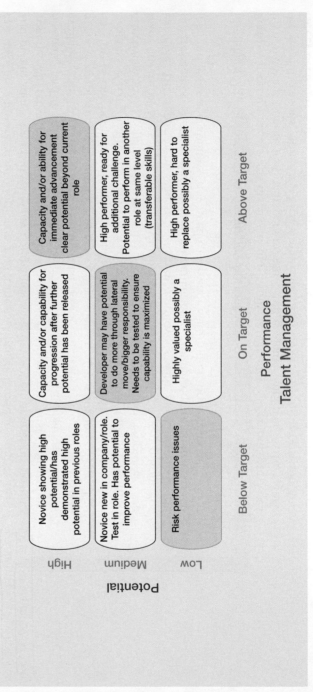

decisions under the pressure of time and also to determine what priority to give each problem.

• *Leaderless group discussions.* With this activity, trainees are gathered in a conference setting to discuss an assigned topic, either with or without designated group roles. The participants are given little or no instruction in how to approach the topic, nor are they told what decision to reach. Leaderless group trainees are evaluated on their initiative, leadership skills, and ability to work effectively in a group setting.

• *Role-playing.* The exercise might involve preparing for and engaging in a customer meeting or a team leader meeting with one's subordinates. A trained assessor then assesses the participant using a structured rating scale.

• *Behavioural interviews.* The interviewer asks the participant a series of question about what he or she would do in particular work circumstances. Sometimes behavioural interviews are combined with videos showing work simulations, and participants are asked at intervals to make choices about what they would do in the situations shown.

At the end of the assessment centre period, the assessors' observations are combined to develop an overall picture of the strengths and needs of the participants. A report is normally submitted to senior management, and feedback is given to the participants. Highlights in HRM 5.2 describes assessment centre activities at the Public Service Commission. Before an assessment is run, however, the characteristics or dimensions to be studied should be determined through job analyses. The exercises used in the centre should reflect the job for which the person is being evaluated.[18] Although assessment centres have proved quite valuable in identifying managerial talent and in helping with the development of individuals, it should be noted that the method tends to favour those who are strong in interpersonal skills

Highlights in HRM 5.2

The Assessment Centre Program of the Public Service Commission

The first step in the use of an assessment centre is to work with managers, who are asked by psychologists to keep a diary of their daily activities and problems. They are then questioned about their work in order to identify the major problems that a manager might face. The focus is on identifying the abilities needed to resolve these problems. This information is used to develop the simulation exercises.

Candidates for managerial positions, playing the role of a manager, are asked to respond to a series of letters, memos, and variance reports (reports detailing how the results varied from the planned results). They then present, in oral and written forms, the approach they would use to resolve the problem. These approaches include the establishment of priorities, plans, solutions, and decisions.

The selection board, composed of the hiring manager, at least one outside manager, and a staffing officer, is trained to understand the simulation and the various effective approaches. The candidates are evaluated on how well they got their ideas across and on how well they plan, monitor, and control programs.

Everyone involved strongly identifies with the realistic nature of the simulation. Candidates get so involved in the simulation that they forget it is a test, and managers feel they can actually visualize these people at work. Even unsuccessful candidates claim they learn about themselves in the process.

Source: The Personal Psychology Centre, Public Service Commission, Government of Canada, Ottawa.

and have the ability to influence others. Some individuals find it difficult to perform at their best in a situation that for them is as threatening as taking a test. The manner in which assessment centre personnel conduct the exercises and provide feedback to the participants will play a major role in determining how individuals react to the experience. On the upside, after having been assessed, candidates are more likely to have a good idea of the job's requirements and be more willing to accept the firm's decision about who gets promoted.

CAREER MANAGEMENT: DEVELOPING TALENT OVER TIME

While we can think of recruitment as a stand-alone activity, limited to a single job at a single point in time, often this is not the case. Inevitably decisions about talent—regardless of whether they pertain to recruiting, transferring, promoting, developing, or deploying people—need to be considered within the context of long-term priorities of the business and the employees. Increasingly, managers are not making these decisions on a "one-off" basis, but rather as part of a comprehensive approach to career management. Integrating career development with other HR programs creates synergies in which all aspects of HR reinforce one another. Figure 5.4 illustrates how HR structures relate to some of the essential aspects of the career management

FIGURE **5.4**

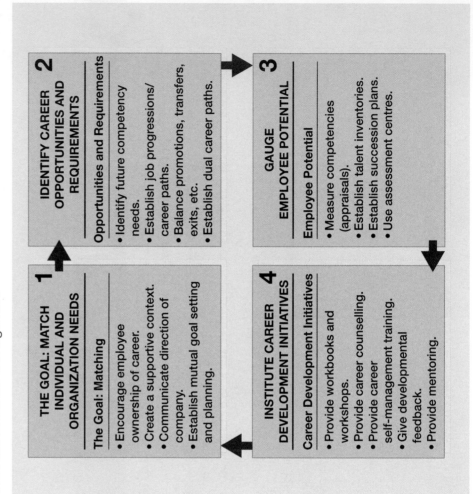

HR's Role in Career Management

THE GOAL: MATCH INDIVIDUAL AND ORGANIZATION NEEDS 1

The Goal: Matching
- Encourage employee ownership of career.
- Create a supportive context.
- Communicate direction of company.
- Establish mutual goal setting and planning.

IDENTIFY CAREER OPPORTUNITIES AND REQUIREMENTS 2

Opportunities and Requirements
- Identify future competency needs.
- Establish job progressions/ career paths.
- Balance promotions, transfers, exits, etc.
- Establish dual career paths.

GAUGE EMPLOYEE POTENTIAL 3

Employee Potential
- Measure competencies (appraisals).
- Establish talent inventories.
- Establish succession plans.
- Use assessment centres.

INSTITUTE CAREER DEVELOPMENT INITIATIVES 4

Career Development Initiatives
- Provide workbooks and workshops.
- Provide career counselling.
- Provide career self-management training.
- Give developmental feedback.
- Provide mentoring.

process. For example, to plan their careers, employees need organizational information that strategic planning, forecasting, succession planning, and skills inventories can provide. Similarly, as they obtain information about themselves and use it in career planning, employees need to know the career paths within the organization and how management views employees' performance.[19]

THE GOAL: MATCHING INDIVIDUAL AND ORGANIZATIONAL NEEDS

In the final analysis, a career development program should be viewed as a dynamic process that matches the needs of the organization with the needs of employees. Each party has a distinctive role to play.

The Employee's Role

Although some firms play a role in the planning of their employees' careers, ultimately, employees are responsible for initiating and managing their own career planning. Because having a successful career involves creating your own career path—not just following a path that has been established by the organization—it is up to each individual to identify his or her own knowledge, skills, abilities, interests, and values, and seek out information about career options in order to set goals and develop career plans. Managers should encourage employees to take responsibility for their own careers. However, they should also offer them continual feedback about their performance and provide them with self-assessment tools, training, and information about the organization and possible career paths within it. General Motors, for example, has prepared a career development guide that groups jobs by fields of work such as engineering, manufacturing, communications, data processing, financial, HR, and scientific. These categories give employees an understanding of the career possibilities in the various fields.

The Organization's Role: Establishing a Favourable Career Development Climate

If career development is to succeed, it must receive the complete support of top management. Ideally, senior line managers and HR department managers should work together to design and implement a career development system. The system should reflect the goals and culture of the organization, and the HR philosophy should be woven throughout. An HR philosophy can provide employees with a clear set of expectations and directions for their own career development. For a program to be effective, managerial personnel at all levels must be trained in the fundamentals of job design, performance appraisal, career planning, and counselling. One of the most important indicators of managerial support is *mentoring*, either formally as part of an ongoing program or informally as merely a kind gesture to a less experienced employee. Dealing with uncertainty is one of the biggest challenges any individual faces in his or her career, so receiving advice from someone who has gone through similar experiences can be invaluable. We devote an entire section to mentoring later in this chapter.

Blending Individual and Organizational Goals

Of course, a career development program should be based on the organization's needs as well. As Figure 5.5 shows, the organization's needs should be linked with the individual career needs of its employees in a way that improves the effectiveness of workers and their satisfaction as well as achieving the firm's strategic objectives.

Before a firm's employees can engage in meaningful career planning, however, they must have not only an awareness of the organization's philosophy, but also a good understanding of the organization's more immediate goals. Otherwise, they might plan for personal change and growth without knowing whether or how their own

Using the Internet

Job sites such as

http://www.workopolis.com

and

http://www.monster.ca

offer assessment tools and career advice

FIGURE **5.5**

Balancing Individual and Organizational Needs

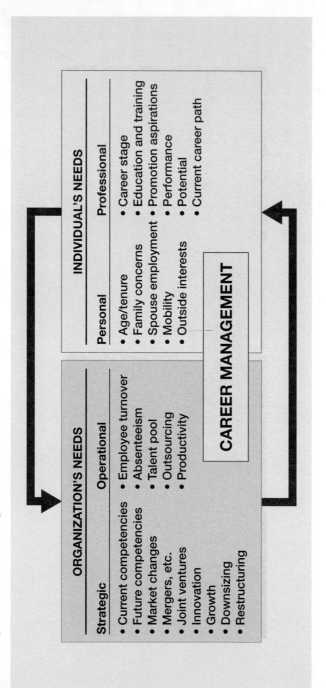

goals match those of the organization. For example, if the technology of a business is changing and new skills are needed, will the organization retrain its employees to meet this need, or hire new talent? Is there growth, stability, or decline in the number of employees needed? How will turnover affect this need? Clearly, an organizational plan that answers these kinds of questions is essential for people's career planning.

At the same time, it would be unrealistic to expect that employees can establish their career goals with *perfect* certainty about where they are going. People change over time and, because of that, their needs and interests change. Similarly, organizations also change their directions and adjust their strategies to cope with change. So while goal setting is critical, building in some flexibility is probably a good idea.

IDENTIFYING CAREER OPPORTUNITIES AND REQUIREMENTS

While talent management integrates a number of related HR activities, those who direct the process have to keep a steady watch on the needs and requirements of the organization. This involves an analysis of the competencies required for jobs, progression among related jobs, and supply of ready (and potential) talent available to fill those jobs. A variety of approaches can be used to do this, including surveys, informal group discussions, and interviews. The process should involve personnel from different groups, such as new employees, managers, long-time employees, minority employees, and technical and professional employees. Identifying the needs and problems of these groups provides the starting point for the organization's career development efforts.

Begin with a Competency Analysis

It is important for an organization to study its jobs carefully in order to identify and assign weights to the knowledge and skills that each one requires. This can be achieved with job analysis and evaluation systems such as those used in compensation programs. The system used at Sears measures three basic competencies for each job: know-how, problem solving, and accountability. Know-how is broken down into three types of job knowledge: technical, managerial, and human relations. Problem solving and accountability also have several dimensions. Scores for each of these three major competencies are assigned to each job, and a total value is computed for each job. For any planned job transfer, the amount of increase (or decrease) the next job represents in each of the skill areas, as well as in the total point values, can be computed. This information is then used to ensure that a transfer to a different job is a move that requires growth on the part of the employee.

Sears designs career development paths to provide the following experiences: (1) an increase in at least one skill area on each new assignment, (2) an increase of at least 10 percent in total points on each new assignment, and (3) assignments in several different functional areas.[20]

Identify Job Progressions

Once the skill demands of jobs are identified and weighted according to their importance, it is then possible to plan **job progressions**. A new employee with no experience is typically assigned to a "starting job." After a period of time in that job, the employee can be promoted to one that requires more knowledge and/or skill. While most organizations concentrate on developing job progressions for managerial, professional, and technical jobs, progressions can be developed for all categories of jobs. These job progressions then can serve as a basis for developing **career paths**—the lines of advancement within an organization—for individuals. Figure 5.6 illustrates a typical line of advancement in the human resources area of a large multinational corporation. It is apparent that one must be prepared to move geographically in order to advance very far in the human resources department of this firm. This would also be true of other career fields within the organization.

Although these analyses can be quite helpful to employees—and are perhaps essential for organizations—a word of caution is appropriate here. Many successful careers are not this methodical, nor do they proceed in a lockstep manner. In today's working world, career progressions often occur as much through creating and capitalizing on arising opportunities as they do through rational planning. So while it is a good idea for organizations to map out a career path and individuals

job progressions
The hierarchy of jobs a new employee might experience, ranging from a starting job to jobs that successively require more knowledge and/or skill

career paths
Lines of advancement in an occupational field within an organization

FIGURE **5.6**

Typical Line of Advancement in HR Management

would do well to establish a strategy for advancement, many successful individuals readily admit that their career paths are quite idiosyncratic to their circumstances. These people often note that they have been fortunate to be "in the right place at the right time." Other people's careers progress quite linearly.

Recognize Lots of Possibilities

Career development and planning systems were once primarily focused on promotions and hierarchical advancement. However, in today's flatter organizations and more dynamic work environment, an individual's career advancement can occur along several different paths: transfers, demotions—even exits—and promotions. HR policies have to be flexible enough to adapt as well as helpful enough to support the career change.

A **promotion** is a change of assignment to a job at a higher level in the organization. The new job normally provides an increase in pay and status, and demands more skill or carries more responsibility. Promotions enable an organization to utilize the skills and abilities of its personnel more effectively and the opportunity to gain a promotion serves as an incentive for good performance. The three principal criteria for determining promotions are merit, seniority, and potential. Often the problem is to determine how much consideration to give to each factor. A common problem in organizations that promote primarily on past performance and seniority is called the Peter Principle. This refers to the situation in which individuals are promoted as long as they have done a good job in their previous job. The trouble is this continues until someone does poorly in his or her new job. Then he or she is no longer promoted. This results in people being promoted to their level of incompetence. There are other intrafirm challenges related to promotions; sometimes extremely good employees are prevented from being promoted to other departments because their current managers are reluctant to lose them. At other firms, an employee who tries, but fails, to advance to a position in another department is earmarked for the next round of layoffs.[21]

In flatter organizations, there are fewer promotional opportunities; therefore, many individuals find career advancement through lateral moves. A **transfer** is the placement of an employee in another job for which the duties, responsibilities, status, and remuneration are approximately equal to those of the previous job (although as an incentive, organizations may offer a salary adjustment). Individuals who look forward to change or want a chance to learn more may seek out transfers. In addition, transfers frequently provide a broader foundation for individuals to prepare them for an eventual promotion. A transfer may require the employee to change work group, workplace, work shift, or organizational unit; it may even necessitate moving to another geographic area. Transfers make it possible for an organization to place its employees in jobs where there is a greater need for their services and where they can acquire new knowledge and skills.

A downward transfer, or *demotion*, moves an individual into a lower-level job that can provide developmental opportunities. Although such a move is ordinarily considered unfavourable, some individuals actually may request it in order to return to their "technical roots." It is not uncommon, for example, for organizations to appoint temporary leaders (especially in team environments) with the proviso that they will eventually step down from this position to resume their former position.

Transfers, promotions, and demotions require individuals to adjust to new job demands and usually to a different work environment. A transfer that involves moving to a new location within Canada or abroad places greater demands on an employee because it requires that employee to adapt not only to a new work environment, but also to new living conditions. The employee with a family has the added responsibility of helping family members adjust to the new living arrangements. Even though some employers provide all types of **relocation services**—including covering moving expenses, helping to sell a home, and providing cultural

promotion
A change of assignment to a job at a higher level in the organization

transfer
Placement of an individual in another job for which the duties, responsibilities, status, and remuneration are approximately equal to those of the previous job

relocation services
Services provided to an employee who is transferred to a new location, which might include help in moving, selling a home, orienting to a new culture, and/or learning a new language

orientation and language training—there is always some loss of productive time. Pretransfer training, whether related to job skills or to lifestyle, has been suggested as one of the most effective ways to reduce lost productivity.

When you consider the numerous changes that may accompany a career move within an organization, it should not surprise you that many individuals are opting to accept career changes that involve *organizational exit*. Given limited career opportunities within firms, coupled with the need for talent in other companies, many individuals are discovering that their best career options may involve switching companies or working for themselves as freelancers, consultants, or entrepreneurs. While some employees leave voluntarily, other employees are forced to leave. Even so, many organizations now provide **outplacement services** to help terminated employees find a job elsewhere. These services can be used to enhance a productive employee's career as well as to terminate an employee who is unproductive. If an organization cannot meet its career development responsibilities to its productive workers, HR policy should provide for assistance to be given them in finding more suitable career opportunities elsewhere. Jack Welch, former chairman of General Electric, was one of the first executives to make a commitment to employees that while the company could no longer guarantee lifetime employment, it would try to ensure *employability*. That is, GE has committed to providing employees with the skills and support they would need to find a job in another organization.[22]

Consider Dual Career Paths for Employees

One of the most obvious places where career paths have been changing is in technical and professional areas. One of the ironies of organizations in the past has been that the most successful engineers, scientists, and professionals were often promoted right out of their area of specialization into management. Instead of doing what they were good at, they were promoted into a job they often did not understand and often did not enjoy. It has become apparent that there must be another way to compensate such individuals without elevating them to a management position. The solution has been to develop dual career paths, or tracks, that provide for progression in special areas such as information technology, finance, marketing, and engineering, with compensation that is comparable to that received by managers at different levels. As we explained in Chapter 2, Microsoft offers software engineers both a management-focused and technical-specialist career track and allows them to move back and forth between the two.

Consider the Boundaryless Career

A generation ago, career success was synonymous with ascending a corporate hierarchy over the course of a lifetime spent in a single firm. Today, however, individuals pursuing *boundaryless careers* may prefer to see themselves as self-directed "free agents" who develop a portfolio of employment opportunities by proactively moving from employer to employer, simultaneously developing and utilizing their marketable skills. As shown in Figure 5.7, it is possible to map the different career profiles. Employees pursuing boundaryless careers develop their human capital along dimensions of industry and occupational knowledge. That is, they may be experts in computer programming or have great insights into trends in the banking industry. In contrast, individuals pursuing more traditional careers develop their knowledge in ways specific to a given firm.

Both approaches can be beneficial, but they are not the same. Under the boundaryless career model, success depends on continually learning new skills, developing new relationships, and capitalizing on existing skills and relationships. These individuals place a premium on flexibility and the capacity to do several different

outplacement services
Services provided by organizations to help terminated employees find a new job

FIGURE **5.7**

Human Capital Profiles for Two Different Careers

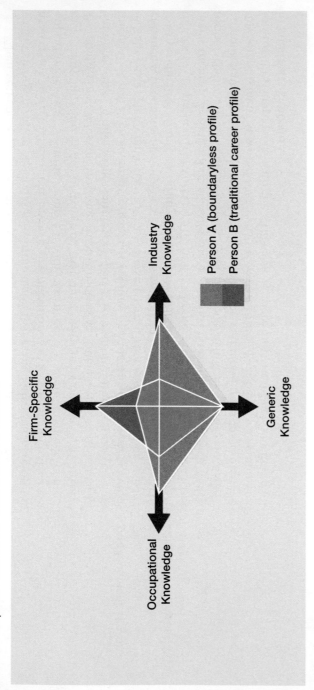

Source: Scott Snell, Cornell University.

types of tasks, learn new jobs, adjust quickly to different group settings and organizational cultures, and move from one firm, occupation, or industry to another. Their employment security depends on their marketable skills rather than their dedication to one organization over time. A number of studies have shown that people with boundaryless careers find them very satisfying. Organizations can also benefit from boundaryless careers because it allows them to attract top talent from all over the world on a project-by-project basis.[23]

Track Career Stages

A person's knowledge, skills, abilities, and attitudes as well as career aspirations change as he or she matures. While the work that individuals in different occupations perform can vary significantly, the challenges and frustrations that they face at the same stage in their careers are remarkably similar. A model describing these stages is shown in Figure 5.8. The stages are: (1) preparation for work, (2) organizational entry, (3) early career, (4) midcareer, and (5) late career. The typical age range and the major tasks of each stage are also presented in the figure.

The first stage—preparation for work—encompasses the period prior to entering an organization, often extending until age 25. It is a period in which individuals must acquire the knowledge, abilities, and skills they will need to compete in the marketplace. It is a time when careful planning, based on sound information, should be the focus. The second stage, typically from ages 18 to 25, is devoted to soliciting job offers and selecting an appropriate job. During this period, one may also be involved in preparing for work. Reality Check outlines how Career Edge solves the problem of finding that first job when employers ask for experience. The next three stages entail fitting into a chosen occupation and organization, modifying goals, making choices, remaining productive, and, finally, preparing for retirement. In the remainder of the chapter we will examine some of the activities of primary concern to the student, who is likely to be in the early stages. Retirement planning will be discussed in Chapter 11.

FIGURE **5.8**

Stages of Career Development

Stage 5: Late Career (ages 55–retirement):
Remain productive in work, maintain self-esteem, prepare for effective retirement.

Stage 4: Midcareer (ages 40–55):
Reappraise early career and early adulthood goals, reaffirm or modify goals, make choices appropriate to middle adult years, remain productive.

Stage 3: Early Career (ages 25–40):
Learn job, learn organizational rules and norms, fit into chosen occupation and organization, increase competence, pursue goals.

Stage 2: Organizational Entry (ages 18–25):
Obtain job offer(s) from desired organization(s), select appropriate job based on complete and accurate information.

Stage 1: Preparation for Work (ages 0–25):
Develop occupational self-image, assess alternative occupations, develop initial occupational choice, pursue necessary education.

Avoid the Plateau Trap

Author Judith Bardwick was the first to label the "plateauing" phenomenon.[24] A **career plateau** is a situation in which, for either organizational or personal, reasons the probability of moving up the career ladder is low. According to Bardwick, only 1 percent of the labour force will not plateau in their working lives. There are three types of plateaus: structural, content, and life. A *structural plateau* marks the end of promotions; one will now have to leave the organization to find new opportunities and challenges. A *content plateau* occurs when a person has learned a job too well and is bored with day-to-day activities. A *life plateau* is more profound and may feel like a midlife crisis. People who experience life plateaus often have allowed work or some other major factor to become the most significant aspect of their lives, and they experience a loss of identity and self-esteem when there is no longer success in that area. Figure 5.9 lists some probing questions employees can ask themselves if they find themselves in, or trying to overcome, a career plateau.

Organizations can help individuals cope with plateaus by providing them with opportunities for lateral growth or allowing them to choose their own assignments when opportunities for advancement do not exist. Companies with international divisions can encourage employees to take assignments abroad to expand their horizons. Career enrichment programs can help people learn more about what gives them satisfaction within a company, as well as what kinds of opportunities will make them happiest if they go elsewhere.

career plateau
A situation in which, for either organizational or personal reasons, the probability of moving up the career ladder is low

Reality CHECK

Career Edge Making a Difference

Career Edge is Canada's youth internship program that helps university, college, and high school graduates launch their careers as full-time paid interns. For recent graduates with no work experience, obtaining that first job can be difficult. They are caught in the cycle of "no experience, no job; no job, no experience." Career Edge helps graduates obtain that first job, which then leads, in most cases, to a permanent job. Career Edge also operates Ability Edge, a national internship program for graduates with disabilities. Career Edge contacts host organizations, which agree to provide an internship combining four elements: employment experience, learning, coaching, and networking. Because the interns are employed by Career Edge, employers do not have to fight for additional positions (a very difficult task in any organization), but can employ the interns from contract budgets. The interns are paid a stipend of $1,500 per month.

All job posting is done electronically. Employers post internships on the Career Edge website (www. careeredge.org). Underemployed or unemployed graduates can sign on and search for internships by sector, company, educational discipline, date of posting, city, length of internship desired, and so on. When a fit is found, the full job description is made available. The site also offers information on job search skills such as résumé and interview preparation.

Frances Randle, former president and CEO of Career Edge, says: "The contact is made directly between the candidate and the host organization, because these students have to learn how to market themselves, and companies have to commit to the intern directly. Interns are looking for practical experience, increased confidence in their abilities, learning about their fields, getting experience in that field, having challenging work, developing a network, and getting feedback on performance, in that order. Companies want recent university graduates who are enthusiastic, flexible, interested in learning, yet with some technical skills and the ability to communicate."

Since opening for business in October 1996, when the youth unemployment rate was nearly 18 percent, Career Edge has placed thousands of interns at over 1,000 companies. About 50 percent of the interns find full-time work with their host organizations.

Source: Interview with Francis Randle, 2006.

FIGURE **5.9**

Career Plateau Questions

1. Do I accept high visibility assignments?
2. Do I continue to advance my education, both formal and vocational?
3. Am I recognized by other leaders in my organization?
4. Am I routinely promoted?
5. Am I known as a versatile employee?
6. Do I continue to get larger-than-normal raises?
7. Do I rate at the high end of the performance ratings?
8. Do I have a plan with measurable objectives, and have I updated it recently?

Source: John Rosche, "Who's Managing Your Career?" *Contract Management* 44, no. 2 (February 2004): 20–22.

CAREER DEVELOPMENT INITIATIVES

Although career management involves a good deal of analysis and planning, the reality is that it needs to provide a set of tools and techniques that help employees gauge their potential for success in the organization. Informal counselling by HR staff and supervisors is used widely. As we mentioned earlier in the chapter, many organizations give their employees information on educational assistance, employment equity programs and policies, salary administration, and job requirements. Career planning workbooks and workshops are also popular means of helping employees identify their potential and the strength of their interests.

In a study undertaken by human resources consulting firm Drake Beam Morin, the six most successful career management practices used within organizations are as follows:

- Placing clear expectations on employees so that they know what is expected of them throughout their careers with the organization
- Giving employees the opportunity to transfer to other office locations, both domestically and internationally
- Providing a clear and thorough succession plan to employees
- Encouraging performance through rewards and recognition
- Giving employees the time and resources they need to consider short- and long-term career goals
- Encouraging employees to continually assess their skills and career direction

Supporting career development activities can help the organization achieve retention and productivity goals as outlined in the Business Case.

The Business CASE

The Value of Career Development Programs

Career development programs may not appear to offer the obvious return on investments that absenteeism or safety management programs offer. However, employers should start to measure the following in order to make the business case for career development:

- *Attraction:* Do organizations establish reputations as "academies" that develop talent through solid career development and mentoring programs?
- *Retention:* Do units with strong career development programs have higher retention rates of top talent than those without?
- *Employability:* If organizations cannot guarantee lifetime employment, do they have a moral responsibility to provide career development programs that ensure that employees are employable?
- *Commitment:* In those organizations with career development programs, is there a correlation between employee commitment and productivity?

One company did measure retention and commitment changes that occurred as a result of a career development program and the ROI was 190 percent. A manufacturer of technical equipment was experiencing a 37-percent turnover among highly valuable engineers. As part of the solution, the company created a high-potential development program. The participants attended workshops, identified learning projects, and were paired with an executive sponsor and an external mentor. Eighteen months later turnover was down from 37 percent to 1 percent, and participants were more productive, as measured by their superiors.

Sources: Jack Ito and Celeste Brotheridge, "Does Supporting Employees Career Adaptability Lead to Commitment, Turnover, or Both?" *Human Resource Management,* Spring 2005, 44, 1, 5–19; Catherine Mossop, "Mentoring Can Drive Business Goals," *Canadian HR Reporter,* July 12, 2004, 6.

In contrast, organizations also need to be mindful of the internal barriers that inhibit employees' career advancement. Generally, these barriers can include such things as the following:

- Lack of time, budgets, and resources for employees to plan their careers and to undertake training and development
- Rigid job specifications, lack of leadership support for career management, and a short-term focus
- Lack of career opportunities and pathways within the organization for employees.[25]

Career Planning Workbooks

Several organizations have prepared workbooks to guide their employees individually through systematic self-assessment of values, interests, abilities, goals, and personal development plans. General Motors' Career Development Guide contains a section called "What Do You Want Your Future to Be?" in which the employee makes a personal evaluation. GE has developed an extensive set of career development programs, including workbooks to help employees explore life issues that affect career decisions.

Some organizations prefer to use workbooks written for the general public. Popular ones include Richard N. Bolles's *What Color Is Your Parachute?*, *Luck Is No Accident: Making the Most of Happenstance in Your Life and Career* by John D. Krumboltz and Al S. Levin, and *Self-Directed* by John Holland.[26] These same books are recommended to students for help in planning their careers.

Career Planning Workshops

Workshops offer experiences similar to those provided by workbooks. However, they have the advantage of providing a chance to compare and discuss attitudes, concerns, and plans with others in similar situations. Some workshops focus on current job performance and development plans. Others deal with broader life and career plans and values. As mentioned earlier, employees should be encouraged to assume responsibility for their own careers; a career workshop can help them do that. It can also help them learn how to make career decisions, set career goals, create career options, seek career planning information, and at the same time build confidence and self-esteem.[27]

Career Counselling

Career counselling involves talking with employees about their current job activities and performance, personal and career interests and goals, personal skills, and suitable career development objectives. While some organizations make counselling a part of the annual performance appraisal, career counselling is usually voluntary. Career counselling may be provided by the HR staff, managers and supervisors, specialized staff counsellors, or outside consultants. Several techniques for career counselling are outlined in this chapter's Appendix. The obligations of employees to return the organization's investments in their development are outlined in Ethics in HRM. As employees approach retirement, they may be encouraged to participate in preretirement programs, which often include counselling along with other helping activities. Preretirement programs will be discussed in Chapter 11.

Determining Individual Development Needs

Because the requirements of each position and the qualifications of each person are different, no two individuals will have identical developmental needs. For one

career counselling
The process of discussing with employees their current job activities and performance, personal and career interests and goals, personal skills, and suitable career development objectives

Ethics in **HRM**

Individual Investment or Organizational Investment?

Organizations such as Procter & Gamble and IBM invest a great deal of time and money in developing their professional sales staff and management personnel. Similarly, the federal government offers new university recruits up to six months of language training and tuition-paid university courses, as well as several weeks of skills training, within the first two years on the job.

Other organizations refuse to invest in the long-term development of their employees. They cite

statistics suggesting that over one-third of university recruits will quit within the first year. In addition, they argue that other corporations will raid these highly trained personnel.

Do employees who have received the benefit of extensive development programs at the employer's expense have an obligation to remain with the organization so that it can realize a return on its investment?

fast-track program

A program that encourages young managers with high potential to remain with an organization by enabling them to advance more rapidly than those with less potential

individual, self-development may consist of developing the ability to write reports, give talks, and lead conferences. For another, it may require developing interpersonal skills in order to communicate and relate more effectively with a diverse workforce. Periodic performance appraisals can provide a basis for determining each employee's progress. Meetings with the employee in which these appraisals are discussed are an essential part of self-improvement efforts.

In helping individuals plan their careers, it is important for organizations to recognize that younger employees today seek meaningful training assignments that are interesting and involve challenge, responsibility, and a sense of empowerment. They also have a greater concern for the contribution that their work in the organization will make to society. Unfortunately, they are frequently given responsibilities they view as rudimentary, boring, and composed of too many "make-work" activities. Some organizations are attempting to retain young managers with high potential by offering a **fast-track program** that enables them to advance more rapidly than

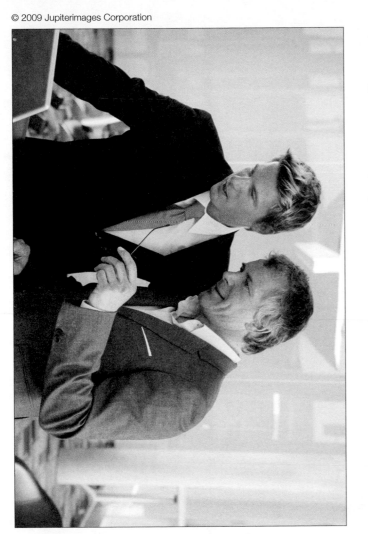

HR managers may act as career counsellors to those at the beginning of their careers.

those with less potential. A fast-track program can provide for a relatively rapid progression—lateral transfers or promotions—through a number of managerial positions designed to expose the employee to different functions within the organization.

Mentoring

It is common to hear people mention individuals at work who influenced them. They frequently refer to their immediate managers who were especially helpful as career developers. But they also mention others at higher levels in the organization who provided them with guidance and support in the development of their careers. Executives and managers who coach, advise, and encourage employees are called **mentors.**

A mentoring relationship need not be formal. In reality, informal mentoring goes on daily within every type of organization. Generally, the mentor initiates the relationship, but sometimes an employee will approach a potential mentor for advice. Most mentoring relationships develop over time on an informal basis. They frequently end that that way, too. However, proactive organizations emphasize formal mentoring plans that assign a mentor to employees considered for upward movement in the organization. GE, for example, selects the top 20 percent of its top performers and allows these people to choose their own mentors from a list of top executives. Under a good mentor, learning focuses on goals, opportunities, expectations, standards, and assistance in fulfilling one's potential.[28]

The top ten myths about mentors are shown in Figure 5.10. Figure 5.11 shows a list of the most effective features of mentors as well as partners. In order to form an effective mentoring relationship, an employee seeking a mentor should follow a few general guidelines.

mentors

Individuals who coach, advise, and encourage individuals of lesser rank

FIGURE **5.10**

Top Ten Myths about Mentors

Myth 1: *Mentors exist only for career development.* Sometimes the mentor focuses on formal career development. Sometimes the mentor is teacher, counsellor, and friend. Some mentors assume all these roles. This enhances both personal and professional development.

Myth 2: *You need only one mentor.* We can have multiple mentors in our lives. Different mentors provide different things and tap different facets of our lives.

Myth 3: *Mentoring is a one-way process.* Learning flows both ways. The mentor often learns from the protégé, so the growth is reciprocal.

Myth 4: *A mentor has to be older than the protégé.* Age does not matter. Experience and wisdom matter. Do not deprive yourself of learning opportunities from others who have rich experiences.

Myth 5: *A mentor has to be the same gender and race as the protégé.* The purpose of mentoring is to learn. Do not deprive yourself. Seek mentors who are different from you.

Myth 6: *Mentor relationships just happen.* Being in the right place at the right time can help, but the key to selecting a good mentor is what (not who) you need. Do not be afraid to actively seek a mentor.

Myth 7: *Highly profiled people make the best mentors.* Prestige and success can be good, but good advice, leadership styles, work ethics, and the like vary by individuals. Good mentors are people who challenge you according to your needs, readiness, and aspirations.

Myth 8: *Once a mentor, always a mentor.* Over time, the mentor should pull back and let the protégé go his or her own way. Although the two may maintain contact, the relationship changes over time.

Myth 9: *Mentoring is a complicated process.* The most complicated part is getting out of a bad mentor relationship. If the relationship is not productive, find a tactful way to disengage.

Myth 10: *Mentor–protégé expectations are the same for everyone.* Individuals seek mentors for the same reasons: resources, visibility, enhanced skills, and counsel. But each individual brings different expectations. The key is understanding where the protégé is now, not where he or she should be.

FIGURE 5.11

Mentoring Functions

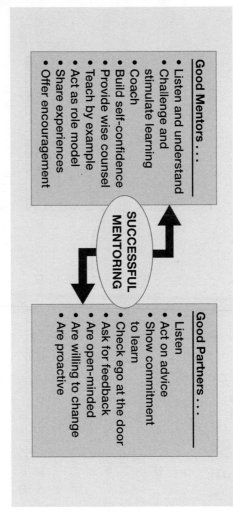

Good Mentors . . .
- Listen and understand
- Challenge and stimulate learning
- Coach
- Build self-confidence
- Provide wise counsel
- Teach by example
- Act as role model
- Share experiences
- Offer encouragement

SUCCESSFUL MENTORING

Good Partners . . .
- Listen
- Act on advice
- Show commitment to learn
- Check ego at the door
- Ask for feedback
- Are open-minded
- Are willing to change
- Are proactive

Source: Matt Starcevich, PhD and Fred Friend, "Effective Mentoring Relationships from the Mentee's Perspective," *Workforce*, supplement (July 1999): 2–3. Used with permission of the Centre for Coaching and Mentoring, Inc., http://coachingandmentoring.com.

1. *Research the person's background.* Do your homework. The more you know about your potential mentor, the easier it will be to approach him or her and establish a relationship that will work for both of you.

2. *Make contact with the person.* Have a mutual friend or acquaintance introduce you, or get involved with your potential mentor in business settings. That will help the mentor see your skills in action.

3. *Request help on a particular matter.* Let the mentor know that you admire him or her, and ask for help in that arena. For example, you might say, "You're good at dealing with customers. Would it be OK if I came to you for advice on my customers?" Keep your request simple and specific.

4. *Consider what you can offer in exchange.* Mentoring is a two-way street. If you can do something for your potential mentor, then, by all means, tell him or her.

5. *Arrange a meeting.* Once your specific request has been accepted, you are ready to meet with your potential mentor. Never go into this meeting cold. Set goals, identify your desired outcomes, and prepare a list of questions. Listen attentively. Then ask your prepared questions and request specific suggestions.

6. *Follow up.* After the meeting, try some of your potential mentor's suggestions and share the results. Express appreciation by identifying something in particular that was significant to you.

7. *Ask to meet on an ongoing basis.* After your potential mentor has had a chance to not only meet and interact with you, but also see the value of what he or she can provide, you are in a good position to request an ongoing relationship. Suggest that you meet with him or her regularly, or ask permission to get help on an ad hoc basis.[29]

When done well, the mentoring process is beneficial for both the pupil and the mentor. One survey found, for example, that 77 percent of companies with successful mentoring programs reported that they effectively increased employee retention.[30]

Even though participants in e-mentoring typically never meet in person, many form long-lasting e-mail connections that tend to be very beneficial. Still, most

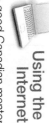

Using the Internet

A good Canadian mentoring resource site that provides links to mentoring sites as well as book and video reviews, article and case study searches, and lots of other resources can be found at http://www.mentors.ca

Highlights in **HRM 5.3**

E-Mentoring

Virtual mentoring is often an excellent way for busy mentors (and equally busy protégés) to deal with time constraints. Those who are comfortable with e-mail and the Internet say that both have many advantages over real-time meetings. Because there are no geographic boundaries to e-mentoring (i.e., no need for the mentor and the protégé to be in the same city), a wider range of possible mentors is accessible. Scheduling is easier, since either party can log on at any time to ask questions or offer counsel. Because the mentor can take time to consider the answers to questions, the individual being mentored gets more reasoned responses. People seeking advice often maintain a log of their questions and the answers to them; these can be shared later with others in similar situations. Because e-mentoring is more efficient in many ways, mentors

can advise more people. The technology can even help match mentors and protégés.

IBM Canada runs a pilot e-mentoring program in which 40 girls from grades seven and eight have been matched with computer programmers, sales personnel, and administrators, the goal being to stimulate their interest in technology careers.

The downside is that e-mentoring uses "flat" technology and so cannot convey emotions or facial expressions that in a face-to-face interaction often alert the partners to underlying problems. That being said, the advantages of e-mentoring—quick feedback, well-considered responses, and more informal communication—make it one of the more popular ways for employees to build organizational know-how.

participants see these connections as supplements to—rather than substitutes for—in-company mentors. Highlights in HRM 5.3 describes the advantages of e-mentoring.

Networking

As the number of contacts grows, mentoring broadens into a process of **career networking.** As a complement to mentoring, in which relationships are more selective, networking relationships tend to be more varied and temporary. The networks can be internal to a particular organization or connected across many different organizations.

According to the Monster Career Advice Center (http://career-advice.monster.com/career-networking/home.aspx), there are many ways to identify networking contacts. Some of the best places to consider are the following:

career networking

The process of establishing mutually beneficial relationships with other businesspeople, including potential clients and customers

- University or college alumni association or career office networking lists
- Extended family
- Friends' parents and other family members
- Professors, advisers, coaches, tutors, and clergy
- Former bosses and friends' and family members' bosses
- Members of clubs, religious groups, and other organizations
- All nearby organizations

Career Self-Management Training

Because the employer–employee relationship has become more transactional and employees are being increasingly encouraged to take responsibility for their own career management, many organizations are establishing programs for employees on how they can engage in *career self-management.* The training focuses on two major objectives: (1) helping employees learn to continuously gather feedback and information about their careers and (2) encouraging them to prepare for mobility.

The training is not geared to skills and behaviours associated with a specific job, but rather toward long-term personal effectiveness. Essentially, career self-management is not a process but an event. Employees typically undertake self-assessments to increase their awareness of their own career attitudes and values. In addition, they are encouraged to widen their viewpoint beyond the next company promotion to broader opportunities in the marketplace, attend conferences, and develop good long-term relationships with their bosses or other mentors. Participants might be encouraged to engage in career networking or to identify other means to prepare for job mobility, such as hearing reports from employees who made transitions to new job opportunities both within and outside the organization.[31]

DEVELOPING A DIVERSE TALENT POOL

RECRUITMENT AND DEVELOPMENT OF WOMEN

In Chapter 3 we discussed some of the current trends in the employment of women in jobs that until recently were held predominantly by men. Included among these jobs are management-level positions. Organizations are continually concerned, as a result of employment equity requirements and because of the need for strong leadership, about increasing the proportion of women they employ as managers.

A major employment obstacle for women, both skilled and unskilled, is the stereotyped thinking that persists within our society. Still another barrier has been that women in the past had fewer years of experience in the workforce and were not as likely as men to have professional training and preparation for entrance or advancement into management positions. This situation is changing, however. Today, there have been significant increases in the enrollment of women in programs leading to degrees in management and other professional fields. In addition, more women are enrolling in management seminars and certification programs that will further prepare them for higher managerial positions.

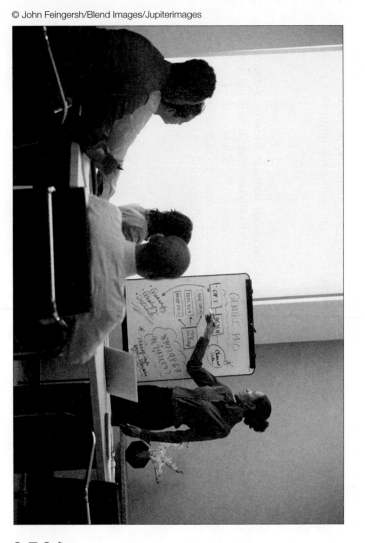

Artificial barriers or "glass ceilings" are being shattered by successful women executives and entrepreneurs.

[OUTCOME]

ELIMINATING WOMEN'S BARRIERS TO ADVANCEMENT

Despite some of the changes taking place, women in management traditionally have been at a disadvantage because they have not been part of the so-called "old boys'" network, an informal network of interpersonal relationships that has traditionally provided a means for senior (male) members of the organization to pass along news of advancement opportunities and other career tips to junior (male) members. Women have typically been outside the network, lacking role models to serve as mentors.

To combat their difficulty in advancing to management positions, women in several organizations have developed their own women's networks. The Bank of Montreal has a women's network that any female employee can join in order to facilitate career development. Corporate officers are invited to regularly scheduled network meetings to discuss such matters as planning, development, and company performance. Network members view these sessions as an opportunity to let corporate officers know of women who are interested in and capable of furthering their careers. Employees who have had a senior manager take an interest in their careers have received more promotions and compensation than those who have not.[32]

As we mentioned previously, several online e-mentoring networks are available. Advancing Women is expressly devoted to working women (www.advancingwomen.com). In addition, an organization devoted to helping employers break down barriers to upward mobility for women is Catalyst, a not-for-profit organization. Catalyst (www.catalystwomen.org) not only courts corporate officers but also offers career advice, job placement, continuing education, and related professional development for women of all ages. Catalyst is regarded as a leading resource for information on women and work.

There is substantial evidence that stereotyped attitudes toward women are changing. As women pursue career goals assertively and attitudes continue to change, the climate for women in management will be even more favourable. Research has shown that newer male managers tend to be more receptive to the advancement of women managers. That said, and despite the fact that more women hold managerial positions than they have in years past, the proportion of women in senior management still remains extremely low, around 15 percent.[33] Although these data suggest that there has been some progress, there is much left to do to break the "glass ceiling"—the invisible barrier of attitudes, prejudices, and old boys' networks that blocks the progress of women who seek important positions in organizations.

GLASS CEILING AUDITS

The glass ceiling can be defined as "those artificial barriers based on attitudinal or organizational bias that prevent qualified individuals from advancing upward in their organizations into management level positions."[34] "Glass ceiling reviews," also known as "corporate reviews," are conducted in order to identify practices that appear to hinder the upward mobility of both qualified women to

- Upper-level management and executive training
- Rotational assignments
- International assignments
- Opportunities for promotion
- Opportunities for executive development programs at universities
- Desirable compensation packages
- Opportunities to participate on high-profile project teams
- Upper-level special assignments

Organizations are increasingly conducting their own glass ceiling audits prior to government review to avoid fines and externally imposed corrective action.

These audits can document any ceilings and the reasons they exist. Self-audits are one step to tapping the potentials of a diversified workforce. A company could have certain promotion goals for women and minorities. For example, if 40 percent of the qualified people who apply for assistant store manager positions are women, 40 percent of those hired should be women. Minorities and women are also breaking through the glass ceiling by starting their own businesses. As one entrepreneur put it, "It's not hard to break through the glass ceiling when you own it."

PREPARING WOMEN FOR MANAGEMENT

As we noted earlier, opportunities for women to move into management positions are improving. In addition to breaking down the barriers to advancement, the development of women managers demands a better understanding of women's needs and the requirements of the management world.

Many employers now offer special training to women who are on a management career path. Organizations may use their own staff or outside firms to conduct this training. Opportunities are also available for women to participate in seminars and workshops that provide instruction and experiences in a wide variety of management topics.

In addition to formal training opportunities, women today are provided with a wealth of information and guidance in books and magazines. Business sections in bookstores are stocked with numerous books written especially for women who want a better idea of the career opportunities available to them. Many books are devoted to the pursuit of careers in specific fields.[35]

ACCOMMODATING FAMILIES

One of the major problems women have faced is that of having both a managerial career and a family. Women managers whose children are at an age requiring close parental attention often experience conflict between their responsibility to the children and their duty to the employer. If the conflict becomes too painful, they may decide to forgo their careers, at least temporarily, and leave their jobs. In recent years, many employers, including BMO and IBM, and the accounting firm KPMG, have inaugurated programs that are mutually advantageous to the career-oriented woman and the employer. The programs, which include alternative career paths, extended leave, flextime, job sharing, and telecommuting, provide new ways to balance career and family. These efforts are paying off. Both IBM and KPMG, for example, report that their programs have helped them retain and increase their numbers of women workers.

ADVANCEMENT OF MINORITIES TO MANAGEMENT

Many organizations have specific career planning programs for minority employees. These programs are intended to equip employees with career planning skills and development opportunities that will help them compete effectively for advancement.

We observed in Chapter 3 that many employers make a special effort to recruit minorities. Once individuals from minority groups are on the job, it is important for employers to provide opportunities for them to move ahead in the organization as they improve their job skills and abilities. The province of Manitoba has a Career Gateway Program that recruits members of visible minorities for term placements in positions where there will be a future recruitment need, and then provides support for training and career development. The province also provides volunteer opportunities, which may then lead to placements. The federal government has a website (www.ncvm.gc.ca) that offers tools for career planning for visible minorities through the National Council of Visible Minorities.

OTHER IMPORTANT TALENT CONCERNS

MANAGING A MULTIGENERATIONAL WORKFORCE

Managing Generational Differences

There is a growing consensus that the labour force can be segmented by age, and divided into four groups: the traditionalists (born 1922–1945), the boomers (1946–1964), the Gen Xers (1965–1980), and the Gen Yers (born after 1981). Each of these groups may possess distinct values, and goals, and thus have different recruitment expectations. Highlights in HRM 5.4 captures some of the differences in recruitment strategies for each of these groups.

Highlights in HRM 5.4

The Four Generations

Generation	Traditionalists Born 1922–1945	Baby Boomers Born 1946–1964	Generation X Born 1965–1980	Generation Y Born after 1981
Life-defining events	Great Depression, WWII, Korean War, rise of labour unions.	Civil rights movement, Cold War, Quebec Crisis, Trudeau era.	Personal computers, AIDS, corporate downsizing, fall of Communism.	Digital age, reality TV, attacks of 9/11, corporate and government scandals.
Attitudes and values	Loyalty, dedication, sacrifice, honour, compliance, hard-working.	Personal growth, youthfulness, equality, ambition, collaboration.	Independence, pragmatism, results-driven, flexibility, and adaptive.	Confident, optimistic, civic minded, innovative, diversity focused, techno-savvy.
Goal	To build a legacy.	To put their stamp on things.	To maintain independence in all areas of their lives	To find work and create a life that has meaning
Recruitment expectations	Formal, traditional methods of recruitment. Employer-driven negotiations.	In-person, relationship building, recruitment. Balanced negotiations.	On-site tours, meeting with current employees. Open employee-driven negotiation.	Review/evaluation of organization's reputation. Valued employee-driven negotiation.
Unique selling proposition	The organization's legacy, stability, and strong loyalty to its employees.	The organization's market leadership and growth.	The organization's career growth, learning, and development opportunities.	The organization's social responsibility, diversity, and creativity.
Key messages	Your experience will be valued here. You will be given the support to learn the organization's IT systems.	You can be a star here. Your personal growth is important to us.	You will work independently.	You will work with experts from across divisions. You will have a variety of experiences.

Source: Giselle Kovary and Adwoa Bauhene, n-gen People Performance Inc., "Recruiting the Four Generations," *Canadian HR Reporter* (May 23, 2005): R6.

Recruiting those under 30 means adapting to these digitally savvy workers. The days of classified ads and job fairs are gone. A better way to find these candidates is to develop engaging and informative websites with blogs and podcasts. To be attractive to these candidates, organizations should provide authentic, uncensored blogs by Gen Y employees, a hiring FAQ page in the form of a wiki, and a method to answer candidates' questions in real-time formats.[36] Retaining them means customizing jobs, providing flexible hours and work places, and having lots of conversations (not lectures) about work for this insatiably curious generation. But most of this generation does not expect to work for the same organization forever, and so smart employers will maintain "alumni" relationships with those who depart. One day they may return and, with insider knowledge of the company, be able to be productive much faster.

EMPLOYING DUAL-CAREER COUPLES

As discussed throughout this book, the employment of both members of a couple has become a way of life in North America. Economic necessity and social forces have encouraged this trend to the point that over 80 percent of all marriages are now **dual-career partnerships** in which both members follow their own careers and actively support each other's career development. As with most lifestyles, the dual-career arrangement has its positive and negative sides. A significant number of organizations are concerned with the problems facing dual-career couples and offer assistance to them. Flexible working schedules are the most frequent organizational accommodation to these couples. Other arrangements include leave policies under which either parent may stay home with a newborn, policies that allow work to be performed at home, day care on an organization's premises, and job sharing.

The difficulties that dual-career couples face include the need for quality child care, time demands, and emotional stress. However, the main problem these couples face is the threat of relocation because gaining the support of a spouse or significant other is crucial for employees. Many large organizations now offer some kind of job-finding assistance for spouses of employees who are relocated, including payment of fees charged by employment agencies, job counselling firms, and executive search firms. Organizations are also developing networking relationships with other employers to find jobs for the spouses of their relocating employees. These networks can provide a way to "share the wealth and talent" in a community while simultaneously assisting in the recruitment efforts of the participating organizations.[37]

Relocating dual-career couples to foreign facilities is a major issue that international employers face. Fewer employees are willing to relocate without assistance for their spouses. Many employers have developed effective approaches for integrating the various allowances typically paid for overseas assignments when husband and wife work for the same employer. Far more complex are the problems that arise when couples work for two different employers. The problems associated with overseas assignments of dual-career couples will be examined in greater detail in Chapter 15.

dual-career partnerships

Couples in which both members follow their own careers and actively support each other's career development

Small Business APPLICATION

Recruiting generally applies to small business much the same way as large business, with the exception of one significant factor: scale. While large companies will have a continuous ongoing need to recruit people into roles, and may require arge numbers of employees, small business may require only one or two persons every now and then. This difference is significant, as small companies may not justify the time and expense associated with developing recruiting strategies to hire few people. Also, because small business hiring needs are lower, the determination

continued

207

of recruitment channels will be based on ensuring a small number of suitable candidates rather than a large number of general candidates.

For example, if a large company needs to hire 20 customer service people because of growth and turnover, the hiring volume would support hiring a designated recruiter, developing and posting an effective posting, screening large numbers of candidates, and developing a set of behavioural competencies for the role to be used in selections. If a small company had the need for 1 customer service person, it certainly would not follow the same approach.

So how do small companies recruit successful staff? Because (1) the hiring needs of small companies are lower, (2) small companies are generally more closely allied with friends and family, and (3) small companies are typically more closely involved with the local community, small companies usually avoid the cost and administration of major promotion of jobs on large job boards or newspapers, and rely on networking through employee referrals or through small targeted industry groups. That does not mean that small companies cannot benefit from recruiting tools such as Web job boards. When small companies need to create a job posting, they can go to these sites to review jobs posted and then tailor an existing posting to reflect their specific requirements. What will be different is that the small company will post that job posting at its place of business, or circulate it to those in its network, rather than posting it on a large-scale job board.

SUMMARY

[OUTCOME 1]   In order to expand the talent pool of organizations—the number and kind of people available for employment—organizations must focus on multiple approaches to recruitment and career management. Outside sources for recruitment are especially useful for filling jobs with special qualifications and to acquire individuals with new skills, ideas, and perspectives. Which outside sources and methods are used in recruiting will depend on the recruitment goals of the organization, conditions of the labour market, and specifications of the jobs to be filled.

[OUTCOME 2]   Employers usually find it advantageous to use internal promotion and transfer to fill as many openings as possible above the entry level. By recruiting from within, an organization can capitalize on the previous investments it has made in recruiting, selecting, training, and developing its current employees. Furthermore, internal promotions reward employees for their past performance and send a signal to other employees that their future efforts will pay off. However, potential candidates from the outside should occasionally be considered in order to prevent the inbreeding of ideas and attitudes.

The legal requirements governing employment equity make it mandatory that employers proactively recruit and promote members of designated groups so that their representation at all levels within the organization will approximate their proportionate numbers in the labour market. These efforts include recruiting not only those members who are qualified, but also those who can be made qualified with reasonable training and assistance.

[OUTCOME 3]   Job opportunities can be identified by studying jobs and determining the knowledge and skills each one requires. Once that is accomplished, key jobs can be identified, and job progressions can be planned. These progressions can then serve as a basis for developing the career paths of employees. Once career paths are developed and employees are identified on the career ladders, it is possible to inventory the jobs and determine where the individuals with the required skills and knowledge are needed or will be needed.

Identifying and developing talent is a responsibility of all managers. In addition to employees' immediate superiors, there should be others in the organization who can nominate and sponsor employees with promise. Many organizations use assessment centres to identify managerial talent and recommend employees engage in developmental activities to reach their full potential. Mentoring has been found to be valuable for providing guidance and support to employees and potential managers.

OUTCOME 4

Beyond recruiting per se, organizations also need to consider the progression and promotion of employees through a series of jobs.

In this way, firms can manage not only the immediate contribution of individuals to the organization, but also the long-term contribution throughout their careers.

A career development program is a dynamic process that should integrate individual employee needs with those of the organization. It is the responsibility of the employee to identify his or her own knowledge, skills, and abilities (KSAs) as well as interests and values, and to seek out information about career options. The organization should provide information about its mission, policies, and plans and what it will provide in the way of training and development for the employee.

OUTCOME 5

In order to be successful, a career management program must receive the support of a firm's top managers. The program should reflect the goals and the culture of the organization, and managerial personnel at all levels must be trained in the fundamentals of job design, performance appraisal, career planning, and counselling. Employees should be aware of the organization's philosophy and its goals; otherwise they will not know how their goals match those of the organization. HRM options.

OUTCOME 6

The first step toward facilitating the career development of women is to eliminate barriers to their advancement. Creating women's networks, providing special training for women, accepting women as valued members of the organization, providing mentors for them, and accommodating families have been found to be effective ways to facilitate women's career development.

A diversified workforce is composed of many different groups, an important segment of which is minority groups. In addition to creating conditions that are favourable for recognizing and rewarding the performance of employees, many organizations have special programs such as internships that provide them with hands-on experience as well as special training opportunities. Other groups that require the attention of management are the multigenerational workforce, and dual-career couples, who often need flexible working

policies, especially those related to the rotation, transfer, and promotion of employees, should be consistent with the firm's goals. The objectives and opportunities of the career development program should be announced widely throughout the organization.

KEY TERMS

9-box grid, 186
assessment centre, 186
career counselling, 198
career networking, 202
career paths, 191
career plateau, 195

dual-career partnerships, 207
fast-track program, 199
job posting and bidding, 185
job progressions, 191
mentors, 200
nepotism, 178

outplacement services, 193
promotion, 192
realistic job preview (RJP), 183
relocation services, 192
transfer, 192
yield ratio, 182

DISCUSSION QUESTIONS

1. In what ways do executive search firms differ from traditional employment agencies?

2. Explain how realistic job previews (RJPs) operate. Why do they appear to be an effective recruitment technique?

3. More than 50 percent of all MBAs leave their first employer within five years. Although the change may mean career growth for these individuals, it represents a loss to the employers. What are some of the probable reasons an MBA would leave his or her first employer?

4. What are the advantages and disadvantages of filling openings from internal sources?

5. How might retired executives in any organization assist in the career management of current employees?

6. The chapter presents the factors that attract students (Figure 5.1). Working with your group, ask 30 students a simple question: What are the key factors that would attract you to a job?" Compile the results and compare your results to the list in Figure 5.1. Then, in groups, develop a recruitment

campaign for a fictional company that would appeal to your group of students.

7. What contributions can a career management program make to an organization that is forced to downsize its operations?

8. What are some of the barriers to advancement opportunities for women in many organizations?

9. The Ottawa Police Services recognized that traditional recruiting practices may not work in a multicultural society. New immigrants may not

view policing as an honourable profession, based on their previous experiences. Sitting in large groups hearing about opportunities in the police force is not effective, as many are reluctant to ask questions. Newcomers also do not know about the "ride along" program that most forces operate as a way to introduce potential recruits to the daily work of a police officer. Design a recruitment campaign for the police force that would be sensitive to the perceptions and needs of a multicultural candidate base.

INTERNET EXERCISE

Think about the job that you would like to obtain when you graduate. Use The Riley Guide (http://www.rileyguide.com/counsel.html) to find articles on

exploring career options, how to research the labour market, etc. Prepare a paper based on your findings for your job.

HRM EXPERIENCE

Career Management

We often think that successful people plan their careers out in advance and then work toward their goals in a very logical, sequential manner. Although some successes are designed and implemented this way, others are created through insight, preparedness, and taking advantages of opportunities as they arise.

Assignment

1. Form teams of four to six members. Identify three different people to interview about their careers. One person should be in the early stages of his or

her career; one should be in midcareer; and one should be in the final stages of his or her career.

2. Ask each person to identify his or her career goals and how they have changed or are expected to change over time.

3. Ask each person to describe the sequence of events that led to where he or she is. How well does that story align with the traditional model of careers?

4. Ask each person what (if anything) he or she would do differently. Ask what advice he or she has for you about how to approach your career.

BIZFLIX EXERCISES

IN GOOD COMPANY: CARTER MANAGES HIS CAREER

This chapter described many ways a company can recruit employees. The scenes from the film *In Good Company* show other ways a company can find new employees. Use the following questions as guides while viewing these scenes.

A corporate takeover brings star advertising executive Dan Foreman (Dennis Quaid) a new boss who is half his age. Carter Duryea (Topher Grace)— Dan's new boss—wants to prove his worth as the new marketing chief at *Sports America,*

Waterman Publishing's flagship magazine. Carter applies his unique approaches while dating Dan's daughter, Alex (Scarlett Johansson).

These scenes come from the "breaking news" segment that appears in the first five minutes of the film. They follow Carter's presentation of his concepts for marketing cell phones to children under age five. Mark Steckle (Clark Greg) tells his staff that Teddy K. (Malcolm McDowell) asked him to take over marketing at the magazine division of Waterman Publishing, Teddy K.'s recent acquisition. Carter Duryea discusses Mark's move to Waterman Publishing and the prospect of Carter following him to head advertising sales for *Sports America*. The film continues with Dan Foreman soon learning that Carter is his new boss.

What to Watch for and Ask Yourself

• Do these scenes show external or internal recruitment?

• Recall an earlier discussion in this chapter of the employee's role in career planning. What does Carter do to help his career?

• Review the earlier section "Career Development Initiatives." Which of those initiatives appear in these scenes? What is Mark Steckle's role in Carter's career development?

CASE STUDY 1

HUMAN RESOURCES CAREER PROGRESSION

If you ask Andrea Taylor how she went from being a part-time clerk to the director of human resources at the White Pages in eight years, without hesitation she will tell you it was "networking." After graduating with a degree in sociology from Brock University, she did what many students do; she travelled in Europe for three months. When she came home, she completed her internship at Timothy's coffee shop and quickly left to join a photocopying service in a large downtown building where Bell Canada was a tenant. Eventually she made a contact in Bell who encouraged her to apply to Tele-Direct, which is commonly known as the Yellow Pages. Since there were no vacancies available, Andrea took a more stable job at Techno-Graph as a shipper and receiver. In the meantime, she persistently called Tele-Direct, once a week for a year, in order to see if there was a spot for her on the team.

Finally, a short-term contract position opened up in Ad Traffic, from 4 p.m. to midnight. Looking for another job before her contract expired, Andrea was encouraged by the same contact to apply to the human resources department because they were looking for a junior administration assistant. She was told not to apply since she was not a permanent employee. Regardless, she put her name in. On the last day of her employment, she was called into the HR department and informed that she got the job. While conducting her various junior duties such as filing, posting job listings, and doing research, she discovered "that I just loved human resources." She checked out a local college offering certificate programs and began to take courses at night.

The contact who originally suggested that she apply was now leaving to become the national manager, and Andrea was selected to replace her as the new HR assistant manager. Moving up the ranks, Andrea became responsible for everything from new hires to collective agreements and the implementation of new human resources initiatives. When the company changed ownership and direction (and HR was outsourced), Andrea left the organization to seek employment where she could practise HR. Her networking served her well again when another contact turned down a job, but recommended Andrea—who became the HR director of a Web designing company. Three years later, another contact in the sales department from the Yellow Pages suggested she apply, and she became the HR director of the White Pages.

Today Andrea finds herself in a position where she is recommended for jobs. Unofficially, Andrea had created mentors out of contacts and the relationships have served both parties well. This happened because she treated every chance encounter with great respect that turned them into lifelong business relationships. "You never know who or where you will meet the next contact that changes your life."

QUESTIONS

1. How did Andrea become so successful in such a short period of time?
2. After reviewing the chapter, suggest all possible ways that Andrea prepared herself for career advancement.

CASE STUDY 2

RECRUITMENT CHANNELS

LoyaltyOne is Canada's leading loyalty marketing organization and the creator and operator of Canada's premier coalition loyalty program, the AIR MILES® Reward Program. As of early 2009, more than 9.8 million Collector accounts, representing approximately two-thirds of all Canadian households, actively participate in the program. AIR MILES reward miles can be redeemed for more than 500 different rewards, such as movie passes, family attractions, electronic merchandise, sports and recreation, travel, and more. Millions of redemptions are made each year. Collectors can shop and collect AIR MILES reward miles at more than 100 brand-name sponsors across the country, representing thousands of retail and service locations. The AIR MILES Reward Program's website is http://www.airmiles.ca.

In addition to operating the AIR MILES Reward Program, LoyaltyOne works with many of North America's leading brands in the retail, financial services, grocery, petroleum retail, travel, and hospitality industries. Through a team of businesses, each specializing in a loyalty discipline, LoyaltyOne designs, delivers, and manages a suite of loyalty marketing services—coalition loyalty programs, advanced analytical marketing, creative services, loyalty consulting, and more. Its loyalty marketing publication *COLLOQUY* provides a worldwide audience of 30,000-plus marketers with news, insights, and best practices from the loyalty marketing industry. LoyaltyOne's website is http://www.loyalty.com.

LoyaltyOne is a unit of Alliance Data Systems Corporation (NYSE:ADS). Alliance Data is a leading provider of marketing, loyalty, and transaction services, managing 120 million consumer relationships for North America's leading brands and expanding its reach into Europe and Asia. With over 1,400 associates across a multitude of functions such as consumer intelligence analysts, marketing specialists, customer care representative, IT, and business developers, LoyaltyOne is continuously looking for top-calibre talent. It is one of the premier organizations to utilize the World Wide Web, job boards such as Workopolis.ca and niche boards such as the HRPA, and maintain a strong staffing division.

LoyaltyOne is looking to proactively source candidates across its lines of business as it suspects its current practices may not be proactive or target both passive and active candidates across the organization and the variety of roles within each business unit.

Currently, LoyaltyOne

- Employs a well-developed recruitment team using traditional methods to source candidates

- Is looking for very specialized segments of the workforce, and these individuals are in limited supply
- Is determined and must work hard to find and hire candidates that meet both job requirements and fit the corporate culture
- Considers its approach somewhat passive and is looking to become more proactive
- Wishes to hire qualified individuals across all age groups
- Would welcome the creative use of social networking tools but currently already uses LinkedIn and Facebook

LoyaltyOne faces challenges:

QUESTION

1. The organization's brand image may not be clearly recognized by candidates as AIR MILES has been historically the company's most predominant brand.

2. Its businesses are diverse as are the knowledge and skills that it would be seeking in its prospective associates.

QUESTION

1. Provide recommendations for proactive best practices and leading-edge sourcing approaches.

CASE STUDY 3

PREPARING A CAREER DEVELOPMENT PLAN

Sue Ann Scott was a receptionist at the headquarters of a large corporation. A high school graduate, she had no particular skills other than an ability to organize her job duties and a pleasant personality. Unfortunately, she did not have any particular plan for career development; nevertheless, she wanted very much to improve her economic position. Recognizing her educational limitations, she began taking accounting courses on a random basis in an evening adult education program.

Scott also took advantage of the corporation's job bidding system by applying for openings that were posted, even though in many instances she did not meet the specifications listed for them. After being rejected several times, she became discouraged. Her depressed spirits were observed by Elizabeth Burroughs, one of the department managers in the corporation. Burroughs invited Scott to come to her office for a talk about the problems she was having. Scott took full advantage of this opportunity to express her frustrations and disappointments. As she unburdened herself, it became apparent both to her and to Burroughs that during interviews she repeatedly apologized for having "only a high school education," an attitude that had probably made it difficult for the interviewers to select her over other candidates who were more positive about their backgrounds and skills. Burroughs suggested that Scott might try taking a more positive approach during her interviews. For example, she could stress her self-improvement efforts at night school and the fact that she was a dependable and cooperative person who was willing to work hard to succeed in the job for which she was applying.

Following Burroughs's advice, Scott applied for a position as invoice clerk, a job for which she felt she was qualified. She made a very forceful and positive presentation during her interview, stressing the favourable qualities she possessed. As a result of this approach, she got the job. While the pay for an invoice clerk was not much more than that for a receptionist, the position did offer an avenue for possible advancement into the accounting field, in which the accounting courses she was taking would be of value.

QUESTIONS

1. What are some of the possible reasons Scott did not seek or receive advice from her immediate supervisor?

2. After reviewing the chapter, suggest all possible ways that Scott can prepare herself for career advancement.

CAREER COUNSEL

Visit the *Managing Human Resources* website at http://www.belcourt6e.nelson .com for assistance in preparing a career plan.

NOTES AND REFERENCES

1. Sherry Sullivan, "The Changing Nature of Careers: A Review and Research Agenda," *Journal of Management* 25, no. 3 (1999): 457–484; Steve Prentice, "A Game Plan for Career Survival," *Canadian HR Reporter* 15, no. 11 (June 3, 2002): 27–28; Mark Tatge, "Prescription for Growth," *Forbes* 171, no. 4 (February 17, 2003): 64–67.

2. Joseph Bower, "Solve the Succession Crisis by Growing Inside-Outside Leaders," *Harvard Business Review* 85, no. 11 (November 2007): 90–96.

3. Douglas P. Shuit, "Monster Board Games," *Workforce Management* 82, no. 2 (November 2003): 37–42; Joe Dysart, "New Directions in Internet Recruiting," *Contractor Magazine* 53, no. 7 (July 2006): 33–36.

4. Rob Yeung, "Finders Keepers," *Accountancy Magazine* 134, no. 1335 (November 2004): 42–44; Dysart, "New Directions in Internet Recruiting," 33–36.

5. Ibid.

6. Jennifer Taylor Arnold, "Employee Referrals at a Keystroke," *HR Magazine* 51, no. 10 (October 2006): 82–88; Victoria Furnes, "The New Frontier," *Personnel Today* (January 22, 2008): 13–16.

7. Mike Martin, "Friends in need," *The Globe and Mail*, April 13, 2005, C1.

8. Keith Swenson, "Maximizing Employee Referrals," *HRfocus* 76, no. 1 (January 1999): 9–10.

9. "In Praise of Nepotism?" *Business Ethics Quarterly* 15, no. 1 (January 2005): 153–161; Richard Reeve and Gavin Sheridan, "Nepotism: Is It Back?" *New Statesman* 135 (September 29, 2003): 22–25.

10. Jennifer Schramm, "Globalizing by Degrees," *HR Magazine* 53, no. 4 (April 2008): 144.

11. J. O'Krafka, "Vancouver Health Region Brands Its Advantages," *Canadian HR Reporter* (April 25, 2005): 8.

12. Max Messmer, "Recognizing Potential Stars by Promoting from Within," *Strategic Finance* 86, no. 5 (October 2004): 9–11; "Retaining vs. Recruiting?" *T+D* 61, no. 8 (August 2007): 74.

13. J. W. Marriott, "Our Competitive Strength: Human Capital," *Executive Speeches* 15, no. 5 (April–May 2001): 18–21.

14. Debbie Mack, "P&G Fights to Protect Its Bounty," *Corporate Legal Times* 13, no. 135 (February 2003): 64.

15. "How to Implement an Effective Process for a New HR Management System," *HRfocus* 82, no. 1 (January 2005): 3–4.

16. Robert Rodriguez, "Filling the HR Pipeline," *HR Magazine* 49, no. 9 (September 2004): 78–84; James W. Walker, "Perspectives," *Human Resource Planning* 25, no. 1 (2002): 12–14; Stanley Ragalevsky, "CEO Succession: Five Best Practices for Internal Candidates," *Community Banker* 17, no. 2 (February 2008): 24–25.

17. "The Pros and Cons of Online Recruiting," *HRfocus* 81 (April 2004 Supplement): S2.

18. Paul W. B. Atkins and Robert E. Wood, "Self versus Others' Ratings as Predictors of Assessment Center Ratings: Validation Evidence for 360-Degree Feedback Programs," *Personnel Psychology* 55, no. 4 (Winter 2002): 871–905; Michelle A. Dean and Philip L. Roth, "Ethnic and Gender Subgroup Differences in Assessment Center Ratings: A Meta-Analysis," *Journal of Applied Psychology* 93, no. 3 (May 2008): 685–691.

19. Ellen Ernst Kossek, Karen Roberts, Sandra Fisher, and Beverly Demarr, "Career Self-Management : A Quasi-Experimental Assessment of the Effects of a Training Intervention," *Personnel Psychology* 51, no. 4 (Winter 1998): 935–962; Shelly Green, "Attracting Top Talent Despite Business Challenges," *Journal of Career Planning and Employment* 62, no. 4 (Summer 2002): 24–28; Cynthia Jones, "Step by Step: Creating a Strategic Management System for Career Services Delivery," *Journal of Career Planning and Employment* 62, no. 3 (Spring 2002): 21–27.

20. Peg O'Herron and Peggy Simonsen, "Career Development Gets a Charge at Sears Credit," *Personnel Journal* 74, no. 5 (May 1995): 103–106. See also Jules Abend, "Behind the Scenes at: Sears," *Bobbin* 39, no. 11 (June 1998): 22–26; Shari Caudron, "The De-Jobbing of America," *IndustryWeek* 243, no. 16 (September 5, 1994): 30–36; Edward E. Lawler III, "From Job-Based to Competency-Based Organizations," *Journal of Organizational Behavior* 15, no. 1 (January 1994): 3–15; Douglas T. Hall, "Accelerate Executive Development—At Your Peril!" *Career Development International* 4, no. 4 (1999): 237–239.

21. "How a Talent Management Plan Can Anchor Your Company's Future," *HRfocus* 81, no. 10 (October 2004): 7–10.

22. Elizabeth Craig, John Kimberly, and Hamid Bouchikhi, "Can Loyalty Be Leased?" *Harvard Business Review* 80, no. 9 (September 2002): 24–34; Edward Potter, "Improving Skills and Employability in the 21st Century," *Industrial and Labor Relations Review* 55, no. 4 (July 2002): 739–745.

23. Suzanne C. de Janasz, Shery E. Sullivan, and Vicki Whiting, "Mentor Networks and Career Success: Lessons for Turbulent Times," *Academy of Management Executive* 17, no. 4 (November 2003): 78–92; Kate Walsh and Judith Gordon, "Creating an Individual Work Identity," *Human Resource Management Review* 18, no. 1 (March 2008): 46–61.

24. Judith Bardwick, *The Plateauing Trap* (New York: AMACOM, 1986). See also Judith Bardwick, *Danger in the Comfort Zone: From Boardroom to Mailroom—How to Break the Entitlement Habit That's Killing American Business* (New York: AMACOM Book Division, 1995); Max Messmer, "Moving beyond a Career Plateau," *National Public Accountant* 45, no. 7 (September 2000): 20–21; John Rosche, "Who's Managing Your Career?" *Contract Management* 44, no. 2 (February 2004): 20–22; "Attention U.S. Workers," *T+D* 61, no. 10 (October 2007): 12.

25. Larry Cambron, "Career Development Pays," *Far Eastern Economic Review* 164, no. 42 (October 25, 2001): 83.

26. For up-to-date career information and guidance as well as an opportunity for self-analysis, see Richard Bolles, *What Color Is Your Parachute 2008: A Practical Manual for Job-Hunters & Career-Changers* (Berkeley, CA: Ten Speed Press, 2007).

27. Susan Wells, "Smoothing the Way," *HR Magazine* 46, no. 6 (June 2001): 52–58; Heath Row, "Market Yourself," *Fast Company* 58 (May 2002): 24.

28. de Janasz, Sullivan, and Whiting, "Mentor Networks and Career Success," 78–92; Carole Gaskell, "Reward Coaching Behavior to Encourage Its Use," *People Management* 14, no. 4 (February 21, 2008): 70.

29. Jeff Barbian, "The Road Best Traveled," *Training* 39, no. 5 (May 2002): 38–42; Kathleen Barton, "Will You Mentor Me?" *Training and Development* 56, no. 5 (May 2002): 90–92.

30. Elaine Biech, "Executive Commentary," *Academy of Management Executive* 17, no. 4 (November 2003): 92–94.

31. Thomas A. Stewart, "What's in It for Me?" *Harvard Business Review* 83, no. 1 (January 2005): 8; Marilyn Clarke and Margaret Patrickson, "The New Covenant of Employability," *Employee Relations* 30, no. 2 (2008): 121–141.

32. A. J. Merrell and E. H. James "Gender and Diversity in Organizations: Past, Present and Future Directions," *Sex Roles* 45, no. 5/6 (September 2001): 243.

33. Catalyst, "Women in Management," (July 2008), http://www.catalyst.org/publication/247/women-in-management-in-canada, retrieved July 30, 2009.

34. Robert Schwab, "Dancing on the Glass Ceiling," *Colorado Biz* 31, no. 5 (May 2004): 18–23. A host of reports on glass ceiling issues can be found on the U.S. Department of Labor's website at http://www.dol.gov.

35. The interested reader should find the following books very informative: Johanna Hunsaker and Phillip Hunsaker, *Strategies and Skills for Managerial Women* (Cincinnati, OH: South-Western, 1991); Marian Ruderman and Patricia Ohlott, *Standing at the Crossroads: Next Steps for High-Achieving Women* (New York: John Wiley and Sons, 2002).

36. D. Tapscott, "How to Hire the Net Generation," *BusinessWeek* (November 24, 2008), http://www.businessweek.com/technology/content/nov2008/tc20081121_828725.htm, retrieved July 30, 2009.

37. Janice Rosenberg, "Dual Career Couples Face Expensive Choices," Bankrate.com (July 2, 2007); Erin White, "Help Increases for Partners of Relocated Workers," *Wall Street Journal* 251, no. 70 (Marcy 25, 2008): D4.

Appendix

PERSONAL CAREER DEVELOPMENT

Because you are likely to spend more time working during your life than doing anything else, it makes sense to plan your career. There are numerous ways for an employer to contribute to an individual employee's career development and at the same time meet the organization's HR needs. Although organizations can certainly be a positive force in the development process, the primary responsibility for personal career growth still rests with the individual. After all, your career is likely to begin before and often continue after a period of employment with a particular organization. To help you, as students and prospective employees, achieve your career objectives, this Appendix is included to provide some background for your personal development and decisions.

DEVELOPING PERSONAL SKILLS AND COMPETENCIES

Planning for a career involves more than simply acquiring specific job knowledge and skills. Job know-how is clearly essential, but you must also develop other skills to be successful as an employee. To succeed as a manager, you must achieve still higher-level skills in the areas of communication, time management, self-motivation, interpersonal relationships, and leadership.

Hundreds of self-help books, professional journals, and magazines have been written on these topics or contain articles about them, and myriad opportunities to participate in workshops are available, often sponsored by employers.[1] For example, the pointers on the basic skills of successful career management listed in Highlights in HRM 5.A1 are taken from a competency assessment conducted at Caterpillar.

CHOOSING A CAREER

Many years ago, when management expert Peter Drucker was asked about career choices, he said, "The probability that the first job choice you make is the right one for you is roughly one in a million. If you decide your first choice is the right one, chances are that you are just plain lazy."[2] The implications of this statement are just as true today. You often have to do a lot of searching and changing to find a career path that is psychologically and financially satisfying.

Highlights in HRM 5.A1

Career Competencies at Caterpillar

During the Caterpillar business unit's career development training process in Joliet, Illinois, the company compiled the following capabilities as necessary for success within the reorganized, changing organization:

- Interpersonal skills. Possesses team-building and leadership skills; can effectively lead groups and facilitate group interaction
- Problem-solving skills. Can analyze and use problem-solving approaches
- Communication skills. Can verbalize articulately, make presentations, and write cogently
- Leadership skills. Is recognized by peers as a natural leader; accomplishes results without formal authority
- Organization and planning skills. Can manage time; sets and achieves goals

- Technical skills. Possesses education specific to assignments and job content; understands and uses appropriate level of technical skills
- Responsibility. Takes initiative; accepts accountability for own work and additional tasks for the good of the group
- Assertiveness. Able and comfortable with communicating openly and directly; demonstrates self-confidence and awareness of others' perceptions
- Flexibility. Can adapt to organizational changes and changing market needs; willingly considers new ideas and implements new ways of doing things
- Judgment. Can determine level of risk and appropriate action; accepts accountability for significant decisions

Source: Peggy Simonsen and Cathy Wells, "African Americans Take Control of Their Careers," *Personnel Journal* 73, no. 4 (April 1994): 99–108; See also David Dubois, "The Seven Stages of One's Career," *Training and Development* 54, no. 12 (December 2000): 45–50.

USE OF AVAILABLE RESOURCES

A variety of resources are available to aid in the process of choosing a satisfying career. Counsellors at colleges and universities, as well as those in private practice, are equipped to assist individuals in evaluating their aptitudes, abilities, interests, and values as they relate to career selection. Placement offices and continuing education centres offer some type of career planning assistance. In addition to career exploration, most of them offer résumé writing help, interview preparation, and job placement assistance. Looking on the Internet is also a great way to jump-start your career planning. Most job-posting websites, including Monster and CareerBuilder. com, contain free career information as well.

ACCURACY OF SELF-EVALUATION

Successful career development depends in part on an individual's ability to conduct an accurate self-evaluation. When you are doing a self-evaluation, you need to consider factors that are personally significant to you. The most important internal factors are your interests, academic aptitude and achievement, occupational aptitudes and skills, social skills, communication skills, and leadership abilities. You also need to consider the salary level, status, opportunities for advancement, and growth for the job you seek. External factors that should be assessed include your family values and expectations, economic conditions, employment trends, and job market information.

THE SIGNIFICANCE OF INTEREST INVENTORIES

Psychologists who specialize in career counselling typically administer a battery of tests. The *Strong Vocational Interest Bank* (SVIB), developed by E. K. Strong, Jr., was among the first of the interest tests.[3] Somewhat later, G. Frederic Kuder

FIGURE **5.A1**

Combination of Career Interests and Skills

developed inventories to measure degree of interest in mechanical, clerical, scientific, and persuasive activities, among others. Both the Strong and the Kuder interest inventories have been used widely in vocational counselling.

Strong found substantial differences in interests that vary from occupation to occupation and that a person's interest pattern, especially after age 21, tends to become quite stable. By taking his test, now known as the *Strong Interest Inventory*, you can learn the degree to which your interests correspond with those of successful people in a wide range of occupations. Your personality type can also be obtained by using a special scoring key on the *Strong Interest Inventory* answer sheet. This key, developed by John Holland, provides scores on six personality types: (1) realistic, (2) investigative, (3) artistic, (4) social, (5) enterprising, and (6) conventional. These categories characterize not only a type of personality, but also the type of working environment that a person would find most satisfying. In the actual application of Holland's theory, combinations of the six types are examined. For example, a person may be classified as realistic-investigative-enterprising (RIE). Jobs in the RIE category include mechanical engineer, line-person, and air traffic controller. To facilitate searching for occupations that match your personality type, such as RIE, Holland devised a series of tables that correlate the Holland categories with jobs in the National Occupational Classification (NOC), described in Chapter 3.[4]

Another inventory that measures both interests and skills is the *Campbell Interest and Skill Survey* (CISS), which can be taken online at a number of sites for a fee, as can the *Strong Interest Inventory*.[5] The CISS can be used not only to help people explore their career path options, but also to help organizations develop their employees or to reassign them because of major organizational changes. In completing the inventory, individuals report their levels of interest and skill using a six-point response scale on 200 interest items and 120 skill items. CISS item responses are translated into seven orientations—influencing, organizing, helping, creating, analyzing, producing, and adventuring—and further categorized into 29 basic scales such as leadership and supervision to identify occupations that reflect today's workplace.

CHOOSING AN EMPLOYER

Once an individual has made a career choice, even if only tentatively, the next major step is deciding where to work. The choice of employer may be based primarily on location, on the immediate availability of a position, on starting salary, or on other basic considerations. Douglas Hall proposes that people frequently choose an organization on the basis of its climate and how it appears to fit their needs. According to Hall, people with high needs for achievement are more likely to choose aggressive, achievement-oriented organizations. Power-oriented people are more likely to choose influential, prestigious, power-oriented organizations. Affiliative people are more likely to choose warm, friendly, supportive organizations. We know that people whose needs fit with the climate of an organization are rewarded more and are more satisfied than those who fit in less well, so it is natural to reason that fit would also be a factor in a person's choice of an organization.[6]

Knowing something about an employer and industry can give you a competitive edge in terms of getting an interview, landing a job, and negotiating a good salary. Numerous company directories containing information about privately and publicly held companies are available. Corporate websites are another source. Often under the "Investors" or "Media" tabs you can find press releases issued by the companies in which you are interested. The releases often highlight the initiatives companies are pursuing and the directions in which they are taking their businesses. Business, industry, and professional publications are a good source, too. Simply "Googling" a company can turn up a great deal of information.

Once you have landed an interview, you have the opportunity to learn more about an employer, including the type of people who work there, its corporate culture, benefits, and so forth. If you are offered a job with the firm, a website such as salary.com can help you determine whether the firm's offer is appropriate. You should ask yourself the following questions before you accept a job offer with a particular company:

QUESTIONS TO ASK YOURSELF BEFORE YOU ACCEPT A JOB OFFER

- Have I been offered a fair salary? Is it comparable to what other people in the same position are making?
- Have I met my potential boss? Does he or she seem like someone with whom I can have a good working relationship?
- What do I know about my potential coworkers?
- Will I be comfortable in this office environment?
- Is the corporate culture in line with my own values, attitudes, and goals?
- Can I handle the commute to this job?

BECOMING AN ENTREPRENEUR

At the opening of the century, no discussion of careers would be complete if entrepreneurship opportunities were not mentioned. Being an **entrepreneur**—someone who starts, organizes, manages, and assumes responsibility for a business or other enterprise—offers a personal challenge that many individuals prefer over being an employee. Small businesses are typically run by entrepreneurs who accept the personal financial risks that go with owning a business but who also benefit directly from the success of the business.[7]

Since the details of organizing a business are beyond the scope of this book, Figure 5.A2 is presented to provide an overview of the basic steps in starting a new business.[8]

entrepreneur
One who starts, organizes, manages, and assumes responsibility for a business or other enterprise

FIGURE 5.A2

Twelve Steps for Starting a New Business

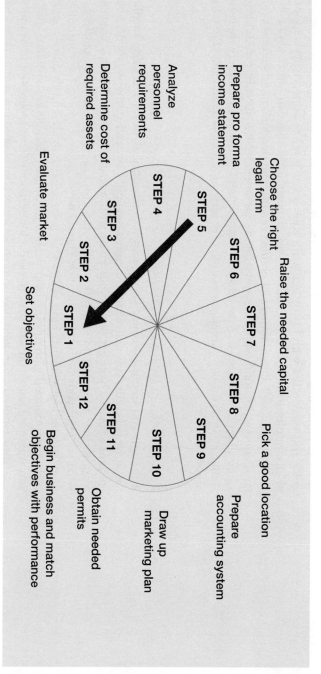

Choose the right legal form

Prepare pro forma income statement

Analyze personnel requirements

Determine cost of required assets

Evaluate market

STEP 6

STEP 5

STEP 4

STEP 3

STEP 2

STEP 1

STEP 7

STEP 8

STEP 9

STEP 10

STEP 11

STEP 12

Raise the needed capital

Pick a good location

Prepare accounting system

Draw up marketing plan

Obtain needed permits

Begin business and match objectives with performance

Set objectives

Source: From *Business in a Changing World*, 3rd edition, by W. Cunningham, R. Aldag, and S. Block: 139 © 1993. Reprinted with permission of South-Western, a division of Cengage Learning: http://www.cengage.com/permissions.

KEEPING A CAREER IN PERSPECTIVE

For most people, work is a primary factor in the overall quality of their lives. It provides a setting for satisfying practically the whole range of human needs and is thus of considerable value to the individual. Nevertheless, it is advisable to keep one's career in perspective so that other important areas of life are not neglected.

DEVELOPING OFF-THE-JOB INTERESTS

Satisfaction with one's life is a product of many forces. Unfortunately, when people complain about not having a good work–life balance, often the problem is not too much work, but too little "life," according to Randall Craig of Pinetree Advisors, a human resources strategy consulting firm.[9] Some of the more important ingredients of "life" are physical health, emotional well-being, financial security, harmonious interpersonal relationships, freedom from too much stress, and achievement of one's goals. While a career can provide some of the satisfaction that one needs, most people find it necessary to turn to interests and activities outside their career. Off-the-job activities not only provide a respite from daily work responsibilities, but also offer satisfaction in areas unrelated to work. With that said, it is up to you to decide what is important to you and how to spend your work and off-the-job time. Your life is yours to live, and it is shorter than you think.

BALANCING MARITAL AND/OR FAMILY LIFE

As we have said, the one event that often poses the greatest threat to family needs is relocation. Families often experience conflicts between the desire to advance the careers of different parents and the desire to stay in one place and put down family roots. Many employers now provide assistance in this area, including relocation counselling, in an effort to reduce the severity of the pain that can accompany relocations. Although relocation is a serious threat to employees with families, there are also other sources of conflict. Some work-related sources of conflict include the number of hours a person must work per week, frequency of the overtime required, and frequency and irregularity of shift work. If an employee is experiencing ambiguity and/or conflict with his or her work role, a low level of supervisory support, or disappointment due to unfulfilled work expectations, this can affect his or her family life as well. Other sources of conflict include the need to spend an unusually large amount of time with a person's family members, either to care for children, aging elders, or a spouse. The different employment patterns in a family and dissimilarity in a couple's career orientations are also commonplace and can take a toll on employees.

PLANNING FOR RETIREMENT

Although you might be many years from retirement, it is never too early to plan for it. In your 20s, you will want to begin a savings plan and perhaps pay off your student loans. As you get older, your goals will probably change. Perhaps you will want to buy a home, and you will need money for a down payment. Regardless of what stage of your life you are in, you should never neglect saving for your retirement throughout your working years. This is because a small sum of money saved early, compounded with interest over years, can amount to millions of dollars. But if you wait until later, you will have to save a lot of money for it to amount to as much.

Your employer can help you with some aspects of retirement planning by providing you with information about tax-advantaged employer and individual savings plans. Your company might even be able to help you project what your health insurance costs will be in retirement, for example, if you are not covered by company-provided insurance. But although employer-sponsored preretirement programs can be helpful (as we will see in Chapter 11), planning for your own retirement is up to you. Do you want to travel or live in another province or country? What kind of retirement does your spouse envision? How much money will all of this require? Your employer will not be able to answer these questions.

However, by reading about the subject of retirement and taking it seriously while you are young, you will be able to answer these questions yourself. Planning early will help you set the stage for a healthy and satisfying retirement as free as possible from worries—especially worries that could have been avoided or minimized had you taken a few easy steps earlier in life.

KEY TERM

entrepreneur, 220

NOTES AND REFERENCES

1. A selection of self-help publications on a variety of topics may be found in any bookstore. College and university bookstores typically have a wide selection in their trade or general books department. Two particularly useful books might be Edward Crip and Richard Mansfield, *The Value-Added Employee: 31 Competencies to Make Yourself Irresistible to Any Company* (London: Butterworth-Heinemann, 2001) and Daniel Goleman, *Emotional Intelligence* (New York: Bantam Books, 1995).
2. Mary Harrington Hall, "A Conversation with Peter Drucker," *Psychology Today* (March 1968): 22.
3. E. K. Strong, Jr., of Stanford University, was active in the measurement of interests from the early 1920s until his death in 1963. Since then his work has been carried on by the staff of the Measurement Research Center, University of Minnesota. The Strong Interest Inventory is distributed by Consulting Psychologists Press, Inc., P.O. Box 60070,

Palo Alto, CA 94306, to qualified people under an exclusive license from the publisher, Stanford University Press.

4. Gary D. Gottfredson and John L. Holland, *Dictionary of Holland Occupational Codes* (Lutz, FL: Psychological Assessment Resources, December 1996); Derek Parker, "The Skills Shortage: Making Headway, But No Easy Answers," *Manufacturers' Monthly* (September 2007).

5. David Lubinski, Camilla P. Benbow, and Jennifer Ryan, "Stability of Vocational Interests among the Intellectually Gifted from Adolescence to Adulthood: A 15-Year Longitudinal Study," *Journal of Applied Psychology* 80, no. 1 (February 1995): 196–200; Hope Samborn, "Left Click, Left Law," *ABA Journal* 92, no. 7 (July 2006): 58.

6. Douglas T. Hall and Jonathan E. Moss, "The New Protean Career Contract: Helping Organizations and Employees Adapt," *Organizational Dynamics* 26, no. 3 (Winter 1998): 22–37. See also Douglas T. Hall, *The Career Is Dead, Long Live the Career: A Relational Approach to Careers* (San Francisco: Jossey-Bass, 1996); Douglas T. Hall, "Protean Careers of the 21st Century," *Academy of Management Executive* 10, no. 4 (1996): 8–16; Douglas T. Hall and Associates, *Career Development in Organizations* (San Francisco: Jossey-Bass, 1986); Yue-Wah Chay and Samuel Aryee, "The Moderating Influence of Career Growth Opportunities on Careerist Orientation and Work Attitudes: Evidence of the Protean Career Era in Singapore," *Journal of Organizational Behavior* 20, no. 5 (September 1999): 613–623.

7. Julie Rose, "The New Risk Takers," *Fortune Small Business* 12, no. 2 (March 2002): 28–34; Jack Howard, "Balancing Conflicts of Interest When Employing Spouses," *Employee Responsibilities & Rights* 20, no. 1 (March 2008): 29–43.

8. For information on starting a business, the interested reader might look into Bob Adams, *Adams Streetwise Small Business Startup* (Holbrook, MA: Adams Media Corporation, 1996); Linda Pinson and Jerry Jinnett, *Anatomy of a Business Plan: Starting Smart, Building a Business and Securing Your Company's Future* (Chicago: Upstart, 1996); Kenneth Cook, *AMA Complete Guide to Strategic Planning for Small Business* (Lincolnwood, IL: NTC Business Books, 1995); Priscilla Y. Huff, *101 Best Small Businesses for Women* (Rocklin, CA: Prima, 1996); Constance Jones, *The 220 Best Franchises to Buy: The Sourcebook for Evaluating the Best Franchise Opportunities* (New York: Bantam Doubleday Dell, 1993).

9. Jamie Eckle, "Randall Craig," *Computerworld* 42, no. 26 (June 23, 2008): 36.

Employee Selection

After studying this chapter, you should be able to

[OUTCOME] **1** Explain the objectives of the personnel selection process.

[OUTCOME] **2** Identify the various sources of information used for personnel selection.

[OUTCOME] **3** Compare the value of different types of employment tests.

[OUTCOME] **4** Illustrate the different approaches to conducting an employment interview.

[OUTCOME] **5** Describe the various decision strategies for selection.

There is perhaps no more important topic in human resources management than employee selection. If it is true that organizations succeed or fail based on the talents of employees, then managers directly influence that success through the people they hire. Regardless of whether the company is large or small, hiring the best and the brightest employees lays a strong foundation for excellence. Alternately, it is common to hear managers who do not recognize this point lament the inordinate amount of time they spend trying to fix bad selection decisions. It is a costly activity, too. A recent study by the Society for HR Management found that the cost of hiring someone for a wrong intermediate position is approximately $20,000, and the cost of hiring the wrong person for a senior manager's position is $100,000. The bottom line is that good selection decisions make a difference. So do bad ones.

MATCHING PEOPLE AND JOBS

In conjunction with the recruiting process, which is designed to increase the number of applicants whose qualifications meet job requirements and the needs of the organization, **selection** is the process of reducing that number and choosing from among those individuals who have the relevant qualifications.

Figure 6.1 shows in broad terms that the overall goal of selection is to maximize "hits" and avoid "misses." Hits are accurate predictions, and misses are inaccurate ones. The cost of one type of miss would be the direct and indirect expense of hiring an employee who turns out to be unsuccessful. The cost of the other type of miss is an opportunity cost—someone who could have been successful did not get a chance. While the overall selection program is often the formal responsibility of the HR department, line managers typically make the final decision about hiring people in their unit. It is important, therefore, that managers understand the objectives, policies, and practices used for selection. In that way, they can be highly involved in the process from the very beginning. Those responsible for making selection decisions should have adequate information upon which to base their decisions.

selection

The process of choosing individuals who have relevant qualifications to fill existing or projected job openings

FIGURE **6.1**

The Goal of Selection: Maximize "Hits"

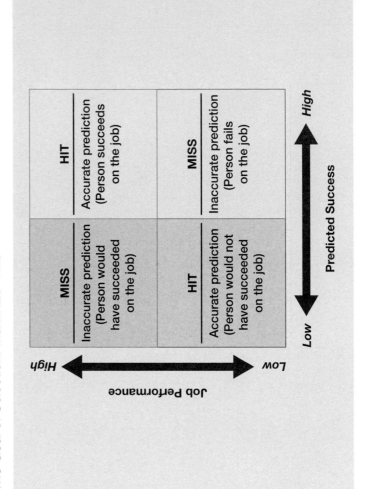

Information about the jobs to be filled, knowledge of the ratio of job openings to the number of applicants, and as much relevant information as possible about the applicants themselves are essential for making sound decisions.

PERSON–JOB FIT: BEGINNING WITH JOB ANALYSIS

In Chapter 4, we discussed the process of analyzing jobs to develop job descriptions and specifications. Job specifications, in particular, help identify the *individual competencies* employees need for success—the knowledge, skills, abilities, and other factors (KSAOs) that lead to superior performance. By identifying competencies through job analysis, managers can then use selection methods such as interviews, references, psychological tests, and the like to measure applicant KSAOs against the competencies required for the job. This is often referred to as *person–job fit*. Research has demonstrated that complete and unambiguous specification of required competencies (via job analysis) reduces the influence of racial and gender stereotypes and helps the interviewer differentiate between qualified and unqualified applicants. Research also shows that applicants whose KSAOs are well matched to the jobs they are hired for perform better and are more satisfied.[1]

PERSON–ORGANIZATION FIT

In addition to the requirements of the job, many organizations also place a priority on finding individuals who meet broader organizational requirements. Companies such as Edward Jones, a Toronto-based brokerage firm, and Intuit, an Edmonton-based financial software company, place a high priority on selecting individuals who match the values and culture of their organizations. Although there are at times potential concerns that this may create an overly uniform workforce (and raises diversity concerns), the need for teamwork and flexibility has created a keen interest in this type of person–organization fit. In many instances, managers will pass up potential employees if they do not embrace the values of the organization—even if they have excellent technical skills for the job.[2]

Ordinarily, managers are well acquainted with the requirements pertaining to the skills, physical demands, and other factors for jobs in their organizations. Interviewers and other members of the HR department who participate in selection should maintain a close liaison with the various departments so that they can become thoroughly familiar with the jobs and competencies needed to perform them.

THE SELECTION PROCESS

In most organizations, selection is an ongoing process. Turnover inevitably occurs, leaving vacancies to be filled by applicants from inside or outside the organization or by individuals whose qualifications have been assessed previously. It is common to have a waiting list of applicants who can be called when permanent or temporary positions become open.

The number of steps in the selection process and their sequence will vary, not only with the organization, but also with the type and level of jobs to be filled. Each step should be evaluated in terms of its contribution to the process. The steps that typically make up the selection process are shown in Figure 6.2. Not all applicants will go through all of these steps. Some may be rejected after the preliminary interview, others after taking tests, and so on.

As Figure 6.2 shows, organizations use several different means to obtain information about applicants. These include application forms, interviews, tests, and background investigations. Regardless of the method used, it is essential that it conform to accepted ethical standards, including privacy and confidentiality, as well as legal requirements. Above all, it is essential that the information obtained be sufficiently reliable and valid.

OUTCOME 1

FIGURE **6.2**

Steps in the Selection Process

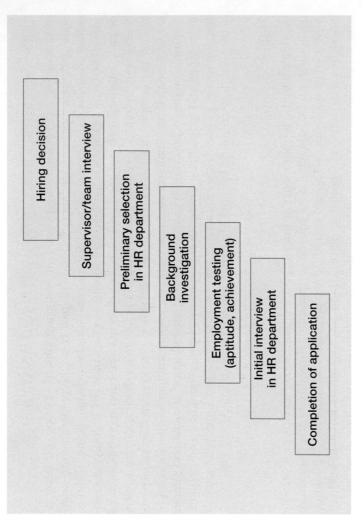

Note: Steps may vary. An applicant may be rejected after any step in the process.

OBTAINING RELIABLE AND VALID INFORMATION

The degree to which interviews, tests, and other selection procedures yield comparable data over a period of time is known as **reliability.** For example, unless interviewers judge the capabilities of a group of applicants to be the same today as they did yesterday, their judgments are unreliable (that is, unstable). Likewise, a test that gives widely different scores when it is administered to the same individual a few days apart is unreliable.

Reliability also refers to the extent to which two or more methods (interviews and tests, for example) yield similar results or are consistent. Interrater reliability—agreement among two or more raters—is one measure of a method's consistency. Unless the data on which selection decisions are based are reliable, in terms of both stability and consistency, they cannot be used as predictors.

In addition to having reliable information pertaining to a person's suitability for a job, the information must be as valid as possible. **Validity** refers to what a test or other selection procedure measures and how well it measures it. In the context of personnel selection, validity is essentially an indicator of the extent to which data from a procedure (interview or test, for example) can predict how well a person performs on the job. Like a new medicine, a selection procedure must be validated before it is used. There are two reasons for validating a procedure. First, validity is directly related to increases in employee productivity, as we will demonstrate later. Second, employment equity regulations require selection procedures to be valid.[3] Although we commonly refer to "validating" a test or interview procedure, validity in the technical sense refers to the inferences made from the use of a procedure, not the procedure itself. There are three recognized approaches to validation: criterion-related validity, content validity, and construct validity.

Criterion-Related Validity

The extent to which a selection tool predicts, or significantly correlates with, important elements of work behaviour is known as **criterion-related validity.** How well a

reliability

The degree to which interviews, tests, and other selection procedures yield comparable data over time and alternative measures

validity

The degree to which a test or selection procedure measures a person's attributes

criterion-related validity

The extent to which a selection tool predicts, or significantly correlates with, important elements of work behaviour person performs on a test, for example, is compared with his or her actual production records, supervisory ratings, training outcomes, and other measures of success that are appropriate to each type of job. In a sales job, for example, it is common to use sales figures as a basis for comparison. In production jobs, the quantity and quality of output are likely to be the best indicators of job success.

There are two types of criterion-related validity: concurrent and predictive. **Concurrent validity** involves obtaining criterion data from *current employees* at about the same time that test scores (or other predictor information) are obtained. For example, a supervisor will be asked to rate a group of clerical employees on the quantity and quality of their performance. These employees are then given a clerical aptitude test, and the test scores are compared with the supervisor's ratings to determine the degree of relationship between them. **Predictive validity**, on the other hand, involves testing *applicants* and obtaining criterion data *after* those applicants have been hired and have been on the job for a certain period of time. For example, applicants are given clerical aptitude tests, which are then filed away for later study. After the individuals have been on the job for several months, supervisors, who should not know the employees' test scores, are asked to rate them on the quality and quantity of their performance. The test scores are then compared with the supervisors' ratings.

Regardless of the method used, cross-validation is essential. **Cross-validation** is a process in which a test or battery of tests is administered to a different sample of people (drawn from the same population) for the purpose of verifying the results obtained from the original validation study.

Correlational methods are generally used to determine the relationship between predictor information such as test scores and criterion data. The correlation scatterplots in Figure 6.3 illustrate the difference between a selection test with zero validity (A) and one with high validity (B). Each dot represents a person. Note that in scatterplot A, there is no relationship between test scores and success on the job; in other words, the validity is zero. In scatterplot B, those who score low on the test tend to have low success on the job, whereas those who score high on the test tend to have high success on the job, indicating high validity. In actual practice we would apply a statistical formula to the data to obtain a coefficient of correlation referred to as a *validity coefficient*. Correlation coefficients range from 0.00, denoting a complete absence of relationship, to +1.00 and to –1.00, indicating a perfect positive and perfect negative relationship, respectively.

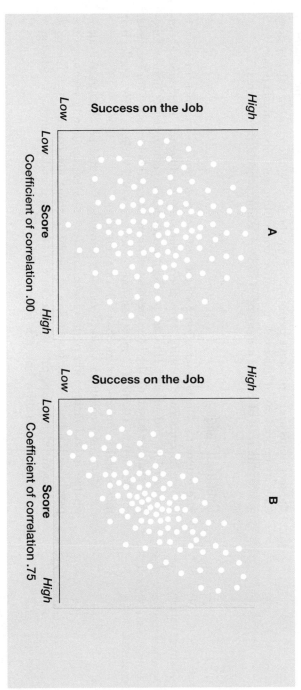

FIGURE **6.3**

Correlation Scatterplots

concurrent validity

The extent to which test scores (or other predictor information) match criterion obtained at about the same time from current employees

predictive validity

The extent to which applicants' test scores match criterion data obtained from those applicants/employees after they have been on the job for some indefinite period

cross-validation

Verifying the results obtained from a validation study by administering a test or test battery to a different sample (drawn from the same population)

A thorough survey of the literature shows that the averages of the maximum validity coefficients are 0.45 when the tests are validated against *training* criteria and 0.35 when the tests are validated against *job proficiency* criteria. These figures represent the predictive power of single tests.[4] A higher validity may be obtained by combining two or more tests or other predictors (an interview or biographical data, for instance), using the appropriate statistical formulas. The higher the overall validity, the greater the chances are of hiring individuals who will be the better performers. The criterion-related method is generally preferred to other validation approaches because it is based on empirical data.

For several decades, personnel psychologists believed that validity coefficients had meaning only for the specific jobs and organizations for which they were being used. However, more recently, as a result of several research studies—many involving clerical jobs—it appears that validity coefficients can often be generalized across situations, hence the term **validity generalization**. When there are adequate data to support the existence of validity generalization, developing selection procedures can become less costly and time consuming. The process involves analyzing jobs and situations and, on the basis of these analyses, consulting tables of generalized validities from previous studies using various predictors in similar circumstances. Because valid custom tests are more defensible in court if applicants challenge them, it is advisable for organizations to hire an industrial-organizational psychologist experienced in test validation to develop selection procedures based on validity generalization.[5]

Content Validity

When it is not feasible to use the criterion-related approach, often because of limited samples of individuals, the content method is used. **Content validity** is assumed to exist when a selection instrument, such as a test, adequately samples the knowledge and skills a person needs to do a particular job.

The closer the content of the selection instrument is to actual work samples or behaviours, the greater its content validity. For example, a civil service examination for accountants has high content validity when it requires applicants to solve accounting problems representative of those found on the job. Asking an accountant to lift a 25-kilogram box, however, is a selection procedure that has content validity only if the job description indicates that accountants must be able to meet this requirement. Content validity is the most direct and least complicated type of validity to assess. It is generally used to evaluate job knowledge and skill tests, to be described later. Unlike the criterion-related method, content validity is not expressed in correlational terms. Instead, an index is computed (from evaluations of an expert panel) that indicates the relationship between the content of the test items and a person's performance on the job.[6] While content validity does have its limitations, it has made a positive contribution to job analysis procedures and to the role of expert judgment in sampling and scoring procedures.

Construct Validity

The extent to which a selection tool measures a theoretical construct, or trait, is known as **construct validity**. Typical constructs are intelligence, mechanical comprehension, and anxiety. They are in effect broad, general categories of human functions that are based on the measurement of many discrete behaviours. For example, the Bennett Mechanical Comprehension Test consists of a wide variety of tasks that measure the construct of mechanical comprehension.

Measuring construct validity requires showing that the psychological trait is related to satisfactory job performance and that the test accurately measures the psychological trait. There is a lack of literature covering this concept as it relates to employment practices, probably because it is difficult and expensive to validate a construct and to show how it is job-related.[7]

---

validity generalization
The extent to which validity coefficients can be generalized across situations

content validity
The extent to which a selection instrument, such as a test, adequately samples the knowledge and skills needed to perform a particular job

construct validity
The extent to which a selection tool measures a theoretical construct or trait

SOURCES OF INFORMATION ABOUT JOB CANDIDATES

Many sources of information are used to provide as reliable and valid a picture as possible of an applicant's potential for success on the job. In this section, we will study the potential contributions of application forms; biographical information blanks; background investigations; polygraph, or lie detector, tests; honesty and integrity tests; and graphology. Because interviewing plays such a major role in selection and because testing presents unique challenges, there will be expanded discussions of these sources of information later in the chapter. Assessment centres, which are often used in managerial selection, were discussed in Chapter 5.

APPLICATION FORMS

Most organizations require application forms to be completed because they provide a fairly quick and systematic means of obtaining a variety of information about the applicant. Application forms serve several purposes. They provide information for deciding whether an applicant meets the minimum requirements for experience, education, and so on. They provide a basis for questions the interviewer will ask about the applicant's background. They also offer sources for reference checks. For certain jobs, a short application form is appropriate. For example, McDonald's uses a form that is quite brief but asks for information that is highly relevant to job performance. The form also provides information regarding the employer's conformity with various laws and regulations. For scientific, professional, and managerial jobs, a more extended form is likely to be used. Even when applicants come armed with elaborate résumés, it is important that they complete an application form early in the process. People, even those in high positions, frequently exaggerate their qualifications on their résumés and omit unflattering information.

Asking applicants to transcribe specific résumé material onto a standardized application form can help alleviate this problem. Far fewer people lie on application forms relative to their résumés, a 2006 survey by CareerBuilder.com found. The applicant is then asked to sign a statement that the information contained on the form is true and that he or she accepts the employer's right to terminate the candidate's employment if any of the information is subsequently found to be false.[8] The consequences of falsifying information on applications and résumés are frequently high, as described in Ethics in HRM.

Many managers remain unclear about the questions they can ask on an application form. While most know when the form was completed and gives them an idea of the marital status, and sexual orientation, other issues are less clear. In addition to consulting the province's employment laws, some of which are more restrictive than others, managers should use the following suggestions for putting together an application form:

- *Application date.* The applicant should date the application. This helps managers know when the form was completed and gives them an idea of the time limit (for example, one year) that the form should be on file.
- *Educational background.* The form should contain blanks for grade school, high school, college, and university attendance—but not the dates attended, since that can be connected with age.
- *Experience.* Virtually any questions that focus on work experience related to the job are permissible.
- *Arrests and criminal convictions.* Questions about arrests, convictions, and criminal records are to be avoided. If bonding is a requirement, the candidate can be asked if she or he is eligible.

OUTCOME 2

Ethics in **HRM**

Writing It Wrong

Most candidates for white-collar jobs prepare a résumé and submit it to prospective employers. They also complete the application form, answering questions required by employers for comparison purposes. Some recruitment agencies noticed during the last recession that résumé padding increased. Applicants were "stretching" the dates of their employment, misleading employers about the nature of their duties, and misrepresenting their salaries. While you are writing a résumé, adding three months to your previous employment, saying you were a night auditor instead of a clerk, and adding $950 to your last salary seem like relatively harmless lies.

What are the facts? Studies of "creative" résumé writing indicate that about 25 percent of résumés contain inaccuracies; one-third report incorrect dates, one-tenth misrepresent reasons for leaving, and the rest exaggerate education attainments or omit criminal records. The probability is that about two-thirds of employers check references. Some former employers give only dates of employment and previous salary ranges.

Most organizations require applicants to sign a statement saying that the information they supply is true, and that if it is not they will be dismissed. Some cases of résumé padding have been heavily publicized. A Toronto Stock Exchange manager was dismissed for lying about having a master's degree. A Member of

Parliament listed an ILB on his résumé, which normally stands for International Baccalaureate of Law, but that he claimed stood for Incomplete Baccalaureate of Law. In one heart-wrenching case, a person who was ready to retire was found to have lied about his age decades earlier to get a job. On discovery, he was dismissed and lost his pension. In another case, a Canadian businessman was sentenced to eight months in jail in New Zealand for lying on his résumé, by listing false qualifications such as an MBA. Academic fraud happens 5 percent of the time. The president of Selection Protection Services, a background check firm, offers this advice to job seekers: "Don't lie." She describes one candidate who wrote "Honours Degree" on her résumé when she did not have one. She did not get the job because dishonesty is a deal breaker.

In a labour market where there are too many people chasing too few jobs, candidates will also lie on their résumés, but do so by dropping experience and educational qualifications. This practice, called "stripping," is used because job seekers are ready to take any job in order to survive or to hold them over until the jobs they really want are available. Knowing that graduate degrees will act as barriers to jobs as labourers or administrative assistants, applicants simply don't list the degrees or previous professional jobs. Understandably, employers don't want to hire those who are overqualified and who would soon quit for better jobs.

Sources: Jason Chow, "Job Shadow," *Financial Post Business*, May 2006: 29; Rick Spence, "Should Executives Do Their Own Reference Checks?" *The Toronto Star*, May 13, 2004; E. Urquhart, "Should We Edit Our Job Skills?" *The Globe and Mail*, June 20, 2003: C1; P. Waldie, "Davy Sentenced to Eight Months in N.Z. Court," *The Globe and Mail*, May 30, 2002: B6; J. Schilder, "Trial by Hire," *Human Resource Professional* 11, no. 2 (March 1994): 21–23.

- *Country of citizenship.* Such questions are not permitted. It is allowable to ask whether the person is legally entitled to work in Canada.
- *References.* It is both permissible and advisable that the names, addresses, and phone numbers of references be provided. (We will cover this in more detail later.)
- *Disabilities.* Employers should avoid asking about disabilities, hospitalization, or if candidates have received workers' compensation.

Many of these issues will be addressed again, particularly in the section on employment interviews. Some organizations use what is referred to as a *weighted application blank (WAB)*. The WAB involves the use of a common standardized employment application that is designed to distinguish between successful and unsuccessful employees. If managers can identify application items that have predicted employee success in the past, they may use that information to screen other applicants. Some evidence suggests that use of the WAB has been especially helpful for reducing turnover costs in the hospitality industry.

ONLINE APPLICATIONS

As we explained in Chapter 5, most large companies accept applications online and are also able to mine résumés, spot qualified applicants, and conduct screening tests online. One of the key advantages of accepting applications online is that companies can recruit candidates and fill their job openings much faster.

Companies report that the downside of posting jobs and accepting online applications is that it can lead to a large volume of them being submitted—many of which fail to meet minimum qualifications. The upside, however, is that generating a larger number of applicants tends to promote greater employee diversity. Home Depot, for example, successfully implemented an online application system called the Job Preference Program to get a broader pool of applicants than it previously had been getting. It ultimately enabled the company to hire more women.[9]

BIOGRAPHICAL INFORMATION BLANKS

One of the oldest methods for predicting job success uses biographical information, or "biodata," about job applicants. As early as 1917, the Life Insurance Agency Management Association constructed and validated a biographical information blank (BIB) for life insurance salespeople. BIBs cover such issues as family life, hobbies, club memberships, sales experience, and investments. Like application forms, BIBs reveal information about a person's history that may have shaped his or her behaviour. Sample questions from a BIB might include the following:

- At what age did you leave home?
- How large was the town/city in which you lived as a child?
- Did you ever build a model airplane that flew?
- Were sports a big part of your childhood?
- Do you play any musical instruments?

Both the BIB and the application form can be scored like tests. Because biographical questions rarely have obviously right or wrong answers, BIBs are difficult to fake. The development of a scoring system requires that the items that are valid predictors of job success (positively or negatively correlated) be identified and that weights be established for different responses to these items. By totalling the scores for each item, it is possible to obtain a composite score on the BIB as a whole for each applicant. Studies have shown that an objective scoring of BIB and application forms is one of the most potentially valid methods of predicting job success. This method has been useful in predicting all types of behaviour, including employee theft, turnover, and performance in jobs such as sales, nursing, and management.[10]

BACKGROUND CHECKS

When the interviewer is satisfied that the applicant is potentially qualified, information about previous employment as well as other information provided by the applicant is investigated. Following 9/11 and a rash of corporate scandals at companies such as Enron, Tyco, and WorldCom, background investigations have become standard procedure for many companies to prevent a variety of problems ranging from embezzlement and theft of merchandise to workplace violence. The vast majority (over 90 percent) of Canadian companies surveyed by the *Canadian HR Reporter* indicated that they conduct background checks for previous employment history (92 percent), academic qualifications (53 percent), criminal record (50 percent), and credit rating (11 percent).[11]

Like the application process, many checks that were once done manually are now being done online using existing computer databases. However, this frequently requires checking many different databases. Information on international applicants is even harder to obtain. Some companies outsource some or all of the checks to third-party screeners.

Some job boards now have online screening tools allowing an applicant to conduct his or her own self-background check and post it online prior to any sort of interview. The idea is to demonstrate upfront to prospective employers that the applicant has a clean criminal record, a good job history, and would make a good employee.[12]

Finally, an increasing number of companies are simply using Internet searches to uncover background information on a potential candidate through social networking sites such as Facebook. Information found on these sites can positively or adversely influence the employer's perspective of a candidate.

Checking References

Organizations check the references of employees in a number of ways. Generally, telephone checks are preferable because they save time and provide for greater candour. But references via faxes, mail, and e-mail are also used. Prescient InfoTech, a computer systems managing company, first calls references to establish contact and then faxes or e-mails them a two-page questionnaire, asking them to numerically rank the applicant's various job-related attributes. There is room at the end of the questionnaire for comments and recommendations.

The most reliable information usually comes from supervisors, who are in the best position to report on an applicant's work habits and performance. Written verification of information relating to job titles, duties, and pay levels from the former employer's HR office is also very helpful. Highlights in HRM 6.1 includes a list of helpful questions to ask about applicants when checking their references.[13]

As a legal protection for all concerned, it is important to ask the applicant to fill out forms permitting information to be solicited from former employers and other reference sources. Even with these safeguards, many organizations are reluctant to put into writing an evaluation of a former employee for fear of being sued by the person. Many employers will verify only former employees' employment dates and positions. Note that there is no legal obligation to provide a reference letter for an employee, unless you have promised in writing to do so. A survey by the SHRM found that although 75 percent of companies do provide references, many reported that the information consists only of employment dates and position. This results in problems for the next employers. A survey of Canadian companies found that the majority had to terminate an employee for reasons that could have been discovered through a reference check. For example, the City of Waterloo fired its chief administrative officer after it uncovered an employment history in which the candidate broke rules and misled his previous employer, all well publicized but not checked either by the recruiting firm or the city.[14]

Using Credit Reports

The use of consumer credit reports by employers as a basis for establishing an applicant's eligibility for employment has become more restricted. For positions of trust, such as those involving financial instruments in banks, credit reports must be used. Applicants must agree in writing to a credit report and have the right to review its contents. More importantly, the reason for the credit report must be job related.

POLYGRAPH TESTS

The polygraph, or lie detector, is a device that measures the changes in breathing, blood pressure, and pulse of a person who is being questioned. It consists of a rubber tube around the chest, a cuff around the arm, and sensors attached to the fingers that record the physiological changes in the examinee as the examiner asks questions that call for

Highlights in **HRM 6.1**

Sample Reference-Checking Questions

Just the Facts

- What were the candidate's dates of employment? What was the candidate's title?
- What were the candidate's general responsibilities?
- What is your relationship to the candidate (peer, subordinate, superior)? How long have you known the candidate?

On the Job

- How would you describe the overall quality of the candidate's work? Can you give me some examples? (For superiors) What areas of performance did you have to work on?
- What would you say are the candidate's strengths? What would you say are the candidate's weaknesses?
- How would you compare the candidate's work to the work of others who performed the same job? What kind of environment did the candidate work in?
- How much of a contribution do you think the candidate made to your company or department? How would you describe the candidate's ability to communicate?
- How does the candidate handle pressure/ deadlines?

- How well does the candidate get along with coworkers? How well does the candidate get along with managers?
- How well does the candidate supervise others? Can you give me your impressions of his or her management style? Describe the candidate's success in motivating subordinates.
- How does the candidate handle conflict situations?
- Based on the candidate's performance with your company, do you think he or she would be good in the type of position we're considering him or her for? How ambitious is he or she?
- What motivates the candidate? How ambitious is he or she?

The Bottom Line

- Why did the candidate leave your company? Would you rehire this person?
- Would you recommend this candidate for this type of position? What type of work is the candidate ideally suited for?
- Were there any serious problems with the candidate that we need to be aware of before making a hiring decision?
- Do you have any additional information to share with us about this candidate?

Source: Carolyn Hirschman, "The Whole Truth," *HR Magazine* 45, no. 6 (June 2000): 86–72. Copyright 2000 by Society for Human Resource Management (SHRM). Reproduced with permission of Society for Human Resource Management (SHRM) in the format Textbook via Copyright Clearance Center. Reprinted with the permission of *HR Magazine* published by the Society for Human Resource Management, Alexandria, VA.

---

an answer of *yes* or *no*. Questions typically cover such items as whether a person uses drugs, has stolen from an employer, or has committed a serious undetected crime.

The RCMP uses a polygraph test to identify candidates who meet its standards of honesty and suitability. However, the use of lie detector tests for employment purposes is prohibited under the *Employment Standards Acts* in both Ontario and New Brunswick. Check provincial legislation before considering the use of a polygraph.

HONESTY AND INTEGRITY TESTS

Many employers have dramatically increased their use of pencil-and-paper honesty and integrity tests. These tests have commonly been used in settings such as retail stores where employees have access to cash or merchandise. Common areas of inquiry include beliefs about frequency and extent of theft in our society, punishment for theft, and perceived ease of theft. For example, Payless ShoeSource has used a paper-and-pencil honesty test to reduce employee theft. When the company began its program, losses totalled nearly $21 million per year among its 4,700 stores.

Within only one year of implementing its screening program, inventory shrinkage fell by 20 percent to less than 1 percent of sales.[15]

Potential items that might be used on an integrity test are shown in Figure 6.4. Although some studies have shown that honesty tests are valid for predicting job performance as well as a wide range of disruptive behaviours such as theft, disciplinary problems, and absenteeism, other studies have questioned their validity.[16] It is possible that the tests "work" not because they predict behaviour but because they deter less than-honest applicants from joining a company. However, applicants sometimes view the tests as an invasion of their privacy. Given these issues, HRM specialists should consider the use of honesty tests very cautiously and most certainly in conjunction with other sources of information.[17]

Nevertheless, honesty tests have come under fire, too. Sobeys, a chain food store based in Stellarton, Nova Scotia, used an integrity test and failed an applicant, even though she had worked for them previously for six years without any incident. The applicant filed a complaint with the Nova Scotia Human Rights Commission. Additionally some candidates find the questions, such as "I like to take chances," offensive. The British Columbia Civil Liberties Union has called for legislation banning integrity tests as an invasion of privacy. Given these events, HRM specialists

FIGURE **6.4**

Integrity Test Question Examples

TO TEST TENDENCY TO	DESCRIPTION
Protect	Contains items that require individuals to indicate whether they would protect friends or co-workers who had engaged in counterproductive behaviours.
	Example: I would turn in a fellow worker I saw stealing money.
Be lenient	Contains items in which test takers indicate whether they would be lenient with respect to the wrongdoings of others.
	Example: An employee should be fired if the employer finds out the employee lied on the application blank.
Admit thought	Includes items that require test takers to indicate the degree to which they would engage in counterproductive thoughts or behaviours.
	Example: I've thought about taking money from an employer without actually doing it.
Admit behaviour	Contains items in which individuals admit to directly participating in actual counterproductive behaviours.
	Example: Over the last three years, what's the total amount of money you've taken without permission from your employer?
Consider common	Includes items that require the individual to indicate whether there are excuses or justifications for stealing or performing other questionable behaviours.
	Example: Most people I've worked with have stolen something at one time or another.
Excuse	Contains items in which individuals indicate whether there are excuses or justifications for stealing or performing other questionable behaviours.
	Example: Someone who steals because his family is in need should not be treated the same as a common thief.
Lie	Contains items that measure the extent to which the test taker is responding in a socially desirable manner.
	Example: Never in my whole life have I wished for anything I was not entitled to.

Note: The number of items in each category was 2, 8, 13, 9, 17, 8, and 7, respectively.

Source: Stephen Dwight and George Alliger, "Reactions to Overt Integrity Test Items," *Educational and Psychological Measurement* 57, no. 6 (December 1977): 937–948, copyright © 1997 by Sage Publications, Inc. Reprinted with the permission of Sage Publications, Inc.

should use the results from honesty tests very cautiously and most certainly in conjunction with other sources of information.

GRAPHOLOGY

Graphology, a term that refers to a variety of systems of handwriting analysis, is used by some employers to make employment decisions. Graphologists obtain a sample of handwriting and then examine such characteristics as the size and slant of letters, amount of pressure applied, and placement of the writing on the page. From their observations, graphologists can allegedly draw inferences about such things as the writer's personality traits, intelligence, energy level, organizational abilities, creativity, integrity, emotional maturity, self-image, people skills, and entrepreneurial tendencies. Graphology is used in Europe and extensively in France, where the practice was developed.[18]

Organizations using handwriting analysis say they prefer it to typical personality tests because it requires only that job candidates take a few minutes to jot down a short essay. By contrast, a battery of personality tests and interviews with psychologists can take several hours and can cost thousands of dollars. In addition, there is some evidence to suggest that graphology can be a reliable predictor of *personality* when compared with other psychological tests. However, graphology's predictive validity for *job performance* and occupational success remains questionable. In the academic community, where formal and rigorous validity studies are customary, the use of graphology for employment decisions has been viewed with considerable skepticism.

EMPLOYMENT TESTS

The formal introduction of psychological selection techniques into the Canadian Army in 1941 represented both a pragmatic response to the contingencies of war and an attempt to make selection decisions more democratic. Prior to 1941, entry into officer training was often based on social status or monetary favours (as opposed to proven ability). Since that time, employment tests have played an important part in the HR programs of both public and private organizations.

One of the drawbacks of pre-employment testing is that it creates the potential for legal challenges, particularly in the United States. There, a small but growing number of companies are being taken to court by candidates claiming that the tests they took were discriminatory. There is also some evidence that the more tests that are required, the higher the likelihood of a lawsuit. The relative frequency of discrimination suits also appears to vary by industry and job type. Police, firefighting, and teaching areas—which generally require applicants to pass more tests—appear to be more prone to discrimination litigation.[19] Because Canadian HR practices often lag U.S. practices, we can expect to see more legal challenges in Canada. Nonetheless, tests have played a more important part in government HR programs in which hiring on the basis of merit is required by law. Although government agencies experienced the same types of problems with their testing programs as did organizations in the private sector, their staffs were forced to improve their testing programs rather than abandon them.

While it is often advisable to use consultants, especially if an organization is considering the use of personality tests, managers should have a basic understanding of the technical aspects of testing and the contributions that tests can make to the HR program. Managers should also do a thorough job analysis to determine the crucial job requirements and related skills that actually need to be tested for and eliminate any unnecessary or duplicate tests.

[OUTCOME 3]

NATURE OF EMPLOYMENT TESTS

An employment test is an objective and standardized measure of a sample of behaviour that is used to gauge a person's knowledge, skills, abilities, and other characteristics (KSAOs) in relation to other individuals.[20] The proper sampling of behaviour—whether verbal, manipulative, or some other type—is the responsibility of the test author. It is also the responsibility of the test author to develop tests that meet accepted standards of reliability.[21] The data concerning a test's reliability are ordinarily presented in the manual for the test. While high reliability is essential, it offers no assurance that the test provides the basis for making valid judgments—that is, that the test actually measures the knowledge, skills, and abilities necessary to do a job successfully. It is the responsibility of the HR staff to conduct validation studies before a test is adopted for regular use. Again, this involves doing a thorough job analysis. One way to measure a test's validity is to test current employees and create a benchmark score to which applicants' scores can be compared. Other considerations are the cost, time, ease of administration and scoring, and apparent relevance of the test to the jobs being tested. This is commonly referred to as "face validity." In other words, how reliable does the test appear on its face? While face validity is desirable, it is no substitute for technical validity. Adopting a test just because it appears relevant is bad practice; many "good-looking" tests have poor validity.

CLASSIFICATION OF EMPLOYMENT TESTS

Employment tests may be classified in different ways. Generally, they are viewed as measuring either aptitude or achievement. **Aptitude tests** measure a person's capacity to learn or acquire skills. **Achievement tests** measure what a person knows or can do right now.

Cognitive Ability Tests

Cognitive ability tests measure mental capabilities such as general intelligence, verbal fluency, numerical ability, and reasoning ability. A host of paper-and-pencil tests measure cognitive abilities, including the General Aptitude Test Battery (GATB), Scholastic Aptitude Test (SAT), Graduate Management Aptitude Test (GMAT), and Bennett Mechanical Comprehension Test. Figure 6.5 provides examples of questions from the General Competency Test (GCT) administered by the Public Service Commission of Canada.

Although cognitive ability tests can be developed to measure very specialized areas such as reading comprehension and spatial relations, many experts believe that the validity of cognitive ability tests simply reflects their connection to general intelligence. However, measures of general intelligence (such as IQ) have been shown to be good predictors of performance across a wide variety of jobs.[22]

Personality and Interest Inventories

Whereas cognitive ability tests measure a person's mental capacity, personality tests measure disposition and temperament. During 1990s, for example, testing by the U.S. Army found that cognitive ability tests were the best predictors of how well soldiers were able to acquire job knowledge and, ultimately, of their technical proficiencies. But personality tests were the better predictors of their motivation, such as their leadership efforts and propensity to adhere to rules. Years of research show that five dimensions can summarize personality traits. The "Big Five" factors are the following:

1. *Extroversion*—the degree to which someone is talkative, sociable, active, aggressive, and excitable
2. *Agreeableness*—the degree to which someone is trusting, amiable, generous, tolerant, honest, cooperative, and flexible

aptitude tests
Measures of a person's capacity to learn or acquire skills

achievement tests
Measures of what a person knows or can do right now

FIGURE 6.5

General Competency Test Level 1

The GCT was developed by the Personnel Psychology Centre, Assessment, Testing and Counselling Directorate, the Public Service Commission of Canada. The GCT 1 has 50 multiple-choice questions and the test takes 85 minutes. There are three types of questions, and an example from each is found below:

Understanding Written Material Example:

Government of Canada

Memorandum

To: All employees

From: Manager

We are pleased to announce that our Ministry's budget has been increased and consequently we will experience an increase in staff size. Because new positions will become available, we will be holding interviews within the next few weeks.

The main focus of this interview is a change concerning:

1. Better ministerial policy   3. More human resources
2. Better budget publicity   4. More office space

Solving Numerical Questions:

You are in charge of financial services and must calculate overtime pay for employees in your division. Due to a heavy workload, an employee had to do 35 hours of overtime in two weeks. Seven of these hours are at "double time" (i.e., twice usual pay), the rest are at "time and a half." The employee's usual pay is $375 a week at $10 an hour. How much overtime money should the employee be paid for the two-week period?

1. $340   3. $560
2. $420   4. $760

Drawing Logical Conclusions:

One of your duties is the selection and disposal of boxes of obsolete files. According to regulations, ordinary files become obsolete after 24 months, confidential files after 36 months, and classified files after 48 months. Which of the following boxes of files can be disposed of?

A box containing ordinary files dated 26 months ago and classified files dated 34 months ago.

A box containing ordinary files dated 38 months ago and confidential files dated 28 months ago.

1. A only   3. Both A and B
2. B only   4. Neither A nor B

Answers can be found on page 269.

Source: General Competency Test: Level 1 – (GCT1) Practice Test: Information (http://www.psc-cfp.gc.ca/gct1_info_e.htm) September 7, 2006. Reproduced with the permission of the Minister of Public Works and Government Services Canada, 2009.

3. *Conscientiousness*—the degree to which someone is dependable and organized and perseveres in tasks

4. *Neuroticism*—the degree to which someone is secure, calm, independent, and autonomous

5. *Openness to experience*—the degree to which someone is intellectual, philosophical, insightful, creative, artistic, and curious[23]

Figure 6.6 illustrates facets and sample items from the well-known California Psychological Inventory (CPI). Other personality tests include the Myers-Briggs Type Indicator (MBTI) and the 180-question Caliper test. Read about testing at Steelcase in Highlights in HRM 6.2.

Although there is some evidence to show that when used in combination with cognitive ability tests, measures of personality traits (such as conscientiousness) can help predict how well a person will perform on the job, historically the connection between the two has been quite low.[24]

FIGURE **6.6**

CPI Personality Facts and Sample Items

Agreeableness

- Consideration—I like to do little things for people to make them feel good.
- Empathy—I take other people's circumstances and feelings into consideration before making a decision.
- Interdependence—I tend to put group goals first and individual goals second.
- Openness—I do not have to share a person's values to work well with that person.
- Thought agility—I think it is vital to consider other perspectives before coming to conclusions.
- Trust—I believe people are usually honest with me.

Conscientiousness

- Attention to detail—I like to complete every detail of tasks according to the work plans.
- Dutifulness—I conduct my business according to a strict set of ethical principles.
- Responsibility—I can be relied on to do what is expected of me.
- Work focus—I prioritize my work effectively so the most important things get done first.

Extroversion

- Adaptability—For me, change is exciting.
- Competitiveness—I like to win, even if the activity isn't very important.
- Desire for achievement—I prefer to set challenging goals, rather than aim for goals I am more likely to reach.
- Desire for advancement—I would like to attain the highest position in an organization some day.
- Energy level—When most people are exhausted from work, I still have energy to keep going.
- Influence—People come to me for inspiration and direction.
- Initiative—I am always looking for opportunities to start new projects.
- Risk-taking—I am willing to take big risks when there is potential for big returns.
- Sociability—I find it easy to start up a conversation with strangers.
- Taking charge—I actively take control of situations at work if no one is in charge.

Neuroticism

- Emotional control—Even when I am very upset, it is easy for me to control my emotions.
- Negative affectivity—I am easily displeased with things at work.
- Optimism—My enthusiasm for living life to its fullest is apparent to those with whom I work.
- Self-confidence—I am confident about my skills and abilities.
- Stress tolerance—I worry about things that I know I should not worry about.

Openness to Experience

- Independence—I tend to work on projects alone, even if others volunteer to help me.
- Innovativeness/creativity—I work best in an environment that allows me to be creative and expressive.
- Social astuteness—I know what is expected of me in different social situations.
- Thought focus—I quickly make links between causes and effects.
- Vision—I can often foresee the outcome of a situation before it unfolds.

Source: Mark J. Schmit, Jenifer A. Kihm, and Chet Robie, "Development of a Global Measure of Personality," *Personnel Psychology* 53, no.1 (Spring 2000): 153–193. Reprinted by permission.

Personality tests can also be problematic if they inadvertently discriminate against individuals who would otherwise perform effectively[25] Rather than being used to make hiring decisions, personality and interest inventories may be most useful for helping people with their occupational selection and career planning.

Physical Ability Tests

In addition to learning about a job candidate's mental capabilities, employers frequently need to assess a person's physical abilities. Particularly for demanding and potentially dangerous jobs such as those held by firefighters and police officers, physical abilities such as strength and endurance tend to be good predictors not only of performance, but also of accidents and injuries.[26]

Highlights in **HRM** 6.2

Testing at Steelcase

Founded in 1912, Steelcase is an office furniture manufacturing company with a mission of transforming the way people work. Steelcase makes it the company's business to study the way that people work and create solutions that allow employees and teams to maximize their potential and have a better work experience. With over 13,000 employees and 30 locations worldwide, Steelcase is able to achieve high standards of excellence in office environments by adhering to Seven Core Values that were displayed by its founders. These are to

- Act with integrity
- Tell the truth
- Keep commitments
- Treat people with dignity and respect
- Promote positive relationships
- Protect the environment
- Excel

According to Gene Lai, vice-president of operations, Steelcase uses tests to ensure that candidates will enact these values. According to Lai, hiring managers can be a costly process. The wrong candidate can not only damage the company's reputation and undermine the company's credibility within the market but also do untold damage to the relationship Steelcase has carefully built with its employees over many years.

As part of the managerial selection process, candidates are given tests, conducted by a qualified industrial psychologist, which assess cognitive abilities, motivation, behaviours, and emotional stability. The use of professional psychologists is stressed because there are too many limitations of readily available selection tests that are too "open" to interpretation, not properly proctored, and based on the assumptions of unqualified personnel. From experience, Lai states that "it's not the technical skills or normal behaviours that get a person into trouble; it is how people react when under stress." The psychological assessment uncovers these potential "de-railers" and also outlines a person's strengths.

Whether or not the candidate is chosen, he or she is given formal feedback from the industrial psychologist. If the candidate is chosen, the assessment data are integrated into a formal personal development plan. The industrial psychologist also works with the individual as a personal coach. From day one, the new employee has a personal development plan that is shared with the individual's manager. The new employee also has access to the coach for any problems that may arise and assistance in overcoming any barriers to success.

Physical ability tests must be used cautiously. In the past, requirements for physical characteristics such as strength, agility, height, and weight were often determined by an employer's unvalidated notion of what should be required. This often put women and disabled job applicants at a disadvantage, a situation that can lead to lawsuits. Evidence suggests that the average man is stronger, faster, and more powerful than the average woman, but women tend to have better balance, manual dexterity, flexibility, and coordination than men. For example, applicants who take the RCMP's Physical Fitness Abilities Requirement Evaluation (PARE) are required to run 350 metres, complete a standing broad jump of about 2 metres, and pick up and carry a heavy bag for 15 metres. According to one RCMP officer, "If you're a bigger person, the PARE test is easier, no doubt." The fact that women fail the test in greater numbers than men has resulted in a complaint before the Canadian Human Rights Commission. The RCMP defended the PARE test on the grounds that it simulates common police activities such as chasing a suspect on foot, carrying an injured person, and forcing open a door. However, the court struck down as illegal a similar test used for firefighters in B.C. because it discriminated against women, who were less likely to meet the standard, which itself was based on a male standard.[27]

On the basis of these differences, it is clear that (as with other methods for screening potential employees) the use of physical ability tests should be carefully validated on the basis of the essential functions of the job.[28]

Job Knowledge Tests

Government agencies and licensing boards usually develop job knowledge tests, a type of achievement test designed to measure a person's level of understanding about a particular job. The uniform CPA Examination used to license certified public accountants is one such test. Most civil service examinations, for example, are used to determine whether an applicant possesses the information and understanding that will permit placement on the job without further training.[29]

Work Sample Tests

Work sample tests, or job sample tests, require the applicant to perform tasks that are actually a part of the work required on the job. Like job knowledge tests, work sample tests are constructed from a carefully developed outline that experts agree includes the major job functions; the tests are thus considered content valid. Organizations that are interested in moving toward *competency-based selection*—that is, hiring based on observation of behaviours previously shown to distinguish successful employees—increasingly use work samples to see potential employees "in action."[30]

Work samples have been devised for many diverse jobs: a map-reading test for traffic control officers, a lathe test for machine operators, a complex coordination test for pilots, an in-basket test for managers, a group discussion test for supervisors, and a judgment and decision-making test for administrators, to name a few. The reports are that this type of test is cost-effective, reliable, valid, fair, and acceptable to applicants.[31]

Related to the job sample test is the job simulation, used by nearly one-third of those surveyed in 2005. Prudential Grand Valley Reality, a real estate firm in Kitchener, Ontario, uses an online video-based assessment that simulates the job of a real estate agent. The candidate plays the role of an agent and interacts with virtual clients who are interested in buying or selling a property. The recruit is taken thorough the entire sales cycle, from building rapport to closing the deal, and must demonstrate the ability to handle objections, negotiate price, understand client needs, and handle periodic rejection.[32]

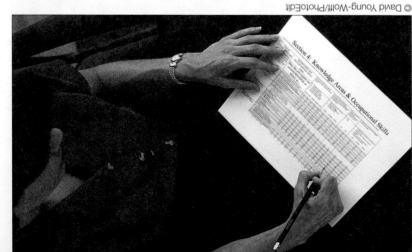

Organizations use a variety of tests to determine an applicant's abilities, knowledge, and skills.

THE EMPLOYMENT INTERVIEW

Traditionally, the employment interview has a central role in the selection process—so much so that it is rare to find an instance in which an employee is hired without some sort of interview. Depending on the type of job, applicants may be interviewed by one person, members of a work team, or other individuals in the organization. While researchers have raised some doubts about its validity, the interview remains a mainstay of selection because (1) it is especially practical when there are only a small number of applicants; (2) it serves other purposes, such as public relations; and (3) interviewers maintain great faith and confidence in their judgments. Nevertheless, the interview can be plagued by problems of subjectivity and personal bias. In those instances, the judgments of different interviewers may vary dramatically, and the quality of the hire can be called into serious question.

In this section, we review the characteristics, advantages, and disadvantages of various types of employment interviews. We highlight the fact that the structure of the interview and the training of interviewers strongly influence the success of the hiring process.[33]

INTERVIEWING METHODS

Interview methods differ in several ways, most significantly in terms of the amount of structure, or control, exercised by the interviewer. In highly structured interviews, the interviewer determines the course that the interview will follow as each question

[OUTCOME]

is asked. In the less structured interview, the applicant plays a larger role in determining the course the discussion will take. An examination of the different types of interviews from the least structured to the most structured reveals these differences.

The Nondirective Interview

In the **nondirective interview**, the interviewer carefully refrains from influencing the applicant's remarks. The applicant is allowed the maximum amount of freedom in determining the course of the discussion. The interviewer asks broad, open-ended questions—such as "Tell me more about your experiences on your last job"—and permits the applicant to talk freely with a minimum of interruption. Generally, the nondirective interviewer listens carefully and does not argue, interrupt, or change the subject abruptly. The interviewer also uses follow-up questions to allow the applicant to elaborate, makes only brief responses, and allows pauses in the conversation; the pausing technique is the most difficult for the beginning interviewer to master. The nondirective interview may be expected to be minimal, because questions and answers cannot be standardized and compared across candidates. This method is most likely to be used in interviewing candidates for high-level positions and in counselling.

The Structured Interview

More attention is being given to the structured interview as a result of employment equity requirements and a concern for maximizing validity of selection decisions.[34] Because a **structured interview** has a set of standardized questions (based on job analysis) and an established set of answers against which applicant responses can be rated, it provides a more consistent basis for evaluating job candidates. For example, staff members of Weyerhaeuser Company's HR department have developed a structured interviewing process with the following characteristics:

1. The interview process is based exclusively on job duties and requirements critical to job performance.

2. It uses four types of questions: situational questions, job knowledge questions, job sample/simulation questions, and worker requirements questions.

3. There are sample (benchmark) answers, determined in advance, to each question. Interviewee responses are rated on a five-point scale relative to those answers.

4. The process involves an interview committee so that interviewee responses are evaluated by several raters.

5. It consistently follows the same procedures in all instances to ensure that each applicant has exactly the same chance as every other applicant.

6. The interviewer takes notes and documents the interview for future reference and in case of a legal challenge.

A structured interview is more likely to provide the type of information needed for making sound decisions. According to one report, structured interviews are twice as likely as nondirective interviews to predict on-the-job performance. Structured interviews are also less likely than nondirective interviews to be attacked in court.[35]

Most employment interviewers will tend toward either a nondirected or a structured format. However, within the general category of structured interviews, there are more specific differences that relate to the format of questions. These include the situational interview and behavioural description interview, discussed next.

The Situational Interview

One variation of the structured interview is called the **situational interview**. With this approach, an applicant is given a hypothetical incident and asked how he or

nondirective interview
An interview in which the applicant is allowed the maximum amount of freedom in determining the course of the discussion, while the interviewer carefully refrains from influencing the applicant's remarks

structured interview
An interview in which a set of standardized questions having an established set of answers is used

situational interview
An interview in which an applicant is given a hypothetical incident and asked how he or she would respond to it

244

Highlights in **HRM 6.3**

Sample Situational Interview Question

QUESTION:

It is the night before your scheduled vacation. You are all packed and ready to go. Just before you get into bed, you receive a phone call from the plant. A problem has arisen that only you can handle. You are asked to come in to take care of things. What would you do in this situation?

RECORD ANSWER:

_____

_____

_____

SCORING GUIDE:

Good: "I would go in to work and make certain that everything is OK. Then I would go on vacation."

Good: "There are no problems that only I can handle. I would make certain that someone qualified was there to handle things."

Fair: "I would try to find someone else to deal with the problem."

Fair: "I would go on vacation."

she would respond to it. The applicant's response is then evaluated relative to pre-established benchmark standards. Interestingly, many organizations are using the situational interview to select new postsecondary graduates. Highlights in HRM 6.3 shows a sample question from a situational interview used to select systems analysts at a chemical plant. Highlights in HRM 6.4 lists some of the funniest statements made by job applicants.

Highlights in **HRM 6.4**

Too Funny for Interviews

Canadian HR Reporter asked its readers to reveal the funniest things they ever heard in an interview. Here is a sample of the responses:

- One candidate asked the president of a company how old she was.
- An applicant applying for an accounting position said, "I'm terrible in math."
- "I've been terminated from the last five companies I've worked for because they don't know what they are doing there."

- "No, I didn't come prepared to make a presentation. I thought you were joking."
- When asked to describe the company's main client group, the candidate said "Well, they're all idiots, aren't they?"
- A candidate was asked how he prepared for the job interview and replied, "I washed my jean jacket."
- A candidate was asked what quick decisions he's had to make and he replied, "I asked my wife to leave and she did."

Adapted from Todd Humber, "What's the Funniest Thing Heard in an Interview?" *Canadian HR Reporter* (May 23, 2005), G2.

The Behavioural Description Interview

In contrast to a situational interview, which focuses on hypothetical situations, a **behavioural description interview (BDI)** focuses on actual work incidents in the interviewee's past. The BDI format asks the job applicant what he or she actually did in a given situation. For example, to assess a potential manager's ability to handle a problem employee, an interviewer might ask, "Tell me about the last time you disciplined an employee." Such an approach to interviewing, based on a critical incidents job analysis, assumes that past performance is the best predictor of future performance. It also may be somewhat less susceptible to applicant faking. In addition, recent research indicates that the BDI is more effective than the situational interview for hiring higher-level positions such as general managers and executives.[36]

See Highlights in HRM 6.5 for behavioural questions posed by BMO Financial. The Business Case outlines the advantages of the behavioural interview.

The Panel Interview

Another type of interview involves a panel of interviewers who question and observe a single candidate. In a typical **panel interview**, the candidate meets with three to five interviewers who take turns asking questions. After the interview, the interviewers pool their observations and their rating scores if the interview is structured to reach a consensus about the suitability of the candidate. HRM specialists using this method at Philip Morris USA and Dominion Virginia Power report that panel interviews provide several significant advantages over traditional one-to-one interviews, including higher reliability because they involve multiple inputs. They can also result in a shorter decision-making period, and applicants are more likely to accept the decisions made. Studies also suggest that if the panels are composed of a diverse group of interviewers, hiring discrimination is minimized.[37]

behavioural description interview (BDI)
An interview in which an applicant is asked questions about what he or she actually did in a given situation

panel interview
An interview in which a board of interviewers questions and observes a single candidate

---

Highlights in **HRM 6.5**

Behavioural Interviews at BMO

The BMO Financial Group has been using behavioural interviewing for almost every position it fills, and after several revisions feels that it is a solid predictive tool in the hiring process. Below is a list of competencies and the questions BMO uses to evaluate them:

Business acumen behaviours
- Tell me about a time when you had to accomplish something that had a tight deadline and when you had to accomplish many things at once.
- Tell me about a challenging assignment that you had in the past year and how you handled this challenge.
- Describe a time when you had to decide what to do about a business situation where no guidelines existed or no precedents had been set.

Analytical and systems thinking behaviours
- Tell me how you approached the most difficult or challenging project that you had to solve.
- Give me an example of a situation where you had to handle a project unlike anything you ever had to do.
- Tell me about a time when your team had to complete a challenging project.

Customer and client service behaviours
- Describe to me a time when you turned around a very angry client and how you did it.
- Give me an example of a particularly difficult situation involving an external client and how you handled it.
- Tell me about a time when you felt particularly effective in establishing or maintaining a business relationship with a client.

Source: Adapted from Todd Humber, "How BMO Financial Selects Employees," *Canadian HR Reporter*, December 6, 2004: G2.

The Business CASE

Behavioural Interviews Bring Big Returns

Fairmont Hotels and Resorts Inc., formerly Canadian Pacific Hotels, with nearly 31,000 employees at 81 hotels in six countries, measures the effectiveness of selection tools. Using a Gallup selection tool, Fairmont has tracked the performance of sales personnel by selecting those who matched the characteristics of the best performers. Those superior employees produce two to three times more revenue than others.

A financial organization decided to assess the ROI (return on investment) of competency-based behavioural interviewing. It focused first on the sales and marketing function, which employed about 100 people, with average annual salaries of $135,000 ($90,000 plus a variable bonus of 50 percent for on-target performance). Turnover was about 20 percent a year. Elementary statistics suggest that the output of a group of workers forms a bell-shaped distribution, resulting in a small portion (about 10 percent) of staff working at above or below acceptable performance, while the majority worked in the acceptable range. The recruiters decided to delineate the competencies that differentiated the superior performers from the average performers and to use these to improve the selection procedure.

Here is how the ROI was calculated:

Assume 20 new recruits a year.

Two recruits, on average, would be superior performers under the current recruiting system.

Under the new system, all 20 would be superior, for a net increase of 18 new superior employees.

Performing above average is worth about 48 percent of the average annual salary to the company.

Therefore: $18 \times (\$135,000 \times .48) = \$1,166,000$

But the recruitment process is not perfect, and so must be discounted by .545 (the consultants' estimate of how good they were at selecting superior candidates and rejecting inferior candidates).

Therefore: $545 \times \$1,166,000 = \$635,000$

The cost of the competency project for sales and marketing was $130,000.

The benefit was $635,000 for an ROI of 488 percent.

The long-term ROI may be higher, as superior recruits may have lower turnover, shorter learning curves, and increasingly effective performance.

Interviews must be as valid as tests because they are so expensive. The average cost per hire of an executive is $43,000, a manager or professional $17,000, a technical person $13,000, and clerical and administrative support around $3,000.

Sources: Adapted from A. Davis, "What Is the Cost of Hiring?" *Canadian HR Reporter* 16, no. 11 (June 2, 2003): 12; T. Tritch, "Fairmont's Talent Strategy Delivers Results," *Gallup Management Journal*, http://www.gmj.gallup.com, May 13, 2003; Lionel LaRoche and Stephen Martin, "Demonstrating the Bottom-Line Impact of HR: A Competencies Case Study," *Canadian HR Reporter* 13, no. 22 (December 18, 2000): 29–31.

The Computer and Virtual Interviews

With advances in information technology, more and more organizations are using computers and the Internet to help with the interviewing process. Nike and Pinkerton Security have developed expert systems to gather preliminary information as well as compare candidates.

Typically, a computer interview requires candidates to answer a series (75 to 125) of multiple-choice questions tailored to the job. These answers are compared either with an ideal profile or with profiles developed on the basis of other candidates' responses. The computer interview can also be used as a screening device to help filter out unqualified applicants applying online who do not merit a personal interview. Depending on the vendor and the software used, a computer interview conducted in conjunction with online tests can measure everything from contradictory responses and latent responses (time delays related to answering a question) to the applicant's typing speed and ability to use different kinds of software. CareerBuilder.com, for example, offers a service called IntelligentHire that screens out the ten most qualified and interested applicants posting for a job on CareerBuilder's site. IntelligentHire then generates a report for the employer that includes the applicants' résumés, answers to questions, background check results, and their overall rankings against one another.[38]

A few years ago, Pic 'n Pay Shoe Stores created a computerized interview that could be conducted over the phone using a toll-free number. The interview focused on honesty, work attitude, drug use, candour, dependability, and self-motivation. After implementing the system, the company cut turnover by 50 percent and reduced employee theft by almost 40 percent. In addition to the benefits of objectivity, some research evidence suggests that applicants may be less likely to engage in "impression management" in computerized interviews than in face-to-face interviews. So far, organizations have used the computer mainly as a complement to, rather than as a replacement for, conventional interviews.[39]

As we explained in Chapter 1, in addition to computerized and telephone tests, some companies are conducting virtual simulation tests, some of which have been developed within the virtual reality game Second Life. As the National City Corp. case at the end of the chapter shows, firms are finding that virtual simulations of this sort are a better way to engage Generation Y and Millennial candidates than handing them a pencil and paper. The simulations can also enhance a company's reputation as a cutting-edge employer.

Video and Digitally Recorded Interviews

Companies such as AT&T, Dell Computer, and Nike are using videoconference technologies to evaluate job candidates. While some use their own in-house systems, others use outside service partners. FedEx Kinko's, for example, rents videoconferencing rooms at a quarter of its 900 stores for about $225 per hour. National Career Centers partnered with Radisson and Hilton to offer videoconferencing to customers in hotels.

Video and digitally recorded interviews have several potential advantages related to flexibility, speed, and cost. Employers can make preliminary assessments about candidates' technical abilities, energy level, appearance, and the like before incurring the costs of a face-to-face meeting. The goal is to enable faster, higher-quality decisions at lower cost.

In this panel interview, one of the participants is connecting by videoconference.

248

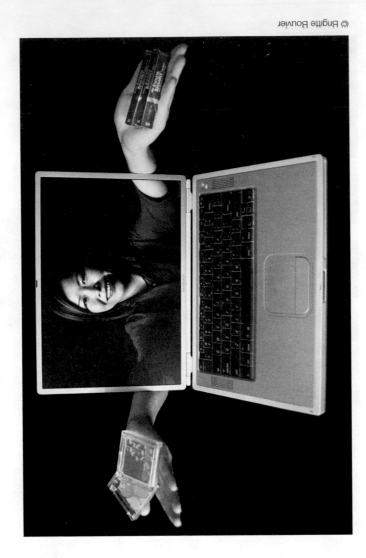

Erica Chean plays a virtual business strategy game that gives winners a shot at working for L'Oreal.

In addition to offering a broad range of candidate assessment services, a number of recruiting companies digitally record job applicants and post their interviews to their websites. Corporations log on to the sites and check out candidates free of charge or for a small fee, depending on the vendor. By recording and playing back the interviews to several companies' executives, firms can eliminate complications involved in setting up many more interviews.[40]

Simulations and Games

Some organizations are creating simulations that mimic the real-world conditions of work. For example, Burnaby-based Re/Max Realty Company uses videos featuring actors posing as home buyers, and candidates must respond to their questions. L'Oreal SA, the French-based cosmetics company, developed a virtual business strategy game in which candidates became general managers of a fictitious cosmetics company, and made all decisions virtually. Since it started using the game six years ago, L'Oreal has hired 186 top players from 28 countries, including two each year from Canada. These simulations tend to attract tech-savvy candidates, and allow them to "try out" the job and the industry to see if there is a fit.[41]

GUIDELINES FOR EMPLOYMENT INTERVIEWERS

Apart from the characteristics of the interviews themselves, there are several important tips for interviewers. Organizations should be cautious in selecting employment interviewers. Qualities that are desirable include humility, the ability to think objectively, maturity, and poise. Given the importance of diversity in the workforce, experience in associating with people from a variety of backgrounds is also desirable. Qualities to avoid in interviewers include overtalkativeness, extreme opinions, and biases.

A Review of the Best

There have been several reviews of research studies on the employment interview.[42] Each of these reviews discusses and evaluates numerous studies concerned with such questions as "What traits can be assessed in the interview?" and "How do interviewers reach their decisions?"

FIGURE **6.7**

Variables in the Employment Interview

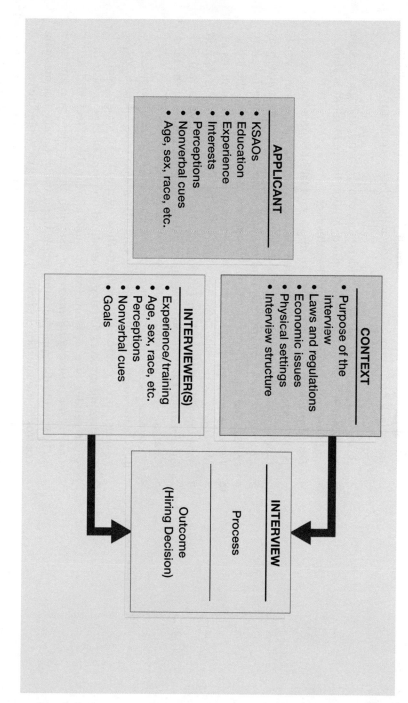

APPLICANT
- KSAOs
- Education
- Experience
- Interests
- Perceptions
- Nonverbal cues
- Age, sex, race, etc.

CONTEXT
- Purpose of the interview
- Laws and regulations
- Economic issues
- Physical settings
- Interview structure

INTERVIEWER(S)
- Experience/training
- Age, sex, race, etc.
- Perceptions
- Nonverbal cues
- Goals

INTERVIEW
Process

Outcome
(Hiring Decision)

Figure 6.7 summarizes the variables and processes involved in the employment interview. The figure shows that a number of applicant characteristics and situational factors can influence the perceptions of the interviewer and thus the hiring decision. For example, the race and sex of an applicant can shape the expectations, biases, and behaviours of an interviewer, which in turn can affect the interview outcome. Even a limited understanding of the variables shown in Figure 6.7 can help increase the interviewing effectiveness of managers and supervisors.

Interviewer Training

Training has been shown to dramatically improve the competence of interviewers. If not done on a continuing basis, training should at least be done periodically for managers, supervisors, and HR representatives who conduct interviews. Interviewer training programs should include practice interviews conducted under guidance. Practice interviews may be recorded and evaluated later in a group training session. Some variation in technique is only natural. However, the following list presents ten ground rules for employment interviews that are commonly accepted and supported by research findings. Their apparent simplicity should not lead one to underestimate their importance.

1. *Establish an interview plan.* Examine the purposes of the interview and determine the areas and specific questions to be covered. Review the job requirements, application form data, test scores, and other available information before seeing the applicant.

2. *Establish and maintain rapport.* This is accomplished by greeting the applicant pleasantly, explaining the purpose of the interview, displaying sincere interest in the applicant, and listening carefully. Keep

non-job-related conversation to a minimum. A common mistake managers make is hiring people who are like themselves—people who went to the same university, enjoy the same activities, and so forth. Although such a strategy can work, it can also lead to bad decisions and a lack of diversity in firms, especially when a company is interviewing global candidates.

3. *Be an active listener.* Strive to understand, comprehend, and gain insight into what is only suggested or implied. A good listener's mind is alert, and face and posture usually reflect this fact.

4. *Pay attention to nonverbal cues.* An applicant's facial expressions, gestures, body position, and movements often provide clues to that person's attitudes and feelings. Be aware of what you are communicating nonverbally.

5. *Provide information as freely and honestly as possible.* Answer fully and frankly the applicant's questions. Present a realistic picture of the job.

6. *Use questions effectively.* To elicit a truthful answer, phrase questions as objectively as possible, giving no indication of what response is desired.

7. *Separate facts from inferences.* During the interview, record factual information. Later, record your inferences or interpretations of the facts. Compare your inferences with those of other interviewers.

8. *Recognize biases and stereotypes.* As we have mentioned, one typical bias is for interviewers to consider candidates who have interests, experiences, and backgrounds similar to their own to be more acceptable. Stereotyping involves forming generalized opinions of how people of a given gender, race, or ethnic background appear, think, feel, and act.

9. *Control the course of the interview.* Establish an interview plan and stick to it. Provide the applicant with ample opportunity to talk, but maintain control of the situation in order to reach the interview objectives.

10. *Standardize the questions asked.* To increase the reliability of the interview and avoid discrimination, ask the same questions of all applicants for a particular job. Keep careful notes; record facts, impressions, and any relevant information, including the applicant was told.

EMPLOYMENT EQUITY: ARE YOUR QUESTIONS LEGAL?

The entire subject of pre-employment questioning is complex. Federal and provincial requirements sometimes vary in the types of questions that may be asked during the interview. However, all jurisdictions forbid direct questions about race, sex, colour, age, religion, and national origin, and most look with disapproval on indirect questions dealing with the same topics. Some of the questions that interviewers once felt free to ask can be potentially hazardous. Human rights commissions have severely limited the areas of questioning. In general, if the question is job related, is asked of everyone, and does not discriminate against a certain class of applicants, it is likely to be acceptable to government authorities. Readers who are interested in a more comprehensive discussion should consult Catano et al., *Recruitment and Selection in Canada,* fourth edition (2010).

Particular care has to be given to questions asked of female applicants about their family responsibilities. It is inappropriate, for example, to ask, "Who will take care of your children while you are at work?" or "Do you plan to have children?" or "What is your husband's occupation?" or "Are you engaged?" It is, in fact, inappropriate to ask applicants of either gender questions about matters that have no relevance to job performance.

Employers have found it advisable to provide interviewers with instructions on how to avoid potentially discriminatory questions in their interviews. The examples of appropriate and inappropriate questions shown in Highlights in HRM 6.6 may serve as guidelines for application forms as well as pre-employment interviews. Complete guidelines may be developed from current information available from

Highlights in **HRM 6.6**

Appropriate and Inappropriate Interview Questions

Subject	Avoid Asking	Preferred
Name	about name change; whether it was changed by court order, marriage, or other reason maiden name	
Address	for addresses outside Canada	ask place and duration of current or recent address
Age	for birth certificates, baptismal records, or about age in general	ask applicants if they are eligible to work under Canadian laws regarding age restrictions
Sex	males or females to fill in different applications about pregnancy, child-bearing plans, or childcare arrangements	
Marital Status	whether applicant is single, married, divorced, engaged, separated, widowed, or living common-law	can ask applicant if the attendance requirements can be met
Family Status	number of children or dependants about childcare arrangements	can ask if the applicant would be able to work the required hours and, where applicable, overtime
Military Service	about military service in other countries	inquiry about Canadian military service where employment preference is given to veterans by law
National or Ethnic Origin	about birthplace, nationality of ancestors, spouse, or other relatives whether born in Canada for proof of citizenship	since those who are entitled to work in Canada must be citizens, permanent residents, or holders of valid work permits, applicants can be asked if they are legally entitled to work in Canada
Race or Colour	any question about race or colour, including colour of eyes, skin, or hair	
Language	mother tongue where language skills obtained	ask if applicant understands, reads, writes, or speaks languages required for the job
Photographs	for photo to be attached to applications or sent to interviewer before interview	
Religion	about religious affiliation, church membership, frequency of church attendance, if applicant will work a specific religious holiday, or for references from clergy or religious leader	explain the required work shift, asking if such a schedule poses problems for the applicant
Height and Weight	no inquiry unless there is evidence they are genuine occupational requirements	
Disability	for listing of all disabilities, limitations, or health problems whether applicant drinks or uses drugs whether applicant has ever received psychiatric care or been hospitalized for emotional problems whether applicant has received workers' compensation	ask if applicant has any condition that could affect ability to do the job ask if the applicant has any condition that should be considered in selection
Medical Information	if currently under physician's care, name of family doctor if receiving counselling or therapy	

continued

Subject	Avoid Asking	Preferred
Pardoned Conviction	whether an applicant has ever been convicted if an applicant has ever been arrested whether an applicant has a criminal record	if bonding is a job requirement ask if applicant is eligible
Sexual Orientation	about the applicant's sexual orientation	
References	The same restrictions that apply to questions asked of applicants also apply to questions asked of the applicant's references.	

Source: Excerpt from "Guidelines to Screening and Selection in Employment" from http://www.chrc-ccdp.ca/publications/screen-preselection.asp. Canadian Human Rights Commission. Reproduced with the permission of the Minister of Public Works and Government Services Canada, 2009.

provincial human rights commissions. Once an individual is hired, the information needed but not asked in the interview may be obtained if there is a valid need for it and if it does not lead to discrimination.

MEDICAL EXAMINATION

A medical examination is generally given to ensure that the health and fitness of applicants is adequate to meet the job requirements. It also provides a baseline against which subsequent medical examinations can be compared and interpreted. The last objective is especially important for determining work-caused disabilities under workers' compensation law.

In the past, requirements for physical characteristics such as strength, agility, height, and weight were often determined by the employer's invalidated notions of what should be required. Many requirements that tend to discriminate against women have been questioned and modified so as to represent typical job demands.

Medical examinations and inquiries about a candidate directed to medical professionals can be conducted only after an offer (preferably written) of employment has been made. The offer can be made conditional on the applicant's ability to perform the essential duties of the job as determined by a job-related medical examination. Any medical inquiries must be directly related to assessing the candidate's abilities to perform the essential duties of the job. This allows the applicant with a disability the opportunity to be considered exclusively on merits during the selection process. Before human rights legislation was introduced, employers would screen out applicants with disabilities based on medical information requested on application forms or obtained through pre-employment medical examinations. These methods are now deemed discriminatory.

An employer may ask a candidate if she or he has any disability-related needs that would require accommodation to enable performance of the essential duties of the job. The interviewer should be cautioned about probing as to the nature of the disability. Later employment-related decisions may be perceived to be based on this information and thereby characterized as discriminatory. To ensure neutrality, and to avoid the possibility of a complaint to the Canadian Human Rights Commission, such information should remain exclusively with the examining physician, not in the personnel file.

If the employee has a disability, the employer has a duty to accommodate his or her needs. The accommodation can be accomplished either by changing some of the essential duties of the position or by providing the appropriate equipment. To determine whether an individual can do the essential duties of a particular position, the employer should conduct a physical demands analysis, checklists for which are available through most provincial ministries of labour.

As mentioned earlier, requirements for physical characteristics such as height were in the past often determined by an employer's notion of what should be required. Under human rights legislation, employers are prohibited from imposing their own standards where it has the effect of excluding members of the designated groups, unless it can be shown that the requirements are reasonable and bona fide. Such standards are often based on the vital statistics of the average white male. There is little evidence to demonstrate that characteristics such as height and weight constitute bona fide occupational requirements.

DRUG TESTING

The Canadian Human Rights Commission and some of its provincial counterparts have issued policies on employment-related drug testing. Addiction to drugs or alcohol is considered a disability, and the employer is to be guided by legislation and by practices such as workplace accommodation. The medical examination cannot be conducted until a conditional offer of employment is made in writing, and the examination can determine only the individual's ability to perform the essential duties. Since drug tests measure neither actual impairment nor the likelihood of a person reporting to work under the influence of drugs, the extent to which they assess the ability to perform essential duties is extremely limited. Therefore, human rights tribunals and courts have imposed very strict limitations on the right of employers to require drug tests.

If the job is a safety-sensitive one, then an employer may be permitted to offer the position conditional on the successful passing of a drug test. The employer then has the right to demand a medical examination of the employee. If an employee refuses, he or she can be dismissed. However, if an employee who fails a drug test is a drug addict, and therefore disabled under human rights statutes, then the employer will be required to accommodate the employee's disability to the point of undue hardship before it can dismiss the employee

The following types of testing are not allowed:

- Pre-employment drug testing
- Pre-employment alcohol testing
- Random drug testing, and
- Random alcohol testing of employees in non-safety-sensitive positions.

There is widespread opposition to drug testing in the workplace, which is why only about 2 percent of companies in Canada do it, compared to about 80 percent of American companies. Canadian companies that operate in both countries, such as those in cross-border trucking, may argue that testing is a bona fide occupational qualification for drivers, otherwise they would be banned from driving in the United States. Syncor Canada, a world leader in mining and extracting crude oil, believes that drug testing of heavy equipment operators could be justified on safety grounds, but not for those in an office environment.

The Canadian Civil Liberties Association takes the position that "no person should be required to share urine with a stranger" as a condition of employment. Employee Assistance Programs (EAPs) play an important role in helping employees with drug and alcohol problems. EAPs will be discussed in Chapter 12.

In the Reality Check, read about how The Bay reaches recruits and reaches selection decisions for its candidates.

REACHING A SELECTION DECISION

The most critical step is the decision to accept or reject applicants. Thus, it requires systematic consideration of all the relevant information about applicants. It is common to use summary forms and checklists to ensure that all of the pertinent information has been included in the evaluation of applicants.

Using the Internet

The Treasury Board Secretariat of the federal government publishes its policies on the accommodation of persons with disabilities at:

http://www.tbs-sct.gc.ca/ pubs_pol/hrpubs/TB_852/ ppaed_e.asp

OUTCOME 5

Reality CHECK

Selection at The Bay

Canada's oldest corporation and largest department store retailer is the Hudson's Bay Company, which was established in 1670 and operates as The Bay and Zellers. Tina Peacock, human resources manager for Merchandise Services and Corporate Offices, has been with HBC for more than 20 years. She helps the company achieve its goals by carefully applying selection methods to identify key potential candidates for many different positions, such as merchandise buyer, financial manager, and systems manager.

"In addition to succession planning," states Peacock, "we follow established trends, such as growth in our business units, turnover, and performance results, to identify those positions that may become vacant during the year. Through a number of training programs provided in-house, we are able to fill our positions internally. In fact, 80 percent are staffed from internal promotions. For the other 20 percent, we hire externally. As a proactive measure in anticipation of those openings, we run recruiting ads so that we always have a 'stable' of competent candidates.

"It is important that we work closely with the managers because they know what is needed to run their business. My role is to provide them with qualified candidates who possess the basic job knowledge with the right competencies to work in our fast-paced, changing environment. For instance, a number of managers are tapped into the marketplace, so they are able to get the ball rolling by identifying candidates in the industry before an ad is placed. Our role is to prescreen those candidates to ensure they have the attributes needed to successfully perform in our environment.

"We work very closely with an ad agency to assist us in preparing the ad and to provide advice on the marketing strategies of where and when to place the ad. They save you a lot of time, especially when they understand your business. Running our ads for a particular position yields us other qualified candidates for other positions we had not counted on.

"Many of our ads yield as many as 250 résumés. Based on the competencies required for a position, we prescreen the résumés. It is not uncommon for me to receive over 50 phone calls per day when an ad is running. If I can delegate some of those calls, I do;

however, if they have asked me for something specific, I make an effort to call them back because they are our customers and they are important to us. Once I have determined a short list, I then conduct a pretty thorough telephone interview before bringing in any candidates. Questions regarding salary expectations, any information that may be missing on the résumé, and some very job-specific questions are reviewed. We are always looking to improve our systems. Our next ad will incorporate a voice response system that has been developed internally by our Information Services Department. Candidates who wish to apply to an ad will be asked to call our system and respond to some basic job-related questions. At the end of the session, the candidate will be advised whether they possess the basic requirements of the job and whether they should apply to this position.

"The questions we ask during the face-to-face interview are open-ended questions that look for behavioural attributes specific to the competencies and key job requirements. For example, we want the candidates to demonstrate how they have gone about performing their job duties in the past. For those candidates who proceed to a final interview, we ask each of them to complete a communications survey. Using an outside consultant, we have developed a prediction performance program profile that has identified benchmark attributes for our buyers, merchandising trainees, and store managers. The results are graphed and compared against the benchmark. This profile is not used as a basis for determining whether we should hire a candidate or not. It provides us with another opportunity to fully assess the individual's capabilities by asking more focused questions. In this way, it ensures that we have fully investigated the individual's background and credentials. We provide each of our candidates with a written assessment of the report, whether they are hired or not, and ask them to comment on the accuracy of the results. Based on these responses, the report has been assessed at an accuracy of over 90 percent."

Peacock says in closing: "Systems in the workplace will continue to change, but the bottom line is that we need the best people to technically do the job and, most importantly, they must be customer focused."

SUMMARIZING INFORMATION ABOUT APPLICANTS

Fundamentally, an employer is interested in what an applicant can do and will do. Evaluating candidates on the basis of information you have assembled should focus on these two factors, as Figure 6.8 shows. The "can-do" factors include a candidate's knowledge and skills, as well as the aptitude (the potential) for acquiring new knowledge and skills. The "will-do" factors include the candidate's motivation, interests, and other personality characteristics. Both factors are essential to successful performance on the job. The employee who has the ability (can do) but is not motivated to use it (will not do) is little better than the employee who lacks the necessary ability.

It is much easier to measure what individuals can do than what they will do. The can-do factors are readily evident from test scores and verified information. What the individual will do can be only inferred. Employers can use the responses to interview and application form questions and references to obtain information for making inferences about what an individual will do.

DECISION-MAKING STRATEGY

The strategy used for making personnel decisions for one category of jobs might differ from that used for another category. The strategy used to select managerial and executive personnel, for example, will be different than the strategy used to select clerical and technical personnel. Although many factors have to be considered in terms of making hiring decisions, the following are some of the questions that managers must consider:

1. Should the individuals be hired according to their highest potential or according to the needs of the organization?
2. At what grade or wage level should the individual be started?
3. Should the selection be concerned primarily with finding an ideal employee to match the job currently open, or should a candidate's potential for advancement in the organization be considered?
4. To what extent should those who are not qualified but are qualifiable (have potential) be considered?
5. Should overqualified individuals be considered?
6. What effect will a decision have on the organization's meeting its employment equity plans and diversity considerations?

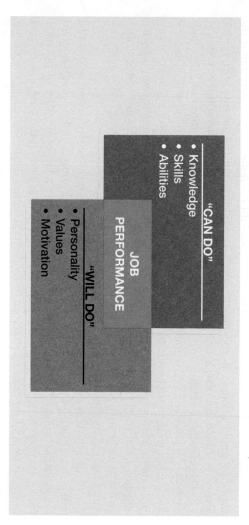

FIGURE 6.8

"Can-Do" and "Will-Do" Factors in Selection Decisions

In addition to these types of factors, managers must also consider which approach they will use in making hiring decisions. There are two basic approaches to selection: clinical (personal judgment) and statistical.

Clinical Approach

In the clinical approach to decision making, those making the selection decision review all the data on the applicants. Then, on the basis of their understanding of the job and the individuals who have been successful in that job, they make a decision. Different individuals often arrive at different decisions about an applicant when they use this approach because each evaluator assigns different weights to the applicant's strengths and weaknesses. Unfortunately, personal biases and stereotypes are frequently covered up by what appear to be rational reasons for either accepting or rejecting a candidate.

Statistical Approach

In contrast to the clinical approach, the statistical approach to decision making is more objective. It involves identifying the most valid predictors and weighting them using statistical methods such as multiple regression.[43] Quantified data such as scores or ratings from interviews, tests, and other procedures are then combined according to their weighted value. Individuals with the highest combined scores are selected. A comparison of the clinical approach with the statistical approach in a wide variety of situations has shown that the statistical approach is superior. Although this superiority has been recognized for many decades, the clinical approach continues to be the one most commonly used.

With a strictly statistical approach, a candidate's high score on one predictor (such as a cognitive ability test) will make up for a low score on another predictor (such as the interview). For this reason, this model is a **compensatory model**. However, it is frequently important that applicants achieve some minimum level of proficiency on all selection dimensions. When this is the case, a **multiple cutoff model** can be used in which only those candidates who score above the minimum cutoff on all dimensions are considered. The selection decision is made from that subset of candidates.[44]

A variation of the multiple cutoff is referred to as the **multiple hurdle model**. This decision strategy is sequential in that after candidates go through an initial evaluation stage, the ones who score well are provisionally accepted and are assessed further at each successive stage. The process continues through several stages (hurdles) before a final decision is made regarding the candidates. This approach is especially useful when either the testing or training procedures are lengthy and expensive.

Each of the statistical approaches requires that a decision be made about where the cutoff lies—that point in the distribution of scores above which a person should be considered and below which the person should be rejected. The score that the applicant must achieve is the cutoff score. Depending on the labour supply and diversity considerations, it may be necessary to lower or raise the cutoff score.

The effects of raising and lowering the cutoff score are illustrated in Figure 6.9. Each dot in the centre of the figure represents the relationship between the test score (or a weighted combination of test scores) and the criterion of success for one individual. In this instance, the test has a fairly high validity, as represented by the elliptical pattern of the dots. Note that the high-scoring individuals are concentrated in the satisfactory job success category, whereas the low-scoring individuals are concentrated in the unsatisfactory category.

If the cutoff score is set at A, only the individuals represented by areas 1 and 2 will be accepted. Nearly all of them will be successful. If more employees are needed, the cutoff score can be lowered to point B. In this case, a larger number of potential failures will be accepted, as shown in quadrants 2 and 4. Even if the cutoff is lowered to C, the total number of satisfactory individuals selected (represented by the dots in areas 1, 3, and 5) exceeds the total number selected who are unsatisfactory (areas 2,

compensatory model
A selection decision model in which a high score in one area can make up for a low score in another area

multiple cutoff model
A selection-decision model that requires an applicant to achieve some minimum level of proficiency on all selection dimensions

multiple hurdle model
A sequential strategy in which only the applicants with the highest scores at an initial test stage go on to subsequent stages

FIGURE 6.9

Test Scores Scatterplot with Hypothetical Cutoffs

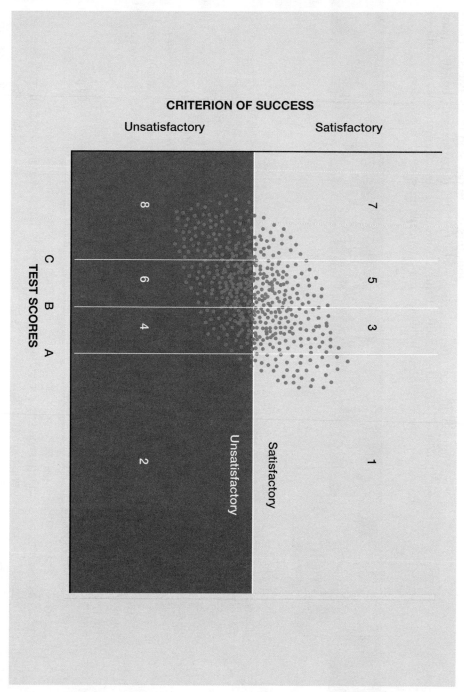

4, and 6). Thus, the test serves to maximize the selection of probable successes and to minimize the selection of probable failures. This is all we can hope for in terms of predicting on-the-job success: the probability of selecting a greater proportion of individuals who will be successful rather than unsuccessful.

Of course, the most valid predictors should be used with any selection strategy. Nonetheless, a related factor contributes to selecting the best qualified people: having an adequate number of applicants or candidates from which to make a selection. It is typically expressed in terms of a **selection ratio**, which is the ratio of the number of applicants to be selected to the total number of applicants. A ratio of 0.10, for example, means that 10 percent of the applicants will be selected. A ratio of 0.90 means that 90 percent will be selected. If the selection ratio is low, only the most promising applicants will be hired. When the ratio is high, very little selectivity will be possible because even applicants with mediocre abilities will have to be hired if the firm's vacancies are to be filled. When this is the situation, a firm's managers can fall prey to what some experts call the "desperation bias"—choosing someone because they are in a pinch. It is a common problem among managers because of the many time and operating constraints they face.

FINAL DECISION

After a preliminary selection/screening by a firm's HR department has been conducted, the applicants who appear most promising are then referred to the departments with vacancies. These people are then interviewed by the managers or supervisors, who usually make the final decision and communicate it to the human

selection ratio
The number of applicants compared with the number of people to be hired.

resources department. Because of the weight that is usually given to their choices, managers and supervisors should be trained so that their role in the selection process does not negate the more rigorous efforts of the firm's HR staff.

In large organizations, notifying applicants of the decision that has been made and making job offers is often the responsibility of HR departments. The HR department should confirm the details of the job, working arrangements, wages, and so on, and specify a deadline by which the applicant must reach a decision.

Small Business APPLICATION

What is different for small business is twofold. Firstly, in all likelihood the person conducting the interview will be the business owner or hiring manager rather than an HR generalist. This will not be true in all cases as there may be times when small businesses work through temporary staffing companies or recruitment agencies, in which case candidates would likely go through an interview with a recruitment specialist prior to being referred for consideration. Secondly, as we outlined in Chapter 3, the nature of working for a small company is that people must fit in with the team and assist in many different capacities. As a result, where selection for positions in large companies balances the importance of person–job fit and person–organization fit, in small companies a greater focus is placed on person–organization fit combined with capability and motivation to do the job candidates are being hired for as well as providing assistance to others when needed.

So how do small companies ensure that their selection process effectively assesses a candidate's fit? With the twin goals of selection being to assess a candidate's skills to perform in the role, as well as his or her ability to fit into the organization, many small companies conduct multiple interviews. One interview is conducted by the functional manager, which focuses

on assessing the required job skill as well as fit with the operational leader. A second interview is conducted by the business owner or another manager, with the aim of assessing the candidate's capacity and demonstrated willingness to support other activities, as well as assessing organizational fit. References then are checked, with a cautionary recognition that references are seldom negative, even if past performance was unsatisfactory, as past employers do not wish to get involved in any controversy as a result of providing negative feedback.

As a final note, in Chapter 5 we identified that employee referrals and hiring family members is a common practice in small companies. Small companies need be very cautious as in the selection process when considering referrals, friends, and family. Such selection creates bias that must be factored in the selection process. This does not mean that small companies should not consider referrals, friends, and family. It just means that all steps should be taken to confirm that candidates are the best candidate for the job based on job fit and organizational fit, and so minimize hiring mistakes that come from incorrectly assuming the skills and fit of referrals, friends, or family.

SUMMARY

[OUTCOME 1]   The employee selection process should provide as much reliable and valid information as possible about applicants so that their qualifications can be carefully matched with the job's specifications. The information that is obtained should be clearly job related or predict success on the job, and be free from potential discrimination. Reliability refers to the consistency of test scores over time and across measures. Validity refers to the accuracy of the measurements taken. Validity can be assessed in terms of whether the measurement is based on a job specification (content validity), whether test scores correlate with performance criteria (predictive validity), and whether the test accurately measures what it purports to measure (construct validity).

OUTCOME 2

Interviews are customarily used in conjunction with application forms, biographical information blanks, references, background investigations, cognitive ability tests, job knowledge tests, and work sample tests.

OUTCOME 3

Cognitive ability tests are especially valuable for assessing verbal, quantitative, and reasoning abilities. Personality and interest tests are perhaps best used for placement or career development. Physical ability tests can be used to prevent accidents and injuries, particularly for physically demanding work. Job knowledge and work sample tests are achievement tests that are useful for determining whether a candidate can perform the duties of the job without further training.

OUTCOME 4

The interview is an important source of information about job applicants. It can be unstructured, wherein the interviewer is free to pursue whatever approach and sequence of topics might seem appropriate, as long as they are job related. Alternatively, an interview can be structured, wherein each applicant receives the same set of questions, which have pre-established answers associated with different scores. Some interviews are situational and can focus on hypothetical situations or actual behavioural descriptions of a candidate's previous work experiences. Interviews can be conducted by a single individual, by a panel, via a computer, or be videotaped or digitally recorded. Regardless of the technique chosen, those who conduct interviews should receive special training to acquaint them with interviewing methods and employment equity considerations. The training should also make them more aware of the major findings from research studies on the interview and how they can apply these findings and avoid biases.

OUTCOME 5

In the process of making decisions, all "can-do" and "will-do" factors should be assembled and weighted systematically so that the final decision can be based on a composite of the most reliable and valid information. Although the clinical approach to decision making is used more than the statistical approach, the former lacks the accuracy of the latter. Compensatory models allow a candidate's high score on one predictor to make up for a low score on another. When the multiple cutoff model is used, only those candidates who score above a minimum cutoff level remain in the running. A variation of the multiple cutoff is the multiple hurdle model, which involves several stages and cutoff levels. Whichever of these approaches is used, the goal is to select a greater proportion of individuals who will be successful on the job.

KEY TERMS

achievement tests, 238
aptitude tests, 238
behavioural description interview (BDI), 245
compensatory model, 256
concurrent validity, 229
construct validity, 230
content validity, 230

criterion-related validity, 228
cross-validation, 229
multiple cutoff model, 256
multiple hurdle model, 256
nondirective interview, 243
panel interview, 245
predictive validity, 229
reliability, 228

selection, 226
selection ratio, 257
situational interview, 243
structured interview, 243
validity generalization, 230
validity, 228

DISCUSSION QUESTIONS

1. What is meant by the term *criterion* as it is used in personnel selection? Give some examples of criteria used for jobs with which you are familiar.

2. What problems might an employer encounter when checking references furnished by job applicants? Are there any solutions to these problems?

3. What characteristics do job knowledge and job sample tests have that often make them more acceptable to the examinees than other types of tests?

4. Personality tests, like other tests used in employee selection, have been under attack for several decades. Why do you think some

applicants find personality tests objectionable? On what basis could their use for selection purposes be justified?

5. Compare briefly the major types of employment interviews described in this chapter. Which type would you prefer to conduct? Why?

6. In what ways does the clinical approach to selection differ from the statistical approach? How do you account for the fact that one approach is superior to the other?

INTERNET EXERCISE

Take an online personality test such as the leadership quiz offered on the Monster.ca website (http://content .monster.ca/tools/quizzes/leadership/). Is this test valid? How could an organization use this test?

HRM EXPERIENCE

Designing Selection Criteria and Methods

Making hiring decisions is one of the most important—and difficult—decisions a manager makes. Without good information, managers have almost no chance of making the right choice. They might as well be using an Ouija board. The process begins with a sound understanding of the job: the tasks, duties, and responsibilities associated with it and the knowledge, skills, and abilities needed to do it. A job analysis should be done to make certain that all managers have assembled all of the information they need to ensure a good person–job fit. However, this information may not be enough. Other information about the company's values and philosophy are likely to be required to ensure that a good person–organization fit results.

Assignment

1. Working in teams of four to six individuals, choose a job with which you are familiar and identify the

most important KSAOs needed for someone doing the job to perform well.

2. Next, identify which methods you would use to find candidates with these qualities. Would you use applications, interviews, cognitive or ability tests, work samples, or something else? Explain why you would use these methods you identified and justify the cost and time required to conduct each.

3. After you have identified your selection criteria and methods, do a "reality check" in a real organization. Interview a manager who employs someone in that job. For example, if the job you selected is salesperson, go to a local business to learn how it selects individuals for sales jobs. Compare what you thought would be a good selection approach with what you learned from the company you visited.

4. Identify the reasons for any discrepancies between your approach and theirs. Are the reasons justified and sound?

BIZFLIX EXERCISES

BOWFINGER: THE LOOKALIKE

Some major learning objectives of this chapter include understanding the goals of an organization's selection process, using different types of information in employee selection and using different employment interview approaches. Watch this humorous scene from *Bowfinger* with those learning objectives in mind.

This film, which brought Steve Martin and Eddie Murphy together for the first time, offers a funny look at Hollywood filmmaking. Bobby Bowfinger (Martin), perhaps the least successful director in films, wants to produce a low-budget film with top star Kit Ramsey (Murphy). Bowfinger's problem: Recruit a crew and cast with almost no budget and trick Kit into appearing in his film.

Bowfinger interviews several candidates for the Kit Ramsey lookalike role. He rejects everyone until—Jefferson, Jiff, Ramsey (Murphy) auditions. This scene is an edited version of "The Lookalike" sequence early in the film. It includes Jiff's audition and interview and a brief look at his first workday.

What to Watch for and Ask Yourself

- Which steps in the employee selection process shown earlier in Figure 6.2 appear in this scene? Which steps did Bobby Bowfinger skip?
- Does Bobby Bowfinger have valid selection criteria for filling the role of the Kit Ramsey lookalike? Do you predict Jiff Ramsey's success as a Kit Ramsey substitute?
- Which type of employment interview did Bowfinger use? See the earlier section "The Employment Interview" for a discussion of different employment interview approaches.

CASE STUDY 1

JOB CANDIDATE ASSESSMENT TESTS GO VIRTUAL

Multistate banking firm National City Corp. had its work cut out if it was going to grow its retail banking division.

One element in the search for everything from branch managers to tellers hinged on the bank's ability to stand out in a cutthroat hiring environment where demand for qualified talent often outstrips the supply. "We were looking for ways to differentiate ourselves among our competitors," says Cheryl Goodman, National City's assessment consultant vice president.

It was among the reasons National City adopted Shaker Consulting Group's Virtual Job Tryout in early 2007. The system does what its name suggests—allows companies to audition candidates by measuring how they react to computerized simulations of specific job-related tasks. Beyond assessment, Goodman is counting on it to give National City a leg up on competitors by creating a distinctive recruiting experience. "This isn't your run-of-the-mill paper-and-pencil assessment test," she explains. "We think it creates a unique impression that lets us stand out among our peers in the industry."

National City, which employs 32,000 people, is part of a growing number of companies that rely on a new wave of virtual simulation tools for more than assessment purposes. They also leverage these platforms to put forth other strategic recruiting practices. Besides differentiation, Goodman says Virtual Job Tryout is also a good way to fortify the National City employer brand. The system works as an educational tool for candidates to learn what it's like to be an employee at the company. "It gives us a way to share our story and what we're all about," she notes. The better acquainted that companies get with virtual tryout tools, the more applications they'll discover for them, says Nov Omana, managing principal of consultancy Collective HR Solutions. He says more employers are realizing the secondary benefits such cutting-edge assessment systems can bring to their recruiting process. Omana anticipates the trend will widen. "Whether it is in the area of Second Life or social networking or virtual tryouts, I think we'll see employers getting more creative in the years to come," he notes.

CREATING A UNIQUE EXPERIENCE

"The days of handing a clipboard and pen to candidates are long over," says Brian Stern of Shaker Consulting. "Innovative companies are now looking for ways to create positive recruiting experiences to successfully vie for talent." The level of interactivity that today's virtual tryout tools deliver is unprecedented, he notes. Employers are able to customize simulations to specific job roles within a company; candidates can get a feel for the job.

In National City's case, Goodman set up individual simulation experiences for call center applicants and potential branch managers. Call center candidates were given scenarios to solve customer service problems, while branch manager applicants had to demonstrate their ability to foster relationships with clients and make quick personnel decisions.

The experiences are interactive—with both video and audio, Stern notes. "Companies are creating a dynamic testing environment that engages the candidates," he says. Delivering this type of innovative recruiting experience is particularly critical when it comes to Gen Y talent, Stern says. "This is a group of individuals that is not going to respond well to the old-school way of recruiting," he notes.

THE GEN Y FACTOR

Recruiting Gen Yers is an ongoing challenge for employers. "They are of a different breed than what recruiters are used to," says Knowledge Infusion CEO Jason Averbook. "You would be surprised at the number of companies that simply don't know how to communicate effectively with them." Averbook says one way of attaining the attention of this segment of the workforce is adopting tools that are interactive in nature, as they stand a better chance of resonating with this audience. "Simulation tools are a good way of letting Gen Yers know that a company has kept up with the times," he notes.

Averbook warns that creating a cutting-edge recruiting experience without having a workplace environment matching that image could be counterproductive. "If you have a fancy assessment tool that impresses the socks off an applicant at the recruiting stage but then hand them a paper and pencil to do their job once you have thrown them over the hiring wall, you're going to be in trouble," he notes. Averbook says employees inevitably will become disappointed and could leave if their initial expectations aren't met. He recommends companies put standards in place, not just during the recruiting phase but throughout an employee's tenure. "This is a group of smart people," he notes. "They'll be able to see through the smoke and mirrors pretty quickly."

IMPORTANT CONSIDERATIONS

While job simulation tools can be instrumental in creating a hallmark recruiting experience, there are certain questions employers should consider before investing in a system, says Shally Steckerl, founder of JobMachine, a recruiting consultancy. "These are great tools to have," he notes. "But they are more beneficial for certain types of employers."

It could backfire for companies targeting high-end white-collar workers. "An MBA is not going to want to take this type of test," Steckerl says. "That candidate is expecting to be wined and dined." He recommends companies take a hard look at the sort of worker being recruited and whether such an assessment would be appropriate in that context. Steckerl also says job simulation may be more of a hindrance at companies handling a large volume of candidates.

"The process gets to be too time-consuming when we are talking about thousands of applicants," he notes. Further, he says such technologies are better suited to test soft skills. It's an important feature, as intangibles are characteristics that are normally difficult to gauge," Stecker] explains. However, when it comes to measuring hard skills, such as engineering or program writing, a company may be better off using conventional aptitude exams.

Before buying such a system, employers should assess virtual job tryout vendors because all are different. "There are several vendors out there, each with its own strength," Stecker] says. "Companies need to do their homework to select the tool that is most compatible with the recruiting experience that they want to create."

In the case of National City, the company already had an established relationship with Shaker Consulting and was familiar with the product's features. The company is still tallying its numbers, but Goodman says she is content with its recruiting performance in 2007. Goodman says the assessment tool enabled National City to hire workers that came from sectors outside banking, so long as they had transferable skills. What's more, she believes retention rates will improve because it provides a way to make hiring decisions that are more educated and scientific. She also sees an added bonus for using the virtual job tryout. "As far as I know, none of our local competitors offers this level of assessment," she says. "I think it gives us an advantage."

Source: Reprinted from Gina Ruiz, "Job Candidate Assessment Tests Go Virtual," *Workforce Management Online*, January 2008. Used by permission.

QUESTIONS

1. What do you think are the prime advantages and disadvantages of National City Corporation's "virtual tryouts"?

2. Do you think there would be any EE concerns regarding this system?

3. Would you suggest the company tailor its system for different types of candidates?

CASE STUDY 2

APTITUDE TESTS AT AN ELECTRONICS CORPORATION

An electronics plant in Midland, Ontario, has begun using aptitude tests as part of its selection process. Before new candidates will be considered for new job openings and for promotions, they must pass eight different aptitude tests. One test for manual dexterity requires applicants to move small metal pegs from holes on one side of a board to holes on the other side as fast as they can. In another test, employees are shown pictures of two cows—one white and the other spotted—and asked, "Which cow would be easier to see from an airplane?"

The company's employees see no relationship between their jobs and the cow test; they also find it humiliating to have to move pegs on a board in order to qualify for jobs they have been doing for years. In one testing session, 80 percent of employees failed. The price of failure is exclusion from higher-paying and more desirable jobs. Even more shameful is the fact that people with less seniority and little plant experience are passing the aptitude tests.

The dispute is deeply rooted. The union feels that the tests are allowing management to replace experienced workers with new hires who work for less pay. The fact that test results are almost always confidential has led to suspicions that the results are being manipulated in some way. After seeing their colleagues fail the tests, some workers are so discouraged that they don't even try for new jobs or promotions. Other changes that have been introduced along with the tests include 12-hour rotating shifts, the "flexible" replacement of workers, and new computerized inspection systems.

Management defends the testing, claiming that new plants and new work methods require aptitudes such as problem solving and flexible thinking. These skills are not usually associated with the stereotype of the senior blue-collar worker. In the past, young people had no need to even graduate from high school if there was a plant in town offering big paycheques for manual labour. The tests that have been introduced discriminate against older workers with less formal education. In demand today are employees who can do many jobs, solve problems, make decisions, provide creative solutions, and function effectively as part of an empowered work team.

Source: Reprinted by permission of the author Megan Terepocki.

QUESTIONS

1. Do you see any problems with the way the company's testing program is being managed? Discuss.

2. Suggest how the program might be modified.

3. The union is fighting to eliminate the testing. On what grounds could the union base its arguments?

4. If an employee files a complaint with the Ontario Human Rights Commission on the grounds that the test discriminated against him as an older worker, what kinds of information will have to be gathered to determine the validity of his claim?

CASE STUDY 3

SEARCHING FOR SPIES

The Canadian Security Intelligence Service (CSIS) is a civilian-run agency, formerly the Security Services of the RCMP. Its role is defensive—to protect Canada from terrorists and foreign spies. It does not send armed spies overseas. Curiously, for a extremely private organization, CSIS has been named a top employer.

Since the 9/11 attacks, CSIS has added about 500 new staff, and now new hires represent about 15 percent of its workforce. Selecting spies used to be a secret process. There was no public knowledge about how spies were recruited, what the job description was, and what the selection criteria and methods were.

Each year, CSIS receives 3,000 unsolicited applicants for about 100 openings. However, most of these applications are from unqualified James Bond wanna-be's. CSIS wants highly qualified, well-educated, multilingual, multiskilled employees. It recruits openly, and its selection criteria and processes are public.

In 2008, CSIS recruited at 53 career fairs, 142 information sessions, and 18 special career events. However, in an effort to recruit more visible minorities, it also uses the Internet, business breakfasts, professional associations, and academic connections. If you want to apply, CSIS looks for Canadian citizens who are university graduates, preferably with advanced degrees. You must have a valid driver's licence and be able to relocate anywhere in Canada at any time. You will have lived or studied abroad, be proficient in English and French, and have a third or fourth language. CSIS looks for generalists—people who are knowledgeable about international and political issues and who have investigative and analytical skills. As a CSIS employee, you will not be able to discuss your work with outsiders at any time.

As an applicant, you must go through the following selection process:

- Submit a résumé
- Complete a 12-page application, which also involves writing a 500-word essay explaining why you want to become an intelligence officer

- Attend a group information session, where recruiters and intelligence officers answer questions
- Attend a suitability interview, where your motivation and verbal and people skills are judged
- Take a battery of psychological and aptitude tests
- Have your language skills tested
- Attend a national assessment panel—veterans will assess your motivation, knowledge of CSIS, and general awareness of public affairs
- Be submitted to security clearance procedures (including a polygraph test, fingerprints, lie detector test, credit check, criminal record check, and references back to teen years), which take three months and cost thousands of dollars
- Go to a final interview

This is a multiple-hurdle model of selection. As a candidate, you will have to pass each hurdle before being allowed to continue to the next. If successful, you will be on probation for five years, undergo 12 weeks of classroom training and language training, and spend two or three years at an operations desk at headquarters, before being transferred to the field under the guidance of a mentor.

Source: Adapted from J. Sallot, "The Spy Masters' Talent Hunt Goes Public," *The Globe and Mail*, June 22, 1999: A1, A10. Reprinted by permission of *The Globe and Mail*. Anonymous. *Financial Post Business*. Toronto: May 2008, pg. 26, 1 pgs. Anonymous. "Wanna be a spy? Your Country Needs You," *The Province*. Vancouver, B.C.: Mar 14, 2008. pg. A.24. Anonymous. "Spies Like Us," *Canadian HR Reporter*. Toronto: May 19, 2003. Vol. 16, Iss. 10; pg. G2.

QUESTIONS

1. Do you think the selection system used by CSIS is valid? Using your knowledge of validity, rate each step in this process.

2. One reason CSIS went public was to increase the representation of women from 10 percent to a target of 50 percent. Are there any possible problems with discrimination in this selection system? Discuss.

CAREER COUNSEL

The résumé preparation exercises on the *Managing Human Resources* website (http://www.belcourt6e.nelson.com) will help you tailor your résumé to the position.

NOTES AND REFERENCES

1. Misty L. Loughry, Matthew W. Ohland, and D. Dewayne Moore, "Development of a Theory-Based Assessment of Team Member Effectiveness," *Educational & Psychological Measurement* 67, no. 3 (June 2007): 505–524; Patrick D. Converse, Fredrick L. Oswald, Michael A. Gillespie, Kevin A. Field, and Elizabeth B. Bizot, "Matching Individual to Occupations Using Abilities and the O*NET," *Personnel Psychology* 57, no. 2 (Summer 2004): 451–488.

2. Wesley Scorggins, "The Relationship between Employee Fit Perceptions, Job Performance and Retention: Implications of Perceived Fit," *Employee Responsibilities and Rights Journal* 20, no. 1 (March 2008); Helene D. Cooper-Thomas, Anelies Van Viannen, and Neil Anderson, "Changes in Person-Organization Fit: The impact of Socialization Tactics on Perceived and Actual P-O Fit" *European Journal of Work and Psychology* 12, no. 1. (March 2004): 52–57.

3. Mary-Kathryn Zachary, "Discrimination without Intent," *Supervision* 64, no. 5 (May 2003): 23–29; Neal Schmitt, William Rogers, David Chan, Lori Sheppard, and Danielle Jennings, "Adverse Impact and Predictive Efficiency of Various Predictor Combinations," *Journal of Applied Psychology* 82, no. 5 (October 1997): 719–730.

4. Daniel A. Biddle and Patrick M. Nooren, "Validity Generalizations versus Title VII: Can Employers Successfully Defend Tests Conducting Local Validation Studies?" *Labor Law Journal* 57, no. 4 (Winter 2006): 216–237; Namok Choi, "A Psychometric Examination of the Personal Attributes Questionnaire," *Journal of Social Psychology* 144, no. 3 (June 2004): 348–352.

5. Jesus F. Salgado and Neil Anderson, "Validity Generalization of GMA Tests across Countries in the European Community," *European Journal of Work & Organizational Psychology* 12, no. 1 (March 2003): 1–17; Calvin C. Hoffman and S. Morton McPhail, "Exploring Options for Supporting Test Use in Situations Precluding Local Validation," *Personnel Psychology* 51, no. 4 (Winter 1998): 987–1003; Leaetta Hough and Frederick Oswald, "Personnel Selection: Looking toward the Future—Remembering the Past," *Annual Review of Psychology* 51 (2000): 631–664.

6. Philip Bobko, Philip L. Roth, and Maury A. Buster, "The Usefulness of Unit Weights in Creating Composite Scores: A Literature Review, Application to Content Validity, and Meta-Analysis," *Organizational Research Methods* 10, no. 4 (October 2007): 689–709; Kobi Dayan, Ronen Kasten, and Shaul Fox, "Entry-Level Police Candidate Assessment Center: An Efficient Tool or a Hammer to Kill a Fly?" *Personnel Psychology* 55, no. 4 (Winter 2002): 827–849.

7. Deniz S. Ones, Chockalingam Viswesvaran, and Frank L Schmidt, "No New Terrain: Reliability and Construct Validity of Job Performance Ratings," *Industrial & Organizational Psychology* 1, no. 2 (June 2008): 174–179; D. Brent Smith and Lill Ellingson, "Substance versus Style: A New Look at Social Desirability in Motivating Contexts," *Journal of Applied Psychology* 87, no. 2 (April 2002): 211–19; Ken Craik et al., "Explorations of Construct Validity in a Combined Managerial and Personality Assessment Programme," *Journal of Occupational and Organizational Psychology* 75, no. 2 (June 2002): 171–193.

8. "Busted," *Training Development* 60, no. 12 (December 2006): 19; Pamela Babock, "Spotting Lies," *HR Magazine* 48, no. 10 (October 2003): 46–51; Tammy Prater and Sara Bliss Kiser, "Lies, Lies, and More Lies," *A.A.M. Advance Management Journal* 67, no. 2 (Spring 2002): 9–14.

9. Connie Walker, "Job Tryouts Go Virtual," *HR Magazine* 51, no. 9 (September 2006): 131–134; "The Pros and Cons of Online Recruiting," *HRfocus* 81 (April 2004): S1; Rob Drew, "Career Portals Boost Online Recruiting," *HR Magazine* 49, no. 4 (April 2004): 111–114; Samuel Greengard, "Smarter Screening Takes Technology and HR Savvy," *Workforce* 81, no. 6 (June 2002): 56–62.

10. Yen Chung, "The Validity of Biographical Inventories for the Selection of Salespeople," *International Journal of Management* 18, no. 3 (September 2001): 322–329; Teri Elkins and James Phillips, "Job Context, Selection Decision Outcome, and the Perceived Fairness of Selection Tests: Biodata as an Illustrative Case," *Journal of Applied Psychology* 85, no. 3 (June 2000): 479–484; Herschel Chait, Shawn Carreher, and M. Ronald Buckley, "Measuring Service Orientation with Biodata," *Journal of Managerial Issues* 12, no. 1 (Spring 2000): 109–120.

11. Todd Humber, "Recruitment Isn't Getting Any Easier," *Canadian HR Reporter*, May 23, 2005: R2, R3.

12. Doug Eisenschenk and Elaine Davis, "Background Checks in Hiring and Compensation: The Next Generation," *Benefits & Compensation Digest* 41, no. 10 (October 2004): 1–4; "What's New," *HR Magazine* 49, no. 4 (April 2004): 153–156; "Why You Should Update Your Background Checks," *HRfocus* (February 2004): 12–13; Merry Mayer, "Background Checks in Focus," *HR Magazine* 47, no. 1 (January 2002): 59–62. In addition, organizations use other resources, such as the following: *The Guide to Background Investigations: A Comprehensive Source Directory for Employee Screening and Background Investigations*, 8th ed. (TISI, 2000).

13. Kira Vermond, "References Done Right," *Profit* 26, no. 2 (May 2007): 101; Kathleen Samey, "A Not-So-Perfect Fit," *Adweek* 44, no. 47 (December 1, 2003): 34; Ann Fisher, "How Can We Be Sure We're Not Hiring a Bunch of Shady Liars?" *Fortune* 147, no. 10 (May 26, 2003).

14. Victor Catano, Willi Wiesner, Rick Hackett, and Laura Methot, *Recruitment and Selection in Canada*, 3rd ed. (Toronto: Thomson Nelson, 2005.)

15. Constance L. Hays, "Tests Are Becoming Common in Hiring," *The New York Times*, November 28, 1997, D1. See also Gregory M. Lousig-Nont, "Avoid Common Hiring

16. Mistakes with Honesty Tests," *Nation's Restaurant News* 31, no. 11 (March 17, 1997): 30; "If the Shoe Fits," *Security Management* 40, no. 2 (February 1996): 11; Michelle Cottle, "Job Testing: Multiple Choices," *The New York Times*, September 5, 1999, 10.

17. Thomas J. Ryan, "Nerves of Steal," *SGB* 37, no. 6 (June 2004): 8–10; D. S. Ones, C. Viswesvaran, and F. L. Schmidt, "Comprehensive Meta-Analysis of Integrity Test Validities: Findings and Implications for Personnel Selection and Theories of Job Performance," *Journal of Applied Psychology* 78 (August 1993): 679–703. See also Deniz S. Ones and Chockalingam Viswesvaran, "Gender, Age and Race Differences on Overt Integrity Tests: Results across Four Large-Scale Job Applicant Data Sets," *Journal of Applied Psychology* 83, no. 1 (February 1998): 35–42.

18. James Krohe Jr., "Are Workplace Tests Worth Taking?" *Across the Board* 43, no. 4 (July–August 2006): 16–23; "Honesty Tests Flawed," *People Management* 3, no. 2 (January 23, 1997): 15; Hays, "Tests Are Becoming Common in Hiring"; Stephen A. Dwight and George M. Alliger, "Reactions to Overt Integrity Test Items," *Educational and Psychological Measurement* 57, no. 6 (December 1997): 937–948.

19. Klass Hogenesch, "A New Science for Finding the Right Employee?" *NZ Business* 18, no. 2 (March 2004): 10; Bill Leonard, "Reading Employees," *HR Magazine* 44, no. 4 (April 1999): 67–73; Steven Thomas and Steve Vaught, "The Write Stuff: What the Evidence Says about Using Handwriting Analysis in Hiring," *S.A.M. Advanced Management Journal* 66, no. 4 (Autumn 2001): 31–35.

20. Elizabeth D. MacGillivray, Juanita H. Beecher, and Diedre M. Golden, "Employment Testing: The New Hot Button Issue for Federal Agencies—and Other Legal Developments," *Global Business & Organizational Excellence* 27, no. 3, (March–April 2008): 68–78.

21. Standards that testing programs should meet are described in *Standards for Educational and Psychological Tests* (Washington, DC: American Psychological Association, 1999). HR managers who want to examine paper-and-pencil tests should obtain specimen sets that include a test manual, copy of the test, answer sheet, and scoring key. The test manual provides the essential information about the construction of the test; its recommended use; and instructions for administering, scoring, and interpreting the test. Test users should not rely entirely on the material furnished by the test author and publisher. A major source of consumer information about commercially available tests—*Mental Measurements Yearbook* (MMY)—is available in most libraries. Published periodically, the MMY contains descriptive information plus critical reviews by experts in the various types of tests. The reviews are useful in evaluating a particular test for tryout in employment situations. Other sources of information about tests include *Test Critiques*, a set of volumes containing professional reviews of tests, and *Tests: A Comprehensive Reference for Assessments in Psychology, Education, and Business*. The latter describes more than 2,000 tests published in the English language.

22. Justin Menkes, "Interviewing for Executive Intelligence," *HR Professional* 25, no. 3 (April–May 2008): 54; Chris Piotrowski and Terry Armstrong, "Current Recruitment and Selection Practices: A National Survey of Fortune 1000 Firms," *North American Journal of Psychology* 8, no. 3 (2006): 489–496; Sara Rynes, Amy Colbert, and Kenneth Brown, "HR Professionals' Beliefs about Effective Human Resource Practices: Correspondence between Research and Practice," *Human Resource Management* 41, no. 2 (Summer 2002): 149–174.

23. Kris Frieswick, "Casting to Type," *CFO* 20, no. 9 (July 2004): 71–73; Timothy Judge and Joyce Bono, "Five-Factor Model of Personality and Transformational Leadership," *Journal of Applied Psychology* 85, no. 5 (October 2000): 751–765; J. Michael Crant and Thomas S. Bateman, "Charismatic Leadership Viewed from Above: The Impact of Proactive Personality," *Journal of Organizational Behavior* 21, no. 1 (February 2000): 63–75.

24. Frederick P. Morgeson, Michael A. Campion, Robert L. Dipboye, John R. Hollenbeck, Kevin Murphy, and Neal Schmitt, "Reconsidering the Use of Personality Tests in Personnel Selection Contexts," *Personnel Psychology* 60, no. 3 (Autumn 2007): 683–729;

Arielle Emmett, "Snake Oil or Science? The Raging Debate on Personality Testing," *Workforce Management* 83, no. 10 (October 2004): 90–93; Gregory Hurtz and John Donovan, "Personality and Job Performance: The Big Five Revisited," *Journal of Applied Psychology* 85, no. 6 (December 2000): 869–879.

25. George B. Yancey, "The Predictive Power of Hiring Tools," *Credit Union Executive Journal* 40, no. 4 (July–August 2000): 12–18; Jeffrey A. Mello, "Personality Tests and Privacy Rights," *HRfocus* 73, no. 3 (March 1996): 22–23.

26. Walter C. Borman, Mary Ann Hanson, and Jerry W. Hedge, "Personnel Selection," *Annual Review of Psychology* 48 (1997): 299–337; Charles Sproule and Stephen Berkley, "The Selection of Entry-Level Corrections Officers: Pennsylvania Research," *Public Personnel Management* 30, no. 3 (Fall 2001): 377–418.

27. British Columbia (Public Service Employee Relations Commission) v. BCGSEU, [1999] 3 S.C.R. 3; http://csc.lexum.umontreal.ca/en/1999/1999rcs3-3/1999rcs3-3.html, retrieved July 30, 2009.

28. M. Brewster "RCMP ease fitness rules for women," *The Globe and Mail*, July 14, 1997, A4.

29. John Bret Becton, Hubert S. Feild, William F. Giles, and Allison Jones-Farmer, "Racial Differences in Promotion Candidate Performance and Reactions to Selection Procedures: A Field Study in a Diverse Top-Management Context," *Journal of Organizational Behavior* 29, no. 3 (April 2008): 265–285.

30. Rachel Suff, "Testing the Water: Using Work Sampling for Selection," *IRS Employment Review* no. 802 (June 18, 2004): 44–49; Leonard D. Goodstein and Alan D. Davidson, "Hiring the Right Stuff: Using Competency-Based Selection," *Compensation & Benefits Management* 14, no. 3 (Summer 1998): 1–10.

31. Noelle Murphy, "Testing the Waters: Employers' Use of Selection Assessments," *IRS Employment Review* 852 (August 4, 2006): 42–48; Florence Berger and Ajay Ghei, "Employment Tests: A Facet of Hospitality Hiring," *Cornell Hotel and Restaurant Administration Quarterly* 36, no. 6 (December 1995): 28–31; Malcolm James Ree, Thomas R. Carretta, and Mark S. Teachout, "Role of Ability and Prior Job Knowledge in Complex Training Performance," *Journal of Applied Psychology* 80, no. 6 (December 1995): 721–730.

32. Igor Kotlyar and Ravit Ableman, "Simulation Turns Recruitment into a Two-Way Street," *Canadian HR Reporter* (December 1, 2003): G6.

33. Amy Maingault, John Sweeney, and Naomi Cossack, "Interviewing, Management Training, Strikes," *HR Magazine* 52, no. 6 (June 2007): 43; James Bassett, "Stop, Thief!" *Gifts & Decorative Accessories* 104, no. 1 (January 2003): 130–134; Richard A. Posthuma, Frederick Morgeson, and Michael Campion, "Beyond Employment Interview Validity: A Comprehensive Narrative Review of Recent Research and Trends over Time," *Personnel Psychology* 55, no. 1 (Spring 2002): 1–8.

34. David E. Terpstra and Bryan R. Kethley, "Organizations' Relative Degree of Exposure to Selection Discrimination Litigation," *Public Personnel Management* 31, no. 3 (February 2002): 277–294; Frank L. Schmidt and Mark Rader, "Exploring the Boundary Conditions for Interview Validity," *Personnel Psychology* 99, no. 2 (Summer 1999): 445–464; Laura G. Williamson, James E. Campion, Stanley B. Malos, and Marc V. Roehling, "Employment Interview on Trial," *Journal of Applied Psychology* 82, no. 6 (December 1997): 900–912.

35. Yen-Chun Chen, Wei-Chi Tsai, and Changya Hu, "The Influences of Interviewer-Related and Situational Factors on Interviewer Reactions to High Structured Job Interviews," *International Journal of Human Resource Management* 19, no. 6 (June 2008): 1056–1071. For an excellent review of research on the structured interview, see Michael A. Campion, David K. Palmer, and James E. Campion, "A Review of Structure in the Selection Interview," *Personnel Psychology* 50, no. 3 (Autumn 1997): 655–702. See also Karen vanderZee, Arnold Bakker, and Paulien Bakker, "Why Are Structured Interviews So Rarely Used in Personnel Selection?" *Journal of Applied Psychology* 87, no. 1 (February 2002): 176–184.

36. Jesus F. Salgado and Silvia Moscoso, "Comprehensive Meta-Analysis of the Construct Validity of the Employment Interview," *European Journal of Work and Organizational Psychology* 11, no. 3 (September 2002): 299–325; Allen Huffcutt, Jeff Weekley, Willi Wiesner, Timothy Degroot, and Casey Jones, "Comparison of Situational and Behavior Description Interview Questions for Higher-Level Positions," *Personnel Psychology* 54, no. 3 (Autumn 2001): 619–644.

37. Peter Herriot, "Assessment by Groups: Can Value Be Added?" *European Journal of Work & Organizational Psychology* 12, no. 2 (June 2003): 131–146; Salgado and Moscoso, "Comprehensive Meta-Analysis"; Amelia J. Prewett-Livingston, John G. Veres III, Hubert S. Field, and Philip M. Lewis, "Effects of Race on Interview Ratings in a Situational Panel Interview," *Journal of Applied Psychology* 81, no. 2 (April 1996): 178–186. See also Damodar Y. Golhar and Satish P. Deshpande, "HRM Practices of Large and Small Canadian Manufacturing Firms," *Journal of Small Business Management* 35, no. 3 (July 1997): 30–38.

38. Jack Welch and Suzy Welch, "Hiring Is Hard Work," *BusinessWeek Online*, no. 4091 (July 7, 2008); Michele V. Rafter, "Candidates for Jobs in High Places Sit for Tests That Size Up Their Mettle," *Workforce Management* 83, no. 5 (May 2004): 70–73; Patricia Buhler, "Computer Interview: Managing in the New Millennium," *Supervision* 63, no. 10 (October 2002): 20–23.

39. Victoria Reitz, "Interview without Leaving Home," *Machine Design* 76, no. 7 (April 1, 2004): 66; Jessica Clark Newman et al., "The Differential Effects of Face-to-Face and Computer Interview Modes," *American Journal of Public Health* 92, no. 2 (February 2002): 294; David Mitchell, "ijob.com Recruiting Online," *Strategic Finance* 80, no. 11 (May 1999): 48–51.

40. Dan Hanover, "Hiring Gets Cheaper and Faster," *Sales and Marketing Management* 152, no. 3 (March 2000): 87

41. Marjo Johne, "Prize for playing the game: A career," *The Globe and Mail*, April 26, 2006, C1.

42. Fay Hansen, "Keeping Interviews on Point to Stay Out of Legal Hot Water," *Workforce Management* no. 85, no. 15 (August 14, 2006): 44–45; Richard A. Posthuma, Frederick P. Morgeson, and Michael A. Campion, "Beyond Employment Interview Validity"; Frank L. Schmidt and Mark Rader, "Exploring the Boundary Conditions for Interview Validity."

43. Multiple regression is a statistical method for evaluating the magnitude of effects of more than one independent variable (e.g., selection predictors) on a dependent variable (e.g., job performance) using principles of correlation and regression

44. Patricia M. Buhler, "Managing in the New Millennium," *Supervision* 68, no. 11 (November 2007): 17–20; David E. Bowen and Cheri Ostroff, "Understanding HRM—Firm Performance Linkages: The Role of the Strengths of the HRM System," *Academy of Management Review* 29, no. 2 (April 2004): 203–222; Ann Marie Ryan, Joshua Sacco, Lynn McFarland, and David Kriska, "Applicant Self-Selection: Correlates of Withdrawal from a Multiple Hurdle Process," *Journal of Applied Psychology* 85, no. 2 (April 2000): 163–179.

Answers to Figure 6.5: 3, 3, 4

Training and Development

After studying this chapter, you should be able to

[OUTCOME] **1** Discuss the systems approach to training and development.

[OUTCOME] **2** Describe the components of training needs assessment.

[OUTCOME] **3** Identify the principles of learning and describe how they facilitate training.

[OUTCOME] **4** Identify the types of training methods used for managers and nonmanagers.

[OUTCOME] **5** Discuss the advantages and disadvantages of various evaluation criteria.

[OUTCOME] **6** Describe the special training programs that are currently popular.

Training has become increasingly vital to the success of modern organizations. Recall that in Chapter 2 we noted that organizations often compete on the basis of their capabilities—the core sets of knowledge and expertise that give them an edge over their competitors. Training plays a central role in nurturing and strengthening the competencies of a firm and in this way has become part of the backbone of strategic management. In addition, rapidly changing technologies require that employees continuously hone their knowledge, skills, and abilities (KSAs) through continuous learning. Greater competition, including that from different firms around the globe, also makes it necessary for a company's employees and managers to develop the skills that enable them to handle new and more demanding assignments.

THE SCOPE OF TRAINING

Many new employees come equipped with most of the KSAs needed to start work. Others require extensive training before they are ready to make much of a contribution to the organization. Almost any employee, however, needs some type of ongoing training to maintain effective performance or to adjust to new ways of work.

The term *training* is often used casually to describe almost any effort initiated by an organization to foster learning among its members. However, many experts distinguish between training, which tends to be more narrowly focused and oriented toward short-term performance concerns, and *development*, which, as you learned in Chapter 5, tends to be oriented more toward broadening an individual's skills for future responsibilities. The two terms tend to be combined into a single phrase—*training and development*—to recognize the combination of activities organizations use to increase the skill base of employees.

INVESTMENTS IN TRAINING

Research shows that an organization's revenues and overall profitability are positively correlated to the amount of training it gives its employees. Here are some interesting training statistics from the Conference Board of Canada's Learning and Development Outlook 2007:

- Canadian businesses spend about $850 per employee on training.
- Over two-thirds of employees received training in 2006, either formally or informally.
- Employees with less experience receive more training.
- Training of managers consumes 44 percent of a company's training budget.

According to the Conference Board of Canada's report, the not-for-profit sector spends the most amount of money per employee ($1229) and the wholesale/retail sector the least ($459). Typically organizations spend about 2 percent of payroll on training.[1] The most profitable companies provide their employees with approximately double that amount of training and sometimes even more. Each employee of the hotel chain the Ritz Carlton, for example, gets nearly 200 hours of training each year. The types of training being offered by Canadian organizations are outlined in Figure 7.1. In addition to the billions of dollars spent by businesses each year on formal training, nearly four times that amount is spent on informal instruction. The types of training given employees range from simple, on-the-job instruction to sophisticated skills training conducted on multimillion dollar simulators.[2]

Ethics in HRM presents the debate about the effectiveness of mandatory training for employees.

Using the Internet

The Canadian Society for Training and Development is the professional association for those working in training and development in Canada

http://www.cstd.ca

FIGURE 7.1

Course content as a percentage of training expenditures, 2006

Management/supervisory skills training	15%
Professional skills training	12
Occupational health and safety/government mandated	10
Technical processes and procedures training	9
Information technology skills training	9
Product knowledge training	7
New employee orientation	7
Executive development	6
Interpersonal communication training	6
Customer relations training	6
Quality, competition, and business practices	5
Sales and dealer training	4
Basic skills training	2
Other	2

Source: P. D. Hughes and M. Grant, *Learning and Development Outlook 2007*, The Conference Board of Canada; http://www.conferenceboard.ca/documents.aspx?DID=1995, retrieved July 30, 2009. Used by permission.

Ethics in HRM

Mandatory or Voluntary?

There is only one payroll training tax in North America. The Quebec government program that forces employers to spend 1 percent of payroll on training may not have the intended consequences of increasing training investments in employees. Using data from a Statistics Canada survey, Alan Saks of the University of Toronto and Robert Haccoun of the Université de Montréal matched Quebec employers with Ontario employers and found that there were no differences in amounts spent on training. The paperwork is so cumbersome that many employers prefer to pay the 1 percent tax rather than go through the thick guidebooks necessary to report the training.

If there is little effect gained by forcing employers to provide training, are there benefits by forcing employees to attend training? The answer is not clear. Some

studies report some slight benefits in outcomes (such as improved job performance) when employees voluntarily attend courses; other studies see no differences.

There may be more serious problems than performance results created by forcing employees to attend courses. Half of the 24 employees of SaskTel who participated in a training program on process re-engineering required psychological counselling, or stress leave, or both in its aftermath. Trainees said they were subjected to a greenhouse environment: Windows were papered over, employees were not allowed to communicate with one another, and all were subjected to verbal abuse from the training consultants. As the president of the Ontario Society for Training and Development commented: "That's not training, that's assault."

continued

Seagulls Pewter and Silversmiths of Pugwash, Nova Scotia, sent its employees to seminars based on the controversial Est therapy. Employees complained to their union that the seminars, in which participants were encouraged to delve into painful emotions, often drove participants to breakdowns. In another example, a large insurance company hired a consultant to conduct management training for hundreds of supervisors and managers. The company did not realize that the consultant was a member of L. Ron Hubbard's Church of Scientology and was teaching management principles developed by

Scientologists. Critics contend that Scientology is a cult, not a religion. Employees resented being subjected to psychological concepts based on "tones" that catalogue emotions, to the ruthless devotion to ferreting out and firing problem employees, and to "religious scriptures."

The employees in these organizations were required to participate in programs that caused them undue stress and sometimes violated their moral or religious beliefs. Those who organized the programs believed that employees with the "right" attitudes would be more effective.

Sources: K. Harding, "A Taxing Way to Train Staff," *The Globe and Mail*, June 4, 2003, C1; D. Brown, "Legislated Training, Questionable Results," *Canadian HR Reporter* 15, no. 9, May 6, 2002: 1; A. Thomlinson, "Mandatory or Voluntary?" *Canadian HR Reporter* 15, no. 6, March 25, 2002: 1; Edward Kay, "Trauma in Real Life," *The Globe and Mail Report on Business Magazine*, November 1996: 82–92; J. Saunders, "How Scientology's Message Came to Allstate," *The Globe and Mail*, April 24, 1995: B1; R. Sharpe, "Agents of intimidation," *The Globe and Mail*, March 28, 1995, B8.

chief learning officer
A high-ranking manager directly responsible for fostering employee learning and development within the firm

A SYSTEMS APPROACH TO TRAINING

From the broadest perspective, the goal of training is to contribute to the organization's overall goals. Training programs should be developed with this in mind. Managers should keep a close eye on their firms' goals and strategies and orient their training accordingly. Unfortunately, many organizations never make the connection between the two. Instead, fads, fashions, or "whatever the competition is doing" can sometimes be the main drivers of an organization's training agenda. As a result, training programs are often misdirected, poorly designed, and inadequately evaluated—not to mention a waste of money.

To ensure that a firm's training and development investment has the maximum impact possible, a systems approach should be used that involves four phases: (1) needs assessment, (2) program design, (3) implementation, and (4) evaluation. A model that is useful to designers of training programs is presented in Figure 7.2. We will use this model as a framework for organizing the material throughout this chapter.

[OUTC1OME]

PHASE 1: CONDUCTING THE NEEDS ASSESSMENT

Because business conditions change rapidly, as does technology, keeping abreast of the types of training a firm's employees need to remain competitive can be a challenge. If employees consistently fail to achieve their productivity objectives, this might be a signal that training is needed. Likewise, if organizations receive an excessive number of customer complaints, this, too, might suggest a firm's training is inadequate. About 30 percent of larger firms, including GE, Walmart, and IBM, have what are called **chief learning officers**. These people are top executives within their firms who are responsible for making certain that a company's training is timely and focused on the firm's top strategic issues. However, regardless of who does the needs assessment within an organization, it should be conducted systematically by utilizing the three different types of analysis shown in Figure 7.3: organization analysis, task analysis, and person analysis. Each of these will be discussed.

Unfortunately, because of the costs, expertise, and time required, a study by the American Society for Training and Development found that organizations conduct needs assessment less than 50 percent of the time. Ironically, as the speed of change

[OUTC2OME]

FIGURE **7.2**

Systems Model of Training

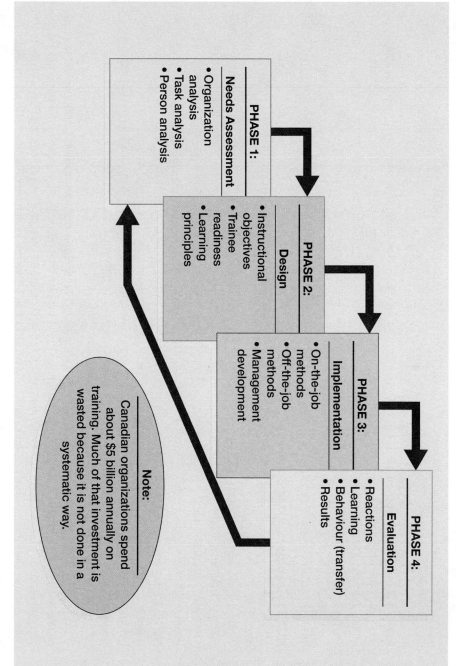

PHASE 1:
Needs Assessment
- Organization analysis
- Task analysis
- Person analysis

PHASE 2:
Design
- Instructional objectives
- Trainee readiness
- Learning principles

PHASE 3:
Implementation
- On-the-job methods
- Off-the-job methods
- Management development

PHASE 4:
Evaluation
- Reactions
- Learning
- Behaviour (transfer)
- Results

Note:
Canadian organizations spend about $5 billion annually on training. Much of that investment is wasted because it is not done in a systematic way.

increases and time and resources are at a premium, the need for good needs assessment increases. In these cases, the process need not be so daunting and laborious. Highlights in HRM 7.1 provides some tips for rapidly assessing training needs.[3]

FIGURE **7.3**

Needs Assessment for Training

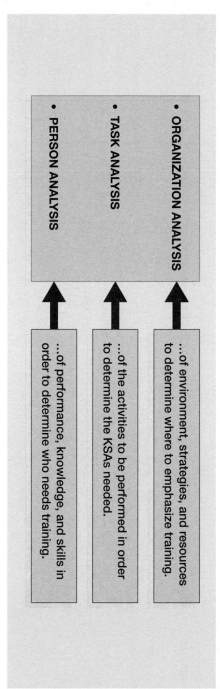

- **ORGANIZATION ANALYSIS** ⟵ ...of environment, strategies, and resources to determine where to emphasize training.

- **TASK ANALYSIS** ⟵ ...of the activities to be performed in order to determine the KSAs needed.

- **PERSON ANALYSIS** ⟵ ...of performance, knowledge, and skills in order to determine who needs training.

Highlights in **HRM 7.1**

Notes on Rapid Needs Assessment

NOTE 1: Look at the problem scope. Common sense suggests that small, local matters may require less information gathering than big problems with a major impact on the organization. Ask managers a series of questions about the nature of the problem and its impact on the organization and gear your analysis accordingly.

NOTE 2: Do organizational scanning. Stay connected with what is going on in the organization in order to anticipate upcoming training needs. If a new technology is about to be launched, the need for training should take no one by surprise. In short, needs assessment isn't an event with a start-and-stop switch. It is the process of being engaged in your business.

NOTE 3: Play "give and take." Get the information you need, but don't drag your feet with excessive analysis before reporting back to managers. Show them that you are sensitive to their need for action by giving them updates on the information you have collected. If necessary, explain that better value may be gained by further analysis.

NOTE 4: Check "lost and found." Often, information gathered for a different purpose may bear on your training issue. Performance data (such as errors, sales, and customer complaints) and staffing data (such as proficiency testing, turnover, and absenteeism) can be very helpful as a starting point.

NOTE 5: Use plain talk. Instead of using clinical terms such as analysis or assessment, use straight talk with managers that tells them what you are doing: (1) identify the problem, (2) identify alternative ways to get there, (3) implement a solution based on cost/benefit concerns, and (4) determine the effectiveness and efficiency of the solution.

NOTE 6: Use the Web. Information technology allows you to communicate with others, perhaps by setting up an electronic mailing list to post questions, synthesize responses, share resources, get feedback, gather information on trends, and the like.

NOTE 7: Use rapid prototyping. Often the most effective and efficient training is that which is "just-in-time, just enough, and just for me." Create a rapid prototype of a training program, evaluating and revising as you implement, and learn more about the problems.

NOTE 8: Seek out exemplars. Find those in the organization that currently demonstrate the performance the organization wants. Bring others together with them to talk about the performance issues, and let the exemplars share their experiences and insights. This avoids the risk of packaging the wrong information, and people learn just what they need to know from each other.

ORGANIZATION ANALYSIS

organization analysis
Examination of the environment, strategies, and resources of the organization to determine where training emphasis should be placed

The first step in a needs assessment is identifying the broad forces that can influence a firm's training needs. An **organization analysis** is an examination of the environment, strategies, and resources the firm faces so as to determine what training it should emphasize.

Economic and public policy issues influence corporate training needs as well. For example, since the September 11 terrorist attacks, the training of airport security personnel has increased substantially. It has also increased for flight crews of airlines, employees in the transportation industry, workers in nuclear power plants, and even security staff at theme parks.[4]

Other training issues tend to revolve around the strategic initiatives of an organization. Mergers and acquisitions, for example, frequently require that employees take on new roles and responsibilities and adjust to new cultures and ways of conducting business. Nowhere is this more prevalent than in grooming new leaders within organizations. Other issues such as technological change, globalization, reengineering, and total quality management all influence the way work is done and the types of skills needed to do it. Still other concerns may be more tactical, but no less important in terms of their impact on training. Organizational restructuring, downsizing, empowerment, and teamwork, for example, have immediate training requirements. Finally, trends in the workforce itself affect a firm's training needs. As older workers near retirement, younger workers need to focus on gaining the skills and knowledge needed to take their place.

Conducting an organization analysis also involves closely examining a firm's resources—technological, financial, and human—available to meet the company's training objectives. HR personnel typically collect data such as information on their companies' direct and indirect labour costs, quality of goods or services, absenteeism, turnover, and number of accidents. The availability of potential replacements and the time required to train them are other important factors in organization analysis.

Organizations continue to keep a tight rein on their costs, including their training budgets. To cope with these resource constraints yet continue to meet their strategic imperatives, firms have become more focused on efficiently using their training budgets. Companies such as Motorola and Merck have found that by using information technology wisely, they cut their training budget by as much as 30 to 50 percent. In order to "do more with less," managers have to plan carefully where they will spend their training dollars, and this means doing a rigorous organization analysis. Other companies outsource their training programs, or at least part of it, to external partners in order to cut costs. A new trend is for companies to partner with other firms in their supply chains so as to jointly train their employees more cost effectively.[5]

TASK ANALYSIS

The second step in training needs assessment is task analysis. **Task analysis** involves reviewing the job description and specifications to identify the activities performed in a particular job and the KSAs needed to perform them. A task analysis often becomes more detailed than a job analysis, but the overall purpose is to determine the exact content of the training program.

The first step in task analysis is to list all the tasks or duties included in the job. The second step is to list the steps performed by the employee to complete each task. Once the job is understood thoroughly, the type of performance required (such as speech, recall, discrimination, and manipulation), along with the skills and knowledge necessary to do it, can be defined. For example, in the task of taking a chest X-ray, a radiologist correctly positions the patient (manipulation), gives special instructions (speech), and checks the proper distance of the X-ray tube from the patient (discrimination). The types of skills and knowledge that trainees need can be determined by observing and questioning skilled jobholders and/or by reviewing job descriptions. This information helps trainers select program content and choose the most effective training methods.

However, like job analysis, task analysis appears to be shifting. Instead of focusing on a fixed sequence of tasks, firms are finding that their employees need more flexible sets of competencies in order to perform in a superior way. Companies such as the RBC Financial Group have found that as jobs begin to involve more teamwork, employees need to be flexible and adjust their behaviour as needed. **Competency assessment** focuses on the sets of skills and knowledge employees need to be

© Noel Hendrickson/Digital Vision/Getty Images

As older workers near retirement, younger workers must be trained in the skills and knowledge needed to take their place. The availability of potential replacements and the time required to train them are two factors that must be considered in organization analysis.

task analysis
The process of determining what the content of a training program should be on the basis of a study of the tasks and duties involved in the job

competency assessment
Analysis of the sets of skills and knowledge needed for decision-oriented and knowledge-intensive jobs

successful, particularly for decision-oriented and knowledge-intensive jobs. But competency assessment goes beyond simply describing the traits an employee must have to successfully perform the work. It also captures elements of how those traits should be used within an organization's context and culture. That might include an employee's motivation levels, personality traits, interpersonal skills, and so on. General Electric, for example, uses a formal competency assessment program based on 45 different employee behaviours. While training programs based on a work-oriented task analysis can become dated as jobs change, training programs based on competency assessment are more flexible and perhaps have more durability. The practice has been adopted extensively in the health care industry.[6] Highlights in HRM 7.2 shows an example of a partial competency assessment tool used for evaluating a manager.

Highlights in HRM 7.2

A Competency Assessment for a Managerial Position

For each item, circle the number that best describes the manager's characteristics. For items that do not apply, circle **NA** (not applicable). For other items for which you lack sufficient observations or documentary evidence, circle **DK** (don't know).

4 – Exemplary

3 – Proficient

2 – Progressing

1 – Needs Assistance

NA – Not Applicable

DK – Don't Know

Competency 1: Behaves professionally and encourages other staff members to do likewise

4   3   2   1   NA   DK

Evidence _____

_____

_____

_____

Competency 2: Behaves ethically and encourages staff members to do likewise

4   3   2   1   NA   DK

Evidence _____

_____

continued

Competency 3: Uses a variety of modes of communication and conveys information fully and clearly

4 3 2 1 NA DK

Evidence _____

_____

_____

Competency 4: Seeks input from all levels and demonstrates fairness and consistency

4 3 2 1 NA DK

Evidence _____

_____

_____

Competency 5: Engages in an open style of management and is open to criticism from supervisors and subordinates

4 3 2 1 NA DK

Evidence _____

_____

_____

Competency 6: Searches for and embraces innovative solutions to improve department's programs and products.

4 3 2 1 NA DK

Evidence _____

_____

_____

PERSON ANALYSIS

Along with organization and task analyses, it is necessary to perform a person analysis. A **person analysis** involves determining which employees require training and, equally important, which do not. In this regard, conducting a person analysis is important for several reasons. First, a thorough analysis helps organizations avoid the mistake of sending all employees into training when some do not need it. In addition, a person analysis helps managers determine what prospective trainees

person analysis
Determination of the specific individuals who need training

are able to do when they enter training so that the programs can be designed to emphasize the areas in which they are deficient.

Companies such as Hewlett-Packard have used performance appraisal information as an input for person analysis. Although performance appraisals might reveal which employees are not meeting the firm's expectations, they typically do not reveal why. If the performance deficiencies are due to ability problems, training is likely to be a good solution. However, if the performance deficiencies are due to poor motivation or factors outside an employee's control, training might not be the answer. Ultimately, managers have to sit down with employees to talk about areas for improvement so that they can jointly determine the developmental approaches that will have maximum benefit.[7]

PHASE 2: DESIGNING THE TRAINING PROGRAM

Once the training needs have been determined, the next step is to design the type of learning environment necessary to enhance learning. The success of training programs depends on more than an organization's ability to identify its training needs. Success hinges on taking the information gained from the needs assessment conducted by the firm and utilizing it to design first-rate training programs. Experts believe that the design of training programs should focus on at least four related issues: (1) the training's instructional objectives, (2) "readiness" of trainees and their motivation, (3) principles of learning, and (4) characteristics of instructors. Next, we discuss each.

INSTRUCTIONAL OBJECTIVES

instructional objectives
Desired outcomes of a training program

After conducting organization, task, and person analyses, managers should have a more complete picture of their firms' training needs. On the basis of this information, they can more formally state the desired outcomes of training through written instructional objectives. Generally, **instructional objectives** describe the skills or knowledge to be acquired and/or the attitudes to be changed. One type of instructional objective, the performance-centred objective, is widely used because it lends itself to an unbiased evaluation of the results. For example, the stated objective for one training program might be that "Employees trained in team methods will be able to perform the different jobs of their team members within six months." Performance-centred objectives typically include precise terms, such as "to calculate," "to repair," "to adjust," "to construct," "to assemble," and "to classify."[8]

TRAINEE READINESS AND MOTIVATION

Two preconditions for learning affect the success of those who are to receive training: readiness and motivation. *Trainee readiness* refers to both maturity and experience of trainees. Prospective trainees should be screened to ensure that they have the background knowledge and the skills necessary to absorb what will be presented to them. Recognizing the individual differences of trainees in terms of their readiness is as important in organizational training as it is in any other teaching situation. Consequently, it is often desirable to group individuals according to their capacity to learn, as determined by test scores or other assessment information, and to provide alternative types of instruction for those who need it.

The receptiveness and readiness of participants in training programs can be increased by having them complete questionnaires about why they are attending training and what they hope to accomplish as a result. Participants can also be asked to *give* copies of their completed questionnaires to their managers.

The other precondition for learning is *trainee motivation*. Individuals who are conscientious, goal oriented, self-disciplined, and persevering are more likely to perceive a link between the effort they put into training and higher performance on the job. For optimum learning to take place, trainees must realize they need new knowledge or skills and maintain a desire to learn as the training progresses. By focusing on the trainees themselves rather than on the trainer or training topic, managers can create a training environment that is conducive to learning. The following six strategies can be essential:

1. Use positive reinforcement.
2. Eliminate threats and punishment.
3. Be flexible.
4. Have participants set personal goals.
5. Design interesting instruction.
6. Break down physical and psychological obstacles to learning.

While most employees are motivated by certain common needs, they differ from one another in the relative importance of these needs at any given time. For example, new college or university graduates often have a high desire for advancement, and they have established specific goals for career progression. The training objectives should therefore be clearly related to trainees' individual needs to succeed.[9]

PRINCIPLES OF LEARNING

As we move from assessing an organization's needs and instructional objectives to employee readiness and motivation, we obviously shift our focus from the organization to employees. Ultimately, however, training has to build a bridge between employees and the organization. One important step in this transition involves giving full consideration to the psychological principles of learning—that is, the characteristics of training programs that help employees grasp new material, make sense of it in their own lives, and transfer it back to their jobs. All things considered, training programs are likely to be more effective if they incorporate the principles of learning shown in Figure 7.4.

Goal Setting

The value of goal setting for focusing and motivating behaviour extends into training. When trainers take the time to explain the training's goals and objectives to trainees—or when trainees are encouraged to set goals on their own—the level of interest, understanding, and effort directed toward the training is likely to increase. In some cases, goal setting can simply take the form of a "road map" of the course/program, its objectives, and its learning points.[10]

Meaningfulness of Presentation

One principle of learning is that the material to be learned should be presented in as meaningful a manner as possible. Quite simply, trainees will be better able to learn new information if they can connect it with things that are already familiar to them. This is the reason that trainers frequently use colourful examples to which trainees can relate. The examples make the material meaningful. In addition, material should be arranged so that each experience builds on preceding ones. In this way, trainees are able to integrate the experiences into a usable pattern of knowledge and skills.

Modelling

The old saying "a picture is worth a thousand words" applies to training. Just as examples increase the meaningfulness of factual material or new knowledge in a training environment, modelling increases the salience of behavioural training. Quite simply, we learn by watching. For example, if you were learning to ride a horse, it would be much easier to watch someone do it—and then try it yourself—than to read a book or listen to a lecture and hope you can do it right.[11]

OUTCOME 3

FIGURE **7.4**

Principles of Learning

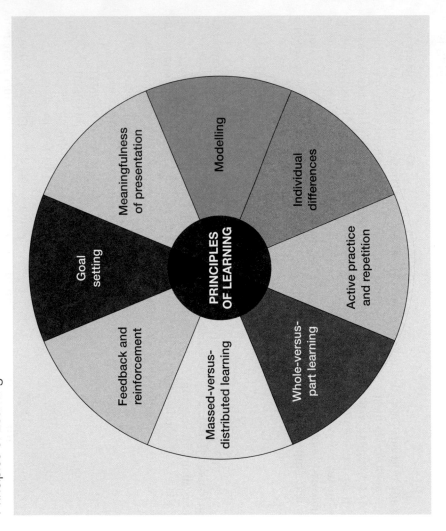

Modelling can take many forms. Real-life demonstrations and demonstrations on DVDs are often helpful; even pictures and drawings can get the visual message across. The point is that modelling demonstrates the desired behaviour or method to be learned. In some cases, modelling the wrong behaviour can even be helpful if it shows trainees what not to do and then clarifies the appropriate behaviour.

Individual Differences

People learn at different rates and in different ways. For example, some people can remember new information after hearing it only once (echoic memory) or seeing it only once (iconic memory). Others may have to work longer or find other techniques for retrieving the information, but this may have nothing to do with their intelligence. Some students do horribly in large lecture settings but then excel in small discussion classes. Others may have the opposite ability. To the extent possible, training programs should try to account for and accommodate these individual differences in order to facilitate each person's style and rate of learning.[12]

Active Practice and Repetition

Those things we do daily become a part of our repertoire of skills. Trainees should be given frequent opportunity to practise their job tasks in the way that they will ultimately be expected to perform them. The individual who is being taught how to operate a machine should have an opportunity to practise on it. The manager who is being taught how to train should be given supervised practice in training.

In some cases, the value of practice is that it causes behaviours to become second nature. For example, when you first learned to drive a car, you focused a great deal on the mechanics: "Where are my hands, where are my feet, and how fast am I going?" As you practised driving, you began to think less about the mechanics and more about the road, the weather, and the traffic. Other forms of learning are no different—by practising, a trainee can forget about distinct behaviours and concentrate on the subtleties of how they are used.

Whole-versus-Part Learning

Most jobs and tasks can be broken down into parts that lend themselves to further analysis. Determining the most effective manner for completing each part then provides a basis for giving specific instruction. Learning to sell a product, for example, is made up of several skills that are part of the total process. Although the process sounds daunting, it can essentially be broken down into a few discrete steps: finding customer opportunities; eliciting a prospective customer's needs by learning the proper questions to ask him or her; presenting the firm's product in a way that meets those needs; and finally, learning how and when to ask the customer to buy the product (closing the deal). In evaluating whole-versus-part learning, it is necessary to consider the nature of the task to be learned. If the task can be broken down successfully, it probably should be broken down to facilitate learning; otherwise, it should probably be taught as a unit.

Massed-versus-Distributed Learning

Another factor that determines the effectiveness of training is the amount of time devoted to practice in one session. Should trainees be given training in 5 two-hour periods or in 10 one-hour periods? It has been found in most cases that spacing out the training will result in faster learning and longer retention. This is the principle of *distributed learning*.

Feedback and Reinforcement

Can any learning occur without feedback? Some feedback comes from trainees themselves via self-monitoring, whereas other feedback comes from trainers, fellow trainees, and the like. Feedback can help individuals focus on what they are doing right and what they are doing wrong. Think about when you first learned how to throw a baseball, ride a bicycle, or swim. Someone, perhaps a parent, told you what you were doing right and what things to correct. As you corrected those things, you likely got better.

In addition to providing participants with information about their performance, feedback also plays an important motivational role. For example, a person's training progress, measured in terms of either mistakes or successes, can be plotted on a chart commonly referred to as a "learning curve." Figure 7.5 presents an example of a learning curve common in the acquisition of many job skills. In many learning situations, there are times when progress does not occur. Such periods show up on the curve as a fairly straight horizontal line called a *plateau*. A plateau can occur because of reduced motivation or because a person gets discouraged when he or she does not always perform a new task as well as hoped. It is a natural phenomenon, and learners usually experience a spontaneous recovery later, as Figure 7.5 shows.

Verbal encouragement or more tangible rewards such as prizes, awards, and ceremonies can help reinforce the behaviour trainees desire of trainees over time as well as help them get over plateaus they might experience. Encouragement is most effective when it is given immediately after a trainee successfully accomplishes a certain task. This is why some employers have instituted spot rewards programs. **Spot rewards** programs award employees "on the spot" when they do something particularly well during training or on the job. The awards can consist of cash, gift cards, time off, or anything else employees value.

spot rewards
Programs that award employees "on the spot" when they do something particularly well during training or on the job

FIGURE **7.5**

A Typical Learning Curve

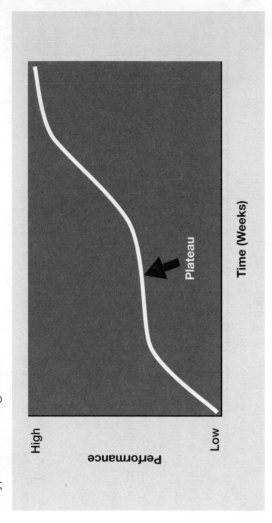

behaviour modification

A technique that operates on the principle that behaviour that is rewarded, or positively reinforced, will be exhibited more frequently in the future, whereas behaviour that is penalized or unrewarded will decrease in frequency

Over the years, organizations have used **behaviour modification**, a technique that operates on the principle that behaviour that is rewarded—positively reinforced—will be exhibited more frequently in the future, whereas behaviour that is penalized or unrewarded will decrease in frequency. For example, in safety training it is possible to identify "safe" behavioural profiles—that is, actions that ensure fewer accidents—as well as unsafe profiles. As a follow-up to training or as part of the training itself, managers can use relatively simple rewards to encourage and maintain desired behaviour. Companies such as Monsanto have found that nothing more than words of encouragement and feedback are needed to strengthen employee behaviours. However, the idea behind behaviour modification is that a person's behaviour can be motivated and gradually shaped toward what managers desire when he or she exhibits positive behaviours and is rewarded for them.[13]

CHARACTERISTICS OF INSTRUCTORS

The success of any training effort will depend in a large part on the teaching skills and personal characteristics of those responsible for conducting the training. What separates good trainers from mediocre ones? Often a good trainer is one who shows a little more effort or demonstrates more instructional preparation. However, training is also influenced by the trainer's personal manner and characteristics. Here is a short list of desirable traits:

1. *Knowledge of subject.* Employees expect trainers to know their job or subject thoroughly. Furthermore, they are expected to demonstrate that knowledge (what some experts call "active intelligence").

2. *Adaptability.* Because some individuals learn faster or slower than others, the instruction should be matched to the trainee's learning ability.

3. *Sincerity.* Trainees appreciate sincerity in trainers. Along with this, trainers need to be patient with trainees and demonstrate tact in addressing their concerns.

4. *Sense of humour.* Learning can be fun; very often a point can be made with a story or anecdote.

5. *Interest.* Good trainers have a keen interest in the subject they are teaching; this interest is readily conveyed to trainees.

6. *Clear instructions.* Naturally, training is accomplished more quickly and retained longer when trainers give clear instructions.

7. *Individual assistance.* When training more than one employee, successful trainers always provide individual assistance.

8. *Enthusiasm.* A dynamic presentation and a vibrant personality show trainees that the trainer enjoys training; employees tend to respond positively to an enthusiastic climate.[14]

For training programs to be most successful, organizations should reward managers who prove to be excellent trainers. Too often, managers are not recognized for their contributions to this important aspect of HRM. Likewise, good training specialists in the HR function should be recognized for their efforts as well.

PHASE 3: IMPLEMENTING THE TRAINING PROGRAM

Despite the importance of needs assessment, instructional objectives, principles of learning, and the like, choices regarding instructional methods are where "the rubber meets the road" in implementing a training program. A major consideration in choosing among various training methods is determining which ones are appropriate for the KSAs to be learned. For example, if the material is mostly factual, methods such as lecture, classroom, or programmed instruction may be fine. However, if the training involves a large behavioural component, other methods such as on-the-job training, simulation, or computer-based training (CBT) might work better.[15]

In order to organize our discussion of various training methods, we will break them down into two primary groups: those used for nonmanagerial employees and those used for managers.

TRAINING METHODS FOR NONMANAGERIAL EMPLOYEES

A wide variety of methods are available for training employees at all levels. Some methods have a long history of being used. Newer methods have emerged over the years out of a greater understanding of human behaviour, particularly in the areas of learning, motivation, and interpersonal relationships. More recently, technological advances, especially in computer hardware and software, have resulted in training devices that in many instances are more effective and economical than the traditional training methods.

On-the-Job Training

By far, the most common method used for training nonmanagerial employees is **on-the-job training (OJT)**. By some estimates, 90 percent of employee learning occurs via OJT. OJT has the advantage of providing hands-on experience under normal working conditions and an opportunity for the trainer—a manager or senior employee—to build good relationships with new employees. OJT is viewed by some to be potentially the most effective means of facilitating learning in the workplace.[16]

Although it is used by all types of organizations, OJT is often one of the most poorly implemented training methods. Three common drawbacks are (1) the lack of a well-structured training environment, (2) poor training skills on the part of managers, and (3) the absence of well-defined job performance criteria. To overcome these problems, training experts suggest the following:

1. Develop realistic goals and/or measures for each OJT area.
2. Plan a specific training schedule for each trainee, including set periods for evaluation and feedback.

[OUTCOME 4]

on-the-job training (OJT)
A method by which employees are given hands-on experience with instructions from their supervisor or other trainer

3. Help managers establish a nonthreatening atmosphere conducive to learning.

4. Conduct periodic evaluations after training is completed to prevent regression.[17]

Figure 7.6 shows the basic steps of an OJT program. The method is used frequently in organizations to ensure that new employees have adequate guidance before taking on work responsibilities on their own. For example, KLM Royal Dutch Airlines uses OJT to train its cabin attendants. The airline started a program that places cabin attendant trainees in the classroom for a certain period and then gives them additional training during an evaluation flight. On these flights, experienced cabin attendants provide the trainees with OJT, based on a list of identified job tasks. Some tasks, such as serving meals and snacks, are demonstrated during the actual delivery of services to passengers. Other tasks are presented to trainees away from passengers between meal service.[18]

Apprenticeship Training

apprenticeship training

A system of training in which a worker entering the skilled trades is given thorough instruction and experience, both on and off the job, in the practical and theoretical aspects of the work

An extension of OJT is **apprenticeship training**. With this method, individuals entering an industry, particularly in the skilled trades such as machinist, laboratory technician, and electrician, are given thorough instruction and experience, both on and off the job. For example, Bonneville Power Administration and General Physics Corporation developed an apprenticeship program for substation operators to give employees both a strong technical foundation in the fundamentals of electricity and a hands-on ability to operate equipment within the power substation. Ultimately, the program was also designed to help future electrical operators respond to emergencies. In Europe, organizations such as BAE Systems and Ford Motor Company use apprenticeship programs extensively for their engineers.[19]

While apprenticeship programs originated in Europe as part of its guild system, they have been adapted for use in Canada. Typically, the programs involve cooperation between organizations and their labour unions, between industry and government, or between organizations and local school systems. For example, Red River College in Winnipeg offers 31 apprenticeship programs, all with long waiting lists because its graduates find work immediately.

FIGURE **7.6**

The PROPER Way to Do On-the-Job Training

P **Prepare.** Decide what employees need to be taught. Identify the best sequence or steps of the training. Decide how best to demonstrate these steps. Have materials, resources, and equipment ready.

R **Reassure.** Put each employee at ease. Learn about his or her prior experience, and adjust accordingly. Try to get the employee interested, relaxed, and motivated to learn.

O **Orient.** Show the employee the correct way to do the job. Explain why it is done this way. Discuss how it relates to other jobs. Let him or her ask lots of questions.

P **Perform.** When employees are ready, let them try the job themselves. Give them an opportunity to practice the job and guide them through rough spots. Provide help and assistance at first, then less as they continue.

E **Evaluate.** Check the employees' performance, and question them on how, why, when, and where they should do something. Correct errors; repeat instructions.

R **Reinforce and Review.** Provide praise and encouragement, and give feedback about how the employee is doing. Continue the conversation and express confidence in his or her doing the job.

Source: Scott Snell, University of Virginia.

However, there are apprenticeships available in a wide range of other industries, including the telecommunications, arts, and health fields. Generally, an apprentice is paid 50 percent of a skilled journey worker's wage to start with, but the wage increases at regular intervals as the apprentice's job skills increase. When the apprentice successfully completes the apprenticeship, he or she becomes a certified journey-level worker earning full pay. According to BAT, many journey workers earn as much as postsecondary graduates, and some earn more.[20]

Cooperative Training, Internships, and Governmental Training

Similar to apprenticeships, **cooperative training programs** combine practical on-the-job experience with formal classes. However, the term *cooperative training* is typically used in connection with high school and college programs that incorporate part- or full-time experiences. In recent years, there has been an increased effort to expand opportunities that combine on-the-job skill training with regular classroom training so that students can pursue either technical work or a college degree program. EnCana, an oil and gas company based in Calgary, has developed the Oil and Gas Production Field Operator Career Pathway program, which offers high school students an opportunity to earn credits while learning about field production work, in alliance with Southern Alberta Institute of Technology. The courses are offered as an option and students graduate with a field operator certificate from SAIT, and have a chance of obtaining a paid internship in the summer.[21] The internship program of a community college is described in Highlights in HRM 7.3. Highlights in HRM 7.4 shows how to make the most from internship opportunities.

The federal government and various provincial governments have begun working with private employers to sponsor a multitude of training programs. For

Highlights in HRM 7.3

Internship Program at Durham College

The work-study program in human resources at Durham College, Ontario, is designed to transition an HR student into an HR practitioner. According to the coordinator of the human resources program, Dr. Carolin Rekar-Munro, each project must allow for the transfer of theories learned in class to a project management format at the field placement location. Students are required to write objectives in a draft proposal, similar to management by objectives, in which the criteria used to measure the success of the placement must be both qualitative and quantitative in content.

For the three-year diploma program, students in their final year will work two days per week from October to April and gain 344 hours of field placement experience. For the one-year post-diploma certificate program, students will attain 200 hours of field placement experience over a five-week block following final exams. Cohorts are also put into teams during the

experience and attend weekly seminars in which the students can share their experiences and get advice on issues they are facing at their respective placements. According to Dr. Rekar-Munro, this peer group process helps to establish a network of HR professionals.

By focusing on application-based projects, students will be in a position to decide if they wish to pursue careers in HR and will have acquired valuable experience in project management. Employers also benefit as they receive both a quality HR project and the chance to preview a potential new staff member. This work-study program gives employers a unique probationary period and 30 to 40 percent of students are hired at their field placements to continue their projects. For example, Dr. Rekar-Munro points to a student who created a health and safety manual for people with English as a Second Language (ESL), who was then hired by her field placement employer to complete the work.

Highlights in HRM 7.4

Making the Most of Internships

Today, many colleges and universities encourage students to apply for internships as part of the curriculum. Done well, internships provide advantages to students, universities, and potential employers.

Benefits for Students

Those who intern with organizations before graduation have higher starting salaries, more job offers, a shorter time in which they obtain their first position, faster movement into jobs with more prestige, greater challenges and financial rewards, and faster promotion. They are better prepared for the world of work.

Benefits for Colleges and Universities

Internships help colleges and universities get in touch with the marketplace. As students succeed in the workplace, student recruitment improves. Strong internship programs increase the retention of students and their placement after graduation.

Benefits for Potential Employers

Interns can provide your organization with competent assistance without a large financial outlay. Internships

also let organizations evaluate a prospective employee nearly risk-free. At the end of the internship, there are no obligations to continue the relationship, but if it's a good match the organization has a leg up on hiring the person—it eliminates recruitment expenses and greatly reduces the cost per hire.

How to Increase the Value of Interns

To increase the internal value of your internship programs, take the following steps:

1. Assign the intern to projects that are accomplishable and provide training as required.
2. Involve the intern in the project-planning process.
3. Appoint a mentor or supervisor to guide the intern.
4. Invite project suggestions from other staff members.
5. Ask interns to keep a journal of their work activities.
6. Rotate interns throughout the organization.
7. Explain the rationale behind work assignments.
8. Hold interns accountable for projects and deadlines.
9. Treat interns as part of the organizational staff and invite them to staff meetings.
10. Establish a process for considering interns for permanent hire.

Source: Condensed from John Byrd and Rob Poole, "Highly Motivated Employees at No Cost? It's Not an Impossible Dream," *Nonprofit World* 19, no. 6 (November/December 2001): 312–32. Reprinted by permission of *Nonprofit World*, http://www.snpo.org, telephone: 734-451-3582.

internship programs

Programs jointly sponsored by colleges, universities, and other organizations that offer students the opportunity to gain real-life experience while allowing them to find out how they will perform in work organizations

example, the federal government has invested money in the Information Technology program at the Nova Scotia Community College, Marconi campus, which installed a high-tech infrastructure to support customized training for the petroleum industry.[22]

Internship programs, jointly sponsored by colleges, universities, and a variety of organizations, offer students the chance to get real-world experience while finding out how they will perform in work organizations. Organizations benefit by getting student-employees with new ideas, energy, and eagerness to accomplish their assignments. Many universities and community colleges allow students to earn credits on the basis of successful job performance and fulfillment of established program requirements. The following are steps firms can take to increase the effectiveness of their internships:

1. Assign the intern to projects that are accomplishable and provide training as required.
2. Appoint a mentor or supervisor to guide the intern.
3. Solicit project suggestions from other staff members.
4. Rotate interns throughout the organization.

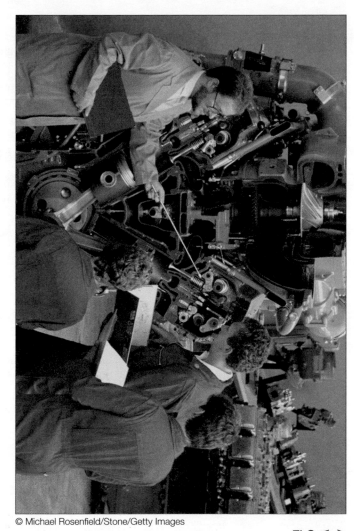

© Michael Rosenfield/Stone/Getty Images

Apprenticeships are a good way to train employees, especially in skilled trade industries.

5. Treat interns as part of the organizational staff and invite them to staff meetings.
6. Establish a process for considering interns for permanent hire.[23]

Classroom Instruction

When most people think about training, they think about classrooms. According to the Conference Board of Canada's Learning and Development Outlook 2007, 75 percent of training still takes place in the classroom. Classroom training enables the maximum number of trainees to be handled by the minimum number of instructors. This method lends itself particularly well to what is called **blended learning** in which lectures and demonstrations are combined with films, DVDs, videotapes, or computer instruction. When it is not possible to obtain video, audio recordings can be very valuable. For example, to instruct flight crew trainees, airlines might play actual cockpit tapes recorded on airplanes involved in accidents. After listening to the recordings, the trainees discuss the behaviour of the crew during the crisis. By listening to the recorded statements of others and, for example, observing their failure to operate as a team, pilot trainees better understand how to balance their sense of self-reliance with an ability to listen to their superiors and subordinates. Despite the rise of many other types of learning—electronic and otherwise—classroom instruction is still the number one training method, as Figure 7.7 shows.[24]

blended learning
The use of multiple training methods to achieve optimal learning on the part of trainees

Programmed Instruction

One method of instruction that is particularly good for allowing individuals to work at their own pace is programmed instruction. Programmed instruction—increasingly referred to as self-directed learning—involves the use of books, manuals, or computers to break down subject matter content into highly organized, logical sequences that demand a continual response on the part of the trainee. After being presented with a small segment of information, the trainee is required to answer a question, either by writing it in a response screen or by pushing a button. If the response is correct, the trainee is told so and is presented with the next step (screen) in the material. If the response is incorrect, further explanatory information is given, and the trainee is told to try again.

FIGURE **7.7**

Delivery Method of Training

Type	Percentage of Canadian Organizations Doing Activity (%)
In-class training	99
On-the-job training	96
Tuition reimbursement	93
Conference attendance	91
Using learning technologies	75
Lunch-and-learn sessions	64
Job rotation or cross training	64
Integrating formal/informal training	55
Job shadowing	51
Train-the-trainer courses	51
Communities of practice	41
Training resource centre	38
Networks	38
Apprenticeship training	38
Virtual training resource centre	36
Industry and customer intelligence	33
Corporate university	29
Mandatory annual training time	28
Line on loan or rotational training staff	26
Workplace flexibility	24
Other programs	6

Source: The Conference Board of Canada, *Learning and Development Outlook 2007*, http://www.conferenceboard.ca/documents.aspx?DID=1995, retrieved July 30, 2009. Used by permission.

A major advantage of programmed instruction is that it incorporates a number of the established learning principles discussed earlier in the chapter. With programmed instruction, training is individualized, trainees are actively involved in the instructional process, and the feedback and reinforcement provided are immediate. Although this type of instruction might not increase the amount an individual learns, it typically increases the speed at which he or she learns.

Audiovisual Methods

To teach skills and procedures for many production jobs, audiovisual devices can be used. For example, video recordings are often used to illustrate the steps in a procedure such as assembling electronic equipment or working with a problem employee. Trainers and trainees can view an on-the-spot recording and to get immediate feedback. Golf and tennis coaches frequently record their students to let them see their mistakes. CDs and DVDs allow trainees to access any segment of the instructional program, which is especially useful for individualized instruction when employees have different levels of knowledge and ability.

Teleconferencing and videoconferencing allow an instructional program to be transmitted to many locations simultaneously as well as permit trainees to interact with one another. Electronic Data Systems has used teleconferencing to train its employees wherever they are in the world rather than having them travel to one location. The company recently conducted a "coaching skills for leaders" program that was disseminated to 1,500 managers in 41 countries via teleconferencing.[25]

Web conferencing is used to conduct live meetings or presentations over the Internet. During a Web conference, trainees sit at their own computers and are connected to other participants via the Web. To attend the conference, they simply enter a website address and also dial in to a toll-free number to talk to one another and the trainer via phone. A *webinar* is a one-way conference, from the speaker to the audience with limited audience interaction. A number of organizations are also using *podcasts* to provide their employees, such sales reps, with information on the go. Podcasts allow reps to learn about new products while they are in the field rather than having to take time off to travel to corporate headquarters to get the information.

There is an old African proverb that states, If you want to go fast, travel alone. If you want to go far, travel together.[26] The latter statement is the idea behind *communities of practice*. This is a new but growing type of training that utilizes social networking tools on the Web that allow people to share their knowledge and collaborate with one another. Blogs and wikis—sites where people can post information like they can on Wikipedia—are examples of the tools used to facilitate learning via the communities of practice method. The method can be particularly helpful for multinational companies whose employees need to be able to share information across time and space. Figure 7.8 shows some of the types of questions posted on communities of practice sites, to which other people post answers that future learners can read.

FIGURE 7.8

Examples of Knowledge-Sharing Learning via Communities of Practice

Problem solving	"Can we work on this design and brainstorm some ideas; I'm stuck."
Requests for information	"Where can I find the code to connect to the server?"
Seeking experience	"Has anyone dealt with a customer in this situation?"
Reusing assets	"I have a proposal for a local area network I wrote for a client last year. I can send it to you, and you can easily tweak it for this new client."
Coordination and synergy	"Can we combine our purchases of solvent to achieve bulk discounts?"
Discussing developments	"What do you think of the new CAD system? Does it really help?"
Documentation projects	"We have faced this problem five times now. Let us write it down once and for all."
Visits	"Can we come and see your after-school program? We need to establish one in our city."
Mapping knowledge and identifying gaps	"Who knows what, and what are we missing? What other groups should we connect with?"

Source: Etienne Wenger, http://www.ewenger.com/theory/index.htm, retrieved July 30, 2009.

Simulation Method

Sometimes it is either impractical or unwise to train employees on the actual equipment used on the job. An obvious example is training employees to operate aircraft, spacecraft, and other highly technical and expensive equipment. The simulation method emphasizes realism in equipment and its operation at minimum cost and maximum safety.

Southwest Airlines boasts perhaps the most technologically advanced flight simulator in the airline industry: a $10.8 million full-motion Boeing 737–700 unit housed in an 110,000-square-foot flight operations training centre. The facility can house up to six 737 simulators and can train up to 300 (of Southwest's 4,100) pilots at one time. The centre has a staff of 110 employees. In addition to the simulators and their associated briefing and computer programming rooms, the training centre houses eight classrooms, each fully equipped with closed-circuit TV, computers, conventional audiovisual equipment, and telephone and Internet hookups. The Canadian Forces uses simulation software to train new recruits about aviation technology. Using the software enables students to disassemble and reassemble a propeller system many times, compared to the traditional training style of observing an instructor do it and perhaps having one opportunity to practice.[27]

Trainees who do poorly in certain situations are then targeted for additional training in those areas. Simulators that represent human patients are being integrated into medical training as well.[28]

As with e-learning and computer-based training, the distinction between simulation and computer-based training has blurred. For example, a simulation developed by Wicat in partnership with Airbus and Singapore Airlines runs on a PC and replicates a cockpit with control displays and throttle/flap controls. Even though the PC-based simulation is relatively inexpensive, it is powerful. Pilots are taken through a self-paced program that simulates "taxi, takeoff, climb, cruise, descent, approach, landing, and go-around." These types of technologies are making it easier to offer training in new and different ways. Given advances in telecommunications, the possibilities seem limitless.[29]

E-Learning and Learning Management Systems (LMS)

The training methods we just discussed are evolving into what trainers today refer to as e-learning. **E-learning** covers a wide variety of applications such as Web and CBT and virtual classrooms. It includes delivery of content via the Internet, intranets and extranets, TV, DVD, CD-ROM, and MP3 players. E-learning makes it possible to provide drill and practice, problem solving, simulation, and gaming forms of instruction, and certain very sophisticated forms of individualized tutorial instruction in a way that is more engaging for learners than traditional classroom instruction. It is also cheaper for employers to administer because, in many instances, it can be delivered cheaply directly to the PCs of multiple employees. Today, one of every three hours of training is now delivered via some form of technology, and companies are reporting that they are saving anywhere from 30 to 70 percent on their training costs by doing so.[30]

E-learning transforms the learning process in several ways. First, as we have said, it allows the firm to bring the training to employees rather than vice versa, which is generally more efficient and cost effective. The nuclear power plant industry is a case in point: Nuclear power plant training is frequent and time consuming. For workers just to remove their protective gear and commute to a separate training venue can take anywhere from an hour or more. One nuclear power company that switched to e-learning reported that it saved nearly $1 million and 10,000 employee hours in just one year by doing so. E-learning also allows employees to search online training libraries in order to customize their own learning in their own time and space. More companies are demanding access to individual training

e-learning

Learning that takes place via electronic media

components for employees to use when and where they need them. This type of training, which is referred to as **just-in-time training**, helps alleviate the boredom trainees experience during full-blown training courses, and employees are more likely to retain the information when they can immediately put it to use. Cisco has thousands of training VoDs (videos on demand) that employees can download off the company's intranet as needed.[31]

E-learning systems need not be overly expensive. Many e-learning training programs use existing applications employees are familiar with such as PowerPoint, Word, and Adobe Acrobat and convert them into Flash programs so they can be easily viewed online with any Web browser. Web-based training can also be revised rapidly, thereby providing continuously updated training material to both small and large groups of people. This not only makes it easier and cheaper to revise training curricula, but also saves travel and classroom costs. When combined with other communications technology such as e-mail, teleconferencing, videoconferencing, and groupware, Web-based training can be even more effective.

Today, large companies—usually those with at least 5,000 employees—are combining their e-learning, employee assessment tools, and other training functions into electronic **learning management systems (LMS)**, also referred to as "virtual learning environments," custom built for them by software vendors. Using the software, managers can assess the skills of employees, register them for courses, deliver interactive learning modules to them directly to their desktops when they need or want them, evaluate and track their progress, and determine when they are ready to be promoted. Purchasing a learning management system does not alleviate HR personnel and a firm's managers from conducting a thorough needs assessment, however—especially because the systems are costly. After conducting a thorough needs analysis, managers have to then address the type of systems that will work best.

METHODS FOR MANAGEMENT DEVELOPMENT

Many of the methods used to train front-line employees are also used to train supervisors and first-level managers. But other methods are used primarily to improve the preparation and development of mid- to senior-level managers. Over the past decade, the importance of management development has grown because so many experienced baby boomer managers have begun retiring and firms are having a hard time replacing the expertise they provided. Most companies reported moderate to major leadership shortages, and many expected the problem to get worse.[32]

As with training for nonmanagerial employees, the methods used for management development differ in terms of the principles of learning they incorporate and their appropriateness for delivering various KSAs.

On-the-Job Experiences

Some skills and knowledge can be acquired just by listening and observing or by reading. But others must be acquired through actual practice and experience. By presenting managers with the opportunities to perform under pressure and to learn from their mistakes, on-the-job development experiences are some of the most powerful and commonly used techniques. However, just as on-the-job training for first-level employees can be problematic if not well planned, on-the-job management development should be well organized, supervised, and challenging to the participants. Methods of providing on-the-job experiences include the following:

1. *Coaching* involves a continuing flow of instructions, comments, and suggestions from the manager to the subordinate. (*Mentoring*, discussed in Chapter 5, is a similar approach to personal and informal management development.)
2. *Understudy assignments* groom an individual to take over a manager's job by gaining experience in handling important functions of the job.

just-in-time training
Training delivered to trainees when and where they need it to do their jobs, usually via computer or the Internet

learning management system (LMS)
On-line system that provides a variety of assessment, communication, teaching, and learning opportunities

3. *Job rotation* provides, through a variety of work experiences, the broadened knowledge and understanding required to manage more effectively.

4. *Lateral transfer* involves horizontal movement through different departments, along with upward movement in the organization.

5. *Special projects* and *junior boards* provide an opportunity for individuals to become involved in the study of current organizational problems and in planning and decision-making activities.

6. *Action learning* gives managers time to work full-time on projects with others in the organization. In some cases, action learning is combined with classroom instruction, discussions, and conferences.

7. *Staff meetings* enable participants to become more familiar with problems and events occurring outside their immediate areas by exposing them to the ideas and thinking of other managers.

8. *Planned career progressions* (discussed in Chapter 5) utilize all these different methods to provide employees with the training and development necessary to progress through a series of jobs requiring higher and higher levels of knowledge and/or skills.[33]

Although these methods are used most often to develop managers for higher-level positions, they also provide valuable experiences for those who are being groomed for other types of positions in the organization. While on-the-job experiences constitute the core of management training and development, other off-the-job methods of development can be used to supplement these experiences.

Seminars and Conferences

Seminars and conferences, like classroom instruction, are useful for bringing groups of people together for training and development. In terms of developing managers, seminars and conferences can be used to communicate ideas, policies, or procedures, but they are also good for raising points of debate or discussing issues (usually with the help of a qualified leader) that have no set answers or resolutions. For this reason, seminars and conferences are often used when attitude change is a goal.

Outside seminars and conferences are often conducted jointly with universities and consulting firms. Caterpillar, the construction and mining equipment manufacturer, is one company that, in conjunction with an outside consulting firm, has developed a training program to groom new managers. The challenge for the company is to get enough leaders and managers in place to effectively run the company by 2020. To meet this challenge, Caterpillar launched a leadership development initiative through its Caterpillar University of Leadership. The effort began with a series of high-level meetings and strategy sessions. Out of those meetings, 11 characteristics were identified that the company seeks in its managers and leaders. So far, some 5,000 managers and executives have gone through the program, which is designed to help them become more self-aware as managers and develop their financial management skills and ability to better formulate strategies to increase Caterpillar's global competitiveness.

Case Studies

A particularly useful method used in classroom learning situations is the case study. Using documented examples, participants learn how to analyze (take apart) and synthesize (put together) facts, become conscious of the many variables on which management decisions are based, and, in general, improve their decision-making skills. Experienced educators and trainers generally point out that the case study is most appropriate when

1. Analytic, problem-solving, and critical thinking skills are most important
2. The KSAs are complex, and participants need time to master them
3. Active participation is desired

4. The process of learning (questioning, interpreting, and so on) is as important as the content

5. Team problem solving and interaction are possible[34]

Even when case studies may be appropriate, they are often mismanaged. As with any other development technique, implementation is crucial for effectiveness.

Management Games and Simulations

Games are now being widely used as a management development method. Generally, players-managers are faced with the task of making a series of management decisions affecting a hypothetical organization. The effects that every decision has on each area within the organization can be simulated with a computer programmed for the game. Bell Canada has its managers play TeleSim, a computer simulation for the telecommunications industry developed by Thinking Tools and Coopers & Lybrand to teach executives how to act in an increasingly open, competitive market.[35] At Marriott International, a computer program called Business Acumen has been used to train its non-U.S. property-level managers on the finer points of hotel operation. The program simulates hotel operations scenarios such as budgetary decisions.[36]

Project managers at L'Oreal Canada are given a "virtual" company to manage after only three months on the job. Working in pairs for four hours a week, employees are introduced to a new topic every week for six weeks. Based on this new content, the pairs make decisions and learn the next day what impact their decisions have on the market share of the imaginary product.[37]

When done on a computer, simulations are sometimes referred to as virtual training. Simulations do not always require a computer, however. Motorola developed a noncomputer-based game called "Equal Employment Opportunity: It's Your Job" to teach the basic principles of equal employment opportunity. The players get caught up in the competitive spirit of a game and at the same time absorb and remember government regulations. They also become aware of how their own daily decisions affect their employer's compliance with these regulations.[38]

Role-Playing

Role-playing consists of assuming the attitudes and behaviour—that is, playing the role—of others, often a supervisor and a subordinate who are involved in a particular problem. By acting out another's position, participants in the role-playing can improve their ability to understand and cope with others. Role-playing should also help them learn how to counsel others by helping them see situations from a different point of view. Role-playing is used widely in training health care professionals to be empathic and sensitive to the concerns of patients. It is also used widely in training managers to handle employee issues relating to absenteeism, performance appraisal, and conflict situations.

At times, participants may be hesitant to try role-playing; therefore, successful role-playing takes planning. Instructors should do the following:

1. Ensure that members of the group are comfortable with each other.
2. Select and prepare the role-players by introducing a specific situation.
3. To help participants prepare, ask them to describe potential characters.
4. Realize that volunteers make better role-players.
5. Prepare the observers by giving them specific tasks (such as evaluation or feedback).
6. Guide the role-play enactment through its bumps (because it is not scripted).
7. Keep it short.
8. Discuss the enactment and prepare bulleted points of what was learned.[39]

Role-playing is a versatile teaching model, applicable to a variety of training experiences. Planned and implemented correctly, role-playing can bring realism and insight into dilemmas and experiences that otherwise might not be shared. Computer programs that simulate role-playing have also been developed. Virtual Leader, a product by SimuLearn, is one such program: Management trainees interact with animated "employees"—some of whom are more cooperative than others. The trainees are then given feedback as to how well they applied their managerial skills to each situation.

Behaviour Modelling

behaviour modelling

An approach that demonstrates desired behaviour and gives trainees the chance to practice and role-play those behaviours and receive feedback

One technique that combines several different training methods, and therefore multiple principles of learning, is the **behaviour modelling** technique. Behaviour modelling involves four basic components:

1. *Learning points.* At the beginning of instruction, the essential goals and objectives of the program are enumerated. In some cases, the learning points are a sequence of behaviours that are to be taught. For example, the learning points might describe the recommended steps for giving employees feedback.

2. *Modelling.* Participants view CDs, DVDs, or downloadable video recordings in which a model manager is portrayed dealing with an employee in an effort to improve his or her performance. The model shows specifically how to deal with the situation and demonstrates the learning points.

3. *Practice and role-play.* Trainees participate in extensive rehearsal of the behaviours demonstrated by the models. The greatest percentage of training time is spent in these skill practice sessions.

4. *Feedback and reinforcement.* As the trainee's behaviour increasingly resembles that of the model, the trainer and other trainees reinforce the behaviour with praise, approval, encouragement, and attention. Videotaping or otherwise digitally recording the sessions can also be very instructive.

Behaviour modelling seems to work, according to various studies. The training can help managers better interact with employees, administer discipline, introduce changes, and increase productivity. Military training is a classic example of how behaviour modelling can work. Drill sergeants model the behaviour expected of new recruits, who, in turn, by emulating them, develop discipline and confidence.[40]

In the final analysis, the most successful training courses for either regular employees or managers do not rely on a single type of training. Instead, utilizing a variety of methods better helps keep the interest of trainees high and accommodates different kinds of learning styles.

PHASE 4: EVALUATING THE TRAINING PROGRAM

[OUTCOME 5]

Training, like any other HRM function, has to be evaluated to determine its effectiveness. A variety of methods are available to assess the extent to which a firm's training programs improve learning, affect behaviour on the job, and impact the bottom-line performance of an organization. Unfortunately, many organizations do not adequately evaluate their training programs. But this is changing. Today, human resources departments are under pressure to calculate the return on their firms' training investment dollars. We will explain how this is done later in this section.

Figure 7.9 shows that four basic criteria are available to evaluate training: (1) reactions, (2) learning, (3) behaviour, and (4) results. Some of these criteria are easier to measure than others, but each is important in that it provides different information about the success of the programs. The combination of these criteria can give a total picture of the training program in order to help managers decide where problem areas lie, what to change about the program, and whether to continue with a program.[41] The Reality Check shows how these four levels have been applied at CONEXUS, the largest credit union in Saskatchewan.

FIGURE 7.9

Criteria for Evaluating Training

CRITERION 1: REACTIONS

One of the simplest and most common approaches to evaluating a training program is assessing participants' reactions. Happy trainees will be more likely to want to focus on training principles and to utilize the information on the job. Trainees can do more than tell you whether they liked a training program. They can give insights into the content and techniques they found most useful. They can critique the instructors or make suggestions about participant interactions, feedback, and the like. Potential questions might include the following:

Reality CHECK

A Classic Four-Level Evaluation

CONEXUS is the largest credit union in Saskatchewan with assets of $1.1 billion. According to Gayle Johnson, CHRP, EVP human resources and corporate secretary, its training and development budget for its 465 employees is 6 percent of payroll. Three percent is spent on university education, and the other 3 percent is spent on training. Its largest training program is one that develops financial service representatives (their title is to be changed to "relationship managers"). The training consists of several steps and each is measured.

In-house and classroom-based modules teach content, such as computer literacy, cash duties, and introduction to CONEXUS's products and services, and progresses through to more advanced training, such as consumer lending practices, estates, and minimal mortgage lending. Each three- to five-day module is followed by a work period of three to 12 months, so that employees can apply their knowledge. The

four levels of measurement of the effectiveness of training are the following:

1. *Reaction.* "Smile sheets" are completed by each participant at the end of the classroom training, asking questions such as "What did you get from this session?"

2. *Comprehensive review.* Exams are given after each module and the results are fed back to the employees and managers.

3. *Employee performance competencies.* Every job family has a number of job-specific competencies, and managers are asked to rate the participants on these performance competencies. The changes in ratings are tracked.

4. *Results.* These vary by module. For example, after the cash-lending module, the performance tracked would be the number of call-outs to customers and the number of sales.

- What were your learning goals for this program?
- Did you achieve them?
- Did you like this program?
- Would you recommend it to others who have similar learning goals?
- What suggestions do you have for improving the program?
- Should the organization continue to offer it?

While evaluation methods based on reactions are improving, too many conclusions about training effectiveness are still based on broad satisfaction measures that lack specific feedback. Furthermore, it should be noted that positive reactions are no guarantee that the training has been successful. It may be easy to collect glowing comments from trainees, but as gratifying as this information is, it may not be useful to the organization unless it somehow translates into improved behaviour and job performance that is measurable. In the final analysis, reaction measures should not stop with assessing the training's entertainment value.[42]

CRITERION 2: LEARNING

Beyond what participants *think* about the training, it might be a good idea to see whether they actually learned anything. Testing the knowledge and skills of trainees before and after a training program will help determine their improvement. The skill and knowledge levels of employees who have undergone a training program can also be compared to employees who have not. FedEx took this approach by studying 20 van drivers who attended a weeklong new-hire training program. The company then compared the performance of these drivers with a control group of 20 drivers who had received only on-the-job training. FedEx found that the drivers who had been formally trained made fewer package processing errors, saving the company about $500 per trained driver.[43]

CRITERION 3: BEHAVIOUR

You might be surprised to learn that much of what is learned in a training program never gets used back on the job. It is not that the training was necessarily ineffective. But for several reasons, trainees do not demonstrate behaviour change back on the job. The **transfer of training** refers to how well employees apply what they have learned to their jobs. To maximize the transfer of training, managers and trainers can take several approaches:

1. *Feature identical elements.* Transferring the training to the job can be facilitated by having conditions in the training program come as close as possible to those on the job. For example, instead of verbally explaining a manufacturing process, it is better to demonstrate it on a factory floor.

2. *Focus on general principles, if necessary.* When jobs change or the work environment cannot be matched exactly, trainers often stress the general principles behind the training rather than focusing on rote behaviour. This approach helps trainees learn how to apply the main learning points to varying conditions on the job.

3. *Establish a climate for transfer.* In some cases, trained behaviour is not implemented because old approaches and routines are still reinforced by other managers, peers, and employees. To prevent this kind of problem, managers need to support, reinforce, and reward trainees for applying the new skills or knowledge. Often this requires firms to train their managers to actively embrace the strategic changes their organizations are seeking to implement.

4. *Give employees transfer strategies.* Particularly in settings that are not conducive to transfer, managers should also provide trainees with strategies and tactics for dealing with their transfer environment. One approach, called relapse prevention (RP), teaches individuals how to anticipate and

transfer of training
Effective application of principles learned to what is required on the job

cope with the inevitable setbacks they will encounter back on the job—that is, a relapse into former behaviours. By identifying high-risk situations that jeopardize transfer and developing coping strategies, relapse prevention can help employees gain better control over maintaining learned behaviours.[44]

There are several methods for assessing transfer of learned skills back to the job. At Xerox, for example, trainers observe trainees once they return to their regular positions, interview the trainees' managers about their progress later on, and examine their post-training performance appraisals.

CRITERION 4: RESULTS, OR RETURN ON INVESTMENT (ROI)

As we have indicated, human resource managers are under pressure to show that their training programs produce "bottom-line" results.[45] Most organizations today measure their training in terms of its return on investment (ROI), which is also sometimes referred to as the *utility* the firm gets for its training dollars. A company's ROI refers to the benefits it derives from training its employees relative to the costs it incurs. HR managers are responsible for calculating and presenting these benefits to the company's top managers. The benefits can include higher revenues generated, increased productivity, improved quality, lower costs, more satisfied customers, higher job satisfaction, and lower employee turnover.

The following are the types of questions HR managers should try to answer as they calculate a training program's benefits:

- How much did quality improve because of the training program?
- How much has it contributed to profits?
- What reduction in turnover and wasted materials did the company get after training?
- How much has productivity increased, and by how much have costs been reduced?

To answer these questions, HR managers use various types of data such as sales data, human resources and financial data, and employee survey and control group data gathered from various sources within the organization. Of course, the costs of the training program need to be measured, too. The ROI formula can then be calculated fairly simply:

ROI = Results/Training Costs

A firm's training costs include the various expenses it incurs related to the training, including the direct costs of the programs (materials, employee travel and meals, meeting site costs, equipment, trainers' salaries or fees, and so on) as well as the indirect costs of the programs (participants' salaries and the productivity they lose while they are attending the training). So, for example, if the ROI ratio of the training is >1, its benefits exceeds its cost; if the ROI ratio is <1, the costs of the training exceed the benefits. Highlights in HRM 7.5 shows some simple examples of ROI calculations. A firm's training ROI can also be measured in terms of how long it takes before the benefits of the training pay off. This analysis is done by adding the costs and dividing the benefits realized in a single month. The result will indicate the overall time required for the training to pay for itself.[46]

The Business Case discusses the return on training investment.

Despite the emphasis on ROI today, some human resources experts think managers can become overly preoccupied with ROI calculations. Why? Because often the benefits of training can be intangible or take a long time to appear. Measuring participants' reactions can be done immediately, of course. However, measuring improved employee skills, customer satisfaction, and so forth can take somewhat longer, and factors other than training can also affect these measures. Finally, the development of ground-breaking new products or processes can also be sparked

Highlights in HRM 7.5

Calculating Training ROI: Examples

If the ROI ratio is >1, the benefits of the training exceed the cost of the program, and if the ratio is <1, the costs of the training program outweigh the benefits.

Example 1: A program to train new machine operators costs $15,000 to develop and implement. After completing the training program, the average number of parts produced each year increased by 3,000, and the profit on each new part is $10, producing a net result of $30,000.

$$ROI = \$30,000/\$15,000 = 2$$

Example 2: A safety program costs the company $25,000 to develop and implement. One year later, there had been a small decrease in accidents, saving the company a total of $10,000.

$$ROI = \$10,000/\$25,000 = 0.4$$

In Example 1, the program resulted in a ROI of 2, indicating that the benefits of the program outweigh its cost. However, in Example 2, the ROI was only 0.4, indicating that the costs of the program outweigh the benefits.

Source: Richard J. Wagner and Robert J. Weigand, "Can the Value of Training Be Measured? A Simplified Approach to Evaluating Training," *The Health Care Manager* 23, no. 1 (January–March 2004): 71–78. Reprinted by permission of Wolters Kluwer Health.

benchmarking

The process of measuring one's own services and practices against the recognized leaders in order to identify areas for improvement

by training but take years to develop, making them hard to attribute to training. Developments such as these nonetheless can transform organizations.

Benchmarking

Closely related to calculating the firm's training ROI is the process of **benchmarking** developmental services and practices against those of recognized leaders in industry.

The Business CASE

Return on Training Investment

Organizations spend about 2 percent of payroll on training, an estimated $750 billion around the globe. Most organizations (four out of five) do not measure the ROI on their training dollars, citing barriers such as the difficulty of doing so, the cost, lack of training, and lack of experience. However, at TD Bank, which has 1,500 branches, 45,000 employees, and 30 different businesses, a focus on measuring the ROI of training captures results such as revenues and profitability. TD has a front-end process—that is, the business units determine the business results expected, the job

performance that will generate these results, and the role that training plays.

According to the Conference Board of Canada, a positive relationship exists between formal training expenditures and performance indicators, such as employee productivity and company profitability. H. J. Heinz Company Canada provided training for its staff in response to increased competition and the need for new technologies. The training costs of $869,000 were repaid within 20 months due to increased productivity, reduced absenteeism, and fewer damaged containers.

Sources: S. Carrigan, "Training: Investment in the Future," *Canadian HR Reporter* 14, no. 11 (June 4, 2001): G1; "What Should You Expect from Your Investment in Training?" *Strategis*, Industry Canada, "Canadian Training Solutions," http://www.strategis.gc.ca.

While no single model for exact benchmarking exists, the simplest models are based on the late W. Edwards Deming's classic four-step process. The four-step process advocates that managers:

1. *Plan.* Conduct a self-audit to define internal processes and measurements; decide on areas to be benchmarked and choose the comparison organization.

2. *Do.* Collect data through surveys, interviews, site visits, and/or historical records.

3. *Check.* Analyze data to discover performance gaps and communicate findings and suggested improvements to management.

4. *Act.* Establish goals, implement specific changes, monitor progress, and redefine benchmarks as a continuous improvement process.

The American Society of Training has developed training benchmarks from hundreds of different companies to which other firms can compare the data on their training costs, staffing, administration, design, development, and delivery of training programs. Benchmarks such as these can help organizations evaluate their current and future training programs.[47] Highlights in HRM 7.6 shows several aspects of training that can be benchmarked against organizations considered superior in the training function and how those aspects are calculated.

The reader might also take special note that these evaluation criteria can also be used as inputs to (further) needs analysis, thereby completing the cycle inherent in the system's approach to training discussed at the beginning of this chapter. By starting the cycle over again, a system's approach to training and development helps to establish an ongoing cycle of continuous assessment and improvement over time.

Highlights in **HRM 7.6**

Benchmarking HR Training

Measurement	How to Calculate
Percentage of payroll spent on training	Total training expenditures ÷ total payroll
Training dollars spent per employee	Total training expenditures ÷ total employees served
Average training hours per employee	Total number of training hours (hours × participants) ÷ total employees served
Percentage of employees trained per year	Total number of employees receiving training ÷ total employee population
HRD staff per 1,000 employees	Number of human resource development staff ÷ total employee population × 1,000
Cost savings as a ratio of training expenses	Total savings in scrap or waste ÷ dollars invested in training
Profits per employee per year	Total yearly gross profits ÷ total number of employees
Training costs per student hour	Total costs of training ÷ total number of hours of training

SPECIAL TOPICS IN TRAINING AND DEVELOPMENT

In addition to training that addresses KSAs reflecting the demands of a particular job, many employers develop training programs to meet the special needs of employees.

In this final section, we summarize some of these programs, including orientation training, basic skills training, team training and cross-training, ethics training, and diversity training. International training will be covered in Chapter 15.

ORIENTATION TRAINING

orientation

The formal process of familiarizing new employees with the organization, their jobs, and their work units

To get new employees off to a good start, organizations generally offer a formal orientation program. **Orientation** is the formal process of familiarizing new employees with the organization, their jobs, and their work units. Most executives, 82 percent in one survey conducted by Robert Half International, believe that formal orientation programs are effective in helping to retain and motivate employees. These and other reported benefits include the following:

1. Lower turnover
2. Increased productivity
3. Improved employee morale
4. Lower recruiting and training costs
5. Facilitation of learning
6. Reduction of the new employee's anxiety [48]

Intuit Canada does an excellent job at employee orientation (See Highlights in HRM 7.7)

The more time and effort spent in helping new employees feel welcome, the more likely they are to identify with the organization and become valuable members of it. Unlike training, which emphasizes the what and the how, orientation often stresses the why. It is designed to influence employee attitudes about the work they will be doing and their role in the organization. It defines the philosophy behind the organization's rules and provides a framework for job-related tasks. As plans, policies, and procedures change in organizations, even current employees need to be kept up to date and continually reoriented to changing conditions.

For a well-integrated orientation program, cooperation between a firm's line and HR staff is essential. The HR department ordinarily is responsible for coordinating orientation activities and for providing new employees with information about conditions of employment, pay, benefits, and other areas not directly under a supervisor's direction. However, the supervisor has the most important role in the orientation program. New employees are interested primarily in what the supervisor says and does and what their new coworkers are like.

Before the arrival of a new employee, the supervisor should inform the work group that a new worker is joining the unit. It is also common practice for supervisors or other managerial personnel to recruit coworkers to serve as volunteer "sponsors," or mentors, for incoming employees. In addition to providing practical help to newcomers, experienced colleagues represent an important source of information about the norms and nuances of the work group, the culture of the organization, and what it expects from its employees. These relationships are vital to the socialization of new employees and contribute significantly to their long-term success within the organization.

Given the immediate and lasting impact of orientation programs, careful planning—with emphasis on program goals, topics to be covered, and methods of organizing and presenting them—is essential. In many cases, organizations devise checklists for use by those responsible for conducting the orientation so that no item of importance to employees is overlooked. The checklist would include such things as (1) an introduction to other employees; (2) an outline of

Highlights in **HRM 7.7**

Wowing the Candidate

Intuit Canada, headquartered in Edmonton, Alberta, is a leading developer of financial software, including personal finance management, small business accounting, and tax preparation, with products such as Quicken. Intuit, like other organizations profiled in this report, is a top employer; it was ranked number two in Canada by *The Globe and Mail* survey and 45th of the 100 Best Companies to Work for in America by *Fortune* magazine in 2002. What makes Intuit special is its success in a highly competitive industry. There are many factors, but evidence of its success is its low attrition rate of 3 percent, which is remarkable in a sector where the average turnover is 20 percent. Ninety-four percent of its employees report that Intuit is a "great place to work," according to their annual surveys.

Intuit is very careful about the first few days of a new employee's work life. There are too many stories about employees in other organizations showing up very excited about their new job, only to discover that no one remembers that they are arriving that day, supplies and offices are not ready, and the reporting manager is absent. Intuit is committed to wowing the candidate—now employee—on the first day. Upon arriving at work, new employees are greeted by name by the receptionist who gives them a stainless steel

coffee mug engraved with their names. The hiring manager is called and arrives promptly. He knows the candidate and takes him to the workstation, showing him the computer, telephone, and office supplies.

The next step is to introduce the new employee to colleagues and other team members and a "buddy" who has volunteered to guide the new employee and answer all questions for the next three weeks. New employees often struggle with simple questions such as: How does the photocopier work? Do most people bring their lunches to work? The IT person arrives next and helps set up voice mail, e-mail, Internet access, etc. Intuit considers it vital that when the new employee goes home that night, he should be able to answer the universal question "How was your first day on the job?" with "Wow, am I ever glad that I took this job!"

This informal orientation is completed by a formal orientation, in which information about the strategy, vision, plans, history—including war stories and all the successes—is shared. A key part of this orientation is a discussion of Intuit values. At the end of the first week, and again at the end of the first month, feedback about the new employee's experiences is solicited. What worked, what was frustrating, how can the orientation be improved.

Source: M. Belcourt and S. Taggar, "Making Government the Best Place to Work: Building Commitment," *IPAC, New Directions Series,* no. 8, 2002.

training; (3) expectations for attendance, conduct, and appearance; (4) the conditions of employment, such as hours and pay periods; (5) an explanation of job duties, standards, and appraisal criteria; (6) safety regulations; (7) a list of the chain of command; and (8) an explanation of the organization's purpose and strategic goals. Highlights in HRM 7.8 shows the types of materials new hires can be given and the various steps that can ease their transition into the workplace.[49]

Some organizations combine orientation programs with computer-based training. Lazarus Department Stores (now Macy's) cut its orientation training time in half this way, orienting 2,500 new employees in just six weeks. New hires at SumTotal Systems, an e-learning company based in Bellevue, Washington, go online for virtual tours of the company's various departments, with introductions to company leaders sprinkled throughout. Of course, these types of programs supplement—but do not replace—the value of face-to-face orientation.[50]

Highlights in **HRM 7.8**

Checklist for Orienting New Employees

Items in Orientation Packet

- Welcome letter with company background
- Map of facility, including parking information
- IDs, keys, and parking decals
- Current organization chart
- Telephone numbers, e-mail addresses, and locations of key personnel
- Copy of employee's specific job goals and descriptions
- List of unique terms in the industry, company, and job
- Training class schedules
- Safety and emergency procedures
- Copy of policy handbook, including office hours and telephone and e-mail rules
- List of employee benefits, including insurance plans
- Holiday schedule

Follow-Up Activities

- Ensure that employee has completed required paperwork, including benefit enrollment forms
- Revisit performance standards
- Schedule first performance appraisal meeting

BASIC SKILLS TRAINING

Job-specific and general skills are both essential for career success.

Businesses report that they are having a harder time finding workers with the basic skills they seek. Almost half of all Canadians have low literacy skills—meaning that they can cope with everyday tasks, but lack the capacity to learn new job skills.[51] Many businesses say it is their top problem. A list of typical basic skills employees need includes the following:

- Reading
- Writing
- Computing
- Speaking
- Listening
- Problem solving
- Managing oneself/self-discipline
- Knowing how to learn
- Working as part of a team
- Leading others

Avon Foods in Nova Scotia and Palliser's Furniture in Manitoba are among the many companies that now offer remedial courses to their employees, many of which are conducted in-house.[52] Recognizing that the skills gap is increasing, colleges and companies have begun teaming up to bridge the gap. To implement a successful program in basic and remedial skills, managers should do the following:

1. Explain to employees why and how the training will help them in their jobs.
2. Relate the training to the employees' goals.
3. Respect and consider participants' experiences, and use these as a resource.
4. Use a task-centred or problem-centred approach so that participants "learn by doing."
5. Give employees feedback on their progress toward meeting their learning objectives.

A workplace education program in the City of Charlottetown won an award of excellence for Municipal Workplace Literacy Achievements by following these principles. The key to developing a successful basic skills program is *flexibility*, reinforcing the principle of individual differences while acknowledging the reality of work and family constraints.

TEAM TRAINING AND CROSS-TRAINING

As we discussed earlier in the book, organizations rely on teams to attain strategic and operational goals. Whether the team is an aircrew, a research team, or a manufacturing or service unit, the contributions of the individual members of the team are not only a function of the KSAs of each individual, but also of the interaction of the team members. Teamwork behaviours that differentiate effective teams are shown in Figure 7.10. They include both process dynamics and behavioural dynamics. The fact that these behaviours are observable and measurable provides a basis for training team members to function more effectively in the pursuit of their goals.[53]

Coca-Cola's Fountain Manufacturing Operation (which makes the syrup for Coke and Diet Coke) developed team training for its manufacturing employees. The program focused on three skill categories: (1) technical, (2) interpersonal, and (3) team action. The technical component, called Four-Deep Training, meant that each individual should learn four different jobs to allow for team flexibility. The interpersonal skills component, called Adventures in Attitudes, focused on listening, conflict resolution, influence, and negotiation. Team action training focused on team leadership, management of meetings, team roles, group dynamics, and problem solving—all skills needed to function effectively as a team. The training not only

FIGURE **7.10**

Team Training Skills

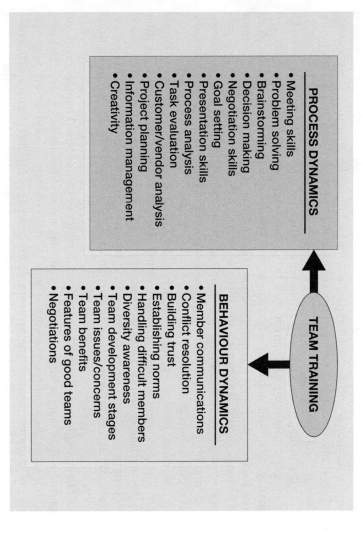

PROCESS DYNAMICS

- Meeting skills
- Problem solving
- Brainstorming
- Decision making
- Negotiation skills
- Goal setting
- Presentation skills
- Process analysis
- Task evaluation
- Customer/vendor analysis
- Project planning
- Information management
- Creativity

TEAM TRAINING

BEHAVIOUR DYNAMICS

- Member communications
- Conflict resolution
- Building trust
- Establishing norms
- Handling difficult members
- Diversity awareness
- Team development stages
- Team issues/concerns
- Team benefits
- Features of good teams
- Negotiations

Source: George Bohlander and Kathy McCarthy, "How to Get the Most from Team Training," *National Productivity Review* (Autumn 1996): 25–35.

increased quality and customer satisfaction, but also helped decrease costs and set up a model for preparing employees for the future.[54]

Closely related to team training is **cross-training**. Cross-trained employees learn how to do different jobs within an organization as well as their own. Part of the motivation for cross-training is that it gives firms flexible capacity. Workers can be dynamically shifted when and where they are needed, unlike specialized workers and equipment, which cannot. Moreover, by keeping workers interested and motivated, cross-training can cut turnover, increase productivity, pare down labour costs, and lay the foundation for careers rather than dead-end jobs.

In a sense, cross-training represents a shift from Henry Ford's assembly line production to flexible production. Some companies are using cross-training to keep their workers and plants in Canada versus offshoring them. Pace Worldwide, a company that sells soldering equipment, watched all of its competitors move offshore. To keep up with the productivity of its low-cost rivals abroad, Pace grouped workers into teams and trained each team to build an entire product as well as different products. "Some of the people could only do certain things, and if they had no work, they would just sit and wait," said one Pace manager. "Now they have ownership of it all." Employees have an incentive to learn because their hourly wages get bumped up as they master more skills. Now Pace builds products to meet actual customer demand, rather than storing inventory, which is more costly, and it has been able to shorten its production times and move its operations into one building versus two. In addition to making them more productive, research shows that cross-training gives employees the "big picture," making them more creative and better problem solvers.[55]

ETHICS TRAINING

Ethics training became more prevalent in companies following the high-profile corporate scandals such as those that occurred at Enron in 2001. As the Enron case showed, ethics training is not just for rank-and-file employees. Top managers also need to attend ethics training and take it seriously or risk jail time, as the high-profile case of Conrad Black demonstrated. For reasons such as these and because the reputational and financial repercussions of ethical lapses can be devastating, many firms have since created ethics codes and developed ethics training programs for their employees.

Top managers play a key role in terms of ethics training because employees take their cues from them and mirror their behaviour. Thus, a firm's top executives and managers should behave in accordance with their companies' values. If this does not happen, no ethics training program within a company can be effective. Senior managers should also broach the topic of ethics often in their speeches and presentations, and a company's ethics training should be a part of the new employee orientation. In addition, a firm's current employees need to undergo ethics training at regular intervals.

Workers who are responsible for areas that expose them to ethical lapses are likely to require special training. Employees who do the purchasing for their firms are one example. Likewise, some firms offer special training to their overseas personnel who work in countries in which corruption and bribery are prevalent. (We will talk more about bribery in Chapter 15, which covers international topics.)

Bringing in an outside expert trained in ethics or values-based management can be helpful as can surveying employees, managers, and sometimes even customers about what they believe the ethical state of the company is and where improvements could be made. Some firms go so far as to appoint **chief ethics officers**—high-ranking managers directly responsible for fostering the ethical climate within their firms.

cross-training
The process of training employees to do multiple jobs within an organization

chief ethics officer
A high-ranking manager directly responsible for fostering the ethical climate within the firm

Hewlett-Packard is one company that has an exemplary ethics program. All employees—from entry-level employees to senior executives—are responsible for holding one another accountable with respect to ethical behaviour. The following are elements of HP's ethics program and training:

- A publicly available ethics code written in 12 languages
- Mandatory ethics training for all employees
- A toll-free ethics hotline complemented by a dedicated electronic mailbox where messages are treated with the highest degree of confidentiality
- An ethics officer with vice president–level leadership and authority
- Conflict resolution procedures
- Communications systems that facilitate and encourage employee feedback without fear of retaliation[56]

DIVERSITY TRAINING

In addition to globalization, the increased emphasis on diversity training has been sparked by an awareness of the varied demographics of the workforce, challenges of employment equity, dynamics of stereotyping, changing values of the workforce, and potential competitive payoffs from bringing different people together for a common purpose. There are basically two types of diversity training: (1) awareness building, which helps employees appreciate the benefits of diversity, and (2) skill building, which provides employees with the KSAs necessary for working with people who are different from them. For example, a skill-building diversity program might teach managers how to conduct performance appraisals with people from different cultures or teach male supervisors how to coach female employees toward better career opportunities. All of the diverse dimensions—race, gender, age, disabilities, lifestyles, culture, education, ideas, and backgrounds—should be considered in the design of a diversity training program.[57]

Increasingly, diversity training is being combined with other training programs, an occurrence that some believe represents the "mainstreaming" of diversity with other strategic issues, such as ethics, facing organizations. Honeywell, for example, subsumes diversity training within a weeklong advanced management program and as part of its sales training programs. PricewaterhouseCoopers operates a one-day program of coaching in cultural traits after it realized that almost all of its 250-person Edmonton office were recruited overseas in places such as Mexico, Russia, the Philippines and China.[58]

To achieve a good outcome in terms of diversity training, managers will want to do the following:

1. *Forge a strategic link.* Begin by establishing the reasons for diversity training. Clarify the links between diversity and a firm's business goals in order to provide a context for training. Employment equity and valuing diversity are not the same thing. Ultimately, diversity enhances differences and unites those differences toward a common goal.

2. *Don't settle for "off-the-shelf" programs.* Each company has somewhat different goals, and its training should reflect this.

3. *Choose your training methods carefully.* Most diversity training is really education (awareness building). Managers may hope they are developing skills, but this requires more in-depth training. Employees may benefit from either awareness or skill building, but they are not the same.

4. *Document the individual and organizational benefits of the training.* Diversity training, when done well, can enhance communications, improve a firm's responsiveness to social issues, reduce lawsuits, create a climate of fairness, improve employee productivity, and increase the company's revenues, profits, and competitiveness.

Using the Internet

For current articles on diversity issues, including training, in Canada, go to

http://www.diversityinthe workplace.ca

The last point—documenting the benefits of diversity training—is particularly important. Often, companies fail to do this, so the training ends up merely being a "feel good" exercise. Diversity training needs to be held to the same rigorous standards as other training programs. If the training is truly working, it should show up eventually in a company's employee demographics and strategy.

Small Business APPLICATION

Training is very important to small businesses because, typically, employee turnover is high, and as a result, the development of new employees quickly and effectively is one of the key success factors for smaller businesses.

To illustrate the role of training for small business, let's draw on the example of a clothing retailer we will call Style Zone. Style Zone has one store, located in a popular shopping mall. It is open seven days per week from 10 a.m. to 9 p.m. It is located close to two high schools, which provide regular customers, as well as staff. Style Zone has 35 staff in addition to the owner and the assistant manager. Generally speaking, turnover is 50 percent per year, meaning that over the course of the year, half of the staff leave, equating to one or two new hires per month. Style Zone supports the regular integration of staff by the standardization of roles and processes for two positions: cashier and stock associate. Within these two roles, the company has clearly defined and documented the responsibilities for the role, from how the employees should groom and dress, to what they do when they arrive, to how they greet customers, to what procedures to follow, to what they do before they leave for the day.

Why is role specialization important for Style Zone or any other small company managing the integration of staff? There are three primary reasons. Firstly, standardization of roles allows many people to be able to train new workers. In Style Zone, with one owner and one assistant manager, it is imperative that existing staff are able to train new staff so that Style Zone is ready on any given day to integrate new staff. Secondly, role standardization allows new workers to be coached and supported by other staff as they learn their roles. Orientation is typically a small part of on-the-job learning, as employees will spend days and weeks becoming proficient in their new roles. Lastly, role specialization is important because it allows new employees to have clear visibility into the expectations of the role, and quickly become proficient.

So how did Style Zone get there? The owner and assistant manager worked together to document the knowledge and skills required for each job. With this written documentation, the manager then started training, which consisted of a systematic review of the required behaviours with the employee, demonstration of these behaviours, and practice of these behaviours with reinforcement—all done on the job.

SUMMARY

Today we find that organizational operations cover a broad range of subjects and involve personnel at all levels, from orientation through management development. In order to have effective training programs, the systems approach is recommended. This approach consists of four phases: (1) needs assessment, (2) program design, (3) implementation, and (4) evaluation.

Needs assessment begins with organization analysis. Managers must establish a context for training by deciding where training is needed, how it connects with their firms' strategic goals, and how their companies' resources can best be used in terms of training. A task analysis is used to identify the knowledge, skills, and abilities employees need. A person analysis is used to identify which people need training.

3 OUTCOME

When designing a training program, managers must consider the two fundamental preconditions for learning: readiness and motivation of trainees. In addition, the principles of learning should be considered in order to create an environment that is conducive to learning. These principles include goal setting, the meaningfulness of presentation, modelling, individual differences, active practice and repetition, whole-versus-part learning, massed-versus-distributed learning, and feedback and reinforcement.

4 OUTCOME

A wide variety of methods are available to train nonmanagerial personnel. On-the-job training is one of the most commonly used methods because it provides trainees with hands-on experience and an opportunity to build a relationship with their supervisor and coworkers. Apprenticeship training and internships are especially effective because they provide both on- and off-the-job experiences. Other off-the-job methods include classroom training, programmed instruction, computer-based training, simulations, and interactive e-learning utilizing teleconferencing, video conferencing, webinars, and the communities of practice method of learning. Using multiple methods, or what is called blended learning, has been found to be most effective.

The training and development of managers is becoming increasingly critical for firms because they are facing increasing competition from across the globe, and the baby boomer generation is retiring. As with nonmanagerial personnel, a wide variety of training methods are used for developing managers.

On-the-job experiences include coaching, understudy assignments, job rotation, lateral transfers, project and committee assignments, and staff meetings. Off-the-job experiences include analysis of case studies, management games and simulations, role-playing, and behaviour modelling.

5 OUTCOME

Evaluation of a training program should focus on several criteria: participant reactions, learning, behaviour change on the job, and bottom-line results such as return on investment. Transfer of training is measured via examination of the degree to which trained skills are demonstrated back on the job. Benchmarking and utility analysis help evaluate the impact of training and provide the information for further needs assessment.

6 OUTCOME

Special issues in training involve programs that are important to a broad range of employees. Orientation training, for example, begins and continues throughout an employee's service with an organization. By participating in a formal orientation program, employees acquire the knowledge, skills, and attitudes that increase the probabilities of their success within the organization. To make an orientation effective, there should be close cooperation between the HR department and other departments in all phases of the program, from initial planning through follow-up and evaluation. Basic skills training, ethics training, and diversity training are also critically important in today's organizations.

KEY TERMS

apprenticeship training, 286
behaviour modelling, 296
behaviour modification, 284
benchmarking, 300
blended learning, 289
chief ethics officer, 306
chief learning officer, 274
competency assessment, 277

cooperative training, 287
cross-training, 306
e-learning, 292
instructional objectives, 280
internship programs, 288
just-in-time training, 293
learning management system (LMS), 293

on-the-job training (OJT), 285
organization analysis, 276
orientation, 302
person analysis, 279
spot rewards, 283
task analysis, 277
transfer of training, 298

DISCUSSION QUESTIONS

1. What economic, social, and political forces have made employee training even more important today than it was in the past?

2. You have been asked by a colleague to teach her how to use Excel. How would you conduct a needs analysis to determine her current knowledge and skill level?

3. Think about the best teacher whom you have ever experienced, and the worst teacher. Go to the list

of characteristics of effective instructors on page 284 and assess each teacher against this list.

4. Indicate what training methods you would use for each of the following jobs. Explain your choices.

    a. File clerk
    b. Computer operator
    c. Automobile service station attendant
    d. Pizza maker
    e. Nurse's aide

5. Compare computer-based instruction and e-learning with the lecture method with regard to the way the two methods involve the different psychological principles of learning.

6. Suppose that you are the manager of an accounts receivable unit in a large company. You are switching to a new system of billing and record keeping and need to train your 3 supervisors

and 28 employees in the new procedures. What training method(s) would you use? Why?

7. Participants in a training course are often asked to evaluate the course by means of a questionnaire. What are the pros and cons of this approach? Are there better ways of evaluating a course?

8. A new employee is likely to be anxious the first few days on the job.

    a. What are some possible causes of this anxiety?
    b. How may the anxiety be reduced?

9. Team up with a classmate and design an orientation program for a new student to your school.

10. Read the interview with the Head of Corporate Human Resources and Organizational Development for Staples http://www.jobquality. ca/interviews/interview_staples.shtml Rate Staples training programs based on the best practices that you have read about in this chapter.

INTERNET EXERCISE

Do students have different learning styles? Listen to Professor Willingham's lecture on learning styles at

http://www.youtube.com/watch?v=sIv9rz2NTUk Do you agree? Why or why not?

HRM EXPERIENCE

Training and Learning Principles

It is surprising how many training programs do not explicitly incorporate the principles of learning into their design (such as goal setting, modelling, individual differences, and feedback). It is not that difficult to do so, even for very simple instructional programs. To prove this point, do the following assignment for building a paper airplane.

Assignment

1. Form teams of four to six members. Identify someone on the team who knows how to make a paper airplane. That person will be the *trainer*.

2. Identify someone who will be the *observer/ recorder*. That person will not participate in the training but will write down how many (and how effectively) principles of learning are used in the instruction:

    a. Goal setting
    b. Modelling
    c. Meaningfulness
    d. Individual differences

    e. Whole-versus-part learning
    f. Mass-versus-distributed learning
    g. Active practice
    h. Feedback

3. Give the trainer 10 to 15 minutes to train the group in making a paper airplane. The observer/ recorder will keep notes of effective and ineffective training techniques (demonstrated learning principles).

4. Have someone from each team—not the trainer— volunteer to come before the class for a friendly competition. The instructor will give each team member two minutes to make a paper airplane. Then just for fun, they can compete by seeing which one flies the farthest. As always, no wagering, please.

5. To finish the exercise, the observers/recorders will lead a discussion of the learning principles that were demonstrated. Discuss also, if they were done in this setting, why they might not be done in other training settings.

BIZFLIX EXERCISES

BACKDRAFT: PROBIE'S TRAINING EXPERIENCES

Watch the scenes from the film *Backdraft* to see examples of the training and development discussions in this chapter. Use the following discussion questions as guides to your viewing of the scenes.

Two brothers follow their late father, a legendary Chicago firefighter, and join the City of Chicago Fire Department. Stephen "Bull" McCaffrey (Kurt Russell) joins first and rises to the rank of lieutenant. Younger brother Brian (William Baldwin) joins later. After graduation from the fire academy, Brian becomes a member of Bull's Engine Company 17. Sibling rivalry tarnishes their work relationships, but they continue to fight Chicago fires successfully. Add a plot element about a mysterious arsonist, and you have the basis for an extraordinary film. The intense, unprecedented special effects give the viewer an unparalleled experience of what it is like to fight a fire. Chicago firefighters applauded the realism of the fire scenes.

These scenes are an edited composite built from two parts of the film. Part I: "On-the-Job Training: Probie's First Day" appears early in *Backdraft* as part of "The First Day" sequence. This part shows Engine Company 17 preparing to fight a garment factory fire. Part II: "Back at Station 17: Probie Continues Training" comes from "The Probie's Life" segment that appears about 30 minutes later in the film. The term *probie* is jargon for a probationary firefighter—someone just starting with the department.

What to Watch for and Ask Yourself

- Which training methods described earlier in this chapter appear in these scenes? Link the training methods discussed to specific moments and examples in the scenes.
- Did Brian McCaffrey receive any classroom instruction?
- Review the earlier section "Phase 4: Evaluating the Training Program." Assess the training Brian received using the criteria discussed in that section.

CASE STUDY 1

SERVICE AT THE CHATEAU WHISTLER

The Chateau Whistler in Whistler, British Columbia, is one of the world's leading hotels and has been named the number one ski resort in North America for the past eight years. The 557-room hotel opened in 1989 and currently has 650 full-time employees.

The orientation program for new employees at the Chateau Whistler reflects the same standards that guests enjoy at the hotel. New recruits have raw talents such as energy and enthusiasm but have to be trained quickly in the art of excellent service.

On day one of the orientation program, an "Orientation Game" is played; then the employees are introduced to the hotel (the types of rooms, the amenities, etc.). Then the following are discussed:

- Salary and benefits, including health care, pension plan, discounted ski passes, staff meals, food discounts, discounted rates at other properties, and health club access
- Employment standards, human rights, and labour relations (although the hotel is not unionized)

- Health and safety, including Workplace Hazardous Materials Information System (WHMIS) and Material Safety Data Sheets (MSDS) and the environmental program
- Harassment policy
- The wellness program
- The incentive program

New employees also receive a tour of the town of Whistler, so that they can talk to guests about the key attractions and establish a network of friends.

Day two is devoted to the Service Plus Program. The Service Plus Code is spelled out this way:

S support
E empathy
R responsiveness
V valuing differences
I interdependence
C caring
E expectations

The day two program focuses on the guest–employee interaction and strives to teach employees how to provide excellent service, deal empathetically and effectively with problems reported by guests, and solve problems creatively. Training consists of role-plays such as "handling the difficult guest." Specifically, the new recruits gain an understanding of the hotel's mission statement and commitment to service, the changing service culture, and the high service expectations of the guests.

The third component of the orientation program is "Guest for a Night," during which employees who have been working at the hotel for three months eat at the restaurants, enjoy the facilities, and spend one night in the hotel as a guest. According to David Roberts, the hotel's general manager, the goal of the Guest for a Night program is to ensure that employees can talk knowledgeably about guest rooms, restaurants, and other facilities, and understand the level of quality that the hotel provides.

As part of this program, employees are asked to fill out a feedback survey, just like a guest. Also at this time, employees are invited to be part of a focus group to express concerns and provide feedback about their work experiences.

Through these orientation and training programs, employees develop knowledge and skills in service excellence. More importantly, they develop a commitment to the company. At a ten-year reunion party given for 600 people, 599 said it was the best working experience of their lives.

QUESTIONS

1. Compare the Chateau Whistler's orientation program to the list of activities presented in Highlights in HRM 7.8. Would you add anything?
2. The hospitality sector has high turnover rates among employees. Why does the Chateau Whistler invest so much time, money, and energy into its orientation program?
3. Describe the activities in the orientation and training programs that would ensure a high degree of transfer of training to the job.
4. How would you measure the success of this program? What results criteria would you try to measure?

CASE STUDY 2

PEOPLE DEVELOPMENT STRATEGIES AT CREDIT UNION CENTRAL OF SASKATCHEWAN

There are 128 credit unions in Saskatchewan, with assets ranging from less than $1 million to more than $1 billion. All of these are affiliated with Credit Union Central of Saskatchewan, which facilitates cooperation among credit unions and provides consulting services, trade association functions, and liquidity management.

Credit Union Central, together with the four largest Saskatchewan credit unions, developed a plan to implement a comprehensive human resources management system to produce, first, a better alignment of employee performance to organizational objectives and, second, more focused training to produce desired business results and an enhanced ability to retain employees through opportunities for professional development. Working with Hay Management Consultants, the first step was to develop a competency glossary, followed by performance management processes and tools, selection and staffing tools, and then succession planning.

Competencies can be defined as attitudes, skills, knowledge, or behaviours that are essential to perform at work and that differentiate superior performers. The competency glossary defines core competencies, which apply to all roles within the organization, and role-specific competencies. Competency target levels indicating superior performance are set for each role.

An example of a core competency, based on the key values and strategies of the organization, is "results orientation":

When your employee tried to improve his or her own performance he or she

1. identified areas of waste or inefficiency but did not take any action

2. made some changes to work methods in order to reach particular goals that had been set for him or her

3. made specific changes in the system and his or her own work methods in order to improve performance beyond goals set

4. set own challenging goals that were accomplished with a significant amount of planning, analysis, and effort

5. set individual goals by thinking through the costs and benefits, and explicitly considered potential profits, risks, and return on investment, in order to make decisions that ended up having a positive organizational impact

6. took a calculated entrepreneurial risk and committed significant organizational resources to act on an idea that ended up significantly improving performance

A role-specific competency might be "concern for order, quality, and compliance" defined as follows:

When your employee demonstrated attention to detail in his or her work, he or she

1. checked on the work to ensure it was accurate, complied with all relevant regulations, and followed all standard practices and procedures

2. monitored the accuracy and quality of his or her own work and others' work consistently and systematically and kept a detailed record of work when it was necessary

3. during the project, monitored the progress of the project against milestones and deliverables, took action to ensure the procedures put in place were effective, and quickly corrected any weaknesses or deficiencies

4. established and utilized a procedure and/or system to facilitate work efficiency and ensure high-quality output; modified and improved the procedure and/or system when a weakness was identified, in order to ensure that high-quality work was being produced

Managers work with employees to assess competency levels. The competency glossary and a competency assessment questionnaire enable managers and employees to discuss skills, abilities, and behaviours using a common framework. Training and development plans are based on gaps between target performance and actual performance. A developmental resource kit, which includes training courses, seminars, books, and work opportunities, all classified by competency, assists with building development plans.

This approach has resulted in clear direction on performance and development plans to move employees toward optimum performance levels.

QUESTIONS

1. Describe the advantages of the approach used to identify performance gaps.
2. Why would managers resist or support this approach?
3. Describe methods that you would use to evaluate the effectiveness of this approach learning level, behaviour level, and organizational-results level.

CASE STUDY 3

ORIENTATION AT BELL CANADA

On May 15th, 2006, Bell Canada began to roll out a new orientation program with a large e-based component for new hires. The website that introduces new employees to their orientation is an upbeat and interactive design where new employees can quickly find much of the information necessary to orient themselves to their new company. The orientation process allows for a consistent message to be delivered to all employees across Canada, in either French or English, and grants the new hire's immediate supervisor more tools that can be used to help welcome the employee over the first few days and months of his career at Bell.

It is only the starting point for a new career at Bell Canada. Bell's corporate culture promotes self-service, where much of the information relating to an individual's options regarding career growth and development is posted on the intranet. This provides each individual private access to only his or her information. This orientation process aligns with the culture of self-service and acquaints new employees with the knowledge of how things get done around Bell and provides links for where they can look for more information. It also encourages the new hires to ask for direction from their managers and to seek information on any items that may have been missed during their first few weeks.

While orientation is a necessary step in welcoming and guiding a new employee, it is a costly endeavour for organizations. Bell's decision to move to a large online orientation component was a conscious decision to find savings where possible. In a national company, the transportation costs of bringing all new hires to a central location may have benefits but other options such as intranet information, conference calls, and other forms of communication should be considered. The current program at Bell gives the same message and without the costs involved in a classroom-dependent process. The extra bonus in this method is that employees have access to information that aids in their education about their work environment, and permits them to begin contributing to their teams as soon as possible.

Given the high cost of hiring new employees, it is important that the employee is able to start being productive as soon as possible. As part of connecting the new employee to the organization, and allowing the transition to occur, Bell has leveraged an already established program using employees known to be Pride Builders. This program identifies employees across all levels and departments who take special pride in their work and display excellent organizational citizenship and desired behaviours. According to Randi Haimovitz, project designer of the orientation program, Pride Builders make it a priority to connect with the new hires within their first few weeks at work and when possible meet them for a coffee in order to provide valuable company information and make the new hire feel more welcomed. New hires are also introduced to other new employees outside their immediate business units via semi-annual forums.

QUESTIONS

1. What are the advantages of the orientation program at Bell? Can you describe some of the limitations?

2. The goals of orientation programs are to explain to new employees the "whys," not just the "whats" and "hows" of their new jobs. What elements in Bell's orientation program would be conducive to meeting this objective? Do you think orientation should be a supplement to a live orientation? Why or why not?

CAREER COUNSEL

Complete the training list on the *Managing Human Resources* website (http://www.belcourt6e.nelson.com).

NOTES AND REFERENCES

1. P. D. Hughes and M. Grant *Learning and Development Outlook 2007*, The Conference Board of Canada.

2. Lori Freifeld, "Best of the Best," *Training* 45, no. 2 (February 2008): 8.

3. David Dubois and William Rothwell, "Competency-Based or a Traditional Approach to Training?" *Training and Development* 58, no. 4 (April 2004): 46–59; See also Irwin L. Goldstein and J. Kevin Ford, *Training in Organizations: Needs Assessment, Development and Evaluation*, 4th ed. (Belmont, CA: Wadsworth, 2002). For the classic citation on needs assessment, see William McGehee and Paul W. Thayer, *Training in Business and Industry* (New York: John Wiley and Sons, 1961).

4. Laurie Bassi and Daniel McMurrer, "How's Your Return on People?" *Harvard Business Review* 8, no. 3 (March 2004): 18; Tracy Mauro, "Helping Organizations Build Community," *Training and Development* 56, no. 2 (February 2002): 25–29; Liam Lahey, "RFIDs Touted as Standard for Airport Security," *Computing Canada* 28, no. 13 (June 21, 2002): 21; Caroline Wilson, "Ensuring a Smooth Ride," *Security Management* 46, no. 8 (August 2002): 92.

5. Brad Long, "Strategic Human Resource Management and the Worker's Experience," *Journal of Individual Employment Rights* 12, no. 3 (2007): 265–282; "E-Learning and Teleconferencing Join Needs Assessment to Control Training Costs," *Managing Training & Development* no. 3 (December 2003): 1; Thomas Gainey, Brian Klaas, and Darla Moore, "Outsourcing the Training Function: Results from the Field," *Human Resource Planning* 25, no. 1 (2002): 16; Sarah Fister Gale, "Creative Training: Doing More with Less," *Workforce* 80, no. 10 (October 2001): 82–88.

6. Scott A. Yorkovich, Gregory S. Waddell, and Robert K. Gerwig, "Competency-based Assessment Systems: Encouragement Toward a More Holistic Approach," *Proceedings of the Northeast Business & Economics Association* (2007): 77–81; Patty Davis, Jennifer Naughton, and William Rothwell, "New Roles and New Competencies for the Profession: Are You Ready for the Next Generation," *Training and Development* 58, no. 4 (April 2004): 26–38; David Dubois and William Rothwell, "Competency-Based or a Traditional Approach to Training?" *Training and Development* 58, no. 4 (April 2004): 46–59.

NEL

7. Thomas Hoffman, "Motivation: These IT Leaders Keep Staffers Upbeat during Lean Times by Targeting What Drives Them: Technology and Training," *Computerworld* 38, no. 1 (January 5, 2004): 39; Elwood Holton, Reid Bates, and Sharon Naquin, "Large-Scale Performance-Driven Training Needs Assessment: A Case Study," *Public Personnel Management* 29, no. 2 (Summer 2000): 249–267.

8. Gail Johnson, "The Development Framework: Booz Allen Hamilton's Holistic Method of Employee Development Gives Its Employee a Roadmap to Success—Both Professionally and Personally," *Training* 40, no. 2 (February 2003): 32–34; Robert Mager, "Contract Training Tips," *Security Management* 45, no. 6 (June 2001): 30.

9. Debbie Schachter, "How to Set Performance Goals: Employee Reviews Are More Than Annual Critiques," *Information Outlook* 8, no. 9 (September 2004): 26–30; "Burger Olympics," *Training* 41, no. 7 (July 2004): 20; Jason A. Colquitt and Marcia J. Simmering, "Conscientiousness, Goal Orientation, and Motivation to Learn during the Learning Process: A Longitudinal Study," *Journal of Applied Psychology* 83, no. 4 (August 1998): 654–665.

10. Annette Towler and Robert Dipboye, "Effects of Trainer Expressiveness, Organization, and Trainee Goal Orientation on Training Outcomes," *Journal of Applied Psychology* 86, no. 4 (August 2001): 664–673; Steve Kozlowski, Stanley Gully, Kenneth Brown, and Eduardo Salas, "Effects of Training Goals and Goal Orientation Traits on Multidimensional Training Outcomes and Performance Adaptability," *Organizational Behavior and Human Decision Processes* 85, no. 1 (May 2001): 1–31.

11. The classics by Albert Bandura include *Social Foundations of Thought and Action: A Social Cognitive Theory* (Englewood Cliffs, NJ: Prentice Hall, 1986) and *A Social Learning Theory* (Englewood Cliffs, NJ: Prentice Hall, 1977). See also Melesa Altizer Bolt, Larry Killough, and Hian Chye Koh, "Testing the Interaction Effects of Task Complexity in Computer Training Using the Social Cognitive Model," *Decision Sciences* 32, no. 1 (Winter 2001): 1–20; Susan Pedersen and Min Liu, "The Transfer of Problem-Solving Skills from a Problem-Based Learning Environment: The Effect of Modeling an Expert's Cognitive Processes," *Journal of Research on Technology in Education* 35, no. 2 (Winter 2002): 303–321.

12. Stanley Gully, Stephanie Payn, K. Lee Kiechel Koles, and John-Andrew Whiteman, "The Impact of Error Training and Individual Differences on Training Outcomes: An Attribute-Treatment Interaction Perspective," *Journal of Applied Psychology* 87, no. 1 (February 2002): 143–155; Steven John Simon, "The Relationship of Learning Style and Training Method to End-User Computer Satisfaction and Computer Use: A Structural Equation Model," *Information Technology, Learning, and Performance Journal* 18, no. 1 (Spring 2000): 41–59.

13. Maya Dollarhide, "Hits the Spot," *Incentive* 181, no. 10 (October 2007): 102–103; "Can Technology Actually Boost Behavior Change?" *Managing Training & Development* no. 3 (November 2003): 3; Don Hartshorn, "Reinforcing the Unsafe Worker," *Occupational Hazards* 62, no. 10 (October 2000): 125–128.

14. Joe M. Ricks, Jacqueline A. Williams, and William A. Weeks, "Sales Trainer Roles, Competencies, Skills, and Behaviors: A Case Study," *Industrial Marketing Management* 37, no. 5 (July 2008): 593–609; John L. Bennett, "Trainers as Leaders of Learning," *Training and Development* 55, no. 3 (March 2001): 42–45; Ruth Palombo Weiss, "Deconstructing Trainers' Self-Image," *Training and Development* 55, no. 12 (December 2001): 34–39.

15. Eduardo Salas and Janis Cannon-Bowers, "The Science of Training: A Decade of Progress," *Annual Review of Psychology* 52 (2001): 471–499.

16. Cohn Terry, "Enabling Staff to Access the Knowledge They Need, When They Need It," *Industrial & Commercial Training* 39, no. 7 (2007): 368–371; Diane Walter, *Training on the Job* (Alexandria, VA: American Society for Training and Development, 2001); Toni Hodges, *Linking Learning and Performance: A Practical Guide to Measuring Learning and On-the-Job Application* (Burlington, MA: Butterworth-Heinemann, 2001); Gary Sisson, *Hands-On Training: A Simple and Effective Method for On-the-Job Training* (San Francisco: Barrett-Koehler, 2001).

17. Teresa M. McAleavy, "U.S. Schools Fail to Provide Job Training," *Knight-Ridder/ Tribune Business News* (June 9, 2004); "Eight Steps to Better On-the-Job Training," *HRfocus* 80, no. 7 (July 2003): 11; Alison Booth, Yu-Fu Chen, and Gylfi Zoega, "Hiring and Firing: A Tale of Two Thresholds," *Journal of Labor Economics* 20, no. 2 (April 2002): 217–248.

18. Ronald L. Jacobs and Michael J. Jones, "Teaching Tools: When to Use On-the-Job Training," *Security Management* 41, no. 9 (September 1997): 35–39.

19. Information found on the Apprenticeship page, Spokane Community College website, February 9, 2005, http://www.scc.spokane.edu/?apprent, retrieved July 30, 2009.

20. For more information about the Bureau of Apprenticeship and Training, see the Bureau's website at http://oa.doleta.gov

21. Uyen Vu, "EnCana Builds Talent Pipeline into High School Classrooms," *Canadian HR Reporter*, April 11, 2005, 3.

22. Major Investment in Training Programs at NSCC, Marconi Campus," News Release Entreprise Cape Breton Corporation, May 17, 2002.

23. John Byrd and Rob Poole, "Highly Motivated Employees at No Cost? It's Not an Impossible Dream," *Nonprofit World* 19, no. 6 (November/December 2001): 312–332.

24. Phil Britt, "E-Learning on the Rise in the Classroom: Companies Move Content Online: Cisco Systems' Employees and Partners Routinely Watch Videos on the Internet," *EContent* 27, no. 11 (November 2004): 36–41; Heather Johnson, "The Whole Picture: When It Comes to Finding Out How Employees Feel about Training, Many Companies Fail to Get a Clear Picture," *Training* 47, no. 7 (July 2004): 30–35.

25. Laura Chubb, "EDS Uses Teleconferencing to Train Leaders in Coaching Skills," *People Management* 13, no. 23 (November 15, 2007): 13; "What Does Teleconferencing Cost?" *T+D* 61, no. 10 (October 2007): 96.

26. Jeane Mesiter, "Communities of Practice 2.0," *Chief Learning Officer* 6, no. 5 (May 2007): 58.

27. Matthew Trevisan "A smart lesson from the Airforce, in 3D," *The Globe and Mail*, May 8, 2008, B11.

28. Ericka Johnson, "Surgical Simulators and Simulated Surgeons: Reconstituting Medical Practice and Practitioners in Simulations," *Social Studies of Science* 37, no. 4 (August 2007): 585–608; "Soup to Nuts: Simulator Manufacturing Is a Lucrative but Risky Business, Which Is Why Market Leader CAE Has Tapped into the More Stable World of Flight Training," *Air Transport World* 40, no. 5 (May 2003): 69–71; "SimsSir: Modeling and Simulation Are Leading the Assault on New Learning Technologies That Are Winning Favor with the U.S. Military," *Training and Development* 57, no. 10 (October 2003): 46–52.

29. Marc J. Rosenberg, "Technology Euphoria?" *T+D* 62, no. 6 (June 2008): 24–27; For applications of simulation training used in the U.S. Navy, see John Flink, "This Is Really Neat Stuff," *United States Naval Institute Proceedings* 128, no. 7 (July 2002): 68–69, For applications of simulation training used in medical schools, see David Noonan, "Is the Cadaver Dead?" *Newsweek* 139, no. 25 (June 24, 2002): 62. For applications of simulation training used in the police force, see Jim Weiss and Mickey Davis, "Deadly Force Decision-Making," *Law and Order* 50, no. 6 (June 2002): 58–62.

30. "What to Do Now That Training Is Becoming a Major HR Force," *HRfocus* (February 2005): 5–6; Tammy Galvin, "The Delivery," *Training* 38, no. 10 (October 2001): 66–72; Kenneth G. Brown, "Using Computers to Deliver Training: Which Employees Learn and Why?" *Personnel Psychology* 54, no. 2 (Summer 2001): 271–296; Bill Roberts, "E-Learning New Twist on CBT," *HR Magazine* 46, no. 4 (April 2001): 99–106.

31. Scott A. Snell, Donna Stueber, and David P. Lepak, "Virtual HR Departments: Getting Out of the Middle," in R. L. Heneman and D. B. Greenberger (eds.), *Human Resource Management in Virtual Organizations* (Greenwich, CT: Information Age Publishing, 2002).

32. Garry Kranz, "E-learning Hits Its Stride," *Workforce Management Online* (February 2008); Martin Delahoussaye, Kristine Ellis, and Matt Bolch, "Measuring Corporate Smarts," *Training* 39, no. 8 (August 2002): 20–35; Daniel Crepin, "From Design to Action: Developing a Corporate Strategy," *Quality Progress* 35, no. 2 (February 2002): 49–56; Brad Miller, "Making Managers More Effective Agents of Change," *Quality Progress* 34, no. 5 (May 2001): 53–57.

33. Yabome Gilpin-Jackson and Gervase R. Bushe, "Leadership Development Training Transfer: A Case Study of Post-Training Determinants," *Journal of Management Development* 26, no. 10 (2007): 980–1004; Joseph Alutto, "Just-in-Time Management Education in the 21st Century," *HR Magazine* 44, no. 11 (1999): 56–57; Gordon Dehler, M. Ann Welsh, and Marianne W. Lewis, "Critical Pedagogy in the 'New Paradigm,'" *Management Learning* 493, no. 4 (December 2001): 493–511.

34. Chris Whitcomb, "Scenario-Based Training to the F.B.I.," *Training and Development* 53, no. 6 (June 1999): 42–46; Anne Hoag, Dale Brickley, and Joanne Cawley, "Media Management

Education and the Case Method," *Journalism and Mass Communication Educator* 55, no. 4 (Winter 2001): 49–59.

35. Jason B. Moats, Thomas J. Chermack, and Larry M. Dooley, "Using Scenarios to Develop Crisis Managers: Applications of Scenario Planning and Scenario-Based Training," *Advances in Developing Human Resources* 10, no. 3 (June 2008): 397–424; A. J. Faria, "The Changing Nature of Business Simulation/Gaming Research: A Brief History," *Simulation and Gaming* 32, no. 1 (March 2001): 97–110.

36. Alli McConnon, "The Games Managers Play," *BusinessWeek* 4040 (June 25, 2007): 12; Matt Bolch, "Games Employees Play: Delta Air Lines Uses a Blended e-Learning Program to Teach Employees the Economic Realities of the Airline Industry," *Training* 40, no. 4 (April 2003): 44–48.

37. Shannon Klie, "L'Oreal Plays Games with Training," *Canadian HR Reporter*, vol. 21, Issue 17, 26.

38. Adam Kirby, "Guest Service Is Fun and Games," *Hotels* 42, no. 5 (May 2008): 71–72; Dan Heilman, "Putting Games to Work: Game-Based Training Is Shaping Up to Be One of This Generation's Primary Teaching Tools, in Business and Elsewhere," *Computer User* 22, no. 2 (February 2004): 14–16.

39. Patricia Robinson, "In Practice: Western Companies Show Asian Counterparts That It Pays to Play," *Chief Learning Officer* 6, no. 12 (December 2007): 30; Christopher Hosford, "Serious Fun: Computer Training Finds a Niche," *Meeting News* 28, no. 7 (December 2004): 16; Rick Sullivan, "Lessons in Smallness," *Training and Development* 56, no. 3 (March 2002): 21–23; James W. Walker, "Perspectives," *Human Resource Planning* 23, no. 3 (2000): 5–7.

40. T. L. Stanley, "Be a Good Role Model for Your Employees," *Supervision* 65, no. 5 (January 2004): 5–8; Gary May and William Kahnweiler, "The Effect of a Mastery Practice Design on Learning and Transfer in Behavior Modeling Training," *Personnel Psychology* 53, no. 2 (Summer 2000): 353–373.

41. Wendy Larlee, "Training Programs: Key to Collections: Companies in the Collections Business Face Significant Challenges: Putting Solid Training Program in Place Can Help," *Collections & Credit Risk* 9, no. 2 (December 2004): 42–44; Heather Johnson, "The Whole Picture: When It Comes to Finding Out How Employees Feel about Training, Many Companies Fail to Get a Clear Picture," *Training* 47, no. 7 (July 2004): 30–35; Martin Delahoussaye, "Show Me the Results," *Training* 39, no. 3 (March 2002): 28–29; Reinout van Brakel, "Why ROI Isn't Enough," *Training and Development* 56, no. 6 (June 2002): 72–74.

42. "Dissatisfaction with Job Training Contributes to Low Job Satisfaction," *Managing Training & Development* (November 2003): 8; James Pershing and Jana Pershing, "Ineffective Reaction Evaluation," *Human Resource Development Quarterly* 12, no. 1 (Spring 2001): 73–90.

43. Andreas Putra, "Evaluating Training Programs: An Exploratory Study of Transfer of Learning onto the Job at Hotel A and Hotel B, Sydney, Australia," *Journal of Hospitality and Tourism Management* 11, no. 1 (April 2004): 77–78; Thomas Hoffman, "Simulations Revitalize e-Learning," *Computerworld* 37, no. 31 (August 4, 2003): 26–28.

44. Jathan Janove, "Use It or Lose It," *HR Magazine* 47, no. 4 (April 2002): 99–104; Max Montesino, "Strategic Alignment of Training, Transfer-Enhancing Behaviors, and Training Usage: A Posttraining Study," *Human Resource Development Quarterly* 13, no. 1 (Spring 2002): 89–108; Siriporn Yamnill and Gary McLean, "Theories Supporting Transfer of Training," *Human Resource Development Quarterly* 12, no. 2 (Summer 2001): 195–208.

45. Delahoussaye, "Show Me the Results," 28–29; van Brakel, "Why ROI Isn't Enough," 72–74.

46. Richard J. Wagner and Robert J. Weigand, "Can the Value of Training Be Measured? A Simplified Approach to Evaluating Training," *The Health Care Manager* 23, no. 1 (January–March 2004): 71–79; van Brakel, "Why ROI Isn't Enough," 72–74; Sarah Fister Gale, "Measuring the ROI of E-Learning," *Workforce* 81, no. 8 (August 2002): 74–77; Earl Honeycutt, Kiran Karande, Ashraf Attia, and Steven Maurer, "A Utility-Based Framework for Evaluating the Financial Impact of Sales Force Training Programs," *Journal of Personal Selling and Sales Management* 21, no. 3 (Summer 2001): 229–238.

47. "Three Quick and Easy Ways to Gauge Your Training Outcomes," *IOMA's Report on Managing Training & Development* (January 2005): 4–5; "Use This Eight-Step Process

to Predict the ROI of Your Training Programs," *IOMA's Human Resource Department Management Report* (December 2004): 4–5; Ellen Drost, Colette Frayne, Keven Lowe, and J. Michael Geringer, "Benchmarking Training and Development Practices: A Multi-Country Comparative Analysis," *Human Resource Management* 41, no. 1 (Spring 2002): 67–86; Daniel McMurrer, Mark Van Buren, and William Woodwell, "Making the Commitment," *Training and Development* 54, no. 1 (January 2000): 41–48.

48. Lisa Bertagnoli, "Basic Training: Orientation Is Proving to Be an Important First Step in Establishing Employee Bonds That Last," *WWD* (September 30, 2004): 40S; Jonathan Thom, "Creating Effective Orientation Programs," *San Diego Business Journal* 25, no. 33 (August 16, 2004): A6; Howard Klein and Natasha Weaver, "The Effectiveness of an Organizational-Level Orientation Training Program in the Socialization of New Hires," *Personnel Psychology* 53, no. 1 (Spring 2000): 47–66.

49. Mike Frost, "Creative New Employee Orientation Programs," *HR Magazine* 47, no. 8 (August 2002): 120–121; Marilyn Moats Kennedy, "Setting the Right Tone, Right Away," *Across the Board* 36, no. 4 (April 1999): 51–52.

50. Emmanuella Plakoyiannaki, Nikolaos Tzokas, Pavlos Dimitratos, and Michael Saren, "How Critical Is Employee Orientation for Customer Relationship Management? Insights from a Case Study," *Journal of Management Studies* 45, no. 2 (March 2008): 268–293.

51. Canadian Council on Learning, June 12, 2008, "Projection: 15 Million Canadian Adults with Low Literacy by 2031," http://www.ccl-cca.ca/CCL/Newsroom/Releases/20080612 ReadingtheFuture.htm, retrieved July 30, 2009.

52. "Corporate America Can't Write," *Work & Family Newsbrief* (January 2005): 4; Matt Bolch, "School at Work," *Training* 39, no. 2 (February 2002); Slav Kanyba, "Community Colleges React to Job-Training Request," *San Fernando Valley Business Journal* 9, no. 2 (June 7, 2004): 1–2.

53. Eduardo Salas, Diana R. Nichols, and James E. Driskell, "Testing Three Team Training Strategies in Intact Teams: A Meta-Analysis," *Small Group Research* (August 2007); "What Makes Teams Work?" *HRfocus* 79, no. 4 (April 2002): S1–S3; John Annett, David Cunningham, and Peter Mathias-Jones, "A Method for Measuring Team Skills," *Ergonomics* 43, no. 8 (August 2000): 1076–1094.

54. "Behavior-Based Sales Team Training Produces a 56% Increase in Revenues," *Managing Training & Development* (April 2004): 1.

55. Lorraine Mirabella, "Productivity Gains in Maryland Mean Less Hiring But More Job Cross-Training," *The Baltimore Sun* (via Knight-Ridder/Tribune Business News) (April 17, 2004).

56. "Ethics Codes and Ethics Training Issue Brief," Business for Social Responsibility (March 2005): www.bsr.org/research/issue-brief-details. cfm?DocumentID=50967; Nan Demars, "Office Ethics: News from the Front Lines," *Office Pro* 68, no. 3 (April 2008): 28–31.

57. Gary Stern, "Small Slights Bring Big Problems," *Workforce* 81, no. 8 (August 2002): 17; Bill Leonard, "Ways to Tell If a Diversity Program Is Measuring Up," *HR Magazine* 47, no. 7 (July 2002): 21.

58. Wallace Immen, "Melting pot gets culture lessons," *The Globe and Mail*, March 26, 2008, C1.

Appraising and Improving Performance

CHAPTER 8

After studying this chapter, you should be able to

[OUTCOME] 1 Explain the purposes of performance appraisals and the reasons they can sometimes fail. Identify the characteristics of an effective appraisal program.

[OUTCOME] 2 Describe the different sources of appraisal information.

[OUTCOME] 3 Explain the various methods used for performance evaluation.

[OUTCOME] 4 Outline the characteristics of an effective performance appraisal interview.

In the preceding chapters, we have discussed some of the most effective methods available to managers for acquiring and developing top-notch employees. But talented employees are not enough—successful organizations are particularly adept at engaging their workforce to achieve goals that benefit the organization as well as the individuals.

In this chapter, we turn to performance appraisal programs, which are a helpful tool organizations can use to maintain and enhance their productivity and facilitate progress toward their strategic goals. Although we will focus mainly on formal performance appraisal procedures, the processes of managing and evaluating performance can be informal as well—and should be. In addition to formally appraising their employees in writing at regular intervals, as you will learn in this chapter, managers should offer them continual on-the-job feedback. It is safe to say that the ultimate success or failure of a performance appraisal program depends on the philosophy underlying it, its connection with the firm's business goals, and the attitudes and skills of those responsible for its administration. Many different methods can be used to gather information about employee performance. Gathering information is only one step in the appraisal process. The information must be evaluated in the context of the organization's needs and communicated to employees so that it will result in high levels of performance.

performance appraisal
A process, typically performed annually by a supervisor for a subordinate, designed to help employees understand their roles, objectives, expectations, and performance success

performance management
The process of creating a work environment in which people can perform to the best of their abilities

PERFORMANCE APPRAISAL PROGRAMS[1]

The **performance appraisal** can be defined as a process—typically delivered annually, biannually, or sometimes quarterly by a supervisor to a subordinate—designed to help employees understand their roles, objectives, expectations, and performance success.

In addition, new employees are often put on probationary status for a period of time and evaluated 30, 60, or 90 days after being hired, with their continued employment contingent upon their performing satisfactorily. **Performance management** is the process of creating a work environment in which people can perform to the best of their abilities. It is a whole work system that begins when a job is defined. Advocates see these HR programs as among the most logical means to appraise, develop, and effectively utilize the knowledge and abilities of employees. However, as we have indicated, a growing number of observers point out that performance appraisals frequently fall short of their potential.

In an ongoing survey of employee attitudes by the HR consulting firm Watson Wyatt, only 30 percent of employees said they thought their company's performance management process actually improved employee performance; only one in five thought it helped poorly performing employees do better.[2]

The push toward teamwork, continuous improvement, learning, and the like has caused numerous organizations to rethink their approach to appraisal. Some have warned that performance appraisal may discourage teamwork because it frequently focuses on individual achievement that produces a self-focus rather than a team focus. Others contend that appraisals are useful only at the extremes—for highly effective or highly ineffective employees—and are not as useful for the majority of employees in the middle. Still others point out that appraisals often focus on short-term achievements rather than long-term improvement and learning. They are sometimes too subjective or inconsistent or autocratic in that they create a distance between managers and employees rather than creating a team environment. Companies such as Xerox, Motorola, and Procter & Gamble have modified their performance appraisals to better acknowledge the importance of teamwork, continuous improvement, quality, and the like. Each of these issues is discussed at greater length throughout the chapter.[3]

THE PURPOSES OF PERFORMANCE APPRAISAL

It might seem at first glance that performance appraisals are used for a rather narrow purpose—to evaluate who is doing a good job (or not). But in reality performance appraisals are one of the most versatile tools available to managers. They can serve many purposes that benefit both the organization and the employee whose performance is being appraised.

Figure 8.1 shows the most common uses of performance appraisals. In general, these can be classified as either *administrative* or *developmental*.

Administrative Purposes

From the standpoint of administration, appraisal programs provide input that can be used for the entire range of HRM activities. For example, research has shown that performance appraisals are used most widely as a basis for compensation decisions. The practice of "pay-for-performance"—basing employees' pay on their achievements—is found in all types of organizations, and studies have shown employees who earn performance-based pay are more satisfied.[4]

Performance appraisals are also directly related to a number of other major HR functions, such as promotions, transfers, and layoff decisions. Performance appraisal data may also be used in HR planning, in determining the relative worth of jobs under a job evaluation program, and as criteria for recruiting particular types of employees and validating selection tests. Performance appraisals also provide a "paper trail" for documenting HRM actions that can result in legal action. Employers must maintain accurate, objective employee performance records in order to defend themselves against possible charges of discrimination when it comes to promotions, salaries, and terminations. Finally, it is important to recognize that the success of the entire HR program depends on knowing how the performance of employees compares with the goals established for them. This knowledge is best derived from a carefully planned and administered HR appraisal program.

Although appraisals often fall short of perfect, good appraisal systems have the capability to influence employee behaviour and improve organizational performance. Indeed, research shows that organizations with strong performance management systems are 40 to 50 percent more likely to outperform their competitors in the areas of revenue growth, productivity, profitability, and market value.[5]

FIGURE 8.1 ▽

Purposes for Performance Appraisal

DEVELOPMENTAL
- Provide performance feedback
- Identify individual strengths/weaknesses
- Recognize individual performance
- Assist in goal identification
- Evaluate goal achievement
- Identify individual training needs
- Determine organizational training needs
- Reinforce authority structure
- Allow employees to discuss concerns
- Improve communication
- Provide a forum for leaders to help

ADMINISTRATIVE
- Document personnel decisions
- Determine promotion candidates
- Determine transfers and assignments
- Identify poor performance
- Decide on retention or termination
- Decide on layoffs
- Validate selection criteria
- Meet legal requirements
- Evaluate training programs/progress
- Personnel planning
- Make reward/compensation decisions

Developmental Purposes

From the standpoint of individual development, appraisal provides the feedback essential for discussing an employee's strengths and weaknesses as well as improving his or her performance. Regardless of the employee's level of performance, the appraisal process provides managers and employees with the opportunity to discuss ways to build on their strengths, eliminate potential weaknesses, identify problems, and set new goals for achieving high performance. Performance appraisals are also used to develop training and development plans for employees. By taking a developmental approach to appraisals, managers help employees understand that the appraisals are being conducted to improve their future competencies and further their careers and are not being conducted simply to judge them based on their past performance. Having a sound basis for improving performance is one of the major benefits of an appraisal program.

Companies such as Best Buy and EDS have redesigned their performance appraisal systems to focus more on employee development and learning. EDS, for example, integrated its performance appraisal system to work in concert with the company's learning and career management objectives. The new system, called the Career Resource System, includes a detailed job description, performance review, and career planner to track employees' long-term goals, as well as access to the company's automated career library. The system is ultimately linked to the company's succession policies. By creating this overall system, EDS hopes to shift the role of manager from that of "judge" to one of "coach."[6]

WHY APPRAISAL PROGRAMS SOMETIMES FAIL

Although performance appraisals can be a very useful and powerful tool to managers, in actual practice and for a number of reasons, formal appraisal programs sometimes yield disappointing results. Figure 8.2 shows that the primary culprits

FIGURE 8.2

Let Me Count the Ways

There are many reasons why performance appraisal systems might not be effective. Some of the most common problems include the following:

- Inadequate preparation on the part of the manager
- Employee is not given clear objectives at the beginning of performance period
- Manager may not be able to observe performance or have all the information
- Performance standards may not be clear
- Inconsistency in ratings among supervisors or other raters
- Manager rating personality rather than performance
- The halo effect, contrast effect, or some other perceptual bias
- Inappropriate time span (either too short or too long)
- Overemphasis on uncharacteristic performance
- Inflated ratings because managers do not want to deal with "bad news"
- Subjective or vague language in written appraisals
- Organizational politics or personal relationships cloud judgments
- No thorough discussion of causes of performance problems
- Manager may not be trained at evaluation or giving feedback
- No follow-up and coaching after the evaluation

Sources: Patricia Evres, "Problems to Avoid during Performance Evaluations," *Air Conditioning, Heating & Refrigeration News* 216, no. 16 (August 19, 2002); 24–26; Clinton Longnecker and Dennis Gioia, "The Politics of Executive Appraisals," *Journal of Compensation and Benefits* 10, no. 2 (1994): 5–11; "Seven Deadly Sins of Performance Appraisals," *Supervisory Management* 39, no. 1 (1994): 7–8.

include lack of top management information and support, unclear performance standards, biased ratings because managers lack training, too many time-consuming forms to complete, and use of the program for conflicting purposes. For example, if an appraisal program is used to determine an employee's future pay and at the same time to motivate the person to perform better, the two purposes can end up conflicting with one another. Often when salary decisions are discussed during a performance appraisal, they tend to become the dominant topic of conversation, and managers spend a lot of time justifying their pay decisions. As a result, ways to improve the employee's future job performance get less discussion.

As with all HR practices, if the support of a firm's top managers is lacking, the appraisal program will not be successful. Even the best-conceived program will not work in an environment where appraisers are not encouraged by their superiors to take the program seriously. To underscore the importance of this responsibility, top management should announce that effectiveness in appraising subordinates is a standard by which the appraisers themselves will be evaluated.

Other reasons performance appraisal programs can fail to yield the desired results include the following:

1. There is little face-to-face discussion between the manager and the employee being appraised.
2. The relationship between the employee's job description and the criteria on the appraisal form is not clear.
3. Managers feel that little or no benefit will be derived from the time and energy they spend on the process, or they are concerned only with bad performances.
4. Managers dislike the face-to-face confrontation of appraisal interviews.
5. Managers are not sufficiently adept at rating employees or providing them with appraisal feedback.
6. The judgmental role of appraisal conflicts with the helping role of developing employees.
7. The appraisal is just a once-a-year event, and there is little follow-up afterward.

In many organizations, performance appraisals are conducted only once a year. And while this is appropriate in many circumstances, an increasing number of organizations are finding value in conducting them on a semiannual and even quarterly basis. An important principle of performance appraisal is that continual feedback and employee coaching must be a regularly occurring activity. The annual or semi-annual performance review should simply be a logical extension of the day-to-day managerial process. It has been found that providing employees with feedback on a continual basis not only improves their performance, but also helps them know where they stand in terms of their performance. As a result, the anxiety they experience during formal appraisals is often alleviated. Some organizations do not perform formal evaluations and use coaching, individual development plans, or other feedback systems instead.

One of the main concerns employees have relates to the fairness of the performance appraisal systems of their firms. Organizational politics, a firm's culture, the orientation of its managers, history, and current competitive conditions can all affect how managers conduct and rate their employees.[7] For example, managers sometimes inflate evaluations because they want to obtain higher salaries for their employees or because higher ratings for their subordinates make them look good as supervisors. Alternatively, managers might want to get rid of troublesome employees by inflating their ratings and passing them off to another department. Even when appraisals are supposed to be confidential, employees often have a keen sense about whether the process is fair or not, or at least they think they do. Employees who believe the system is unfair are likely to consider the appraisal interview a waste of time and leave the interview feeling frustrated and cynical. Also, they may view compliance with the appraisal system as perfunctory and thus play only a passive role during the interview process. By addressing these employee concerns during the planning stage of the appraisal process and reassuring them that they can meet the requirements, and will be rewarded accordingly, an appraisal program is more likely to be successful.[8]

DEVELOPING AN EFFECTIVE APPRAISAL PROGRAM

The HR department ordinarily has the primary responsibility for overseeing and coordinating a firm's appraisal program. However, managers from the company's operating departments must also be actively involved, particularly when it comes to helping establish the objectives for the program. Furthermore, employees are more likely to accept and be satisfied with the performance appraisal program when they have the chance to participate in its development. Their concerns about the fairness and accuracy of the program insofar as it determines their raises, promotions, and the like tend to be alleviated somewhat when they have been involved at the planning stage and have helped develop the performance standards themselves.

WHAT ARE THE PERFORMANCE STANDARDS?

Before any appraisal is conducted, the standards by which performance is to be evaluated should be clearly defined and communicated to the employee. As discussed in Chapter 4, these standards should be based on job-related requirements derived from job analysis and reflected in an employee's job description and job specifications. When performance standards are properly established, they help translate an organization's goals and objectives into job requirements that communicate to employees the definitions of acceptable and unacceptable performance levels.

As shown in Figure 8.3, there are four basic considerations in establishing performance standards: strategic relevance, criterion deficiency, criterion contamination, and reliability.

Strategic Relevance

Strategic relevance refers to the extent to which the standards of an appraisal relate to the strategic objectives of the organization in which they are applied. For example, if an organization has established a standard that "95 percent of all customer complaints are to be resolved in one day," then it is relevant for the customer service representatives to be held to this standard when they are evaluated. Companies such as 3M have strategic objectives to the effect that 25 to 30 percent of their sales are to be generated from products developed within the past five years. These objectives are then translated into performance standards for their employees. General Motors and Whirlpool's strategic objectives include cost, quality, and speed, and the two companies have developed metrics to identify and compare their performance around the world on these measures. A strategy-driven performance appraisal process also provides the documentation HR managers need to justify various training expenses in order to close any gaps between employees' current skills and those they will need in the future to execute the firm's strategy.[9]

Criterion Deficiency

A second consideration in establishing performance standards is the extent to which the standards capture the entire range of an employee's responsibilities.

FIGURE **8.3**

Establishing Performance Standards

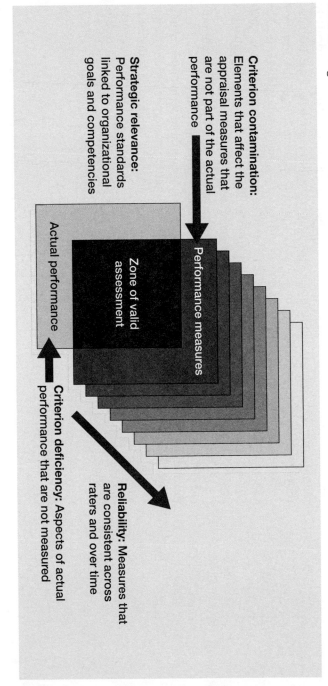

Criterion contamination: Elements that affect the appraisal measures that are not part of the actual performance

Strategic relevance: Performance standards linked to organizational goals and competencies

Performance measures

Zone of valid assessment

Actual performance

Reliability: Measures that are consistent across raters and over time

Criterion deficiency: Aspects of actual performance that are not measured

When performance standards focus on a single criterion (such as sales revenues) to the exclusion of other important but less quantifiable performance dimensions (such as customer service), then the appraisal system is said to suffer from criterion deficiency.[10]

Criterion Contamination

Just as performance criteria can be deficient, they can also be contaminated. There are factors outside an employee's control that can influence his or her performance. A comparison of performance of production workers, for example, should not be contaminated by the fact that some work with newer machines than others do. A comparison of the performance of travelling salespeople should not be contaminated by the fact that territories differ in sales potential.[11]

Reliability

As we discussed in Chapter 6, reliability refers to the stability or consistency of a standard, or the extent to which individuals tend to maintain a certain level of performance over time. In terms of appraisal ratings, reliability can be measured by correlating two sets of ratings made by a single rater or by two different raters. For example, two managers would rate the same individual and estimate his or her suitability for a promotion. Their ratings would then be compared to determine interrater reliability.

A new process some companies are now using to make sure managers are rating employees consistently is called **calibration**. During calibration meetings, a group of supervisors, led by their managers and facilitated by a HR professional, discuss the performance of individual employees to ensure all managers apply similar standards to all of the firm's employees. The supervisors begin the process by rating employees whose performances are especially good or especially poor. They then attempt to rate employees who lie more in the middle and try to achieve a

calibration
A process whereby managers meet to discuss the performance of individual employees to ensure their employee appraisals are in line with one another

consensus on their performance. Initially, the ratings are likely to vary considerably simply because some managers are hard raters and others are not. Over subsequent evaluation periods and calibration meetings, however, the ratings should begin to converge, or become more similar. Calibration meetings can be particularly helpful after a merger or acquisition—especially one that is global. Why? Because differences in the corporate cultures and the appraisal standards of the formerly separate companies can cause the same employees to be rated quite differently. For example, when Lawson Software grew from 1,400 employees in 3 countries to 4,000 employees in 30 countries, it successfully used calibration to be sure its managers across the globe were assessing employees accurately.[12]

Performance standards also permit managers to specify and communicate precise information to employees regarding quality and quantity of output. This is why the standards should be defined in quantifiable and measurable terms and written down. For example, "the ability and willingness to handle customer orders" is not as good a performance standard as "all customer orders will be filled in four hours with a 98 percent accuracy rate." When the standard is expressed in specific, measurable terms, comparing an employee's performance against the standard results in a more accurate and justifiable appraisal.

Specific, measurable job standards help remove vagueness and subjectivity from performance appraisals.

LEGAL ISSUES

Since some performance appraisals are used for HRM actions, they must meet certain legal requirements. Employers might face legal challenges to their appraisal systems when appraisals indicate an employee's performance is acceptable or above-average performance, but then the person is later passed over for promotion, disciplined for poor performance, discharged, or laid off from the organization. In these cases, the performance appraisals can undermine the legitimacy of the subsequent personnel decision. Intel, for example, was taken to court by a group of former employees on grounds that the performance appraisal system (used for layoff decisions) was unreliable and invalid. Other companies such as Goodyear and Ford have also faced legal battles in the United States because their performance appraisals were viewed as discriminatory against older workers.[13] In light of cases such as these, performance appraisals should meet the following legal guidelines:

- Performance ratings must be job related, with performance standards developed through a job analysis.
- Employees must be given a written copy of their job standards in advance of their appraisals.
- Managers who conduct the appraisals must be able to observe the behaviour they are rating. This implies having measurable standards with which to compare employee behaviour.
- Supervisors should be trained to use the appraisal form correctly. They should be instructed as to how to apply the appraisal standards when making judgments.
- The appraisals should be discussed openly with employees and counselling or corrective guidance offered to help poor performers improve their performance.
- An appeals procedure should be established to enable employees to express their disagreement with the appraisals.[14]

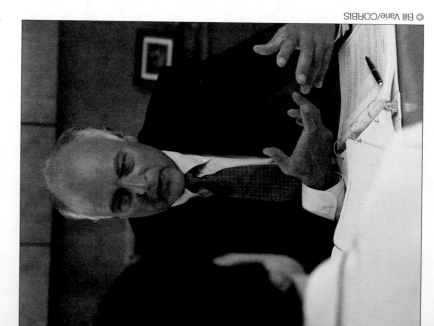

Employers must ensure that managers and supervisors document appraisals and reasons for subsequent HRM actions. This information may prove decisive should an employee take legal action. An employer's credibility is strengthened when it can support performance appraisal ratings by documenting instances of poor performance.

WHO SHOULD APPRAISE PERFORMANCE?

Just as there are multiple standards by which to evaluate performance, there are also multiple candidates for appraising performance. Given the complexity of today's jobs, it is often unrealistic to presume that one person can fully observe and evaluate an employee's performance. At IBM, employees with high potential are regularly reviewed by a broad cross-section of the company's leaders, not just their immediate bosses. As shown in Figure 8.4, raters may include supervisors, peers, team members, self, subordinates, customers, vendors, and suppliers. Each may be more or less useful for the administrative and developmental purposes we discussed earlier. Companies such as Cigna, Black & Decker, and Disney have used a multiple-rater approach—or 360-degree appraisal—to evaluate employee performance.[15] We will talk more about 360-degree appraisal at the end of this section.

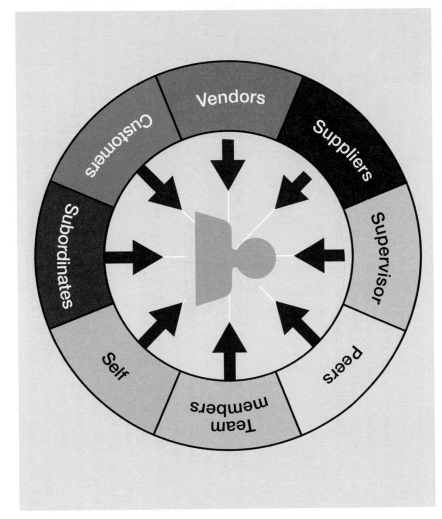

FIGURE 8.4

Alternative Sources of Appraisal

OUTCOME 2

Manager/Supervisor Appraisal

Manager and/or supervisor appraisal has been the traditional approach to evaluating an employee's performance. In most instances, supervisors are in the best position to perform this function, although it may not always be possible for them to do so. Managers often complain that they do not have the time to fully observe the performance of employees. These managers must then rely on performance records to evaluate an employee's performance. If reliable and valid measures are unavailable, the appraisal may be less than accurate. (Recall our earlier discussion of criterion deficiency and criterion contamination.) In addition, research has shown that the ratings managers give employees they have known for less than one year are less reliable.[16]

When a supervisor appraises employees independently, provision is often made for a review of the appraisals by the supervisor's superior. Having appraisals reviewed by a supervisor's superior reduces the chance of superficial or biased evaluations.

manager and/or supervisor appraisal
A performance appraisal done by an employee's manager and often reviewed by a manager one level higher

Self-Appraisal

Sometimes employees are asked to evaluate themselves on a self-appraisal form. The **self-appraisal** is beneficial when managers seek to increase an employee's involvement in the review process. A self-appraisal system requires an employee to complete the appraisal form prior to the performance interview. At a minimum, this gets the employee thinking about his or her strengths and weaknesses and may lead to discussions about barriers to effective performance. During the performance interview, the manager and the employee discuss job performance and agree on a final appraisal. This approach also works well when the manager and the employee jointly establish future performance goals or employee development plans. Critics of self-appraisal argue that self-raters are more lenient than managers in their assessments and tend to present themselves in a highly favourable light. There is also evidence that self-appraisals can lead employees to believe that they will have more influence over the appraisal's outcome. If that expectation is not met, the employee can become frustrated. For this reason, self-appraisals may be best for developmental purposes rather than for administrative decisions. Used in conjunction with other methods, self-appraisals can be a valuable source of appraisal information. They at least serve as a catalyst for discussion during the appraisal.[17]

self-appraisal
A performance appraisal done by the employee being evaluated, generally on an appraisal form completed by the employee prior to the performance interview

Subordinate Appraisal

Subordinate appraisals have been used by both large and small organizations to give managers feedback on how their subordinates view them.[18] Subordinates are in a good position to evaluate their managers because they are in frequent contact with their superiors and occupy a unique position from which to observe many performance-related behaviours. Subordinate appraisals have also been shown to improve the performance of managers. The performance dimensions judged most appropriate for subordinates to appraise include a manager's leadership, oral communication, delegation of authority, coordination of team efforts, and interest in his or her subordinates. However, dimensions related to managers' specific job tasks, such as planning and organizing, budgeting, creativity, and analytical ability, are not usually considered appropriate dimensions for subordinates to appraise. Because subordinate appraisals give employees power over their bosses, managers may be hesitant to endorse such a system, particularly when it might be used as a basis for compensation decisions. However, when the information is used for developmental purposes, managers tend to be more open to the idea. Available evidence suggests that when managers heed

subordinate appraisal
A performance appraisal of a superior by an employee, which is more appropriate for developmental than for administrative purposes

the advice of their subordinates, their own performance can improve substantially. Nevertheless, to avoid potential problems, subordinate appraisals should be submitted anonymously and combined across several individual raters.[19]

Peer Appraisal

Individuals of equal rank who work together are increasingly asked to evaluate each other. A **peer appraisal** provides information that differs to some degree from ratings by a superior, since an employee's peers often see different dimensions of his or her performance. Peers can readily identify leadership and interpersonal skills along with other strengths and weaknesses of their coworkers. For example, a superior asked to rate a patrol officer on a dimension such as "dealing with the public" might not have had much opportunity to observe it. Fellow officers, on the other hand, have the opportunity to observe this behaviour regularly.

One advantage of peer appraisals is the belief that they furnish more accurate and valid information than appraisals by superiors. The supervisor often sees employees on their best behaviour, while those who work with their fellow employees on a regular basis may see a more realistic picture. With peer appraisals, coworkers complete an evaluation on the employee. The forms are then usually compiled into a single profile, which is given to the supervisor for use in the final appraisal. For employees who have trouble confronting their coworkers about problems, the reviews provide a forum in which to address issues and resolve conflicts. They also provide an opportunity to hand out praise.[20]

Despite the evidence that peer appraisals are possibly the most accurate method of judging employee behaviour, there are reasons that they have not been used more frequently.[21] The reasons commonly cited include the following:

1. Peer ratings are simply a popularity contest.
2. Managers are reluctant to give up control over the appraisal process.
3. Those receiving low ratings might retaliate against their peers.
4. Peers rely on stereotypes in ratings.

When peers, such as sales associates, for example, are in competition with one another, peer appraisals should not be used to make administrative decisions such as those involving salary or bonuses. Employers using peer appraisals must also be sure to safeguard confidentiality in handling the review forms. Any breach of confidentiality can create interpersonal rivalries or hurt feelings and foster hostility among fellow employees.

Team Appraisal

An extension of the peer appraisal is the **team appraisal**. In a team setting, it may be nearly impossible to separate out an individual's contribution. Advocates of team appraisals argue that, in such cases, individual appraisals can be dysfunctional because they detract from the critical issues of the team. To address this issue, organizations have begun developing team appraisals to evaluate the performance of their teams as a whole. These companies believe that team appraisals can help break down barriers between individual employees and encourage a joint effort on their part.

Much of the interest in team appraisals grew out of company commitments to total quality management (TQM) in the 1980s. But the principles and practices are no less relevant today. At its root, TQM is a control system that involves setting standards (based on customer requirements), measuring a firm's performance against those standards, and identifying opportunities for continuous improvement. In this regard, TQM and performance appraisals complement one another. However,

peer appraisal

A performance appraisal done by one's fellow employees, generally on forms that are compiled into a single profile for use in the performance interview conducted by the employee's manager

Using the Internet

Review the advantages and limitations of the peer appraisal used by nurses at:

http://nursing.advanceweb .com/editorial/content /editorial.aspx?cc=191092

team appraisal

A performance appraisal, based on TQM concepts, that recognizes team accomplishment rather than individual performance

Some managers give their teams autonomy but hold them accountable for results.

customer appraisal

A performance appraisal that, like team appraisal, is based on TQM concepts and seeks evaluation from both external and internal customers

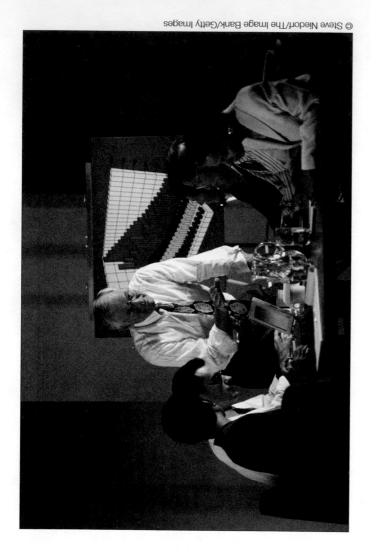

© Steve Niedorf/The Image Bank/Getty Images

a basic tenet of TQM is that a firm's performance is best understood at the level of the system as a whole, whereas performance appraisals traditionally focus on individual performance.[22] Frequently, the system is complemented by the use of team incentives or group variable pay. (See Chapters 10 and 16.)

Customer Appraisal

Also driven by TQM concerns, an increasing number of organizations use internal and external **customer appraisals** as a source of performance appraisal information. External customers' evaluations, of course, have been used for some time to appraise restaurant personnel. However, companies such as FedEx and BMW Canada are among the companies that have utilized external customers as well. Poor customer appraisals undoubtedly explain why some firms, including Dell and others, have reconsidered offshoring their customer service functions. Other companies survey their vendors and suppliers as part of the appraisal process. By including the firm's business partners in the performance reviews, managers hope to produce more objective evaluations, more effective employees, more satisfied customers, and better business performance.[23]

In contrast to external customers, internal customers include anyone inside the organization who depends on an employee's work output. For example, managers who rely on the HR department for selection and training services would be candidates for conducting internal customer evaluations of that department. For both developmental and administrative purposes, internal customers can provide extremely useful feedback about the value added by an employee or team of employees.

PUTTING IT ALL TOGETHER: 360-DEGREE APPRAISAL

As mentioned previously, companies combine various sources of performance appraisal information to create multirater—or 360-degree—appraisal and feedback systems. Jobs are multifaceted, and different people see different things. As the name implies, 360-degree feedback is intended to provide employees with as accurate a view of their performance as possible by getting input from all angles: supervisors, peers, subordinates, customers, and the like. Although in the beginning, 360-degree systems were purely developmental and were restricted mainly to management and career development, they have migrated to performance appraisal and other administrative applications.

Because the system combines more information than a typical performance appraisal, it can become administratively complex. For that reason, organizations have recently begun using performance management software to compile and aggregate the information.[24] For example, Workstream 7.0 developed by Workstream, Inc. gives managers a single view of all their talent management information: performance reviews, 360-degree assessments, compensation planning, development data, and succession planning, all unified in one application.[25] Figure 8.5 shows a list of pros and cons of 360-degree appraisal. When Intel established a 360-degree system, the company observed the following safeguards to ensure its maximum quality and acceptance:

- *Assure anonymity.* Make certain that no employee ever knows how any evaluation team member responded. (The supervisor's rating is an exception to this rule.)
- *Make respondents accountable.* Supervisors should discuss each evaluation team member's input, letting each member know whether he or she used the rating scales appropriately, whether his or her responses were reliable, and how other participants rated the employee.
- *Prevent "gaming" of the system.* Some individuals may try to help or hurt an employee by giving either too high or too low an evaluation. Team members may try to collude with one another by agreeing to give each other uniformly high ratings. Supervisors should check for obviously invalid responses.

FIGURE **8.5** √

Pros and Cons of 360-Degree Appraisal

PROS

- The system is more comprehensive in that responses are gathered from multiple perspectives.
- Quality of information is better. (Quality of respondents is more important than quantity.)
- It complements TQM initiatives by emphasizing internal/external customers and teams.
- It may lessen bias/prejudice since feedback comes from more people, not one individual.
- Feedback from peers and others may increase employee self-development.

CONS

- The system is complex in combining all the responses.
- Feedback can be intimidating and cause resentment if an employee feels the respondents have "ganged up."
- There may be conflicting opinions, though they may all be accurate from the respective standpoints.
- The system requires training to work effectively.
- Employees may collude or "game" the system by giving invalid evaluations to one another.
- Appraisers may not be accountable if their evaluations are anonymous.

Sources: Compiled from David A. Waldman, Leanne E. Atwater, and David Antonioni, "Has 360-Degree Feedback Gone Amok?" *Academy of Management Executive* 12, no. 2 (May 1998): 86–94; Bruce Pfau, Ira Kay, Kenneth Nowak, and Jai Ghorpade, "Does 360-Degree Feedback Negatively Affect Company Performance?" *HR Magazine* 47, no. 6 (June 2002): 54–59; Maury Peiperl, "Getting 360-Degree Feedback Right," *Harvard Business Review* 79, no. 1 (January 2001): 142–147; Joyce E. Bono and Amy E. Colbert, "Understanding Responses to Multi-Source Feedback: The Role of Core Self-Evaluations," *Personnel Psychology* 58, no. 1 (Spring 2005): 171–205.

- *Use statistical procedures.* Use weighted averages or other quantitative approaches to combining evaluations. Supervisors should be careful about using subjective combinations of data, which could undermine the system.

- *Identify and quantify biases.* Check for prejudices or preferences related to age, gender, ethnicity, or other group factors.[26]

Based on the experiences of companies such as Canadian Tire, described in the Reality Check, it appears that 360-degree feedback can provide a valuable approach to performance appraisal. Its success, as with any appraisal technique, depends on how managers use the information and how fairly employees are treated.

Reality CHECK

Canadian Tire 360-Degree Matrix

"Accentuate the positive; build on leadership strengths" is the principal theme of leadership performance evaluation and development conducted by the Canadian Tire Corporation as described by Janice Wismer, vice-president of human resources. Canadian Tire is a network of interrelated businesses with retail, financial, and petroleum interests. About 45,000 employees work in 1,000 retail stores across Canada.

The customized 360-degree feedback process used at Canadian Tire is research based and designed to build a cadre of great leaders. The first step in the design of the 360-degree feedback instrument was to benchmark other organizations that had effective 360-degree feedback processes. Twenty-seven key employees at Canadian Tire were interviewed to identify the attributes of their great leaders as measured by the standards of the organization. These key leadership attributes were then discussed and evaluated in workshops with important stakeholders. A total of 16 competencies were identified: seven related to "who one is"—characteristics such as *trustworthy, passionate, and curious.* Nine others focused on "what one can do for the team, business, and enterprise"—such as make *strategic choices, motivate and celebrate, communicate authentically.*

To date, about 170 managers have been assessed by an average of nine colleagues, including peers, subordinates, and bosses. Colleagues complete a self-survey, and all feedback assessment is analyzed relative to their own organization and to industry standards, which are maintained in a database. A confidential feedback report is given to each individual.

In addition to the generation of individual reports, an aggregate one-page executive summary is produced. The report, presented as a matrix, provides a visual summary colour-coded under each competency comparing aggregate feedback data for all individuals in a defined business unit. The sample 360-degree matrix shown below lists key attributes across the horizontal axis and the employee's feedback along the vertical axis. In order to maintain confidentiality, identifiers are assigned to the supervisors and managers so that they can see their relative standing but without knowing the identity of the other employees. In the colour-coding, red signifies a weak performance, yellow is an average performance, and green indicates exceptional strengths. By using this 360-degree matrix, HR can identify areas where groups of employees need professional development, thus investing training dollars where it matters most. In the example, Executives A, B, and C are perceived as generally excellent across most of the eight areas of interest, while Executives M, N, and O are experiencing considerable difficulty. In addition, most of the executive team performed well in areas 1, 2, and 3, having most difficulty in area 8. In this case, individual development plans may work well for executives having problems in areas 1, 2, and 3, while a group development solution may be best designed for area 8.

According to Ed Haltrecht, Ph.D., CHRP, who specializes in measurement and organizational leadership development, in most organizations when performance feedback is presented, both the employee and the manager focus on the reds—the weaknesses—and try to work out methods of development to improve this

continued

Executive	1. Treats others with respect.	2. Gives credit to others who have contributed or performed well.	3. Shows consistency between words and action.	4. Models the core values of the corporation; leads by example.	5. Treats team members as individuals based on knowledge of their strengths and development needs.	6. Takes actions that build a high level of commitment to work group goals and objectives.	7. Obtains resources so that the team has the knowledge, skills, and experience required to deliver results.	8. Where there is underlying conflict, helps parties involved bring up their issues and get to the heart of the problem.	Mean
A	5.0	4.9	4.9	4.6	4.8	4.6	4.6	4.5	4.7
B	5.0	4.8	4.9	4.9	4.9	4.8	4.3	3.7	4.7
C	5.0	4.7	4.9	4.7	4.7	4.8	4.5	4.2	4.6
D	4.8	4.6	4.2	4.7	4.3	4.7	4.5	4.6	4.4
E	4.7	5.0	4.7	4.2	4.0	4.3	4.6	4.1	4.4
F	4.8	4.3	4.3	4.5	4.4	4.3	4.5	4.2	4.2
G	4.6	4.2	4.2	4.2	4.2	4.1	4.1	4.2	4.2
H	4.5	4.4	4.1	4.2	4.3	3.9	3.9	4.2	4.2
I	4.4	3.8	4.0	4.0	4.0	4.3	4.5	4.1	4.2
J	4.4	4.3	4.3	4.3	4.1	4.2	3.9	3.7	4.2
K	4.6	4.2	4.5	4.0	4.5	4.2	3.6	4.3	4.2
L	3.8	4.4	4.3	4.3	3.7	4.1	4.5	3.9	4.1
M	4.4	4.2	4.4	4.1	4.2	4.0	4.0	4.2	4.1
N	4.3	3.8	4.1	3.9	4.0	4.0	3.5	2.9	3.9
O	3.3	4.1	4.0	3.6	3.8	3.8	3.9	3.3	3.6
Mean	4.5	4.3	4.4	4.2	4.2	4.2	4.1	4.2	

area. What is unique about Canadian Tire is that the focus is on the positive. It has found that improvements in weak areas (provided it is not a fundamental flaw) do not affect overall performance, while improvements in areas of strength bring managers from good to extraordinary. The goal is to identify and strengthen attributes so employees will distinguish and present themselves as extraordinary. Individuals first address any "fundamental flaws"—either a very weak attribute of the individual or, more importantly, elements regarded as critical to the organization. In the sample 360-degree matrix, Executives I, L, N, and C have potential fundamental flaws in areas 1 and 2. If there are no fundamental flaws, then development focuses on building strengths.

This combination has resulted in measurable gains in performance.

This approach is research based. A recently published book, *The Extraordinary Leader: Turning Good Managers into Great Leaders* by John Zenger and Joseph Folkman, presents several significant findings based on 225,000 evaluations of 20,000 people. Poor leaders were identified as those scoring in the bottom 10 percent; extraordinary leaders scored in the top 10 percent. Employee turnover in a call centre was 19 percent for the units managed by the poor managers, 14 percent for the middle group, and 9 percent for the extraordinary leaders. In another case that looked at a bank, net incomes for the bank generated by those groups whose managers were

continued

extraordinary, average, and poor were $7 million, $3.7 million, and $1.9 million respectively. Employee satisfaction indices were at the 80th percentile for top managers compared to the 18th percentile for the bottom-scoring managers. Likewise, union vulnerability indices, which measure how attractive the organization is to a union's membership drive, reflected the 91st percentile for the top-scoring managers compared to the 10th percentile for the poor managers—that is, poorer managers are more likely to attract union interest. Although the pay structure was the same across different departments, those led by the top-scoring managers had employees who were at the 65th percentile in satisfaction with company pay and job security; the employees of average managers were in the 50th percentile; and poor managers' employees scored at the 37th percentile for satisfaction with company pay and job security.

Canadian Tire's leadership development system also recognizes two other significant research findings: first, extraordinary leaders have about three

competencies that they excel at, and developing a few strengths to very high performance levels has a greater impact than improving several competencies from poor to average. Second, competencies travel together and improvement in one leads to significant progress in others. Identifying these companion competencies has proven to be extremely worthwhile. In a nutshell, these are the findings: start with the right set of competencies or attributes; focus on strengths; eliminate any fundamental flaws; and pay attention to companion attributes.

The assessment feedback process at Canadian Tire is seen as a tool for dialogue and for focusing on what makes a great company and what matters in leadership. Those employees who try to improve are given a developmental opportunities guidebook. Canadian Tire has discovered that the best development methods are stretch challenging assignments, coaching and mentoring, personal feedback, talks with consultants, and training programs.

Source: Interview with Janice Wismer and Ed Haltrecht.

TRAINING APPRAISERS

A weakness of many performance appraisal programs is that managers and supervisors are not adequately trained for the appraisal task, and so the feedback they provide their subordinates is not as useful as it might be and can often be meaningless, if not destructive. This is perhaps one reason that some experts believe firms should no longer conduct performance appraisals of their employees. However, training appraisers can vastly improve the performance appraisal process. According to one HR manager: "What's not important is the (appraisal) form or the (measuring) scale. What's important is that managers can objectively observe people's performance and objectively give feedback on that performance." Notwithstanding, in a survey of 55 HR managers from medium and large companies, more than half said their companies did either little or no evaluation of how well their managers do appraisals.[27]

Establishing an Appraisal Plan

A training program for raters is most effective when it follows a systematic process that begins with an explanation of the objectives of the firm's performance appraisal system. It is also important for the rater to know the purpose for which the appraisal is to be used. For example, using the appraisal for compensation decisions rather than development purposes can affect how the rater evaluates the employee, and it may change the rater's opinion of how the appraisal form should be completed. The mechanics of the rating system should also be explained, including how frequently the appraisals are to be conducted, who will conduct them, and what are the standards of performance. In addition, appraisal training should alert raters to the weaknesses and problems of appraisal systems so that they can be avoided.

Eliminating Rater Error

Appraisal training should focus on eliminating the subjective errors made by managers in the rating process. Gary Latham of the University of Toronto and Kenneth Wexle, an American industrial psychologist, stress the importance of performance appraisal training by noting that

[R]egardless of whether evaluations are obtained from multiple appraisers or from only the employee's immediate superior, all appraisers should be trained to reduce errors of judgment that occur when one person evaluates another. This training is necessary because to the degree to which a performance appraisal is biased, distorted, or inaccurate, the probability of increasing the productivity of the employee is greatly decreased. Moreover, wrong decisions could be made regarding whom to promote, retain, or replace, which in turn will penalize the organization's bottom line. In addition, when a performance appraisal is affected by rating errors, the employee may be justified in filing a discrimination charge.[28]

With any rating method, certain types of errors can arise that should be considered. The "halo error" is common with respect to rating scales, especially those that do not include carefully developed descriptions of the employee behaviours being rated. Provision for comments on the rating form tends to reduce halo error. The "horn error" is the opposite of the halo effect. It occurs when a manager focuses on one negative aspect about an employee and generalizes it into an overall poor appraisal rating. A personality conflict between a manager and his or her employees increases the probability of the horn effect, which can lead to a high level of frustration on the employee's part if it is not corrected.[29] Some types of rating errors are *distributional errors* in that they involve a group of ratings given across various employees. For example, raters who are reluctant to assign either extremely high or extremely low ratings commit the **error of central tendency**. In this case, all employees are rated about average. To such raters, it is a good idea to explain that, among large numbers of employees, one should expect to find significant differences in their behaviour, productivity, and other characteristics. In contrast to central tendency errors, it is also common for some raters to give unusually high or low ratings. For example, a manager may erroneously assert, "All my employees are excellent" or "None of my people are good enough." These beliefs give rise to what is called **leniency or strictness error**.[30]

One way to reduce this error is to clearly define the characteristics or dimensions of performance and to provide meaningful descriptions of behaviour, known as "anchors," on the scale. Another approach is to require ratings to conform to a *forced ranking*, a type of system initially developed by GE, purportedly with good results. Managers appraising employees under a *forced distribution* system are required to place a certain percentage of employees into various performance categories. For example, it may be required that 10 percent of ratings be poor (or excellent). This is similar to the requirement in some schools that instructors grade on a curve. A variation of this is *peer ranking*, a system whereby employees in a work group are ranked against one another from best to worst. Although forced distribution and peer ranking may solve leniency and strictness errors, they can create other rating errors—particularly if most employees are performing above standard. Even so, more organizations are using forced ranking systems. However, other companies, including Ford and Goodyear, described in the Business Case, abandoned their forced ranking systems after lawsuits, lower morale, decreased teamwork, and destructive employee competition ensued following their use. In addition, not all corporate cultures are conducive to forced rankings systems. For example, at Starbucks, which fosters a corporate climate based on teamwork, using a forced ranking system would probably be counterproductive. Because of

error of central tendency
A performance rating error in which all employees are rated about average

leniency or strictness error
A performance rating error in which the appraiser tends to give employees either unusually high or unusually low ratings

The Business CASE

Rank and Yank

Research shows that performance appraisals can have a positive financial impact, but there is the potential to lose money if the wrong system is chosen. Goodyear Tire & Rubber Co. abandoned a performance-rating system for salaried employees just as discrimination attorneys were planning to file a class-action lawsuit over it. Goodyear said it was dropping major parts of its program, including its so-called 10-80-10 feature, which essentially graded all salaried employees on a curve. The top 10 percent were rated A, the middle 80 percent were rated B, and the bottom 10 percent were rated C. Those falling in the bottom 10 percent weren't eligible for raises or bonuses and were warned that they might lose their jobs.

The lawsuit alleged that the workers who got C ratings were humiliated and stigmatized among their peers and managers. The legal arm of the AARP, formerly known as the American Association of Retired Persons, joined the lawsuit as co-counsel. Most of the plaintiffs who got C rankings in the case were Goodyear employees who were over 50 years old. "This case will send a clear message that performance rating schemes that target older workers for unfair treatment are illegal and will not be tolerated," said Laurie McCann of AARP.

Jack McGilvrey, a 59-year-old salaried employee, was one of those named in the suit. He claimed that he always received ratings of at least "good/effective performer" in his formal performance reviews up through the late 1990s. In 2000, he was ranked "highly effective." But in February 2001, he was transferred to a new department and shortly thereafter was given a C rating in his performance review. The suit asserted that Mr. McGilvrey didn't deserve the rating and received it as part of Goodyear's plan to discriminate against older employees. He was later dismissed.

The lawsuit against Goodyear has many parallels to one filed in 2001 against Ford Motor Co. In that case, also joined by AARP, the company modified its plans in the face of a legal challenge. The Ford case was eventually settled.

In modifying its white-collar ranking system, Goodyear said it would replace those A, B, and C rankings with the terms *exceeds expectations*, *meets expectations*, and *unsatisfactory*. There will be no requirement to assign those ratings to set percentages of employees. The company also said it was stepping up training for managers so they learn to do a better job of conducting performance reviews. Goodyear has about 28,000 salaried employees around the world.

Source: Timothy Aeppel, "Goodyear Ends Ratings System Ahead of Discrimination Suit," *The Wall Street Journal Online*, September 12, 2002: B8. Copyright © 2002 Dow Jones & Company, Inc. Reprinted with permission of Dow Jones & Company, Inc. in the format Textbook, via Copyright Clearance Center.

recency error

A performance rating error in which the appraisal is based largely on the employee's most recent behaviour rather than on behaviour throughout the appraisal period

the legal issues related to forced ranking, companies that use these methods obviously need to carefully train their appraisers.[31]

Some rating errors are *temporal* in that the performance review is biased either favourably or unfavourably, depending on the way performance information is selected, evaluated, and organized by the rater over time. For example, when the appraisal is based largely on the employee's recent behaviour, good or bad, the rater has committed the **recency error**. Managers who give higher ratings because they believe an employee is "showing improvement" may unwittingly be committing recency error. Without work record documentation for the entire appraisal period, the rater is forced to recall recent employee behaviour to establish the rating. Having the rater routinely document employee accomplishments and failures throughout the whole appraisal period can minimize the recency error. One way for managers to do this is by keeping a diary or a log. Rater training also will help reduce this error.

Contrast error occurs when an employee's evaluation is biased either upward or downward because of another employee's performance, evaluated just previously. For example, an average employee may appear especially productive when compared with a poor performer. However, that same employee may appear unproductive when compared with a star performer. Contrast errors are most likely when raters are required to rank employees in order from the best to the poorest. Employees are evaluated against one another, usually on the basis of some organizational standard or guideline. For example, they may be compared on the basis of their ability to meet production standards or their "overall" ability to perform their job. As with other types of rating errors, contrast error can be reduced through training that focuses on using objective standards and behavioural anchors to appraise performance.[32]

The **similar-to-me error** occurs when appraisers inflate the evaluations of people with whom they have something in common. For example, if both the manager and the employee are from small towns, the manager may unwittingly have a more favourable impression of the employee. The effects of a similar-to-me error can be powerful, and when the similarity is based on race, religion, or gender, it can result in discrimination.

Furthermore, raters should be aware of any stereotypes they may hold toward particular groups—such as male/female or white/black—because the observation and interpretation of performance can be clouded by these stereotypes. For example, one study found that men who experience conflicts between family and work received lower overall performance ratings and lower reward recommendations than men who did not experience such conflicts. Women, on the other hand, were judged no differently, whether they experienced family–work conflicts or not. A host of organizations such as Avenor, a Montreal-based pulp and paper company, have developed formal training programs to reduce the subjective errors commonly made during the rating process. This training can pay off, particularly when participants have the opportunity to (1) observe other managers making errors, (2) actively participate in discovering their own errors, and (3) practise job-related tasks to reduce the errors they tend to make.[33]

Feedback Training

Finally, a training program for raters should provide some general points to consider for planning and providing feedback during the appraisal interview. Managers need to understand that employees want feedback—that is, they want to know how they are doing and how they can improve. They are less eager to be appraised or judged. This is why it is important for their managers to provide them with ongoing feedback and not just "dump on them" during a formal appraisal. Feedback training should cover at least three basic areas: (1) communicating effectively, (2) diagnosing the root causes of performance problems, and (3) setting goals and objectives. A checklist like the one in Highlights in HRM 8.1 can be used to assist supervisors in preparing for the appraisal interview.[34]

PERFORMANCE APPRAISAL METHODS

In the discussion that follows, we will examine in some detail the methods that have found widespread use, and we will briefly touch on other methods that are used less frequently. Performance appraisal methods can be broadly classified as measuring traits, behaviours, or results. Trait approaches continue to be more popular despite their inherent subjectivity. Behavioural approaches provide more action-oriented information to employees and therefore may be best for development. The results-oriented approach is gaining popularity because it focuses on the measurable contributions that employees make to the organization.

[OUTCOME 3]

---

contrast error

A performance rating error in which an employee's evaluation is biased either upward or downward because of comparison with another employee just previously evaluated

similar-to-me error

A performance rating error in which an appraiser inflates the evaluation of an employee because of a mutual personal connection

Highlights in HRM 8.1

Supervisor's Checklist for the Performance Appraisal

Scheduling

1. Schedule the review and notify the employee ten days to two weeks in advance.

2. Ask the employee to prepare for the session by reviewing his or her performance, job objectives, and development goals.

3. Clearly state that this will be the formal annual performance appraisal.

Preparing for the Review

1. Review the performance documentation collected throughout the year. Concentrate on work patterns that have developed.

2. Be prepared to give specific examples of above- or below-average performance.

3. When performance falls short of expectations, determine what changes need to be made. If performance meets or exceeds expectations, plan to discuss this and how to reinforce it.

4. After the appraisal is written, set it aside for a few days and then review it again.

5. Follow whatever steps are required by your organization's performance appraisal system.

Conducting the Review

1. Select a location that is comfortable and free of distractions. The location should encourage a frank and candid conversation.

2. Discuss each topic in the appraisal one at a time, considering both strengths and shortcomings.

3. Be specific and descriptive, not general and judgmental. Report occurrences rather than evaluating them.

4. Discuss your differences and resolve them. Solicit agreement with the evaluation.

5. Jointly discuss and design plans for taking corrective action for growth and development.

6. Maintain a professional and supportive approach to the appraisal discussion.

TRAIT METHODS

Trait approaches to performance appraisal are designed to measure the extent to which an employee possesses certain characteristics—such as dependability, creativity, initiative, and leadership—that are viewed as important for the job and the organization in general. The fact that trait methods are the most popular is due in a large part to the ease with which they are developed. However, if not designed carefully on the basis of job analysis, trait appraisals can be notoriously biased and subjective.

Graphic Rating Scales

graphic rating scale method

A trait approach to performance appraisal whereby each employee is rated according to a scale of characteristics

In the **graphic rating scale method**, each trait or characteristic to be rated is represented by a scale on which a rater indicates the degree to which an employee possesses that trait or characteristic. An example of this type of scale is shown in Highlights in HRM 8.2. There are many variations of the graphic rating scale. The differences are to be found in (1) the characteristics or dimensions on which individuals are rated, (2) the degree to which the performance dimension is defined for the rater, and (3) how clearly the points on the scale are defined. In Highlights in HRM 8.2, the dimensions are defined briefly, and some attempt is made to define the points on the scale. Subjectivity bias is reduced somewhat when the dimensions on the scale and the scale points are defined as precisely as possible. This can be achieved by training raters and by including descriptive appraisal guidelines in a performance appraisal reference packet.[35]

Highlights in **HRM 8.2**

Graphic Rating Scale with Provision for Comments

Appraise employee's performance in PRESENT ASSIGNMENT. Check (✔) most appropriate square. Appraisers are *urged to freely use the* "Remarks" sections for significant comments descriptive of the individual.

1. KNOWLEDGE OF WORK: Understanding of all phases of his/her work and related matters	Needs instruction or guidance ☐	Has required knowledge of own and related work ☐	✔	Has exceptional knowledge of own and related work ☐
	Remarks: *Is particularly good on gas engines.*			
2. INITIATIVE: Ability to originate or develop ideas and to get things started	Lacks imagination ☐	Meets necessary requirements ✔		Unusually resourceful ☐
	Remarks: *Has good ideas when asked for an opinion, but otherwise will not offer them. Somewhat lacking in self-confidence.*			
3. APPLICATION: Attention and application to his/her work	Wastes time Needs close supervision ☐	Steady and willing worker ✔		Exceptionally industrious ☐
	Remarks: *Accepts new jobs when assigned.*			
4. QUALITY OF WORK: Thoroughness, neatness, and accuracy of work	Needs improvement ☐	Regularly meets recognized standards ☐	✔	Consistently maintains highest quality ☐
	Remarks: *The work he turns out is always of the highest possible quality.*			
5. VOLUME OF WORK: Quantity of acceptable work	Should be increased ☐	Regularly meets recognized standards ✔		Unusually high output ☐
	Remarks: *Would be higher if he did not spend so much time checking and rechecking his work.*			

Also, the rating form should provide sufficient space for comments on the behaviour associated with each scale. These comments improve the accuracy of the appraisal because they require the rater to think in terms of observable employee behaviours while providing specific examples to discuss with the employee during the appraisal interview.

Mixed-Standard Scales

mixed-standard scale method

A trait approach to performance appraisal similar to other scale methods but based on comparison with (better than, equal to, or worse than) a standard

The **mixed-standard scale method** is a modification of the basic rating scale method. Rather than evaluating traits according to a single scale, the rater is given three specific descriptions of each trait. These descriptions reflect three levels of performance: superior, average, and inferior. After the three descriptions for each trait are written, they are randomly sequenced to form the mixed-standard scale. As shown in Highlights in HRM 8.3, supervisors evaluate employees by indicating whether their performance is better than, equal to, or worse than the standard for each behaviour.

Forced-Choice Method

forced-choice method

A trait approach to performance appraisal that requires the rater to choose from statements designed to distinguish between successful and unsuccessful performance

The **forced-choice method** requires the rater to choose from statements, often in pairs, that appear equally favourable or equally unfavourable. The statements, however, are designed to distinguish between successful and unsuccessful performance. The rater selects one statement from the pair without knowing which statement correctly describes successful job behaviour. For example, forced-choice pairs might include the following:

1. ____ a) Works hard   ____ b) Works quickly
2. ____ a) Shows initiative   ____ b) Is responsive to customers
3. ____ a) Produces poor quality ____ b) Lacks good work habits

The forced-choice method is not without limitations, the primary one being the cost of establishing and maintaining its validity. The fact that it has been a source of frustration to many raters has sometimes caused the method to be eliminated from appraisal programs. In addition, it cannot be used as effectively as some of the other methods as a tool for developing employees.

Highlights in HRM 8.3

Example of a Mixed-Standard Scale

DIRECTIONS: Please indicate whether the individual's performance is above (+), equal to (0), or lower than (–) each of the following standards.

1. ____ Employee uses good judgment when addressing problems and provides workable alternatives; however, at times does not take actions to prevent problems. *(medium PROBLEM SOLVING)*

2. ____ Employee lacks supervisory skills; frequently handles employees poorly and is at times argumentative. *(low LEADERSHIP)*

3. ____ Employee is extremely cooperative; can be expected to take the lead in developing cooperation among employees; completes job tasks with a positive attitude. *(high COOPERATION)*

4. ____ Employee has effective supervision skills; encourages productivity, quality, and employee development. *(medium LEADERSHIP)*

5. ____ Employee normally displays an argumentative or defensive attitude toward fellow employees and job assignments. *(low COOPERATION)*

6. ____ Employee is generally agreeable but becomes argumentative at times when given job assignments; cooperates with other employees as expected. *(medium COOPERATION)*

7. ____ Employee is not good at solving problems; uses poor judgment and does not anticipate potential difficulties. *(low PROBLEM SOLVING)*

8. ____ Employee anticipates potential problems and provides creative, proactive alternative solutions; has good attention to follow-up. *(high PROBLEM SOLVING)*

9. ____ Employee displays skilled direction; effectively coordinates unit activities; is generally a dynamic leader and motivates employees to high performance. *(high LEADERSHIP)*

Essay Method

Unlike rating scales, which provide a structured form of appraisal, the **essay method** requires the appraiser to compose a statement that best describes the employee being appraised. The appraiser is usually instructed to describe the employee's strengths and weaknesses and to make recommendations for his or her development. Often the essay method is combined with other rating methods. Essays may provide additional descriptive information on an employee's performance that cannot be generated with a structured rating scale, for example.

The essay method provides an excellent opportunity to point out the unique characteristics of the employee being appraised. This aspect of the method is heightened when a supervisor is instructed to describe specific points about the employee's promotability, special talents, skills, strengths, and weaknesses. A major limitation of the essay method is that composing an essay that attempts to cover all of an employee's essential characteristics is a very time-consuming task (though when combined with other methods, this method does not require a lengthy statement). Another disadvantage of the essay method is that the quality of the performance appraisal may be influenced by the supervisor's writing skills and composition style. Good writers may simply be able to produce more favourable appraisals. A final drawback of this appraisal method is that it tends to be subjective and may not focus on the relevant aspects of a person's job performance.

BEHAVIOURAL METHODS

As we mentioned, one of the potential drawbacks of a trait-oriented performance appraisal is that traits tend to be vague and subjective. We discussed earlier that one way to improve a rating scale is to have descriptions of behaviour along a scale, or continuum. These descriptions permit the rater to readily identify the point where a particular employee falls on the scale. Behavioural methods have been developed to specifically describe which actions should (or should not) be exhibited on the job. They are often used to provide employees with developmental feedback.

Critical Incident Method

The critical incident method, described in Chapter 4 in connection with job analysis, is also used as a method of appraisal. Recall that a **critical incident** occurs when employee behaviour results in unusual success or unusual failure in some part of the job. An example of a favourable critical incident occurs when a janitor observes that a file cabinet containing classified documents has been left unlocked at the close of business and calls the firm's security officer to correct the problem. An example of an unfavourable incident occurs when a mail clerk fails to deliver an Express Mail package immediately, instead putting it in with regular mail to be routed two hours later. The manager keeps a log or diary for each employee throughout the appraisal period and notes specific critical incidents related to how well they perform. When completing the appraisal form, the manager refers to the critical incident log and uses this information to substantiate an employee's rating of outstanding, satisfactory, or unsatisfactory in specific performance areas and overall. This method can also help a manager counsel employees when they are having performance problems while the problem is still minor. It also increases the objectivity of the appraisal by requiring the rater to use job performance criteria to justify the ratings.[36]

Behavioural Checklist Method

One of the oldest appraisal techniques is the behavioural checklist method. It consists of having the rater check the statements on a list that the rater believes are characteristic of the employee's performance or behaviour. A checklist developed for computer salespeople might include a number of statements such as the following:

essay method
A trait approach to performance appraisal that requires the rater to compose a statement describing employee behaviour

critical incident
An unusual event that denotes superior or inferior employee performance in some part of the job

_____ Is able to explain equipment clearly

_____ Keeps abreast of new developments in technology

_____ Tends to be a steady worker

_____ Reacts quickly to customers' needs

_____ Processes orders correctly

Behaviourally Anchored Rating Scale (BARS)

behaviourally anchored rating scale (BARS)

A behavioural approach to performance appraisal that consists of a series of vertical scales, one for each important dimension of job performance

A **behaviourally anchored rating scale (BARS)** consists of a series of five to ten vertical scales—one for each important dimension of performance identified through job analysis. These dimensions are anchored by behaviours identified through a critical incident job analysis. The critical incidents are placed along the scale and are assigned point values according to the opinions of experts. A BARS for the job of firefighter is shown in the upper portion of Highlights in HRM 8.4. Note that this particular scale is for the dimension described as "Firefighting Strategy: Knowledge of Fire Characteristics."

A BARS is typically developed by a committee that includes both subordinates and managers. The committee's task is to identify all the relevant characteristics or dimensions of the job. Behavioural anchors in the form of statements are then established for each of the job dimensions. Several participants are asked to review the anchor statements and indicate which job dimension each anchor illustrates. The only anchors retained are those that at least 70 percent of the group agrees belong with a particular dimension. Finally, anchors are attached to their job dimensions and are placed on the appropriate scales according to values that the group assigns to them.

At present there is no strong evidence that a BARS reduces all of the rating errors mentioned previously. However, some studies have shown that scales of this type can yield more accurate ratings. One major advantage of a BARS is that personnel outside the HR department participate with HR staff in its development.

Highlights in HRM 8.4

BARS and BOS Examples

Example of a BARS for Municipal Fire Companies

FIREFIGHTING STRATEGY: Knowledge of Fire Characteristics. This area of performance concerns the ability of a firefighter to understand fire characteristics to develop the best strategy for fighting a fire.

HIGH   7 — Finds the fire when no one else can

        6 — Correctly assesses best point of entry for fighting fire

AVERAGE 5 — Uses type of smoke as indicator of type of fire

        4 — Understands basic hydraulics

        3 — Cannot tell the type of fire by observing the color of flame

        2 — Cannot identify location of the fire

LOW   1 — Will not change firefighting strategy in spite of flashbacks and other signs that accelerants are present

Source: Adapted from Landy, Jacobs, and Associates. Reprinted with permission.

Employee participation can lead to greater acceptance of the performance appraisal process and of the performance measures that it uses.

The procedures followed in developing a BARS also result in scales that have a high degree of content validity. The main disadvantage of a BARS is that it requires considerable time and effort to develop. In addition, because the scales are specific to particular jobs, a scale designed for one job might not apply to another.

Behaviour Observation Scale (BOS)

A **behaviour observation scale (BOS)** is similar to a BARS in that they are both based on critical incidents. However, Highlights in HRM 8.5 shows that rather than asking the evaluator to choose the most representative behavioural anchor, a BOS is designed to measure how frequently each of the behaviours has been observed.

The value of a BOS is that this approach allows the appraiser to play the role of observer rather than of judge. In this way, he or she can more easily provide constructive feedback to the employee, who will be more willing to accept it. Research shows that users of the system frequently prefer it over the BARS or trait scales for (1) maintaining objectivity, (2) distinguishing good performers from poor performers, (3) providing feedback, and (4) identifying training needs.[37]

RESULTS METHODS

Rather than looking at the traits of employees or the behaviours they exhibit on the job, many organizations evaluate employee accomplishments—the results they achieve through their work. Advocates of results appraisals argue that they are more objective and empowering for employees. Looking at results such as sales figures and production output involves less subjectivity and therefore may be less open to bias. Furthermore, results appraisals often give employees responsibility for their outcomes, while giving them discretion over the methods they use to accomplish them (within limits). This is empowerment in action.

behaviour observation scale (BOS)
A behavioural approach to performance appraisal that measures the frequency of observed behaviour

Highlights in **HRM 8.5**

Sample Items from Behaviour Observation Scales

For each behaviour observed, use the following scale:

5 represents *almost always*　　95–100% of the time
4 represents *frequently*　　85–94% of the time
3 represents *sometimes*　　75–84% of the time
2 represents *seldom*　　65–74% of the time
1 represents *almost never*　　0–64% of the time

SALES PRODUCTIVITY

	NEVER				ALWAYS
1. Reviews individual productivity results with manager	1	2	3	4	5
2. Suggests to peers ways of building sales	1	2	3	4	5
3. Formulates specific objectives for each contact	1	2	3	4	5
4. Focuses on product rather than customer problem	1	2	3	4	5
5. Keeps account plans updated	1	2	3	4	5
6. Follows up on customer leads	1	2	3	4	5

Productivity Measures

A number of results measures are available to evaluate performance. Salespeople are evaluated on the basis of their sales volume (both the number of units sold and the dollar amount in revenues). Production workers are evaluated on the basis of the number of units they produce and perhaps the scrap rate or number of defects that are detected. Executives are frequently evaluated on the basis of company profits or growth rate. Each of these measures directly links what employees accomplish and results that benefit the organization. In this way, results appraisals can directly align employee and organizational goals.

But there are some problems with results appraisals. First, recall our earlier discussion of criterion contamination. Results appraisals can be contaminated by external factors that employees cannot influence. Sales representatives who have extremely bad markets or production employees who cannot get materials will not be able to perform up to their abilities. In this case, it is unfair to hold these employees accountable for results that are contaminated by circumstances beyond their control. Furthermore, results appraisals can inadvertently encourage employees to "look good" on a short-term basis, while ignoring the long-term ramifications. Line supervisors, for example, might let their equipment suffer to reduce maintenance costs. If the appraisal focuses on a narrow set of results criteria to the exclusion of other important process issues, the system may suffer from criterion deficiency and unintentionally foster the attitude that "what gets measured gets done." In fact, in any job involving interaction with others, it is not enough to simply look at production or sales figures. Factors such as cooperation, adaptability, initiative, and concern for human relations are important to the job success of employees, too. If these factors are important job standards, they should be added to the appraisal review. Thus, to be realistic, both the results and the methods or processes used to achieve them should be considered.[38]

management by objectives (MBO)

A philosophy of management that rates performance on the basis of employee achievement of goals set by mutual agreement of employee and manager

Management by Objectives

One method that attempts to overcome some of the limitations of results appraisals is **management by objectives (MBO)**. MBO is a philosophy of management first proposed by Peter Drucker in 1954 that has employees establish objectives (such as production costs, sales per product, quality standards, and profits) through consultation with their superiors and then uses these objectives as a basis for evaluation.[39] MBO is a system involving a cycle (Figure 8.6) that begins with setting the organization's common goals and objectives and ultimately returns to that step. The system acts as a goal setting process whereby objectives are established for the organization (Step 1), departments (Step 2), and individual managers and employees (Step 3).

As Figure 8.6 illustrates, a significant feature of the cycle is the establishment of specific goals by the employee, but those goals are based on a broad statement of the employee's responsibilities prepared by the person's supervisor. Employee-established goals are discussed with the supervisor and jointly reviewed and modified until both parties are satisfied with them (Step 4). The goal statements are accompanied by a detailed account of the actions the employee proposes to take in order to reach the goals. During periodic reviews, as objective data are made available, the progress that the employee is making toward the goals is then assessed (Step 5). Goals may be changed at this time as new or additional data are received. At the conclusion of a period of time (usually six months or one year), the employee makes a self-appraisal of what he or she has accomplished, substantiating the self-appraisal with factual data wherever possible. The "interview" is an examination of the employee's self-appraisal by the supervisor and the employee together (Step 6). The final step (Step 7) is reviewing the connection between individual and organizational performance. To ensure success, MBO programs should be viewed as part of a total system for managing, not as merely an addition to the manager's job.

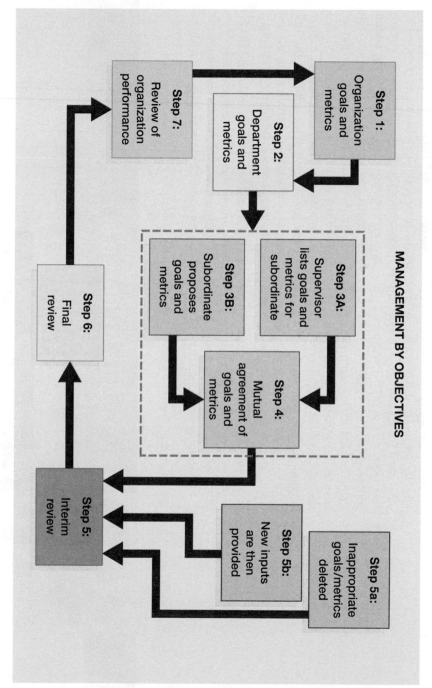

FIGURE 8.6

Performance Appraisal under an MBO Program

MANAGEMENT BY OBJECTIVES

Step 1: Organization goals and metrics

Step 2: Department goals and metrics

Step 3A: Supervisor lists goals and metrics for subordinate

Step 3B: Subordinate proposes goals and metrics

Step 4: Mutual agreement of goals and metrics

Step 5a: Inappropriate goals/metrics deleted

Step 5b: New inputs are then provided

Step 5: Interim review

Step 6: Final review

Step 7: Review of organization performance

Managers must be willing to empower employees to accomplish their objectives on their own, giving them discretion over the methods they use (but holding them accountable for outcomes). The following guidelines may be especially helpful:

1. Managers and employees must be willing to establish goals and objectives together. Goal setting has been shown to improve employee performance, typically ranging from 10 to 25 percent. Goal setting works because it helps employees focus on important tasks and makes them accountable for completing these tasks. It also establishes an automatic feedback system that aids learning because employees can regularly evaluate their performance against their goals.[40]

2. The objectives should be quantifiable and measurable for the long and short terms. However, goal statements should be accompanied by a description of how that goal will be accomplished.

3. The results that are expected must be under the employee's control. Recall our early discussion of criterion contamination.

4. The goals and objectives must be consistent for each employee level (top executive, manager, and employee).

5. Managers and employees must establish specific times when the goals are to be reviewed and evaluated.

The Balanced Scorecard

The balanced scorecard (BSC), which we first discussed in Chapter 2, can be used to appraise individual employees, teams, business units, and the corporation itself. The idea behind the balanced scorecard model was shown in Chapter 2. The appraisal takes into account four related categories: (1) financial, (2) customer, (3) processes, and (4) learning. These internal processes—product development, service, and the like—are critical for creating customer satisfaction and loyalty. In turn, creating value for customers is what drives a firm's financial performance and profitability. Highlights in HRM 8.6 shows an example of how a BSC translates to a personal scorecard for an employee. As you can see, the corporation's objectives have already been spelled out on the scorecard. Then the various business unit targets are added, followed by the target objectives of the firm's teams and individual employees. The value of this is that each individual can see more clearly how his or her performance ties into the overall performance of the firm. Similar in some ways to MBO, the BSC enables managers to translate broad corporate goals into divisional, departmental, and team goals in a cascading fashion. Many firms have adopted the BSC approach, but it is neither a flawless nor a simple performance management system. Some recommendations for ensuring the method's success include the following:

- *Translate the strategy into a scorecard of clear objectives.* Because the BSC process begins with strategic objectives, unless these are clear, the rest of the system is doomed to ambiguity and potential failure. Translating a strategy into objectives provides managers and front-line employees with

Highlights in **HRM 8.6**

Personal Scorecard

CORPORATE OBJECTIVES
• Double our corporate value in seven years.
• Increase our earnings by an average of 20% per year.
• Achieve an internal rate of return 2% above the cost of capital.
• Increase both production and reserves by 20% in the next decade.

☑ Corporate
☐ Business Unit
☐ Team/Individual

Corporate Targets				Scorecard Measures	Bus. Unit Targets				Team/Individual Objectives
2005	2006	2007	2008		2005	2006	2007	2008	
				Financial					
100	120	160	180	Earnings (millions of dollars)					1.
100	450	200	210	Net cash flow					
100	85	75	70	Overhead and operating costs					2.
				Operating					
100	75	73	70	Production costs/barrel					3.
100	97	93	90	Development costs/barrel					
100	105	108	110	Total annual production					4.

Team/Individual Measures	Targets				
1.					
2.					
3.					
4.					

Source: Reprinted by permission of *Harvard Business Review*. [Excerpt]. From Robert Kaplan and David Norton, "Using the Balanced Scorecard as a Strategic Management System," *Harvard Business Review* (January–February 1996): 75–85. Copyright © 1996 by the Harvard Business School Publishing Corporation; all rights reserved.

- goals that are more understandable and attainable. Typically, having fewer goals adds clarity and focus.

- *Attach measures to each objective.* In order for managers and employees to know if and when the objectives are achieved, clear measures must be attached to each goal. Each objective should be given at least one metric that can be measured either by a pre-existing system or manually within an organization.

- *Cascade scorecards to the front line.* It is often said that the real strategic work happens at the front line. In order for all employees to understand how their roles and job duties are aligned with the firm's higher-level goals, the scorecards should be cascaded to the individual level. Cascading score-cards ensures that strategy then becomes "everyone's" job.

- *Provide performance feedback based on measures.* As with other perfor-mance management systems, unless managers provide employees with solid feedback on how they are doing, the system is likely to be ineffective. As part of this process, employees must know that they are accountable for achieving their objectives and providing an explanation when they do not hit their targets.

- *Empower employees to make performance improvements.* Individuals, on their own or working in teams, may understand ways of achieving higher performance. One of the benefits of a results-based system such as the BSC is that it gives employees the latitude to continuously improve best practices methods.

- *Reassess strategy.* One of the key benefits of the BSC is that it is a con-tinuous loop process. Managers should monitor performance and use this information to reassess the strategy and make continuous adjustments. Those who have had the best success with the BSC argue that the system helps improve communication and learning rather than fixing in place a mechanical set of controls.[41]

WHICH PERFORMANCE APPRAISAL METHOD TO USE?

The method chosen should be based largely on the purpose of the appraisal. Figure 8.7 lists some of the strengths and weaknesses of trait, behaviour, and results approaches to appraisal. Note that the simplest and least expensive techniques often yield the least accurate information. However, research has not always sup-ported a clear choice among appraisal methods. While researchers and HR man-agers generally believe that the more sophisticated and more time-consuming methods offer more useful information, this may not always be the case. Ronald Gross, an industrial psychologist and human resources consultant, states: "I can't judge a performance appraisal system just by looking at the paperwork. The back of an envelope can work just fine. I've seen many systems fail miserably because they're too complex, too time consuming, and too burdensome. I've never seen a system fail because it was too simple."[42] One way to assess whether an organi-zation's appraisal system is effective is by doing an annual, or at least periodic, audit of the process using a survey instrument that both managers and employees complete on a periodic basis. This should give HR a better sense of whether the appraisal processes is improving.

Of course, having a first-rate appraisal method does no good if the manager simply "shoves it in a drawer." Even a rudimentary system, when used properly, can initiate a discussion between managers and employees that genuinely leads to supe-rior performance. These issues are discussed next under the topic of performance appraisal interviews. In addition, as we have explained, performance appraisals should not be just for middle managers and rank-and-file employees. If the orga-nization's goals are to cascade downward, the firm's top executives need to be involved in the appraisal process as well.

FIGURE **8.7**

Summary of Various Appraisal Methods

	ADVANTAGES	DISADVANTAGES
Trait Methods	1. Are inexpensive to develop	1. Have high potential for rating errors
	2. Use meaningful dimensions	2. Are not useful for employee counselling
	3. Are easy to use	3. Are not useful for allocating rewards
		4. Are not useful for promotion decisions
Behavioural Methods	1. Use specific performance dimensions	1. Can be time consuming to develop/use
	2. Are acceptable to employees and superiors	2. Can be costly to develop
	3. Are useful for providing feedback	3. Have some potential for rating error
	4. Are fair for reward and promotion decisions	
Results Methods	1. Have less subjectivity bias	1. Are time consuming to develop/use
	2. Are acceptable to employees and superiors	2. May encourage a short-term perspective
	3. Link individual performance to organizational performance	3. May use contaminated criteria
	4. Encourage mutual goal setting	4. May use deficient criteria
	5. Are good for reward and promotion decisions	

APPRAISAL INTERVIEWS

The appraisal interview is perhaps the most important part of the entire performance appraisal process. The appraisal interview gives a manager the opportunity to discuss a subordinate's performance record and to explore areas of possible improvement and growth. Unfortunately, the interviewer can become overburdened by attempting to discuss too much, such as the employee's past performance and future development goals. Dividing the appraisal interview into two sessions, one for the performance review and the other for the employee's growth plans, can be helpful. Moreover, by separating the interview into two sessions, the interviewer can give each session the proper attention it deserves. It can be difficult for a supervisor to perform the role of both evaluator and counsellor in the same review period. Dividing the sessions can also improve the communication and cooperation between the parties, thereby reducing any stress and defensiveness that might arise.

The format for the appraisal interview will be determined in a large part by the purpose of the interview, type of appraisal system used, and organization of the interview form. Most appraisal interviews attempt to give feedback to employees on how well they are performing their jobs and on planning for their future development. Interviews should be scheduled far enough in advance to allow the interviewee, as well as the interviewer, to prepare for the discussion. Usually ten days to two weeks is a sufficient amount of lead time.

THREE TYPES OF APPRAISAL INTERVIEWS

The individual who as probably studied different approaches to performance appraisal interviews most thoroughly is Norman R. F. Maier. In his classic book *The Appraisal Interview*, he analyzes the cause-and-effect relationships in three types of appraisal interviews: tell and-sell, tell-and-listen, and problem solving.

Tell-and-Sell Interview

The skills required in the tell-and-sell interview include the ability to persuade an employee to change in a prescribed manner. This may require the development of new behaviours on the part of the employee and skillful use of motivational incentives on the part of the appraiser/supervisor.

Tell-and-Listen Interview

In the tell-and-listen interview, the skills required include the ability to communicate the strong and weak points of an employee's job performance during the first part of the interview. During the second part of the interview, the employee's feelings about the appraisal are thoroughly explored. The tell-and-listen method gives both managers and employees the opportunity to release and iron out any feelings of frustration they might have. Today, most experts advise supervisors to encourage their employees to speak freely and to listen closely to what they have to say, emphasizing the fact that the communication during performance appraisals should be a two-way street.

Problem-Solving Interview

The skills associated with the problem-solving interview are consistent with the nondirective procedures of the tell-and-listen method. Listening, accepting, and responding to feelings are essential elements of the problem-solving interview. However, this method goes beyond an interest in the employee's feelings. It seeks to stimulate growth and development in the employee by discussing the problems, needs, innovations, satisfactions, and dissatisfactions the employee has encountered on the job since the last appraisal interview. Maier recommends this method because the objective of appraisals is normally to motivate employees and stimulate their growth and development. Managers should not assume that only one type of appraisal interview is appropriate for every review session. Rather, they should be able to use one or more of the interview types, depending on the topic being discussed or on the behaviour of the employee being appraised. The interview should be seen as requiring a flexible approach.

CONDUCTING THE APPRAISAL INTERVIEW

While there are probably no hard-and-fast rules for how to conduct an appraisal interview, some guidelines can increase an employee's willingness to discuss his or her performance and improve it, accept feedback from his or her supervisors, and increase the person's overall satisfaction with the interview. Many of the principles of effective interviewing discussed in Chapter 6 apply to performance appraisal interviews as well. Here are some other guidelines that should also be considered.

Ask for a Self-Assessment

As we noted earlier in the chapter, it is useful to have employees evaluate their own performance prior to the appraisal interview. Even if this information is not used to determine the final rating on the review, the self-appraisal starts the employee thinking about what criteria he or she is being evaluated, thus eliminating any potential surprises. Self-appraisal also ensures that the employee knows against his or her accomplishments. Self-appraisal also ensures that the employee knows against what criteria he or she is being evaluated, thus eliminating any potential surprises.

Recent research evidence suggests that employees are more satisfied and view the appraisal system as providing more *procedural justice* when they have input into the process.

©Thomas Barwick/The Image Bank/Getty Images

There are different approaches to performance appraisal interviews. A problem-solving approach may be the best.

When the employee has evaluated his or her own performance, the interview can be used to discuss areas in which the manager and the employee have reached different conclusions—not so much to resolve the "truth," but to work toward a resolution of problems.

Invite Participation

The core purpose of a performance appraisal interview is to initiate a dialogue that will help an employee improve his or her performance. To the extent that an employee is an active participant in that discussion, the more likely it is that the root causes and obstacles to performance will be uncovered and the more likely it is that constructive ideas for improvement will be raised. In addition, research evidence suggests that participation is strongly related to an employee's satisfaction with the appraisal feedback, the extent to which the employee believes it is fair and useful, and his or her intention to improve performance. As a rule of thumb, supervisors should spend only about 30 to 35 percent of the time talking during the interview. They should spend the rest of the time listening to the information their employees volunteer and their responses to questions.

Express Appreciation

Praise is a powerful motivator, and in an appraisal interview, particularly, employees are seeking positive feedback. It is frequently beneficial to start the appraisal interview by expressing appreciation for what the employee has done well. In this way, he or she may be less defensive and more likely to talk about aspects of the job that are not going so well. However, supervisors should try to avoid the obvious use of the "sandwich technique" in which positive statements are followed by negative ones, which are then followed by positive statements. This approach may not work for several reasons. Praise often alerts the employee that criticism will be coming. If managers follow an appraisal form, the problem of the sandwich technique will often be avoided. Furthermore, if employees are kept informed of their behaviour on a regular basis, there will be no need to use this appraisal technique.

Minimize Criticism

Even the most stoic employees can absorb only so much criticism before they start to get defensive. If an employee has many areas in need of improvement, managers should focus on those few objective issues that are most problematic or most important to the job. In other words, criticism should be given in small doses.

Some tips for using criticism constructively include the following:

- *Consider whether it is really necessary.* Frustration with performance problems sometimes leads to criticism that is little more than a manager "letting off steam." Make certain that the criticism focuses on a recurrent problem or a consistent pattern of behaviour over which the employee has control.
- *Consider the needs of the employee.* Everyone handles criticism differently. Some people are able to handle it well. Others react very negatively to even the slightest criticism.
- *Be specific and do not exaggerate.* Even managers who dislike criticizing may find that, once they get started, they tend to overdo it. Sometimes we overstate problems in order to be convincing or to demonstrate our concern. Try to keep criticism simple, factual, and to the point. Avoid using terms such as *always, completely,* and *never.*

- *Watch your timing*. Properly timed criticism can often mean the difference between success and failure. Even good criticism given late in the day, for example, can touch a raw nerve if the employee is tired.

- *Make improvement your goal*. Frankly, it is hard to change a person's behaviour with a single conversation, so "laying it on the line" is not probably a good idea. Moreover, any criticism needs to be complemented with managerial support. This point is elaborated on next.[43]

Change the Behaviour, Not the Person

Managers frequently try to play psychologist, to "figure out" why an employee has acted a certain way. Empathy is a good thing, and attempts to understand the employee's point of view can be very helpful. However, when dealing with a problem area, in particular, remember that it is not the person who is bad, but the actions exhibited on the job. Avoid making suggestions to employees about personal traits to change; instead suggest more acceptable ways of performing. For example, instead of focusing on a person's "unreliability," a manager might focus on the fact that the employee "has been late to work seven times this month." It is difficult for employees to change who they are; it is usually much easier for them to change how they act.

Focus on Solving Problems

When addressing performance issues, it is also frequently tempting to get into the "blame game" in which both manager and employee enter into a potentially endless discussion of why a situation has arisen. Frequently, solving problems requires an analysis of the causes, but ultimately the appraisal interview should be directed at devising a solution to the problem.

Be Supportive

One of the better techniques for engaging an employee in the problem-solving process is for the manager to ask: "What can I do to help?" Employees frequently attribute performance problems to either real or perceived obstacles (such as bureaucratic procedures or inadequate resources). By being open and supportive, the manager conveys to the employee that he or she will try to eliminate roadblocks and will work with the employee to achieve a higher standard of performance.

Establish Goals

Since a major purpose of the appraisal interview is to make plans for improvement, it is important to focus the interviewee's attention on the future rather than the past. Toward that goal, managers should

- Emphasize strengths on which the employee can build rather than weaknesses to overcome and how the employee's efforts will contribute to the organization during the coming year.

- Concentrate on opportunities for growth that exist within the framework of the employee's present position and drop unproductive tasks.

- Limit plans for growth to a few important items that can be accomplished within a reasonable period of time.

- Establish specific action plans that spell out how each goal will be achieved. The plans may also include a list of contacts, resources, and timetables for follow-up.

Many managers are as nervous about administering appraisals as employees are about receiving them. Some supervisors may be tempted to establish difficult goals with their subordinates. The ethical issues surrounding unreasonable goals are discussed in Ethics in HRM.

Ethics in HRM

Stretch Goals

Employees are being asked to set performance goals, labelled "stretch goals," that ask them to do such things as double their sales or increase response time to customers threefold. Research has shown that the establishment of goals results in higher productivity. So if goals are good, are super goals better?

"Not necessarily," says Steve Kerr, General Electric's chief learning officer. In his opinion, most managers do not know how to manage stretch targets. Companies set ambitious goals for their employees but fail to provide them with the resources they need to achieve them. They are saying, in effect, "We aren't going to give you any more people or money, so your solution is to work smarter and be creative." The only resource left to employees is their personal time, and so North Americans are working harder than employees in any other developed country. They are working evenings and weekends, with fewer vacations. "That's immoral," says Kerr. "Companies have a moral obligation to provide the tools to meet tough goals.". The other risk is that stretch goals may lead to risk taking behaviour on the part of employees. For instance, U.S. banks set numerical goals for mortgages that resulted in selling mortgages to high-risk customers, who subsequently defaulted, causing a massive meltdown in the home real estate market.

How should stretch goals be managed? The goal must be seen as achievable, and not provoke a reaction of "You've got to be kidding." People must also realize that creative energy can be increased. For example, in one innovation training program, teams are given an orange and told that each person must handle the orange, but that the orange must end up in the hands of the person who started with it. All teams start by throwing the orange to team members; this takes nine seconds. They try to reduce the time to seven seconds by throwing faster or in tighter circles. When told that it is possible to do this task in one second, they get creative: they stack their hands and the first person drops the orange through the stacked but open hands and catches it at the bottom.

If the stretch goals are not achieved, then punishment should not be used. Be careful with high achievers who are already stretching, or these winners will feel like losers if they can not meet impossible goals. Provide the tools; asking people to double their quota without ensuring backup is demoralizing. Finally, share the wealth. If the achievement results in additional funds flowing to the organization, split the incremental savings or gains.

Some employees, masters at the politics of organizations, play games with stretch goals. They negotiate hard for modest, achievable goals, while arguing that these are stretch targets. Others, with high needs for achievement, accept the stretch targets. At bonus time, the modest goal setters have met or surpassed their goals and receive merit increases. Having failed to achieve impossible targets, the less Machiavellian employees receive nothing.

Source: Adapted from S. Sherman, "Stretch Goals: The Dark Side of Asking for Miracles," *Fortune*, November 13, 1995: 231; W. Immen, "The Goal: To Set Goals That Really Can Be Met," *The Globe and Mail*, March 20, 2009, B12.

Follow Up Day to Day

As you have learned, feedback is most useful when it is immediate and specific to a particular situation. Unfortunately, both managers and employees are frequently happy to finish the interview and file away the appraisal form. A better approach is to have informal talks periodically, perhaps quarterly, to follow up on the issues raised in the appraisal interview. Levi Strauss, for example, offers employees informal feedback and coaching sessions on an ongoing basis. This puts managers in more of a coaching role versus that of a judge.

IMPROVING PERFORMANCE

In many instances, the appraisal interview will provide the basis for noting deficiencies in employee performance and for making plans for improvement. Unless these deficiencies are brought to the employee's attention, they are likely to continue until they become quite serious. Sometimes underperformers do not understand exactly what is expected of them. However, once their responsibilities are clarified, they are in a position to take the corrective action needed to improve their performance.

Identifying Sources of Ineffective Performance

A person's performance is a function of several factors, but perhaps it can be boiled down to three primary concerns: ability, motivation, and environment. Each individual has a unique pattern of strengths and weaknesses that play a part. But talented employees with low motivation are not likely to succeed. In addition, other factors in the work environment—or even in the external environment, which includes personal, family, and community concerns—can affect a person's performance either positively or negatively. Figure 8.8 provides a better picture of how these three factors (ability, motivation, and environment) can influence people's performance.

It is recommended that a diagnosis of poor employee performance focus on these three interactive elements. As Figure 8.9 shows, if an employee's performance is not up to standard, the cause could be an ability problem (knowledge, skills, technical competencies), a motivation problem (effort to get the job done), and/or some problem in the work environment (poor economic conditions, worker shortages due to downsizing, difficult sales territories).[44] Any one of these problem areas could cause performance to suffer.

Performance Diagnosis

Although performance appraisal systems can often tell us who is not performing well, they typically cannot reveal why. Unfortunately, managers often assume that poor performance is first due to lack of ability, second to poor motivation, and then to external conditions an employee faces. Ironically, research also suggests that we tend to make just the opposite attributions about our own performance. We first attribute poor performance to external constraints such as bad luck or factors out of our control. If the problem is internal, then we typically attribute it to temporary

FIGURE 8.8

Factors That Influence Performance

ABILITY	MOTIVATION	ENVIRONMENT
• Technical skills	• Career ambition	• Equipment/materials
• Interpersonal skills	• Employee conflict	• Job design
• Problem-solving skills	• Frustration	• Economic conditions
• Analytical skills	• Fairness/satisfaction	• Unions
• Communication skills	• Goals/expectations	• Rules and policies
• Physical limitations		• Management support
		• Laws and regulations

factors such as motivation or energy ("I had a bad day") and only as a last resort admit that it might be due to ability.

So what can be done to diagnose the real reasons for poor performance? More specifically, how can managers identify the root causes and get to work on a solution that improves performance? By comparing different performance measures, managers can begin to get an idea of the underlying causes of performance problems. For example, as shown in Figure 8.9, results measures cannot distinguish between ability, motivation, and environmental determinants of performance. So if someone is not achieving desired results, it could be due to ability, motivation, or external constraints. On the other hand, behavioural measures are less affected by external constraints. So if someone is demonstrating all the desired behaviours but is not achieving the desired results, logic suggests that it might be due to factors beyond his or her control.

Other kinds of diagnoses are possible by comparing different measures of performance. Only by correctly diagnosing the causes of performance problems can managers—and employees—hope to improve them.

Managing Ineffective Performance

Once the sources of performance problems are known, a course of action can be planned. This action may lie in providing training in areas that would increase the knowledge and/or skills needed for effective performance. A transfer to another

FIGURE 8.9

Performance Diagnosis

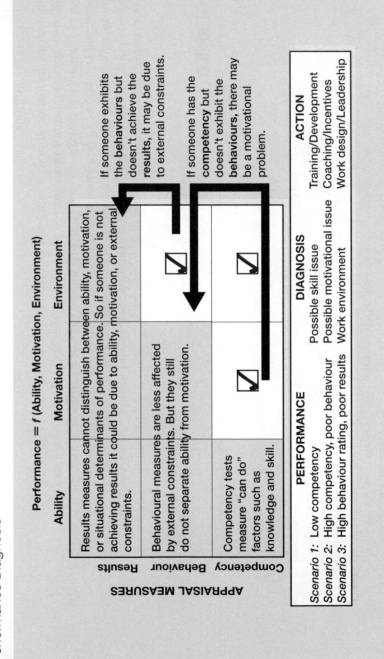

Performance = *f* (Ability, Motivation, Environment)

APPRAISAL MEASURES	Ability	Motivation	Environment
Results	Results measures cannot distinguish between ability, motivation, or situational determinants of performance. So if someone is not achieving results it could be due to ability, motivation, or external constraints.		
Behaviour	Behavioural measures are less affected by external constraints. But they still do not separate ability from motivation.		
Competency	Competency tests measure "can do" factors such as knowledge and skill.		

If someone exhibits the behaviours but doesn't achieve the results, it may be due to external constraints.

If someone has the competency but doesn't exhibit the behaviours, there may be a motivational problem.

PERFORMANCE	DIAGNOSIS	ACTION
Scenario 1: Low competency	Possible skill issue	Training/Development
Scenario 2: High competency, poor behaviour	Possible motivational issue	Coaching/Incentives
Scenario 3: High behaviour rating, poor results	Work environment	Work design/Leadership

Source: Scott Snell, University of Virginia.

job or department might give an employee a chance to become a more effective member of the organization. In other instances, greater attention may have to be focused on ways to motivate the individual.

If the ineffective performance persists, it may be necessary to transfer the employee, take disciplinary action, or discharge the person from the organization. The ineffective behaviour is likely affecting not only the manager and the organization as a whole, but also the person's coworkers. Whatever action is taken, however, should be done objectively, fairly, and with an understanding of the feelings of the individual involved. A new manager is likely to need training in this area because it is one of the most difficult of aspects of being a manager.

A final word of caution when it comes to managing performance problems: Because research consistently shows that managers often attribute poor performance to characteristics of the individuals (ability or motivation), while employees themselves typically blame external factors for their miscues, this can establish a negative cycle if not handled properly. Managers who assume that employees are not motivated or not capable may begin to treat them differently (perhaps supervising them too closely or watching for their next mistake). This can actually decrease an employee's motivation and cause him or her to withdraw. Seeing this, the manager may confirm his or her initial beliefs that the employee does not "measure up." As you can probably tell, this "set-up-to-fail" syndrome can be self-fulfilling and self-reinforcing. We hope the ideas and suggestions in this chapter will help managers accurately identify who is performing well (and why) and give them some focus for improving the productivity of their employees.[45]

Small Business **APPLICATION**

In this chapter we have covered many appraisal methods under the broad categories of trait, behavioural, and results models. Depending on the context, any of these may be suitable for a small business. However, in a small business where one's role is unique, a results-based model is likely going to be the most suitable model. For clarity, a results-based model considers the employee's objective outcomes against pre-established objectives. Let's use the example of a carpenter named John working for a small contracting company. While there are periods where there is enough carpentry work for him to be occupied for the full day, the company regularly also turns to John for assistance on client calls, as well as other miscellaneous work such as painting. So how does one evaluate John's performance? In essence, John's core responsibility is carpentry, so John will be evaluated based on the effectiveness of his carpentry in terms

of quantity, quality, and the manner in which it was delivered. This is a results-based assessment. The other components of John's role fall into the category of "other duties as required." Recognizing that these, even though are unstructured, form a regular part of John's role, John's manager will likely speak to John regarding his performance in these areas, drawing upon the behavioural methods we have reviewed, likely the critical incident method.

Finally, while small business typically employs a less formal and less structured approach to performance appraisal programs, the legal considerations outlined in this chapter apply equally to small business as to large companies. Small companies looking for assistance in training in or development of effective performance appraisal may consider working with outside training companies or human resources consultants to effectively establish performance appraisal processes.

SUMMARY

[OUTCOME 1]

Performance appraisal programs serve many purposes but, in general, those purposes can be clustered into two categories: administrative and developmental. The administrative purposes include decisions about who will be promoted, transferred, or laid off. Appraisals are also conducted in order to make compensation decisions. Developmental decisions include those related to improving and enhancing an individual's capabilities. These include identifying a person's strengths and weaknesses, eliminating external performance obstacles, and establishing training needs.

Some human resource experts and firms believe performance appraisals are ineffective. In other organizations, performance appraisals are seen as a necessary evil. Managers frequently avoid conducting appraisals because they dislike passing judgment on people. Furthermore, if managers are not adequately trained, subjectivity and organizational politics can distort employee reviews. Managers do not develop good feedback skills and are often not prepared to conduct an appraisal. As a consequence, the appraisal is done begrudgingly once a year and then forgotten. The ultimate success or failure of a performance appraisal program depends on the philosophy underlying it, its connection with the firm's business goals, and the attitudes and skills of those responsible for its administration.

[OUTCOME 2]

To determine the contributions of each individual, it is necessary to have a formal appraisal program with clearly stated objectives. Carefully defined performance standards that are reliable, strategically relevant, and free from either criterion deficiency or criterion contamination are essential foundations for evaluation. Appraisal systems must also comply with the law and, like selections tests, be valid and reliable. For example, ratings must be job related, employees must understand their performance standards in advance, appraisers must be able to observe job performance, appraisers must be trained, feedback must be given, and an appeals procedure must be established. Some companies now hold calibration meetings to ensure their managers are accurately rating employees. Using multiple raters is frequently a good idea because different individuals see different facets of an employee's performance. The supervisor, for example, has legitimate authority over an employee and is in a good position to discern whether he or she is contributing to the goals of the organization. Peers and team members, on the other hand, often have an unfiltered view of an employee's work activity, particularly related to issues such as cooperation and dependability. Subordinates often provide good information about whether an employee is facilitating their work, and customers (both internal and external) can convey the extent to which an employee adds value and meets their requirements. Self-appraisal is useful, if for no other reason than it encourages employees to think about their strengths, weaknesses, and future goals. An increasing number of organizations are using multiple raters—or 360-degree appraisal—to get a more comprehensive picture of employee performance. Regardless of the source of appraisal information, appraisers should be thoroughly trained in the particular methods they will use in evaluating their subordinates. Participation in developing rating scales, such as a BARS, automatically provides such training.

[OUTCOME 3]

Several methods can be used for performance appraisals. These include trait approaches (such as graphic rating scales, mixed-standard scales, forced-choice forms, and essays), behavioural methods (such as critical incident ratings, checklists, BARS, and BOS), and results methods (MBO). The choice of method depends on the purpose of the appraisal. Trait appraisals are simple to develop and complete, but they have problems in subjectivity and are not useful for feedback. Behavioural methods provide more specific information for giving feedback but can be time consuming and costly to develop. Results appraisals are more objective and can link individual performance to the organization as a whole, but they may encourage a short-term perspective (such as annual goals) and may not include subtle yet important aspects of performance.

[OUTCOME 4]

The degree to which a performance appraisal program benefits an organization and its members is directly related to the quality of the appraisal interviews that are conducted. Interviewing skills are best developed through instruction and supervised practice. Although there are various approaches to the interview, research suggests that employee participation and goal setting lead to higher satisfaction and improved performance. Discussing problems, showing support, minimizing criticism, and rewarding effective performance are also beneficial practices. During the interview, performance deficiencies can be discussed and plans for improvement can be made.

KEY TERMS

behaviour observation scale (BOS), 345
behaviourally anchored rating scale (BARS), 344
calibration, 327
contrast error, 327
critical incident, 343
customer appraisal, 332
error of central tendency, 337

essay method, 343
forced-choice method, 343
graphic rating scale method, 340
leniency or strictness error, 337
management by objectives (MBO), 346
manager and/or supervisor appraisal, 330
mixed-standard scale method, 342

peer appraisal, 331
performance appraisal, 322
performance management, 322
recency error, 338
self-appraisal, 330
similar-to-me error, 339
subordinate appraisal, 330
team appraisal, 331

DISCUSSION QUESTIONS

1. Eighty percent of Canadian organizations have performance appraisal systems. List some reasons that 20 percent would not choose to implement one.

2. Develop a list of the characteristics of effective service for fast-food servers at places such as Tim Hortons. Over your next five visits, rate the servers against the criteria that you have developed. Did your criteria meet the performance standards of relevant and reliable, or were they subject to criterion deficiency or contamination?

3. Develop a ten-item checklist to be used to rate student behaviour (e.g., *Always submits assignments on time*.) Rate your own behaviour against this list. Then ask friends and family members to rate your behaviour. Are there differences? If so, how would you explain them?

4. Take two of the items from question 3, and develop a behaviourally anchored rating scale for each of these items. Then rate yourself and ask others to rate you using the BARS. Did the ratings change? If so, why?

5. Think of a friend or a family member whose behaviour you wish to change (e.g., your friend is usually late for events that you have organized). Using the problem-solving interview, and the suggestions for conducting an effective appraisal interview, provide appraisal feedback to your friend.

6. What sources could be used to evaluate the performance of people working in the following jobs?
   a. Sales representative
   b. TV repairer
   c. Director of nursing in a hospital
   d. HR manager
   e. Air traffic controller

7. In many organizations, evaluators submit ratings to their immediate superiors for review before discussing them with the individual employees they have rated. What advantages are there to this procedure?

8. What are the pros and cons of trait, behaviour, and results appraisals?

9. Three types of appraisal interviews are described in this chapter.
   a. What different skills are required for each type of appraisal interview? What reactions can one expect from using these different skills?
   b. How can one develop the skills needed for the problem-solving type of interview?
   c. Which method do you feel is the least desirable? Why?

10. A member of your study team usually misses the deadline for submitting his part of the assignment. Using Figure 8.9, conduct a performance diagnosis.

INTERNET EXERCISE

Using the Oxy-gen website, http://www.oxy-gen.com/360-degree-feedback/what-is-360-degree-feedback.asp, prepare a performance evaluation exercise for your group work (at school or work)

1. Determine the purpose of your providing feedback.

2. Select sample rating items from the forms provided.

3. Provide feedback using the recommendations in this chapter.

HRM EXPERIENCE

Performance Diagnosis

Managing performance is an important—yet delicate—process for managers to undertake. They need to make tough calls at times regarding who is performing well or not. Also, they need to play the role of coach to help each employee improve his or her performance. One of the toughest aspects of performance management is assessing why someone is not performing well. Although it may be easy to spot who is not performing well, it is not always easy to diagnose the underlying causes of poor performance (such as ability, motivation, and environment). But without a correct diagnosis, it is nearly impossible to cure the problem.

Assignment

The following are descriptions of three different employees. Describe the potential causes of poor performance in each case. For each potential cause, identify appropriate solutions to enhance performance.

1. Carl Spackler is the assistant greenskeeper at Bushwood Country Club. Over the past few months, members have been complaining that gophers are destroying the course and digging holes in the greens. Although Carl has been working evenings and weekends to address the situation, the problem persists. Unfortunately, his boss is interested only in results, and because the gophers are still there, he contends that Carl is not doing his job. He has accused Carl of "slacking off" and threatened his job.

2. Susan Griswold works in research and development for a chemical company that makes nonnutritive food additives. Her most recent assignment has been the development of a nonstick aerosol cooking spray, but the project is way behind schedule and seems to be going nowhere. CEO Frank Shirley is decidedly upset and has threatened that if things do not improve, he will suspend bonuses again this year, as he did last year. Susan feels dejected because without the bonus she will not be able to take her family on vacation.

3. Bonnie Molloy is the host of a local television talk show called *Morning Metro*. Although she is a talented performer and comedienne, Bonnie has an unacceptable record of tardiness. The show's producer, David Bellows, is frustrated because the problem has affected the quality of the show. On several occasions, Bonnie was unprepared when the show went on the air. Bellows has concluded that Bonnie is not a morning person and has thought about replacing her with a different host.

BIZFLIX EXERCISES

SEABISCUIT: GEORGE RIDES SEABISCUIT

This scene will show you several aspects of appraising and improving performance. Watch for performance standards, peer appraisal, behaviour shaping, and coaching.

Combine a jockey who is blind in one eye with an undersized, ill-tempered thoroughbred and an unusual trainer. The result: the Depression-era champion racehorse Seabiscuit. This engaging film shows the training and development of Seabiscuit by trainer "Silent" Tom Smith (Chris Cooper) and jockey Red Pollard (Tobey Maguire). The enduring commitment of owner Charles Howard (Jeff Bridges) ensures the ultimate success of Seabiscuit on the racing circuit.

The *Seabiscuit* scene is a composite edited from DVD Chapter 21 toward the end of the film. In earlier scenes, Red severely injured a leg—he cannot ride Seabiscuit in the competition against War Admiral. Samuel Riddle (Eddie Jones), War Admiral's owner, has described any new rider as immaterial to the race's result. The scene begins with Red giving George Wolff (Gary Stevens), Seabiscuit's new jockey, some tips about riding him.

What to Watch for and Ask Yourself

- Does Red set clear performance standards for George? If he does, what are they?
- Red and George are both jockeys who competed against each other in earlier races. Do these scenes show peer appraisal or appraisal by people of different rank or position? Which characteristics of the performance appraisal process does this scene show?
- An earlier section, "Performance Appraisal Methods," discussed many approaches to performance appraisal. Which method or methods most closely match(es) what occurs in these scenes? Identify examples in the scenes that match the performance appraisal method or methods you picked.

CASE STUDY 1

JUST-IN-TIME FEEDBACK

Critics of formal performance evaluation programs cite "timeliness" as the major disadvantage of the annual formal performance appraisal interview. This criticism is gaining force as more people become accustomed to instant dialogue on BlackBerries, Facebook, and Twitter. The second criticism of the traditional performance appraisal interview is the one-way nature of the communication. The Net generation wants dialogue, not lectures. They want instant feedback and information about everything. The traditional process does not deliver what employees want: constant, timely and interactive feedback. Daily feedback is more important and effective than annual feedback.

Technology may be the answer. A Canadian company, Rypple, has created a Web-based service to replace the performance review. Instead of waiting one year to sit down with a boss, employees choose some advisers who could be mentors, coworkers, managers, or clients. These employees can then contact the advisers with direct questions (How do I prepare for the report to the board?) or career queries (How can I be more effective on my job?). The advisers can respond quickly and anonymously to provide real-time, just-in-time performance feedback.

Source: Adapted from Dan Tapscott, "The Just-in-Time Performance Review," *The Globe and Mail*, February 13, 2009, B15; Malcolm Gabriel, Pierre Robitaille, "Sustaining High Performance with Generation-Y Employees," *Canadian HR Reporter* (January 14, 2008), vol. 21, iss. 1: 13.

QUESTIONS

1. What are the advantages and limitations of this kind of performance feedback?

2. Who would you choose as mentors in your current job, and why?

3. What questions would you ask them?

CASE STUDY 2

BANK OF MONTREAL'S BALANCED SCORECARD

In 1990, the Bank of Montreal (BMO) had one major goal: to focus the entire workforce on success. It's a simple idea, but not so easy in execution. How would the company get entry-level tellers to think of their work not just as a means to a paycheque, but as a direct contribution to BMO shareholders? How would it remind corporate executives that their jobs were not just to boost the bottom line, but to charm entire communities?

The answer was BMO executives' balanced scorecard approach. To be competitive, executives decided, the bank had to meet the needs of four stakeholders: BMO shareholders, customers, employees, and communities. Executives translated that idea into four goals: Shareholders needed a return on equity, customers needed good service, employees needed to feel loyal and satisfied, and communities needed to feel that the bank made a difference in their neighbourhoods. Return on investment would determine satisfaction for shareholders; surveys and feedback would determine satisfaction for customers, employees, and communities.

Every single department and every employee in every department had to understand how their work contributed to the success of those four goals. So each employee's and each department's performance ratings were revised to reflect their contribution toward each goal. Employees in the customer service department, for instance, were rated by their return on equity (judged by their cost-effectiveness), their customer satisfaction (judged by customer feedback), and their community involvement (judged by any outreach programs or increase in customers). In some cases, departments were assigned a specific stakeholder. For example, HR was put in charge of the employee piece, ensuring competent, committed workers in a cost-effective way. Similarly, the company's senior vice-president of HR was responsible for training and education aspects to ensure competency and work–life and career development programs to help with employee commitment. At the end of the year, the scores from everyone's performance ratings were translated into indexes, ratings from 1 to 10. The index for the employee stakeholder piece was determined by ratings for competency, commitment, and cost-effectiveness. The four indexes for BMO shareholders, customers, employees, and communities were then rolled up into one figure of merit to determine the bonus of BMO's CEO.

QUESTIONS

1. What are the strengths and weaknesses of a balanced scorecard approach to performance appraisal?

2. Do you think it is fair to base the bonus paid to BMO's CEO on the four indexes comprising the firm's balanced scorecard?

3. Do you believe that a balanced scorecard approach would be more effective for the administrative or for the developmental purposes of appraisal discussed in this chapter?

CAREER COUNSEL

Obtain a rating of your performance by consulting http://www.belcourt6e.nelson .com.

NOTES AND REFERENCES

1. Susan Scherreik, "Your Performance Review: Make It Perform," *Business Week*, no. 3762 (December 17, 2001): 139; Dick Grote, "Performance Evaluations: Is It Time for a Makeover?" *HRfocus* 77, no. 11 (November 2000): 6–7; "Employers Need to Do a Better Job of Performance Management," *Managing Training & Development* (April 2003): 8; Christopher D. Lee, "Feedback, Not Appraisal," *HR Magazine* 51, no. 11 (November 2006): 111–114.

2. Matthew Boyle, "Performance Reviews: Perilous Curves Ahead," *Fortune* 143, no. 11 (May 28, 2001): 187–188; Susanne Scott and Walter Einstein, "Strategic Performance Appraisal in Team-Based Organizations: One Size Does Not Fit All," *Academy of Management Executive* 15, no. 2 (May 2001): 107–116, "Study Questions Performance Appraisal," *Australasian Business Intelligence* (May 1, 2003); Drew Robb, "Building a Better Workforce: Performance Management Software Can Help You Identify and Develop High-Performing Workers," *HR Magazine* 49, no. 10 (October 2004): 86–93.

3. Jonathan A. Segal, "86 Your Appraisal Process?" *HR Magazine* 45, no. 10 (October 2000): 199–206; Barry Witcher and Rosie Butterworth, "Honshin Kanri: How Xerox Manages," *Long-Range Planning* 32, no. 3 (June 1999): 323–332.

4. Janet Wiscombe, "Can Pay for Performance Really Work?" *Workforce* 80, no. 8 (August 2001): 28–34; Charlotte Garvey, "Meaningful Tokens of Appreciation: Cash Awards Aren't the Only Way to Motivate Your Workforce," *HR Magazine* 49, no. 8 (August 2004): 101–106; Lisa D. Sprenkle, "Forced Ranking: A Good Thing for Business?" Workforce.com.

5. David Allen and Rodger Griffeth, "Test of a Mediated Performance-Turnover Relationship Highlighting the Moderating Roles of Visibility and Reward Contingency," *Journal of Applied Psychology* 86, no. 5 (October 2001): 1014–1021; Charles Pettijohn, Linda Pettijohn, and Michael D'Amico, "Characteristics of Performance Appraisals and Their Impact on Sales Force Satisfaction," *Human Resource Development Quarterly* 12, no. 2 (Summer 2001): 127–146; Scott and Einstein, "Strategic Performance Appraisal in Team-Based Organizations," 107–116; "Organizations Seek Stronger Performance Management—and PFP," *Pay for Performance Report* 4, no. 6 (June 2004): 2–4.

6. Donna Doldwasser, "Me a Trainer?" *Training* 38, no. 4 (April 2001): 60–66; Rebecca Ganzel, "Mike Carter," *Training* 38, no. 7 (July 2001): 28–30; Carla Joinson, "Making Sure Employees Measure Up," *HR Magazine* 46, no. 3 (March 2001): 36–41; Morton D. Rosenbaum, "Gratitude Adjustment: When a Pat on the Back Isn't Enough," *Meetings & Conventions* 39, no. 7 (June 2004): 20; James W. Smither, Manuel London, and Richard R. Reilly, "Does Performance Improve Following Multisource Feedback?" *Personnel Psychology* 58, no. 1 (Spring 2005): 33–67.

7. Kathryn Bartol, Cathy Durham, and June Poon, "Influence of Performance Evaluation Rating Segmentation on Motivation and Fairness Perceptions," *Journal of Applied Psychology* 86, no. 6 (December 2001): 1106–1019; Anne P. Hubbell, "Motivating Factors: Perceptions of Justice and Their Relationship with Managerial and Organizational Trust," *Communication Studies* 56, no. 1 (March 2005): 47; Rebecca M. Chory-Assad, "Room for Improvement," *Training* 40, no. 11 (December 2003): 18–20; Deanna M. Merritt, "Appraising the Performance Appraisal," *Supervision* 68, no 4 (April 2007): 3–5.

8. John Newman, J. Mack Robinson, Larry Tyler, David Dunbar, and Joseph Zager, "CEO Performance Appraisal: Review and Recommendations/Practitioner Application," *Journal of Healthcare Management* 46, no. 1 (January/February 2001): 21–38; Bob Losyk, "How to Conduct a Performance Appraisal," *Public Management* 84, no. 3 (April 2002): 8–12; Arup Varma and Shaun Pichler, "Interpersonal Affect: Does It Really Bias Performance Appraisals?" *Journal of Labor Research* 28, no. 2 (Spring 2007): 397–412.

9. Doug Cederblom, "From Performance Appraisal to Performance Management: One Agency's Experience," *Public Personnel Management* 31, no. 2 (Summer 2002): 131–140; "Anonymous 360-Feedback Drives Vauxhall Strategy," *Personnel Today* (August 19, 2003): 16; Cindy Romaine, "Staying Relevant: Competencies and Employee Reviews," *Information Outlook* 8, no. 7 (April 2004): 21–25; Jerry K. Palmer and James M. Loveland, "The Influence of Group Discussion on Performance Judgments: Rating Accuracy, Contrast Effects, and Halo," *Journal of Psychology* 142, no. 2 (March 2008): 117–130.

10. Jason D. Shaw and Nina Gupta, "Job Complexity, Performance, and Well-Being: When Does Supplies-Values Fit Matter?" *Personnel Psychology* 57, no. 4 (Winter 2004): 847–880.

11. Joel Lefkowitz, "The Role of Interpersonal Affective Regard in Supervisory Performance Ratings: A Literature Review and Proposed Causal Model," *Journal of Occupational and Organizational Psychology* 73, no. 1 (March 2000): 67–85; Scott Highhouse, "Assessing the Candidate As a Whole: A Historical and Critical Analysis of Individual Psychological Assessment for Personnel Decision Making," *Personnel Psychology* 55, no. 2 (Summer 2002): 363–397.

12. Joanne Sammer, "Calibrating Consistency," *HR Magazine* 53, no. 1 (January 2008): 73–75.

13. Timothy Aeppel, "Goodyear Ends Ratings System ahead of Lawsuit," *The Wall Street Journal*, September 12, 2002, B8; "How to Stay 'Legal' with Performance Evaluation and Testing," *Managing Training & Development*, no. 4 (February 2004): 9.

14. Gillian Flynn, "Getting Performance Reviews Right," *Workforce* 80, no. 5 (May 2001): 76–78; David C. Martin, Kathryn M. Bartol, and Patrick E. Kehoe, "The Legal Ramifications of Performance Appraisal: The Growing Significance," *Public Personnel Management* 29, no. 3 (Fall 2000): 381; Deanna M Merritt, "Appraising the Performance Appraisal," *Supervision* 68, no 4 (April 2007): 3–5; Kevin R. Murphy, "Perspectives on the Relationship Between Job Performance and Ratings of Job Performance," *Industrial & Organizational Psychology* (June 2008): 197–205.

15. Joan Brett and Leanne Atwater, "360-Degree Feedback: Accuracy, Reactions, and Perceptions of Usefulness," *Journal of Applied Psychology* 86, no. 5 (October 2001): 930–942; Bruce Pfau, Ira Kay, Kenneth Nowak, and Jai Ghorpade, "Does 360-Degree Feedback Negatively Affect Company Performance?" *HR Magazine* 47, no. 6 (June 2002): 54–59; Maury Peiperl, "Getting 360-Degree Feedback Right," *Harvard Business Review* 79, no. 1 (January 2001): 142–147; Robert Gandossy and Tina Kao, "Talent Wars: Out of Mind, Out of Practice," *Human Resource Planning* 27, no. 4 (December 2004): 15–20.

16. Corey E. Miller and Carl L. Thornton, "How Accurate Are Your Performance Appraisals?" *Public Personnel Management* (Summer 2006): 153–162; Edward J. Inderrieden, Robert E. Allen, and Timothy J. Keaveny, "Managerial Discretion in the Use of Self-Ratings in an Appraisal System: The Antecedents and Consequences," *Journal of Managerial Issues* 16, no. 4 (Winter 2004): 460–484.

17. Bob Rosner, "Squeezing more respect out of your team" *Workforce* 79, no. 7 (July 2000): 78–79; Dick Grote "The secrets of Performance Appraisal: Best Practices from the Masters" *Across the Board* 37, no. 5 (May 2000): 14–20; Edward J. Inderrieden, Robert E. Allen, and Timothy J. Keaveny "Managerial Discretion in the use of self-ratings in an appraisal system: The use of antecedents and consequences" *Journal of Managerial Issues*, 16. no. 4, (winter 2004): 460–484.

18. Jeffrey Seglin, "Reviewing Your Boss," *Fortune* 143, no. 12 (June 11, 2001): 248; Ann Harrington, "Workers of the World, Rate Your Boss!" *Fortune* 142, no. 6 (September 18, 2000): 340–342; Robert Thompson, "Management Lite: Less Control, More Innovation," *HR Magazine* 44, no. 8 (August 1999): 10.

19. Brett and Atwater, "360-Degree Feedback," 930–942; Paula Silva and Henry L. Tosi, "Determinants of the Anonymity of the CEO Evaluation Process," *Journal of Managerial Issues* 16, no. 1 (Spring 2004): 87–103.

20. Ann Pomeroy, "Great Places, Inspired Employees: The Nation's Best Employers Show That Inspiring Employee Involvement through Good HR Practices Makes Good Business Sense," *HR Magazine* 49, no. 7 (July 2004): 44–64; Sue Browness, "Full-Circle Feedback," *Profit* 25, no. 2 (May 2006): 77.

21. John Drexler, Jr., Terry Beehr, and Thomas Stetz, "Peer Appraisals: Differentiation of Individual Performance on Group Tasks," *Human Resource Management* 40, no. 4 (Winter 2001): 333–345.

22. Scott and Einstein, "Strategic Performance Appraisal in Team-Based Organizations," 107–116; Debbie Kibbe and Jill Casner-Lotto, "Ralston Foods: From Greenfield to Maturity in a Team-Based Plant," *Journal of Organizational Excellence* 21, no. 3 (Summer 2002): 57–67; Simon Taggar and Mitchell Neubert, "The Impact of Poor Performers on Team Outcomes: An Empirical Examination of Attribution Theory," *Personnel Psychology* 57, no. 4 (Winter 2004): 935–969; Bradley Kirkman and Benson Rosen, "Powering Up Teams," *Organizational Dynamics* 28, no. 3 (Winter 2000):

48–66; Matthew Valle and Kirk Davis, "Teams and Performance Appraisal: Using Metrics to Increase Reliability and Validity," *Team Performance Management* 5, no. 8 (1999): 238–243; Ebrahim Soltani, Robert Van der Meer, Terry M. Williams, and Pei-chun Lai, "The Compatibility of Performance Appraisal Systems with TQM Principles: Evidence from Current Practice," *International Journal of Operations & Production Management* 26, no. 1 (2006): 92–112.

23. Michael Cohn, "Best Buy Beefs Up Customer Value at the Call Center," *Internet World* 8, no. 6 (June 2002): 42–43; Joe Kohn, "Isuzu Has IDEA for Boosting Sales," *Automotive News* 76, no.5973 (March 4, 2002): 41; D. L. Radcliff, "A New Paradigm of Feedback," *Executive Excellence* 19, no. 4 (April 2002): 20; Neeraj Bharadwaj and Anne Roggeveen, "The Impact of Offshored and Outsourced Call Service Centers on Customer Appraisals," *Marketing Letters* 19, no. 1 (January 2008): 13–23.

24. Pfau, Kay, Nowak, and Ghorpade, "Does 360-Degree Feedback Negatively Affect Company Performance?" 54–59; Peiperl, "Getting 360-Degree Feedback Right," 142–147; Jack Kondrasuk, and Matt Graybill, "From Paper to Computer," *The Human Resource Professional* 13, no. 6 (November/December 2000): 18–19.

25. Gary Meyer, "Performance Reviews Made Easy, Paperless," *HR Magazine* 45, no. 10 (October 2000): 181–184; Douglas P. Shuit, "Huddling with the Coach—Part 2," *Workforce Management* 84, no. 2 (February 1, 2005): 5; "Ceridian and Softscape Announce an Agreement to Deliver Employee Performance and Development Solutions," *Payroll Manager's Report* (May 2004): 13; K. Sanwong, "The Development of a 360-Degree Performance Appraisal System: A University Case Study," *International Journal of Management* 25, no. 1 (March 2008): 16–22.

26. "Performance Appraisal," *HR Magazine* 47, no. 10 (October 2002): 146; Frank E. Kuzmits, Arthur J. Adams, Lyle Sussman, and Louis E. Raho, "360-Feedback in Health Care Management: A Field Study," *The Health Care Manager* 23, no. 321 (October–December 2004): 321–329; Jerry K. Palmer and James M. Loveland, "The Influence of Group Discussion on Performance Judgments: Rating Accuracy, Contrast Effects, and Halo. Preview," *Journal of Psychology* 142, no 2 (March 2008): 117–130; S. Bartholomew Craig and Kelly Hannum, "Research Update: 360-Degree Performance Assessment," *Consulting Psychology Journal: Practice & Research* 58, no. 2 (Spring 2006): 117–124.

27. Gary E. Roberts, "Perspectives on Enduring and Emerging Issues in Performance Appraisal," *Public Personnel Management* 27, no. 3 (Fall 1998): 301–320; William Hubbartt, "Bring Performance Appraisal Training to Life," *HR Magazine* 40, no. 5 (May 1995): 166, 168; Filip Lie vens, "Assessor Training Strategies and Their Effects on Accuracy, Interrater Reliability, and Discriminant Validity," *Journal of Applied Psychology* 86, no. 2 (April 2001): 255–264; Dick Grote, "Performance Appraisals: Solving Tough Challenges," *HR Magazine* 45, no. 7 (July 2000): 145–150; Leslie A. Weatherly, "Performance Management: Getting It Right from the Start," *HR Magazine* 49, no. 3 (March 2004): S1–S12.

28. Gary P. Latham and Kenneth N. Wexley, *Increasing Productivity through Performance Appraisal*, 2nd ed. (Reading, MA: Addison-Wesley, 1994), 137.

29. Lefkowitz, "The Role of Interpersonal Affective Regard in Supervisory Performance Ratings," 67–85; Edwin Arnold and Marcia Pulich, "Personality Conflicts and Objectivity in Appraising Performance," *The Health Care Manager* 22, no. 3 (July–September 2003): 227; Krista Uggersly and Lorne M. Suksy, "Using Frame-of-Reference Training to Understand the Implications of Rater Idiosyncrasy for Rating Accuracy," *Journal of Applied Psychology*, 93, no. 3 (May 2008): 711–719.

30. Deidra J. Schleicher and David V. Day, "A Cognitive Evaluation of Frame-of-Reference Rater Training: Content and Process Issues," *Organizational Behaviour and Human Decision Processes* 73, no. 1 (January 1998): 76–101; Wanda Smith, K. Vernard Harrington, and Jeffery Houghton, "Predictors of Performance Appraisal Discomfort: A Preliminary Examination," *Public Personnel Management* 29, no. 1 (Spring 2000): 21–32; Krista L. Uggerslev and Lorne M. Sulsky, "Using Frame-of-Reference Training to Understand the Implications of Rater Idiosyncrasy for Rating Accuracy," *Journal of Applied Psychology* 93, no. 3 (May 2008): 711–719.

31. Gail Johnson, "Forced Ranking: The Good, the Bad, and the Alternative," *Training* 41, no. 5 (May 2004): 24–31; Christine A. Amalfe and Eileen Quinn Steiner, "Forced Ranking Systems: Yesterday's Legal Target?" *New Jersey Law Journal* (March 28, 2005);

Jessica Marquez, "Is GE's Ranking System Broken?" *Workforce Management* 86, no. 12 (June 25, 2007): 1–3;

32. Lisa Keeping and Paul Levy, "Performance Appraisal Reaction: Measurement, Modeling, and Method Bias," *Journal of Applied Psychology* 85, no. 5 (October 2000): 708–723.

33. Adam B. Butler and Amie Skattebo, "What Is Acceptable for Women May Not Be for Men: The Effect of Family Conflicts with Work on Job-Performance Ratings," *Journal of Occupational and Organizational Psychology* 77, no. 4 (December 2004): 553–564; Cheri Ostroff, Leanne E. Atwater, and Barbara J. Feinberg, "Understanding Self-Other Agreement: A Look at Rater and Ratee Characteristics, Context, and Outcomes," *Personnel Psychology* 57, no. 1 (Summer 2004): 333–337; Mike Schraeder and Jim Simpson, "How Similarity and Liking Affect Performance Appraisals," *Journal for Quality & Participation* 29, no. 1 (Spring 2006): 34–40.

34. Kristina E. Chirico, M. Ronald Buckley, Anthony R. Wheeler, Jeffrey D. Facteau, H. John Bernardin, and Danielle S. Beu, "A Note on the Need for True Scores in Frame-of-Reference (FOR) Training Research," *Journal of Managerial Issues* 16, no. 3 (Fall 2004): 382–398; Christopher D. Lee, "Feedback, Not Appraisal," *HR Magazine* 51, no. 11 (November 2006): 111–114.

35. Stephen C. Behrenbrinker, "Conducting Productive Performance Evaluations in the Assessor's Office," *Assessment Journal* 2, no. 5 (September/October 1995): 48–54; Aharon Tziner, Christine Joanis, and Kevin Murphy, "A Comparison of Three Methods of Performance Appraisal with Regard to Goal Properties, Goal Perception, and Ratee Satisfaction," *Group & Organization Management* 25, no. 2 (June 2000): 175–190.

36. Elaine Pulakos, Sharon Arad, Michelle Donovan, and Kevin Plamondon, "Adaptability in the Workplace: Development of a Taxonomy of Adaptive Performance," *Journal of Applied Psychology* 85, no. 4 (August 2000): 612–624; Weatherly, "Performance Management: Getting It Right from the Start," S1–S12; Edwin Arnold and Marcia Pulich, "Personality Conflicts and Objectivity in Appraising Performance," *The Health Care Manager* 22, no. 3 (July–September 2003): 227.

37. Latham and Wexley, *Increasing Productivity*; Tziner, Joanis, and Murphy, "A Comparison of Three Methods of Performance Appraisal," 175–190; Simon Taggar and Travor Brown, "Problem-Solving Team Behaviours: Development and Validation of BOS and a Hierarchical Factor Structure," *Small Group Research* 32, no. 6 (December 2001): 698–726; Paul Falcone, "Big-Picture Performance Appraisal," *HRfocus* 84, no. 9 (September 2007): 1–15.

38. Daniel Bachrach, Elliot Bendoly, and Philip Podsakoff, "Attributions of the 'Causes' of Group Performance as an Alternative Explanation of the Relationship between Organizational Citizenship Behavior and Organizational Performance," *Journal of Applied Psychology* 86, no. 6 (December 2001): 1285–1293; Susan Leandri, "Measures That Matter: How to Fine-Tune Your Performance Measures," *Journal for Quality and Participation* 24, no. 1 (Spring 2001): 39–41.

39. Peter F. Drucker, *The Practice of Management* (New York: Harper & Brothers, 1954); reissued by HarperCollins in 1993; Janice S. Miller, "High Tech and High Performance: Managing Appraisal in the Information Age," *Journal of Labor Research* 24, no. 3 (Summer 2003): 409–425.

40. E. Locke and G. Latham, *A Theory of Goal Setting and Task Performance* (Englewood Cliffs, NJ: Prentice Hall, 1990). See also John J. Donovan and David J. Radosevich, "The Moderating Role of Goal Commitment on the Goal Difficulty-Performance Relationship: A Meta-Analytic Review and Critical Reanalysis," *Journal of Applied Psychology* 83, no. 2 (April 1998): 308–315; Cindy Romaine, "Staying Relevant: Competencies and Employee Reviews," *Information Outlook* 8, no. 4 (April 2004): 21–25; Gail Johnson, "Room for Improvement," *Training* 40, no. 11 (December 2003): 18–20.

41. Jack Steele, "Transforming the Balanced Scorecard into Your Strategy Execution System," *Manage* 53, no. 1 (September/October 2001): 22–23. See also Robert Kaplan and David Norton, "Strategic Learning and the Balanced Scorecard," *Strategy & Leadership* 24, no. 5 (September/October 1996): 18–24; Robert Kaplan and David Norton, "Using the Balanced Scorecard as a Strategic Management System," *Harvard Business Review* (January–February 1996): 75–85; Joe Mullich, "Get in Line: People Talk about Aligning Corporate, Departmental and Employee Goals, But Not Many Actually Do It," *Workforce Management* 82, no. 13 (43) (December 2003); "Good Appraisal Is

Simple, Happens Often, Experts Say," *The Orlando Sentinel* (Knight-Ridder/Tribune News Service), December 3, 2003; Li-cheng Chang, "The NHS Performance Assessment Framework as a Balanced Scorecard Approach," *International Journal of Public Sector Management* 20, no 2 (2007): 101–117.

42. Deloris McGee Wanguri, "A Review, an Integration, and a Critique of Cross-Disciplinary Research on Performance Appraisals, Evaluations, and Feedback," *Journal of Business Communications* 32, no. 3 (July 1995): 267–293; Tziner, Joanis, and Murphy, "A Comparison of Three Methods of Performance Appraisal," 175–190; "Good Appraisal Is Simple, Happens Often, Experts Say"; Joanna Haworth, "Measuring Performance," *Nursing Management*—UK 15, no. 3 (June 2008): 22–28.

43. Kwok Leung, Steven Su, and Michael Morris, "When Is Criticism Not Constructive? The Roles of Fairness Perceptions and Dispositional Attributions in Employee Acceptance of Critical Supervisory Feedback," *Human Relations* 54, no. 9 (September 2001): 1155–1187; Ted Pollock, "Make Your Criticism Pay Off," *Electric Light & Power* 81, no. 1 (January 2003): 31; "Five Ways to Tackle Poor Performers," *Law Office Management & Administration Report* 6, no. 12 (December 2006): 9.

44. "Focus on Success," *Aftermarket Business* 115, no. 2 (February 2005): 1.

45. Helen Wilkie, "The Tricky Art of Criticism," *HR Magazine* 49, no. 12 (December 2004): 77–83.

NEL

Managing Compensation

CHAPTER

After studying this chapter, you should be able to

[OUTCOME] 1 Explain employer concerns in developing a strategic compensation program.

[OUTCOME] 2 Indicate the various factors that influence the setting of wages.

[OUTCOME] 3 Differentiate the mechanics of each of the major job evaluation systems.

[OUTCOME] 4 Explain the purpose of a wage survey.

[OUTCOME] 5 Define the wage curve, pay grades, and rate ranges as parts of the compensation structure.

[OUTCOME] 6 Identify the major provisions of the laws and regulations affecting compensation.

[OUTCOME] 7 Discuss the current issues of equal pay for work of equal value and pay compression.

An extensive review of the literature indicates that important work-related variables leading to job satisfaction include challenging work, interesting job assignments, equitable rewards, competent supervision, and rewarding careers.[1] It is doubtful, however, whether many employees would continue working were it not for the money they earn. Employees desire compensation systems that they perceive as being fair and commensurate with their skills and expectations.

Furthermore, in today's business environment of low wage and salary increases, pay has become an increasingly significant consideration for employees as they strive to maintain their standard of living.[2] Therefore, pay is a major consideration in HRM because it provides employees with a tangible reward for their services, as well as a source of recognition and self-esteem. Employee compensation includes all forms of pay and rewards received by employees for the performance of their jobs. *Direct compensation* encompasses employee wages and salaries, incentives, bonuses, and commissions. *Indirect compensation* comprises the many benefits supplied by employers, and *nonfinancial compensation* includes employee recognition programs, rewarding jobs, organizational support, work environment, and flexible work hours to accommodate personal needs.

Both managers and scholars agree that the way compensation is allocated among employees sends a message about what management believes is important and the types of activities it encourages.[3] Furthermore, for an employer, the payroll constitutes a sizable operating cost. Ravin Jesuthasan, compensation specialist at Towers Perrin, notes, "Labour costs are a significant portion of expenses for any organization and a very substantial portion for some, but companies continue to spend on pay programs without any evidence of business relevance."[4] A strategic compensation program, therefore, is essential so that pay can serve to motivate employee production sufficiently and keep labour costs at an acceptable level. This chapter will be concerned with the management of a compensation program, job evaluation systems, and pay structures for determining compensation payments. Included will be a discussion of laws and regulations that affect wage and salary rates. Chapter 10 will review financial incentive plans for employees. Employee benefits that are part of the total compensation package are discussed in Chapter 11.

STRATEGIC COMPENSATION PLANNING

[OUTCOME 1]

What is strategic compensation planning? Simply stated, it is the compensation of employees in ways that enhance motivation and growth, while at the same time aligning their efforts with the objectives, philosophies, and culture of the organization. Strategic compensation planning goes beyond determining what market rates to pay employees—although market rates are one element of compensation planning—to purposefully linking compensation to the organization's mission and general business objectives. For example, in 2006, Microsoft Corporation, in the wake of managerial discontent, boosted the efficiency of its pay system by linking compensation payments to important business needs. An employee survey conducted in 2007 showed that employees now saw a stronger connection between pay and performance and the accomplishment of business goals and objectives.[5] Commenting on the importance of strategic compensation planning to organizational success, compensation specialists note, "Companies throughout the economy have begun to rethink their compensation systems in search for competitive advantage."

Additionally, strategic compensation planning serves to mesh the monetary payments made to employees with specific functions of the HR program. For example, in the recruitment of new employees, the rate of pay for jobs can increase or limit the supply of applicants. A compensation specialist speaking to one of the authors noted, "The linkage of pay levels to labour markets is a strategic policy issue because it serves to attract or retain valued employees while affecting the organization's relative payroll budget." For example, community colleges and universities know that they cannot attract or retain qualified professors unless their pay strategy is linked to competitive market rates.

Many fast-food restaurants, such as Burger King and Taco Bell—traditionally low-wage employers—have needed to raise their starting wages to attract a sufficient number of job applicants to meet staffing requirements. If pay rates are high, creating a large applicant pool, then organizations may choose to raise their selection standards and hire better-qualified employees. This in turn can reduce employer training costs. When employees perform at exceptional levels, their performance appraisals may justify an increased pay rate. For these reasons and others, an organization should develop a formal HR program to manage employee compensation. We will discuss three important aspects of strategic compensation planning: linking compensation to organizational objectives, the pay-for-performance standard, and motivating employees through compensation.

LINKING COMPENSATION TO ORGANIZATIONAL OBJECTIVES

Compensation has been revolutionized by heightened domestic competition, globalization, increased employee skill requirements, and new technology. Therefore, an outcome of today's dynamic business environment is that managers have needed to change their pay philosophies from paying for a specific position or job title to rewarding employees on the basis of their individual competencies or work contributions to organizational success. One study showed that 91 percent of responding organizations had a company compensation philosophy linking their pay strategy with organizational performance. As the authors of this study noted, "A written compensation philosophy indicates senior management understands and is committed to aligning their business strategy with pay," suggesting that alignment can have a positive impact on organizational effectiveness.[6]

Increasingly, compensation specialists are asking which components of the compensation package (benefits, base pay, incentives, and so on), both separately and in combination, create value for the organization and its employees. Managers are asking questions such as, "How will this pay program help to retain and motivate valued employees?" and "Does the benefit or pay practice affect the administrative cost?" Payments that fail to advance either the employee or the organization are removed from the compensation program.[7]

It is not uncommon for organizations to establish very specific goals for joining their organizational objectives to their compensation program.[8] Formalized compensation goals serve as guidelines for managers to ensure that wage and benefit policies achieve their intended purpose. The more common goals of a strategic compensation policy include the following:

1. To reward employees' past performance[9]
2. To remain competitive in the labour market
3. To maintain salary equity among employees
4. To mesh employees' future performance with organizational goals
5. To control the compensation budget
6. To attract new employees
7. To reduce unnecessary turnover[10]

To achieve these goals, policies must be established to guide management in making decisions. Formal statements of compensation policies typically include the following:

1. The rate of pay within the organization and whether it is to be above, below, or at the prevailing market rate
2. The ability of the pay program to gain employee acceptance while motivating employees to perform to the best of their abilities

3. The pay level at which employees may be recruited and the pay differential between new and more senior employees

4. The intervals at which pay raises are to be granted and the extent to which merit and/or seniority will influence the raises

5. The pay levels needed to facilitate the achievement of a sound financial position in relation to the products or services offered

THE PAY-FOR-PERFORMANCE STANDARD

This quote from compensation specialist Stephen E. Gross, global leader for Mercer Performance, Measurement, and Rewards consulting, illustrates the importance of pay-for-performance as a strategic pay practice: "Companies are looking for ways to pay for performance and segmenting their workforce helps them identify their most valuable contributors. Rewarding top performers is essential for the ongoing success of the company."[11] Why is this statement significant? A pay-for-performance standard serves to raise productivity and lower labour costs in today's competitive economic environment. It is agreed that managers must tie at least some reward to employee effort and performance. Without this standard, motivation to perform with greater effort will be low, resulting in higher wage costs to the organization. Additionally, most employees believe that their compensation should be directly linked to their relative performance.

The term *pay for performance* refers to a wide range of compensation options, including merit-based pay, bonuses, salary commissions, job and pay banding, team/group incentives, and various gainsharing programs. (Gainsharing plans are discussed in Chapter 10.) Each of these compensation systems seeks to differentiate between the pay of average performers and that of outstanding performers. When Plum Creek Timber Company merged with The Timber Company, it emphasized a pay-for-performance philosophy by forming new salary ranges based on each job's impact on the business and incentive rewards linked more directly to individual and company performance.

Unfortunately, designing a sound pay-for-performance system is not easy. Consideration must be given to how employee performance will be measured. For example, measuring an employee's output may be relatively easy and objective on an assembly line but more difficult (and subjective) when the employee works in a service environment. Other concerns include the monies to be allocated for compensation increases, which employees to cover, the payout method, and the periods when payments will be made.

Perhaps the most critical concern for a successful pay-for-performance system is the amount of money allocated by organizations for annual salary increases.[12] Although differences exist as to how large a wage or salary increase must be before it is perceived as meaningful, a pay-for-performance program will lack its full potential when pay increases only approximate rises in the cost of living.

pay-for-performance standard

A standard by which managers tie compensation to employee effort and performance

MOTIVATING EMPLOYEES THROUGH COMPENSATION

Pay constitutes a quantitative measure of an employee's relative worth. For most employees, pay has a direct bearing not only on their standard of living, but also on the status and recognition they may be able to achieve both on and off the job. Because pay represents a reward received in exchange for an employee's contributions, it is essential, according to the equity theory, that the pay be equitable in terms of those contributions. It is essential also that an employee's pay be equitable in terms of what other employees are receiving for their contributions.

Pay Equity

Simply defined, equity embraces the concept of fairness. Equity theory, also referred to as *distributive fairness*, is a motivation theory that explains how people respond to situations in which they feel they have received less (or more) than they deserve.[13]

Central to the theory is the role of perception in motivation and the fact that individuals make comparisons.[4] It states that individuals form a ratio of their inputs (abilities, skills, experiences) in a situation to their outcomes (salary, benefits) in that situation. They then compare the value of that ratio with the value of the input/output ratio for other individuals in a similar class of jobs either internal or external to the organization. If the value of their ratio equals the value of another's, they perceive the situation as equitable, and no tension exists. However, if they perceive their input/output ratio as inequitable relative to others', this creates tension and motivates them to eliminate or reduce the inequity. The strength of their motivation is proportional to the magnitude of the perceived inequity. Figure 9.1 illustrates pay equity and feelings of being fairly paid.

For employees, pay equity is achieved when the compensation received is equal to the value of the work performed. Research clearly demonstrates that employees' perceptions of pay equity, or inequity, can have dramatic effects on their motivation for both work behaviour and productivity. Managers must therefore develop strategic pay practices that are both internally and externally equitable. Compensation policies are *internally* equitable when employees believe that the wage rates for their jobs approximate the job's worth to the organization. Perceptions of *external* pay equity exist when the organization is paying wages that are relatively equal to what other employers are paying for similar types of work.

Expectancy Theory and Pay

The expectancy theory of motivation predicts that one's level of motivation depends on the attractiveness of the rewards sought and the probability of obtaining those rewards.[5] The theory has developed from the work of psychologists who consider humans as thinking, reasoning people who have beliefs and anticipations concerning future life events. Expectancy theory therefore holds that employees

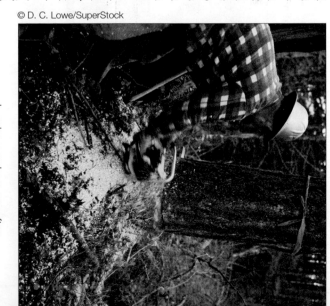

© D. C. Lowe/SuperStock

Lumber workers are often paid on a pay-for-performance basis.

pay equity
An employee's perception that compensation received is equal to the value of the work performed

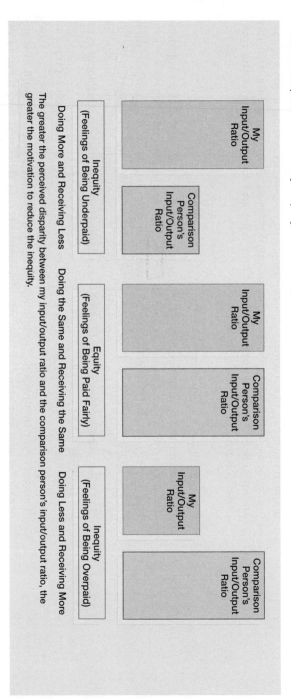

FIGURE 9.1

Relationship between Pay Equity and Motivation

My Input/Output Ratio	Comparison Person's Input/Output Ratio
Inequity (Feelings of Being Underpaid)	

Doing More and Receiving Less

My Input/Output Ratio	Comparison Person's Input/Output Ratio
Equity (Feelings of Being Paid Fairly)	

Doing the Same and Receiving the Same

My Input/Output Ratio	Comparison Person's Input/Output Ratio
Inequity (Feelings of Being Overpaid)	

Doing Less and Receiving More

The greater the perceived disparity between my input/output ratio and the comparison person's input/output ratio, the greater the motivation to reduce the inequity.

FIGURE **9.2**

Pay-for-Performance and Expectancy Theory

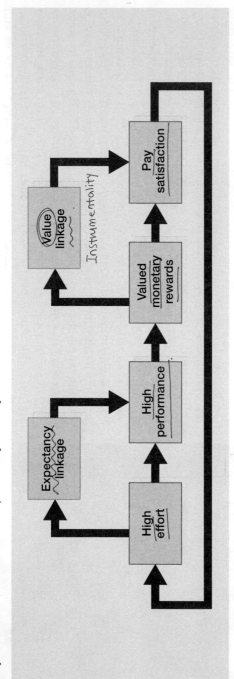

should exert greater work effort if they have reason to expect that it will result in a reward that is valued.[16] To motivate this effort, the value of any monetary reward should be attractive. Employees also must believe that good performance is valued by their employer and will result in their receiving the expected reward.

Figure 9.2 shows the relationship between pay-for-performance and the expectancy theory of motivation. The model predicts, first, that high effort will lead to high performance (expectancy). For example, if an employee believes she has the skills and abilities to perform her job and if she works hard (effort), then her performance will improve or be high. Second, high performance should result in rewards that are appreciated (valued). Elements of the compensation package are said to have instrumentality when an employee's high performance leads to monetary rewards that are valued. As we previously stated that pay-for-performance leads to a feeling of pay satisfaction, this feeling should reinforce one's high level of effort.

Thus, how employees view compensation can be an important factor in determining the motivational value of compensation. Furthermore, the effective communication of pay information together with an organizational environment that elicits employee trust in management can contribute to employees having more accurate perceptions of their pay. The perceptions employees develop concerning their pay are influenced by the accuracy of their knowledge and understanding of the compensation program's strategic objectives.

Pay Secrecy

Misperceptions by employees concerning the equity of their pay and its relationship to performance can be created by secrecy about the pay that others receive. There is reason to believe that secrecy can generate distrust in the compensation system, reduce employee motivation, and inhibit organizational effectiveness. Yet pay secrecy seems to be an accepted practice in many organizations. Employers may have overt or implicit prohibitions on sharing pay information, and some even put the policies in writing.[17]

Managers may justify secrecy on the grounds that most employees prefer to have their own pay kept secret. Probably one of the reasons for pay secrecy that managers may be unwilling to admit is that it gives them greater freedom in compensation management because pay decisions are not disclosed and there is no need to justify or defend them.[18] Employees who are not supposed to know what others are being paid have no objective base for pursuing complaints about their own pay. Secrecy also serves to cover up inequities existing within the internal pay structure. Furthermore, secrecy surrounding compensation decisions may lead employees to believe that there is no direct relationship between pay and performance.

Managers wishing to maintain pay secrecy among employees may encounter problems with Internet salary survey data. Ready access to free online salary surveys gives employees an approximate idea of how their salary compares to others nationally or locally. This information could put managers "on the spot" should employees discover that their salaries are lower than those of other employees at comparable organizations.

THE BASES FOR COMPENSATION

Work performed in most private, public, and not-for-profit organizations has traditionally been compensated on an hourly basis. It is referred to as **hourly work**, in contrast to **piecework**, in which employees are paid according to the number of units they produce. Hourly work is far more prevalent than piecework as a basis for compensating employees.

Employees compensated on an hourly basis are classified as *hourly employees*, or *wage earners*. Those whose compensation is computed on the basis of weekly, biweekly, or monthly pay periods are classified as *salaried employees*. Hourly

hourly work
Work done on an hourly basis

piecework
Work paid according to the number of units produced

Ethics in **HRM**

Working for Free

Two restaurants in Ontario, one in Port Hope, and the other in Belleville were benefiting from the services of more than 20 people (called volunteers or agents) who were not being paid wages but made their money on the tips customers left for them. The province's *Employment Standards Act* stipulates that waiters must be paid $5.95 an hour (less than the minimum wage, due to tips), and that every employer must pay a minimum wage. The restaurants argued that they provided a location where workers could act as service agents and undertake their business, relying on tips for income. Were the waiters working for free?

Elaine Chu worked at a local fast-food restaurant to earn enough money to support herself while she attended university part-time. Her job title was night manager, and she worked the 4 p.m. to 11 p.m. shift. During this shift she was the only employee on duty, and she did all of the food preparation, serving, and

cleanup. Most nights, customers arrived after the movies (around 11 p.m.), and Chu was expected to work into the next shift until the crowd dispersed. She received no overtime pay for these extra hours because employers were not required to pay overtime for managers. Did Chu's employer misuse the title "manager" in order to circumvent its obligations with respect to overtime pay? To be deemed a true manager, an individual should have staff reporting to him or her, should have responsibility for a major aspect of the business, and should provide counselling to more junior staff through performance appraisal. Was Chu working for free?

According to a Statistics Canada survey, one-fifth of all employees put in extra hours at work, and 60 percent of these are unpaid, with workers averaging nine unpaid hours per week. White-collar employees are working for free, and they know why: they are afraid of losing their jobs.

Sources: http://www.jobquality.ca/indicator, retrieved June 30, 2006; Bruce Little, "Canadians Work Overtime for Free," *The Globe and Mail*, July 14, 1997: B6; Susan Bourette, "Volunteer Waiters Work Only for Tips," *The Globe and Mail*, July 27, 1997: A7.

employees are normally paid only for the time they work. Salaried employees, by contrast, are generally paid the same for each pay period, even though they occasionally may work more hours or fewer than the regular number of hours in a period. They also usually receive certain benefits not provided to hourly employees.

Employment practices are a provincial jurisdiction, and each province has its own employment standards act. Each of these acts contains a provision that requires the employer to reimburse the employee at a specified rate after he or she has worked the minimum required hours. This rate is usually 1.5 times the employee's base hourly rate of pay. Some employers offer overtime pay that is more generous than what the act specifies. Some acts provide for time in lieu of overtime; thus, four hours of overtime paid at 1.5 would be the equivalent of six hours in either pay or time off in lieu of payment. Supervisory and management personnel are not usually paid overtime; still other personnel work overtime for free (see Ethics in HRM). Each of the employment standards acts includes a list of people who are exempt from the overtime provision.

Because so many American companies are operating in Canada, the terms *exempt* (to describe employees not covered in the overtime provisions of the *U.S. Fair Labor Standards Act*) and *nonexempt* (to describe employees covered by the overtime provisions of the *U.S. Fair Labor Standards Act*) are often heard, although neither has any relevance in Canadian legislation. These terms are used specifically to denote *supervisory* and *nonsupervisory* roles. U.S. legislation stipulates that only nonexempt (i.e., nonsupervisory) workers are entitled to overtime pay.

Using the Internet

You can determine the salary of almost any job by using sites such as

http://www.workopolis.ca

[OUTCOME 2]

DETERMINING COMPENSATION—THE WAGE MIX

Employees may inquire of their managers: "How are the wages for my job determined?" In practice, a combination of *internal* and *external* factors can influence, directly or indirectly, the rates at which employees are paid. Through their interaction, these factors constitute the wage mix, as shown in Figure 9.3. For example, the area wage rate for administrative assistants might be $11.50 per hour. However, one employer may elect to pay its administrative assistants $14.25 per hour because of their excellent performance. The influence of government legislation on the wage mix will be discussed later in the chapter.

INTERNAL FACTORS

The internal factors that influence wage rates are the employer's compensation strategy, the worth of a job, an employee's relative worth in meeting job requirements, and an employer's ability to pay.

Employer's Compensation Strategy

Highlights in HRM 9.1 illustrates the compensation strategies of two organizations, Tri Star Performance and Preventive Health Care. The pay strategy of Preventive Health Care is to be an industry pay leader, while Tri Star Performance seeks to be wage-competitive. Both employers strive to promote a compensation policy that is internally fair.

Tri Star Performance and Preventive Health Care, like other employers, will establish numerous compensation objectives that affect the pay employees receive. As a minimum, both large and small employers should set pay policies reflecting (1) the internal wage relationship among jobs and skill levels, (2) the external

FIGURE 9.3

Factors Affecting the Wage Mix

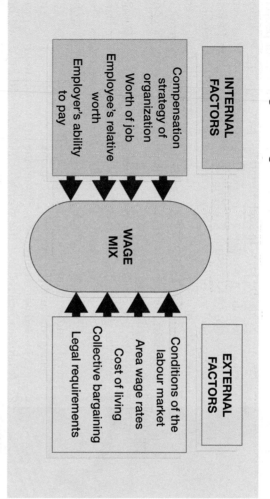

competition or an employer's pay position relative to what competitors are paying, (3) a policy of rewarding employee performance, and (4) administrative decisions concerning elements of the pay system such as overtime premiums, payment periods, and short-term or long-term incentives.

Highlights in HRM 9.1

Comparison of Compensation Strategies

Compensation strategies and objectives can differ widely across large and small employers as well as across employers in the private and public sectors. Here are the compensation strategies at Tri Star Performance and Preventive Health Care.

Tri Star Performance	Preventive Health Care
• Promote pay-for-performance practices	• Be a pay leader in the health care industry
• Pay market-competitive compensation	• Promote open and understandable pay practices
• Achieve internal and external pay equity	• Ensure fair employee treatment
• Achieve simplicity in compensation programs	• Offer benefits promoting individual employee needs
• Strive for employee commitment and a collaborative work environment	• Offer compensation rewarding employee creativity and achievements
• Promote gender fairness in pay and benefits	• Offer compensation to foster the strategic mission of the organization
• Comply with all governmental compensation regulations	• Obtain employee input when developing compensation practices
• Minimize increased fixed costs	• Emphasize performance through variable pay and stock options

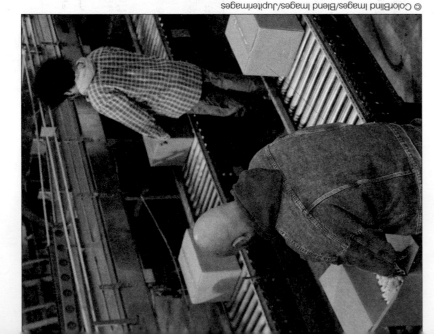

Assembly-line workers have little opportunity to influence their individual pay.

© ColorBlind Images/Blend Images/Jupiterimages

Worth of a Job

Organizations without a formal compensation program generally base the worth of jobs on the subjective opinions of people familiar with the jobs. In such instances, pay rates may be influenced heavily by the labour market or, in the case of unionized employers, by collective bargaining. Organizations with formal compensation programs, however, are more likely to rely on a system of job evaluation to aid in rate determination. Even when rates are subject to collective bargaining, job evaluation can assist the organization in maintaining some degree of control over its wage structure.

The use of job evaluation is widespread in both the public and the private sector. The City of Mississauga and Star Data Systems use job evaluation in establishing wage structures. The jobs covered most frequently by job evaluation are clerical, technical, and various blue-collar groups. Other jobs covered are managerial and top executive positions.

In today's competitive environment, compensation professionals believe that the worth of a job should be based on more than market prices or using only an internally driven job evaluation program. Rather, a job's value should be based on the total value delivered to the organization. That is, some jobs may simply be more important to organizational success than others regardless of how they are internally evaluated. Valuing work not only properly enables organizations to price "important" jobs effectively, but also provides insight into how a job relates to overall organizational success. Additionally, valuing work properly serves to attract and retain the right talent to drive organizational performance.[19]

Employee's Relative Worth

In both hourly and salary jobs, employee performance can be recognized and rewarded through promotion and with various incentive systems. (The incentive systems used most often will be discussed in Chapter 10.) Superior performance can also be rewarded by granting merit raises on the basis of steps within a rate range established for a job class. If merit raises are to have their intended value, however, they must be determined by an effective performance appraisal system that differentiates between employees who deserve the raises and those who do not. This system, moreover, must provide a visible and credible relationship between performance and any raise received. Unfortunately, too many so-called merit systems provide for raises to be granted automatically. As a result, employees tend to be rewarded more for merely being present than for being productive on the job. Also, as previously noted, most increases may lack motivational value to employees when organizational salary budgets are low.[20]

Employer's Ability to Pay

Pay levels are limited by earned profits and other financial resources available to employers. This is clearly illustrated by financially burdened companies that ask their employees for pay cuts. Furthermore, an organization's ability to pay is determined in part by the productivity of its employees. This productivity is a result not only of their performance, but also of the amount of capital the organization has invested in labour-saving equipment. Generally, increases in capital investment reduce the number of employees required to perform the work and increase an employer's ability to provide higher pay for those it employs.

affect the rates they are able to pay. Competition and recessions can force prices down and reduce the income from which compensation payments are derived. In such situations, employers have little choice but to reduce wages and/or lay off employees or, even worse, to go out of business.

General Motors and Chrysler have had to both reduce wages and lay off employees.

EXTERNAL FACTORS

The major external factors that influence wage rates include labour market conditions, area wage rates, cost of living, collective bargaining if the employer is unionized, and legal requirements. The legal requirements of compensation will be discussed later in the chapter.

Labour Market Conditions

The labour market reflects the forces of supply and demand for qualified labour within an area. These forces help influence the wage rates required to recruit or retain competent employees. It must be recognized, however, that counterforces can reduce the full impact of supply and demand on the labour market. The economic power of unions, for example, may prevent employers from lowering wage rates even when unemployment is high among union members. Government regulations also may prevent an employer from paying at a market rate less than an established minimum set by each province. The meltdown of the auto sector has resulted in the government's intervening in the compensation agreements in return for giving financial assistance. The goal is to avoid the collapse of the auto sector, as described in the Business Case.

The Business CASE

Labour Market Rates

On average, hourly wages for a typical manufacturing job in Canada are $21.66. Hourly wages at the Big Three auto manufacturers in Canada were about $76.00. (The hourly wages for dentists are $60 and for scientists $50).

Both the Canadian and American governments demanded that GM and Chrysler renegotiate these compensation arrangements in return for loans and subsidies. The goal is to align the GM and Chrysler wage rates with those paid to Honda and Toyota auto workers, which average $57.00 an hour. For Chrysler alone, labour costs would be cut $240 million

annually. In addition, the CAW (Canadian Auto Workers)—the union that negotiated the original collective agreements—would have to forego automatic cost-of-living raises, and significant overtime payments. These new rates have helped GM and Chrysler avoid bankruptcy and liquidation.

The unions are disputing the numbers given for the hourly wages, stating that they are inflated by including retiree benefits. Ken Lewenza, the president of CAW, also points out that wages represent 7 percent of the cost of a car, yet the public perception is that labour rates are 100 percent of the problem.

Source: B. McKenna, "Meet the New Board of Directors," *Globe and Mail Online*, April 29, 2009; G. Keenan, "Auto Workers Agree to Historic Concession," *Globe and Mail Online*, April 27, 2009; Jeff Sanford, "Kenny's Last Stand," *Canadian Business*. Toronto: April 13, 2009. Vol. 82, Iss. 6: 26.

Area Wage Rates

A formal wage structure should provide rates that are in line with those being paid by other employers for comparable jobs within the area. Data pertaining to area wage rates may be obtained from local wage surveys. Wage survey data also may be obtained from a variety of sources, including compensation consulting firms such as Mercer Management Consulting and free from some companies such as Monster.ca. The Conference Board of Canada also conducts an annual compensation survey. Smaller employers use government or local board of trade surveys to establish rates of pay for new and senior employees. Others engage in a cooperative exchange of wage information or rely on various professional associations for these data.

Wage surveys (discussed fully later in the chapter) serve the important function of providing external wage equity between the surveying organization and other organizations competing for labour in the surrounding labour market. Importantly, data from area wage surveys can be used to prevent the rates for jobs from drifting too far above or below those of other employers in the region. When rates rise above existing area levels, an employer's labour costs may become excessive. Conversely, if they drop too far below area levels, it may be difficult to recruit and retain competent personnel. Wage survey data must also take into account indirect wages paid in the form of benefits.

Cost of Living

Because of inflation, compensation rates have had to be adjusted upward periodically to help employees maintain their purchasing power. Employers make these changes with the help of the **consumer price index (CPI)**. The CPI is a measure of the average change in prices over time in a fixed "market basket" of goods and services. The consumer price index is based on prices of food, clothing, shelter, and fuels; transportation fares;; and prices of other goods and services that people buy for day-to-day living. Statistics Canada collects price information on a monthly basis and calculates the CPI for the nation as a whole and various Canadian cities. Employers in a number of communities monitor changes in the CPI as a basis for compensation decisions.

CPI figures can have important consequences for organizational morale and productivity. Granting wages based largely on "cost-of-living" figures will not inspire higher employee performance and may cause valued employees to leave the organization. Cost-of-living payments, when traditionally given, may be seen by employees as "entitlements" unrelated to individual performance. Furthermore, should cost-of-living increases be discontinued, managers can expect disgruntled employees, particularly those not likely to receive merit raises.

Employees who work under a union contract may receive wage increases through **escalator clauses** found in their collective agreement. These clauses provide for cost-of-living adjustments (COLA) in wages based on changes in the CPI. The most common escalator clauses are 1 cent per hour for each 0.3 or 0.4-point change in the CPI. COLAs are favoured by unions during particularly high periods of inflation.

Collective Bargaining

One of the primary functions of a labour union, as emphasized in Chapter 14, is to bargain collectively over conditions of employment, the most important of which is compensation.[21] The union's goal in each new agreement is to achieve increases in **real wages**—wage increases larger than the increase in the CPI—thereby improving the purchasing power and standard of living of its members. This goal includes gaining wage settlements that equal or exceed the pattern established by other unions within the area.

The agreements negotiated by unions tend to establish rate patterns within the labour market. As a result, wages are generally higher in areas where organized

consumer price index (CPI)

A measure of the average change in prices over time in a fixed "market basket" of goods and services

escalator clauses

Clauses in collective agreements that provide for quarterly cost-of-living adjustments in wages, basing the adjustments on changes in the consumer price index

real wages

Wage increases larger than rises in the consumer price index, that is, the real earning power of wages labour is strong. To recruit and retain competent personnel and avoid unionization, nonunion employers must either meet or exceed these rates. The union scale also becomes the prevailing rate that all employers must pay for work performed under government contract. The impact of collective bargaining therefore extends beyond the segment of the labour force that is unionized.

JOB EVALUATION SYSTEMS

As we discussed earlier, one important component of the wage mix is the worth of the job. Organizations formally determine the value of jobs through the process of job evaluation. Job evaluation is the systematic process of determining the *relative* worth of jobs in order to establish which jobs should be paid more than others within the organization. Job evaluation helps establish internal equity between various jobs. The relative worth of a job may be determined by comparing it with others within the organization or by comparing it with a scale that has been constructed for this purpose. Each method of comparison, furthermore, may be made on the basis of the jobs as a whole or on the basis of the parts that constitute the jobs. [22]

Three traditional methods of comparison provide the basis for the principal systems of job evaluation. We will begin by discussing the simpler nonquantitative approaches and conclude by reviewing the more popular quantitative system. Also discussed is a newer method of job evaluation. Regardless of the methodology used, it is important to remember that all job evaluation methods require varying degrees of managerial judgment.

JOB RANKING SYSTEM

The simplest and oldest system of job evaluation is the job ranking system, which arrays jobs on the basis of their relative worth. One technique used to rank jobs consists of having the raters arrange cards listing the duties and responsibilities of each job in order of the importance of the jobs. Job ranking can be done by a single individual knowledgeable about all jobs or by a committee composed of management and employee representatives.

The basic disadvantage of the job ranking system is that it does not provide a very precise measure of each job's worth. Another weakness is that the final ranking of jobs indicates the relative importance of the job, not the differences in the degree of importance that may exist between jobs. A final limitation of the job ranking method is that it can be used only with a small number of jobs, probably no more than fifteen. Its simplicity, however, makes it ideal for use by smaller employers.

JOB CLASSIFICATION SYSTEM

In the job classification system, jobs are classified and grouped according to a series of predetermined grades. Successive grades require increasing amounts of job responsibility, skill, knowledge, ability, or other factors selected to compare jobs. For example, Grade GS-1 from the federal government grade descriptions reads as follows:

GS-1 includes those classes of positions the duties of which are to perform, under immediate supervision, with little or no latitude for the exercise of independent judgment (A) the simplest routine work in office, business, or fiscal operations; or (B) elementary work of a subordinate technical character in a professional, scientific, or technical field.

The descriptions of each of the job classes constitute the job classes against which the specifications for the various jobs are compared. Managers then evaluate jobs

job evaluation
A systematic process of determining the relative worth of jobs in order to establish which jobs should be paid more than others within an organization

job ranking system
The simplest and oldest system of job evaluation by which jobs are arrayed on the basis of their relative worth

job classification system
A system of job evaluation in which jobs are classified and grouped according to a series of predetermined wage grades

by comparing job descriptions with the different wage grades in order to "slot" the job into the appropriate grade. While this system has the advantage of simplicity, it is less precise than the point system because the job is evaluated as a whole.

POINT SYSTEM

The point system is a quantitative job evaluation procedure that determines a job's relative value by calculating the total points assigned to it.[23] It has been successfully used by high-visibility organizations such as the Province of Alberta.

Although point systems are rather complicated to establish, once in place they are relatively simple to understand and use. The principal advantage of the point system is that it provides a more refined basis for making judgments than either the ranking or classification systems and thereby can produce results that are more valid and less easy to manipulate.

The point system permits jobs to be evaluated quantitatively on the basis of factors or elements—commonly called *compensable factors*—that constitute the job.[24] The skills, efforts, responsibilities, and working conditions that a job usually entails are the more common major compensable factors that serve to rank one job as more or less important than another. More contemporary factors might include fiscal accountability, leadership, teamwork, and project accountability. The number of compensable factors an organization uses depends on the nature of the organization and the jobs to be evaluated. Once selected, compensable factors will be assigned weights according to their relative importance to the organization. For example, if responsibility is considered extremely important to the organization, it could be assigned a weight of 40 percent. Next, each factor will be divided into a number of degrees. Degrees represent different levels of difficulty associated with each factor.

point system

A quantitative job evaluation procedure that determines the relative value of a job by the total points assigned to it

The Point Manual

The point system requires the use of a point manual. The point manual is, in effect, a handbook that contains a description of the compensable factors and the degrees to which these factors may exist within the jobs. A manual also will indicate—usually by means of a table—the number of points allocated to each factor and to each of the degrees into which these factors are divided. The point value assigned to a job represents the sum of the numerical degree values of each compensable factor that the job possesses.

For example, the job factors illustrated in Highlights in HRM 9.2 represent those covered by the American Association of Industrial Management point manual. Each of the factors listed in this manual has been divided into five degrees. The number of degrees into which the factors in a manual are to be divided, however, can be greater or smaller than this number, depending on the relative weight assigned to each factor and the ease with which the individual degrees can be defined or distinguished. A statement is provided defining each of the degrees, as well as each factor as a whole. The definitions should be concise and yet distinguish the factors and each of their degrees. Highlights in HRM 9.3 represents another portion of the point manual used by the American Association of Industrial Management to describe each of the degrees for the education factor. These descriptions enable those conducting a job evaluation to determine the degree to which the factors exist in each job being evaluated.

Using the Point Manual

Job evaluation under the point system is accomplished by comparing the job descriptions and job specifications, factor by factor, against the various factor-degree descriptions contained in the manual. Each factor within the job being evaluated is then assigned the number of points specified in the manual. When the points for

Highlights in **HRM 9.2**

Point Values for Job Factors of the American Association of Industrial Management

FACTORS	1ST DEGREE	2ND DEGREE	3RD DEGREE	4TH DEGREE	5TH DEGREE
Skill					
1. Education	14	28	42	56	70
2. Experience	22	44	66	88	110
3. Initiative and ingenuity	14	28	42	56	70
Effort					
4. Physical demand	10	20	30	40	50
5. Mental or visual demand	5	10	15	20	25
Responsibility					
6. Equipment or process	5	10	15	20	25
7. Material or product	5	10	15	20	25
8. Safety of others	5	10	15	20	25
9. Work of others	5	10	15	20	25
Job Conditions					
10. Working conditions	10	20	30	40	50
11. Hazards	5	10	15	20	25

Source: American Association of Industrial Management.

Highlights in **HRM 9.3**

Description of Education Factor and Degrees of the American Association of Industrial Management

1. EDUCATION

This factor measures the basic trades training, knowledge or "scholastic contact" essential as background or training preliminary to learning the job duties. This job knowledge or background may have been acquired either by formal education or by training on jobs of lesser degree or by any combination of these approaches.

1st Degree   **14 points**

Requires the use of simple writing, adding, subtracting, whole numbers and the carrying out of instructions; and the use of fixed gauges and direct reading instruments and devices in which interpretation is not required.

continued

2nd Degree

Requires the use of commercial English, grammar and arithmetic such as addition, subtraction, multiplication and division, including decimals and fractions; simple use of formulas, charts, tables, drawings, specifications, schedules, wiring diagrams, together with the use of adjustable measuring instruments, graduates and the like requiring interpretation in their various applications; or the posting, preparation, interpretation, use and checking of reports, forms, records and comparable data.

28 points

3rd Degree

Requires the use of shop mathematics together with the use of complicated drawings, specifications, charts, tables, various types of adjustable measuring instruments and the training generally applicable in a particular or specialized occupation. Equivalent to one to three years applied trades training.

42 points

4th Degree

Requires the use of advanced shop mathematics, together with the use of complicated drawings, specifications, charts, tables, handbook formulas, all varieties of adjustable measuring instruments and the uses of broad training in a recognized trade or craft. Equivalent to complete, accredited, indentured apprenticeship or equivalent to high school plus a two-year technical college education.

56 points

5th Degree

Requires the use of higher mathematics involved in the application of engineering principles and the performance of related, practical operations, together with a comprehensive knowledge of the theories and practices of mechanical, electrical, chemical, civil or like engineering field. Equivalent to complete four years of technical college or university education.

70 points

Source: American Association of Industrial Management.

work valuation

A job evaluation system that seeks to measure a job's worth through its value to the organization

each factor have been determined from the manual, the total point value for the job as a whole can be calculated. The relative worth of the job is then determined from the total points that have been assigned to that job.

WORK VALUATION

Work valuation is a relatively new job evaluation system championed to meet the demands of a dynamic business environment. The cornerstone for **work valuation** is that work should be valued relative to the business goals of the organization rather than by an internally applied point-factor job evaluation system.[25] As noted by one compensation specialist, "Valuing work properly enables organizations to not only price individual jobs effectively, but provides insight into how jobs relate to overall organizational goals and objectives and how roles ultimately contribute to organizational success."[26] Additionally, work valuation serves to direct compensation dollars to the type of work pivotal to organizational goals.

With work valuations, work is measured through standards that come directly from business goals. For example, jobs might be valued relative to financial, operational, or customer service objectives. All forms of work, employee roles, and ways of organizing work (such as teams) are valued. The work evaluation process ends with a work hierarchy—that is an array of work by value to the organization. The work hierarchy is eventually priced through wage surveys to determine individual pay rates.

JOB EVALUATION FOR MANAGEMENT POSITIONS

Because management positions are more difficult to evaluate and involve certain demands not found in jobs at the lower levels, some organizations do not attempt to include them in their job evaluation programs for hourly employees. Rather, they employ either a standardized (purchased) program or customize a point method to fit their particular jobs. However, regardless of the approach adopted, point plans for executive and managerial employees operate similarly to those for other groups of employees.

One of the better-known standardized job evaluation programs for evaluating executive, managerial, and professional positions is the Hay profile method, developed by Edward N. Hay. The three broad factors that constitute the evaluation in the "profile" are knowledge (or know-how), mental activity (or problem solving), and accountability. The Hay method uses only three factors because it is assumed that these factors represent the most important aspects of all executive and managerial positions. The profile for each position is developed by determining the percentage value to be assigned to each of the three factors. Jobs are then ranked on the basis of each factor, and point values that make up the profile are assigned to each job on the basis of the percentage-value level at which the job is ranked.

THE COMPENSATION STRUCTURE

Job evaluation systems provide for internal equity and serve as the basis for wage rate determination. They do not in themselves determine the wage rate. The evaluated worth of each job in terms of its rank, class, points, or monetary worth must be converted into an hourly, daily, weekly, or monthly wage rate. The compensation tool used to help set wages is the wage and salary survey.

WAGE AND SALARY SURVEYS

The wage and salary survey is a survey of the wages paid by employers in an organization's relevant labour market—local, regional, or national, depending on the job. The labour market is frequently defined as the area from which employers obtain certain types of workers. The labour market for office personnel would be local, whereas the labour market for engineers would be national. It is the wage and salary survey that permits an organization to maintain external equity—that is, to pay its employees wages equivalent to the wages similar employees earn in other establishments.

When job evaluation and wage survey data are used jointly, they link the likelihood of both internal and external equity. Although surveys are conducted primarily to gather competitive wage data, they can also collect information on employee benefits or organizational pay practices (such as overtime rates or shift differentials).

Collecting Survey Data

While many organizations conduct their own wage and salary surveys, a variety of "preconducted" pay surveys are available to satisfy the requirements of most public and not-for-profit or private employers. Companies such as Watson Wyatt (http://www.watson.wyatt.com), Hewitt Associates (http://www.hewitt.com), Mercer Human Resources Consulting (http://www.mercerHR.com) Hay Management Associates (http://www.haygroup.com), and the Conference Board of Canada (http://www.conferenceboard.ca) conduct annual surveys.

Highlights in HRM 9.4 describes the results of compensation surveys for those working in human resources management.

Many provinces and cities conduct surveys and make them available to employers. Besides these government surveys, boards of trade and professional associations conduct special surveys tailored to their members' needs.

Employers with global operations can purchase international surveys through large consulting firms. The overseas compensation survey offered by *TPF&C* reports on payment practices in 20 countries. While all of these third-party surveys provide

Hay profile method

A job evaluation technique using three factors—knowledge, mental activity, and accountability—to evaluate executive and managerial positions

wage and salary survey

A survey of the wages paid to employees of other employers in the surveying organization's relevant labour market

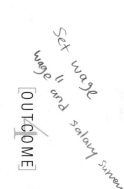

Set wage
wage and salary survey

[OUTCOME]

Highlights in HRM 9.4

Compensation Surveys for HR Professionals

Salaries for HR professionals and managers are as follows:

Title	Low ($)	Median ($)	High ($)
HR Assistant	32,000	37,817	42,000
Recruiter	37,400	44,827	54,292
Manager, Compensation	62,609	78,164	100,353
Director	88,700	100,714	114,473
VP HR	113,768	135,517	159,416

A study done by the Human Resources Professionals Association of Ontario showed the value of professional certification. Those people working in HR who had achieved the CHRP (Certified Human Resources Professional) earned on average $17,000 more than those without a CHRP. Clearly, the CHRP has an economic value in employers' minds.

Sources: http://workopolis.ca, retrieved May 12, 2009; D. Brown, "More Respect, Better Pay for HR: Toronto Study," *Canadian HR Reporter* 15, no. 20 (November 18, 2002): 2; M. Belcourt and A. Templer, "The CHRP Edge," *HR Professional* (April/May 2002): 30; M. Belcourt and A. Templer, "The CHRP Edge: Part 2," *HR Professional* (December 2002/January 2003): 36.

certain benefits to their users, they also have various limitations. Two problems with all published surveys are that (1) they are not always compatible with the user's jobs and (2) the user cannot specify what specific data to collect. To overcome these problems, organizations may collect their own compensation data.

HRIS and Salary Surveys

Wage and benefits survey data can be found on numerous websites. Also readily available are commercial products such as those offered at http://www.salary.com: the Salary Wizard, Comp Analyst, and Survey Finder surveys. Survey Finder has a database of hundreds of compensation surveys offered by more than 50 independent vendors. Managers and compensation specialists can search for applicable surveys for either purchase or participation.[27]

Employer-Initiated Surveys

Employers wishing to conduct their own wage and salary survey must first select the jobs to be used in the survey and identify the organizations with which they actually compete for employees. Since it is not feasible to survey all the jobs in an organization, normally only key jobs, also called benchmark jobs, are used. Characteristics of key jobs include the following:

1. They are important to employees and the organization.
2. They contain a large number of positions.
3. They have relatively stable job content.
4. They have the same job content across many organizations.
5. They are acceptable to employees, management, and unions as appropriate for pay comparisons.

The survey of key jobs will usually be sent to 10 or 15 organizations that represent a valid sample of other employers likely to compete for the employees of the surveying organization. A diversity of organizations should be selected—large and small, public and private, new and established, and union and nonunion—since each classification of employer is likely to pay different wage rates for surveyed jobs.

After the key jobs and the employers to be surveyed have been identified, the surveying organization must decide what information to gather on wages, benefit types, and pay policies. For example, when requesting pay data, it is important to specify whether hourly, daily, or weekly pay figures are needed. In addition, those conducting surveys must state whether the wage data are needed for new hires or for senior employees. Precisely defining the compensation data needed will greatly increase the accuracy of the information received and the number of purposes for which it can be used.[28] Once the survey data are tabulated, the compensation structure can be completed.

THE WAGE CURVE

The relationship between the relative worth of jobs and their wage rates can be represented by means of a wage curve. This curve may indicate the rates currently paid for jobs within an organization, new rates resulting from job evaluation, or rates for similar jobs currently being paid by other organizations within the labour market. A curve may be constructed graphically by preparing a scattergram consisting of a series of dots that represent the current wage rates. As shown in Figure 9.4, a freehand curve is then drawn through the cluster of dots in such a manner as to leave approximately an equal number of dots above and below the curve. The

NEL

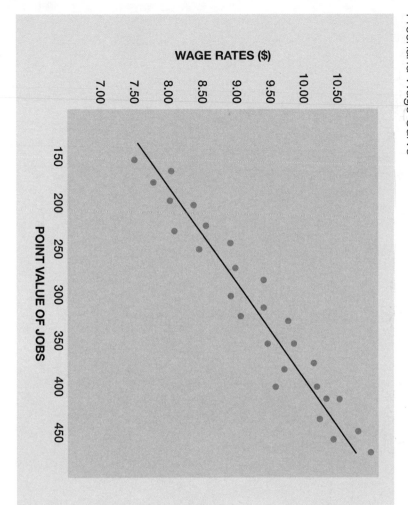

FIGURE 9.4

Freehand Wage Curve

WAGE RATES ($)

10.50
10.00
9.50
9.00
8.50
8.00
7.50
7.00

POINT VALUE OF JOBS

150   200   250   300   350   400   450

OUTCOME 5

wage curve
A curve in a scattergram, representing the relationship between relative worth of jobs and wage rates

wage curve can be relatively straight or curved. This curve can then be used to determine the relationship between the value of a job and its wage rate at any given point on the line.

PAY GRADES

pay grades
Groups of jobs within a particular class that are paid the same rate

From an administrative standpoint, it is generally preferable to group jobs into pay grades and to pay all jobs within a particular grade the same rate or rate range. When the classification system of job evaluation is used, jobs are grouped into grades as part of the evaluation process. When the point system is used, however, pay grades must be established at selected intervals that represent either the point or the evaluated monetary value of these jobs. The graph in Figure 9.5 illustrates a series of pay grades designated along the horizontal axis at 50-point intervals.

The grades within a wage structure may vary in number.[29] The number is determined by factors such as the slope of the wage curve, the number and distribution of the jobs within the structure, and the organization's wage administration and promotion policies. The number utilized should be sufficient to permit difficulty levels to be distinguished, but not so great as to make the distinction between two adjoining grades insignificant.

FIGURE **9.5**

Single Rate Structure

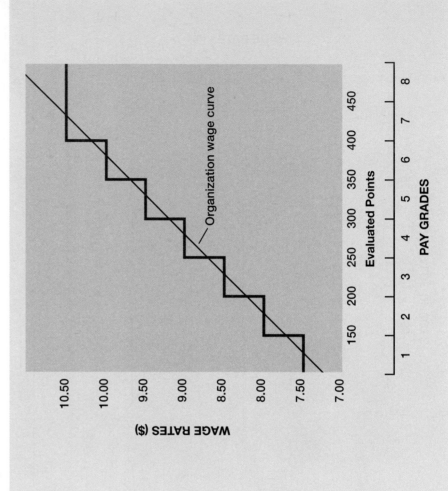

RATE RANGES

Although a single rate may be created for each pay grade, as shown in Figure 9.6, it is more common to provide a range of rates for each pay grade. The rate ranges may be the same for each grade or proportionately greater for each successive grade, as shown in Figure 9.6. Rate ranges constructed on the latter basis provide a greater incentive for employees to accept a promotion to a job in a higher grade.

Rate ranges generally are divided into a series of steps that permit employees to receive increases up to the maximum rate for the range on the basis of merit or seniority or a combination of the two. Most salary structures provide for the ranges of adjoining pay grades to overlap. The purpose of the overlap is to permit an employee with experience to earn as much as or more than a person with less experience in the next higher job classification.

The final step in setting up a wage structure is to determine the appropriate pay grade into which each job should be placed on the basis of its evaluated worth. Traditionally, this worth is determined on the basis of job requirements without regard to the performance of the person in that job. Under this system, the performance of those who exceed the requirements of a job may be acknowledged by

FIGURE 9.6

Wage Structure with Increasing Rate Ranges

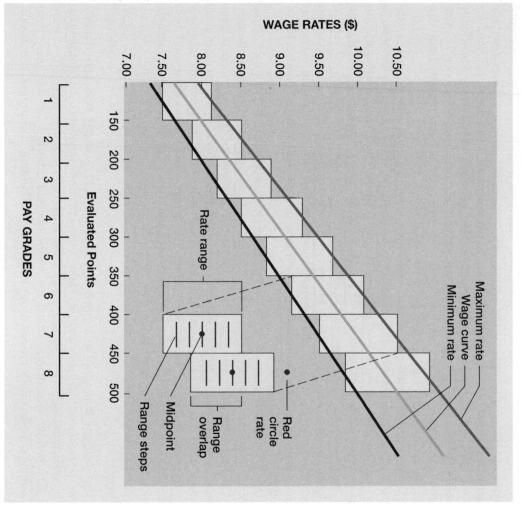

merit increases within the grade range or by promotion to a job in the next higher pay grade.[30]

Organizations may pay individuals above the maximum of the pay range when employees have high seniority or promotional opportunities are scarce. Wages paid above the range maximum are called **red circle rates.** Because these rates are exceptions to the pay structure, employers often "freeze" these rates until all ranges are shifted upward through market wage adjustments.

red circle rates
Payment rates above the maximum of the pay range

COMPETENCE-BASED PAY

The predominant approach to employee compensation is still the job-based system. Unfortunately, such a system often fails to reward employees for their skills or the knowledge they possess or to encourage them to learn a new job-related skill. Additionally, job-based pay systems may not reinforce an organizational culture stressing employee involvement or provide increased employee flexibility to meet overall production or service requirements. Therefore, organizations such as Nortel Networks and Honeywell have introduced competence-based pay plans.

Competence-based pay, also referred to as skill-based pay or knowledge-based pay, compensates employees for the different skills or increased knowledge they possess rather than for the job they hold in a designated job category.[31] Regardless of the name, these pay plans encourage employees to earn higher base wages by learning and performing a wider variety of skills (or jobs) or displaying an array of competencies that can be applied to a variety of organizational requirements. For example, in a manufacturing setting, new tasks might include various assembly activities carried out in a particular production system or a variety of maintenance functions. Within service organizations, employees might acquire new knowledge related to advanced computer systems or accounting procedures. Organizations will grant an increase in pay after each skill or knowledge has been mastered and can be demonstrated according to a predetermined standard.

Competence-based pay systems represent a fundamental change in the attitude of management regarding how work should be organized and how employees should be paid for their work efforts. The most frequently cited benefits of competence-based pay include greater productivity, increased employee learning and commitment to work, improved staffing flexibility to meet production or service demands, and reduced effects of absenteeism and turnover, because managers can assign employees where and when needed. Competence-based pay also encourages employees to acquire training when new or updated skills are needed by an organization.

Unfortunately, competence-based plans bring some long-term difficulties. Some plans limit the amount of compensation employees can earn, regardless of the new skills or competencies they acquire. Thus, after achieving the top wage, employees may be reluctant to continue their educational training. Perhaps the greatest challenge in paying individuals for their skills, knowledge, and competencies is developing appropriate measures. It is difficult to write specific knowledge and skill descriptions for jobs that employees perform and then establish accurate measures of acquired skills or knowledge.

competence-based pay
Pay based on an employee's skill level, variety of skills possessed, or increased job knowledge

Broadbanding

Organizations that adopt a competency-based or skill-based pay system frequently use *broadbanding* to structure their compensation payments to employees. Broadbanding simply collapses many traditional salary grades into a few wide salary bands. Broadbands may have midpoints and quartiles, or they may have extremely wide salary ranges or no ranges at all. Banding encourages lateral skill

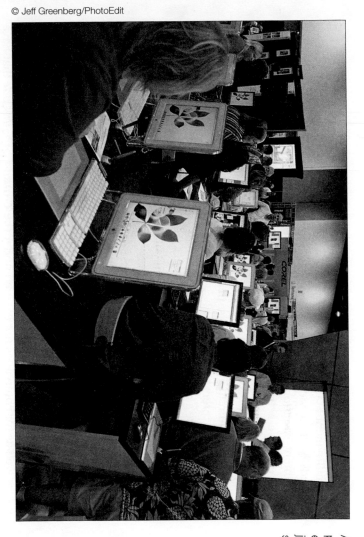

A competency-based pay program will encourage employees to increase their job-related knowledge and skills.

building while addressing the need to pay employees performing multiple jobs with different skill level requirements. Additionally, broadbands help eliminate the obsession with grades and, instead, encourage employees to move to jobs in which they can develop in their careers and add value to the organization. Paying employees through broadbands enables organizations to consider job responsibilities, individual skills and competencies, and career mobility patterns in assigning employees to bands.[32]

GOVERNMENT REGULATION OF COMPENSATION

Compensation management, like the other areas of HRM, is subject to provincial and federal regulations. Each province has an employment standards act that establishes minimum requirements with respect to wages, hours of work, and overtime. Provincial as well as federal minimum requirements can be obtained by contacting the appropriate federal or provincial office.

THE CANADA LABOUR CODE

Part III of the *Canada Labour Code* and the *Canada Labour Standards Regulations* set minimum labour standards for all employees and employers in works or undertakings that fall within federal jurisdiction, including interprovincial highway and rail transportation, pipelines, telecommunications, air transport, fishing, and banking. Federal Crown corporations are covered by the *Canada Labour Code*, but federal public service employees are not. Employees working under these classifications are subject to a 40-hour workweek. Managerial and professional employees are not covered by the hours-of-work provisions and may be required to exceed those hours. Revisions are constantly being made to these standards; HR managers must keep abreast of these changes to ensure compliance in the workplace.

Using the Internet

Canada's Labour Code can be found at http://laws.justice.gc.ca

[O U T C O M E]

EMPLOYMENT STANDARDS ACTS

The Employment Standards acts of each province and territory establish minimum standards with a view to protecting both employees and employers in certain employment situations. Collective agreements are permitted to override the provisions of these acts as long as employees are not being provided with less than what the acts have stipulated, and as long as these overrides benefit the employee. Employers who operate in more than one province must become fully informed of the different requirements that exist in each province. This information is generally available on the Internet.

Each province's act contains a provision that stipulates that an overtime rate of 1.5 times the base rate must be paid for all hours worked in excess of the set minimum prescribed in the province. For example, if an employee works 45 hours in a province that legislates the minimum workweek as 40 hours, he or she is entitled to overtime for the extra 5 hours at 1.5 times his or her base rate. Particular groups, including lawyers, doctors, engineers, and managers, are exempt from overtime requirements.

OTHER LEGISLATION

Employment equity is under federal jurisdiction for all federally regulated companies, as well as for companies not covered under the *Canada Labour Code* that have dealings with federally legislated companies. Pay equity is covered provincially where applicable. As we discussed in Chapter 3, legislation relating to employment equity and pay equity is designed to ensure that fair employment practices are applied to all members of designated groups.

SIGNIFICANT COMPENSATION ISSUES

As with other HR activities, compensation management operates in a dynamic environment. We will discuss two of these issues here: (1) equal pay for work of equal value and (2) wage rate compression.

EQUAL PAY FOR WORK OF EQUAL VALUE

One of the most important gender issues in compensation is equal pay for work of equal value. In Ontario, the definition is "equal pay for work of equal or comparable value." The issue stems from the fact that jobs performed predominantly by women are paid less than those performed by men.

This practice results in what critics term *institutionalized sex discrimination*, causing women to receive lower pay for jobs that may be different from but comparable in worth to those performed by men. The issue of equal pay for work of equal value goes beyond providing equal pay for jobs that involve the same duties for women as for men. It is not concerned with whether a female secretary should receive the same pay as a male secretary. Rather, the argument for comparable worth is that jobs held by women are not compensated the same as those held by men, even though both job types may contribute equally to organizational success.

MEASURING COMPARABILITY

Advocates of comparable worth argue that the difference in wage rates for predominantly male and female occupations rests in the undervaluing of traditional female occupations. To remedy this situation, they propose that wages should be

Using the Internet

Pay equity legislation in Canada by jurisdiction can be found at

http://www.hrsdc.gc.ca/ eng/labour/labour_law/esl/ pay_equit_tb.shtml

OUT C O ME

Reality CHECK

Pay Equity

Linda Sullivan, program specialist of the Ontario Pay Equity Commission, talks about current issues in pay equity: "Most private-sector employers should have implemented pay equity by now, and our role is to monitor them for compliance. However, organizations with 10 to 99 employees have the highest rate of noncompliance because they do not have resources, including a dedicated HR professional, and some positions are held by family members. Last year we monitored the food services sector. A family-owned bakery, for example, would need to identify female and male jobs, compare them, and make the required pay adjustments. In these family-owned enterprises, one can find the traditional breakdown where, for example, the bakers are male, and the customer service positions (i.e., the [people] working at the counter) are female. The bakers are paid more than positions in customer service. The multitude of tasks needed in customer service, such as communication skills, organizational skills, dealing with people who are upset, and dealing with customers quickly are typically overlooked in female-dominated jobs and are not credited. These tasks within each job must be carefully identified and compensated.

"Smaller organizations in the public sector have different types of problems. In the public sector, it is difficult to do pay equity in a lot of organizations, because these organizations only have jobs held by women. For example, women usually hold all jobs in a day care centre. These organizations can not compare male and female jobs because there are no male jobs. So, in 1993, when the pay equity

act was amended, another method of comparing jobs for these types of organizations was added: a proxy comparison method. The proxy comparison method allowed organizations to take key jobs, such as a day care supervisor or an early childhood educator, and compare these to similar jobs in a larger public-sector employer, such as a large municipal day care centre. The municipal sector had already done pay equity, comparing male and female jobs in the day care centre to male jobs in the municipality. The small day care centre could compare the early childhood educator job and borrow the pay equity results, i.e., through a proxy comparison method.

"A third issue is, without a doubt, the degree of emotion felt by those who believe that they are being paid unfairly. For example, I had an e-mail from a woman about her work situation, where she had been hired and was doing what she felt was an equivalent job to a male colleague, but was being paid less. So she went to her manager and raised the issue with her, and a change was made to her wage, which she felt was justified. Then she realized once again, while they had raised her wage, she was still being paid considerably less than her male colleague doing work of equal or less value. The employer has not done pay equity. To me, what was striking about this situation was how emotional and betrayed the woman felt. The employers don't realize that employees feel so strongly about this unfair treatment. In a lot of these situations, women end up looking for other work, leaving the organization and costing the employer thousands of dollars required to recruit and train new employees."

Source: Personal interview with Linda Sullivan.

---

equal for jobs that are "somehow" equivalent in total worth or compensation to the organization. Unfortunately, there is no consensus on a comparable worth standard by which to evaluate jobs, nor is there agreement on the ability of current job evaluation techniques to remedy the problem. Indeed, organizations may dodge the comparable-worth issue by using one job evaluation system for clerical and secretarial jobs and another system for other jobs. Reality Check outlines some of the issues that face pay equity specialists. Furthermore, the advocates of comparable worth argue that current job evaluation techniques simply serve to continue the differences in pay between the sexes. However, others believe that job evaluation systems can be designed to measure different types of jobs, in the same way that apples and oranges can be compared (see Figure 9.7). The Business Case describes two large settlements that have resulted from pay equity issues.

FIGURE **9.7**

How Can You Compare Apples and Oranges?

	150.0 grams	150.0 grams
Weight		
Calories	87	73
Carbohydrates	21.7 grams	18.3 grams
Protein	0.3 grams	1.5 grams
Fibre	1.5 grams	1.8 grams
Vitamin A	140 IU	300 IU

Source: M. Belcourt, "Human Resource Management," in *Introduction to Canadian Business*, ed. J. Pilnuissen (Toronto: McGraw-Hill Ryerson and Captus Press, 1994), 410.

The Business CASE

Cashing Out

Bell Canada had to pay out $100 million in cash and added pension benefits to over 4,000 mostly female employees, to settle a pay equity dispute started in the early 1990s. The union argued that thousands of Bell employees, who were mostly women, were underpaid compared with those in male-dominated positions. Those working in female-dominated jobs were making, on average, $2 to $5 less an hour than men in comparable jobs. The request for salary adjustments was based on a study of the work performed by telephone operators, clerical staff, sales associates, and others. Most of those employees were women. Their salaries were compared with other job functions that were dominated by men.

In July 1998, the Canadian Human Rights Tribunal ruled that there was a substantial and illegal wage gap between job categories dominated by men and those jobs dominated by women in the federal government.

For example, Canada Post could not explain the wide wage gap between clerical workers, who were mostly women, and male-dominated employees in an operations group and so had to pay 6,000 current and former clerical workers about $150 million in back pay. (Note that Canada Post is appealing this ruling, in a case which is approaching its 23rd year in court!) The tribunal determined that the federal government had underpaid those mainly female workers in administrative support occupational categories. Each employee was entitled to about $30,000 in pay retroactive to March 1985. The Public Service Alliance of Canada, the union representing the workers affected by the tribunal ruling, calculates that the average annual pension of workers from these groups is only $10,000 per year. The pay equity settlement would make an important difference in the standard of living for these workers and their families now and in the future.

Sources: Colin Freeze, "Bell Settles Pay Equity Dispute," *The Globe and Mail*, May 16, 2006, A5; Neco Cockburn, "Tribunal Rules Systemic Sex Discrimination at Canada Post," *CanWest News*, October 8, 2005, 1; Uyen Vu, "22 Years and Counting," *Canadian HR Reporter* (November 7, 2005): 1.

THE ISSUE OF WAGE-RATE COMPRESSION

Pay compression is a compensation problem that has its roots in low salary budgets. **Wage-rate compression** occurs when less experienced, often junior employees, earn as much or more than experienced employees due to high starting salaries for new employees. For example, the scarcity of qualified applicants in computers, engineering, and other professional and technical fields has forced starting salaries for these occupations to be at or near the salaries paid employees with considerable experience and seniority. Pay compression can also occur when hourly employees, at the top of their pay grades, earn only slightly less than managers at the low end of their pay grades.

Identifying wage-rate compression and its causes is far simpler than implementing organizational policies to alleviate its effect. Organizations wishing to minimize the problem may incorporate the following ideas into their pay policies:

- Reward high performance and merit-worthy employees with large pay increases.
- Design the pay structure to allow a wide spread between hourly and supervisory employees.
- Prepare high-performing employees for promotions to jobs with higher salary levels.
- Provide equity adjustments for selected employees hardest hit by pay compression.[33]

Since wage rate compression is largely an internal pay equity concern, if not addressed fairly, it can cause low employee morale, leading to issues of reduced employee performance, hard feelings between employees, higher absenteeism and turnover, and even delinquent behaviour such as employee theft.

Wage-rate compression

Compression of differentials between job classes, particularly the differential between hourly workers and their managers

---

Small Business APPLICATION

In Chapter 3 we addressed the issue of legal compliance for small business as it applies to pay equity. The focus of this chapter is on the application of internal and external compensation equity within the context of small companies.

Typically, threats to internal equity come as a result of wage compression resulting from (1) hiring someone new at a higher salary than existing employees as a result of market forces, or (2) redeploying an employee into a potentially lower-value job without adjusting his or her wages as a result of requirement changes, or (3) long-service employees wages getting high relative to hiring wages as a result of historical salary adjustments. While these challenges are normal, they can be managed by small enterprises by freezing wages for employees in such conditions until other wages catch up.

Secondly, while small companies typically cannot justify the expense of time and money to invest in wage analysis or purchasing surveys, small business can use free online data sources such as those mentioned in this chapter to provide an indication of comparator wages. Other strategies include networking with other business owners in the area to share salary ranges for positions. Lastly, interviewing candidates and asking them their salary expectations will provide a gauge of the market value for positions in your area.

Finally, as we have spoken to many times through this book, one of the inherent challenges with small companies is that general roles require a different approach than specialist roles. When it comes to compensation, the challenge for the small business

continued

owner is to determine what roles of comparable knowledge, skills, and abilities are worth at other organizations, balanced with the value of the position to the company. That being said, small business owners have the visibility and flexibility to align compensation recognizing the individual contributions of members, which provides small companies a competitive advantage against large companies that lack the visibility or resources to be able to employ a bespoke approach.

SUMMARY

[OUTCOME 1] Establishing compensation programs requires both large and small organizations to consider specific goals—employee retention, compensation distribution, and adherence to a budget, for instance. Compensation must reward employees for past efforts (pay for performance) while motivating employees' future performance. Internal and external equity of the pay program affects employees' concepts of fairness. Organizations must balance each of these concerns while still remaining competitive. The ability to attract qualified employees while controlling labour costs is a major factor in allowing organizations to remain viable in the domestic or international markets.

[OUTCOME 2] The basis on which compensation payments are determined and the way they are administered can significantly affect employee productivity and the achievement of organizational goals. Internal influences include the employer's compensation policy, worth of the job, performance of employee, and the employer's ability to pay. External factors influencing wage rates include labour market conditions, area wage rates, cost of living, outcomes of collective bargaining, and legal requirements.

[OUTCOME 3] Organizations use one of four basic job evaluation techniques to determine the relative worth of jobs. The job ranking system arranges jobs in numerical order on the basis of the importance of the job's duties and responsibilities to the organization. The job classification system slots jobs into pre-established grades. Higher-rated grades will require more responsibilities, and more important job duties. The point system of job evaluation uses a point scheme based on the compensable job factors of skill, effort, responsibility, and working conditions. The more compensable factors a job possesses, the more points are assigned to it. Jobs with higher accumulated points are considered more valuable to the organization. The work valuation system evaluates jobs based on their value relative to organizational goals—financial, customer service, and so on—and the job's contribution to organization success.

[OUTCOME 4] Wage surveys determine the external equity of jobs. Data obtained from surveys will facilitate establishing the organization's wage policy while ensuring that the employer does not pay more, or less, than needed for jobs in the relevant labour market.

[OUTCOME 5] The wage structure is composed of the wage curve, pay grades, and rate ranges. The wage curve depicts graphically the pay rates assigned to jobs within each pay grade. Pay grades represent the grouping of similar jobs on the basis of their relative worth. Each pay grade will include a rate range. Rate ranges will have a midpoint and minimum and maximum pay rates for all jobs in the pay grade.

[OUTCOME 6] The federal and provincial governments regulate compensation through the *Canada Labour Code*, Employment Standards acts, and employment equity/pay equity legislation.

[OUTCOME 7] The concept of equal pay for work of equal value seeks to overcome the fact that jobs held by women are compensated at a lower rate than those performed by men. This happens even though both types of jobs may contribute equally to organizational productivity. Wage-rate compression largely affects managerial and senior employees as the pay given to new employees or the wage increases gained through collective agreements erode the pay differences between these groups.

KEY TERMS

competence-based pay, 390
consumer price index (CPI), 380
escalator clauses, 380
Hay profile method, 385
hourly work, 375
job classification system, 381
job evaluation, 381

job ranking system, 381
pay equity, 373
pay-for-performance standard, 372
pay grades, 388
piecework, 375
point system, 382
real wages, 380

red circle rates, 390
wage and salary survey, 385
wage curve, 387
wage-rate compression, 395
work valuation, 384

DISCUSSION QUESTIONS

1. Tomax Corporation has 400 employees and wishes to develop a compensation policy to correspond to its dynamic business strategy. The company wishes to employ a high-quality workforce capable of responding to a competitive business environment. Suggest different compensation objectives to match Tomax's business goals.

2. Most students work, during the summer, with full-time employees and are paid on an hourly basis until the job is done. Typically, the students will work productively, loading sacks of fertilizer, for example, as quickly as possible. They are soon reprimanded by their older workers to slow down, so that the time to do the job is increased. Has this happened to you? What is the best response?

3. What is job evaluation? Explain the differences between the major job evaluation systems, noting the advantages and disadvantages of each.

4. Describe the basic steps in conducting a wage and salary survey. What are some factors to consider?

5. One of the objections to granting wage increases on a percentage basis is that the lowest-paid employees, who are having the most trouble making ends meet, get the smallest increase, while the highest-paid employees get the largest increase. Is this objection a valid one? Explain.

6. Federal laws governing compensation raise important issues for both employers and employees. Discuss the following:
   a. The effect of mandatory overtime
   b. The effects of raising the minimum wage

7. The Pay Equity Commission proposes three methods to make pay equity comparisons:
   - The job-to-job comparison method
   - The proportional value comparison method
   - The proxy comparison method.

Read about these methods on http://www.payequity.gov.on.ca/peo/english/pubs/proxycomp.html. What are some of the problems of developing a pay system based on each of these methods?

INTERNET EXERCISE

Test your knowledge of pay equity provisions by taking the Pay Equity Quiz found at http://www.payequity.gov.on.ca/peo/english/quiz/start.html.

HRM Experience

Why This Salary?

A question frequently asked is, "Why is that person paid more than I am when we both perform the same job?" The answer to this question lies in understanding the components of the wage mix as discussed in this chapter. While we may disapprove of the idea that someone is paid more or less than we are for similar work, nevertheless, factors both internal and external to the organization influence the final salary paid to a

continued

job or a specific person. Often we have little control over the wage mix factors. However, at other times, we can improve our wage by gaining additional job experience or seniority, or by obtaining increases in job knowledge or skills. This project is designed to give you experience in understanding why jobs are paid different salaries.

Assignment

The website of http://www.workopolis.ca provides a salary calculator for the Canadian market, giving salary ranges for jobs and a comparison tool for the national average. For example, a HR assistant working in Brandon, Manitoba, earned a median salary of $34,069. Using this site, determine the salaries paid to these occupations, nationally, and then answer the questions that follow as to why the differences in salaries exist. Relate these reasons to the internal and external factors of the wage mix that are discussed in the text.

Occupation	National Median Annual Salary ($)	Low ($)	High ($)
HR Assistant	37,242	32,607	42,439
Librarian			
Construction labourer			
Computer systems administrator			
Police officer			
Motor coach operator			
Lawyer			

1. What factors may account for the wide differences among salaries for different occupations?
2. Now check on compensation rates in your city and compare these to Toronto or Vancouver and Lethbridge, Alberta. What factors account for the differences among salaries for identical occupations in different cities?
3. What factors may account for the differences among salaries for the identical occupation in different organizations?

You may work individually or in teams to complete this skill-building exercise.

BIZFLIX EXERCISES

THE WEDDING DATE: HOW MUCH IS NICK MERCER'S JOB WORTH?

These scenes from *The Wedding Date* occur in two parts. Watch Part I, "Nick's Job," first. Apply the job evaluation concepts discussed in this chapter to decide the worth of Nick Mercer's (Dermot Mulroney) job.

Kat Ellis (Debra Messing) wants a date to accompany her to her sister Amy's (Amy Adams) wedding. She also wants to show her ex-fiancé that she can recover from him dumping her two years earlier. These requirements become part of her frantic search of the male escort classified advertisements. She hires Nick Mercer, who turns out to be much more dashing and charming than she expected. This lighthearted romantic comedy will entertain you from beginning to end.

There are two sets of scenes with a chalkboard between them. Part I comes from the "Trying too Hard" segment that appears in the first ten minutes of the film. Kat and Nick have arrived at Heathrow Airport, London, England. Part II comes from the "A Simple Business Transaction" segment that appears a few minutes later. They have arrived at the cocktail party honouring Amy and her fiancé, Edward Fletcher-Wooten (Jack Davenport).

The Part I chalkboard reads, "Nick's Job"; the Part II chalkboard reads, "Nick's Pay." Pause the scenes at the start of Part II to consider the first question below. Kat and Nick return to the cocktail party after Kat straightens the coats in the closet.

What to Watch for and Ask Yourself

- From your viewing of Part I, how much is Nick Mercer's job as Kat's date worth? If you have seen this film, do not try to recall how much Nick received.

- The opening of this chapter includes the following observation: "Employees desire compensation systems that they perceive as being fair and commensurate with their skills and expectations." Does Nick believe he is paid fairly in Part II of the scenes? Does he place any conditions on his job and its compensation?

- Review the earlier section "Significant Compensation Issues." Do any issues raised in that section apply to these scenes? Why or why not?

CASE STUDY 1

PAY DECISIONS AT PERFORMANCE SPORTS

Katie Perkins's career objective while attending university was to obtain a degree in small-business management and to start her own business after graduation. Her ultimate desire was to combine her love of sports and a strong interest in marketing to start a mail-order golf equipment business aimed specifically at beginning golfers.

In February 2009, after extensive development of a strategic business plan and a loan in the amount of $75,000 from the Federal Business Development Bank, she started Performance Sports. Based on a marketing plan that stressed fast delivery, error-free customer service, and large discount pricing, Performance Sports grew rapidly. At present the company employs 16 people: eight customer service representatives earning between $11.75 and $13.25 per hour; four shipping and receiving associates paid between $10.50 and $11.50 per hour; two clerical employees each earning $9.75 per hour; an assistant manager earning $14.10 per hour; and a general manager with a wage of $18.00 per hour. Both the manager and assistant manager are former customer service representatives.

Perkins intends to create a new managerial position, purchasing agent, to handle the complex duties of purchasing golf equipment from the company's numerous equipment manufacturers. Also, the mail-order catalogue will be expanded to handle a complete line of tennis equipment. Since the position of purchasing agent is new, Perkins is not sure how much to pay this person. She wants to employ an individual with five to eight years of experience in sports equipment purchasing.

While attending an equipment manufacturers' convention in Las Vegas, Nevada, Perkins learns that a competitor, East Valley Sports, pays its customer service representatives on a pay-for-performance basis. Intrigued by this compensation philosophy, Perkins asks her assistant manager, George Balkin, to research the pros and cons of this payment strategy. This request has become a priority because only last week two customer service representatives expressed dissatisfaction with their hourly wage. Both complained that they felt underpaid relative to the large amount of sales revenue each generates for the company.

QUESTIONS

1. What factors should Perkins and Balkin consider when setting the wage for the purchasing agent position? What resources are available for them to consult when establishing this wage?

2. Suggest advantages and disadvantages of a pay-for-performance policy for Performance Sports.

3. Suggest a new payment plan for the customer service representatives.

CASE STUDY 2

CANADA POST

Canada Post Corporation employs 67,000 workers, which makes it one of Canada's largest employers. In 1997 it revised its job evaluation system for postmasters and assistants. The old system, which had been in place since 1976, did not take into account changes that had arisen since 1981, when Canada Post became a Crown corporation.

A human resources consulting firm, Watson Wyatt Worldwide, was hired to assist with the entire process. According to Linda Tremblay of Organization Planning and Development, Canada Post, the job evaluation system was revised to incorporate employee input, to be responsive to federal pay equity legislation, and—most importantly—to reflect corporate culture and values.

The new job evaluation system measured the content and relative value of jobs. The system evaluated jobs according to their "typical" or "normal" components—that is, tasks that were done on a regular basis. These compensable factors were a function of the job itself, not of the performance of the person doing the job.

The four factors considered and their relative weights were as follows:

A: Responsibilities—What type of responsibilities does the job entail?
60 percent

B: Skills—What particular skills are needed to accomplish the job?
25 percent

C: Working Conditions—What working conditions apply to the job?
11 percent

D: Effort—What amount of effort does the job require? 4 percent

Total 100 percent

AN EXAMPLE OF AN ITEM UNDER C: WORKING CONDITIONS:

This factor measures the surroundings or physical conditions under which your work must be done and the extent to which they make your job disagreeable. Consider whether elements such as those listed are present, and the relative amount and continuity of exposure:

Place a checkmark beside all those that apply:

- Adverse weather conditions
- Confined work space
- Dirt/dust
- Fumes
- Inadequate lighting

- Lack of privacy
- Noisy conditions
- Temperature extremes
- Verbal abuse/public harassment
- Other

Job evaluation criteria, such as in the above example, were used in each of the four areas and are summarized as below:

JOB EVALUATION CRITERIA

Compensable factors	Components
Responsibilities	Internal and external contacts
	Decision making
	Supervision of employees
	Responsibility for property maintenance
	Responsibility for rural routes, suburban services, and/or stage services
	Points of call
	Responsibility for contractor invoices
	Responsibility for a till and/or authorized allowance
Skills	Knowledge areas (such as budget process, collective agreement, contacted services in mail operations or property management, financial practices, procedures knowledge, product knowledge, primary sortation, final sortation, sales and customer service techniques, personnel management techniques)
	Job-related experience
Working conditions	Physical work environment
	Travel
Effort	Physical effort
	Multiple demands

Employees completed the job evaluation questionnaire for their own jobs. The completed questionnaires were reviewed by supervisors, managers, and human resources staff.

Total points were then allocated to each job, which corresponded to one of six job bands. Collective agreement negotiations were used to set the rates of pay for each of the six job bands.

Source: Interview and correspondence with Linda Tremblay, Canada Post Corporation, April 2006.

QUESTIONS

1. What type of job evaluation did Canada Post use?
2. What are the advantages and limitations of this system?
3. If you were asked to review both the questionnaire and the process used to obtain the job information, what recommendations for changes would you make?

CAREER COUNSEL

To find out what compensation you can expect to receive in your career, visit the *Managing Human Resources* website (http://www.belcourt6e.nelson.com).

NOTES AND REFERENCES

1. Don Hellriegel and John W. Slocum, Jr., *Organizational Behavior*, 11th ed. (Mason, OH: South-Western, 2007).

2. "Pay to be Stable, PFP Usage Lags," *HRfocus* 84, no. 12 (December 207): 12.

3. Debra L. Nelson and James Campbell Quick, *Understanding Organizational Behavior*, 3rd ed. (Mason, OH: South-Western, 2008), Chapter 5.

4. For a frequently referenced book on strategic compensation planning, see Edward E. Lawler III, *Strategic Pay: Aligning Organizational Strategies and Pay Systems* (San Francisco: Jossey-Bass, 1990). See also Susan E. Jackson and Randall S. Schuler, *Managing Human Resources: Through Strategic Partnerships*, 9th ed.(Mason, OH: South-Western, 2006): Chapter 9.

5. Fay Hansen, "Lackluster Performance," *Workforce Management* 86, no. 19 (November 2007): 39.

6. Fay Hansen, "Control and Customization," *Workforce Management* 86, no. 19 (November 2007): 42.

7. Hai-Ming Chen and Yi-Hua Hsien, "Key Trends in the Total Reward System of the 21st Century," *Compensation and Benefits Review* 38, no. 6 (November/December 2006): 64.

8. George T. Milkovich and Jerry M. Newman, *Compensation*, 9th ed. (Boston: McGraw-Hill Irwin, 2008).

9. Patricia K. Zingheim and Jay R. Schuster, "What Are Key Issues Right Now?" *Compensation and Benefits Review* 39, no. 3. (June 2007): 51. See also "Reward 'Stars' and Pay for Performance Lead in Pay Control Strategies," *HRfocus* 84, no. 11 (November 2007): 3.

10. Valerie L. Myers and Janice L. Dreachslin, "Recruitment and Retention of a Diverse Workforce: Challenges and Opportunities," *Journal of Healthcare Management* 52, no. 5 (September/October 2007): 290.

11. Stephen Miller, "2008 Pay: More Ties to Performance," *HR Magazine* 52, no. 10 (October 2007): 26. See also Jay Schuster, Paul Weatherhead, and Patricia Zingheim, "Pay for Performance Works: The United States Postal Service Presents a Powerful Business Case," *WorldatWork* 15, no. 1 (First Quarter 2006): 24.

12. Rose Stanley, Project Manager, Benefits, *WorldatWork*, Scottsdale, Arizona, interview by author, December 14, 2007; Jude Sotherlund and Chris Gokturk, "Paying for Performance: Walking a Legal Fine Line," *Workspan* (January 2007): 37.

13. For one of the classic articles on equity theory, see J. Stacey Adams, "Integrity in Social Exchange," in L. Berkowitz (ed.), *Advances in Experimental Social Psychology* (New York: Academic Press, 1965): 276–299.

14. Andrew J. DuBrin, *Fundamentals of Organization Behavior*, 4th ed. (Mason, OH: South-Western, 2007), Chapter 6.

15. Victor H. Vroom, *Work and Motivation* (San Francisco: Jossey-Bass, 1994). This landmark book, originally published in 1964, integrates the work of hundreds of researchers seeking to explain choice of work, job satisfaction, and job performance

16. Joseph Champoux, *Organizational Behavior: Integrating Individuals, Groups, and Organizations*, 3rd ed. (Mason, OH: South- Western, 2006), Chapter 8.

17. "Supreme Court Decision Touches on Employees Sharing Pay Data," *HRfocus* 84, no. 10 (October 2007): 12.

18. Brian Hindo, "Mind If I Peek at Your Paycheck?" *BusinessWeek*, June 18, 2007: 40.

19. James R. Bowers, "Valuing Work: An Integrated Approach," *WorldatWork* 12, no. 2 (Second Quarter 2003): 28–39. See also Robert L. Heneman, Peter V. LeBlanc, and Tim L. Reynolds, "Using Work Valuation to Identify and Protect the Talent Pool," *WorldatWork* 11, no. 2 (Third Quarter 2002): 31–41.

20. Kathryn Cohen and Alison Avalos, "Salary Budget Increases: Slow but Steady," *Workspan* (September 2007): 29.

21. William H. Holley, Jr., Kenneth H. Jennings, and Rogert W. Wolters, *The Labor Relations Process*, 9th ed. (Mason, OH: South-Western, 2009), Chapter 6.

22. Robert L. Heneman, "Job and Work Evaluation," *Public Personnel Management* 32, no. 1 (Spring 2003): 1–25.

23. Emin Kahya, "Revising the Metal Industry Job Evaluation System for Blue-Collar Jobs," *Compensation and Benefits Review* 38, no. 6 (November/December 2006): 49.

24. Lance A. Berger and Dorothy R. Berger, *The Compensation Handbook*, 5th ed. (Boston: McGraw-Hill, 2008).

25. Robert L. Heneman, Peter V. LeBlanc, and Howard Risher, "Work Valuation Addresses Shortcomings of Both Job Evaluation and Market Pricing," *Compensation and Benefits Review* 35, no. 1 (January–February 2003): 7–11.

26. James R. Bowers, "Valuing Work," *WorldatWork* 12, no. 1 (Second Quarter 2003): 28.

27. Nona Tobin, "Can Technology Ease the Pain of Salary Surveys?" *Public Personnel Management* 31, no. 1 (Spring 2002): 65–76.

28. Charles H. Fey and Madhura Tare, "Market Pricing Concerns," *WorldatWork* 16, no. 2 (Second Quarter 2007): 61.

29. Curt Finch, "How to Create an Effective Pay Structure," *Employee Benefit Plan Review* 61, no. 10 (April 2007): 26. See also Gregory A. Stoskopf, "Choosing the Best Salary Structure for Your Organization," *WorldatWork* 11, no. 4 (Fourth Quarter 2004): 28–36.

30. Organizations may have a compensation program that pays a differential based on geographic location. See Thomas J. Atchison, "Branch Office Salary Structure," *Compensation and Benefits Review* 39, no. 3 (June 2007): 35.

31. Carri Baca and Gary Starzmann, "Clarifying Competencies: Powerful Tools for Driving Business Success, Part Two," *Workspan* (April 2006): 53.

32. Howard Risher, "Second-Generation Banded Salary Systems," *WorldatWork* 16, no. 1 (First Quarter 2007): 20.

33. Susan Ladika, "Decompression Pay," *HR Magazine* 50, no. 10 (December 2005): 79.

Pay-for-Performance: Incentive Rewards

CHAPTER 10

After studying this chapter, you should be able to

[OUTCOME] **1** Discuss the basic requirements for successful implementation of incentive programs.

[OUTCOME] **2** Identify the types of and reasons for implementing individual incentive plans.

[OUTCOME] **3** Explain why merit raises may fail to motivate employees adequately and discuss ways to increase their motivational value.

[OUTCOME] **4** Indicate the advantage of each of the principal methods used to compensate salespeople.

[OUTCOME] **5** Differentiate how gains may be shared with employees under the Scanlon and Improshare gainsharing systems.

[OUTCOME] **6** Differentiate between profit-sharing plans and explain advantages and disadvantages of these programs.

[OUTCOME] **7** Describe the main types of ESOPs and discuss the advantages of ESOP to employers and employees.

In Chapter 9, we emphasized that organizations design their compensation programs—strategic compensation planning—to encourage employee (motivation) and (growth). The goal is to motivate employees to perform to their full capacity. Recognizing this fact, many organizations offer some form of (incentive) to workers. According to the *WorldatWork* 2007/2008 salary budget survey, 80 percent of reporting organizations use variable pay as a cornerstone of their pay philosophy.[1] These organizations are attempting to get more motivational mileage out of employee compensation by tying it more closely to organizational objectives and employee performance. Jessica Smilko and Kathy Van Neck, compensation specialists, note this fact about variable pay: "Employees are embracing variable compensation as a means of (aligning employee behaviour with organizational goals)." When incentives are linked with output, workers will increasingly apply their skills and knowledge to their jobs and will be encouraged to work together as a team. Therefore, in their attempt to raise productivity, managers are focusing on the many variables that help determine the effectiveness of pay as a motivator.[2]

In this chapter, we will discuss incentive plans in terms of the (objectives) they hope to achieve and the (various factors) that may affect their success. Because many organizations have implemented broad-based incentive programs, for discussion purposes we have grouped incentive plans into three broad categories: individual incentive plans, group incentive plans, and enterprise incentive plans, as shown in Figure 10.1.[3]

variable pay

Tying pay to some measure of individual, group, or organizational performance

STRATEGIC REASONS FOR INCENTIVE PLANS

A major element of strategic compensation management is the use of incentive plans, also called (variable pay) programs, for employees throughout the organization. Ken Abosch, compensation specialist with Hewitt Associates LLC, notes, "There's no question that most corporations have turned away from fixed forms of compensation in favour of variable forms. There has been an abandonment of entitlement programs."[4]

FIGURE **10.1**

Types of Incentive Plans

Individual	Group	Enterprise
Piecework	Team compensation	Profit sharing
Standard hour plan	Scanlon Plan	Stock options
Bonuses	Improshare	Employee stock ownership plans (ESOPs)
Merit pay		
Lump-sum merit pay		
Incentive awards		
Sales incentives		
Incentives for professional employees		
Executive compensation		

Incentive rewards are based entirely upon a pay-for-performance philosophy (see Chapter 9). Incentive pay programs establish a performance "threshold" (a baseline performance level) that an employee or group of employees must reach in order to qualify for incentive payments. According to one compensation manager, "The performance threshold is the minimum level an employee must reach in order to qualify for variable pay." Additionally, incentive plans emphasize a shared focus on organizational objectives by broadening the opportunities for incentives to employees throughout the organization. Incentive plans create an operating environment that champions a philosophy of shared commitment through the belief that every individual contributes to organizational performance and success.

INCENTIVE PLANS AS LINKS TO ORGANIZATIONAL OBJECTIVES

Contemporary arguments for incentive plans focus on linking compensation rewards, both individual and group, to organizational goals. Specific company goals or objectives might be to lower labour costs, improve customer satisfaction, expand product markets, or maintain high levels of productivity and quality, which in turn improve the market for the company's goods and services in a global economy. By meshing compensation and organizational objectives, managers believe that employees will assume "ownership" of their jobs, thereby improving their effort and overall job performance. Incentives are designed to encourage employees to put out more effort to complete their job tasks—effort they might not be motivated to expend under hourly and/or seniority-based compensation systems. Also, incentive pay is highly valued as a compensation strategy to attract and retain top-performing employees.[5]

Figure 10.2 summarizes the major advantages of incentive pay programs as noted by researchers and HR professionals.

Do incentive plans work? The answer is both yes and no. Various studies, along with reports from individual organizations, show a measurable relationship between incentive plans and improved organizational performance.[6] However, the degree of success obtained depends on several factors including (1) identifying important organizational metrics by which to measure employee performance and (2) a customized incentive plan that effectively measures employee output and rewards exceptional employee performance.[7] For example, at one

FIGURE 10.2

Advantages of Incentive Pay Programs

- Incentives focus employee efforts on specific performance targets. They provide real motivation that produces important employee and organizational gains.
- Incentive payouts are variable costs linked to the achievement of results. Base salaries are fixed costs largely unrelated to output.
- Incentive compensation is directly related to operating performance. If performance objectives (quantity and/or quality) are met, incentives are paid. If objectives are not achieved, incentives are withheld.
- Incentives foster teamwork and unit cohesiveness when payments to individuals are based on team results.
- Incentives are a way to distribute success among those responsible for producing that success.
- Incentives are a means to reward or attract top performers when salary budgets are low.

hospital, health care employees are eligible for up to a 10 percent merit raise depending on whether or not they meet or exceed important hospital performance expectations. Importantly, in a survey designed to assess the hospital's incentive pay program, employee responses showed a high relationship between hospital goals and the linkage between pay and performance.[8] At an insurance company, salespeople who achieve sales targets receive significant bonuses, merchandise awards, and recognition through the company's website and in-house publications.[9]

Unfortunately, studies also show that variable pay plans may not achieve their proposed objectives or lead to organizational improvements. First, incentive plans sometimes fail to satisfy employee expectations for pay gains. Second, management may have failed to give adequate attention to the design and implementation of the plan, leaving employees confused about how incentive payments are calculated. Third, employees may have little ability to affect performance standards. Furthermore, the success of an incentive plan will depend on the environment that exists within an organization. A plan is more likely to work in an organization where morale is high, employees believe they are being treated fairly, and there is harmony between employees and management.

REQUIREMENTS FOR A SUCCESSFUL INCENTIVE PLAN

For an incentive plan to succeed, employees must have some desire for the plan. This desire can be influenced in part by how successful management is in introducing the plan and convincing employees of its benefits. Encouraging employees to participate in developing and administering the plan is likely to increase their willingness to accept it.

Employees must be able to see a clear connection between the incentive payments they receive and their job performance. This connection is more visible if there are objective quality or quantity standards by which they can judge their performance. Commitment by employees to meet these standards is also essential for incentive plans to succeed. This requires mutual trust and understanding between employees and their supervisors, which can be achieved only through open, two-way channels of communication. Management should never allow incentive payments to be seen as an entitlement. Instead, these payments should be viewed as a reward that must be earned through effort. This perception can be strengthened if the incentive money is distributed to employees in a separate cheque. Compensation specialist Joanne Sammer notes the following as characteristics of a successful incentive plan:[10]

- Identify important organizational metrics that encourage employee behaviour.
- Involve employees. Incentive programs should seem fair to employees.
- Find the right incentive payout. Payout formulas should be simple and understandable.
- Establish a clear link between performance and payout.

Furthermore, the best-managed incentive pay programs are clearly and continuously communicated to employees. This is true during both good and bad economic periods. According to one compensation consultant, "Communicate what you are doing and why it is critical to success. Everyone needs to know what the goals are and what the rewards are for achieving those goals."[11] Proactive organizations find it advisable to continually evaluate the operation and administration of their variable pay programs.

[OUTCOME 1]

SETTING PERFORMANCE MEASURES

Measurement is key to the success of incentive plans because it communicates the importance of established organizational goals. What gets measured and rewarded gets attention.[12] For example, if the organization desires to be a leader in quality, then performance indexes may focus on customer satisfaction, timeliness, or being error-free. If being a low-priced producer is the goal, then emphasis should be on cost reduction or increased productivity with lower acceptable levels of quality. While a variety of performance options are available, most focus on quality, cost control, or productivity. Highlights in HRM 10.1 provides five proven guidelines on how to establish and maintain an effective performance measurement program.

For some organizations, linking incentive payments to formalized performance measures has not obtained positive results for either employees or the organization. Failure can often be traced to the choice of performance measures.[13] Therefore, measures that are quantitative, simple, and structured to show a clear relationship to improved performance are best. Overly quantitative, complex measures are to be avoided. Also, when selecting a performance measure, it is necessary to evaluate the extent to which the employees involved can actually influence the measurement. Finally, employers must guard against "ratcheting up" performance goals by continually trying to exceed previous results. This eventually leads to employee frustration and employee perception that the standards are unattainable. The result will be a mistrust of management and a backlash against the entire incentive program.

Highlights in **HRM 10.1**

Setting Performance Measures—The Keys

Both large and small organizations have established performance measures to improve operational success while rewarding employees for their performance outcomes. Establishing meaningful performance measures is one of the important and difficult challenges facing management today. Before managers or supervisors develop and implement organizational measures, they should consider the following guidelines.

- *Performance measures—at all organizational levels—must be consistent with the strategic goals of the organization.* Avoid irrelevant measures or metrics that are not closely linked to the business or what employees do in their work.

- *Define the intent of performance measures and champion the cause relentlessly.* Demonstrate that performance measures are, in fact, good business management and hold managers and employees accountable for their success.

- *Involve employees.* A critical step in any measurement program is the development of an employee involvement strategy outlining the

nature of employee participation, implementation, and ongoing management of the performance management program. Segment the workforce based on nature of work and potential for impact. Consider which metrics require customization. Acceptance of a performance measurement program is heightened when employees "buy into" the process.

- *Consider the organization's culture and workforce demographics when designing performance measures.* For example, organizations with a more traditional hierarchical structure may need more time to introduce performance metrics compared to flatter organizations, which are more fluid and less steeped in control and command characteristics.

- *Widely communicate the importance of performance measures.* Performance messages are the principles and guidelines that communicate to employees about required performance levels and why the organization needs to achieve those levels of success.

ADMINISTERING INCENTIVE PLANS

While incentive plans based on productivity can reduce direct labour costs, to achieve their full benefit they must be carefully thought out, implemented, and maintained. A cardinal rule is that thorough planning must be combined with a "proceed with caution" approach. Compensation managers repeatedly stress a number of points related to the effective administration of incentive plans. Three of the more important points are, by consensus, as follows:

1. Incentive systems are effective only when managers are willing to grant incentives based on differences in individual, team, or organizational performance. Allowing incentive payments to become pay guarantees defeats the motivational intent of the incentive. The primary purpose of an incentive compensation plan is not to pay off under almost all circumstances, but rather to motivate performance. Thus, if the plan is to succeed, poor performance must go unrewarded.

2. Annual salary budgets must be large enough to reward and reinforce exceptional performance. When compensation budgets are set to ensure that pay increases do not exceed certain limits (often established as a percentage of payroll or sales), these constraints may prohibit rewarding outstanding individual or group performance.

3. The overhead costs associated with plan implementation and administration must be determined. These may include the cost of establishing performance standards and the added cost of record keeping. The time consumed in communicating the plan to employees, answering questions, and resolving any complaints about it must also be included in these costs.

INDIVIDUAL INCENTIVE PLANS

In today's competitive world, one word—flexibility—describes the design of individual incentive plans.[14] For example, technology, job tasks and duties, and/or organizational goals (such as being a low-cost producer) impact the organization's choice of incentive pay programs. Incentive payments may be determined by the number of units produced, achievement of specific performance goals, or productivity improvements in the organization as a whole. In addition, in highly competitive industries such as food and retailing, low profit margins will affect the availability of monies for incentive payouts. All of these considerations suggest that tradition and philosophy, as well as economics and technology, help govern the design of individual incentive systems.

PIECEWORK

One of the oldest incentive plans is based on piecework. Under straight piecework, employees receive a certain rate for each unit produced. Their compensation is determined by the number of units they produce during a pay period. At Steelcase, an office furniture maker, employees can earn more than their base pay, often as much as 35 percent more, through piecework for each slab of metal they cut or chair they upholster. Under a differential piece rate, employees whose production exceeds the standard output receive a higher rate for all of their work than the rate paid to those who do not exceed the standard.

Employers include piecework in their compensation strategy for several reasons. The wage payment for each employee is simple to compute, and the plan permits an organization to predict its labour costs with considerable accuracy, since these costs are the same for each unit of output. The piecework system is more likely to succeed when units of output can be measured readily, the quality of the product is less critical, the job is fairly standardized, and a constant flow of work can be maintained.

[OUTCOME 2]

straight piecework
An incentive plan under which employees receive a certain rate for each unit produced

differential piece rate
A compensation rate under which employees whose production exceeds the standard amount of output receive a higher rate for all of their work than the rate paid to those who do not exceed the standard amount

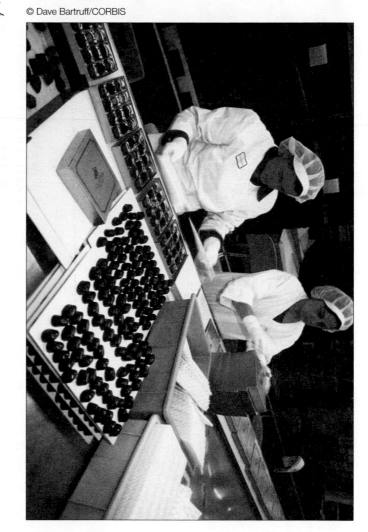

Employees in manufacturing plants often work under individual incentive plans such as piecework.

Computing the Piece Rate

Although time standards establish the time required to perform a given amount of work, they do not by themselves determine what the incentive rate should be. The incentive rates must be based on hourly wage rates that would otherwise be paid for the type of work being performed. For example, the standard time for producing one unit of work in a job paying $12.75 per hour was set at 12 minutes. The piece rate would be $2.55 per unit, computed as follows:

$$\frac{60 \text{ (minutes per hour)}}{12 \text{ (standard time per hour)}} = 5 \text{ (units per hour)}$$

$$\frac{\$12.75 \text{ (hourly rate)}}{5 \text{ (units per hour)}} = 2.55 \text{ per unit}$$

Piecework: The Drawbacks

Despite their obvious advantages—including their direct tie to a pay-for-performance philosophy—piecework systems have a number of disadvantages that offset their usefulness. One of the most significant weaknesses of piecework, as well as of other incentive plans based on individual effort, is that it may not always be an effective motivator. If employees believe that an increase in their output will provoke disapproval from fellow workers (often referred to as rate busting), they may avoid exerting maximum effort because their desire for peer approval outweighs their desire for more money. Also, jobs in which individual contributions are difficult to distinguish or measure or in which the work is mechanized to the point that the employee exercises very little control over output may be unsuited to piecework. Piecework may also be inappropriate in the following situations:

- When quality is more important than quantity.
- When technology changes are frequent.
- When productivity standards on which piecework must be based are difficult to develop.

Importantly, piecework incentive systems can work against an organizational culture promoting workforce cooperation, creativity, or problem solving because each of these goals can infringe on an employee's time and productivity and, therefore, total incentive earned.

STANDARD HOUR PLAN

standard hour plan
An incentive plan that sets rates based on the completion of a job in a predetermined standard time

Another common incentive technique is the **standard hour plan**, which sets incentive rates on the basis of a predetermined "standard time" for completing a job. If employees finish the work in less than the expected time, their pay is still based on the standard time for the job multiplied by their hourly rate. Standard hour plans are popular in service departments in automobile dealerships. For example, if the standard time to install an engine in a truck is five hours and the mechanic completes the job in four and a half hours, the payment would be the mechanic's hourly rate times five hours. Standard hour plans are particularly suited to long-cycle operations or jobs or tasks that are nonrepetitive and require a variety of skills. However, while standard hour plans can motivate employees to produce more, employers must ensure that equipment maintenance and product quality do not suffer as employees strive to do their work faster to earn additional income.

BONUSES

bonus
An incentive payment that is supplemental to the base wage

A **bonus** is an incentive payment that is given to an employee beyond one's normal base wage. It is frequently given at the end of the year and does not become part of base pay. Bonuses have the advantage of providing employees with more pay for exerting greater effort, while at the same time the employees still have the security of a basic wage. Bonus payments are common among managerial and executive employees, but recent trends show that they are increasingly given to employees throughout the organization.[15]

Depending on who is to receive the bonus, the incentive payment may be determined on the basis of cost reduction, quality improvement, or performance criteria established by the organization. At the executive level, for example, performance criteria might include earnings growth or enterprise-specific agreed-on objectives.

spot bonus
An unplanned bonus given for employee effort unrelated to an established performance measure

When some special employee contribution is to be rewarded, a **spot bonus** is used. A spot bonus, as the name implies, is given "on the spot," normally for some employee effort not directly tied to an established performance standard. For example, a customer service representative might receive a spot bonus for working long hours to fill a new customer's large order. Spot bonuses are championed as useful retention and motivational tools for overburdened employees, especially during lean financial times. Lauren Sejen, compensation expert with Watson Wyatt Worldwide, notes, "I think spot bonuses are one of the most underutilized forms of rewards, given how well employees respond to them. These plans make perfect sense."[16]

MERIT PAY

merit pay program (merit raise)

A **merit pay program** (merit raise) links an increase in base pay to how successfully an employee performs his or her job. The merit increase is normally given on the basis of an employee's having achieved some objective performance standard—although a superior's subjective evaluation of subordinate performance may play a large role in the increase given. Merit raises can serve to motivate if employees perceive the raise to be related to the performance required to earn it.[17]

Theories of motivation, in addition to behavioural science research, provide justification for merit pay plans as well as other pay-for-performance programs.[18] However, research shows that a merit increase in the range of 7 to 9 percent is necessary to serve as a pay motivator.[19] Employees may welcome lower percentage amounts, but low salary increases may not lead to significantly greater effort on the part of employees to drive business results. Consequently, with low salary budgets (see Chapter 9), organizations wishing to reward top performers will be required to distribute a large portion of the compensation budget to these individuals.[20] A meaningful merit increase will catch the attention of top performers while sending a signal to poor-performing employees. A strategic compensation policy *must differentiate* between outstanding and good or average performance. Furthermore, increases granted on the basis of merit should be distinguishable from cost-of-living or other general increases.

Problems with Merit Raises

Merit raises may not always achieve their intended purpose. Unlike a bonus, a merit raise may be perpetuated year after year even when performance declines. When this happens, employees come to expect the increase and see it as an entitlement, unrelated to their performance. Furthermore, what are referred to as merit raises often turn out to be increases based on seniority or favouritism. A superior's biased evaluation of subordinate performance may play a large role in the increase given. Even when merit raises are determined by performance, the employee's gains may be offset by inflation and higher income taxes. Compensation specialists also recognize the following problems with merit pay plans:

1. Money available for merit increases may be inadequate to satisfactorily raise all employees' base pay.

2. Managers may have no guidance in how to define and measure performance; there may be vagueness regarding merit award criteria.

3. Employees may not believe that their compensation is tied to effort and performance; they may be unable to differentiate between merit pay and other types of pay increases.

4. Employees and their managers may hold different views of the factors that contribute to job success.

5. Merit pay plans may create feelings of pay inequity.[21]

While there are no easy solutions to these problems, organizations using a true merit pay plan often base the percentage pay raise on merit guidelines tied to performance appraisals. For example, a certain pay increase, "3 percent," will be tied to a certain performance evaluation, "above average." The percentages may change each year, depending on various internal or external concerns such as profit levels or national economic conditions as indicated by changes in the consumer price index. To prevent all employees from being rated outstanding or above average, managers may be required to distribute the performance rating according to some preestablished formula (such as only 10 percent can be rated outstanding). Additionally, when setting merit percentage guidelines, organizations should consider individual performance along with such factors as training, experience, and current earnings.

LUMP-SUM MERIT PAY

To make merit increases more flexible and visible, some organizations have implemented a lump-sum merit program. Under this type of plan, employees receive a single lump-sum increase at the time of their review, an increase that is not added to their base salary. Lump-sum merit programs offer several advantages. For employees, an advantage is that receiving a single lump-sum merit payment can provide a clear link between pay and performance. For example, a 5 percent merit increase granted to an industrial engineer earning $72,000 a year translates into a weekly increase of $69.23—a figure that looks small compared with a lump-sum payment of $3,600. For employers, lump-sum payments essentially freeze base salaries, thereby maintaining annual salary and benefit costs, since the level of benefits are normally calculated from salary levels. Organizations using a lump-sum merit program will want to adjust base salaries upward after a certain period of time. These adjustments should keep pace with the rising cost of living and increases in the general market wage.

[OUTCOME 3]

merit guidelines
Guidelines for awarding merit raises that are tied to performance objectives

lump-sum merit program
Program under which employees receive a year-end merit payment, which is not added to their base pay

INCENTIVE AWARDS AND RECOGNITION

Incentive awards and employee recognition are an important part of an employer's pay-for-performance compensation strategy. Awards are used to recognize productivity gains, special contributions or achievements, and service to the organization. Popular noncash incentive awards include merchandise, personalized gifts, theatre or sports tickets, vacations, dining out, gift certificates or gift cards, and personalized clothing. Tangible awards presented with the right message and style can make employees feel appreciated while at the same time underscoring a company value. Research clearly shows that noncash incentive awards are most effective as motivators when the award is combined with a meaningful employee recognition program. Tyler Gentry, employee recognition specialist, notes this about the importance of noncash incentive awards, "Recognition and rewards aren't so much about recognizing someone for going 'above and beyond' and giving gifts as they are about letting employees know that they are *valued* and *appreciated*. Recognition is a conduit that shows employees that the company appreciates their efforts, their unique gifts, and their contributions."[22] Employers should take care to tie awards to performance and deliver awards in a timely, sincere, and specific way. Generally, the more public the recognition, the more powerful the effect.[23]

Importantly, noncash incentive awards should support business goals and objectives. Greg Boswell, a director of performance recognition, notes, "Employers are now thinking of awards and employee recognition more strategically with programs closely aligned to their business goals."[24] For example, if quality improvement is a business goal, then recognition needs to be tied to those behaviours that further the achievement of quality. Additionally, incentive awards work best when awards are appreciated and valued by employees. At one advertising agency, the employee-of-the-month is allowed to drive the president's car for one month—the car is a Maserati. Highlights in HRM 10.2 provides suggestions for noncash incentive awards based on the generational grouping of employees.

Highlights in **HRM 10.2**

Customize Your Noncash Incentive Awards

Compensation specialists recognize that a successful noncash incentive program will offer employees a wide selection of awards—awards that appeal to a diverse workforce and the uniqueness of individual employees. "One-size-fits-all" is not the approach to take. What appeals to younger employees may not be attractive to older employees. For example, one marketing firm characterizes recognition and rewards based on generations as follows:

- Traditionalists (61+). These individuals are less likely to spend money on themselves. Attractive awards include entertainment venues, vacations, and technology items. They also appreciate health and wellness opportunities.
- Boomers (41–60). Personal recognition is important. These individuals want to feel appreciated for their

work contributions and are likely to change jobs if they feel undervalued or go unrecognized. Boomers favour incentive rewards in the areas of travel, luxury gifts, health and wellness options, and personalized plaques and awards.

- Generation X (25–41). This group values a balanced lifestyle of work and play. Generation X employees value gadgets and high-tech items along with flexible schedules and discretionary time off. A flexible "day-off-work" would appeal to this group.
- Generation Y (14–25). These employees desire immediate performance feedback. Employee-of-the-month programs appeal to these employees as do "spot" recognition plans. Gift cards, gift certificates to "trendy" stores, and movie tickets are appropriate as rewards for the immediate recognition of performance.

Source: Adapted from Alison Avalos, "Recognition: A Critical Component of the Total Reward Mix," *Workspan* (July 2007): 33. Reprinted by permission of WorldatWork.

[OUTCOME] ✗ 415

SALES INCENTIVES

The enthusiasm and drive required in most types of sales work demand that sales employees be highly motivated. This fact, as well as the competitive nature of selling, explains why financial incentives for salespeople are widely used. These incentive plans must provide a source of motivation that will elicit cooperation and trust. Motivation is particularly important for employees away from the office who cannot be supervised closely and who, as a result, must exercise a high degree of self-discipline.

Unique Needs of Sales Incentive Plans

Incentive systems for salespeople are complicated by the wide differences in the types of sales jobs. These range from department store clerks who ring up customer purchases to industrial salespeople who provide consultation and other highly technical services. Salespeople's performance may be measured by the dollar volume of their sales and by their ability to establish new accounts. Other measures are the ability to promote new products or services and to provide various forms of customer service and assistance that do not produce immediate sales revenues.[25]

Performance standards for sales employees are difficult to develop, however, because their performance is often affected by external factors beyond their control. Economic and seasonal fluctuations, sales competition, changes in demand, and the nature of the sales territory can all affect an individual's sales record.[26] Sales volume alone therefore may not be an accurate indicator of the effort salespeople have expended.

In developing incentive plans for salespeople, managers are also confronted with the problem of how to reward extra sales effort and at the same time compensate for activities that do not contribute directly or immediately to sales. Furthermore, sales employees must be able to enjoy some degree of income stability.[27] Many schemes to reward employees for reaching sales goals are threatened by instances of unethical behaviour where the needs of employees are not aligned with the needs of the customers, as reported in Ethics in HRM.

Ethics in **HRM**

Counter-Productive Compensation

I started worrying about the corrupting influence of incentive schemes when, in a period of one month, I was asked by three employees at three different companies to help them achieve their bonuses. The first case happened after I purchased a car and was asked by the sales representative to complete an evaluation form and to give him high ratings so that he would get his bonus. The second instance took place after I had another car serviced and was told by the mechanic that I would be contacted by an agency that conducted independent ratings on employee performance, and that I had better rate him as a "ten" because no other mark would get him the bonus.

Then, a few days later, I wanted to move some money from one bank to another bank where I could receive a higher interest rate. I was asked by the financial adviser to delay the transfer of my money until the following month (even though it would cost me money) because her bonus was calculated at the end of the month.

Apparently my experience is not unique. At one company, employees were given a small bonus for every voluntary and spontaneous complementary letter received about their performance. Of course, employees began asking clients to send them these types of letters.

continued

Incentives may create conflict between the best interests of employees and the best interests of customers. In order to receive commissions and bonuses, many employees engage in unethical conduct. When Alberta Government Telephones rewarded employees for customers adopting a new phone optional service, some employees simply added the option to the customer's line, and the customer would have to notice this, and then phone the company to have it removed.

According to one study, almost half of the respondents, who were sales personnel, had lied on a sales call, a third had made unrealistic promises, and about one-fifth had sold products that customers did not need. Another study reported that employees working in call centres, whose performance targets included handling a customer in ten seconds, would "accidentally" disconnect those who spoke English poorly (and thus slowed the call). Sears had introduced commissions for auto-service employees, and employees began to cheat to meet their quotas. An undercover investigation revealed that customers were being charged for unnecessary repairs.

Unions have concerns about incentive programs, and are usually not supportive of them. For example, Toronto Hydro tried to implement an incentive program that would include gift certificates, extra breaks, and prizes such as cameras. The union, Local 1 of the Canadian Union of Public Employees, was invited to participate in the committee to design the rewards program, but declined because the allocation of rewards was seen to be inherently subjective. The program was going to reward people for "going above and beyond," but this may mean different things to different people. The union argued that if going "above and beyond" means carrying a larger than normal workload, such as journalists covering an election campaign, or a group of nurses working through the SARS epidemic, then paying for overtime is how the organization should reward these workers. Also some organizations reward employees for attendance, but again the union says: "If someone is blessed with good health, why should somebody else with poor health be treated differently?" The union is particularly opposed to incentive programs linked to health and safety. If the unit is depending on a cash payout for reaching X days without an injury, the first person to be injured can be coerced into covering up the injury, so that his peers qualify for the reward. Furthermore, assessing and compensating employees outside the performance appraisal provisions of the collective agreement is in breach of the collective agreement.

Sources: Adapted from Uyen Vu, "Morale Booster or Minefield," *Canadian HR Reporter,* August 9, 2004, 13; M. Choquette, "Compensation That Corrupts," The Conference Board of Canada, 1999: 254–299.

Types of Sales Incentive Plans

Compensation plans for sales employees may consist of a straight salary plan, a straight commission plan, a combination salary and commission plan, or a sales plus bonus plan.[28] A **straight salary plan** permits salespeople to be paid for performing various duties not reflected immediately in their sales volume. It enables them to devote more time to providing services and building up the goodwill of customers without jeopardizing their income. The principal limitation of the straight salary plan is that it may not motivate salespeople to exert sufficient effort in maximizing their sales volume.

On the other hand, the **straight commission plan,** based on a percentage of sales, provides maximum incentive and is easy to compute and understand. For example, total cash compensation might equal total sales volume times some percentage of total sales, perhaps 2 percent. Straight commission plans encourage aggressive selling, which might be needed in highly competitive industries. Under a straight commission plan, salespeople may be allowed a salary draw. A *draw* is a cash advance that must be paid back as commissions are earned.

However, the straight commission plan is limited by the following disadvantages:

1. Salespeople will stress high-priced products.
2. Customer service after the sale is likely to be neglected.

straight salary plan
A compensation plan that permits salespeople to be paid for performing various duties that are not reflected immediately in their sales volume

straight commission plan
A compensation plan based on a percentage of sales

3. Earnings tend to fluctuate widely between good and poor periods of business, and turnover of trained sales employees tends to increase in poor periods.

4. Salespeople are tempted to grant price concessions.

The **combined salary and commission plan** is the most widely used sales incentive program. For example, the most common pay mix for salespersons responsible for *new* accounts is 50 percent base pay and 50 percent variable pay. For salespersons servicing *existing* accounts, a pay distribution of 70 percent base pay and 30 percent commission is typical.[29] The ratio of base salary to commission can be set to fit organizational objectives. The following advantages indicate why the combination salary and commission plan is so widely used:

1. The right kind of incentive compensation, if linked to salary in the right proportion, has most of the advantages of both the straight salary and the straight commission forms of compensation.

2. A salary-plus-incentive compensation plan offers greater design flexibility and can therefore be more readily set up to help maximize company profits.

3. The plan can develop the most favourable ratio of selling expense to sales.

4. The field sales force can be motivated to achieve specific company marketing objectives in addition to sales volume.

Sales representative at Glaxo Pharmaceuticals are paid on a salary plus bonus program. Under **salary plus bonus plans** the payout can be paid on a monthly, quarterly, or yearly schedule contingent upon the salesperson achieving targeted sales goals such as number of sales calls made, account servicing, or quality of sales.

INCENTIVES FOR PROFESSIONAL EMPLOYEES

Like other salaried workers, professional employees—engineers, scientists, and attorneys, for example—may be motivated through bonuses and merit increases. In some organizations, unfortunately, professional employees cannot advance beyond a certain point in the salary structure unless they are willing to take an administrative assignment. When they are promoted, their professional talents are no longer utilized fully. In the process, the organization may lose a good professional employee and gain a poor administrator. To avoid this situation, some organizations have extended the salary range for professional positions to equal or nearly equal that for administrative positions. The extension of this range provides a double-track wage system, as illustrated in Chapter 5 whereby professionals who do not aspire to become administrators still have an opportunity to earn comparable salaries. Professional employees can receive compensation beyond base pay. For example, scientists and engineers employed by high-tech firms are included in performance-based incentive programs such as profit sharing or stock ownership. These plans encourage greater levels of individual performance. Cash bonuses can be awarded to those who complete projects on or before deadline dates. Payments may also be given to individuals elected to professional societies, granted patents, or meeting professional licensing standards.

THE EXECUTIVE PAY PACKAGE

Executive compensation plans consist of five basic components: (1) base salary, (2) short-term incentives or bonuses, (3) long-term incentives or stock plans, (4) benefits, and (5) perquisites.[30] Each of these elements may receive different emphasis in the executive's compensation package depending on various organizational goals and executive needs.[31]

---

combined salary and commission plan
A compensation plan that includes a straight salary and a commission

salary plus bonus plan
A compensation plan that pays a salary plus a bonus achieved by reaching targeted sales goals.

Executive Base Salaries

Executive base salaries represent between 30 and 40 percent of total annual compensation.[32] An analysis of executive salaries shows that the largest portion of executive pay is received in long-term incentive rewards and bonuses. Regardless, executives of Fortune 500 firms routinely earn an annual base salary in excess of $500,000, with executives in very large corporations earning considerably more. The levels of competitive salaries in the job market exert perhaps the greatest influence on executive base salaries. An organization's compensation committee—normally members of the board of directors—will order a salary survey to find out what executives earn in comparable enterprises.[33] For example, by one estimate, 96 percent of companies in the Standard & Poor's 500 stock index use a technique called *competitive benchmarking* when setting executive pay or to remain competitive for executive talent. As noted in *BusinessWeek*, company boards reason that a CEO who does not earn as much as his or her peers is likely to "take a hike." Comparisons may be based on organization size, sales volume, or industry groupings. Thus, by analyzing the data from published studies, along with self-generated salary surveys, the compensation committee can determine the equity of the compensation package outside the organization.

© Digital Vision/Getty Images

A straight commission plan can lead to the aggressive selling favoured by highly motivated individuals.

Executive Short-Term Incentives

Annual bonuses represent the main element of executive short-term incentives.[34] A bonus payment may take the form of cash or stock and may be paid immediately (which is frequently the case), deferred for a short time, or deferred until retirement. Most organizations pay their short-term incentive bonuses in cash (in the form of a supplemental cheque), in keeping with their pay-for-performance strategy. By providing a reward soon after the performance and thus linking it to the effort on which it is based, they can use cash bonuses as a significant motivator. Deferred bonuses are used to provide a source of retirement benefits or to supplement a regular pension plan.

Incentive bonuses for executives should be based on the contribution the individual makes to the organization. A variety of formulas have been developed for this purpose. Incentive bonuses may be based on a percentage of a company's total profits or a percentage of profits in excess of a specific return on stockholders' investments. In other instances, the payments may be tied to an annual profit plan whereby the amount is determined by the extent to which an agreed-on profit level is exceeded. Payments may also be based on performance ratings or the achievement of specific objectives established with the agreement of executives and the board of directors.

In a continuing effort to monitor the pulse of the marketplace, more organizations are tying operational yardsticks to the traditional financial gauges when computing executive pay. Called *balanced scorecards*, these yardsticks may measure things such as customer satisfaction, the ability to innovate, or product or service leadership.[35] Notes David Cates, a compensation principal with Towers Perrin, a balanced scorecard "allows companies to focus on building future economic value, rather than be driven solely by short-term financial results." Mobil Oil uses a balanced scorecard that better indicates exactly where the company is successful and where improvement is needed.

Executive Long-Term Incentives

Stock options are the primary long-term incentive offered to executives.[36] The principal reason driving executive stock ownership is the desire of both the company and outside investors for senior managers to have a significant stake in the success of the business—to have their fortunes rise and fall with the value they create for shareholders. Stock options can also be extremely lavish for executives. In 2008, the average CEO in Canada received $5.1 million, which was a combination of salary of $863,000, a cash bonus of $1.2 million and stock options of $2.4 million. The highest paid executives in 2008 were Thomas Glocer of Thomson Reuters at $39,010,519 (including stock options of $30 million) and George Cope of BCE at $19,551,345 (including stock options of $11 million).[37] Not surprisingly, the creativity in designing a stock option program seems almost limitless. Figure 10.3 highlights several common forms of long-term incentives.

Short-term incentive bonuses are criticized for causing top executives to focus on quarterly profit goals to the detriment of long-term survival and growth objectives. Therefore, corporations such as Sears and Manulife have adopted compensation strategies that tie executive pay to long-term performance measures. Each of these organizations recognizes that compensation strategies must also take into account the performance of the organization as a whole. Important to stockholders are such performance results as growth in earnings per share, return on stockholders' equity, and, ultimately, stock price appreciation.

A variety of incentive plans, therefore, have been developed to tie rewards to these performance results, particularly over the long term. Additionally, stock options can serve to retain key executive personnel when exercising the options is linked to a specified vesting period, perhaps two to four years (this type of incentive is called "golden handcuffs").

Stock options are under attack.[38] The Canadian Coalition for Good Governance, which represents Canada's largest institutional shareholders, is having meetings with large organizations to change their compensation packages and tie them more closely to long-term goals. Many object to the sheer magnitude of these incentive

FIGURE 10.3

Types of Long-Term Incentive Plans

Stock options	Rights granted to executives to purchase shares of their organization's stock at an established price for a fixed period of time. Stock price is usually set at market value at the time the option is granted.
Stock appreciation rights (SARs)	Cash or stock award determined by increase in stock price during any time chosen by the executive in the option period; does not require executive financing.
Stock purchase	Opportunities for executives to purchase shares of their organization's stock valued at full market or a discount price, often with the organization providing financial assistance.
Phantom stock	Grant of units equal in value to the fair market value or book value of a share of stock; on a specified date the executive will be paid the appreciation in the value of the units up to that time.
Restricted stock	Grant of stock or stock units at a reduced price with the condition that the stock not be transferred or sold (by risk of forfeiture) before a specified employment date.
Performance units	Grants analogous to annual bonuses except that the measurement period exceeds one year. The value of the grant can be expressed as a flat dollar amount or converted to a number of "units" of equivalent aggregate value.
Performance shares	Grants of actual stock or phantom stock units. Value is contingent on both predetermined performance objectives over a specified period of time and the stock market.

rewards. The link between pay and performance that options are championed to provide can also be undermined when compensation committees grant additional options to executives even when company stock prices fall or performance indexes decline. Peter Clapman, chief counsel for TIAA-CREF, the world's largest pension system, notes, "It's sort of heads you win, tails let's flip again." Even worse for shareholders is the dilution problem. Every option granted to executives makes the shares of other stockholders less valuable.

Executive Benefits

The benefits package offered executives may parallel one offered to other groups of employees. Various programs for extended health insurance, life insurance, retirement plans, and vacations are common. However, unlike other employee groups, the benefits offered executives are likely to be broader in coverage and free of charge. Additionally, executives may be given financial assistance in the form of trusts for estate planning, payment of mortgage interest, and legal help.[39]

Executive Perquisites

perquisites

Special nonmonetary benefits given to executives; often referred to as perks

Perquisites are nonmonetary rewards given to executives. Perquisites, or *perks*, are a means of demonstrating the executive's importance to the organization. The status that comes with perks—both inside and outside the organization—shows a pecking order and conveys authority. Corporate executives may simply consider perks a "badge of merit."

The dark side of perks is that they are viewed as wasteful spending and overly lavish. A recent study, however, shows that perks can facilitate company productivity by saving executive time (for example, private planes and chauffeur service) or improve or maintain executive health (for example, spas, health clubs, and company cabins). Therefore, the cost of perks should be weighed against the added efficiency and managerial effectiveness they generate.[40] Highlights in HRM 10.3 shows the more common perks offered to executives.

EXECUTIVE COMPENSATION: ETHICS AND ACCOUNTABILITY

The top executive paycheques for 2007 were, as usual, off-the-chart amazing.[41] Consider the total compensation drawn in 2007 by the following executives.[42]

John A. Thain, Merrill Lynch	$78,520,000
Lloyd C. Blanfein, Goldman Sachs	$68,500,000
Ray R. Irani, Occidental Petroleum	$60,980,000
Kenneth I. Chenault, American Express	$46,230,000
Richard S. Fuld Jr., Lehman Brothers Holding	$40,000,000

Interestingly, respected management expert Peter F. Drucker argued in a 1984 essay that CEO pay had rocketed out of control and implored compensation committees to hold CEO compensation to no more than 20 times what rank-and-file employees made. He warned that the growing pay gap between CEOs and employees would threaten the very credibility of leadership, particularly when CEOs fire thousands of their workers and their companies underperform.[43]

Given the large amount of various compensation packages, the question asked by many is, "Are top executives worth the salaries and bonuses they receive?" The answer may depend on who you ask. Corporate compensation committees justify big bonuses in the following ways:[44]

1. Large financial incentives are a way to reward superior performance.
2. Business competition is pressure-filled and demanding.

Highlights in **HRM 10.3**

The "Sweetness" of Executive Perks

Compensation consulting firms such as Coopers and Lybrand LLP, *WorldatWork*, and Hewitt Associates regularly survey companies nationwide to identify the perks they provide for executives and other top managers. The following are popular executive perks.

- Company car
- Company plane
- Executive eating facilities
- Financial consulting
- Company-paid parking
- Personal liability insurance
- Estate planning
- First-class air travel
- Physical exams
- Mobile phones
- Large insurance policies
- Income tax preparation
- Country club membership
- Luncheon club membership
- Personal home repairs
- Loans
- Legal counseling
- Vacation cabins
- Home computers
- Chauffeur service
- Children's education
- Spouse travel

3. Good executive talent is in great demand.
4. Effective executives create shareholder value.

Others justify high compensation as a fact of business life, reflecting market compensation trends.

Nevertheless, in an era of massive downsizing, low wage increases, and increased workloads for layoff survivors, strong criticism is voiced regarding the high monetary awards given to senior executives. Furthermore, with the large compensation packages awarded to senior managers and top-level executives, cries for performance accountability and openness abound. In 2007, *Forbes* noted that while some high-paid executives do improve performance measures, such as return on equity, earnings per share, and return to shareholders, clearly, many others do not, and their pay far exceeds their performance outcomes.[45] While not all executive pay is exorbitant and not all executive performance is poor, angry employees, union groups, government officials, and stockholders argue for change.

GROUP INCENTIVE PLANS

The emphasis on cost reduction and total quality management has led many organizations to implement a variety of group incentive plans. Group plans enable employees to share in the benefits of improved efficiency realized by major organizational units or various individual work teams. These plans encourage a cooperative—rather than individualistic—spirit among all employees and reward them for their total contribution to the organization. Such features are particularly desirable when working conditions make individual performance difficult, if not impossible, to measure.

TEAM COMPENSATION

Team incentive plans reward team members with an incentive reward when agreed-on performance standards are met or exceeded. Team incentives seek to establish a psychological climate that fosters team member cooperation and a collective desire to fulfill organizational goals and objectives. While team incentive plans promote a

team incentive plan

A compensation plan in which all team members receive an incentive bonus payment when production or service standards are met or exceeded

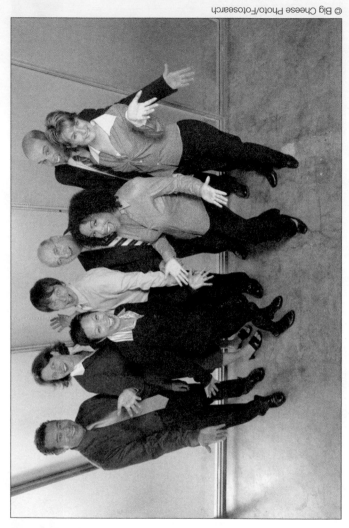

Although top management support is critical, the incentive program requires the support of those directly involved with it in order for it to be successful.

pay-for-performance philosophy, unfortunately, establishing an effective organization-specific incentive team plan is not easy.

One catch with setting team compensation is that not all teams are alike (see Chapter 4). For example, cross-functional teams, self-directed teams, and task force teams make it impossible to develop one consistent type of team incentive plan. With a variety of teams, managers find it difficult to adopt uniform measurement standards or payout formulas for team pay.[46] According to Steven Gross, Hay manager, "Each type of team requires a specific pay structure to function at its peak." Highlights in HRM 10.4 lists important considerations when designing a team incentive plan.

When team compensation is decided upon, organizations typically use the three-step approach to establishing team incentive payments. First, they set performance measures on which incentive payments are based. Improvements in efficiency, product quality, or reduction in materials or labour costs are common benchmark criteria. For example, if labour costs for a team represent 30 percent of the organization's sales dollars and the organization pays a bonus for labour cost savings, then whenever team labour costs are less than 30 percent of sales dollars, a portion of those savings are paid as an incentive bonus to team members. Information on the size of the incentive bonus is reported to employees on a weekly or monthly basis, explaining why incentive pay was or was not earned.

Second, the size of the incentive bonus must be determined. At one insurance company, health insurance underwriters can receive team incentive bonuses of up to 10 percent of base salary; however, the exact level of incentive pay depends on overall team performance and the company's performance over one year. Team incentives are paid annually.

Third, a payout formula is established and fully explained to employees. The team bonus may be distributed to employees equally, in proportion to their base pay, or on the basis of their relative contribution to the team. With discretionary formulas, managers, or in some cases team members themselves, agree on the payouts to individual team members.

Highlights in **HRM** 10.4

Lessons Learned: Designing Effective Team Incentives

Will your team incentive program be successful? While there are no exact keys to success, team compensation specialists cite the following as important components of a meaningful team incentive plan.

- Are organizational members—employees and managers—predisposed to a team incentive reward system? Is there a "cultural readiness" for team compensation? If change is indicated, what information needs to be given to all organizational employees?
- Enlist total employee and managerial support for the incentive effort. While top management support is critical, without the encouragement of employees and middle and lower-level managers (those directly involved in the program implementation), team incentive programs invariably fail.
- When developing new programs, include representatives from all groups affected by the incentive effort—labour, management, employees. Inclusion, not exclusion, serves to build trust and understanding of the program's intent and its overall importance to organizational success.

- Establish effective, fair, and precise measurement standards. Selected performance measures should be key indicators of organizational success. Do not attempt to measure everything. Employees should be able to directly influence the performance measures selected. Furthermore, performance measures should be challenging but realistic and obtainable. Standards must encourage increased effort without becoming entitlements.
- Incentive payout formulas must be seen as fair, be easy for employees to calculate, offer payouts on a frequent basis, and be large enough to encourage future employee effort. The goal is to create a pay-for-performance environment. When standards are not met, explain why the reward was not earned.
- Determine how incentive rewards will be distributed. Will team members receive equal dollar awards, or will team members receive differential payments based on such factors as seniority, skill levels, rates of pay, member contributions, and so forth?
- Communicate, communicate, communicate. Constantly champion the benefits of the incentive awards to employees and their contribution to organizational success.

Team incentive programs are not without their problems. The following are some noted problems associated with team compensation.

- Individual team members may perceive that "their" efforts contribute little to team success or to the attainment of the incentive reward.
- Intergroup social problems. Team members may be afraid that one individual may make the others look bad, or that one individual may put in less effort than others but share equally in team rewards, the "free-rider" effect.
- Complex payout formulas or insufficient payout rewards.

GAINSHARING INCENTIVE PLANS

Gainsharing plans are organizational programs designed to increase productivity or decrease labour costs and share monetary gains with employees. These plans are based on a mathematical formula that compares a baseline of performance with actual productivity during a given period. When productivity exceeds the baseline, an agreed-on savings is shared with employees. Inherent in gain sharing is the idea that involved employees will improve productivity through more effective use of organizational resources.

Although productivity can be measured in various ways, it is usually calculated as a ratio of outputs to inputs. Sales, pieces produced, pounds, total standard costs,

gainsharing plans

Programs under which both employees and the organization share financial gains according to a predetermined formula that reflects improved productivity and profitability direct labour dollars earned, and customer orders are common output measures. Inputs frequently measured include materials, labour, energy, inventory, purchased goods or services, and total costs. An increase in productivity is normally gained when:

- Greater output is obtained with less or equal input.
- Equal production output is obtained with less input.

There are many variations of gainsharing plans; however, the Scanlon Plan and Improshare are representative of gainsharing programs. The Scanlon Plan emphasizes participative management and encourages cost reductions by sharing with employees any savings resulting from those reductions. Improshare is based on the number of finished goods that the employee work teams complete in an established period.

The Scanlon Plan

The philosophy behind the **Scanlon Plan** is that employees should offer ideas and suggestions to improve productivity and, in turn, be rewarded for their constructive efforts. According to Scanlon's proponents, effective employee participation, which includes the use of committees on which employees are represented, is the most significant feature of the Scanlon Plan. Improvement or gains largely come from "working smarter, not harder." Figure 10.4 illustrates the Scanlon Plan suggestion

Scanlon Plan

A bonus incentive plan using employee and management committees to gain cost-reduction improvements

FIGURE **10.4**

Scanlon Plan Suggestion Process

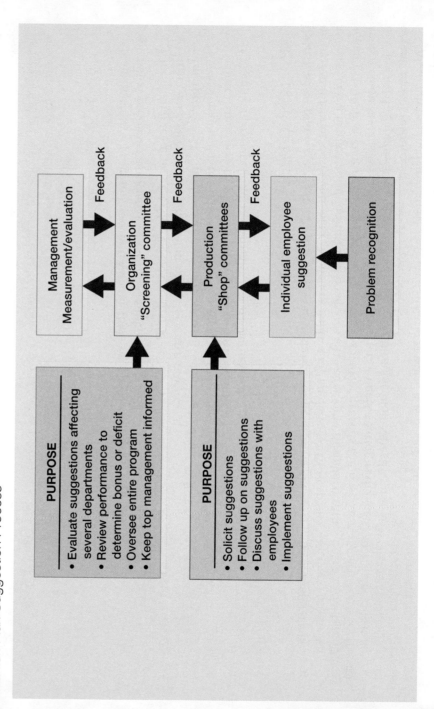

process, including the duties and responsibilities of two important groups—the *shop* and *screening* committees.

Financial incentives under the Scanlon Plan are ordinarily offered to all employees (a significant feature of the plan) on the basis of an established formula. This formula is based on increases in employee productivity as determined by a norm that has been established for labour costs.[47] Specific information on the Scanlon Plan can be obtained at the Scanlon Leadership Network, which has helped organizations in manufacturing, transportation, health care, communications, warehousing, and other industries establish Scanlon Plans.[48]

The Network Improshare

Improshare—improved productivity through sharing—is another gainsharing program. Individual production bonuses are typically based on how much an employee produces above some standard amount, but Improshare bonuses are based on the overall productivity of the work team. Improshare output is measured by the number of finished products that a work team produces in a given period. Both production (direct) employees and nonproduction (indirect) employees are included in the determination of the bonus.[49]

The bonus is based on productivity gains that result from reducing the time it takes to produce a finished product. The employees and the company each receive payment for 50 percent of the improvement. Since a cooperative environment benefits all, Improshare promotes increased interaction and support between employees and management. Companies such as Hinderliter Energy Equipment pay the bonus as a separate cheque to emphasize that it is extra income.

Lessons from the Scanlon Plan and Improshare

Perhaps the most important lesson to be learned from the Scanlon Plan and Improshare—or any gainsharing program—is that any management expecting to gain the cooperation of its employees in improving efficiency must permit them to become involved psychologically as well as financially in the organization. If employees are to contribute maximum effort, they must have a feeling of involvement and identification with their organization, which does not come out of the traditional manager-subordinate relationship. Consequently, it is important for organizations to realize that while employee cooperation is essential to the successful administration of gainsharing plans, the plans themselves do not necessarily stimulate this cooperation. Furthermore, the attitude of management is of paramount importance to the success of gainsharing plans. For example, when managers show little confidence and trust in their employees, the plans tend to fail.

ENTERPRISE INCENTIVE PLANS

Enterprise incentive plans differ from individual and group incentive plans in that all organizational members participate in the plan's compensation payout. Enterprise incentive plans reward employees on the basis of the success of the organization over an extended time period—normally one year, but the period can be longer. Enterprise incentive plans seek to create a "culture of ownership" by fostering a philosophy of cooperation and teamwork among all organizational members. Common enterprise incentive plans include profit sharing, stock options, and employee stock ownership plans (ESOPs).

Improshare
A gainsharing program under which bonuses are based on the overall productivity of the work team

Using the Internet
Read about gainsharing plans at
http://www.qualitydigest.com/jul/gainshre.html

profit sharing

Any procedure by which an employer pays, or makes available to all regular employees, in addition to base pay, special current or deferred sums based on the profits of the enterprise

PROFIT-SHARING PLANS

Profit sharing is any procedure by which an employer pays, or makes available to all regular employees, special current or deferred sums based on the organization's profits. As defined here, profit sharing represents cash payments made to eligible employees at designated time periods, as distinct from profit sharing in the form of contributions to employee pension funds.

Profit-sharing plans are intended to give employees the opportunity to increase their earnings by contributing to the growth of their organization's profits. These contributions may be directed toward improving product quality, reducing operating costs, improving work methods, and building goodwill rather than just increasing rates of production. Profit sharing can help stimulate employees to think and feel more like partners in the enterprise and thus to concern themselves with the welfare of the organization as a whole. Its purpose therefore is to motivate a total commitment from employees rather than simply to have them contribute in specific areas.

A popular example of a highly successful profit-sharing plan is the one in use at Lincoln Electric Company, a manufacturer of arc welding equipment and supplies. This plan was started in 1934 by J. F. Lincoln, president of the company. Each year the company distributes a large percentage of its profits to employees in accordance with their salary level and merit ratings. It is not uncommon for employees' annual bonuses to exceed 50 percent of annual wages. The success of Lincoln Electric's incentive system depends on a high level of contribution by each employee. Unquestionably there is a high degree of respect among employees and management for Lincoln's organizational goals and for the profit-sharing program.

Variations in Profit-Sharing Plans

Profit-sharing plans differ in the proportion of profits shared with employees and in the distribution and form of payment. The amount shared with employees may range from 5 to 50 percent of the net profit.

In most plans, however, about 20 to 25 percent of the net profit is shared. Profit distributions may be made to all employees on an equal basis, or they may be based on regular salaries or some formula that takes into account seniority and/or merit. The payments may be disbursed in cash, deferred, or made on the basis of combining the two forms of payments.

Weaknesses of Profit-Sharing Plans

In spite of their potential advantages, profit-sharing plans are also prone to certain weaknesses. The profits shared with employees may be the result of inventory speculation, climatic factors, economic conditions, national emergencies, or other factors over which employees have no control. As one HR manager noted to the authors, "Since there is little linkage between what employees do and their profit bonus, there is an absence of any employee involvement initiatives." Conversely, losses may occur during years when employee contributions have been at a maximum. The fact that profit-sharing payments are made only once a year or deferred until retirement may reduce their motivational value. If a plan fails to pay off for several years in a row, this can have an adverse effect on productivity and employee morale.

EMPLOYEE STOCK OPTION PLANS

What do the following companies—Apple Computer, Yahoo, Coca-Cola, Starbucks, Nike, Quaker Oats, and Sara Lee—have in common? The answer: Each of these diverse organizations offers a stock option program to its employees. According to

WorldatWork, a compensation association, the use of stock options is a very prevalent method of motivating and compensating hourly employees, as well as salaried and executive personnel. This appears true regardless of the industry surveyed or the organization's size.[50]

Stock option programs are sometimes implemented as part of an employee benefit plan or as part of a corporate culture linking employee effort to stock performance. However, organizations that offer stock option programs to employees do so with the belief that there is some incentive value to the systems. By allowing employees to purchase stock, the organization hopes they will increase their productivity, assume a partnership role in the organization, and thus cause the stock price to rise.[51] Furthermore, stock option programs have become a popular way to boost morale of disenfranchised employees caught in budget cuts and downsizing.

Stock option plans grant to employees the right to purchase a specific number of shares of the company's stock at a guaranteed price (the option price) during a designated time period. Although there are many types of options, most options are granted at the stock's fair market value. Not uncommon are plans for purchasing stock through payroll deductions. Highlights in HRM 10.5 explain employee stock

Highlights in **HRM 10.5**

Employee Stock Option Plans

Traditionally, stock option plans have been used as a way to reward company executives or "key" employees and to link their interests with those of the company and their shareholders. Today companies use employee stock option plans to reward, retain, and attract all levels of employees. Stock options are an effective way to share ownership with employees and to gain commitment to organizational goals.

What Is a Stock Option?

A stock option gives an employee the right to buy a certain number of shares in the company at a fixed price for a certain number of years. The price at which the option is provided is called the "grant" price and is usually the market price at the time the options are granted. Employees who have been granted stock options hope that the share price will go up and that they will be able to "cash in" by exercising (purchasing) the stock at the lower grant price and then selling the stock at the current market price.

How Stock Option Plans Work

Here is an example of a typical employee stock option plan. An employee is granted the option to purchase 1,000 shares of the company's stock at the current market price of $5 per share. The employee can exercise the option at $5 per share—typically the exercise price will be equal to the price when the options are granted. Plans allow employees to exercise their options after a certain number of years or when the company's stock reaches a certain price. If the price of the stock increases to $20 per share, for example, the employee may exercise his or her options to buy 1,000 shares at $5 per share and then sell the stock at the current market price of $20 per share.

Companies sometimes revalue the price at which the options can be exercised. This may happen, for example, when a company's stock price has fallen below the original exercise price. Companies revalue the exercise price as a way to retain their employees.

Source: Adapted from Employee Stock Options Fact Sheet, National Center for Employee Ownership at http://www.nceo.org, retrieved August 26, 2009.

Reality CHECK

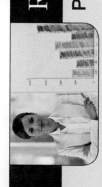

Pay-for-Performance at Lombard Canada

Recently promoted to HR Director from Manager of Compensation & Benefits at Lombard Canada, Sandy Bernier is ever aware that pay policies are critical to ensuring a stable and productive workforce. Lombard's overall compensation strategy is to lead the marketplace at the 75th percentile for base pay and to have an incentive plan that is based on performance. This mixed approach to compensation allows Lombard to pay competitively and to reward high performers based on the value they add to the company. For example, an individual's bonus will depend partly on his or her own achievements and partly on corporate performance. According to Bernier, corporate performance has exceeded its target every year for the last four years, which has permitted full bonuses to be awarded to all employees.

In order to ensure all systems and processes are up to date, a thorough job analysis for all positions under the senior management team has been conducted using a hybrid point-factor system. All jobs are then graded and employees are paid within the salary range for the position they are performing. Lombard has 11 salary ranges and regularly participates in external salary surveys to ensure that the company is using the most up-to-date salary information. Furthermore, each time a new hire is recruited, the job description is reviewed to ensure its accuracy and relevance to the position and any updates needed are made immediately. For all senior-level positions, an individual ad hoc analysis is conducted annually that compares each position to the marketplace. This is an effective approach to executive compensation as it looks at each position and its uniqueness and is not trying to slot a senior position into a restrictive salary range.

According to Bernier, one of the greatest challenges facing today's compensation and benefits teams is the soaring costs of health care—many companies are seeing double-digit premium increases each year. There are also a lot of psychological claims being introduced; these are challenging as they are difficult to manage. To add to this challenge, with the new privacy legislation many companies find it difficult to administer their short-term disability in-house. One way to combat rising health care costs is to educate employees about their benefits plan and ways to contain costs. Bernier has done these types of presentations to employees across Canada.

As a major insurance company, Lombard is fairly traditional in its approach to benefits, but being an employee of this type of company provides its own unique perks. Along with a flexible extended health and dental plan, Lombard offers its employees a stock ownership plan in which 1 to 10 percent of an employee's salary can be voluntarily deducted from payroll; the company matches this amount by 30 percent. If company ROE targets are met for the year, the company will then put an additional 20 percent into the plan for a total 50 percent match. This plan provides employees with an opportunity to invest in the company's long-term performance, and employees have a vested interest in how the company is doing. To add to this perk, the money in the fund can also be withdrawn once a year at any time, without penalty, and the employee can use it or place it in an individual RRSP for additional tax savings. Finally, employees are offered a perk that is not easily attained in today's market place: after four years of service they are eligible to apply for the mortgage subsidy program, and are also given a 40 percent discount on home and auto insurance if they have their insurance coverage with Lombard.

option plans in greater detail. Reality Check describes stock option and other pay-for-performance plans at Lombard Canada.

Unfortunately, in the wake of various corporate scandals, employee stock option plans have come under attack from stockholder groups, government officials, and the general public. Criticism largely focuses on the extravagance of executive stock option plans and dubious corporate accounting procedures.[52]

Nevertheless, despite these faults, stock options continue to be a popular and efficient way to pay for the performance of employees and managers. When stock prices rise, employee stock plans can be financially rewarding to employees.

EMPLOYEE STOCK OWNERSHIP PLANS (ESOPs)

Canadian Tire and Sears Canada have established **employee stock ownership plans (ESOPs)**—stock plans in which employees can acquire shares in the firm that employs them. There are three main types of employee stock plans. An employee stock bonus plan is the simplest. An employer provides company shares to employees at no cost to the employee by just granting them or by linking the granting to some kind of performance pay plan. An employee stock purchase plan allows employers to purchase shares, but not pay full market price for these shares. Under an employee stock option plan, employees are given the option to purchase shares in the company at some future date, at a set price, which they would exercise if the market price rises to exceed this price.

Advantages of ESOPs

ESOPs can increase employees' pride of ownership in the organization, providing an incentive for them to increase productivity and help the organization prosper and grow. Employees may become more interested in how the company is managed, and hold managers to higher and different performance standards, such as maximizing share value. Stock plans have the additional advantage of not requiring companies to pay out in cash, and so firms can reward employees with shares. For employees, the advantages include a form of saving for retirement, and in some cases, such as Microsoft, employees could become millionaires.

Problems with ESOPs

Generally, ESOPs are more likely to serve their intended purposes in publicly held companies than in privately held ones. A major problem with the privately held company is its potential inability to pay back the shares of employees when they retire. These employees do not have the alternative of disposing of their shares on the open market. Thus, when large organizations suffer financial difficulties and the value of the companies' shares falls, so does the value of the employees' retirement plan. Other problems with ESOPs include the following:

- The more retirement income comes from these plans, the more dependent a pensioner becomes on the price of company shares. Future retirees are vulnerable to stock market fluctuations as well as to management mistakes.
- Employees may become demotivated and frustrated if the share price falls, even though they have worked productively.
- Finally, although studies show that productivity improves when ESOPs are implemented, these gains are not guaranteed. ESOPs help little unless managers are willing to involve employees in organizational decision making. Unfortunately, ESOPs are sometimes set up in ways that restrict employee decision making and expose the ESOP to risk, though providing investors with large potential gains.

Overall, do incentive plans work? The answer can be found in the Business Case.

Using the Internet

The ESOP Association Canada outlines four main motives for implementing stock ownership plans in Canada:

http://www.esop-canada.com

OUTCOME 7

employee stock ownership plans (ESOPs)

Stock plans in which an organization contributes shares of its stock to an established trust for the purpose of stock purchases by employees

The Business CASE

Organizational Benefits of Incentive Plans

Incentive pay is a strategic tool used most often to attract and retain employees and to improve organizational outcomes. Organizations spend an average of 9 percent of total payroll dollars on variable compensation programs. Is this money well spent?

- Four out of five organizations report that incentive compensation is an effective tool for attracting and retaining employees.

- About one-third of employers reported that compensation had a positive effect on operating results. In another study, retail stores that used the Scanlon Plan had higher sales performance, more favourable customer satisfaction scores, and lower turnover than a control group. Higher-performing companies are more likely to provide stock options and feel strongly that these options influence behaviour among professional ranks.

- The offering of stock options is associated with improved company performance. Bonuses seem to be more tightly linked to increased profits than are long-term incentives.

- Companies that had CEOs who earned above median salary increases delivered a return to shareholders of 29.4 percent compared to an 8.6-percent return for those companies that had CEOs who earned below median salary increases.

Sources: Business BC, "More Firms Tie Executive Pay to Performance," *The Vancouver Sun*, December 1, 2005; D. Scott, *WorldatWork Journal*, "Survey of Compensation Policies and Practices," http://www.worldatwork.org/research, March 2003, retrieved August 26, 2009; D. Scott, J. Floyd, P. G. Benson, and J. W. Bishop, "The Impact of the Scanlon Plan on Retail Store Performance," *WorldatWork Journal* 11, no. 3 (Third Quarter, 2002); D. J. Gherson, "Getting the Pay Thing Right," *Workspan* 43, no. 6 (June 2000): 47–51; K. H. Van Neek and J. E. Smilko, "Variable Pay Plans," *WorldatWork Journal* 11, no. 4 (Fourth Quarter 2002).

Small Business APPLICATION

While in this chapter we have seen a variety of different forms of incentive plans, the three most common incentives employed in small companies are (1) discounts, (2) commissions, and (3) profit sharing or bonuses.

If you think of the variety of small businesses, be they restaurants, retail stores, or product manufacturing or distribution companies, a significant proportion of these businesses deliver consumer products or services. As a result, it is very common for company employees to also be customers of the product. As such, restaurant, retail, and consumer product companies usually offer their product to staff at a discount. While this incentive comes at little or no cost to the company, it encourages employee loyalty to company products or services and provides promotional value. We must note one caution, however. Small companies typically need to put guidelines in place so that employees may purchase product only for themselves and family and friends, otherwise, enterprising employees might engage in purchasing and reselling discounted product, with negative consequences for the company.

In many small companies in which the sale of product is tied to the effectiveness of sales staff, formal commission plans are frequently used. The purpose of commissions is to encourage profitable revenue-generating activity. These are seen in retail jobs where store salespeople receive commissions for sales volumes or upselling complementary products. An example of upselling might be the sale of a belt to someone purchasing a pair of pants. In other sales roles where an employee may have responsibility for a sales territory, the commissions might be based on sales volumes, profitability targets, new sales, or any combination of these.

continued

The key is that commission plans reward organizationally identified goals with monetary compensation based on goal accomplishment. As such, critical to successful commission programs is setting effective targets and having a mechanism to measure results.

Finally, recognizing that many employees in small companies are not in sales roles, commission plans reward the contributions of only a few. To reward the contributions of all employees for the achievement of profitability, many small companies pay annual or even quarterly bonuses to employees. Such payments are usually based on company profitability, as well as individual contributions. Even when such payments are small, they can act as powerful tools for recognition and appreciation of employee commitment, helping to foster positive organizational climate.

SUMMARY

OUTCOME 1

The success of an incentive pay plan depends on the organizational climate in which it must operate, employee confidence in it, and its suitability to employee and organizational needs. Importantly, employees must view their incentive pay as being equitable and related to their performance. Performance measures should be quantifiable, be easily understood, and bear a demonstrated relationship to organizational performance.

OUTCOME 2

Piecework plans pay employees a given rate for each unit satisfactorily completed. Employers implement these plans when output is easily measured and when the production process is fairly standardized. Bonuses are incentive payments above base wages paid on either an individual or team basis. A bonus is offered to encourage employees to exert greater effort. Standard hour plans establish a standard time for job completion. An incentive is paid for finishing the job in less than the preestablished time These plans are popular for jobs with a fixed time for completion.

OUTCOME 3

Merit raises will not serve to motivate employees when they are seen as entitlements, which occurs when these raises are given yearly without regard to changes in employee performance. Merit raises are not motivational when they are given because of seniority or favouritism or when merit budgets are inadequate to sufficiently reward employee performance. To be motivational, merit raises must be such that employees see a clear relationship between pay and performance, and the salary increase must be large enough to exceed inflation and higher income taxes.

OUTCOME 4

Salespeople may be compensated by a straight salary, a combination of salary and commission, salary plus bonus, or a commission only. Paying employees a straight salary allows them to focus on tasks other than sales, such as service and customer goodwill. A straight commission plan causes employees to emphasize sales goals. A combination of salary and commission or bonus provides the advantages of both the straight salary and the straight commission form of payments.

OUTCOME 5

The Scanlon and Improshare gain-sharing plans pay bonuses to employees unrelated to profit levels. Each of these plans encourages employees to maximize their performance and cooperation through suggestions offered to improve organizational performance. The Scanlon Plan pays an employee a bonus based on saved labour cost measured against the organization's sales value of production. The Improshare bonus is paid when employees increase production output above a given target level.

OUTCOME 6

Profit-sharing plans pay to employees sums of money based on the organization's profits. Cash payments are made to eligible employees at specified times, normally yearly. The primary purpose of profit sharing is to provide employees with additional income through their participation in organizational achievement. Employee commitment to improved productivity, quality, and customer service will contribute to organizational success and, in turn, to their compensation. Profit-sharing plans may not achieve their stated gains when employee performance is unrelated to organizational success or failure. This may occur because of economic conditions, other competition, or environmental conditions. Profit-sharing plans can have a negative effect on employee morale when plans fail to consistently reward employees.

[OUTCOME 7]

With an ESOP, each year the organization contributes stock or cash to buy stock that is then placed in an ESOP trust. The ESOP holds the stock for organizational improvement. Employees, however, may lose their retirement income should the company fail or stock prices fall.

KEY TERMS

bonus, 412
combined salary and commission plan, 417
differential piece rate, 410
employee stock ownership plans (ESOPs), 429
gainsharing plans, 423

Improshare, 425
lump-sum merit program, 413
merit guidelines, 413
perquisites, 420
profit sharing, 426
salary plus bonus plan, 417
Scanlon Plan, 424

spot bonus, 412
standard hour plan, 412
straight commission plan, 416
straight piecework, 410
straight salary plan, 416
team incentive plan, 421
variable pay, 406

DISCUSSION QUESTIONS

1. Working individually or in groups, identify the factors necessary for a successful incentive plan.
2. List all the ways that a manager at a fast-food retail outlet can reward exceptional performance. Which ways would you prefer and why? Compare your answers to those of other students.
3. The City of Toronto pays a bonus of up to 3 percent to managers who meet performance goals. In 2007, 3,500 of 3,800 managers received this "merit" pay. Should merit pay be given for meeting objectives or exceeding objectives?
4. Using your employee experience or an online salary locator, determine the salary of the CEO and the lowest-paid employee for a public organization. What is the ratio? How does it compare

with the American ratio of 301:1 or the Japanese ratio of 15:1? How would you explain the ratio to employees who are asking questions about the reasons for their levels of compensation?
5. Many students are attracted to companies that promote themselves as "green" or environmentally friendly. What kinds of incentives could a "green" company offer to its employees?
6. Because of competitive forces within your industry, you have decided to implement a profit-sharing plan for your employees. Discuss the advantages of profit sharing and identify specific characteristics that will ensure success for your plan.
7. What are some reasons for the implementation of ESOPs? Cite some of the potential problems concerning their use.

INTERNET EXERCISE

Watch the video about CEO compensation on http://www.growinggap.ca/node/150. What are the arguments

given against the increases in CEO compensation? If you were a CEO, how would you justify your salary?

HRM EXPERIENCE

Awarding Salary Increases

Because pay-for-performance is an important factor governing salary increases, managers must be able to defend the compensation recommendations they make for their employees. Merit raises granted under a pay-for-performance policy must be based on objective appraisals if they are to achieve their intended purposes of rewarding outstanding employee performance. As managers know, however, they must deal with other factors that can affect salary recommendations. These may include the opinions of the employee's peers or extenuating circumstances such as illness or family responsibilities. The purpose of this exercise is to provide you with the experience of granting salary increases to employees based on their work performance and other information.

Assignment

Following are the work records of five employees. As their supervisor, you have just completed their annual appraisal reviews, and it is now time to make recommendations for their future salary. Your department budget has $5,780 allocated for salary increases. Distribute the $5,780 among your employees based on the descriptions for each subordinate.

a. Janet Jenkins currently earns $41,000. Her performance appraisal rating was very high. She is respected by her peers and is felt to be an asset to the work group. She is divorced and has three young children to support.

b. Russell Watts earns a salary of $36,000. His annual performance appraisal was average. Several members of the work group have spoken to you about the difficulty involved in Russell's job. They feel that it is a tough and demanding job and that he is doing his best.

c. Jack Perkins earns $31,250. His performance appraisal was below average, and he seems to have difficulty adjusting to his coworkers. Jack has had a difficult time this past year. His wife passed away early in the year, and his father has recently been diagnosed as terminally ill.

d. Rick Jacobson earns $28,000. His performance appraisal was above average. He is respected by his peers and is generally considered to be a "good guy."

e. Paula Merrill earns $28,850. Her performance appraisal was very high. Her peers are upset because they feel that she is working only to provide a second income to her household. Moreover, her peers see her as trying to "show them up."

Share your results with other class members. Be prepared to explain your allocation of money.

BIZFLIX EXERCISES

SCENT OF A WOMAN: FREDDIE BISCO'S INCENTIVES

The scene from *Scent of a Woman* shows many aspects of incentive rewards and employee performance discussed in this chapter. Watch for types of incentives and the positive and negative effects of incentives as you view the scene.

Young Charlie Simms (Chris O'Donnell) wants to earn extra money over Thanksgiving weekend for airfare to go home during his Christmas break. He becomes a guide and caretaker for ill-tempered, retired, blind Lt. Col. Frank Slade (Al Pacino). Charlie, from Gresham, Oregon, is quiet and reserved and has had little experience with the opposite sex. He attends the exclusive Baird Preparatory School on a scholarship. His wild New York City weekend with Frank Slade bonds them forever. This film is a remake of *Profumo di Donna*, a 1974 Italian film. This scene is an edited version from the end of the "Tango Lessons" segment and the beginning of "The Ferrari" segment that appear about halfway through the film. It follows the despondent hotel room scene and the tango lesson scene Slade gave Donna (Gabrielle Anwar) in the Waldorf Astoria restaurant. It begins shortly after Freddie

Bisco (Leonard Gaines), the Ferrari salesman, says to Charlie, "Yeah, this is a valid Oregon driver's license, … " Freddie does not want to let either Charlie or Slade test-drive a Ferrari. The scene ends after Slade says, "I'm a gray ghost too." The film cuts to the Ferrari rounding a New York City street corner with Charlie driving.

What to Watch for and Ask Yourself

- Assume that Freddie Bisco receives a sales incentive for each Ferrari he sells. Does Freddie appear highly motivated by this incentive reward system? What is the evidence from the scene?
- Freddie does not work for Frank Slade. Is the $2,000 that Slade gives Freddie the same as a bonus discussed earlier in this chapter? If yes, which type of bonus is it?
- Did you perceive any negative effects of Freddie Bisco's incentives that he experienced in this scene?

CASE STUDY 1

OUT BUT RICH AT HOME DEPOT

The clamor over sky-high executive paychecks and CEO severance or retirement pay packages is a hot topic of national debate. Shareholder groups, union leaders, political officials, and activists from hedge funds all demand change. The controversy over gargantuan executive pay reached a boiling point in 2009, when Robert Pritchard, CEO of the *Toronto Star*, received a severance payment of $9.6 million. Since his appointment in 2002, Pritchard had received a total compensation of $24 million. Union activists went to Torstar's Board of Directors, asking them to take back the severance pay. The union argues that the payment is both inappropriate and unearned. Profits have been falling at the media-based company, and the company is slashing budgets and laying off staff.

QUESTIONS

1. Are CEOs and key corporate executives worth the large pay packages they receive? Explain.

2. Do you agree with Peter Drucker that corporate executives should receive compensation packages no larger than a certain percentage of the pay of hourly workers? Explain.

3. How can the board of directors of Torstar justify a severance package when corporate performance is weak?

Source: Adapted from http://www.newswire.ca, retrieved June 4, 2009; J. Sturgeon, "Torstar CEO Departs as Losses Widen," *Financial Post*, May 7, 2009.

CASE STUDY 2

TEAM-BASED INCENTIVE REWARDS: IT'S NOT ALL ROSES

Network Cable, Inc. is a service provider for cable TV and high-speed Internet connections. Network Cable operates in an area described as a "high-growth market."

In January 2003, Tara Gilbert, vice-president of human resources for Network Cable, convinced company president and CEO Jeff Lesitner that restructuring the organization workforce into teams would benefit both Network Cable and its employees. Cost savings, improved morale, and team synergy were cited as inherent benefits of teams. Based on these assessments, in June 2003 a select group of three senior managers, plus Tara Gilbert and the company's financial officer, implemented teams within the company's installation department. Here, 40 service installers were formed into eight teams of five installers each. Management set performance goals for the installation teams linked to attractive incentive rewards (cash bonuses above base salaries) when performance goals were reached. Performance measures included indexes for improved installation time, customer satisfaction scores, additional sales, equipment maintenance, and repair/callback problems. Each team could earn incentive bonuses up to a maximum of $15,000 annually with cash bonuses shared equally by each team member—a possible cash reward of $3,000 for each installer. Team bonuses after the first year were as follows: two teams, $15,000; one team, $12,500; one team, $7,300; one team, $3,150.

During August 2008, Tara Gilbert sent to all installers and their supervisors a survey requesting feedback on the satisfaction with teams and, specifically, the incentive rewards program. While survey results were generally positive, not all was rosy. Problems could be grouped into the following categories:

QUESTIONS

1. Some installers believed that various team members did not "buy into" the team concept and were simply "free riders"—average employees who benefited from the efforts of superior employees.

2. There was a general feeling that several teams were routinely assigned difficult installations that prevented them from achieving high performance goals.

3. Teams did not always display the motivation and synergy expected, since "bickering" was prevalent between average performers and super performers. Average performers complained that high performers made them look bad.

4. A high percentage of survey respondents (29 percent) felt the incentive rewards program was unfair and asked for a return to fixed across-the-board salary increases.

QUESTIONS

1. Do results from the survey illustrate typical complaints about teams and specifically about team incentive rewards? Explain.

2. If appropriate, what changes would you recommend to improve the incentive reward program? Be specific.

3. Would management have benefited from employee involvement in the initial design and implementation of the program? Explain.

CAREER COUNSEL

Take the incentive survey on the *Managing Human Resources* website to discover what types of incentives are motivating for you (http://www.belcourt6e.nelson.com).

NOTES AND REFERENCES

1. *2007–2008 Salary Budget Survey*, 34th annual (Scottsdale, AZ: WorldatWork Press 2007), 9.

2. Anjali Athavaley, "More Raises to Be Tied to Performance," *The Wall Street Journal*, December 13, 2007, D3.

3. Patricia K. Zingheim and Jay R. Schuster, "Designing Pay and Rewards in Professional Service Companies," *Compensation and Benefits Review* 39, no 1 (January/February 2007): 55.

4. "Reward 'Stars' and Pay-for-Performance Lead in Pay Control Strategies," *HRfocus*, 84, no. 11 (November 2007): 3.

5. John A. Menefee and Ryan O. Murphy, "Rewarding and Retaining the Best," *Benefits Quarterly* 20, no. 3 (Third Quarter 2004): 13–21.

6. Enno Siensen, Sridhar Balasubramanian, and Aleda V. Roth, "Incentives That Induce Task-Related Effort, Helping, and Knowledge Sharing in Workgroups," *Management Science* 53, no. 10 (October 2007): 1533.

7. Fay Hansen, "Control and Customization," *Workforce Management* 86, no. 19 (November 5, 2007): 42.

8. Corey Helm, Courtney L. Holladay, Frank R. Tortorella, and Christine Candio, "The Performance Management System: Applying and Evaluating a Pay-for-Performance Initiative," *Journal of Healthcare Management* 52, no. 1 (January/February 2007): 49.

9. Leo Jakobson, "All It's Quacked Up To Be," *Incentive* 181, no. 9 (September 2007): 24.

10. Joanne Sammer, "Weighing Pay Incentives," *HR Magazine* 52, no. 6 (June 2007): 64.

11. Roisin Woolnough, "How to Set Up an Incentive Scheme," *Personnel Today*, February 14, 2005, 22.

12. Ann Pomeroy, "Business Strategy, Not Just HR Strategy," *HR Magazine* 52, no. 11 (November 2007): 46.

13. Jim McCoy, "How to Align Employee Performance with Business Strategy," *Workforce Management* 86, no. 12 (June 27, 2007): 55.

14. George T. Milkovich and Jerry M. Newman, *Compensation*, 9th ed. (Boston: McGraw Hill Irwin, 2008).

15. Patty Kujawa, "Private Firms Recognize Value of Cash Bonuses," *Workforce Management* 86, no. 21 (December 10, 2007): 11.

16. Chris Taylor, "On-the-Spot Incentives," *HR Magazine* 49, no. 5 (May 2004): 80–84.

17. Don Hellriegel and John W. Slocum, Jr., *Organizational Behavior*, 12th ed. (Mason, OH: South-Western, 2009), Chapter 6.

18. Debra L. Nelson and James Campbell Quick, *Organizational Behavior: Science, The Real World, and You*, 6th ed. (Mason, OH: South-Western, 2009).

19. Employee perceptions of appropriate pay raises likely depend on the employer's ability to pay and the economics of the period. For example, when it is known that an employer's ability to pay is great and the economics of the industry are strong, then employees will expect larger percentage merit raises.

20. Susan J. Wells, "No Results, No Raise," *HR Magazine* 50, no. 5 (May 2005): 76.

21. David E. Terpstra and Andre L. Honoree, "Employees Responses to Merit Pay Inequity," *Compensation and Benefits Review* 37, no. 1 (January/February 2005): 51.

22. Tyler Gentry, "Re-engineering Recognition," *Workspan* (February 2007): 47. See also Ann Norman, "Airs Budget Group: Using Recognition to Foster Engagement," *Workspan* (November 2007): 75.

23. Alison Avalos, "Recognition: A Critical Component of the Total Reward Mix," Workspan (July 2007): 33. See also Scott Dow, Tom McMullen, Richard S. Sperling, and Bill Bowbin, "Reward Programs: What Works and What Needs to be Improved," *WorldatWork* 16, no. 3 (Third Quarter 2007): 6.

24. Charlotte Garvey, "Meaningful Tokens of Appreciation," *HR Magazine* 49, no. 9 (August 2004): 102.

25. Michele Marchetti, "Rethinking Compensation Plans," *Sales and Marketing Management* 159, no. 7 (September 2007): 14.

26. Paul R. Dorf and Lisette F. Masur, "The Tough Economy Prompts Companies to Shift Their Approach to Sales Compensation," *Journal of Organizational Excellence* 23, no. 2 (Spring 2004): 35–42.

27. Joseph Dimisa, "How to Sell Your Sales Compensation Plan," *Workspan* (December 2007): 25.

28. Jim Stockmann, "Change on the Horizon: An Analysis of Sales Compensation Practices," *Workspan* (April 2007): 41.

29. Donald L. Caruth and Gail D. Handloggten-Caruth, "The Formula for Compensating Sales Personnel," *The American Salesman* 51, no. 4 (April 2006): 6.

30. Mark Reilly and Brian Enright, "A New Approach to Executive Compensation," Workspan (August 2007): 45.

31. Seymour Burchman and Blair Jones, "Executive Compensation as a Support for Growth Strategy," *WorldatWork* 15, no. 3 (Third Quarter 2006): 39.

32. Total annual compensation is the sum of an executive's annual and long-term compensation. Annual compensation consists of salary, bonus, and other yearly pay. Long-term

compensation consists of stock awards, the value of any stock options exercised during the year, and any other long-term compensation (such as payouts from long-term incentive plans, director's fees, and special bonuses).

33. Edward E. Lawler III and David Finegold, "CEO Compensation: What Board Members Think," *WorldatWork Journal* 16, no. 3 (Third Quarter 2007): 38.

34. Brandon Cherry, "Executive Bonus Plans: Recent Trends in Equity Compensation," *Workspan* (January 2007): 22.

35. Darrell Rigby and Barbara Bilodeau, "Selecting Management Tools Wisely," *Harvard Business Review* 85, no. 12 (December 2007): 20.

36. Brad Hill and Christine Tande, "What's Next for Executive Incentives Now That Options Are Limited?" *Workspan* (September 2007): 47.

37. J. McFarland, "Executive compensation," *The Globe and Mail*, June 23, 2009, B1, B11.

38. Peter Burrows, "He's Making Hay as CEOs Squirm," *BusinessWeek*, January 15, 2007, 64. See also Saado Abboud, "Best Buy Uses Flexibility and Choice to Improve Long-Term Incentive Design," *Workspan* (October 2007): 32.

39. Pam Delaney, "Filling the Executive Benefits Gap," *Workspan* (November 2007): 69.

40. "An Unfair Rap for CEO Perks?" *BusinessWeek*, June 7, 2004: 32.

41. Anne Tergesen, "How Much Are Execs Really Paid?" *BusinessWeek*, March 20, 2006: 96.

42. Joann S. Lublin, "CEO Compensation Survey (A Special Report): Persistent Pay Gains: A Survey Overview," *The Wall Street Journal*, April 14, 2008: R.I. 112; Leigh Rivenback, "Responsible Executive Compensation for a New Era of Accountability," *HR Magazine* 48, no. 9 (September 2004): 178. See also Michael Savage and Terry Adamson, "Employee Stock Options: New Valuation Responsibilities and Planning Opportunities," *Benefits Quarterly* 20, no. 3 (Third Quarter 2004): 34.

43. John A. Byrne, "The Man Who Invented Management: Why Peter Drucker's Ideas Still Matter," *BusinessWeek*, November 2004, 97.

44. Steven N. Kaplan, "Are CEOs Overpaid?" *WorldatWork Journal* 16, no. 3 (Third Quarter 2007): 22. See also Ira Kay and Steve Van Putten, *Myths and Realities of Executive Pay* (Cambridge, MA: Cambridge University Press, 2007); Jessica Marquez, "5 Questions: in Defense of CEO Pay," *Workforce Management* 86, no. 16 (September 27, 2007): 8.

45. "CEO Compensation," 112.

46. Milkovich and Newman, *Compensation*.

47. Scott Dow, Paul Davis, and Chuck Cockburn, "Scanlon Principles and Processes: Building Excellence at Watermark Credit Union," *WorldatWork Journal* 16, no. 1 (First Quarter 2007): 29.

48. The Scanlon Leadership Network can be found at http://www.scanlonleader.org.

49. The standard of Improshare's measurement system is the base productivity factor (BPF), which is the ratio of standard direct labour hours produced to total actual hours worked in a base period. The productivity of subsequent periods is then measured by enlarging standard direct labour hours earned by the BPF ratio to establish Improshare hours (IH). The IH is then compared with actual hours worked in the same period. If earned hours exceed actual hours, 50 percent of the gain is divided by actual hours worked to establish a bonus percentage for all employees in the plan.

50. Jason Kovac, "Stock Options," *Workspan* (August 2006): 23. See also Seymour Burchman and Blair Jones, "The Future of Stock Options: From Starring Role to Ensemble Player," *WorldatWork Journal* 13, no. 1 (First Quarter 2004): 29–38.

51. Ira T. Kay and Steve Seelig, "Revising the Use of a Management Stock Purchase Plan to Increase Management Ownership," *Journal of Deferred Compensation* 11, no. 3 (Spring 2006): 24.

52. Raquel Meyer Alexander, Mark Hirchey, and Susan Scholz, "Backdating Employee Stock Options: Tax Implications," *The CPA Journal* 77, no. 10 (October 2007): 24. See also T. Thomas Cottingham III, "The Stock Options Backdating Scandal: Critical First Response," *Risk Management* 54, no. 6 (June 2007): 12.

CHAPTER 11

Employee Benefits

After studying this chapter, you should be able to

[OUTCOME 1] Describe the characteristics of a sound benefits program.

[OUTCOME 2] Indicate management concerns about the costs of employee benefits, and discuss ways to control those costs.

[OUTCOME 3] Identify and explain the employee benefits required by law.

[OUTCOME 4] Discuss suggested ways to control the costs of health care programs.

[OUTCOME 5] Describe benefits that involve payment for time not worked.

[OUTCOME 6] Discuss recent trends in retirement policies and programs.

[OUTCOME 7] Indicate the major factors involved in managing pension plans.

[OUTCOME 8] Describe the types of work–life benefits employers can provide.

What is the best-kept secret in Canada today? According to surveys, it is the hidden payroll, i.e., employee benefits. Compensation surveys indicate that most employees are unable to name accurately the benefits they receive, and about 50 percent of employees underestimate the value of their benefits.[1] Though benefits are largely undervalued and misidentified, they are still an important issue for both employers and employees. It is clear that benefits are not a "fringe" but rather an integral part of the compensation package. Additionally, since most benefits are provided voluntarily by employers, they become a significant cost and an employment advantage for employers, while providing needed psychological and physical assistance to employees. The importance of benefits to both sides cannot be overstated.

Virtually all employers provide a variety of benefits to supplement the wages or salaries they pay their workers. These benefits, some of which are required by law, must be considered a part of total compensation. Therefore, in this chapter we look at the characteristics of employee benefits programs. We will study the types of benefits required by law, the major discretionary benefits that employers offer, the employee services they provide, and the retirement programs in use. The chapter concludes with a discussion of popular and highly important work–life benefit programs.

EMPLOYEE BENEFITS PROGRAMS

Employee benefits constitute an indirect form of compensation intended to improve the quality of work lives and personal lives of employees. As discussed later, benefits typically represent up to 40 percent of total payroll costs to employers.[2] In return, employers generally expect employees to be supportive of the organization and to be productive. Since employees have come to expect an increasing number of benefits, the motivational value of these benefits depends on how the benefits program is designed and communicated. Once viewed as a gift from the employer, benefits are now considered rights to which all employees are entitled.

HRIS AND EMPLOYEE BENEFITS

With the large number of benefits offered to employees today, administering an organization's benefits program can be both costly and time consuming. Even for small employers with 30 to 40 employees, keeping track of each employee's use of a benefit or request for a change of benefits can be cumbersome. For example, even rather straightforward tasks, such as monitoring employees' sick leave, become complex as the size of the organization grows.

Fortunately, interactive employee benefit systems are becoming mainstream for most employers. Employees at TransAlta Corporation in Calgary can obtain information about their pension plans and enroll in a flexible benefits plan by logging onto the company website. For the third of its employees without access to computers, TransAlta has installed kiosks on company premises. The benefits of a human resources information system (HRIS) (explained in Chapter 1) are reduced costs, increased efficiencies, and accuracy.[3] Online benefits programs create a form of self-service administration. One intent of online programs is to eliminate the annual open enrollment period for various benefits, thereby providing greater flexibility in benefits selection. An important advantage to an interactive benefits program is the significant savings in administration costs. Once an online system is operational, it is easy and inexpensive to adapt to employer and employee demands. However, while the Internet can be used effectively in benefits administration, security must always be a concern when transmitting benefits information.[4]

Perhaps no part of the HR function is more technologically advanced than benefits administration. A wide variety of commercially developed software packages

[OUTCOME 1]

Using the Internet

A broad view of benefits in Canada can be found at:

http://www.benefitscanada.ca

have been developed that serve to facilitate benefits administration in such areas as pensions, variable pay, workers' compensation, health benefits, and time-off programs. Descriptions of and advertisements for a variety of benefits software programs are regularly found in HR journals such as *Canadian HR Reporter* and *Human Resource Professional.* Software programs represent a cost-effective way to manage employee benefits programs when employers lack the resources or expertise.

REQUIREMENTS FOR A SOUND BENEFITS PROGRAM

The soundness of a benefits program hinges on two factors: (1) selecting benefits that target important employee needs while promoting strategic organizational objectives and (2) effective administration of benefits programs. The objectives an organization establishes will depend on many factors, including the size of the firm; its location; its degree of unionization; its profitability; and industry patterns. Most important, these aims must be compatible with the organization's strategic compensation plan (see Chapter 9), including its philosophy and policies.

Strategic Benefits Planning

Like any other component of the HR program, an employee benefits program should be based on specific objectives. The objectives an organization establishes will depend on many factors, including the size of the firm; its location; its degree of unionization; its profitability; and industry patterns. Most important, these aims must be compatible with the organization's strategic compensation plan (see Chapter 9), including its philosophy and policies.

The chief objectives of most benefits programs are to

- Improve employee work satisfaction
- Meet employee health and security requirements
- Attract and motivate employees
- Retain top-performing employees
- Maintain a favourable competitive position

In a 2009 survey of employees, about half stated that a good benefits plan would make them stay with their current employer and would prefer their health benefits over increased compensation.[5] Another survey found that four out of ten employers use wellness programs and subsidized fitness programs as a retention strategy.[6] Furthermore, these objectives must be considered within the framework of cost containment—a major issue in today's programs.

Unless the organization plans to develop a flexible benefits plan (to be discussed later), a uniform package of benefits should be developed. This involves carefully considering the various benefits that can be offered, the relative preference shown for each benefit by management and the employees, the estimated cost of each benefit, and the total amount of money available for the entire benefits package.

Allowing for Employee Involvement

Before a new benefit is introduced, the need for it should first be established. Many organizations create committees composed of managers and employees to administer, interpret, and oversee their benefits policies. Opinion surveys are also used to obtain employee input. Having employees participate in designing benefits programs helps to ensure that management is moving in the direction of satisfying employee wants. Pan Canadian Petroleum formed 11 focus groups of randomly selected employees to provide insights and valuable feedback on its pension investments.[7]

The soundness of a benefits program hinges on two factors: (1) selecting benefits that target important employee needs while promoting strategic organizational objectives and (2) effective administration of benefits programs. Gone are the days of providing a particular benefit because other employers are doing it, because someone in authority believes it is a good idea, or because the benefit is "popular" at the moment. Therefore, benefit specialists recommend paying attention to certain basic considerations.

441

Benefits for a Diverse Workforce

To serve their intended purpose, employee benefits programs must reflect the social changes that Canada is constantly facing. Particularly significant are changes in the diversity and lifestyles of the workforce; the changes make it necessary to develop new types of benefits to meet shifting needs. Therefore, more employers are tailoring their benefits programs to be family-friendly. (Specific family-friendly benefits are discussed later in the chapter.) For example, as we have indicated throughout this book, the number of women in the workforce is continuing to grow. Which benefits are most valuable to them (and to men) will be determined largely by whether they have dependent children and whether they have a spouse who has benefits coverage.

Unfortunately, benefits plans sometimes provide little advantage to employees, limiting the organization's ability to attract and retain quality employees. For example, many employers provide unneeded medical benefits to the young and single in the form of dependants' coverage. Likewise a well-designed—and costly—defined-benefits pension program may not serve the needs of employees or the employer of a predominantly younger workforce. Similarly, the employer's contribution to the pension plan for a 30-year-old employee is roughly one-quarter the contribution for a 50-year-old employee for the same amount of pension commencing at age 65. This difference in funds spent on older workers in effect discriminates against younger workers, although in legal terms it is not regarded as discriminatory.

Providing for Flexibility

To accommodate the individual needs of employees, many organizations are embracing **flexible benefits plans**, also known as cafeteria plans. When Zabeen Hirji, senior vice-president of human resources for RBC, surveyed 16,000 of the bank's 65,000 employees about their benefits preferences, the number one request was for flexibility.[8] These plans enable individual employees to choose the benefits that are best suited to their particular needs. They also prevent certain benefits from being wasted on employees who have no need for them. Typically, employees are offered a basic or core benefits package of life and health insurance, sick leave, and vacation. Requiring a core set of benefits ensures that employees have a minimum level of coverage to protect against unforeseen financial hardships. Employees are then given a specified number of credits that they may use to "buy" whatever other benefits they need. Other benefits options might include prepaid legal services, financial planning, or long-term-care insurance.[9] Compensation specialists often see flexible benefits plans as ideal. Employees select the benefits of greatest value to them, while employers manage benefits costs by limiting the dollars employees have to spend.

Honeywell Canada considered three types of flexible benefits programs: cafeteria-style, whereby employees could choose any benefits they wanted; a module approach, whereby employees could select among prepackaged sets of benefits; and a core-plus-options plan, whereby employees could choose among options to augment a basic level of protection. Employees were able to select health and dental benefits that suited their life stages and that matched well with the plans their spouses had. Figure 11.1 lists the most commonly cited advantages and disadvantages of flexible benefits programs.

Because cafeteria plans increase the complexity of administering the entire benefits program, organizations may elect to outsource the handling of this function to a professional benefits vendor. About one-third of Canadian firms rely on third parties to perform these types of transactional services for their plans.[10] Paying a service or contract fee to these firms may be particularly cost-effective for the smaller employer. Furthermore, benefits programs must be flexible enough to accommodate the constant flow of new laws and regulations that affect them. A number of consulting firms specializing in benefits can help managers track changes in all phases of the programs they oversee.

flexible benefits plans (cafeteria plans)

Benefits plans that enable individual employees to choose the benefits that are best suited to their particular needs

FIGURE 11.1

Flexible Benefits Plans: Advantages and Disadvantages

Advantages

- Employees select benefits to match their individual needs.
- Benefit selections adapt to a constantly changing (diversified) workforce.
- Employees gain greater understanding of the benefits offered to them and the costs incurred.
- Employers maximize the psychological value of their benefits program by paying only for the highly desired benefits.
- Employers limit benefit costs by allowing employees to "buy" benefits only up to a maximum (defined) amount.
- Employers gain competitive advantage in the recruiting and retention of employees.

Disadvantages

- Poor employee benefits selection results in unwanted financial costs.
- There are certain added costs to establishing and maintaining the flexible plan.
- Employees may choose benefits of high use to them that might increase employer premium costs.

COMMUNICATING EMPLOYEE BENEFITS INFORMATION

Many employees do not believe what their employers tell them about soaring benefits costs, and employees and employers are at loggerheads over how effectively benefits are used. Therefore, it becomes critical that organizations effectively—and frequently—communicate the benefits package to employees. Court cases in Canada have established that it is the employer's responsibility to properly inform and disclose information about benefits. In *Spinks v. Canada*, an employee was not advised of certain pension options when he started with a new employer—specifically, that he was eligible to purchase past service in connection with his prior employment. The Federal Court of Appeal ruled that the employee had been poorly advised. In other cases, such as *Schmidt v. Air Products of Canada*, the courts have ruled that employee brochures, which usually are not considered to be legal documents, may in fact be legally binding.[11]

While it is important to communicate information about employee benefits, there is no legislation that mandates how this is to be done. Various provincial pension benefits acts and federal laws regulating pension benefits state that employers operating a pension plan must provide specific information to employees. However, there are differences among provinces about what must be communicated. The sponsor of a registered retirement plan (RPP) has until six months after the end of the plan's fiscal year to provide active plan members with statements of their pension benefits. (Quebec regulations require annual pension statements for retired and deferred vested members.) The employee's name, date of birth, and date of hire must be included in the pension statement, along with the pension plan membership date, vesting date, and normal retirement date. Most provinces also require the name of the employee's spouse and/or pension plan beneficiary.[12]

Employers use a number of methods to communicate benefits to employees such as the following:

- In-house publications (employee handbooks and organizational newsletters)
- Group meeting and training classes

444

- Online modules
- Bulletin boards
- Payroll inserts/pay stub messages
- Specialty brochures

The City of Regina, Saskatchewan, arranged to deliver pension presentations to all its 300 firefighters, a group of employees who are difficult to reach because of their shift work, by arranging these presentations on different days of the week at fire halls.[13] Also, the topic is usually covered in new-hire orientation programs. Managers who are conducting orientations should be allowed plenty of time to inform new employees of the benefits program and to answer any questions. The Calgary Health Region solved the problem of communicating benefits to thousands of works in 115 locations who did not have ready access to computers by providing free-standing interactive information kiosks in more than 100 high-traffic areas. Using a touch-screen display, employees can access e-mail, website and personal information.[14]

Highlights in HRM 11.1 provides a list of recommendations for communicating benefits.

Employee self-service systems have made it possible for employees to gather information about their benefits plans, enroll in their plans of choice, change their benefits coverage, or simply inquire about the status of their various benefits accounts without ever contacting an HR representative. Coopers & Lybrand uses a benefits information line to provide its employees with instant access to a wide variety of HR and benefits information by telephone. Employees can access their individual account

© Perov Stanislav/Shutterstock

Employees can access their benefit plans online.

Highlights in HRM 11.1

Crafting an Effective Benefits Communication Program

A well-designed benefits communication program will greatly enhance employees' appreciation of their benefits while ensuring that employers receive the intended value of these offerings. An effective program provides information to employees frequently and in a timely and cost-effective manner. Compensation specialists recommend the following when administering a benefits communication program.

In building an identity:

- Design materials that are eye-catching and of high interest to employees.
- Develop a graphic logo for all material.
- Identify a theme for the benefits program.

In writing benefits materials:

- Avoid complex language when describing benefits. Clear, concise, and understandable language is a must.

- Provide numerous examples to illustrate benefits specifics.
- Explain all benefits in an open and honest manner. Do not attempt to conceal unpleasant news.
- Explain the purpose behind the benefit and the value of the benefit to employees.

In publicizing benefits information:

- Use all popular employee communication techniques.
- Maintain employee self-service (ESS) technology to disseminate benefits information and to update employee benefits selections.
- Use voice mail to send benefits information.
- Employ presentation software to present information to groups of employees.
- Maintain a benefits hot line to answer employee questions.

information by entering a personal identification number (PIN). Other organizations use networked PCs or multimedia kiosks to the same purpose. These latter approaches enable employees to click on icons to access different benefits and to type in new information to update their records. Once an update or change has been made, the new information is permanently entered into the organization's HR information system without the need for paperwork.

It is also important for each employee to have a current statement of the status of her or his benefits. The usual means is a personalized computer-generated statement, as illustrated in Figure 11.2.

FIGURE 11.2

Communicating Benefits as Part of Total Rewards

Your 2009 Total Rewards

This statement summarizes the scope and value of your total rewards package at ABC. It was prepared with data current as of December 31, 2009, and it includes your 2010 benefit elections. We encourage you to review this statement carefully and to share it with your family.

81%	Base Compensation
3%	Variable Compensation
5%	Benefits
5%	Retirement
6%	Government Benefits

	ABC Pays	You Pay
Base Compensation	$49,000	—
Variable Compensation		
• Long-term incentive plan	$ 1,500	—
• Other bonus/incentive plan	$ 0	—
	$ 1,500	—
Benefits		
• Health and dental plans	$ 2,954	$ 1,412
• Flexible spending account	$ 1,797	$ 576
• Long-term disability plan	—	$ 500
• Basic life/AD&D insurance	$ 346	—
• Optional life/AD&D insurance	$ 201	—
• Optional dependant life insurance	—	$ 183
• Other benefits	—	$ 153
	$ 610	—
Retirement		
• Pension Plan	$ 2,944	$ 998
• Savings Plan	$ 2,495	—
	$ 499	$ 998
Government Benefits	$ 3,808	$ 2,620
Your 2009 Total Rewards	$60,256	

Source: Made available with permission from Mercer (Canada) Limited. Copyright 2009. (http://www.mercer.ca)

As the field of benefits becomes increasingly complex, and as employees become more sophisticated about financial planning, the need to hire and train benefits experts also grows. For those interested in specializing in this field, a good career move would be to become a certified employee benefit specialist (CEBS). In cooperation with the Wharton School at the University of Pennsylvania, Dalhousie University in Halifax sponsors a program leading to the CEBS designation. This ten-course program covers total compensation, health benefits, and strategic human resources.

CONCERNS OF MANAGEMENT

Managing an employee benefits program requires close attention to the many forces that must be kept in balance if the program is to succeed. Management must consider union demands, the benefits other employers are offering, tax consequences, and rising costs, which are discussed in the Business Case.

The escalating cost of health care benefits is a concern to employers, who must strike an appropriate balance between offering quality benefits and keeping costs under control. The shift in benefit planning from entitlement to self-responsibility is discussed in Reality Check.

The Conference Board of Canada has published a list of cost-containment strategies, which include the following:

- Contribution changes, such as increasing deductibles.
- Dollar limits, such as a dollar cap on specific benefits such as eyeglasses.

[OUTC2OME]

The Business CASE

Managing the Costs of Benefits

Mandatory benefits cost employers a minimum of 14 percent of payroll; when voluntary benefits are included, these costs may rise to 50 percent of payroll. These costs continue to increase at rates higher than inflation. The main area of concern is health care costs. While governments pay for about 70 percent of health care expenditures, employers and individuals pay for the rest, and these costs are escalating. For example, drug costs have been rising by 16 percent annually (higher than any other country) and drug costs represent as much as 70 percent of health care costs (excluding dental and vision care costs). These benefits represent a fixed rather than a variable cost, so management must decide whether it will be able to afford this cost in bad economic times. As managers can readily attest, if an organization is forced to discontinue a benefit, the negative effects of cutting it often outweigh any positive effects that accrued from providing it.

A current trend (and one not universally liked by employees) is for employers to require employees to pay part of the costs of certain benefits (e.g., through co-payments or higher deductibles). RBC used to pay 100 percent of benefits but now requires employees to pay a small deductible. At all times, benefit plan administrators are expected to select vendors of benefit services that have the most to offer for the cost. Furthermore, besides the actual costs of employee benefits, there are the costs of administering them, including direct labour costs, overhead charges, office space, and technology. But a big part of the escalating costs is the employee attitude of entitlement. Employees think that they are "entitled" to 12 days of sick leave so they take it, or that they since they have paid $50 for $600 of vision care they should use it.

Sources: Gloria Gonzalez, "Canadian Firms Seek to Stem Rising Costs of Benefits," *Business Insurance*, March 22, 2004, 3; D. Brown, "Runaway Drug Costs Make Benefit Upgrades Impractical," *Canadian HR Reporter* 16, no. 12 (June 16, 2003): 2; S. Felix, "Gimme Gimme," *Benefits Canada* 24, no. 7 (July 2000): 20–21.

- Coverage changes (e.g., limits on hospital upgrades).
- Benefit caps (e.g., on dispensing fees).
- Use of preferred providers and flexible benefits.[15]

Reality CHECK

Benefits Planning: From Entitlement to Self-Responsibility

In recent years, we have witnessed major upheavals in the area of benefits. Never before have there been such large increases in the cost of providing benefits as senior executives in companies throughout Canada try to change the "entitlement mindset" so prevalent in employees. Human resources professionals and senior executives can no longer make decisions regarding benefits plans without the assistance of benefits consultants. We met with Daphne Woolf of William H. Mercer Limited to discuss trends in benefit coverage.

Woolf specializes in the design and implementation of flexible benefits plans, strategic planning as it relates to compensation and benefits, and the design and monitoring of programs for promoting workplace health. She brings extensive experience in evaluating funding, administration, and utilization for the purpose of identifying ways to contain benefit plan costs. A visionary in her own right, she leads the national and central region task forces on flexible benefits for Mercer.

"First of all, we need to look at the drivers of change. We see five things happening: our demographics are changing as people age; we have double-income families; the workplace is becoming increasingly diverse; benefits are being taxed to greater extents; and human rights legislation is changing with respect to who should be covered. Due to the high costs of providing benefit coverage, we are seeing a shift in responsibility from the provinces to third parties and individuals. The provinces are covering less, and this trend will continue to grow. The final, most important, underlying issue is increased sensitivity to the magnitude of these trends and the resulting benefit cost impacts.

"The entitlement mindset stems from the fact that, 15 years ago, benefits were considered fringe. Now they are viewed as part of total compensation, which is a change in mentality. Employers are starting to move away from this entitlement mindset to self-responsibility. Employees are not used to making their own health care decisions, and it is a challenge for employers to educate their employees sufficiently and sway them to a different way of thinking. As the population ages,

employees' needs for benefits are increasing; at the same time, the quality of their benefits must decrease in response to the high costs. Based on some of our studies, what we are seeing for the first time is that employees are making employment decisions based on benefits. Employers look at dealing with these benefit trends by revisiting their philosophy and benefits objectives. For example, does an employer pay for smoking cessation, include high deductibles, offer choice, or provide coverage for dependants?

"We are seeing an increase in flexible benefit plans. Our belief is that in five years the majority of plans will be flexible, and an employer who waits may be disadvantaged. Employers are better off as flex leaders than flex followers. You want to create your own plan, not have to base your program design on what someone else has done. Now you can 'anti-select' the benefit costs of the spouse's plan, allowing your employee to 'cash out' or allocate flex credits to stock plans or an RRSP (registered retirement savings plan). In the future, however, employees and their dependants may not opt out of your plan, and this would potentially increase your costs. So going flex sooner than later, if it's in keeping with corporate objectives, makes sense for many employers who have employees with spouses who work elsewhere. It is going to be a much tougher sell in the future if employees don't learn what the costs are today—and their provincial medicare does not cover as much.

"Managers have to start watching the cost of illness and absenteeism and realize the lost production costs of paying for time off. These costs add to the overall cost of benefits and should be tied to compensation so that employees can appreciate those benefits. We are also moving toward managed care. We have to look at providing the same level of health care at the same cost. That means putting caps on dispensing fees where drugs are concerned and getting second opinions to ensure that unnecessary procedures are not being administered.

continued

"Americans have moved to a two-tiered system, and Canada is not far behind. While this is not currently a problem, it will be soon. For instance, if a patient wants a second opinion for something serious such as cancer, he or she may have to wait to see another specialist. In a two-tiered system, the patient can pay to have a second opinion immediately. This would not be reimbursed by the provincial health plan. We are beginning to see the collapse of provincial medicare as we now know it.

"There is an increase in health promotion. We are talking about wellness programs, which may focus on stress reduction, fitness in the workplace, and smoking-cessation programs. Employers are seeing the value in keeping employees healthy and productive, that is, preventing the claims costs. In one of my presentations, 'Taking the Fluff Out of Health Promotion,' I specifically outline the advantages of introducing health promotion programs to target cost pressures within the organization. Employers can yield a favourable return on investment if they ensure the right steps are taken to implement health promotion to secure effective cost containment. We are also diverging from traditional medicine to naturopathy and other paramedic services.

"In essence, employers are revisiting the extension of benefits to part-timers, retirees, and dependants. There is a movement toward providing incentive-based benefits—that is, using benefits to reward performance—and, with this, bringing things back to the overall compensation strategy. Employee expectations have become unrealistic mainly because they have not been educated. Once informed, we find that employees become a valuable resource. They need to understand the numbers. Employee focus groups are fast becoming the way to heed the transition from entitlement mindset to self-responsibility.

"[Finally], the trends are moving somewhere in the middle between the American health care system and Canada's. [In the future], flexible benefit plans will be the plan of choice so that educating the employee will be paramount if we are to move from an entitlement mindset to self-responsibility. Your plan should be devised considering an overall philosophy with particular attention to the strategic plan of your organization. Benefits can no longer be taken for granted as the costs of providing this commodity are at a premium. What constitutes benefits must be expanded beyond the basic dental, life insurance, and drug plans. Benefits strategies cannot be short term, but rather must be long range, and in this regard benefit consultants can provide value-added advice. Selecting the right consultant to work with you is just as important as determining your overall benefits philosophy. This philosophy is key to the design of your program as it sets the stage for what your benefit plan will entail."

About 20 percent of employers are choosing at least one of these methods to control costs. Lafarge Canada is one of those employers trying to contain the costs of benefits for its 8,000 employees, which have been rising at 6 to 10 percent per year. The organization's goal is to keep the escalation in costs at the annual rate of inflation. Stelco stopped reimbursing its employees for over-the-counter medicines such as cold remedies and ended coverage for private or semi-private hospital rooms. Air Canada is requiring its employees to pay 30 percent of the costs of the benefits.[16] All employers should try to uncover instances of fraudulent claims, as discussed in Ethics in HRM.

EMPLOYEE BENEFITS REQUIRED BY LAW

Legally required employee benefits amount to 12 percent of the benefits packages that Canadian employers provide.[17] These benefits include employer contributions to the Canada and Quebec pension plans, employment insurance, workers' compensation insurance, and (in some provinces) provincial medicare.

CANADA AND QUEBEC PENSION PLANS (CPP/QPP)

The Canada and Quebec pension plans cover almost all Canadian employees between the ages of 18 and 70. (Certain migratory and casual workers who earn less than the specified amount may be excluded.) To receive a retirement benefit,

[OUTCOME 3]

Ethics in **HRM**

Benefits Fraud

Employers are acutely aware of the rising costs of benefits, but they may not be aware of the amount of fraudulent claims, a contributor to high costs. The Canadian Health Care Anti-Fraud Association estimates that about 2 to 10 percent of health care dollars in North America are spent fraudulently. According to this association, the most common type of frauds are

- Malingering—exaggerating illnesses or injuries to collect additional disability benefits
- Doctor shopping—collecting multiple prescriptions
- Misrepresenting dependants—making claims for children who are no longer dependent or not
- coordinating spousal plans
- Submitting false claims

The association estimates that this costs plan sponsors, members, and insurers from $1 to $5 billion dollars each year.

One way to discover fraudulent claims is through the use of a whistle-blower or tips line. The City of Toronto has one, and through it was able to find nine cases of city employees accused of making false claims on the benefits plans, all of which are under investigation. Other options to reduce fraud are to establish a code of ethical conduct for employees, alert employees in communication materials about these types of inappropriate claims, and ensure that your organization's benefits provider has fraud detection mechanisms in place.

Source: A. Hanes, "Audit Reveals Alleged Scams by City Staff," *The National Post*, February 21, 2009, A15; S. Maxwell, "Fraud Squad," *Benefits Canada* vol. 32, Iss. 10 (2008): 25.

an individual must apply to Human Resources and Social Development Canada at least six months in advance of retirement.

Although similar in concept, the CPP and QPP differ in how much they pay out to participants. Both plans require employers to match the contributions made by employees. The revenues generated by these contributions are used to pay three main types of benefits: retirement pensions, disability benefits, and survivors' benefits. Governments do not subsidize these plans; all contributions come from employers and employees. Self-employed individuals can also contribute to the plan. With Canada's population aging, funds from the CPP will not be able to meet the needs of retirees unless those currently working, and their employers, significantly increase their contributions.

Canada has cross-border agreements with several countries to protect the acquired social security rights of people who have worked and lived in both countries and who meet the minimum qualifications for benefits from either country. A contributor's rights to benefits under CPP or QPP are not affected or impaired in any way by a change of employment or residence in Canada. All Canadian workers have "universal portability"—that is, the right to claim benefit credits wherever they are employed in Canada.

EMPLOYMENT INSURANCE (EI)

Employment Insurance (EI) benefits are payable to claimants who are unemployed and are actively seeking employment. A person who becomes unemployed is usually entitled to what most Canadians still call "Unemployment Insurance" (or UI), which was what this program used to be called. The new name reflects a change in focus from basic income support to active employment measures.[18]

The amount of benefit paid is determined by the number of hours of employment in the past year and the regional unemployment rate. Individuals are entitled to unemployment insurance after they have contributed enough for a qualifying period and after a waiting period. The waiting period may vary with the individual's situation. Also, employees who resign from their jobs or who are terminated for cause may be ineligible for benefits unless they can prove there was no reasonable alternative to leaving their jobs. Just causes include sexual harassment, health concerns, and moving to another town or city because of a spouse's reassignment.

Additional benefits may be extended for situations involving illness, injury, or quarantine, or for maternity, parental, or adoption leave. If an organization does not offer sick leave benefits, the employee may have to apply to EI for sick benefits. The benefit amount, which is calculated on the same basis as the regular benefit, varies across jurisdictions. Sickness or disability benefits are available for up to 15 weeks. A combination of maternity, parental, or adoptive benefits may be available up to a cumulative maximum of one year in some provinces.

Employees and employers both contribute to the EI fund. An EI premium reduction is available to employers who cover their employees under an approved wage-loss plan. The amount of the reduction depends on the supplement being given to the employee and therefore varies from company to company. Work-sharing programs have recently come into existence as a means of reducing the overall burden on EI. Under work sharing, an organization reduces the workweek of all employees in a particular group instead of laying them off. The company pays for the time worked, and the employee draws EI for the rest of the workweek.

WORKERS' COMPENSATION INSURANCE

Workers' compensation insurance is based on the theory that compensation for work-related accidents and illnesses should be considered one of the costs of doing business and should ultimately be passed on to the consumer. Individual employees should not be required to bear the cost of their treatment or loss of income; nor should they be subjected to complicated, delaying, and expensive legal procedures.

Workers' compensation is a form of insurance. It was created by an act of Parliament to help workers injured on the job return to the workplace. Each provincial and territorial board is empowered by the relevant legislation to amend and collect assessments (i.e., insurance premiums), to determine the right to compensation, and to pay the amount due to the injured worker. This system of collective liability is compulsory. Employers' contributions are assessed as a percentage of their payroll. The percentage varies with the nature of the industry. For example, in a high-risk industry such as mining, the assessment rates are higher than in knowledge-based industries.

Workers' compensation is based on the following principles:

- Employers share collective liability, though contributions may vary among employers in the same industry (e.g., some provinces punish employers who do not maintain a safe and healthy work environment by levying additional fines).
- This compensation is based on loss of earnings.
- The system is no-fault and nonadversarial, and thus offers no recourse to the courts.

Benefits are paid out of an employer-financed fund and include medical expenses stemming from work-related injuries, survivors' benefits (including burial expenses and pensions), and wage-loss payments for temporary, total, or partial disability. Permanent disability benefits may be disbursed as a lump-sum payment or as a permanent disability pension with rehabilitation services. The amount paid depends on the employee's earnings and provincial legislation.

Employees cannot be required either to make contributions toward a workers' compensation fund or to waive their right to receive compensation benefits. Payments made to claimants are effectively nontaxable. Premiums paid for by the employer may be deducted as expenses and are not deemed a taxable benefit for employees.

workers' compensation insurance

Insurance provided to workers to defray the loss of income and cost of treatment resulting from work-related injuries or illness

Figure 11.3 lists the steps that an HR department can take to control workers' compensation costs.

PROVINCIAL HOSPITAL AND MEDICAL SERVICES

People who have been resident in a Canadian province for three months are eligible to receive health care benefits. Applications must be made and approval given before coverage starts. Benefits include services provided by physicians, surgeons, and other qualified health professionals; hospital services such as standard ward accommodation and laboratory and diagnostic procedures; and hospital-administered drugs. Many employers offer third-party benefit coverage, which entitles their employees to additional benefits such as semi-private or private accommodation, prescription drugs, private nursing, ambulance services, out-of-country medical expenses that exceed provincial limits, vision and dental care, and paramedic services. Depending on the employer, all or just a portion of the services may be covered.

FIGURE **11.3**

Reducing Workers' Compensation Costs: Key Areas

1. Perform an audit to assess high-risk areas in the workplace.
2. Prevent injuries by proper ergonomic design of the workplace and effective assessment of job candidates.
3. Provide quality medical care to injured employees from physicians with experience and preferably with training in occupational health.
4. Reduce litigation by ensuring effective communication between the employer and the injured worker.
5. Manage the care of the injured worker from time of injury until return to work.
6. Keep a partially recovered employee at the worksite.
7. Provide extensive worker training in all related health and safety areas.

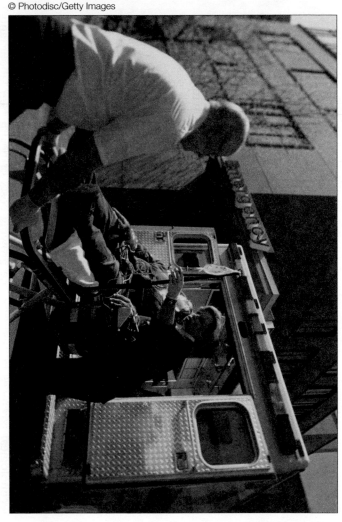

© Photodisc/Getty Images

Injured employees have their incomes protected through sick leave provisions.

DISCRETIONARY MAJOR EMPLOYEE BENEFITS

Besides the mandated benefits, most employers offer other benefits such as health care and dental plan; payment for time not worked, life insurance, retirement programs, and pension plans.

HEALTH CARE BENEFITS

The benefits receiving the most attention from employers today, owing to sharply rising costs and employee concerns, are health care benefits. In the past, health insurance plans covered only medical, surgical, and hospital expenses. Today employers are under pressure to include prescription drugs as well as dental, optical, and mental health care benefits in the packages they offer their workers. Drugs now represent the second largest health expenditures, second only to hospital costs.

Cost Containment

The growth in health care costs can be attributed to a number of factors, including the greater need for health care by an aging population, the costs associated with technological advances in medicine, the growing costs of health care labour, and the overuse of costly health care services.

With the significant rise in health care costs, it is understandable that employers seek relief from these expenses. The approaches used to contain the costs of health care benefits include reductions in coverage, increased deductibles or co-payments, and increased coordination of benefits to ensure that the same expense is not paid by more than one insurance reimbursement. A list of cost-containment strategies is provided in Figure 11.4.

Employee assistance programs and wellness programs can help organizations cut the costs of health care benefits. Highlights in HRM 11.2 focuses on a team approach to cost reduction.

[OUTCOME]

FIGURE **11.4**

Cost-Containment Strategies

Employers can reduce the cost of benefits in the following ways:

1. Education and Motivation
   - Communicate the costs of benefits.
   - Provide incentives to employees to reduce costs.
   - Teach employees how to live healthy lifestyles, and how to plan for retirement.
2. Change Coverage
   - Introduce dollar limits on benefits.
   - Eliminate duplicate coverage for spouses.
   - Remove upgrades.
   - Introduce minimum fees to be paid by employees.
3. Change the System
   - Form partnerships with pharmacies to provide discounts.
   - Move to defined-contribution plans.
   - Move to a claims management approach, and audit claims.

Other Health Benefits

In the past two decades, more and more employees have been receiving dental care insurance as a benefit. Besides their obvious purpose, dental plans encourage employees to receive regular dental attention. Typically, the insurance pays a portion of the charges and the subscriber pays the remainder.

Another fairly new benefit that many employers are offering is optical care. Typically, the coverage includes visual examinations and a percentage of the costs of lenses and frames.

Highlights in HRM 11.2

A Team Approach to Cost Containment

The University of New Brunswick (UNB) in Fredericton has long done what so many other organizations are only starting to do: The Fringe Benefits Review Committee was established to assist in devising strategies to combat increases in benefits costs. According to Jim O'Sullivan, the university's vice-president of finance and administration, the committee was organized in "an effort to repair relations with angry faculty representatives after the university's board of governors was perceived to have unilaterally eliminated an existing benefit."

The committee, comprising management as well as unionized and nonunionized employees, had the task of reviewing the university's group health and long-term disability (LTD) plans. Although the board of governors still holds the final decision-making authority, the committee alone is responsible for making benefits recommendations and working out the details; its efforts have resulted in a $3.8 million benefits surplus.

For more than 20 years, the employees have shared the costs of the university's group insurance plan, thus allowing the university to maintain effective cost control and to plan redesigns. Because the plan costs are shared, employees are aware that increasing benefits will mean higher contributions for both sides. To keep LTD claims down, employees have allowed the university to follow up directly with workers on disability claims to help them return to work faster. Compared to other universities with similar workforces, UNB has the lowest claims. For many other organizations, the price tag for health care, drug, and dental benefits has grown annually, but UNB has managed to hold benefit costs below the general rate of inflation. O'Sullivan attributes the savings to the cost-sharing partnership.

As in many other organizations, the employee assistance program is fully paid for by the employer. However, because the development of this program was discussed with the committee, employees played a major role in selling this plan to their coworkers. O'Sullivan believes that the plan is cost-effective in the long term. "Failure to seek treatment for personal problems," he notes, "would eventually affect job performance and lead to higher costs for health and LTD insurance."

The university has been self-insuring benefits—that is, paying for and managing its own risk, rather than contracting with an external insurance provider—with a pay-as-you-go philosophy, since the 1970s. Commercial insurance is purchased only to provide protection against catastrophic losses. For example, the LTD plan is self-insured for the first ten years of any claim, after which commercial insurance coverage comes into effect.

Employer and employee representative groups each have control over their half share of surplus funds. When there has been a surplus, consideration has been given to declaring contribution holidays or to implementing new benefits, but both sides, concerned that the good times could come to an end, have decided to act conservatively. The surplus funds are invested by the university's endowment fund investment managers; investment income is used to improve employees' benefits.

"I do believe we have developed a realistic balance between the operation of a responsive and competitive benefits package and the need to maintain effective cost controls," states O'Sullivan. "In this way, we have not only helped meet our overall financial objectives but have created positive spinoffs for labour–management relations generally."

Source: Personal interview with Jim Sullivan.

PAYMENT FOR TIME NOT WORKED

The "payment for time not worked" category of benefits includes the following: statutory holiday pay and vacation pay; time off for bereavement, jury duty, and military duty; rest periods and coffee breaks; and maternity/paternity benefits (which usually involve some form of salary continuance).

Vacations with Pay

It is generally agreed that vacation time is essential to the well-being of employees. Eligibility for vacations varies by industry, locale, and size of the organization. To qualify for longer vacations of three, four, or five weeks, one may expect to work for 5, 10, or 15 years. The average annual number of vacations days in Canada is 19, but about one in four employees does not take all of his or her vacation allotment and a surprising 10 percent never take their vacation time allotment. The reasons? They did not schedule in advance, prefer cash in lieu of time, and are too busy at work.[19] However, some companies are now forcing employees to take time off, as an internal control to avoid fraud. For example, Deutsche Bank has a global policy to force traders to take 10 consecutive days of work off a year, so that any concealed positions (secret trading) becomes evident in their absence. This was a result of the $79 million that a trader placed in undetected gambling bets, and he only took 4 vacation days a year.[20]

Paid Holidays

Both hourly and salaried workers can expect to be paid for statutory holidays as designated by each province. The standard statutory holidays are New Year's Day, Good Friday, Canada Day (Memorial Day in Newfoundland), Labour Day, and Christmas Day. Other holidays commonly recognized by the various provinces are Victoria Day and Thanksgiving Day. Some provinces have their own special statutory holidays. Many employers give workers an additional one to three personal days off (i.e., personal use days).

Sick Leave

Employees who cannot work because of illness or injury are compensated in various ways. Most employers offer short-term disability and long-term disability plans. Short-term disability plans include salary continuance programs, sick leave credits, and weekly indemnity plans. Most public employees, and many in private firms—especially in white-collar jobs—receive a set number of sick leave days each year to cover such absences. Sometimes employees are permitted to accumulate the sick leave they do not use to cover prolonged absences. Accumulated vacation leave is sometimes treated as a source of income when sick leave benefits have been exhausted. Group insurance that provides income protection during a long-term disability is also becoming more common. LTD plans normally provide a disabled employee with 50 to 70 percent of pre-disability income. Yet another alternative, depending on the situation, is workers' compensation insurance, which was discussed earlier in the chapter.

Severance Pay

An employee who is being terminated is sometimes given a one-time payment. Known as **severance pay**, it can amount to anywhere from a few days' wages to several months', with the exact payment depending on length of service. There are not strict rules for severance pay, but the following are guidelines based on court decisions:

- Two weeks per year of service for those working as labourers, production workers, and administrative support staff.
- Three weeks per year of service for those employed in technical, professional, supervisor, and managerial jobs.
- Four weeks per year of service for those employed as senior managers.[21]

severance pay
A lump-sum payment given to terminated employees by an employer at the time of an employer-initiated termination

Employers that are downsizing often use severance pay to soften the impact of unexpected termination on employees. An employee is not entitled to severance pay if a reasonable offer of alternative employment is refused.

LIFE INSURANCE

Group life insurance is the benefit most commonly provided by an employer. The purpose is to provide financial security to the dependants of the employee, in case of his or her death.

RETIREMENT PROGRAMS

Retirement is an important part of life and requires careful preparation. When convincing job applicants to come work for them, employers usually emphasize the retirement benefits that can be expected after a certain number of years of employment. As we noted earlier, it is common for each employee, once a year, to receive a personalized statement of benefits that contains information about projected retirement income from pensions and employee investment plans.

Retirement Policies

Canadian employees may retire at age 55 and begin drawing a reduced pension from CPP/QPP as well as funds from other sources such as RRSPs. Alternatively, some individuals can work until 71 in some provinces, at which time they must retire. Mandatory retirement at age 65 in Canada is slowly being abolished. Statistics Canada reported that 61 is the average age of retirement, with women leaving work at 58 and men at 62. The higher the household income, the lower the age of retirement.[22] Many are retiring because they have lost their jobs and cannot find other work. However, as we have seen, there is a growing trend for individuals in their 60s to take on part-time employment as a means of supplementing their income.

To avoid making layoffs and to reduce salary and benefits costs, employers often encourage early retirement. This encouragement often takes the form of increased pension benefits or cash bonuses, sometimes referred to as the **silver handshake**. Some companies, including IBM Canada, have given generously to encourage the early retirement of workers. Ontario Hydro presented its employees with various options to retire early; these included an early retirement allowance, a voluntary separation allowance, a special retirement program, and a voluntary retirement program. The incentives succeeded; most employees with 25 years of service opted for the special retirement program.[23] An employer can offset the cost of retirement incentives by paying lower compensation to replacements and/or by reducing its workforce.

For employees, the main factors in a decision to retire early are health, personal finances, and job satisfaction. Lesser factors include an attractive pension and the possibility of future layoffs.

Preretirement Programs

Most people are eager to retire; some are bitterly disappointed once they do. In an attempt to lessen the disappointment, some employers offer programs to help employees prepare for retirement. These programs typically include seminars and workshops, where lectures, videos, and printed materials are offered. Usually they cover topics such as how to live on a reduced, fixed income and how to cope with

silver handshake
An early retirement incentive in the form of increased pension benefits for several years or a cash bonus

lost prestige, family conflict, and idleness. Also discussed are more concrete topics such as pension plans, health insurance coverage, retirement benefits and provincial health care, and personal financial planning.

At Consumers Gas, employees between 50 and 53 can attend, with their spouses, a three-day seminar that covers six subject areas: positive outlook, leisure time, health, home, financial planning, and estate planning. At other organizations, these programs have a more individual focus. CIBC, which has over 40,000 employees at 1,800 different locations, provides its employees with tools such as tapes, books, videos, and computer programs. The Retirement Council of Canada recommends that 1 percent of a company's pension program be earmarked for retirement planning programs.[24]

Some organizations now offer retirement seminars to their younger employees as well. For instance, at Siemens Canada, employees as young as 35 are being offered the same financial sessions as employees 55 and over.

To help older workers get used to the idea of retirement, some organizations are experimenting with retirement rehearsal. Polaroid offers employees an opportunity to try out retirement through an unpaid three-month leave program. The company offers another program that permits employees to cut their hours gradually before retirement. Employees are paid only for hours worked, but receive full medical insurance and prorated pension credits. Most experts agree that preretirement planning is a much-needed, cost-effective employee benefit.[25]

PENSION PLANS

Originally, pensions were based on a *reward philosophy*; in other words, employers viewed pensions mainly as a reward to employees who stayed with them until retirement. Employees who quit or were terminated before retirement were not seen as deserving retirement benefits. Since then, most unions have negotiated vesting requirements into their contracts, and vesting has become required by law. Put another way, pensions are now based on an *earnings philosophy*; they are seen as deferred income that employees accumulate during their working lives; in other words, the pension belongs to the employee after a specified number of years of service, whether or not she or he remains with the employer until retirement.

Since the CPP/QPP legislation was enacted in 1966, pension plans have been used to supplement the protection provided by government-sponsored programs. Most private pension plans and a significant number of public plans now integrate their benefits with CPP/QPP benefits.

It is up to the employer whether to offer a pension plan. Because these plans are so expensive, companies are always looking for the least expensive ways to provide them to their employees.

Types of Pension Plans

Pensions can be categorized in two basic ways: according to contributions made by the employer and according to the amount of pension benefits to be paid. In a **contributory plan**, contributions to a pension plan are made jointly by employees and employers. In a **noncontributory plan**, the contributions are made solely by the employer. Most plans in privately held organizations are contributory.

When pension plans are classified by the amount of pension benefits to be paid, there are two basic types: the defined-benefit plan and the defined-contribution plan. Under a **defined-benefit plan**, the retirement benefit is determined according to a predefined formula. This amount is usually based on the employee's years of service, average earnings during a specific period of time, and age at time of retirement. A variety of formulas exist for determining pension benefits; the one used most often is based on the employee's average earnings (usually over a three- to

contributory plan
A pension plan in which contributions are made jointly by employees and employers

noncontributory plan
A pension plan in which contributions are made solely by the employer

five-year period immediately preceding retirement) multiplied by the number of years of service with the organization. A deduction is then made for each year the retiree is under 65. As noted earlier, pension benefits are usually integrated with CPP/QPP. Very few employers introduce this type of plan, because it places them under the legal obligation to pay benefits regardless of the performance of the pension plan.

A **defined-contribution plan** establishes the basis on which an employer will contribute to the pension fund. These plans come in a variety of forms: some involve profit sharing; others are employer-sponsored RRSP plans. The size of the pension the employee will get is determined by the funds in his or her account at the time of retirement and what retirement benefits (usually in the form of an annuity) these funds will purchase. These plans are not as predictable (i.e., secure) as defined-benefit plans. However, even under defined-benefit plans, retirees may not receive the benefits promised them if the plan is not adequately funded.

Defined-benefit plans, with their fixed payouts, are falling out of use and have dropped to 40 percent of companies.[26] They are less popular with employers nowadays because they cost more and because they require compliance with complicated government rules.[27] All new pension plans in Canada, such as those introduced by MacMillan Bloedel and Molson Breweries, are defined-contribution plans.

Registered retirement savings plans (RRSPs) have experienced tremendous growth in recent years because the funds in these plans are allowed to accumulate tax-free until they are withdrawn. RRSPs have annual contribution limits; also, if withdrawals are made from them before retirement, tax must be paid on them. Some employers offer group RRSPs, which have some advantages over individual RRSPs: they are deducted from payroll and have mass-purchasing power.

Federal Regulation of Pension Plans

Registered pension plans (RPPs) are subject to federal and provincial regulations. The federal *Income Tax Act* prescribes limits and standards that affect the amount of contributions that can be deducted from income; it also mandates how pension benefits can be taxed. In the federal jurisdiction and most provincial ones, there are laws that state how pension plans must be operated. For example, the actuarial assumptions on which the funding is based must be certified by an actuary at specified intervals.

An important issue to employees is vesting. **Vesting** is a guarantee of accrued benefits to participants at retirement age, regardless of their employment status at that time. Vested benefits that have been earned by the employee cannot be revoked by the employer. Employees with two years of service in an organization are considered, with regard to their pension plans, fully vested and locked in.

Pension Portability

For a long time, most pension plans lacked portability; in other words, employees who changed jobs were unable to maintain equity in a single pension. Unions addressed this concern by encouraging multiple-employer plans. These plans cover the employees of two or more unrelated organizations in accordance with a collective agreement. They are governed by boards of trustees on which both the employers and the union are represented. Multiple-employer plans tend to be found in industries in which few companies have enough employees to justify an individual plan. They are also found often in industries in which employment tends to be either seasonal or irregular. These plans are found in the following manufacturing sectors: apparel, printing, furniture, leather, and metalworking. They are also found in nonmanufacturing industries such as mining, construction, transport, entertainment, and private higher education.

defined-benefit plan
A pension plan in which the amount an employee is to receive on retirement is specifically set forth

defined-contribution plan
A pension plan that establishes the basis on which an employer will contribute to the pension fund

vesting
A guarantee of accrued benefits to participants at retirement age, regardless of their employment status at the time

Employees who leave an organization can leave their locked-in funds in their current pension plan, or they can transfer those funds into a locked-in RRSP or into their new employer's pension plan (if one exists).

Pension Funds

A pension fund can be administered through a trusted plan or through an insured one. In a *trusted* plan, the pension contributions are placed in a trust fund. The fund is then invested and administered by trustees. The trustees are appointed by the employer; but if there is a union, the union sometimes appoints them. Contributions to an *insured* pension plan are used to purchase insurance annuities. These funds are administered by the insurance company that is providing the annuities.

Government benefits such as CPP/QPP and Old Age Security will be stretched thin as baby boomers grow older, and some private pensions may be vulnerable to poorly performing investments. It should also be noted that the pension funds of some organizations are not adequate to cover their obligations. Here is another interesting question: "Whose money is it?" When a pension fund has generated a surplus over plan (and many of them have), management tends to see this surplus as part of the organization's portfolio of assets; not surprisingly, employees tend to view it as their own money. Highlights in HRM 11.3 describes this debate.

Highlights in HRM 11.3

Whose Money Is It?

Ray Bekeris worked 12-hour shifts as a steelworker for 30 years for Cold Metal Products, a steel manufacturing plant based in Hamilton, Ontario. Cold Metal Products went bankrupt, and Ray discovered that his pension plan was gone too. After the banks and other secured creditors got their money, there was almost none left for the employees. Canadian bankruptcy laws favour secured creditors, and employees are at the bottom of the list. Actuaries view this as reasonable, because creditors would not risk their investment if they were not at the top of the list to be repaid. This is not heartless because banks are investing people's money and want some expectation of a return. But this means that employees become unwitting investors. To illustrate, a company is in trouble and the employer stops making its contributions to the pension plan. They use this money to finance the company, perhaps prolonging the bankruptcy. The employees, who are likely unaware

of this, become unintentional investors, but with no rights or no voice. And it is not just private companies using pension plan funds as if the funds were their own money. There is a case before the courts that is deemed the most important pension court case in history. Legal firms representing 670,000 public service employees and retirees are suing the federal government because it appropriated the pension surplus (of $30 billion in 1999). Employees believed that they were paying into a pension plan where the money would be held safely and then distributed to them, not to the general coffers of the government.

Bankruptcies and appropriation of pension surpluses are not the only threats to pension plans. Most pension plans can cover only 80 percent of their obligations. These facts should stimulate employees to not rely on organizational pension plans, but to save wisely for their own retirements.

Source: Diane Swain, "How Safe Is Your Pension?" *CBC News Online*, November 15, 2004, retrieved March 10, 2006, from http://www.cbc.ca/news/background/pension and from "Public Service Pension Plan: Pension Grab Court Case Begins," http://www.pipsc.ca/english/newsletters/c-dec05/5.html.

EMPLOYEE SERVICES: CREATING A WORK–LIFE SETTING

Employee services, like other benefits, represent a cost to the employer. But they are often well worth the cost. More and more different services are being offered by employers to make life at work more rewarding and to enhance the well-being of employees. "Wellness is good for business," says Ann Coll of Husky Injection Molding Systems. The employees at Husky's plant in Bolton, Ontario, enjoy a subsidized cafeteria with organic vegetarian meals, a $500 stipend for vitamins, and a fitness centre that is open around the clock.

CREATING A FAMILY-FRIENDLY SETTING

Eddie Bauer, an outdoor clothing and equipment supplier, offers its employees takeout dinners and one paid "balance day" off a year. Alta Gas, based in Calgary, offers many benefits: a share purchase plan, extra vacation days; quarterly corporate events such as cross-country skiing, emergency short-term day care, and discounts on home computers.[28] These organizations, and many others, are seeking to create a family-friendly organizational environment that allows employees to balance work and personal needs. Programs like these help employees manage their time; employers benefit by attracting good workers and by reducing the various interruptions that affect workplace productivity.[29] Figure 11.5 lists some of the more popular employer-sponsored work-life benefits.

EMPLOYEE ASSISTANCE PROGRAMS

To help workers cope with a wide variety of problems that interfere with their work performance, organizations have developed **employee assistance programs (EAPs)**. Typically, an EAP provides diagnosis, counselling, and referral services for alcohol or drug problems, emotional problems, and financial or family crises. (EAPs will be discussed in more detail in Chapter 12.) It has been estimated that employees' stress adds as much as 8 percent to payroll costs. The point of EAPs is to help employees solve their personal problems, or at least to prevent those problems from turning into crises that affect their ability to work productively. To handle crises, many EAPs offer 24-hour hotlines. Between 7 and 10 percent of employees use EAPs.[30] The Public Service Commission of the Yukon Government provides a summary of employee and employer responsibilities when using the employee assistance program to deal with the personal problems of employees that affect their work performance (see Highlights in HRM 11.4).

employee assistance programs (EAPs)

Services provided by employers to help workers cope with a wide variety of problems that interfere with the way they perform their jobs

FIGURE 11.5

Family-Friendly Benefits: Balancing Work and Home Needs

- Child care/elder care referral services
- Time off for children's school activities
- Employer-paid on-site or near-site child-care facilities
- Flexible work hours scheduling
- Employee-accumulated leave days for dependant care
- Subsidized temporary or emergency dependant care
- Extended leave policies for child/elder care
- Sick child programs (caregiver on call)
- Work-at-home arrangements/telecommuting
- Partial funding of child-care costs
- Customized career paths

Highlights in HRM 11.4

Yukon Government's Public Service Commission

Employee Assistance Program

To assist employees to deal with personal problems that are affecting or have the potential to affect their work performance.

Employee Rights and Responsibilities

- To maintain work performance at an acceptable level.
- To voluntarily seek or accept confidential assistance or advice when deteriorating or impaired work performance is being caused by a personal, health, or behavioural problem.
- To cooperate in any treatment program that is established and continue the program to completion.
- An employee who accepts the referral, counseling, and rehabilitation available under EAP does so without prejudice to job security.

Supervisory Responsibilities

- Recognize that a problem exists.
- Document the facts.
- Confront the employee with the facts.
- Try to find a solution within the work situation without diagnosing the underlying personal/behavioural problem.
- Refer employee to EAP if the problem cannot be resolved in the workplace.
- Follow up with the EAP adviser on the employee's progress.
- Work with the EAP adviser in establishing course of action to reintegrate employee into work environment.
- Monitor the work performance of the employee against clearly established objectives and support the employee in the integration process.

Source: Printed with the permission of the Government of Yukon, Public Service Commission.

COUNSELLING SERVICES

An important part of an EAP is the counselling services it provides to employees. While most organizations expect managers to counsel subordinates on work-related issues, some employees will have problems that require professional counselling. Most organizations refer such individual employees to outside services such as family counselling services, marriage counsellors, and mental health clinics. Some organizations have a clinical psychologist, counsellor, or comparable specialist on staff to whom employees may be referred.

CHILD AND ELDER CARE

Consider these statistics:

- About 32 percent of Canadians have elder care responsibilities.
- Employees spend an average of 23 hours each month on elder care.[31]

Those responsible for care giving are more likely to miss work because of the emotional and physical fatigue associated with care giving.[32] Great West Life Insurance Company, based in Winnipeg, has hired a family services coordinator to help its employees with family issues. The coordinator recommends products, such as personal alarm systems, or services, such as adult day care in the community.[33] In the past, working parents had to make their own arrangements with sitters or with nursery schools for pre-school children. Today, benefits may include financial assistance, alternative work schedules, and family leave. For many employees, on-site or near-site child care centres are the most visible, prestigious, and desired solutions.

Ontario Hydro has provided the space and is paying the occupancy costs for a program it calls Hydro Kids. This program encompasses three on-site day care centres, which are open to company employees. These nonprofit centres are operated by the parents themselves, who hire the child care staff and manage day-to-day operations. Parents pay market rates for the child care services.[34] Ford Motor Company of Canada offers its employees as much as $2000 a year in child care assistance.

A growing benefit offered employees with children experiencing a short illness is called mildly ill child care. Medical supervision is the primary difference between these facilities and traditional day care arrangements. Mildly ill care facilities serve children recovering from colds, flu, ear infections, chicken pox, or other mild illnesses that temporarily prevent them from attending regular school or day care. See Highlights in HRM 11.5 for the benefits of these arrangements as cited by CIBC.

Responsibility for the care of aging parents and other relatives is another fact of life for more and more employees. The term **elder care**, as used in the context of employment, refers to situations in which an employee provides care to an elderly relative while remaining actively at work. Most caregivers are women.

There is no doubt that elder care responsibilities detract from work efficiency: from time lost to take a parent to the doctor, to loss of concentration due to worry, work time being spent making care arrangements, never knowing when an emergency will occur, and calls from neighbours and relatives disrupting the workday. When combined, these responsibilities lead to a situation where neither the caregiver nor the employee role is filled adequately. Lost productivity due to absenteeism of those caring for elders can cost a 1,000-employee company without an elder care program as much as $400,000 per year. TransAmerica Corporation, an insurance and financial services organization, reported that 1,600 missed workdays per year were attributed to 22 percent of its employees who were caring for an elderly relative, for an annual loss to the corporation of $250,000. For larger companies, these costs can run into the millions.[35]

To reduce the negative effects of care giving on productivity, organizations can offer elder care counselling, educational fairs and seminars, printed resources,

Highlights in **HRM 11.5**

CIBC Cares

CIBC was the first Canadian corporation to open an employer-sponsored centre dedicated to backup child care. Every parent has faced the hardship of finding emergency care, when regular child-care arrangements break down due to a caretaker's illness, or when schools are closed for professional development days or snow days. The CIBC Children's Centre offers special play areas for children of different ages and is licensed under the *Day Nurseries Act*. The centre is operated by ChildrenFirst, which designs, develops, and operates innovative backup child-care facilities in North America. Nearly 800 parents used the CIBC

Children's Centre in the first six months of operation, with a resultant saving of 2528 employee days. At an average daily rate of about $200, the productivity saving was estimated to be over $0.5 million. The intangible benefits include increased attraction and retention of employees, allowing them to achieve better work–life family balance. CIBC discovered through surveys that 90 percent of Canadians want organizations to focus on more than profits, 60 percent form an impression of a company based on its social responsibility, and 17 percent have avoided a company's products because of its lack of social responsibility.

Sources: David Brown, "CIBC Day Care Saves 2500 Absence Days," *Canadian HR Reporter*, November 17, 2003: 1; ChildrenFirst, http://www.childrenfirst.com; CIBC, http://www.cibc.com; presentation made by Joyce M. Phillips, Executive Vice-President human resources, CIBC, in April 2003.

support groups, and special flexible schedules and leaves of absence. Schering-Plough, a pharmaceuticals manufacturer, uses an 800-line for elder care referrals. IBM has established a nationwide telephone network of more than 200 community-based referral agencies. Some employers band together to come up with better solutions to the challenge of elder care.

AT&T has given grants to community organizations to recruit, train, and manage elder care volunteers where its employees live and work. Travellers Corporation, a financial services company, is part of a consortium of employers that trains family care workers; it also shares with employees the cost of three days' in-home care for family emergencies.[36] Interest in and demand for elder care programs will increase dramatically as baby boomers age and find themselves managing organizations and experiencing elder care problems with their own parents.

OTHER SERVICES

The variety of benefits and services that employers offer today could not have been imagined a few years ago. Some are fairly standard, and we will cover them briefly. Some are unique and obviously grew out of specific concerns, needs, and interests. Some of the more creative and unusual benefits are group insurance for employee pets, free baseball tickets for families and friends, on-site barbers and car washers, and dropoffs for dry cleaning. Highlights in HRM 11.6 describes the perks at Intuit Canada.

Legal Services

Legal service plans are generally of two types: access plans and comprehensive plans. *Access plans* provide free telephone or office consultation and document review, as well as discounts on legal fees for more complex matters. *Comprehensive plans* cover other services such as representation in divorce cases, real estate transactions, and civil and criminal trials.

© Susan Van Etten/PhotoEdit

Caring for one's aging parents and relatives is a growing concern for employees.

Highlights in HRM 11.6

Perks at Intuit

Intuit Canada, which develops financial software, employs about 400 employees at its Edmonton offices and is rated one of Canada's top employers. The benefits program it offers employees is one of the reasons for its success. First, Intuit offers the standard benefits package, for which it pays 100 percent of the premiums. Then the fun stuff begins. There is a staff lounge with pool table, foozball, ping pong, and a gas fireplace. Down the hall, employees work out in the company gym, playing volleyball, basketball, and floor hockey. A complete fitness centre, with a free towel service, is greatly valued by employees. For the long hours and stress, Intuit even provides three nap rooms after listening to employees who said they just wanted a place to crash for an hour or two. Intuit pays for employees and their families to relax at the annual corporate retreat at Alberta's Jasper Park Lodge. For Intuit, the benefit of these benefits is the ability to attract and retain the best people.

Source: T. Humber, "Perquisites No Longer a Prerequisite?" *Canadian HR Reporter* 16, no. 3 (February 10, 2003): G7–G9.

Covered employees normally pay a monthly or annual fee to be enrolled in the plan. When the need for legal assistance arises, the employee may choose a lawyer from a directory of providers and incur no legal fees. Prepaid legal programs are typically offered as part of an employer's cafeteria benefits plan.

Financial Planning

One of the newer benefits is financial planning. Primarily available to executives and middle managers, it will likely become available to more employees through flexible benefits programs. Financial planning programs cover investments, tax planning and management, estate planning, and similar needs.

Housing and Moving Expenses

The days of "company" houses are now past, except in some remote areas and the armed forces. However, a variety of housing services is usually provided in nearly all organizations that move employees from one office or plant because of a transfer or a relocation. These services may include helping employees find living quarters, paying for travel and moving expenses, and protecting transferred employees from loss when selling their homes.

Transportation Pooling

Daily transportation to and from work is a major concern of employees. The result may be considerable time and energy devoted to organizing car pools and scrambling for parking spaces. Employer-organized van pooling is common among private and public organizations in metropolitan areas. For example, Molson Breweries introduced transportation pooling after the company consolidated its facilities and moved to a remote location. Employees appreciated the savings on expenses and the reduced commuting stress. Many employers report that tardiness and absenteeism are reduced by van pooling.

Credit Unions

Credit unions exist in many organizations to serve the financial needs of employees. They offer a variety of deposits as well as other banking services and make loans to their members. Although the employer may provide office space and a payroll deduction service, credit unions are operated by the employees under federal and provincial legislation and supervision.

Recreational and Social Services

Many organizations offer some type of sports programs in which personnel may participate on a voluntary basis. Bowling, softball, golf, baseball, and tennis are often provided as intramural programs. In addition to intramurals, many organizations have teams that represent them in competitions with other local organizations. Memberships at health clubs and fitness centres or discounts on memberships are also popular offerings (see Chapter 12).

Many social functions are organized for employees and their families. Employees should play a major role in the planning if these functions are to succeed. However, the employer should retain control of all events associated with the organization, because of possible legal liability. For example, employers can be held liable for injuries to third persons caused by an employee's actions arising from employment. "Employment" in this context can include attending a company party, if the employee was urged or obligated to attend it. Thus, an employer could be held responsible for an accident occurring while an employee is driving to or from an employer-sponsored event.

Small Business APPLICATION

Small business aims to address three issues with the prevalence of benefit programs in Canada. First, such programs help employees remain healthy, reducing the cost of absenteeism. Second, such programs help keep small businesses competitive with other employers. Third, these programs provide a tax advantage as contributions to such programs may be tax exempt, whereas compensation is taxable.

So what options are available to small business? From the standpoint of benefits programs, many insurance providers have benefit programs available for as few as one or two employees. Such programs can be employer-paid, employee-paid, or cost-shared. Coverage can be 100 percent, 80 percent, or any other level. Plans may cover full-time employees, part-time employees, or both. It is critical to identify the plan that

best meets the objectives and budget of the organization. Regarding retirement plans, assuming the set-up and management of pension plans is cost-prohibitive and administratively burdensome, small employers may wish to provide an incentive to employees to contribute to a Retirement Savings Plan (RSP) managed by the employee. Simple programs where a company matches employee contributions to an RSP up to a certain maximum can have the same positive effect of a company pension, with much lower cost and program administration challenges.

In conclusion, not all small companies have benefit or retirement programs. However, recognizing the benefit of such programs and that many can be implemented with relative ease and low cost, small companies certainly should consider them.

SUMMARY

[OUTCOME 1] Benefits are an established and integral part of the total compensation package. In order to have a sound benefits program, there are certain basic considerations. It is essential that a program be based on specific objectives that are compatible with the organization's philosophy and policies, as well as affordable. Through committees and surveys, a benefits package can be developed to meet employees' needs. Through the use of flexible benefits plans, employees are able to choose those benefits that are best suited to their individual needs. An important factor in how employees view the program is the full communication of benefits information through meetings, printed materials, and annual personalized statements of benefits.

[OUTCOME 2] Since many benefits represent a fixed cost, management must pay close attention in assuming more

benefit expense. Increasingly, employers are requiring employees to pay part of the costs of certain benefits. Employers also shop for benefits services that are competitively priced.

[OUTCOME 3] Nearly one-quarter of the benefits packages provided by employers are legally required. These benefits include employer contributions to retirement plans, employment insurance, and workers' compensation insurance.

[OUTCOME 4] The cost of health care programs has become the major concern in the area of employee benefits. Several approaches can be used to contain health care costs, including reduction in coverage, increased coordination of benefits, and increased deductibles. Employee assistance programs (EAPs) and wellness programs can also help cut the costs of health care benefits.

CHAPTER 11 Employee Benefits

OUTCOME 5

Included in the category of benefits that involve payments for time not worked are vacations with pay, paid holidays, sick leave, and severance pay. Most Canadian workers receive 10 to 15 days' vacation leave plus statutory holidays. In addition to vacation time, most employees—especially in white-collar jobs—receive a set number of sick leave days. A one-time payment of severance pay may be given to employees who are being terminated.

OUTCOME 6

Many provinces have abolished mandatory retirement, and now employees can choose when to retire. However, many employers provide incentives for early retirement in the form of increased pension benefits or cash bonuses. Some organizations now offer preretirement programs, which typically include seminars, workshops, and informational materials.

OUTCOME 7

Once a pension plan has been established, it is subject to federal and provincial regulation to ensure that benefits will be available when the employee retires. While two types of plans are available—defined benefit and defined contribution—most employers now opt for the latter. The amount an employee receives on retirement is based on years of service, average earnings, and age at time of retirement. Usually, pension benefits are integrated with CPP/QPP. Pension funds are administered through either a trustee or an insurance plan.

OUTCOME 8

The types of service benefits that employers typically provide include EAPs, counselling services, child care, and elder care. Other benefits are prepaid legal services, financial planning, housing and moving, transportation pooling, credit unions, and social and recreational opportunities.

KEY TERMS

defined benefit plan, 456
defined contribution plan, 457

employee assistance programs (EAPs), 459
flexible benefits plans (cafeteria plans), 442
noncontributory plan, 456

workers' compensation insurance, 450

DISCUSSION QUESTIONS

1. You are a small employer wishing to establish a benefits program for your employees. What things should you consider to ensure that the program is a success for your employees?

2. Many organizations are concerned about the rising cost of employee benefits and question their value to the organization and to the employees.
   a. In your opinion, what benefits are of greatest value to employees? to the organization? Why?
   b. What can management do to increase the value to the organization of the benefits provided to employees?

3. Benefits may total from 23 to 36 percent of total payroll costs. Name three ways in which you, as an employer, would try to reduce the costs of benefits.

4. This chapter leaves the impression that it is the responsibility of the government and the employer to look after an employee's health. What is the employee's responsibility? More

than half of Canadians are overweight and about 15 percent are obese. The costs to Canada's health care system are $2 billion a year and growing. Overweight employees typically cost 140 percent more than others in health services. An emerging viewpoint is that employees who smoke or do not exercise or are obese should pay a larger percentage of health benefits. Outline the rationale for and against this perspective.

5. Do you agree with the argument that the benefits for time not worked are the ones most readily available to reduce employer costs? Explain.

6. Employers used to prescribe a mandatory retirement age—usually 65. What do you think are the advantages and disadvantages of a mandatory retirement age? What factors may affect an individual's decision to retire at a particular time, and what factors may affect his or her ability to adjust to retirement?

7. Should the government guarantee private company's pension plans, when these companies go bankrupt? Why or why not?

8. Assume your team has been hired as a benefits consultant by a small business with 50 to 60 employees. What benefits do you believe this employer should offer, given its limited resources? Explain why you would offer these benefits.

INTERNET EXERCISE

Using key search terms such as *employee benefits* and *perks*, discover what employers are offering their employees in terms of innovative or unusual benefits. Make a list of these. Try to assess their cost to the employer, and then describe the potential benefits of each perk. At the end of this analysis, decide if you think the benefit is worth the cost.

HRM EXPERIENCE

Understanding Employer Benefit Programs

Compensation surveys indicate that a majority of employees are unable to accurately name the benefits they receive, and employees vastly underestimate the cost of benefits paid by their employers.

This exercise will help you more fully understand the benefits discussed in this chapter. Additionally, you will explore, in detail, the benefits and services offered by your employer and other employers in your area.

Assignment

Working in teams of four to six individuals, obtain information on the benefits package offered by your employer or other employers in your area. Once the information is gathered, be able to identify (1) each benefit offered, (2) what the benefit provides the employee, (3) employee eligibility (if required), and (4) how the benefit is paid for (employer, employee, or a combination of both). Compare benefit packages. Be prepared to discuss your findings with the class.

BIZFLIX EXERCISES

ERIN BROCKOVICH: ERIN GETS BENEFITS, WITH DENTAL

The chapter discussed the important role of employee benefits in the employment relationship. Watch this scene from *Erin Brockovich* and assess the importance of benefits to Erin.

Erin Brockovich (Julia Roberts), a single mother of three, needs a job and convinces skeptical attorney Ed Masry (Albert Finney) to hire her. She quickly discovers a potentially large case against Pacific Gas & Electric Company (PG&E) for environmental pollution. Based on a true story, the film has many dramatic and funny moments. Roberts received the 2000 Best Actress Academy Award.

The scene comes from the "Ed Comes Over" segment that appears about 45 minutes into the film. It follows Erin's discussion with her neighbour George (Aaron Eckhart) about her one-year reign as Miss Wichita. This scene ends with Ed Masry saying he is drawing the line on benefits. The film continues with Ed reviewing the limited information Erin got from the Lohantan Regional Water Board office. Erin and her three children revisit the office to copy more information for the case.

What to Watch for and Ask Yourself

- The first section of this chapter, "Employee Benefits Programs," opened with this sentence: "Employee benefits constitute an indirect form of compensation intended to improve the quality of work lives and personal lives of employees." Does this quotation apply to Erin in this scene? If so, in what way does it apply to her and her life situation?

- Erin and Ed are unclear about what benefits, except medical and dental, his firm provides. Which benefits discussed in this chapter would a typical small law firm give to its employees? See the earlier section "Discretionary Major Employee Benefits" for some ideas.

- Erin negotiates a 10 percent pay raise from Ed, suggesting that pay is important to her. Does the scene suggest that benefits are also important to Erin? Why or why not?

CASE STUDY 1

EVALUATE THE WORK–LIFE CLIMATE IN YOUR COMPANY

What is the quality of the work–life environment in your company? The following survey provided by the Work and Family Connection will help provide a "case analysis" of the climate in your organization. Answers to the 20 questions will provide clear insights about your company's position in the work–life area.

Agree or Disagree with the Following Statements:

1. My manager/supervisor treats my work–life needs with sensitivity.

2. It is usually easy for me to manage the demands of both work and home life.

3. My career path at this company is limited because of the pressure of home life demands.

4. My job at this company keeps me from maintaining the quality of life I want.

5. My manager/supervisor is supportive when home life issues interfere with work.

6. My manager/supervisor focuses on results, rather than the time I am at my desk.

7. My manager/supervisor has a good understanding of flexible work hour practices.

8. If I requested a flexible work arrangement my manager/supervisor would support me.

9. My manager/supervisor is often inflexible or insensitive about my personal needs.

10. I believe my manager/supervisor treats me with respect.

11. My manager/supervisor allows me informal flexibility as long as I get the job done.

12. My manager/supervisor tends to treat us like children.

13. My manager/supervisor seldom gives me praise or recognition for the work I do.

14. My manager/supervisor seems to care about me as a person.

15. I would recommend this company to others.

16. The work I do is not all that important to this company's success.

17. If I could find another job with better pay, I would leave this organization.

18. If I could find another job where I would be treated with respect, I would take it.

19. If I could find another job where I could have more flexibility, I would take it.

20. I am totally committed to this company.

For a perfect score, you should answer "Disagree" to questions 3, 4, 9, 12, 13, 16, 17, 18, and 19 and "Agree" to all the rest (questions 1, 2, 5, 6, 7, 8, 10, 11, 14, 15, and 20).

To score, begin by giving yourself 20 points. Then deduct one point for every "wrong" response from the total score.

If your score is 18 to 20: Congratulations! Your organization is leading the nation in flexibility and supportiveness.

If your score is 14 to 17: Your organization is probably more supportive and flexible than most, but you have room to grow.

If your score is 11 to 13: You could be open to other job offers in the race for talent among employees.

If your score is 10 or less: Your managers will need help to manage the 21st century workforce.

Source: Used with permission of the Work and Family Connection, 5195 Beachside Drive, Minnetonka, Minnesota 55343; phone 1-800-487-7898 or http://www.workfamily.com.

CASE STUDY 2

TRUE NORTH'S FAMILY-FRIENDLY BENEFITS: AN UNEXPECTED BACKLASH

True North Consulting Services (TNCS), a provider of HR software application systems, prides itself on the variety of benefits it offers employees. In addition to health care, pension, and vacation benefits, the company also offers an attractive family-friendly benefits package including flexible schedules, child and elder care assistance, counselling services, adoption assistance, and extended parental leave. Unfortunately, in recent months, the company's progressive work–life policy has experienced a backlash from several employees, as the following case illustrates.

In March 2004, Teresa Wheatly was hired by True North as a software accounts manager. With excellent administrative and technical skills, plus four years of experience at Adaptable Software, True North's main competitor, Teresa became a valued addition to the company's marketing team. As a single mother with two grade-school children, Teresa received permission to take Fridays off. She was also allowed to leave work early or come in late to meet the demands of her children. Teresa is one of 11 software account managers at True North.

The problem for True North, and particularly Janis Blancero, director of marketing, began in the fall of 2004. On September 15, Dorothy McShee, citing "personal reasons"—which she refused to discuss—requested a four-day workweek for which she was willing to take a 20 percent cut in pay. When Dorothy asked for the reduced work schedule, she sarcastically quipped, "I hope I don't have to have kids to get this time off." On October 3, Juan Batista, a world-class marathon runner, requested a flexible work hours arrangement in order to accommodate his morning and afternoon training schedule. Juan is registered to run the London, England, marathon. Just prior to Juan's request, Susan Woolf asked for, and was granted, an extended maternity leave to begin after the birth of her first child in December. If these unexpected requests were not enough, Blancero has heard comments from senior account managers about how some employees seem to get "special privileges," while the managers work long hours that often require them to meet around-the-clock customer demands. Janis has adequate reason to believe that there is hidden tension over the company's flexible work hours program. Currently, True North has no formal policy on flexible schedules. Furthermore, with the company's growth in business combined with the increasing workload of some customers, Blancero realizes managers and the constant service demands of some customers, Blancero realizes that she simply cannot grant all the time-off requests of her employees.

Source: Adapted from Alden M. Hayashi, "Mommy-Track Backlash," *Harvard Business Review* 79, no. 3 (March 2001): 33–42.

QUESTIONS

1. Do managers like Janis Blancero face a more complicated decision when evaluating the personal requests of employees versus evaluating employees' individual work performance?

2. a. Should True North establish a policy for granting flexible work schedules? Explain.

   b. If you answered yes, what might that policy contain?

3. If you were Janis Blancero, how would you resolve this dilemma? Explain.

CAREER COUNSEL

Design your own benefits package by completing the Flexible Benefits exercise on the *Managing Human Resources* website (http://www.belcourt6e.nelson.com).

NOTES AND REFERENCES

1. J. Taggart, "Putting Flex Benefits through Their Paces," *Canadian HR Reporter* 15, no. 21 (December 2, 2002): G3.
2. The Canadian Payroll Association, "Compensation Planning 2003," *Dialogue* [online magazine] http://www.payroll.ca. November/December 2002: 14–17.
3. S. Felix, "Techno Benefits," *Benefits Canada* 24, no. 1 (January 2000): 27–34.
4. Jan Everett, "Internet Security," *Employee Benefits Journal* 23, no. 3 (September 1998): 14–18. See also Alan R. Parham, "Developing a Technology Policy," *Employee Benefits Journal* 23, no. 3 (September 1998): 3–5.
5. http://www.benefitscanada.ca, retrieved June 11, 2009.
6. Jeff Holloway, "Recruiting On Principle: Selling A Company's Values," *Canadian HR Reporter*, November 22, 2004, 7; Jacqueline Taggart and Joy Sloane, "If the Pitch Is Total Rewards, Flex Benefits Are the Home Run," *Canadian HR Reporter*, February 23, 2004 G3.
7. Dian Cohen, "Parallel Goals," *Benefits Canada* 22, no. 6 (June 1998): 98.
8. Todd Humber, "RBC Organizes Pay, Benefits Training, Work Environment into a Single Package," *Canadian HR Reporter*, February 23, 2004, G1.

9. Ronald W. Perry and N. Joseph Cayer, "Cafeteria Style Health Plans in Municipal Govt.," *Public Personnel Management* 28, no. 1 (Spring 1999): 107–117; Jon J. Meyer, "The Future of Flexible Benefit Plans," *Employee Benefits Journal* 25, no. 2 (June 2000): 3–7. See also Carolyn Hirschman, "Kinder, Simpler Cafeteria Rule," *HR Magazine* 46, no. 1 (January 2001): 74–79.

10. L. Byron and R. Dawson, "Flex Benefits Are More Popular Than Ever with Employers and Employees," *Benefits, Benefits Canada,* http://www.benefitscanada.com/magazine/article.jsp?content= 20030624_134506_4312, April 2003.

11. "Communication Break Down: Employers Must Properly Inform Employees of Their Entitlement Benefits or Face Expensive and Time Consuming Court Challenges," *Benefits Canada* 21, no. 1 (January 1997): 27, 29.

12. M. Paterson, "Making a Statement: Are You Ready to Turn an Obligation into an Opportunity?" *Benefits Canada,* February 1995: 19–21.

13. "Great Communication Challenge," *Benefits Canada* 21, no. 9 (October 1997): 25–26.

14. T. Belford "The 24/7 Personnel office," *The Globe and Mail,* November 20, 2007, B13.

15. J. MacBride-King, *Managing Corporate Health Care,* Conference Board of Canada, October 1995, Report 158–195: 10.

16. David Brown, "Employees Willing to Help Defray the Costs of Benefits," *Canadian HR Reporter,* June 14, 204, 1; Uyen Vu, "HR Responds to Cost Crunch with Workforce Cuts," *Canadian HR Reporter,* May 31, 2004, 1; Greg Keenan, "Stelco cuts benefits for salaried workers," *The Globe and Mail,* May 15, 2006, B3; Gloria Gonzalez, "Canadian Firms Seek to Stem Rising Costs of Benefits," *Business Insurance,* March 22, 2004, 3; Jacqueline Taggart, "No Easy Answer for Cost Conundrum," *Canadian HR Reporter,* April 19, 2004, 11.

17. Taggart, "No Easy Answer for Cost Conundrum," 11.

18. "FTNT Employment Insurance: More Than a New Name," *Work Life Report* 10, no. 2 (1996): 1–4, 5.

19. Wallance Immen, "Working life blues: Can't shake the job," *The Globe and Mail,* May 17, 2006, C1.

20. "Deutsche Bank traders told to take time off," *The Globe and Mail,* March 23, 2008, B1.

21. Richard Long, *Strategic Compensation in Canada,* 3rd ed. (Toronto: Nelson Thomson, 2006).

22. Dorothy Lipovenko, "Job losses force early retirement," *The Globe and Mail,* September 8, 1995, A8.

23. Doug Burn, "Wheel of Fortune: How Much Should an Organization Gamble on Early Retirement Planning?" *Human Resources Professional* 11, no. 4 (May 1994): 13–17.

24. David McCabe, "Retiring the Side: Approaches to Retirement Planning Range From the Conservative to the Revolutionary," *Human Resources Professional* 11, no. 4 (May 1994).

25. Catherine D. Fyock, "Crafting Secure Retirements," *HR Magazine* 35, no. 7 (July 1990): 30–33.

26. Ron Robins, "Moral Investing," *HR Professional,* April/May 2005: 16.

27. Larry Light, "The Power of the Pension Funds," *BusinessWeek,* November 6, 1999: 154–158.

28. S. Dobson" Benefits go beyond financials" *Canadian HR Reporter* 21, no. 15 (2008): 15, 20.

29. "Employers Help Workers Achieve Balance in Life," *HRfocus* 75, no. 11 (November 1998): S3.

30. T. Humber, "Stress Attack," *Canadian HR Reporter* 16, no. 3 (February 10, 2003): G1, G10.

31. A. Tomlinson, "Trickle Down Effect of Retiring Boomers," *Canadian HR Reporter* 15, no. 11 (June 3, 2002): 1, 12.

32. G. Joseph, "Embracing Elder Care" *Benefits Canada* 2, no. 4, 2008: 57.

33. Betty Healey, "Support for Employees Providing Support," *Canadian HR Reporter,* September 13, 2004: 17; Uyen Vu, "At Great-West There's Elder Care Help on Staff," *Canadian HR Reporter,* September 13, 2004: 18.

34. Sonya Felix, "Running on Empty," *Benefits Canada* 21, no. 16 (June 1997): 109–114.

35. Elaine Davis and Mary Kay Krouse, "Elder Care Obligations Challenge the Next Generation," *HR Magazine* 41, no. 7 (July 1996): 98–103; Rodney K. Platt, "The Aging Workforce," *Workspan* 44, no. 1 (January 2001): 26.

36. Sue Shellenbarger, "Firms Try Harder, but Often Fail, to Help Workers Cope with Elder-Care Problems," *Wall Street Journal*, June 23, 1993: B1.

CHAPTER

12

Safety
and Health

After studying this chapter, you should be able to

[OUTCOME] 1 Summarize the common elements of federal and provincial occupational health and safety legislation.

[OUTCOME] 2 Describe what management can do to create a safe work environment.

[OUTCOME] 3 Identify the measures that should be taken to control and eliminate health hazards.

[OUTCOME] 4 Describe the organizational services and programs for building better health.

[OUTCOME] 5 Explain the role of employee assistance programs in HRM.

[OUTCOME] 6 Indicate methods for coping with stress.

Occupational safety and health accidents are both numerous and costly to employers. To prevent losses such as these, employers are concerned with providing working conditions—in all areas of employment—that provide for the safety and health of their employees.

While the laws safeguarding employees' physical and emotional well-being are certainly an incentive, many employers are motivated to provide desirable working conditions by virtue of their sensitivity to human needs and rights. The more cost-oriented employer recognizes the importance of avoiding accidents and illnesses wherever possible. One in every 21 workers can expect to be injured at work each year.[1] Costs associated with sick leave, disability payments, replacement of employees who are injured or killed, and workers' compensation far exceed the costs of maintaining a safety and health program. A recent study found that employers saved $1.95 and $3.75 for each $1 invested in workplace safety.[2] Accidents and illnesses attributable to the workplace may also have pronounced effects on employee morale and on the goodwill that the organization enjoys in the community and in the business world.

Managers at all levels are expected to know and enforce safety and health standards throughout the organization. They must ensure a work environment that protects employees from physical hazards, unhealthy conditions, and unsafe acts of other personnel. Through effective safety and health programs, the physical and emotional well-being of employees may be preserved and even enhanced.

After discussing the legal requirements for safety and health, the rest of the chapter will focus on the creation of a safe and healthy work environment and on the management of stress.

SAFETY AND HEALTH: IT'S THE LAW

Consider these facts:

- According to the Association of Workers' Compensation Boards of Canada statistics, in 2002 there were 900 workplace-related deaths, which means about four Canadian workers die every working day.
- There are over 1 million work-related injuries each year.
- There are 340,000 injuries serious enough to cause the worker to miss at least one day of work.
- Over $12 billion is paid out to injured workers and their families, annually.[3]

The burden on Canada's commerce as a result of lost productivity and wages, medical expenses, and disability compensation is staggering. And there is no way to calculate the human suffering involved.

Occupational health and safety is regulated by the federal, provincial, and territorial governments. Statutes and standards vary slightly from jurisdiction to jurisdiction, although attempts have been made to harmonize the various acts and regulations. An occupational injury is any cut, fracture, sprain, or amputation resulting from a workplace accident. The worker's involvement in the accident can be direct, or the worker can simply be near enough to the accident to be injured as a result of it. An occupational illness is any condition or disorder (other than one resulting from an occupational injury) caused by the work environment. An occupational illness can be acute or chronic; it can result from inhaling, absorbing, ingesting, or directly contacting an illness-causing agent. Those working in the field agree that occupational illnesses are underreported because few diseases are caused solely by work-related factors, and cause and effect can be difficult to determine. Consider, for example, the case of a mine worker who has contracted a lung disease, but who also smokes heavily.

[OUTCOME 1]

occupational injury

Any cut, fracture, sprain, or amputation resulting from a workplace accident or from an exposure involving an accident in the work environment.

occupational illness

Any abnormal condition or disorder, other than one resulting from an occupational injury, caused by exposure to environmental factors associated with employment.

ACTS AND REGULATIONS

All HR managers should become familiar with the occupational health and safety laws that apply to their organization. The various acts and government departments that enforce the legislation are listed in Figure 12.1.

DUTIES AND RESPONSIBILITIES

The fundamental duty of every employer is to take every reasonable precaution to ensure employee safety. The motivating forces behind workplace legislation were effectively articulated in the landmark case *Cory v. Wholesale Travel Group*.

Regulatory legislation is essential to the operation of our complex industrial society; it plays a legitimate and vital role in protecting those who are most vulnerable and least able to protect themselves. The extent and importance of that role has increased continuously since the onset of the Industrial Revolution.

FIGURE 12.1

Occupational Health and Safety in Canada

Jurisdiction	Legislation	Enforcement	Source
Canada	Canada Labour Code	Ministry of Labour	http://www.hrsdc.gc.ca/eng/lp/lo/ohs/publications/overview.shtml
Alberta	Occupational Health and Safety Act	Occupational Health and Safety Council (OHSC)	http://employment.alberta.ca/documents/WHS/WHS-LEG_ohsc_2009.pdf
British Columbia	Workers Compensation Act	WorkSafeBC	http://www.worksafebc.com/
Manitoba	The Workplace Safety and Health Act	Workplace Safety and Health Division (WSHD)	http://safemanitoba.com/about.aspx
New Brunswick	Occupational Health and Safety Act	WorkSafeNB	http://www.worksafenb.ca/emp12_e.asp
Newfoundland and Labrador	Occupational Health and Safety Act	Occupational Health and Safety Branch	http://www.gs.gov.nl.ca/ohs/about.stm
Nova Scotia	Occupational Health and Safety Act	The Department of Labour and Workforce Development	http://www.gov.ns.ca/lwd/
Ontario	Occupational Health and Safety Act	Ministry of Labour	http://www.labour.gov.on.ca/english/hs/
Prince Edward Island	Occupational Health and Safety Act	Workers Compensation Board of PEI	http://www.wcb.pe.ca/index.php3?number=58768&lang=E
Quebec	An Act Respecting Occupational Health and Safety (AOHS)	Commission de la santé et de la sécurité du travail (CSST)	http://www.csst.qc.ca/Portail/en/lois_politiques/index_loi.htm
Saskatchewan	Occupational Health and Safety Act	Saskatchewan Labour	http://www.labour.gov.sk.ca/overview-hs
Northwest Territories	Safety Act	Workers' Safety and Compensation Commission	http://www.wcb.nt.ca/safety_and_training/occupational_safety_health.html
Nunavut	Safety Act	For information only; not an official act	http://www.wcb.nt.ca/your_wcb/Legislation/General_Safety.pdf

Before effective workplace legislation was enacted, labourers—including children—worked unconscionably long hours in dangerous and unhealthy surroundings that evoke visions of Dante's inferno. It was regulatory legislation with its enforcement provisions which brought to an end the shameful situations that existed in mines, factories and workshops in the 19th century. The differential treatment of regulatory offences is justified by their common goal of protecting the vulnerable.

Duties of Employers

Besides providing a hazard-free workplace and complying with the applicable statutes and regulations, employers must inform their employees about safety and health requirements. Employers are also required to keep certain records, to compile an annual summary of work-related injuries and illnesses, and to ensure that supervisors are familiar with the work and its associated hazards, (the supervisor, in turn, must ensure that workers are aware of those hazards). An organization with many employees may have a full-time health and safety officer.

In all jurisdictions, employers are required to report to the Workers' Compensation Board all accidents that cause injuries and diseases. Accidents resulting in death or critical injuries must be reported immediately; the accident must then be investigated and a written report submitted. In addition, employers must provide safety training and be prepared to discipline employees for failing to comply with safety rules. Employers are increasingly being required to prove due diligence. This includes establishing a comprehensive occupational health and safety management system; providing competent supervision, training, and instruction; and taking every reasonable precaution in the workplace for the health and safety of workers. Highlights in HRM 12.1 provides a list of health and safety procedures for new employees.

Duties of Workers

Employees are required to comply with all applicable acts and regulations, to report hazardous conditions or defective equipment, and to follow all employer safety and health rules and regulations, including those prescribing the use of protective equipment.

Workers have many rights that pertain to requesting and receiving information about safety and health conditions. They also have the right to refuse unsafe work without fear of reprisal. (Some professionals such as police, firefighters, teachers, and health care workers have only a limited right of refusal, the logic being that their work is inherently dangerous.) An employee who suspects that work conditions are hazardous can report this concern to his or her supervisor; this will trigger an investigation by the supervisor and a worker representative.

A work refusal investigation can result in either the employee's return to work or his or her continued refusal. In the latter case, the appropriate ministry is notified and an investigator is dispatched to the job site to provide a written decision. If a replacement worker is used, he or she must be notified of the previous employee's refusal to work.

Duties of Supervisors

A supervisor is generally defined as a person (with or without a title) who has charge of a workplace and authority over a worker. Occupational health and safety acts require supervisors to do the following: advise employees of potential workplace hazards; ensure that workers use or wear safety equipment, devices, or clothing; provide written instructions where applicable; and take every reasonable precaution to guarantee the safety of workers.

Using the Internet

For a description of the best features of a health and safety program, go to the website for the Canadian Centre for Occupational Health and Safety and click on Basic OH&S Program Elements:

http://www.ccohs.ca/
oshanswers/hsprograms/
basic.html

Using the Internet

The Industrial Accident Prevention Association (IAPA) offers diploma programs for workers, supervisors, and health and safety representatives:

http://www.iapa.ca

Highlights in **HRM 12.1**

Health and Safety Checklist for New Employees

By the end of a new employee's first week, an employee should be familiar with the following health and safety procedures and issues:

1. Fire Safety
   - Identify the evacuation alarm sound.
   - Show his or her evacuation route and assembly point, and any alternative route.
   - Show where the extinguishers are in the work area.
   - Explain when water and other extinguishers can and cannot be used.
   - Show how to use extinguishers and what to do after use.
   - Show where the alarm point is and how to sound it.
   - Explain use of elevators and lifts in fire situation.

2. Housekeeping and Access
   - Explain reasons for maintaining clear access.
   - Explain hazards caused by obstructing gangways.

3. Smoking
   - State where smoking is and is not allowed, and give reasons.

4. Accidents and Abnormal Occurrence
   - Explain reporting procedure and reasons.
   - Show the way to casualty (or first aid).
   - Explain action in case of serious injury to oneself or another.
   - Give two examples of abnormal occurrence.
   - Include any hazard special to the job.

5. Lifting (manual handling)
   - Demonstrate correct manual handling methods.

6. Uniforms, Overalls
   - Explain issue, care, and cleaning arrangements.

7. Personal Clothing—Contamination
   - Explain action in the event of clothing being contaminated (give two examples).

8. Protective Equipment
   - Show how to wear equipment issued in department, and explain need for it.

9. Personal Hygiene
   - Explain reasons for attention to personal hygiene.

10. Absence
    - Know what to do in the event of sickness or other absence.

11. Electrics
    - Demonstrate checks required before using electrical equipment.
    - Explain action if faults found.

12. Material Hazards
    - Identify any dangerous materials or objects, and explain how to handle them.
    - Supply workplace hazardous information sheets.

13. Chemical Hazards
    - Demonstrate safe handling methods for corrosive liquids, compressed gases, flammable solvents, other classes (appropriate to immediate workplace) (WHMIS).

14. Spillages
    - Explain what must be done in the event of spillages.

15. Disposal
    - Show waste/rubbish disposal system and explain hazards.

16. Machine Equipment Hazards
    - Explain correct handling of equipment.
    - Explain lock out/tagging procedures (appropriate to immediate workplace).

17. Health and Safety Management
    - Explain the role of the Occupational Health Department.
    - Identify the health and safety representatives and explain their roles.
    - Explain the correct procedure if a hazard or problem is identified.
    - Explain the functions of the safety committee.
    - Describe the responsibilities of employees in health and safety.

- Give two examples of risk of cross-infection.
- Explain why it is necessary to report contact with notifiable diseases, and give examples of diseases.
- Know to consult Occupational Health staff.

Source: Adapted from B. Pomfret, "Sound Employee Orientation Program Boosts Productivity and Safety," *Canadian HR Reporter* (January 25, 1999): 17.

Duties of Joint Health and Safety Committees

Most jurisdictions require that health and safety committees be set up, with both union and management representation. The point of these joint committees is to establish a nonadversarial climate for creating safe and healthy workplaces. In Ontario, at least one management rep and one worker rep must be certified. The certification program provides training in the following subjects: safety laws, sanitation, general safety, rights and duties, and indoor air quality.

Read about how a world leader in H&S structures the committees to produce award-winning safety environments (see Highlights in HRM 12.2).

Highlights in HRM 12.2

A World Leader in H&S

When Novopharm merged with Teva Pharmaceuticals to become the world's largest producer of generic drugs, the company decided to pursue an aggressive growth strategy. Part of the strategy as the leader in the manufacture of pharmaceuticals was also to become the leader in environmental health and safety. The objectives were to develop a safety culture and a safety management system, to improve occupational safety compliance with internal standards, reduce the number of accidents, and improve Novopharm's management rating. According to Roberto Ocon, the corporate director of environmental health, safety, and security at Novopharm, a series of high-level initiatives, processes, and procedures were developed in order to achieve this goal.

The Teva Global Group hired a new vice president of global environmental health and safety to assess the current state of programs and support operations and EHS personnel.

At Novopharm, the environment health and safety department was transitioned into the operations department. This move ensured that environmental health and safety would become a part of the culture at Novopharm and also part of the day-to-day operations.

The environment health and safety (EHS) manager position was elevated to a director position reporting directly to the executive VP of operations. The new position sits on the senior operations leadership management team. This increased the visibility of the environmental health and safety resources.

H&S coordinators became managers positioned directly at the sites of each of the three manufacturing facilities in Ontario. In addition to having health and

safety experience, these managers were also specialized in other disciplines (industrial hygiene, ergonomics, training).

The EHS managers within each of the site locations reported in a dotted line to the site operations directors and directly to the EHS director. Being on-site and "walking" the floor on a regular basis allowed these new EHS managers to become an integral part of daily operations and encouraged an open dialogue with employees who were able to openly express their concerns regarding health and safety.

As a further measure to support health and safety, the occupational health nurse visited each site at least one day each week, to address and promote employee wellness programs.

Moving forward, three hierarchal levels of environmental health and safety committees were established to promote this culture throughout Novopharm. At the highest level, an environmental health and safety council was established as a champion of new initiatives and to set strategy. Meeting two to three times per year, this council includes all senior management, the president and CEO of Novopharm, the VP of human resources, the executive VP of commercial development, the global VP of EHS and the executive VP of operations. The next level is the steering committee; Ocon chairs quarterly meetings with the heads of operations, the labour relations director, corporate director of engineering, technical services director and the director of quality assurance. At this level, a work plan is established and targets are set. Furthermore, to ingrain the new initiatives across Novopharm, health and safety targets are included in each director's project management plan

continued

where they are accountable for their performance in attaining health and safety mandates. At the third level, the employee committee meets monthly and explores methods in which to execute the directives. At this level, employees, the site manager, the site director, and the health and safety committee explore creative ideas and behaviour-based changes to promote health and safety.

As a result of implementing this new infrastructure into the culture of Novopharm, health and safety initiatives in its Ontario locations reached new levels of excellence. In a period of two years, Novopharm went from a reactive culture with poor involvement in safety activities to a very proactive culture with employee involvement in safety activities at all levels of the organization a 40 percent compliance improvement; a 90 percent reduction in accidents, which was the best in Teva in 2005; as well as one of the best accident rates in the industry. The company also went from an average risk management rating to superior.

This won its sites the Health and Safety Award of Excellence for Teva worldwide as well as a prestigious

Superior Risk Management Award. The award was based on performance from the work plan objectives and for the reduction in workplace accidents. An outside risk management group that rates the facilities' programs and compliance with regulations grants this last award through a yearly audit. Where health and safety has often been seen as an outside "policing" group, it has now become an integral part of operations and culture at Novopharm. Furthermore, instead of HR being used as a reference group in this process, it is now a contributing partner to the health and safety of the organization's employees. To demonstrate the level of commitment across the organization to its new programs, when a site director posted his commitment to health and safety on a large white board, every employee signed it. When the global CEO visited Canada, he signed it too and in doing so, demonstrated the level of commitment, buy-in, and dedication to the health and safety of employees at Novopharm.

Source: Personal interview with Robert Ocon.

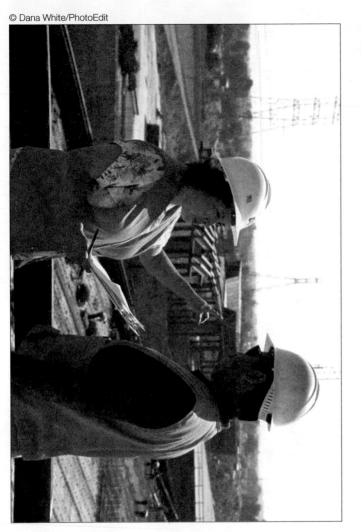

© Dana White/PhotoEdit

Supervisors are required to advise employees of potential workplace hazards and ensure that workers wear safety equipment.

PENALTIES FOR EMPLOYER NONCOMPLIANCE

The penalties for violating occupational health and safety regulations vary across provinces and territories. Most health and safety acts provide for fines up to $500,000, and offenders can be sent to jail. Hershey Canada was fined $50,000 for a violation that resulted in a serious hand injury to an employee.[4] Bill C-45, also known as the corporate killing law, makes it possible for criminal charges to be brought against coworkers, supervisors, and executives when a worker is killed or injured on the job.

WORKERS' COMPENSATION

Under workers' compensation, injured workers can receive benefits in the form of a cash payout (if the disability is permanent) or wage loss payments (if the worker can no longer earn the same amount of money). Unlimited medical aid is also provided, along with vocational rehabilitation, which includes physical, social, and psychological services. The goal is to return the employee to his or her job (or some modification thereof) as soon as possible. Sun Life Assurance Company of Canada has a return-to-work awards program, which gives premium credits to employers that allow injured workers to change jobs or duties to enable these employees to return to work. A person who has been off work for six months has a 50 percent chance of returning; after 12 months, a 20 percent chance; and after two years, a 10 percent chance. Weyerhaeuser Co. Ltd of Vancouver's coordinated back-to-work program resulted in a 47 percent reduction in duration of claims and a 39 percent reduction in the costs of the claims.

Compensation has become a complex issue. The definitions of accidents and injuries have recently been expanded to include industrial diseases and stress. An **industrial disease** is a disease resulting from exposure to a substance relating to a particular process, trade, or occupation in industry.

Equally problematic is compensation for stress, which is discussed in more detail later in the chapter. Stress-related disabilities are usually divided into three groups: physical injuries leading to mental disabilities (e.g., clinical depression after a serious accident); mental stress resulting in a physical disability (ulcers or migraines); and mental stress resulting in a mental condition (anxiety over work-load or downsizing leading to depression). Most claims, it should be pointed out, result from accidents or injuries.

The emphasis in workers' compensation has been shifting away from simply making assessments and payments toward creating safety-conscious environments where there will be fewer work-related accidents, disabilities, and diseases. In some industrial sectors, employers are working together to establish rules and training programs to further the cause of accident prevention.

CREATING A SAFE WORK ENVIRONMENT

We have seen that employers are required by law to provide safe working conditions for their employees. To achieve this objective, the majority of employers have a formal safety program. Typically, the HR department or the industrial relations department is responsible for the safety program. While the success of a safety program depends largely on managers and supervisors of operating departments, the HR department typically coordinates the safety communication and training programs, maintains safety records required by legislation, and works closely with managers and supervisors in a cooperative effort to make the program a success. As Dennis Locking, the HR manager for Calgary-based Volker Stevin, a growing road building company with more than 1,000 employees, states, "Safety is all about the way that you run your business. Wherever you see poor safety, there is always a poorly run company. If a company has a poor attitude towards safety, then it makes us wonder if that attitude is indicative of other aspects of their business."[5]

Organizations with formal safety programs generally have an employee–management safety committee that includes representatives from management, each department or manufacturing/service unit, and employee representatives. Committees are typically involved in investigating accidents and helping to publicize the importance of safety rules and their enforcement.

Using the Internet

The National Institute of Disability Management and Research was established by business, labour, government, insurance, and rehabilitation representatives to promote best practices in disability management:

http://www.nidmar.ca

industrial disease

A disease resulting from exposure to a substance relating to a particular process, trade, or occupation in industry

Using the Internet

Find more information at the Workplace Safety and Insurance Board website:

http://www.wsib.ca

[OUTCOME]

PROMOTING SAFETY AWARENESS

Probably the most important role of a safety awareness program is motivating managers, supervisors, and subordinates to be champions of safety considerations. In one study conducted, "survey results showed a direct correlation between an increase in management's commitment to safety in the workplace and a decrease in accidents."[6]

If managers and supervisors fail to demonstrate awareness, their subordinates can hardly be expected to do so. Unfortunately, many managers and supervisors wear their "safety hats" far less often than their "production, quality control, and methods of improvement hats."

Most organizations have a safety awareness program that entails the use of several different media. Safety lectures, commercially produced films, specially developed videocassettes, and other media such as pamphlets are useful for teaching and motivating employees to follow safe work procedures.

The Key Role of the Supervisor

One of a supervisor's major responsibilities is to communicate to an employee the need to work safely. Beginning with new-employee orientation, safety should be emphasized continually. Proper work procedures, the use of protective clothing and devices, and potential hazards should be explained thoroughly. Furthermore, employees' understanding of all these considerations should be verified during training sessions, and employees should be encouraged to take some initiative in maintaining a concern for safety. Since training by itself does not ensure continual adherence to safe work practices, supervisors must observe employees at work and reinforce safe practices. Where unsafe acts are detected, supervisors should take immediate action to find the cause. Supervisors should also foster a team spirit of safety among the work group.

Proactive Safety Training Program

Safety training is not only good business; in certain occupational areas safety and health training is legally required. When training is mandated, employers must keep accurate records of all employee education. Violations can incur criminal penalties.

In companies that voluntarily undertake safety and health training, one study found the most frequent topics to be (1) first aid, (2) defensive driving, (3) accident prevention techniques, (4) hazardous materials, and (5) emergency procedures.[7] Most programs emphasize the use of emergency first-aid equipment and personal safety equipment.

HR professionals, and safety directors in particular, advocate employee involvement when designing and implementing safety programs.[8] Employees can offer valuable ideas regarding specific safety and health topics to cover, instructional methods, and proper teaching techniques.[9] Furthermore, acceptance for safety training is heightened when employees feel a sense of ownership in the instructional program.

Information Technology and Safety Awareness and Training

Several reasons are advanced for the use of the Internet and information technology in safety and health training. First, enhanced delivery modes facilitate the development of both managers and employees.[10] Videos, PowerPoint presentations, and interactive CD-ROM training are ideal methods for standardized safety, environmental, and health instruction. Second, information technology allows organizations to customize their safety and health training needs.[11] At Stanley Works, the company's Internet is the number one tool for reducing health and safety problems. According to Kevin Nelson, employee health and safety director, "The Internet functions as the organization's SWAT team to develop and implement timely and

© Kathy Ferguson-Johnson/PhotoEdit

Safety begins with proper instruction, as these firefighters demonstrate in this training exercise.

efficient health and safety programs." Third, information technology is ideally suited for regulatory instruction.[12]

ENFORCING SAFETY RULES

Specific rules and regulations concerning safety are communicated through supervisors, bulletin board notices, employee handbooks, and signs attached to equipment. Safety rules are also emphasized in regular safety meetings, at new-employee orientations, and in manuals of standard operating procedures.[13]

Penalties for violation of safety rules are usually stated in the employee handbook. In a large percentage of organizations, the penalties imposed on violators are the same as those for violations of other rules. They include an oral or written warning for the first violation, suspension for repeated violations, and, as a last resort, dismissal. However, for serious violations—such as smoking around volatile substances—even the first offence may be cause for termination.

While discipline may force employees to work safely, safety managers understand that the most effective enforcement of safety rules occurs when employees willingly obey and "champion" safety rules and procedures. This can be achieved when management actively encourages employees to participate in all aspects of the organization's safety program. For example, opportunities for employee involvement include (1) jointly setting safety standards with management, (2) participation in safety training, (3) involvement in designing and implementing special safety training programs, (4) involvement in establishing safety incentives and rewards, and (5) inclusion in accident investigations. There are many workable incentives—for example, gift certificates, cash awards, trips, dinners, and gifts such as clothing or jewellery. Economy Carriers, a transportation company based in Edmonton, offers an employee points program. It audits 18 operational areas for safety; on the basis of that audit, employees accumulate safety points, which they can use for purchases. Two researchers looked at 24 studies where positive reinforcement and feedback were used to enhance safe behaviour. In all the studies, incentives were found to improve safety conditions or reduce accidents.[14]

The Procter & Gamble plant in Belleville, Ontario, won an award for its novel approach to incentives. The plant manager calculated that P&G would receive a refund from workers' compensation of about $200,000 a year if injuries were eliminated at the plant. He then set up a plan that would allow this refund to go to the local hospital if the target of zero injuries was achieved. With this community-based incentive, P&G employees met the target and the hospital received a large donation.[15]

Figure 12.2 provides the steps recommended for launching a successful safety incentive program.

FIGURE 12.2

Steps in a Successful Safety Incentive Program

- Obtain the full support and involvement of management by providing cost benefits.
- Review current injury and health statistics to determine where change is needed.
- Decide on a program of action and set an appropriate budget.
- Select a realistic safety goal such as reducing accidents by a set percentage, improving safety suggestions, or achieving a length of time without a lost-time injury. Communicate your objectives to everyone involved.
- Select incentive rewards on the basis of their attractiveness to employees and their fit with your budget.
- Develop a program that is both interesting and fun. Use kickoff meetings, posters, banners, quizzes, and/or games to spark employee interest. Give all employees a chance to win.
- Communicate continually the success of your program. Provide specific examples of positive changes in behaviour.
- Reward safety gains immediately. Providing rewards shortly after improvements reinforces changed behaviour and encourages additional support for the safety program.

INVESTIGATING AND RECORDING ACCIDENTS

Every accident, even those considered minor, should be investigated by the supervisor and a member of the safety committee. Such an investigation may determine the factors contributing to the accident and reveal what corrections are needed to prevent it from happening again. Correction may require rearranging workstations, installing safety guards or controls, or, more often, giving employees additional safety training and reassessing their motivation for safety.[16]

Employers are required to keep certain records and to compile and post annual summaries of work-related injuries and illnesses. From these records, organizations can compute their incidence rates (i.e., the number of injuries and illnesses per 100 full-time employees during a given year). The standard equation for computing the incidence rate is shown below; 200,000 constitutes the base for 100 full-time workers who work 40 hours a week, 50 weeks a year:

$$\text{Incidence rate} = \frac{\text{Number of injuries and illnesses} \times 200{,}000}{\text{Total hours worked by all employees during period covered}}$$

The same formula can be used to compute incidence rates for (1) the number of workdays lost because of injuries and illnesses, (2) the number of nonfatal injuries and illnesses without lost workdays, and (3) cases involving only injuries or only illnesses.

Incidence rates are useful for making comparisons between work groups, between departments, and between similar units in the same organization. They also provide a basis for making comparisons with other organizations doing similar work. The occupational health and safety departments in each province and Human Resources and Social Development Canada compile data that employers can use to measure their safety records against those of other organizations. As noted in Ethics in HRM, organizations that report and investigate their own accidents often face more inspections, higher insurance premiums, and possible lawsuits. Reality Check provides an overview of H&S issues in Canada today.

Ethics in **HRM**

Bury the Record

A supervisor was instructing a group of new recruits in the cleaning of metal parts in an assembly plant. She was attempting to demonstrate the cleaning technique to two employees at one workstation, while at another workstation another new employee was trying to clean the parts himself. The cleaning liquid was highly toxic. The employee felt restricted by his safety gloves and so removed them. His eyes started to water, and instinctively he rubbed them with his solution-soaked hands. The pain was overwhelming, and no water was immediately available with which he could rinse his eyes. The employee suffered some temporary vision loss.

Who is to blame? The worker who started to clean without receiving full instructions and without using the issued gloves? The supervisor who could have forbidden the worker to start work until she explained the safety aspects? Or the company that failed to post warning signs about the hazardous nature of the cleaning solvent and did not have an eye-washing facility available?

Because workplace accidents increase workers' compensation premiums and the number of inspections, the company had an interest in not reporting the accident. Furthermore, because the company had instituted

continued

a reward program that provided incentives to employees for accident-free days, even the employees did not want to report the accident. Thus, the supervisor and the employees agreed to "bury the record." According to one survey of Canadian workers, 30 percent are afraid to report accidents, 29 percent know someone who reports false claims, and 27 percent know that their employers are not reporting accidents. This is illegal. Another company was fined $600,000 for misleading the Workplace Health and Safety Insurance Board after it deliberately chose not to report that injured workers had missed time at work. In a highly publicized case in 2003, a young worker fell five storeys to his death, landing just one metre from the supervisor, who was his uncle. The first thing the supervisor did was call 911, and he was overheard telling workers, "Workers' comp will be here right away, so you get that railing up right now."

Source: Adapted from Ipsos Reid, July 2003, as described in *Canadian HR Reporter* (April 19, 2004): 17.

Reality CHECK

CN Centre for Occupational Health and Safety

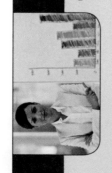

The CN Centre for Occupational Health and Safety is a research institute founded at Saint Mary's University in Halifax, Nova Scotia, through an endowment from CN. According to Kevin Kelloway, the director of the CN Centre, the mandate of the centre is (1) to coordinate and conduct research in occupational health and safety; (2) to build capacity for occupational health and safety research in Nova Scotia; and (3) to provide mechanisms for training and education in occupational health and safety.

Professor Kelloway, as co-author of the book *Managing Occupational Health and Safety*, says, "The hottest issue in safety is the role of human resources. We have taken engineering approaches to their limit. It is no longer the case that if we provide protective wear or put guards on equipment, that workers are safe. Engineering approaches are not sufficient. Now we are looking at these issues from a people perspective: How do we get people to work safely? What does it mean to work safely?

"There is another shift in thinking about safety and it is the recognition that compliance with legislation and standards is also not enough. We know that the old motto 'If you are compliant with the law, you have a safe workplace' is not true. Let me give you an example. WHMIS training is compulsory across Canada and all employers give WHMIS training to their employees. These organizations are fully compliant. But does that mean that the employees remember what they have learned? Does this guarantee that they pay attention to all the symbols? An employer can comply and still have unsafe work practices.

"The focus now is on safety initiative. How do we keep people and companies focused on safety? There is a role for leaders. One thing we found in our research is that active leadership which is continually promoting safety is necessary. When leaders stop talking—the minute they stop promoting safety—safety declines. There is a role for HR, to create a culture in which employees feel secure talking about safety, and mechanisms for channelling safety concerns exist. For example, do employees raise safety issues about potential safety hazards? If they raise concerns, are they treated as complainers? Is there a process to identify safety hazards? Part of the role of HR is to create that environment and provide those channels.

"It is always difficult to motivate safety, because it is the absence of something (an accident, an injury). From employees' perspective, they want to get their work done, and the organization encourages this. Of course, they want to work safely, but to get work done, shortcuts are more efficient. A good analogy is that we all want to drive safely but many of us will take risks to get home quickly. Rationally, driving safely is the most important goal, but behaviourally people drive as if saving 15 seconds was important."

Source: Personal interview with Kevin Kelloway.

CONTROLLING AND ELIMINATING HEALTH HAZARDS

From the title alone, occupational health and safety legislation was clearly designed to protect the health, as well as the safety, of employees. Because of the dramatic impact of workplace accidents, however, managers and employees alike may pay more attention to these kinds of immediate safety concerns than to job conditions that are dangerous to their health. It is essential, therefore, that health hazards be identified and controlled.[17] Furthermore, pressure from the federal government and unions, as well as increased public concern, has given employers a definite incentive to provide the safest and healthiest work environment possible.

HEALTH HAZARDS AND ISSUES

At one time health hazards were associated primarily with jobs found in industrial processing operations. In recent years, however, hazards in jobs outside the plant, such as in offices, health care facilities, and airports, have been recognized and preventive methods adopted. Substituting materials, altering processes, enclosing or isolating a process, issuing protective equipment, and improving ventilation are some of the common preventions. This section will review several of the more important health concerns to employees and employers.

Chemical Hazards

When a boiler maker at Teck Cominco Ltd., a smelter plant in Trail, British Columbia, started to experience symptoms that resembled motion sickness, he never associated it with exposure to poisonous thallium metal. Like many workers, he had limited awareness of the chemicals in the workplace. And it is not only workers in industrial settings who are exposed to chemicals. Many teachers work in prefabricated temporary classrooms, which may contain mouldy material. It is estimated that more than 65,000 different chemicals are currently in use with which humans may come into contact. Many of these chemicals are harmful, lurking for years in the body with no outward symptoms until the disease they cause is well established. Increasingly, employees are complaining of physiological reactions to low-level chemical exposures in the environment, such as headaches, dry nasal passages, and nausea. These complaints have several labels, such as total allergy symptom, 20th-century disease, and multiple chemical sensitivity. (For a full discussion of chemical hazards, read Chapter 5 in *Management of Occupational Health and Safety* 4th ed., by Kevin Kelloway, Lori Francis, and James Montgomery.)

Workplace Hazardous Materials Information Systems

In the belief that workers have the right to know about potential workplace hazards, industry, labour, and government have joined forces to develop a common information system for labelling hazardous substances. The Workplace Hazardous Materials Information System (WHMIS) is based on three elements:

1. *Labels.* Labels are designed to alert the worker that the container holds a potentially hazardous substance. The two types of labels (supplier labels and workplace labels) must contain specified and regulated information, including product identifiers and data on safe handling and material safety. WHMIS class symbols and subclass designations are shown in Figure 12.3 on page 486.

2. *Material Safety Data Sheets (MSDSs).* A **Material Safety Data Sheet** identifies the product and its potentially hazardous ingredients and suggests procedures for handling the product safely. The MSDS information must be comprehensive, current, and available in English and French.

Material Safety Data Sheets (MSDSs)
Documents that contain vital information about hazardous substances

FIGURE **12.3**

Class Symbols and Subclass Designations

The subclass designations are shown below the class designation.

CLASS AND SUBCLASS DESIGNATIONS

COMPRESSED GAS

POISONOUS AND
INFECTIOUS MATERIAL
Materials Causing
Immediate and
Serious Toxic Effects

CORROSIVE MATERIAL

Materials Causing
Other Toxic Effects

FLAMMABLE AND
COMBUSTIBLE MATERIAL
Flammable Gas
Flammable Liquid
Flammable Solid
Flammable Aerosol
Reactive Flammable Material

OXIDIZING MATERIAL

Biohazardous
Infectious Material

DANGEROUS REACTIVE
MATERIAL

Source: *Solvents in the Workplace*, Cat. no. B01230 (Toronto Industrial Accident Prevention Association, March).

3. *Training.* Workers must be trained to check for labels and to follow spe-
    cific procedures for handling spills. Training workers is part of the due
    diligence required of employers; it also becomes an important factor
    in the event of a lawsuit. The Peel Board of Education in Ontario has
    developed a computer-based program to train workers in WHMIS. This
    program allows illiterate workers to respond to audio commands by
    touching the screen.

Indoor Air Quality

Between 60 and 70 percent of all workers now spend their days in offices, and many complain about headaches, dizziness, disorientation, fatigue, and eye, ear, and throat irritation. As a consequence of energy concerns, commercial and residential construction techniques have been changed to increase energy efficiency of heating, ventilating, and air-conditioning systems. This has included sealing windows, reducing outside air intake, and generally "buttoning up" buildings—thus resulting in the "sick building syndrome" (SBS) and "building-related illnesses" (BRI) that give rise to such employee complaints. One expert estimates that between 10 and 25 percent of buildings have the characteristics of SBS.[18] Popular office equipment, including photocopying machines, computer terminals, fax machines, and laser printers, contributes to these health complaints.

Four basic ways to overcome polluted buildings are to (1) eliminate tobacco smoke, (2) provide adequate ventilation, (3) maintain the ventilating system, and (4) remove sources of pollution. It is now common practice in both office and industrial settings, as well as public facilities (airports, hotels, schools, and so on), to monitor and manage the quality of indoor air.

Tobacco Smoke

For the past ten years probably the most heated workplace health issue has been smoking. In a study published in the *Journal of the American Medical Association*, findings showed that "in businesses that permitted smoking, more than 60 percent of the office air samples contained nicotine levels above the 'significant risk' level of 6.8 micrograms per cubic metre."[19] Because of findings such as these, smokers have been banned from lighting up on airplanes, at work, and in restaurants and hotels. Furthermore, nonsmokers, fuelled by studies linking "passive smoking" (inhaling other people's smoke) with disease and death, and irritated by smoke getting in their eyes, noses, and clothes, have demanded a smoke-free environment. Employers will benefit from this ban. Smokers on average miss 6.16 days of work per year, nearly double the rate of nonsmokers.[20] A Labour Canada study found that employees who smoke cost companies about $2,500 more per year (than nonsmoking employees) in increased absenteeism, lost productivity, and increased health and life insurance premiums.[21] It has been documented that health care costs are higher for smokers; for this reason, some employers are charging smokers more for extended health insurance or are reducing their benefits. Many employers, however, prefer positive reinforcement through wellness programs to encourage employees to stop smoking.

A British Columbia arbitrator has ruled that smoking is as addictive as cocaine and so constitutes a drug dependency.[22] Under human rights legislation, employers may have to allow workers with a substance abuse problem to take a leave of absence to seek treatment. If nicotine addiction is accepted as a disability, companies may have to provide stop-smoking programs and refrain from disciplining addicted employees who smoke.

Video Display Terminals

The expanding use of computers and video display terminals (VDTs) in the workplace has generated intense debate over the possible hazards to which VDT users may be exposed. Many fears about VDT use have been shown to be unfounded, but serious health complaints remain an issue. Problems that managers have to confront in this area fall into three major groups:

1. *Visual difficulties.* VDT operators frequently complain of blurred vision, sore eyes, burning and itching eyes, and glare.

2. *Muscular aches and pains.* Pains in the back, neck, and shoulders are common complaints of VDT operators.

3. *Job stress.* Eye strain, postural problems, noise, insufficient training, excessive workloads, and monotonous work are complaints reported by three-quarters of VDT users.

To capitalize on the benefits of VDTs while safeguarding employee health, Dr. James Sheedy, a VDT and vision expert, offers these tips on how to minimize the negative effects of computer use on the eyes and body:

- Place the computer screen 10 to 25 cm (4 to 9 inches) below eye level.
- Keep the monitor directly in front of you.
- Sit in an adjustable-height chair and use a copyholder that attaches to both the desk and the monitor.
- Use a screen with adjustable brightness and contrast controls.
- Use shades or blinds to reduce the computer-screen glare created by window lighting.

Cumulative Trauma Disorders

cumulative trauma disorders

Injuries involving tendons of the fingers, hands, and arms that become inflamed from repeated stresses and strains

Meat cutters, fish filleters, cooks, dental hygienists, textile workers, violinists, flight attendants, office workers at computer terminals, and others whose jobs require repetitive motion of the fingers, hands, or arms are reporting injuries in growing percentages. Known as **cumulative trauma disorders** or repetitive motion injuries, these musculoskeletal disorders (MSDs) are injuries of the muscles, nerves, tendons, ligaments, joints, and spinal discs caused by repeated stresses and strains. One of the more common conditions is *carpal tunnel syndrome,* which is characterized by tingling or numbness in the fingers occurring when a tunnel of bones and ligaments in the wrist narrows and pinches nerves that reach the fingers and the base of the thumb. Without proper treatment, employees with carpal tunnel syndrome can lose complete feeling in their hands. Another cumulative trauma disorder prevalent among tennis players is tennis elbow.

In Chapter 4, we discussed job design and ergonomics considerations as one way to accommodate the capabilities and limitations of employees. Ergonomics techniques are also successfully used to improve or correct workplace conditions that cause or aggravate cumulative trauma disorders.[23] Continuous developments in office furniture, video display terminals, tool design, computer keyboards, and adjustable workstations are all attempts to make the work setting more comfortable—and, it is hoped, more productive—but also to lessen musculoskeletal disorders. Mini-breaks involving exercise and the changing of work positions have been found helpful. Importantly, these kinds of injuries often go away if they are caught early. If they are not, they may require months or years of treatment or even surgical correction. Also, when cumulative trauma disorders result from work activities, they serve to lower employee productivity, increase employer health costs, and incur workers' compensation payments.

Key elements of successful ergonomic programs are shown in Figure 12.4.[24]

Communicable Diseases

Provisions for dealing with communicable diseases such as herpes simplex (cold sores), influenza, athlete's foot, and AIDS (acquired immune deficiency syndrome) are covered in public health legislation, not occupational health and safety legislation. Epidemics such as SARS (severe acute respiratory syndrome) and swine flu (H1N1) put pressure on employers to develop emergency programs to deal with these. Employers in Canada have to have plans about travel bans, quarantines, the right to refuse work, and what constituted a safe work environment. Provincial legislation provides certain rights for employees affected by pandemics, including job-protected leave, no penalties for emergency leave, payment for those not working because of quarantines, and work refusal processes. Highlights in HRM 12.3 describes how some employers cope with pandemics.

Companies with award-winning ergonomics programs list the "following as common elements of success:

- *Provide notice and training for employees.* Implement a well-publicized ergonomics policy or present ergonomic information in safety policies or training programs. Train employees, supervisors, and managers in basic workplace ergonomics.

- *Conduct pre-injury hazard assessment.* Survey the workplace and work processes for potential hazards and adopt measures to lessen the exposure to ergonomic risk factors. Answer the question, "Are certain work areas more prone to ergonomic hazards than others?"

- *Involve employees.* Include employees in risk assessment, recognition of MSD symptoms, design of work-specific equipment or tools, and the setting of work performance rules and guidelines.

- *Plan and execute.* Integrate ergonomic responsibilities into the performance plans for all personnel. Demand accountability for program success.

- *File injury reports.* Encourage early reporting of MSD symptoms or injuries. Refer employees to the company's medical facilities or to the employee's personal physician for treatment.

- *Evaluate and assess the ergonomics program.* Periodically review the effectiveness of the ergonomics program. If the program appears to be ineffective, determine the underlying causes for failure and propose corrective changes.

FIGURE **12.4**

Key Elements for a Successful Ergonomics Program

Highlights in **HRM 12.3**

Are You Ready?

The last decade will be remembered for the necessity to develop disaster recovery planning and business continuity planning. Events that disrupted business included ice storms, Y2K, 9/11, strikes, and blackouts. The greatest fear is a pandemic, where it is estimated that absenteeism will run at 20 to 60 percent for a period of two to four weeks. Companies such as UPS and FedEx would be seriously affected by a pandemic, and have contingency plans in place. But a true pandemic would cross all business sectors. HR needs to own this issue.

Canadian human resource professionals, particularly those working in hospitals, faced a crisis in the spring of 2003 that none had seen in their working lifetimes. For the first time in the memory of most hospital employees at Sunnybrook and Women's College Health Sciences Centre in Toronto and London Health Sciences Centre in London, Ontario, there was a code orange crisis—in other words, the most serious level. People looked to the HR team to initiate action plans to deal with sick employees, quarantined employees, and scared employees. Unlike crises such as the events of September 11, 2001, where there was one dramatic event, SARS was an escalating event, with every day

creating new problems. At Sunnybrook, the HR director took every decision with the thought, "What are the repercussions? Long after SARS ends, the employees and the unions will remember how they were treated."

The escalating pace was difficult. HR people had to train employees to screen 12,000 people a day and had just one weekend to design the process and hire and train staff. Communication had to be objective and immediate, not only with employees but also with their worried families. For the first time, health care workers could not leave their work behind, with most having to wear masks at home and avoid contact with their families. To deal with these concerns, staff forums were held (employees needed to talk about their concerns). The London Health Sciences Centre faced similar issues. Both vice-presidents of HR emphasized the need for visible leadership. One immediate problem that was soon evident was the folly of any absenteeism program that motivated employees to come to work sick, which of course increased the risk of communicable diseases spreading throughout the workforce. Some employees continued to come to work even when they were not feeling well because they were worried they would lose

continued

income, so a policy that had to be developed immediately was a commitment to maintain the wages of workers in quarantine. Another unusual problem was that certain categories of workers, such as nurses, have limited rights to refuse work. When Mount Sinai Hospital in Toronto asked employees to staff screening stations, a librarian refused to do this work as she deemed it to be unsafe. A lesson learned is the importance of preparing for an emergency by stockpiling personal protective equipment and training all staff in its use.

It is not just hospitals that have to be prepared for outbreaks of communicable diseases. Hewlett-Packard has a workforce of 8,000 employees, with 3,200 of them at ten sites in the Greater Toronto Area. Two HP employees were hospitalized with SARS, and one site was forced to close. Fortunately, because the site had always required employees and visitors to sign in, and access was controlled with a pass card, all those known to have been at the site were easy to trace and all pass cards were revoked. Also, because HP is a

high-tech company, with all employees online all the time, communication with employees was not difficult. However, the nature of the highly mobile workforce posed problems for health care officials. The public health department required lists of all employees who were absent, but HR does not track absences because most HP employees work from home or offsite.

Avian flu may be the next pandemic, with an estimate of up to 58,000 deaths and 138,000 hospitalizations in Canada. HINI (swine flu) is another pandemic expected to cause deaths and hospitalizations. Experts suggest that senior management, along with HR, drive the emergency preparedness program, and that a program team be established that would create a plan to protect human life, eliminate or minimize risk and injury, protect physical assets, minimize losses, and resume operations as quickly as possible. The plan must be communicated in advance and every employee needs to know what to do. There must be a test and practice phase, with emergency drills. Are you ready?

Sources: Michael Bennet, "Are You Ready?" *HR Professional* (October/November 2005); 21–26; Phillip Quinn, "Plan for Pandemic," *The National Post* (March 29, 2006); WK 1 and 5; B. Orr, "SARS Outbreak Teaches Valuable Lessons on a New 'Normal' State for HR Management," *Canadian HP Reporter* 16, no. 11 (June 2, 2003): 5; Ministry of Labour, "Workplace Laws and SARS," http://www.gov .on.ca/LAB; A. Picard, "Mommy, Are You Going to Die?" *The Globe and Mail*, April 5, 2003; http://www.andrepicard.com/stories/ mommy.html, retrieved August 27, 2009

WORKPLACE VIOLENCE

Many people think of workplace violence as a physical assault. But there are many forms including

- Threatening behaviour such as shaking fists or throwing objects
- Verbal or written threats
- Harassment—any behaviour that demeans, embarrasses, or humiliates
- Verbal abuse including swearing, insults, or condescending language
- Physical attacks including hitting, shoving, pushing, or kicking[25]

Manon Blanc at Queen's University and Kevin Kelloway, director of the CN Centre for Occupational Health and Safety at Saint Mary's University, have identified the job characteristics that put workers at risk for aggression and violence in the workplace:

- Interacting with the public.
- Making decisions that influence other people's lives (e.g., terminating an employee or assigning a failing grade) or denying the public a service or request
- Supervising and/or disciplining others
- Working nights; working alone
- Handling cash, handling or guarding valuables, collecting or delivering items of value
- Caring for the physical or emotional needs of others, going to clients' homes
- Serving or selling alcohol; dealing with individuals under the influence of mind-altering substances[26]

Exposure to workplace violence results in employees fearing more incidents of violence, leading to personal strains (such as stress) and organizational strains (reduced commitment, neglect of job duties).

The Canadian Centre for Occupational Health and Safety suggests that preventive measures should include

- *Workplace design*, such as locks or physical barriers (pass-through windows or bulletproof enclosures), lighting, and electronic surveillance.
- *Administrative practices*, such as keeping cash register funds to a minimum, varying the time of day that cash is emptied, and using a security firm to deliver cash.
- *Work practices* (particularly for those working alone away from an office, such as home care workers and real estate agents) that might include having a designated contact kept informed of the employee's schedule and checking the credentials of clients.[27]

Employers in all Canadian jurisdictions are bound to take all reasonable precautions to protect the safety and health of their workers. At this time, however, only British Columbia and Saskatchewan have specific laws requiring employers to protect their workers from violence. However, under common law an employer may be held liable for the actions of employees. Nurses are victims of violence at a rate that is 16 times higher than other service workers; almost 70 percent of nurses have been physically assaulted.[28] Managers and supervisors can be trained to recognize violence indicators such as those given in Figure 12.5. Awareness of these threatening behaviours can provide an opportunity to intervene and prevent disruptive, abusive, or violent acts. Managers must effectively communicate a zero-tolerance

FIGURE 12.5

Violence Indicators: Know the Warning Signs

Most people leave a trail of indicators before they become violent. Similarly, disgruntled former employees who commit acts of violence leave warning signs of their intent before and after termination. The following behaviours should be taken seriously when assessing situations of potential violence:

- Direct or veiled threatening statements
- Recent performance declines, including concentration problems and excessive excuses
- Prominent mood or behaviour changes; despondence
- Preoccupation with guns, knives, or other weapons
- Deliberate destruction of workplace equipment; sabotage
- Fascination with stories of violence
- Reckless or antisocial behaviour; evidence of prior assaultive behaviour
- Aggressive behaviour or intimidating statements
- Written messages of violent intent; exaggerated perceptions of injustice
- Serious stress in personal life
- Obsessive desire to harm a specific group or person
- Violence against a family member
- Substance abuse

Sources: Adapted from *Violence in the Workplace: Risk Factors and Prevention Strategies*, NIOSH Bulletin #59; Gillian Flynn, "Employers Can't Look Away from Workplace Violence," *Workforce* 79, no. 7 (July 2000): 68–70; Dannie B. Fogleman, "Minimizing the Risk of Violence in the Workplace," *Employment Relations Today* 87, no. 1 (Spring 2000): 83–98.

policy for violence and encourage employees to report any possible or observed incidents of workplace violence. A meaningful reporting procedure with clear lines of responsibility can ensure that management is promptly notified of potential security risks in order to take immediate steps to resolve the issues. Finally, organizations have formalized workplace violence–prevention policies, informing employees that aggressive employee behaviour will not be tolerated.

TERRORISM

Once largely confined to foreign countries, terrorism is now a major concern to Canadian employers, particularly those in high-target categories such as airlines, sporting facilities, energy plants and dams, high-tech companies, financial institutions, and public and commercial buildings. The heightened security procedures at these facilities show the importance employers place on the prevention of terrorist attacks, including those involving conventional explosives, nuclear devices, dirty bombs, chemical weapons, and bioweapons.

Many of the points recommended to prevent workplace violence apply equally to preventing terrorism—background checks, violence prevention policy, and so on. Additionally, counterterrorism experts recommend the following to deter terrorist attacks:

- Heightened ID checks and baggage screening
- Increased video monitoring with threat-recognition software to back up human surveillance
- Blast-resistant glass to reduce casualties
- Offsite emergency offices
- Tightened garage security with stepped-up inspections
- Staggered deliveries to reduce truck traffic[29]
- Emergency evacuation procedures, including escape routes, emergency equipment, and gathering locations[30]

At a minimum, these procedures would include escape routes, emergency equipment and gathering locations, and special assistance for disabled people and individuals responsible for the movement of employees. Practice evacuation drills at unannounced times ensure that employees know how to respond to an evacuation while preventing unnecessary confusion should a real attack occur. Although Canadians have yet to encounter a colossal domestic catastrophe, Canadian workplaces should be prepared against such an eventuality.

Crisis Management Teams

Most large organizations have formal crisis management teams. These teams, composed of both hourly and managerial employees, conduct initial risk assessment surveys, develop action plans to respond to violent situations, and, importantly, perform crisis intervention during violent, or potentially violent, encounters. For example, a crisis management team would investigate a threat reported by an employee. The team's mandate would be to gather facts about the threat, decide whether the organization should intervene, and, if so, determine the most appropriate method of doing so. Occasionally, a member of the team or an individual manager will be called upon to intervene and calm an angry employee.[31] When this occurs, the steps given in Figure 12.6 will help to defuse a volatile situation.

When violent incidents, such as the death of a coworker, happen at work, employees can experience shock, guilt, grief, apathy, resentment, cynicism, and a host of other emotions.[32] Such incidents may require the crisis management team to perform crisis intervention through positive counselling techniques.[33]

Using the Internet

The Canadian Initiative on Workplace Violence, a social research firm, offers information at

http://www
.workplaceviolence.ca

If you try to defuse a tense situation, remember that anger frequently results from a person's feeling of being wronged, misunderstood, or unheard. Keep the following tips in mind to guide you:

- Strive to save the employee's dignity during an angry confrontation. Do not attack a person's rash statements or continue a muddled line of thinking.
- Hold all conversations in private. Do not allow the employee to create an embarrassing public situation for himself or herself, yourself, or other employees.
- Always remain calm. Anger or aggressiveness on your part will trigger a similar response in the employee.
- Listen to the employee with an open mind and nonjudgmental behaviour. Give the employee the benefit of hearing him or her out.
- Recognize the employee's legitimate concerns or feelings. Agree that the employee has a valid point and that you will work to correct the problem.
- If the employee is very emotional or if the engagement seems out of control, schedule a delayed meeting so people can calm down.
- Keep the discussion as objective as possible. Focus on the problem at hand, not the personalities of individuals. A cornerstone of conflict resolution is to "attack the problem, not the personality."
- If the employee appears overly aggressive, withdraw immediately and seek professional help before any further discussion with the employee.
- If your efforts fail to calm the employee, report the incident to your manager, security, or human resource personnel.

Source: Adapted from professional literature on crisis management and seminars attended by the authors.

FIGURE 12.6

Calming an Angry Employee

BUILDING BETTER HEALTH

Along with improving working conditions that are hazardous to employee health, many employers provide health services and have programs that encourage employees to improve their health habits. It is recognized that better health not only benefits the individual, but also pays off for the organization in reduced absenteeism, increased efficiency, better morale, and other savings. An increased understanding of the close relationship between physical and emotional health and job performance has made broad health-building programs attractive to employers as well as to employees.

ENSURING HEALTHFUL EMPLOYEES

The size of the organization determines the kind of health services that can be provided to employees. Small organizations are likely to have only limited facilities, such as those required to handle first aid; many larger firms offer complete diagnostic, treatment, and emergency surgical services. Since employers are required to provide medical services after an injury, larger companies usually have nurses and physicians on full-time duty. Medium-size and smaller organizations will have one or more physicians on call.

We noted in Chapter 6 that some employers give medical examinations to prospective employees after a job offer has been made. The examination should include a medical history with specific reference to previous hazardous

OUTCOME 4

exposures. Exposure to hazards whose effects may be cumulative, such as noise, lead, and radiation, are especially relevant. For jobs involving unusual physical demands, the applicant's muscular development, flexibility, agility, range of motion, and cardiac and respiratory functions should be evaluated. Many organizations also give periodic examinations on a required or voluntary basis. Such examinations can help determine the effects of potential hazards in the workplace, and detect any health problems to which the employee's lifestyle or health habits may contribute.

PROMOTING WORKPLACE FITNESS AND HEALTH

Many organizations have developed programs that emphasize regular exercise, proper nutrition, weight control, and avoidance of substances harmful to health. Xerox gives its employees a publication called *Fitbook* that includes chapters on the hazards of smoking and the effects of alcohol and drug abuse, facts on nutrition and weight control, and guidelines for managing stress and learning to relax. The City of Victoria encourages its employees to bike to work.

Importantly, wellness programs produce measurable cost savings to employers, as described in the Business Case. Figure 12.7 gives nine steps for launching a successful wellness program, even on a limited budget.

The Business **CASE**

Investing in Employee Health

For the 2,800 employees at Husky Injection Molding Systems of Bolton, Ontario, work seems like play as they visit their children over lunch; eat fresh, healthy cafeteria food; play table tennis on their breaks; and receive an extra vacation day for staying fit. Husky spends more than $4 million a year on employee benefits, but this investment more than pays for itself in higher productivity, lower turnover, and lower absenteeism. The voluntary turnover rate is about 8 percent, which is below the industry average of 10 percent. The absenteeism rate is 3.7 days, less than half of the manufacturing industry average of 9.1 days. Injury claims are 1.5 for every 200,000 hours worked, compared with an industry average of 7.2. The annual drug benefit costs are $255 per employee compared to the industry average of $507. The estimated savings are $8.4 million a year.

Husky is not the only company seeing returns on investments in workplace well-being. Organizations in Atlantic Canada found that employees who participated in a three-month wellness program reduced the risk of

heart disease and stroke, for an estimated return on the investment of $1.64 for every dollar spent. In one of the largest studies done on return on investment of health care programs, the National Wellness program delivered wellness programs consisting of smoking cessation workshops, lifestyle and nutrition counselling, and on-site fitness to 90,000 employees in 30 locations. Those who participated had lower health care costs of between $5 and $16 per month. Even a one-time inexpensive program can show returns. TELUS introduced a flu immunization program and saw absences due to respiratory illness drop from 33 to 22 percent. Overall, studies of wellness programs document cost-benefit ratios of between $3 and $8 for every dollar spent. The benefits to organizations include decreased lost workdays, decreased workers' compensation costs, increased employee morale and productivity, reduced overtime costs, and reduced workplace injuries. Yet, only 60 percent of Canadian workplaces offer wellness programs. Why aren't more companies getting it?

Sources: Vera N. Held, "Husky's Andrée Brière on Productivity and Stress Free Employees," *HR Professional* (August/September 2005): 19–25; T. Grant, "Husky Woos Workers with Unique Perks," *The Globe and Mail* (August 20, 2001); S. Kee, "The Bottom Line on Wellness," *Canadian Health Care Manager* 9, no. 1 (Fall 2002): 23; G. Lowe, "The Dollars and Sense of Health Promotion," *Canadian HR Reporter* (September 23, 2002): 7–8.

FIGURE 12.7

Tips for Starting a Successful Wellness Program

1. Conduct a health risk assessment of employees.
2. Create incentives for employees to achieve a healthy lifestyle.
3. Create opportunities for regular physical activities during the day or before or after work.
4. Provide nutritional advice from a registered dietitian.
5. Include healthy, low-fat choices among snacks and meals provided in cafeterias and through vending machines.
6. Eliminate smoking from the work setting.
7. Negotiate discounts from area health clubs.
8. Start a health and fitness newsletter.
9. Focus on reducing one or two high-risk factors among employees.

Source: Adapted from "The Surgeon General's Call to Action to Prevent and Decrease Overweight and Obesity 2001." See http://www.surgeongeneral.gov/topics/obesity.

EMPLOYEE ASSISTANCE PROGRAMS

A broad view of health includes the emotional as well as the physical aspects of one's life. While emotional problems, personal crises, alcoholism, and drug abuse are considered personal matters, they become organizational problems when they affect behaviour at work and interfere with job performance.[34] Mental illness accounts for about 40 percent of disability claims, resulting in about $8.5 billion dollars in long-term disability claims.[35] To be able to handle such problems, organizations offer an employee assistance program (EAP). Typically, such a program refers employees in need of assistance to in-house counsellors or outside professionals.[36] Supervisors are often given training and policy guidance in the type of help they can offer their subordinates. However, some employees are reluctant to accept help as they risk being stigmatized. At Canadian Forces Base Winnipeg, anyone taking treatment for stress is said to be taking the "Crazy Train to the North Side." Soldiers fear that they will be unjustly accused of faking post-traumatic stress disorder.

Personal Crises

The most prevalent problems among employees are personal crises involving marital, family, financial, or legal matters. EAPs have been directing increased attention to the problem of domestic violence. Such problems often come to a supervisor's attention. In most instances, the supervisor can usually provide the best help simply by being understanding and supportive and by helping the individual find the type of assistance he or she needs.[37] In many cases, in-house counselling or referral to an outside professional is recommended. In recent years, crisis hotlines have been set up in many communities to provide counselling by telephone for those too distraught to wait for an appointment with a counsellor.

Emotional Problems

While personal crises are typically fraught with emotion, most of them are resolved in a reasonable period of time and the troubled individual's equilibrium is restored. Unfortunately, when personal crises linger, stress and tension may cause or intensify a mood disorder such as depression. Depression is a decrease in functional activity

OUTCOME 5

depression
Negative emotional state marked by feelings of low spirits, gloominess, sadness, and loss of pleasure in ordinary activities

Highlights in HRM 12.4

Depression in the Workplace

When a depressed mood persists for a few weeks, deepens, and eventually starts interfering with work and other aspects of everyday life, it has likely become an illness—or a clinical depression. In the workplace, a person with depression will exhibit many of the following signs:

Recognizing Depression

Personal Changes

- Irritability, hostility
- Hopelessness, despair
- Slowness of speech
- Chronic fatigue
- Withdrawal from or extreme dependency on others
- Alcohol or drug abuse

Workplace Changes

- Difficulty in making decisions
- Decreased productivity
- Inability to concentrate
- Decline in dependability
- Unusual increase in errors in work
- Accident proneness
- Frequent tardiness, increased "sick" days
- Lack of enthusiasm for work

Someone who has been experiencing many of these signs for a few weeks or more should seek help immediately.

Source: Reprinted by permission of Canadian Mental Health Association, Toronto.

---

accompanied by symptoms of low spirits, gloominess, and sadness. Highlights in HRM 12.4 lists the symptoms of depression.

About 5 percent of Canadians experience depression. With available treatment, however, 70 percent of these individuals will significantly improve, usually within a matter of weeks.

Since depression lowers individual productivity, causes morale problems, increases absenteeism, and contributes to substance abuse, it is important for managers to identify signs of depression on the job and to learn to deal with depressed employees. The more likely workplace signs of depression are decreased energy, concentration and memory problems, guilt feelings, irritability, and chronic aches and pains that don't respond to treatment. When confronted with depressed employees, managers and supervisors are encouraged to be concerned with the employee's problem, be an active listener, and—should the depression persist—suggest professional help.[38] Under no circumstances should managers attempt to play amateur psychologist and try to diagnose an employee's condition. Mood disorders such as depression are complex in nature and do not lend themselves to quick diagnoses. Furthermore, in reviewing such cases, the organization should pay particular attention to workplace safety factors, because there is general agreement that emotional disturbances are primary or secondary factors in a large portion of industrial accidents and violence.

Alcoholism

Alcoholism affects workers in every occupational category—blue-collar and white-collar. In confronting the problem, employers must recognize that alcoholism is a disease that follows a rather predictable course. Thus, they can take specific actions to deal with employees showing symptoms of the disease at particular stages of its progression. Alcoholism typically begins with social drinking getting out of control. As the disease progresses, the alcoholic loses control over how much to drink and eventually cannot keep from drinking, even at inappropriate times. The person uses denial to avoid facing the problems created by the abuse of alcohol and often blames others for these problems. The first step in helping the alcoholic is to awaken the person to the reality of his or her situation.

To identify alcoholism as early as possible, it is essential that supervisors monitor the performance of all personnel regularly and systematically. A supervisor should carefully document evidence of declining performance on the job and then confront the employee with unequivocal proof that the job is suffering. The employee should be assured that help will be made available without penalty. Since the evaluations are made solely with regard to lagging job performance, a supervisor can avoid any mention of alcoholism and allow such employees to seek aid as they would for any other problem.[39]

Abuse of Illegal Drugs

The abuse of drugs by employees is one of the major employment issues today. Drug abuse is now a national problem and has spread to every industry, occupation, and employee level. Estimates of the costs of substance abuse by employees vary considerably. Besides lost productivity, there are the costs of increased numbers of accidents and injuries, and rising rates of employee theft. The costs of substance abuse can have a dramatic impact on the bottom line. Drug testing remains a controversial issue. In general, pre-employment drug or alcohol testing or random testing of current employees is prohibited by human rights laws. Furthermore, human rights legislation prohibits discrimination on the basis of disability, and drug and alcohol dependency is generally considered to be a disability.

While attention is usually focused on the abuse of illegal drugs, it should be noted that the abuse of legal drugs can also pose a problem for employees. Employees who abuse legal drugs—those prescribed by physicians—often do not realize they have become addicted or how their behaviour has changed as a result of their addiction. Also, managers should be aware that some employees may be taking legal sedatives or stimulants as part of their medical treatment and that their behaviour at work may be affected by their use of these drugs.

MANAGEMENT OF STRESS

HR professionals are well aware of the negative effects of workplace stress on employees' health and job performance. For example, job stress places both women and men at risk for cardiovascular problems and depression, and increases employee susceptibility to infectious diseases. All of these contribute to higher health care costs, and can lower productivity, job satisfaction, and retention. Importantly, in a study on the magnitude of stress in the workplace, 54 percent of respondents indicated that they "often" or "always" come home from work in a state of fatigue, and nearly 50 percent come in to work tired.[40]

WHAT IS STRESS?

Stress is any demand on the individual that requires coping behaviour. Stress comes from two basic sources: physical activity and mental or emotional activity. The physical reaction of the body to both types of stress is the same. Psychologists use two separate terms to distinguish between positive and negative forms of stress, even though reactions to the two forms are the same biochemically. Eustress is positive stress that accompanies achievement and exhilaration. Eustress is the stress of meeting challenges such as those found in a managerial, technical, or public contact job. Eustress is regarded as a beneficial force that helps us to forge ahead against obstacles. What is harmful is distress. Stress becomes distress when we begin to sense a loss of our feelings of security and adequacy. Helplessness, desperation, and disappointment turn stress into distress.

stress
Any adjustive demand caused by physical, mental, or emotional factors that require coping behaviour.

eustress
Positive stress that accompanies achievement and exhilaration

distress
Harmful stress characterized by a loss of feelings of security and adequacy

The stress reaction is a coordinated chemical mobilization of the entire body to meet the requirements of fight-or-flight in a situation perceived to be stressful. The sympathetic nervous system activates the secretion of hormones from the endocrine glands that places the body on a "war footing." This response, commonly referred to as the **alarm reaction**, basically involves an elevated heart rate, increased respiration, elevated levels of adrenaline in the blood, and increased blood pressure. It persists until one's estimate of the relative threat to well-being has been re-evaluated. If distress persists long enough, it can result in fatigue, exhaustion, and even physical and/or emotional breakdown.[41] Some research has linked stress to heart disease. Other studies have shown a connection between chronic stress and hypertension (high blood pressure). High blood pressure, the most common cause of strokes, contributes to heart disease.

JOB-RELATED STRESS

Although the body experiences a certain degree of stress (either eustress or distress) in all situations, here we are primarily concerned with the stress related to the work setting. It is in this setting that management can use some preventive approaches.

Sources of Job-Related Stress

Causes of workplace stress are many. However, according to a study by Luminari, a national health care company, four factors have a major influence on employee stress:

- *High demand:* having too much to do in too short a time.
- *High effort:* having to expend too much mental or physical energy over too long a period.
- *Low control:* having too little influence over the way a job is done on a day-to-day basis.
- *Low reward:* receiving inadequate feedback on performance and no recognition for a job well done.[42]

Other recognized job stressors include layoffs and organizational restructuring; disagreements with managers or fellow employees; prejudice because of age, gender, race, or religion; inability to voice complaints; and poor working conditions. Even minor irritations such as lack of privacy, unappealing music, and other conditions can be distressful to one person or another.

Burnout

Burnout is a severe stage of distress. Career burnout generally occurs when a person begins questioning his or her own personal values. Quite simply, one no longer feels that what he or she is doing is important. Depression, frustration, and a loss of productivity are all symptoms of burnout. Burnout is due primarily to a lack of personal fulfillment in the job or a lack of positive feedback about performance.[43] In organizations that have downsized, remaining employees can experience burnout because they must perform more work with fewer coworkers. Overachievers can experience burnout when unrealistic work goals are unattainable.[44]

COPING WITH STRESS

Many employers have developed stress management programs to teach employees how to minimize the negative effects of job-related stress. A typical program might include instruction in relaxation techniques, coping skills, listening skills, methods of dealing with difficult people, time management, and assertiveness. All of these techniques are designed to break the pattern of tension that accompanies stress situations and to help participants achieve greater control of their

alarm reaction

Response to stress that basically involves an elevated heart rate, increased respiration, elevated levels of adrenaline in the blood, and increased blood pressure

burnout

Most severe stage of distress, manifesting itself in depression, frustration, and loss of productivity

© Photodisc

Many Canadians report experiencing stress on the job.

lives. Organizational techniques such as clarifying the employee's work role, redesigning and enriching jobs, correcting physical factors in the environment, and effectively handling interpersonal factors, should not be overlooked in the process of teaching employees how to handle stress. Stress management counsellors recommend several ways to resolve job-related stress as described in Figure 12.8.

Before concluding this discussion, we should observe that stress that is harmful to some employees may be healthy for others.[45] Most managers learn to handle distress effectively and find that it actually stimulates better performance. However, there will always be those who are unable to handle stress and need assistance in learning to cope with it. The increased interest of young and old alike in developing habits that will enable them to lead happier and more productive lives will undoubtedly be beneficial to them as individuals, to the organizations where they work, and to a society where people are becoming more and more interdependent.

FIGURE 12.8

Tips for Reducing Job-Related Stress

- Build rewarding relationships with coworkers.
- Talk openly with managers or employees about job or personal concerns.
- Prepare for the future by keeping abreast of likely changes in job demands.
- Do not greatly exceed your skills and abilities.
- Set realistic deadlines; negotiate reasonable deadlines with managers.
- Act now on problems or concerns of importance.
- Designate dedicated work periods during which time interruptions are avoided.
- When feeling stressed, find time for detachment or relaxation.
- Do not let trivial items take on importance; handle them quickly or assign them to others.
- Take short breaks from your work area as a change of pace.

Small Business APPLICATION

While small companies may be too small to justify a designated health and safety officer in their organization, they still must ensure that health and safety practices are adhered to. As such, small companies may draw upon outside organizations such as consultants or local workplace safety boards for assistance in the establishment and monitoring of safe workplace practices.

Managers frequently say that dealing with people-related issues, such as sickness, problems at home, problems with other workers, or any other issues impacting the success of team members, takes a significant portion of their time. As such, small companies that are able to have managers address the personal issues of employees help foster an organizational climate conducive to success.

Effective management is a balance between (1) fair, respectful treatment of and communication with employees, (2) sensitivity to individual employees' situations and needs, while (3) providing direction to employees to ensure the accomplishment of organizational needs.

So how does a manager accomplish this? To be successful, managers need to (1) genuinely care about their staff, (2) have a close enough working relationship to have visibility into each employee's work satisfaction and productivity, (3) have effective dialogue with their staff to know what is important to each employee as well as what is required to support their individual needs, (4) provide fair counsel to employees regarding their specific needs, (5) have the power to meet individual needs when warranted, and (6) maintain the role of providing support while maintaining organizational fairness and success as the primary goal.

In smaller organizations, managers are able to observe employees more frequently and may be able to detect when these employees are experiencing stress. As a first step in the process of employee assistance, a manager may be able to listen to an employee and provide a supportive work environment. In some cases, of course, a manager may have to refer employees for professional help, through local hospitals or social workers.

SUMMARY

[OUT**1**OME]   Occupational health and safety legislation is designed to assure, so far as possible, safe and healthful working conditions for every working person. In general, the act extends to all employers and employees. This legislation sets standards, ensures employer and employee compliance, and provides safety and health consultation and training where needed. Both employers and employees have certain responsibilities and rights under these acts. Employers not only are required to provide a hazard-free work environment, but also must keep employees informed about legislative requirements and must require their employees to use protective equipment when necessary. Employers are required to keep employees informed of hazardous substances and instruct them in avoiding the dangers presented. Employees, in turn, are required to comply with safety standards, report hazardous conditions, and follow all employer safety and health regulations.

[OUT**2**OME]   In order to provide safe working conditions for their employees, employers typically establish a formal program that, in a large percentage of organizations, is under the direction of the HR manager. The program may have many facets, including providing safety knowledge and motivating employees to use it, making employees aware of the need for safety, and rewarding them for safe behaviour. Incentives such as praise, public recognition, and awards are used to involve employees in the safety program. Maintenance of required records from accident investigations provides a basis for information that can be used to create a safer work environment.

[OUTCOME 3]

Job conditions that are dangerous to the health of employees are now receiving much greater attention than in the past. There is special concern regarding toxic chemicals that proliferate at a rapid rate and may lurk in the body for years without outward symptoms. Health hazards other than those found in industrial processing operations—such as video display terminals and cumulative trauma disorders—present special problems that must be addressed. Today tobacco smoke is not tolerated in the work environment.

[OUTCOME 4]

Along with providing safer and healthier work environments, many employers establish programs that encourage employees to improve their health habits. Wellness programs that emphasize exercise, nutrition, weight control, and avoidance of harmful substances serve employees at all organizational levels.

[OUTCOME 5]

Virtually all of larger organizations and many of smaller ones have found an

employee assistance program beneficial to all concerned. While emotional problems, personal crises, alcoholism, and drug abuse are often viewed as personal matters, it is apparent that they affect behaviour at work and interfere with job performance. An employee assistance program typically provides professional assistance by in-house counsellors or outside professionals where needed.

[OUTCOME 6]

An important dimension to health and safety is stress that comes from physical activity and mental or emotional activity. While stress is an integral part of being alive, when it turns into distress it becomes harmful. We have seen that many sources of stress are job related. In recognizing the need for reducing stress, employers can develop stress-management programs to help employees learn techniques for coping with stress. In addition, organizations need to redesign and enrich jobs, clarify the employee's work role, correct physical factors in the environment, and take any other actions that will help reduce stress on the job.

KEY TERMS

alarm reaction, 498
burnout, 498
cumulative trauma
  disorders, 488
depression, 495

distress, 497
eustress, 497
industrial disease, 480
Material Safety Data Sheets
  (MSDSs), 485

occupational illness, 474
occupational injury, 474
stress, 497

DISCUSSION QUESTIONS

1. Ergonomics-related injuries now account for over 40 percent of lost-time injuries in the province of Ontario. Prepare a list of the most common types of ergonomics-related injuries, and then make suggestions about how employers could reduce these types.

2. Visit a local fast food restaurant and interview the manager. Prepare a list of the occupational health and safety issues. Prepare a training plan to teach workers about these dangers.

3. An unhealthy work environment can lower productivity, contribute to low morale, and increase medical and workers' compensation costs. Working individually or in teams, list specific ways managers can
  a. Help individual employees avoid repetitive strain injuries caused by prolonged computer usage
  b. Deal with employee complaints about sick building syndrome.
  c. Address employee fears caused by pandemics

4. Conduct an office hazards assessment by using the checklist provided at http://www.esao.on.ca/downloads/checklist_pdfs/office_checklist.pdf or conduct a PC Workstation Assessment by completing the checklist at http://www.esao.on.ca/downloads/checklist_pdfs/ergo_checklist.pdf

5. Go to the website of Human Resources and Social Development Canada, and discover what the experts (including your authors!) have to say about work–life family balance, and what organizations are doing about this: http://www.hrsdc.gc.ca/eng/lp/spila/wlb/ell/24monica_belcourt.shtml. Prepare a list of the key initiatives that would make your life as an employee less stressful.

6. Both unions and management express concern for the well-being of their employees. However, union reaction to the proposed introduction of wellness initiatives is not always positive. Unions fear that information collected—for example, as part of an

EAP—will be kept and used against the employee experiencing performance problems. They also state that the real culprit in any employee health issue is the work context, not employee behaviour or lifestyle. So even if the employees exercise and stop smoking, work hazards still remain. They also fear reprisals for those employees unwilling to participate in programs, particularly where groups are provided with incentives for achieving program aims. As the HR manager responsible for the introduction of a wellness initiative, how would you deal with these union concerns?

INTERNET EXERCISE

The Canadian Labour and Business Centre (CLBC) (http://www.clbc.ca/Research_and_Reports/Case_ Studies.asp) presents 12 case studies on the health and wellness initiatives of Canadian companies such as Irving Paper, Dofasco, American Express Canada, Petro-Canada, Burrard Products Terminal, City of performance. Regina Transit Department, and Seven Oaks Hospital in Winnipeg. In groups, prepare a summary report that outlines the motivations for introducing the initiatives, the roles of managers and employees, and the impact on employee health and workplace

HRM EXPERIENCE

Reducing Employee Stress

Job stress and its negative effect on both employees and the organization are a growing concern for managers and supervisors. As this text discusses, employee distress costs employers staggering amounts of money in lost productivity, absenteeism, turnover, increased workers' compensation claims, and health care costs. The cost of distress on the personal lives of employees is unmeasurable. Not surprisingly, stress management is an important aspect of any manager's job.

Stress-management programs typically focus on three things to reduce workplace stress: (1) They identify factors in jobs that create stress; (2) they discuss specific techniques and managerial practices that help elevate workplace stress; and (3) they help individuals identify personal characteristics that serve to increase or decrease stress for them.

Assignment

1. Working in groups of four to six individuals, identify personal experiences that caused workplace stress. Explain exactly why these incidents were stressful. Suggest ways to reduce or eliminate these stressful conditions.

2. Stress management often begins by having individuals identify their skills and abilities and jobs that will help them succeed. Assessing our preferences and skills can help us understand why some tasks or roles are more stressful than others. Identify work-related stress by answering these questions:

   - What skills that I enjoy using am I currently using in my job?
   - What skills that I enjoy using am I currently not using?
   - What specific things about my job do I really like?
   - What things about my job do I dislike?
   - Based on my personal skills and abilities, what would my perfect job be?

BIZFLIX EXERCISES

8 MILE: WORKING AT NORTH DETROIT STAMPING

When you view these scenes, watch for the safety of Jimmy's job and his work environment. Many aspects of safety and health discussed in this chapter appear in these scenes.

Jimmy "B-Rabbit" Smith, Jr. (Eminem) wants to succeed as a rapper and to prove that a white man can create moving sounds. His job at the North Detroit Stamping (NDS) plant fills his days while he pursues his music at night—and sometimes on the plant's grounds. The film's title refers to Detroit's northern city boundary, well known to local people. *8 Mile* is a gritty look at Detroit's hip-hop culture in 1995 and Jimmy's desire for acceptance by it.

The scene is an edited composite of two brief NDS plant sequences that appear in different places in the film. Part 1 appears early in the film in the sequence "The Franchise." Part II appears in the last 25 minutes of the film in the "Papa Doc Payback" sequence. Jimmy arrives late for work in the first part of the scene, after riding the city bus because his car did not start. The second part occurs after his beating by Papa Doc (Anthony Mackie) and Papa Doc's gang.

What to Watch for and Ask Yourself

- What is your perception of the safety of Jimmy's job and his work environment? What has management done about job and work environment safety at North Detroit Stamping?
- Could this job and work environment create stress for Jimmy and his co-workers? Why or why not?
- How would you react to this type of work experience?

CASE STUDY 1

WORKPLACE SAFETY AND YOUNG WORKERS

Every year about 50 young Canadians are killed on the job and about 60,000 more suffer injuries serious enough to be reported to safety officials. Young workers are six times more likely to be killed or have a workplace injury than any other group. About 95 percent of those affected workers are men. This means that 1 in 11 young men can expect to suffer a workplace injury. Typically, these young men are employed at small manufacturing businesses, fast-food restaurants, convenience stores, and warehouses. The accidents usually happen within the first six months on the job. These young men lose fingers while slicing meat at the deli counter, are crushed by equipment they do not know how to operate, are electrocuted on metal ladders that touch hydro poles, or are burned handling chemicals with no protective equipment. The top five causes of injuries to young workers are slips and falls, overexertion, being struck by an object, exposure to toxic chemicals, and burns.

Less than half receive any job training. Only about 30 percent of teenagers receive instruction in first aid and CPR in their safety training, but most learn nothing about the law, their rights, hazards on the job, or safety management. Young workers are especially vulnerable because they feel invincible and lack experience. They believe the following myths:

- I can take risks; I won't die.
- I can handle anything; I am young and fit.
- Nothing will happen to me; I am safe at work.
- I must do any job my employer tells me to do.
- I am not responsible for workplace safety.

Most will not ask for safety training because they are unaware of risks, are anxious to please, or are fearful of losing their jobs.

Many provinces, recognizing these risks, have added health and safety training to the high school curriculum. Most such programs discuss workplace hazards, employer rights and responsibilities, health and safety laws, and the workers' right of refusal. Alberta has the most advanced training course for young workers in Canada: Job Safety Skills, which consists of 75 hours of instruction, divided into three modules:

- Personal safety management (first aid, back care, safety, and the law)
- Workplace safety practices (ergonomics, confined space entry, transportation of dangerous goods, and farm safety)
- Safety management systems (loss control, accident investigation, and a mock workshop in which students develop an entire safety program)

QUESTIONS

1. Why are there more workplace injuries among those aged 16 to 25?

2. By law, workplace safety is the responsibility of the employer and employee. Why have nearly all provinces created courses in occupational health and safety as part of the high school curriculum? Should these be mandatory courses or electives?

3. Check the website of the Industrial Accident Prevention Association (http://www.iapa.ca), which has excellent information on occupational health and safety (OH&S) training programs. Design a training program that an employer could provide to young workers.

Sources: Adapted from Peter Cheney, "Focus," *The Globe and Mail* (April 25, 2006): F1 and 8; S. Singh, "HR's Role in Health and Safety for Young Workers," *HR Professional* 18, no. 5 (November 2001): 17–18; L. Ramsay, "Work Can Kill You," *National Post* (September 27, 1999): C12; L. Young, "Young Workers: Changing the Face of Safety," *Occupational Health and Safety* 14, no. 4 (June–July 1998): 24–30; "Workplace Safety," *The Globe and Mail* (Friday, May 12, 2000); Government of Canada, "Youth Path, Health and Wellness," www.youth.gc.ca/healsafe.

CASE STUDY 2

RETURN TO WORK: WHAT WORKS?

Employer costs for health-related absenteeism are rising, mainly due to rising claims for mental conditions, such as depression, anxiety, or stress. The payments for disabilities in an organization of 1,000 employees are estimated to be in the range of $2 million per year. But with effective disability management and return-to-work programs, these costs can be cut by 50 percent. Two methods of managing return-to-work programs illustrate effective practices.

In the 1990s, CIBC was dealing with increasing levels of short-term disability claims that were slowly turning into long-term disability claims. The traditional medical model was that the employee would produce a doctor's note providing evidence of a disability, and then the manager would hear nothing for a long time. Employees on disability felt isolated and managers felt resentful. CIBC wanted to change this model and started by focusing on what the employee could do rather than what the employee could not do. So the bank started a new process. As soon as an employee is absent for six days, the file is downloaded into CIBC Health Services department, where the coordinator calls the employee's manager and then the employee. A meeting is arranged to discuss the employee's abilities, not the medical condition. Then the manager and the employee work out a return-to-work plan. Any resources needed for accommodation are provided by a central accommodation fund, not from the manager's budget. CIBC spends its money on rehabilitation, not checking on whether the person is really sick or not. Through the use of this facilitated return-to-work program, CIBC has reduced its lost days by 30 percent and has won awards for its disability management program.

The traditional medical model is still prevalent, and is working well for some organizations. The disability management program at Ontario Power Generation (OPG), an employer of 11,000 in highly diverse positions from nuclear engineers to receptionists, is resource-intensive but effective. The OPG process is based on the premise that early return to work is beneficial to employees and that accommodating these employees is paramount. A team of 23 full- and part-time occupational health nurses manage about 1,400 major medical absences a year. The program is mandatory for any employee absent for more than 5 days. On day 5 of an absence, the supervisor notifies the nurse care coordinator that the organization has a major medical absence. The employee receives a medical absence form to be completed by the physician, who then submits it to OPG within 14 days. The nurse care coordinator works with the employee to develop a plan for return to work. As long as the employee is cooperating, or there are valid reasons why he or she cannot cooperate with the plan, then the sick benefits continue.

QUESTIONS

1. If you were an employee with a major medical absence, which model would you prefer and why?

2. What do you think the role of the union should be under each model?

Source: Adapted from David Brown, "True Costs of Disability Make Clear Case for Return-to-Work," Canadian HR Reporter (May 31, 2004): 12; Andrea Davis, "DM Diagnosis," Benefits Canada (March 2006): 38–43; Uyen Vu, "Physical Disability Going Down; Mental Disability Going Up," Canadian HR Reporter (March 22, 2004): 6.

CASE STUDY 3

THE SILENT SAFETY ISSUE

Have you experienced any of the following at work?

- Implied threats of termination
- Repeated screaming or yelling
- Constant criticism in front of others
- Assignment of trivial tasks below the level of the job
- The silent treatment by others

These are all examples of bullying or harassing behaviour at work. Bullying is malicious behaviour that is designed to undermine the employee through intimidation, cruelty, or humiliation. The behaviour is hurtful and repetitive. Adult bullying can be classified in these ways:

- Threats to professional status, such as belittling your opinion
- Threats to personal standing, such as name calling
- Isolation (not including you in meetings or ignoring your comments)
- Overwork, such as impossible deadlines
- Destabilization, such as meaningless tasks or constant reminders of previous errors

A UK employer was found liable for not stopping, despite repeated requests for help from a female employee, bullying by four coworkers. The bullying consisted mainly of isolation-type behaviours:

- Bursting out laughing when she walked by
- Pretending they could not hear her when she spoke
- Crude and lewd comments that made her feel uncomfortable
- Removing her name from circulation lists and removing paper from her desk
- Ignoring her or staring at her silently, with arms crossed

The court ruled that the claimant was subjected to a campaign of mean and spiteful behaviour; i.e., a deliberate campaign of bullying. Targets of bullying suffer long-term psychological and occupational impairment. Total damages awarded were estimated to be Cdn$1.7 million.

Provincial occupational health and safety acts state that the employer is responsible for ensuring a safe workplace. Two provinces (Quebec and Saskatchewan) have introduced legislation to "protect workers from psychological harassment." Since Quebec introduced this legislation in 2004, there have been about 7,000 complaints filed by nonunion workers. Most of those being harassed are women, and they state that the harassment is repetitive and being done by the employer or its representative.

But are there more effective ways to deal with a workplace bully? The answer is yes. Brian Smeenk, President of the Toronto chapter of the Human Resources Professionals Association of Ontario, states that his members, many of whom work in the headquarters of national organizations, have a responsibility for developing the policies and programs to eradicate bullying.

Studies on bullying show that three relatively simple measures can be put into place to discourage and prevent workplace bullying. The first of these is to provide a list of behaviours that constitute harassment. By naming and labelling these acts as wrong, the workplace bully is suddenly in the spotlight, and also has been made aware that the organization will not tolerate this conduct.

The second method is to develop flexible channels of reporting, beyond the supervisor, and that might include a designated HR professional and an ombudsman. It makes no sense to ask an alleged victim to report the harassment to her supervisor, if her supervisor is the harasser. However, before any unacceptable behaviour is reported, the employee should begin a log, noting the time, date, persons present, and most importantly, a behaviourly based description of the harassment. The behaviour cannot be described as *"be bullied me"* or *"be humiliated me in front of some customers."* The behaviour must be described as, for example, *"The manager told me to get some products off the shelf for the customer. When I proceeded to do this, be yelled at me, 'Hurry up fatso, We don't have all day,' and then said to the customer, while I retrieved the box, 'If she didn't eat so many donuts, you would have your item already,' and then laughed."*

This log should consist of several instances of the harassment. The courts will look at the duration and frequency of the bullying and would not normally consider one or two incidents. Then the log should be discussed with the supervisor or his or her manager or the HR representative. The interview is conducted exactly like any disciplinary investigation, with an outline of the consequences if the harassment continues.

The victim should not be the only one monitoring bullies. The HR department might also want to monitor disability leaves by unit. Many victims of bullying are afraid of retaliation if they report it, so instead go on disability leave as the only solution to the distress that they are experiencing. There are other "canaries in the mineshaft" indicators that a toxic boss is in the organization. HR should track grievances, complaints, absenteeism, and turnover by unit. Any indication that these are higher than similar units may be cause for further investigation. HR should also incorporate a few questions about employee experiences of bullying in organizational surveys. The final step is a conflict dispute mechanism, such as a mediator.

The consequences of not dealing with harassment at work include higher than average turnover, lower productivity, and less creativity. No one can work in an atmosphere of fear. By putting anti-bullying programs in place, the organization can expect reductions in absenteeism rates, disability claims, grievances, and legal costs.

QUESTIONS

1. Determine if there is bullying at your workplace by using the Workplace Violence Employee Assessment checklist provided at http://www.esao.on.ca/downloads/checklist_pdfs/WORKPLACE%20VIOLENCE%20EMPLOYEE%20RISK%20FORM.dot.

2. Then, prepare a list of what you and your employer can do to prevent bullying in the workplace by using the prescriptions offered by the Canadian Centre for Occupational Health and Safety at http://www.ccohs.ca/oshanswers/psychosocial/bullying.html.

CAREER COUNSEL

The Job Stress Assessment on the *Managing Human Resources* website (http://www.belcourt6e.nelson.com) is designed to help you measure the amount of stress you are experiencing. Visit this site to measure your stress level and learn about strategies for managing stress.

NOTES AND REFERENCES

1. http://atlantic.psac.com/what/healthsafety/documents/BRIEF_Independent%20Review_WHSCC_ENG1.pdf, retrieved August 27, 2009.

2. Adrian Gostick, "Delivering Timely Safety Recognition," *Occupational Safety and Health* 73, no. 9 (September 2004): 94; "Developing Tomorrow's Leaders," *Canadian Business* 78, no. 2 (2005): 59.

3. http://www.awcbc.org and http://www.iapa.ca, retrieved July 19, 2006.

4. "Lear Corporation Canada Ltd Fined $125,000 for Health and Safety Violation," *Canada News Wire*, May 23, 2006; "Hershey Canada Fined $50,000 for Health and Safety Violation," *Canada News Wire*, August 11, 2005.

5. Rob Stewart, "The Challenge of Creating a Culture of Safety," *Canadian HR Reporter* (March 28, 2005): 11.

6. M.J. Colligan and A. Cohen, "The Role of Training in Promoting Workplace Safety and Health" in M. J. Barling and M. Frone (Eds.) *Handbook of Workplace Safety* (pp. 223–248).

7. Todd Nighswonger, "Is First-Aid First in Your Workplace?" *Occupational Hazards* 64, no. 4 (April 2002): 45–47.

8. Tim W. McDaniel, "Employee Participation: A Vehicle for Safety by Design," *Occupational Hazards* 6, no. 5 (May 2002): 71–76.

9. John P. Spath, "How to Get Employees Involved in the Safety Program," *Occupational Hazards* 66, no. 9 (September 2004): 63.

10. Craig Miller, "Can the Internet Improve Safety?" *Occupational Safety and Health* 73, no. 6 (June 2004): 98.

11. G. C. Shah, "Five Steps to Digital Safety," *Occupational Safety and Health* 71, (March 2002): 22–25.

12. Roger Brooks, "OSHA's E-Tool for Lockout/Tagout," *Occupational Safety and Health* 71, no. 4 (April 2002): 22–24.

13. Larry Hansen, "How Will They Know?" *Occupational Hazards* 66, no. 10 (October 2004): 39.

14. R. Bruce McAfee and Ashley R. Winn, "The Use of Incentives/Feedback to Enhance Work Place Safety: A Critique of the Literature," *Journal of Safety Research* 20 (1989): 7–19. See also Thomas R. Krause, John H. Hidley, and Stanley J. Hodson, "Broad-Based Changes in Behavior Key to Improving Safety Culture," *Occupational Health and Safety* 59, no. 7 (July 1990): 31–37, 50; Matthew P. Weinstock, "Rewarding Safety,"

Occupational Hazards 56, no. 3 (March 1994): 73–76; Susan J. Marks, "Incentives that Really Reward and Motivate," *Workforce* 80, no. 6 (June 2001): 108–113.

15. Tara Neal, "Tools of the Trade," *Occupational Health and Safety* 18, no. 2 (March 2002): 60–68.

16. Diana McCrohan, "Add Impact to Your Program," *Occupational Safety and Health* 73, no. 2 (February 2004): 52.

17. Terese Steinback, "Workplace Strategies for Removing Obstacles to Employee Health," *Employee Benefits Journal* 25, no. 1 (March 2000): 9–10.

18. David Brown, "Sick Buildings Lower Productivity," *Canadian HR Reporter*, March 22, 2004, 11.

19. "Smoke Gets in Your Lungs," *HRfocus* 73, no. 2 (February 1996): 17.

20. Todd Humber, "Snuffing out Smoking," *Canadian HR Reporter* (April 11, 2005): 19.

21. D. Dyck, "Wrapping Up the Wellness Package," *Benefits Canada* 23, no. 1 (January 1999): 16–20.

22. http://www.courts.gov.bc.ca/jdb-txt/ca/04/02/2004bcca0269.htm, retrieved August 27, 2009.

23. Greta Thornbory, "Dealing with MSDs," *Occupational Health* 56, no. 5 (May 2004): 18. See also Dave Heidorn, "Where Ergo Needs to Go," *Professional Safety* 49, no. 7 (July 2004): 14.

24. James M. Stewart, "Critical Elements for Effective Ergonomics," *Occupational Safety and Health* 71, no. 1 (January 2002): 43–45.

25. Canadian Centre for Occupational Health and Safety, http://www.ccohs.ca, retrieved July 18, 2006.

26. Kevin Kelloway, "Predictors and Outcomes of Workplace Violence," *HR Professional* 20, no. 1 (February/March 2003): 50.

27. http://www.ccohs.ca, retrieved July 19, 2006.

28. Andre Picard, "Remedy is needed for violence against nurses," *The Globe and Mail*, March 30, 2006, A17.

29. Richard S. Dunham, Rick Miller, Aren Therese Palmer, and Michael Arndt, "The War on Terror: What Companies Need to Do," *BusinessWeek* (August 16, 2004): 26. See also Lawrence D. Mankin and Ronald W. Perry, "Terrorism Challenges for Human Resource Management," *Review of Public Personnel Management* 24, no. 1 (March 2004): 3–17.

30. Stephen V. Magyar Jr., "Do You Have an Evacuation Plan That Works?" *Occupational Safety and Health* 72, no. 12 (December 2003): 44. See also Susanne M. Bruyère and William G. Stothers, "Enabling Safe Evacuations," *HR Magazine* 47, no. 1 (January 2002): 65–67.

31. John C. DelBel, "Workplace Aggression," *Nursing Management* 34, no. 9 (July 2003): 30. See also Bruce T. Blythe and Terri Butler Stivarius, "Assessing and Defusing Workplace Threats of Violence," *Occupational Safety and Health* 73, no. 2 (February 2004): 20.

32. Claire Ginther, "A Death in the Family," *HR Magazine* 46, no. 5 (May 2001): 55–58.

33. Bruce T. Blythe, "The Human Side of Crisis Management," *Occupational Hazards* 66, no. 7 (July 2004): 37.

34. Paul Falcone, "Dealing with Employees in Crisis," *HR Magazine* 48, no. 5 (May 2003): 117.

35. Andre Picard "The working wounded," *The Globe and Mail* (June 23, 2008), A8.

36. Maryann Hammers, "Banking on an In-House EAP," *Workforce* 82, no. 4 (April 2003): 18.

37. Kristi D. Willbanks, "The Role of Supervisory Referral in Employee Assistance Programs," *Employee Assistance Quarterly* 15, no. 2 (1999): 13–28.

38. Zachary Meyer, "Combating Employee Depression by Integrating Behavioral, Medical, and Pharmaceutical Benefits," *Employee Benefit Plan Review* 59, no. 2 (August 2004): 13.

39. Susan K. McFarlin, William Fals-Stewart, Debra A. Major, and Elaine M. Justice, "Alcohol Use and Workplace Aggression: An Examination of Perpetration and Victimization," *Journal of Substance Abuse* 13, nos. 1–2 (2001): 303–321.

40. "Change Your Culture and Lower Your Benefit Costs," *HRfocus* 81, no. 11 (November 2004): 6.

41. Lee Ann Jackson, "Relax, Relate, Release," *Black Enterprise* 35, no. 2 (September 2004): 61.

42. "Change Your Culture and Lower Your Benefit Costs," 6.

43. Max Messmer, "Are You Burning Out Your Best Employees?" *Strategic Finance* 85, no. 11 (May 2004): 12. See also Bob Gunn, "The Antidote to Burnout," *Strategic Finance* 86, no. 3 (September 2004): 8.

44. "Stop Burnout—Before It Stops Your Employees," *HRfocus* 79, no. 2 (February 2002): 3–4.

45. Sora Song, "The Price of Pressure," *Time* (July 19, 2004): 68.

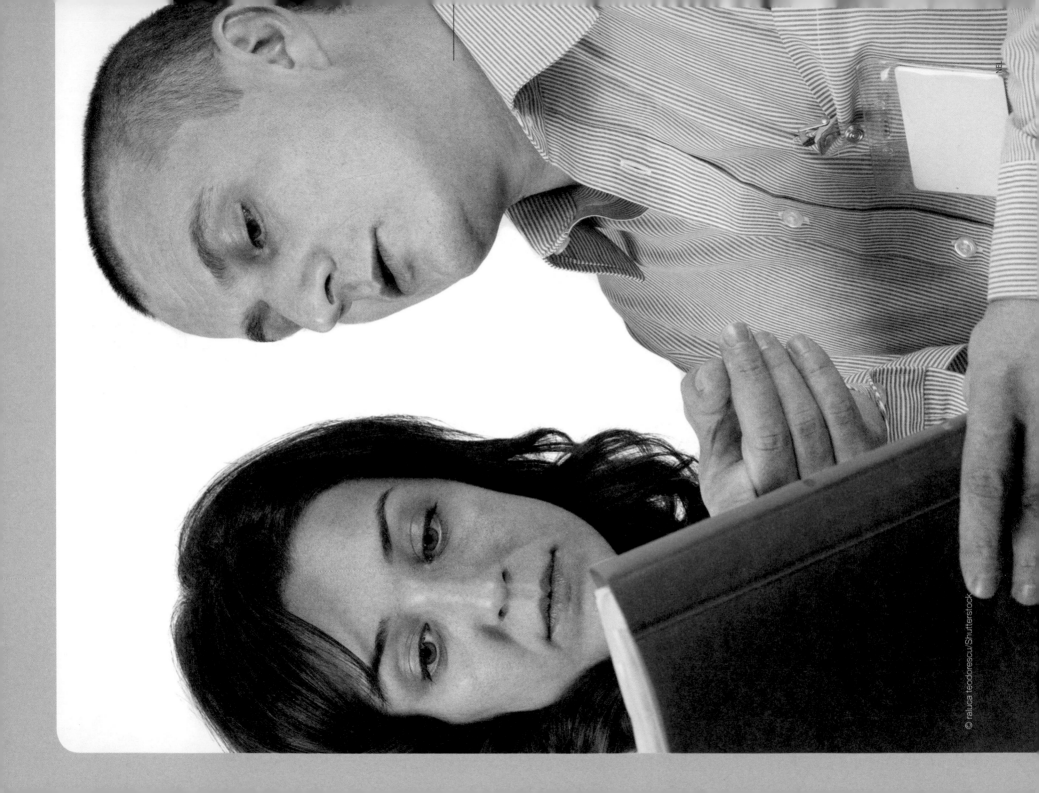

Employee Rights and Discipline

CHAPTER 13

After studying this chapter, you should be able to

[OUTCOME 1] Explain the different regimes that govern the employment relationship.

[OUTCOME 2] Explain the difference between expressed and implied terms of employment contracts.

[OUTCOME 3] Explain the rules governing the dismissal of employees.

[OUTCOME 4] Identify and explain the privacy rights of employees.

[OUTCOME 5] Explain the process of establishing disciplinary policies, including the proper implementation of organizational rules.

[OUTCOME 6] Discuss the meaning of discipline and how to investigate a disciplinary problem.

[OUTCOME 7] Differentiate between the two approaches to disciplinary action.

[OUTCOME 8] Identify the different types of alternative dispute resolution procedures.

[OUTCOME 9] Discuss the role of ethics in the management of human resources.

In this chapter we discuss employee rights, workplace privacy, and employee discipline. At a general level, the rights of employees are those described in the employment contract. However, that is a very incomplete description. First, many employment contracts are not written down, but are oral contracts, so the precise terms may not be obvious to the employee or the employer. Second, many important aspects of the employment relationship appear in the form of customs or practices, rather than as noted contract terms. Third, common law judges have long shaped the scope of the employment contract by "implying" contract terms. "Implied" contract terms may not be known to either party to the contract, but are nevertheless treated by the courts as enforceable contract terms. Fourth, employment contracts may be limited, altered, or voided by a range of employment legislation through which the government intervenes in the employment relationship. The true scope of employee rights and employer obligations is therefore influenced by all of these factors.

Furthermore, managers are discovering that the right to discipline and discharge employees—a traditional responsibility of management—is more difficult to exercise in light of the growing attention to employee rights. Disciplining employees is a difficult and unpleasant task for most managers and supervisors; many of them report that taking disciplinary action against an employee is the most stressful duty they perform. Balancing employee rights and employee discipline may not be easy, but it is a universal requirement and a critical aspect of good management.

Because the growth of employee rights issues has led to an increase in the number of lawsuits filed by employees, we include in this chapter a discussion of alternative dispute resolution as a way to foster organizational justice. Because disciplinary actions are subject to challenge and possible reversal through governmental agencies or the courts, management should make a positive effort to prevent the need for such action. When disciplinary action becomes impossible to avoid, however, that action should be taken in accordance with carefully developed HR policies and practices. Because ethics is an important element of organizational justice, the chapter concludes with a discussion of organizational ethics in employee relations.

THE THREE REGIMES OF EMPLOYMENT LAW

At the outset of our discussion in this chapter, it is important to understand the different sources of employee rights in the law of employment. There are three different legal regimes that govern the employment relationship: (1) the common law; (2) statutory regulation; and (3) collective bargaining and arbitration law. This chapter deals primarily with the first two, whereas Chapter 14 considers the third regime in greater detail. However, we will consider all three in this chapter, particularly in regards to how they govern the rules of employee discipline and dismissal.

THE COMMON LAW OF EMPLOYMENT

The rights and obligations of employers and employees are determined firstly by the terms of the employment contract. However, often there is no written contract, or the terms of the contract are vague or fail to address a particular situation at all. As such, it is common for disagreements to arise under employment contracts. Whenever a dispute arises about the meaning and application of an employment contract, either party to the contract may file a lawsuit in the courts and ask a judge (and sometimes a jury) to decide what the contract means or how it was intended to apply in a particular circumstance. The judges' decisions are recorded in law books, and more recently, in electronic legal databases, and considered in future disputes involving similar issues. Over time, a huge body of "case law" has been compiled that considers the meaning and application of employment contracts to an endless

OUTCOME [1]

array of employment scenarios. This body of law is known as the **common law of employment**.

It is crucial for HR managers to understand how the common law of employment influences the terms and conditions of employment and the interpretation of employment contracts. Common law judges have developed a long list of implied **contract terms** that are incorporated into all employment contracts, unless there is a written term in the contract that overrides the implied term. For example, probably the most well-known implied term is the requirement for both the employer and the employee to give reasonable notice that they are terminating the employment contract. If the written contract includes a clause specifying how much notice of termination is required, then the implied term requiring reasonable notice will not apply (providing the contractual notice clause complies with the notice provisions in employment standards legislation).

Important terms courts have implied into employment contracts include

- Obligation of the employer and the employee to provide reasonable notice that they are terminating the contract
- Obligation on the employer to maintain a safe workplace
- Obligation on the employer to treat employees with decency, civility, respect, and dignity
- Obligation on the employee to serve the employer with loyalty and fidelity
- Obligation on the employee to perform competently
- Obligation on the employee to advance the employer's economic interests
- Obligation on the employee to avoid insubordination and insolence

Breach of an implied term has the same effect as breach of a written term. Therefore, it is crucial that HR managers are familiar with the scope of implied terms applied by the courts to employment contracts.

STATUTORY EMPLOYMENT REGULATION

Unhappy with the outcomes of the common law model of employment, governments in Canada have over the past century intervened by passing a large variety of legislation aimed at influencing the employment relationship. As we saw in Chapter 3, employment equity legislation is intended to address systemic discrimination against women, Aboriginal people, people with disabilities, and visible minorities. Human rights legislation prohibits discrimination in employment on certain designated grounds, including sex, age, religion, and skin colour. Pay equity legislation addresses inequities in how men and women are compensated; employment standards legislation regulates the content of employment contracts by imposing minimum contract standards, such as minimum wage, maximum hours of work, and overtime pay; occupational health and safety legislation attempts to ensure safe working conditions; labour relations laws give employees the right to form and belong to unions, and to bargain for better working conditions, and restricts the right of employers to dismiss or discipline employees for exercising rights protected by the legislation (see Chapter 14). And this is only a sampling of the wide range of legislation in Canada that addresses aspects of the employment relationship.

Statutory regulation operates alongside the common law, co-existing with it, but also often modifying it. Usually, it is not permissible to contract out of protective employment legislation, with the result that regulation acts as a default minimum amount of protection required. For example, while the common law includes an implied obligation on the parties to provide reasonable notice of termination of the contract, employment standards regulation also imposes an obligation on employers to provide notice of termination. The employment standards' notice requirement is considered a "minimum" that must be provided to an employee, and a contract term providing "less notice will be unenforceable (see Highlights in HRM 13.1).

common law of employment

The body of case law in which courts interpret employment contracts, and the legal principles taken from those cases that guide the interpretation of employment contracts

implied contract terms

Terms judges read into employment contracts when the written contract does not expressly deal with the matter

Highlights in **HRM 13.1**

Take Notice!

What happens if the employment contract includes a notice of termination clause that provides for less notice than required by employment standards legislation? That was the issue in a case called *Machtinger v. HOJ Industries*. The contract included a written term permitting the employer to terminate the contract without notice. At the time of dismissal, the employee was entitled to four weeks' notice under the Ontario *Employment Standards Act*. The issue before the Supreme Court of Canada was, what happens when a contractual notice of termination clause provides for less notice than the minimum notice required by employment standards legislation? The employer argued that the statutory minimum notice should be applied, while the employee argued that reasonable notice should be applied.

The Supreme Court ruled that reasonable notice applies, since the effect of including the illegal notice clause in the contract was to void the contract term altogether. If the contract notice term is void, then it is as if there was not notice term at all, in which case, the implied term requiring reasonable notice is read into the contract. As a result, rather than receiving the four week's statutory notice he was entitled to, the employee was awarded reasonable notice amounting to 7.5 months.

Source: Machtinger v. HOJ Industries Ltd., [1992] 1 S.C.R. 986.

collective agreement
An employment contract between an employer and a union that sets out the terms of employment of a group of the employer's employees represented by the union

---

Thus, an employee may be entitled to 12 months notice of termination according to the implied contractual requirement to pay reasonable notice, but entitled to only 8 weeks' notice under employment standards legislation. An employer may opt to provide only the minimum notice under the legislation. While legally the employee is contractually entitled to the larger reasonable notice, in practice, recovering it would require the employee to file a lawsuit (known as a "wrongful dismissal" case), which is expensive and time consuming. As a result, many employees simply accept the statutory minimum notice and do not pursue their common law entitlement to reasonable notice.

COLLECTIVE BARGAINING LEGISLATION AND LABOUR ARBITRATION

Collective bargaining legislation, such as the Ontario *Labour Relations Act*, seeks to improve conditions of work by empowering workers to join together and bargain a better contract for themselves than is usually possible when an individual employee bargains with his or her employer. It does this by facilitating a right of workers to organize into unions and bargain collectively with the employer with the aid of a professional union bargainer, and by permitting workers to strike and employers to "lock out" the employees in limited circumstances in order to apply pressure to reach an agreement. This process is discussed further in Chapter 14.

For now, it is important to note some crucial differences between the rules that govern unionized and nonunionized workplaces in Canada. The contract that is bargained in a unionized workplace is known as a collective agreement. The common law of employment does not apply to a collective agreement. Therefore, for example, the implied term permitting an employer to terminate an employee by giving reasonable notice does not apply when the employees are unionized. This is an important difference between unionized and nonunionized workplaces. Whereas a nonunion employer can terminate an employee for any reason, or no reason at all (subject to statutes that prevent discriminatory dismissals) by simply giving the proper notice, a unionized employer usually needs just cause to dismiss a worker, unless the dismissal is due to purely economic reasons (a permanent layoff). In other words, unlike a nonunion employer, a unionized employer usually needs a valid reason to fire an employee.

Another important difference between a collective agreement and an individual employment contract is the method of enforcement. A nonunion employee must sue the employer in a court for breach of the employment contract. That process is often costly (since the employee will usually retain a lawyer) and very time consuming. A unionized employee, on the other hand, must file a grievance alleging that the collective agreement has been violated, and that grievance, if not settled or resolved, may be referred to a labour arbitrator instead of a court. Arbitration is much quicker than a lawsuit, and the costs are covered by the union as part of the benefit paid for by employees in the form of union dues. Labour arbitrators have built up their own form of common law, known as "arbitration law," which helps guide the interpretation and application of collective agreements. While, on some issues, arbitration law may be the same or similar to the approach of common law judges interpreting individual employment contracts, the two bodies of law should not be confused.

UNDERSTANDING THE INDIVIDUAL EMPLOYMENT CONTRACT

Since the individual employment contract is a type of contract, the general rules of contract law developed in the common law apply. One important rule of contract law is that a valid contract requires "mutual consideration." This means that both parties to the contract must receive some benefit in the exchange. This has important implications for HR managers. For example, it means that once an employee has commenced employment, the employer cannot unilaterally change or introduce new terms of employment, unless the employee agrees to the change and receives some new benefit in exchange. Employers frequently run into this problem when they permit an employee to start working before presenting the employment contract to the employee for his or her signature. When that happens, the employee has started work under a verbal contract. If the employer later presents a written contract that includes terms beneficial to the employer (such as a notice of termination clause that provides less than reasonable notice), those new terms will not be enforceable, even if the employee signs the contract, if the employee was not also given some new benefit (such as a raise, a new holiday, etc.) in exchange for signing the contract.

The fact that the rules of contract law apply to the employment relationship has other important implications. For example, it means that the employee can insist that the employer comply with the terms of the contract. This might seem obvious, yet many HR managers mistakenly believe that the employer has the right to unilaterally make changes to the conditions of employment. If an employer unilaterally changes a term of the employment contract, it will usually have breached the contract, enabling the employee to sue for breach and, if they so choose, to claim that he or she has been constructively dismissed.

A constructive dismissal occurs when an employer commits a significant or fundamental breach of the contract, such as by eliminating a important benefit enjoyed by the employee, reducing compensation, or demoting an employee. In that case, the employee may treat the contract as having been terminated by the employer, quit, and sue the employer to recover either contractual notice or implied reasonable notice. This highlights the need for HR managers to be careful when attempting to make a change to employees' terms and conditions of employment.

[OUTCOME 2]

[OUTCOME 3]

labour arbitrator
A person assigned to interpret and decide disputes ("grievances") about the meaning, interpretation, and application of a collective agreement governing employees in a unionized workplace

constructive dismissal
When an employer commits a fundamental breach of the contract, such as by unilaterally changing a key term of the contract, the employee can treat the breach as a termination

The Business CASE

The Danger of Changing a Contract Term Without the Employee's Agreement

What if the employee just will not agree to a contract amendment that the employer wants? In *Wronko v. Western Inventory Service*, the employer wanted to change a term in the employment contract that required the employer to pay two years' salary to the employee in the event the employee was terminated. The employer asked Mr. Wronko to sign a revised contract that reduced the payment required from two years to 30 weeks. Wronko refused to sign and indicated he did not agree to the change. The employer then gave Wronko two years' notice that it was amending the term accordingly. After two years, the employer again gave Wronko a revised contract and told him that this new contract was now "in effect," and that if Wronko did not sign the new contract, then the company did "not have a job for [him]."

Wronko quit and sued the employer for wrongful dismissal, alleging he was entitled to two years' salary as per the original contract. The employer argued that

it was permitted to give notice of the change to a term in the contract, which it had done. The Ontario Court of Appeal disagreed. It ruled that when faced with an employee who will not agree to a proposed change to the employment contract, an employer must either withdraw the proposed amendment or terminate the entire contract by giving the required notice, and then offer the employee a new contract including the revised terms. The employer here had not given notice that it was terminating the contract, it had given only notice of its intention to make a unilateral change to one term of the contract. Therefore, the court ruled that the employee was entitled to two years' salary (minus money earned by the employee during that period). The employer should seek to make the amendment palatable to the employee by offering some benefit to the employee in exchange for the benefit it seeks to obtain from the amendment. This could avoid the costs associated with having to terminate the contract in its entirety.

To make a change to the terms of an employment contract without breaching the contract, the employer should do *either* of the following:

1. Obtain the employee's agreement to the change and provide the employee with some *new* consideration (benefit); or
2. Terminate the employment contract in its entirety by giving the required notice of termination, and then offer a new contract on the revised terms. See the Business Case, above.

HR managers need to understand the terms of the employment contracts in order to appreciate the scope of their managerial authority. For example, does an employer have a contractual right to suspend an employee without pay as a form of progressive discipline or to put an employee on temporary layoff during an economic downturn? In both cases, the employer is essentially preventing the employee from performing his or her end of the bargain. That would be a breach of the contract, unless the employer can point to a contract term that empowers it to suspend or layoff. Most contracts do not confer these rights on employers, with the result that suspensions and layoffs are usually contract breaches, and the employees affected could opt to quit and sue for constructive dismissal.

THE RULES GOVERNING DISMISSAL

DISMISSAL OF A NONUNION EMPLOYEE: WRONGFUL DISMISSAL

Under the common law of employment, either the employer or the employee can terminate the employment contract by providing the other side with the amount of notice specified in the contract, or if the contract does not include a notice term or includes a term requiring less notice than required by employment standards legislation, with reasonable notice. What amount of notice is "reasonable" is determined by the court, applying a variety of criteria judges have developed over the years, including the employee's age and the availability of alternative similar employment given the employee's experience and training. However, the two most important factors in assessing notice are (1) length of service with the employer and (2) the nature of the job performed by the employee. Generally, the longer an employee has worked for an employer, the longer the period of notice. In addition, the courts have developed a form of cap on the length of reasonable notice that is tied to the job performed by the employee: nonmanagerial employees are usually not entitled to more than 12 months' notice, whereas managerial employees may be entitled as much as 24 months' notice.[1]

Notably, a nonunion employer does not need a reason to dismiss an employee. It can dismiss an employee at any time, for any reason (that is not a violation of a statute, such as human rights legislation), or for no reason at all. It just needs to give the employee the proper contractual or reasonable notice. Most dismissals in Canada are done by means of the employer providing the employee with notice, which can be working notice or a payment of wages equal to what the employee would have received for working during the notice period.

However, an employer may also dismiss a nonunion employee without any notice, if the employee has committed a serious breach of the contact, such as engaging in significant dishonesty, gross incompetence, sexual harassment, or workplace bullying or violence. When a nonunion employer dismisses an employee for cause, without notice, it is called a **summary dismissal.**

One comprehensive study of summary dismissal cases found that employers won 40 percent of the time when the charge was dishonesty, theft, substance abuse, or abusive behaviour; 54 percent of the time when the charge was insubordination; 65 percent of the time when the charge was conflict of interest or competing with the employer; and just 25 percent of the time when the charge was poor performance.[2]

Whenever an employee believes he or she should have received more notice than that provided, the employee may file a **wrongful dismissal lawsuit.** This is a claim filed in court alleging that the employer breached the employment contract by failing to provide the required notice of termination. Although in a case of summary dismissal the court will have to decide whether the employer had cause sufficient to warrant the employee forfeiting his or her entitlement to notice, it is important to note that the court will not question whether the employer had a legal right to dismiss the employee. The issue in a wrongful dismissal case is whether notice should have been given and, if so, how much. It is not whether the employer had just cause to dismiss the employee, which is the issue usually at stake in a unionized arbitration case. Therefore, the remedy in a successful wrongful dismissal case is usually money; courts do not overturn the decision to dismiss, and they virtually never order the employer to reinstate the employee.

Statutory Regulation of Dismissal

The common law entitlement of employers to dismiss a nonunion employee for any reason by giving proper notice has been restricted in a number of ways by government intervention. Statutes prohibit employers from dismissing employees for certain reasons. For example, human rights legislation prohibits dismissals based on discriminatory reasons. Labour relations legislation prohibits an employer from dismissing an employee involved in organizing a union. Many types of employment statutes prohibit dismissals and punishment as a reprisal against employees who exercise their statutory rights. For example, employment standards and occupational health and safety statutes usually prohibit employers from punishing employees in any way as a reprisal for the employee making claims under the statute. The tribunals responsible for enforcing the statutes usually have the authority to

---

summary dismissal
When a nonunion employer terminates an employee without notice because the employee has committed a serious breach of the contract

wrongful dismissal
A lawsuit filed in a court by an employee alleging that he or she was dismissed without proper contractual or reasonable notice

statutory rights
Legal entitlements that derive from government legislation

order the employer to reinstate the employee, with full back pay and benefits, if they find that the reason for the dismissal was prohibited by the statute.

As noted earlier, employment standards legislation in Canada imposes a minimum amount of notice of termination required. For example, in Ontario, the amount of notice required in the *Employment Standards Act* is linked directly to years of service; one week's notice per year of service to a maximum of 8 weeks, but that amount goes up in the case of mass layoffs, to as much as 18 weeks' when 500 or more employees are terminated. In addition, the legislation imposes a separate obligation to pay "severance pay" when the employer has an annual payroll of $2.5 million or more or when 50 or more employees are being terminated in a 6-month period due to the closure of all or part of a business. Severance pay is one week's pay per year of service to a maximum of 26 weeks. Other provinces have similar requirements with variations. HR managers should be knowledgeable about the statutory provisions that govern the employment contract and dismissals in order to avoid costly and potentially embarrassing complaints by employees.

DISMISSAL OF A UNIONIZED EMPLOYEE: JUST CAUSE

Most collective agreements in unionized workplaces confer a right on employers to lay off workers, although they regulate the selection of the employees to be laid off, and the order of recalls. Therefore, a unionized employer usually has the option of laying off workers for economic reasons. In addition, collective agreements usually include a management rights clause that grants employers the right to impose discipline short of dismissal, such as unpaid suspensions. As we noted previously, since most individual employment contracts do not include expressed management rights to impose temporary layoffs or unpaid suspensions, these actions are usually considered breaches of the individual employment contract amounting to a constructive dismissal.

However, while unionized employers may have these additional managerial rights, they are also significantly more restrained than nonunion employers in other ways. Most notably, in stark contrast with most individual employment contracts, collective agreements usually include a term requiring that the employer have just cause to impose discipline or dismiss an employee. As a result, unlike a nonunion employer, a unionized employer usually needs a reason to dismiss an employee. That reason can then be challenged by the employee and the union through the grievance procedure in the collective agreement, rather than in the courts. The implied common law right of employers to dismiss employees for any reason by giving them reasonable notice does not apply to unionized employees. Moreover, a labour arbitrator has the statutory power to substitute a lesser penalty than the one imposed by the employer. That means that labour arbitrators can (and often do) reinstate employees when they rule that the employer did not have just cause to dismiss the employee.

As a result, it is particularly crucial in a unionized setting that HR managers keep careful records of employee misconduct. Labour arbitrators expect employers to apply progressive discipline before dismissing a unionized employee, except when the employee's misconduct is particularly serious. It is very common for arbitrators to reinstate dismissed unionized employees and to substitute an unpaid suspension of some duration. In considering the appropriate penalty for employee misconduct, arbitrators consider the entirety of the situation looking for "mitigating" factors, which include the employee's length of service and past disciplinary record, the manner in which the employer treated other similar incidents involving other employees, and even the employee's personal circumstances, such as the impact the dismissal would have the employee and his or her dependants.

We can see, therefore, that nonunion employers face similar challenges to unionized employers when they attempt to summarily dismiss an employee without providing notice. The nonunion employer must convince a court that the employee's

FIGURE 13.1

Tips to Consider When Dismissing a Nonunion Employee with Cause or a Unionized Employee with Just Cause

- *Terminate an employee for cause only if there is a clear and articulated reason.* An employer should have clearly articulated, easily understandable reasons for discharging an employee. The reasons should be stated as objectively as possible and should reflect company rules, policies, and practices.
- *Set and follow termination rules and schedules.* Ensure every termination follows a documented set of procedures. Procedures can be from an employee handbook, a supervisory manual, or even an intra-office memorandum. Before terminating, give employees notices of unsatisfactory performance and improvement opportunities through a system of warnings and suspensions.
- *Nonunion employers should consider bargaining a contractual right to suspend an employee.* The right to suspend an employee without pay is a key component of progressive discipline in unionized workplaces, but that right rarely appears in nonunion employment contracts. Nonunion employers could include greater disciplinary rights in the contract language to give it more disciplinary options.
- *Document all performance problems.* A lack of documented problems in an employee's personnel record may be used as circumstantial evidence of pretextual discharge if the employee is "suddenly" discharged.
- *Be consistent with employees in similar situations.* Document reasons given for all disciplinary actions, even if they do not lead to termination. Terminated employees may claim that exception-to-the-rule cases are discriminatory. Detailed documentation will help employers explain why these "exceptions" did not warrant termination.

Using the Internet

A large number of arbitration and labour law–related tribunal decisions can be found at the website of the Canadian Labour Law Project:

http://www.canlii.org/en/blog/index.php?/archives/23-CanLII-Labour-Law-Project.htm

misconduct was sufficiently serious to warrant forfeiting notice of termination. A unionized employer needs to convince a labour arbitrator that it had just cause to dismiss the employee. In meeting these tests, employers face common challenges; similar advice can therefore be applied to both unionized and nonunion employers in regards to properly preparing for and implementing discipline, as outlined in Figure 13.1. (Figure 13.2 describes this process from the employee's perspective.) However, it is important to recall that the nonunion employer always has the option of dismissing the employee with notice (not asserting cause), which is an option not available to a unionized employer.

EMPLOYEE PRIVACY RIGHTS

There are many instances in which the interests of employees can come into conflict with those of the employer. An important example relates to employee privacy rights at work and outside the workplace. To what extent should employees be entitled to privacy in their relationship with the employer?

[OUTCOME]

PRIVACY ISSUES AT THE WORKPLACE

Employers have a legitimate interest in ensuring their employees work efficiently and avoid improper conduct at work, such as theft, harassment, or misuse of company computers. Surveillance of the workplace is a common method for managing these challenges. However, employer surveillance can also have the feel of "Big Brother" to employees, who may feel entitled to some measure of privacy at work. Balancing managerial rights and employee expectations about their entitlement to privacy can be a difficult job for HR managers.

A right of privacy at work has been recognized in various degrees under all three regimes of employment law. The strongest protections of employee rights are probably those recognized by labour arbitrators interpreting collective agreements.

FIGURE **13.2**

Firing Back!

Once you have received either verbal or written warnings about performance, a decision has usually been made to fire you. What can you do? If you are a unionized employee, you can file a grievance challenging the discipline. But a nonunion employee will not usually have that option. Writing back to pick holes in the accusations is the least effective defense. Using the same weapons as management, you must prove that the just cause will not hold.

Howard Levitt, a legal expert on dismissal, offers the following advice:

- Establish in writing that you were unaware of the standards of performance or conduct. You can argue that the standards are new or were not part of the initial job offer, position description, performance evaluations, or previous warnings. The company must prove that you were grossly incompetent, so any letters of praise or good performance review should be used. Any aspects of performance that may override the weak areas should be noted. For example, if you are being dismissed for poor communication skills but your productivity figures are increasing, this should be documented. As soon as you commence employment, start a file containing all performance evaluations; letters of praise from customers, coworkers, internal clients, and supervisors; and all other examples of performance achievements. Establish a paper trail of good performance.
- Argue that the company, while complaining about poor performance, has not stated specifically what is required to improve performance.
- Assert that you were not given the time, training, assistance, or learning opportunities necessary to improve performance.
- Establish, if true, that the employer hired you knowing that you did not possess the necessary skills. Note any understanding that you would receive the appropriate training.
- State, if applicable, that the skills desired now were not part of your original job description.
- Attribute your poor performance to factors outside your control, such as a decline in sales in all regions, or poorly priced products, or a temporary illness. If possible, establish that the company contributed to the performance problem by failing to respond to your (documented) suggestions for improvement.

Levitt further advises that letters and all other documentation be written with the assistance of a specialist. In the end, a nonunion employee will not get his or her job back if dismissed for performance problems, but if successful, they may receive an attractive severance package.

Source: Howard Levitt, Counsel, Lang Michener, Toronto, "How Employees Can Fight Firing for Just Cause," *Toronto Star*, August 17, 1992, C1. Reprinted by permission of the author.

Highlight in **HRM 13.2**

Overview of Regimes Governing Dismissals

HR managers are usually responsible for implementing dismissals of employees. This is a stressful part of the profession. However, it helps significantly to understand the basic legal rules governing the process. Here is a quick summary of the key issues and regimes discussed in this chapter.

Common Law (Nonunion Employees)

The common law rules of contract govern the employment relationship between individual employees and

nonunion employers. Every contract includes a notice of termination clause. The clause is either expressed (written) into the contract, or the courts imply a requirement for both parties to provide reasonable notice of termination. The courts decide how much notice is "reasonable" by applying a list of criteria. An expressed notice term supercedes the implied "reasonable notice" requirement, but courts will not enforce an expressed term if it requires less notice than required under employment standards legislation. A nonunion employer does

continued

not need a reason to dismiss an employee, provided it gives proper notice. Summary dismissal—dismissal without notice—is permitted only when the employee has committed a serious breach of the contract. Disputes about contracts in nonunion workplaces are resolved in courts after one of the parties files a lawsuit for breach of contract. The usual remedy is lost wages and benefits during the notice period that should have been given (not reinstatement).

Statutory Regulation (Union and Nonunion Employees)

Employment standards regulation explains the minimal notice of termination required, which usually applies only to the employer. The length of notice in employment standards regulation is often less than the common law reasonable notice. Employment standards regulations also often require "severance" pay in addition to notice, when the employer is large or there has been a mass termination. Various pieces of legislation prohibit dismissals for certain public policy reasons, such as for discriminatory reasons or as retaliation for the employee exercising statutory rights. Claims alleging a violation of a statute are decided by administrative tribunals, not courts, and the remedy can include lost wages and benefits and also reinstatement.

Collective Bargaining and Labour Arbitration

Unionized employees enjoy greater protection from dismissals. They are governed by the rules of collective agreements, not contract law; the common law does not apply to collective agreements. A unionized employer can usually lay off or dismiss an employee for economic reasons by giving at least the statutory minimum notice or a longer period in the collective agreement. But collective agreements usually require the employer to have just cause in all other situations, so that a unionized employer must have a reason to dismiss someone. A dismissed unionized employee challenging the employer's decision must filing a grievance that may be litigated before a labour arbitrator (not a court). An arbitrator has power to overturn the employer's decision and impose a lesser penalty (such as suspension) or reinstate the employee.

Arbitration law usually requires employers to establish both that there is a pressing need for surveillance and that the surveillance is conducted in a reasonable manner that balances the employee's interest in a reasonable amount of privacy with the employer's business concerns. In applying this balancing test, arbitrators have sometimes prohibited surveillance cameras; personal searches of people, bags, and clothing; and employer searches of employee e-mails and Internet usage. However, when the employer can show a strong reason justifying the surveillance, and that there was no other reasonable, less intrusive means of obtaining the information, arbitrators have tended to permit surveillance.[3]

Governments have sometimes passed legislation to protect employee privacy rights. For example, the British Columbia *Personal Information Protection Act* applies to the private sector in British Columbia and requires a similar balancing of employer and employee interests in assessing whether an employer can conduct surveillance on employees. An important recent piece of legislation is the federal *Personal Information Protection and Electronic Documents Act* (PIPEDA), which, among other things, regulates an employer's collection and dissemination of information about employees, as well as the right of employees to access their personnel files in some circumstances. It applies to federally regulated workplaces, but also to some "commercial activities" engaged in by provincially regulated companies. (commercial activities include the selling of information, such as employee lists or information about employees.)

Organizations covered by PIPEDA must obtain an individual's consent when they collect, use, or disclose the individual's personal information. The individual has a right to access personal information held by an organization and to challenge its accuracy, if necessary. Any organization that collects personal information can use that information only for the purpose for which it was collected. If an organization wants to use it for another purpose, it must obtain the individual's consent

Using the Internet

For further information on PIPEDA, see the federal Privacy Commissions Guide for Businesses and Organizations at **http://www.priv.gc.ca/leg_c/leg_c_p_e.cfm#contenttop**

© Digital Vision/Getty Images

Monitoring employee behaviour is an important deterrent to inappropriate conduct of employees.

again. Individuals must also be assured by the organization that their information will be protected by adequate safeguards. Recent interpretations of the PIPEDA indicate that the legislation requires a balancing of employer and employee rights similar to that required by labour arbitrators and other privacy legislation such as that in British Columbia. For example, employers covered by the legislation are now restricted in their ability to secretly monitor employee computer use unless they can prove that less intrusive means of monitoring computer use were used and did not solve the problem.[4]

Because privacy laws often oblige corporations to obtain consent from the individual whose personal information is being gathered, HR professionals should conduct an audit to determine if the organization's practice conforms to the legislation. For example, one organization collected information about the birth country of employees in order to facilitate international transfers. However, collecting this information for clerks, who will not be transferred, is unnecessary and would not meet the new standards.[5] Sources of information from selection interviews, employee evaluations, and disciplinary reports may have to be made available to employees.[6]

Employers have traditionally enjoyed a greater latitude under the common law to monitor their employees' behaviour. For example, court cases governing e-mail and the Internet have granted employers the right to monitor materials created, received, or sent at work on the premise that the employer owns the computer, the employee is expected to be performing only work-related tasks while at work, and there is no reasonable expectation of privacy when using the employer's computers and equipment. Two recent court cases have made this very clear. In one case, the employee, with 18 years of service, was terminated for using the company Internet for personal purposes, including accessing pornography. In another case, an employee with 15 years of service was found to have been using the company Internet to manage his own unrelated travel business, for up to two hours a day on company time, using the company's computers.[7]

However, even under the common law, an employer's right to monitor its employees' conduct at work is not absolute. In fact, common law judges appear to be slowly recognizing an implied right to privacy at work. In one recent case, an employer installed a hidden camera in the office of one of its employees. When the

FIGURE **13.3**

Employee Monitoring Practices

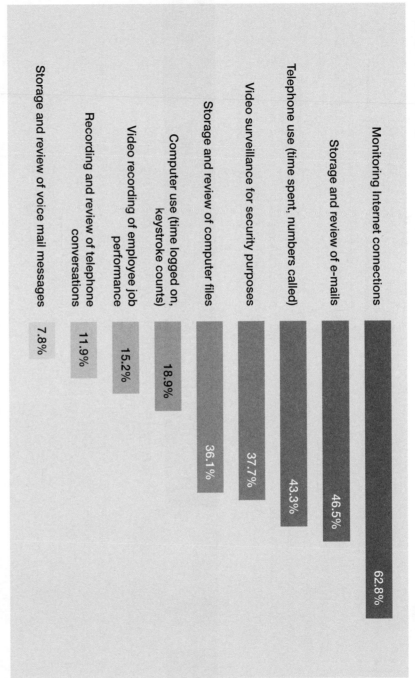

Practice	%
Monitoring Internet connections	62.8%
Storage and review of e-mails	46.5%
Telephone use (time spent, numbers called)	43.3%
Video surveillance for security purposes	37.7%
Storage and review of computer files	36.1%
Computer use (time logged on, keystroke counts)	18.9%
Video recording of employee job performance	15.2%
Recording and review of telephone conversations	11.9%
Storage and review of voice mail messages	7.8%

Source: Uyen Vu, "Employee Resistant to Any Form of Computer Video Monitoring, Study Says," *Canadian HR Reporter* (March 8, 2004): 2.

employee found out, she quit and sued for constructive dismissal. The employer defended its actions by claiming it had a legal right to install surveillance cameras. The court disagreed and found that the employer violated an implied term in the contract that it would treat its employees in good faith and fairly. Installing a hidden camera without any strong justification violated that term. The court ordered 7.5 months' reasonable notice damages.[8]

As you can see, employee surveillance can raise legal concerns. Nevertheless, surveillance of employees in various forms is quite common (see Figure 13.3).

HR experts and legal authorities strongly encourage employers to develop clear policies and guidelines that explain to employees how e-mail, the Internet, and voice mail are to be used, including when and under what conditions employees can be monitored[9] (see Figure 13.4). As with other employment policies, employees should sign a form indicating that they have read and understand the policy. The employer's surveillance and monitoring practices have a greater chance of being upheld by a court or tribunal if the rules have been clearly explained to the employees and implemented in accordance with the company's own guidelines. Reality Check describes the privacy issues facing the courts and Ethics in HRM outlines the issues raised through monitoring employees.

EMPLOYEE CONDUCT OUTSIDE THE WORKPLACE

Consider the following situation. On Monday morning the owner of ABC Corporation reads in the newspaper that a company employee has been charged with robbery and assault on a local convenience store owner. The employee has been released

FIGURE **13.4**

E-Mail, Computer, and Voice Mail: Policy Guidelines

- Ensure compliance with applicable legislation and common law rules.
- Specify the circumstances, if any, under which the system can be used for personal business.
- Specify that confidential information not be sent on the network.
- Set forth the conditions under which monitoring will be done—by whom, how often, and with what notification to employees.
- Specify that e-mail and voice mail information be sent only to users who need it for business purposes.
- Expressly prohibit use of e-mail or voice mail to harass others or to send anonymous messages.
- Make clear that employees have no privacy rights in any material delivered or received through e-mail or voice mail.
- Specify that employees who violate the policy are subject to discipline, including dismissal.

Reality CHECK

Privacy Issues with New Technologies

Paul Boniferro, partner, head of the Ontario labour and employment group at McCarthy Tétrault, Canada's largest law firm with offices in Vancouver, Calgary, London, Ottawa, Montreal, and Quebec City and London UK describes a case involving the use of biometric scanning.

"We have a client in the property management industry. The security officers and building maintenance staff were being asked to no longer use access passes and punch cards, but to have their hands scanned by a biometric system.

The idea of using a biometric scanning device started with 9/11. The problem for landlords was that no one knew who was in the towers of the World Trade Center. Property managers are responsible for knowing who is in the building for security purposes and for emergency events.

Swipe cards can be exchanged or stolen, and so are not reliable methods of identification. Furthermore, the employer had heard that employees were giving each other their punch cards for logging in, and effectively stealing time from the employer.

The employer wanted to install a biometric entry system for security, for emergency contact, and for tracking employee time for payroll purposes. The biometric system scans and reads handprints, which are unique to every individual, and therefore solved both the problems of employee identification and time theft.

The employees refused, saying that it was an invasion of their privacy. They felt that "Big Brother" wanted

to control their whereabouts and know where they were at all times. In another case where a unionized employer introduced a similar system, the union filed a grievance alleging a breach of the collective agreement's protection of worker privacy. The case went to a labour arbitrator. The arbitrator agreed with the union (and the employees) and based her decision on these factors:

1. The employer has to first establish that there is an issue and a problem that needs to be controlled. In this case, the theft of time was not established as an issue that needed to be addressed.

2. The company has to establish that there is no other reasonable and less intrusive method to manage the three issues.

3. The employer has to establish that all necessary precautions have been taken to protect the privacy of the employees.

4. Furthermore, the employer must consult with the union about the implementation and the protection of employees' privacy.

The employer was not allowed to use the system. However, in another similar situation, in a manufacturing environment, the current employees were allowed to keep their passes, but all new employees were required to use the biometric system. Existing employees, on a voluntary basis, could use the system. The company also charged $25 to replace lost cards, and over time employees no longer wanted the hassle of the cards. Now, 100 percent of its employees are using the biometric system.

Source: Interview with Paul Boniferro.

Ethics in **HRM**

Supervising or Super-Spying?

Cameras monitor much of our everyday life, often without our knowledge. Surveillance systems may be monitoring you as you leave the lobby of your apartment building, as you enter the underground garage, as you drive on the highway to work, as you purchase a coffee at the variety store, and even at some workplaces. Pinhole cameras the size of a quarter can fit into a picture on the wall, a telephone, or a ceiling device that looks like a water sprinkler. They can catch an employee loading up on office supplies; they can even determine whether the employee is using chat lines or the Internet for personal reasons. Some employers keep records of the calls employees make and their duration. A standard feature on network-management software enables the administrator to pull up the screen of any employee on the network.

Employees who work as customer representatives, handling 60 to 80 calls a day, may have their conversations monitored by supervisors or a trainer to ensure that the information given is accurate and that service standards are maintained. At one firm that raises money for charities, employees are required to make 8,500 keystrokes an hour; failure to achieve this standard

is noted electronically. (Distractions are minimized by covering windows, forbidding conversation unrelated to business, and facing all desks in the same direction.) Eight cameras are capable of zooming in on any desk, in case any employee is displaying materials unrelated to work.

Even babysitters and nannies are being targeted for electronic monitoring. Cameras hidden in books watch the children and the babysitter or nanny while anxious parents are at work. Parents insist that this surveillance enables them to ensure the safety and emotional security of their children; babysitters and nannies are outraged at the lack of trust and invasion of their privacy.

According to a national director with the Canadian Union of Postal Workers, "Surveillance and monitoring is really about power, and the uneven levels of power in the workplace. If it is abused by employers, then it really becomes a powerful weapon that is used to control the behaviour of workers, or as a source of discipline." A 2,000 study found that people consider these electronic monitoring systems highly invasive and unfair.

Sources: David Zwieg, "The Line Between Benign and Invasive Monitoring Technologies," *HR Professional* 19, no. 4 (August/September, 2002): 36–38; J. Powell, "Keeping an Eye on the Workplace," *Financial Post*, September 6, 1997, 24; M. Gooderham, "Rise in Technology Lets Everyone Be a Spy," *The Globe and Mail*, June 7, 1995, A1; A. M. Stewart, "For a Nervous Breakdown, Please Press One," *The Globe and Mail*, June 1, 1994, A25; G. Arnaut, "Electronic Big Brother Is on the Job," *The Globe and Mail*, October 22, 1996, C1; R. Fulford, "Tolerating Electronic Sweatshops," *The Globe and Mail*, December 14, 1994, C1.

pending trial. A phone call to the employee's supervisor reveals that the employee has reported to work. What should the owner do? What is the owner legally entitled to do? What can an employer do if it believes that an employee is lying about his or her inability to work due to sickness or disability? Can the employer spy on the employee outside the workplace? What if an employee writes damaging things about the company on his or her personal blog?

These are questions that commonly arise. Generally, an employer has no reach over the private lives of its employees; when an employee "punches out," he or she is no longer subject to the employer's control. Thus, both unionized and nonunion employers have been found to have lacked proper cause to dismiss employee who are arrested for activities unrelated to the workplace. However, when the employer can establish that the employee's off-duty conduct adversely impacts the economic interests of the employer, such as business reputation, or the employee's ability to perform his or her job, then the employer may be justified in taking action in response to that conduct. Therefore, an employee who writes slanderous or damaging comments about the employer, or who discloses confidential information on a personal blog or social networking website such as Facebook, will usually be subject to summary dismissal by a nonunion employer. See Highlights in HRM 13.3.

Employers that wish to conduct secret surveillance on employees during off hours need to be particularly careful. Both courts and arbitrators have required employers to show a valid business reason that the surveillance is necessary and to establish that the surveillance was conducted in a reasonable manner without violating common law and statutory rules protecting property rights and prohibiting nuisance. For example, recent court cases have suggested that videotaping an employee inside his or her home is an unreasonable invasion of privacy and constitutes the tort of nuisance. Videotaping in a public place was found reasonable in other cases. Labour arbitrators have been more strict in limiting outside employer surveillance than courts, usually requiring the employer to show that there was no other less intrusive means of obtaining the necessary information.[10] Employers covered by privacy legislation discussed earlier are also more restricted in the scope of their right to conduct employee surveillance than those governed solely by the common law.[11]

Highlights in HRM 13.3

The Long Arm of the Employer

Employees usually are not subject to the authority of their employer during nonworking hours. Nor are employers expected to act as morality police. Of course, a nonunion employer can always dismiss an employee whose off-duty conduct it does not like by giving the employee proper notice. However, if the nonunion employer wants to summarily dismiss the employee without notice, or if the employer is covered by a collective agreement, it will need to prove that the off-duty conduct amounts to proper cause for dismissal.

Sometimes off-duty employee behaviour can have an adverse impact on the employer's interests, or can directly impede the ability of the worker to perform his or her job. An example of the latter scenario is a case in which an employee is incarcerated and unable to come to work, or a truck driver loses his driver's licence. If the employee cannot work as a result of off-duty behaviour,

this would usually amount to cause for summary dismissal without notice.

Even if the employee's behaviour does not physically prevent him or her from working, it is possible that the employer's interest are nevertheless adversely effected by the behaviour. For example, in a recent case, a court found that an employer had cause to summarily dismiss an employee without notice who was convicted of possession of child pornography on his personal computer at home. There was no problem with the employee's job performance and the offensive conduct took place entirely during the employee's nonworking hours. Nevertheless, the court found that the company's very visible public reputation as the largest employer in town and as a prominent contributor to local children's activities had been damaged by its association with the employee's illegal conduct.

Source: Kelly v. Linamar Corp. (2005, Ontario Superior Court of Justice).

DISCIPLINARY POLICIES AND PROCEDURES

The rights of managers to discipline and discharge employees are increasingly limited. There is thus a great need for managers at all levels to understand discipline procedures. Disciplinary action taken against an employee must be for justifiable reasons, and there must be effective policies and procedures to govern its use. Such policies and procedures assist those responsible for taking disciplinary action and help ensure that employees will receive fair and constructive treatment.

Disciplinary policies and procedures should extend to a number of important areas to ensure thorough coverage. Figure 13.5 presents a disciplinary model that illustrates the areas where provisions should be established. The model also shows the logical sequence in which disciplinary steps must be carried out to ensure enforceable decisions.

A major responsibility of the HR department is to develop, and to have top management approve, its disciplinary policies and procedures. The HR department is also responsible for ensuring that disciplinary policies, as well as the disciplinary action taken against employees, are consistent with the collective agreement (if one exists) and conform to current laws. However, the primary responsibility for preventing or correcting disciplinary problems rests with an employee's immediate supervisor. This person is best able to observe evidence of unsatisfactory performance and to discuss the matter with the employee. Should discipline become necessary, the employee's immediate supervisor is the logical person to apply the company's disciplinary procedure and monitor employee improvement.

THE RESULTS OF INACTION

Figure 13.6 on page 528 lists the more common disciplinary problems identified by managers. Failure to take disciplinary action in any of these areas serves only to aggravate a problem that eventually must be resolved. Failure to act implies that the performance of the employee concerned has been satisfactory. If disciplinary action is eventually taken, the delay will make it more difficult to justify the action if challenged by the employee. A unionized employee can "grieve" the discipline, and a nonunion employee can treat the discipline as breach of contract, and perhaps even a constructive dismissal, and sue the employer in a court for wrongful dismissal.

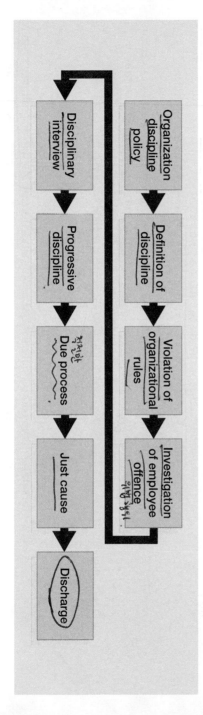

FIGURE **13.5**

A Disciplinary Model

OUTCOME 5

Using the Internet

Further legal resources on the topics discussed in this chapter can be found on the website of Canada Law Book at
http://www.canadalawbook.ca

FIGURE **13.6**

Common Disciplinary Problems

Attendance Problems

- Unexcused absence
- Chronic absenteeism
- Unexcused/excessive tardiness
- Leaving without permission

Dishonesty and Related Problems

- Theft
- Falsifying employment application
- Willfully damaging organizational property
- Punching another employee's time card
- Falsifying work records

Work Performance Problems

- Failure to complete work assignments
- Producing substandard products or services
- Failure to meet established production requirements

On-the-Job Behaviour Problems

- Intoxication at work
- Insubordination
- Horseplay
- Smoking in unauthorized places
- Fighting
- Gambling
- Failure to use safety devices
- Failure to report injuries
- Carelessness
- Sleeping on the job
- Using abusive or threatening language with supervisors
- Possession of narcotics or alcohol
- Possession of firearms or other weapons
- Sexual harassment

In defending against such a challenge to the employer's discipline, the employer is likely to be asked why an employee who had not been performing or behaving satisfactorily was kept on the payroll. Or an even more damaging question might be, "Why did that employee receive satisfactory performance ratings [or perhaps even merit raises]?"

Such contradictions in practice can only aid employees in successfully challenging management's corrective actions. Unfortunately, some supervisors try to build a case to justify their corrective actions only after they have decided that a particular employee should be discharged. The following are common reasons given by supervisors for their failure to impose a disciplinary penalty:[12]

1. The supervisor had failed to document earlier actions, so no record existed on which to base subsequent disciplinary action.

2. Supervisors believed they would receive little or no support from higher management for the disciplinary action.

3. The supervisor was uncertain of the facts underlying the situation requiring disciplinary action.

4. Failure by the supervisor to discipline employees in the past for a certain infraction caused the supervisor to forgo current disciplinary action in order to appear consistent.

5. The supervisor wanted to be seen as a likable person.

SETTING ORGANIZATIONAL RULES

The setting of organizational rules is the foundation for an effective disciplinary system. These rules govern the type of behaviour expected of employees. Organizations as diverse as Gerber Products, Steelcase, and Pitney Bowes have written policies explaining the type of conduct required of employees. Because employee behaviour standards are established through the setting of organizational rules and regulations, the following suggestions may help reduce problems in this area:

1. Rules should be widely disseminated and known to all employees. It should not be assumed that employees know all the rules.
2. Rules should be reviewed periodically—perhaps annually—especially those rules critical to work success.
3. The reasons for a rule should always be explained. Acceptance of an organizational rule is greater when employees understand the reasons behind it.
4. Rules should always be written. Ambiguity should be avoided, as this can result in different interpretations of the rules by different supervisors.
5. Rules must be reasonable and relate to the safe and efficient operation of the organization. Rules should not be made simply because of personal likes or dislikes.
6. If management has been lax in the enforcement of a rule, the rule must be restated, along with the consequences for its violation, before disciplinary action can begin.
7. Employees should sign a document stating that they have read and understand the organizational rules.

When seeking reasons for unsatisfactory behaviour, supervisors must keep in mind that employees may not be aware of certain work rules. Before initiating any disciplinary action, therefore, it is essential that supervisors determine whether they have given their employees careful and thorough orientation in the rules and regulations relating to their jobs. In fact, the proper communication of organizational rules and regulations is so important that arbitrators cite *neglect in communicating rules* as a major reason for reversing the disciplinary action taken against an employee by unionized employers.13

THE HOT-STOVE APPROACH TO RULE ENFORCEMENT

Regardless of the reason for the disciplinary action, it should be taken as soon as possible after the infraction has occurred and a complete investigation has been conducted. HR professionals often use the **hot-stove rule** to explain the correct application of discipline. A hot stove gives warning that it should not be touched. Those who ignore the warning and touch it are assured of being burned. The punishment is an immediate and direct consequence of breaking the rule never to touch a hot stove. Likewise, a work rule should apply to all employees and should be enforced consistently and in an impersonal and unbiased way. Employees should know the consequences of violating the rule, so that it has preventive value.

DEFINING DISCIPLINE

In management seminars conducted by the authors of this text, when managers are asked to define the word *discipline*, their most frequent response is that discipline means punishment. Although this answer is not incorrect, it is only one of three possible meanings. As normally defined, **discipline** has these meanings:

1. Treatment that punishes
2. Orderly behaviour in an organizational setting
3. Training that moulds and strengthens desirable conduct—or corrects undesirable conduct—and develops self-control

To some managers, *discipline* is synonymous with punishment. They equate the term with the punishment of employees who violate rules or regulations. Other managers think of discipline as a general state of affairs—a condition of orderliness in which employees conduct themselves according to standards of acceptable behaviour.

[OUTCOME]

hot-stove rule
A rule of discipline that can be compared with a hot stove in that it gives warning, is effective immediately, is enforced consistently, and applies to all employees in an impersonal and unbiased way.

discipline
(1) Treatment that punishes, (2) orderly behaviour in an organizational setting, or (3) training that moulds and strengthens desirable conduct—or corrects undesirable conduct—and develops self-control

Discipline viewed in this manner can be considered positive when employees willingly practise self-control and respect organizational rules.

The third definition considers discipline a management tool used to correct undesirable employee behaviour. Discipline is applied as a constructive means of getting employees to conform to acceptable standards of performance. Many organizations define *discipline* in their policy manuals as training that "corrects, moulds, or perfects knowledge, attitudes, behaviour, or conduct." Discipline is thus viewed as a way to correct poor employee performance.

When taken against employees, disciplinary action should never be thought of as punishment. Discipline can embody a penalty as a means of obtaining a desired result; however, punishment should not be the intent of disciplinary action. Rather, discipline must have as its goal the improvement of the employee's future behaviour. To apply discipline in any other way—as punishment or as a way of getting even with employees—can only invite problems for management, including possible wrongful discharge suits.

INVESTIGATING THE DISCIPLINARY PROBLEM

It is a rare manager who has a good, intuitive sense of how to investigate employee misconduct. Too frequently, investigations are conducted in a haphazard manner; worse, they overlook one or more investigative concerns.[14] In conducting an employee investigation it is important to be objective and to avoid the assumptions, suppositions, and biases that often surround discipline cases. Figure 13.7 lists seven questions to consider in investigating an employee offence. Attending to each question will help ensure a full and fair investigation while providing reliable information free from personal prejudice.[15]

Documentation of Employee Misconduct

"It's too complicated." "I just didn't take time to do it." "I have more important things to do." These are some of the frequent excuses used by managers who have failed to document cases of employee misconduct. The most significant cause of inadequate documentation, however, is that managers have no idea of what constitutes good documentation. Unfortunately, the failure of managers to record employee misconduct accurately can result in the reversal of any subsequent disciplinary action. The maintenance of *accurate* and *complete* work records, therefore, is an essential part of an effective disciplinary system. For documentation to be complete, the following eight items should be included:

1. Date, time, and location of the incident(s)
2. Negative performance or behaviour exhibited by the employee—the problem
3. Consequences of that action or behaviour on the employee's overall work performance and/or the operation of the employee's work unit
4. Prior discussion(s) with the employee about the problem
5. Disciplinary action to be taken and specific improvement expected
6. Consequences if improvement is not made and a follow-up date
7. The employee's reaction to the supervisor's attempt to change behaviour
8. The names of witnesses to the incident (if appropriate)

When preparing documentation, it is important for a manager to record the incident immediately after the infraction takes place, when the memory of it is still fresh, and to ensure that the record is complete and accurate. Documentation need not be lengthy, but it must include the eight points in the preceding list. Remember, a manager's records of employee misconduct are considered business documents, and as such they are admissible as evidence in arbitration hearings, administrative proceedings, and courts of law. As noted by one manager at a seminar on discipline,

FIGURE **13.7**

Considerations in Disciplinary Investigations

1. In very specific terms, what is the offence charged?
   - Is management sure it fully understands the charge against the employee?
   - Was the employee really terminated for insubordination, or did the employee merely refuse a request by management?

2. Did the employee know he or she was doing something wrong?
   - What rule or provision was violated?
   - How would the employee know of the existence of the rule?
   - Was the employee warned of the consequence?

3. Is the employee guilty?
   - What are the sources of facts?
   - Is there direct or only indirect evidence of guilt?
   - Has anyone talked to the employee to hear his or her side of the situation?

4. Are there extenuating circumstances?
   - Were conflicting orders given by different supervisors?
   - Does anybody have reason to want to "get" this employee?
   - Was the employee provoked by a manager or another employee?

5. Has the rule been uniformly enforced?
   - Have all managers applied this rule consistently?
   - What punishment have previous offenders received?
   - Were any other employees involved in this offence?

6. Is the offence related to the workplace?
   - Is there evidence that the offence hurt the organization?
   - Is management making a moral judgment or a business judgment?

7. What is the employee's past work record?
   - How many years of service has the employee given the organization?
   - How many years or months has the employee held the present job?
   - What is the employee's personnel record as a whole, especially his or her disciplinary record?

An investigative interview should always be held in private and should elicit the comments and concerns of the employee.

"When taking corrective action against an employee, the importance of compiling a complete and objective disciplinary record simply cannot be overstated."

The Investigative Interview

Before any disciplinary action is initiated, an investigative interview should be conducted to make sure employees are fully aware of the offence.[16] This interview is necessary because the supervisor's perceptions of the employee's behaviour may not be entirely accurate.[17] The interview should concentrate on how the offence violated the performance and behaviour standards of the job. It should avoid getting into personalities or areas unrelated to job performance. Most important, the employee must be given a full opportunity to explain his or her side of the issue so that any deficiencies for which the organization may be responsible are revealed.

APPROACHES TO DISCIPLINARY ACTION

If a thorough investigation shows that an employee has violated some organization rule, disciplinary action must be imposed. Two approaches to disciplinary action are progressive discipline and positive discipline.

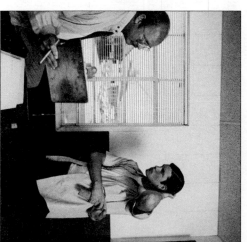

© Deborah Schwartz/Getty Images

Progressive Discipline

Generally, discipline is imposed in a progressive manner. By definition, **progressive discipline** is the application of corrective measures by increasing degrees. Progressive discipline is designed to motivate an employee to correct his or her misconduct voluntarily. The technique is aimed at nipping the problem in the bud, using only enough corrective action to remedy the shortcoming. However, the sequence and severity of the disciplinary action vary with the type of offence and the circumstances surrounding it. Because each situation is unique, a number of factors must be considered in determining how severe a disciplinary action should be.

The typical progressive discipline procedure includes four steps. From an oral warning (or counselling) that subsequent unsatisfactory behaviour or performance will not be tolerated, the action may progress to a written warning, to a suspension with pay, and ultimately to discharge.

It would usually be a breach of contract and a constructive dismissal for an employer to suspend a nonunion employee without pay, unless the contract includes an expressed term permitting this (and most do not).

The "capital punishment" of discharge is utilized only as a last resort. Organizations normally use lower forms of disciplinary action for less severe performance problems. It is important for managers to remember that three important things occur when progressive discipline is applied properly:

1. Employees always know where they stand regarding offences.
2. Employees know what improvement is expected of them.
3. Employees understand what will happen next if improvement is not made.

Positive Discipline

Some HR professionals believe that progressive discipline has certain flaws, including its intimidating and adversarial nature, that prevent it from achieving the intended purpose. For these reasons, some organizations are using an approach called **positive, or nonpunitive, discipline**. Positive discipline is based on the concept that employees must assume responsibility for their personal conduct and job performance.[18]

Positive discipline requires a cooperative environment in which the employee and the supervisor engage in joint discussion and problem solving to resolve incidents of employee irresponsibility. The approach focuses on early correction of misconduct, with the employee taking total responsibility for resolving the problem. Nothing is imposed by management; all solutions and affirmations are jointly reached. HR managers often describe positive discipline as "nonpunitive discipline that replaces threats and punishment with encouragement."

While positive discipline appears similar to progressive discipline, its emphasis is on giving employees reminders rather than reprimands as a way to improve performance. The technique is implemented in three steps. The first is a conference between the employee and the supervisor. The purpose of this meeting is to find a solution to the problem through discussion, with oral agreement by the employee to improve his or her performance. The supervisor refrains from reprimanding the employee or threatening him or her with further disciplinary action. Supervisors may document this conference, but a written record of this meeting is not placed in the employee's file unless the misconduct occurs again.

If improvement is not made after this first step, the supervisor holds a second conference with the employee to determine why the solution agreed to in the first

progressive discipline

Application of corrective measures by increasing degrees

positive, or nonpunitive, discipline

A system of discipline that focuses on early correction of employee misconduct, with the employee taking total responsibility for correcting the problem conference did not work. At this stage, however, a written reminder is given to the employee. This document states the new or repeated solution to the problem, with an affirmation that improvement is the responsibility of the employee and a condition of continued employment.

When both conferences fail to produce the desired results, the third step is to give the employee a one-day *decision-making leave* (a paid leave). The purpose of this paid leave is for the employee to decide whether he or she wishes to continue working for the organization. The organization pays for this leave to demonstrate its desire to retain the person. Also, paying for the leave eliminates the negative effects for the employee of losing a day's pay. Employees given a decision-making leave are instructed to return the following day with a decision either to make a total commitment to improve performance or to quit the organization. If a commitment is not made, the employee is dismissed with the assumption that he or she lacked responsibility toward the organization. The fact that the employer goes through this process would not necessarily mean that it has cause to dismiss the employee. There is a strong likelihood that the employer would still be required to give the employee reasonable notice, or such other notice required in the written terms of the contract, since it is very hard to prove common law cause based solely on inadequate performance. Therefore, another strategy might be to give the employee a working notice of termination after the second conference, and then offer to reemploy the employee on a new contract if the performance improves over the notice period.

The positive discipline process used by Volkswagen Canada is described in Highlights in HRM 13.4.

INFORMING THE EMPLOYEE

Regardless of the reasons for a discharge, it should be done with personal consideration for the employee affected. Every effort should be made to ease the trauma a discharge creates.[19] The employee must be informed honestly, yet tactfully, of the exact reasons for the action. Such candour can help the employee face the problem and adjust to it in a constructive manner.

Managers may wish to discuss, and even rehearse, with their peers the upcoming termination meeting. This practice can ensure that all important points are covered while giving confidence to the manager. While managers agree that there is no single right way to conduct the discharge meeting, the following guidelines will help make the discussion more effective:

1. Come to the point within the first two or three minutes, and list in a logical order all reasons for the termination.

2. Be straightforward and firm, yet tactful, and remain resolute in your decision.

3. Make the discussion private, businesslike, and fairly brief.

4. Do not mix the good with the bad. Trying to sugarcoat the problem sends a mixed message to the employee.

5. Avoid making accusations against the employee and injecting personal feelings into the discussion.

6. Avoid bringing up any personality differences between you and the employee.

7. Provide any information concerning severance pay and the status of benefits and coverage.

8. Explain how you will handle employment inquiries from future employers.[20]

534

Highlights in HRM 13.4

Volkswagen Canada's Positive Discipline Program

Positive discipline is a method for attempting to solve employee problems before they develop into serious situations. Positive discipline relies on frontline coaching and counselling to help employees identify inappropriate behaviour; it also suggests ways of turning that behaviour around. Positive discipline allows supervisors to treat their fellow employees in a fair and consistent manner, and as adults. Most employees will respond to coaching and counselling. For employees who do not correct their behaviour—or who are involved in an incident so serious that coaching or counselling is deemed inappropriate—there are steps in place to impress on every employee the seriousness of their actions and the consequences of continued poor behaviour. The following is a general outline of the program.

There are five general methods used in the Positive Discipline Program:

- Coaching and Counselling
- Step 1: Verbal Reminder
- Step 2: Written Warning
- Step 3: Decision Making
- Step 4: Termination

There are three categories of work rule violations:

- Work Performance
- Attendance
- Misconduct

There are three degrees of severity of workplace violations:

- Minor
- Major
- Grave

There are two other major ingredients of the Positive Discipline Program:

- Praise
- Goal Setting

Guidelines

- The union, if requested, may be involved in every step of the discipline process, but must be involved in Step 1 and higher.
- An employee may, under certain circumstances, be sent home with or without pay pending an investigation into the incident. The union should be involved in any investigation into serious incidents.
- Counselling should be the preferred method of correcting behaviour when a problem first appears.
- Praise should be used often, whenever an employee has corrected a potential problem, had a step deactivated, performed beyond his or her normal duties, or any other time the supervisor feels it is appropriate. This praise should be done both orally and in writing.
- Goal setting should be used at every step in the disciplinary process in order to ensure both the supervisor and the employee know exactly what is expected of them.
- This program is aimed at those very few employees who insist on conducting themselves in an inappropriate manner. The vast majority of our employees may never have to encounter the various steps of this program.

Termination meetings should be held in a neutral location, such as a conference room, to prevent the employee from feeling unfairly treated. When discussing the termination, management must never provoke the employee or allow the employee to become belligerent toward management. Should the employee become agitated, or show signs of hostility, the meeting should be stopped immediately with notification given to security or the HR department.

Finally, when terminated employees are escorted off the premises, the removal must not serve to defame the employee. Managers should not give peers

Source: Donald McQuirter, Manager of Human Resources, Volkswagen Canada Inc.

the impression that the terminated employee was dishonest or untrustworthy. Furthermore, managers are advised never to discuss the discharge or "bad-mouth" the terminated employee with other employees, customers, or other individuals.

ALTERNATIVE DISPUTE RESOLUTION PROCEDURES

In unionized workplaces, grievance procedures are stated in virtually all collective agreements. In nonunion organizations, however, **alternative dispute resolution (ADR)** procedures are a developing method to address employee complaints.[21] The employer's interest stems from the desire to meet employees' expectations for fair treatment in the workplace while guaranteeing them due process—in the hope of minimizing discrimination claims or wrongful discharge suits.[22]

Step-Review Systems

As Figure 13.8 illustrates, a **step-review system** is based on a pre-established set of steps—normally four—for the review of an employee complaint by successively higher levels of management. These procedures are patterned after the union grievance systems we will discuss in Chapter 14. For example, they normally require that the employee's complaint be formalized as a written statement. Managers at each step are required to provide a full response to the complaint within a specified time period, perhaps three to five working days.

An employee is sometimes allowed to bypass the meeting with his or her immediate supervisor if the employee fears reprisal from this person. Unlike grievance procedures in unionized organizations, however, nonunion appeal procedures ordinarily do not provide for a neutral third party—such as an arbitrator—to serve as the judge of last resort. In most step-review systems, the president, chief executive officer, vice-president, or HR director acts as the final authority, and this person's decision is not appealable. Some organizations give employees assistance in preparing their complaint cases. For example, an employee who desires it may be able to get advice and counsel from a designated person in the HR department before discussing the issue with management.

alternative dispute resolution (ADR)
A term applied to different types of employee complaint or dispute resolution procedures

step-review system
A system for reviewing employee complaints and disputes by successively higher levels of management

A peer review system can create a sense of justice among employees.

FIGURE **13.8**

Conventional Step-Review Appeal Procedure

| Employee | → | Supervisor | → | Department head | → | HR department | → | Top management |

peer-review system

A system for reviewing employee complaints that utilizes a group composed of equal numbers of employee representatives and management appointees, which functions as a jury because its members weigh evidence, consider arguments, and, after deliberation, vote independently to render a final decision

open-door policy

A policy of settling grievances that identifies various levels of management above the immediate supervisor for employee contact

Unfortunately, step-review systems may not yield their intended benefits. Employees may believe that management is slow in responding to complaints and that management's response often does not solve the problem. Furthermore, employees may believe that, regardless of policies forbidding reprisal, supervisors would still hold it against them if they exercised their rights as spelled out in the step-review system. These concerns should not lead to the conclusion that all step-review systems are ineffective, but rather that management must take special precautions to ensure that the systems work and provide the benefits intended.

Peer-Review Systems

A **peer-review system**, also called a complaint committee, is composed of equal numbers of employee representatives and management appointees. Employee representatives are normally elected by secret ballot by their coworkers for a rotating term, whereas management representatives are assigned, also on a rotating basis. A peer-review system functions as a jury because its members weigh evidence, consider arguments, and, after deliberation, vote independently to render a final decision.

Organizations consider one of the benefits of the peer-review system to be the sense of justice that it creates among employees. The peer-review system can be used as the sole method for resolving employee complaints, or it can be used in conjunction with a step-review system. For example, if an employee is not satisfied with management's action at step 1 or 2 in the step-review system, the employee can submit the complaint to the peer-review committee for final resolution.

Open-Door Policy

The open-door policy is an old standby for settling employee complaints. The traditional **open-door policy** identifies various levels of management above the immediate supervisor that an aggrieved employee may contact; the levels may extend as high as a vice-president, president, or chief executive officer. Typically the person who acts as "the court of last resort" is the HR director or a senior staff official.

The problems with an open-door policy are well documented. Two of its major weaknesses are the unwillingness of managers to listen honestly to employee complaints and worker reluctance to approach managers with their complaints. As an employee once told the authors of this text, "My manager has an open-door policy but the door is only open one inch." Obviously this employee felt he had little opportunity to get through to his manager. Other problems are attributed to this system as well. The open-door policy generally fails to guarantee consistent decision making because what is fair to one manager may seem unfair to another. Higher-level managers tend to support supervisors for fear of undermining authority. And, as a system of justice, open-door policies may lack credibility with employees. Still, the open-door policy is often successful when it is supported by all levels of management and when management works to maintain a reputation for being fair and open-minded.

Ombudsperson System

An **ombudsperson** is a designated individual from whom employees may seek counsel for the resolution of their complaints. The ombudsperson listens to an employee's complaint and attempts to resolve it by seeking an equitable solution between the employee and the supervisor. This individual works cooperatively with both sides to reach a settlement, often employing a problem-solving approach to the issue. Because the ombudsperson has no authority to finalize a solution to the problem, compromises are highly possible and all concerned tend to feel satisfied with the outcome.

To function successfully, ombudspeople must be able to operate in an atmosphere of confidentiality that does not threaten the security of the managers or subordinates who are involved in a complaint. For example, complaints of sexual harassment, abuse of power, or issues that deal with circumstances that violate the law or unethical behaviour (whistleblowing) require high degrees of confidentiality to protect those involved. While ombudspeople do not have the power to decide employee complaints, it is recommended that they have access to high levels of management to ensure that employee complaints receive fair treatment.

ombudsperson
A designated individual from whom employees may seek counsel for resolution of their complaints

Mediation

Along with arbitration, mediation is fast becoming a popular way to resolve employee complaints. **Mediation** employs a third-party neutral (called a mediator) to help employees and managers reach voluntary agreement acceptable to both parties. The essence of mediation is compromise. The **mediator** holds a meeting with the employee and management, listens to the position of each side, gathers facts, then, through discussion, suggestions, and persuasion obtains an agreement that will satisfy the needs and requirements of both sides. A mediator serves primarily as a fact finder and to open up a channel of communication between the parties. Unlike arbitrators, mediators have no power or authority to force either side toward an agreement. They must use their communication skills and the power of persuasion to help the parties resolve their differences. A cornerstone of mediation is that the parties maintain control over the settlement outcome.

Mediation is a flexible process that can be shaped to meet the demands of the parties. Also, it can be used to resolve a wide range of employee complaints, including discrimination claims or traditional workplace disputes.[23] Employees like the process because of its informality. According to one authority, "Mediation might be described as a private discussion assisted by an impartial third party."[24] Settlements fashioned through mediation are readily acceptable by the parties, thus promoting a favourable working relationship.

mediation
The use of an impartial neutral to reach a compromise decision in employment disputes

mediator
A third party in an employment dispute who meets with one party and then the other in order to suggest compromise solutions or to recommend concessions from each side that will lead to an agreement

Arbitration

At the 1996 Summer Olympics, the athletes were required by the International Olympic Committee (IOC) to agree to take any Olympic dispute (including those over drug testing) to a special arbitration panel for a binding decision. The point of this was to avoid costly and disruptive battles in U.S. courts.[25] (Arbitration is discussed in depth in Chapter 14.) Arbitration can save litigation costs and avoid time delays and unfavourable publicity. However, to ensure that their arbitration policies are legal, employers must

- Have a clear, well-defined, and widely communicated arbitration policy
- Specify those topics subject to arbitration
- Inform employees of the rights they are relinquishing by signing an arbitration agreement
- Provide a procedurally fair arbitration system
- Allow for the nonbiased selection of an arbitrator or arbitration panel.[26]

[OUTCOME]

ethics

A set of standards of conduct and moral judgments that help to determine right and wrong behaviour

MANAGERIAL ETHICS IN EMPLOYEE RELATIONS

Throughout this text we have emphasized the legal requirements of HRM. Laws, agency rulings, and court decisions impact all aspects of the employment process—recruitment, selection, performance appraisal, safety and health, labour relations, and testing. Managers must comply with governmental regulations to promote an environment free from litigation.

However, beyond what is required by the law is the question of organizational ethics and the ethical—or unethical—behaviour engaged in by managers. **Ethics** can be defined as a set of standards of acceptable conduct and moral judgment. Ethics provides cultural guidelines—organizational or societal—that help us decide between proper or improper conduct. Therefore, ethics, like the legal aspects of HR, permeates all aspects of the employment relationship. For example, managers may adhere to the organization's objective of hiring members from the designated groups, but how those employees are supervised and treated once employed gets to the issue of managerial ethics. We have presented Ethics in HRM boxes in each chapter of this book to illustrate the complexity of ethical dilemmas.

Compliance with laws and the behavioural treatment of employees are two completely different aspects of the manager's job. While ethical dilemmas will always occur in the supervision of employees, it is how employees are treated that largely distinguishes the ethical organization from the unethical one. Interestingly, a recent research study, *Employee Trust and Organizational Loyalty,* sponsored by the Society for Human Resource Management, showed that employee perceptions of ethical behaviour by their organizational leadership may be the most important driver of employee trust and loyalty. According to the study, of critical interest to employees is the consistent and credible communication of information about the organization's ethical standards and its values, the organization's mission, and its workplace policies.[27] We believe that managerial ethics in employee relations requires honesty in all dealings between employees and their managers, including mutual respect throughout the performance of workplace duties.

Many organizations have their own code of ethics that governs relations with employees and the public at large.[28] This written code focuses attention on ethical values and provides a basis for the organization, and individual managers, to evaluate their plans and actions. HR departments have been given a greater role in communicating the organization's values and standards, monitoring compliance with its code of ethics, and enforcing the standards throughout the organization. Organizations now have ethics committees and ethics ombudspeople to provide training in ethics to employees. The ultimate goal of ethics training is to avoid unethical behaviour and adverse publicity; to gain a strategic advantage; and, most of all, to treat employees in a fair and equitable manner, recognizing them as productive members of the organization.

Small Business APPLICATION

Issues of employee rights and discipline will be discussed in the context of a small advertising business. The company at hand is a company with 75 employees, made up of sales staff, customer service staff, copy staff, and printers. The company produces a weekly free publication and generates revenue through the sale of advertising space. While the company used to be profitable, currently the company is starting to lose money. If sales continue to decline, the company could be rendered insolvent in two years, putting all employees at risk. There are two reasons the company is losing money. First, advertising sales are down, not just for this company, but for all companies in this business. Second, a key client has reduced its business volume and complained that the service it has been receiving from staff was sub-par.

So what is the company to do? First, while this company would like to preserve the employment of all of its staff, if sales volumes have been reduced to the point of incurring losses, the company has no choice but to reduce costs or find ways to increase sales. If

work volumes are down with these sales volumes, the company may elect to reduce staff or hours to address this reality.

The second issue here is the issue of the client raising concerns about staff, which has resulted in business decline. In such a situation, the company will need to investigate the situation thoroughly and identify a remedy. The company would likely ask the client if it has examples of the issues of concern. The company also would likely draw from other sources of interaction between staff and the client, which may include order records. Then the company may discuss the situation with management responsible for supporting this client. Finally, if specific staff have been identified, and evidence has been produced, a meeting with the staff in question to further explore this situation would be required. If the conduct of staff has been found to be unacceptable, the lessons learned in this chapter regarding discipline of staff should provide guidance on steps to take depending on the magnitude of the offence.

SUMMARY

OUTCOME 1

There are three regimes of employment law. The common law is a body of rules made by judges in the course of interpreting employment contracts. Employment legislation is legislation enacted by governments to regulate the terms of the employment contract and is enforced by administrative tribunal. Collective bargaining law includes the rules that govern unionized employees. The employment contract for unionized employees is called a collective agreement, and it is interpreted and enforced by labour arbitrators rather than courts.

OUTCOME 2

An employment contract between an employee and an employer may comprise expressed, written terms and a series of "implied terms" imposed by common law judges. Sometimes there are no written terms at all, in which case the contract is an oral one that includes all of the implied terms judges have created over the years. A written term

usually supercedes an implied term, provided the written term does not violate a statutory minimum standard.

OUTCOME 3

A nonunion employer can dismiss an employee for any reason it likes provided it gives either the required contractual notice or implied reasonable notice (as long as the reason for the dismissal is not prohibited by a statute). It can also dismiss an employee with no notice, if the employee has committed a serious breach of contract. A unionized employer, on the other hand, usually needs to prove it had just cause to dismiss an employee.

OUTCOME 4

PIPEDA provides employees some rights about the use of their personal information. Employers should establish policies regarding privacy issues. Employers have the right, under certain conditions, to monitor the work of employees, including their use of e-mail and the Internet.

[OUTCOME] 5

The HR department, in combination with other managers, should establish disciplinary policies. This will help achieve both acceptance of the policy and its consistent application. To reduce the need for discipline, organizational rules and procedures should be widely known, reviewed on a regular basis, and written and explained to employees. The rules must relate to the safe and efficient operation of the organization. When managers overlook the enforcement of rules, they must re-emphasize the rule and its enforcement before disciplining an employee.

[OUTCOME] 6

The term *discipline* has three meanings—punishment, orderly behaviour, and training of employee conduct.

When used with employees, discipline not be punishment; it should serve to correct undesirable employee behaviour, creating within the employee a desire for self-control. This third definition of discipline can be achieved only when managers conduct a complete and unbiased investigation of employee misconduct. Investigation of employee misconduct begins with proper documentation of wrongdoing. When managers are investigating employee problems, they need to know specifically the infraction of the employee, whether the employee knew of the rule violated, and any extenuating circumstances that might justify the employee's conduct. When employees are to receive

discipline, the rule must be uniformly enforced and the past work record of the employee must be considered.

[OUTCOME] 7

The two approaches to discipline are progressive discipline and positive discipline. Progressive discipline follows a series of steps based on increasing the degrees of corrective action. The corrective action applied should match the severity of the employee misconduct. Positive discipline, based on reminders, is a cooperative discipline approach in which employees accept responsibility for the desired employee improvement. The focus is on coping with the unsatisfactory performance and dissatisfactions of employees before the problems become major.

[OUTCOME] 8

Alternative dispute resolution (ADR) procedures present ways by which employees exercise their due-process rights. The most common forms of ADR are step-review systems, peer-review systems, the open-door policy, the ombudsperson system, mediation, and arbitration.

[OUTCOME] 9

Ethics in HRM extends beyond the legal requirements of managing employees. Managers engage in ethical behaviour when employees are treated in an objective and fair way, and when an employee's personal and work-related rights are respected and valued.

KEY TERMS

alternative dispute resolution (ADR), 535
constructive dismissal, 515
collective agreement, 514
common law of employment, 513
discipline, 529
ethics, 538

hot-stove rule, 529
implied contract terms, 513
labour arbitrator, 515
mediation, 537
mediator, 537
ombudsperson, 537
open-door policy, 537
peer-review system, 536

positive, or nonpunitive, discipline, 533
progressive discipline, 532
statutory rights, 513
step-review system, 535
summary dismissal, 517
wrongful dismissal, 517

DISCUSSION QUESTIONS

1. Do you have a right to your job? What rights do you have with respect to employment?

2. In what ways, if any, does a unionized employee have greater protection from dismissal than a non-union employee in the Canadian model? Do you think that is fair or not, and why?

3. What is the difference between just cause in a unionized environment and cause for summary dismissal in a nonunion environment?

4. Under what conditions can an employer monitor employees? Ask a group of working students the following questions:

- Are you monitored at work?
- What types of monitoring are used?
- For what purposes does your employer monitor the workplace?
- Do you object to the monitoring? If so, why? If not, why not?

5. Millions of people have created their own blogs, and many of these are employees who describe their working conditions, colleagues, and bosses. While employers should have a reasonable expectation that employees would not publicly criticize or defame the organization, do they have a right to control the "diaries" of employees?

6. You have discovered that an employee has not been keeping client files updated, as is required by your company policy. Outline the steps that you would use to deal with this performance problem.

7. Discuss why documentation is so important to the disciplinary process. What constitutes correct documentation?

8. What do you think would constitute an effective alternative dispute resolution system? What benefits would you expect from such a system? If you

9. In groups, discuss whether the following situations are fair or not fair:

   a. Zabeen was using the company Internet to locate a nursing home for her increasingly handicapped father. Her supervisor observed this and verified it with the Information Technology unit. Zabeen was given a written reprimand. Meanwhile, Sonia used the company telephone to do her personal banking and bill paying and was not reprimanded.

   b. Anthony spent his lunch hour at the gym, consisting of a strenuous workout program with a personal trainer. Meanwhile, Nicholas met his friends for lunch, sharing several beers at the local pub. Both employees felt fatigued in the afternoon, and their diminished productivity was noticed by their supervisor. Nicholas was asked to meet with his supervisor to review performance standards and received a verbal warning. Anthony was not.

were asked to rule on a discharge case, what facts would you analyze in deciding whether to uphold or reverse the employer's action?

INTERNET EXERCISE

In many ways, being a human resources manager can be a legal mine field, since so much of the employment relationship is governed by common law rules, written and implied contract terms, and a vast volume of employment-related statutes. Can an employer temporarily lay off an employee? Is there an implied duty to treat employees fairly? Can an employer amend the terms of the employment contract? Go to Professor Doorey's Workplace Law Blog and review his entry entitled "Developments in Employment & Labour Law: 5 Things Every HR Manager Should Know" (http://www.yorku.ca/ddoorey/lawblog/?p=949), which discusses these issues and more.

HRM EXPERIENCE

Learning about Employee Rights

In the constantly changing field of human resources it is imperative that both HR managers and supervisors be aware of changes that affect the organization and the process of managing employees. Nowhere is this more true than in the growing field of employee rights. As employees demand more job and employment rights regarding monitoring, unjust dismissals, and off-duty conduct, employers must be knowledgeable

about new laws, court rulings, and the policies of other organizations that influence each area. This knowledge will enable managers to respond to these employee concerns in a positive and proactive manner. Failure to provide employees their rights could lead to costly and embarrassing lawsuits, resulting in diminished employee loyalty or morale. The purpose of this exercise, therefore, is to familiarize yourself with issues of employee rights.

continued

Assignment

Working individually or in teams, for each of the following employee rights topics, identify and discuss the concerns and interests at stake for both employees and employers. Answer the questions pertaining to each topic.

- Wrongful dismissal lawsuits
- Employee searches and monitoring
- Employee conduct away from the workplace

- E-mail and Internet use at work and at home

1. What are the employer's interests?
2. What are the employee's interests?
3. What do you think is a fair balance between these interests?
4. What, if any, laws or court cases affect this right?
5. Generally, how are employers responding to this employee right?

BIZFLIX EXERCISES

IN GOOD COMPANY: FIRING AN EMPLOYEE

This scene from the film *In Good Company* shows Mark Steckle's (Clark Greg) efforts to fire Dan Foreman (Dennis Quaid) and Carter Duryea (Topher Grace). Carefully assess Mark's behaviour against the discussion of employee rights and discipline in this chapter.

A corporate takeover brings star advertising executive Dan Foreman a new boss who is half his age. Carter Duryea—Dan's new boss—wants to prove his worth as the new marketing chief at *Sports America*, Waterman Publishing's flagship magazine. Carter applies his unique approaches while dating Dan's daughter, Alex (Scarlett Johansson).

This scene comes from the "Teddy K. Is Coming" sequence near the film's end. It starts with Mark Steckle saying to Dan Foreman, "Look, we've been carrying your fat, bloated salary for way too long." This scene follows Teddy K.'s (Malcolm McDowell) synergy speech to the assembled employees of his recent acquisition, Waterman Publishing. The film continues with Carter and Dan carrying out their plan to get some new magazine advertising.

What to Watch for and Ask Yourself

- This chapter opened with the observation that managers and supervisors find it hard to discipline employees. Does this observation apply to Mark Steckle? Why or why not?
- Does Mark follow the suggestions shown in Figure 13.1 in trying to end the employment of Dan and Carter?
- The section "Disciplinary Policies and Procedures" in this chapter offered guidelines and observations on correct approaches to employee discipline. Does Mark follow any of those procedures? If not, which aspects of his behaviour deviate from the procedures described earlier?

CASE STUDY 1

DISMISSING AN EMPLOYEE FOR ABSENTEEISM

Supervisors report that discharging an employee is one of the toughest tasks they perform as managers. Termination for absenteeism can be particularly difficult, since if the absenteeism is related to a disability, the employer will need to consider not only the rules governing dismissal with notice and with cause, but also requirements in human rights legislation.

Mr. Keays was hired in 1986 by Honda as an assembly-line worker. In 1997, he was diagnosed with chronic fatigue syndrome and consequently went on disability benefits until the insurer declared that he was fit to return to work. When he returned, the employer put him into its disability program, which required him to submit medical reports for every absence from work. The employer began to doubt the veracity of Mr. Keays's doctor's reports and, therefore, in 2000, ordered him to see a doctor it had selected. Mr. Keays obtained legal advice recommending he not see the employer's doctor unless the employer clearly indicated the purpose of the examination. The employer ignored the lawyer's request and summarily dismissed Mr. Keays for cause (without notice) when he refused to meet with the employer's doctor. The employer claimed this was insubordination, entitling it to dismiss Mr. Keays without notice.

Mr. Keays sued for wrongful dismissal. He argued that his employer did not have a contractual right to force him to attend a different doctor chosen by the employer simply because the employer did not like the opinion of the employee's own doctor. Therefore, he was not being insubordinate by refusing an order that the employer had no right to make. Moreover, he argued that the requirement to submit medical letters for every absence and to submit to a medical exam by the employer's doctor amounted to harassment and discrimination on the basis of his disability and was part of a conspiracy between the employer and the doctor intended to enable the employer to dismiss him for cause after the doctor issued a report saying Mr. Keays was able to work. Therefore, he argued that, in addition to reasonable notice damages, he should be entitled to damages for bad faith in the manner in which he was dismissed and to punitive damages to punish the employer for its egregious conduct.

QUESTIONS

1. Do you think the employer should be entitled to dismiss Mr. Keays without giving him reasonable notice?

2. Does an employer have a right to insist that employees submit to medical exams by doctors chosen by the employer?

3. If the doctors inform the employer that Mr. Keays's absences are due to his chronic fatigue syndrome and that they are likely to continue in the future, should the employer be entitled to dismiss Mr. Keays?

4. If Mr. Keays wins his wrongful dismissal case, will the court order Honda to reinstate him to his previous employment? Should it do that?

CASE STUDY 2

IMPROVING PERFORMANCE THROUGH A PROGRESSIVE DISCIPLINE POLICY

Simon Ouellet, former president of the Human Resources Professionals Association of Ontario, was recruited by Fantom Technologies to be vice-president of Human Resources. Fantom is a manufacturer of state-of-the-art floor care products, based in southern Ontario.

One of the first issues he faced in his new job was an unacceptable absenteeism rate. There were about 250 employees on the three assembly lines, operating two shifts a day. The average employee was absent 13 or 14 days a year. The benchmark for other manufacturing sites was 8 or 9 days. Simon calculated that Fantom was employing between 30 and 35 extra people to cover absences. This hurt the bottom line.

A related problem was punctuality. Employees were habitually five or ten minutes late on their shifts. In a white-collar environment with flextime, this would not have been as critical. But tardiness in this situation meant that the assembly line could not operate and that the other employees on the three lines were forced to remain idle.

The solution was to develop a system of progressive discipline. Simon prepared a simple two-page policy. Page 1 dealt with culpable absenteeism—the behaviour in the control of employees such as arriving late, leaving work without permission, calling in sick but playing golf, and so on. Page 2 dealt with legitimate or innocent absences. Simon met with the unions and notified them that this policy would come into effect as of December 1998. All employees started at zero absences at this time.

The policy assumed that all absences were innocent. However, if an employee was absent five times in a 12-month period, the supervisor met with that employee to express concern over the absences and to identify any need for counselling or assistance. The goal of the meeting was to express legitimate concerns, reinforce that the employee was needed, and ensure that the employee accepted responsibility for managing his or her own attendance. Following this meeting, if the employee had fewer than two absences in the ensuing six months, the employee was no longer part of the program. However, if the absence pattern continued, the employee was counselled a second and third time. If no improvements resulted, a level 4 employment status review was conducted. This was done on a case-by-case basis. For example, a frequently absent employee with 28 years of good service would be treated differently from another employee with the same absenteeism record but only 2 years of employment.

The results were impressive. About 70 employees entered the program. Of these, 8 to 10 advanced to step 2, 2 to step 3, and none to step 4. The absenteeism rate dropped to an average of fewer than 10 days, and punctuality was no longer an issue. Labour costs were reduced, because it meant that 20 fewer employees were needed.

QUESTIONS

1. "The policy assumed that all absences were innocent." What do you think this means?

2. Do you think the application of the policy would be affected if the absences were due to a disability as defined in the Human Rights Code?

3. The policy was active as of December 1998, and all employees were treated equally from that date, regardless of their previous absenteeism records. Was this fair?

4. Could a policy of this type be developed to manage student punctuality and absenteeism?

CAREER COUNSEL

Visit the *Managing Human Resources* website (http://www.belcourt6e.nelson.com) for tips on negotiating a formal employment contract.

NOTES AND REFERENCES

1. *Cronk v. Canadian General Insurance* (1995), 19 O.R. (3rd) 515 (Ontario Court of Appeal).
2. T. Wagar, "Wrongful Dismissal: Perception vs. Reality," *Human Resources Professional* 8, no. 10 (1996).
3. *Doman Forest Products Ltd.* (1990), 13 Labour Arbitration Cases (4th) 275.
4. G. England, *Individual Employment Law* (Irwin Law, 2008), 205–208.

5. S. Cohen and A. V. Campbell, "It's Time to Face the Inevitable and Comply with Privacy Laws," *Canadian HR Reporter* 15, no. 2 (January 28, 2002): 9–10.

6. David Brown, "10 Months to Get Ready," *Canadian HR Reporter* 16, no. 4 (February 24, 2003): 1, 11.

7. Dan J. Shields and Valerie Jepson, "When Internet Use Turns to Abuse," *HR Professional*, April–May 2006, 28.

8. *Colwell v. Cornerstone Properties* (Ontario Superior Court of Justice, 2008).

9. Gillian Flynn, "Internet Issues at Work," *Workforce-Vendor Directory* 80, no. 10 (2002): 33–34.

10. *Prestressed Systems Inc.* (2005), 137 Labour Arbitration Cases (4th), 193.

11. *Doman Forest Products Ltd.* (1990), 13 Labour Arbitration Cases (4th), 275, considering the impact of the *British Columbia Privacy Act* on the right of employers to conduct surveillance of employees.

12. One of the original studies on this topic can be found at Edward L. Harrison, "Why Supervisors Fail to Discipline," *Supervisory Management* 30, no. 4 (April 1985): 17.

13. George W. Bohlander and Donna Blancero, "A Study of Reversal Determinants in Discipline and Discharge Arbitration Awards: The Impact of Just Cause Standards," *Labor Studies Journal* 21, no. 3 (Fall 1996): 3–18.

14. "Steps to Take before Recommending Disciplinary Action," *PM Public Management* 86, no. 6 (July 2004): 43.

15. "22 Tips for Avoiding Employee Lawsuits," *HRfocus* 80, no. 12 (December 2003): 4.

16. Jathan W. Janove, "Private Eye 101," *HR Magazine* 49, no. 7 (July 2004): 127.

17. Kelly Mollica, "Perceptions of Fairness," *HR Magazine* 49, no. 6 (June 2004): 169.

18. Readers interested in the pioneering work on positive discipline should see James R. Redeker, "Discipline, Part I: Progressive Systems Work Only by Accident," *Personnel* 62, no. 10 (October 1985): 8–12; James R. Redeker, "Discipline, Part 2: The Nonpunitive Approach Works by Design," *Personnel* 62, no. 11 (November 1985): 7–14.

19. Richard Bayer, "Firing: Letting People Go with Dignity Is Good for Business," *HRfocus* 77, no. 1 (January 2000): 10. See also Paul Falcone, "Give Employees the (Gentle) Boot," *HR Magazine* 46, no. 4 (April 2001): 121–128.

20. "The New Rules of Termination," *HRfocus* 78, no. 5 (May 2001): 1, 11–15.

21. Elizabeth Hill, "AAA Employment Arbitration: A Fair Forum at Low Cost," *Dispute Resolution Journal* 58, no. 2 (May–June 2003): 8.

22. Theodore Eisenberg and Elizabeth Hill, "Arbitration and Litigation of Employment Claims," *Dispute Resolution Journal* 58, no. 4 (November 2003–January 2004): 44.

23. Margaret M. Clark, "EEOC's Effort to Expand Mediation Gains Momentum," *HR Magazine* 48, no. 5 (May 2003): 32.

24. "How Best to Avoid Mediation Mistakes," *HRfocus* 77, no. 9 (September 2000): 2. See also Nancy Kauffman and Barbara Davis, "What Type of Mediation Do You Want?" *Dispute Resolution Journal* 53, no. 2 (May 1998): 10.

25. Norm Frauenheim, "Clause Alarms Athletes," *Arizona Republic*, May 10, 1996, C1.

26. George W. Bohlander, Robert J. Deeny, and Mishka L. Marshall, "Alternative Dispute Resolution Policies: Current Procedural and Administrative Issues," *Labor Law Journal* 47, no. 9 (September 1996): 619–626; Thomas R. Kelly and Danielle L. Berke, "What's New in ADR?" *HRfocus* 73, no. 4 (April 1996): 15.

27. Jennifer Schramm, "Perception on Ethics," *HRfocus* 79, no. 11 (November 2004): 176.

28. "Ethical Corporate Behavior Begins with a Code of Conduct," *HRfocus* 49, no. 7 (July 2002): 8–9.

The Dynamics of Labour Relations

CHAPTER 14

After studying this chapter, you should be able to

[OUTCOME 1] Identify and explain the federal and provincial legislation that provides the framework for labour relations.

[OUTCOME 2] Explain why employees join unions.

[OUTCOME 3] Describe the process by which unions organize employees and gain recognition as their bargaining agent.

[OUTCOME 4] Discuss the bargaining process and the bargaining goals and strategies of a union and an employer.

[OUTCOME 5] Differentiate the forms of bargaining power that a union and an employer may utilize to enforce their bargaining demands.

[OUTCOME 6] Describe a typical union grievance procedure and explain the basis for arbitration awards.

Mention the word union and most people will have some opinion, positive or negative, regarding Canadian labour organizations. To some, the word evokes images of labour–management unrest—grievances, strikes, picketing, boycotts. To others, the word represents industrial democracy, fairness, opportunity, equal representation. Many think of unions as simply creating an adversarial relationship between employees and managers.

Regardless of attitudes toward them, since the mid-1800s unions have been an important force shaping organizational practices, legislation, and political thought in Canada. Today unions remain an interest because of their influence on organizational productivity and HR policies and practices. Like business organizations themselves, unions are undergoing changes in both operation—such as mergers and coalitions—and philosophy.

In spite of the long history of unions, the intricacies of labour relations are unfamiliar to many individuals. Therefore, this chapter describes government regulation of labour relations, the labour relations process, the reasons that workers join labour organizations, and the structure and leadership of unions. Importantly, according to labour law, once the union is certified to negotiate for bargaining-unit members, it must represent everyone in the unit equally. Therefore, in the latter sections of the chapter, we discuss the important topics of contract administration, particularly the handling of employee grievances and arbitration.

About 27 percent of all employees are unionized, with rates higher in the public sector (71 percent) than the private sector (17 percent).[1] Unions and other labour organizations can affect significantly the ability of managers to direct and control the various functions of HRM. For example, union seniority provisions in the collective agreement may influence who is selected for job promotions or training programs. Pay rates may be determined through union negotiations, or unions may impose restrictions on management's employee appraisal methods. Therefore, it is essential that managers in both the union and nonunion environment understand how unions operate and be thoroughly familiar with the important body of law governing labour relations. Remember, ignorance of labour legislation is no defence when managers and supervisors violate labour law. Before reading further, test your knowledge of labour relations law by answering the questions in Highlights in HRM 14.1.

GOVERNMENT REGULATION OF LABOUR RELATIONS

[OUTCOME 1]

Labour relations in Canada are regulated by a multiplicity of federal and provincial laws. There are specific laws, or acts, for different sectors, industries, and workers. It is a highly decentralized system. For example, interprovincial transportation and communications are under federal jurisdiction, while manufacturing and mining are provincial. However, 90 percent of workers are governed by provincial legislation.

THE INDUSTRIAL RELATIONS DISPUTES AND INVESTIGATION ACT

The *Industrial Relations Disputes and Investigation Act* (1948) specified the right of workers to join unions, allowed unions to be certified as bargaining agents by a labour relations board, required management to recognize a certified union as the exclusive bargaining agent for a group of employees, required both unions and management to negotiate in good faith, outlined unfair labour practices by both unions and management, and created a two-stage compulsory conciliation process that was mandatory before strikes or lockouts became legal.[2]

The federal government later incorporated these rights into a more comprehensive piece of legislation known as the *Canada Labour Code*. At the same time, the Canada Industrial Relations Board (CIRB) was established to administer and enforce the code. Similarly, each province has a labour relations board that administers labour

Using the Internet

For a history of labour, read the article "The Cradle of Collective Bargaining: History of Labour" at:

http://www.humanities
.mcmaster.ca/-cradle

Highlights in **HRM 14.1**

Test Your Labour Relations Know-How

1. During a labour organizing drive, supervisors questioned individual employees about their union beliefs. Was this questioning permissible?

   Yes _____   No _____

2. While an organizing drive was underway, an employer agreed—as a social gesture—to furnish refreshments at a holiday party. Was the employer acting within the law?

   Yes _____   No _____

3. A company distributed to other anti-union employers in the area a list of job applicants known to be union supporters. Was the distribution unlawful?

   Yes _____   No _____

4. During a union organizing drive, the owner of Servo Pipe promised her employees a wage increase if they would vote against the union. Can the owner legally make this promise to her employees?

   Yes _____   No _____

5. John Green, a maintenance engineer, has a poor work record. Management wishes to terminate his employment; however, Green is a union steward and is highly critical of the company. Can management legally discharge this employee?

   Yes _____   No _____

   Answers on page 581.

THE LABOUR RELATIONS PROCESS

Individually, employees may be able to exercise relatively little power in their relationship with employers. Of course, if they believe they are not being treated fairly, they have the option of quitting. However, employees can also correct this situation by organizing and bargaining with the employer collectively. When employees pursue this option, the labour relations process begins. As Figure 14.1 illustrates, the **labour relations process** consists of a logical sequence of four events: (1) workers desire collective representation, (2) the union begins its organizing campaign, and (3) collective negotiations lead to a contract, and (4) the contract is administered. Laws and administrative rulings influence each of the separate events by granting special privileges to, or imposing defined constraints on, workers, managers, and union officials.[4]

WHY EMPLOYEES UNIONIZE

The majority of research on why employees unionize comes from the study of blue-collar employees in the private sector. These studies generally conclude that employees unionize as a result of economic need, and because of a general dissatisfaction with managerial practices, and thereby seek to have a voice in the

---

and the provincial labour law statutes, such as the Ontario *Labour Relations Act*. (The exception is Quebec, which has a labour court and commissioners.) Members of the labour relations boards are generally government appointees. Labour relations boards are generally autonomous from the federal government and have representatives from both labour and management. The duties of the LRB include

- Administering the statutory procedures for the acquisition, transfer, and termination of bargaining rights
- Hearing complaints related to unfair labour practices
- Supervising strikes and lockout votes
- Determining whether bargaining was done in good faith
- Remedying violations of labour legislation.[3]

---

law

labour relations process
Logical sequence of four events: (1) workers desire collective representation, (2) union begins its organizing campaign, which may lead to certification and recognition, (3) collective negotiations lead to a contract, and (4) the contract is administered

OUTCOME 2

FIGURE **14.1**

The Labour Relations Process

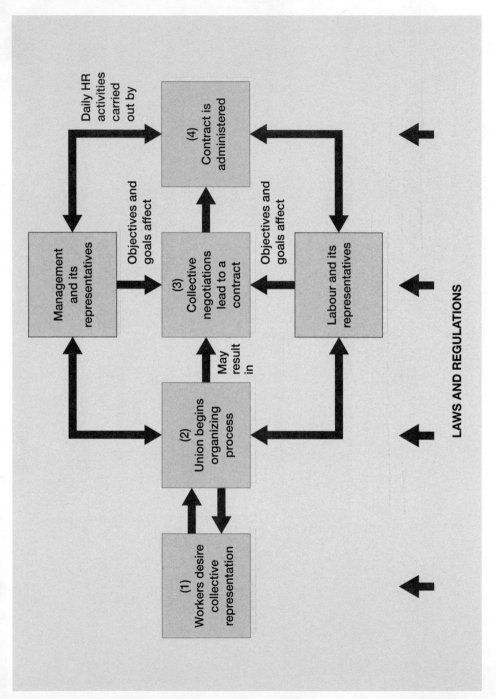

LAWS AND REGULATIONS

union shop

Provision of the collective agreement that requires employees to join the union as a condition of their employment

setting of working conditions and/or as a way to fulfill social and status needs. In short, employees see unionism as a way to achieve results they cannot achieve acting individually. As Highlights in HRM 14.2 illustrates, some segments of the labour force are very difficult to unionize. It should be pointed out that some employees join unions because of the union-shop provisions. A union shop is a provision of the collective agreement that requires employees to join as a condition of employment.

Economic Needs

Whether employees select unionization will greatly depend on whether the employees perceive the union as likely to be effective in improving various economic conditions of employment—often referred to as the union's instrumentality. Dissatisfaction with wages, benefits, and working conditions appears to provide the strongest reason to join a union. This point is continually supported by research studies that find that both union members and nonmembers have their highest expectations of union performance regarding the "bread and butter" issues of collective bargaining.[5] Hourly earnings were $23 for those in unions and $18.50 for those not in a union.[6] It is these traditional issues of wages, benefits, and working conditions on which unions are built.

Highlights in **HRM 14.2**

Homeworkers: Canada's Invisible Labour Force

Rosanna Gonzalez (not her real name) works in the basement of her home in a small room crowded with industrial sewing machines. Rosanna is in the process of making 410 sweatshirts. To meet her deadline she will have to put in 40 hours of work in two days. There is no natural light in the airless basement room, no way to escape the flying dust and thread particles. Last week the assignment was T-shirts. Rosanna received 38 cents per shirt. She can churn one out in five minutes, but even at that speed, she still earns only about $4.50 per hour—the minimum wage a decade ago.

In most provinces the law requires that homeworkers be paid at least one dollar above minimum wage to compensate them for the use of space and equipment in their homes. But enforcement of the law is

rare. Canadians are quick to condemn working conditions in developing countries, yet they are notably silent about abuses in their own country. Joining a union is a traditional response to abysmal working conditions. For homeworkers, unionization is a remote possibility at best. These individuals (most of whom speak no English) work in scattered and unlicensed locations and are usually unaware of their rights. Those who are aware are afraid that if they complain, they will suffer retribution at the hands of the retailers, contractors, and subcontractors with whom they do business. These women have few employment options and are often the sole providers for their children. For them the choice is clear: put up with the exploitation or don't work at all.

Involving employees in decision making may reduce the desire to seek representation through unionization.

Dissatisfaction with Management

Employees may seek unionization when they perceive that managerial practices regarding promotion, transfer, shift assignment, or other job-related policies are administered in an unfair or biased manner. Employees cite favouritism shown by managers as a major reason for joining unions. This is particularly true when the favouritism concerns the HR areas of discipline, promotion, job assignments, and training opportunities.

We have noted throughout this book that today's employees are better educated than those of the past, and they often express a desire to be more involved in decisions affecting their jobs. Chapter 4 discussed the concept of employee empowerment and highlighted various employee involvement techniques. The failure of employers to give employees an opportunity to participate in decisions affecting their welfare may encourage union membership. It is widely believed that one reason managers begin employee involvement programs and seek to empower their employees is to avoid collective action by employees. For example, employers in the auto, semiconductor, and financial industries involve employees in collaborative programs as a means to stifle unionization. In one organizing effort by the United Auto Workers at a Nissan plant, the union lost the election because workers were satisfied with the voice in decision making that Nissan's participatory style of management gave them.

Social and Leadership Concerns

Employees whose needs for recognition and social affiliation are being frustrated may join unions as a means of satisfying these needs. Through their union, they have an opportunity to fraternize with other employees who have similar desires, interests, problems, and gripes. Simply, employees may join unions for the same reason

© Getty Images

they would join a civic organization, club, or sports team, namely to enjoy the companionship of others and to benefit in the prestige and value that organization may provide. Additionally, the union also enables them to put leadership talents to use as officers of the union and representatives of fellow employees. One study found that employees became union stewards so that they could be seen as "a fellow your buddies look to" and as a person who "stands up to the boss."[7]

ORGANIZING CAMPAIGNS

Once employees desire to unionize, a formal organizing campaign may be started either by a union organizer or by employees acting on their own behalf.[8] Contrary to popular belief, most organizing campaigns are begun by employees rather than by union organizers. Large national unions such as the United Auto Workers, the United Brotherhood of Carpenters, the United Steelworkers, and the Teamsters, however, have formal organizing departments whose purpose is to identify organizing opportunities and launch organizing campaigns.

[OUT3COME]

Organizing Steps

The organizing process normally includes the following steps:

1. Employee/union contact
2. Initial organizational meeting
3. Formation of in-house organizing committee
4. Application to labour relations board
5. Issuance of certificate by labour relations board
6. Election of bargaining committee and contract negotiations.

Step 1. The first step begins when employees and union officials make contact to explore the possibility of unionization. During these discussions, employees investigate the advantages of representation, and union officials begin to gather information on employee needs, problems, and grievances. Union organizers also seek specific information about the employer's financial health, supervisory styles, and organizational policies and practices. To win employee support, labour organizers must build a case *against* the employer and *for* the union. Typically there are signs, reported in Highlights in HRM 14.3, that an organizing drive is occurring. Note also that most organizing drives take place inside the company.

Highlights in HRM 14.3

Is a Union Being Organized?

Senior management is sometimes the last to know that a union has targeted the company. Often the process starts after employees call a union with complaints, and want to understand their legal rights and responsibilities. Listed here below are a few common signs that an organization drive is happening:

- Unusual employee behaviour of any kind
- An increase in the number of complaints about working conditions

- Demands for detailed information about employment policies
- Gatherings of employees that appear larger in number than usual, or that involve employees whose jobs are unrelated or who would usually have no common interests
- Changes in how employees interact with their supervisors
- The presence of union leaflets or other union material

Step 2. As an organizing campaign gathers momentum, the organizer schedules an initial union meeting to attract more supporters. The organizer uses the information gathered in Step 1 to address employee needs and explain how the union can secure these goals. Two additional purposes of organizational meetings are (1) to identify employees who can help the organizer direct the campaign and (2) to establish communication chains that reach all employees.

Step 3. The third important step in the organizing drive is to form an in-house organizing committee composed of employees willing to provide leadership to the campaign. The committee's role is to interest other employees in joining the union and in supporting its campaign. An important task of the committee is to have employees sign an authorization card indicating their willingness to be represented by a union in collective bargaining with their employer. Union membership cards, once signed, are confidential, and only the labour relations board has access to them. The number of signed authorization cards demonstrates the potential strength of the labour union.[9] Legislation across Canada requires as a first step in the union certification process that a union collect authorization cards.

There are then two different processes for union certification used in Canada. One method is known as a card-check. Under that method, a union is certified to represent the workers if the union submits to the labour board authorization cards on behalf of some majority of workers (such as 55 percent) in an appropriate bargaining unit. The second method, known as a mandatory ballot, is a two-step process. First, the union must obtain authorization cards on behalf of a certain number of workers (in Ontario, it is 40 percent or more) in order to obtain a vote. Then, the labour board orders a vote of employees in the bargaining unit, which the union must win. In other words, those who do not cast ballots are not assumed to be voting against the certification of the union.

Step 4. When the union has collected sufficient authorization cards to satisfy the requirements under the applicable certification model, it will file an application for certification. It submits to the labour board its authorization cards, but the employer does not get to see them. The labour board then applies the model, either certifying the union on the basis of a card-check, ordering a vote in provinces that use a mandatory ballot model, or dismissing the application if the union does not submit the required number of authorization cards.

Step 5. Once the labour board has applied the process, it will declare whether or not the union has been successful in its application for certification. If the union is successful, the board will "certify" the union. If the union fails to meet the required test, the board will dismiss the application.

Step 6. Once the labour relations board determines that the union is certified, the bargaining committee is put in place to start negotiating a collective agreement. If the union is a national union, such as the Canadian Auto Workers (CAW), usually a national representative works with the bargaining committee to negotiate a collective agreement with the company. Labour relations legislation imposes a duty on employers and unions to bargain in good faith and make reasonable efforts to complete a collective agreement.

Employer Tactics

Employers must not interfere with the labour relations process of certification. They are prohibited by law from dismissing, disciplining, or threatening employees for exercising their right to form a union. Employers cannot promise better conditions, such as increased vacation days, if the employees vote for no union or choose one union over another. Nor can they threaten to close the business, as one company did as workers were voting.[10] They cannot unilaterally change wages and working conditions during certification proceedings or during collective bargaining. Like unions, they must bargain in good faith, meaning that they must demonstrate a commitment to bargain seriously and fairly. In addition, they cannot participate in the formation, selection, or support of unions representing employees (see Figure 14.2).

authorization card
A statement signed by an employee authorizing a union to act as his or her representative for the purposes of collective bargaining

FIGURE 14.2

Employer "Don'ts" During Union Organizing Campaigns

Union organizing drives are emotionally charged events. Furthermore, labour law, labour relation board rulings, and court decisions greatly affect the behaviour and actions of management and union representatives. During the drive, managers and supervisors should avoid the following:

- Attending union meetings, spying on employee–union gatherings, and questioning employees about the content of union meetings

- Questioning current employees about their union sentiments—especially about how they might vote in a union election

- Threatening or terminating employees for their union support or beliefs

- Changing the working conditions of employees because they actively work for the union or simply support its ideals

- Supplying the names, addresses, and phone numbers of employees to union representatives or other employees sympathetic to the union or opposed to the union

- Promising employees improvements in working conditions (e.g., wage increases, benefit improvements, etc.) if they vote against the union

- Accepting or reviewing union authorization cards or pro-union petitions, since employees' names are listed on these documents

- Providing financial or any other support to employees opposed to unionization

bargaining unit
Group of two or more employees who share common employment interests and conditions and may reasonably be grouped together for purposes of collective bargaining

unfair labour practices (ULPs)
Specific employer and union illegal practices that deny employees their rights and benefits under federal and provincial labour law

None of these prohibitions prevents an employer from making the case that the employees have the right not to join a union and that they can deal directly with the employer on any issue. Employer resistance to unionization is the norm in Canada and opposition has been found to decrease the probability of successfully organizing.[11] When Walmart consolidated its entry into Canada by buying 122 non-unionized Woolco stores, the company was widely viewed as anti-union. However, Walmart spokespeople insist that they are not anti-union, but rather "pro-associate" (the Walmart term for the retail salesclerk).[12]

Employers' attempts to influence employees are scrutinized closely by officials of the organizing union and by the labour relations board. In one case, an employer committed a serious unfair labour practice with the organizing process and the union was automatically recognized by the labour board, even though only 5 percent of the employees had signed authorization cards.[13] Magna International has developed unique HR practices to remain union free, as described in Reality Check.

Union Tactics

Unions also have a duty to act in accordance with labour legislation. Unions are prohibited from interfering with the formation of an employer's organization. They cannot intimidate or coerce employees to become or remain members of a union. Nor can they force employers to dismiss, discipline, or discriminate against nonunion employees. They must provide fair representation for all employees in the bargaining unit whether in collective bargaining or in grievance procedure cases. Unions cannot engage in activities such as strikes before the expiration of the union contract.

Any of the prohibited activities noted above for both employers and unions are considered unfair labour practices (ULPs). Charges of ULPs are filed with the labour relations board, whose duty it is to enforce labour relations legislation. A summary of ULPs is presented in Highlights in HRM 14.4.

Reality CHECK

Magna's Unique HR Culture

Magna International is a successful automotive supplier with over 82,000 employees in 224 plants in 22 countries. In 2009, Magna announced plans to become an auto manufacturer, in light of the impending collapses of GM and Chrysler. In Canada, Magna employs about 18,000 employees in 60 plants. Researchers have studied Magna's success and focused on the HR strategies used to remain union free. One strategy is to have many channels for workers to have a voice and to resolve conflicts. There are weekly departmental meetings and daily line meetings in which the workforce is encouraged to solve any problems raised. Promotions and compensation are based on a worker's positive attitudes to productivity and quality. Each plant operates as a profit centre and is generally much smaller than other auto makers'. The location of the plant is also strategic. Magna builds its plants in semi-peripheral labour markets where wages and job security are much lower than those in urban areas. Wages are much lower at Magna than at the Big Three, averaging 40 percent lower for assemblers and 15 percent lower for skilled categories. The feeling among Magna workers is that they are paid well for what they do, in

the context of the external labour market and compared to previous jobs that they have held. Magna recruits mainly immigrants, who may face inequalities in the external labour market, and thus value the job security based on productivity at Magna. Moreover, most immigrants have no experience with unionized workplaces in their home countries. Magna recruits through family referrals, thus reinforcing the attitudes of ethnic labour pools. The most effective strategy may be to offer employees access to a deferred profit sharing plan, from which they are not allowed to make withdrawals for 10 years. Profit sharing aligns workers' interests with management interests.

In a surprise move in 2007, Magna opened the door to unions. The deal was that there were to be no strikes, and binding arbitration would be used to settle differences. Annual wage increases would depend on the performance of the plant, a manufacturing wage increase, and competitive factors. The traditional union grievance procedure would be replaced by a resolution subcommittee. The goal was to retain the unique human resources culture at Magna, and end decades of hostility between Magna and the CAW.

Source: G. Keenan, "Magna's Union Deal: No Strikes," *The Globe and Mail*, October 6, 2007, B7; W. Lewchuck and D. Wells, "When Corporations Substitute for Adversial Unions," *Relations Industrielles* 61, 4 (Autumn 2006): 639–66c; CBCA Business: 639.

Highlights in HRM 14.5 on page 556 lists the key strategies identified by HR specialists to reduce workers' motivation to join unions. Since these strategies are under the direct control of management, they can be used to help discourage or prevent unionization.

HOW EMPLOYEES BECOME UNIONIZED

The procedures for union certification vary across Canadian jurisdictions. As mentioned earlier, the common practice is for unions to present documentation to the appropriate labour relations board for certification. The labour relations board must certify a union before it can act as a bargaining unit for a group of employees. As noted, in order to acquire certification, the union must demonstrate that it has obtained the minimum level of membership support required by the labour relations board. It is also possible for a union to obtain the right to represent workers through voluntary recognition, a process in which the employer simply agrees to recognize the union as the representative of the employees.

Voluntary Recognition

All employers, except those in Quebec, may voluntarily recognize and accept a union. This rarely happens, except in the construction industry, where there is a great reliance on union hiring halls.

Highlights in HRM 14.4

Unfair Labour Practices

Unfair labour practices by employers include

- Helping to establish or administer a union
- Altering the working conditions of the employees while a union is applying for certification without the union's consent
- Using intimidation, coercion, threats, promises, or exercising undue influence while a union is being organized
- Failing to recognize or bargain with the certified union
- Hiring professional strike breakers

Unfair labour practices by unions include

- Contributing financial or other support to an employer's organization
- Not representing fairly the employees in the bargaining unit
- Bargaining or negotiating a collective agreement with an employer while another union represents the employees in the bargaining unit
- Calling or authorizing an unlawful strike or threatening to do so
- Threatening or intimidating workers to influence their support for the union

Highlights in HRM 14.5

Strategies to Remain Union-Free

- Offer competitive wages and benefits based on labour market comparisons and salary and benefit surveys.
- Train supervisors in progressive human relations skills, including employee motivation, job design, and employment law.
- Institute formal procedures to resolve employee complaints and grievances; these may include peer review committees, step-review complaint systems, or open-door policies.
- Involve employees in work decisions affecting job performance or the quality or quantity of the product or service provided.

- Give attention to employee growth and development needs; recognize that the workforce is growing older, more female, more vocal, better educated, less patient, and more demanding.
- Draft HR policies that reflect legal safeguards and that are fair and equitable in employment conditions such as discipline, promotions, training, and layoffs.

The best work environment, and the least receptive to unionization, is one that treats the individual with respect, dignity, and fairness, while encouraging participation in decision making.

CONTRACT NEGOTIATION

Once a bargaining unit has been certified by the labour relations board, the employer and the union are legally obligated to bargain in good faith over the terms and conditions of a collective agreement. Usually the terms of a collective agreement apply for a minimum of one year and a maximum of three years, although there is no legally mandated maximum. As the contract expiry date approaches, either party must notify the other of its intention to bargain for a renewal collective agreement or contract negotiation.

DECERTIFICATION

All legislation allows for the decertification of unions under certain conditions. If the majority of employees indicate that they do not want to be represented by the union, or that they want to be represented by another union, or if the union has failed to bargain, an application for decertification can be made to the labour relations board. If a collective agreement has been reached with the employer, this application can be made only at specified times, such as a few months before the agreement expires. Workers at seven Starbucks in Vancouver voted to decertify from the CAW. Employees can initiate an application for decertification if the union fails to bargain.

IMPACT OF UNIONIZATION ON MANAGERS

Why would employers oppose the unionization of their employees? First, studies from the field of labour economics routinely show that wages and benefits are higher in union organizations compared to similar nonunion organizations. Second, unions can have a significant effect on the rights exercised by management in making decisions about employees. Third, unionization restricts the freedom of management to formulate HR policy unilaterally and can challenge the authority of supervisors.

Challenges to Management Decisions

Unions typically attempt to achieve greater participation in management decisions that affect their members. Specifically, these decisions may involve such issues as the subcontracting of work, productivity standards, and job content. Employers quite naturally seek to claim many of these decisions as their exclusive **management rights**—decisions over which management claims exclusive rights. However, the union may challenge and erode these prerogatives at the bargaining table, through the grievance procedure, and through strikes.

Loss of Supervisory Authority

At a recent labour–management conference a union official commented, "Contract terms covering wages, benefits, job security, and working hours are of major importance to our membership." However, for managers and supervisors, the focal point of the union's impact is at the operating level (the shop floor or office facility), where the terms of the collective agreement are implemented on a daily basis. For example, these terms can determine what corrective action is to be taken in

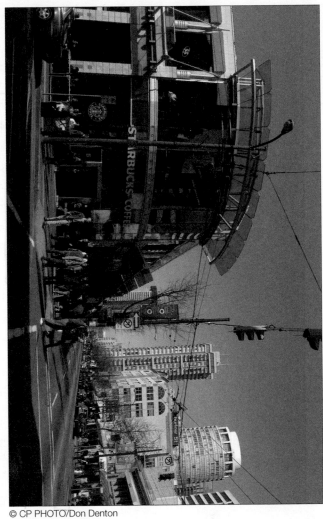

© CP PHOTO/Don Denton

Workers at seven Starbucks outlets in Vancouver voted to decertify.

management rights
Decisions regarding organizational operations over which management claims exclusive rights

directing and in disciplining employees. When disciplining employees, supervisors must be certain they can demonstrate *just cause* (see Chapter 13) for their actions, because these actions can be challenged by the union and the supervisor called as defendant during a grievance hearing. If the challenge is upheld, the supervisor's effectiveness in coping with subsequent disciplinary problems may be impaired. Specific contract language can also reduce the supervisor's ability to manage in such areas as scheduling, training, transfers, performance evaluation, and promotions. Under provisions of the collective agreement, supervisors may have to promote employees by seniority rather than by individual merit.

STRUCTURES, FUNCTIONS, AND LEADERSHIP OF LABOUR UNIONS

Unions that represent skilled craft workers, such as carpenters or masons, are called **craft unions.** Craft unions include the International Association of Iron Workers, the United Brotherhood of Carpenters, and the United Association of Plumbers and Pipefitters. Unions that represent unskilled and semiskilled workers employed along industry lines are known as **industrial unions.** The Canadian Union of Postal Workers is an industrial union, as are the United Auto Workers, the United Steelworkers, and the Office and Professional Employees International Union. While this distinction still exists, technological changes, union mergers, and competition among unions for members have helped reduce it. Today skilled and unskilled workers, white-collar and blue-collar workers, and professional groups are being represented by both types of unions.

Besides unions, **employee associations** represent various groups of professional and white-collar employees. Examples of employee associations include the Federation of Quebec Nurses and the Alberta Teachers Association. In competing with unions, these associations, for all purposes, may function as unions and become just as aggressive as unions in representing members.

Regardless of their type, labour organizations are diverse organizations. Each will have its own structure, objectives, and methods of governance. When describing labour organizations, most researchers divide them into three levels: (1) central labour congresses, (2) international and national unions, and (3) local unions belonging to a parent national or international union. Each level has its own reason for existence and its own operating policies and procedures.

THE CANADIAN LABOUR CONGRESS

The Canadian Labour Congress (CLC) is a central federation of unions. In 2007, the total membership of the CLC was over 3 million Canadians and represented the majority of all unions in Canada.[14] Because of its size and resources, the CLC is considered the most influential labour federation in Canada. It is mainly a service organization representing over 90 international and national unions; these finance the CLC through dues based on membership size. Like the AFL-CIO, the CLC attempts to influence legislation and promote programs that are of interest to labour. It does this by lobbying, resolving jurisdictional disputes, maintaining ethical standards, providing education and training to its members, conducting research, and representing Canadian interests in the international labour movement.

INTERNATIONAL AND NATIONAL UNIONS

International unions tend to be affiliates of American unions, with headquarters in the United States. In Canada, there are 39 international unions (with membership of about 1.3 million workers) and 175 national unions (with membership of nearly

craft unions
Unions that represent skilled craft workers

industrial unions
Unions that represent all workers — skilled, semiskilled, unskilled — employed along industry lines

employee associations
Labour organizations that represent various groups of professional and white-collar employees in labour–management relations

3 million). The large membership base offers a good deal of leverage to local unions engaged in strike action.

Both international and national unions are made up of local unions. The objectives of these "umbrella" unions are to help organize local unions, to provide strike support, and to assist local unions with negotiations, grievance procedures, and the like. These unions also represent their members' interests with internal and external constituents. By ensuring that all employers pay similar wages to their unionized workers, they also remove higher wages as a competitive disadvantage.

In Canada, most of the decision-making authority in national unions is vested in the local unions or at the bargaining-unit level. This is often referred to as bottom-up unionism. However, many international unions, especially craft unions, are more likely to retain a greater degree of control over the affairs of local unions. This is often referred to as top-down unionism. The officers of both types of union typically include a president, a secretary-treasurer, and several vice-presidents, all officially elected. These officers make up the executive board, which is the top policy-making body. Other positions at the national level include lawyer, economist, statistician, and public relations officer. An economics director gathers, analyzes, and disseminates economic and other information of value in collective bargaining. Many national unions also have an education director, whose job is to provide training for local union officers and stewards.

International and national unions often have social and political objectives outside their traditional goal of representing member interests. This contentious issue is discussed in Ethics in HRM.

LOCAL UNIONS

Employees of any organization can form their own union, with no affiliation to a national or international union. In situations like this, the local is the union. There are about 605 independent local unions in Canada. However, most local unions are

Ethics in **HRM**

Inflation

Members of unions and associations pay dues to support union activities. Most of this money is used to fund traditional union activities such as labour and economic research, contract negotiation, and the handling of grievances. However, sometimes the union, especially at the international and national levels, dedicates some of these funds to causes such as opposing human rights violations in China or supporting gun control in Canada. For example, the CLC is actively involved with social justice groups such as the women's movement, anti-poverty activities, churches, peace activists, and environmentalists. The Canadian Union of Public Employees (CUPE) lobbies for safe clean water, and

its Water Watch campaign to fight the privatization of water is a national priority for this union.

In 1991, a union member challenged, under the Canadian *Charter of Rights and Freedoms*, his obligation to contribute part of his union dues to political causes with which he disagreed. The Supreme Court ruled that trade unions are not in violation of the *Charter* if they use union dues for purposes other than collective bargaining in the narrow sense, since the requirement to pay union dues advances important social and democratic objectives, namely the participation of unions in broader democratic discourse as well as collective bargaining.

Sources: Canadian Labour Congress, http://www.cupe.ca/www/WaterWatch, retrieved August 28, 2009; P. E. Larson, "Fighting for Labour," *Canadian Business Review* 13. no. 4 (1986): 8–12; P. Poiter, "Court Dashes Labour's Hopes of More Rights," *The Globe and Mail*, June 25, 1993, A5.

members of national or international unions or the CLC, which make available to them financial resources and advice.

Unionized employees pay union dues that finance the operation of the local union. Local unions tend to make their own decisions, but turn to the national union for collective bargaining help, research, and assistance when handling certain types of grievances. Many national unions also provide training for local unions on the roles and responsibilities of union officers. The officers of a local union are usually responsible for negotiating the local collective agreement, ensuring the agreement is adhered to, and investigating and processing member grievances. Most importantly, they help prevent their members from being treated by their employers in ways that run counter to management-established HR policies.[15] They also keep members informed through meetings and newsletters.

Role of the Union (Shop) Steward

The union (shop) steward represents the interests of union members in their relations with immediate supervisors and other members of management. Stewards are usually elected by the union members in their own department and serve without union pay. Since stewards are full-time employees of the organization, they often spend considerable time after working hours investigating and handling members' problems. When stewards represent members during grievance meetings on organizational time, their lost earnings are often paid by the local union.

A union steward can be viewed as a "person in the middle," caught between conflicting interests and groups. It cannot be assumed that stewards will always champion union members and routinely oppose managerial objectives. Union stewards are often insightful people working for the betterment of employees and the organization. So supervisors and managers at all levels are strongly encouraged to develop a professional working relationship with stewards and all union officials. This relationship can have a major bearing on union–management cooperation and on the efficiency and morale of the workforce.

Role of the Business Agent

Negotiating and administering the collective agreement and working to resolve problems arising in connection with it are major responsibilities of the business agent. In performing these duties, business agents must be all things to all people in their unions. They are often required to assume the role of counsellor in helping union members with both personal and job-related problems. They are also expected to satisfactorily resolve grievances that cannot be settled by the union stewards. Administering the daily affairs of the local union is another significant part of the business agent's job.

LABOUR RELATIONS IN THE PUBLIC SECTOR

Collective bargaining among federal, provincial, and municipal government employees, and among employees in parapublic agencies (private agencies or branches of government acting as extensions of government programs) has been an area of important activity for the union movement. More than 70 percent of public employees are now unionized.

The three largest unions in Canada represent public-sector employees. The Canadian Union of Public Employees (CUPE) is the largest union in Canada, with 548,000 members. The second-largest union, with 340,000 members, is the National Union of Public and General Employees (NUPGE). The largest union representing employees at the federal level is the Public Service Alliance of Canada (PSAC), with 166,000 members. PSAC comprises 17 different unions representing various groups

---

union (shop) steward
Employee who as a nonpaid union official represents the interests of members in their relations with management

Using the Internet

A description of a union steward's job can be found on the website of the Canadian Union of Public Employees:

http://www.cupe.ca/
www/351/volunteers

business agent
Normally a paid labour official responsible for negotiating and administering the collective agreement and working to resolve union members' problems

such as the Professional Institute of the Public Service of Canada (PIPS), the Social Science Employees Association (SSEA), and air traffic controllers. Growth in these unions is threatened by increased cost-cutting efforts of governments at all levels, resulting in employee reductions.

While public-sector collective bargaining is quite similar to bargaining in the private sector, a number of differences are worth noting. We explore these differences in two contexts: (1) the political nature of the labour-management relationship, and (2) public-sector strikes.

POLITICAL NATURE OF THE LABOUR-MANAGEMENT RELATIONSHIP

Government employees are not able to negotiate with their employers on the same basis as their counterparts in private organizations. It is doubtful that they will ever be able to do so because of inherent differences between the public and private sectors.

One of the significant differences is that labour relations in the private sector has an economic foundation, whereas in government its foundation tends to be political. Since private employers must stay in business in order to sell their goods or services, their employees are not likely to make demands that could bankrupt them. A strike in the private sector is a test of the employer's economic staying power, and usually the employer's customers have alternative sources of supply. Governments, on the other hand, must stay in business because alternative services are usually not available.

Another difference between the public and private sectors relates to the source of management authority. In a private organization, authority flows downward from the board of directors and, ultimately, from the shareholders. In contrast, authority in the public sector flows upward from the public at large to their elected representatives and to the appointed or elected managers. It follows that public employees can exert influence not only as union members but also as pressure groups and voting citizens.

STRIKES IN THE PUBLIC SECTOR

Strikes by government employees create a problem for lawmakers and for the general public. Because many of the services that government employees provide, such as policing and firefighting, are considered essential to the well-being of the public, public policy is opposed to strikes by these people. However, various provincial legislatures have granted public employees the right to strike. Where striking is permitted, the right is limited to specific groups of employees—those performing nonessential services—and the strike cannot endanger the public's health, safety, or welfare. Public-sector unions contend, however, that denying them the same right to strike as employees in the private sector greatly reduces their power during collective bargaining.

Public employees who perform essential services do in fact strike. Teachers, sanitation employees, police, transit employees, firefighters, and postal employees have all engaged in strike action. To avoid potentially critical situations, various arbitration methods are used for resolving collective bargaining deadlocks in the public sector. One is **compulsory binding arbitration** for employees such as police officers, firefighters, and others in jobs where strikes cannot be tolerated; in this case, a neutral third party is appointed to resolve the deadlock. Another method is **final offer arbitration**, under which the arbitrator must select one or the other of the final offers submitted by the disputing parties. With this method, the arbitrator's award is more likely to go to the party whose final bargaining offer has moved the closest to a reasonable settlement. The government can also enact back-to-work legislation, an option being used with increasing frequency.

Using the Internet

The Public Service Labour Relations Board oversees employer–employee relations in the federal public service:

http://www.pslrb-crtfp.gc.ca

compulsory binding arbitration

Binding method of resolving collective bargaining deadlocks by a neutral third party

final offer arbitration

Method of resolving collective bargaining deadlocks whereby the arbitrator has no power to compromise but must select one or another of the final offers submitted by the two parties

THE BARGAINING PROCESS

Those unfamiliar with contract negotiations often view the process as an emotional conflict between labour and management, complete with marathon sessions, fist pounding, and smoke-filled rooms. In reality, negotiating a collective agreement entails long hours of extensive preparation combined with diplomatic manoeuvring and the development of bargaining strategies. Furthermore, negotiation is only one part of the **collective bargaining process**. (See Figure 14.3.) Collective bargaining also may include the use of economic pressures in the form of strikes and boycotts by a union. Lockouts, plant closures, and the replacement of strikers are similar pressures used by an employer. In addition, either or both parties may seek support from the general public or from the courts as a means of pressuring the opposing side.

PREPARING FOR NEGOTIATIONS

Preparing for negotiations includes assembling data to support bargaining proposals and forming the bargaining team. This permits collective bargaining to be conducted on an orderly, factual, and positive basis with a greater likelihood of achieving desired goals. Negotiators often develop a bargaining book that serves as a cross-reference file to determine which contract clauses would be affected by a demand. The bargaining book also contains a general history of contract terms and their relative importance to management.[16] Assuming that the collective agreement is not the first to be negotiated by the parties, preparation for negotiations ideally start soon after the current agreement has been signed. This practice allows negotiators to review and diagnose weaknesses and mistakes made during the previous negotiations while the experience is still current in their minds.

Gathering Bargaining Data

Employers gather economic data primarily in the areas of wages and benefits. However, internal data relating to grievances, disciplinary actions, transfers,

---

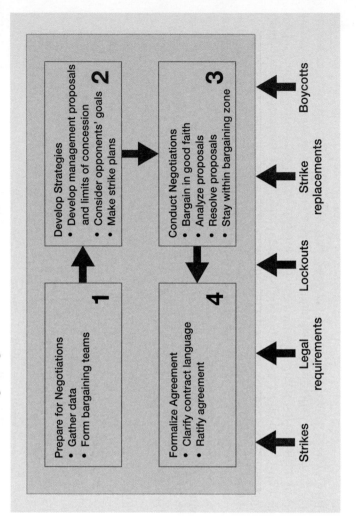

FIGURE 14.3

The Collective Bargaining Process

[OUT**C**OME]

collective bargaining process

Process of negotiating a collective agreement, including the use of economic pressures by both parties promotions, overtime, and former arbitration awards are useful in formulating and supporting the employer's bargaining position. The supervisors and managers who must live with and administer the collective agreement can be very important sources of ideas and suggestions concerning changes that are needed in the *next* agreement. Their contact with union members and representatives provides them with a first-hand knowledge of the changes that union negotiators are likely to propose.

When negotiating contracts, union bargainers talk about "taking wages out of competition." This term refers to having similar contract provisions—particularly concerning wages and benefits—between different companies in order to prevent one employer from having a favourable labour cost advantage over another. For example, the United Auto Workers representing workers at both General Motors and Ford will seek similar contract provisions. Furthermore, this allows unions to show their members that they are receiving wages and benefits comparable to those of other employees doing like work. Other negotiated collective agreements, particularly at the local and regional levels, play a significant part in settling the terms of the collective agreement.

Bargaining Teams

Normally, each side has four to six representatives at the negotiating table. The chief negotiator for management is the vice-president or manager for labour relations or, most often, a hired labour lawyer; the chief negotiator for the union is usually the local union president or national union representative or business agent. Others making up management's team may include representatives from accounting or finance, operations, human resources, legal, or training. The local union president is likely to be supported by the chief steward, various local union vice-presidents, and a representative from the national union.

The initial meeting of the bargaining teams is a particularly important one because it establishes the climate that will prevail during the negotiations that follow. According to one experienced negotiator, "The conduct of negotiations largely depends on the relationship and attitude of negotiators toward one another. If you want conflict in your bargaining sessions, just start off attacking the other side." This *attitudinal structuring* is done to change the attitudes of the parties toward each other, often with the objective of persuading one side to accept the other side's demands.[17]

DEVELOPING BARGAINING STRATEGIES AND TACTICS

Both management and union negotiators approach bargaining with a defined strategy. In tough economic periods, the employer's strategy might be cost containment or specific reductions in wages or benefits. Conversely, in times of economic growth—when a union strike would harm sales—the employer will be more willing to meet union demands. The employer's strategy should also consider proposals the union is likely to submit, goals the union is striving to achieve, and the extent to which it may be willing to make concessions or to resort to strike action in order to achieve these goals. At a minimum, the employer's bargaining strategy must address these points:

- Likely union proposals and management responses to them
- A listing of management demands, limits of concessions, and anticipated union responses
- Development of a database to support management bargaining proposals and to counteract union demands
- A contingency operating plan should employees strike

Certain elements of strategy are common to both the employer and the union. Generally, the initial demands presented by each side are greater than those it actually may hope to achieve.[18] This is done in order to provide room for concessions. Moreover, each party usually avoids giving up the maximum it is capable of conceding in order to allow for further concessions that may be needed to break a bargaining deadlock.

The negotiation of a collective agreement can have some of the characteristics of a poker game, with each side attempting to determine its opponent's position while not revealing its own.[19] Each party normally tries to avoid disclosing the relative importance that it attaches to a proposal so that it will not be forced to pay a higher price than is necessary to have the proposal accepted. As in buying a new car, the buyer and seller employ a lot of strategy in order to obtain the best outcome possible.

Negotiating the Collective Agreement

While there is no "exact" way to negotiate a collective agreement, typically each side focuses on one issue or several related issues until agreement is reached. For each bargaining issue to be resolved satisfactorily, the point at which agreement is reached must be within limits that the union and the employer are willing to accept. In a frequently cited bargaining model, Ross Stagner and Hjalmar Rosen call the area within these two limits the **bargaining zone**. In some bargaining situations, such as the one illustrated in Figure 14.4, the solution desired by one party may exceed the limits of the other party. Thus, that solution is outside the bargaining zone. If that party refuses to modify its demands sufficiently to bring them within the bargaining zone or if the opposing party refuses to extend its limit to accommodate the demands of the other party, a bargaining deadlock results.[20] For example,

bargaining zone
Area within which the union and the employer are willing to concede when bargaining

FIGURE **14.4**

The Bargaining Zone and Negotiation Influences

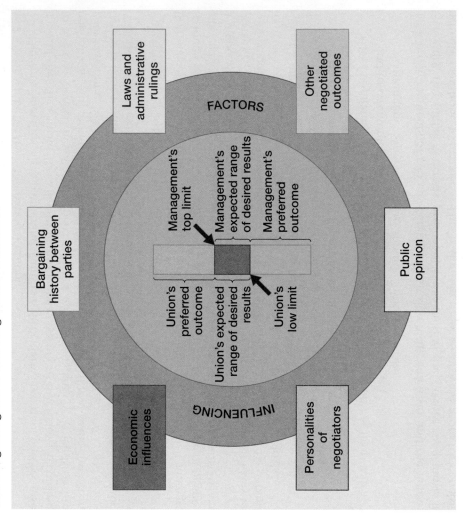

Source: From *Psychology of Union–Management Relations*, First Edition by Stagner/Rosen, © 1996 Wadsworth, a part of Cengage Learning, Inc. Reproduced by permission. http://www.cengage.com/permissions.

when bargaining a wage increase for employees, if the union's lowest limit is a 4 percent increase and management's top limit is 6 percent, an acceptable range—the bargaining zone—is available to both parties. If management's top limit is only 3 percent, however, a bargaining zone is not available to either side and a deadlock is likely to occur. Figure 14.4, which is based on the original model by Stagner and Rosen, shows that as bargaining takes place, several important variables influence the negotiators and their ability to reach agreement within the bargaining zone.

An employer is obligated to negotiate in good faith with the union's representatives over conditions of employment (the same obligation applies to the union representatives). Good faith requires meetings to be held at reasonable times and places to discuss employment conditions. It requires also that the proposals submitted by each party be realistic. In discussing the other party's proposals, each side could offer reasonable counterproposals for those it is unwilling to accept. The counterproposal can be "no change" or "we don't agree to that"—there is no requirement to agree to all or part of the other sides' proposals. Finally, both parties must sign the written document containing the agreement reached through negotiations.

INTEREST-BASED BARGAINING

Sometimes labour–management negotiations are characterized as adversarial. With adversarial bargaining, negotiators start with defined positions and, through deferral, persuasion, trade, or power, the parties work toward the resolution of individual bargaining demands. With traditional bargaining—and its give-and-take philosophy—the results may or may not be to the complete satisfaction of one or both parties.[21] In fact, when one side feels it received "the short end of the stick," bitter feelings may persist throughout the life of the agreement. As noted by one labour negotiator, "adversarial bargaining does little to establish a long-term positive relationship based on open communications and trust. By its nature, it leads to suspicion and compromise."[22] To overcome these negative feelings, labour and management practitioners may use a nonadversarial approach to negotiating.

Interest-based bargaining (IBB) is based on the identification and resolution of mutual interests rather than the resolve of specific bargaining demands.[23] Interest-based bargaining is "a problem-solving process conducted in a principled way that creates effective solutions while improving the bargaining relationship."[24] The focus of bargaining strategy is to discover mutual bargaining interests with the intent of formulating options and solutions for mutual gain.

Interest-based bargaining is novel in both its philosophy and its bargaining process. Also distinct are the bargaining tools used to expedite a successful nonadversarial negotiating experience. Rather than using proposals and counterproposals as a means of reaching agreement (as with adversarial negotiations), participants use brainstorming, consensus decision making, active listening, process checking, and matrix building to facilitate the settlement of issues. An underlying goal of interest-based bargaining is to create a relationship for the future based on trust, understanding, and mutual respect, a process described in Highlights in HRM 14.6. The Business Case outlines how IBB can save money.

MANAGEMENT AND UNION POWER IN COLLECTIVE BARGAINING

Fortunately, the great majority of labour–management negotiations are settled peacefully. However, should negotiations become deadlocked, bargaining can become highly adversarial as each side will now employ its bargaining power to achieve its desired ends. The party's **bargaining power** consists of its economic, political, and social influence to achieve its demands at the expense of the other side.

OUTCOME 5

interest-based bargaining (IBB)
Problem-solving bargaining based on a win–win philosophy and the development of a positive long-term relationship

bargaining power
The power of labour and management to achieve their goals through economic, social, or political influence

565

Highlights in HRM 14.6

Building Trust Through IBB

The *Ottawa Citizen*, a newspaper with a circulation of 145,000 newspapers, is the largest daily newspaper in Ottawa, and the eighth largest in Canada. Approximately 65 percent of its 595 full-time employees are unionized and belong to one of three unions: the Communication Energy & Paperworkers (CEP), the Graphic Communications Union (GCU), and the Newspaper Guild. These bargaining units are also called chapels (and the shop steward is called chapel chairman) in recognition of the time when it was illegal to hold union meetings so groups of employees wishing to meet collectively would say they were going to a "chapel [or church] meeting."

The *Ottawa Citizen* won a Vision award, a recognition by the Ottawa chapter of the Human Resources Professionals Association of Ontario, for outstanding HR practices for the innovative design and implementation of an HR program based on its successful implementation of IBB. Debbie Bennett, vice-president of human resources and finance for the newspaper, describes the process: "In my opinion, IBB works when you have a good relationship that you want to improve upon, or when things are so bad that something has to change. I approached the [Newspaper] Guild, the largest union, with whom we already had a good relationship, about IBB. At the time, it had about 325 members. I started by buying them some IBB books (*Getting to Yes* and *Getting Together*) to determine if there was interest. There was. Union and management advertised for, jointly selected, and paid for a facilitator, who took us through a three-day training and relationship-building session. The entire bargaining team from both parties took part in the workshop to make sure we all understood the differences between IBB and traditional bargaining.

"For example, one difference was the ways in which we communicated, both internally to build trust and externally to our stakeholders. In IBB, we brainstormed, with the rule that no repercussions would follow if an idea was presented that everyone liked but subsequently was not found workable. In traditional bargaining, if an idea is placed on the table and then removed, it could be seen as reneging or bargaining in bad faith. The agreement to brainstorm led to very little caucus time, and a much faster bargaining pace, because the respective teams did not have to ask for a break to discuss new ideas in the hallway before presenting it to the other party.

"The tone of communications was also different. The objective at the table is to discuss issues in an open and honest manner. This objective would be hard to achieve if some of the more direct comments were quoted in public communiqués. Therefore, the parties agreed that communications to both management and union members were for the purpose of keeping everyone informed, not for the purpose of embarrassing the other party or belittling their position. The tone of communications was respectful.

"We started bargaining, with the facilitator at table, to ensure that we practised what we learned. After the third day, we no longer needed the facilitator. Usually our bargaining sessions took four to five months; this time, we finished in four to five days. Usually the changes to the collective agreement were mainly monetary; this time there were a lot of language changes. For example, like most organizations, when an employee is disciplined, a disciplinary letter is placed on file. The union wanted a sunset clause requiring automatic removal of the discipline letter after a period of time. The union's view was that a transgression should not be held against an employee forever. However, management felt a record of a serious infraction, like hitting another employee, should never be removed from the file nor should records of a repetitive problem. Through IBB, the teams came up with a clause, which said that a disciplinary letter will not automatically be removed, but will be taken to the VP who will decide on its removal based on clear criteria, such as the seriousness of the act and the repetitiveness of the behaviour.

"Overall, the effect of IBB on the labour relations climate, although always good, was to improve it."

Union Bargaining Power

The bargaining power of the union may be exercised by striking, picketing, or boycotting the employer's products or services. A strike is the refusal of a group of employees to perform their jobs. Canadians are often surprised to learn that

The Business CASE

The Benefits of IBB

Eleanor Gallant, manager of HR for the City of Charlottetown, Prince Edward Island, worked closely with PANS (Police Association of Nova Scotia—PEI local 301) and CUPE to establish a process of IBB. The goal was not to repeat the past when negotiations dragged on for four years, ending in strikes and arbitration (for those without the right to strike). The process began before the contract opened again in 2002. In preparation, to encourage the interest of the parties, the director of HR for the city of Saint John, New Brunswick, was invited to speak about the success of IBB in that city. Some basic rules for the process of negotiating the collective agreement were put into place, including no lawyers would be present, there would be no discussion about the bargaining mandate with outsiders, and union and management officials would sit next to each other at the table, not on opposing sides.

The issue of time off in lieu of overtime serves as an example of how IBB worked in the City of Charlottetown. When the police officers were required to work overtime, they wanted to be compensated with time off instead of overtime pay. Management had refused this request due to bookkeeping complexities. However, the IBB process demonstrated the value of this arrangement to both parties. The two parties reached an agreement to hire part-time officers when extra hours were needed. The police officers were less stressed because of less overtime, and the city saved money, because part-time police officers were less costly than full-time police officers being paid overtime rates.

Here are the savings produced by IBB for negotiations with PANS:

	Traditional bargaining	IBB
Time to reach agreement	4 years	8 days
Number of grievances	0	0
Amount that would have been spent on arbitration	$30,000	0

Here are the savings produced by IBB for negotiations with CUPE:

	Traditional bargaining	IBB
Time to reach agreement	4 years	8 days
Number of grievances	275	1
Amount that would have been spent on arbitration	$180,000	0

Canada has the second highest rates of days lost to strikes in the world.[25] It is a legal requirement that unions hold and win a strike vote as a condition of striking lawfully. A strike vote by the members does not mean they actually want or expect to go out on strike. Rather, it is intended as a vote of confidence to strengthen the position of their leaders at the bargaining table.

Of critical importance to the union is the extent, if any, to which the employer will be able to continue operating through the use of supervisory and nonstriking personnel and employees hired to replace the strikers. In some jurisdictions, employers face restrictions to their right to hire replacement workers. In the 1990s the use of "scabs" at the Royal Oak Mine in Yellowknife so infuriated a striking miner that he blew up the mine, killing nine workers. (Employers have the right to dismiss workers who engage in sabotage or violence during a strike.) The violence and strife associated with the use of replacement workers has caused Quebec and British Columbia to forbid their use.

In organizations with high levels of technology and automation, and consequently fewer employees, continuing service with supervisors and managers is more likely. Among the highly automated telephone companies, most services can be maintained by supervisors during a strike. According to one authority, "Because

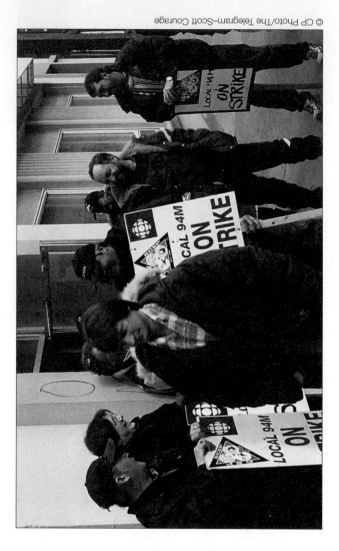

Picketing is used by unions to publicize their disputes and discourage people from entering the premises.

of technological change, striking in many industries no longer has the effect of curtailing the employer's operations significantly."[26] Consequently, the greater the ability of the employer to continue operating, the less the union's chances of gaining its demands through a strike.

When a union goes on strike, it often pickets the employer by placing people at business entrances to advertise the dispute and to discourage others from entering the premises. Because unions often refuse to cross another union's picket line, the pickets may serve to prevent the delivery and pickup of goods or performance of other services. For example, a Teamster truck driver may refuse to deliver produce to a food store whose employees are out on strike with the United Food and Commercial Workers Union. In 2008, IBM workers in Italy organized a picket line, and were joined by 1,850 avatars from 30 countries and the strike was carried out in the virtual environment Second Life.[27] Once a strike has been settled, the workers are entitled to return to their jobs, though not necessarily their previous positions. The right to return to work is often an issue to be negotiated. Although laws vary, employees are often required to submit in writing their intention to return to their jobs once a strike is finalized.

Another economic weapon of the union is the *boycott*, which is a refusal to patronize the employer. For example, production employees on strike against a hand tool manufacturer might picket a retail store that sells the tools made by the struck employer. Unions will also use handbills, radio announcements, e-mail campaigns, and newspaper ads to discourage the purchase of the employer's product or service.

Management Bargaining Power

When negotiations become deadlocked, the employer's bargaining power largely rests on being able to continue operations in the face of a strike *or* to shut down operations entirely.

Another prevalent bargaining strategy is for the employer to continue operations by using managers and supervisors to staff employee jobs. In one case, nearly 30,000 managers left their offices to serve as operators, technicians, and customer service representatives during a strike between Verizon and the Communications Workers of America. As noted previously, technological advances enhance the employer's ability to operate during a strike.

NEL

The employer may elect to lock out its employees. The lockout is a bargaining strategy by which the employer denies employees the opportunity to work by closing its operations. In a highly publicized case, during the 2004–2005 National Hockey League season, management locked out players represented by the National Hockey League Players Association. Besides being used in bargaining impasses, lockouts may be used by employers to combat union slowdowns, damage to their property, or violence within the organization that may occur in connection with a labour dispute.[28] Employers may still be reluctant to resort to a lockout, however, because of their concern that denying work to regular employees (employees who are not members of the union who may be locked out; they may or may not be members of another union) might hurt the organization's image.

RESOLVING BARGAINING DEADLOCKS

Unions and employers in all types of industries—sports, transportation, entertainment, manufacturing, communication, and health care—have used mediation and arbitration to help resolve their bargaining deadlocks. As discussed in Chapter 13, mediation is a voluntary process that relies on the communication and persuasive skills of a mediator to help the parties resolve their differences. In all Canadian jurisdictions, conciliation is compulsory before a legal strike or lockout. The conciliator, appointed by the provincial or federal ministry of labour, attempts to reach a workable agreement.

Unlike a mediator, an **interest arbitrator** assumes the role of a decision maker and determines what the settlement between the two parties should be. In other words, interest arbitrators write a final contract that the parties *must* accept. Compared with mediation, arbitration is not often used to settle private-sector bargaining disputes. In the public sector, where strikes are often prohibited, the use of *interest arbitration* is a common method to resolve bargaining deadlocks. Generally, one or both parties are reluctant to give a third party the power to make the settlement for them. Consequently, a mediator typically is used to break a deadlock and assist the parties in reaching an agreement. An arbitrator generally is called on to resolve disputes arising in connection with the administration of the agreement, called *rights arbitration* or *grievance arbitration*, which will be discussed shortly.

THE COLLECTIVE AGREEMENT

When negotiations are concluded, the collective agreement becomes a formal *binding* document listing the terms, conditions, and rules under which employees and managers agree to operate. Highlights in HRM 14.7 shows some of the major articles in a collective agreement and also provides examples of some new and progressive contract clauses. Two important items in any collective agreement pertain to the issue of management rights and the forms of security afforded the union.

THE ISSUE OF MANAGEMENT RIGHTS

Management rights have to do with the conditions of employment over which management is able to exercise exclusive control. Almost without exception, the collective agreement contains a *management rights* clause. This clause states that "management's authority is supreme in all matters except those it has expressly conceded in the collective agreement, or in those areas where its authority is restricted by law." Management rights might include the right of management to determine the products to produce, to determine the location of production or service facilities, or to select production equipment and procedures. The following is an example of a clause defining management rights in one collective agreement:

interest arbitrator

Third-party neutral who resolves labour dispute by issuing a final decision in the disagreement

Using the Internet

One of the newer forms of mediation is online mediation. Check out how experts can be used by visiting these sites:

http://www.mediate.com/odr
http://www.adr.com

Highlights in HRM 14.7

Items in a Collective Agreement

Typical clauses will cover

- Wages
- Grievance procedures
- Vacations
- No strike/no lockout clause
- Holidays
- Overtime
- Work schedules
- Safety procedures
- Management rights
- Severance pay
- Union security
- Seniority
- Transfers
- Pensions and benefits
- Discipline
- Outsourcing

Progressive clauses will cover

- Employee access to records
- Limitations on use of performance evaluation
- Elder care leave, child care, work–family balance provisions
- Flexible medical spending accounts
- Protection against hazards of technology equipment
- Limitations against electronic monitoring
- Bilingual stipends
- Domestic partnership benefits

It is agreed that the company possesses all of the rights, powers, privileges, and authority it had prior to the execution of this agreement; and nothing in this agreement shall be construed to limit the company in any way in the exercise of the regular and customary functions of management and the operation of its business, except as it may be specifically relinquished or modified herein by an express provision of this agreement.[29]

UNION SECURITY AGREEMENTS

As we noted at the beginning of this chapter, unions must represent all bargaining-unit members equally regardless of whether employees join the union or not. In exchange for this obligation, union officials will seek to negotiate some form of compulsory membership as a condition of employment. Union officials argue that compulsory membership precludes the possibility that some employees will receive the benefits of unionization without paying their fair share of the costs. A standard union security provision is dues checkoff, which gives the employer the responsibility of withholding union dues from the paycheques of union members who agree to such a deduction.

Other common forms of union security found in collective agreements are different types of "shop" agreements. These agreements—in varying degrees—attempt to require employees to join the union. For example, a *union shop* agreement may provide that any employee who is not a union member upon employment must join the union within 30 days or be terminated. Another, the *agency shop*, provides for voluntary membership. However, all bargaining-unit members must pay union dues.

ADMINISTRATION OF THE COLLECTIVE AGREEMENT

Negotiation of the collective agreement, as mentioned earlier, is usually the most publicized and critical aspect of labour relations. Strike deadlines, press conferences, and employee picketing help create this image. Nevertheless, as managers in unionized organizations know, the bulk of labour relations activity comes from the day-to-day administration of the agreement, because no agreement could possibly anticipate all the forms that disputes may take. In addition, once the agreement is signed, each side will naturally interpret ambiguous clauses to its own advantage.[30] These differences are traditionally resolved through the grievance procedure.

NEGOTIATED GRIEVANCE PROCEDURES

The **grievance procedure** typically provides for the union to represent the interests of its members (and nonmembers as well) in processing a grievance. It is considered by some authorities to be the heart of the bargaining agreement, or the safety valve that gives flexibility to the whole system of collective bargaining.[31]

The grievance process is normally initiated by the union—or an individual employee—when it feels management has violated some article of the collective agreement. In one case, the union filed a grievance against a supervisor when it believed the supervisor promoted an employee out of seniority order—called a bypass grievance. A significant benefit of the grievance procedure is that it provides a formal and orderly procedure for the union to challenge the actions of management without resorting to strikes. One authority has noted, "The grievance procedure fosters cooperation, not conflict, between the employer and the union."[32]

The operation of a grievance procedure is unique to each individual collective bargaining relationship, but it is usually required under Canadian labour relations statutes. For example, grievance procedures normally specify how the grievance is to be initiated, the number and timing of steps that are to compose the procedure, and the identity of representatives from each side who are to be involved in the hearings at each step. When a grievance cannot be resolved at one of the specified steps, most agreements provide for the grievance to be submitted to a third party—usually an arbitrator—whose decision is final. Some collective agreements provide for mediation as a way to resolve employee grievances. When used, *grievance mediation* will be listed as a formal step in the grievance procedure preceding arbitration.[33]

THE GRIEVANCE PROCEDURE IN ACTION

In order for an employee's grievance to be considered formally, it must be expressed orally and/or in writing, ideally to the employee's immediate supervisor. Because grievances are often the result of an oversight or a misunderstanding, many of them can be resolved at this point. Whether it is possible to resolve a grievance at the initial step will depend on the supervisor's ability and willingness to discuss the problem with the employee and the steward. Additionally, HR professionals acknowledge that grievance handling is more successful when supervisors are trained formally in resolving grievances, including familiarization with the terms of the collective agreement and the discussion of the problem in a rational and objective manner. A grievance should not be viewed as something to be won or lost. Rather, both sides must view the situation as an attempt to solve a human relations problem.

In some instances, a satisfactory solution may not be possible at the first step because there are legitimate differences of opinion between the employee and the supervisor or because the supervisor does not have the authority to take the action required to satisfy the grievant. Personality conflicts, prejudices, emotionalism, stubbornness, or other factors may also be barriers to a satisfactory solution at this step.

RIGHTS ARBITRATION

The function of **rights arbitration** is to provide the solution to a grievance that a union and an employer have been unable to resolve by themselves. As mentioned earlier, arbitration is performed by a neutral third party (an arbitrator or impartial umpire). This third party's decision dictates how the grievance is to be settled.[34] Both parties are obligated to comply with the decision.

The Decision to Arbitrate

In deciding whether to use arbitration, each party must weigh the costs involved against the importance of the case and the prospects of gaining a favourable award. It would

---

grievance procedure
Formal procedure that provides for the union to represent members and nonmembers in processing a grievance

rights arbitration
Arbitration over interpretation of the meaning of contract terms or employee work grievances

seem logical that neither party would allow a weak case to go to arbitration if there were little possibility of gaining a favourable award. Logic, however, does not always prevail. For example, it is not unusual for a union to take a weak case to arbitration in order to demonstrate to the members that the union is willing to exhaust every remedy in looking out for their interests. Union officers also are not likely to refuse to take to arbitration the grievances of members who are popular or politically powerful in the union, even though their cases are weak. Moreover, unions have a legal obligation to provide assistance to members who are pursuing grievances. Because members can bring suit against their unions for failing to process their grievances adequately, many union officers are reluctant to refuse taking even weak grievances to arbitration.

Management, on the other hand, may allow a weak case to go to arbitration to demonstrate to the union officers that management "cannot be pushed around." Also, managers at lower levels may be reluctant to risk the displeasure of top management by stating that a certain HR policy is unworkable or unsound. Stubbornness and mutual antagonism also may force many grievances into arbitration because neither party is willing to make concessions to reach an agreement, even when it may recognize that it is in the wrong.

The Arbitration Process

In our experience, employees unfamiliar with arbitration find the process confusing and often stressful. Arbitration hearings have the appearance of a court hearing but without many of the formalities of a court proceeding.

The process begins with the swearing-in of witnesses, The parties then make opening statements, followed by the presentation of facts and evidence, and the oral presentation of witnesses. The hearing concludes with each side making summary statements that are arguments in support of its position.

In arbitrating a dispute, it is the responsibility of the arbitrator to ensure that each side receives a fair hearing during which it may present all of the facts it considers pertinent to the case. The primary purpose of the hearing is to assist the arbitrator in obtaining the facts necessary to resolve a human relations problem rather than a legal one. The arbitrator, therefore, has a right to question witnesses or to request additional facts from either party. After conducting the hearing and receiving post-hearing briefs (should the parties choose to submit them), the arbitrator considers the evidence and renders an award. In the majority of cases, the costs of arbitration are shared equally by the parties.

The Arbitration Award

The **arbitration award** is a formal written document given to both sides. As in grievance procedures, there is no specific format to an arbitration award but typically the award contains five parts: (1) the submission to arbitrate, (2) the facts of the case, (3) the positions of the parties, (4) the opinion of the arbitrator, and (5) the decision rendered. As might be expected, the decision of the arbitrator is of major importance to the parties. However, the reasoning behind the decision—the opinion—is equally important as it can provide guidance concerning the interpretation of the collective agreement and the resolution of future disputes arising from its administration. In pointing out the merits of each party's position, the reasoning that underlies the award can help lessen the disappointment and protect the self-esteem of those representing the unsuccessful party. The opinion will also evaluate the evidence presented by each side in support of its position and, in discipline cases, whether management had just cause for the action taken against an employee. (See Chapter 13 for a discussion of just cause in arbitration.) Importantly, in deciding a case, the arbitrator has the power to modify the outcome requested by both sides. It is not uncommon, for example, for an arbitrator to reduce a discharge to a suspension without pay for a specific time period.

arbitration award
Final and binding award issued by an arbitrator in a labour–management dispute

Because of the importance and magnitude of arbitration in the union setting, the process by which arbitrators make decisions and the factors that influence those decisions are of continuing interest to managers. Typically, arbitrators use four factors when deciding cases:

1. The wording of the collective agreement (or employment policy in non-union organizations)
2. The submission agreement as presented to the arbitrator
3. Testimony and evidence offered during the hearing
4. Arbitration criteria or standards (similar to standards of common law) against which cases are judged

When deciding the case of an employee discharged for absenteeism, for example, the arbitrator would consider these factors separately and/or jointly. Arbitrators are essentially constrained to decide cases on the basis of the wording of the collective agreement, or employment policy, and the facts, testimony, and evidence presented at the hearing.

In practice, arbitration decision making is not an exact science. In fact, the decisions of arbitrators can be rather subjective. Arbitrators can, and do, interpret contract language differently (for example, What does "just-cause discharge" actually mean?), they assign varying degrees of importance to testimony and evidence, they judge the truthfulness of witnesses differently, and they give arbitration standards greater or lesser weight as they apply to facts of the case. Each of these influences introduces subjectivity into the decision-making process.

Small Business APPLICATION

Unions impose procedural requirements, just as other regulators do. What is different about unionization is that the legal requirements regarding the behaviour of employers regarding union activity is often not as clear-cut as with other legal compliance. Additionally, and most significantly, is that errors in interpretation can have long-lasting implications as labour relations boards have the power to certify unions without a membership vote if the labour relations board has concerns that the employees' right to union representation has somehow been impeded.

So what is a small employer to do? Assuming that small employers prefer the flexibility associated with being nonunionized, they should provide employees with competitive wages and treat employees fairly and with respect, to have little or no risk of becoming unionized. The fact that a company is small decreases the probability of a union targeting a company, since in such cases the cost to the union to certify, bargain, and represent workers would likely be greater than the collected union dues from a small membership. That being said, a small company can still become unionized. For

employers in small businesses who sense discontent in the workplace, actions should be taken to understand and address this situation. If this discontent festers to the point where an employer hears of unionization attempts, he or she would be well advised to consult with a human resources or labour relations consultant, or labour relations lawyer, to get assistance in establishing an appropriate course of action, as well as review the sections in this text on unfair labour practices.

So far we have spoken from the standpoint of a small company dealing with unionization attempts. But what does a small employer do if it has a union? In this case, it follows the same process as large companies. It must bargain with the union and negotiate a collective agreement that outlines the employment terms and conditions for a period of time. The company must also collect and submit union dues to the union representing employees. Finally, it must follow the legislative requirements set for represented employees, including grievance management and arbitration. The type of union we are referring to is one in which the bargaining unit is

continued

limited to the company, rather than a craft union. Small businesses such as construction companies may have staff represented by craft unions such as the bricklayers union. In craft unions, the craft will dictate employment terms and conditions for its members, but individual small companies do not bargain with the union, and simply pay wages in accordance with the craft rates.

SUMMARY

OUTCOME 1
Labour relations legislation in Canada recognizes the right of employees to form and join unions, and prohibits both unions and employers from engaging in unfair labour practices. Provincial labour relations laws are administered and enforced by labour relations boards.

OUTCOME 2
Studies show that workers unionize for different economic, psychological, and social reasons. While some employees may join unions because they are required to do so, most belong to unions because they are convinced that unions help them improve their wages, benefits, and various working conditions. Employee unionization is largely caused by dissatisfaction with managerial practices and procedures.

OUTCOME 3
A formal organizing campaign is used to solicit employee support for the union. Once employees demonstrate their desire to unionize, the union will file an application with the labour relations board for approval of the union as the certified bargaining agent.

OUTCOME 4
Negotiating a collective agreement is a detailed process. Each side prepares a list of proposals it wishes to achieve while additionally trying to anticipate proposals desired by the other side. Bargaining teams must be selected and all proposals must be analyzed to determine their impact on and cost to the organization. Both employer and union negotiators are sensitive to current bargaining patterns within the industry, general cost-of-living trends, and geographical wage differentials. Managers establish goals that seek to retain control over operations and to minimize costs. Union negotiators focus their demands around improved wages, hours, and working conditions. An agreement is reached when both sides compromise their original positions and final terms fall within the limits of the parties' bargaining zone.

Currently, there is an increased interest in nonadversarial negotiations—negotiations based on mutual gains and a heightened respect between the parties. Interest-based bargaining is one form of nonadversarial negotiations.

OUTCOME 5
The collective bargaining process includes not only the actual negotiations but also the power tactics used to support negotiating demands. When negotiations become deadlocked, bargaining becomes a power struggle to force from either side the concessions needed to break the deadlock. The union's power in collective bargaining comes from its ability to picket, strike, or boycott the employer. The employer's power during negotiations comes from its ability to lock out employees or to operate during a strike by using managerial or replacement employees.

OUTCOME 6
When differences arise between labour and management they are normally resolved through the grievance procedure. Grievance procedures are negotiated and thus reflect the needs and desires of the parties. The typical grievance procedure consists of three, four, or five steps—each step having specific filing and reply times. Higher-level managers and union officials become involved in disputes at the higher steps of the grievance procedure. The final step of the grievance procedure may be arbitration. Arbitrators render a final decision to problems not resolved at lower grievance steps.

The submission to arbitrate is a statement of the issue to be solved through arbitration. It is simply the problem the parties wish to have settled. The arbitrator must answer the issue by basing the arbitration award on four factors: the contents of the collective agreement (or employment policy), the submission agreement as written, testimony and evidence obtained at the hearing, and various arbitration standards developed over time to assist in the resolution of different types of labour-management disputes. Arbitration is not an exact science, because arbitrators give varying degrees of importance to the evidence and criteria by which disputes are resolved.

KEY TERMS

arbitration, 561
arbitration award, 572
authorization card, 553
bargaining power, 565
bargaining unit, 554
bargaining zone, 564
business agent, 560
collective bargaining process, 562

compulsory binding, 561
craft unions, 558
employee associations, 558
final offer arbitration, 561
grievance procedure, 571
industrial unions, 558
interest arbitrator, 569
interest-based bargaining (IBB), 565

labour relations process, 549
management rights, 557
rights arbitration, 571
unfair labour practices (ULPs), 555
union shop, 550
union steward, 560

DISCUSSION QUESTIONS

1. About 16 percent of working Canadians are self-employed. Some see this as a positive sign (i.e., of an increase in entrepreneurial activity); others see it as a response to the lack of permanent employment opportunities. The labour laws in each province effectively ignore independent workers. For many of them, wages (i.e., contract rates) are low, working conditions are difficult, and income security does not exist. Prepare to debate solutions to this issue, taking one of two sides: "Governments should change labour laws to recognize and protect self-employed workers," or, "Unions should organize these independent contractors and fight for better treatment by the employers."

2. *Fast Food High* is a film produced by CTV and inspired by the real story about how a group of teenage workers tried to organize a union at McDonald's in Orangeville, Ontario. Watch the film, and discuss in groups the reasons that these workers want to form a union, and the effectiveness of their efforts.

3. Contrast the arguments concerning union membership that are likely to be presented by a union with those likely to be presented by an employer. What are your reasons for joining a student union, and how do they compare with the reasons for joining a labour union?

4. The president of North America's largest union, the Service Employees International Union (SEIU) uses business-savvy techniques to organize workers and is now in Canada using them.

5. A group of students wants a Burger King fast-food franchise on their university campus. University administrators want a health-food restaurant. Resources allow for only one food outlet. Divide the class into bargaining teams, with one team representing the students, and the other team representing the university administrators. (If there is another issue on your campus use the real and current issue instead.) After the groups have started bargaining, consult the Career Counsel website to assess the negotiating styles employed by each team.

6. The negotiations between Data Services International and its union have become deadlocked. What form of bargaining power does each side possess to enforce its bargaining demands? What are the advantages and disadvantages of each form of bargaining power for both the employer and union?

7. Indira Singh has decided to file a grievance with her union steward. The grievance alleges that she

For example, he had great difficulty organizing office cleaners, who are mainly women and immigrants. When he realized that office buildings are financed by large employee retirement funds, he persuaded one to insert a "responsible contractor" clause into each financing policy, and then in one fast way, organized all the office cleaners. Is this a fair labour practice? What other "nontraditional" organizing tactics are unions using to increase their memberships?

was "bypassed" by a junior employee for a promotion to senior technician.

a. Explain the steps her grievance will follow in a formal union–management grievance procedure.

b. Should her grievance go to arbitration, explain the process of an arbitration hearing and identify the criteria used by the arbitrator to resolve her claim.

INTERNET EXERCISE

Access to technology has changed the dynamics in bargaining power. Go to http://www.slunions.org/category/faqs, which is a Second Life virtual environment designed to help union activists use social networking and virtual reality sites to aid their causes.

Outline how the use of Web 2.0 technology, such as slunions, Facebook, and Twitter can impact labour relations.

HRM EXPERIENCE

Learn about Unions

Unions, like business organizations, are dynamic and varied organizations. Some unions are very large, such as the Canadian Auto Workers (CAW) and represent workers nationally. Others are smaller in size and represent only specific groups of employees or organize only in a designated geographic area. This exercise will help you learn more about unions.

Assignment

Working individually or in teams, select four or five different unions or employee associations and report on the following. Vary your selections (large/small, public/private, and so on) to widen your understanding of labour organizations.

- History of the union
- Membership size and type of employees represented
- Mission of the union
- Structure of the union, including its major departments
- National officers
- Names of employers with whom they have an agreement
- Special benefits they offer members
- Other interesting or pertinent information

National unions and their locals along with library research can also provide information. Be prepared to present your findings during a class discussion.

BIZFLIX EXERCISES

BREAD & ROSES: JOIN THE UNION, GET BREAD AND ROSES
Make sure you have read this chapter before watching this scene from *Bread & Roses*. Before viewing the scene, note your perceptions of unions. Do the same after watching the scene. It strongly relates to discussions of why employees unionize and of union-organizing campaigns.

"Justice for Janitors" is the union-organizing slogan that drives Sam Shapiro's (Adrien Brody) efforts to organize the janitors who work for Angel Services in Los Angeles. Unionized janitors earn over $8.00 an hour plus benefits; nonunionized janitors earn $5.75 an hour with no benefits. These nonunionized janitors are mainly immigrants from different countries. Maya (Pilar Padilla) becomes an early supporter of the cause, although she risks losing her job and getting deported. Director Ken Loach launches a political polemic that grippingly tells the story of workers calling for fair wages and fair treatment by their employers.

This scene comes from the "Standing Strong" segment near the end of the film. Sam has worked untiringly to organize the Angel Services workers who work in a building with a prominent law firm as a major tenant. A large group of janitors, both union and nonunion, have marched to the building's lobby. Sam rallies them to continue their fight for fair wages, benefits, and reinstatement of the workers fired by Perez (George Lopez) at Angel Services. The film continues after this scene to show that the workers won. Angel Services agrees to reinstate all fired workers with higher wages and benefits.

What to Watch for and Ask Yourself

- What was your perception of unions and union organizers before you watched this scene? What was your perception after you watched this scene? If your perception changed, why do you think it changed?

- An earlier chapter section, "Why Employees Unionize," describes several factors that motivate people to become union members. Based on this scene, which factors do you think drive these janitors to want to join a union? You also can refer to Figure 14.1 on page 550 for guidance with this question.

- An earlier section in this chapter, "Organizing Campaigns," describes many parts of a union-organizing campaign. Sam Shapiro is the union organizer in the movie. Compare the chapter section to this scene, and infer which steps occurred. Also, assess Sam Shapiro's effectiveness as a union organizer.

CASE STUDY 1

UNIONIZATION IN THE SERVICE SECTOR

The percentage of Canadian workers who belong to a union has dropped from 38 percent in 1981 to about 30 percent in 2008, and the impact on younger workers is even more dramatic. Job losses in the manufacturing sector have been particularly bad for young workers (defined as ages 17 to 24) as they are the last hired/first fired. Only about 13 percent of young workers work in manufacturing while about 84 percent of young workers work in the service sector. The jobs in this sector, unlike the manufacturing sector, tend to consist of low paid, part-time, and temporary workers. There are few benefits. Service-sector employees tend to be scattered among many small retail stores and bank branches, for example, and are more difficult to organize than a manufacturing plant of thousands of workers. Young workers in the service sector tend to see these jobs as steps to other jobs, or as a source of income while attending school. Turnover is high and many would not see the advantages to them of joining a union.

Source: Lorna Harris, "Youthful Proposition from Unions," *Canadian HR Reporter*, Vol. 21, Iss. 18 (October 20, 2008): 31–32.

QUESTIONS

1. In groups, discuss the issues that would interest young workers in joining a union.

2. What approaches could a union use to organize young workers in the service sector?

CASE STUDY 2

WALMART STORES IN CANADA

In 2006, Walmart was operating more than 6,500 stores with 1.8 million employees around the world. In the early 1990s Walmart Stores Inc. expanded into Canada, with the purchase of 122 stores from the failing Woolco chain. Walmart had refused to purchase nine Woolco stores, which were unionized.

Walmart tries to distinguish itself from other retailers by its culture. For example, it calls its workers "associates," not employees. Every day at 8:45 a.m., a compulsory meeting is held at each store during which company managers share financial information and performance targets, and respond to questions. The meeting ends with the Walmart cheer. The company operates an open-door policy, whereby any employee can talk to any member of management about issues and receive answers, without being threatened with reprisal. The sundown rule ensures that management responds to the questions before sundown the same day.

The first Walmart store ever to be unionized was in Windsor, Ontario, where the United Steelworkers (Retail and Wholesale Division) was certified by the Ontario Labour Relations Board. On April 14, 1997, the United Steelworkers began its organizing drive. On April 26, the store manager became aware that associates were being approached to sign unionization cards. The district manager was told of the organizing drive and the next morning attended the morning meeting. The district manager asked the associates why they would want to join a union and spent the day circulating through the store to discuss their problems or concerns. By April 27, 84 associates had signed cards. On April 29, an associate asked to speak at the morning meeting, and there expressed her opposition to the union, ending with the statement, "A union will only cause discontentment in our store, and I assure you as I am standing here, Walmart will not put up with it." (Management did not ask, nor did the associate reveal, why she wanted to speak.) An inside organizer was prevented from responding because it was 9 a.m. and customers were waiting to enter the store.

Between May 4 and May 9, Walmart managers—including managers from outside the store—responded to questions placed in a question-and-answer box, and to those raised while they wandered about the store. Most of the questions focused on compensation and hours of work. However, questions were also raised about whether Walmart would close the store and dismiss the employees if the union was successful. Walmart answered that "It would be inappropriate for your company to comment on what it will or will not do if the store is unionized." It repeated that line when employees asked the same question in person. One associate testified that one manager said that things would change if the employees were unionized—for example, the profit-sharing plan would be revoked. On May 9, the union lost the vote, with 151 employees voting against it, and 43 voting for it.

The Ontario Labour Relations Board (OLRB) nonetheless certified the union, because the employer violated the *Labour Relations Act* by not disassociating itself from the remarks made by the associate at the meeting; by not allowing the inside organizer to respond; soliciting questions about the impact of unionization but then refusing to tell employees that they would not all be fired if the union won; and by using senior outside managers to engage employees in frequent and repetitive discussions about the unionization drive in the days leading up to the vote. The OLRB stated that the union had 84 cards signed before the managers' visits, and a week later, this support had dropped. A second vote would not change the outcome, because the threat to job security could not be erased from employees' minds. After Walmart's illegal conduct was remedied by a certification order, the Ontario government changed the law to take away that remedial option from the labour board. However, the right to certify a union as a remedy for a unfair labour practice has once again been restored in Ontario and exists in other Canadian jurisdictions.

Despite numerous organizing drives, Walmart continues to try to be union free. The United Food and Commercial Workers Union (UFCW) charged Walmart with unfair labour practices in thwarting a union organizing drive in British Columbia by discrediting the key organizer and by advising employees that if he turned up at their homes, they could call the police. The B.C. Labour Board said, "Walmart has an anti-union history . . . and simply cannot resist the temptation to get involved in certification campaigns. While Walmart has tended not to repeat its mistakes, there is no shortage of new ones that it finds ways to make." In the company's view, not being able to answer employee concerns about unionization is not part of its culture of open communication. But two labour relations boards believe that the company has gone too far in communication, by, for example, distributing anti-union literature at a store in Quesnel, B.C. Walmart is seeking to change labour laws to allow it to address employee concerns.

QUESTIONS

1. What were the rights of Walmart, the employer, during these two organizing drives?

2. The certification of the first Walmart was hailed by labour as a milestone event. Why?

3. In your opinion, can Walmart remain union free indefinitely? Why or why not?

4. Should foreign companies that operate in Canada use their resources to try to weaken Canadian labour laws, or rather accept the legal culture of the country and comply with those laws?

Sources: Adapted from Uyen Vu, "Wal-Mart Seeks to Change Labour Laws," *Canadian HR Reporter* (September 13, 2004): 1; V. Galt, "Wal-Mart Must Give Union Access," *The Globe and Mail*, May 13, 2003, B5; J. Hobel, "Allegation of Union Vote Rigging Investigated at Wal-Mart," *Canadian HR Reporter* (September 20, 1999): 1, 19; "Employer Interference: The Wal-Mart Case," *Worklife Report* 11, no. 2: 1–4.

CASE STUDY 3

THE NEGOTIATING CLIMATE

It was difficult, in 2009, being a union leader in the automotive sector. The role of a union is to negotiate increased wages, benefits, and job security. In 2009, two of Canada's largest employers, GM (at 12,000 employees) and Chrysler (8,000 employees), faced bankruptcy. In order to survive and receive government bailout funds (of about $10 billion), both GM and Chrysler had to negotiate with the CAW (Canadian Auto Workers) to reduce wages, benefits, and job security. As a result of these (often-government-mandated) negotiations, auto workers saw their hourly wages reduced from $76.00 to $57.00, their benefits of $31 per hour reduced, and the prospect of a loss of 10,800 jobs by 2011.

The ripple effect on auto parts suppliers was immediate. At the TRW feeder plant in Windsor, Ontario, the CAW agreed to a package that included no wage increases under a three-year contract. Management at the Navistar truck plant in Chatham, Ontario, negotiated with CAW for job cuts.

The ability to compromise doing negotiation has an international effect. If American unions agree to bigger concessions than Canadian unions (and thus offer lower labour costs), then companies with operations in both markets may choose to consolidate their operations in the market with the lower wage rates. As Ken Lowenza, President of the CAW, stated, "We could have a nice collective agreement and no jobs."

Meanwhile public-sector employees in many Canadian cities are striking for increased wages and benefits, while thousands of others in the same cities are losing their jobs. Governments are facing increased costs due to the increased number of people on welfare and decreased revenues from businesses. Politicians are stating that municipal workers have to be realistic about the current economic client. At least one union employee agrees, "What more do they want? We make a decent living. People in my neighbourhood are losing their jobs. They're losing their houses."

Source: Gord Henderson, "Lewenza's Two Roles," *The Windsor Star* (March 11, 2008): A3; Nicolas Van Praet, "Chrysler Crisis Pulls Union into Reverse; Negotiations," *National Post* (April 25, 2009): FP1.

QUESTIONS

1. The employer's ability to pay is one factor in negotiating a collective agreement. When the employer makes money, workers negotiate a share. When the employer loses revenues, should workers adjust their demands downward?

2. Compare and contrast the differences in the negotiating climates for the private and public sectors, and describe the impact of these on both management and union options to settle disputes.

CAREER COUNSEL

For feedback on how you handle conflict, complete the Managing Conflict Questionnaire on the *Managing Human Resources* website (http://www.belcourt6e.nelson.com). You can also learn about six negotiating strategies and how they can be used in salary negotiations.

NOTES AND REFERENCES

1. "Union Membership in Canada," Workplace Information Directorate, Labour Program, Human Resources and Skills Development Canada, January 1, 2007.

2. Bruce E. Kaufman, "Reflections on Six Decades in Industrial Relations: An Interview with John Dunlop," *Industrial and Labor Relations Review* 55, no. 2 (January 2002): 324–348; C. Heron, *The Canadian Labour Movement: A Short History* (Toronto: James Lorimer & Company, 1989); M. Gunderson, A. Ponak, and D. Gottlieb Taras, *Union Management Relations in Canada*, 4th ed. (Toronto: Addison Wesley Longman, 2001).

3. Gunderson, et al., *Union Management Relations in Canada*, 4th ed.

4. Readers interested in reading more about the labour relations process can consult Gunderson, et al., *Union Management Relations in Canada*, 4th ed.; J. Godard, *Industrial Relations: The Economy and Society* (Toronto: McGraw-Hill Ryerson, 1994).

5. Maureen Hannay, "The Unionization of Professionals," *Journal of Labor Research* 23, no. 3 (Summer 2002): 487–498. See also John A. McClendon, Hoyt N. Wheeler, and Roger D. Weikle, "The Individual Decision to Unionize," *Labor Studies Journal* 23, no. 3 (Fall 1998): 34–54.

6. Statistics Canada, "Perspectives on Labour and Income," http://www.statcan.gc.ca/pub/75-001-x/commun/421933-eng.pdf, retrieved August 28, 2009.

7. For a pioneering study on why workers unionize, see E. Wight Bakke, "Why Workers Join Unions," *Personnel* 22, no. 7 (July 1947): 3.

8. Kate Bronfenbrenner and Robert Hickey, "Successful Union Organizing in the United States—Clear Lessons, Too Few Examples," *Multinational Monitor* 24, no. 6 (June 2003): 9.

9. William H. Holley, Kenneth M. Jennings, and Roger S. Wolters, *The Labor Relations Process*, 8th ed. (Mason, OH: South-Western, 2005).

10. Lorna Harris, "Labour Board Punishes Employer for Heavy Handed Efforts to Block Union," *Canadian HR Reporter* 15, no. 9 (May 6, 2002): 6.

11. K. J. Bentham, "Employer Resistance to Union Certification: A Study of Canadian Jurisdictions," *Relations Industrielles* (Winter 2002): 159–187.

12. J. Heinz, "Union Attempts to Organize Walmart Stores in Ontario," *The Globe and Mail*, June 3, 1995, B3.

13. Discussion with CAW business representative, July 1995.

14. "Union Membership in Canada," Workplace Information Directorate, Labour Program, Human Resources and Skills Development Canada, January 1, 2007.

15. E. Kevin Kelloway and Julian Barling, "Members' Participation in Local Union Activities: Measurement, Prediction, and Replication," *Journal of Applied Psychology* 78, no. 2 (April 1993): 262–278.

16. John A. Fossum, *Labor Relations: Development, Structure, Process*, 6th ed. (Homewood, IL: BPI-Irwin, 1995): 312.

17. For the original description of attitudinal structuring, see Richard E. Walton and Robert B. McKersie, *A Behavioral Theory of Labor Negotiations* (New York: McGraw-Hill, 1965). This book is considered a classic in the labour relations field.

18. Leigh Thompson, *The Mind and Heart of the Negotiator*, 3rd ed. (Upper Saddle River, NJ: Prentice Hall, 2004).

19. Thomas R. Colosi, "The Principles of Negotiation," *Dispute Resolution Journal* 57, no. 1 (February–April 2002): 28–31.

20. Ross Stagner and Hjalmar Rosen, *Psychology of Union-Management Relations* (Belmont, CA: Wadsworth, 1965): 95–97. This is another classic in the field of labour–management relations.

21. Nils O. Fonstad, Robert B. McKersie, and Susan C. Eaton, "Interest-Based Negotiations in a Transformed Labor–Management Setting," *Negotiation Journal* 20, no. 1 (January 2004): 5. See also Robert B. McKersie, Susan E. Eaton, and Thomas A. Kochan, "Kaiser Permanente: Using Interest-Based Negotiations to Craft a New Collective Bargaining Agreement," *Negotiation Journal* 20, no. 1 (January 2004): 13.

22. Joe Stanley, interview by author, Phoenix, Arizona, January 5, 2005.

23. The FMCS has a complete and comprehensive program to train labour and management negotiators in the art and techniques of interest-based bargaining (IBB). Information on the IBB program can be obtained from the FMCS national headquarters at 2100 K Street, N.W., Washington, DC 20427, or from FMCS district offices.

24. *Interest-Based Negotiations: Participants' Guidebook* (Washington, DC: Federal Mediation and Conciliation Service, 1998): 11.

25. H. Scoffield, "Canada a world leader in hitting the bricks," *The Globe and Mail*, June 4, 2007, B3.

26. Bill McDonough, president of United Food and Commercial Workers Union Local 99, interview by author, January 12, 2005, Phoenix, Arizona.

27. N. Paton "You won't touch me, I'm part of the . . . avatars" *The Globe and Mail*, May 16, 2008, C3.

28. Bill Coffin, "Labor Lockout Hurts More Than Shipping," *Risk Management* 49, no. 12 (December 2002): 8.

29. Labor agreement, Wabash Fibre Box Company and Paperworkers.

30. John B. Larocco, "Ambiguities in Labor Union Contracts: Where Do They Come From?" *Dispute Resolution Journal* 59, no. 1 (February–April 2004): 38.

31. *Grievance Guide*, 11th ed. (Washington, DC: BNA Books, 2003).

32. Vera Riggs, Labor-Management Relations Conference, August 11, 2004, Phoenix, Arizona.

33. Peter J. Conodeca, "Ready . . . Set . . . Mediate," *Dispute Resolution Journal* 56, no. 4 (November 2001–January 2002): 32–38.

34. Arbitration awards are not final in all cases. Arbitration awards may be overturned through the judicial process if it can be shown that the arbitrator was prejudiced or failed to render an award based on the essence of the agreement.

Answers to **Highlights in HRM 14.1**

1. No. Individual questioning of employees about their union membership or activities is unlawful.

2. Yes. However, this must be part of normal conduct and cannot be interpreted as a gesture to buy votes.

3. Yes. Blacklisting of job applications or employees is against labour law.

4. No. During an organizing drive, an employer cannot promise improvements in wages or benefits as a means of defeating the union.

5. Yes. Employees can be disciplined or discharged for work-related misconduct but not solely because of their union affiliations or union sentiments.

International Human Resources Management

After studying this chapter, you should be able to

[OUTCOME] **1** Identify the types of organizational forms used for competing internationally.

[OUTCOME] **2** Explain the economic, political-legal, and cultural factors in different countries that HR managers need to consider.

[OUTCOME] **3** Explain how domestic and international HRM differ.

[OUTCOME] **4** Discuss the staffing process for individuals working internationally.

[OUTCOME] **5** Identify the unique training needs for international assignees and their employees.

[OUTCOME] **6** Identify the characteristics of a good international compensation plan.

[OUTCOME] **7** Reconcile the difficulties of home- and host-country performance appraisals.

[OUTCOME] **8** Explain how labour relations differ around the world.

When you pick up a newspaper or turn on the TV, you will notice that stories are constantly being told about companies competing globally. These stories might include mergers of North American and international companies, such as the Dutch brewer InBev's bid to take over Anheuser Busch in 2008. Or they might highlight companies expanding into other markets, such as Research In Motion in Asia or Scotiabank in the Dominican Republic. Or the stories might focus on international companies gaining dominance here in Canada, such as ING or Walmart. "No matter what kind of business you run, no matter what size you are, you're suddenly competing against companies you've never heard of all around the world that make a very similar widget or provide a very similar service," as one global manager put it. In fact, nearly three-quarters of HR professionals from companies large and small in a wide range of industries and countries say they expect their company's international business to grow in the coming years.[1] Some of these companies are handling the challenge well. Others are failing miserably as they try to manage across borders. More often than not, the difference boils down to how people are managed, the adaptability of cultures, and the flexibility of organizations.

Up until this point in the book, we have emphasized HRM practices and systems as they exist in Canada. This is not so much an oversight on our part as it is a deliberate decision to explain the HR practice in the most fundamental manner possible. Nonetheless, the topic of international HRM is so important that we wanted to dedicate an entire chapter to its discussion. In this chapter we will observe that much of what has been discussed throughout this text can be applied to international operations, provided one is sensitive to the requirements of a particular international setting.

The first part of this chapter presents a brief introduction to international business firms. In many important respects, the way a company organizes its international operations influences the type of managerial and human resources issues it faces. In addition, we briefly describe some of the environmental factors that also affect the work of managers in a global setting. Just as with domestic operations, the dimensions of the environment form a context in which HRM decisions are made. A major portion of this chapter deals with the various HR activities involved in the recruitment, selection, development, and compensation of employees who work in an international setting.

MANAGING ACROSS BORDERS

International business operations can take several different forms. A large percentage carry on their international business with only limited facilities and minimal representation in foreign countries. Others, particularly Fortune 500 corporations, have extensive facilities and personnel in various countries of the world. Dell, for example, employs more people outside the United States than within it. Managing these resources effectively and integrating their activities to achieve global advantage is a challenge to the leadership of these companies.

Figure 15.1 shows four basic types of organizations and how they differ in the degree to which international activities are separated to respond to the local regions and integrated to achieve global efficiencies. The **international corporation** is essentially a domestic firm that builds on its existing capabilities to penetrate overseas markets. Companies such as Honda, General Electric, and Procter & Gamble used this approach to gain access to Europe—they essentially adapted existing products for overseas markets without changing much else about their normal operations. (One such adaptation, for example, was P&G's extremely successful introduction of a detergent brick used on washboards in India.)

A **multinational corporation (MNC)** is a more complex form that usually has fully autonomous units operating in multiple countries. Shell, Philips, and ITT are

[OUTCOME 1]

international corporation
A domestic firm that uses its existing capabilities to move into overseas markets

multinational corporation (MNC)
A firm with independent business units operating in multiple countries

FIGURE 15.1

Types of Organizations

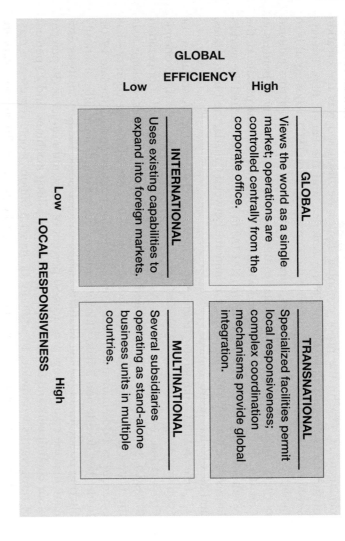

GLOBAL EFFICIENCY

Low — High

LOCAL RESPONSIVENESS Low — High

GLOBAL
Views the world as a single market; operations are controlled centrally from the corporate office.

TRANSNATIONAL
Specialized facilities permit local responsiveness; complex coordination mechanisms provide global integration.

INTERNATIONAL
Uses existing capabilities to expand into foreign markets.

MULTINATIONAL
Several subsidiaries operating as stand-alone business units in multiple countries.

three typical MNCs. These companies have traditionally given their foreign subsidiaries a great deal of latitude to address local issues such as consumer preferences, political pressures, and economic trends in different regions of the world. Frequently these subsidiaries are run as independent companies, without much integration. The **global corporation**, on the other hand, can be viewed as a multinational firm that maintains control of operations back in the home office. Japanese companies, such as Matsushita and NEC, tend to treat the world market as a unified whole and try to combine activities in each country to maximize efficiency on a global scale. These companies operate much like a domestic firm, except that they view the whole world as their marketplace.

Finally, a **transnational corporation** attempts to achieve the local responsiveness of an MNC while also achieving the efficiencies of a global firm. To balance this "global/local" dilemma, a transnational uses a network structure that coordinates specialized facilities positioned around the world. By using this flexible structure, a transnational provides autonomy to independent country operations but brings these separate activities together into an integrated whole. For most companies, the transnational form represents an ideal, rather than a reality. However, companies such as Ford, Unilever, and Shell have made good progress in restructuring operations to function more transnationally.[2]

Although various forms of organization exist, in this chapter we will generally refer to any company that conducts business outside its home country as an international business. Canada, of course, has no monopoly on international business. International enterprises are found throughout the world. A number of European and Pacific Rim companies have been conducting business on an international basis much longer than their Canadian counterparts. The close proximity of European countries, for example, makes them likely candidates for international trade. Many of these companies generate more revenue annually than do entire small nations.

global corporation
A firm that has integrated worldwide operations through a centralized home office

transnational corporation
A firm that attempts to balance local responsiveness and global scale via a network of specialized operating units

HOW DOES THE GLOBAL ENVIRONMENT INFLUENCE MANAGEMENT?

In Chapter 1, we highlighted some of the global trends affecting human resources management. One of the major economic issues we discussed was the creation of free-trade zones within Europe, North America, and the Pacific Rim. Twenty-seven member countries now comprise the European Union (EU), whose goal is to facilitate the flow of goods, services, capital, and human resources across national borders in Europe in a manner similar to the way they cross provincial borders in Canada.[3] A similar transition occurred within North America with the passage of the North American Free Trade Agreement (NAFTA) in 1994. NAFTA created the world's largest free market. Since its passage, commerce between Canada, the United States, and Mexico has nearly tripled.

Like NAFTA, numerous trade agreements, including the Association of Southeast Asian Nations (ASEAN), East Asia Economic Group, Asia-Pacific Economic Cooperation (APEC), and South Asian Association for Regional Cooperation (SAARC), have significantly facilitated trade among Asian countries, making Asia the fastest-growing region in the world. China—its fastest-growing country—has emerged as a dominant trade leader since instituting trade reforms in the late 1970s. In the last decade and a half, China's economy has grown dramatically, drastically altering political and trading relations among nations. Some industry analysts estimate that the country now produces 50 percent of the world's cameras, 30 percent of air conditioners and televisions, 25 percent of washing machines, and 20 percent of refrigerators worldwide. In addition, China's 1.3 billion people represent a massive, largely untapped consumer market for global companies. Today more cars are sold in China than in Europe, for example. Driving this trend are big MNCs such as General Electric, Toyota, and Intel, which are building or expanding their manufacturing units in the country. But many smaller firms are heading to China as well. "It's not so much that [companies] want to go East: They feel that they have no choice," said one international HR staffing consultant. "They must be in China. It's not a question of if, but a question of how." In addition to China, India's economy is also growing very quickly, as is Brazil's.[4]

The fact that international corporations can choose the countries in which they do business or relocate operations generally results in the selection of countries that have the most to offer. In addition to economic factors, political-legal factors are a huge consideration. In many countries, particularly those in Africa, property rights are poorly protected by governments. Whoever has the political power or authority can seize others' property with few or no repercussions. Civil unrest can also lead to the poor enforcement of property rights. This gives companies less incentive to locate factories or invest there. Another issue relates to intellectual property rights—rights related to patents, trademarks, and so forth. Despite the fact that private property rights are now generally enforced in China, intellectual property rights have seen little protection. For example, when General Motors formed a joint venture with a Chinese company to produce and sell a new automobile in the country, a knockoff version of the car could be seen on China's streets even before GM and its partner were able to manufacture their first car. Environmental restrictions also make some countries more attractive to do business in than others.

Beyond the economic and political-legal issues just mentioned, a country's **cultural environment** (communications, religion, values and ideologies, education, and social structure) also has important implications when it comes to a company's decision about when and how to do business there. Because of language and culture similarities, many Canadian companies are finding the United States, Ireland, and the United Kingdom attractive places to locate their facilities, particularly call centres. Eastern Europe has also begun to attract interest because citizens there are well educated and largely possess English-speaking skills.

[OUT2COME]

cultural environment
The communications, religion, values and ideologies, education, and social structure of a country

Figure 15.2 summarizes the complexity of the cultural environment in which HR must be managed. Culture is an integrated phenomenon. By recognizing and accommodating taboos, rituals, attitudes toward time, social stratification, kinship systems, and the many other components listed in Figure 15.2, managers stand a better chance of understanding the culture of a **host country**—a country in which an international business operates. Different cultural environments require different approaches to human resources management. Highlights in HRM 15.1 describes some of these cultural differences. Strategies, structures, and management styles that are appropriate in one cultural setting may lead to failure in another. Even in countries that have close language or cultural links, HR practices can be dramatically different. In some countries night shifts are taboo. In other countries employers are expected to provide employees with meals and transportation between home and work. In India, workers generally receive cash bonuses on their wedding anniversaries with which to buy their spouses gifts, and dating allowances are provided to unmarried employees. These are practices that would never occur to Canadian managers and HR practitioners.[5] For example, in many countries, bribes are considered

host country
A country in which an international corporation operates

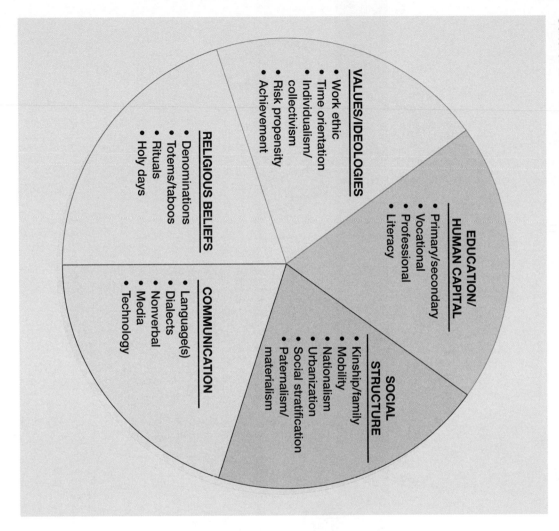

FIGURE **15.2**

Cultural Environment of International Business

VALUES/IDEOLOGIES
- Work ethic
- Time orientation
- Individualism/ collectivism
- Risk propensity
- Achievement

EDUCATION/ HUMAN CAPITAL
- Primary/secondary
- Vocational
- Professional
- Literacy

RELIGIOUS BELIEFS
- Denominations
- Totems/taboos
- Rituals
- Holy days

COMMUNICATION
- Language(s)
- Dialects
- Nonverbal
- Media
- Technology

SOCIAL STRUCTURE
- Kinship/family
- Mobility
- Nationalism
- Urbanization
- Social stratification
- Paternalism/ materialism

Highlights in **HRM** 15.1

Understanding the Importance of Cultural Differences

A North American company decided to open an office in Paris and sent the future manager to find office space and hire employees. The manager found a great location at a good price on the outskirts of Paris. Then she advertised the vacant positions in French business magazines. When she interviewed her first candidate, an alumnus of the École Polytechnique de Paris, she asked the candidate for a copy of his transcript and his grade point average. At first, he evaded the request. Then he refused, saying that he was a graduate of the most prestigious Grande école, and added, as he left the office, "Besides, your company's offices are not exactly in the best part of town." That same day, all other alumni of the École Polytechnique who were scheduled for interviews cancelled their appointments.

The manager, from the home country, had failed to understand cultural differences between North Americans and the French. In France, the location of the office is important, and the most desirable locations are the city centres. Only second-rate companies locate offices in the suburbs of Paris. Second, the French educational system is hierarchical and highly selective, and those attending the École Polytechnique de Paris are considered to be the very best graduates. These graduates are in high demand and a North American company would be very fortunate to hire one. Networking in France is done through alumni associations, and so word would spread quickly about this failed interview. The lesson to be learned is that hiring local talent requires sensitivity to local culture and customs.

Source: Adapted from Lionel Laroche, "Hiring Abroad," *CMA Management* 76, 1: 57.

Ethics in **HRM**

Bribery Abroad

Ikea has refused to open stores in Russia because of continuing concerns about bribery and corruption. Canadian employees sent to other countries to conduct business and negotiate deals are not immune to bribery attempts. Two employees from the Calgary office of Enbridge were pitched about doing business with an unrelated company while discussing royalty rates with a U.S. government agency that collects royalties from energy companies.

While businesses wish to be productive and profitable, it is unacceptable to achieve these goals through unethical behaviour. Transparency International, a global coalition against corruption, estimates that systemic corruption can add 20 to 25 percent to the costs of

government procurement and may result in the purchase of inferior goods or unnecessary services.

Every organization that does business internationally should have a code of ethics which should contain specific clauses forbidding bribery.

Experts recommend that any employee sent abroad to negotiate deals should review the *Corruption of Foreign Public Officials Act*. Under this act, any employee caught bribing foreign officials could face five years in jail and unlimited fines. The CEO could also face jail time, even if he was unaware of the bribe. Knowledge of this act will make it easier for an employee to state to corrupt negotiators, that if he gave a bribe, he could go to jail.

Source: B. Best, "Battling Bribery, Corruption Abroad," *Canadian HR Reporter* (April 9, 2007): 17, 20.

a normal business practice (see Ethics in HRM). Throughout this chapter we will discuss several HR issues related to adapting to different cultural environments.

DOMESTIC VS. INTERNATIONAL HRM

International HRM differs from domestic HRM in several ways. In the first place, it necessarily places a greater emphasis on functions and activities such as relocation, orientation, and translation services to help employees adapt to new and different environments outside their own countries and to help newly hired employees in foreign countries adapt to working for companies headquartered outside their borders. In years past, the internationalization has grown at a faster pace than the internationalization of the HRM profession, causing executives in the very best of companies to lament that their HR policies have not kept pace with the demands of global competition. But this is changing. Today, global HR management has become a front-and-centre issue for a wide variety of firms. Many larger corporations, and even smaller ones doing business in key international markets, now have full-time HR managers devoted solely to assisting with the globalization process. British Airways, for example, has a team of HR directors who travel around the world to help country managers stay updated on international concerns, policies, and programs. Coca-Cola provides support to its army of HR professionals working around the world. A core HR group in the company's Atlanta headquarters holds a two-week HR orientation twice a year for the international HR staff. This program helps international HR practitioners share information about HR philosophies, programs, and policies established either in Coca-Cola's headquarters or in another part of the world that can be successfully adopted by others.[6] Because doing business internationally can be extremely complex, many companies also hire international staffing firms such as Boston Global Consulting. These firms have expertise when it comes to relocating employees, establishing operations abroad, and helping with import/export and foreign tax issues.

HR information systems (HRIS) have also come a long way in terms of helping firms improve their international coordination. A good HRIS can facilitate communication, record keeping, and a host of other activities worldwide. Some HRIS are designed to track the whereabouts of employees travelling or on assignment. This can be important in the event of a transportation accident, a natural disaster such as a tsunami, a terrorist attack, or civil strife if evacuation plans must be implemented. Occasionally, however, even the seemingly simplest of cultural differences can be difficult to overcome when a company attempts to set up a global HRIS: When Lucent first rolled out a PeopleSoft system to more than 90 countries, the company's managers found that the order of employees' names was so important—and so varied—that it took two months to settle on a name format allowing employees to be entered into the system. As you can see, even seemingly small cultural differences can create major headaches for the international HR manager.[7]

INTERNATIONAL STAFFING

When a company expands globally, HR managers are generally responsible for ensuring that operations are staffed. There are three main ways a company can staff a new international operation. First, the company can send people from its home country. These employees are often referred to as **expatriates,** or **home-country nationals.** Second, it can hire natives of the host country, called

© Andy Nelson/The Christian Science Monitor/Getty Images

Global companies have the challenge of managing operations and people in many different countries.

expatriates, or home-country nationals

Employees from the home country who are on international assignment

[OUTCOME 3]

Reality CHECK

Selecting for Service

Four Seasons Hotels, with a staff of over 25,000, manages 50 hotels and luxury resorts around the world, from Bali to Boston. The Four Seasons brand is synonymous with luxury and first-class service standards. The execution of the strategy of being the best in the world starts with leaders who are passionate about the corporation's customer service and employee relations values. These leaders can take a concept such as "We will deliver exceptional personal service" and paint a picture for employees that is clear and motivational and that results in the delivery of that exceptional personal service.

Does the perception of service excellence depend on the country or culture in which Four Seasons operates? John Young, executive vice-president of human resources, states that the Four Seasons guest is typically a sophisticated global traveller who has acquired a sensitivity to differences in culture without negative preconceptions. Nevertheless, Four Seasons trains service staff to be sensitive to guests' needs and to minimize or avoid culture and language problems. For example, in Asia, when an English-speaking guest gives a food or beverage order, the service staff are trained to repeat the order. This is done not only to prevent a potential service error, but also to avoid loss of face for the employee. In North America, a repetition of the order would be seen as redundant.

So that employees can meet these high performance expectations, Four Seasons selects employees based on their service attitudes. Candidates for employment must undergo four behaviourally based interviews (including one with the general manager) to determine their service attitudes and current skills and knowledge. As Young says: "Customer service is the heart and soul of our business, and we need to assess if a candidate has sensitivity to the needs and wants of others. Of course, we also look at high levels of knowledge, skill, and experience, but these can be trained. We continuously adapt our service to match guest needs. For example, many years ago, in our Seattle hotel, one of the valet parking attendants noted that on weekends our guests were disproportionately families with children. On his own initiative, he put chocolate chip cookies and milk in cars that he was returning to

these departing guests. They loved it. This practice has now become one of Four Seasons' standards."

Four Seasons does not have a rigid formula for selecting home country nationals or expatriates for any given country. The ratios depend on three factors: regulations, economics, and corporate management development needs. Young continues: "For example, Indonesia used to have a rule that no more than three expatriates could be employed per hotel. So we set expatriate reduction targets to meet this regulation. Economically it made sense for us, since an expatriate general manager could cost us as much as 75 or 80 local employees. And finally, we will choose candidates based on their need for global exposure and professional development, to match our targeted needs for international expansion.

"Our biggest challenge in international HR now is management development in the context of our growth plans. We need to develop culturally appropriate leadership in preparation for specific new locations on a defined time line. If we cannot find managers who can speak the language, and understand the culture, then our ability to grow is limited. Recently we opened a hotel in Puerto Vallarta. We found a Spanish-speaking general manager from Colombia who, over time, was able to integrate the Mexican culture. Business culture in Mexico tends to be very rule and policy driven. Employees continuously asked, 'What is the policy ...' in HR, sales, everything." Over time, the general manager learned to deal with the questions by no longer looking to home office for all the rules, but by asking himself and his team, "What should the rule be in our situation?"

This attention to the selection and development of high-performance employees has resulted in Four Seasons being named by *Fortune* magazine one of the 100 best employers for three consecutive years. Consequently, Four Seasons is now able to attract more and better applicants. Furthermore, the turnover rate at Four Seasons is one of the lowest in the hospitality sector. Even those employees who have left are often recaptured as they elect to return to the kind of culture that treats them as they treat the guests.

Source: "Why Canadians Are Sent on Global Assignments," *Canadian HR Reporter* (December 1, 2003): 22.

FIGURE 15.3

Changes in International Staffing over Time

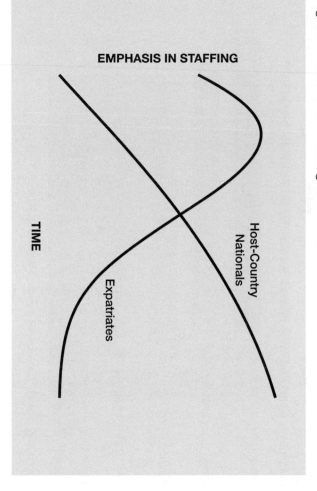

EMPHASIS IN STAFFING

Host-Country Nationals

Expatriates

TIME

host-country nationals
Employees who are natives of the host country

third-country nationals
Employees who are natives of a country other than the home country or the host country

host-country nationals, to do the managing. Third, it can hire **third-country nationals**, natives of a country other than the home country or the host country.

Each of these three sources of overseas workers provides certain advantages and certain disadvantages. Most corporations, such as the Four Seasons Hotel (described in Reality Check), use all three sources for staffing their multinational operations, although some companies exhibit a distinct bias for one or another of the three sources.[8]

As shown in Figure 15.3, at early stages of international expansion, organizations often send home-country expatriates to establish activities (particularly in less-developed countries) and to work with local governments. This is generally very costly. Traditionally, expatriates have received generous salaries, automobiles, full relocation services, private schooling for their children, trips home, and other perks. These services frequently end up costing more than $300,000 yearly, on average, making the cost of a typical three-year expatriate assignment more than $1 million. Companies are taking greater pains to more clearly outline the overall goal of the foreign assignment and its timetable for completion. Ingersoll-Rand, an international equipment maker, now carefully documents in detail what should be accomplished during an assignment abroad—whether the assignment is designed to enhance an assignee's leadership skills, improve productivity and sales targets abroad, transfer specific technology to a foreign operation, or staff it with local, expatriate, or third-country nationals.

Nearly 70,000 Canadians are working abroad, mainly in the United States (44 percent), followed by Europe (33 percent), then Asia/Pacific (15 percent), and Central and South America (8 percent). Most employees now consider foreign work credentials essential or extremely useful.[9] Figure 15.4 lists the reasons that Canadians are sent on global assignments.

In recent years, there has also been a trend to send expatriates on shorter, project-based assignments (2 to 12 months versus one to three years) and to shift more quickly toward hiring host-country nationals. This has three main advantages:

1. Hiring local citizens is generally less costly than relocating expatriates.
2. Since local governments usually want good jobs for their citizens, foreign employers may be required to hire locally.
3. Most customers want to do business with companies (and people) they perceive to be local versus foreign.

FIGURE 15.4

Why Canadians Are Sent on Global Assignments

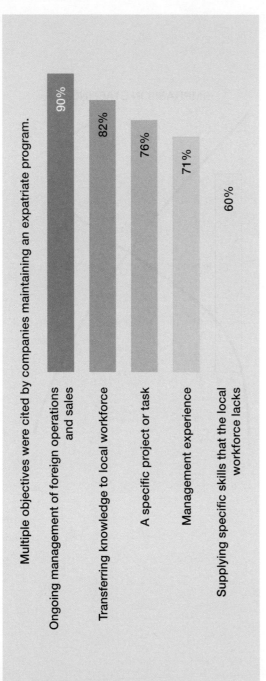

Source: "Why Canadians Are Sent on Global Assignments," *Canadian HR Reporter* (December 1, 2003): 22.

Because Canadian companies want to be viewed as true international citizens, there has also been a trend away from hiring expatriates to head up operations in foreign countries, especially European countries. Bombardier and Four Seasons, which have strong regional organizations, tend to replace their expatriate managers with local managers as quickly as possible. Highlights in HRM 15.2 describes some of the issues in checking references of locals. In addition to hiring local managers to head their foreign divisions and plants, more companies are using third-country nationals. Third-country nationals are often multilingual and already acclimated to the host country's culture—perhaps because they live in a nearby region. Thus, they are also less costly to relocate and sometimes better able to cope culturally with the foreign environment.

Companies tend to continue to use expatriates only when a specific set of skills is needed or when individuals in the host country require development. For example, after embarking on a joint venture in China with a formerly state-owned enterprise, Ingersoll-Rand discovered that it had to educate its Chinese employees not only on the company's practices and culture, but also on free-market, Western business practices. This required the company's expatriates to stay in China longer than planned.[10] It is important to note, however, that while top managers may prefer one source of employees over another, the host country may place pressure on them that restricts their choices. Such pressure takes the form of sophisticated government persuasion through administrative or legislative decrees designed to employ host-country individuals. Tax incentives, tariffs, and quotas are frequently implemented by the host country to encourage local hiring.

RECRUITING INTERNATIONALLY

Improved telecommunications and travel have made it easier to match up employers and employees of all kinds worldwide. Rolls-Royce, headquartered in the United Kingdom, hires 25 percent of its 25,000 employees abroad. Because its customers come from around the globe, Rolls-Royce figures its workforce should as well. Airbus, the European commercial jet maker, recruits engineers from universities and colleges all over Europe. American-based Boeing's need for engineers is so great that it also recruits internationally and has even opened a design centre in Moscow.

Using the Internet

Canadian employers wishing to assess over 15,000 academic credentials of foreign-born employees can consult the not-for-profit World Education Services at http://www.wes.org/ca

Highlights in **HRM 15.2**

Reference Checking

An American company was very impressed with the 20-page résumé of a candidate for a management position for its new Japanese office. The promising candidate had worked on a wide variety of deals. However, upon checking his references, the company learned that indeed he had been involved in all these deals—as the interpreter!

Those checking references in foreign countries have to be aware of privacy regulations. For example, in Canada and the United States, there are privacy laws that govern what data is and is not allowed to be accessed and used by potential employers. An employee working in the Indian office of a Canadian company is covered by the laws of India, not Canada. There are also cultural differences in the ways references are checked. If you wanted to know if a

candidate had a criminal history in Latin America, you would need to know the name of the applicant's mother. It is also helpful to understand the political context in which reference checking is done. One candidate who had worked in a country that had just recently become a democracy supplied the name of his former supervisor as a reference. However, when the supervisor was contacted, he claimed to have never known the candidate. After the call, the supervisor phoned the applicant and said, "A company called asking about you, but don't worry, I told them that I don't know you and that you never worked for us." Based on the practices of the former government, the supervisor was sensitive to any kinds of investigative questions.

Source: Adapted from Traci Canning, "Hiring Global," *HR Professional* (June/July 2006): 34.

The trend is likely to continue as the populations in developed countries age and HR managers search for talent elsewhere.

HR departments must be particularly responsive to the cultural, political, and legal environments both domestically and abroad when recruiting internationally. Companies such as Starbucks, Levi Strauss, and Honeywell have made a special effort to create codes of conduct for employees throughout the world to ensure that standards of ethical and legal behaviour are known and understood. PepsiCo has taken a similar approach to ensuring that company values are reinforced (even while recognizing the need for adapting to local cultures). The company has four core criteria that are viewed as essential in worldwide recruiting efforts: (1) personal integrity, (2) a drive for results, (3) respect for others, and (4) capability. Zurich, a Swiss financial and insurance company with operations in North America and Europe, makes sure its inbound North American assignees take diversity and sexual harassment courses. This training is rarely provided in other parts of the world.[11]

In general, however, employee recruitment in other countries is subject to more government regulation than it is in Canada. Regulations range from those that cover procedures for recruiting employees to those that govern the employment of foreign labour or require the employment of the physically disabled, war veterans, or displaced people. Many Central American countries, for example, have stringent regulations about the number of foreigners that can be employed as a percentage of the total workforce. Virtually all countries have work permit or visa restrictions that apply to foreigners. A **work permit or visa** is a document issued by a government granting authority to a foreign individual to seek employment in that government's country. Whatever the employee's destination, HR managers need to ensure that work permits and visas are applied for early in the relocation process.

At the executive level, companies use search firms such as Korn/Ferry in North America or Spencer Stuart in the United Kingdom. At lower levels, more informal

work permit or visa
A government document granting a foreign individual the right to seek employment

approaches tend to be useful. At lower levels, companies recruiting abroad often need to advertise their firms and employment "brand" to recruits who are not familiar with it. In countries such as India and China, an employer's reputation is extremely important to candidates' families—sometimes more important than pay.

Many employers have learned that the best way to find workers in these countries is through referrals and radio announcements because many people lack sufficient reading or writing skills. Some countries, in fact, require the employment of locals if adequate numbers of skilled people are available. Specific exceptions are sometimes granted (officially or unofficially) for contrary cases, as for Mexican farm workers in Canada and for Italian, Spanish, Greek, and Turkish workers in Germany and the Benelux countries (Belgium, the Netherlands, and Luxembourg). Read Highlights in HRM 15.3 to learn why the hospitality industry in Canada employs foreign workers. Foreign workers invited to perform needed labour are usually referred to as **guest workers**. Although hiring nonnationals may result in lower direct labour costs for a company, the indirect costs—those related to housing, language training, health services, recruitment, transportation, and so on—can be substantial. Some companies competing in industries with acute talent shortages are nonetheless finding the expenditures worthwhile. Nursing is one such industry.

Apprenticeships

A major source of trained labour in European nations is apprenticeship training programs (described in Chapter 7). On the whole, apprenticeship training in Europe is superior to that in Canada. In Europe, a dual-track system of education directs a

guest workers
Foreign workers invited to perform needed labour

Highlights in HRM 15.3

Importing Culture

The Inn at Manitou in Ontario's Muskoka District has a staff of about 70, half of whom are not Canadian. The decision to recruit outside Canada for this Relais et Chateux luxury hotel and spa was made after years of trying to find Canadian workers and train them to offer the type of service that a luxury inn must offer.

Ben Wise, the inn's owner, gives several reasons for employing non-Canadians. The first is culture: "We hire Europeans, who have a culture of hospitality. To serve people is not perceived by Europeans to be denigrating. Canadians berate the job of a waiter, saying that they are not waiters, but on their way to be stockbrokers. Being a waiter is a profession in Europe. Chefs are celebrities in Europe."

In Europe, jobs in the hospitality sector are seen as professions for which extensive training is necessary. Europeans arrive at Wise's inn with four to five years of training and experience at some of the best hotels. Canadian candidates cannot compete. Wise tried to train Canadians, but four weeks of on-the-job training could not match the extensive training Europeans

receive. Besides, he did not think it was fair to ask the inn's clients to put up with the mistakes and deficiencies of workers in training.

Another reason was the seasonal nature of the hospitality industry in Muskoka District: "Canadians have a summer job mentality to these positions. Consequently, a report on their performance is of no value to them. There is little we can do to motivate them to meet our service expectations. Europeans are serious. Their future employment depends on our performance evaluations and our references."

So each year The Inn at Manitou places ads in trade magazines, screens hundreds of applicants, interviews and selects those with training and experience at the best resorts and hotels, and finally arranges work permits for the lucky 30. Why lucky? "Canada has a fascinating appeal for Europeans, especially the French, who must have all read books about a charming little cabin in the woods, with mountains, space, and fresh water."

Source: Personal interview with Ben Wise.

large number of youths into vocational training. The German system of apprenticeship training, one of the best in Europe, provides training for office and shop jobs under a three-way responsibility contract between the apprentice, his or her parents, and the organization. At the conclusion of their training, apprentices can work for any employer but generally receive seniority credit with the training firm if they remain in it. France has been able to draw on its "Grandes écoles" for centuries. Created during the Renaissance to fulfill a need that universities weren't meeting at the time, the Grandes écoles educate prospective engineers up to the equivalent level of Master of Engineering. Snecma, an international equipment supplier headquartered in Paris, hires about 80 percent of its employees from the Grandes écoles.[12]

Staffing Transnational Teams

In addition to focusing on individuals, it is also important to note that companies are increasingly using transnational teams to conduct international business. **Transnational teams** are composed of members of multiple nationalities working on projects that span multiple countries. General Electric's LightSpeed VCT, a state-of-the art medical scanner, was designed with input from cardiologists around the world. The machine's innards were designed by GE engineers in four different countries, and the software to run it written by multiple teams working together from India, Israel, France, and the United States.[13] Teams such as these are especially useful for performing tasks that the firm as a whole is not yet structured to accomplish. For example, they may be used to transcend the existing organizational structure to customize a strategy for different geographic regions, transfer technology from one part of the world to another, and communicate between headquarters and subsidiaries in different countries. In GE's case, the company realized its competitors were developing their own medical scanning technology more quickly. GE decided it could no longer afford to duplicate its efforts in different divisions around the world—that these groups would have to work together as a team.

Sometimes companies send employees on temporary assignments abroad as part of transnational teams lasting, say, a few months. This might be done to break down cultural barriers between international divisions or disseminate new ideas and technologies to other regions. In other instances, employees are transferred for extended periods of time. Years ago, Fuji sent 15 of its most experienced engineers from Tokyo to a Xerox facility in Webster, New York. Over a five-year period, the engineers worked with a team of American engineers to develop the "world" copier. The effort led to a joint venture that has lasted for decades. Fuji-Xerox now employs approximately 34,000 people globally at 60 member companies around the world.[14]

The fundamental task in forming a transnational team is assembling the right group of people who can work together effectively to accomplish the goals of the team. For GE's LightSpeed team, this frequently meant holding eight-hour global conference calls encompassing numerous time zones. (The call times were rotated so that no single team had to stay up all night for every call.) Many companies try to build variety into their teams in order to maximize responsiveness to the special needs of different countries. For example, when Heineken formed a transnational team to consolidate its production facilities, it ensured that team members were drawn from each major region within Europe. Team members tended to have specialized skills, and members were added only if they offered some unique skill that added value to the team.

SELECTING EMPLOYEES INTERNATIONALLY

As you might imagine, selection practices vary around the world. In Canada, managers tend to emphasize merit, with the best-qualified person getting the job. In other countries, however, firms tend to hire on the basis of family ties, social status, language, and common origin. The candidate who satisfies these criteria may get

transnational teams
Teams composed of members of multiple nationalities working on projects that span multiple countries

Expatriate employees receive intensive training on their host countries, the cultural differences, negotiation tactics, business practices, everyday living, and other aspects of working and living successfully in a foreign country.

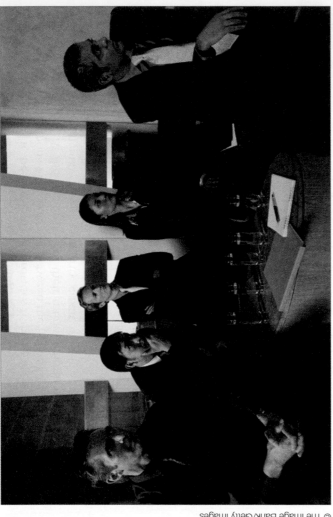

© The Image Bank/Getty Images

global manager
A manager equipped to run an international business

the job even if otherwise unqualified. Much of this is changing—there has been a growing realization among organizations in other nations that greater attention must be given to hiring those most qualified. In addition to a person's qualifications, various other hiring laws, particularly those related to discrimination, are enforced around the world. Labour union restrictions, which we will discuss later in the chapter, can also have an impact on hiring.

Selecting Global Managers

Selecting a global manager depends on a variety of different employment factors, including the extent of contact the manager will have with local citizens and the government and the degree to which the foreign environment differs from the home environment. For example, if the job involves extensive contacts with the community, as with a chief executive officer, this factor should be given appropriate weight. The magnitude of differences between the political, legal, socioeconomic, and cultural systems of the host country and those of the home country should also be assessed.[15]

Levi Strauss has identified the following six skill categories for the **global manager**, or manager equipped to run an international business:

- Ability to seize strategic opportunities
- Ability to manage highly decentralized organizations
- Awareness of global issues
- Sensitivity to issues of diversity
- Competence in interpersonal relations
- Skill in building community[16]

If a candidate for expatriation is willing to live and work in a foreign environment, an indication of his or her tolerance of cultural differences should be obtained. On the other hand, if local nationals have the technical competence to carry out the job successfully, they should be carefully considered for the job before the firm launches a search (at home) for a candidate to fill the job. As stated previously, most corporations realize the advantages to be gained by staffing international operations with host-country nationals wherever possible.

FIGURE **15.5**

Comparison of Advantages in Sources of Overseas Managers

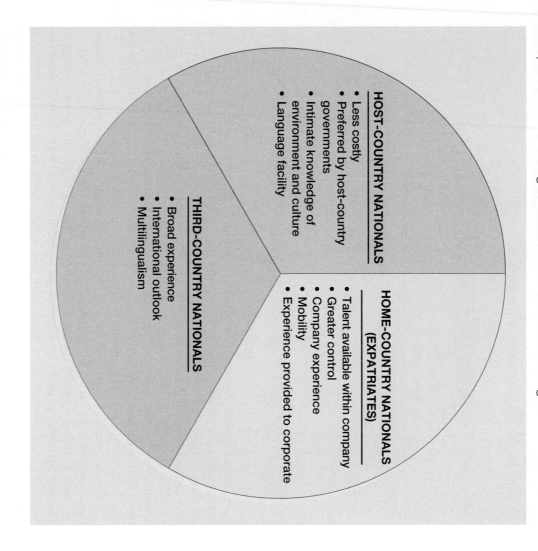

HOST-COUNTRY NATIONALS

- Less costly
- Preferred by host-country governments
- Intimate knowledge of environment and culture
- Language facility

HOME-COUNTRY NATIONALS (EXPATRIATES)

- Talent available within company
- Greater control
- Company experience
- Mobility
- Experience provided to corporate

THIRD-COUNTRY NATIONALS

- Broad experience
- International outlook
- Multilingualism

Selecting home-country and third-country nationals requires that more factors be considered than in selecting host-country nationals. While the latter must of course possess managerial abilities and the necessary technical skills, they have the advantage of familiarity with the physical and cultural environment and the language of the host country. Figure 15.5 compares the advantages and disadvantages of hiring global managers from these three different groups. The discussion that follows, however, will focus on the selection of expatriate managers from the home country, along with their compensation and performance appraisals.

Colgate-Palmolive, Whirlpool, and Dow Chemical have further identified a set of **core skills** that they view as critical for success abroad and a set of **augmented skills** that help facilitate the efforts of expatriate managers. These two types of skills are shown in Highlights in HRM 15.4. Many of these skills are not significantly different from those required for managerial success at home. Although in years past the average expatriate manager was a North American-born Caucasian, more companies today are seeing the advantages of assigning expatriates depending on their ethnicity. But such a decision needs to be considered carefully. For example, an Indian-Canadian candidate applying for a position in India may never have actually visited the country or may not relate well to the culture. Ultimately, the candidate best qualified for the job should be sent. Unfortunately, talented women are frequently overlooked for global

core skills
Skills considered critical to an employee's success abroad

augmented skills
Skills helpful in facilitating the efforts of expatriate managers

Highlights in HRM 15.4

Skills of Expatriate Managers

CORE SKILLS	AUGMENTED SKILLS
Experience	Technical skills
Decision making	Negotiation skills
Resourcefulness	Strategic thinking
Adaptability	Delegation skills
Cultural sensitivity	Change management
Team building	
Maturity	

For many reasons, women often make very successful expatriates.

managerial positions—perhaps because companies believe they will fare poorly in foreign, male-dominated societies or because they believe women have less desire to go abroad. However, many women who have been given international assignments have performed well. Because locals know how unusual it is for a woman to be given a foreign assignment, they frequently assume that the company would not have sent a woman unless she was the very best. In addition, because women expatriates are novel (particularly in managerial positions), they are very visible and distinctive and may even receive special treatment not given to their male colleagues.[17]

Several steps are involved in selecting individuals for an international assignment, and the sequencing of these activities can make a big difference:

Step 1: Begin with self-selection. Employees should begin the process years in advance by thinking about their career goals and interest in international work. By beginning with self-selection, companies can more easily avoid the problems of forcing otherwise promising employees into international assignments where they would be unhappy and unsuccessful. For individuals with families, decisions about relocation are more complicated. Employees should seek information to help them predict their chances of success living abroad. Companies such as EDS and Deloitte & Touche give their employees self-selection instruments to help them consider the pros and cons of international assignments. Other companies give these tools to candidates' spouses as well. At Solar Turbines, a San Diego–based manufacturer of industrial gas turbines, a candidate's spouse and sometimes his or her children undergo a day of assessment to see how well they are likely to respond to an international assignment.[18]

Step 2: Create a candidate pool. After employees have self-selected, organizations can build a database of candidates for international assignments. Information in the database might include availability, languages, country preferences, and skills.

Step 3: Assess core skills. From the short list of potential candidates, managers can assess each candidate on technical and managerial readiness relative to the needs of

© Photodisc/Getty Images

FIGURE 15.6

Expatriate Selection Criteria

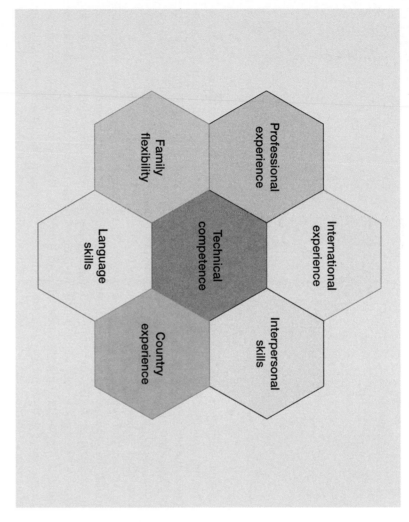

the assignment. Although many factors determine success abroad, the initial focus should be on the requirements of the job.

Step 4: Assess augmented skills and attributes. As shown in Figure 15.6, expatriate selection decisions are driven typically by technical competence as well as professional and international experience. In addition, however, an increasing number of organizations have also begun considering an individual's ability to adapt to different environments. Satisfactory adjustment depends on flexibility, emotional maturity and stability, empathy for the culture, language and communication skills, resourcefulness and initiative, and diplomatic skills.[19]

Even companies that believe they have selected the best candidates frequently experience high expatriate **failure rates.** Figure 15.7 shows the major causes of assignment failure. By far, the biggest factor tends to be a spouse's inability to adjust to his or her new surroundings.[20] There are a number of ways to improve the success of expatriate assignments. One important step is to involve spouses early on in the process. In addition, training and development for both expatriates and their spouses can have a big impact. We discuss this next.

TRAINING AND DEVELOPMENT

Although companies try to recruit and select the very best people to send abroad, once they are selected it is often necessary to provide them with some type of training. This type of training is important not only for expatriate managers, but also for the foreign employees they will ultimately supervise. To know and understand how the Japanese or Chinese negotiate contracts or how businesspeople from Latin America view the enforcement of meeting times, for example, can help expatriate managers and their employees deal with each other more successfully. The biggest

failure rate
The percentage of expatriates who do not perform satisfactorily

[OUTCOME 5]

FIGURE **15.7**

Causes of Expatriate Assignment Failure

- Family adjustment
- Poor performance
- Lifestyle issues
- Other opportunities arise
- Work adjustment
- Business reasons
- Bad selection
- Repatriation issues

Using the Internet

The Outpost Expatriate Network is an online information centre for Shell expatriates and their families:

http://www.outpostexpat.nl

mistake managers can make is to assume that people are the same everywhere. Corporations that are serious about succeeding in global business are tackling these problems head-on by providing intensive training. At Motorola, this type of training is conducted at divisions worldwide by Motorola University, the company's educational arm. All employees, including division heads, receive 40 hours of training each year to learn, in part, how to work together as "Motorola People."[21]

Apart from developing talent for overseas assignments, most companies have found that good training programs also help them attract needed employees from the host countries. In less-developed countries especially, individuals are quite eager to receive the training they need to improve their work skills. Increasingly, organizations such as the World Bank, ExxonMobil, and Petroleos de Venezuela are entering into partnerships with university executive education programs to customize the training experiences to the specific needs of expatriate managers and foreign nationals.

CONTENT OF TRAINING PROGRAMS

Lack of training is one of the principal causes of failure among employees working internationally. Those working internationally need to know as much as possible about (1) the country where they are going, (2) that country's culture, and (3) the history, values, and dynamics of their own organizations. Figure 15.8 gives an overview of what one needs to study for an international assignment. In many cases, the

FIGURE **15.8**

Preparing for an International Assignment

To prepare for an international assignment, individuals should become acquainted with the following aspects of the host country:

1. Social and business etiquette
2. History and folklore
3. Current affairs, including relations between the host country and Canada
4. Cultural values and priorities
5. Geography, especially its major cities
6. Sources of pride and great achievements of the culture
7. Religion and the role of religion in daily life
8. Political structure and current players
9. Practical matters such as currency, transportation, time zones, hours of business
10. The language

employee and his or her family can obtain a great deal of general information about the host country, including its culture, geography, social and political history, climate, food, and so on, via the Internet, books, lectures, videotapes, and DVDs. The knowledge gained will at least help the participants have a better understanding of their assignments. Sensitivity training can also help expatriates overcome ethnic prejudices they might harbour. Expatriates can simulate a field experience in sensitivity training by visiting a nearby subculture in their native countries or by actually visiting the foreign country prior to relocating there.

However, at least five essential elements of training and development programs prepare employees for working internationally: (1) language training, (2) cultural training, (3) assessing and tracking career development, (4) managing personal and family life, and (5) repatriation—a final, but critical, step.

Language Training

Communication with individuals who have a different language and a different cultural orientation is extremely difficult. Most executives agree that it is among the biggest problems for the foreign business traveller. Students who plan careers in international business should start instruction in one or more foreign languages as early as possible. The top-ranked China Europe International Business School (CEIBS), jointly founded by the Chinese government and the European Union in 1994, also offers language training.[22] Some companies do their own language training. Multinational companies as well as businesses that outsource work abroad stand to benefit from this type of training.

Fortunately for most Canadians, English is almost universally accepted as the primary language for international business. Particularly when many people from different countries are working together, English is usually the designated language for meetings and formal discourse. Many companies provide instruction in English for those who are required to use English in their jobs. Dow Chemical requires that all employees across the globe be fluent in English so they can communicate more easily with one another. At Volkswagen's Shanghai operation, only after workers pass German-language examinations do they become eligible for further training in Germany. Learning the language is only part of communicating in another culture, though. Even with an interpreter, much is missed.

Cultural Training

Cross-cultural differences represent one of the most elusive aspects of international business but successfully done, it tends to improve the satisfaction and success of expatriates and their employers.[23] Brazilians tend to perceive North Americans as always in a hurry, serious, reserved, and methodical, whereas the Japanese view North Americans as relaxed, friendly, and impulsive. Why do these different perceptions exist and how do they affect the way we do business across borders?

People's attitudes and behaviours are influenced, in large part, by the society in which they have received their education and training. Each culture has its expectations for the roles of managers and employees. On her first day on the job abroad, one expatriate manager recalls her boss ordering a bottle of wine to split between the two of them at lunch. Although this is a common practice in Britain, the expatriate manager was initially taken aback. Likewise, what one culture encourages as participative management another might see as managerial incompetence: An American manager in Asia once complained that meetings held in his foreign place of employment accomplished nothing. He was used to arriving at a final decision during meetings. But to his Asian co-workers, meetings were solely a place in which to share ideas. Decisions were to be made only later. Being successful depends on one's ability to understand the way things are normally done and to recognize that changes cannot be made abruptly without considerable resistance, and possibly antagonism, on the part of local nationals.

A wealth of data from cross-cultural studies reveals that nations tend to cluster according to similarities in certain cultural dimensions such as work goals, values, needs, and job attitudes. Using data from eight comprehensive studies of cultural differences, Simcha Ronen and Oded Shenkar have grouped countries into the clusters shown in Figure 15.9.

Ronen and Shenkar point out that while evidence for the grouping of countries into Anglo, Germanic, Nordic, Latin European, and Latin American clusters appears to be quite strong, clusters encompassing the Far Eastern and Arab countries are ill defined and require further research, as do clusters of countries classified as independent. Many areas, such as Africa, have not been studied much at all. It should

FIGURE **15.9**

A Synthesis of Country Clusters

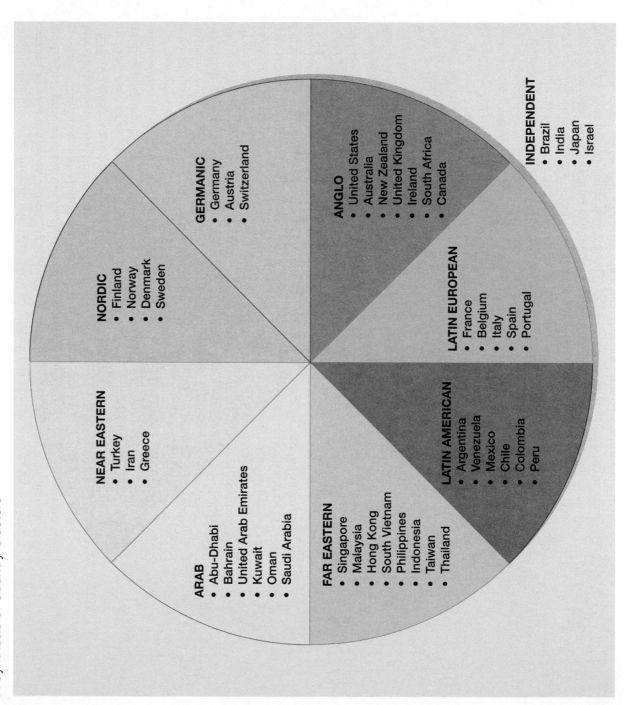

Source: Simcha Ronen and Oded Shenkar. "Clustering Countries on Attitudinal Dimensions: A Review and Synthesis," *Academy of Management Review* 10, no. 3 (July 1985): 435–454. Copyright © 1985 by Academy of *Management Review*. Reproduced with permission of *Academy of Management (NY)* in the format Textbook via Copyright Clearance Center.

also be noted that the clusters presented in Figure 15.9 do not include Russia and the former satellites of the Soviet Union. Those countries, if added to the figure, would likely fall between the Near Eastern and Nordic categories. Studying cultural differences can help managers identify and understand work attitudes and motivation in other cultures. When compared with the Japanese, for example, North Americans may feel little loyalty to their organizations. In Japan, employees are more likely to feel a strong loyalty to their company, although this may be changing. Japanese companies no longer universally guarantee an employee a job for life, and layoff decisions are increasingly being made based on merit, not seniority—a practice unthinkable in the country in the past. Latin Americans tend to view themselves as working not only for a particular company but also for an individual manager. Thus, managers in Latin American countries can encourage performance only by using personal influence and working through individual members of a group. In North America, competition has been the name of the game; in Japan, Taiwan, and other Asian countries, cooperation is more the underlying philosophy.[24]

One of the important dimensions of leadership, whether in international or domestic situations, is the degree to which managers invite employee participation in decision making. While it is difficult to find hard data on employee participation across different countries, careful observers report that Canadian managers are about in the middle on a continuum of autocratic to democratic decision-making styles. Scandinavian and Australian managers also appear to be in the middle. South American and European managers, especially those from France, Germany, and Italy, are toward the autocratic end of the continuum; Japanese managers are at the most participatory end. Because Far Eastern cultures and religions tend to emphasize harmony, group decision making predominates there.[25]

Assessing and Tracking Career Development

International assignments provide some definite developmental and career advantages. For example, working abroad tends to increase a person's responsibilities and influence within the corporation. In addition, it provides a person with a set of experiences that are uniquely beneficial to both the individual and the firm. In this way, international assignments enhance a person's understanding of the global marketplace and offer the opportunity to work on a project important to the organization.[26]

To maximize the career benefits of a managerial assignment, a candidate should ask two key questions before accepting a foreign post:

1. Do the organization's senior executives view the firm's international business as a critical part of their operation? Research shows that expatriates with clear goals that truly need to be accomplished are likely to find their assignments more rewarding. Realizing this, fewer companies are sending expatriates abroad for career development purposes only.

2. Within top management, how many executives have a foreign-service assignment in their background, and do they feel it's important to have overseas experience? Colgate-Palmolive sees a foreign assignment as part of an extended career track rather than as a one-off assignment. A successful foreign assignment tends to lead to another and another. "Our top priority is to identify, develop, and retain the next two to three generations of leaders," said one Colgate-Palmolive manager. Part of that strategy includes directly using the knowledge of the company's current and former expatriates.

Managing Personal and Family Life

As noted previously, one of the most frequent causes of an employee's failure to complete an international assignment is personal and family stress. **Culture shock**—a

culture shock
Perpetual stress experienced by people who settle overseas

disorientation that causes perpetual stress—is experienced by people who settle overseas for extended periods. The stress is caused by hundreds of jarring and disorienting incidents such as being unable to communicate, having trouble getting the telephone to work, being unable to read the street signs, and a myriad of other everyday matters that are no problem at home. Soon minor frustrations become catastrophic events, and one feels helpless and drained, emotionally and physically. Highlights in HRM 15.5 shows some of the primary sources of stress at different stages of an international assignment, as well as some of the responses that individuals and organizations use to cope with these types of stress.

Highlights in **HRM 15.5**

Stressors and Coping Responses in the Developmental Stages of Expatriate Executives

	Primary Response	Executive Coping Response	Employer Coping Response
Expatriate selection	Cross-cultural unreadiness	Engage in self-evaluation	Encourage expatriate's self- and family evaluation Perform an assessment of potential and interests
Assignment	Unrealistic evaluation of stressors to come Hurried time frame	Think of assignment as a growth opportunity rather than an instrument to vertical promotion	Do not make hard-to-keep promises Clarify expectations
Pre- and post-arrival training	Ignorance of cultural differences	Do not make unwarranted assumptions of cultural competence and cultural rules	Provide pre-, during, and post-assignment training Encourage support-seeking behaviour
Arrival	Cultural shock Stressor reevaluation Feelings of lack of fit and differential treatment	Do not construe identification with the host and parent cultures as mutually exclusive Seek social support	Provide post-arrival training Facilitate integration in expatriate network
Novice	Cultural blunders or inadequacy of coping responses Ambiguity owing to inability to decipher meaning of situations	Observe and study functional value of coping responses among locals Do not simply replicate responses that worked at home	Provide follow-up training Seek advice from locals and expatriate network
Transitional	Rejection of host or parent culture	Form and maintain attachments with both cultures	Promote culturally sensitive policies at host country Provide Internet access to family and friends at home Maintain constant communication and periodic visits to parent organization
Mastery	Frustration with inability to perform boundary-spanning role Bothered by living with a cultural paradox	Internalize and enjoy identification with both cultures and walking between two cultures	Reinforce rather than punish dual identification by defining common goals
Repatriation	Disappointment with unfulfilled expectations Sense of isolation Loss of autonomy	Realistically re-evaluate assignment as a personal and professional growth opportunity	Arrange pre-repatriation briefings and interviews Schedule post-repatriation support meetings

Source: J. Sanchez, P. Spector, and C. Cooper, "Adapting to a Boundaryless World: A Developmental Expatriate Model," *Academy of Management Executive* 14, no. 2 (May 2000): 96–106.

In Chapter 5, we observed that more and more employers are assisting two-career couples in finding suitable employment in the same location. To accommodate dual-career partnerships, some employers are providing informal help finding jobs for the spouses of international transferees. However, other companies are establishing more formal programs to assist expatriate couples. These include career- and life-planning counselling, continuing education, intercompany networks to identify job openings in other companies, and job-hunting/fact-finding trips. In some cases, a company may even create a job for the spouse—though this is not widely practised. The available evidence suggests that while a spouse's career may create some problems initially, in the long run it actually may help ease an expatriate's adjustment process.[27]

Repatriation

An increasing number of companies such as Enbridge are developing programs specifically designed to facilitate **repatriation**—that is, helping employees make the transition back home. Coming back is often difficult. An employee recently repatriated from Colombia walked outside his Edmonton office and waited for his driver, not remembering that he had driven his own car to work. Another family, repatriated from Kazakhstan, had to be restrained from purchasing all the fresh vegetables at the supermarket, because there, if there was fresh produce, you hoarded it because it might not be there next week. Repatriation programs are designed to prepare employees for adjusting to life at home (which at times can be more difficult than adjusting to a foreign assignment). ExxonMobil employees are given a general idea of what they can expect following a foreign assignment even before they leave home. Unfortunately, not all companies have career development programs designed for repatriating employees. Several studies have found that the majority of companies do not do an effective job of repatriation. Here are some general findings:

1. About 36 percent of Canadian companies have a repatriation plan.
2. Another one-third have programs to facilitate appropriate career positions upon repatriation.
3. Over two-thirds provide career planning assistance toward the end of assignment, while 8 percent provide this assistance after repatriation.
4. About one-fifth of companies start planning for repatriation even before the candidate leaves.[28]

Employees often lament that their organizations are vague about repatriation, their new roles within the company, and their career progression. In many cases, employees abroad have learned how to run an entire international operation—or at least significant parts of it. When they return home, however, their responsibilities are often significantly diminished. In fact, the evidence suggests that only a fraction of them are actually promoted. It is also not at all uncommon for employees to return home after a few years to find that there is *no* position for them in the firm and that they no longer know anyone who can help them—their longtime colleagues have moved to different departments or even different companies. This frequently leaves the repatriated employee feeling alienated.

Even when employees are successfully repatriated, their companies often do not fully utilize the knowledge, understanding, and skills developed on their assignments. This hurts the employee, of course, but it also hurts the firm's chances of utilizing the employee's expertise to gain a competitive advantage. Not surprisingly, expatriates frequently leave their companies within a year or two of coming home. Some experts say the number of expatriates who do so is as high as 50 percent.

repatriation
The process of employee transition home from an international assignment

At companies with good repatriation processes, employees are given guidance about how much the expatriate experience may have changed them and their families. Some firms introduce former expatriates and their spouses to other former expatriates at special social events. And more companies are making an effort to keep in touch with expatriates while they are abroad, which has been made easier by e-mail, instant messaging, and videoconferencing. Colgate's division executives and other corporate staff members frequently visit international transferees. Dow appoints a high-level manager who serves as a home-country contact for information about organizational changes, job opportunities, and anything related to salary and compensation. Monsanto's repatriation program is designed not only to smooth the employee's return to the home organization but also to ensure that the expatriate's knowledge and experience are fully utilized. To do so, returning expatriates get the chance to showcase their new knowledge in debriefing sessions. Some companies also create databases of expatriates to help other employees who go abroad later.[29] A repatriation checklist is shown in Highlights in HRM 15.6.

Highlights in HRM 15.6

Repatriation Checklist

Before they go:

- Make sure there is a clear need for the international assignment. Do not send someone abroad unnecessarily. Develop a clear set of objectives and expectations and timeframes in which they should be met.
- Make sure that your selection procedures are valid. Select the employee and also look at and involve the employee's family.
- Provide (or fund) language and cultural training for the employee and the employee's family.
- Offer counselling and career assistance for the spouse.
- Establish career-planning systems that reward international assignments and lead to promotion and knowledge sharing.

While they are away:

- Jointly establish a developmental plan that focuses on the goal to be achieved.
- Tie performance objectives to the achievement of the goal.

- Identify mentors who can be a liaison and support person from home.
- Keep communications open so that the expatriate is aware of job openings and opportunities.
- Arrange for frequent visits back home (for the employee and the family). Make certain they do not lose touch with friends and relatives.

When they come back home:

- Throw a "welcome home" party and arrange for a meeting with other former expatriates.
- Offer counselling to ease the transition.
- Arrange conferences and presentations to make certain that knowledge and skills acquired away from home are identified and disseminated.
- Set up an expatriate database to help other employees who go abroad later.
- Get feedback from the employee and the family about how well the organization handled the repatriation process.

Sources: Adapted from Bennet & Associates, Price Waterhouse, and Charlene Marmer Solomon, "Repatriation Planning Checklist," *Personnel Journal* 14, no. 1 (January 1995): 32; Charlene Marmer Solomon, "Global HR: Repatriation Planning," *Workforce* 2001, special supplement, 22–23.

COMPENSATION

One of the most complex areas of international HRM is compensation. Different countries have different norms for employee compensation. For North Americans, while nonfinancial incentives such as prestige, independence, and influence may be motivators, money is likely to be the driving force. Other cultures are more likely to emphasize respect, family, job security, a satisfying personal life, social acceptance, advancement, or power. Since there are many alternatives to money, the rule is to match the reward with the values of the culture. In individualistic cultures, such as Canada, pay plans often focus on individual performance and achievement. However, in collectively oriented cultures such as Japan and Taiwan, pay plans focus more on internal equity and personal needs.[30]

In general, a guiding philosophy for designing pay systems might be "think globally and act locally." That is, executives should normally try to create a pay plan that supports the overall strategic intent of the organization but provides enough flexibility to customize particular policies and programs to meet the needs of employees in specific locations. After a brief discussion of compensation practices for host-country employees and managers, we will focus on the problems of compensating expatriates.

COMPENSATION OF HOST-COUNTRY EMPLOYEES

As shown in Figure 15.10, hourly wages vary dramatically from country to country, from more than $40 on average in Norway to less than a dollar in developing countries. Host-country employees are generally paid on the basis of productivity, time spent on the job, or a combination of these factors. In industrialized countries, pay is generally by the hour; in developing countries, by the day. The piece-rate method is quite common. In some countries, including Japan, seniority is an important element in determining employees' pay rates. When companies commence operations in a foreign country, they usually set their wage rates at or slightly higher than the prevailing wage for local companies. Eventually, though, they are urged by other businesses, government, or even headquarters to reduce costs to conform to local practices to avoid "upsetting" local compensation practices. In Italy, Japan, and some other countries, it is customary to add semiannual or annual lump-sum payments equal to one or two months' pay. These payments are not considered profit sharing but an integral part of the basic pay package. Profit sharing is legally required for certain categories of industry in Mexico, Peru, Pakistan, India, and Egypt among the developing countries, and in France among the industrialized countries. Compensation patterns in Eastern Europe are in flux as these countries make the adjustment to more-capitalistic systems.

Employee benefits can range dramatically from country to country as well. In France, for example, benefits are about 70 percent, compared with around 30 percent in Canada. Whereas in North America most benefits are awarded to employees by employers, in other industrialized countries most of them are legislated or ordered by governments. Some of these plans are changing. Defined contribution plans are on the rise, sex equality is becoming important, and stock ownership is being tried.[31]

Because the largest cost for most companies is labour, it plays a prime role in international HR decision making. However, some people believe that companies are overcapitalizing on worldwide compensation differences. Many firms (Nike included) have generated bad press for charging hundreds of dollars for their individual products while the people who make them—sometimes children in developing countries working under terrible conditions—earn only a few cents. This has led to international political protests and pressure on firms to exercise

OUTCOME

FIGURE **15.10**

Hourly Wages in Different Countries*

COUNTRY	$/HOUR
Norway	41.05
Denmark	35.45
Germany	34.21
Netherlands	32.34
Belgium	31.85
Sweden	31.80
Switzerland	30.67
Austria	30.46
Finland	29.90
Luxembourg	27.74
United Kingdom	27.10
Australia	26.14
Ireland	25.96
Canada	25.74
Italy	25.07
France	24.90
United States	23.82
Japan	20.20
Spain	18.83
Greece	16.10
Korea, Republic of	14.72
New Zealand	14.47
Israel	12.98
Singapore	8.55
Portugal	7.65
Czech Republic	6.77
Taiwan	6.43
Hungary	6.29
Hong Kong SAR (1)	5.78
Poland	4.99
Brazil	4.91
Mexico	2.75
Philippines	1.07
Sri Lanka	0.54

*Hourly compensation costs in U.S. dollars for production workers in manufacturing.

Source: U.S. Department of Labor, Bureau of Labor Statistics, January 2008.

greater global social responsibility. As Nike discovered, it is pressure companies can not afford not to take seriously. Starbucks clearly takes good corporate citizenship seriously. Among Starbucks' many initiatives is its association with Fair Trade and Conservation International to help farmers in developing countries get a premium for the coffee they grow. We will discuss more on the fair treatment of workers in developing countries toward the end of the chapter.

COMPENSATION OF HOST-COUNTRY MANAGERS

In the past, remuneration of host-country managers has been ruled by local salary levels. However, increased competition among different companies with subsidiaries in the same country has led to a gradual upgrading of host-country managers' salaries. Overall, international firms are moving toward a narrowing of the salary gap between the host-country manager and the expatriate. Unilever, for example, used to leave the compensation arrangements largely to the boss of a region or a big country. Now brand managers in different countries increasingly compare notes, so they see potential discrepancies based on market differences and expatriate assignments. So the company moved from a narrow grading structure to five global work levels. Managers' pay is still based on the country they work in, but there will be regional convergence so that in time there will be a pan-European rate.[32]

COMPENSATION OF EXPATRIATE MANAGERS

If the assignment is going to be successful, the expatriate's compensation plan must be competitive, cost-effective, motivating, fair, easy to understand, consistent with international financial management, relatively easy to administer, and simple to communicate. To be effective, an international compensation program must:

1. Provide an incentive to leave Canada
2. Allow for maintaining a North American standard of living
3. Provide for security in countries that are politically unstable or present personal dangers
4. Include provisions for good health care
5. Take into account the foreign taxes the employee is likely to have to pay (in addition to domestic taxes) and help him or her with tax forms and filing
6. Provide for the education of the employee's children abroad, if necessary
7. Allow for maintaining relationships with family, friends, and business associates via trips home and other communication technologies
8. Facilitate re-entry home
9. Be in writing[33]

For short-term assignments, usually those that are project-based, expatriates are frequently given per-diem (per-day) compensation. These managers might reside in hotels and service apartments instead of leasing houses. They are also less likely to bring their family members with them. The assignment becomes more like a commuting assignment in which the expatriate spends the week in the host country and returns home on the weekend.

For longer-term assignments, there are two basic types of compensation systems. The first is **home-based pay**, based on the **balance-sheet approach**, a system designed to equalize the purchasing power of employees at comparable positions living overseas and in the home country and to provide incentives to offset qualitative differences between assignment locations.[34] The balance-sheet approach generally comprises the following steps:

Step 1: Calculate base pay. Begin with the home-based gross income, including bonuses. Deduct taxes and pension contributions.

Step 2: Figure cost-of-living adjustment (COLA). Add a cost-of-living adjustment to the base pay. Typically, companies do not subtract when the international assignment has a lower cost of living. Instead, they allow the expatriate to benefit from the negative differential. Often a housing allowance is added in here as well.

home-based pay
Pay based on an expatriate's home country's compensation practices

balance-sheet approach
A compensation system designed to match the purchasing power in a person's home country

Step 3: Add incentive premiums. General mobility premiums and hardship premiums compensate expatriates for separation from family, friends, and domestic support systems, usually 15 percent of base salary, although in recent years, some companies have reduced this amount. Sometimes incentive premiums are paid for hazardous duty or harsh conditions the expatriate might experience while abroad.

Step 4: Add assistance programs. These additions are often used to cover added costs such as moving and storage, automobile, and education expenses.

The differences in compensation paid to those working overseas are intended to correct for the higher costs of overseas goods and services so that in relation to their domestic peers expatriates neither gain purchasing power nor lose it. A myriad of calculations are required to arrive at a total differential figure, but in general, as we have said, the cost typically runs between three and five times the home-country salary. Fortunately, employers do not have to do extensive research to find comparative data. They typically rely on data published quarterly by federal government departments, such as External Affairs, for use in establishing allowances to compensate civilian employees for costs and hardships related to assignments abroad. Alternately, they consult international relocation experts to make sure all of the relocation bases are covered.

The second type of compensation system is **host-based pay**. Companies are under pressure to move expatriates to host-based pay because it is generally less costly. Host-based pay is compensation that is equivalent to that earned by employees in the country where the expatriate is assigned. This process is called **localization**. When an employee is localized, his or her compensation is set on par with local standards and practices. Incentive premiums are generally phased out, and the employee pays only local taxes and falls under the social benefit programs established by the government of the host country. Some companies localize only certain aspects of the pay package or do so gradually over a course of three to five years.

Usually the decision to localize an employee depends on whether he or she will ultimately remain abroad or return home. In many companies the decision depends on whether the employee or the employer is the driving force behind the localization. An expatriate employee with a strong desire to remain in the host country beyond the planned length of assignment (perhaps because he or she married a local or has simply fallen in love with the country), is likely to be more amenable to localization. Localization should not be viewed as a cost-saving panacea, however. There are many countries in which expatriates would refuse to "go local." Forcing an employee to do so can ultimately result in a failed assignment costing the company much more money than it would have saved by localizing him or her.

Recently, **split-pay** plans have become popular among companies. Under a split pay system, expatriates are given a portion of their pay in the local currency to cover their day-to-day expenses. The rest of their pay is distributed in their home currency to safeguard their earnings should changes in foreign exchange rates or inflation adversely affect their pay.

Another serious issue related to expatriate compensation is medical care. Employees are unlikely to consent to going abroad if they cannot get health care comparable to what is available in their home countries. Often Canadian-based plans can not cover expatriate employees or efficiently deal with claims that need to be reimbursed in foreign currency. One solution is to transfer the employee to a global employment company that can provide these types of benefits. Basically, the employee is transferred to the global employment company, which administers all of his or her benefits as well as those of numerous employees working for other companies. Still another issue is the need to provide expatriates and employees who travel abroad with security. Citigroup hires private drivers for employees doing business in countries such as Mexico—even for employees on extended stays. Companies can also purchase travel-related insurance covering a range of services

host-based pay
Expatriate pay comparable to that earned by employees in a host country

localization
Adapting pay and other compensation benefits to match that of a particular country

split pay
A system whereby expatriates are given a portion of their pay in the local currency to cover their day-to-day expenses and a portion of their pay in their home currency to safeguard their earnings from changes in inflation or foreign exchange rates

such as evacuation and disability or travel-related injuries.[35] HR managers are generally responsible for evaluating and implementing these different types of programs.

PERFORMANCE APPRAISAL

As we noted earlier, individuals frequently accept international assignments because they know that they can acquire skills and experiences that will make them more valuable to their companies. Frequently, however, it can be difficult for the home office to evaluate the performance of employees working abroad. Even the notion of performance evaluation is indicative of a North American management style that focuses on the individual, which can cause problems in Asian countries such as China, Japan, and Korea, and Eastern European countries such as Hungary and the Czech Republic. Performance appraisal problems can contribute to failure rates among expatriates and actually derail an individual's career rather than enhance it.[36]

WHO SHOULD APPRAISE PERFORMANCE?

In many cases, an individual working internationally has at least two allegiances: one to his or her home country (the office that made the assignment) and the other to the host country in which the employee is currently working. Superiors in each location frequently have different information about the employee's performance and may also have very different expectations about what constitutes good performance. For these reasons, the multirater (360-degree) appraisal discussed in Chapter 8 is gaining favour among global firms. There are exceptions, however. Thai workers do not see it as their business to evaluate their bosses, and Thai managers do not think subordinates are in any way qualified to assess them. Before implementing a different appraisal process, HR managers need to understand how the process is likely to be received in the host country.[37]

HOME- VS. HOST-COUNTRY EVALUATIONS

Domestic managers are frequently unable to understand expatriate experiences, value them, or accurately measure their contribution to the organization. Geographical distances create communication problems for expatriates and home-country managers, although e-mail, instant messaging, and other HR information systems technologies have begun to help close the gap.[38] Still, local managers with daily contact with the expatriate are more likely to have an accurate picture of his or her performance. Host-country evaluations can sometimes be problematic, though. First, local cultures may influence one's perception of how well an individual is performing. As noted earlier in the chapter, participative decision making may be viewed either positively or negatively, depending on the culture. Such cultural biases may not have any bearing on an individual's true level of effectiveness. In addition, local managers sometimes do not have enough of a perspective on the entire organization to know how well an individual is truly contributing to the firm as a whole.

Given the pros and cons of home-country and host-country evaluations, most observers agree that performance evaluations should try to balance the two sources of appraisal information. Although host-country employees are in a good position to view day-to-day activities, in many cases the individual is still formally tied to the home office. Promotions, pay, and other administrative decisions are connected there, and as a consequence, the written evaluation is usually handled by the home-country manager. Nevertheless, the appraisal should be completed only after vital input has been gained from the host-country manager. As discussed in Chapter 8, multiple sources of appraisal information can be extremely valuable for providing

OUTCOME 7

independent points of view—especially if someone is working as part of a team. If there is much concern about cultural bias, it may be possible to have people of the same nationality as the expatriate conduct the appraisal.

PERFORMANCE CRITERIA

Because expatriate assignments are so costly, many HR managers are increasingly under pressure to calculate the return on investment (ROI) of these assignments. What did the firm get for the million dollars it spent to send an expatriate abroad? Has the expatriate achieved the goals set forth in the assignment in the appropriate time frame? Obviously, the goals and responsibilities inherent in the job assignment are among the most important criteria used to evaluate an individual's performance, and different goals necessitate measuring different criteria. The criteria are tied to the various reasons employees were sent abroad in the first place—whether the goal was to transfer technical skills or best practices, improve a division's financial performance, or develop managerial talent.[39] The Business Case outlines the costs of employee expatriates and initiatives companies can undertake to improve ROI.

There are five steps related to calculating the ROI of an assignment:

1. Defining the assignment's objectives
2. Agreeing on the quantifiable measurements for the assignment
3. Developing an equation that converts qualitative behaviour into quantifiable measurements
4. Evaluating the expatriate's performance against these measurements
5. Calculating the ROI, which can be a complex cost accounting or a simple calculation to see if the expatriate covered the cost of keeping him or her on assignment.

The danger with ROI calculations, however, is that there is a temptation to resort to using "easy" criteria such as productivity, profits, and market share to measure an expatriate's performance. These criteria may be valid—but they are still deficient if they do not capture the full range of an expatriate's responsibility. Other, more subtle factors should be considered as well. Leadership development, for example, involves a much longer-term value proposition. In many cases, an expatriate is an ambassador for the company, and a significant part of the job is cultivating relationships with citizens of the host country. As we discussed at the beginning of this chapter, an individual's success or failure is affected by a host of technical and personal factors. For example, as one might guess, it is much easier to adjust to similar cultures than to dissimilar ones. A Canadian can usually travel to the United Kingdom or Australia and work with locals almost immediately. Send that same individual to Hungary or Malaysia, and the learning curve is more steep. And the expatriate's adjustment period may be even longer if the company has not yet established a good base of operations in the region. The first individuals transferred to a country have no one to show them the ropes or to explain local customs. Even relatively simple activities such as navigating the transit system can prove to be problematic. The U.S. State Department has developed rating systems that attempt to distinguish the different degrees of difficulty associated with different regional assignments. These difficulty factors need to be considered and built into the appraisal system.[40]

PROVIDING FEEDBACK

Performance feedback in an international setting is clearly a two-way street. Although the home-country and host-country superiors may tell an expatriate how well he or she is doing, it is also important for expatriates to provide feedback regarding the support they are receiving, the obstacles they face, and the suggestions they have about the assignment. More than in almost any other job situation, expatriates are in the very best position to evaluate their own performance.

The Business CASE

The Costs of Employing Expatriates

Organizations typically make selection decisions on the basis of a match between job requirements and the candidates' skills and abilities. But selection decisions in international assignments must always compare the costs of employing locals versus expatriates. The chart below compares the cost of employing a Canadian manager in the United Kingdom to employing a U.K. manager. The case involves a manager, based in Ontario, who earns about $85,000 a year, with a $17,000 bonus, who is to be sent on a three-and-a-half-year assignment to London, England. He is married with one school-age child who attends private school. This manager receives an automobile allowance as well as a trip home per year. The company pays for the relocation, household goods storage, and tax return preparations.

Total cost of assignment for 3.5 years:

Cost Element	$
Base salary	297,500
Bonus	59,500
Gross income	357,000
Cost of living allowance	92,800
Housing allowance	135,000
Education allowance	61,500
Automobile allowance	55,300
Home leaves	32,400
Relocation, storage, and tax return	76,300
Additional tax expenses	175,500
Total Cost	**$985,800**

The costs of sending this manager on an international assignment are nearly a million dollars, compared to the approximately $300,000 it would cost to employ a U.K.-based manager.

Below is a list of initiatives that would improve return on investment (ROI) of expatriates:

Better candidate selection	32%
Career-planning skills	26%
Communicating objectives	24%
Assignment preparation	20%
Monitoring program	17%
Cross-cultural training	10%
Developing or expanding intranet	7%
Communication/recognition	6%
Web-based cultural training	5%
Mandating destination support	4%
Other	17%

Sources: Andrea Poe, "Selection Savvy," *HR Magazine* 47, no. 4 (April 2002): 77–83; Jeff Bitten, "Compensation Strategies for International Assignments," *Canadian HR Professional* 18, no. 2 (April/May 2001): 29–31.

In addition to ongoing feedback, an expatriate should have a debriefing interview immediately on returning home from an international assignment. These repatriation interviews serve several purposes:

1. They help expatriates reestablish old ties with the home organization and may prove to be important for setting new career paths.
2. The interview can address technical issues related to the job assignment itself.
3. The interview may address general issues regarding the company's overseas commitments, such as how relationships between the home and host countries should be handled.
4. The interview can be very useful for documenting insights an individual has about the region. These insights can then be incorporated into training programs for future expatriates. However, if the learning is not shared, then each new expatriate to a region may have to go through the same cycle of adjustment.[41]

THE LABOUR ENVIRONMENT WORLDWIDE

A country's labour environment plays a large role in international business and HR decisions. As we have said, wages and benefits vary dramatically across the world as do safety, child labour, and other legal regulations. In many countries, the state's regulation of labour contracts is profound and extensive. Labour unions around the world differ significantly as well. Differences exist not only in the collective bargaining process but also in the political-legal conditions. For example, the EU prohibits discrimination against workers in unions, but in many other countries, including countries in Central America and Asia, labour unions are illegal. China has only one union, the All-China Federation of Trade Unions, an 80-year-old Communist Party institution that for decades has aligned itself more closely with management than workers. In some countries, only workers at larger firms are allowed to organize.[42]

Union strength depends on many factors, such as the level of employee participation, per capita labour income, mobility between management and labour, homogeneity of labour (racial, religious, social class), and unemployment levels. These and other factors determine how well a union will be able to represent labour effectively. Nearly all of Sweden's workers are organized, giving the unions in this country considerable strength and autonomy. By contrast, in countries with relatively high unemployment, low pay levels, and no union funds with which to support social welfare systems, unions are driven into alliance with other organizations: political party, church, or government. This is in marked contrast to Canada, where the union selected by the majority of employees bargains only with the employer, not with other institutions. By contrast, the unions in many European countries (such as Sweden) have a great deal of political power and are often allied with a particular political party. When employers in these countries deal with unions, they are, in effect, dealing indirectly with governments.

In a number of countries, however, including Japan, Germany, New Zealand, and the United Kingdom, unions have been losing some of their power. Ironically, the power of the unions to gain high wages and enforce rigid labour rules has been blamed for hurting competitiveness, particularly in European countries. Laws make it difficult to fire European employees, so workers are hired only sparingly. Unemployment benefits are very generous, so people tend to remain unemployed for longer rather than seek work. But because companies are increasingly tempted to offshore jobs to lower-labour-cost countries, unionized workers are beginning to make more concessions. For example, at Bosch in France, union bosses opposed management's plan to lengthen the workweek. But fearful workers overruled the union bosses, voting instead for the longer workweek.[43] As the power of unions declines a bit, the trend has been to demand compensation in other ways—through benefits or through greater participation in company decision making. Various approaches to participation will be discussed later.

COLLECTIVE BARGAINING IN OTHER COUNTRIES

We saw in Chapter 14 how the collective bargaining process is typically carried out in companies operating in Canada. When we look at other countries, we find that the process can vary widely, especially with regard to the role of government. Collective bargaining can take place at the firm, local, or national level. In Australia and New Zealand, for most of the 20th century labour courts had the authority to impose wages and other employment conditions on a broad range of firms (many of which were not even privy to the suits brought before the courts). In the United Kingdom and France, the government intervenes in all aspects of collective bargaining. Government involvement is only natural where parts of industry are nationalized. Also, in countries with heavy nationalization government involvement is more likely to be accepted, even in the nonnationalized companies. At Renault, the French government-owned automobile manufacturer, unions use political pressures in their bargaining with managers, who are essentially government employees. The resulting agreements then set the standards for other firms. This is true in spite of the fact that union membership rates in France have declined dramatically since the 1970s. In developing countries governments commonly have representatives present during bargaining sessions to ensure that unions with relatively uneducated leaders are not disadvantaged in bargaining with skilled management representatives. Still, in these countries a union may do little more than attempt to increase wages and leave the rest of the employment contract unchanged. In more-developed countries, goals related to other aspects of the employment relationship, such as workweek lengths, safety requirements, and grievance procedures, are more likely to be pursued.

INTERNATIONAL LABOUR ORGANIZATIONS

The most active of the international union organizations has been the International Confederation of Free Trade Unions (ICFTU), which has its headquarters in Brussels. The ICFTU is a confederation of 215 national trade union groups, representing 125 million trade union members in 145 countries and territories. Cooperating with the ICFTU are numerous International Trade Secretariats (ITSs), which are really international federations of national trade unions operating in the same or related industries. In addition to the ITSs, the ICFTU also cooperates with the European Trade Union Confederation (ETUC). The ETUC represents 60 million trade unionists from 82 trade unions in 36 Western, Central, and Eastern Europe countries. Another active and influential organization is the International Labour Organization (ILO), a specialized agency of the United Nations created in 1919. The ILO perhaps has had the greatest impact on the rights of workers throughout the world. It promotes the rights of workers to organize, the eradication of forced and child labour, and the elimination of discrimination. Over the decades, 182 countries have voluntarily committed to nearly 200 international conventions proposed by the ILO. The organization has been effective because it involves nation-states as well as workers and their employers. In recent years, the ILO has redefined its mission based on the "Decent Work Agenda." The Decent Work Agenda promotes the idea that there is an ethical dimension of work. This ethical dimension includes decent homes, food, education, the right to organize, and social programs to protect workers when they are elderly, disabled, or unemployed. Moreover, the agenda pertains to workers worldwide, including the self-employed—a situation common in agricultural-based, developing countries. Given the fact that half of the world's population lives on $2 a day or less, that 250 million children around the world are forced to work, and only 20 percent of people globally are covered by any sort of social insurance programs, these are worthy goals. Some companies, however, oppose the decent pay initiative, believing it promotes unionization.[44]

LABOUR PARTICIPATION IN MANAGEMENT

In many European countries, provisions for employee representation are established by law. An employer may be legally required to provide for employee representation on safety and hygiene committees, worker councils, or even boards of directors. While their responsibilities vary from country to country, worker councils basically provide a communication channel between employers and workers. The legal codes that set forth the functions of worker councils in France are very detailed. Councils are generally concerned with grievances, problems of individual employees, internal regulations, and matters affecting employee welfare.

A higher form of worker participation in management is found in Germany, where representation of labour on the board of directors of a company is required

codetermination
Representation of labour on the board of directors of a company

by law. This arrangement is known as **codetermination** and often by its German word, *Mitbestimmung*. While sometimes puzzling to outsiders, the system is fairly simple: Company shareholders and employees are required to be represented in equal numbers on the supervisory boards of large corporations. Power is generally left with the shareholders, and shareholders are generally assured the chairmanship. Other European countries and Japan either have or are considering minority board participation.[45]

Each of these differences makes managing human resources in an international context more challenging. But the crux of the issue in designing HR systems is not choosing one approach that will meet all the demands of international business. Instead, organizations facing global competition must balance multiple approaches and make their policies flexible enough to accommodate differences across national borders. Throughout this book we have noted that different situations call for different approaches to managing people, and nowhere is this point more clearly evident than in international HRM.

Small Business APPLICATION

At first glance, one might question whether international human resources management applies to small business. Certainly from the standpoint of sending expatriates from a home country to a host country with expatriate allowances and incentives, such practices are unlikely to find their way into small companies. However, international work, whether producing goods or products in one country and selling them in another, is as likely to be embraced by small business as by large companies. In fact, recognizing that small business is by its nature more likely to be responsible for only portions of a supply chain, with other suppliers and partners involved, it may be that small companies are more likely to be involved in international business, which may involve dimensions of international work. Accordingly, small business owners must learn to support staff requirements in this international context.

Small businesses support international work requirements though visa compliance, supplier relations, partnership, global delivery, and tariffs and exchange rates. Let us exemplify this through the review of a sporting goods distributor and manufacturer. This company has 30 employees responsible for the distribution of goods across Canada. The products they distribute are manufactured in China and in Europe. As such, on occasion some staff need to travel to China or Europe and require visitor or work visas

depending on the nature of their visit. Employees in this business regularly work with international suppliers. The company also partners with Chinese manufacturers to produce goods abroad for sale in Canada. This company has some clients whose orders are so large that an entire order is manufactured, packaged, and shipped directly from offshore to the customer, without ever being received in the home country. Finally, with this much international trade, the impact of tariffs, shipping costs, and exchange rates can make the difference between profit and loss.

So how does this company address international human resources? Each employee who is involved in the international supply chain must learn to work with the complexities of international business. This includes business travel into regions with different language, culture, and legal systems, requiring preparation and training to deal with these complexities. This also includes working within a framework of global delivery and the confines of time zone differences that, on occasion, require participating in evening conference calls to accommodate business hours in China. International human resources also involves managing the volatile fluctuations of currency exchange in the timing of ordering, pricing, and paying for goods, as well as adapting business practices to accommodate different business styles

continued

in different countries. These adaptations create challenges for employees. However, once employees learn to be interested in and sensitive to the legal, cultural, and language differences in working across geographical boundaries, they quickly appreciate that the world is in fact very small, with people being able to seamlessly collaborate with people around the globe. In this company, it is the international nature of the business that makes the company an interesting place for employees.

SUMMARY

OUTCOME 1

There are four basic ways to organize for global competition: (1) the international corporation is essentially a domestic firm that has leveraged its existing capabilities to penetrate overseas markets; (2) the multinational corporation has fully autonomous units operating in multiple countries in order to address local issues; (3) the global corporation has a world view but controls all international operations from its home office; and (4) the transnational corporation uses a network structure to balance global and local concerns.

OUTCOME 2

In addition to economic considerations, political-legal and cultural factors in different parts of the world make some countries more desirable to do business in than others.

OUTCOME 3

International HRM places greater emphasis on a number of responsibilities and functions such as relocation, orientation, and translation services to help employees adapt to a new and different environment outside their own country.

OUTCOME 4

Many factors must be considered in the selection and development of employees. Though hiring host-country nationals or third-country nationals automatically avoids many potential problems, expatriates are preferable, but more costly, in some circumstances. When expatriates are hired, most companies try to minimize their stay. Operations are handed off to host-country nationals as soon as possible.

OUTCOME 5

Once an expatriate is selected, an intensive training and development program is essential to qualify that person and his or her spouse for the assignment. Wherever possible, development should extend beyond information and orientation training to include sensitivity training and field experiences that will enable the manager to understand cultural differences better. Those in charge of the international program should provide the help needed to protect managers from career development risks, re-entry problems, and culture shock.

OUTCOME 6

Compensation systems should support the overall strategic intent of the organization but be customized for local conditions. Compensation plans must give expatriates an incentive to leave Canada; meet their standard-of-living, health care, and safety needs; provide for the education of their children, if necessary; and facilitate repatriation.

OUTCOME 7

Although home-country managers frequently have formal responsibility for appraising individuals on foreign assignments, they may not be able to fully understand expatriate experiences because geographical distances pose communication problems. Host-country managers may be in the best position to observe day-to-day performance but may be biased by cultural factors and may not have a view of the organization as a whole. To balance the pros and cons of home-country and host-country evaluations, one option is performance evaluations that combine the two sources of appraisal information.

[OUTCOME]

In many European countries—Germany, for one—employee representation is established by law. Organizations typically negotiate the agreement with the union at a national level, frequently with government intervention. In other countries, union activity is prohibited or limited to only large companies. European unions have much more political power than many other unions around the world, although their power has declined somewhat, due to globalization forces. The International Confederation of Free Trade Unions (ICFTU), the European Trade Union Confederation (ETUC), and the International Labour Organization (ILO) are among the major worldwide organizations endeavouring to improve the conditions of workers.

KEY TERMS

augmented skills, 597
balance-sheet approach, 609
codetermination, 616
core skills, 597
cultural environment, 586
culture shock, 603
expatriates, or home-country nationals, 589
failure rate, 599

global corporation, 585
global manager, 596
guest workers, 594
home-based pay, 609
host-based pay, 610
host country, 587
host-country nationals, 591
international corporation, 584
localization, 610

multinational corporation (MNC), 584
repatriation, 605
split pay, 610
third-country nationals, 591
transnational corporation, 585
transnational teams, 595
work permit or visa, 593

DISCUSSION QUESTIONS

1. Identify a Canadian company attempting to open offices in Asia. Interview one of the decision-making managers to determine the kinds of problems the company will face, and the preparations they are undergoing to deal with these.

2. If you were starting now to plan for a career in international HRM, what steps would you take?

3. What cultural differences exist between North Americans, Asians, and South Americans that would affect HR policies?

4. Scotiabank operates in 50 countries and employs Canadians to staff its New Delhi office. What are the advantages of employing Canadians with roots in the host country? Would you use expatriate managers or host country nationals to staff Scotiabank offices? Why?

5. In what ways are North American managers likely to experience difficulties in their relationships with employees in foreign operations? How can these difficulties be minimized?

6. Talk with a foreign student on your campus; ask about his or her experience with culture shock on first arriving in Canada. What did you learn from your discussion?

7. If the cost of living is lower in a foreign country than in Canada, should expatriates be paid less than they would be at home? Explain your position. Who should ultimately decide whether an employee should be localized or not?

8. The most common reason for failure of an expatriate assignment is the spouse. Go to http://www.expat.or.id/info/mythsofexpatlife.html and summarize the problems faced by spouses. What HR policies and practices would help reduce the magnitude of these problems?

9. Recently, as part of a restructuring, the CAW now owns a piece of GM and a place on the board. Do you think that codetermination will become popular in Canada? Explain.

INTERNET EXERCISE

About 25,000 young Canadians (18 to 30 years of age) found overseas work through the Department of Foreign Affairs youth program last year. Having international experience is a very useful credential. Think about a country in which you would like to acquire work or educational experience.

Using the Foreign Affairs and International Trade Canada website at http://www.voyage.gc.ca, determine what documentation you would need to work or study in your country of choice. Click on Country Profiles and prepare a list of cultural differences between Canada and your chosen country.

HRM Experience

A Canadian (Expatriate) in Paris

There is often a great deal of work involved in setting up expatriate assignments. The administrative requirements can be far ranging and extend beyond the employee to also include family issues. Suppose you were faced with the following scenario. What would be the most pressing considerations that you would need to address?

Assignment

Working in teams of four to six individuals, put together the package that would allow Jim to move his family to Paris while still maintaining his present lifestyle (his current annual salary is $140,000 plus incentives). Address at least the following issues:

1. Visas and permits
2. Relocation allowance and housing
3. Language and culture training
4. Spousal employment concerns
5. Health/medical/insurance issues
6. Compensation and incentives
7. Education for the children

The following websites may be helpful to you, but other resources may prove valuable as well.

- Canadian Embassy in Paris (http://www.international .gc.ca/canada-europa/France/menu-en.asp)
- French Embassy in Canada (http://www.ambafrance-ca.org)
- Expatica.com (http://www.expatica.com/france.asp)
- The Paris France Guide (http://www.parisfranceguide .com)
- Centers for Disease Control (http://www.cdc.gov/ travel)
- Travlang (currency calculator) (http://www.travlang .com/money)

The Scenario

You are the head of HR for Sarip International, a consulting firm specializing in hotel and restaurant management. Your firm is opening an office in Paris, and Jim Verioti, director of sales and marketing, has been asked to assume responsibilities for the expansion. Jim understands that the expatriate assignment will last two to three years, and although he has travelled to Europe for work on several occasions, this is his first long-term assignment overseas. He has a lot of questions about what he can expect and also some personal constraints.

Jim and his wife Betty have just moved into their new home (their mortgage is around $1,500 per month). In addition, Betty is an elementary school teacher and does not really know how the move will affect her job security. Their three children, Veronica (14), Reggie (12), and Archie (10), are of ages at which school considerations are very important. A friend told them about the American School in Paris, and this is a consideration. None of the Veriotis speak French.

BIZFLIX EXERCISES

MR. BASEBALL: TOLERANCE OF CULTURAL DIFFERENCES

This chapter emphasized the importance of tolerance of cultural differences for success as an expatriate. Watch this *Mr. Baseball* scene carefully while considering the questions below.

The New York Yankees trade aging baseball player Jack Elliot (Tom Selleck) to the Chunichi Dragons, a Japanese team. This lighthearted comedy traces Elliot's bungling entry into Japanese culture. It exposes his cultural misconceptions, which almost cost him everything—including his new girlfriend, Hiroko Uchiyama (Aya Takanashi). After Elliot slowly begins to understand Japanese culture and Japanese baseball, his teammates finally accept him. This film shows many examples of Japanese culture, especially its love for baseball.

This scene is an edited version of the "Welcome to Japan" sequence that appears early in the film. Jack Elliot arrives at Nogoya International Airport, Tokyo, Japan. Yoji Nishimura (Toshi Shioya) meets him and acts as Jack's interpreter and guide. The film continues after this scene with the unfolding adventure of Jack Elliot playing for the Chunichi Dragons.

What to Watch for and Ask Yourself

- Is Jack Elliot culturally sensitive or culturally insensitive?
- Does he make any cross-cultural errors on his arrival in Japan? If yes, what are they?
- Review the earlier chapter section "Training and Development." What type of training would you recommend for Jack Elliot?

CASE STUDY 1

CULTURAL CONUNDRUM

Anna has enjoyed great success in the Toronto office of a global company. When she was offered an assignment in Tokyo, she approached the job with the full confidence of her employer that she could oversee the reorganization of the subsidiary. By asking her extensive network of colleagues about Japan, she learned a few tips. For example, she learned that when a Japanese businessman hands you his business card, it is proper to read the card before taking it, and to never throw it on the desk. Even with tips like these, however, Anna's assignment was heading toward failure.

After six months, she was very discouraged and when she returned home for the holidays, she reported the following problems:

- Although everyone spoke English, there were communication problems.
- Everything took too long to complete, with deadlines missed and employees not following schedules.
- Although she asked her employees for feedback and information, and received promises that these would be forthcoming, no data arrived.

The company's response was to give her cross-cultural training, in which Anna learned the following:

- In Japanese culture, group identity supersedes individual identity. Loyalty is to the group, and criticisms of performance are taboo. Group meetings are the norm, and one-on-one meetings designed to facilitate feedback make employees very uncomfortable.
- Japanese culture is based on hierarchy and is organized to recognize the power differentials between superiors and subordinates. Japanese workers do not expect to have input into decisions; their only expectation is to be told what to do. If forced to participate in decision making, the typical Japanese will avoid uncertainty by accumulating every possible item of information to support the decision.
- Japan is a masculine society and women are employed in low-status positions. Anna's credibility as a decision maker would be questioned, and male employees would be uncomfortable working for her.

The communication problems only compounded the difficulty of the situation. Yes, the employees spoke English. But there were cultural differences. To a direct request to meet a deadline that they perceived as impossible, employees would save face (for themselves and the person making the request) by saying that they would do their best. Saying no is not part of Japanese culture.

Anna made the mistake of transferring her management style, which was successful in Toronto, to Tokyo, without understanding the cultural differences.

QUESTIONS

1. Exactly what preparation should Anna's company have given her before she started her assignment?

2. In general, what should a candidate for an international assignment do to prepare for a job, in the absence of company orientation and training?

3. Many believe that women on international assignments prove to be very effective, because they are both task oriented (a North American cultural imperative) and relationship oriented (an important attribute in Asian and other cultures). Why did these two sets of skills not help Anna?

Source: Adapted from Z. Fedder, "Same Language, Different Meanings," *Canadian HR Reporter* 13, no. 11 (June 5, 2000): 9, 13; S. McKay, "Women Going Global," *Financial Post Magazine*, December 1998, 38–54.

CASE STUDY 2

RECRUITING AND RETAINING INTERNATIONAL EMPLOYEES

Cambior, based in Longueil, Quebec, is one of Canada's largest gold producers, employing 2,700 people at mines in Quebec, Peru, French Guyana, and Surinam. Of these, over 1,000 are based outside Canada. Their HR policies for managing these international employees are described below:

STAFFING

Cambior has had no problems recruiting employees for its operations. They find that candidates who are attracted to international assignments tend to apply to organizations where these are possible.

Cambior uses three types of postings in order to staff its mines:

- Short-term assignments that are used for special projects or during construction of the mine.

- Home-based assignments where employees will spend periods of time at the mine and then return home for rest and recuperation. The longest period that an employee is on-site is 30 days, followed by 26 days of recuperation.

- Long-term assignments, usually for executives, who move with their families close to the mine. The biggest problems with these assignments are the education of the children and the careers of working spouses.

COMPENSATION

Cambior uses a tax equalization policy that guarantees an employee on assignment will be no better or worse off as a result of taxes. If the taxes are higher in the host country, then the company absorbs the costs of these extra payments. If they are lower, the excess reverts to the company. Employees are also given hardship allowances. Cambior has established an Employee Leasing Company that hires the employees for these international secondments, which allows the employee to retain home-based benefits such as pension plans and employment insurance.

HEALTH AND SAFETY

Cambior has found that safety standards are consistent across their international operations, but health issues are more complex. For example, employees need to be educated about malaria, and special provisions are made for other diseases not normally found in Canada. Employees have to feel assured that if there is a serious health issue, that they will receive rapid medical treatment. Each site has a complete medical facility. Medical evacuations are done when the condition is life threatening.

Violence is an issue in developing countries. Special sessions on topics such as kidnap training and emergency evacuation are provided.

QUESTIONS

1. Describe the advantages and limitations of Cambior's staffing policies. How would you compare these to the advantages and limitations of employing host country nationals?

2. What kinds of hardships would Cambior employees face? What would be appropriate compensation for these conditions?

3. What benefits required by law in Canada would be unlikely to be provided in developing countries?

Sources: Adapted from N. Bedard, "Human Resources for a Global Company," *CIM Bulletin*, 97, 1978, 2004, 99–100, http://www.cambio.com.

CAREER COUNSEL

Take the culture quiz on the *Managing Human Resources* website (http://www .belcourt6e.nelson.com) to assess your sensitivity to other cultures.

NOTES AND REFERENCES

1. Peter Dowling, Denice E. Welch, and Randall S. Schuler, *International Human Resource Management: Managing People in a Multinational Context*, 3rd ed. (Cincinnati, OH: South-Western, 1999); Nancy J. Adler, *International Dimensions of Organizational Behaviour* (Cincinnati, OH: South-Western, 1997); J. Michael Geringer, Colette Frayne, and John Milliman, "In Search of 'Best Practices' in International Human Resource Management: Research Design and Methodology," *Human Resource Management* 41, no. 1 (Spring 2002): 5–30; "Cendant Mobility Survey Shows Continued Challenges around Repatriation Management; Focus on Cost Control Also Driving New Approaches to Global Assignments, Say Global Mobility Practitioners," *PR Newswire* (April 28, 2004).

2. Abagail McWilliams, David Van Fleet, and Patrick Wright, "Strategic Management of Human Resources for Global Competitive Advantage," *Journal of Business Strategies* 18, no. 1 (Spring 2001): 1–24.

3. M.F. Wolff, "Innovation and Competitiveness among EU Goals for Knowledge Economy," *Research Technology Management* 44, no. 6 (November/December 2001): 2–6; Tony Emerson, "The Great Walls: The United States and Europe Are Leading the Race to Carve Up the Trading World," *Newsweek* (April 23, 2001): 40. For more information about the European Union online, see the Europa website at http://europa.eu.int.

4. Sadanand Dhume, "Just Quit It," *Far Eastern Economic Review* 165, no. 36 (September 12, 2002): 46–50; George Koo, "Fast Lane to China: Companies That Never Thought of Doing Business Overseas Are Now Looking to the Thriving Chinese Economy," *Computer Technology Review* 24, no. 4 (April 2004): 42.

5. Beth McConnell, "Global Forum Speakers to Share Insights on International HR," *HR Magazine* 48, no. 3 (March 2003): 115–117.

6. DeeDee Doke, "Perfect Strangers: Cultural and Linguistic Differences between U.S. and U.K. Workers Necessitate Training for Expatriates," *HR Magazine* 49, no. 12 (December 2004): 62.

7. Readers interested in codes of conduct and other ethical issues pertaining to international business might read the following: Bill Roberts, "Going Global," *HR Magazine* 45, no. 8 (August 2000): 123–128.

8. Carla Joinson, "No Returns," *HR Magazine* 47, no. 11 (November 2002): 70–77; Frank Jossi, "Successful Handoff," *HR Magazine* 47, no. 10 (October 2002): 48–52; Steve Bates, "Study Discovers Patterns in Global Executive Mobility," *HR Magazine* 47, no. 10 (October 2002): 14; Morgan McCall and George Hollenbeck, "Global Fatalities: When International Executives Derail," *Ivey Business Journal* 66, no. 5 (May/June 2002): 74–78; Leslie Gross Klass, "Fed Up with High Costs, Companies Thin the Ranks of Career Expats," *Workforce Management* 83, no. 10 (October 1, 2004): 84.

9. Wallace Immen, "Going abroad to get ahead," *The Globe and Mail*, February 22, 2006, C1.

10. David Lipschultz, "Bosses from Abroad," *Chief Executive* 174 (January 2002): 18–21.

11. Readers interested in codes of conduct and other ethical issues pertaining to international business might read Nadar Asgary and Mark Mitschow, "Toward a Model for International Business Ethics," *Journal of Business Ethics* 36, no. 3 (March 2002): 238–246; Diana Winstanley and Jean Woodall, "The Adolescence of Ethics in Human Resource Management," *Human Resource Management Journal* 10, no. 4 (2000): 45; J. Brooke Hamilton and Stephen Knouse, "Multinational Enterprise Decision Principles for Dealing with Cross-Cultural Ethical Conflicts," *Journal of Business Ethics* 31, no. 1 (May 2001): 77–94; Michael Maynard, "Policing Transnational Commerce: Global Awareness in the Margins of Morality," *Journal of Business Ethics* 30, no. 1 (March 2001): 17–27.

12. "Keeping Out the Wrong People: Tightened Visa Rules Are Slowing the Vital Flow of Professionals into the U.S.," *BusinessWeek* no. 3902 (October 4, 2004): 90; "Security Delays Hurt U.S. Business," *Legal Times*, August 23, 2004.

13. Anne E. Kornblut, "Bush Cites Political Hurdles in Plan for 'Guest Workers,'" *The New York Times*, March 24, 2005, A6.

14. "Society: Affirmative Action? Oui! At Long Last, France Takes a Page from America in Order to Manage Diversity—and Bring Minorities into Elite Schools," *Newsweek International*, April 12, 2004, 30.

15. Snell et al., "Designing and Supporting Transnational Teams: The Human Resource Agenda," *Human Resource Management* 37, no. 2: 147–158; Debra Shapiro, Stacie Furst, Gretchen Spreitzer, and Mary Ann Von Glinow, "Transnational Teams in the Electronic Age: Are Team Identity and High Performance at Risk?" *Journal of Organizational Behaviour* 23 (June 2002): 455–467; Claude Philipps, Harold Sirkin, Duane Filtz, and Scott Kirsner, "Time [Zone] Travelers: They Bounce from Beijing to Bangalore at a Moment's Notice," *Fast Company* no. 85 (August 2004): 60–67.

16. Snell et al., "Designing and Supporting Transnational Teams," 147–158; Leslie Gross Klass, "Fed Up with High Costs, Companies Thin the Ranks of Career Expats," *Workforce Management* 83, no. 10 (October 1, 2004): 84.

17. Andrea Poe, "Selection Savvy," *HR Magazine* 47, no. 4 (April 2002): 77–83; "Exploiting Opportunity: Executives Trade Stories on Challenges of Doing Business in Global Economy," *Business Mexico* 15, no. 2 (February 2005): 54–58.

18. Yehuda Baruch, "No Such Thing as a Global Manager," *Business Horizons* 45, no. 1 (January/February 2002): 36–42.

19. Sheree R. Curry, "Offshoring Swells Ranks of 'Returnees' Working Back in Their Native Countries," *Workforce Management* 84, no. 2 (February 1, 2005): 59; Margaret Linehan and Hugh Scullion, "Selection, Training, and Development for Female International Executives," *Career Development International* 6, no. 6 (2001): 318–323; Nancy Lockwood, "The Glass Ceiling: Domestic and International Perspectives," *HR Magazine* 49, no. 6 (June 2004): S1–11.

20. Nancy Wong, "Mark Your Calendar! Important Tasks for International HR," *Workforce* 79, no. 4 (April 2000): 72–74; Robert O'Connor, "Plug the Expat Knowledge Drain," *HR Magazine* 47, no. 10 (October 2002): 101–107; Andrea Graf and Lynn K. Harland, "Expatriate Selection: Evaluating the Discriminant, Convergent, and Predictive Validity of Five Measures of Interpersonal and Intercultural Competence," *Journal of Leadership & Organizational Studies* 11, no. 2 (Winter 2005): 46–63.

21. McCall and Hollenbeck, "Global Fatalities: When International Executives Derail," 74–78; Poe, "Selection Savvy," 77–83; Juan Sanchez, Paul Spector, and Cary Cooper, "Adapting to a Boundaryless World: A Developmental Expatriate Model," *Academy of Management Executive* 14, no. 2 (May 2000): 96–106; Eric Krell, "Evaluating Returns

on Expatriates: Though Difficult to Ascertain, Measuring the Return on the Cost of Expatriate Assignments Is Necessary to Justify the Expensive Investment," *HR Magazine* (March 2005): 12.

22. Riki Takeuchi, Seokhwa Yun, and Paul Tesluk, "An Examination of Crossover and Spillover Effects of Spousal and Expatriate Cross-Cultural Adjustment on Expatriate Outcomes," *Journal of Applied Psychology* 87, no. 4 (August 2002): 655–666; Poe, "Selection Savvy," 77–83; Talya Bauer and Sully Taylor, "When Managing Expatriate Adjustment, Don't Forget the Spouse," *Academy of Management Executive* 15, no. 4 (November 2001): 135–137; Iris I. Varner and Teresa M. Palmer, "Role of Cultural Self-Knowledge in Successful Expatriation," *Singapore Management Review* 27, no. 1 (January–June 2005): 1–25.

23. "Motorola to Increase Operations in China," *The New York Times*, November 8, 2001, C4; Peter J. Buckley, Jeremy Clegg, and Hui Tan, "Knowledge Transfer to China: Policy Lessons from Foreign Affiliates," *Transnational Corporations* 13, no. 1 (April 2004): 31–73.

24. Lionel Laroche, John Bing, and Catherine Mercer Bing, "Beyond Translation," *Training & Development* 54, no. 12 (December 2000): 72–73; Sabrina Hicks, "Successful Global Training," *Training & Development* 54, no. 5 (May 2000): 95.

25. Jared Wade, "The Pitfalls of Cross-Cultural Business," *Risk Management* 51, no. 3 (March 2004): 38–43.

26. Vipin Gupta, Paul Hanges, and Peter Dorman, "Cultural Clusters: Methodology and Findings," *Journal of World Business* 37, no. 1 (Spring 2002): 11–15; Jane Terpstra-Yong and David Ralston, "Moving toward a Global Understanding of Upward Influence Strategies: An Asian Perspective with Directions for Cross-Cultural Research," *Asia Pacific Journal of Management* 19, no. 2 (August 2002): 373–404.

27. Ping Ping Fu, et al., "The Impact of Societal Cultural Values and Individual Social Beliefs on the Perceived Effectiveness of Managerial Influence Strategies: A Meso Approach," *Journal of International Business Studies* 35, no. 4 (July 2004): 33; Geert Hofstede, *Culture's Consequences: Comparing Values, Behaviors, Institutions, and Organizations across Nations* (Thousand Oaks, CA: Sage, 2001).

28. Lisa Bohannon, "Going Global," *Career World* 29, no. 6 (April/May 2001): 28–30; Aimin Yan, Guorgong Zhu, and Douglas T. Hall, "International Assignments for Career Building: A Model of Agency Relationships and Psychological Contracts," *Academy of Management Review* 27, no. 3 (July 2002): 373–391; Justin Martin, "The Global CEO: Overseas Experience Is Becoming a Must on Top Executives' Resumes, According to This Year's Route to the Top," *Chief Executive* no. 195 (January–February 2004): 24–31.

29. "Prudential Relocation Survey Finds Spouses' Experiences a Key Factor in the Success of International Work Assignments," *Canadian Corporate News* (December 7, 2004).

30. Virginia Galt, "It's Not Easy to Come Home Again," *The Globe and Mail*, February 22, 2006, C6.

31. Mila Lazarova and Paula Caligiuri, "Retaining Repatriates: The Role of Organizational Support Practices," *Journal of World Business* 36, no. 4 (Winter 2001): 389–401; "Expatriate Administration: New Realities and HR Challenges," *Employee Benefit News* (March 1, 2005): 1; "For Those Working Abroad, Moving Home Can Be Jarring," *The Kansas City (Missouri) Star* (via Knight-Ridder/Tribune Business News), February 22, 2005.

32. Calvin Reynolds, *Guide to Global Compensation and Benefits* (New York: Harcourt, 2001); Gary Parker, "Establishing Remuneration Practices across Culturally Diverse Environments," *Compensation & Benefits Management* 17, no. 2 (Spring 2001): 23–27; Timothy Dwyer, "Localization's Hidden Costs," *HR Magazine* 49, no. 6 (June 2004): 135–141.

33. Caroline Fisher, "Reward Strategy Linked to Financial Success: Europe," *Benefits & Compensation International* 32, no. 2 (September 2002): 34–35; "Comparative Analysis of Remuneration: Europe," *Benefits & Compensation International* 31, no. 10 (June 2002): 27–28; Fay Hansen, "Currents in Compensation and Benefits: International Trends," *Compensation and Benefits Review* 34, no. 2 (March/April 2002): 20–21.

34. Chao Chen, Jaepil Choi, and Shu-Cheng Chi, "Making Justice Sense of Local-Expatriate Compensation Disparity: Mitigation by Local Referents, Ideological Explanations, and Interpersonal Sensitivity in China-Foreign Joint Ventures," *Academy of Management Journal* 45, no. 4 (August 2002): 807–817.

35. Patricia Zingheim and Jay Schuster, "How You Pay Is What You Get," *Across the Board* 38, no. 5 (September/October 2001): 41–44; "Benefits for Expatriate Employees: International," *Benefits & Compensation International* 31, no. 10 (June 2002): 26–27; Steven P. Nurney, "The Long and Short of It: When Transitioning from a Short-Term to a Long-Term Expatriate Assignment, Consider the Financial Implications," *HR Magazine* 50, no. 3 (March 2005): 91–95.

36. Stephan Kolbe, "Putting Together an Expat Package: As More and More Companies Adopt an International Outlook, They Are Increasingly Sending Staff on Overseas Assignments—Usually Involving a Complex Relocation Package," *International Money Marketing* (September 2004): 33.

37. The U.S. State Department Index of Living Costs Abroad can be found at http://www. state.gov/travel.

38. Barbara Hanrehan and Donald R. Bentivoglio. "Safe Haven: Accommodating the Needs of Employees and Families in Hostile Environments Can Increase Expenses and Alter Tax Liability," *HR Magazine* 47, no. 2 (February 2002): 52–54.

39. Paul Hempel, "Differences between Chinese and Western Managerial Views of Performance," *Personnel Review* 30, no. 2 (2001): 203–215.

40. "Cross-Cultural Lessons in Leadership: Data from a Decade-Long Research Project Puts Advice to Managers in Context, Country by Country," *MIT Sloan Management Review* 45, no. 1 (Fall 2003): 5–7.

41. Paula Caligiuri, "The Big Five Personality Characteristics as Predictors of Expatriate's Desire to Terminate the Assignment and Supervisor-Rated Performance," *Personnel Psychology* 53, no. 1 (Spring 2000): 67–88; Calvin Reynolds, "Global Compensation and Benefits in Transition," *Compensation and Benefits Review* 32, no. 1 (January/February 2000): 28–38; Charlene Marmer Solomon, "The World Stops Shrinking," *Workforce* 79, no. 1 (January 2000): 48–51; Stephenie Overman, "Mentors without Borders: Global Mentors Can Give Employees a Different Perspective on Business Matters," *HR Magazine* 49, no. 3 (March 2004): 83–87.

42. Frank Jossi, "Successful Handoff," *HR Magazine* 47, no. 10 (October 2002): 48–52; Paula Caligiuri and David Day, "Effects of Self-Monitoring on Technical, Contextual, and Assignment-Specific Performance," *Group & Organization Management* 25, no. 2 (June 2000): 154–174.

43. Mark Mendenhall and Gary Oddou, eds., *Readings and Cases in International Human Resource Management* (Cincinnati, OH: South-Western, 1999).

44. Ariane Berthoin, "Expatriates' Contributions to Organizational Learning," *Journal of General Management* 26, no. 4 (Summer 2001): 62–84; Peter J. Buckley, Jeremy Clegg, and Hui Tan, "Knowledge Transfer to China: Policy Lessons from Foreign Affiliates," *Transnational Corporations* 13, no. 1 (April 2004): 31–73.

45. Bernhard Ebbinghaus and Jelle Visser, *The Societies of Europe: Trade Unions in Western Europe since 1945* (London, England: Palgrave Macmillan, 2000); John Pencavel, "Unionism Viewed Internationally," *Journal of Labor Research* 26, no. 1 (Winter 2005): 65–98.

46. Christopher Rhoads, "Germany Faces Storm over Tech Staffing—Labor Groups Are Enraged by Proposal to Import Badly Needed Workers," *The Wall Street Journal*, March 7, 2000, A23; "European Workplaces Tighten Policies as Countries Struggle to Compete Worldwide," *Pittsburgh (Pennsylvania) Post-Gazette* (via Knight-Ridder/Tribune Business News), November 28, 2004.

47. Dharam Gahi, "Decent Work: Universality and Diversity" (discussion paper, International Institute for Labour Studies 2005), 1–22; Jean-Michael Servais, "Globalization and Decent Work Policy: Reflections upon a New Legal Approach," *International Labour Review* 143, no. 1–2 (Spring–Summer 2004): 104–108; "Philosophical and Spiritual Perspectives on Decent Work," *International Labour Review* 143, no. 3 (Autumn 2004): 290–292. Interested readers can find more information about international trade unions by checking out the websites of the ICFTU (http://www.icftu.org) and the ILO (http://www.ilo.org).

48. Dirk Kolvenbach and Ute Spiegel, "The Reform of the Works Council Constitution Act in Germany and Its Effects on the Co-Determination Rights of the Works Council," *International Financial Law Review* (2001): 59–65; Pencavel, "Unionism Viewed Internationally," 65–98.

Creating High-Performance Work Systems

After studying this chapter, you should be able to

[OUTCOME] Discuss the underlying principles of high-performance work systems.

[OUTCOME] Identify the components that make up a high-performance work system.

[OUTCOME] Describe how the components fit together and support strategy.

[OUTCOME] Recommend processes for implementing high-performance work systems.

[OUTCOME] Discuss the outcomes for both employees and the organization.

This chapter is available on the *Managing Human Resources* website (http://www.belcourt6e.nelson.com).

Excalibur Cases

EXCALIBUR
Excellence ■ calibre

INTRODUCTION

Excalibur, the Canadian University Tournament in Human Resources, is held annually in March in Montreal, Québec. This case competition attracts entrants from universities across Canada. Teams of three students, coached by their professors, are asked to demonstrate their knowledge of human resources management to a jury of practitioners and professors. The teams analyze the HR issues facing real Canadian companies and are given 90 minutes to prepare their cases, and another 20 minutes to present their recommendations to the jury. The top three winning teams receive cash awards. The tournament is managed by the Québec HR Association L'Ordre des CRHA et CRIA du Québec, supported by the Canadian Council of Human Resources Association. The following cases have been used in previous Excalibur Tournaments.

Source: Cases from Excalibur, the Canadian University Tournament in Human Resources (from 2000 to 2009) Le Cirque du Soleil: How to Manage Growth (2001); Avon: Leader and Trendsetter (2008); Garda: A Company on a Winning Course! (2007); Ambulance New Brunswick (2009); Labatt Breweries: A Hot Summer in Store (2003).

LE CIRQUE DU SOLEIL: HOW TO MANAGE GROWTH

CASE 1

Founded in 1984 by a group of young street performers, Cirque du Soleil has been in constant evolution since its creation. The company enjoys excellent international recognition and is said to have reinvented circus arts. In 1984 Cirque du Soleil had sales of $1.7 million, 50 employees, and 23 performers; in 2000, sales were expected to reach $407 million and it would employ 1370 people and 445 performers. It planned to present seven shows in 2000 on three continents: North America, Europe, and Asia. Also, in order to adequately manage all its personnel, it had four separate headquarters. Besides international headquarters in Montreal, it has four other head offices: Montreal (called Headquarters—America), Amsterdam (Headquarters—Europe), Las Vegas (Headquarters—Las Vegas), and Singapore (Headquarters—Asia-Pacific).

While Cirque du Soleil wanted to find and exploit new niches related to presenting shows, the majority of its revenues came from ticket sales. Thus, the vital nucleus of the Cirque remained presenting shows. The Cirque had four fixed shows, two touring shows in Asia, one in North America, and another in Europe. A touring show comprised 150 to 200 people, including 50 to 70 performers, and it had to relocate on average every six weeks, which demanded very skilled logistics and effective planning of the entry authorizations for the different countries on the tour. Relocating meant moving personnel, their baggage, and the Cirque's equipment from town to town. It also meant lodging all these people and ensuring they obtained the required visas and work permits in order to be able to practise their art in the countries the tour was visiting.

To attain the level of excellence set by Cirque du Soleil, talent scouts and recruiters travelled the globe in search of artists, creators, coaches, musicians, etc. Consequently, the Cirque's performers and personnel came from more than 30 countries and spoke many languages. Also, while the average age of employees was relatively young at 32, the age of the performers and employees ranged from 3 to 62.

In short, Cirque du Soleil was an international company that reflected the level of excellence it had achieved in the past and its constant desire to push the limits.

DEVELOPMENT PROJECT

As well as continuing to create and produce new shows, Cirque du Soleil wanted to diversify its commercial activities. Indeed, it wanted to see itself develop the production of audiovisual works such as the soundtracks of the different shows, explore the field of publishing, and continue to promote some strategic agreements with partners in the hotel business. Cirque du Soleil had also set itself the objective of adding two or three tours within five years, which would have the effect of bringing the number of employees required to achieve such an objective to about 2,000.

MANAGEMENT

Cirque du Soleil had adopted a management style in its own image, that is, dynamic, vibrant, and imaginative. The organic nature of how it operated put each employee in a position that allowed him or her to contribute to a common work. Cirque du Soleil firmly believed that, by appealing to everyone's intelligence, all objectives are achievable. Also, communications were extremely open and the authority that certain hierarchical titles could impose was practically nonexistent. And a Cirque du Soleil core value was respect for cultural diversity.

In spite of the continuous growth the company had experienced, it had always known how to ensure cohesion among employees and maintain a strong sense of belonging.

CHALLENGES TO BE MET

Given its growth plans, in relation to both the number of shows presented and the establishment of new commercial activities, Cirque du Soleil needed to apply itself to adapting its structure and, above all, to ensuring that its managers have the ability to support such development. In this respect, several managers who had grown up with Cirque du Soleil and who had thus acquired broad operating experience were having some difficulty moving to a strategic management mode. Given their extensive knowledge of how the Cirque operated, they too often remained occupied or preoccupied with operating questions, rather than investing their energy more in strategic planning.

Also, given the increased number of tours planned, another problem that already existed was likely to get bigger. Due to the difficult touring conditions, such as the frequent relocations, the increased number of shows per week, and challenging working conditions in general, the turnover rate among employees was very high. On average, they worked for the Cirque between 19 and 24 months, which created a turnover rate of 18 to 22 percent. In spite of the efforts made to reduce the inconveniences inherent in touring, problems still remained. For example, the Cirque offered the services of a tutor to child performers and to the children of performers. However, because of the costs this would have entailed, this service could not be offered to all the children of its personnel. Despite the attractive salaries, Cirque du Soleil was experiencing some difficulties in retaining its touring personnel.

Finally, it is important to note that, both in the touring shows and in International Headquarters in Montreal, the presence of many people of different nationalities, speaking different languages, was a challenge. Indeed, while the presence of Quebec and Canadian performers at International Headquarters and on tours was often secondary, dealing with several nationalities greatly influenced the quality of communications. And, depending on the cultural baggage of each person, the perception of the message communicated could differ greatly. Since cultural references are very divergent, what are innocuous gestures to some have unexpected implications for others. However, despite these difficulties in perception, Cirque du Soleil had always greatly valued cultural diversity and had always emphasized the richness it brought, rather than the differences it created. Nonetheless, Cirque du Soleil had to constantly manage stereotypes and prejudices. This situation was even more palpable at International Headquarters in Montreal since the performers who worked there were, for the most part, passing through, either with the aim of learning a new number or to take up training again following an injury. Also, people of the same nationality often grouped together without mixing too much with other performers of different nationalities.

Questions

You have been given a mandate by Cirque du Soleil to propose solutions to the problems raised by the facts described above.

To do so, you must

1. State your understanding of the situation at Cirque du Soleil;
2. Precisely determine the needs of Cirque du Soleil in the short and medium term;
3. In the light of those needs, make provisions for the obstacles envisaged;
4. Finally, establish a plan of action by formulating possible solutions to the problems you have identified. You must then justify the proposed solutions, taking into account the values transmitted by Cirque du Soleil.

AVON: LEADER AND TRENDSETTER

CASE 2

Avon is the world's leading direct seller of beauty and related products, operating in over 100 countries. Launched in 1886 when David H. McConnell founded the California Perfume Company, the organization was renamed Avon Products in 1939. Over the years, the company expanded its horizons and was listed on the New York Stock Exchange in 1964. Avon has 5.4 million Sales Representatives worldwide and 40,000 employees, 75 percent of whom are women.

Avon Canada, founded in 1914, moved to Montreal's West Island in 1961. It has a head office staff of 900, commonly known as "associates," including the District Managers. The 72,000 Sales Representatives across Canada are self-employed. Seventy-five percent of its employees and 99.8 percent of its Representatives are women. Representative turnover is known to be high at 80 percent; the company therefore has to recruit about 57,000 new Representatives each year.

Avon Products Inc is the number one direct seller in the world, posting sales of $9.9 billion in the United States. In Canada, sales reached CAD$300 million, 44 percent of which are derived from beauty products and 56 percent from non-beauty products.

Since 2000, Avon Products has adopted a more global approach to its operational structure, clustering markets in five main geographic regions. Avon Canada has therefore been working with its North American partners, the United States, Puerto Rico, and the Dominican Republic, to optimize work processes and business opportunities. One of the roadblocks to this optimization has been the fact that Canada sells 18 campaigns in a year, compared to 26 campaigns for its partners.

In 2006, the direction to take was clear: migrate from the current 18 annual sales campaigns to 26 as per the U.S. model. This was identified as a key driver of growth for the company and a creator of significant efficiencies achieved through harmonization of the structures, products, processes, and size of product lines. As for the Sales Representatives, albeit more work, a 26-campaign approach would result in more sales opportunities and better, less complex work schedules. It was the opportunity to redesign all business processes and to create a more simplified, more harmonized and more intense experience for the Sales Representatives, especially with the top players in terms of sales revenues.

Such a decision required major changes for employees in every department throughout the company, as well as major investments to support systems and operations. For example, the marketing department plans, designs, and produces the sales brochure; each campaign became quite a challenge for all employees involved in this business process. Additionally, one questions whether the distribution channel of independent contractors would be able to deliver products as usual within the compressed time frame. Furthermore, the finance department had to look into the risk factors facing a possible drop in sales volume. Finally, the information technology group had to evaluate the need to redesign technology or adjust its platforms to support such a change.

Today, all key concerns have been addressed and the project plan is on target to launch the final phases in April 2008. The company has always abided by the same five values since its inception: trust, respect, belief, humility, and integrity. Avon has carved a niche with products exclusively for women and has extended this focus through generous donations in support of the crusade against breast cancer.

The Human Resources department had its role to play throughout the overall process. Its action plan was targeted primarily towards communications, mobilization, retention, recruiting, and change management. The Canadian Avon HR structure is composed of one Vice-President, two generalists, one recruiter, and two nonmanagement employees. They chose to assume a leadership role where close partnerships with all departments were required to form strategic teams able to direct the magnitude and realities of changes to come.

The main HR targets for an organizational development intervention were the District Managers, who represent the critical link to help the Sales Representatives get over the emotional impact of the proposed changes. This includes identifying the obstacles the Representatives would face and communicating the rationale behind the changes in order to ensure the continuity of sales activities. This was viewed as quite a challenge since the Sales Representatives are not Avon employees; they have no company benefits and there is no employee-employer relationship.

Therefore, Avon is depending on the strong leadership capabilities of their District Managers to maintain the integrity of the sales process and to continue to recruit and motivate their Sales Representatives, who are viewed as the key stakeholders in undertaking the change and ensuring a success for Avon. As Avon employees, the District Managers receive a compensation package that includes a base pay plus commissions on sales. As part of the original HR action plan, the compensation and reward programs had to be reviewed and adapted, while engagement and training had to be reinforced.

From idea to reality: 2008 represents the crucial year to complete the migration from 18 to 26 sales campaigns, and have it become an operational reality. However, Avon still faces a number of strategic challenges. Among these, its operating structure needs to be well established to face growing competitive global markets and overall organization effectiveness remains to be achieved. Furthermore, it had determined a key success factor that a strong leadership culture of trendsetters must remain in place and present at all times.

Assuming that the key concerns related to the original 2006 migration project were properly identified and that the critical organizational development steps undertaken have been successful, it is now time to plan the activities necessary to support the "aftermath" to ensure ongoing engagement, stability and success for the whole change initiative, while continuing to respect the original Avon values.

In the light of the HR action plan implemented so far:

1. Identify five activities that should be reinforced throughout the next year (2008) and why.

2. What would you recommend to the HR team in terms of activities for the oncoming two years to ensure success and sustained sales results?

3. Provide an impact assessment of your recommendations as it pertains to all "associates" in Canada and the company itself.

GARDA: A COMPANY ON A WINNING COURSE!

CASE 3

In light of your consulting firm's reputation, the President and CEO of Garda has asked you to recommend HR management strategies to build a sense of commitment and loyalty among the company's employees. At the same time, he would like to maintain the firm's growth objectives and management philosophy. You thus held several meetings with various management representatives and retained the following information.

BACKGROUND

Founded in 1970, Garda changed hands several times before being bought by its current President and CEO in 1999. The company is active in the following four operating segments: consulting and investigations, pre-employment screening, physical security and cash handling.

Garda has a well-established reputation: not only as a leader on the international scene, where it has operations in Europe, Mexico, and the Middle East, but also as the second largest cash-handling firm in North America. In addition, the company is considered to be the top Canadian player in consulting and investigations, pre-employment screening and physical security. The corporation counts on 28,000 employees worldwide, mainly in the security and cash-handling sectors, about 15 percent of whom work part-time. Most of these employees are security officers. Garda generally favours a decentralized approach for each entity, apart from a number of shared functions such as finance, marketing and communications, information technology, and purchasing, which are managed from its head office in Montreal. It has an administrative staff of 450 employees working in various branches across Canada. Of these, 180 are based in the Montreal head office.

Listed on the stock exchange for the past seven years, the corporation has focused heavily on sales and profit growth in recent years and is now financially sound. Its success is largely due to its substantial growth and the creation of synergies between certain administrative and operational cost centres. Since 1999, Garda has posted an average revenue growth of 91.74 percent. Moreover, it hopes to reach its target annual revenue of CAN$1.4 billion in 2008.

While internal growth explains a large part (65 percent) of the corporation's success in the last five years, its acquisitions have also boosted its earnings. In all, Garda has made 26 acquisitions in Canada, the United States, and Europe since its inception. These acquisitions have enabled the corporation to secure an advantageous position on the global market, propelling it to fifth place in the physical security and cash-handling sectors. The firm is thus close to attaining its CEO's goal—to become one of the three largest players on the global market within seven years.

Garda's executive team includes some 30 vice presidents, each with clearly defined roles and responsibilities. The company's human resources management is decentralized, with teams in Canada, the United States, and Europe in order to comply with the legislation and culture in each region. Up to now, Garda has applied a rigorous management approach, maintaining the same organizational structure across the board. It now realizes that it will have to adapt this structure to meet these new challenges.

CHALLENGES

Industry observers believe Garda is on a winning course. Extremely targeted, in terms of both geography and activities, its acquisitions have been well-received by the financial community, shareholders, and clients. Not only has the firm enhanced its value through these acquisitions, but it has also been able to successfully integrate these newly acquired firms into its overall operations.

To achieve this success, management focused on the following four steps: adaptation of the existing structure, elimination of duplication, job maintenance, and job improvement. All of these steps can be quickly implemented. Each acquisition is managed according to its specific context and employees are kept informed very early on in the process.

Changes are communicated in collaboration with the management of the acquired entities since Garda understands the importance of both informal and formal modes of communication. The President/CEO and his management team play an active role in making sure the new employees are integrated in a positive environment. The result is that these workers are almost immediately familiar with the company's code of ethics and its values of team spirit, client focus, responsibility, integrity, effectiveness, simplicity, flexibility, and commitment.

However, because of the corporation's sustained growth strategy, the HR department at Garda Canada has to apply a short-term management approach, while planning for the longer term. Given the 30 collective agreements in effect, their potential legal implications and regional economic realities, it is becoming more and more difficult to recruit a stable workforce. Turnover in the security industry is higher than in other sectors; when the unemployment rate drops, it is harder to recruit good candidates.

In fact, employee recruitment and retention represent significant challenges for the company, particularly in Canada. Furthermore, the rate at which new public protection legislation is being introduced does not suggest the situation will improve in the near future. Garda is currently counting on the dynamism of its existing team to develop its employees' loyalty and enhance their sense of commitment in the organization.

Your team of consultants is required to analyze the situation and make recommendations on the strategies and priority actions to implement in order to build employees' sense of commitment and loyalty. Any recommendations for improving Garda's workforce recruitment and retention should take into account the company's growth strategy, its desire to keep costs to a minimum, and the need for rapid results.

YOUR ROLE

You are required to:

1. Explain your understanding of the main issue facing Garda Canada;
2. Determine the appropriate approach and priority actions that would build and even increase employees' sense of commitment and loyalty, taking into account the expectation of immediate results;
3. Explain the potential impact of your recommendations on HR management and on the organization;
4. List at least five conditions that will quickly contribute to workplace commitment across the organization.

AMBULANCE NEW BRUNSWICK

CASE 4

BACKGROUND

Ambulance New Brunswick (ANB) is a public company created by the Government of New Brunswick in June 2007 to operate a standardized, province-wide emergency medical service.

SITUATION BEFORE ANB:

Emergency medical services in New Brunswick were delivered through dozens of separate contractors. There were for-profit operators, non-profit operators (including provincial government systems managed by Regional Health Authorities [RHAs]), municipal ambulance services, and First Nations ambulance services. A private sector company provided air ambulance services. Some operations were subject to collective agreements and some were not.

- There was no centralized dispatch. Three regional centres in the province received emergency calls and dispatched ambulances. There was no accepted standard for response times.
- Thirty-five different medical directors set patient care protocols, resulting in different standards of patient care.
- Paramedic training differed greatly. Most paramedics were trained as Emergency Medical Technicians, but only some were trained as Primary Care Paramedics (who have additional skills, such as the ability to intervene in cardiac and respiratory emergencies).
- Many ambulance operators provided on-call service during non-peak hours. At these times, paramedics had to be called into work when calls were received.

GOALS OF ANB

- Unify all ambulance services under a single body;
- Create an improved, standardized response time for the province. The target is 90 percent compliance with a 9-minute response time in urban areas and 90 percent compliance with a 22-minute response time in rural areas;
- Elevate training standards for all paramedics until 100 percent are trained as Primary Care Paramedics. Introduce Advanced Care Paramedics at a later date;
- Improve consistency of care through a centralized approach to emergency care protocols;
- Have 24-hour on-site schedules, eliminating on-call systems.

ANB RESPONSIBILITIES

The province expects ANB to:

- Operate land ambulance services, including patient transfers within and outside the province (for example, for specialized care in Halifax, Nova Scotia, or elsewhere);
- Deliver air ambulance service, including patient transfers within and outside the province;
- Operate the Medical Communications Management Centre (MCMC)—a province-wide medical emergency communications and dispatch centre;
- Develop and maintain continual quality improvement processes;
- Acquire and maintain assets required to operate the ambulance service;
- Develop, test, and update the provincial disaster response plan for ambulance services, including an MCMC disaster and business continuity plan and emergency operations centre;
- Respond to customer, media, and public inquiries and complaints and manage community and stakeholder relations;
- Work with related departments, organizations and agencies, including medical first responders (e.g., fire services) and 911.

THE CORE COMPANY—ANB

Ambulance New Brunswick is a public sector corporation under the *Public Service Labour Relations Act*. The province is technically the employer of ANB front-line personnel.

ANB bought required assets (stations, trucks) from former operators following negotiations for the transfer of responsibilities to ANB.

Employees of the former operators who were not already public servants were offered employment with ANB and became public servants.

THE MANAGEMENT COMPANY: NEW BRUNSWICK EMERGENCY MEDICAL SERVICES INC.

Following a public tender, the province selected Medavie Blue Cross to develop the plan for ANB and to operate the provincial ambulance service. Medavie Blue Cross established a wholly owned subsidiary, New Brunswick Emergency Medical Services Inc. (NB EMS) for this purpose. The province negotiated a ten-year performance-based contract with NB EMS to manage Ambulance New Brunswick and its personnel.

NB EMS employs the managers within ANB. The NB EMS managers act as agents of the province to manage ANB's public service employees.

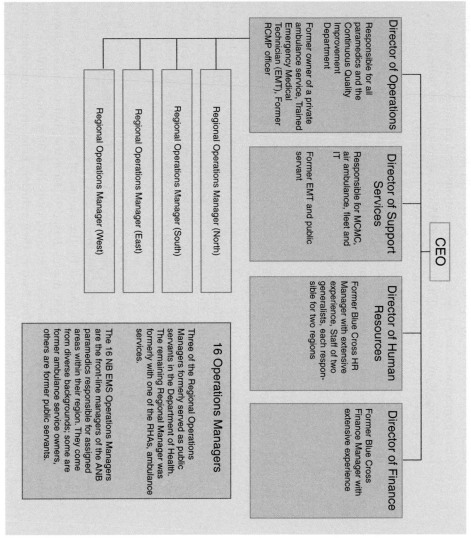

Organization of NB EMS org chart:

CEO

Director of Operations — Responsible for all paramedics and the Continuous Quality Improvement Department. Former owner of a private ambulance service, Trained Emergency Medical Technician (EMT), Former RCMP officer

Director of Support Services — Responsible for MCMC, air ambulance, fleet and IT. Former EMT and public servant

Director of Human Resources — Former Blue Cross HR Manager with extensive experience, Staff of two generalists, each responsible for two regions

Director of Finance — Former Blue Cross Finance Manager with extensive experience

16 Operations Managers — Three of the Regional Operations Managers formerly served as public servants in the Department of Health. The remaining Regional Manager was formerly with one of the RHAs, ambulance services.

The 16 NB EMS Operations Managers are the front-line managers of the ANB paramedics responsible for assigned areas within their region. They come from diverse backgrounds; some are former ambulance service owners, others are former public servants.

Regional Operations Manager (North)
Regional Operations Manager (South)
Regional Operations Manager (East)
Regional Operations Manager (West)

COLLECTIVE BARGAINING STRUCTURE

The approximately 900 employees of ANB consist of 850 paramedics, 40 dispatchers, and 15 nurses.

Since the employees who were previously employed within the RHAs remained provincial government employees, little changed when ANB was formed.

The paramedics and dispatchers formerly employed by other operators were integrated into the Canadian Union of Public Employees (CUPE) local when they joined ANB. They were credited with seniority based on continuous service with their previous employer.

The New Brunswick Nurses' Union represents the 15 nurses, who are all associated with the air ambulance service.

A province-wide local of CUPE represents the paramedics and MCMC personnel.

COLLECTIVE BARGAINING RELATIONSHIPS

ANB personnel are covered by collective agreements written to cover the entire health system of the province—RHAs plus ANB. The agreements' focus remains hospital operations, and ANB is scarcely mentioned.

NB EMS places fewer demands on the province for HR support than the RHAs did, but must still work with the Provincial Department of Human Resources for job classification and for legal support in the arbitration of grievances. Management's pre-ANB experience affects early approaches to labour relations:

- In the RHAs, human resources management was reactive, and many HR affairs such as classification and labour relations were controlled closely by the province's Department of Human Resources. The labour relations climate between the RHAs and CUPE was mildly adversarial. The focus for management was always on hospital operations, and paramedicine was something of an afterthought. Former RHA managers came to believe that the union's view of issues would prevail over management's.

- The Department of Health had little direct responsibility for labour relations matters. Any internal departmental issues were directed to the provincial Department of Human Resources. ANB managers who were formerly government employees also came to believe that the union's view of issues would prevail over management's.

CONTEXT OF YOUR MANDATE

The NB EMS management team has done an outstanding job at putting together a functioning, highly professional, state-of-the-art service in a year.

During the first year, they hired more than 100 new paramedics, most of the flight nurses, dozens of dispatchers, upgraded the ambulance fleet, created new maintenance standards, developed new standard operating procedures, transferred and equipped more than 800 employees, negotiated for the takeover of services from 39 contractors with more than 50 contracts, assisted in the negotiation of a new collective agreement, and established a central office and MCMC.

But with the huge workload, NB EMS senior managers have not been able to work on a strategic human resources plan. They have not been blind to this need; they have simply been unable to find the time.

Employee relations are hampered by the nature of the business. The MCMC and air ambulance employees are mainly based in Moncton, but other employees are scattered across New Brunswick. There are more than 60 stations, and for most of the day paramedics are on the road in their vehicles. Employee communications and personal leadership are difficult. Front-line managers have a heavy burden of administrative tasks, such as scheduling paramedics. It is easy to revert to management by e-mail.

Assume that the following symptoms have begun to emerge, reflecting the organization's difficulty to date in giving HR the priority that management knows it must have in the future:

- There are concerns over the level of engagement by paramedics. It is obvious that there are pockets of front-line staff who have not bought into the new system. Paramedics are not generally motivated by career progression, since they have fairly limited opportunities to move up in their organizations. However, they take intense pride in their skills, abilities, and technology and are critical of anything that may take away from their public image. They sometimes express uncertainty about the new system.
- Managers are reverting to their former employers' business styles and there is a danger of multiple disconnected cultures emerging:

    - Managers who were previously private operators acutely feel their lack of freedom now that they are in a larger organization. They can no longer just buy a new truck when they want to. They can not have their own administrative assistants. They have to adapt to new and different standard procedures. In many cases they were non-union and now they have to comply with a collective agreement.
    - Many managers who were public servants believe that "nothing can be done" about many HR issues, because their former managers often did not deal with labour relations issues effectively. They believe the union is able to "win" any time they take a stand.

- The employee experience differs across the organization, based on differing management styles among the operations managers or regional managers. Some are described as blunt and black-and-white about issues, while others are more like friends. Some hold information meetings with staff and others do not. In some cases, policies are discussed and in some, they are issued.

- In a number of cases, HR has learned about serious issues too late to have an influence. Front-line managers have already taken a position. HR has sometimes had to modify the manager's position at a later date. As a result, there has begun to be some friction between HR and operations.

Tensions exist between dispatch and paramedics. While this is a common state of affairs in emergency services, it is undesirable and may be growing.

YOUR MANDATE

Your team of consultants has been engaged by NB EMS to develop a plan to build a progressive, positive workplace culture and harmonious labour relations. Note that given the difficult economic times, assume a modest budget.

You are required to:

1. After identifying the main issues and challenges, outline a concrete two-year plan for NB EMS to i) create a unified and positive ANB culture and ii) improve labour relations.

   Your plan will describe specific actions, expected outcomes, and timelines.

2. Recommend three things that NB EMS can do to instill confidence in the new emergency medical services system, especially among paramedics.

LABATT BREWERIES: A HOT SUMMER IN STORE

CASE 5

In 1847, John Kinder Labatt laid the foundations of a brewing company in London, Ontario, that would later become Labatt Breweries. The company quickly branched out. In 1878, it established an agency in Montreal to distribute its products. Twenty years later, the company took steps to satisfy growing demand in the Toronto area and opened a sales office and a small warehouse. When Prohibition was introduced in the United States in 1900, the company's expansion was temporarily delayed. It survived, however, and in 1946 began a series of acquisitions that made it one of the largest breweries in Canada. The launch of Labatt Blue in 1951 helped cement the company's status as Canadian industry leader. In 1995 the world-renowned company was sold to Belgium's Interbrew SA, the third-largest brewing consortium in the world.

Today Labatt produces over 60 beers, employs 3,800 employees, and operates eight breweries from coast to coast, in St. John's, Halifax, Montreal, Toronto, London, Edmonton, Creston, and New Westminster. Its most popular brands are Labatt Blue, Budweiser, Keith's, Labatt Wildcat, and Kokanee. In Quebec alone, 893 million 341-mL bottles are produced each year, an amount equal to 3.1 million hL, or 23 percent of the total Canadian production of 13.64 million hL. Labatt's products are distributed to over 22,000 outlets, and 20 percent of the production is exported. The Montreal brewery is the largest in Canada, closely followed by the London, Ontario, plant, which produces 2.97 million hL. Worldwide, Interbrew produces 180 beers that are distributed in more than 110 countries in Europe,

North America, and the Asia-Pacific region. Interbrew's most popular brands are Stella Artois, Bass, and Beck's.

Innovation has set Labatt apart from other breweries. In fact, it was Labatt that marketed the first twist-off cap, the first light beer, and the first non-alcoholic beer in Canada. More recently, the company made history by creating the first lemonade-flavoured malt beer. Shortly after, in 1997, to address ever-growing demand for and popularity of specialty beers and imported beers, Labatt created the Oland Specialty Beer Company (OSBC).

The quest for innovation that has characterized the company since its early days is entirely consistent with its mission statement to deliver superior quality products made from the finest ingredients using proven methods. The company's stated goal is to become Canada's leading brewer, a goal that plays out in market share points, given the intense competition in national and world markets. From 1997 to 2001, the brewing industry was characterized by a wave of mergers. Since then, the number of players on the market has fallen considerably and the remaining companies have gotten larger. To remain competitive and make further inroads, Interbrew has been using a strategy called "The World's Local Brewer" to become a larger presence in mature and emerging markets through strategic acquisitions and internal growth.

CULTURE SHOCK

With its background of family tradition, Labatt had managed through the years to foster a strong sense of belonging among its employees. Staff members were genuine ambassadors for the company's products, always eager to represent the company during community events, for example. The culture of excellence, perfor-mance, and quality that built the company's reputation was widely shared by a vast majority of employees—managers, representatives, and shop workers alike.

When Interbrew bought the company in the mid-1990s, harsher market condi-tions had chipped away at the relationship between the employees and their com-pany. To function in an ultra-competitive world market, the organization has worked very hard over the last few years to optimize productivity. To achieve this, it reduced its workforce and increased the work load. The new operating methods have caused much discontent among unionized employees in the plants and fostered a feeling of nostalgia for the way things were.

In Quebec, the last round of labour negotiations in 1996 intensified the cul-ture shock that accompanied the acquisition. When the collective agreement was reopened, management proposed retirement incentives in an effort to reduce pro-duction manpower and increase the company's competitiveness. Although the older workers hailed the proposal, it caused deep dissatisfaction among younger employees, whose main goal was access to permanent positions. This was a very controversial issue, as indicated by the fact that the proposal passed by a mere 52 percent. The collective agreement was to be in effect for six years.

It is important to note that 90 percent of Labatt's Quebec employees are union-ized, and the company's 150 managers are not. In all, there were nine bargaining units belonging to the Teamsters Union, a number that had remained unchanged since the beginning of unionization within the company. So far the company has had no strikes and only one lockout. The current HR managers agree that labour relations on the whole are still very good.

But the discontent caused by the last agreement has turned things upside down. Over the last three years there has been an increase in the number of grievances filed. Most of the grievances were about tighter management and fewer workers.

NEGOTIATION ON THE HORIZON

Given that the collective agreement was expiring in December of 2002, Labatt started negotiating with its various bargaining units in Quebec in the fall. The Montreal-area plant and delivery workers—traditionally the strongest unit—had always been the first unit to start the round of negotiations. This time around, however, the scenario has changed. Following a period of union raiding in July of 2002, the Montreal unit left the Teamsters Union and joined the ranks of the Confederation of National Trade Unions (CNTU) on February 28, 2003. The CNTU, it should be noted, is based primarily in Quebec and has always adopted a more confrontational and left-leaning stance than other labour unions. The Teamsters, for their part, prefer using a business approach.

The switch raised many questions. Not only does the employer have to face a brand-new union, but it also has to learn to work with a labour union whose philosophy is entirely different from that of its predecessor. In fact, this will be the very first collective agreement the CNTU negotiates with the brewing industry. Representation on the employer's side remains unchanged. Only one negotiator is appointed to conclude an agreement with all the unions, including the new one.

It is already understood that worker status (regular, temporary, casual) will be at the heart of the upcoming debates. Worker expectation on the issue is running very high, because many workers are still considered temporary despite having logged ten or so years of continuous service with the company. The aging of the worker population is a fact that will put the issue of early retirement back on the table.

Meanwhile, the employer has entered into an agreement with another large bargaining unit that could possibly pave the way for upcoming discussions. The agreement was conducted with the other union and was satisfactory for most of the distribution workers in the province. In fact, the final proposal received 93-percent approval. This new collective agreement has already come into effect and expires only in seven years. Under the agreement, many employees will retire over the next few months owing to improvements to the pension plan; consequently, the same number of temporary employees will receive permanent employee status.

Despite this happy ending, there are many unanswered questions. In particular, the company is unsure about the impact of the new situation over the near, medium, and long term. Will other units join the ranks of the CNTU? Will negotiations lead to a conflict during the summer season, which is somewhat of a peak season for the company? Will the agreement concluded with the first unit create a domino effect during upcoming negotiations? Given the atmosphere of uncertainty, management decides to send a memo to all employees to advise them of the new CNTU unit. The letter also describes the agreement with the unit belonging to the Teamsters Union and the main gains the employees made. The company also states its intention to step up production to increase inventory and thus avoid a shortage if a conflict should occur over the summer.

Questions

It is in this context that your consulting team is to conduct an analysis and issue recommendations on an appropriate communications and negotiation strategy to adopt in the near and long term.

To do this, you must

1. Briefly explain your understanding of Labatt's overall situation;
2. Establish a diagnosis of the challenges that Labatt is facing in the area of labour relations;
3. In light of the main challenges, formulate two to four possible strategies and the main obstacles to implementing them over the near term (2003), the medium term (four years), and the long term (seven years);
4. Propose and justify your action plan by presenting tangible solutions that are viable and consistent with Labatt's values.

GLOSSARY

9-box grid
A comparative diagram that includes appraisal and assessment data to allow managers to easily see an employee's actual and potential performance

A

achievement tests
Measures of what a person knows or can do right now

alarm reaction
Response to stress that basically involves an elevated heart rate, increased respiration, elevated levels of adrenaline in the blood, and increased blood pressure

alternative dispute resolution (ADR)
A term applied to different types of employee complaint or dispute resolution procedures

apprenticeship training
A system of training in which a worker entering the skilled trades is given thorough instruction and experience, both on and off the job, in the practical and theoretical aspects of the work

assessment centre
A process by which individuals are evaluated as they participate in a series of situations that resemble what they might be called on to handle on the job

attrition
A natural departure of employees from organizations through quits, retirements, and deaths

augmented skills
Skills helpful in facilitating the efforts of expatriate managers

authorization card
A statement signed by an employee authorizing a union to act as his or her representative for the purposes of collective bargaining

B

balanced scorecard (BSC)
A measurement framework that helps managers translate strategic goals into operational objectives

balance-sheet approach
A compensation system designed to match the purchasing power in a person's home country

bargaining power
The power of labour and management to achieve their goals through economic, social, or political influence

bargaining unit
Group of two or more employees who share common employment interests and conditions and may reasonably be grouped together for purposes of collective bargaining

bargaining zone
Area within which the union and the employer are willing to concede when bargaining

behaviour modelling
An approach that demonstrates desired behaviour and gives trainees the chance to practice and role-play those behaviours and receive feedback

behaviour modification
A technique that operates on the principle that behaviour that is rewarded, or positively reinforced, will be exhibited more frequently in the future, whereas behaviour that is penalized or unrewarded will decrease in frequency

behaviour observation scale (BOS)
A behavioural approach to performance appraisal that measures the frequency of observed behaviour

behavioural description interview (BDI)
An interview in which an applicant is asked questions about what he or she actually did in a given situation

behaviourally anchored rating scale (BARS)
A behavioural approach to performance appraisal that consists of a series of vertical scales, one for each important dimension of job performance

benchmarking
The process of comparing the organization's processes and practices with those of other companies

blended learning
The use of multiple training methods to achieve optimal learning on the part of trainees

bona fide occupational qualification (BFOQ)
A justifiable reason for discrimination based on business reasons of safety or effectiveness

bonus
An incentive payment that is supplemental to the base wage

burnout
Most severe stage of distress, manifesting itself in depression, frustration, and loss of productivity

business agent
Normally a paid labour official responsible for negotiating and administering the collective agreement and working to resolve union members' problems

C

calibration
A process whereby managers meet to discuss the performance of individual employees to ensure their employee appraisals are in line with one another

career counselling
The process of discussing with employees their current job activities and performance, personal and career interests and goals, personal skills, and suitable career development objectives

career networking
The process of establishing mutually beneficial relationships with other businesspeople, including potential clients and customers

career paths
Lines of advancement in an occupational field within an organization

career plateau
A situation in which, for either organizational or personal reasons, the probability of moving up the career ladder is low

chief ethics officer
A high-ranking manager directly responsible for fostering the ethical climate within the firm

chief learning officer
A high-ranking manager directly responsible for fostering employee learning and development within the firm

codetermination
Representation of labour on the board of directors of a company

collective agreement
An employment contract between an employer and a union that sets out the terms of employment of a group of the employer's employees represented by the union

collective bargaining process
Process of negotiating a collective agreement, including the use of economic pressures by both parties

combined salary and commission plan
A compensation plan that includes a straight salary and a commission

common law of employment
The body of case law in which courts interpret employment contracts, and the legal principles taken from those cases that guide the interpretation of employment contracts

compensatory model
A selection decision model in which a high score in one area can make up for a low score in another area

competence-based pay
Pay based on an employee's skill level, variety of skills possessed, or increased job knowledge

competency assessment
Analysis of the sets of skills and knowledge needed for decision-oriented and knowledge-intensive jobs

compulsory binding arbitration
Binding method of resolving collective bargaining deadlocks by a neutral third party

concentration
Term applied to designated groups whose numbers in a particular occupation or level are high relative to their numbers in the labour market

concurrent validity
The extent to which test scores (or other predictor information) match criterion obtained at about the same time from current employees

construct validity
The extent to which a selection tool measures a theoretical construct or trait

constructive dismissal
When an employer commits a fundamental breach of the contract, such as by unilaterally changing a key term of the contract, the employee can treat the breach as a termination

consumer price index (CPI)
A measure of the average change in prices over time in a fixed "market basket" of goods and services

content validity
The extent to which a selection instrument, such as a test, adequately samples the knowledge and skills needed to perform a particular job

contrast error
A performance rating error in which an employee's evaluation is biased either upward or downward because of comparison with another employee just previously evaluated

contributory plan
A pension plan in which contributions are made jointly by employees and employers

cooperative training
Training program that combines practical on-the-job experience with formal educational classes

core capabilities
Integrated knowledge sets within an organization that distinguish it from its competitors and deliver value to customers

core skills
Skills considered critical to an employee's success abroad

core values
The strong and enduring beliefs and principles that the company uses as a foundation for its decisions

corporate social responsibility
The responsibility of the firm to act in the best interests of the people and communities affected by its activities

craft unions
Unions that represent skilled craft workers

criterion-related validity
The extent to which a selection tool predicts, or significantly correlates with, important elements of work behaviour

critical incident
An unusual event that denotes superior or inferior employee performance in some part of the job

critical incident method
A job analysis method by which important job tasks are identified for job success

cross-training
The process of training employees to do multiple jobs within an organization

cross-validation
Verifying the results obtained from a validation study by administering a test or test battery to a different sample (drawn from the same population)

cultural audits
Audits of the culture and quality of work life in an organization

cultural environment
The communications, religion, values and ideologies, education, and social structure of a country

culture shock
Perpetual stress experienced by people who settle overseas

cumulative trauma disorders
Injuries involving tendons of the fingers, hands, and arms that become inflamed from repeated stresses and strains

customer appraisal
A performance appraisal that, like team appraisal, is based on TQM concepts and seeks evaluation from both external and internal customers

D

defined-benefit plan
A pension plan in which the amount an employee is to receive on retirement is specifically set forth

defined-contribution plan
A pension plan that establishes the basis on which an employer will contribute to the pension fund

depression
Negative emotional state marked by feelings of low spirits, gloominess, sadness, and loss of pleasure in ordinary activities

designated groups
Women, visible minorities, Aboriginal people, and persons with disabilities who have been disadvantaged in employment

differential piece rate
A compensation rate under which employees whose production exceeds the standard amount of output receive a

higher rate for all of their work than the rate paid to those who do not exceed the standard amount

discipline
(1) Treatment that punishes, (2) orderly behaviour in an organizational setting, or (3) training that moulds and strengthens desirable conduct—or corrects undesirable conduct—and develops self-control

distress
Harmful stress characterized by a loss of feelings of security and adequacy

diversity management
The optimization of an organization's multicultural workforce in order to reach business objectives

downsizing
Planned elimination of jobs

dual-career partnerships
Couples in which both members follow their own careers and actively support each other's career development

E

elder care
Care provided to an elderly relative by an employee who remains actively at work

e-learning
Learning that takes place via electronic media

employee assistance programs (EAPs)
Services provided by employers to help workers cope with a wide variety of problems that interfere with the way they perform their jobs

employee associations
Labour organizations that represent various groups of professional and white-collar employees in labour-management relations

employee empowerment
Granting employees power to initiate change, thereby encouraging them to take charge of what they do

employee involvement groups (EIs)
Groups of employees who meet to resolve problems or offer suggestions for organizational improvement

employee leasing
The process of dismissing employees who are then hired by a leasing company (which handles all HR-related activities)

and contracting with that company to lease back the employees

employee stock ownership plans (ESOPs)
Stock plans in which an organization contributes shares of its stock to an established trust for the purpose of stock purchases by employees

employee teams
An employee contributions technique whereby work functions are structured for groups rather than for individuals and team members are given discretion in matters traditionally considered management prerogatives, such as process improvements, product or service development, and individual work assignments

employment equity
The employment of individuals in a fair and nonbiased manner

entrepreneur
One who starts, organizes, manages, and assumes responsibility for a business or other enterprise

environmental scanning
Systematic monitoring of the major external forces influencing the organization

ergonomics
An interdisciplinary approach to designing equipment and systems that can be easily and efficiently used by human beings

error of central tendency
A performance rating error in which all employees are rated about average

escalator clauses
Clauses in collective agreements that provide for quarterly cost-of-living adjustments in wages, basing the adjustments on changes in the consumer price index

essay method
A trait approach to performance appraisal that requires the rater to compose a statement describing employee behaviour

ethics
A set of standards of conduct and moral judgments that help to determine right and wrong behaviour

eustress
Positive stress that accompanies achievement and exhilaration

expatriates, or home-country nationals
Employees from the home country who are on international assignment

external fit
The situation in which the work system supports the organization's goals and strategies

F

failure rate
The percentage of expatriates who do not perform satisfactorily

fast-track program
A program that encourages young managers with high potential to remain with an organization by enabling them to advance more rapidly than those with less potential

final offer arbitration
Method of resolving collective bargaining deadlocks whereby the arbitrator has no power to compromise but must select one or another of the final offers submitted by the two parties

flexible benefits plans (cafeteria plans)
Benefits plans that enable individual employees to choose the benefits that are best suited to their particular needs

flextime
Flexible working hours that permit employees the option of choosing daily starting and quitting times, provided that they work a set number of hours per day or week

flow data
Data that provide a profile of the employment decisions affecting designated groups

forced-choice method
A trait approach to performance appraisal that requires the rater to choose from statements designed to distinguish between successful and unsuccessful performance

G

gainsharing plans
Programs under which both employees and the organization share financial gains according to a predetermined formula that reflects improved productivity and profitability

global corporation
A firm that has integrated worldwide operations through a centralized home office

global manager
A manager equipped to run an international business

globalization
The trend toward opening up foreign markets to international trade and investment

graphic rating scale method
A trait approach to performance appraisal whereby each employee is rated according to a scale of characteristics

grievance procedure
Formal procedure that provides for the union to represent members and nonmembers in processing a grievance

guest workers
Foreign workers invited to perform needed labour

H

hay profile method
A job evaluation technique using three factors—knowledge, mental activity, and accountability—to evaluate executive and managerial positions

high-performance work system (HPWS)
A specific combination of HR practices, work structures, and processes that maximizes employee knowledge, skill, commitment, and flexibility

hiring freeze
A practice whereby new workers are not hired as planned, or workers who have left the organization are not replaced

home-based pay
Pay based on an expatriate's home country's compensation practices

host-based pay
Expatriate pay comparable to that earned by employees in a host country

host country
A country in which an international corporation operates

host-country nationals
Employees who are natives of the host country

hot-stove rule
A rule of discipline that can be compared with a hot stove in that it gives warning, is effective immediately, is enforced consistently, and applies to all employees in an impersonal and unbiased way

hourly work
Work paid on an hourly basis

human capital
The knowledge, skills, and capabilities of individuals that have economic value to an organization

human capital readiness
The process of evaluating the availability of critical talent in a company and comparing it to the firm's supply

human resources management (HRM)
The process of managing human talent to achieve an organization's objectives

human resources information system (HRIS)
A computerized system that provides current and accurate data for purposes of control and decision making

human resources planning (HRP)
The process of anticipating and providing for the movement of people into, within, and out of an organization

I

implied contract terms
Terms judges read into employment contracts when the written contract does not expressly deal with the matter

Improshare
A gainsharing program under which bonuses are based on the overall productivity of the work team

industrial disease
A disease resulting from exposure to a substance relating to a particular process, trade, or occupation in industry

industrial engineering
A field of study concerned with analyzing work methods and establishing time standards

industrial unions
Unions that represent all workers—skilled, semiskilled, unskilled—employed along industry lines

instructional objectives
Desired outcomes of a training program

interest arbitrator
Third-party neutral who resolves labour dispute by issuing a final decision in the disagreement

interest-based bargaining (IBB)
Problem-solving bargaining based on a win–win philosophy and the development of a positive long-term relationship

internal fit
The situation in which all the internal elements of the work system complement and reinforce one another

international corporation
A domestic firm that uses its existing capabilities to move into overseas markets

internship programs
Programs jointly sponsored by colleges, universities, and other organizations that offer students the opportunity to gain real-life experience while allowing them to find out how they will perform in work organizations

J

job
A group of related activities and duties

job analysis
The process of obtaining information about jobs by determining the duties, tasks, or activities of jobs

job characteristics model
A job design theory that purports that three psychological states (experiencing meaningfulness of the work performed, responsibility for the work performed, knowledge of the results of the work performed) of a jobholder result in improved work performance, internal motivation, and lower absenteeism and turnover

job classification system
A system of job evaluation in which jobs are classified and grouped according to a series of predetermined wage grades

job description
A statement of the tasks, duties, and responsibilities of a job to be performed

job design
An outgrowth of job analysis that improves jobs through technological and human considerations in order to enhance organization efficiency and employee job satisfaction

job enrichment
Enhancing a job by adding more meaningful tasks and duties to make the work more rewarding or satisfying

job evaluation
A systematic process of determining the relative worth of jobs in order to establish which jobs should be paid more than others within an organization

job family
A group of individual jobs with similar characteristics

job posting and bidding
Posting vacancy notices and maintaining lists of employees looking for upgraded positions

job progressions
The hierarchy of jobs a new employee might experience, ranging from a starting job to jobs that successively require more knowledge and/or skill

job ranking system
The simplest and oldest system of job evaluation by which jobs are arrayed on the basis of their relative worth

job sharing
The arrangement whereby two part-time employees perform a job that otherwise would be held by one full-time employee

job specification
A statement of the needed knowledge, skills, and abilities of the person who is to perform the job

just-in-time training
Training delivered to trainees when and where they need it to do their jobs, usually via computer or the Internet

K

knowledge workers
Workers whose responsibilities extend beyond the physical execution of work to include planning, decision making, and problem solving

L

labour arbitrator
A person assigned to interpret and decide disputes ("grievances") about the meaning, interpretation, and application of a collective agreement governing employees in a unionized workplace

labour relations process
Logical sequence of four events: (1) workers desire collective representation, (2) union begins its organizing campaign, which may lead to certification and recognition, (3) collective negotiations lead to a contract, and (4) the contract is administered

learning management system (LMS)
Online system that provides a variety of assessment, communication, teaching, and learning opportunities

leniency or strictness error
A performance rating error in which the appraiser tends to give employees either unusually high or unusually low ratings

localization
Adapting pay and other compensation benefits to match that of a particular country

lump-sum merit program
Program under which employees receive a year-end merit payment, which is not added to their base pay

M

management by objectives (MBO)
A philosophy of management that rates performance on the basis of employee achievement of goals set by mutual agreement of employee and manager

management forecasts
The opinions (judgments) of supervisors, department managers, experts, or others knowledgeable about the organization's future employment needs

management rights
Decisions regarding organizational operations over which management claims exclusive rights

manager and/or supervisor appraisal
A performance appraisal done by an employee's manager and often reviewed by a manager one level higher

managing diversity
Being aware of characteristics common to employees, while also managing employees as individuals

Markov analysis
A method for tracking the pattern of employee movements through various jobs

Material Safety Data Sheets (MSDSs)
Documents that contain vital information about hazardous substances

mediation
The use of an impartial neutral to reach a compromise decision in employment disputes

mediator
A third party in an employment dispute who meets with one party and then the other in order to suggest compromise solutions or to recommend concessions from each side that will lead to an agreement

mentors
Individuals who coach, advise, and encourage individuals of lesser rank

merit guidelines
Guidelines for awarding merit raises that are tied to performance objectives

mission
The basic purpose of the organization as well as its scope of operations

mixed-standard scale method
A trait approach to performance appraisal similar to other scale methods but based on comparison with (better than, equal to, or worse than) a standard

multinational corporation (MNC)
A firm with independent business units operating in multiple countries

multiple cutoff model
A selection-decision model that requires an applicant to achieve some minimum level of proficiency on all selection dimensions

multiple hurdle model
A sequential strategy in which only the applicants with the highest scores at an initial test stage go on to subsequent stages

N

nepotism
A preference for hiring relatives of current employees

noncontributory plan
A pension plan in which contributions are made solely by the employer

nondirective interview
An interview in which the applicant's allowed the maximum amount of freedom in determining the course of the discussion,

while the interviewer carefully refrains from influencing the applicant's remarks

O

occupational illness
Any abnormal condition or disorder, other than one resulting from an occupational injury, caused by exposure to environmental factors associated with employment

occupational injury
Any cut, fracture, sprain, or amputation resulting from a workplace accident or from an exposure involving an accident in the work environment

offshoring
The business practice of sending jobs to other countries

ombudsperson
A designated individual from whom employees may seek counsel for resolution of their complaints

on-the-job training (OJT)
A method by which employees are given hands-on experience with instructions from their supervisor or other trainer

open-door policy
A policy of settling grievances that identifies various levels of management above the immediate supervisor for employee contact

organization analysis
Examination of the environment, strategies, and resources of the organization to determine where training emphasis should be placed

organizational capability
The capacity of the organization to act and change in pursuit of sustainable competitive advantage

orientation
The formal process of familiarizing new employees with the organization, their jobs, and their work units

outplacement services
Services provided by organizations to help terminated employees find a new job

outsourcing
Contracting outside the organization to have work done that formerly was done by internal employees

P

panel interview
An interview in which a board of interviewers questions and observes a single candidate

pay equity
An employee's perception that compensation received is equal to the value of the work performed

pay-for-performance standard
A standard by which managers tie compensation to employee effort and performance

pay grades
Groups of jobs within a particular class that are paid the same rate

peer appraisal
A performance appraisal done by one's fellow employees, generally on forms that are compiled into a single profile for use in the performance interview conducted by the employee's manager

peer-review system
A system for reviewing employee complaints that utilizes a group composed of equal numbers of employee representatives and management appointees, which functions as a jury because its members weigh evidence, consider arguments, and, after deliberation, vote independently to render a final decision

performance appraisal
A process, typically performed annually by a supervisor for a subordinate, designed to help employees understand their roles, objectives, expectations, and performance success

performance management
The process of creating a work environment in which people can perform to the best of their abilities

perquisites
Special nonmonetary benefits given to executives; often referred to as perks

person analysis
Determination of the specific individuals who need training

piecework
Work paid according to the number of units produced

point system
A quantitative job evaluation procedure that determines the relative value of a job by the total points assigned to it

position
The different duties and responsibilities performed by only one employee

position analysis questionnaire (PAQ)
A questionnaire covering 194 different tasks that, by means of a five-point scale, seeks to determine the degree to which different tasks are involved in performing a particular job

positive, or nonpunitive, discipline
A system of discipline that focuses on early correction of employee misconduct, with the employee taking total responsibility for correcting the problem

predictive validity
The extent to which applicants' test scores match criterion data obtained from those applicants/employees after they have been on the job for some indefinite period

proactive change
Change initiated to take advantage of targeted opportunities

process audit
Determining whether the high-performance work system has been implemented as designed

profit sharing
Any procedure by which an employer pays, or makes available to all regular employees, in addition to base pay, special current or deferred sums based on the profits of the enterprise

progressive discipline
Application of corrective measures by increasing degrees

promotion
A change of assignment to a job at a higher level in the organization

R

reactive change
Change that occurs after external forces have already affected performance

real wages
Wage increases larger than rises in the consumer price index, that is, the real earning power of wages

realistic job preview (RJP)
Informing applicants about all aspects of the job, including both its desirable and undesirable facets

reasonable accommodation
Attempt by employers to adjust the working conditions or schedules of employees with disabilities or religious preferences

recency error
A performance rating error in which the appraisal is based largely on the employee's most recent behaviour rather than on behaviour throughout the appraisal period

red circle rates
Payment rates above the maximum of the pay range

reengineering
Fundamental rethinking and radical redesign of business processes to achieve dramatic improvements in cost, quality, service, and speed

reliability
The degree to which interviews, tests, and other selection procedures yield comparable data over time and alternative measures

relocation services
Services provided to an employee who is transferred to a new location, which might include help in moving, selling a home, orienting to a new culture, and/or learning a new language

repatriation
The process of employee transition home from an international assignment

replacement charts
Listings of current jobholders and people who are potential replacements if an opening occurs

rights arbitration
Arbitration over interpretation of the meaning of contract terms or employee work grievances

S

salary plus bonus plan
A compensation plan that pays a salary plus a bonus achieved by reaching targeted sales goals.

Scanlon Plan
A bonus incentive plan using employee and management committees to gain cost-reduction improvements

selection
The process of choosing individuals who have relevant qualifications to fill existing or projected job openings

selection ratio
The number of applicants compared with the number of people to be hired

self-appraisal
A performance appraisal done by the employee being evaluated, generally on an appraisal form completed by the employee prior to the performance interview

severance pay
A lump-sum payment given to terminated employees

severance pay
A lump-sum payment given to terminated employees by an employer at the time of an employer-initiated termination

sexual harassment
Unwelcome advances, requests for sexual favours, and other verbal or physical conduct of a sexual nature in the working environment

silver handshake
An early retirement incentive in the form of increased pension benefits for several years or a cash bonus

similar-to-me error
A performance rating error in which an appraiser inflates the evaluation of an employee because of a mutual personal connection

situational interview
An interview in which an applicant is given a hypothetical incident and asked how he or she would respond to it

Six Sigma
A process used to translate customer needs into a set of optimal tasks that are performed in concert with one another

skill inventories
Files of personnel education, experience, interests, skills, and so on that allow managers to quickly match job openings with employee backgrounds

split pay
A system whereby expatriates are given a portion of their pay in the local currency to cover their day-to-day expenses and a portion of their pay in their home currency to safeguard their earnings from changes in inflation or foreign exchange rates

spot bonus
An unplanned bonus given for employee effort unrelated to an established performance measure

spot rewards
Programs that award employees "on the spot" when they do something particularly well during training or on the job

staffing tables
Graphic representations of all organizational jobs, along with the numbers of employees currently occupying those jobs and future (monthly or yearly) employment requirements

standard hour plan
An incentive plan that sets rates based on the completion of a job in a predetermined standard time

statutory rights
Legal entitlements that derive from government legislation

step-review system
A system for reviewing employee complaints and disputes by successively higher levels of management

stock data
Data showing the status of designated groups in occupational categories and compensation levels

straight commission plan
A compensation plan based on a percentage of sales

straight piecework
An incentive plan under which employees receive a certain rate for each unit produced

straight salary plan
A compensation plan that permits salespeople to be paid for performing various duties that are not reflected immediately in their sales volume

strategic human resources management (SHRM)
The pattern of human resources deployments and activities that enable an organization to achieve its strategic goals

strategic planning
Procedures for making decisions about the organization's long-term goals and strategies

strategic vision
A statement about where the company is going and what it can become in the future; clarifies the long-term direction of the company and its strategic intent

stress
Any adjustive demand caused by physical, mental, or emotional factors that require coping behaviour

structured interview
An interview in which a set of standardized questions having an established set of answers is used

subordinate appraisal
A performance appraisal of a superior by an employee, which is more appropriate for developmental than for administrative purposes

succession planning
The process of identifying, developing, and tracking key individuals for executive positions

summary dismissal
When a nonunion employer terminates an employee without notice because the employee has committed a serious breach of the contract

systemic discrimination
The exclusion of members of certain groups through the application of employment policies or practices based on criteria that are not job related

T

task analysis
The process of determining what the content of a training program should be on the basis of a study of the tasks and duties involved in the job

task inventory analysis
An organization-specific list of tasks and their descriptions used as a basis to identify components of jobs

team appraisal
A performance appraisal, based on TQM concepts, that recognizes team accomplishment rather than individual performance

team incentive plan
A compensation plan in which all team members receive an incentive bonus payment when production or service standards are met or exceeded

telecommuting
Use of personal computers, networks, and other communications technology to do work in the home that is traditionally done in the workplace

termination
Practice initiated by an employer to separate an employee from the organization permanently

third-country nationals
Employees who are natives of a country other than the home country or the host country

total quality management (TQM)
A set of principles and practices whose core ideas include understanding customer needs, doing things right the first time, and striving for continuous improvement

transfer
Placement of an individual in another job for which the duties, responsibilities, status, and remuneration are approximately equal to those of the previous job

transfer of training
Effective application of principles learned to what is required on the job

transnational corporation
A firm that attempts to balance local responsiveness and global scale via a network of specialized operating units

transnational teams
Teams composed of members of multiple nationalities working on projects that span multiple countries

trend analysis
A quantitative approach to forecasting labour demand based on an organizational index such as sales

U

underutilization
Term applied to designated groups that are not utilized or represented in the employer's workforce proportional to their numbers in the labour market

unfair labour practices (ULPs)
Specific employer and union illegal practices that deny employees their rights and benefits under federal and provincial labour law

union shop
Provision of the collective agreement that requires employees to join the union as a condition of their employment

union (shop) steward
Employee who as a nonpaid union official represents the interests of members in their relations with management

V

validity
The degree to which a test or selection procedure measures a person's attributes

validity generalization
The extent to which validity coefficients can be generalized across situations

value creation
What the firm adds to a product or service by virtue of making it; the amount of benefits provided by the product or service once the costs of making it are subtracted

variable pay
Tying pay to some measure of individual, group, or organizational performance

vesting
A guarantee of accrued benefits to participants at retirement age, regardless of their employment status at the time

virtual team
A team with widely dispersed members linked together through computer and telecommunications technology

W

wage and salary survey
A survey of the wages paid to employees of other employers in the surveying organization's relevant labour market

wage curve
A curve in a scattergram representing the relationship between relative worth of jobs and wage rates

wage-rate compression
Compression of differentials between job classes, particularly the differential between hourly workers and their managers

work permit or visa
A government document granting a foreign individual the right to seek employment

work valuation
A job evaluation system that seeks to measure a job's worth through its value to the organization

workers' compensation insurance
Insurance provided to workers to defray the loss of income and cost of treatment resulting from work-related injuries or illness

wrongful dismissal
A lawsuit filed in a court by an employee alleging that he or she was dismissed without proper contractual or "reasonable" notice

Y

yield ratio
The percentage of applicants from a recruitment source that make it to the next stage of the selection process

NAME INDEX

A

Abosch, Ken, 406
Argyris, Chris, 153
Arian, Mark, 19
Avalos, Alison, 412
Averbook, Jason, 262

B

Balkin, George, 399
Bardwick, Judith, 195
Barksdale, Jim, 156
Bascomb, Andrea, 82
Batten, Brenda, 168–169
Benimadhu, Prem, 124
Bennett, Debbie, 566
Bernier, Sandy, 428
Bethune, Gordon, 69
Black, Conrad, 306
Blake, Gary, 16
Blanc, Manon, 490
Blanfein, Lloyd C., 420
Bolles, Richard N., 198
Boniferro, Paul, 424
Bontis, Nick, 8
Boswell, Greg, 412, 414
Bower, Joseph, 178
Brakon, Lois, 159
Bray, Douglas, 186
Broedling, Laurie, 15
Buckman, Robert, 13
Buckner, Marilyn, 12
Budnick, Peter, 154

C

Cates, David, 418
Chean, Erica, 248
Chenault, Kenneth I., 420
Chu, Elaine, 375
Clapman, Peter, 420
Cope, George, 419
Craig, Randall, 221

D

Dart, Beatrix, 125
Deming, W. Edwards, 14, 301
Dhesi, Arvinder, 14

Ding, Bill, 82
Drucker, Peter F., 217, 420
Duff, Calvin, 82
Duff, Michael, 35–36
Durack, Deena, 5

E

Eaton, Martin, 168–169

F

Fairbanks, Richard, 83
Fitzenz, Jac, 76
Florida, Richard, 8
Folkman, Joseph, 335
Foot, David, 50, 51
Francis, Lori, 485
Frank, Evelyn, 83
Fuld, Richard S., Jr., 420

G

Gallant, Eleanor, 567
Gates, David, 418
Gentry, Tyler, 414
Gilbert, Tara, 434–435
Glocer, Thomas, 419
Goodman, Cheryl, 261–263
Green, Bill, 36
Gretzky, Wayne, 80
Gross, Ronald, 349
Gross, Stephen E., 372
Gross, Steven, 422
Gubman, Ed, 4

H

Haccoun, Robert, 273
Hackman, Richard, 151
Hagen, Sue, 86
Haimovitz, Randi, 315
Hall, Douglas, 220
Haltrecht, Ed, 334
Hay, Edward N., 385
Hedge, Alan, 154
Hemphill, Barbara, 162
Herzberg, Frederick, 150
Hirji, Zabeen, 130

Hoffman, Sandra, 11
Holland, John, 198, 219
Hubbard, L. Ron, 274
Huselid, Mark, 77
Hyson, Ron, 72

I

Irani, Ray R., 420

J

Jesuthasan, Ravin, 370
Jobs, Steve, 11
Johnson, Gayle, 297

K

Kanter, Rosabeth Moss, 11
Kaplan, Robert, 65
Keays, 543
Kelloway, Kevin, 485, 490
Kerr, Steve, 354
Krumboltz, John D., 198

L

Lafley, Alan, 11–12
Lai, Gene, 241
Latham, Gary, 337
Lawrence, Aloma, 115
Lesitner, Jeff, 434
Levin, Al S., 198
Levitt, Howard, 520
Levy, Leah, 116
Lewenza, Ken, 379
Lincoln, J. F., 426
Lowenza, Ken, 579
Lynch, Merrill, 420

M

Maier, Norman R. F., 350
McCann, Laurie, 338
McGilvrey, Jack, 338
McKay, Dawn Rosenberg, 220
Mentzer, Mark, 107
Montgomery, James, 485
Moore, Gordon, 13

N

Norton, David, 65

O

Oldham, Greg, 151
Omana, Nov, 261–262
Ouellet, Simon, 543

P

Peacock, Tina, 254
Perkins, Katie, 398, 399
Perrin, Towers, 418
Platt, Lew, 13
Pritchard, Robert, 434

Q

Quinn, James Brian, 50

R

Radjou, Navi, 159
Randle, Frances, 196
Rekar-Munro, Carolin, 287
Roberts, David, 312
Rochon, Robert, 108
Ronen, Simcha, 602
Rosen, Hjalmar, 564

Ruiz, Gina, 263
Ryan, Dave L., 119

S

Saks, Alan, 273
Sallot, J., 265
Sammer, Joanne, 408
Sasaki, Virginia, 148
Schuyler, Matthew, 84–85
Sejen, Lauren, 412
Sheedy, James, 488
Shenkar, Oded, 602
Smilko, Jessica, 406
Spinks, Nora, 28, 163
Stagner, Ross, 564
Steckerl, Shally, 262–263
Steiner, Jo, 125
Stern, Brian, 262
Sullivan, Linda, 393
Sullivan, Stacy, 138

T

Tapscott, Dan, 8
Taylor, Andrea, 211–212
Tellier, Marie, 123
Tétrault, McCarthy, 424
Thain, John A., 420
Tichenor, Paulette, 159
Tierro, Annbel, 36

Traynor, Jason, 36–37
Tremblay, Linda, 399

U

Ulrich, David, 13–14

V

Van Neck, Kathy, 406
Vashistha, Atul, 19
Verioti, Betty, 619
Verioti, Jim, 619

W

Walker, James, 45
Ware, Edgar, 123
Watson, Thomas J., 4
Weatherbee, Don, 142
Welch, Jack, 13
Wexle, Kenneth, 337
Wise, Ben, 594
Wismer, Janice, 334
Wyatt, Watson, 385

Y

Young, John, 590

Z

Zenger, John, 335

ORGANIZATION INDEX

A

Accenture, 35–36, 50
Ad Traffic, 211
Adaptable Software, 211
Aetna Life and Casualty, 28
AFL-CIO, 558
Air Canada, 73, 125, 140, 448
Air Canada Jazz, 140
Airbus, 292
Alberta Teachers Association, 558
All-China Federation of Trade
    Unions, 614
Alliance Data Systems Corporation, 212
Allstate Insurance, 274
Amazon.com, 45, 185
American Airlines, 152
American Association of Industrial
    Management, 382, 383f
American Association of Retired Persons
    (AARP), 338
American Express, 338
American Express Canada, 502
American Society for Training and
    Development, 274, 301
Anheuser Busch, 584
Apple Computer, 11, 69, 426
Asia-Pacific Economic Cooperation
    (APEC), 7, 586
Association of Southeast Asian Nations
    (ASEAN), 586
Association of Workers' Compensation
    Boards of Canada, 474
AstraZeneca, 14
AT&T, 186, 247, 462
Avenor, 339
Aviva, 14
Avon Foods, 304

B

BAE Systems, 286
Bank of America, 6
Bank of Montreal, 123, 362
Bata Shoe Company, 178
The Bay and Zellers, 25, 48, 254
B.C. Hydro, 119
BCE, 419
Bell Canada, 295, 314–315, 394

Best Buy, 324
BHP Ekati Diamond Mine, 23
Black & Decker, 329
Blackhawk Aironics, 468
BMO Financial Group, 124, 205, 245
BMW, 6
BMW Canada, 332
Boeing, 292, 592
Boeing Satellite Systems, 14
Bosch, 614
Boston Global Consulting, 589
British Airways, 589
British Columbia, Office of
    the Auditor, 54
British Columbia Civil Liberties
    Union, 236
British Columbia Government and
    Services Employees
    Union, 131
British Columbia Ministry of
    Forestry, 131
Brock University, 211
Buckman Laboratories, 13
Burger King, 371
Burrard Products Terminal, 502

C

Calgary Health Region, 444
Cambior, 621
Cameco Corporation, 111
Canada Industrial Relations Board
    (CIRB), 548–549
Canada Post Corporation, 394, 400
Canadian Armed Forces, 119, 292, 495
Canadian Auto Workers (CAW), 380,
    553, 555, 557, 576, 579
Canadian Centre for Occupational
    Health and Safety, 166, 491
Canadian Civil Liberties
    Association, 253
Canadian Coalition for Good
    Governance, 419
Canadian Employment Lawyers
    Network, 516
Canadian Health Care Anti-Fraud
    Association, 449
Canadian HR Reporter, 233, 441

Canadian Human Rights Commission,
    121–122, 241, 252–253
Canadian Human Rights Tribunal,
    118, 394
Canadian Initiative on Workplace
    Violence, 492
Canadian Labour and Business Centre
    (CLBC), 502
Canadian Labour Congress (CLC),
    558, 559, 560
Canadian Labour Law Project, 519
Canadian Nurses Association, 58
Canadian Pacific, 138
Canadian Pacific Hotels, 138
Canadian Security Intelligence Service
    (CSIS), 264–265
Canadian Society for Training and
    Development, 272
Canadian Tire Corporation,
    334–336, 429
Canadian Union of Postal Workers,
    525, 558
Canadian Union of Public Employees
    (CUPE), 416, 559, 560, 567
Capital One, 83–85
Career Edge, 196
CareerBuilder.com, 218, 231, 246–247
Catalyst, 204
Caterpillar, 218, 294
Caterpillar University of Leadership, 294
Centre de recherche industrielle du
    Quebec (CRIQ), 110
Charles Schwab and Company, 70
Chateau Whistler, B.C., 311
Chemico, 63
China Europe International Business
    School (CEIBS), 601
Chrysler, 379, 380, 555, 579
Church of Scientology, 274
CIBC, 456, 461, 504
Cigna, 329
Citigroup, 610
City of Calgary, 138
City of Charlottetown, 305, 567
City of Mississauga, 378
City of Regina, 444
City of Regina Transit
    Department, 502

City of Richmond, 119
City of Toronto, 114, 123, 449
City of Waterloo, 234
CN, 123, 175
CN Centre for Occupational Health and Safety, 484, 490
CNA Financial Corp., 44
Coca-Cola, 305, 426, 589
Cold Metal Products, 458
Colgate-Palmolive, 597, 603, 606
Commission de la Santé et de la Sécurité du Travail, 475
Communication Energy & Paperworkers, 566
Communications Workers of America, 568
Compaq Computer, 154
Compass Group, 109
CONEXUS, 296, 297
Conference Board of Canada, 6, 124, 132, 272, 300, 380, 385, 446
Connaught Laboratories, 125
Conservation International, 608
Consumers Gas, 456
Continental Airlines, 69
Coopers & Lybrand, 295, 421, 444
Cornell University, 154
Corning, Inc., 9–10, 60
Credit Union Central of Saskatchewan, 313

D

Dalhousie University, 446
Dell Computer, 247, 332, 584
Deloitte & Touche, 21, 598
Department of Labour and Workforce Development, 475
Dexter, 72
Digital Equipment of Canada, 123
Disney, 52, 329
Dofasco, 502
Dole Food Company, 85–86
Dow Chemical, 14, 15, 597, 601, 606
Drake Beam Morin, 197
Ducks Unlimited, 138, 167–168
Durham College, Ontario, 287

E

East Asia Economic Group, 586
Ebco, 123
École Polytechnique de Paris, 588
Economy Carriers, 482
EDS, 142, 324, 598
Edwards School of Business, 107
Electronic Data Systems, 291
Enbridge, 52

EnCana, 287
Enron, 233
ErgoWeb, Inc., 154
ESOP Association Canada, 429
European Trade Union Confederation (ETUC), 615
ExxonMobil, 600, 605

F

Fair Trade, 608
Fairmont Hotels and Resorts Inc., 246
Families and Work Institute, 159
Fantom Technologies, 543
FAO Schwartz, 48
Federal Business Development Bank, 399
Federation of Quebec Nurses, 558
FedEx, 52, 53, 69, 156, 298, 332, 489
FedEx Kinko's, 247
First Nations University, 110
Ford Motor Company, 14, 15, 31, 116, 152, 178, 286, 326, 328, 337, 563, 585
Four Seasons Hotels, 52, 69, 590, 591, 592
Fuji-Xerox, 595

G

Gallup Polls, 246
General Electric, 13, 14, 45, 53, 67, 185, 193, 200, 274, 278, 337, 354, 584, 586, 595
General Motors (GM), 36–37, 72–73, 189, 326, 379, 380, 555, 563, 579, 586
Genpact, 181
Glaxo Pharmaceuticals, 417
Goldman Sachs, 420
Goodyear, 15, 16, 326, 328, 337, 338
Google, 45, 138
Graphic Communications Union (GCU), 566
Great West Life Insurance Company, 460

H

H. J. Heinz Company, 300
Harley-Davidson, 149–150
Harvard Business School, 178
Hay Management Associates, 313, 385, 422
Heineken, 596
Hershey, 479
Hewitt Associates LLC, 19, 28, 385, 406, 421
Hewlett-Packard, 13, 156, 280, 307, 490
Hilton Hotels, 247
Hinderliter Energy Equipment, 425

Holt Renfrew, 69
Home Depot, 434
Home Depot Canada, Inc., 11, 22, 152
Honda, 380, 543, 584
Honeywell Limited, 14, 307, 390, 442
Hudson's Bay Company. *See* The Bay and Zellers
Human Resource Professional, 441
Human Resource Professional Association (HRPA), 5, 180, 212
Human Resource Professionals Association of Ontario, 386, 506, 543, 566
Human Resources and Skills Development Canada (HRSDC), 180
Human Resources and Social Development Canada, 449
Human Resources Development Canada, 108
Husky Injection Molding Systems, 459, 494

I

IBM, 4, 9, 45, 50, 53, 66–67, 158, 199, 202, 205, 274, 329, 329, 455, 462, 568
Ikea, 588
Imperial Oil, 125
InBevs, 584
Indigo, 45
Industrial Accident Prevention Association, 504
ING, 584
Ingersoll-Rand, 591
Inn at Manitou, 594
Intel, 13, 66, 328, 333, 586
IntelligentHire, 247
International Association of Iron Workers, 558
International Confederation of Free Trade Unions (ICFTU), 615
International Labour Organization (ILO), 615
International Olympic Committee (IOC), 537
Intuit Canada, 227, 302, 303, 462
Irving Paper, 502
ITT, 584

J

JobMachine, 262
Journal of American Medical Association, 487

K

KB Toys, 48
KLM Royal Dutch Airlines, 286
Knowledge Infusion, 262
Korn/Ferry International, 178, 593
KPMG, 205
Kraft Foods, 152

L

L. L. Bean, 17, 76
Labour Canada, 487
Lafarge Canada, 448
Law Society of Upper Canada, 109
Lawson Software, 328
Lazarus Department Stores, 303
Lehman Brothers, 420
Lenovo, 67
Levi Strauss & Co., 126, 254, 354, 596
Life Insurance Agency Management Association, 233
Lincoln Electric Company, 426
Loblaws, 26, 183
Lombard Canada, 428
London Health Sciences Centre, 489
L'Oreal, 248, 248f, 295
LoyaltyOne, 212–213
LucasFilm, 156
Lucent Technologies, 589

M

Macy's, 303
Magna International, 119, 554, 555
Manpower Inc., 9, 181
Manulife, 419
MAPICS, 11
Marriott, 21, 295
Matsushira, 585
McCarthy Tétrault, 524
McDonald's Restaurants of Canada, 22, 52, 68
Mediacorp, 125
Mercer Human Resources Consulting, 385
Mercer Management Consulting, 380
Mercer Performance, Measurement, and Rewards, 372
Merck, 9, 10, 31, 277
Merrill Lynch, 420
Microsoft Corporation, 52, 66, 193, 370, 429
Ministry of Labour, 475
Molson Breweries, 463
Monsanto, 284, 606
Monster.ca, 25, 202, 218, 260, 380
Motorola, 14, 15, 277, 295, 322, 600

N

National Bank of Canada, 124, 125
National Career Centers, 247
National Center for Employee Ownership, 427
National City Corp., 247, 261–263
National Council of Visible Minorities, 205
National Grocer Company, 108
National Hockey League Players Association, 569
National Institute of Disability Management and Research, 480
National Union of Public and General Employees (NUPGE), 560
National Wellness program, 494
Navistar, 579
NBC, 67
NEC, 585
Netscape Communications, 156
Network Cable Inc., 434
Newspaper Guild, 566
Nike, 247, 426, 607–608
Nissan, 551
Nokia, 159
Nortel Networks, 123, 390
North Shore Health Region, 183
Nova Scotia Community College, 72, 288
Nova Scotia Human Rights Commission, 236
Novapharm, 478–479

O

Occidental Petroleum, 420
Occupational Health and Safety Council (OHSC), 475
Office and Professional Employees International Union, 558
Ontario Human Rights Commission, 264
Ontario Hydro, 74, 461
Ontario Labour Relations Board (OLRB), 578
Ontario Pay Equity Commission, 393
Ontario Power Generation (OPG), 505
Ontario Society for Training and Development, 273
Oracle-PeopleSoft, 61
Organizational Renaissance, 159
Ottawa Citizen, 566

P

Pace Worldwide, 306
PageNet, 149–150
Palliser's Furniture, 304
Pan Canadian Petroleum, 441
Payless ShoeSource, 235
PeopleSoft, 185
Peregrine, Inc., 36–37
Performance Sports, 399
Petro-Canada, 502
Petroleos de Venezuela, 600
Philips, 584
Pic 'n Pay Shoe Stores, 247
Pinetree Advisors, 221
Plum Creek Timber Company, 372
Polaroid, 456
Police Association of Nova Scotia (PANS), 567
The Portables, 18
Pratt & Whitney, 111, 154
Preventive Health Care, 376, 377
PricewaterhouseCoopers, 76, 307
Proctor & Gamble, 12, 13, 18, 184–185, 199, 322, 482, 584
Professional Institute of the Public Service of Canada (PIPS), 561
Province of Alberta, 382
Prudential Grand Valley Reality, 242
Public Service Alliance of Canada (PSAC), 394, 560
Public Service Commission of Canada (PSC), 115, 238
Public Service Commission of the Yukon Government, 459, 460

Q

Quaker Oats, 426
Queen's University, 490
Qwest, 161

R

Radisson Hotels, 247
Ray Bernstein, 178
RBC Financial Group, 130, 152, 183, 277, 442
Red River College, Winnipeg, 286
Re/Max Company, 248
Research In Motion, 584
Retirement Council of Canada, 456
Reuters, 6
Ritz Carlton, 272
Roffey Park research institute, 12
Rogers Communications, Inc., 18
Rotman School of Management, 125

Royal Bank of Canada (RBC), 25, 446
Royal Canadian Mounted Police (RCMP), 235, 264
Royal Dutch Shell, 52
Royal Oak Mine, 567
Rypple, 361

S

Saint Mary's University, 484
SAP, 61, 185
Sara Lee, 426
Saratoga Institute, 76
Sarip International, 619
Sask Tel, 273
Saskatchewan Labour, 475
Saskatchewan Wheat Pool, 108
Schering-Plough, 462
Scotiabank, 108, 584
Seagulls Pewter and Silversmiths, 274
Sears, 51, 119, 190–191, 419, 429
Selection Protection Services, 232
Seven Oaks Hospital, Winnipeg, 502
Shaker Consulting, 262, 263
Shell International, 584, 585
SimuLearn, 296
Singapore Airlines, 292
SkyCable, 118
SNC-Lavalin, 123
Snecma, 596
Sobeys, 236
Social Science Employees Association (SSEA), 561
Society for Human Resource Management, 538
Solar Turbines, 598
South Asian Association for Regional Cooperation (SAARC), 586
Southern Alberta Institute of Technology, 287
Southwest Airlines, 52, 292
Spencer Stuart, 593
Standard & Poor, 418
Star Data Systems, 378
Starbucks, 52, 77, 426, 557, 608
Statistics Canada, 22, 24, 27, 50, 97, 112, 375, 376, 380
Steelcase, 241
Stelco, 448
SumTotal Systems, 303
Sun Life Assurance Company, 480
Sunnybrook and Women's College Health Sciences Centre, 125, 489
Syncor Canada, 253

T

Taco Bell, 371
TD Bank Financial Group, 6, 300
Teamsters, 552, 568
Techno-Graph, 211
Teck Cominco Ltd., 485
Tele-Direct, 211
TELUS, 494
Teva Global Group, 478, 479
Teva Pharmaceuticals, 478
Texas Instruments, 13
Thinking Tools, 295
Thomson Reuters, 419
3M Company, 326
TIAA-CREF, 420
The Timber Company, 372
Toronto Police Force, 114
Toronto Star, 434
Towers Perrin, 370, 418
Toyota Motor, 19–20, 380, 586
Toys "R" Us, 48
TransAlta Corporation, 440
TransAmerica Corporation, 461
Travellers Corporation, 462
Tri Star Performance, 376, 377
True North Consulting Services (TNCS), 468–469
Tyco, 233

U

Unilever, 585
United Association of Plumbers and Pipefitters, 558
United Auto Workers, 551, 552, 558, 563
United Brotherhood of Carpenters, 552, 558
United Food and Commercial Workers Union, 568, 579
United Steelworkers of America, 552, 558
United Steelworkers of Ontario, 578
Université de Montréal, 273
University of Michigan, 14
University of New Brunswick (UNB), 453
University of Pennsylvania, 446
University of Saskatchewan, 107
University of Toronto, 8, 51, 273, 337
University of Victoria, 131
UPS, 489

UPS Canada, 31
U.S. Air Force, 145

V

Verizon, 568
Victoria Tea Company, Ontario, 118
Virtual Job Tryout, 261
Volker Stevin, 480
Volkswagen, 533, 534, 601

W

Walmart Stores, 48, 185, 274, 554, 578–579
Warner-Lambert, 123
Watson Wyatt Worldwide, 17, 322, 385, 400, 412
WestJet, 47, 49
Weyerhaeuser Co. Ltd., 480
Wharton School, 446
Whirlpool, 326, 597
Wicat, 292
Wikipedia, 291
William H. Mercer Limited, 447
Workers' Compensation Board, 475, 476
Workers' Safety and Compensation Commission, 475
Work–Life Harmony Enterprises, 28, 163
Workplace Health and Safety Insurance Board, 484
Workplace Safety and Health Division (WSHD), 475
WorkSafeNB, 475
Workstream, Inc., 333
World Bank, 600
World Trade Organization (WTO), 7
WorldatWork, 406, 421
WorldCom, 233

X

Xerox, 14, 299, 322, 596

Y

Yahoo, 426
Yellow Pages. *See* Tele-Direct

Z

Zero Knowledge Systems, 25
Zurich, 593

A

Ability Edge internship program, 196
ability tests
  cognitive, 238
  physical, 240–241
Aboriginal people, 97–98, 100, 102f, 111
absenteeism, 5, 528f
  calculating turnover, 90–91
  costs of, 93
  dismissal for, 542–543
  employee absenteeism rates, 91–92
  HR planning and, 93
  returning to work, 504–505
abuse, of illegal drugs, 253, 528f
Accenture People, 35–36
accessible workplace, 116f
accommodations industry, 27
active practice, repetition and, 282–283
adaptability
  jobs and work unit, 138
  of training instructors, 284
Adobe Acrobat, 293
advertisements, 175–176
advice and counsel, as HR manager's
  responsibility, 29
age
  median retirement age, 50
  prohibited discrimination by, 103f
  young workers' health and safety
    risks, 503–504
age distribution
  analysis of, 47
  imbalance in, 21–23, 23f
  impacting overall framework for
    HRM, 6f
  managing multigenerational
    workforce, 206–207
  at Peregrine Inc., 36–37
  social issues arising from, 21
AIDS (acquired immune deficiency
    syndrome), 488
alarm reaction, 498
alcoholism, 253, 496–497
  intoxication at job, 528f
alignment, external and internal fit, 70,
  78–79, 79f
alliance partners, 55

alternative dispute resolution (ADR),
  534–538, 536f
  defined, 535
alternative work schedules, 21, 159
  compressed workweek, 160
  flextime, 21, 160–161, 163
  job sharing, 161
  keys for successful telecommuting,
    161–162, 162f
  telecommuting, 161–162, 162f
  why students value, 160
  work–life balance, 163
ancestry/place of origin, prohibited
  discrimination by, 104f
anger, managing employee's, 493f
annual earnings
  educational levels v., 23–25, 24f
  women v. men, 24f
annual maintenance costs, 11
anti-bullying programs, 505–507
APEC. See Asia-Pacific Economic
    Cooperation
appraisal, in overall framework for HRM, 6f
appraisal interviews, 350–357, 351f, 356f
  asking for self-assessment, 351–352
  be supportive, 353
  change behaviour/not person, 353
  establish goals, 353
  express appreciation, 352
  focus: solving problems, 353
  follow up day to day, 354
  invite participation, 352
  minimize criticism, 352–353
  problem-solving interview, 351
  "stretch goals," 354
  tell-and-listen interview, 351
  tell-and-show interview, 351
appraiser training, 336–339
  eliminating rater error, 337–339
  error of central tendency, 337
  establishing appraisal plan, 336
  feedback training, 339
  forced distribution system, 337
  forced ranking, 337
  leniency or strictness error, 337
appreciation, 352
apprenticeship training, 286–287, 289f
  international cases, 594–595
  for international guest workers,
    594–595

arbitration, 537
  business case/avoiding strikes and
    arbitration, 567
collective bargaining legislation and
  labour arbitration, 514–515,
  521, 539
  compulsory binding arbitration, 561
  decision to arbitrate, 571–572
  disciplinary policies and
    procedures, 537–538
  final offer arbitration, 561
  labour arbitration, 514–521, 519f,
    520f, 561
  legality of arbitration policies, 538
  negotiated grievance procedure, 571
  rights arbitration, 571–573
arbitration award, 572
arbitration law, 515
arbitrator
  interest arbitrator, 569
  labour arbitrator, 515, 518, 521,
    524, 525
Asia-Pacific Economic Cooperation
    (APEC), 7
assessment centres, 186, 188
  Public Service Commission
    Assessment Centre, 187
assistance programs, international
  cases, 610
  see also employee assistance
    programs
attendance problems, 528f
  see also absenteeism
attitude, towards work, 26–28, 27f
  on-the-job behaviour problems,
    528f
audiovisual method, of training, 290–291
augmented skills, 597
authorization card, 553

B

Babe, 35
Baby Boomers, 22–23, 49
  customized noncash incentive
    awards for, 414
  managing multigenerational
    workforce, 206–207
  pension funds for, 458

background checks, 233–234
background diversity
in overall framework for HRM, 6f
balanced scorecard (BSC)
evaluation of firm's performance, 77–78
performance appraisal using, 347–349, 348f
in strategic planning and HR linkage, 46f
balance-sheet approach, international cases, 609
bargaining data, 562–563
bargaining deadlock, 569
bargaining power, 565–566
bargaining process. See collective bargaining process
bargaining strategies/tactics, 563–565
bargaining teams, 563
bargaining unit, 554
bargaining zone, 562f, 564f, 565, 574
defined, 564
base pay, international cases, 609
basic skills training (new employee), 304–305
behavioural interviews, 187
behaviourally anchored rating scale (BARS), 344–345
behavioural methods, of performance appraisal, 343–345, 345f
behavioural checklist method, 343–344
behaviourally anchored rating scale, 344–345
behaviour observation scale, 345
critical incident method, 145, 343
behaviour modeling, 296
behaviour modification, 284
behaviour observation scale (BOS), 345
benchmarking
defined, 300
four-step process of, 301
in strategic planning and HR linkage, 46f
training in, measurement and calculation, 301
benefits. See employee benefits
Bennett Mechanical Comprehension Test, 230, 238
Bill C-45 (corporate killing law), 479
biographical information blank (BIB), 233
biometric scanning device, 524
Blacks, in Canada's population composition, 22f
blended learning, 289
bonus, 408, 413–415, 424, 431
counter-productive, 415–416

defined, 412
executive, 418–421
in executive pay package, 417–418
Improshare, 406f, 425
at Lombard Canada, 428
as part of sales incentive plan, 416–417
spot, 412
in team incentive plan, 421–422
types of incentive plans, 406f
weaknesses of profit-sharing plans, 426
boundaryless careers, 193–194
Boychuk, 260–261
boycott, 568
Bread and Roses, 576–577
bribery, 587–589
broadbanding, 390–391
building-related illness (BRI), 487
bullying
as harassment, 120, 122
as safety issue, 505–507
burnout, 498
business acumen, 31f
business agent, labour union, 560
business strategy
cultural environment of international business, 587f
differentiation strategy: compete on value added, 69–70, 69f
HR linking to, 46f
low-cost strategy: compete on productivity/efficiency, 68–69, 69f
reasons for diversity management, 127f
steps for starting new business, 221f
business unit, in personal scorecard, 348

C

cafeteria plans. See flexible benefit plans
calibration, 327–328
California Psychological Inventory (CPI), 239
Caliper test, 239
Campbell Interest and Skill Survey (CISS), 219
Canada
invisible labour force of, 551
population composition, 22f
worker output, 20
Canada and Quebec Pension Plans (CPP/QPP), 448–449
Canada Labour Code, Part III, 391
Canada Labour Standards Regulations, 391

Canadian Human Rights Act (CHRA), 101–105
1978 amendment to, 106
enforcement of, 106
career counseling, 198–199, 199f
career development
choosing career, 217–219, 219f
choosing employer, 219–220
developing skills and competencies, 217
entrepreneurs, 220
international assignments, 603
marital/family life balanced with, 221–222
off-the-job interests, 221
personal, 217–219, 219f
questions to ask before accepting job offer, 220
retirement planning, 222
steps for starting new business, 221f
career development initiatives
career counseling, 198–199, 199f
career development programs, 197–198
career planning workbooks, 198
career planning workshops, 198
career self-management training, 202–203
case study, 213–214
determining individual development needs, 198–200
e-mentoring, 202
fast-track program, 199–200
individual investment v. organizational investment, 199
mentoring, 200–202, 200f, 201f
networking, 202
career development programs, 197–198
Career Gateway Program, 205
career management
see also external recruitment; internal recruitment
career development initiatives, 197–203, 199f, 200f, 201f
dual-career couples, 207
HR's role in, 188f
identifying career opportunities/requirements, 190–197, 191f, 194f, 195f, 196f
matching individual and organizational needs, 189–190, 190f
talent concerns, 206–207
career opportunities/requirements
avoid career plateau trap, 195, 196f
boundaryless careers, 193–194
competency analysis, 190–191
demotion, 192

dual career paths, 193, 194f
identify job progressions, 191–192, 211–212
promotion, 192
recognize possibilities, 192
relocation services, 192
track career stages, 194, 195f
transfer, 192
typical line of advancement in HR management, 191f
career planning workbooks, 198
career planning workshops, 198
career progression, 191–192, 211–212
career self-management training, 202–203
career stages, 194, 195f
carelessness, 528f
certified employee benefit specialist, 446
change
change management planning, 12
competency in managing, 30
as downsizing, 17, 18–19, 28, 33
as reengineering, 15f, 16–17, 138
in strategic planning and HR linkage, 46f
technological, 9–11
types of, 11–12
Charter of Rights and Freedoms (*Constitution Act of 1982*), 101
checklist
behavioural checklist method, 343–344
for orienting new employees, 304
as performance appraisal method, 340
chemical hazards, 485
chief ethics officer, 29, 306
chief executive officer (CEO), 174–175
compensation for, 420, 434
on value/impact of human capital, 13
chief learning officer, 274
child care, 47, 460–462, 462f
child pornography case, 526
Chinese, 99
in Canada's population composition, 22f
cigarette smoking, 487, 528f

Civil Rights movement, 206
civil service examinations, 242
civil status, prohibited discrimination by, 104f
classroom instruction, trainee, 289
coaching, productivity enhancement through, 20f
code orange, 489–490
codetermination, 616
cognitive ability tests, 238
Cold War, 206
collective agreement, 206
administration of, 570–574
items in, 570
management's, 569–570
negotiation of, 564–565
union security agreements, 570
collective bargaining
defined, 562
developing bargaining strategies/tactics, 563–565
gathering bargaining data, 562–563
interest arbitrator, 569
interest-based bargaining, 565
management power in, 568–569
negotiating collective agreements, 564–565
picketing, 568, 568f
preparing for negotiations, 562–563
replacement workers, 567
resolving bargaining deadlocks, 569
union power in, 565–568, 568f
combined salary and commission incentive plan, 417
common disciplinary problems, 528f
common law, 512–513
employer's right to monitor employees, 522–523, 522f, 523f
regimes governing dismissals, 520–521
common law of employment, 513
communicable diseases, 488, 489–490
communication
of employee benefits program, 444
host country's cultural environment, 587–589, 587f
in overall framework for HRM, 6f
performance appraisal and, 323f
in strategic planning and HR linkage, 46f

communications industries, 9
Communism, fall of, 206
communities of practice, 291, 291f
commuting, 28
tele-, 21, 161–162, 162f
Comp Analyst, 386
compensation, 5
see also strategic compensation planning
bases for, 375–377, 377f
costs of employing expatriates, 613
direct, 370
employing expatriates, 613
equal pay for work of equal value, 392–394
of expatriate managers, 609–611
external factors determining, 379–380, 380f
government regulation of, 391–392
of host-country employees, 607–609, 608f
of host-country managers, 609
hourly wages in different countries, 608f
indirect, 370
internal factors determining, 377–379, 377f
international HRM recruitment, 621–622
job evaluation systems, 381–385, 383f
in overall framework of HRM, 6f
performance appraisal and, 323f
wage and salary survey, 385–391, 387f, 388f, 389f
wage-rate compression, 395–396
wage structure with increasing rate ranges, 389f
compensation management, 139
compensation analysis, 190–191
compensatory model, 256
competency assessment
defined, 277
managerial position, 278–279
in strategic planning and HR linkage, 46f
competency-based pay, 390–391, 391f
defined, 390
competency glossary, 313
competitive challenges
competing, recruiting, and staffing globally, 6–8
employee concerns balanced with, 4
new technology, 8–11, 10f
worker output/productivity, 20
competitive environment, 47
customers, 48
five forces framework, 48–49, 48f

competitive environment (*continued*)
  new entrants, 49
  replacement workers, 567
  rival firms, 48
  substitutes, 49
  suppliers, 49
competitor/industry analysis, 46f
compressed workweek, 160
compulsory binding arbitration, 561
computer-based training programs, 285
computer interview, 246–247
computer use, 523f
  see also Internet
  digital age, 206
  ergonomic considerations, 154, 155f
  Generation X's, 206
  policy guidelines for, 524f
concentration, 113
concurrent validity, 229
conferences, employee training
  through, 294
conflict resolution procedures, 307
constructive dismissal, 515
construct validity, 229
consumer price index (CPI), 380, 397
content plateau, 195
content validity, 230
continuous improvement, as TQM core
  idea, 14
contract
  changing, without employee's
    agreement, 516
  Employment Standards Act, 514
  implied contract terms, 513
  labour arbitrator, 515, 518
  Machtinger v. HOJ Industries, 514
  "mutual consideration," 515
contract negotiation, 556
contrast error, 339
contributory plan, 456
cooperative training, 287–288
core employee, 54–55
core skills
  assessment of, 598–599
  defined, 597
  of expatriate managers, 598
core values, 46
Corporate Events Committee, 5
corporate executives, 44
corporate social responsibility, 7
corporate strategy, 46f
  growth and diversification, 66–67
  mergers and acquisitions, 67
  strategic alliances and joint
    ventures, 68
corporations
  corporate executives, 44
  economy based on brains not
    brawn, 8

HR linking to, 46f
  international, 584, 585f
corporation scandals, Generation Y's
  life-defining events, 206
correlation scatterplots, 229, 229f
Corruption of Foreign Public Officials Act, 588
cost containment
  downsizing, 17–18
  as HRIS choice factor, 11
  as HRM challenge, 6f
  outsourcing/offshoring/employee
    leasing, 18–19, 21, 50
  as overall HR challenge, 17–20, 20f
  productivity enhancements,
    19–20, 21f
cost-of-living adjustment, 609
counseling services, 460, 495
counter-productive bonus, 415–416
country clusters, 602f
courage, 31f
course content, as percentage of training
  expenditures, 273f
CPA Examination, 242
CPI Personality Facts and Sample Items,
  240f
CPP/QPP. *See* Canada and Quebec
  Pension Plans
craft unions, 558
creativity/innovativeness, 31f
credibility, 30, 31f
credit union, 463
criminal conviction, 105f
criterion deficiency, 326–327, 327f
critical incident, 145, 344, 345, 357, 358
  defined, 343
criticism. *See* appraisal interviews
cross-cultural differences, 601–603, 602f,
  620–621
cross-training, 306
cross-validation, 229
cultural changes, 24–25
cultural environment, 586–587, 589
  host country, 588
  of international business, 587f
  understanding of, 588
cultural training, 601
culture, workplace, productivity
  enhancement through, 20f
culture shock, 603–604
cumulative trauma disorders, 488
customer, 48
  orientation, 31f
  satisfaction, as benefit from
    avoiding downsizing, 18
customer appraisal, 332
customer needs
  five forces framework, 48,
    48f, 49
  as TQM core idea, 14

D

day care, 21
deadlines, for strikes, 570
deadlocks, in collective bargaining
  process, 569
Decent Work Agenda, 615
decertification, 556–557, 557f
decision-making leave, 533
defect reduction, Six Sigma process
  and, 15
defined benefit plan, 456
defined contribution plan, 457
delivery method, of training, 290f
Delphi technique, 57f, 60
demographic changes, social issues
  arising from, 21
demotion, 192
dental and optical care, 453
depression, 495
  recognizing, in workplace, 496
designated groups
  Aboriginals, 97–98, 100,
    102f, 111
  Chinese, 22f, 99
  defined, 97
  First Nations, 97
  Indians, 99
  Inuit, 97
  Latin Americans, 22f, 99
  in management, 205
  Métis, 97
  Pakistanis, 99
  people with disabilities, 99,
    114–116, 116f, 232, 307
  prohibited discrimination toward,
    102f
  Southeast Asians, 99
  visible minorities, 22f, 98–100
  women, 97
differential piece rate (piecework), 410
digital age, 206
direct compensation, 370
disabilities, 232, 307
  Barrier Free Access program, 114
  nondisclosure of disabilities, 111
  prohibited discrimination toward,
    103f
  reasonable accommodation for,
    114–116
  suggestions for accessible
    workplace, 116f
disciplinary policies and procedures
  see also dismissal
  alternative dispute resolution,
    535–538, 536f
  arbitration, 537–538
  collective bargaining legislation,
    514–515

common disciplinary problems, 528f
decision-making leave, 533
discipline defined, 529–530
documentation of misconduct, 530–531
employment termination, 533–535
ethics in, 538
hot-stove approach to enforcement, 529
investigating problems, 530–531, 531f
investigative interview, 531, 531f, 535f
management's, 527, 527f
mediation, 537
neglect in communicating rules, 529
nonpunitive discipline, 532
ombudsperson system, 537
open-door policy, 536–537
peer-review system, 536
positive discipline, 532–533
progressive discipline, 532
results of inaction, 527–528
setting organization rules, 527–528
step-review system, 535–536, 536f
disciplinary problems, common, 528f
discipline, 529–530
discretionary major, 452–458, 452f
discrimination, prohibited, 102f, 103f, 104f
diseases, 489–490
dishonesty
bribery, 587–589
burying/falsifying work records, 483–484, 528f
honesty and integrity tests, 235–237, 236f
dismissal
for absenteeism, 542–543
collective bargaining legislation, 514–515
as disciplinary action, 533–535
employee's response, 520f
lawsuit for wrongful dismissal, 527
of nonunion and unionized employees, 519f
nonunion employee: wrongful dismissal, 516–518
overview of regimes governing, 520–521
statutory regulation of, 517–518
unionized employee: just cause, 518–519, 519f
distress, 497
distributive fairness, 373
diversity, 6f
see also employment equity
challenge of immigration and, 21, 22f

cross-cultural differences, 601–603, 602f
cultures/languages/nationalities/ethnic groups, 96
common law of employment, 513
compensation of host-country employees, 607–609, 608f
conduct outside workplace, 523, 525–526
diversity of, social issues arising from, 21
empowered, 20f, 152, 153f, 345–349, 347f
forecasting demand for, 58–60, 59f
health care costs for, 21, 452, 452f
how employees become unionized, 555
implied contract terms, 513
individual development needs, 198–200
outsourcing/offshoring/leasing, 18–19, 21, 50
PIPEDA and, of, 522
Pride Builders, 315
productivity enhancement, 20f
reasonable notice given to, 514
response to threat of dismissal, 520f
statutory employment regulation, 513–514
employee advocacy, as HR manager's responsibility, 30
employee assistance programs (EAPs), 5, 253, 459
alcoholism, 253, 496–497
domestic violence, 495
drug abuse, 253, 497, 528f
emotional problems, 495–496
international cases, 610
laws and legislation, 462–463
personal crises, 495
stress management, 497–500, 499f, 502
employee associations, 558
employee benefit programs
small business, 464
employee benefits, 5, 27f
Canada and Quebec Pension Plans, 448–449
certified employee benefit specialist, 446
concerns of management, 446–448
crafting of benefits communication program, 444
dental and optical care, 453
discretionary major, 452–458, 452f
employment insurance, 449–450
from entitlement to self-responsibility, 447–448

diversity management, 24, 82, 123
managing diversity, 24, 82, 122–123, 127f
race/gender/age/disabilities/lifestyles/culture/education/ideas/backgrounds, 307
reasons for diversity management, 127f
training, 307–308
diversity management, 24, 82, 123
defined, 122
primary business reasons for, 127f
documentation
of benefits from diversity training, 308
learning from case studies, 294–295
of misconduct, 530–531
of personnel decisions, 323f
"doing things right the first time," as TQM core idea, 14
domestic violence, 495
downsizing, 18–19, 28, 33
defined, 17
drug abuse, 253, 497, 528f
dual-career partnerships, 207
dual career paths, 193, 194f

E

"echo boom" generation, 22–23
educational institutions, as recruiting source, 179, 179f
educational levels
annual earnings v., 23–25, 24f
in overall framework for HRM, 6f
educational priorities
as external issue to analyze, 47
education factor, 383–384f
8 Mile, 503
elder care, 21, 28, 460–462, 462f, 465
defined, 461
as external issue to analyze, 47
e-learning, 292–293
e-mail
employee's use of, at work, 522, 523f
policy guidelines for, 524f
e-mentoring, 202
emotional problems, 495–496, 528f
employability, 193
employee(s), 25
see also employer/employee; privacy
advantages of part-time, 26
angry, 493f

attitudes towards work, 26–28, 27f
calming angry employees, 493f
common disciplinary problems, 528f

employee benefits (continued)
flexible plans: advantages/
disadvantages, 442, 443f
groundworkers' v. skywalkers', 27
health care cost containment, 21,
452, 452f
HRIS and, 440–441
legally required, 448–449
life insurance, 455
managing costs of, 446
mandated, 21
noncontributory plan, 456
in overall framework for HRM, 6f
paid holidays, 454
payoff upon severance, 18, 454–455
pension plans, 456–458
preretirement policies, 455–456
provincial hospital and medical
services, 451
reducing workers' compensation
costs, 451f
registered retirement plan, 443
requirements for, 441–443
retirement policies, 455
severance pay, 18, 454–455
sick leave, 454
team approach to cost containment,
453
total rewards package, 445f
trusted pension plan, 458
vacations with pay, 18, 454
workers' compensation, 450–451, 451f
employee concerns
competitive challenges balanced
with, 4
in overall framework for HRM, 6f
performance appraisal and, 323f
employee involvement groups (EIs),
155–156
employee leasing, 19
employee referrals, as internal recruiting
source, 176–178
employee selection. See selection
employee services
see also employee assistance
programs
child and elder care, 460–462, 462f
CIBC's, 461
counseling services, 460
credit unions, 463
family-friendly work-life setting,
27f, 28, 459, 459f, 467–469
financial planning, 463
housing and moving expenses, 463
legal, 462–463
recreational and social, 463
Retirement Savings Plan, 464
small business, 464

transportation pooling, 463
Yukon government's public service
commission, 460
employee stock ownership plans
(ESOPs)
advantages of, 429
problems with, 429–430
in small business, 430
employee training programs, for
management
behaviour modeling, 296
documented case studies,
294–295
games and simulations, 295
on-the-job training, 293–294
role-playing, 295–296
seminars and conferences, 294
employee training programs,
nonmanagerial, 289–293, 290f, 291f
apprenticeship training, 286–287,
289f
cooperative training, 287–288
internship programs, 287, 288–289
on-the-job training, 285–286, 286f
employer(s)
choosing your, 219–220
common law of employment, 513
dismissal of nonunion employee,
516–518
dismissal of unionized employee,
518–519, 519f
employee termination, 519f
implied contract terms, 513
liability of, in bullying/harassment
cases, 505–507
neglect in communicating rules,
529
PIPEDA and, 522
professional employer
organizations, 19
statutory employment regulation,
513–514
strategies to remain union free, 556
unfair labour practices of, 556
employer/employee relationship, 21
see also labour relations
collective bargaining legislation,
514–515
constructive dismissal, 515–516
employer's right to monitor
employees, 522–523, 522f, 523f
ethics in, 538
/ethics/whistle-blowing, 21
HRM competency model and, 31f
informing employee of termination,
533–535
labour arbitrator, 515, 518, 521,
524, 525

Labour Relations Act, 514
lawsuits, 18, 30, 514–518
"mutual consideration," 515
overview of regimes governing
dismissal, 520–521
performance appraisal failure
and, 325
supervising v. super-spying, 525
surveillance outside workplace, 523,
525–526
value placed on, 27f
employer-initiated surveys, 386–387
employment equity, 97
see also pay equity
advantages of diversity initiatives,
125–126
Air Canada's achievements, 125
Barrier Free Access program, 114
benefits of, 101
defined, 96
in Department of National Defense,
125
economic values of diversity, 124
Employment Equity Act of 1995,
107–108, 127
Federal Contractors Program, 108
fighting fires, 131
implementation of, in
organizations, 108–118, 110f
incorporating diversity, 123–125
leadership in incorporating
diversity, 124–125, 125f
model of diversity management
strategy, 126f
myths about, 129
sexual harassment, 118–122, 119f,
120f, 130, 132
small business, 127–128
status of designated groups,
97–100
step 1: senior management
commitment to, 109–111
step 2: data collection and analysis,
111–113
step 3: employment systems review,
113–116, 116f
step 4: establishment of workplan,
117
step 5: implementation, 117
step 6: evaluation/monitoring/
revision, 117–118
suggestions for accessible
workplace, 116f
Employment Equity Act of 1995, 107–108,
127
Employment Equity (EE) program, 115
employment insurance, 449–450
employment interview

appropriate/inappropriate interview questions, 251f
behavioral description interview, 245
computer and virtual interviews, 246–247
employment equity: are your questions legal?, 250–252, 251f
funniest candidate responses, 244
guidelines for interviewers, 248–250, 249f
interviewer training, 249–250
nondirect method, 243
panel interview, 243
simulations and games, 248, 248f
situational interview, 243–244, 245
structured interview, 243
variables in, 249f
video and digitally recorded interviews, 247–248, 247f
employment law
  see also privacy
collective agreement, 514
common law of employment, 512–513
constructive dismissal, 515–516
implied contract terms, 513
Labour Relations Act, 514
"mutual consideration," 515
statutory employment regulation, 513–514
statutory regulation of dismissal, 517–518
three regimes of, 512
Employment Standards Acts, 235, 392, 514
employment tests
aptitude tests at electronics corporation, 263–264
cognitive ability tests, 238
CPI Personality Facts and Sample Items, 240f
General Competency Test, 238, 239f
job knowledge tests, 242
nature of, 238
personality and interest inventories, 238–240
physical ability tests, 240–241
testing at Steelcase, 241
virtual, 261–263
work sample tests, 242
empowered employees, 20f
enterprise incentive plans, 425–432
common types of, 425, 426
job design resulting in, 152, 153f
"culture of ownership," 425
employee stock ownership plans, 406f, 429–432
profit sharing, 406f, 426–431
stock options, 406f, 426–429

entitlement
incentive payments v., 408
self-responsibility v., 447–448
entrepreneur, 220
steps for starting new business, 221f
entry barriers, 49
environment
analysis of, in strategic planning, 46–50, 48f
building-related illness, 487
competitive, 47–49, 48f
cultural, 586–589, 587f
labour, 614–617
productivity enhancement via, 20f
reengineering of global business, 138
safe work environment, 474–480, 475f, 479f, 500
working conditions, in job evaluation, 400
environmental scanning, 46f
equal pay for work of equal value, 21, 392–394
equity legislation, 101
ergonomics program key elements, 489f
Erin Brockovich, 466–467
error of central tendency, 337
escalator clauses, 380
essay method, of performance appraisal, 343
ethics
chief ethics officers, 29
defined, 538
in disciplinary policies and actions, 538
as employee selection factor, 255
employer/employee relationship, 21
executive compensation plans, 420–421, 434
skywalkers v. groundworkers, 27
training program in, 306–307
whistle-blowing, 21
work attitudes/work ethic, 6f, 587–589, 587f
eustress, 497
evaluation, of firm's performance
assessing internal fit (functional cohesion/workforce objectives), 70, 78–79, 79f
balanced scoreboard, 77–78
benchmarking, 76–77
building Metrics Model, 78f
ensuring strategic flexibility for future, 79–80
issues in, 75–77
measuring firm's strategic alignment, 77–79, 78f

evaluation, of training programs' effectiveness, 296–301
assessing participants' reactions, 297f
criterion 1: reactions, 297–298
criterion 2: actual learning, 298
criterion 3: behaviour, 298–299
criterion 4: results (return on investment), 299–301
four-level evaluation, 297
executive compensation incentive plan, 406f
executive incentive plans, 406f
base salaries, 418
benefits, 420
ethics and accountability, 420–421, 434
executive bonus, 418–421
executive pay package, 417–418
long-term incentives, 418–420, 419f
perquisites, 420
short-term incentives, 420
executive search firms, 178
exempt, 376
expatriate employees, 595–596, 596f
Canadian in Paris, 619
expatriate executives, stressors and coping responses, 604
expatriate managers, 597–599, 598f
expatriate compensation of, 609–611
expatriates
causes of assignment failure, 600f
compensation of expatriate managers, 609–611
costs of employing, 613
defined, 589
expatriate assignment failure, 600f
expatriate repatriation, 604–606
stressors and coping responses, 604
expatriate selection process, 599f
expectancy theory, 373–374
external issues, 46
external recruitment
advertisements, 175–176
of CEOs, 174–175
costs of, 182
educational institutions, 179, 179f
employee referrals, 176–178
executive search firms, 178
global labour market, 181
improving effectiveness of, 181–182
Internet, 176
labour unions, 180
nepotism, 178
organizational recruiters, 182–183
private employment agencies, 180–181
professional associations, 180

external recruitment (continued)
public employment agencies, 180
realistic job previews, 183
temporary employment agencies, 180–181
unsolicited applications and résumés, 176
yield ratios, 182
external relations, 31f

F

"face validity," 238
failure rate, 599
family concerns
accommodating women employees, 205
child care, 47, 460–462, 462f
domestic violence, 495
drug abuse, 253, 497, 528f
elder care, 21, 28, 47, 460–462, 462f
emotional problems, 495–496, 528f
host country's, 587–589, 587f
in overall framework for HRM, 6f
personal and family life in foreign country, 603–605
pregnancy leave, 28, 207, 207
spouse, 28
family-friendly work-life setting, 27f, 28, 459, 459f, 467–469
family life, career balanced with, 221–222
family status, prohibited discrimination by, 104f
fast-track program, 199–200
Federal Contractors Program, 108
Federal Crown corporations, 391
feedback
productivity enhancement via, 20f
providing, for international assignments, 612–613
reinforcement and, 283–284
spot rewards, 283
feedback training, 339
fighting, 528f
Filipinos, in Canada's population composition, 22f
final decision (employee selection), 258
final offer arbitration, 561
financial planning, 463
firearms, possession of, 528f
First Nations, 97
five forces framework, 48f, 49
Flash programs, 293
flexibility
firm's, 79–80
in strategic planning, 46f
flexible benefit plans, 442

advantages/disadvantages, 443f
flexible work schedules
alternative work schedules, 21, 159–163, 162f
compressed workweek, 160
flextime, 21, 160–161, 163
flextime and work–life balance, 163
job sharing, 161
keys for successful telecommuting, 162f
telecommuting, 21, 161–162, 162f
why students value, 160
flextime, 21, 160–161, 163
flow data, 111
food and beverage industry, 27
forced-choice method, of performance appraisal, 342
forecasting
Delphi technique, 57f, 60
external factors' influencing, 61–62, 62f
HR planning and strategy questions to ask, 60
human capital readiness, 62–63, 63f, 64f
management forecasts, defined, 60
model of HR forecasting, 57, 57f
predicting demand for employees, 58–60, 59f
predictive validity, 229
qualitative approaches, 59–60
quantitative approaches, 59
skill inventories and management inventories, 61
staffing tables and Markov analysis, 61, 61f
succession planning, 61–62, 62f, 64f
trend analysis, 59
four-day workweek, 28
freehand wage curve, 387f
free-trade agreements, 7

G

gainsharing incentive plans, 423–425
gambling, 528f
The Game Changer (Lafley), 12
games, learning from, 295
GATT. See General Agreement on Tariffs and Trade
gender issues
see also women
in overall framework for HRM, 6f
prohibited employment discrimination by gender, 103f
General Agreement on Tariffs and Trade (GATT), 7
General Aptitude Test Battery (GATB), 238

General Competency Test (GCT), 238, 239f
Generation X
customized noncash incentive awards for, 414
managing multigenerational workforce, 206–207
Generation Y
customized noncash incentive awards for, 414
job recruiting of, 262
managing multigenerational workforce, 206–207
glass ceiling audits, 204–205
global corporation, 585
global economic issues, 46
cultural environment impacting, 586
labour environment, 614–617
globalization, 7, 35–36
see also international human resources management
Canadians on global assignments, 592, 592f
competing/recruiting/staffing influenced by, 6–8
country clusters, 602f
defined, 7
global corporations, 585, 585f
guest workers, 594
hourly wages in different countries, 608f
HRM challenges from, 6f
impact on management, 586–589
international corporations, 584, 585f
managing across borders, 584–589, 585f, 587f
multinational corporations, 584–585, 585f
recruiting internationally, 592–594
social issues arising from, 21
staffing transnational teams, 595
transnational corporations, 585, 585f
understanding host country's culture, 587
work permit/visa, 593
global labour market, 181
global manager, 596
goal setting, 281, 323f
government, as external issue for analysis, 47
government regulation
see also laws and legislation
Canada Labour Code Part III, 391
Canada Labour Standards Regulations, 391
of compensation, 391–392
Employment Standards acts, 392

government scandals, as Generation Y's life-defining events, 206
Graduate Management Aptitude Test (GMAT), 238
graphic rating scale method, 340–341, 341f
graphology, 341f
Great Depression, 237
grievance procedure, 206
groundworkers, 571
group incentive plans. *See* gainsharing incentive plans, 423–425
  lessons from Scanlon Plan and Improshare, 425
  network Improshare, 425
  Scanlon Plan, 406f, 424–425, 424f
  team compensation, 421–423, 422f, 434–435
guest workers, 594

H

handicap, prohibited discrimination by, 103f
  see also disabilities
harassment, bullying as, 120, 122
harassment/bullying
  see also sexual harassment requiring disciplinary action, 528f
  as safety issue, 505–507
Hay profile method, 385
hazardous materials information systems, 485–486, 486f
hazardous materials symbols, 486f
health and safety. *See* occupational health and safety
health care, cost containment, 21, 452, 452f
health habits
  see also employee assistance programs
  building better, 493
  promoting workplace fitness, 494, 495f
herpes simplex, 488
hidden cameras, 522–523, 522f
hidden payroll. *See* employee benefits
home-based pay, 609
home-country nationals. *See* expatriates
honesty and integrity tests, 235–237, 236f
host-based pay, 610
host country, 587
host-country nationals, 591
hot-stove approach, to rule enforcement, 529
hourly wages, in different countries, 608f

hourly work, 375
housing expenses, 463
HRIS. *See* human resources information systems
HRM. *See* human resources management
human capital, 12
  CEOs on value/impact of, 13
  defined, 13
  host country's cultural environment and, 587–589, 587f
  HRM and, 13–14
  human capital architecture, 53–57
  as overall HRM challenge, 6f
  readiness, 62–63, 63f, 64f
  in strategic planning and HR linkage, 46f
human resources information systems (HRIS), 9, 10f
  defined, 9
  employee benefits, 440–441
  factors in choosing, 10–11
  job analysis and, 146
  salary surveys, 386
  technology, 9–11, 10f
  time implementation, 11
human resources management (HRM)
  see also international human resources management
  challenge 1: competing, recruiting, and staffing globally, 6–8
  challenge 2: new technology, 8–11, 10f
  challenge 3: managing change, 11–12, 12f
  challenge 4: managing talent/ human capital, 12–14
  challenge 5: responding to the market, 14–17, 15f, 16f
  challenge 6: cost containment, 17–20, 20f
  competencies of HR manager, 30–31
  competency model, 31f
  corporate executives on expenditures for, 44
  defined, 4
  domestic v. international, 589
  international staffing, 589–592, 591f
  line managers' partnership with, 29–30
  overall framework for, 6f
  performance appraisal function, 322
  recruiting internationally, 592–594
  relationship of job requirements and, 138–140
  in small businesses, 32
  social issues in, 21
  study of, 4
human resources planning (HRP), 44

I

ideologies, host country, 587–589, 587f
immigration, 50
  diversity from, 21
  as external issue for analysis, 47
  immigrant recruits at Magna, 555
implementation, of training programs, 285–296, 286f, 289f, 291f
  computer-based training, 285
  on-the-job training, 285–286
implied contract terms, 512
Improshare, 406f, 425
in-basket exercises, 186
incentive awards, 406f, 414
  customized noncash, 414
incentive pay programs, 407f
incentive plans
  administering, 410
  as links to organizational objectives, 371–372
  enterprise, 425–432
  group, 421–425, 422f, 424f
  individual, 410–417, 411f
  linking compensation to organizational objectives, 407–408
  professional employees', 417–421, 418f, 419f
  requirements for, 408–410
  setting performance standards, 409, 409f
  strategic reasons for, 406–408, 406f, 407f
  types of, 406f
incentive premiums, 610
Indians, 99
indirect compensation, 370
individual differences, in learning, 282
individual incentive plans, 410–417, 411f
indoor air quality, 487
industrial disease, 480
industrial engineering, 153
industrial unions, 558
influenza, 488
In Good Company, 210–211, 542
injury, occupational, 474–480, 475f, 479f
injury/illness incidence rate calculation, 483
  in overall framework for HRM, 6f
instructional objectives, 280
instructors, characteristics of, 284–285
insubordination, 528f

interest arbitrator, 569
interest-based bargaining, 565
  benefits of, 567
  building trust through, 566
internal analysis
  composition: human capital
    architecture, 53–57, 53f, 55f
  core capabilities: people as strategic
    resource, 52–53, 53f
  culture: auditing values, beliefs, and
    attitudes, 51–52
  forecasting, 57–62, 57f, 59f, 61f, 62f
  internal fit, 70, 78–79, 79f
  three Cs: culture/capabilities/
    composition, 50–57, 53f, 55f
internal fit (functional cohesion), 70, 78–79, 79f
  workforce objectives), 70, 78–79, 79f
internal recruitment
  advantages and limitations of,
    183–185, 184f
  methods for identifying qualified
    candidates, 185–188, 186f
  warning signs of weak talent
    "bench," 184f
internal recruitment methods
  9-box grid, 186, 186f
  identifying talent through
    performance appraisals,
    185–186, 186f
  inventorying management talent,
    185
  job posting and bidding, 185
  using assessment centres, 186–188
international corporation, 584, 585f
international guest workers, 594–595
international human resources
    management
  apprenticeship training, 594–595
  assessing and tracking career
    development, 603
  assistance programs, 610
  balance-sheet approach, 609
  base pay, 609
  Canadians on global assignments,
    592, 592f
  causes of expatriate assignment
    failure, 600f
  codetermination, 616
  compensation of expatriate
    managers, 609–611
  compensation of host-country
    employees, 607–609, 608f
  compensation of host-country
    managers, 609
  content of training programs, 600–
    606, 600f, 602f, 604f
  Corruption of Foreign Public Officials
    Act, 588

cost-of-living adjustment, 609
costs of employing expatriates, 613
cross-cultural differences, 601–603,
    602f
cultural training, 601
culture shock, 603–604
employee selection, 595–596
expatriate employees, 595–596, 596f
expatriate managers, 597–599, 598f
expatriate selection process, 599f
guest workers, 594
home-based pay, 609
hourly wages in different countries,
    608f
incentive premiums, 610
language training, 601
localization, 610
managing personal and family life,
    603–605
performance appraisal, 611–613
recruitment, 621
reference checking, 593
repatriation, 604–606
selecting global managers, 596–599,
    597f, 598f, 599f
split-pay, 610
staffing transnational teams, 595
stressors and coping responses:
    expatriate executives, 604
synthesis of country clusters, 602f
training and development, 599–606,
    600f, 602f, 604f
understanding of cultural
    environment, 588
visa/work permits, 593
international labour organizations,
    615–616
International labour unions, 558–559
Internet
  e-based orientation training, 314
  e-learning, 292–293
  e-mail, 522, 523f
  e-mail and voice mail policy
    guidelines, 524f
  e-mentoring, 202
  employee's use of, 522, 523f
  external recruitment using, 176
  online employment applications,
    233
  online job applications, 233
  online job posting system, 177
  online learning, 292–293
  online reservation systems, 49
  PIPEDA, 25, 521–522, 522f
  Voice-Over-the-Internet Protocol, 49
internship programs, 287, 289
  Ability Edge internship program, 196
  defined, 288

interview, employment, 5
  see also employment interview
Intolerable Cruelty, 167
intoxication, 496–497, 528f
Inuit, 97
inventories
  California Psychological Inventory,
    239
  management inventories, 61
  of management talent, 185
  personality and interest inventories,
    238–240
  skill inventories, 61
  task inventory analysis, 145, 146f
  Wronko v. Western Inventory Service,
    516
investigation
  of disciplinary problem, 530–531,
    531f
  and recording of accidents, 483
investigative interview, 531, 531f, 535f
investment, in training and
    development, 272–274, 273f
issue of management, 569–570

J
job, 138
  classification system, 381
  defined, 138
  downsizing, 17–18
  enrichment/productivity
    enhancement through, 20f
  point value of (in freehand wage
    curve), 387f
  questions to ask before accepting
    job offer, 220
  and work unit adaptability, 138
job analysis
  competency-based analysis,
    145–146
  controlling accuracy of job
    information, 142–143
  critical incident method, 145, 343
  defined, 140
  at EDS Canada Inc., 142
  gathering job information, 140–142
  HRIS and, 146
  NOC and, 143, 219
  position analysis questionnaire
    system, 143–145
  process of, 141f
  task inventory analysis, 145, 146f
job characteristics model, 151
job classification system, 381–382
job description, 139
  defined, 139
  for HR employment assistant, 148

job duties/essential functions section, 147
job identification section, 147
job specifications section, 147, 149
job title, 147
  problems with, 149
job design, 31f, 149
  basis for, 150f
  behavioural concerns, 150-153, 153f
  defined, 49
  empowered employees, 152, 153f
  ergonomic considerations, 154, 155f
  flexible work schedules, 21, 159-163, 162f
  forms of employee teams, 158f
  industrial engineering considerations, 153
  job characteristics model, 151-152
  job enrichment, 150-151
  nonstandard jobs, 25-26
  in overall framework for HRM, 6f
  synergistic team characteristics, 158f
  virtual teams, 158
  work for group/team contributions, 154, 155-157
job evaluation, 382-385, 383f
  defined, 381
job fairs, 5
job family, 5
job posting and bidding, 185
job previews, 183
job progression, 191-192, 211-212
job ranking system, 381
job requirements, small business, 164
job rotation, 21
job security, 27f
  downsizing impacting, 18
  in overall framework for HRM, 6f
job sharing, 21, 28, 161
job specification, 138-139
just cause, required for dismissal, 515, 518-519, 519f
just-in-time training, 293

K
knowledge, skills and abilities (KSAs), 5
  CEOs on human capital, 13
  continual development/retraining, 21
  as employee selection factor, 255
  job knowledge tests, 242
  on-the-job development of, 27f
  productivity enhancement through improved, 20f
knowledge-based training, 9
knowledge-sharing learning, 291, 291f

knowledge workers, 27
  defined, 8
Korean War, 206
KSAs. See knowledge, skills, and abilities

L
labour arbitration
  employee dismissal, 514-521, 519f, 520f
  politics of labour-management relationship, 561
labour arbitrator, 518, 521
  defined, 515
  in privacy cases, 524, 525
labour market
  linked to HR strategic planning, 47
  linked to multigenerational workforce, 206-207
labour relations
  in SHRM analysis, 49-50
  Canada's invisible labour force, 551
  contract negotiation, 556
  decertification, 556-557, 557f
  government regulation of, 548-549

impact of unionization, 557-558
Labour Relations Act, 514
labour relations process, 549-558, 550f, 551f, 554f, 557f
layoffs, 18, 30, 323f
organizational productivity/HRM linked to, 548
in overall framework for HRM, 6f
in public sector, 560-561
Labour Relations Act, 514
labour relations process, 514
  551f, 554f, 557f
  defined, 549
organizing campaigns, 552-555, 554f
why employees unionize, 549-552
labour union, 30
  allocation of union dues, 559
  bargaining process, 562-569, 562f, 564f, 567f, 568f
  Canadian Labour Congress, 558
  collective bargaining legislation, 514-515
  history of, 206
  how employees become unionized, 555
  International and national, 558-559
  just cause required for dismissal, 518-519, 519f
  Labour Relations Act, 514
  local, 559-560
  management v., 557

overview of regimes governing dismissal, 520-521
recruitment from, 180
role of business agent, 560
role of union steward, 560
structures/functions/leadership of, 558-560
unfair labour practices of, 556
union power in collective bargaining, 565-568, 568f
small businesses and, 573-574
strategies to remain union free, 556
Walmart's union-free drives, 578-579
language
  abusive, requiring disciplinary action, 528f
  ethics code in relevant languages, 307
  host country's, 587-589, 587f
  learning second, 8
  prohibited employment discrimination by, 104f
  training, 601
language training, 601
Latin Americans, 99
  in Canada's population composition, 22f
laws and legislation
  see also government regulation
  Bill C-45, 479
  Canada Industrial Relations Board, 548-549
  Canada Labour Code, 548-549
  Canada Labour Code, Part III, 391
  Canada Labour Standards Regulations, 391
  Canadian Human Rights Act, 101-105, 106
  collective bargaining in other countries, 614-615
  collective bargaining legislation, 514-515
  Corruption of Foreign Public Officials Act, 588
  Decent Work Agenda, 615
  employee assistance programs, 462-463
  employee benefits, 448-449
  employer/employee relationship, 21
  Employment Equity Act of 1995, 107-108
  as external issues to analyze, 47
  Federal Contractors Program, 108
  implied contract terms, 512
  Industrial Relations Disputes and Investigation Act of 1948, 548-549

laws and legislation (*continued*)
 international labour organizations, 615
 labour relations, 548–549
 Labour Relations Act, 514
 Ontario *Labour Relations Act*, 549
 performance appraisal requirements, 328–329
 safe work environment, 474–480, 475f, 479f, 500
 small businesses and unionization, 573–574
 status of designated groups, 97–100
 tort of nuisance, 526
laws and regulations
 Personal Information Protection and Electronic Documents Act, 25, 521–522, 522f
lawsuits
 breach of employment contract, 515
 layoffs and potential, 18, 30, 323f
 "wrongful dismissal" cases, 514, 517–518
layoffs, 30
 see also dismissal
 performance appraisal and, 323f
 survivors' psychology after, 18
leaderless group discussions, 187
leadership
 labour union, 558–560
 productivity enhancement through leader support, 20f
 in strategic planning and HR linkage, 46f
learning, principles of, 280, 282f
 active practice and repetition, 282–283
 behaviour modification, 284
 feedback and reinforcement, 283–284
 goal setting, 281
 incorporation of, 310
 individual differences, 282
 Massed v. Distributed learning, 283
 modeling, 281–282
 spot rewards, 283
 typical learning curve, 284f
 Whole v. Part learning, 283
learning curve, typical, 284f
learning management systems (LMS), 292–293
leasing, employee, 19
Legally Blonde, 130–131
leniency or strictness error, 337
lie detector tests, 235
life insurance, 455
life plateau, 195

line manager
 partnership with HR department, 29–31, 31f
 role of, 31–32
line of advancement, in HR management, 191f
literacy
 as external issue to analyze, 47
 host country's, 587–589, 587f
 lived values, 31f
 localization, 610
 local labour unions, 559–560
 lockout, 548, 549, 562, 562f, 569, 570
 loyalty, 18
Luck Is No Accident: Making the Most of Happenstance in Your Life and Career (Krumboltz and Levin), 198
lump-sum merit pay, 406f, 413

M

Machtinger v. HOJ Industries, 514
management
 calibration process among, 327–328
 compensation of expatriate managers, 609–611
 compensation of host-country managers, 609
 disciplinary of, 527, 527f
 in disciplinary policies/procedures, 527
 employee benefit concerns, 446–448
 ethics in employee relations, 538
 expatriate managers, 596–599, 598f
 expatriate selection criteria, 599f
 globalization impact on, 584–589, 585f, 587f
 impact of unionization on, 557–558
 international labour organizations, 615–616
 length of reasonable notice for, 517
 minorities in, 205
 overseas managers, 596–599, 597f
 performance appraisal by, 330
 performance appraisal failure, 325
 politics of labour-management relationship, 561
 power in collective bargaining process, 568–569
 strategies to remain union free, 556
 women in, 205
management by objectives (MBO), 346–347, 347f
management inventories, 61
Management of Occupational Health and Safety (Kelloway, Francis, Montgomery), 485

management rights, 557
managing diversity, 24, 82, 122–123
marital status, prohibited discrimination by, 104f
Markov analysis, 61, 61f
Massed v. Distributed learning, 283
Material Safety Data Sheets (MSDs), 485
median retirement age, 50
mediation, 537
mediator, 537
medical examination, 252
memory, loss of institutional, from layoffs, 18
mentoring, 200–202, 200f, 201f
merit guidelines, 413
merit pay, 406f, 412–413
Métis, 97
minorities
 see also designated groups; visible minorities
 in management, 205
National Council of Visible Minorities, 205
mission, 45
Mitbestimmung (codetermination), 616
mixed-standard scales, 342, 358
mobility, host country's, 587–589, 587f
modeling, 281–282
motivation
 distributive fairness theory, 373–374
 as employee selection factor, 255
 expectancy theory and pay, 373–374
 linking compensation to organizational objectives, 371–372
 pay equity and, 374f
 pay-for-performance standard, 372–373
 productivity enhancement through, 20f
 strategic compensation planning, 373–375
 trainee readiness and, 280–281
moving expenses, 463
Mr. Baseball, 619–620
multigenerational workforce, 206–207
multinational corporation (MNC), 584–585
 defined, 584
multiple cutoff model, 256, 257f
multiple hurdle model, 256
Municipal Workplace Literacy Achievements award, 305
"mutual consideration," 515
Myers-Briggs Type Indicator (MBTI), 239

N

NAFTA. *See* North American Free Trade Agreement
nationalism
  host country's, 587–589, 587*f*
national labour unions, 558–559
  see also labour union
National Occupational Classification (NOC), 143, 219
needs assessment, 274–280, 275*f*, 277*f*
  chief learning officer, 274
  competency assessment, 277–279
  organization analysis, 276–277
  person analysis, 279–280
  rapid, 276
  task analysis, 277–280
neglect, in communicating rules, 529
negotiated grievance procedure, 571
negotiations
  see also collective bargaining process
  bargaining zone, 562*f*, 564, 564*f*, 565, 574
  CAW and government-mandated, 579–580
  preparation for, 562–563
nepotism, 178
network Improshare, 406*f*, 425
networking, 202
new business, steps for starting, 221*f*
new entrarts, 49
9-box grid, 186, 186*f*
no-layoff policy, 18
noncontributory plan, 456
nonexempt, 376
nonfinancial compensation, 370
nonpunitive discipline, 532
nonstandard jobs, 25–26
North American Free Trade Agreement (NAFTA), 7

O

occupational health and safety
  see also health habits
  burying/falsifying records, 483–484, 528*f*
  calming angry employees, 493*f*
  chemical hazards, 485
  code orange, 489–490
  communicable diseases, 488
  creation of, 480–484, 481*f*, 482*f*
  cumulative trauma disorders, 488
  enforcing safety rules, 482
  ergonomics program key elements, 489*f*
  indoor air quality, 487
  injury/illness incidence rate calculation, 483
  investigating and recording accidents, 483
  laws and legislation, 474–480, 475*f*, 479*f*
  promoting safety awareness, 481–482, 481*f*
  research on, 484
  small business, 500
  steps in safety incentive program, 482*f*
  symbols for hazardous materials, 486*f*
  terrorist crisis management teams, 492
  video display terminals, 487–488
  workers' compensation, 450–451, 451*f*, 480
  workplace hazardous materials information systems, 485–486, 486*f*
  workplace violence, 490–492, 491*f*
occupational illness, 474–480, 503–504
  young workers, 503–504
occupational injury, 474
  laws and legislation on, 474–480, 475*f*, 479*f*
  supervisor's role in preventing, 479*f*
  world leader in environmental health and safety, 478–479
offshoring, 18–19, 21, 50
off-the-job development, 294
off-the-job interests, 221
Old Age Security, 458
ombudsperson system, 458
online employment applications, 537
online job applications, 233
online job posting system, 177
online learning, 292–293
online reservation systems, 49
on-the-job behaviour problems, 528*f*
on-the-job training (OJT)
  for managerial positions, 293–294
  for nonmanagerial positions, 285–286, 286*f*
open-door policy, 536–537
opportunities and threats (OT), 46*f*
optimal tasks, 14–16
organizational capability, 80
organizational exit, 193
organizational productivity/HRM linked to, 548
organizational recruiters, 182–183
organization analysis, 276–277
organization design, 31*f*
organizing labour campaign
  employer tactics, 553–554, 554*f*
  organizing steps, 552–553
  union tactics, 554–555
orientation, 302
orientation training, 302–304
  case study, 311–312
  checklist for new employees, 304
  e-based, 314
outsourcing, 18, 21, 50
overtime, working, 375–376

P

paid holidays, 454
Pakistanis, 99
parental leave, 21, 207
part-time employees, 26, 27, 49
pay equity, 373, 374
  see also compensation; employment equity
  1978 amendment to *Canadian Human Rights Act*, 106
  equal pay for work of equal value, 107, 392–394
pay-for-performance standard, 372, 373*f*
  government regulation of, 391–392
  wage-rate compression, 395–396
pay grades, 388
  single rate structure, 388*f*
pay package, executive, 417
peer appraisal, 360, 361
  defined, 331
peer-review system, 536
pension plans, 456–458
pensions, 18, 456–458
  Canada and Quebec Pension Plans, 448–449
performance
  threats to, 458
performance appraisal
  improving, 355–357, 355*f*, 356*f*
  relevance of standards, 326
  360-degree appraisal, 332–334, 333*f*
  administrative purposes of, 323, 323*f*
  appraisal interviews, 350–357, 351*f*, 356*f*
  appraiser training, 336–339
  at Canadian Tire, 334–336
  common problems of, 324–326, 324*f*
  compensation and, 323*f*
  contrast error, 339
  criterion deficiency, 326–327, 327*f*
  customer appraisal, 332
  defined, 322

performance appraisal (continued)
developmental purposes of, 323f, 324
establishing performance standards, 327f
failure, 325
Goodyear's program, 338
in HR competency model, 31f
improving performance, 355–357, 355f, 356f
as internal recruitment method, 185–186, 186f
international assignments, 611–613
international cases, 611–613
legal issues, 328–329
manager/supervisor appraisal, 330
peer appraisal, 331
raters, 329, 329f, 337–339
recency error, 338
relevance of performance standards, 326
reliability/consistency of standards, 327–328
self-appraisal, 330
similar-to-me error, 339
small business, 357
stereotyping v., 339
subordinate appraisal, 330–331
team appraisal, 331–332, 332f
zone of valid assessment, 327f
performance appraisal methods, 339
behavioural methods, 145, 343–345, 345f
checklist, 340
essay method, 343
forced-choice method, 342
graphic rating scale method, 340–341, 341f
mixed-standard scales, 342
results methods, 345–349, 347f, 348f
simplicity and use of, 349
summary of, 350f
supervisor's checklist, 340
performance improvement
identifying sources of ineffectiveness, 355, 355f
managing ineffective performance, 356–357
performance diagnosis, 355–356, 356f, 360
performance management, 322
performance standards, 327f
perquisites ("perks"), 420
"sweetness" of, 421
personal career development
choosing career, 217–219, 219f
choosing employer, 219–220

developing skills and competencies, 217
entrepreneur, 220
marital/family life balanced with, 221–222
off-the-job interests, 221
questions to ask before accepting job offer, 220
retirement planning, 222
steps for starting new business, 221f
personal credibility, 30, 31f
personal crises, 495
Personal Information Protection and Electronic Documents Act (PIPEDA), 25, 521–522, 522f
person analysis, 279–280
personnel planning, performance appraisal and, 323f
Peter Principle, 192
physical ability tests, 240–241
Physical Fitness Abilities Requirement Evaluation (PARE), 241
picketing, 568, 568f
piecework, 375, 406f, 410, 411f
computing piece rate, 411
differential piece rate, 410
drawbacks/weaknesses of, 411–412
straight, 410
PIPEDA. See Personal Information Protection and Electronic Documents Act
planning, in overall framework for HRM, 6f
point manual, 382–383
point system, 382
policy formulation and implementation see also disciplinary policies and procedures
guidelines for e-mail/computer/voice mail, 524f
as HR manager's responsibility, 29
no-layoff policy, 18
open-door policy, 536–537
against sexual harassment, 122
political association, prohibited discrimination by, 105f
politics, of labour-management relationship, 561
polygraph tests, 234–235
poor performance, 323f
population
Canada's diversity, 21, 22f, 307
challenge of immigration and diversity, 21, 22f
cross-cultural differences, 601–603, 602f
cultures/languages/nationalities/ethnic groups, 96

designated groups, 97–100, 205
diversity training, 307
managing diversity, 24
reasons for diversity management, 127f
position, 138
position analysis questionnaire (PAQ), 143–145, 144f
positive discipline, 532–533
PowerPoint, 293
predictive validity, 229
pregnancy leave, 28, 207
premiums, 5
preretirement benefit policies, 455–456
Pride Builders, 315
principles, business/corporate, 46f
principles of learning, 281–284, 282f, 284f
incorporation of, 310
privacy
employer/employee relationship, 21
in job evaluation system, 400
labour arbitrator, 524, 525
in overall framework for HRM, 6f
PIPEDA, 25, 521–522, 522f
policy guidelines: e-mail/computer/voice mail, 524f
supervising v. super-spying, 515
workplace issues, 519, 521–523, 522f, 523f
private employment agencies, 180–181
proactive change, 11
problem-solving skills, 31f
productivity
counter-productive sales incentive plans, 415
enhancements, 19–20, 20f
labour relations HRM linked to, 548
low-cost strategy: compete on productivity/efficiency, 68–69, 69f
measures, 346
Six Sigma process and, 15, 15f
professional associations, 558
recruiting from, 180
professional employees incentive plans, 406f
base salaries, 418
benefits, 420
long-term incentives, 418–420, 419f
pay package, 417
perquisites, 420
short-term incentives, 418
professional employer organizations (PEOs), 19
profit sharing, 406f, 427–431
defined, 426

programmed instruction, 289–290
progressive discipline, 532
promotion, 192
  case study, 543–544
  performance appraisal and, 323f
  productivity enhancement through, 20f
protection, from dismissal, 521
provincial employment equity, 108
provincial hospital and medical services, 451
provincial human rights legislation, 235, 236
  enforcement of, 106
public employment agencies, 180
public sector, labour relations in, 560
  compulsory binding arbitration, 561
  final offer arbitration, 561
  political nature of labour-management relationship, 561
  strikes, 561
public service commission, 460

Q
qualitative approaches, to forecasting, 59–60
quality management. *See* total quality management
quantitative approaches, to forecasting, 59
Quebec Crisis, 206

R
rapid needs assessment, 276
rate ranges, per pay grade, 389–390
  wage structure with increasing rate ranges, 389f
raters, 329, 329f, 337–339
reactive change, 11
real wages, 380
reasonable accommodation, 114–116
reasonable notice, 514, 517, 520–521
reassigning, 18
recency error, 338
records, burying/falsifying, 483–484, 528f
recreational benefits, 463
recruitment, 29, 36–37
  case study, 212–213
  edge in, from avoiding downsizing, 18
  globalization influencing, 6–8
  job specification and, 138–139
  in overall framework for HRM, 6f, 138–139

recruiting external talent, 174–175
recruiting internationally, 592–594, 621
red circle rates, 390
reengineering, 15f
  global business environment requiring, 138
  HRM and, 16–17
reference checking, 231–233, 234
  globalization's impact on, 593
  international cases, 593
regional economic issues, 46
registered retirement plan, 443
religion
  see also diversity
  host country's, 587–589
  Sabbath absences from work, 102f, 116, 587f
relocation services, 192
repatriation, 604–605
  checklist, 606
replacement charts, 61–62, 62f
replacement strikers, 562, 562f, 567
replacement workers, 567
resources
  in overall framework for HRM, 6f
  people as strategic resource, 52–53, 53f
  in strategic planning and HR linkage, 46f
respect, 27f
responsiveness, as HRM challenge, 6f
results methods, of performance appraisal, 345
  balanced scorecard, 347–349, 348f
  management by objectives, 346–347, 347f
  productivity measures, 346
"results orientation," 313
résumés
  advice on, 232
  KSAs in, 5
  unsolicited, 176
retirement
  median age of, 50
  planning, 222
  policies, 455
  preretirement benefit policies, 455–456
  strategies, 21
Retirement Savings Plan (RSP), 464
retraining, 18
return on investment (ROI), 299–300
  costs of employing expatriates, 613
  international assignments, 612
  return on training investment, 300

rewards, 31f
  productivity enhancement through, 20f
  spot, 283
  total rewards package, 445f
rights arbitration, 572–573
Riley Guide, 210
rival firms, 48
  five forces framework, 48–49, 48f
role-playing, 187, 295–296

S
safety and health accidents, 474
  see also occupational health and safety
safety awareness, 481–482, 481f
safety incentive program, 482f
safe work environment
  bullying v., 505–507
  case study, 484
  creation of, 480–484, 481f, 482f
  enforcement of safety rules, 482
  ergonomics program key elements, 489f
  indoor air quality, 487
  injury/illness incidence rate calculation, 483
  investigating and recording accidents, 483
  laws and legislation, 474–480, 475f, 479f, 500
  safety awareness program, 481–482, 481f
  safety incentive program, 482f
  video display terminals, 487–488
  workers' compensation, 450–451, 451f, 480
salary
  awarding increases in, 433
  combined salary and commission incentive plan, 417
  HRIS and salary surveys, 417
  salary plus bonus incentive plan, 417
  Salary Wizard, 386
  straight salary incentive plan, 416
  wage and salary survey, 385–391, 387f, 388f, 389f
salary plus bonus plan, 417
Salary Wizard, 386
sales incentive plans, 406f, 415
  behaviour observation scale, 345
  combined salary and commission incentive plan, 417
  counter-productive, 415
  salary plus bonus plans, 417

sales incentive plans (continued)
    types of, 416–417
    unique needs of, 415–416
SARS epidemic, 488
Scanlon Plan, 406f, 424–425, 424f
Scent of a Woman, 433–434
scheduling/attendance issues, 5
selection
    see also interview, employment
    compensatory model, 256
    criterion-related validity, 228–230
        for CSIS, 264–265
    decision-making strategy, 255–257,
        255f, 257f
    defined, 226
    designing criteria and methods for,
        260
    drug testing, 253
    employment interview, 242–253
    employment tests, 237–242, 239f,
        240f, 242f
    final decision, 257–258
    of global managers, 596–599, 597f,
        598f, 599f
    goal of, 226f
    at Hudson's Bay Company, 254
    job descriptions as basis for, 139
    job proficiency, 230
    line managers and, 226
    medical examination, 252–253
    multiple cutoff model, 256
    multiple hurdle model, 256
    performance appraisal and criteria
        for, 323f
    person-job fit, 227
    person-organization fit, 227
    process of, 227, 228f
    reliability of information, 228–229
    selection ratio, 257
    validity of information, 228–229
selection information sources
    application forms, 231–233
    background checks, 233–234
    candidate dishonesty, 232
    credit reports, 234
    graphology, 237
    honesty and integrity tests, 235–237,
        236f
    online applications, 233
    résumés, 232
selection ratio, 257
self-appraisal, 330
Self-Directed (Holland), 198
seminars, 294
sense of accomplishment, 27f
September 11 attacks, 206
service activities, HR manager's
    responsibilities in, 30

service sector, 49
    unionization in, 577
severance pay, 18, 454–455, 465
    defined, 454
sexual harassment, 119f, 120f
    case study, 132
    components of effective policy
        against, 122
    cost of, 118
    defined, 119
    necessity of confidentiality, 120
    Ontario Human Rights Code, 119–120
    policies to deal with, 119–120
        as prevalent and problematic,
        121–122
    preventing, 130
    questions asked in auditing, 120
sexual orientation, prohibited
    discrimination by, 104f
"sick building syndrome," 487
sick leave, 454
silver handshake, 455
similar-to-me error, 339
simulations, learning from, 292, 295
sincerity, of instructors, 284
situational interview, 243–244, 245
Six Sigma
    defined, 14
    importance of HR to, 14–15, 15f
    reality check/derivation of, 16
skill inventories, 61
skywalkers, 27
sleeping, on job, 528f
small business
    benefit programs, 464
    compensation equity, 395–396
    discipline and employee, 539
    employee selection, 258
    employee services, 464
    employment equity, 127–128
    HR responsibilities, 32
    job requirements in, 164
    performance appraisal, 357
    recruitment, 207–208
    safety and health practices, 500
    strategic planning, 80
    training/development, 308
social concerns, analysis of, 47
social stratification, host country's,
    587–589, 587f
software
    factors in choosing, 10–11
    Microsoft's software engineers, 193
    for succession planning/talent
        management, 62
South Asians, in Canada's population
    composition, 22f

Southeast Asians, 99
    in Canada's population
        composition, 22f
split-pay, 610
spot bonus, 412
spot rewards, 283
spouse, 28
staffing, 31f
    Capital One case study, 83–85
    globalization influencing, 6–8
    international HRM recruitment,
        621
    layoffs impacting, 18
    in overall framework for HRM, 6f
    transnational teams, 595
staffing tables, 61, 61f
staff parties scheduling, 5
Staff Recognition Committee, 5
standard hour plan, 406f, 412
standards
    reliability/consistency of, 327–328
statutory regulation, 512
    of employee dismissals, 517–518
statutory rights, 513
step-review system, 535–536, 536f
stereotyping
    performance appraisal v., 339
stock data, 111
stock option incentive plan, 426
    for all levels of employees, 427
    criticism of, 428–429
    example of, 427
    pay-for-performance at Lombard
        Canada, 428
straight commission incentive plan,
    416–417
straight piecework, 410
straight salary incentive plan, 416
strategic compensation planning
    expectancy theory and pay,
        373–374, 374f
    linking compensation to
        organizational objectives,
        371–372
    motivating employees through,
        373–375, 373f
    pay equity, 374
    pay-for-performance standard, 372–373
    pay secrecy, 375
    see also strategic compensation
        planning
    business strategy, 68–72, 69f, 71f
    corporate strategy, 66–68
    defined, 44
    functional strategy: ensuring
        alignment, 70
strategic knowledge worker, 55
strategic planning, 44

HR planning linked to, 45
small business, 80
step 1: mission, vision, values, 45–46, 47
step 2: environmental analysis, 46–50, 48f
step 3: internal analysis, 50–64, 53f; 55f, 57f, 59f, 61f, 62f, 63f, 64f; references from, 234
step 4: formulating strategy, 64–70, 65f, 66f, 69f
step 5: strategy implementation, 70–75, 71f
step 6: evaluation and assessment, 75–80, 78f, 79f
SWOT analysis, 65–66, 66f
strategic vision, 45
  linked to strategic planning and HR, 46f
stress
  burnout, 498
  defined, 497
  distress, 497
  how job candidates react to, 241
  job-related, 487–488, 498–499, 499f
stress management, 497–500, 502
  stressors and coping responses: expatriate executives, 604
  tips for reducing job-related stress, 499f
"stretch goals," 354
strikes, 554, 555, 561, 574
  as challenge to management decisions, 557
  boycotts and, 568
  in collective bargaining process, 557
  deadlines for, 570
  defined, 566
  lockouts and, 548, 549, 562, 562f, 569, 570
  in public v. private sectors, 561
  replacement of strikers, 562, 562f, 567
  strike breakers, 556
  violence during, 567
"stripping," 232
Strong Interest Inventory, 219
structured interview, 243
subordinate appraisal, 330–331
substitutes, 49
  five forces framework, 48f, 49
succession planning, 61–62, 62f
  checklist, 64f
  software for, 62
summary dismissal, 517
supervising v. super-spying, 515

supervisor
  calming angry employees, 493f
  checklist for performance appraisal, 340
  notification of medical absence, 505
  open-door policy, 536–537
  performance appraisal by, 330
  references from, 234
  role in preventing occupational injury, 479f
  supervising v. super-spying, 515
  unions v. authority of, 557–558
suppliers, 49
  five forces framework, 48f, 49
supply, 60
  supply and demand, 46f, 85
supporting labour, 54–55
Survey Finder, 386
suspension, without pay, 519
swine flu (H1N1), 519
SWOT analysis, 65–66, 66f, 488
symbols, for hazardous materials, 486f
systemic discrimination, 113
systems approach, to training programs, 274, 275f

T
talent management
  automation of functions, 10f
  case study, 85–86
  software for, 62
tardiness, 528f
task analysis, 277–280
task inventory analysis, 145
team appraisal, 331–332, 332f
team approach to cost containment, 453
team compensation, 406f, 421–423, 422f
team incentive plan, 406f, 421–423, 422f
  case study, 434–435
  designing effective, 423
team training, 305–306, 305f
teamwork
  as approach to cost containment, 453
  productivity enhancement, 20f
  transnational teams, 595
technical support, as HRIS choice, 11
technology
  competitive challenges from new, 8–11, 10f
  as external issue to analyze, 47
  host country's, 587–589, 587f
  HRIS, 9–11, 10f
  HRM challenges from, 6f
  see also computer use; Internet
  workplace of future, 8
  technology industries, 9

telecommuting, 21, 161–162, 162f
telephone use, monitoring of, 523f
television, 206
temporary employment agencies, 180–181
terrorist crisis management teams, 492
  September 11 attacks, 206
Test of Workplace Essential Skills (TOWES), 24
third-country nationals, 591
360-degree appraisal, 332–334, 333f
time
  host country's orientation toward, 587f
  implementation, as HRIS choice factor, 11
tobacco smoke, 487, 528f
  off, 567
tort of nuisance, 526
total quality management (TQM), 14–16, 15f
total rewards package, 445f
TQM. See total quality management
Traditionalists
  customized noncash incentive awards for, 414
  managing multigenerational workforce, 206–207
trainee readiness, 139
training and development, 280–281
  basic skills training, 304–305
  checklist for orienting new employees, 304
  chief ethics officer, 306
  competency assessment for managerial position, 278–279
  course content as percentage of training expenditures, 273f
  cross-training, 306
  diversity training, 306
  ethics training, 307
  international cases, 599–606, 600f
  international HRM, 599–606, 600f
  investment in, 272–274, 273f
  orientation training, 302–304
  in overall framework for HRM, 6f
  Phase 1: assessing needs, 274–280, 275f, 277f
  Phase 2: designing training program, 280–285, 282f, 284f
  Phase 3: implementation, 285–296, 286f, 289f, 291f
  Phase 4: evaluation of effectiveness, 296–301, 297f
  small business, 308

training and development (*continued*)
systems approach to, 274
team training, 305–306, 305f
work is more than paycheque, 27f, 29
training needs, 323f
training programs, 280–285, 282f, 284f
characteristics of instructors,
284–285
implementation of, 285–296, 286f,
289f, 291f
instructional objectives, 280
international cases, 600f
for international cases, 600–606,
602f, 604f
for international employees, 600f
methods for nonmanagerial
employees, 285–293, 286f,
289f, 290f, 291f
performance appraisal and, 323f
principles of learning, 281–284,
282f, 284f
trainee readiness and motivation,
280–281
training instructor's adaptability,
284
transactional-based v. relationship
employment, 21
transfer, 192
transfer of learning, 298
transnational corporation, 585, 585f
transnational teams, 595
transportation industries, 9
transportation pooling, 463
trend analysis, 59
trends
analysis of HR demand, 59f
demographic and labour market, 47
industry, 46
Trudeau era, 206
trust, 31f
interest-based bargaining, 566
layoffs v., 18
trusted pension plan, 458

U

U-571, 83
underutilization, 113
unemployment, 27, 50
unfair labour practices (ULP), 556
union. *See* credit union; labour union
union dues, allocation of, 559
union security agreements, 570
union (shop) steward, 560
United States, most productive nation, 20
unsolicited applications and résumés,
176
upgrade, software, 11

urbanization, host country's, 587–589,
587f
U.S. Fair Labor Standards Act, 376
user friendliness, 11
utilities industries, 9
utility (return on training investment),
300

V

vacation payouts, 18
vacations with pay, 454
validity
construct validity, 230
content validity, 230
criterion-related validity, 228–230
defined, 228
validity coefficient, 229, 229f
validity generalization, 230
values, host country, 587–589, 587f
variable pay, 406–408, 417
defined, 406
vesting, 457
video display terminals (VDTs), 487–488
video surveillance, 523f
of employee conduct outside
workplace, 523, 525–526
violent behaviour, 490–492, 491f
fighting, 528f
possession of weapons, 528f
during strikes, 567
warning signs, 491f
virtual interview, 246–247
virtual learning, 9
learning management systems,
292–293
virtual office, 161
visa/work permits, 593
visible minorities, 22f, 98–100, 102f
National Council of Visible
Minorities, 205
vision, strategic, 45
linked to strategic planning and
HR, 46f
voice mail, policy guidelines for, 524f
Voice-Over-the-Internet Protocol
(VOIP), 49

W

wage and salary survey, 387f, 388–391,
388f, 389f
collecting survey data, 385–386,
386f
compensation for HR professionals,
386f
defined, 385
employer-initiated surveys, 386–387

wage curve, 387–388
freehand wage curve, 387f
wage rate compression, 392, 396
defined, 395
wage structure
with increasing rate ranges, 389f
single rate, 388f
weak talent "bench," 184f
weapons, possession of, 528f
weighted application blank
(WAB), 232
wellness programs, 494
tips for starting, 495f
What Color Is Your Parachute? (Bolles),
198
whistle-blowing, 21
white-collar workers. *See* skywalkers
Whites
in Canada's population
composition, 22f
myths about employment equity,
129
Whole v. Part learning, 283
women, 97
see also family concerns; sexual
harassment
as designated group, 97
educational level v. annual earnings,
24f
eliminating barriers to
advancement, 204
employed, 49
employment equity: fighting fires,
131
equal pay for work of equal value,
106, 392–394
gender distribution of workforce, 23
glass ceiling audits, 204–205
in management, 205
pregnancy leave, 28, 207
prohibited discrimination toward,
103f
recruitment and development of,
203
social issues arising from, in
workforce, 21
work attitudes/work ethic
host country's, 587–589, 587f
in overall framework for HRM, 6f
workers' compensation
for injured workers, 480
insurance, 450–451, 451f
reducing costs of, 451f
workers' compensation insurance, 450
working
for free, 275
is more than paycheque, 27f, 29
overtime, 375–376

working conditions, in job evaluation, 400

work-life balance, 221–222, 603–605
evaluating your company, 467–468
family-friendly work-life setting, 27f, 28, 459, 459f, 467–469
flextime and, 21, 160–163
privacy issues, 519, 521–523, 522f, 523f

True North's, 468–469
work permit, 593
workplace fitness, promoting, 494, 495f
Workplace Hazardous Materials Information Systems (WHMIS), 485–486, 486f
work schedules

alternative work schedules, 21, 159–163, 162f
compressed workweek, 160
flextime, 21, 160–161, 163
job sharing, 161
keys for successful telecommuting, 162f
telecommuting, 161–162, 162f
why students value, 160
work–life balance, 163
work valuation, 396
workweek
defined, 384
33 hours per, 50
compressed, 160
four-day, 28

World War II, 206
writing analysis, 237
wrongful dismissal, nonunion employee, 514, 516–518
defined, 517
lawsuit for, 517
Wronko v. Western Inventory Service, 516

Y
yield ratios, 182

Z
zone of valid assessment, 327f